The Bare Facts Video Guide

2nd Edition

Craig Hosoda

Additional copies of this book (volume purchases also available)
can be purchased from:

> The Bare Facts
> P.O. Box 3255
> Santa Clara, CA 95055-3255

ISBN 0-9625474-2-5

HOW TO USE THIS BOOK

The book is divided into three sections: Actresses, Actors and Titles. In the People sections, everyone is listed alphabetically by last name. Under each name are films, TV shows and magazines that the person has appeared in. The non-nudity titles are listed to help you remember who a particular person is. If they have appeared nude in a film or magazine, the title is in bold face. Following the title is the year the film was released, then the character name or article title. Under the title is the time or the page number the nudity occurs. Then there is a brief description of how the person appears in the scene followed by a one to three star rating.

In the Title section, Films or Made for Cable TV Movies that have nude scenes (of someone in the People section) are listed. Under each entry, are the cast and charater names. All the nude scenes for each cast member are listed under their names. If a person is listed in the Title section, they have a listing in the Actor or Actress section. Note that a film can have more nude scenes than are listed—I only list nude scenes of people who are in the Actress or Actor section.

Time definitions:
Very, very brief:	Need to use PAUSE to see one frame
Very brief:	Use SLOW MOTION to see under 1 second
Brief:	About 1 second
No comment:	2 to 15 seconds
Long scene:	Longer than 15 seconds

Rating definitions:
•	Yawn. Usually too brief or hard to see for some reason.
••	Okay. Check it out if you are interested in the person.
•••	Wow! Don't miss it. The scene usually lasts for a while.

The ratings are approximate guides to how much nudity an actor or actress has in a scene. More weight is given on how famous a person is, how well lit and clear the scene is, if it's a close shot and the length of time they stay still so you can see clearly. So if someone has an erotic love scene but they don't show any skin or they are topless but their backs are toward the camera, it won't get rated.

To help you find the nude scenes quickly and accurately, the location on video tape is specified in hours and minutes rather than counter numbers since different VCR's have different counters. The time starts at 0:00 minutes after the last film company logo disappears (Universal, Paramount, etc.).

Actresses that have appeared nude in only one film and are never seen anywhere else are not included because this book helps you locate someone you've seen somewhere else before, unclothed on another video tape. "One timer" actors are listed though, without them, the Actors section would be woefully thin!

Some film titles have bold type with no descriptions and others have bold type with descriptions and no time. These are video tapes that readers have sent as additions that aren't on video tape or I haven't had time to verify. These titles are listed so as not to waste people's time sending me duplicate additions.

INTRODUCTION

It used to be that people did nude scenes in films at the beginning of their careers trying to get their "big break." Once they established themselves, they announced they would not be doing any more nudity and hoped that everybody would forget their earlier performances. Daryl Hannah and Phoebe Cates for example. But more and more actors and actresses are surprising us and doing nudity in films much later in their careers (Sigourney Weaver and Julie Andrews). Fortunately, there are a few who do nudity in just about every film they are in. Bo Derek and Sylvia Kristel for example. This book compiles all of these unbashful actors and actresses into one reference to help you locate their nude scenes on video tape to save you time and money. I have listed a few close calls like Janine Turner in *Monkey Shines* or Christina Applegate in *Streets*.

Some actresses that have done *Playboy* and *Penthouse* pictorials are included because not all actresses do nude scenes in films. Unrevealing pictorials that would be rated PG are not listed (Janet Jones and Jayne Kennedy for example). Only pictorials from *Playboy* and *Penthouse* are listed since they are the easiest men's magazines to find. I haven't finished reviewing all of the back issues in this edition but I will for the next edition.

Actresses that *look* like they have done nudity in films, but have used body doubles instead, are also noted. A body double is a stand-in that is used for nude shots when an actor or actress is too modest. You can usually spot a body double being used when there is a nude body without seeing a face.

I have tried to limit each person's filmography to between ten to fifteen films. This book is starting to get too large now that there is a cross reference by film title. It doesn't take too many films for someone to remember who Meryl Streep or Jack Nicholson are. If you need complete filmographies for people, please consult *The Motion Picture Guide*. Your local library probably carries it.

I have spent my time concentrating on getting the greatest number of celebrities into this book as possible. Therefore, you'll find the entries for some people like Natassja Kinski or Claudia Jennings, incomplete since it's relatively easy to locate films they have nude scenes in. Obviously, I haven't been able to view all the movies ever made (yet), so there will be films with nude scenes that I have missed. (I haven't even started looking at Russ Meyers' films!)

If you find any mistakes or have additions, please write to me and they will be corrected in the next edition. I have a long, long list of nude scenes compiled from letters sent in by readers. I need to verify each nude scene because occasionally, readers send me scenes they have incorrectly remembered. For example, one person wrote that Lesley Ann Warren has nude scenes in *Pretty Baby*—obviously mistaking her for Susan Sarandon.

I only review video tapes, not the theatrical release in movie theaters, so you won't see times for *Inner Sanctum* or *The Doors* listed in this edition because they weren't on video tape when this book was being prepared. But you can be assured that they will be in the next edition!

Enjoy!

THANKS, THANKS AND MORE THANKS!

First of all, I need to thank my wife, Marie, for her help and patience putting up with all my video tape viewing. I also need to thank my children, Christopher and Melanie, for taking their naps so I can watch video tapes. Thanks also to my parents and parents in-laws and the rest of my family for all their help and support.

Secondly, a big thank you to Dave Dell'Aquila, who is my 4th Dimension Consultant. Without his help, I couldn't have set up the database, imported the data or generated the Title cross reference section of this book. Also big thanks to Ron Dell'Aquila who programmed the export from 4th Dimension into FrameMaker.

Thanks to Greg Romankiw & Kevin Rose/Roman Video, Kenny Preston/LaserForce and Irv Slifkin for letting me borrow some of their hard-to-find video tapes and laser discs.

Thanks to the personalities who have provided additional information:
Michelle Bauer, Jennifer Delora, Matt Devlin, Donald Farmer, Kathleen Kinmont, Becky LeBeau, Shelley Michelle, Melissa Moore, Fred Olen Ray, Brinke Stevens and Ingrid Vold.

Thanks to all my friends and the media people who have enabled me to spread word about *The Bare Facts* through newspapers, magazines, radio and television:
David Brandt, Joe Bob Briggs, Marty Burden/New York Post, Anne Marie Calzolari/Associated Press, Tim Connelly/Adam Film World, Kathy Couturie, S. C. Dacy, Sharon Dizenhuz, Cindy Farello, Deborah Fernandez, John A. Gallagher, Roy Harvey, Andrea Hill, David Klinghoffer/Washington Times, Bruce Kluger/Playboy Magazine, Jean-Pierre Lebrun, Craig Ledbetter/European Trash Cinema, Michelle Lee (not the actress), Judith Markey/Chicago-Sun Times, Dan O'Day, Mark Ouimet, David Pearce/Video Trader, Jim Pehling, Dawn Reshen/Media Management, Neil Reshen/Media Management, Debbie Richard/Entertainment Tonight, Gene Ross/Adult Video News, Mike Santomauro, Valerie Smith, Adam Stokke, Carolyn Turek, Richard von Busack/Metro and Michael J. Weldon/Psychotronic Video.

Thanks to all the people who have sent me additions and corrections:

These individuals have gone beyond the call of duty:
Nicolas Barbano, Jim Bereza, Wallace C. Clopton, David Grubka, John Heckel, Martin Hundley, Bertil Lundgren, Mitch Martens, Dennis W. Moore, Gary D. Mullings, Everett Osborne, Matt Pachosa, Stephen H. Peratt, George M. St. George, Lawrence Stewart and Thomas G. Valachovic.

A big thank you also to:
Lloyd Allen, Daniel Bates, Matt Bear, Roy Benson, Kevin M. Burns, Dwight L. Chambers, Kris Clark, Frank Combes, Luther Cruthers, Edward Dolan, Robert T. Dolsay, Steve Draper, Michael Duck, Mark S. Duemmel, James Embree, Larry Estrin, Joseph P. Falco, H. T. Forbes, George Forresi, W. T. Furgerson, Ward Gambrell, Michael G. Grey, Don Hart, F. Hillman, Greg Hotchkiss, Norm Howsmon, Bill Hunt, Thomas P. Johnson, Terry Kaegin, Jim Klein, Michael Klossner, Dave Lachance, Dan Leone, Philip Long, Bill Luhman, Robert Mallory, T. J. Manning, Frank Marulli, David McKee, Stan Melton, Don Metz, Jamie Murray, Robert Neill, Tom North, Dov O'Nuanain, Roger E. Opie, Duane Oyen, Gordon Panei, Ernest N. Peloquin, William C. Pollard, R. L. Porter, Rafael Prata, Martin Praul, William J. Pullin, John Reeks, James J. Rhodes, John E. Robertson, D. M. Robinson, Judson Rosebush, T. R. Rouff, E. G. Sackman, Jr., Daniel Satlow, P. Simpson, Erik Smith, Robin Stumbo, Richard Suttle, Fender Tucker, Alexander Verrone, David Voigt, Stephen White, John Wiemer and Wm. F. Williams.

Actresses

Aames, Angela

Films:

Fairytales (1979). . . . . Little Bo Peep
••• 0:14 - Nude with The Prince in the woods.
H.O.T.S. (1979) . . . . Boom-Boom Bangs
• 0:21 - Topless parachuting into pool.
• 0:39 - Topless in bathtub playing with a seal.
• 1:33 - Topless playing football.
...All the Marbles (1981). . . . . .Louise
a.k.a. The California Dolls
•• 0:20 - Topless in Peter Falk's motel room talking with Iris, then sitting on the bed.
The Best of Sex and Violence (1981)
. . . . Little Bo Peep
• 0:18 - Brief topless in scene from *Fairytales*.
• 0:20 - Brief right breast in scene from *Fairytales*.
Famous T & A (1982) . . . . Little Bo Peep
(No longer available for purchase, check your video store for rental.)
•• 0:50 - Topless scene from *Fairytales*.
The Lost Empire (1983) . . . . Heather McClure
••• 0:31 - Topless and buns taking a shower while Angel and White Star talk to her.
Scarface (1983). . . . . .Woman at the Babylon Club
Bachelor Party (1984) . . . . .Mrs. Klupner
Basic Training (1984). . . . . Cheryl
• 0:19 - Brief topless in bathtub.
Chopping Mall (1986) . . . . .Miss Vanders

Abigail

Films:

Alvin Purple (1973; Australian) . . . . Girl in See-Through
0:01 - On bus in see-through top. Hard to see anything.
Alvin Rides Again (1974; Australian) . . . . Mae
••• 0:12 - Topless in store with Alvin.
The Adventures of Eliza Fraser (1976; Australian)
. . . . .Buxom Girl
• 0:01 - Topless when Martin pulls the sheets off her.
Breaking Loose (1988; Australian) . . . . Helen

Abril, Victoria

Films:

Comin' At Ya! (1982) .Abilene
The Moon in the Gutter (1983; French/Italian) . . . . Bella
On the Line (1984; Spanish) . . . . Engracia
••• 0:16 - Topless getting undressed to make love with Mitch.
• 0:29 - Very brief topless, making love in bed with Mitch.
0:54 - In white lingerie getting dressed.
L'Addition (1985; French) . . . . .Patty
Padre Nuestro (1987) . . . .
Tie Me Up! Tie Me Down! (1990; Spanish)
. . . . .Marina Osorio
••• 0:24 - Full frontal nudity playing with a frogman toy in the bathtub.

• 0:34 - Buns and brief side of right breast, getting dressed.
•• 0:44 - Topless changing clothes, then on TV while Maximo watches.
•• 1:09 - Topless changing clothes.
••• 1:16 - Right breast, then topless in bed making love with Ricky.
Magazines:
Playboy (Nov 1987). . . . . Sex in Cinema 1987
• 143: Topless in bed.

Ackerman, Leslie

Films:

The First Nudie Musical (1979) . . . . Susie
Hardcore (1979) . . . . .Felice
• 0:44 - Topless in porno house with George C. Scott.
Blame it on the Night (1984) . . . . Shelly
TV:
Skag (1980) . . . . .Barbara Skagska

Adams, Brooke

Films:

Shock Wave (1977) . . . . Rose
Days of Heaven (1978). Abby
Invasion of the Body Snatchers (1978)
. . . . Elizabeth Driscoll
0:49 - All covered in pod gunk in her bedroom when Donald Sutherland discovers her. Don't really see anything.
•• 1:43 - Brief topless behind plants when Sutherland sees her change into a pod person. Hard to see because plants are in the way.
• 1:48 - Topless walking through the pod factory pointing out Sutherland to everybody. Long shot, hard to see.
Cuba (1979) . . . . Alexandra Pulido
Tell Me a Riddle (1980) . . . . Jeannie
The Dead Zone (1983). . . . . Sarah Bracknell
Utilities (1983) . . . . Marion
Almost You (1984) .Erica Boyer
Key Exchange (1985) . . . . Lisa
0:10 - Nude on bicycle with her boyfriend, but you can't see anything because of his strategically placed arms.
• 0:45 - Very brief right breast getting into the shower with her boyfriend, then hard to see behind the shower curtain.
Miniseries:
Lace (1984) . . . . Pagan
Lace II (1985). . . . . Pagan
Made for TV Movies:
Bridesmaids (1989) . . . . .Pat
Stephen King's "Sometimes They Come Back" (1991)
. . . . .Sally
TV:
O.K. Crackerby (1965-66) . . . . .Cynthia Crackerby

Adams, Maud

Films:
The Christian Licorice Store (1971) . . . Cynthia Vicstrom
The Girl in Blue (1973; Canadian) . . . . . . .Paula/Tracy
a.k.a. U-turn
- 1:16 - Side view of right breast, while sitting on bed with Scott.
  1:19 - In two piece swimsuit getting out of lake.
The Man with the Golden Gun (1974; British)
. . . . Andrea Anders
Killer Force (1975; Swiss/Irish). . . . . . . .Claire Chambers
Rollerball (1975) . . . . Ella
Laura (1979). . . . . Sarah
a.k.a. Shattered Innocence
Tattoo (1981) . . . . Maddy
- 0:22 - Very brief topless taking off clothes and putting a bathrobe on.
- •• 0:23 - Topless opening bathrobe so Bruce Dern can start painting.
- •• 0:25 - Brief topless getting into the shower to take off body paint.
- •• 0:58 - Brief topless and buns getting out of bed.
- •• 1:04 - Topless, knocked out on table before Dern starts tattooing her.
- ••• 1:07 - Topless looking at herself in the mirror with a few tattoos on.
- •• 1:24 - Topless lying on table masturbating while Dern watches through peep hole in the door.
- ••• 1:36 - Full frontal nudity taking off robe then making love with Dern (her body is covered with tattoos).
Target Eagle (1982). Carmen
Octopussy (1983; British) . . . . Octopussy
  1:06 - Very brief nude getting out of swimming pool while Bond watches. Long, long shot.
Hell Hunters (1985). . . . . Amanda Hoffman
Nairobi Affair (1986). . . . . Anne Malone
Jane and the Lost City (1987; British) . . . . . .Lola Pagola
The Women's Club (1987) . . . . .Angie Blake
  0:17 - In black panties, garter belt and stockings making out with Michael Paré.
Angel III: The Final Chapter (1988) . . . . Nadine
Intimate Power (1989) . . . . Sineperver
Silent Night, Deadly Night 4: Initiation (1990) . . . .Fima
Made for TV Movies:
Playing for Time (1980). . . . . .Mala
TV:
Chicago Story (1982) . . . . .Dr. Judith Bergstrom
Emerald Point N.A.S. (1983-84) . . . . Maggie Farrell
Magazines:
Playboy (Oct 1981). . . . . .Tattooed Woman
••• 100-107: Topless photos from *Tattoo*.
Playboy (Dec 1981). . . . . .Sex Stars of 1981
  238: Right breast, holding pink robe against herself.
Playboy (Aug 1983) . . . . . The Spy They Love To Love
  92: Topless on pier.
Playboy (Sep 1987). . . . . 25 Years of James Bond
•• 131: Left breast.

Adjani, Isabelle

Films:
Story of Adele H. (1975; French) . . . . Adele Hugo
The Tenant (1976; French). . . . . Stella
The Driver (1978). . . . . The Player
The Bronte Sisters (1979; French). . . . . Emily
Nosferatu, The Vampire (1979; French/German)
. . . . Lucy Harker
Possession (1981; French/German) . . . . . . Anna/Helen
- 0:04 - Topless in bed.
- 0:16 - Topless lying in bed when Sam Neill pulls the covers over her.
- ••• 0:47 - Right breast, then topless lying in bed with Neill.
- 1:08 - Right breast, while lying on the floor with Neill, then sitting up.
Quartet (1981; British/French) . . . . Marya Zelli
- •• 1:06 - Topless in bed with Alan Bates.
Next Year if All Goes Well (1983; French). . . Isabelle
- 0:27 - Brief right breast, lying in bed with Maxime.
One Deadly Summer (1984; French) . . . . .Eliane
- •• 0:21 - Brief topless changing in the window for Florimond.
- ••• 0:32 - Nude, walking in and out of the barn.
- 0:36 - Brief left breast lying in bed when Florimond gets up.
- 0:40 - Buns and topless taking a bath.
- 1:41 - Part of right breast, getting felt up by an old guy, then right breast then brief topless.
- •• 1:47 - Topless in bedroom with Florimond.
  1:49 - In white bra and panties talking with Florimond.
Subway (1985; French) . . . . .Helena
Ishtar (1987) . . . . Shirra Assel
- 0:27 - Very brief left breast flashing herself to Dustin Hoffman at the airport while wearing sunglasses.
Camille Claudel (1989; French) . . . . Camille Claudel

Agbayani, Tetchie

Films:
The Emerald Forest (1985). . . . . Caya
- 1:48 - Topless in the river when Kachiri is match making all the couples together.
Gymkata (1985). . . . . .Princess Rubali
Rikky & Pete (1988; Australian). . . . . Flossie
- 0:58 - Brief upper half of left breast in bed with Pete when Rikky accidentally sees them in bed.
- ••• 1:30 - Topless in black panties dancing outside the jail while Pete watches from inside.
Mission Manila (1989) . . . . .Maria

Agutter, Jenny

Films:
East of Sudan (1964; British) . . . . Asua
A Man Could Get Killed (1966) . . . . Linda Frazier
Gates to Paradise (1968; British/German). . . . . . Maud
I Started Counting (1970; British). . . . . .Wynne
The Railway Children (1971; British). . . . . .Bobbie

Walkabout (1971; Australian/U.S.) . . . . Girl
(Hard to find this video tape.)
Nude several times.

Logan's Run (1976) . . . . .Jessica
• 1:05 - Very brief topless and buns changing into fur
coat in ice cave with Michael York.

The Eagle Has Landed (1977; British) . . . . . . Molly Prior

Equus (1977) . . . . Jill Mason
••• 2:00 - Nude in loft above the horses in orange light,
then making love with Alan.

China 9, Liberty 37 (1978; Italian). . . . . . . Catherine
(Hard to find this video tape.)

Dominique is Dead (1978; British). . . . . . . Miss Ballard

Survivor (1980; Australian) . . . . .Hobbs

Sweet William (1980; British). . . . . Ann
0:27 - Buns, standing on balcony with Sam Water-
ston.
•• 0:28 - Topless sitting on edge of the bed while talking with Waterston.
• 0:44 - Brief left breast when Waterston takes her
blouse off in the living room.

An American Werewolf in London (1981)
. . . . Alex Price
• 0:41 - Brief right breast in bed with David Naughton.
Dark, hard to see.

Riddle of the Sands (1984; British). . . . . . Clara Dollman

Secret Places (1984; British) . . . . .Miss Lowrie

Dark Tower (1987) . . . . Carolyn Page
0:05 - In black teddy in her office while a window
washer watches from outside.

Child's Play 2 (1990) . . . . Joanne Simpson

Made for TV Movies:

Silas Marner (1985; British) . . . . Nancy Lammeter

Albert, Laura

Films:

Angel III: The Final Chapter (1988) . . . Nude Dancer
• 0:00 - Brief topless dancing in a casino. Wearing red
G-string.
• 0:01 - Brief topless dancing in background.
• 0:06 - Side view of left breast and buns yelling at
Molly for taking her picture.

Bloodstone (1988) . . . . Kim Chi
• 0:05 - Very brief side view of left breast turning
around in pool to look at a guy.

Glitch (1988) . . . . Topless
• 0:35 - Brief topless auditioning for two guys by tak-
ing off her top.

The Jigsaw Murders (1988). . . . . .Blonde Stripper
••• 0:19 - Topless and buns in black G-string, stripping
during bachelor party in front of a group of policemen.

Party Plane (1988) . . . uncredited Auditioning Woman
•• 0:30 - Topless, taking off blue dress during audition.
She's wearing a white ribbon in her ponytail.

The Unnameable (1988) . . . . .Wendy Barnes
•• 0:46 - Left breast while lying on floor kissing John,
then brief buns when he pulls her panties down.

Blood Games (1989) . . . . Babe
0:03 - Pitching in baseball game in braless T-shirt.
0:16 - In white bra and black shorts in locker room.

Dr. Alien (1989) . . . . .Rocker Chick #3
a.k.a. I Was a Teenage Sex Mutant
••• 0:21 - Topless in black outfit during dream sequence
with two other rocker chicks.

Dr. Caligari (1989). . . . . Mrs. Van Houten
••• 0:05 - Topless taking off yellow towel, then sitting in
bathtub.
•• 0:07 - Lying down, making love with guy wearing a
mask.
••• 0:10 - Topless taking orange bra off, then lying back
and playing with herself.
•• 0:11 - More topless, lying on the floor.
•• 0:12 - More topless, lying on the floor again.
• 0:30 - Brief left breast with big tongue.

Roadhouse (1989) . . . . Strip Joint Girl
•• 0:45 - Topless and buns dancing on stage, wearing a
hat.

Made for Cable TV:

Tales From the Crypt: The Man Who was Death
(1989; HBO). .Go-Go Dancer
• 0:20 - Brief topless a couple of times dancing in a
cage in a nightclub.

Dream On: The First Episode (1990; HBO)
. . . . Whipped Cream Girl
0:22 - Covered with whipped cream in bed with
Martin.

Dream On: Pants on Fire (1991; HBO) . . . . . . .Tanya
•• 0:16 - Topless sitting up on the couch, talking to
Martin.

Magazines:

Playboy (Nov 1989) . . . . Sex in Cinema 1989
•• 136: Right breast in still from *Roadhouse*.

Alexander, Jane

Films:

A Gunfight (1971) . . . . .Nora Tenneray

The New Centurions (1972). . . . . .Dorothy

The Betsy (1978) . . . . Alicia Hardeman

Kramer vs. Kramer (1979) . . . . Margaret Phelps

Brubaker (1980). . . . . .Lillian

Night Crossing (1981) . . . . Doris Strelzyks

Testament (1983). . . . . .Carol Wetherly

City Heat (1984) . . . . Addy

Sweet Country (1985). Anna
• 1:39 - Brief side view of left breast after getting out
of bed.

Square Dance (1987) . . . . Juanelle
a.k.a. Home is Where the Heart Is

Made for TV Movies:

Playing for Time (1980) . . . . Alma Rose

Alexander, Nina

See: Parton, Julie.

Alhanti, Iris

Films:
Kramer vs. Kramer (1979) . . . .
Partners (1982) . . . . Jogger
•• 0:21 - Topless in the shower when Ryan O'Neil opens
the shower curtain.

Aliff, Lisa

Films:
Dragnet (1987) . . . . April
Remote Control (1987) . . . . Heroine
Playroom (1989) . . . . Jenny
•• 0:23 - Topless making love on top of Christopher.
Damned River (1990) . . . . .Anne
0:28 - Silhouette topless undressing in tent.
• 0:32 - Very, very brief top of right breast in open
blouse, then half of right breast in wet blouse washing her hair.
• 0:50 - Very brief topless struggling with Ray when he
rips her top open. Don't see her face.

Alise, Esther

a.k.a. Esther Elise.
Films:
Deathrow Game Show (1988) . . . . Groupie
•• 0:08 - Topless in bed with Chuck.
Hollywood Chainsaw Hookers (1988) . . . . .Lisa
••• 0:25 - Topless playing with a baseball bat while a
John photographs her.
Vampire at Midnight (1988) . . . . .Lucia Giannini
••• 1:01 - In black lingerie, then topless and buns while
taking off clothes to wish Roger a happy birthday.

Allen, Ginger Lynn

Former adult film actress.
Films:
Vice Academy (1988) . . . . .Holly
1:20 - Buns, in white lingerie outfit when graduation
robe gets torn off.
Wild Man (1988) . . . . .Dawn Hall
•• 0:24 - Topless taking off her dress in front to Eric,
then making love with him.
Cleo/Leo (1989) . . . . Karen
••• 0:39 - Full frontal nudity getting out of the shower,
getting dried with a towel by Jane Hamilton, then in
nightgown.
••• 0:57 - Full frontal nudity getting out of the shower
and dried off again.
Dr. Alien (1989) . . . . Rocker Chick #1
a.k.a. I Was a Teenage Sex Mutant
••• 0:21 - Topless in red panties during dream sequence
with two other rocker chicks.
Edgar Allan Poe's "Buried Alive" (1989) . . . . Debbie

Hollywood Boulevard II (1989) . . . . Candy Chandler
•• 0:33 - Topless in screening room with Woody, the
writer.
Vice Academy, Part 2 (1990) . . . . Holly
• 0:44 - Buns in black bra, panties, garter belt and
stockings.
•• 1:04 - Buns in G-string, then topless dancing with
Linnea Quigley on stage at club.
Young Guns II (1990) . . . . Dove
Magazines:
Playboy (Jul 1989) . . . . B-Movie Bimbos
••• 137: Full frontal nudity, standing in a car.

Allen, India

Video Tapes:
Playboy Video Centerfold: India Allen
. . . . Playmate of the Year
Playmates of the Year—The '80's . . . . Playmate
Playboy Video Calendar 1989 (1988) . . . . . . January
••• 0:01 - Nude.
Playmates at Play (1990) . . . . Hoops, Hardbodies
Magazines:
Playboy (Dec 1987) . . . . Playmate

Allen, Karen

Films:
National Lampoon's Animal House (1978)
. . . . Katherine "Katy" Fuller
1:21 - Brief buns putting on shirt when Boone visits
her at her house.
Manhattan (1979; B&W) . . . . TV Actor
The Wanderers (1979) . . . . Nina
Cruising (1980) . . . . Nancy
A Small Circle of Friends (1980) . . . . Jessica
• 0:47 - Brief topless in bathroom with Brad Davis.
Don't see her face.
• 0:48 - Very brief topless, pushing Davis off her. Then
very, very brief half of left breast turning around to
walk to the mirror.
Raiders of the Lost Ark (1981) . . . . . Marion Ravenwood
Shoot the Moon (1982) . . . . Sandy
Split Image (1982) . . . . .Rebecca
Starman (1984) . . . . Jenny Hayden
Until September (1984) . . . . Mo Alexander
•• 0:41 - Topless in bed making love with Thierry Lhermitte.
•• 1:13 - Topless and buns walking from bed to Lhermitte.
• 1:25 - Brief topless jumping out of bathtub.
Backfire (1987) . . . . Mara
• 0:48 - Lots of buns, then brief topless with Keith Carradine in the bedroom.
• 1:00 - Brief topless in the shower.
The Glass Menagerie (1987) . . . . Laura
Scrooged (1988) . . . . .Claire Phillips

Made for Cable Movies:
Secret Weapon (1990) . . . . Ruth
   1:12 - In black slip in room with Griffin Dunne.
   1:27 - In black slip again in another room.
   1:28 - Putting on white slip in bathroom.
Made for TV Movies:
Challenger (1990). . . . . Christa McAuliffe
TV:
East of Eden (1981). . . . . Abra

Allen, Nancy

Films:
The Last Detail (1973). . . . . .Nancy
Forced Entry (1975) . . . . .Hitchhiker
  • 0:44 - Topless and buns tied up by Carl on the beach.
Carrie (1976). . . . . .Chris Hargenson
  •• 0:01 - Nude, in slow motion in girls' locker room behind Amy Irving.
I Wanna Hold Your Hand (1978) . . . . Pam
1941 (1979) . . . . Donna
   0:17 - Wearing red bra in cockpit of airplane with Tim Matheson.
   1:12 - In red bra again with Matheson, but this time the airplane is in the air.
Dressed to Kill (1980) . . . . Liz Blake
   1:21 - In black bra, panties and stockings in Michael Caine's office.
  • 1:36 - Topless (from above), buns and brief right breast in shower.
Home Movies (1980) . . . . .Kristina
Blow Out (1981). . . . . Sally
  • 0:58 - Brief upper half of right breast with the sheet pulled up in B&W photograph that John Travolta examines.
Strange Invaders (1983) . . . . Betty Walker
The Buddy System (1984). . . . . Carrie
Not for Publication (1984) . . . . Lois Thorndyke
The Philadelphia Experiment (1984) . . . . Allison
Robocop (1987) . . . . .Ann Lewis
Sweet Revenge (1987) . . . . Jillian Grey
Poltergeist III (1988) . . . . Patricia Gardner
Limit Up (1989) . . . . Casey Falls
Robocop 2 (1990). . . . . .Anne Lewis
Made for Cable Movies:
Memories of Murder (1990; Lifetime) . . . .

Alley, Kirstie

Wife of actor Parker "The Big One" Stevenson.
Films:
Star Trek II: The Wrath of Kahn (1982) . . . . . . Lt. Saavik
Blind Date (1984). . . . . Claire Parker
(Not the same 1987 *Blind Date* with Bruce Willis.)
  • 0:12 - Brief topless making love in bed with Joseph Bottoms. Dark, hard to see anything.
Runaway (1984) . . . . Jackie
   1:04 - Briefly in white bra getting scanned at the police station for bugging devices.
Summer School (1987). . . . . Robin Bishop

Shoot to Kill (1988) . . . . Sarah
Look Who's Talking (1989). . . . . .Molie
Loverboy (1989) . . . . Joyce Palmer
Look Who's Talking Too (1990) . . . . Mollie
Madhouse (1990) . . . . .Jessie
   0:02 - In white slip in bedroom with John Laroquette.
   0:18 - Brief bra shots while doing a sexy strip tease for Laroquette.
   1:16 - In bra under blazer throwing everybody out of her house.
Sibling Rivalry (1990) . . . . Marjorie Turner
Made for Cable TV:
The Hitchhiker: Out of the Night . . . . Angelica
Miniseries:
North and South (1985) . . . . Virgilia Hazard
North and South, Book II (1986) . . . . Virgilia Hazard
Made for TV Movies:
Stark: Mirror Images (1986) . . . . Maggie
TV:
Masquerade (1983-84) . . . . Casey Collins
Cheers (1987-) . . . . .Rebecca Howe

Almgren, Susan

Films:
Separate Vacations (1985). . . . . Helene Gilbert
  •• 1:05 - Topless and buns in bed with David Naughton.
Shades of Love: Lilac Dream (1987) . . . .
Made for Cable Movies:
Deadly Surveillance (1991; Showtime) . . . . Rachel
   0:00 - Very, very brief right breast getting dressed. Don't see her face. B&W.
  • 0:12 - Topless in the shower. Long shot.
  •• 0:34 - Topless in the shower with Nickels.
  ••• 0:54 - Buns, in black panties and bra, then topless in room with Michael Ironside.

Alonso, Maria Conchita

Miss Teen World 1975.
Miss Venezuela 1981.
Films:
Fear City (1984). Silver Chavez
Moscow on the Hudson (1984) . . . . .Lucia Lombardo
  •• 1:17 - Topless in bathtub with Robin Williams.
Touch and Go (1984). . . . . .Denise
A Fine Mess (1986) . . . . Claudia Pazzo
Extreme Prejudice (1987) . . . . Sarita Cisneros
  •• 0:27 - Brief topless in the shower while Nick Nolte is in the bathroom talking to her.
The Running Man (1987). . . . . Amber Mendez
Colors (1988) . . . . Louisa Gomez
  ••• 0:48 - Topless making love in bed with Sean Penn.
Con el Corazón en la Mano (1988; Mexican) . . . . . .
  • 0:38 - Very, very brief right breast, turning over in bed with her husband.
  • 0:39 - Topless several times, taking a bath.
  •• 1:15 - Topless ripping off her dress. Long shot, side view, standing while kissing a guy.

Vampire's Kiss (1989) . . . . Alva
   0:47 - In white bra, ironing her clothes in her living room.
   0:59 - In white bra getting attacked by Nicholas Cage.
Predator 2 (1990) . . . . Leona
Made for Cable Movies:
Blood Ties (1986; Italian; Showtime). . . . . . . Caterina
  •• 0:35 - Brief topless when Vincent Spano rips her dress off.

Alphen, Corinne
a.k.a. Corinne Wahl.
Films:
Hot T-shirts (1980) . . . . Judy
   0:55 - In braless T-shirt as a car hop.
  • 1:10 - In yellow outfit dancing in wet T-shirt contest. Brief topless flashing her breasts at the crowd.
Brainwaves (1983) . . . . Lelia
C.O.D. (1983). . . . . Cheryl Westwood
  • 0:21 - Brief topless changing clothes in dressing room while talking to Zacks.
  • 1:25 - Brief topless taking off her blouse in dressing room scene.
   1:26 - In green bra, talking to Albert.
   1:28 - In green bra during fashion show.
New York Nights (1983) . . . . The Debutante
  •• 0:10 - Topless, making love in the back seat of a limousine with the rock star.
  ••• 1:38 - Topless dancing in the bedroom while the Financier watches from the bed.
Spring Break (1983; Canadian) . . . . Joan
   0:32 - Taking a shower in a two piece bathing suit in an outdoor shower at the beach.
Equalizer 2000 (1986). . . . . Karen
Amazon Women on the Moon (1987) . . . . Shari
  ••• 1:13 - In black bra, then topless on TV while Ray watches.
Screwball Hotel (1988) . . . . Cherry Amour
   0:46 - Buns, in black outfit on bed with Norman.
Magazines:
Penthouse (Jun 1978) . . . . Pet
  99-111:
Penthouse (Aug 1981) . . . . Pet
  83-101:
Penthouse (Nov 1982) . . . . Pet of the Year
  123-139:

Alt, Carol
Model.
Films:
Portfolio (1983) . . . . herself
  • 0:28 - Brief right breast, while adjusting black, see-through blouse.
   0:31 - Brief side view of a little bit of right breast while changing clothes backstage at a fashion show.

Bye Bye Baby (1989) . . . . Sandra
   0:09 - Part of right breast, while in the shower.
   0:22 - Wearing a white bra, while taking off her blouse in the doctor's office.

Always, Julie
Films:
Hardbodies (1984) . . . . Photo Session Hardbody
  •• 0:40 - Topless with other girls posing topless getting pictures taken by Rounder. She's wearing blue dress with a white belt.
The Rosebud Beach Hotel (1985) . . . . Bellhop
  •• 0:22 - Topless, in open blouse, undressing with two other bellhops. She's the blonde on the left.
  •• 0:44 - Topless, playing spin the grenade, with two guys and the two other bellhops. She's on the left.

Amis, Suzy
Films:
Fandango (1985) . . . . The Girl
The Big Town (1987) . . . . Aggie Donaldson
Plain Clothes (1988). . . . . Robin Torrence
Rocket Gibraltar (1988) .Aggie
Where the Heart Is (1990) . . . . Chloe McBain
  • 0:08 - Topless during her art film. Artfully covered with paint, with a bird. Topless again in the third segment.
  • 0:09 - Topless during the film again. Hard to see because of the paint. Last segment while she narrates.

Amore, Gianna
Films:
Screwball Hotel (1988). . . . . Mary Beth
Video Tapes:
Playboy's Wet and Wild (1989). . . . .
Playmates at Play (1990)
  . . . . Free Wheeling, Gotta Dance
Magazines:
Playboy (Aug 1989) . . . . Playmate

Anderson, Erika
Films:
The Nightmare on Elm Street 5: The Dream Child
  (1989) . . . . .Greta
Zandalee (1991) . . . . Zandalee Martin
  ••• 0:02 - Nude, taking off robe and dancing around the room.
  ••• 0:21 - Nude, undressing, then in bed with Judge Reinhold. Long scene.
  •• 0:30 - Right breast, then topless making love in bed with Nicholas Cage.
  •• 0:32 - Topless as Cage paints on her with his finger.
  ••• 0:45 - Left breast, then topless and lower frontal nudity on floor with Cage.
  •• 0:47 - Nude, getting massaged by Cage with an oil and cocaine mixture.

- 0:48 - Brief topless getting into bed with Reinhold. Slightly out of focus.
- •• 1:09 - Topless opening her dress for Reinhold while lying on a river bank, then making love with him at night in bed.

TV:

Twin Peaks . . . .

Magazines:

Playboy (Nov 1991) . . . . Sex in Cinema 1991
- 144: Full frontal nudity in mirror. From *Zandalee*.

Anderson, Melody

Films:

Flash Gordon (1980) . . . . Dale Arden
Dead and Buried (1981) . . . . Janet
The Boy in Blue (1986; Canadian) . . . . Dulcie
  0:07 - Brief cleavage making love with Nicholas Cage, then very brief top half of right breast when a policeman scares her.
Firewalker (1986) . . . . Patricia Goodwyn
Final Notice (1989) .Kate Davis

Made for Cable Movies:

Hitler's Daughter (1990) . . . .

Made for TV Movies:

Policewoman Centerfold (1983) . . . .
Ladies of the Night (1986) . . . . .Claudia

TV:

Manimal (1983) . . . . Brooke McKenzie

Anderson, Pamela

Video Tapes:

Playboy Video Calendar 1991 (1990) . . . . .July
  ••• 0:26 - Nude.
Playboy's Sexy Lingerie II (1990) . . . .

Magazines:

Playboy (Feb 1990) . . . . Playmate
  ••• 102-113: Nude.

Andersson, Bibi

Films:

The Seventh Seal (1956; Swedish/B&W) . . . . .Mia
Brink of Life (1957; Swedish/B&W) . . . . Hjordis
Wild Strawberries (1957; Swedish/B&W) . . . . Sara
The Magician (1959; B&W) . . . . Sara
Duel at Diablo (1966) . . . . Ellen Grange
Persona (1966; Swedish/B&W) . . . . .Nurse Alma
The Touch (1971; U.S./Swedish) . . . . . . Karen Vergerus
- 0:31 - Topless in bed with Elliott Gould.
- ••• 0:56 - Topless kissing Gould.
  1:13 - Very, very brief right breast washing Gould's hair in the sink.
Scenes from a Marriage (1973; Swedish). . . . . . Katarina
I Never Promised You a Rose Garden (1977) . . . Dr. Fried
Quintet (1979) . . . . Ambrosia

Twice a Woman (1979). . . . . .Laura
- 0:05 - Topless taking off her bra and putting a blouse on.
- 0:06 - Brief side view of left breast, getting into bed, brief left breast lying back in bed.
Exposed (1983) . . . . Margaret
Babette's Feast (1987; Danish)
. . . . Swedish Court Lady-in-Waiting

Made for TV Movies:

Wallenberg: A Hero's Story (1985) . . . . Maj

Andreeff, Starr

Films:

Dance of the Damned (1988) . . . . Jodi
- •• 0:03 - Topless dancing in black bikini bottoms on stage in a club.
  1:06 - In black bra, panties, garter belt and stockings dancing in bar just for the vampire.
- •• 1:08 - Topless in the bar with the vampire.
Ghoulies II (1988) . . . . Alice
Out of the Dark (1988) . . . . Camille
The Terror Within (1988) . . . . Sue
Streets (1989) . . . . Policewoman on Horse

Andress, Ursula

Films:

Dr. No (1962; British). Honey
  1:19 - Almost very, very brief topless after going through shower to remove any radioactivity.
Four for Texas (1963) . . . . Maxine Richter
Fun in Acapulco (1963) . . . . Margarita Douphine
Nightmare in the Sun (1964) . . . . .Marsha Wilson
What's New, Pussycat? (1965; U.S./French) . . . . Rita
The Blue Max (1966) . . . . .Countess Kasti
Casino Royale (1967; British) . . . . .Vesper Lynd
Anyone Can Play (1968; Italian) . . . . .Norma
The Southern Star (1969; French/British) . . Erica Kramer
Perfect Friday (1970; British) . . . . . .Lady Britt Dorsett
  Nude a lot.
Red Sun (1972; French/Italian/Spanish) . . . . Cristina
  1:12 - Almost side view of right breast, then left breast changing tops in room while Charles Bronson watches.
Loaded Guns (1975) . . . . .Laura
  0:32 - Buns, lying in bed with a guy.
- ••• 0:33 - Topless and buns getting out of bed. Full frontal nudity in elevator.
- •• 0:40 - Nude getting out of bed and putting dress on.
- ••• 0:48 - Nude getting into bathtub, topless in tub, nude getting out and drying herself off.
  1:00 - Buns while getting undressed and hopping in to bed.
- 1:02 - Brief side view of right breast while getting dressed.
Stateline Motel (1975; Italian) . . . . . .Michelle Nolton
  a.k.a. Last Chance for a Born Loser
- ••• 0:34 - Left breast, then topless on bed with Oleg.

The Loves and Times of Scaramouche (1976; Italian)
. . . . Josephine
The Sensuous Nurse (1979). . . . . .Anna
- •• 0:16 - Topless and buns in bed after making love with Benito.
- •• 0:22 - Nude swimming in pool while Adonais watches.
- ••• 0:50 - Nude slowly stripping and getting in bed with Adonais.
- ••• 1:10 - Nude getting into bed.
Slave of the Cannibal God (1979; Italian) . . . .
- •• 0:33 - Topless taking off shirt and putting on a T-shirt.
- ••• 1:07 - Nude getting tied to a pole by the Cannibal People and covered with red paint.
  1:20 - Brief peek at buns under her skirt when running away from the Cannibal People.
Tigers in Lipstick (1979)
. . . . The Stroller and The Widow
  0:02 - In black bra, panties and garter belt and stockings opening her fur coat to cause an accident.
  0:48 - In slip posing for photographer.
- • 0:50 - Very brief topless when top of slip accidentally falls down.
- • 0:51 - More topless with the photographer.
Clash of the Titans (1981). . . . . .Aphrodite
Famous T & A (1982) . . . . herself
(No longer available for purchase, check your video store for rental.)
- ••• 0:15 - Full frontal nudity scenes from *Slave of the Cannibal God*.
Made for TV Movies:
Man Against the Mob: The Chinatown Murders (1989)
. . . . Betty Starr
Magazines:
Playboy (Nov 1973) . . . . Encore
  102-109: Topless and buns.
Playboy (Apr 1976) . . . . .Incomparably Ursula
- ••• 91-95: Photos from the film *The Loves and Times of Scaramouche*. Full frontal nudity.
Playboy (Jan 1979) . . . . 25 Beautiful Years
- •• 158: Topless in a stream.
Playboy (Jan 1989) . . . . Women of the Sixties
- ••• 163: Topless running her fingers through her hair sitting by a pond.

Andrews, Julie

Films:
Americanization of Emily (1964) . . . . Emily
Mary Poppins (1964) . . . . Mary Poppins
(Academy Award for Best Actress.)
The Sound of Music (1965). . . . . Maria
Hawaii (1966). . . . . Jerusha Bromley
Thoroughly Modern Millie (1967). . . . . Millie Dillmount
Darling Lili (1970). . . . . Lili Smith
The Tamarind Seed (1974) . . . . Judith Farrow
10 (1979). . . . . Sam
Little Miss Marker (1980) . . . . Amanda

S.O.B. (1981) . . . . Sally Miles
- •• 1:19 - Topless pulling the top off her red dress during the filming of a movie.
Victor/Victoria (1982). . . . . Victor/Victoria
The Man Who Loved Women (1983) . . . . . . .Marianna
That's Life! (1986) . . . . Gillian Fairchild
Duet for One (1987) . . . . .Stephanie Anderson
- • 0:28 - Very brief left breast in gaping blouse in bathroom splashing water on her face because she feels sick, then wet T-shirt.
- ••• 1:06 - Topless stretching, lying in bed.
- • 1:07 - Very brief buns and very brief right breast, when she rolls off the bed onto the floor.
  1:30 - In wet white blouse from perspiring after taking an overdose of pills.
Made for TV Movies:
Our Sons (1991) .Audrey Grant
TV:
The Julie Andrews Hour (1972-73) . . . . hostess

Angel, Vanessa

Films:
Spies Like Us (1985). . . . . . .Russian Rocket Crewmember
  1:31 - In bra, putting on her snow outfit, coming out of tent after Dan Aykroyd.
Another Chance (1989) . . . . Jacky Johanssen
- • 0:26 - Sort of topless under water in spa. Hard to see because of the bubbles.
King of New York (1990) . . . . British Female

Ann-Margret

Films:
Pocketful of Miracles (1961). . . . . Louise
State Fair (1962) . . . . .Emily Porter
Bye Bye Birdie (1963). . . . . .Kim McAfee
The Pleasure Seekers (1964). . . . . Fran Hobson
Viva Las Vegas (1964). . . . . Rusty Martin
Bus Riley's Back in Town (1965) . . . . Laurel
The Cincinnati Kid (1965) . . . . Melba
Murderer's Row (1966) . . . . .Suzie Solaris
The Swinger (1966). . . . . .Kelly Olsson
Tiger and the Pussycat (1967; U.S./Italian) . . . . .Carolina
C. C. & Company (1970). . . . . .Ann
R.P.M. (1970) . . . . Rhoda
- •• 0:07 - Brief left breast and buns getting out of bed talking with Anthony Quinn.
  0:30 - In fishnet top.
Carnal Knowledge (1971) . . . . .Bobbie
- •• 0:48 - Topless and buns making love in bed with Jack Nicholson, then getting out of bed and into shower with Jack.
- • 1:07 - Brief side view of left breast putting a bra on in the bedroom.
The Outside Man (1973; U.S./French) . . . . Nancy
The Train Robbers (1973). . . . . Mrs. Lowe
Tommy (1975; British) . . . . Nora Walker

The Twist (1976) . . . . Charlie Minerva
- 0:24 - Left breast when Claire daydreams someone is sticking a pin into Ann-Margret's breast. A little bloody. Body double.
- 1:24 - Very, very brief left breast during Bruce Dern's daydream. Seen from above, body double again.

Joseph Andrews (1977; British/French) . . . . . Lady Boaby
The Last Remake of Beau Geste (1977)
. . . . Lady Flavia Geste
The Cheap Detective (1978) . . . . Jezebel Desire
Magic (1978) . . . . Peggy Ann Snow
••• 0:44 - Right breast, lying on her side in bed talking to Anthony Hopkins.
The Villain (1979) . . . . Charming Jones
Middle Age Crazy (1980; Canadian) . . . . Sue Ann
I Ought to be in Pictures (1982) . . . . Stephanie
Return of the Soldier (1983; British) . . . . Jenny
Twice in a Lifetime (1985) . . . . Audrey
52 Pick-Up (1986) . . . . Barbara Mitchell
A New Life (1988) . . . . Jackie
A Tiger's Tale (1988) . . . . Rose
- 0:45 - Side view of left breast in bra, then topless jumping up after fire ants start biting her. Brief buns running along a hill. Long shot, probably a body double.

Made for TV Movies:
Our Sons (1991) . . . . Luanne Barnes
Magazines:
Playboy (Feb 1981) . . . . The Year in Sex
•• 146: Left breast in still from *Magic*.

Annen, Glory

Films:
Felicity (1978; Australian) . . . . Felicity
•• 0:02 - Topless taking off leotard in girl's shower room, then nude taking a shower.
- 0:05 Buns, then left breast, then right breast undressing to go skinny dipping.
•• 0:10 - Topless and buns at night at the girl's dormitory.
•• 0:15 - Topless undressing in room with Christine.
- 0:16 - Left breast, while touching herself in bed.
••• 0:20 - Lots of lower frontal nudity trying on clothes, bras and panties in dressing room. Brief topless.
••• 0:25 - Buns and topless taking a bath. Full frontal nudity when Steve peeks in at her.
- 0:31 - Brief full frontal nudity losing her virginity on car with Andrew.
••• 0:38 - Full frontal nudity in bath with Mei Ling and two other girls. Long scene. Hot!
••• 0:58 - Full frontal nudity in bed with Miles.
••• 1:13 - Full frontal nudity with Mei Ling making love on bed. Long scene.
- 1:20 - Left breast, while making love standing up.
•• 1:21 - Topless and buns making love with Miles.
•• 1:27 - Nude making love again with Miles.
1:29 - Buns, in the water with Miles.

Spaced Out (1980; British) . . . . Cosia
••• 0:23 - Topless talking to the other two space women. Long scene.
- 0:31 - Very brief topless changing clothes while dancing.
•• 0:43 - Topless in bed with Willy.
••• 1:08 - Topless lying down.
The Lonely Lady (1983) . . . . Marion
- 0:07 - Brief left breast in back seat of car with Joe. Dark, hard to see.
Alien Prey (1984; British) . . . . Jessica
- 0:22 - Topless unbuttoning blouse to sunbathe.
•• 0:34 - Topless taking off top, getting into bed with Josephine, then making love with her.
0:36 - Buns, rolling on top of Josephine.
••• 0:38 - More topless when Josephine is playing with her.
0:39 - More buns in bed. Long shot.
- 0:46 - Left breast and buns standing up in bathtub.
•• 1:05 - Topless getting out of bed and putting a dress on.
•• 1:19 - Topless in bed with Anders. Brief buns when he rips her panties off.
Supergirl (1984; British) . . . . Midvale Protestor

Annis, Francesca

Films:
Macbeth (1972) . . . . Lady Macbeth
1:41 - Buns, walking around after the bad guys have attacked and looted the castle. Side view of left breast, hard to see because it's covered by her hair.
Dune (1984) . . . . Lady Jessica
Under the Cherry Moon (1986; B&W) . . Mrs. Wellington
Miniseries:
Masterpiece Theatre: Lilli (1979) . . . . Lilli Langtree
Made for TV Movies:
The Richest Man in the World: The Story of Aristot (1988) . . . . Jacqueline Kennedy Onassis
Magazines:
Playboy (Feb 1972) . . . . The Making of "Macbeth"
80:
Playboy (Nov 1972) . . . . Sex in Cinema 1972
- 167: Right breast, sticking out of hair. Photo from *MacBeth*.

Anspach, Susan

Films:
Five Easy Pieces (1970) . . . . Catherine Van Oost
The Landlord (1970) . . . . Susan
Play It Again Sam (1972) . . . . Nancy
Blume in Love (1973) . . . . Nina Blume
The Big Fix (1978) . . . . Lila
Running (1979) . . . . Janet Andropolis
Gas (1981; Canadian) . . . . Jane Beardsley
Montenegro (1981; British/Swedish) . . . Marilyn Jordan
•• 1:08 - Full frontal nudity taking a shower.
- 1:28 - Right breast making love with Montenegro.
Blood Red (1988) . . . . Widow

Into the Fire (1988) . . . . Rosalind Winfield
•• 0:22 - Left breast, under trench coat when she first comes into the house, briefly again in the kitchen.
•• 0:31 - Topless in bedroom standing up with Wade.
Back to Back (1990) . . . . Madeline Hix
Made for Cable Movies:
Gone Are the Days (1984; Disney) . . . .
Made for Cable TV:
The Hitchhiker: Dead Man's Curve . . . . .Claudia
(Available on *The Hitchhiker, Volume II*.)
0:14 - Buns (probably a body double) in a hotel room with a guy.
TV:
The Yellow Rose (1983) . . . . Grace McKenzie

Anthony, Lysette

Films:
Krull (1983). . . . . .Lyssa
Looking for Eileen (1988; Dutch)
. . . . Marjan/Eileen/Karnen
(Not available on video tape.)
Topless.
Without a Clue (1988) . . . . Fake Leslie
Switch (1991) . . . .
Made for Cable Movies:
A Ghost in Monte Carlo (1990). . . . .
Made for TV Movies:
Ivanhoe (1982) . . . . Lady Rowena
Jack the Ripper (1988). . . . . .Mary Jane Kelly
The Lady and the Highwayman (1989)
. . . . Lady Panthea Vyne
TV:
Dark Shadows (1991) . . . . .Angelique
Magazines:
Playboy (Dec 1988). Lysette
• 166-173: Topless B&W photos.

Antonelli, Laura

Films:
Dr. Goldfoot and the Girl Bombs (1966; Italian)
. . . . Rosanna
Man Called Sledge (1971; Italian). . . . . Ria
Docteur Popaul (1972; French) . . . . Martine
How Funny Can Sex Be? (1973)
. . . . Miscellaneous Personalities
• 0:01 - Brief topless taking off swimsuit.
• 0:04 - Brief topless in bathtub covered with bubbles.
0:13 - Lying in bed in sheer nightgown.
0:18 - Lying in bed again.
• 0:26 - Topless getting into bed.
• 0:36 - Topless making love in elevator behind frosted glass. Shot at fast speed.
• 1:08 - In sheer white nun's outfit during fantasy sequence. Brief topless and buns. Nice slow motion.
1:16 - In black nightie.
• 1:24 - In black bra and panties, then topless while changing clothes.

Malicious (1974; Italian). . . . . .Angela
• 1:14 - Topless after undressing while two boys watch from above.
•• 1:27 - Topless, undressing under flashlight. Hard to see because the light is moving around a lot.
• 1:29 - Topless and buns running around the house.
Till Marriage Do Us Part (1974; Italian). . . . . Eugenia
•• 0:58 - Topless in the barn lying on hay after guy takes off her clothes.
•• 1:02 - Full frontal nudity standing up in bathtub while maid washes her.
•• 1:07 - Right breast with chauffeur in barn.
•• 1:36 - Topless surrounded by feathers on the bed while priest is talking.
The Innocent (1976; Italian) . . . . Julianna
••• 0:41 - Topless in bed with her husband.
••• 0:53 - Full frontal nudity in bed when her husband lifts her dress up.
The Divine Nymph (1977; Italian)
. . . . Manoela Roderighi
•• 0:10 - Full frontal nudity reclining in chair.
• 0:18 - Right breast in open blouse sitting in bed. Pubic hair while getting up.
Wifemistress (1977; Italian) . . . . Antonia De Angelis
0:50 - In lacy nightgown in her bedroom.
1:22 - Brief upper half of left breast in bed with Clara and her husband.
1:25 - In sheer lacy nightgown leaning out the window.
1:29 - Almost right breast making love with a guy in bed.
Tigers in Lipstick (1979) . . . . The Pick Up
0:24 - In brown lingerie lying in bed, then getting dressed.
0:34 - In same lingerie, getting undressed, then in bed.
Secret Fantasy (1981) . . . . Costanza Vivaldi
(Topless a lot. Only the best are listed.)
••• 0:16 - In black bra in Doctor's office, then left breast, then topless getting examined.
•• 0:18 - In black bra and panties in another Doctor's office. Topless and buns.
•• 0:19 - Topless getting X-rayed. Brief topless lying down.
•• 0:32 - Topless and buns when Nicolo drugs her and takes Polaroid photos of her.
•• 0:49 - Topless and buns posing around the house for Nicolo while he takes Polaroid photos.
•• 0:53 - Topless and buns during Nicolo's dream.
••• 1:12 - Topless in Doctor's office.
•• 1:14 - Topless and buns in room with another guy.
•• 1:16 - Topless on train while workers "accidentally" see her.
•• 1:20 - Topless on bed after being carried from bathtub.
•• 1:25 - Topless dropping dress during opera.
•• 1:27 - More topless scenes from 0:49.

Passion of Love (1982) . . . . .Clara
a.k.a. Passion D'Amor
  0:05 - Brief side of right breast, undressing by the
  fire. Long shot.
La Venexiana (1986) . . . . Angela
Collector's Item (1988) . . . . Marie Colbert
  0:18 - In white lingerie with Tony Musante.
  • 0:20 - Lower frontal nudity, then right breast making
  love with Musante. Dark.
  0:37 - In black bra, garter belt and stockings in open
  robe undressing for Musante.
  0:41 - In the same lingerie again dropping robe and
  getting dressed.
Magazines:
Playboy (Nov 1979) . . . . Sex Stars of 1979
••• 250: Topless.
Playboy (Nov 1980) . . . . Sex in Cinema 1980
••• 179: Full frontal nudity.

Anulka

See: Dziubinska, Anulka.

Apollonia

Real name is Patty Kotero.
Singer.
Films:
Amor Ciego (1980; Mexican) . . . . .Patty
  • 0:32 - Topless getting out of hammock.
  ••• 0:52 - Right breast, standing up, then topless kissing
  Daniel. More topless in bed.
  ••• 0:59 - Buns, making love in bed, then topless afterwards.
  •• 1:11 - Topless, taking off her towel and putting
  Daniel's hand on her left breast.
  •• 1:15 - Topless, turning over, then lying in bed.
Heartbreaker (1983) . . . . Rose
Purple Rain (1984) . . . . Apollonia
  •• 0:20 - Brief topless taking off jacket before jumping
  into lake.
  0:41 - In lingerie making love with Prince.
  1:06 - In black lingerie and stockings singing on
  stage.
Back to Back (1990) . . . . .Jesse Duro
Black Magic Woman (1990) . . . . Cassandra Perry
  0:18 - Brief side of left breast with Mark Hamill. Don't
  see her face.
  0:25 - Very brief upper half of left breast, while in
  shower with Hamill.
TV:
Falcon Crest (1985-86) . . . . Apollonia
Magazines:
Playboy (Jan 1985) . . . . The Girls of Rock 'n' Roll
  98: In leather bikini, rated PG.

Applegate, Christina

Films:
Streets (1989) . . . . Dawn
  1:09 - Very, very brief almost side view of left breast
  kissing her boyfriend. His hand is over her breast. I
  don't think this is really a nude scene, but I'm including it because some people might consider it and
  send this in.
Don't Tell Mom the Babysitter's Dead (1991) . . . .
TV:
Married ...with Children . . . . Kelly Bundy

Applegate, Colleen

a.k.a. Adult film actress Shauna Grant.
Films:
Penthouse Love Stories (1986)
. . . . Service Station Woman
••• 0:10 - Nude, making love in a bedroom. Long scene.

Archer, Anne

Films:
The All-American Boy (1973) . . . . .Drenna Valentine
Lifeguard (1975) . . . . Cathy
  • 1:04 - Very brief nipple while kissing Sam Elliott.
  Need to crank the brightness on your TV to the max-
  imum. It appears in the lower right corner of the
  screen as the camera pans from right to left.
Paradise Alley (1978) .Annie
Good Guys Wear Black (1979) . . . . Margaret
Hero at Large (1980) . . . . .J. Marsh
Raise the Titanic (1980; British) . . . . Dana Archibald
The Naked Face (1984) . . . . Ann Blake
The Check is in the Mail (1986) . . . . Peggy Jackson
Fatal Attraction (1987) . . . . Ellen Gallagher
  0:51 - In white bra, sitting in front of mirror, getting
  ready for a party.
Love at Large (1990) . . . . .Miss Dolan
Narrow Margin (1990) . . . . Hunnicut

Ariane

Model.
Full name is Ariane Koizumi.
Films:
The Year of the Dragon (1985) . . . . Tracy Tzu
  • 0:59 - Very brief topless when Mickey Rourke rips her
  blouse off in her apartment.
  •• 1:14 - Nude, taking a shower in her apartment.
  •• 1:18 - Topless straddling Rourke, while making love
  on the bed.
King of New York (1990) . . . . Dinner Guest
Made for Cable Movies:
Women & Men 2: Three Short Stories (1991; HBO)
. . . . Alice

Armstrong, Bess

Films:
Four Seasons (1981) . . . . .Ginny Newley
    0:26 - In two piece swimsuit on boat putting lotion
    on herself.
    • 0:38 - Brief buns twice skinny dipping in the water
    with Nick.
    0:40 - In one piece swimsuit.
Jekyll & Hyde...Together Again (1982) . . . . .Mary
High Road to China (1983) . . . . Eve
Jaws 3 (1983) . . . . Kathryn Morgan
The House of God (1984) . . . . .Dr. Worthington
  (Not available on video tape.)
  Topless.
Nothing in Common (1986) . . . . Donna Mildred Martin
Second Sight (1989) . . . . Sister Elizabeth
Made for TV Movies:
The Lakeside Killer (1979) . . . .
TV:
On Our Own (1977-78) . . . . Julia Peters
All Is Forgiven (1986) . . . . Paula Russell
Married People (1990-91) . . . . .Elizabeth Meyers

Armstrong, Rebekka

Films:
Hider in the House (1989). . . . . . . .Attractive Woman
    • 0:47 - Brief topless in bed with Mimi Roger's hus-
    band when she surprises them.
Immortalizer (1990) . . . . June
    • 0:16 - Topless getting blouse taken off by nurse.
    ••• 0:29 - Topless when a worker fondles her while she's
    asleep.
Instant Karma (1990) . . . . Jamie
Video Tapes:
Playboy Video Centerfold: Rebekka Armstrong .
  Playmate
Playboy Video Magazine, Volume 10 . . . . Playmate
Playboy Video Calendar 1987 (1986) . . . . Playmate
Playboy's Sexy Lingerie (1988). . . . .
Playboy's Wet and Wild (1989) . . . .
Playboy Video Centerfold: Kerri Kendall (1990)
  . . . . Playmate
    ••• 0:33 - Nude.
Playmates at Play (1990) . . . . .Gotta Dance
Magazines:
Playboy (Sep 1986) . . . . Playmate

Arnett, Sherry

Video Tapes:
Playboy Video Centerfold: Sherry Arnett
  . . . . Playmate
Playboy Video Calendar 1987 (1986) . . . . Playmate
Playboy Video Calendar 1988 (1987) . . . . Playmate
Magazines:
Playboy (Jan 1986) . . . . Playmate

Aronson, Judie

Films:
Friday the 13th, Part IV—The Final Chapter
  (1984) . . . . Samantha
    • 0:26 - Brief topless and very brief buns taking clothes
    off to go skinny dipping.
    • 0:29 - Brief topless under water pretending to be
    dead.
    •• 0:39 - Topless and brief buns taking off her T-shirt to
    go skinny dipping at night.
American Ninja (1985). . . . . Patricia
Weird Science (1985) . . . . .Hilly
After Midnight (1989) . . . . Jennifer
Cool Blue (1990) . . . . Cathy
    •• 1:03 - Topless in bed on top of Woody Harrelson.
The Sleeping Car (1990) . . . . Kim
    •• 0:42 - Brief topless on top of David Naughton mak-
    ing love. Brief topless three times after he halluci-
    nates.

Arquette, Rosanna

Sister of actress Patricia Arquette.
Films:
Gorp (1980). . . . . .Judy
S.O.B. (1981) . . . . Babs
    • 0:21 - Brief topless taking off white T-shirt on the
    deck of the house. Long shot, hard to see.
The Executioner's Song (1982) . . . . Nicole Baker
  (European Version.)
    ••• 0:30 - Brief topless in bed, then getting out of bed.
    Buns, walking to kitchen.
    ••• 0:41 - Topless in bed with Tommy Lee Jones.
    ••• 0:48 - Topless on top of Jones making love.
    •• 1:36 - Right breast and buns, standing up getting
    strip searched before visiting Jones in prison.
Off the Wall (1982) . . . . .Pam
Baby, It's You (1983) . . . . Jill
    •• 1:17 - Left breast, making love in bed with Vincent
    Spano.
The Aviator (1984). . . . . .Tilly Hansen
After Hours (1985) . . . . Marcy
    0:48 - In bed, dead, in panties. Arm covers breasts.
Desperately Seeking Susan (1985) . . . .Roberta Glass
    • 0:46 - Topless getting dressed when Aidan Quinn
    sees her through the fish tank. Long shot, hard to
    see.
Silverado (1985). . . . . Hannah
8 Million Ways to Die (1986) . . . . Sarah
    1:00 - In a bra in Jeff Bridges' apartment.
Nobody's Fool (1986) . . . . Cassie
Amazon Women on the Moon (1987) . . . . .Karen
The Big Blue (1988) . . . . .Johana
    1:00 - Brief right breast in bra in water when Jacques
    helps her out of the dolphin tank and her sweater
    gets pulled up.

Black Rainbow (1989; British) . . . . Martha Travis
   0:48 - In black bra, panties, garter belt and stockings
   in while talking to Tom Hulce.
  ••• 0:50 - Topless in bed with Hulce, then walking to
   bathroom.
New York Stories (1989) . . . . Paulette
...Almost (1990; Australian) . . . . Wendy
Flight of the Intruder (1991) . . . . Callie
Made for Cable Movies:
Sweet Revenge (1990) . . . . Kate
Miniseries:
Son of Morning Star (1991) . . . . Libbie Custer
Magazines:
Playboy (Sep 1990) . . . . Rosanna
  ••• 126-137: B&W and color photos nude in the surf.
   Some are out of focus.

Arth, Emily
Video Tapes:
Playboy Video Calendar 1990 (1989) . . . . May
  ••• 0:23 - Nude.
Magazines:
Playboy (Jun 1988) . . . . Playmate

Ashley, Elizabeth
Films:
The Carpetbaggers (1964) . . . . Monica Winthrop
The Marriage of a Young Stockbroker (1971) . . . . . Nan
Paperback Hero (1973; Canadian). . . . . Loretta
  ••• 0:37 - Nude in shower with Keir Dullea. Long scene.
  ••• 0:39 - Topless, straddling Dullea in the shower.
Rancho Deluxe (1975) . . . . Cora Brown
The Great Scout and Cathouse Thursday (1976)
. . . . Nancy Sue
Coma (1978) . . . . Mrs. Emerson
Paternity (1981) . . . . Sophia Thatcher
Split Image (1982) . . . . Diana
Dragnet (1987). . . . Police Commissioner Jane Kilpatrick
Vampire's Kiss (1989) . . . . Dr. Glaser
TV:
Evening Shade . . . .

Ashley, Jennifer
Films:
Your Three Minutes Are Up (1973) . . . . . Teenage Driver
The Centerfold Girls (1974) . . . . Charly
  • 0:34 - Topless taking off blouse while changing
   clothes.
  •• 0:49 - Topless and buns posing for photographer
   outside with Glory.
The Pom Pom Girls (1976) . . . . Laurie
Tintorera (1977) . . . .
Horror Planet (1980; British) . . . . Holly
  a.k.a. Inseminoid
Partners (1982) . . . . Secretary
Chained Heat (1983; U.S./German) . . . . Grinder
The Man Who Loved Women (1983) . . . David's Mother

Magazines:
Playboy (Nov 1978) . . . . Sex in Cinema 1978
  • 187: Topless above the water.

Astley, Pat
Films:
Playbirds (1978; British). . . . . Doreen Hamilton
  •• 0:00 - Topless posing for photo session.
Don't Open 'Till Christmas (1984; British) . . . . . . Sharon

Austin, Lynne
Video Tapes:
Playboy Video Centerfold: Lynne Austin
. . . . Playmate
Playboy Video Calendar 1989 (1988) . . . . May
  ••• 0:17 - Nude.
Playboy's Sexy Lingerie (1988) . . . .
Playboy's Wet and Wild (1989) . . . .
Magazines:
Playboy (Jul 1986) . . . . Playmate

Austin, Teri
Films:
Terminal Choice (1985; Canadian) . . . . Lylah Crane
  0:14 - Full frontal nudity, covered with blood on operating table. Long shot.
  0:21 - Right breast, on table being examined by Ellen
   Barkin. Dead, covered with dried blood.
  0:26 - Very brief left breast under plastic on table,
   hard to see.
Vindicator (1986; Canadian) . . . . Lauren Lehman
  a.k.a. Frankenstein '88
  • 0.30 - Very brief left breast and buns in mirror getting
   out of the bubble bath covered with bubbles. Long
   shot, hard to see anything.
Dangerous Love (1988) . . . . Dominique
Made for TV Movies:
False Witness (1989) . . . . Sandralee
TV:
Knots Landing (1985-) . . . . Jill Bennett

Axelrod, Nina
Films:
Roller Boogie (1979) . . . . Bobby's Friend
Motel Hell (1980) . . . . Terry
  0:58 - In wet white T-shirt, tubin' with Ida.
  •• 1:01 - Topless sitting up in bed to kiss Vincent.
  • 1:04 - Very brief topless in tub when Bruce breaks the
   door down, then getting out of tub.
Time Walker (1982) . . . . Susie
Brainstorm (1983) . . . . Simulator Technician
Cross Country (1983; Canadian) . . . . Lois Hayes
  0:28 - Brief buns and sort of topless, getting fondled
   by Richard.
  1:05 - Very, very brief topless fighting outside the
   motel in the rain with Johnny.
Cobra (1986) . . . . Waitress

Ayer, Lois

a.k.a. Adult film actress Lois Ayers or Sondra Stilman.
Films:
In Search of the Perfect 10 (1986) . . Perfect Girl #2
(Shot on video tape.)
••• 0:08 - In swimsuit, then topless exercising by the
pool.
Tougher Than Leather (1988) . . . . Charlotte

Ayres-Hamilton, Leah

Films:
All That Jazz (1979) . . . . Nurse Capobianco
The Burning (1981) . . . . Michelle
Eddie Macon's Run (1983) . . . . Chris
Bloodsport (1987) . . . . Janice
Hot Child in the City (1987) . . . . Rachel
0:38 - In braless white T-shirt walking out by the pool
and inside her sister's house.
• 1:12 - Very brief topless in the shower with a guy.
Long shot, hard to see anything.
TV:
9 to 5 (1983) . . . . Linda Bowman

Bach, Barbara

Wife of singer/former *Beatles* drummer Ringo Starr.
Films:
Black Belly of the Tarantula (1972; Italian) . . . . Jenny
Stateline Motel (1975; Italian) . . . . Emily
a.k.a. Last Chance for a Born Loser
The Spy Who Loved Me (1977; British)
. . . . Major Anya Amosova
1:21 - Brief side view of right breast in shower on
submarine. Don't see her face.
Force Ten from Navarone (1978) . . . . Maritza
• 0:32 - Brief topless taking a bath in the German offic-
er's room.
Screamers (1978; Italian) . . . . Amanda
a.k.a. The Island of the Fishmen
a.k.a. Something Waits in the Dark
The Humanoid (1979; Italian) . . . .
Jaguar Lives (1979) . . . . Anna
Great Alligator (1980; Italian) . . . .
Caveman (1981) . . . . Lana
The Unseen (1981) . . . . Jennifer
Up the Academy (1981) . . . . Bliss
Give My Regards to Broad Street (1984; British)
. . . . Journalist
Miniseries:
Princess Daisy (1983) . . . .
Magazines:
Playboy (Jun 1977) . . . . Bonded Barbara
•• 106-109: In lingerie, partial buns and topless.
Playboy (Jan 1981) . . . . Barbara Bach
••• 120-127: Full frontal nudity.
Playboy (Sep 1987) . . . . 25 Years of James Bond
•• 130: Left breast.
Playboy (Jan 1989) . . . . Women of the Seventies
212-213: Buns.

Bagdasarian, Carol

Films:
The Strawberry Statement (1970) . . . . . . Telephone Girl
Charge of the Model T's (1979) . . . .
The Octagon (1980) . . . . Aura
• 1:18 - Brief side view of right breast, while sitting on
bed next to Chuck Norris and taking her blouse off.
The Aurora Encounter (1985) . . . . Alain

Baker, Carroll

Films:
Baby Doll (1956; B&W) . . . . Baby Doll
Giant (1956) . . . . Luz Benedict II
How the West was Won (1963) . . . . Eve Prescott
The Carpetbaggers (1964) . . . . Rina
Harlow (1965) . . . . Jean Harlow
Sylvia (1965) . . . . Sylvia West
Orgasmo (1968) . . . .
The Sweet Body of Deborah (1968) . . . . . . Deborah
(Not available on video tape.)
Topless.
Andy Warhol's Bad (1977; Italian) . . . .
The World is Full of Married Men (1979; British)
. . . . Linda Cooper
• 0:19 - Brief left breast sitting up in bathtub covered
with bubbles.
My Father's Wife (1981; Italian) . . . . Lara
• 0:03 - Right breast making love in bed with her hus-
band, Antonio.
•• 0:06 - Topless standing in front of bed talking to An-
tonio.
••• 0:18 - Topless kneeling in bed, then getting out and
putting a robe on while wearing beige panties.
The Watcher in the Woods (1981) . . . . Helen Curtis
Star 80 (1983) . . . . Dorothy's Mother
The Secret Diary of Sigmund Freud (1984)
. . . . Mama Freud
Ironweed (1987) . . . . Annie Phelan
Kindergarten Cop (1990) . . . . Eleanor Crisp
Magazines:
Playboy (Jun 1980) . . . . Grapevine
• 300: Left breast in bathtub in B&W still from *The
World is Full of Married Men*.

Baker, Cheryl

Films:
Lethal Weapon (1987) . . . . Girl in Shower #1
Die Hard (1988) . . . . Woman with Man
• 0:22 - Brief topless in office with a guy when the ter-
rorists first break into the building.
Roadhouse (1989) . . . . Well-Endowed Wife
L.A. Story (1991) . . . . Changing Room Woman
• 0:18 - Brief topless in dressing room, when Steve
Martin sees her.

Baker, Cynthia
Films:
Sector 13 (1982)..............................
Risky Business (1983) .... Test Teacher
Blood Diner (1987)...................... Cindy
••• 0:44 - Nude outside by fire with her boyfriend, then fighting a guy with an axe.

Baker, Kirsten
Films:
California Dreaming (1978)................. Karen
Teen Lust (1978)...................... Carol Hill
• 0:45 - Brief side view of left breast changing clothes in her bedroom.
Friday the 13th, Part II (1981).............. Terry
•• 0:45 - Topless and buns taking off clothes to go skinny dipping.
• 0:47 - Very brief topless jumping up in the water.
• 0:48 - Full frontal nudity and buns getting out of the water. Long shot.

Baker, LeeAnne
Films:
Breeders (1986) .... Kathleen
••• 0:28 - Nude, undressing from her nurse outfit in the kitchen, then taking a shower.
• 0:59 - Brief topless in alien nest. (She's the blonde in front.)
•• 1:08 - Topless in alien nest.
•• 1:09 - Topless in alien nest again. (Behind Alec.)
• 1:11 - Topless behind Alec again. Then long shot when nest is electrocuted. (On the left.)
Mutant Hunt (1987) .... Pleasure Droid
Necropolis (1987)........................ Eva
• 0:04 - Right breast, dancing in skimpy black outfit during vampire ceremony.
• 0:38 - Brief topless in front of three evil things. (Before she has special make up to make it look like she has six breasts).
Galactic Gigolo (1989) .... Lucy
a.k.a. Club Earth

Baker, Marina
Video Tapes:
Playboy Video Calendar 1988 (1987) .... Playmate
Playboy's Wet and Wild (1989) ....
Magazines:
Playboy (Mar 1987)..................... Playmate

Baker, Penny
Films:
Real Genius (1985) .... Ick's Girl at Party
The Men's Club (1986)..................... Lake
•• 1:13 - Topless in bed with Treat Williams.
Million Dollar Mystery (1987) .... Charity

Video Tapes:
Playboy Video Magazine, Volume 4 ..... Playmate
Playboy's Wet and Wild (1989)................
Magazines:
Playboy (Jan 1984)..................... Playmate
Playboy (Nov 1986) .... Sex in Cinema
• 128: Topless in bed with Treat Williams.
Playboy (Jan 1989).......... Women of the Eighties
••• 253: Full frontal nudity.

Bakke, Brenda
Films:
Last Resort (1985).................... Veroneeka
•• 0:36 - Topless in the woods with Charles Grodin.
Hardbodies 2 (1986).................... Morgan
•• 0:34 - Buns, getting into bathtub, then topless, taking a bath.
Dangerous Love (1988) .... Chris
Scavengers (1988) .... Kimberly Blake
Fist Fighter (1989) .... Ellen
Nowhere to Run (1989) .... Joanie

Balaski, Belinda
Films:
Bobbie Jo and the Outlaw (1976)... Essie Beaumont
• 0:29 - Topless in pond with Marjoe Gortner and Lynda Carter.
Cannonball (1976; U.S./Hong Kong) .... Maryanne
Food of the Gods (1976) .... Rita
Piranha (1978)............................ Betsy
Till Death (1978) ....
The Howling (1981).................. Terry Fisher
Amazon Women on the Moon (1987) ....Bernice Pitnik
Gremlins 2: The New Batch (1990)
.... Movie Theatre Mom
Made for TV Movies:
Deadly Care (1987) .... Terry

Baldwin, Janit
Films:
Prime Cut (1972)........................ Violet
• 0:25 - Very brief nude, being swung around when Gene Hackman lifts her up to show to Lee Marvin.
• 0:41 - Brief topless putting on a red dress.
Gator Bait (1973) ....
•• 0:27 - Topless and buns walking into a pond, then getting out and getting dressed.
• 0:35 - Very brief right breast twice popping out of her dress when the bad guys hold her.
• 0:40 - Brief left breast struggling against two guys on the bed.
Ruby (1977)...................... Leslie Claire
Where the Buffalo Roam (1980) ....
Humongous (1982; Canadian)........ Carla Simmons

Baldwin, Judy

Films:

The Seven Minutes (1971) . . . . Fremont's Girlfriend
Evel Knievel (1972) . . . . Sorority Girl
No Small Affair (1984). . . . . Stephanie
  ••• 0:36 - In white bra, panties and garter belt, then top-
  less in Jon Cryer's bedroom trying to seduce him.
Talking Walls (1987) . . . .
Made in U.S.A. (1988). Dorie
Pretty Woman (1990) . . . . Susan
TV:
The Bold and the Beautiful (1987). . . . . Beth Logan

Barbeau, Adrienne

Films:

The Fog (1980). Stevie Wayne
The Cannonball Run (1981) . . . . Marcie
Escape from New York (1981) . . . . Maggie
Swamp Thing (1981) . . . . Alice Cable
  • 1:03 - Side view of left breast washing herself off in
  the swamp. Long shot.
Creepshow (1982) . . . . Wilma Northrup
The Next One (1983) . . . . Andrea Johnson
Back to School (1986). . . . . Vanessa
Open House (1987) . . . . Lisa Grant
  • 0:27 - In black lace lingerie, then very brief half of left
  breast making love with Joseph Bottoms on the
  floor.
  •• 1:15 - Brief side view of right breast getting out of
  bed at night to look at something in her briefcase.
  ••• 1:16 - Brief topless taking off bathrobe and getting
  back into bed. Kind of dark.
Cannibal Women in the Avocado Jungle of Death (1988)
. . . . Dr. Kurtz

Made for Cable Movies:
Doublecrossed (1991; HBO) . . . . Debbie Seal
TV:
Maude (1972-78) . . . . Carol

Barber, Glynnis

Films:

Terror (1979; British). Carol
Yesterday's Hero (1979; British). . . . . Susan
The Wicked Lady (1983; British) . . . . Caroline
  ••• 0:58 - Topless and buns making love with Kitt in the
  living room. Possible body double.
Edge of Sanity (1988) . . . . Elisabeth Jekyll
TV:
Dempsey and Makepeace (1984-86)
. . . . Detective Sergeant Harriet Makepeace

Bardot, Brigitte

Films:

Doctor at Sea (1955; British). . . . . Helene Colbert
...and God created woman (1957; French) . . Juliette
  • 0:40 - Very brief side view of right breast getting out
  of bed.

A Very Private Affair (1962; French/Italian) . . . . Jill
Contempt (1963; French/Italian) . . . . Camille Javal
  0:04 - Buns.
  0:52 - Almost buns walking through door after bath.
  0:54 - Buns, while lying on rug.
  1:30 - Buns, while lying on beach. Long shot.
Dear Brigitte (1965). . . . . Herself
Shalako (1968; British) . . . . Countess Irini Lazaar
Ms. Don Juan (1973) . . . . Joan
  • 0:19 - Left breast in bathtub.
  •• 1:19 - Topless through fish tank. Buns and left breast,
  then brief topless in mirror with Paul.
Famous T & A (1982) . . . . Joan
  (No longer available for purchase, check your video
  store for rental.)
  • 0:25 - Buns, then brief topless in scene from *Ms. Don
  Juan.*

Barkin, Ellen

Wife of actor Gabriel Byrne.
Films:

Diner (1982) . . . . Beth
Eddie and the Cruisers (1983) . . . . Maggie
Tender Mercies (1983) . . . . Sue Anne
The Adventures of Buckaroo Banzai, Across the 8th
  Dimension (1984) . . . . Penny Priddy
Harry and Son (1984) . . . . Katie
Terminal Choice (1985; Canadian) . . . . . Mary O'Connor
Desert Bloom (1986) . . . . Starr
Down by Law (1986) . . . . Bobbie
The Big Easy (1987) . . . . Anne Osborne
  0:21 - White panties in lifted up dress in bed with
  Dennis Quaid.
  0:32 - Brief buns jumping up in kitchen after pinching a guy who she thinks is Quaid.
Made in Heaven (1987) . . . . Lucille
Siesta (1987) . . . . Diane
  ••• 0:03 - Brief full frontal nudity long shot taking off red
  dress, topless, brief buns standing up, then full frontal nudity lying down.
  1:23 - Right nipple sticking out of dress making love
  and getting raped by taxi driver. Lower frontal nudity then brief buns. Dark, hard to see.
  1:28 - Very brief side view of right breast putting on
  dress in bed just before Isabella Rossellini comes into
  the bedroom to attack her. Long distance shot.
Johnny Handsome (1989) . . . . Sunny Boyd
Sea of Love (1989). . . . . Helen Cruger
  0:56 - Side view of left breast of body double, then
  buns standing up making out with Al Pacino in his
  apartment.
  0:59 - Back view wearing panties, putting blouse on
  in bathroom.
  1:13 - Brief upper half of buns, lying in bed with Pacino.
Switch (1991) . . . . Amanda/Steve

Barnes, Priscilla

Films:

Delta Fox (1977) . . . . Karen
> 0:36 - Left breast undressing in room for David. Very dark, hard to see.
- 0:38 - Very brief topless struggling with a bad guy and getting slammed against the wall.
> 0:39 - Very brief blurry left breast running in front of the fireplace.
- 0:40 - Topless sneaking out of house. Brief topless getting into Porsche.
- 0:49 - Brief right breast reclining onto bed with David. Side view of left breast several times while making love.
> 1:29 - Very brief side view of left breast in David's flashback.

Texas Detour (1977) . . . . Claudia Hunter
- ••• 1:03 - Topless, changing clothes and walking around in bedroom. Wearing white panties. This is her best topless scene.
- 1:11 - Topless sitting up in bed with Patrick Wayne.

Tintorera (1977) . . . .
- 1:12 - Very brief topless dropping her beer into the water.
- 1:14 - Topless, on the beach after the shark attack (on the left).

Seniors (1978) . . . . Sylvia
- •• 0:18 - Topless at the top of the stairs while Arnold climbs up the stairs while the rest of the guys watch.

The Last Married Couple in America (1980)
. . . . Helena Dryden
Sunday Lovers (1980; Italian/French) . . . . Donna
Traxx (1988) . . . . Mayor Alexandria Cray
License to Kill (1989) . . . . Della Churchill
Lords of the Deep (1989) . . . . Claire
Little Devils (1991) . . . .

TV:

The American Girls (1978) . . . . Rebecca Tomkins
Three's Company (1981-84) . . . . Terri Alden

Magazines:

Penthouse (Mar 1976) . . . . Pet
(Used the name Joann Witty.)
77-89:

Barrault, Marie-Christine

Films:

My Night at Maud's (1970; French) . . . . Francoise
Cousin, Cousine (1975; French) . . . . Marthe
- •• 1:05 - Topless in bed with her lover, cutting his nails.
- 1:07 - Brief side view of right breast, while giving him a bath.
- ••• 1:16 - Topless with penciled tattoos all over her body.
> 1:33 - Braless in see-through white blouse saying "good bye" to everybody.

The Daydreamer (1975; French) . . . . Lisa
The Medusa Touch (1978; British) . . . . Patricia
Stardust Memories (1980; B&W) . . . . Isabel
Table for Five (1983) . . . . Marie

A Love in Germany (1984; French/German)
. . . . Maria Wyler
- 0:23 - Right breast, in bed with her lover when Pauline peeks from across the way.
- •• 0:28 - Right breast in bedroom with Karl. Very brief lower frontal nudity getting into bed. Long scene.
- ••• 0:43 - Topless in bedroom with Karl. Subtitles get in the way! Long scene.
Swann in Love (1984; French/German)
. . . . Madame Verdunn

Barrese, Katherine

Films:

Homer & Eddie (1989) . . . . Waitress
Jezebel's Kiss (1990) . . . . Jezebel
- •• 0:36 - Full frontal nudity washing herself off in kitchen after having sex with the sheriff.
- 0:42 - Brief buns, swimming in the ocean. Dark.
- ••• 0:48 - Topless taking off her robe in front of Hunt, then making love with him.
- 0:58 - Brief right breast and buns while Malcolm McDowell watches through slit in curtain. Long shot.
- 1:09 - Right breast and buns getting undressed. Long shot. Closer shot of buns, putting robe on.
- ••• 1:12 - Topless making love with McDowell. More topless after.

Barrett, Jamie

Films:

Club Life (1987) . . . . Sissy
House of the Rising Sun (1987) . . . . Janet
- 1:04 - Very brief topless making love with Louis.

Barrett, Nitchie

Films:

Prepplies (1984) . . . . Roxanne
- 0:11 - Brief topless changing into waitress costumes with her two friends.
She-Devil (1989) . . . . Bob's Secretary

Barrett, Victoria

Films:

Hot Resort (1984) . . . . Jane
Hot Chili (1985) . . . . Victoria Stevenson
- 0:55 - Very brief close up shot of right breast when it pops out of her dress. Don't see her face.
Three Kinds of Heat (1987) . . . . Terry O'Shea

Barrington, Rebecca

Films:

Dance or Die (1988) . . . .
The Newlydeads (1988) . . . .
Living to Die (1990) . . . . Married Woman
- 0:23 - In red bra, blindfolded and tied to a lounge chair, then topless while getting photographed.
- 0:27 - Topless in chair talking to Wings Hauser.

17

Barry, Wendy

Films:
3:15—The Moment of Truth (1986) . . . . Lora
Knights of the City (1986). . . . . Jasmine
Young Lady Chatterley II (1986)
. . . . Sybil "Maid in Hot House"
 • 0:12 - Topless in hot house with the Gardener.

Basinger, Kim

Films:
Hard Country (1981) . . . . Jodie Lynn Palmer
Motherlode (1982) . . . . Andrea Spalding
The Man Who Loved Women (1983) . . . . Louise "Lulu"
Never Say Never Again (1983) . . . . Domino Vitale
The Natural (1984) . . . . Memo Paris
Fool For Love (1985) . . . . May
9 1/2 Weeks (1986) . . . . Elizabeth
 • 0:27 - Blindfolded while Mickey Rourke plays with an
   ice cube on her. Brief right breast.
   0:36 - Masturbating while watching slides of art.
   0:41 - Playing with food at the refrigerator with
   Rourke. Messy, but erotic.
 • 0:54 - Very brief left breast rolling over in bed.
   0:58 - Making love with Rourke in clock tower.
 ••• 1:11 - In wet lingerie, then topless making love in a
   wet stairwell with Rourke.
   1:19 - Doing a sexy dance for Rourke in a white slip.
   1:22 - Buns, showing off to Rourke on building.
No Mercy (1986) . . . . Michel Duval
Blind Date (1987) . . . . Nadia Gates
Nadine (1987) . . . . Nadine Hightower
My Stepmother Is An Alien (1988) . . . . . Celeste Martin
   0:40 - Dancing very seductively in a white slip in
   front of Dan Aykroyd while he lies in bed. No nudity,
   but still very exciting.
Batman (1989) . . . . Vicki Vale
The Marrying Man (1991). . . . . Vicki Anderson
Miniseries:
From Here to Eternity (1979) . . . . Lorene Rogers
Made for TV Movies:
Katie: Portrait of a Centerfold (1978). . . . .
TV:
Dog and Cat (1977) . . . . Officer J.Z. Kane
Magazines:
Playboy (Feb 1983) . . . . Betting on Kim
 ••• 82-89: Nude.
Playboy (Dec 1983). . . . . Sex Stars of 1983
 •• 211: Topless.
Playboy (Dec 1984). . . . . Sex Stars of 1984
 ••• 208: Topless walking in water.
Playboy (Sep 1987) . . . . 25 Years of James Bond
 •• 130: Topless.
Playboy (Jan 1988) . . . . Kim
 ••• 78-85: Topless and buns from Feb 1983.
Playboy (Jan 1989) . . . . Women of the Eighties
   256: Buns.
Playboy (Dec 1990). . . . . Sex Stars of 1990
 • 173: Buns, lying in water. B&W.

Bates, Jo Anne

Films:
Perfect Timing (1984) . . . . Karen
 ••• 0:21 - Nude, getting ready to get her picture taken.
Heavenly Bodies (1985) . . . . Girl in Locker Room
Immediate Family (1989) . . . . Home Buyer

Bauer, Belinda

Films:
The American Success Company (1979) . . . . Sarah
Winter Kills (1979) . . . . Yvette Malone
 •• 0:46 - Topless making love in bed with Jeff Bridges,
   then getting out of bed.
 • 1:25 - Topless, dead as a corpse when sheet uncovers
   her body.
Flashdance (1983) . . . . Katie Hurley
Timerider (1983) . . . . Clair Cygne
The Rosary Murders (1987) . . . . Pat Lennon
UHF (1989) . . . . Mud Wrestler
Act of Piracy (1990) . . . . Sandy Andrews
Robocop 2 (1990) . . . . Juliette Faxx
Made for Cable TV:
The Hitchhiker: Love Sounds . . . . Veronica Hoffman
 • 0:15 - Brief topless, making love in the house with
   Kerry.
 •• 0:22 - Topless, making love in the boat.
Made for TV Movies:
Starcrossed (1985) . . . . Mary

Bauer, Jaime Lyn

(Yes, her name is spelled Jaime.)
Films:
The Centerfold Girls (1974). . . . . Jackie
 •• 0:04 - Topless getting out of bed and walking around
   the house.
 ••• 0:14 - Topless getting undressed in the bathroom.
 •• 0:15 - Brief topless and buns putting on robe and
   getting out of bed, three times.
Young Doctors in Love (1982) . . . . cameo
TV:
The Young and the Restless (1973-82) . . . .
Lauralee (Laurie) Brooks Prentiss
Bare Essence (1983) . . . . Barbara Fisher
Magazines:
Penthouse (May 1974) . . . .
(Used the name Jessica Lyn.)

Bauer, Michelle

a.k.a. Michelle McClellan briefly when her ex-husband
  threatened to sue for using "Bauer."
a.k.a. Former adult film actress Pia Snow.
The easiest adult video tape to find is *Cafe Flesh*.
Films:
Best Chest in the West (1984). . . . . Michelle
 ••• 0:24 - In two piece swimsuit, then topless and buns.

Cave Girl (1985) . . . . Locker Room Student
- •• 0:05 - Topless with four other girls in the girls' locker room undressing, then running after Rex. She's the first to take her top off, wearing white panties, running and carrying a tennis racket.

Armed Response (1986) . . . . Stripper
- • 0:41 - Topless, dancing on stage.

Centerfold Screen Test, Take 2 (1986) . . . . . Marsha
- ••• 0:12 - Topless taking off her dress for Mr. Johnson. Then full frontal nudity. Nice, long scene.

Cyclone (1986) . . . . uncredited Shower Girl
- • 0:06 - Very brief buns and side of left breast walking around in locker room. (Passes several times in front of camera.)

In Search of the Perfect 10 (1986)
. . . . Perfect Girl #10
(Shot on video tape.)
- ••• 0:53 - In yellow outfit stripping in office. Topless and buns in G-string bottom.

Penthouse Love Stories (1986). . . .Therapist's Patient
- ••• 0:45 - Nude, making love in Therapist's office with his assistant.

Reform School Girls (1986)
. . . . .uncredited Shower Girl
- •• 0:25 - Topless, then nude in the shower.

Roller Blade (1986) . . . . .Bod Sister
- • 0:11 - Topless, being held by Satacoy's Devils.
- ••• 0:13 - More topless and buns in G-string during fight. Long scene.
- • 0:16 - Brief topless twice, getting saved by the Sisters.
- •• 0:33 - Topless during ceremony with the other two Bod Sisters. Buns also.
- ••• 0:35 - Full frontal nudity after dip in hot tub. (Second to leave the tub.)
- •• 0:40 - Nude, on skates with the other two Bod Sisters. (She's on the left.)

Screen Test (1986) . . . . Dancer/Ninja Girl
- •• 0:04 - Topless dancing on stage.
- ••• 0:42 - Nude, with Monique Gabrielle, making love in a boy's dream.

Commando Squad (1987) . . . .

Night of the Living Babes (1987). . . . . .Sue
- •• 0:44 - Topless chained up with Chuck and Buck.
- ••• 0:46 - More topless chained up.
- • 0:50 - Topless getting rescued with Lulu.

Nightmare Sisters (1987) . . . . Mickey
(This is the best video tape for viewing all three "Scream Queens.")
- ••• 0:39 - Topless standing in panties with Melody and Marci after transforming from nerds to sexy women.
- ••• 0:40 - Topless in the kitchen with Melody and Marci.
- ••• 0:44 - Full frontal nudity in the bathtub with Melody and Marci. Excellent, long scene.
- ••• 0:47 - Topless in the bathtub. Nice close up.
- ••• 0:48 - Still more topless in the bathtub.
- •• 0:53 - Topless in bed with J.J.

Phantom Empire (1987). . . . . .Cave Bunny
- 0:32 - Running around in the cave a lot in two piece loincloth swimsuit.
- •• 1:13 - Finally topless after losing her top during a fight, stays topless until Andrew puts his jacket on her.

The Tomb (1987). . . . . Nefartis

Demonwarp (1988). .Betsy
- •• 0:41 - Topless, taking off her T-shirt to get a tan in the woods.
- •• 0:43 - Left breast, lying down, then brief topless getting up when the creature attacks.
- •• 0:47 - Topless putting blood-stained T-shirt back on.
- •• 1:19 - Topless, strapped to table, getting ready to be sacrificed.
- • 1:22 - Topless on stretcher, dead.

Hollywood Chainsaw Hookers (1988) . . . .Mercedes
- ••• 0:09 - Nude in motel room with a John just before chainsawing him to pieces.

The Jigsaw Murders (1988) . . . . Cindy Jakulski
- 0:20 - Brief buns on cover of puzzle box during bachelor party.
- • 0:21 - Brief topless in puzzle on underside of glass table after the policemen put the puzzle together.
- • 0:29 - Very brief topless when the police officers show the photographer the puzzle picture.
- • 0:43 - Very brief topless long shots in some pictures that the photographer is watching on a screen.

Sorority Babes in the Slimeball Bowl-O-Rama
(1988) . . . . Lisa
- 0:07 - In panties getting spanked with Linnea Quigley.
- ••• 0:12 - Topless brushing herself in the front of mirror while Quigley takes a shower.
- • 0:14 - Brief full frontal nudity when the three nerds fall into the bathroom.
- 0:33 - In black bra, panties, garter belt and stockings asking for Keith.
- 0:35 - Wearing the same lingerie, on top of Keith in the locker room.
- ••• 0:40 - Topless taking off her bra.
- ••• 0:43 - More topless undoing garter belt.
- •• 0:46 - More topless in locker room.
- •• 0:47 - More topless taking off stockings.
- • 1:04 - Full frontal nudity sitting on the floor by herself.
- •• 1:05 - Full frontal nudity getting up after the lights go out. Kind of dark.

Warlords (1988) .Harem Girl
- ••• 0:14 - Topless, getting her top ripped off, then shot by a bad guy.

Wild Man (1988) . . . . Trisha Collins
- 1:02 - In sheer white lingerie with Eric. Buns also.
- ••• 1:06 - Topless on couch making love with Eric. Brief lower frontal nudity.

Assault of the Party Nerds (1989) . . . . Muffin
- 0:16 - Side view of left breast kissing Bud.
••• 0:20 - Topless lying in bed seen from Bud's point of view, then sitting up by herself.
- 1:15 - Brief right breast, then topless in bed with Scott.

Beverly Hills Vamp (1989) . . . . Kristina
- 0:12 - Buns and brief side view of right breast in bed biting a guy.
  0:33 - In red slip, with Kyle.
•• 0:38 - Topless trying to get into Kyle's pants.
  1:09 - In black lingerie attacking Russell in bed with Debra Lamb and Jillian Kesner.
  1:19 - In black lingerie enticing Mr. Pendleton into bedroom.
  1:22 - In black lingerie, getting killed as a vampire by Kyle.

Deadly Embrace (1989) . . . . Female Spirit of Sex
•• 0:22 - Topless caressing herself during fantasy sequence.
••• 0:28 - Topless taking off tube top and caressing herself.
••• 0:40 - Topless and buns kissing blonde guy. Nice close up of him kissing her breasts.
- 0:42 - Side of left breast lying down with the guy.
- 1:03 - Buns and side of right breast with the guy.

Dr. Alien (1989) . . . . Coed #1
a.k.a. I Was a Teenage Sex Mutant
••• 0:53 - Topless taking off her top (she's on the left) in the women's locker room after another coed takes hers off in front of Wesley.

Murder Weapon (1989) . . . . Girl in Shower on TV
- 1:00 - Brief left breast on TV that the guys are watching. Scene from *Nightmare Sisters*.

Virgin High (1990) . . . . Miss Bush
The Dwelling (1991) . . . .
Evil Toons (1991) . . . .
Inner Sanctum (1991) . . . . body double
Does some topless body doubling for Mariel Hemingway.
Little Devils (1991) . . . .
Scream Queen Hot Tub Party (1991) . . . .
Terror Night (1991) . . . .
Magazines:
Penthouse (Jul 1981) . . . . Pet
Playboy (Jul 1989) . . . . B-Movie Bimbos
•• 138: Topless and buns lying in a car that looks like a shark.
Playboy (Nov 1991) . . . . Grapevine
••• 183: Topless, kneeling. B&W.

Baxter, Amy

Films:
Summer's Games (1987) . . Boxer/Girl from Penthouse
•• 0:04 - Topless opening her swimsuit top after contest. (1st place winner.)
•• 0:18 - Topless during boxing match.

Wet Water T's (1987) . . . . herself
••• 0:33 - Topless in black lingerie bottoms, then buns in G-string, dancing on stage in a contest.
•• 0:38 - Topless during judging.
•• 0:39 - Topless during semi-finals.
••• 0:40 - Topless dancing with the other women during semi-final judging.
••• 0:43 - Topless during finals.
•• 0:47 - Topless during final judging.
••• 0:48 - Topless dancing after winning first place.
Spring Fever USA (1988) . . . . Amy (Car Wash Girl)
Summer Job (1989) . . . . .Susan
•• 0:10 - Topless changing in room with the other three girls. More topless sitting on bed.
  0:15 - In white bra, looking at herself in mirror.
- 0:34 - Brief topless when her swimsuit top pops off after saving a guy in swimming pool.
- 0:45 - In white lingerie, brief topless on stairs, flashing her breasts (wearing curlers).
  1:00 - Brief buns in two piece swimsuit turning around.
- 1:23 - Topless pulling her top down talking to Mr. Burns.

Beacham, Stephanie

Films:
The Games (1970) . . . . Angela Simmonds
The Nightcomers (1971; British)
. . . . Miss Margaret Jessel
- 0:13 - Brief left breast lying in bed having her breasts fondled.
••• 0:30 - Topless in bed with Marlon Brando while a little boy watches through the window.
•• 0:55 - Topless in bed pulling the sheets down.
The Devil's Widow (1972; British) . . . . Janet
Dracula A.D. 1972 (1972; British) . . . .Jessica Van Helsing
And Now the Screaming Starts (1973; British)
. . . . .Catherine Fengrifen
The Confessional (1977; British) . . . . Vanessa
Schizo (1977; British) . . . . Beth
a.k.a. Amok
a.k.a. Blood of the Undead
Horror Planet (1980; British) . . . . .Kate
a.k.a. Inseminoid
Troop Beverly Hills (1989) . . . . Vicki Sprantz
Miniseries:
Napolean and Josephine (1987) . . . . Therese
TV:
The Colbys (1985-89) . . . . Sable Scott Colby
Sister Kate (1989-90) . . . . Sister Katherine Lambert
Magazines:
Playboy (Nov 1972) . . . . Sex in Cinema 1972
•• 160: Right breast, B&W photo from *The Nightcomers*.
Playboy (Feb 1987) . . . .
•• 112-121: Color photos taken in 1972.

Beal, Cindy
Films:
My Chauffeur (1986) . . . . .Beebop
Slavegirls from Beyond Infinity (1987). . . . . . .Tisa
(Wearing skimpy outfits during most of the movie.)
    0:25 - Walking around in white bra and panties.
  ••• 0:36 - Topless on beach wearing white panties.
  • 1:05 - Left breast leaning back on table while getting
    attacked by Zed.

Beall, Sandra
Films:
Easy Money (1983) . . . . Maid of Honor
A Night in Heaven (1983) . . . . Slick
  • 1:09 - Brief close up of left breast in shower with
    Christopher Atkins.
The Cotton Club (1984) . . . . Myrtle Fay
Birdy (1985) . . . . Shirley
Key Exchange (1985) .Marcy
  ••• 1:14 - Topless on bed taking off her clothes and talk-
    ing to Daniel Stern.
Loverboy (1989) . . . . Robin
State of Grace (1990) . . . . Steve's Date

Beals, Jennifer
Films:
Flashdance (1983). . . . . Alex
The Bride (1985). . . . . Eva
    0:21 - Lower frontal nudity and buns of body double
    coming down stairs and to kneel down and talk to
    Sting.
    0:53 - Standing in wet white nightgown in the rain
    talking to Sting.
Split Decisions (1988) . . . . Barbara Uribe
Vampire's Kiss (1989) . . . . Rachel
    0:14 - Almost topless in bed with Nicholas Cage.
    Squished left breast against Cage while she bites
    him. In one shot, you can see the beige pastie she
    put over her left nipple.
    0:27 - In bed again with Cage.
    0:41 - In black lingerie taking her dress off for Cage.
Club Extinction (1990) . . . . Sonja Vogler
  • 1:16 - Brief side of left breast rolling over in bed with
    Hartmann. Don't see her face, but probably her.
  •• 1:17 - Brief topless in bed with Hartmann when he
    kisses her right breast, then brief right breast.

Béart, Emmanuelle
Films:
Date with an Angel (1987) . . . . Angel
Manon of the Spring (1987; French) . . . . Manon
  • 0:11 - Brief nude dancing around a spring playing a
    harmonica.

Beck, Kimberly
Films:
Massacre at Central High (1976) . . . . Theresa
  • 0:32 - Nude romping in the ocean with David. Long
    shot, dark, hard to see anything.
  •• 0:42 - Topless on the beach making love with An-
    drew Stevens after a hang glider crash.
Roller Boogie (1979) . . . . Lana
Friday the 13th, Part IV—The Final Chapter (1984)
. . . . Trish
Maid to Order (1987) . . . . Kim
TV:
Peyton Place (1965). . . . . Kim Schuster
Lucas Tanner (1974-75) . . . . Terry Klitsner
General Hospital (1975) . . . . Samantha Chandler
Rich Man, Poor Man—Book II (1976-77) . . Diane Porter
Capitol (1982-83) .Julie Clegg

Becker, Desiree
Films:
Good Morning, Babylon (1987; Italian/French)
. . . . Mabel
  • 1:06 - Brief topless in the woods making love.
Made for Cable TV:
The Hitchhiker: Out of the Night . . . . .Kathy
  •• 0:12 - Brief topless lying in the steam room talking to
    Peter, then close up topless.

Bedelia, Bonnie
Films:
The Gypsy Moths (1969) . . . . .Annie Burke
(Not available on video tape.)
Lovers and Other Strangers (1970) . . . .Susan Henderson
The Big Fix (1978) .Suzanne
Heart Like a Wheel (1983) . . . . Shirley Muldowney
The Boy Who Could Fly (1986) . . . . Charlene
The Stranger (1986) . . . . Alice Kildee
  • 0:15 - Brief right breast sticking up from behind her
    lover's arm making love in bed during flashback se-
    quence (B&W).
  • 0:19 - Brief left breast turning over in hospital bed
    when a guy walks in. Long shot, hard to see.
  •• 0:38 - Right breast again making love (B&W).
Violets Are Blue (1986). . . . . Ruth Squires
Die Hard (1988) .Holly McClane
The Prince of Pennsylvania (1988) . . . . . Pam Marshetta
    0:12 - In black bra in open blouse in kitchen. Long
    scene.
Fat Man and Little Boy (1989) . . . . . Kitty Oppenheimer
Die Hard 2 (1990) . . . . .Holly McClane
Presumed Innocent (1990). . . . . .Barbara Sabich
Made for Cable Movies:
Somebody Has to Shoot the Picture (1990; HBO)
. . . . .Hannah McGrath
    1:15 - Upper half of left breast, lying in bed with Roy
    Scheider.
Made for TV Movies:
Switched at Birth (1991) . . . . .Regina Twigg

Bell, Jeannie
Films:
Black Gunn (1972) . . . . .Lisa
Mean Streets (1973) . . . . Diane
• 0:07 - Topless dancing on stage with pasties on.
• 1:00 - Topless backstage wearing pasties.
The Klansman (1974) . . . . Mary Anne
TNT Jackson (1975). . . . . TNT Jackson
Sex on the Run (1979; German/French/Italian)
. . . . Slave Girl

a.k.a. Some Like It Cool
a.k.a. Casanova and Co.
Magazines:
Playboy (Oct 1969) . . . . Playmate

Beller, Kathleen
Films:
The Betsy (1978) . . . . Betsy Hardeman
••• 0:12 - Brief nude getting into swimming pool.
•• 1:14 - Topless in bed with Tommy Lee Jones.
Movie Movie (1978) . . . . Angie Popchik
Promises in the Dark (1979) . . . . .Buffy Koenig
Surfacing (1980). . . . . Kate
0:22 - Very brief buns, pulling down pants to
change. Dark, hard to see.
0:23 - Very brief right breast undressing. Dark, hard
to see.
• 0:24 - Very, very brief topless turning over in bed.
0:25 - Buns, standing next to bed.
••• 1:23 - Topless washing herself in the water. One long
shot, one side view of right breast.
Fort Apache, The Bronx (1981) . . . . .Theresa
The Sword and the Sorcerer (1982) . . . . Alana
• 0:54 - Side view of buns, lying face down getting oil
rubbed all over her.
Touched (1982) . . . . .Jennifer
Time Trackers (1989). . . . . R. J. Craig
Miniseries:
Blue and the Gray (1982) . . . . .Kathy Reynolds
Made for TV Movies:
Mary White (1977) . . . .
TV:
Search for Tomorrow (1971-74) . . . . .Liza Walton
Dynasty (1982-84) . . . . .Kirby Anders
Bronx Zoo (1988-89) . . . . Callahan

Belli, Agostina
Films:
Bluebeard (1972) . . . . Caroline
• 1:31 - Brief left breast lying on grass getting a tan.
•• 1:32 - Topless taking off clothes and lying on the
couch.
Blood in the Streets (1974; French/Italian) . . . . . . Maria
The Seduction of Mimi (1974; Italian) . . . .
The Purple Taxi (1977; French/Italian/Irish)
. . . . .Anne Taubelman
Holocaust 2000 (1978) . . . . Sara Golen
•• 0:50 - Topless in bed making love with Kirk Douglas.

Bellwood, Pamela
Films:
Two-Minute Warning (1976) . . . . Peggy Ramsay
Airport '77 (1977) . . . . Lisa
Hanger 18 (1980) . . . . .Sarah
Serial (1980) . . . . .Carol
The Incredible Shrinking Woman (1981) . Sandra Dyson
Cellar Dweller (1987). . . . . .Amanda
Made for TV Movies:
Double Standard (1988) . . . . .Joan
TV:
W.E.B. (1978). . . . . .Ellen Cunningham
Dynasty (1981-86). . . . . Claudia Blaisdel
Magazines:
Playboy (Apr 1983) . . . . .Going Native
• Covered with mud and body paint.

Bening, Annette
Films:
The Great Outdoors (1988) . . . . Kate Craig
Valmont (1989) . . . . .Marquise de Merteuil
0:10 - Very brief, hard to see right breast, reaching
up to kiss Jeffrey Jones.
The Grifters (1990) . . . . .Myra Langtry
•• 0:36 - In bra and panties in her apartment, then topless lying in bed "paying" her rent. Kind of dark.
••• 1:06 - Nude, walking down the hall to the bedroom
and into bed.
1:30 - Very brief right breast, dead in morgue. Long
shot.
Postcards from the Edge (1990) . . . . Evelyn Ames
Guilty by Suspicion (1991). . . . .
Regarding Henry (1991). . . . .
Magazines:
Playboy (Nov 1991) . . . . Sex in Cinema 1991
• 143: Topless, lying in bed, in scene from *The Grifters.*

Bennett, Angela
Films:
Fatal Games (1984). . . . . .Sue Allen Baines
•• 0:21 - Full frontal nudity in the sauna with Teal Roberts.
• 0:23 - Nude, running around the school, trying to
get away from the killer. Dark.
Punchline (1988) . . . . Nurse

Benson, Vickie
Films:
Private Resort (1985) . . . . .Bikini Girl
• 0:28 - In blue two piece swimsuit, showing her buns,
then brief topless with Reeves.
1:11 - Buns, in locker room, trying to slap Reeves.
Las Vegas Weekend (1986). . . . .
My Chauffeur (1986) .Party Girl
The Wraith (1986) . . . . .Waitress
Cheerleader Camp (1988) . . . . Miss Tipton
a.k.a. Bloody Pom Poms

Bentley, Dana
Films:
Bad Girls from Mars (1990) . . . . Martine
- •• 0:28 - Topless taking off her blouse in office.
- •• 0:59 - Topless several times wrestling with Edy Williams.

Invisible Maniac (1990) . . . . Newscaster
- • 1:22 - Brief topless on monitor doing the news.

Nightie Nightmare (1991) . . . .

Benton, Barbi
Films:
Hospital Massacre (1982) . . . . Susan Jeremy
- 0:29 - Undressing behind a curtain while the Doctor watches her silhouette.
- ••• 0:31 - Topless getting examined by the Doctor. First sitting up, then lying down.
- ••• 0:34 - Great close up shot of breasts while the Doctor uses stethoscope on her.

Deathstalker (1983) . . . . Codille
- •• 0:39 - Topless struggling while chained up and everybody is fighting.
- • 0:47 - Right breast, struggling on the bed with Deathstalker.

TV:
Hee Haw (1971-76) . . . . Regular
Sugar Time! (1977-78) . . . . Maxx
Video Tapes:
Playboy Video Magazine, Volume 9 . . . . herself
Magazines:
Playboy (Dec 1973) . . . . Barbi's Back
- ••• 143-149: Nude.

Playboy (Jan 1989) . . . . Women of the Seventies
- ••• 210: Topless.

Benton, Suzanne
Films:
That Cold Day in the Park (1969) . . . . Nina
- • 0:38 - Side view of left breast putting top on. Long shot.
- • 1:05 - Topless taking off her clothes and getting into the bathtub. Another long shot.

Catch-22 (1970) . . . . Dreedle's WAC
A Boy and His Dog (1976) . . . . Quilla June
- •• 0:29 - Nude, getting dressed while Don Johnson watches.
- • 0:45 - Right breast lying down with Johnson after making love with him.

Bentzen, Jane
Films:
Nightmare at Shadow Woods (1983) . . . . Julie
a.k.a. Blood Rage
- 0:38 - In red lingerie, black stockings and garter belt in her apartment with Phil.

Made for Cable Movies:
A Breed Apart (1984; HBO) . . . . Reporter
- ••• 0:55 - Left breast in bed with Powers Booth, then full frontal nudity getting out of bed and putting her clothes on.

Benz, Donna Kei
Films:
Looker (1981) . . . . Ellen
The Challenge (1982) . . . . Akiko
- • 1:23 - Topless making love with Scott Glenn in motel room. Could be a body double. Dark, hard to see anything.

Pray for Death (1986) . . . . Aiko Saito
Moon in Scorpio (1987) . . . . Nurse Mitchell
Magazines:
Playboy (Nov 1982) . . . . Sex in Cinema 1982
- • 161: Topless.

Berenson, Marisa
Films:
Death in Venice (1971; Italian/French)
. . . . Frau Von Aschenbach
Cabaret (1972) . . . . Natalia Landauer
Barry Lyndon (1975; British) . . . . Lady Lyndon
Topless in bathtub.
Killer Fish (1979; Italian/Brazilian) . . . . Ann
Sex on the Run (1979; German/French/Italian) . . . .
a.k.a. Some Like It Cool
a.k.a. Casanova and Co.
- 1:23 - Almost right breast, while in bed with Tony Curtis when she rolls over him.

S.O.B. (1981) . . . . Mavis
- •• 1:20 - Topless in bed with Robert Vaughn.

The Secret Diary of Sigmund Freud (1984)
. . . . Emma Herrmann
White Hunter Black Heart (1990) . . . . Kay Gibson
Miniseries:
Sins (1986) . . . .
Made for TV Movies:
Playing for Time (1980) . . . .
Magazines:
Playboy (Dec 1973) . . . . Sex Stars of 1973
- • 210: Right breast.

Playboy (Nov 1976) . . . . Sex in Cinema 1976
- • 114: Left breast in a shot that wasn't used in *Barry Lyndon.*

Berg, Carmen
Video Tapes:
Playboy Video Calendar 1989 (1988) . . . . July
- ••• 0:25 - Nude.

Playboy's Sexy Lingerie (1988) . . . .
Playboy's Wet and Wild (1989) . . . .
Magazines:
Playboy (Jul 1987) . . . . Playmate

Bergen, Candice

Wife of French director Louis Malle.
Films:
The Group (1966) . . . . .Lakey Eastlake
The Adventurers (1970) . . . . Sue Ann
Getting Straight (1970). . . . . Jan
Soldier Blue (1970) . . . . Cresta Marybelle Lee
Carnal Knowledge (1971) . . . . Susan
The Hunting Party (1971; British) . . . . Melissa Ruger
T. R. Baskin (1971) . . . . T.R. Baskin
Bite the Bullet (1975) . . . . .Miss Jones
The Wind and the Lion (1975) . . . . Eden Pedecaris
A Night Full of Rain (1978; Italian) . . . . .Lizzy
   (Not available on video tape.)
   Topless.
Oliver's Story (1978) . . . . Marcie Bonwit
Starting Over (1979) . . . . .Jessica Potter
      1:01 - In a sheer blouse sitting on couch talking to
      Burt Reynolds.
   • 1:29 - Very, very brief left breast in bed with Reynolds
      when he undoes her top. You see her breast just be-
      fore the scene dissolves into the next one. Long
      shot, hard to see.
Rich and Famous (1981) . . . . Merry Noel Blake
Gandhi (1982) . . . . Margaret Bourke-White
Made for TV Movies:
Mayflower Madam (1987) . . . . . Sydney Biddle Barrows
TV:
Murphy Brown (1988-) . . . . Murphy Brown

Berger, Sophie

Films:
Emmanuelle IV (1984) . . . . Maria
   •• 0:46 - Full frontal nudity putting on robe.
      0:49 - Buns, taking off robe in front of Mia Nygren.
Love Circles Around the World (1984) . . . . Dagmar
   ••• 0:38 - Topless in women's restroom in casino making
      love with a guy in a tuxedo.
   ••• 0:43 - Topless in steam room wearing a towel around
      her waist, then making love.

Bergman, Sandahl

Films:
All That Jazz (1979) . . . . Sandra
   •• 0:52 - Topless dancing on scaffolding during a dance
      routine.
Xanadu (1980) . . . . .A Muse
Airplane II: The Sequel (1982) . . . . Officer
Conan the Barbarian (1982). . . . . Valeria
   •• 0:49 - Brief left breast making love with Arnold
      Schwarzenegger.
She (1983) . . . . .She
   •• 0:22 - Topless getting into a pool of water to clean
      her wounds after sword fight.
Red Sonja (1985) . . . . Queen Gedren
Hell Comes to Frogtown (1987) . . . . Spangle
Kandyland (1987) . . . . .Harlow Divine

Programmed to Kill (1987) . . . . .Samira
   a.k.a. The Retaliator
   • 0:11 - Brief side view of right breast taking off T-shirt
      and leaning over to kiss a guy. Don't see her face.
Stewardess School (1987) . . . . Wanda Polanski
Raw Nerve (1991) . . . .
Made for TV Movies:
Getting Physical (1984) . . . .
Magazines:
Playboy (Mar 1980) . . . . .All That Fosse
   •• 174-175: Topless stills from *All That Jazz.*
Playboy (Dec 1981) . . . . .Sex Stars of 1981
   •• 239: Topless.

Bernard, Sue

Films:
Faster, Pussycat! Kill! Kill! (1966; B&W). . . . . .Linda
   Russ Meyer film.
The Killing Kind (1973) .Tina
   • 0:00 - Topless during gang rape.
   • 0:19 - Topless again during flashback.
   • 1:12 - Brief topless again several times during flash-
      backs.
The Witching (1983). . . . . .Nancy
   a.k.a. Necromancy
   • 1:03 - Brief topless in bed with Michael Ontkean.
Magazines:
Playboy (Dec 1966) . . . . Playmate

Bernhard, Sandra

Comedienne.
Films:
King of Comedy (1983) . . . . Masha
Track 29 (1988; British) . . . . Nurse Stein
Heavy Petting (1989) . . . . herself/Comedienne
Without You I'm Nothing (1990)
   . . . . .Miscellaneous Characters
   Dancing in pasties and G-string near the end of the film.
Hudson Hawk (1991) . . . .
Magazines:
Playboy (May 1991) . . . . Grapevine
   • 182: Upper half of right breast in open dress. B&W.

Berridge, Elizabeth

Films:
The Funhouse (1981) .Amy
   •• 0:03 - Brief topless taking off robe to get into the
      shower, then very brief topless getting out to chase
      Joey.
Amadeus (1984) . . . . Constanze
Five Corners (1988) . . . . Melanie

Besch, Bibi

Films:
The Long Dark Night (1977) . . . . Marge
Hardcore (1979) . . . . .Mary
The Beast Within (1982) . . . . Caroline MacCleary
  •• 0:06 - Topless, getting her blouse torn off by the
    beast while she is unconscious. Dark, hard to see her
    face.
Star Trek II: The Wrath of Kahn (1982)
  . . . . .Dr. Carol Marcus
The Lonely Lady (1983). . . . . Veronica
Who's That Girl? (1987) . . . . Mrs. Worthington
Kill Me Again (1989) . . . . Jack's Secretary
Steel Magnolias (1989) . . . . Belle Marmillion
Tremors (1989) . . . . Megan - The Doctor's Wife
Betsy's Wedding (1990) . . . . .Nancy Lovell
Made for TV Movies:
Death of a Centerfold: The Dorothy Stratten Story
  (1981). . . . . .Hilda
TV:
Secrets of Midland Heights (1980-81)
  . . . . Dorothy Wheeler
The Hamptons (1983). . . . . Adrienne Duncan Mortimer

Beswicke, Martine

Films:
From Russia with Love (1963; British) . . . . Zora
Thunderball (1965; British) . . . . Paula Caplan
One Million Years B.C. (1966; U.S./British) . . . .Nupondi
Dr. Jekyll and Sister Hyde (1971) . . . . Sister Hyde
The Happy Hooker Goes Hollywood (1980)
  . . . . Xaviera Hollander
  •• 0:05 - Brief topless in bedroom with Policeman.
  ••• 0:22 - Brief buns, jumping into the swimming pool,
    then topless next to the pool with Adam West.
  • 0:27 - Topless in bed with West, then topless waking
    up.
Melvin and Howard (1980) . . . . .Real Estate Woman
Cyclone (1986) . . . . Waters
The Offspring (1986) . . . . Katherine White
Miami Blues (1990) . . . . Noira
Evil Spirits (1991) . . . .
Trancers II (1991) . . . . Nurse Trotter
TV:
Aspen (1977) .Joan Carolinian

Binoche, Juliette

Films:
Hail Mary (1985). . . . . .Juliette
Rendez-Vous (1986; French) . . . . . Anne "Nina" Larrieu
  • 0:07 - Brief topless in dressing room when Paulot sur-
    prises her and Fred.
  ••• 0:25 - Side of left breast, then topless and buns in
    empty apartment with Paulot.
  •• 0:32 - Full frontal nudity in bed with Quentin.
  •• 0:35 - Buns, then brief topless in bed with Paulot and
    Quentin. Full frontal nudity getting out.

  •• 1:08 - Topless taking off her top in front of Paulot in
    the dark, then topless lying on the floor.
  • 1:11 - Right breast, making love on the stairs. Dark.
The Unbearable Lightness of Being (1988)
  . . . . Tereza
    0:22 - In white bra in Tomas' apartment.
  • 1:33 - Brief topless jumping onto couch.
    1:36 - Buns, sitting in front of fire being photo-
    graphed, then running around, trying to hide.
  • 2:18 - Left breast in The Engineer's apartment.
Made for Cable Movies:
Women & Men 2: Three Short Stories (1991; HBO)
  . . . . Mara
Magazines:
Playboy (Nov 1987) . . . . Sex in Cinema 1987
  • 143: Side view of right breast from *Rendez-vous*.

Bird, Minah

Films:
Oh, Alfie! (1975; British). . . . . Gloria
  a.k.a. Alfie Darling
The Stud (1978; British) . . . . .Molly
  •• 0:26 - Topless in bed when Tony is talking on the
    telephone.

Birkin, Jane

Films:
Blow-Up (1966; British/Italian) . . . . Teenager
  Nude.
Ms. Don Juan (1973) . . . . Clara
    0:58 - Lower frontal nudity lying in bed with Brigitte
    Bardot.
    1:00 - Brief topless in bed with Bardot. Long shot.
  •• 1:01 - Full frontal nudity getting dressed. Brief top-
    less in open blouse.
Dark Places (1974; British) . . . . Alta
Catherine & Co. (1975; French) . . . . Catherine
  • 0:07 - Topless, standing up in the bathtub to open
    the door for another woman.
  •• 0:09 - Side view of left breast, while taking off her
    blouse in bed.
  ••• 0:10 - Topless, sitting up and turning the light on,
    smoking a cigarette.
  •• 0:17 - Right breast, while making love in bed.
  •• 0:24 - Topless taking off her dress, then buns jump-
    ing into bed.
  •• 0:36 - Buns and left breast posing for a painter.
  • 0:45 - Topless taking off dress, walking around the
    house. Left breast, inviting the neighbor in.
Stuntwoman (1981). . . . .
Kung Fu Master (1989; French) . . . . Mary-Jane
  a.k.a. Le Petit Amour

Bisignano, Jeannine

Films:
Body Rock (1984) . . . . Girl
My Chauffeur (1986) . . . . Party Girl
Ruthless People (1986) . . . . Hooker in Car
    0:17 - Topless, hanging out of the car. Long, long
    shot, don't see anything.
    • 0:40 - Topless in the same scene three times on TV
    while Danny De Vito watches.
    • 0:49 - Left breast hanging out of the car when the
    Chief of Police watches on TV. Closest shot.
    1:15 - Same scene again in department store TV's.
    Long shot, hard to see.
Stripped to Kill II (1988) . . . . Sonny
    0:06 - Buns, while wearing a black bra in dressing
    room.
    ••• 0:38 - Topless and buns during strip dance routine in
    white lingerie.
License to Kill (1989) . . . . Stripper
Magazines:
Playboy (Nov 1986) . . . . Sex in Cinema 1986
    •• 131: Topless in a photo from *Ruthless People*, leaning
    out of the car.

Bisset, Jacqueline

Films:
Cul-de-sac (1966) . . . . Jacqueline
Casino Royale (1967; British) . . . . Miss Goodthighs
Two for the Road (1967; British) . . . . Jackie
Bullitt (1968) . . . . Cathy
The Detective (1968) . . . . Norma McIver
The Sweet Ride (1968) . . . . Vicki Cartwright
    (Not available on video tape.)
    Topless.
The Secret World (1969; French) . . . . Wendy
Airport (1970) . . . . Gwen Meighen
The Grasshopper (1970) . . . . Christine Adams
    0:21 - In flesh colored Las Vegas-style showgirl cos-
    tume. Dark, hard to see.
    0:27 - More showgirl shots.
    1:14 - In black two piece swimsuit.
    1:16 - Almost left breast while squished against Jay in
    the shower.
Believe in Me (1971) . . . . Pamela
The Mephisto Waltz (1971) . . . . Paula Clarkson
    • 0:48 - Very brief right and side view of left breast in
    bed with Alan Alda.
    1:36 - Sort of left breast getting undressed for witch-
    craft ceremony. Long shot side views of right breast,
    but you can't see her face.
    •• 1:45 - Very brief topless twice under bloody water in
    blood covered bathtub, dead. Discovered by Kath-
    leen Widdoes.
Secrets (1971) . . . . Jenny
    0:49 - Very brief lower frontal nudity, putting panties
    on while wearing a black dress.
    ••• 1:02 - Brief buns and a lot of topless on bed making
    love with Raoul.

The Life and Times of Judge Roy Bean (1972)
    . . . . Rose Bean
The Thief Who Came to Dinner (1973) . . . . Laura
The Magnificent One (1974; French/Italian)
    . . . . Tatiana/Christine
Murder on the Orient Express (1974; British)
    . . . . Countess Andrenyi
The Spiral Staircase (1975; British) . . . . Helen
St. Ives (1976) . . . . Janet Whistler
The Deep (1977) . . . . Gail Berke
    ••• 0:01 - Scuba diving underwater in a wet T-shirt.
    • 0:08 - More wet T-shirt, getting out of water, onto
    boat.
The Greek Tycoon (1978) . . . . Liz Cassidy
Who is Killing the Great Chefs of Europe? (1978)
    . . . . Natasha
When Time Ran Out! (1980) . . . . Kay Kirby
Inchon (1981) . . . . Barbara Hallsworth
Rich and Famous (1981) . . . . Liz Hamilton
Famous T & A (1982) . . . . Jenny
    (No longer available for purchase, check your video
    store for rental.)
    ••• 0:31 - Topless scene from *Secrets*.
Class (1983) . . . . Ellen
Under the Volcano (1984) . . . . Yvonne Firmin
High Season (1988; British) . . . . Katherine Shaw
    • 0:56 - Brief topless doing the backstroke in the water
    with Rick, then left breast while lying down. Hard to
    see, everything is lit with blue light.
Scenes from the Class Struggle in Beverly Hills (1989)
    . . . . Clare
The Maid (1990) . . . . Nicole Chantrelle
    0:47 - In lingerie, changing clothes in front of Martin
    Sheen while talking to him.
    1:13 - Very, very brief side of left breast shadow on
    wall, leaping out of bed with Sheen.
Wild Orchid (1990) . . . . Claudia
    1:21 - Dancing in braless white tank top during car-
    nival.
Made for Cable Movies:
Forbidden (1985) . . . . Nina von Halder
    0:25 - In bra and slip in villa with her Jewish lover.
    0:47 - Squished breasts against Jurgen Prochnow in
    bed making love.
Miniseries:
Anna Karenina (1985) . . . . Anna Karenina
Napolean and Josephine (1987)
    . . . . Josephine de Beauharnais
    Lots of cleavage.

Black, Karen

Films:
Easy Rider (1969) . . . . Karen
Five Easy Pieces (1970) . . . . Rayette Dipesto
    0:48 - In sheer black nightie in bathroom, then walk-
    ing to bedroom with Jack Nicholson.
Cisco Pike (1971) . . . . Sue

Drive, He Said (1972). .Olive
  • 1:05 - Brief topless screaming in the bathtub when
    she gets scared when a bird flies in.
    1:19 - Brief lower frontal nudity running out of the
    house in her bathrobe.
Little Laura and Big John (1972) . . . . Laura
Portnoy's Complaint (1972) . . . . The Monkey
Airport 1975 (1974) . . . . .Nancy
The Great Gatsby (1974). . . . . Myrtle Wilson
The Day of the Locust (1975) . . . . Faye
Nashville (1975) . . . . Connie White
Burnt Offerings (1976) . . . . Marion
Capricorn One (1978). . . . . Judy Drinkwater
In Praise of Older Women (1978; Canadian) . . Maya
  •• 0:35 - Topless in bed with Tom Berenger.
Separate Ways (1979) . . . . Valentine Colby
  • 0:04 - Topless and in panties changing while her hus-
    band talks on the phone, then in bra. Long shot.
  •• 0:18 - Topless in bed, while making love with Tony
    Lo Bianco.
  •• 0:36 - Topless taking a shower, then getting out.
Chanel Solitaire (1981) . . . . .Emilienne D'Alencon
Killing Heat (1981). . . . . Mary Turner
  •• 0:41 - Full frontal nudity giving herself a shower in
    the bedroom.
Come Back to the Five and Dime, Jimmy Dean, Jimmy
(1982). . . . . Joanne
Can She Bake a Cherry Pie? (1983) . . . . .Zec
    0:40 - Sort of left breast squished against a guy, while
    kissing him in bed.
  • 1:02 - Very brief upper half of left breast in bed when
    she reaches up to touch her hair.
Cut and Run (1985) . . . . .Karin
Invaders from Mars (1986) . . . . Linda
Eternal Evil (1987). . . . .
Miss Right (1987). . . . . Amy
  • 0:47 - Brief topless jumping out of bed and running
    to get a bucket of water to put out a fire.
The Invisible Kid (1988) . . . . Mom
Out of the Dark (1988) . . . . .Ruth
Bad Manners (1989) . . . . .Mrs. Fitzpatrick
Homer & Eddie (1989) . . . . Belle
Night Angel (1989). . . . . .Rita
Overexposed (1990) . . . . .Mrs. Trowbridge
Twisted Justice (1990). . . . . Mrs. Granger
Blood Money (1991). . . . . Barrett
Made for Cable TV:
The Hitchhiker: Hired Help . . . . Mrs. Kay Mason
  (Available on *The Hitchhiker, Volume 1.*)
Made for TV Movies:
Trilogy of Terror (1974). . . . .
TV:
The Second Hundred Years (1967-68)
. . . . Marcia Garroway
Magazines:
Playboy (Dec 1973). . . . . Sex Stars of 1973
  • 207: Peak at left breast.
Playboy (Dec 1976). . . . . Sex Stars of 1976
  •• 185: In pink see-through night gown.

Blackburn, Greta

Films:
48 Hours (1982). . . . . Lisa
  •• 0:13 - Topless and buns in bathroom in hotel room
    with James Remar.
The Concrete Jungle (1982) . . . . Lady in Bar
Time Walker (1982) . . . . .Sherri
Chained Heat (1983; U.S./German) . . . . .Lulu
Yellowbeard (1983) . . . . .Mr. Prostitute
Death Feud (1989). . . . . .Jenny
    0:29 - In sexy black dress talking to Frank Stallone.
    1:04 - In black lingerie on couch.
Under the Boardwalk (1989) . . . . Mrs. Vorpin
My Blue Heaven (1990) . . . . Stewardess

Blackman, Joan

Films:
Vengeance of Virgo (1972). . . . .
Macon County Line (1974) . . . . Carol Morgan
Pets (1974). . . . . .Geraldine Mills
  • 0:46 - Brief side view of left breast, while getting out
    of bed after making love with Bonnie.
Moonrunners (1975) . . . . Reba
One Man (1979; Canadian) . . . .
Return to Waterloo (1986) . . . .

Blackwood, Nina

Films:
Vice Squad (1982) . . . . .Ginger
TV:
Entertainment Tonight . . . . Music Correspondent
Music Television . . . . Video Jockey
Magazines:
Playboy (Aug 1978) . . . . The Girls in the Office
  ••• 142: Full frontal nudity (with brunette hair).

Blair, Linda

Films:
Way We Live Now (1970). . . . . Sara Aldridge
The Sporting Club (1971) . . . . .Barby
The Exorcist (1973) . . . . Regan
Airport 1975 (1974). . . . . .Janice Abbott
Exorcist II: The Heretic (1977) . . . . Regan
Roller Boogie (1979) . . . . Terry Barkley
Hell Night (1981). . . . . Marti
Chained Heat (1983; U.S./German). . . . . Carol
  ••• 0:30 - Topless in the shower.
  •• 0:56 - In bra, then topless in the Warden's office
    when he rapes her.
Night Patrol (1985). . . . . Sue
  • 1:19 - Brief left breast, in bed with The Unknown
    Comic.
Savage Island (1985) .Daly
Savage Streets (1985). . . . . .Brenda
  ••• 1:05 - Topless sitting in the bathtub thinking.
Night Force (1986) . . . .
Grotesque (1987). . . . . Lisa

Red Heat (1987; U.S./German) . . . . Chris Carlson
   0:09 - In blue nightgown in the bedroom with her
   boyfriend, almost topless.
  ••• 0:56 - Topless in shower room scene.
  ••• 1:01 - Brief topless getting raped by Sylvia Kristel
   while the male guard watches.
Silent Assassins (1988). Sara
   0:48 - Very brief, wearing light blue bra struggling on
   couch with a masked attacker.
Up Your Alley (1988). . . . . .Vickie Adderly
W. B., Blue and the Bean (1988) . . . . .Nettie
  a.k.a. Bail Out
Witchery (1988) . . . . .Jane Brooks
Bedroom Eyes II (1989) . . . . Sophie Stevens
   0:31 - Buns, in bed with Wings Hauser.
  • 0:33 - Brief left breast under bubbles in the bathtub.
   Don't see her face.
A Woman Obsessed (1989). . . . . Evie Barnes
Repossessed (1990). . . . . Nancy Aglet
Made for TV Movies:
Born Innocent (1974) . . . .
Sarah T.: Portrait of a Teenage Alcoholic (1975)
  . . . . Sarah
Magazines:
Playboy (Dec 1983). . . . . Sex Stars of 1983
  ••• 209: Topless.
Playboy (Dec 1984). . . . . Sex Stars of 1984
  ••• 207: Topless in the water up to her breasts.

Blaisdell, Deborah
a.k.a. Adult film actress Tracey Adams.
Films:
The Lost Empire (1983). . . . . Girl Recruit
Screen Test (1986) . . . . Dancer
  •• 0:04 - Topless dancing on stage.
Student Affairs (1987) . . . . Kelly
  ••• 0:26 - Topless sitting up in bed talking to a guy.
Wildest Dreams (1987) . . . . Joan Peabody
  • 1:10 - Brief topless during fight on floor with two
   other women.
Wimps (1987) . . . . .Roxanne Chandless
  • 1:22 - Brief topless and buns taking off clothes and
   getting into bed with Francis in bedroom.
Enrapture (1989) . . . . .Martha
  ••• 0:10 - Topless undressing in her apartment with Keith.
  •• 0:17 - Left breast, in bed with Keith, then brief topless.

Blake, Stephanie
Films:
The Big Bet (1985). . . . . Mrs. Roberts
  ••• 0:04 - Topless sitting on bed, then making love with
   Chris.
  •• 0:37 - Nude on bed with Chris. Shot at fast speed, he
   runs between bedrooms.
  •• 0:59 - Full frontal nudity in bed again. Shot at fast
   speed.

Ferris Bueller's Day Off (1986) . . . . Singing Nurse
Danger Zone II: Reaper's Revenge (1988)
  . . . . Tattooed Topless Dancer
  ••• 0:47 - Dancing on stage in bikini bottoms.

Blakely, Susan
Films:
Savages (1972) . . . . Cecily
The Way We Were (1973). . . . . Judianne
The Lords of Flatbush (1974) . . . . .Jane Bradshaw
The Towering Inferno (1974) . . . . Patty Simmons
Capone (1975) . . . . Iris Crawford
  (Not available on video tape.)
  Topless.
Report to the Commissioner (1975). . . . . . . Patty Butler
Airport '79: The Concorde (1979) . . . . Maggie
Over the Top (1987) . . . . Christine Hawk
Made for Cable TV:
The Hitchhiker: Remembering Melody. . . . Melody
  ••• 0:17 - Right breast in shower with Ted and brief top-
   less in the bathtub.
Miniseries:
Rich Man, Poor Man (1976)
  . . . . Julie Prescott Abbott Jordache
Made for TV Movies:
Broken Angel (1988) . . . . Catherine Coburn
Murder Times Seven (1990). . . . . .Gert Kiley
And the Sea Will Tell (1991) . . . . .Gail Bugliosi
Magazines:
Playboy (Mar 1972) . . . . Savages
  • 142: Topless.
  • 145: Topless.

Blanchard, Vanessa
Films:
Witchfire (1986) . . . . Liz
  •• 0:52 - Brief topless in bed and then the shower.
Uphill All the Way (1987). . . . . Velma

Blee, Debra
Films:
The Beach Girls (1982) . . . . .Sarah
  ••• 1:22 - Brief topless opening her swimsuit top on the
   beach.
Sloane (1984). . . . . Cynthia Thursby
  • 0:15 - Very brief topless during attempted rape.
The Malibu Bikini Shop (1985). . . . . .Jane
Savage Streets (1985) . . . . Rachel
  0:20 - In a bra in the girls locker room.
Hamburger—The Motion Picture (1986) . . . . .Mia Vunk
  0:25 - Briefly in wet dress in the swimming pool.

Bloom, Claire
Films:
The Illustrated Man (1969). . . . . Felicia
Three into Two Won't Go (1969; British)
  . . . . .Frances Howard

A Severed Head (1971; British) . . . . Honor Klein
  • 1:10 - Topless leaning up then right beast while sit-
    ting up in bed with Richard Attenborough.
A Doll's House (1973) . . . . Nora Helmer
Islands in the Stream (1977) . . . . Audrey
Deja Vu (1984) . . . .
Miniseries:
Brideshead Revisited (1981; British). . . .Lady Marchmain
Made for TV Movies:
Promises to Keep (1985) . . . . Sally

Bloom, Lindsay

Films:
Six Pack Annie (1975) . . . . Annie
Texas Detour (1977) . . . . Sugar McCarthy
French Quarter (1978)
  . . . . "Big Butt" Annie/Policewoman in Bar
H.O.T.S. (1979) . . . . Melody Ragmore
  • 0:28 - Very brief right breast on balcony.
  • 1:34 - Brief topless during football game throwing
    football as quarterback.
The Main Event (1979) . . . . Girl in Bed
The Happy Hooker Goes Hollywood (1980) . . . . . .Chris
TV:
Dallas (1982) . . . . Bonnie Robertson
Mike Hammer (1984-87) . . . . Velda

Blount, Lisa

Films:
9/30/55 (1977). . . . . Billie Jean
Dead and Buried (1981) . . . . Girl on the Beach
  • 0:06 - Brief topless on the beach getting her picture
    taken by a photographer.
An Officer and a Gentleman (1982) . . Lynette Pomeroy
  1:25 - In a red bra and tap pants in a motel room
    with David Keith.
Radioactive Dreams (1984) . . . . Miles Archer
Cease Fire (1985) . . . . .Paula Murphy
Cut and Run (1985) . . . . .Fran Hudson
What Waits Below (1986) . . . . Leslie Peterson
Nightflyers (1987). . . . . Audrey
Prince of Darkness (1987) . . . . Catherine
South of Reno (1987) . . . . Anette Clark
  1:02 - In black bra getting blouse torn open while ly-
    ing down.
Great Balls of Fire (1989). . . . . Lois Brown
Out Cold (1989) . . . . .Phyllis
Blind Fury (1990) . . . . Annie Winchester
Femme Fatale (1990) . . . . Jenny
Made for Cable TV:
The Hitchhiker: One Last Prayer . . . . Miranda
  0:06 - Briefly in a black bra putting a new homemade
    outfit on.
Made for TV Movies:
Unholy Matrimony (1988) . . . . Karen Stockwell
TV:
Sons and Daughters (1990-91) . . . . Mary Ruth

Bockrath, Tina

Video Tapes:
Playboy Video Calendar 1991 (1990). . . . . . January
  ••• 0:01 - Nude.
Playboy's Sexy Lingerie II (1990) . . . .
Magazines:
Playboy (May 1990). . . . . Playmate

Bohrer, Corinne

Films:
The Beach Girls (1982). . . . . Champagne Girl
I, the Jury (1982) . . . . Soap Opera Actress
My Favorite Year (1982). . . . .
Zapped! (1982) . . . . Cindy
Joysticks (1983) . . . . Patsy Rutter
Surf II (1984) . . . . Cindy Lou
Police Academy 4: Citizens on Patrol (1987) . . . . .Laura
Stewardess School (1987) . . . . .Cindy Adams
Vice Versa (1988) . . . . .Sam
Made for Cable Movies:
Dead Solid Perfect (1988; HBO). . . . . . .Janie Rimmer
  ••• 0:31 - Nude, getting out of bed to get some ice for
    Randy Quaid. Nice scene!
Made for Cable TV:
Dream On: What I Did for Lust (1991; HBO) . . . . Chloe
TV:
E/R (1984-85) . . . . Nurse Cory Smith
Free Spirit (1989-90) . . . . Winnie Goodwin
Man of the People (1991-) . . . .

Bolling, Tiffany

Films:
Tony Rome (1967). Photo Girl
The Marriage of a Young Stockbroker (1971)
  . . . . .Girl in the Rain
Bonnie's Kids (1973) . . . . Ellie
  •• 0:21 - Topless, modeling in office.
  • 1:16 - Brief right breast making love in bed.
Wicked, Wicked (1973) . . . . Lisa James
The Centerfold Girls (1974). . . . . .Vera
  • 1:02 - Brief topless in photograph.
  ••• 1:12 - Topless in the shower.
  • 1:21 - Brief topless in motel bed getting raped by
    two guys after they drug her beer.
The Wild Party (1975) . . . . .Kate
Kingdom of the Spiders (1977) . . . . Diane Ashley
The Vals (1982) . . . . .Valley Attorney and Parent
Love Scenes (1984) . . . . .Val
  •• 0:01 - Side view of left breast in bed with Peter.
  ••• 0:06 - Topless getting photographed by Britt Ekland
    in the house.
  • 0:09 - Brief topless opening her bathrobe to show
    Peter.
  • 0:12 - Topless in bathtub with Peter.
  ••• 0:19 - Topless lying in bed talking with Peter, then
    making love.
  •• 0:43 - Topless acting in a movie when Rick opens her
    blouse.

•• 0:57 - Nude behind shower door, then topless getting out and talking to Peter.
•• 0:59 - Topless making love tied up on bed with Rick during filming of movie.
•• 1:07 - Topless, then full frontal nudity acting with Elizabeth during filming of movie.
•• 1:17 - Full frontal nudity getting out of pool.
•• 1:26 - Topless with Peter on the bed.
Open House (1987) . . . . Judy Roberts
Made for TV Movies:
Key West (1973) . . . . Ruth
TV:
The New People (1969-70) . . . . Susan Bradley
Magazines:
Playboy (Apr 1972) . . . . Tiffany's A Gem
••• 153-159:
Playboy (Dec 1972). . . . . Sex Stars of 1972
••• 210: Topless.
Playboy (Nov 1973) . . . . Sex in Cinema
• 152: Left breast in red light.
Playboy (Dec 1973). . . . . Sex Stars of 1973
• 208: Left breast.

Bonet, Lisa

Films:
Angel Heart (1987) . . . . Epiphany Proudfoot
••• 1:27 - Topless in bed with Mickey Rourke. It gets kind of bloody.
• 1:32 - Topless in bathtub.
• 1:48 - Topless in bed, dead.
TV:
The Cosby Show (1984-87). . . . . Denise Huxtable
A Different World (1987-89) . . . . Denise Huxtable
The Cosby Show (1989-). . . . Denise Huxtable -Kendall

Bonet, Nai

Films:
The Greatest (1977; U.S./British) . . . . Suzie Gomez
Fairytales (1979). . . . . Sheherazade
• 0:29 - Buns and very brief left breast doing a belly dance and rubbing oil on herself.
Nocturna (1979). Nocturna

Boorman, Katrine

Films:
Excalibur (1981; British) . . . . Igrayne
• 0:14 - Right breast, then topless in front of the fire when Uther tricks her into thinking that he is her husband and makes love to her.
Dream One (1984; British/French)
. . . . Duchka/Nemo's Mother

Botsford, Sara

Films:
By Design (1982; Canadian) . . . . Angie
• 0:23 - Full frontal nudity in the ocean. Long shot, hard to see anything.

• 1:08 - Brief side view of left breast making love in bed while talking on the phone.
Deadly Eyes (1982) . . . . Kelly Leonard
Still of the Night (1982) . . . . Gail Phillips

Bouche, Sugar

Films:
Heavenly Bodies (1985) . . . . Stripper
• 0:16 - Topless doing stripper-gram for Steve.
Graveyard Shift (1987). . . . . Fabulous Frannie
••• 0:12 - Topless doing a stripper routine on stage.
• 0:24 - Brief topless in the shower.

Bouchet, Barbara

Films:
A Global Affair (1964) . . . . Girl
Good Neighbor Sam (1964). . . . . .Receptionist
Sex and the Single Girl (1964) . . . . Frannie
What a Way to Go (1964) . . . . Girl on Plane
In Harm's Way (1965; B&W). . . . . Liz Eddington
• 0:05 - Very, very brief right breast waving to a guy from the water.
Agent for H.A.R.M. (1966) . . . . Ava Vestak
Casino Royale (1967; British) . . . . .Moneypenny
Danger Route (1968; British) . . . . Mari
Sweet Charity (1969) . . . . Ursula
Black Belly of the Tarantula (1972; Italian)
. . . . .Maria Zani
Down the Ancient Staircase (1975; Italian). . . . . . . Carla
Blood Feast (1976; Italian) . . . .
Duck in Orange Sauce (1976; Italian). . . . . Patty
Sex with a Smile (1976; Italian)
. . . . "One for the Money" segment
••• 0:50 - Topless sitting up in bed with a guy in bed, then lying down, wearing glasses.
Death Rage (1978; Italian) . . . .
Maniac Mansion (1978; Italian) . . . .
Magazines:
Playboy (Nov 1972) . . . . Sex in Cinema
• 161: Buns.

Boulting, Ingrid

Films:
The Last Tycoon (1976) . . . . .Kathleen Moore
Deadly Passion (1985) . . . . .Martha Greenwood
• 0:46 - Brief buns taking off clothes and jumping into pool. Long shot.
•• 0:47 - Topless getting out of pool and kissing Brent Huff. Right breast in bed.
• 0:54 - Topless in whirlpool bath with Huff.
••• 1:02 - Topless, wearing white panties and massaging herself in front of a mirror.
•• 1:31 - Topless taking off clothes and jumping into bed with Huff.

Bouquet, Carole

Model for *Chanel* cosmetics.
Films:
That Obscure Object of Desire
(1977; French/Spanish) . . . . .Conchita
••• 0:53 - Topless in bedroom.
••• 1:01 - Topless in bed with Fernando Rey.
For Your Eyes Only (1981) . . . . Melina Havelock
Bingo Bongo (1983) . . . . Laura
Dream One (1984; British/French) . . . . Rals-Akrai
Too Beautiful for You (1990; French)
. . . . Florence Barthelemy

Boushel, Joy

Films:
Pick-Up Summer (1979; Canadian) . . . . Sally
••• 0:56 - Topless playing pinball, then running around.
Terror Train (1980; Canadian) . . . . Pet
•• 0:49 - Topless wearing panties in sleeper room on
train with Mo.
Quest For Fire (1981) . . . . Tribe Member
Humongous (1982; Canadian) . . . . Donna Blake
•• 0:09 - Topless looking out the window. More topless
in the room in the mirror.
• 0:48 - Topless undoing her top to warm up Bert.
The Fly (1986) . . . . .Tawny
• 0:54 - Very brief topless viewed from below when Jeff
Goldblum pulls her by the arm to get her out of bed.
Keeping Track (1988) . . . . Judy
Look Who's Talking (1989) . . . . Melissa

Bowser, Sue

Films:
Stripes (1981) . . . . Mud Wrestler
Doctor Detroit (1983) . . . . Dream Girl
Into the Night (1985) . . . . Girl on Boat
•• 0:24 - Topless taking off blouse with Jake on his boat
after Michelle Pfeiffer leaves.

Boyd, Tanya

Films:
Black Shampoo (1976) . . . . Brenda
Ilsa, Harem Keeper of the Oil Sheiks (1978) . . . . . . .Satin
The Happy Hooker Goes Hollywood (1980) . . Sylvie
• 0:39 - Brief topless in jungle room when an older cus-
tomer accidentally comes in.
Wholly Moses (1980) . . . . Princess
Jo Jo Dancer, Your Life Is Calling (1986) . . . . Alicia

Bracci, Teda

Films:
C. C. & Company (1970) . . . . Pig
R.P.M. (1970) . . . .

The Big Bird Cage (1972) . . . . .Bull Jones
•• 0:15 - Topless in front of the guard, Rocco.
• 0:51 - Very brief right breast, then left breast during
fight with Pam Grier. Brief left breast standing up in
rice paddy.
The Centerfold Girls (1974) . . . . Rita
• 0:18 - Topless taking off her clothes in the living
room in front of everybody.
The Trial of Billy Jack (1974) . . . . Teda
The World's Greatest Lover (1977) . . . .

Brady, Janelle

Films:
Class of Nuke 'Em High (1986) . . . . .Chrissy
•• 0:26 - Topless sitting on bed in the attic with Warren.
• 0:31 - Brief topless scene from 0:26 superimposed
over Warren's nightmare.
Teen Wolf Too (1987). . . . . History Student

Braga, Sonia

Films:
Dona Flor and Her Two Husbands (1978; Brazilian)
. . . . Flor
• 0:13 - Buns and brief topless with her husband.
•• 0:15 - Topless lying on the bed.
0:17 - Buns, getting out of bed.
••• 0:54 - Topless making love on the bed with her husband.
•• 0:57 - Topless lying on the bed.
••• 1:41 - Topless kissing her first husband.
Lady on the Bus (1978; Brazilian) . . . .
• 0:11 - Brief left breast.
••• 0:12 - Topless, then buns, then full frontal nudity in
bed getting her slip torn off by her newlywed husband. Long struggle scene.
•• 0:39 - Right breast standing with half open dress,
then topless lying in bed, then getting into the pool.
••• 0:48 - Topless and buns on the beach after picking
up a guy on the bus.
• 0:54 - Brief topless in bed dreaming.
• 1:02 - Brief topless in waterfall with bus driver.
•• 1:05 - Topless in cemetery after picking up another
guy on the bus.
• 1:13 - Topless on the ground with another guy from
a bus.
• 1:16 - Left breast sitting on sofa while her husband
talks.
I Love You (1982; Brazilian) . . . . .Maria
••• 0:34 - Full frontal nudity making love with Paulo.
•• 0:36 - Topless sitting on the edge of the bed.
• 0:49 - Topless running around the house teasing
Paulo.
•• 0:50 - Brief nude in strobe light. Don't see her face.
• 0:53 - Topless eating fruit with Paulo.
••• 0:54 - Topless wearing white panties in front of windows with Paulo. Long scene.
• 1:03 - Left breast standing talking to Paulo.
• 1:10 - Left breast talking to Paulo.

••• 1:23 - Topless with Paulo during an argument. Dark, but long scene.
•• 1:28 - Topless walking around Paulo's place with a gun. Dark.
•• 1:33 - Various topless scenes.
Gabriela (1984; Brazilian) . . . . Gabriela
•• 0:26 - Topless leaning back out the window making love on a table with Marcello Mastroianni.
••• 0:27 - Nude, taking a shower outside and cleaning herself up.
• 0:32 - Right breast in bed.
•• 0:38 - Nude, making love with Mastroianni on the kitchen table.
•• 0:45 - Nude, getting in bed with Mastroianni.
1:13 - Full frontal nudity, on bed with another man, then getting beat up by Mastroianni.
••• 1:17 - Nude, changing clothes in the bedroom.
•• 1:32 - Topless and buns making love outside with Mastroianni. Lots of passion!
Kiss of the Spider Woman (1985; U.S./Brazilian)
. . . . Leni/Marta/Spider Woman
The Milagro Beanfield War (1988) . . . . . . Ruby Archuleta
Moon Over Parador (1988) . . . . Madonna Mendez
The Rookie (1990) . . . . Liesl
Magazines:
Playboy (May 1979) . . . . Foreign Sex Stars
•• 165: Topless.
Playboy (Nov 1983) . . . . Sex in Cinema 1983
••• 149: Topless.
Playboy (Oct 1984) . . . . The Girls from Brazil
••• 86-91: Nude.
Playboy (Dec 1984) . . . . Sex Stars of 1984
••• 205: Full frontal nudity leaning against bed.
Playboy (Dec 1987) . . . . Sex Stars of 1987
••• 153: Full frontal nudity.
Playboy (Dec 1988) . . . . Sex Stars of 1988
••• 183: Full frontal nudity leaning against bed.

Brandt, Brandi

Films:
Wedding Band (1989) . . . . Serena (Gypsy Wedding)
Video Tapes:
Playboy Video Calendar 1989 (1988) . . . November
••• 0:41 - Nude.
Glamour Through Your Lens—Outdoor Techniques (1989) . . . . herself
0:42 - In white lingerie on couch.
Playmates at Play (1990) . . . . Easy Rider
Magazines:
Playboy (Oct 1987) . . . . Playmate

Bremmer, Leslee

Films:
Best Chest in the West (1984) . . . . Leslee
••• 0:29 - In black, two piece swimsuit, then topless and buns.
• 0:32 - More topless during judging and winning the 2nd round.

Hardbodies (1984) . . . . Photo Session Hardbody
• 0:02 - Topless in the surf when her friends take off her swimsuit top during the opening credits.
•• 0:40 - Topless with other topless girls posing for photographs taken by Rounder. She takes off her dress and is wearing a black G-string.
Centerfold Screen Test (1985) . . . . herself
0:22 - Topless under fishnet top. (Practically see-through top.)
•• 0:24 - Dancing, wearing the fishnet top and black G-string.
••• 0:28 - Closer shot, dancing, while wearing the top.
Paradise Motel (1985)
. . . . uncredited Girl Leaving Room
• 0:38 - Topless buttoning her pink sweater, leaving motel room.
School Spirit (1985) . . . . Sandy
Best Chest in the West II (1986) . . . . herself
0:49 - Dancing in pink top. Buns, in G-string.
My Chauffeur (1986) . . . . Party Girl
Reform School Girls (1986) . . . . uncredited Shower Girl
•• 0:25 - Brief topless in the shower three times. Walking from left to right in the background, full frontal nudity by herself with wet hair, topless walking from left to right.
Another Chance (1989) . . . Girl in Womanizer's Meeting

Brennan, Eileen

Films:
The Last Picture Show (1971; B&W) . . . . Genevieve
Scarecrow (1973) . . . . Darlene
• 0:27 - Brief topless in bed when Gene Hackman takes off her bra and grabs her breasts.
The Sting (1973) . . . . Billie
Daisy Miller (1974) . . . . Mrs. Walker
Hustle (1975) . . . . Paula Hollinger
The Great Smokey Roadblock (1976) . . . . Penelope
Murder by Death (1976) . . . . Tess Skeffington
The Cheap Detective (1978) . . . . Betty DeBoop
FM (1978) . . . . Mother
Private Benjamin (1980) . . . . Captain Doreen Lewis
Clue (1985) . . . . Mrs. Peacock
The New Adventures of Pippi Longstocking (1988)
. . . . Miss Bannister
White Palace (1990) . . . . Judy
Made for TV Movies:
Deadly Intentions...Again? (1991) . . . . Charlotte

Brentano, Amy

Films:
Breeders (1986) . . . . Gail
• 0:59 - Long shot of buns, getting into the next.
• 1:07 - Topless in nest, throwing her head back.
•• 1:08 - Brief topless, writhing around in the nest, then topless, arching her back.
• 1:11 - Topless, long shot, just before the nest is destroyed.
Robot Holocaust (1986) . . . . Irradiated Female

Bresee, Bobbie

Films:
Mausoleum (1983) . . . . Susan Farrell
••• 0:25 - Topless and buns wrapping a towel around herself in her bedroom.
•• 0:26 - Topless on the balcony showing herself to the gardener.
• 0:29 - Topless in the garage with the gardener. Brief, dark, hard to see.
• 0:32 - Brief left breast, while kissing Marjoe Gortner.
• 1:10 - Topless in the bathtub talking to Gortner. Long shot.
Armed Response (1986) . . . . Anna
Star Slammer—The Escape (1986) . . . . Marai
Surf Nazis Must Die (1986) . . . . Smeg's Mom
Evil Spawn (1987) . . . . Lynn Roman
0:14 - Very brief half of right breast in bed with a guy.
0:26 - In red one piece swimsuit.
••• 0:36 - Topless in bathroom looking at herself in the mirror, then taking a shower.
Magazines:
Playboy (Jul 1989) . . . . B-Movie Bimbos
••• 133: Full frontal nudity leaning on a car.

Brighton, Connie

Video Tapes:
Playboy's Playmate Review 3 (1985) . . . . . Playmate
Playboy Video Centerfold: Kerri Kendall (1990)
. . . . Playmate
••• 0:31 - Nude.
Magazines:
Playboy (Sep 1982) . . . . Playmate

Brimhall, Cynthia

Films:
Hard Ticket to Hawaii (1987) . . . . Edy
•• 0:47 - Topless changing out of a dress into a blouse and pants.
•• 1:33 - Topless during the end credits.
Picasso Trigger (1989) . . . . Edy
•• 0:59 - Topless in weight room with a guy.
Guns (1990) . . . . Edy Stark
0:26 - Buns, in G-string singing and dancing at club.
•• 0:27 - Topless in dressing room.
0:53 - Buns, in black one piece outfit and stockings, singing in club. Nice legs!
Video Tapes:
Playboy Video Magazine, Volume 10 . . . . Playmate
Playboy Video Calendar 1987 (1986) . . . . Playmate
Playboy's Sexy Lingerie (1988) . . . .
Playmates at Play (1990) . . . . Easy Rider
Magazines:
Playboy (Oct 1985) . . . . Playmate

Brisebois, Danielle

Films:
The Premonition (1976) . . . . Janie
King of the Gypsies (1978) . . . . Young Tita
Big Bad Mama II (1987) . . . . Billy Jean McClatchie
••• 0:12 - Topless with Julie McCullough playing in a pond underneath a waterfall.
0:36 - In a white slip standing at the door talking to McCullough, then talking to Angie Dickinson.
Kill Crazy (1989) . . . . Libby
•• 0:39 - Topless taking off top to go skinny dipping with Rachel.
TV:
All In the Family (1978-83) . . . . Stephanie Mills
Knots Landing (1983-84) . . . . Mary-Frances Summer

Brittany, Tally

See: Chanel, Tally.

Broady, Eloise

Films:
Dangerous Love (1988) . . . . Bree
••• 0:06 - Topless changing into lingerie in the mirror.
To Die For (1988) . . . . Girl at Party
Troop Beverly Hills (1989) . . . . Starlet at Party
Video Tapes:
Playboy Video Calendar 1989 (1988) . . . . December
••• 0:45 - Nude.
Magazines:
Playboy (Apr 1988) . . . . Playmate
92:

Brooke, Sandy

Films:
Bits and Pieces (1985) . . . . Mrs. Talbot
••• 1:03 - Topless in bathtub washing herself before the killer drowns her. Very brief right breast when struggling.
• 1:09 - Brief topless under water in bathtub, dead.
Star Slammer—The Escape (1986) . . . . Taura
••• 0:21 - Topless in jail putting a new top on. In braless white T-shirt for most of the rest of the film.
•• 1:09 - Topless changing into a clean top.
The Terror on Alcatraz (1986) . . . . Mona
• 0:05 - Right breast on bed getting burned with a cigarette by Frank.
Nightmare Sisters (1987) . . . . Amanda Detweiler
Deep Space (1988) . . . . Woman in House

Brooks, Elizabeth

Films:
The Howling (1981) . . . . Marsha
- •• 0:46 - Full frontal nudity taking off her robe in front of a campfire.
- • 0:48 - Topless sitting on Bill by the fire.

The Forgotten One (1989) . . . . Carla
TV:
Doctors' Hospital (1975-76)
. . . . Nurse Connie Kimbrough
Magazines:
Playboy (Nov 1980) . . . . Sex in Cinema 1980
- ••• 174: Full frontal nudity.

Brooks, Randi

Films:
Looker (1981) . . . . Girl in Bikini
Deal of the Century (1983) . . . . Ms. Della Rosa
The Man with Two Brains (1983) . . . . Fran
- •• 1:11 - Brief topless showing Steve Martin her breasts in front of the hotel. Buns, changing in the hotel room, then wearing black see-through negligee.

Tightrope (1984) . . . . Jamie Cory
- ••• 0:20 - Topless taking off her robe and getting into the spa.
- 0:24 - Buns, dead in the spa while Clint Eastwood looks at her.

Hamburger—The Motion Picture (1986)
. . . . Mrs. Vunk
- •• 0:52 - Brief topless in helicopter with a guy.

Cop (1988) . . . . Jeanie Pratt
- 0:32 - In a bra making love in her kitchen with James Woods.
TV:
Wizards and Warriors (1983) . . . . Witch Bethel
The Last Precinct (1986) . . . . Officer Mel Brubaker
Magazines:
Playboy (Nov 1983) . . . . Sex in Cinema 1983
- • 150: See-through negligee.
Playboy (Dec 1983) . . . . Sex Stars of 1983
- • 210: Side view of right breast and buns.

Brown, Blair

Films:
The Choirboys (1977) . . . . Mrs. Lyles
Altered States (1980) . . . . Emily Jessup
- • 0:10 - Brief left breast making love with William Hurt in red light from an electric heater.
- •• 0:34 - Topless lying on her stomach during Hurt's mushroom induced hallucination.
- 1:39 - Buns, sitting in hallway with Hurt after the transformations go away.

One Trick Pony (1980) . . . . Marion
Continental Divide (1981) . . . . Nell
A Flash of Green (1984) . . . . . Catherine "Kat" Hubble
- • 1:30 - Very brief right breast moving around in bed with Ed Harris.

Strapless (1990) . . . . Dr. Lillian Hempel

Made for Cable TV:
Days and Nights of Molly Dodd . . . . Molly Dodd
Miniseries:
Space (1986) . . . .
Made for TV Movies:
Hands of a Stranger (1987) . . . . Diane Benton
Extreme Close-Up (1990) . . . .
TV:
Captains and the Kings (1976) . . . .
Elizabeth Healey Hennessey
Wheels (1978) . . . . Barbara Lipton
Days and Nights of Molly Dodd (1987-88) . . Molly Dodd

Brown, Julie

Comedienne.
Singer–"The Homecoming Queen's Got a Gun."
Not to be confused with MTV Video Jockey "Downtown" Julie Brown.
Films:
Any Which Way You Can (1980) . . . . Candy
Bloody Birthday (1980) . . . . Beverly
- ••• 0:13 - Dancing in red bra, then topless while two boys peek through hole in the wall, then buns. Nice, long scene.
- 0:48 - In bedroom wearing red bra.
- 1:03 - In bedroom again in the red bra.

Police Academy II: Their First Assignment (1985)
. . . . Chloe
Earth Girls are Easy (1989) . . . . Candy
TV:
Just Say Julie (1990-) . . . . host

Bruce, Andi

Films:
Summer's Games (1987) . . . . News Anchor
- 0:12 - Brief right breast turning around to look at monitor.
- • 0:42 - Topless turning around to look at the monitor.
Magazines:
Penthouse (Aug 1987) . . . . Pet

Bryant, Pamela Jean

Films:
H.O.T.S. (1979) . . . . Teri Lynn
- • 1:33 - Topless during football game.

Separate Ways (1979) . . . . Cocktail Waitress
Don't Answer the Phone (1980) . . . . Sue
Looker (1981) . . . . Reston Girl
Lunch Wagon (1981) . . . . Marcy
- •• 0:04 - Topless changing tops in room in gas station with Rosanne Katon while a guy watches through key hole.
- • 0:55 - Left breast, several times, in van with Bif.

Private Lessons (1981) . . . . Joyce
- • 0:03 - Very brief right breast, changing in the house while Billy and his friend peep from outside.

Made for TV Movies:
B.J. and the Bear (1978) . . . .
Magazines:
Playboy (Sep 1977) . . . . Girls of the Big Ten
•• 148: Topless.
Playboy (Apr 1978) . . . . Playmate
118:

Buckman, Tara

Films:
Rollercoaster (1977) . . . . Coaster Attendant
Hooper (1978) . . . . Debbie
The Cannonball Run (1981) . . . . Jill
Silent Night, Deadly Night (1984) . . . . Mother (Ellie)
  • 0:12 - Brief right breast twice when the killer dressed
    as Santa Claus, rips her blouse open. Topless lying
    dead with slit throat.
  • 0:18 - Very, very brief topless during Billy's flashback.
  • 0:43 - Brief topless a couple of times again in another
    of Billy's flashbacks.
Never Too Young to Die (1986) . . . . . Sacrificed Punkette
Silent Night, Deadly Night, Part 2 (1986)
 . . . . Mother
  • 0:09 - Very brief right breast, with Santa Claus during
    flashback.
  • 0:14 - Very brief topless on ground during flashback.
  • 0:22 - Very, very brief blurry topless during flashback.
  • 0:47 - Very, very brief topless during flashback.
Terminal Exposure (1988) . . . .
The Loves of a Wall Street Woman (1989)
 . . . . Brenda Baxter
  Private Screenings.
  • 0:00 - Topless taking a shower, opening the door and
    getting a towel.
  •• 0:06 - Topless changing clothes in locker room in
    black panties. Nice legs!
  ••• 0:18 - Topless in bed making love with Alex.
  •• 0:31 - Topless in bed with Alex making love.
  •• 0:40 - Topless in black panties dressing in locker
    room.
  • 0:46 - Brief topless lying in bed, talking to her lover,
    side view of buns. Long shot.
  ••• 1:16 - Topless making love in bed with Alex.
The Marilyn Diaries (1990) . . . . Jane
  Private Screenings.
  •• 0:53 - Topless and buns, taking off robe and getting
    into bathtub. Left breast, in tub reading diary.
  •• 0:54 - Topless in and getting out of tub. Very brief
    lower frontal nudity.
  •• 1:27 - Topless in bathtub talking with John.
Xtro 2, The Second Encounter (1991) . . . .

Bujold, Genevieve

Films:
King of Hearts (1966; French/Italian) . . . . Colombine
The Thief of Paris (1967; French/Italian) . . . . . Charlotte
Anne of the Thousand Days (1969; British)
 . . . . Anne Boleyn

The Trojan Women (1972) . . . . Cassandra
Kamouraska (1973; Canadian/French) . . . . . Elisabeth
  Nude in long shot.
Earthquake (1974) . . . . Denise
Obsession (1976)
 . . . . Elizabeth Courtland/Sandra Portinari
Swashbuckler (1976) . . . . Jane Barnet
  • 1:00 - Very brief side view nude, diving from the ship
    into the water. Long shot, don't really see anything.
  • 1:01 - Buns and brief side of left breast seen from un-
    der water.
Coma (1978) . . . . Dr. Susan Wheeler
  0:03 - Nude behind frosted glass shower door, so
    you can't see anything.
Murder by Decree (1979) . . . . Annie Crook
Last Flight of Noah's Ark (1980) . . . . . Bernadette Lafleur
Monsignor (1982) . . . . Clara
  ••• 1:05 - Topless getting undressed and climbing into
    bed while talking to Christopher Reeve.
Choose Me (1984) . . . . Dr. Love
Tightrope (1984) . . . . Beryl Thibodeaux
Trouble in Mind (1986) . . . . Wanda
Dead Ringers (1988) . . . . Claire Niveau
  •• 0:49 - Very brief right breast in bed with Jeremy
    Irons, then brief topless reaching for pills and water.
    Dark, hard to see.
The Moderns (1988) . . . . Libby Valentin
Made for TV Movies:
Red Earth, White Earth (1989) . . . . Madeline

Burger, Michele

Films:
Party Plane (1988) . . . . Carol
  • 0:31 - Topless, squirting whipped cream on herself
    for her audition.
  •• 0:38 - Topless doing a strip tease routine on plane.
  ••• 1:02 - Topless mud wrestling with Renee on the
    plane.
  • 1:09 - Topless in the cockpit, covered with mud.
  •• 1:17 - Topless in serving cart.
Payback (1988) . . . . Laura
  • 0:08 - Brief topless sitting up in bed just before get-
    ting shot, then brief topless twice, dead in bed.
Roadhouse (1989) . . . . Strip Joint Girl
Ninja Academy (1990) . . . . Nudist

Burkett, Laura

Films:
Avenging Angel (1985) . . . . Blonde Hooker
Daddy's Boys (1988) . . . . Christie
  ••• 0:17 - Topless in room with Jimmy.
  •• 0:20 - Left breast, while making love with Jimmy in
    bed again.
  • 0:21 - Brief topless during Jimmy's nightmare.
  • 0:43 - Brief topless in bed again, then getting
    dressed.
  • 0:53 - Brief topless in bed consoling Jimmy.
  • 1:11 - Left breast, while in bed with Jimmy.

Rush Week (1989) . . . . Rebecca Winters
- •• 0:43 - Topless in the shower, talking to Jonelle.
- • 0:55 - Brief topless getting dressed after modeling session.

Burns, Bobbi

Films:
I, the Jury (1982). . . . . Sheila Kyle
Q (1982). . . . . .Sunbather
- •• 0:06 - Topless taking off swimsuit top and rubbing lotion on herself.

New York Nights (1983) . . . . .The Authoress
- •• 0:16 - Topless on the couch outside with the rock star, then topless in bed.

Burstyn, Ellen

Films:
The Last Picture Show (1971; B&W) . . . . . . .Lois Farrow
The Exorcist (1973). . . . . .Chris
Harry and Tonto (1974) . . . . Shirley
Alice Doesn't Live Here Anymore (1975) . . . . Alice Hyatt
  (Academy Award for Best Actress.)
A Dream of Passion (1978) . . . . Brenda
Same Time Next Year (1978). . . . . .Doris
Resurrection (1980). . . . . .Edna McCauley
The Ambassador (1984) . . . . Alex Hacker
- ••• 0:06 - Topless opening her robe to greet her lover.
- ••• 0:07 - Brief topless making love in bed.
- ••• 0:29 - Topless in a movie while her husband, Robert Mitchum, watches.

Twice in a Lifetime (1985). . . . . Kate
Hanna's War (1988) . . . . Katalin Senesh
TV:
The Iron Horse (1967-68) . . . . Julie Parsons
The Ellen Burstyn Show (1986-88) . . . . Ellen Brewer

Butler, Cher

Video Tapes:
Playboy's Wet and Wild (1989) . . . .
Playmates at Play (1990) . . . . .Bareback
Magazines:
Playboy (Aug 1985) . . . . Playmate

Byrd-Nethery, Miriam

Films:
Lies (1984; British) . . . .
The Offspring (1986). . . . . Eileen Burnside
- • 0:26 - Topless in bathtub filled with ice while her husband tries to kill her with an ice pick.
- 0:29 - Very brief right breast, dead in bathtub while he is downstairs.

Walk Like a Man (1987). . . . . Toy Store Clerk
Stepfather 2 (1989). . . . . Sally Jenkins
The Raven Red Kiss-Off (1990) . . . . .Motel Manager
TV:
Mr. T and Tina (1976). . . . . .Miss Llewellyn

Byrne, Patti T.

Films:
Fuzz (1972) . . . . .Abigail
Night Call Nurses (1972) . . . . Barbara
a.k.a. Young LA Nurses 2
- •• 0:59 - Topless several times in bed with the Doctor.

Cable, Tawnni

Video Tapes:
Playboy Video Calendar 1990 (1989). . . . . . . March
- ••• 0:13 - Nude.

Playmates at Play (1990) . . . . Gotta Dance
Magazines:
Playboy (Jun 1989). . . . . Playmate

Cadell, Ava

Films:
Happy Housewives . . . . Schoolgirl
  0:39 - Buns, getting caught by the Squire and getting spanked.
Spaced Out (1980; British). . . . . .Partha
- •• 0:41 - Left breast making love on bed with Cliff.
- •• 0:42 - Nude wrestling on bed with Cliff.
- • 0:43 - Brief left breast lying in bed alone.
- •• 1:08 - Topless sitting on bed.

Smokey and the Bandit III (1983). . . . . .Blond
Commando (1985) . . . . Girl in Bed
- • 0:46 - Very brief topless three times in bed when Arnold Schwarzenegger knocks a guy through the motel door into her room.

Jungle Warriors (1985). . . . . Didi Belair
- • 0:50 - Brief topless getting yellow top ripped open by a bad guy.

Not of This Earth (1988) . . . . Second Hooker
- •• 0:41 - Topless in cellar with Paul just before getting killed with two other hookers. Wearing a gold dress.

Made for Cable TV:
Pillow Previews. . . . . Hostess
Magazines:
Playboy (Jun 1989). . . . . Grapevine
  187: Buns, on bear skin rug in B&W photo.

Caffaro, Cheri

Films:
Ginger (1970) . . . . .Ginger
The Abductors (1971) . . . . Ginger
A Place Called Today (1972) . . . . . .Cindy Cartwright
- •• 0:14 - Full frontal nudity covered with oil or something writhing around on the bed.
- • 1:21 - Brief side view of right breast undressing in the bathroom.
- • 1:23 - Brief full frontal nudity getting kidnapped by two guys.
- •• 1:30 - Nude when they take off the blanket.
- • 1:35 - Brief topless just before getting killed.

Girls Are For Loving (1973) . . . . .Ginger
Savage Sisters (1974) . . . . Jo Turner

Too Hot To Handle (1975). . . . . .Samantha Fox
- •• 0:06 - Topless wearing a black push-up bra and buns in black G-string.
- • 0:13 - Full frontal nudity lying on boat.
- ••• 0:39 - Topless making love in bed with Dominco.
- ••• 0:55 - Full frontal nudity taking off clothes and lying in bed.
- • 1:06 - Brief left breast in bed with Dominco.

Magazines:
Playboy (Nov 1972) . . . . Sex in Cinema 1972
- • 168: Left breast, lit with red light in a photo from *A Place Called Today*.

Playboy (Dec 1972). . . . . Sex Stars of 1972
- ••• 216: Frontal nudity.

Playboy (Nov 1973) . . . . Sex in Cinema
- • 156: Left breast.

Cain, Sharon

a.k.a. Adult film actress Sharon Kane.
Films:
Slammer Girls (1987). .Rita
- • 0:23 - Brief topless changing clothes under table in the prison cafeteria.
- •• 1:02 - Topless walking around an electric chair trying to distract a prison guard.

Calabrese, Gina

Films:
Goin' All the Way (1981) . . . .
- •• 0:12 - Left breast, in the girls' locker room shower. Standing on the left.

The Vals (1982). . . . . Annie
- • 0:04 - Topless changing clothes in bedroom with three of her friends. Long shot, hard to see.
- • 0:15 - Right breast making love with a guy at a party.
0:32 - In black bra with her friends in a store dressing room.

Cameron, Cissie

See: Colpitts-Cameron, Cissie.

Cameron, Joanna

Films:
B.S. I Love You (1971) . . . . Marilyn Michele
(Not available on video tape.)

Camp, Colleen

Films:
Smile (1974). . . . . Connie Thompson
0:47 - Side profile of right breast and buns in dressing room while Little Bob is outside taking pictures.
The Swinging Cheerleaders (1974) . . . . Mary Ann
Fox Fire (1976) . . . .

Death Game, The Seducers (1977) . . . . .Donna
a.k.a. Mrs. Manning's Weekend
0:16 - Buns, in spa with Sondra Locke trying to get George in with them.
- • 0:47 - Brief topless jumping up and down on the bed while George is tied up.
- •• 1:16 - Topless behind stained glass door taunting George. Hard to see.

Cat in the Cage (1978) . . . . .Gilda Riener
- • 0:36 - Very brief left breast twice, while making love in bed with Bruce.

Apocalypse Now (1979). . . . . Playmate
The Game of Death (1979) . . . . .Anne Morris
Cloud Dancer (1980) . . . . Cindy
1:02 - In bra, driving a convertible car while Joseph Bottoms flies a plane over her.
They All Laughed (1981) . . . . .Christy Miller
The Seduction (1982) . . . . .Robin
Smokey and the Bandit III (1983) . . . . Dusty Trails
Valley Girl (1983) . . . . .Sarah Richman
Doin' Time (1984) . . . . .Catlett
The Joy of Sex (1984). . . . . Liz Sampson
D.A.R.Y.L. (1985) . . . . .Elaine
Police Academy II: Their First Assignment (1985)
. . . . Kirkland
The Rosebud Beach Hotel (1985) . . . . Tracy
0:07 - In white lingerie in hotel room with Peter Scolari.
0:28 - In black one piece swimsuit on lounge chair, then walking on the beach.
Police Academy 4: Citizens on Patrol (1987)
. . . . .Mrs. Kirkland-Tackleberry
Walk Like a Man (1987) . . . . Rhonda
Illegally Yours (1988) . . . . Molly Gilbert
Track 29 (1988; British) . . . . Arlanda
Wicked Stepmother (1989) . . . . .Jenny
My Blue Heaven (1990) . . . . Margaret Snow
Made for TV Movies:
Addicted to his Love (1988) . . . . Ellie Snyder
Magazines:
Playboy (Oct 1979) . . . . "Apocalypse" Finally
- ••• 118-119: Topless.

Playboy (Nov 1979) . . . . Sex in Cinema 1979
- • 175: Side view of right breast.

Cannon, Dyan

Films:
Such Good Friends (1971) . . . . Julie Messinger
(Not available on video tape.)

Capri, Ahna

Films:
Company of Killers (1970)......... Mary Jane Smythe
Darker than Amber (1970) .... Del
Payday (1972)......................... Mayleen
• 0:20 - Left breast in bed sleeping, then right breast
with Rip Torn.
••• 0:21 - Topless sitting up in bed smoking a cigarette
and talking to Torn. Long scene.
Enter the Dragon (1973)................. Tania
• 0:47 - Very brief left breast three times in open
blouse in bed with John Saxon.
The Specialist (1975)...................... Londa

Cara, Irene

Films:
Aaron Loves Angela (1975) .... Angela
Sparkle (1976) .... Sparkle
Fame (1980) .... Coco
1:16 - In leotard, dancing and talking to Hillary.
• 1:57 - Brief topless during "audition" on a B&W TV
monitor.
D.C. Cab (1983) .... Herself
City Heat (1984) .... Ginny Lee
Certain Fury (1985) .... Tracy
0:32 - Getting undressed to take a shower.
• 0:36 - Topless behind shower door while Sniffer
comes into the bathroom. Brief topless in quick cuts
when he tries to rape her.
Killing 'Em Softly (1985) ....
Caged in Paradiso (1990) .... Eva
Miniseries:
Roots: The Next Generation (1979)
.... Bertha Palmer Haley

Cardan, Christina

Films:
Chained Heat (1983; U.S./German) .... Miss King
Glitch (1988)........................ Non SAG
• 0:47 - Brief topless in spa taking off her swimsuit top.

Carl, Kitty

Films:
Your Three Minutes Are Up (1973) .... Susan
The Centerfold Girls (1974) .... Sandi
•• 0:45 - Topless taking off her top while sitting on the
bed with Perry.
0:51 - Topless on the beach, dead. Long shot, hard
to see.
Kitty Can't Help It (1975) ....
Carhops (1980)...............................

Carlisi, Olimpia

Films:
Catch-22 (1970)........................ Luciana
• 1:04 - Topless lying in bed talking with Alan Arkin.
Casanova (1976; Italian).................... Isabella
Rendez-Vous (1986; French)......................

Carlisle, Anne

Films:
Liquid Sky (1984)................. Margaret/Jimmy
Perfect Strangers (1984) ....Sally
• 0:34 - Left breast, while making love in bed with
Johnny.
Desperately Seeking Susan (1985) .... Victoria
Suicide Club (1988) .... Catherine
Magazines:
Playboy (Sep 1984) .... Cult Queen
•• 80-85: Nude.
Playboy (Dec 1984) ....Sex Stars of 1984
• 203: Right breast and lower frontal nudity, standing
in bra, garter belt and stockings.

Carlson, Karen

Films:
Shame, Shame, Everybody Knows Her Name (1969)
.... Susan Barton
The Student Nurses (1970) ....Phred
a.k.a. Young LA Nurses
• 0:08 - Topless in bed with the wrong guy.
0:19 - In bra, on sofa with Dr. Jim Casper.
••• 0:50 - In bed with Jim, topless and buns getting out,
then topless sitting in chair. Long scene.
• 1:02 - Brief topless in bed.
The Candidate (1972) .... Nancy McKay
Black Oak Conspiracy (1977) .... Lucy
Matilda (1978)................... Kathleen Smith
The Octagon (1980) .... Justine
Fleshburn (1984) .... Shirley Pinter

Carlton, Hope Marie

Films:
Hard Ticket to Hawaii (1987) ....Taryn
•• 0:07 - Topless taking a shower outside while talking
to Dona Speir.
••• 0:23 - Topless in the spa with Speir looking at diamonds they found.
••• 0:40 - Topless and buns on the beach making love
with her boyfriend, Jimmy John.
•• 1:33 - Topless during the end credits.
A Nightmare on Elm Street 4: The Dream Master
(1988) ....Pin-Up Girl
• 0:21 - Brief topless swimming in a waterbed.
Slaughterhouse Rock (1988) .... Krista Halpern
• 0:09 - Brief right breast, taking off her top in bedroom with her boyfriend.
•• 0:49 - Topless, getting raped by Richard as he turns
into a monster.

Terminal Exposure (1988) . . . . Christie
••• 1:11 - Topless in bathtub licking ice cream off a guy.
How I Got Into College (1989) . . . . Game Show Hostess
Picasso Trigger (1989) . . . . Taryn
   0:17 - In white lingerie on boat with Dona Speir.
••• 0:56 - Topless and buns in spa with a guy.
Savage Beach (1989) . . . . Taryn
   0:06 - Almost topless in spa with the three other
      women.
 • 0:32 - Topless changing clothes in airplane with
      Dona Speir.
•• 0:48 - Nude, going for a swim on the beach with
      Speir.
Side Out (1990) . . . . Vanna
Ghoulies III, Ghoulies Go To College (1991) . . . .
Video Tapes:
Playboy Video Magazine, Volume 9 . . . . . Playmate
Playmate Playoffs . . . . Playmate
Playmates at Play (1990) . . . . Flights of Fancy
Magazines:
Playboy (Jul 1985) . . . . Playmate
   96:

Carol, Jean

a.k.a. Jeannie Daly.
Films:
Payback (1988) . . . . Donna Nathan
••• 0:24 - Topless opening her pink robe for Jason while
      reclining on couch.
TV:
The Guiding Light . . . . Nadine Cooper

Carol, Linda

Films:
School Spirit (1985) . . . . Hogette
Reform School Girls (1986) . . . . Jennifer Williams
•• 0:05 - Nude in the shower.
 • 0:56 - Topless in the back of a truck with Norton.
•• 1:13 - Topless getting hosed down by Edna.
Future Hunters (1987) . . . .
Carnal Crimes (1991) . . . .

Carpenter, Linda

Films:
Apocalypse Now (1979) . . . . Playmate
A Different Story (1979) . . . . Chastity
 • 1:33 - Very brief topless in shower, shutting the door
      when Meg Foster discovers her with Perry King.

Carr, Laurie

Video Tapes:
Playboy Video Magazine, Volume 12 . . . . Playmate
Playboy's Wet and Wild (1989) . . . .
Magazines:
Playboy (Dec 1986) . . . . Playmate

Carrera, Barbara

Films:
Embryo (1976) . . . . Victoria
   0:36 - Almost topless meeting Rock Hudson for the
      first time. Hair covers breasts.
   1:09 - In see through top in bedroom with Hudson.
•• 1:10 - Brief buns and topless in the mirror after mak-
      ing love with Hudson.
 • 1:11 - Left breast sticking out of bathrobe.
The Island of Dr. Moreau (1977) . . . . Maria
When Time Ran Out! (1980) . . . . Iolani
Condorman (1981) . . . . Natalia
I, the Jury (1982) . . . . Dr. Charolette Bennett
••• 1:02 - Nude on bed making love with Armand As-
      sante. Very sexy.
 • 1:46 - Brief topless in hallway kissing Assante.
Lone Wolf McQuade (1983) . . . . Lola
Never Say Never Again (1983) . . . . Fatima Blush
Wild Geese II (1985) . . . . Kathy
The Underachievers (1987) . . . . Katherine
Love at Stake (1988) . . . .
Loverboy (1989) . . . . Alex Barnett
Wicked Stepmother (1989) . . . . Priscilla
 • 1:14 - Very, very brief upper half of right breast peek-
      ing out of the top of her dress when she flips her
      head back while seducing Steve.
Miniseries:
Masada (1981) . . . . Sheva
TV:
Centennial (1978-79) . . . . Clay Basket
Dallas (1985-89) . . . . Angelica Nero
Video Tapes:
Playboy Video Magazine, Volume 1 . . . . herself
Magazines:
Playboy (Jul 1977) . . . . Acting Beastly
••• 93-97: Topless.
Playboy (Mar 1982) . . . . Aye, Barbara
••• 148-155: Nude, also photos from *I, the Jury*.
Playboy (Sep 1987) . . . . 25 Years of James Bond
•• 129: Topless.

Carrere, Tia

Films:
Fatal Mission (1990) . . . . Mai Chang
 • 0:22 - Side view of right breast while changing tops.
      Dark.
Harley Davidson & The Marlboro Man (1991) . . . .
Showdown in Little Tokyo (1991) . . . .

Carrillo, Elpidia

Films:
The Border (1982) . . . . Maria
 • 1:19 - Right breast, opening her blouse in shack with
      Jack Nicholson.
Beyond the Limit (1983) . . . . Clara
•• 0:31 - Topless making love with Richard Gere. Long
      scene.
•• 1:08 - Topless talking to Gere. Another long scene.

Under Fire (1983) . . . . Sandanista (Leon)
Let's Get Harry (1986). . . . . Veronica
Salvador (1986) . . . . Maria
  • 0:21 - Very brief right breast, lying in a hammock
  with James Woods.
Predator (1987) . . . . .Anna
The Assassin (1989). . . . . Elena
Predator 2 (1990) . . . . .Anna
Made for TV Movies:
Dangerous Passion (1990). . . . . Angela

Carroll, Jill

Films:
The Vals (1982). . . . . Sam
The Man Who Loved Women (1983)
  . . . . Sue the Baby Sitter
The Unholy (1988) . . . . Millie
  • 1:10 - Very brief upper half of left breast talking in the
  courtyard with Ben Cross.
Made for TV Movies:
American Harvest (1987). . . . . Calla Bergstrom

Carroll, Regina

Films:
Brain of Blood (1971; Philippines) . . . .
Blazing Stewardesses (1975) . . . .
Jessi's Girls (1976) . . . . Claire
  •• 0:58 - Topless and buns in hay with Indian guy. Don't
  see her face.

Carter, Helena Bonham

Films:
A Room with a View (1986; British)
  . . . . Lucy Honeychurch
Lady Jane (1987; British) . . . . Lady Jane Grey
  • 1:19 - Topless kneeling on the bed with Guilford.
  • 2:09 - Side view of right breast and very, very brief
  topless sitting by fire with Guilford.
Maurice (1987; British) . . . Young Lady at Cricket Match
Getting It Right (1989) . . . . Minerva Munday
  •• 0:18 - Topless a couple of times in bed talking to
  Gavin. It's hard to recognize her because she has lots
  of makeup on her face.
Hamlet (1990) . . . . Ophelia
Made for TV Movies:
A Hazard of Hearts (1987). . . . .

Carter, Lynda

Miss World U.S.A. 1973.
Films:
Bobbie Jo and the Outlaw (1976)
  . . . . Bobbie Jo Baker
  •• 0:17 - Brief left breast making love with Marjoe Gortner.
  •• 0:27 - Brief left breast making love with Gortner.
  • 0:29 - Very brief breasts in pond with Gortner experimenting with mushrooms.

Made for TV Movies:
Rita Hayworth: The Love Goddess (1983)
  . . . . Rita Hayworth
Mickey Spillane's Mike Hammer: Murder Takes All
  (1989) . . . . .Helen Durant
TV:
Wonder Woman (1976-79)
  . . . . Yeoman Diana Prince/Wonder Woman
Partners in Crime (1984) . . . . Carole Stanwyck

Cartwright, Nancy

Films:
Flesh + Blood (1985) . . . . Kathleen
  • 0:28 - Brief topless showing Jennifer Jason Leigh how
  to make love. Long shot.
Going Undercover (1988; British) . . . . Stephanie

Cartwright, Veronica

Films:
Inserts (1976). . . . . Harlene
  •• 0:16 - Topless sitting on bed with Richard Dreyfus.
  ••• 0:31 - Nude on bed with Stephen Davies making a
  porno movie for Dreyfus. Long scene.
Goin' South (1978) . . . . Hermine
Invasion of the Body Snatchers (1978)
  . . . . Nancy Bellicec
Alien (1979). . . . . .Lambert
Nightmares (1983) . . . . .Claire
The Right Stuff (1983) . . . . Betty Grissom
Flight of the Navigator (1986) . . . . Helen Freeman
My Man Adam (1986). . . . . .Elaine Swit
  • 1:09 - Side view of right breast lying on tanning table
  when Adam steals her card keys. Long shot, hard to
  see.
Wisdom (1986) . . . . .Samantha Wisdom
The Witches of Eastwick (1987) . . . . Felicia Alden
Valentino Returns (1988). . . . . .Pat Gibbs
  ••• 0:33 - Topless sitting in bed with Frederic Forrest.
  Fairly long scene.
Made for Cable Movies:
Hitler's Daughter (1990). . . . .
TV:
Daniel Boone (1964-66). . . . . Jenima Boone

Case, Catherine

Films:
The Jigsaw Murders (1988) . . . . Stripper #2
  • 0:27 - Brief topless in black peek-a-boo bra posing for
  photographer.
Dr. Caligari (1989) . . . . Patient with Extra Hormones

Cash, Rosalind

Films:
Klute (1971) . . . . Pat
The Omega Man (1971) .Lisa
- •• 1:09 - Side view of left breast and upper half of buns getting out of bed. Buns and topless sitting in bed.
- • 1:21 - Side view topless in beige underwear while trying on clothes.
Hickey and Boggs (1972) . . . . Nyona
The New Centurions (1972) . . . . Lorrie
The All-American Boy (1973). . . . . .Poppy
Uptown Saturday Night (1974). . . . . Sarah Jackson
Wrong is Right (1982). . . . . Mrs. Ford
The Adventures of Buckaroo Banzai, Across the 8th Dimension (1984) . . . . John Emdall
Go Tell It On the Mountain (1984) . . . . . . Aunt Florence

Cassidy, Joanna

Films:
Bank Shot (1974) . . . . El
The Laughing Policeman (1974) . . . . .Monica
The Stepford Wives (1975) . . . .
Stay Hungry (1976). . . . . Joe Mason
The Late Show (1977). . . . . .Laura Birdwell
Stunts (1977) . . . . Patti Johnson
Our Winning Season (1978) . . . . Sheila
The Glove (1980) . . . . .Sheila Michaels
Night Games (1980). . . . . Julie Miller
    0:44 - Buns, skinny dipping in the pool with Cindy Pickett.
- •• 0:45 - Brief full frontal nudity sitting up.
Blade Runner (1982) . . . . Zhora
- •• 0:54 - Topless getting dressed after taking a shower while talking with Harrison Ford.
Under Fire (1983) . . . . Claire
Club Paradise (1986). . . . . .Terry Hamlin
The Fourth Protocol (1987; British). . . . . . . Vassilieva
- • 1:39 - Brief left breast. She's lying dead in Pierce Brosnan's bathtub.
- • 1:49 - Same thing, different angle.
1969 (1988) . . . . Ev
Who Framed Roger Rabbit (1988). . . . . .Dolores
May Wine (1990) . . . . Lorraine
Where the Heart Is (1990). . . . . Jean McBain
Don't Tell Mom the Babysitter's Dead (1991) . . . .
Made for Cable Movies:
Wheels of Terror (1990) . . . . Laura
Miniseries:
Hollywood Wives (1988). . . . . Maralee Gray
TV:
Shields and Yarnell (1977). . . . . regular
The Roller Girls (1978) . . . . Selma "Books" Cassidy
240 Robert (1979-80) . . . . . Deputy Morgan Wainwright
Buffalo Bill (1983-84) . . . . JoJo White
Falcon Crest (1983). . . . . .Katherine Demery
The Family Tree (1983) . . . . Elizabeth Nichols
Codename: Foxfire (1985) . . .Elizabeth "Foxfire" Towne

Cates, Phoebe

Wife of actor Kevin Kline.
Films:
Paradise (1981) . . . . .Sarah
- •• 0:23 - Buns and topless taking a shower in a cave while Willie Aames watches.
    0:36 - In wet white dress in a pond with Aames.
- • 0:40 - Very brief left breast caressing herself while looking at her reflection in the water.
    0:43 - Buns, getting out of bed to check out Aames' body while he sleeps.
    0:46 - Buns, washing herself in a pond at night.
- •• 0:55 - Side view of her silhouette at the beach at night. Nude swimming in the water, viewed from below.
- ••• 1:11 - Topless making love with Aames.
- ••• 1:12 - Full frontal nudity swimming under water with Aames.
- ••• 1:16 - Topless making love with Aames again.
Fast Times at Ridgemont High (1982)
. . . . Linda Barrett
- ••• 0:50 - Topless getting out of swimming pool during Judge Reinhold's fantasy.
Private School (1983). . . . . Christine
    1:21 - Brief buns lying in sand with Mathew Modine.
    1:24 - Upper half of buns flashing with the rest of the girls during graduation ceremony.
Gremlins (1984). . . . . .Kate
Date with an Angel (1987). . . . . Patty Winston
Bright Lights, Big City (1988). . . . . .Amanda
Heart of Dixie (1989) .Aiken
Shag (1989). . . . . .Carson McBride
Gremlins 2: The New Batch (1990) . . . . . .Kate Beringer
I Love You to Death (1990) . . . . . Uncredited Girl in Bar
Drop Dead Fred (1991) . . . .
Miniseries:
Lace (1984) Lili
Lace II (1985). Lili

Cattrall, Kim

Films:
Rosebud (1975) . . . . Joyce
Tribute (1980; Canadian) . . . . Sally Haines
Porky's (1981; Canadian) . . . . Honeywell
- • 0:58 - Brief buns, then very brief lower frontal nudity after removing skirt to make love in the boy's locker room.
Ticket to Heaven (1981; Canadian) . . . . .Ruthie
City Limits (1984) . . . . Wickings
- •• 1:02 - Right breast, while sitting up in bed with a piece of paper stuck to her.
Police Academy (1984) . . . . .Karen Thompson
Turk 182 (1985) . . . . Danny Boudreau
Big Trouble in Little China (1986). . . . . .Gracie Law
Mannequin (1987). . . . . Emmy
Masquerade (1988) . . . . Mrs. Brooke Morrison
- ••• 0:04 - Topless in bed with Rob Lowe.
    0:47 - In white teddy after having sex with Lowe.

Midnight Crossing (1988) . . . . Alexa Schubb
    0:39 - In wet white blouse, arguing in the water with
    her husband.
Smoke Screen (1988) . . . . Odessa Muldoon
    0:31 - Brief half of right breast sitting in bed with
    sheet pulled up on her.
  •• 1:16 - Topless in bed on top of Gerald.
  ••• 1:17 - Topless lying in bed under Gerald while he
    kisses her breasts.
The Return of the Musketeers (1989) . . . . Justine
The Bonfire of the Vanities (1990) . . . . Judy McCoy
Honeymoon Academy (1990) . . . . .Chris
Made for TV Movies:
Sins of the Past (1984) . . . . Paula
TV:
Scruples (1980) . . . . .Melanie Adams
Magazines:
Playboy (Nov 1987) . . . . Sex in Cinema 1987
  • 138: Left breast lying in bed with Rob Lowe.

Cayer, Kim
Films:
Screwballs (1983) . . . . Brunette Cheerleader
Loose Screws (1986) . . . . .Pig Pen Girl
Graveyard Shift (1987) . . . . Suzy
  •• 0:06 - In black bra, then brief left breast when vam-
    pire rips the bra off.
  • 0:53 - Brief topless in junk yard with garter belt, black
    panties and stockings.
Psycho Girls (1987) . . . .

Cayton, Elizabeth
See: Kaitan, Elizabeth.

Celedonio, Maria
Films:
One Man Force (1989) . . . . Maria
  • 0:30 - Brief topless, twice, hiding John Matuzak in
    her apartment. Long shot.
Backstreet Dreams (1990) . . . . Maria M.

Cellier, Caroline
Films:
Life Love Death (1969; French/Italian). . . . .
This Man Must Die (1970) . . . . Helene Lawson
Femmes de Persone (1986; French) . . . . .Isabelle
Petit Con (1986; French). . . . . Annie Choupon
L'Annee Des Meduses (1987; French)
. . . . Claude, Chris' Mother
  •• 0:02 - Topless taking off top at the beach.
  •• 0:56 - Topless on boat at night with Romain.
  ••• 1:06 - Topless on the beach with Valerie Kaprisky.
  • 1:14 - Left breast, lying on beach with Romain at
    night.

Chadwick, June
Films:
The Golden Lady (1979; British). . . . . Lucy
Forbidden World (1982) . . . . Dr. Barbara Glaser
  •• 0:29 - Topless in bed making love with Jesse Vint.
  •• 0:54 - Topless taking a shower with Dawn Dunlap.
The Last Horror Film (1984) . . . . Reporter
This is Spinal Tap (1984) . . . . .Jeanine Pettibone
Headhunters (1988). . . . . Denise Giuliani
Rising Storm (1989) . . . . Mila Hart
Backstab (1990) . . . . Mrs. Caroline Chambers
The Terror Below (1991) . . . .
TV:
V: The Series (1984-85) . . . . Lydia
Riptide (1986) . . . . Lt. Joanna Parisi

Chambers, Marilyn
Former adult film actress.
Films:
Rabid (1977) . . . . Rose
  •• 0:14 - Topless in bed.
  •• 1:04 - Topless in closet selecting clothes.
  •• 1:16 - Topless in white panties getting out of bed.
Angel of H.E.A.T. (1981). . . . . Angel Harmony
a.k.a. The Protectors, Book I
  •• 0:15 - Full frontal nudity making love with an intrud-
    er on the bed.
  • 0:17 - Topless in a bathtub.
  •• 0:40 - Topless in a hotel room with a short guy.
  • 0:52 - Topless getting out of a wet suit.
  •• 1:01 - Topless sitting on floor with some robots.
  • 1:29 - Topless in bed with Mark.
My Therapist (1983) . . . . .Kelly Carson
Shot on video tape.
  •• 0:01 - Topless in sex therapy class.
  •• 0:07 - Topless, then full frontal nudity undressing for
    Rip. Long scene.
  ••• 0:10 - Topless undressing at home, then full frontal
    nudity making love on couch. Long scene. Nice.
    Then brief side view of right breast in shower.
  • 0:18 - Topless on sofa with Mike.
  •• 0:21 - Topless taking off and putting red blouse on at
    home.
  ••• 0:26 - Nude in bedroom by herself masturbating on
    bed.
  ••• 0:32 - Topless exercising on the floor, buns in bed
    with Mike, topless in bed getting covered with
    whipped cream.
  •• 0:41 - Left breast and lower frontal nudity fighting
    with Don while he rips off her clothes.
  •• 1:08 - Topless and brief buns in bed.
    1:12 - In braless pink T-shirt at the beach.
Up 'n' Coming (1987) . . . . Cassie
(R-rated version reviewed, X-rated version available.)
  ••• 0:01 - Nude, getting out of bed and taking a shower.
  •• 0:08 - Topless making love in bed with the record
    producer.
  • 0:30 - Brief topless in bed with two guys.

•• 0:47 - Full frontal nudity getting suntan lotion rubbed on her by another woman.

• 0:55 - Topless taking off her top at radio station.

Party Incorporated (1989) . . . . Marilyn Sanders

••• 0:56 - In lingerie, then topless in bedroom with Weston. Nice!

• 1:11 - Brief topless on the beach when Peter takes her swimsuit top off.

The Marilyn Diaries (1990) . . . . Marilyn

Private Screenings.

•• 0:02 - Topless in bathroom with a guy during party.

•• 0:26 - In bra and panties in studio, then topless.

••• 0:27 - Topless in panties and open blouse.

•• 0:45 - Topless in trench coat, opening it up to give the Iranian secret documents.

• 0:47 - Topless when the Rebel Leader opens her trench coat.

• 0:48 - Topless with Colonel South.

•• 0:57 - Topless opening her top for the producer.

• 1:10 - In swimsuit, then topless with Roger.

••• 1:13 - In black lingerie, then topless making love with Chet.

• 1:19 - Left breast, in flashback with Roger.

•• 1:25 - In slip, then right breast, then topless with Chet.

Magazines:

Playboy (Aug 1973). . . . . Porno Chic

••• 141: Full frontal nudity.

Playboy (Jan 1989) . . . . Women of the Seventies

••• 214: Topless.

Playboy (Nov 1989) . . . . Sex in Cinema 1989

••• 134: Topless still from *Party Incorporated*.

Chanel, Tally

Films:

Bits and Pieces (1985) . . . . Jennifer

0:58 - In the woods with the killer, seen briefly in bra and panties before and after being killed.

Free Ride (1986) . . . . Candy

• 0:57 - Brief topless in bedroom with Dan.

Sex Appeal (1986) . . . . Corinne

• 1:22 - Brief topless at the door of Tony's apartment when he opens the door while fantasizing about her.

The Nightstalker (1987) . . . . Brenda

• 0:54 - Brief frontal nudity lying dead in bed covered with paint. Long shot, hard to see anything.

Slammer Girls (1987) . . . . Candy Treat

0:57 - Doing a dance routine wearing feathery pasties for the Governor in the hospital.

Warrior Queen (1987) . . . . Vespa

••• 0:09 - Topless hanging on a rope, being auctioned.

••• 0:20 - Topless and buns with black slave girl.

•• 0:37 - Nude, before attempted rape by Goliath.

•• 0:57 - Topless during rape by Goliath.

Hollywood Hot Tubs 2—Educating Crystal (1989)

. . . . Mindy Wright

Magazines:

Penthouse (May 1990) . . . . Dry as Dust

40-49:

Chaplin, Geraldine

Daughter of actor Charlie Chaplin.

Granddaughter of Eugene O'Neill.

Films:

Doctor Zhivago (1965) . . . . Tonya

Dr. Zhivago (1965). . . . . Tonya

The Three Musketeers (1973). . . . . Anne of Austria

Nashville (1975). . . . . Opal

Buffalo Bill and the Indians (1976) . . . . Annie Oakley

Roseland (1977). . . . . Marilyn

Welcome to L.A. (1977) . . . . Karen Hood

•• 1:28 - Full frontal nudity standing in Keith Carradine's living room.

Remember My Name (1978) . . . . Emily

• 1:23 - Very brief left breast, lying in bed, then right breast, with Anthony Perkins.

A Wedding (1978) . . . . Rita Billingsley

The Moderns (1988) . . . . Nathalie de Ville

White Mischief (1988) . . . . Nina

The Return of the Musketeers (1989) . . . . . Queen Anne

Charbonneau, Patricia

Films:

Desert Hearts (1986) . . . . Cay Rivvers

••• 1:09 - Brief topless making love in bed with Helen Shaver.

Manhunter (1986) . . . . Mrs. Sherman

Call Me (1988) . . . . Anna

•• 1:18 - Brief left breast making love in bed with a guy, then topless putting blouse on and getting out of bed.

Shakedown (1988). . . . . Susan Cantrell

Brain Dead (1989) . . . . Dana Martin

0:13 - Buns, on table with Bill Paxton. Briefly almost see side of left breast.

Robocop 2 (1990) . . . . uncredited Engineer

Charlie

See: Spradling, Charlie.

Chen, Joan

Films:

Tai-Pan (1986) . . . . May May

0:55 - In sheer top sitting on bed talking to Bryan Brown.

• 0:56 - Brief left breast washing herself, hard to see anything.

1:14 - Sheer top again.

1:30 - Sheer top again.

The Last Emperor (1987) . . . . Wan Jung

The Nightstalker (1987) . . . . Mai Wong

The Blood of Heroes (1989) . . . . Kidda

TV:

Twin Peaks (1990-91) . . . . Jocelyn Packard

Chevalier, Catherine

Films:
Hellraiser II—Hellbound (1988) . . . . Tiffany's Mother
Riders of the Storm (1988) . . . . Rosita
Stormy Monday (1988) . . . . Cosmo's Secretary
Night Breed (1990) . . . . Rachel
  • 1:12 - Topless in police jail, going through a door
    and killing a cop.

Chiles, Lois

Films:
The Way We Were (1973) . . . . Carol Ann
Coma (1978) . . . . Nancy Greenly
Moonraker (1979). . . . . Dr. Holly Goodhead
Raw Courage (1983). . . . . Ruth
Sweet Liberty (1986). Leslie
Broadcast News (1987). . . . . Jennifer Mack
Creepshow 2 (1987). . . . . Annie Lansing
  •• 0:59 - Brief topless getting out of boyfriend's bed,
    then getting dressed.

TV:
Dallas (1982-84) . . . . Holly Harwood

Chin, Lonnie

Films:
Star 80 (1983). . . . . Playboy Mansion Guest
Video Tapes:
Playboy's Playmate Review 3 (1985). . . . . Playmate
Magazines:
Playboy (Jan 1983) . . . . Playmate

Chong, Rae Dawn

Daughter of comedian/actor Tommy Chong.
Wife of actor C. Thomas Howell.
Films:
Quest For Fire (1981) . . . . Ika
    0:37 - Topless and buns, running away from the bad
    tribe.
    0:40 - Topless and buns, following the three guys.
    0:41 - Brief topless behind rocks.
  • 0:43 - Brief side view of left breast, healing Noah's
    wound.
  • 0:50 - Right breast, while sleeping by the fire.
    0:53 - Long shot, side view of left breast after making
    love.
  • 0:54 - Topless shouting to the three guys.
  • 1:07 - Topless standing with her tribe.
  • 1:10 - Topless and buns, walking through camp at
    night.
  • 1:18 - Topless in a field.
  • 1:20 - Left breast, turning over to demonstrate the
    missionary position. Long shot.
  • 1:25 - Buns and brief left breast running out of bear
    cave.
Beat Street (1984). . . . . Tracy
City Limits (1984) . . . . Yogi

Fear City (1984) . . . . .Leila
  ••• 0:26 - Topless and buns, dancing on stage.
  • 0:50 - Brief topless in the hospital getting a shock to
    get her heart started.
American Flyers (1985) .Sarah
The Color Purple (1985). . . . . Squeak
Commando (1985) . . . . Cindy
Running Out of Luck (1986) . . . . Slave Girl
  •• 0:42 - Left breast, while hugging Mick Jagger, then
    again while lying in bed with him.
  •• 1:12 - Left breast painting some kind of drug laced
    solution on herself.
  •• 1:14 - Right breast, while in prison office offering her
    breast to the warden.
  • 1:21 - Buns and left breast, in bed with Jagger during
    a flashback.
Soul Man (1986) . . . . .Sarah
The Squeeze (1987). . . . . Rachel Dobs
Curiosity Kills (1990) . . . . .Jane
Far Out Man (1990). Herself
Tales From the Darkside, The Movie (1990)
. . . . Carola
  • 1:09 - Left breast in blue light, twice, with James Re-
    mar. Don't see her face.
Denial (1991). . . . . .Julie
Made for Cable Movies:
Prison Stories, Women on the Inside (1990; HBO)
. . . . Rhonda
  • 0:26 - Very brief right breast several times in prison
    shower with Annabella Sciorra.
Magazines:
Playboy (Apr 1982) . . . . Quest For Fire

Christian, Claudia

Films:
The Hidden (1987). . . . . Brenda Lee
Arena (1988) . . . . Quinn
Clean and Sober (1988). . . . . Iris
Never on Tuesday (1988) . . . . Tuesday
  (There are a lot of braless T-shirt shots of her throughout
  the film.)
  • 0:43 - Brief side view of right breast in the shower
    with Eddie during his fantasy.
Mad About You (1990) . . . . .Casey
    0:56 - On boat in a white, fairly transparent one
    piece swimsuit.
Maniac Cop 2 (1990). . . . . Susan Riley
Think Big (1990) . . . . Dr. Marsh
Made for TV Movies:
Danielle Steel's "Kaleidoscope" (1990). . . . . . . .Meagan
TV:
Berrengers (1985) . . . . Melody Hughes

Christie, Julie

Films:
Billy Liar (1963) . . . . Liz
Darling (1965). . . . . Diana Scott
Doctor Zhivago (1965) . . . . Lara

Fahrenheit 451 (1967) . . . . Linda/Clarisse
Petulia (1968; U.S./British) . . . . Petulia Danner
McCabe and Mrs. Miller (1971) . . . . Mrs. Miller
Don't Look Now (1973) . . . . Laura Baxter
    • 0:27 - Brief topless in bathroom with Donald Sutherland.
    •• 0:30 - Topless making love with Sutherland in bed.
Shampoo (1975) . . . . Jackie
Demon Seed (1977) . . . . Susan Harris
    • 0:25 - Side view of left breast, getting out of bed.
    •• 0:30 - Topless and buns getting out of the shower while the computer watches with its camera.
Heaven Can Wait (1978) . . . . Betty Logan
Heat and Dust (1982) . . . . Anne
Return of the Soldier (1983; British) . . . . Kitty
Power (1986) . . . . Ellen Freeman
Miss Mary (1987) . . . . Miss Mary Mulligan
Made for TV Movies:
Dadah is Death (1988) . . . . Barbara

Clark, Anna

Video Tapes:
Playboy Video Calendar 1988 (1987) . . . . Playmate
Playboy's Wet and Wild (1989) . . . .
Magazines:
Playboy (Apr 1987) . . . . Playmate

Clark, Candy

Films:
Fat City (1972) . . . . Faye
American Graffiti (1973) . . . . Debbie
The Man Who Fell to Earth (1976; British)
. . . . Mary-Lou
(Uncensored version.)
    •• 0:42 - Topless in the bathtub, washing her hair and talking to David Bowie.
    •• 0:55 - Topless sitting on bed and blowing out a candle.
    ••• 0:56 - Topless in bed with Bowie.
    ••• 1:26 - Full frontal nudity climbing into bed with Bowie after he reveals his true alien self.
       1:56 - Nude with Bowie making love and shooting a gun.
Citizen's Band (1977) . . . . Electra/Pam
The Big Sleep (1978; British) . . . . . Camilla Sternwood
    ••• 0:18 - Topless, sitting in a chair when Robert Mitchum comes in after a guy is murdered.
    • 0:30 - Brief topless in photo that Mitchum is looking at.
       0:38 - Topless in the photos again. Out of focus.
    •• 0:39 - Topless sitting in chair during recollection of the murder.
    •• 1:03 - Very brief full frontal nudity in bed, throwing open the sheets for Mitchum.
       1:05 - Very, very brief buns, getting up out of bed.
When Ya Comin' Back Red Ryder (1979) . . . . Cheryl
(Not available on video tape.)
Q (1982) . . . . Joan

Blue Thunder (1983) . . . . Kate
Hambone and Hillie (1984) . . . . Nancy
Cat's Eye (1985) . . . . Sally Ann
At Close Range (1986) . . . . Mary Sue
The Blob (1988) . . . . Fran Hewitt
Magazines:
Playboy (Nov 1978) . . . . Sex in Cinema 1978
    • 181: Topless.

Clark, Dawn

Films:
The Happy Hooker Goes to Washington (1977)
. . . . Candy
    • 1:18 - Topless, covered with spaghetti in a restaurant.
Stripes (1981) . . . . Mud Wrestler

Clark, Marlene

Films:
The Landlord (1970) . . . .
Slaughter (1972) . . . . Kim Walker
    • 0:11 - Very brief buns and right breast, getting thrown out of room by Jim Brown.
Night of the Cobra Woman (1974; U.S./Philippines)
. . . . Lena
Switchblade Sisters (1975) . . . .

Clark, Sharon

a.k.a. Sharon Weber or Sharon Clark Weber.
Films:
Lifeguard (1975) . . . . Tina
    • 0:07 - Brief side view of right breast undressing and getting into the shower.
    • 0:08 - Buns and brief topless wrestling with Sam Elliott on the bed.
Lisa (1989) . . . . Porsche Passenger
Magazines:
Playboy (Aug 1970) . . . . Playmate

Clark, Susan

Films:
Coogan's Bluff (1968) . . . . Julie
Tell Them Willie Boy is Here (1969) . . . . Liz
       0:21 - Very brief buns when Robert Redford turns her over in bed.
       0:57 - In slip, after taking off dress for Redford.
Skin Game (1971) . . . . Ginger
Valdez is Coming (1971) . . . . Gay Erin
The Apple Dumpling Gang (1975)
. . . . Magnolia Dusty Clydesdale
Night Moves (1975) . . . . Ellen
    • 1:09 - Brief topless in bed with Gene Hackman.
French Quarter (1978) . . . . Bag Stealer/Sue
Deadly Companion (1979) . . . . Paula West
    • 0:19 - Brief left breast, while consoling Michael Sarrazin in bed, then brief side view of left breast.
    • 0:20 - Brief topless sitting up in bed.

The North Avenue Irregulars (1979) . . . . .Anne
Promises in the Dark (1979) . . . . Fran Koenig
Nobody's Perfekt (1981) . . . . Carol
Porky's (1981; Canadian) . . . . Cherry Forever
Made for TV Movies:
Babe (1975) . . . . Babe Didrickson Zaharias
(Emmy Award for Best Actress in a Special.)
TV:
Webster (1983-89)
 . . . . .Katherine Calder Young Papadapolis
Magazines:
Playboy (Feb 1973) . . . . The Ziegfeld Girls
•• 75: Right breast.

Clarke, Caitlin
Films:
Dragonslayer (1981) . . . . Valerian
 0:27 - Body double's very brief side of left breast from
 under water.
Penn & Teller Get Killed (1989) . . . . Carlotta
TV:
Once a Hero (1979) . . . . Emma Greely

Clarkson, Lana
Films:
Fast Times at Ridgemont High (1982) . . . . . .Mrs. Vargas
Deathstalker (1983). . . . . .Kaira
•• 0:26 - Topless when her cape opens, while talking to
 Deathstalker and Oghris.
••• 0:29 - Topless lying down by the fire when Deathstalker comes to make love with her.
• 0:49 - Brief topless with gaping cape, sword fighting
 with a guard.
Scarface (1983). . . . . .Woman at the Babylon Club
Blind Date (1984). . . . . Rachel
(Not the same 1987 *Blind Date* with Bruce Willis.)
• 0:52 - Brief topless rolling over in bed when Joseph
 Bottoms sneaks in. Dark, hard to see.
 1:11 - In two piece swimsuit during a modeling assignment.
 1:18 - In two piece swimsuit by pool.
Barbarian Queen (1985) . . . . .Amethea
•• 0:38 - Brief topless during attempted rape.
••• 0:48 - Topless being tortured with metal hand then
 raped by torturer.
Amazon Women on the Moon (1987). . . . . . Alpha Beta
Haunting of Morella (1990). . . . . Miss Deveroux
Wizards of the Lost Kingdom, Part 2 (1991) . . . .

Clayburgh, Jill
Films:
Portnoy's Complaint (1972) . . . . Naomi
The Thief Who Came to Dinner (1973) . . . . Jackie
The Terminal Man (1974) . . . . .Angela Black
Silver Streak (1976). . . . . Hilly Burns
Semi-Tough (1977). . . . . Barbara Jane Bookman

An Unmarried Woman (1978). . . . . Erica
 0:05 - Dancing around the apartment in white long
 sleeve T-shirt and white panties.
•• 0:12 - Brief topless getting dressed for bed, kind of
 dark and hard to see.
•• 1:10 - In bra and panties in guy's apartment, then
 brief topless lying on bed.
Luna (1979). . . . . .Caterina Silveri
Starting Over (1979). . . . . Marilyn Holmberg
• 0:45 - Very brief upper half of breasts taking a shower
 while Burt Reynolds waits outside.
It's My Turn (1980) . . . . Kate Gunzinger
• 1:10 - Brief upper half of left breast in bed with
 Michael Douglas after making love.
First Monday in October (1981). . . . . Ruth Loomis
I'm Dancing as Fast as I Can (1981) . . . .Barbara Gordon
Where Are the Children? (1986). . . . . . Nancy Eldgridge
Shy People (1988) . . . . .Diana
Made for TV Movies:
Hustling (1975) . . . . .Wanda
Female Instinct (1985) . . . . Mary
Reason for Living: The Jill Ireland Story (1991)
 . . . . Jill Ireland

Clery, Corrine
Films:
Kleinhoff Hotel (1973) . . . .
The Story of "O" (1975; French). . . . . .O
•• 0:09 - Topless in bedroom with two women.
•• 0:12 - Topless being made love to.
•• 0:20 - Frontal nudity making love with two men.
•• 0:29 - Topless taking a bath while a man watches.
••• 0:42 - Buns, on a sofa while her boyfriend lifts her
 dress up, then topless while another man plays with
 her, then nude except for white stockings.
••• 0:51 - Brief topless chained by wrists and gagged.
••• 1:22 - Nude making love with a young guy.
Covert Action (1978) . . . .
The Switch (1978) .Charlotte
a.k.a. The Con Artists
The Humanoid (1979; Italian) . . . .
Moonraker (1979) . . . . Corinne Dufour
I Hate Blondes (1981) . . . . Angelica
Yor: The Hunter from the Future (1983) . . . . .Ka-Laa
Dangerous Obsession (1990; Italian)
 . . . . .Carol Simpson
• 0:14 - Right breast sticking out of lingerie while lying
 in bed.
•• 0:36 - Full frontal nudity lying in bed waiting for her
 husband, then with him, then getting out of bed.
Magazines:
Playboy (Sep 1987) . . . . 25 Years of James Bond
•• 131: Topless.

Close, Glenn
Films:
World According to Garp (1982) . . . . Jenny Fields
The Big Chill (1983) . . . . Sara
• 0:27 - Topless sitting down in the shower crying.
The Natural (1984) . . . . Iris Gaines
The Stone Boy (1984) . . . . Ruth Hillerman
Jagged Edge (1985) . . . . Teddy Barnes
0:46 - Side view of left breast, making love in bed
with Jeff Bridges.
1:38 - Very brief side view of right breast running
down the hall taking off her blouse. Back is toward
camera. Blurry shot.
Maxie (1985) . . . . Jan/Maxie
Fatal Attraction (1987) . . . . .Alex Forrest
•• 0:17 - Left breast when she opens her top to let
Michael Douglas kiss her. Then very brief buns, falling into bed with him.
• 0:20 - Brief right breast in freight elevator with Douglas.
••• 0:32 - Topless in bed talking to Douglas. Long scene,
sheet keeps changing positions between cuts.
Dangerous Liaisons (1988) . . . . . . Marquise de Merteuil
Immediate Family (1989) . . . . Linda Spector
Hamlet (1990) . . . . .Gertrude
Reversal of Fortune (1990) . . . . Sunny von Bülow
Made for TV Movies:
Sarah, Plain and Tall (1991) . . . . .Sarah Wheaton

Cochrell, Elizabeth
a.k.a. Liza Cochrell.
Films:
The Big Bet (1985) . . . . Sister in Stag Film
••• 1:05 - Topless and buns, undressing and getting into
bathtub in a video tape that Chris is watching.
•• 1:08 - Topless again on video tape, when Chris
watches it on TV at home.
Free Ride (1986) . . . . Nude Girl #1
• 0:25 - Brief buns taking a shower with another girl.
Sunset Strip (1986) . . . . Stripper

Cole, Debra
Films:
Crossing Delancey (1988) . . . . Waitress
The Hot Spot (1990) . . . . Irene Davey
• 1:26 - Topless sunbathing next to Jennifer Connelly
at side of lake. Long shot.
•• 1:27 - Topless talking with Connelly some more.

Coleman, Renee
Films:
After School (1987) . . . . September Lane
•• 0:35 - Topless and buns getting into bathtub. Almost
lower frontal nudity.
Rocket Gibraltar (1988) . . . . Waitress
Who's Harry Crumb? (1989) . . . . Jennifer Downing

Collings, Jeannie
Films:
Happy Housewives . . . . Mrs. Wain
• 0:16 - Very, very brief right breast with the Newsa-
gent's Daughter and Bob in the bathtub.
Confessions of a Window Cleaner (1974; British)
. . . . .Baby Doll
Carry on England (1976; British) . . . . . . Private Edwards
Emily (1976; British) .Rosalind
• 1:05 - Brief topless on the couch with Gerald while
Richard watches.

Collins, Alana
a.k.a. Alana Collins, Alana Hamilton or Alana Stewart.
Ex-wife of singer Rod Stewart.
Ex-wife of actor George Hamilton.
Films:
Evel Knievel (1972) . . . . Nurse
Night Call Nurses (1972) . . . . .Janis
a.k.a. Young LA Nurses 2
•• 0:12 - Topless in bed with Zach.
0:24 - In white two piece swimsuit on boat.
•• 0:28 - Topless and buns on bed with Kyle.
• 0:52 - Brief right breast twice in shower with Kyle.
The Ravagers (1979) . . . . .Miriam
Swing Shift (1984) . . . . Frankie Parker
0:11 - Buns in B&W photo that Christine Lahti shows
to Fred Ward. Possible photo composite.
Where the Boys Are '84 (1984) . . . . Maggie

Collins, Candace
Films:
Class (1983) . . . . Buxom Girl
Smokey and the Bandit III (1983) . . . . Maid
Magazines:
Playboy (Dec 1979) . . . . Playmate
198:

Collins, Joan
Films:
Decameron Nights (1953) . . . . .Maria
Stopover Tokyo (1957) . . . . .Tina
Subterfuge (1969) . . . . .Anne Langley
The Executioner (1970; British) . . . . .Sarah Booth
Quest for Love (1971) . . . . Ottilie
Fear in the Night (1972; British) . . . . Molly Charmichael
a.k.a. Dynasty of Fear
Tales From the Crypt (1972) . . . . Joanne Clayton
Dark Places (1974; British) . . . . .Sarah
Oh, Alfie! (1975; British) . . . . Fay
a.k.a. Alfie Darling
0:28 - In white bra and panties, running to answer
the phone, then talking to Alfie.
••• 1:00 - Topless lying in bed after Alfie rolls off her.
Bawdy Adventures of Tom Jones (1976) . . . . . Black Bess
Empire of the Ants (1977) . . . . Marilyn Fryser
The Big Sleep (1978; British) . . . . .Agnes Lozelle

Fearless (1978) . . . . Bridgitte
- • 0:01 - In bra and panties, then brief right breast during opening credits.
- •• 0:41 - Topless after doing a strip tease routine on stage.
- • 1:17 - Undressing in front of Wally in white bra and panties, then right breast.
- • 1:20 - Brief right breast lying dead on couch.

The Stud (1978; British) . . . . Fontaine
- • 0:10 - Brief left breast making love with Tony in the elevator.
-   0:27 - Brief buns in panties, stockings and garter belt in Tony's apartment.
-   0:58 - Brief black bra and panties under fur coat in back of limousine with Tony.
- • 1:03 - Brief topless taking off dress to get in pool.
- • 1:04 - Nude in the pool with Tony.

The Bitch (1979; British) . . . . Fontaine Khaled
-   0:01 - In long slip getting out of bed and putting a bathrobe on.
- • 0:03 - Brief topless in the shower with a guy.
- •• 0:24 - Brief topless taking black corset off for the chauffeur in the bedroom, then buns getting out of bed and walking to the bathroom.
-   0:39 - Making love in bed wearing a blue slip.
- • 1:01 - Left breast after making love in bed.

Sunburn (1979) . . . . Nera
Homework (1982). . . . . Diana
Body double used for Joan's nude scene.
Miniseries:
Sins (1986) . . . .
Made for TV Movies:
Her Life as a Man (1984). . . . .
The Cartier Affair (1985) . . . .
Monte Carlo (1986) . . . . Katrina Petrovna
TV:
Dynasty (1981-89) . . . . Alexis Carrington Colby
Magazines:
Playboy (Nov 1978) . . . . Sex in Cinema 1978
- • 185: Left breast and lower frontal nudity.

Playboy (Dec 1983). . . . .
Playboy (Dec 1984). . . . . Sex Stars of 1984
- ••• 209: Topless in bed.

Playboy (Jan 1989) . . . . Women of the Eighties
- •• 250: Buns and side view of right breast in B&W photo.

Collins, Pamela

Films:
Sweet Sugar (1972) . . . . Dolores
- • 0:26 - Brief topless when doctor tears her bra off.
- ••• 0:50 - Topless in the shower with Phyllis Davis.

So Long, Blue Boy (1973) . . . . Cathy

Collins, Pauline

Films:
Secrets of a Windmill Girl (1966; British) . . . . . . Pat Lord
Shirley Valentine (1989). . . . . Shirley Valentine
(If you like older women, check this out.)
- • 0:13 - Brief left breast giving Joe a shampoo in the bathtub.
- •• 1:17 - Topless jumping from the boat into the water in slow motion. Very brief topless in the water.
- •• 1:19 - Buns, hugging Tom Conti, left breast several times kissing him.

Collins, Roberta

Films:
The Big Doll House (1971) . . . . Alcott
- ••• 0:33 - Topless in shower. Seen through blurry window by prison worker, Fred. Blurry, but nice.
- • 0:34 - Brief left breast, while opening her blouse for Fred.

Unholy Rollers (1972). . . . . Jennifer
The Roommates (1973) . . . . Beth
Caged Heat (1974) . . . . Belle
a.k.a. Renegade Girls
- • 0:11 - Very brief topless getting blouse ripped open by Juanita.
- ••• 1:01 - Topless while the prison doctor has her drugged so he can take pictures of her.

Death Race 2000 (1975). . . . . Matilda the Hun
- •• 0:27 - Topless being interviewed and arguing with Calamity Jane.

Train Ride to Hollywood (1975) . . . .
Death Wish II (1982) . . . . Woman at Party
Hardbodies (1984). . . . . Lana
School Spirit (1985) . . . . Helen Grimshaw
Hardbodies 2 (1986) . . . . Lana Logan
Vendetta (1986). . . . . Miss Dice

Collins, Ruth Corrine

Films:
Sexpot (1986) . . . . Ivy Barrington
- •• 0:09 - Topless on table, taking her dress off for Phillip.
- • 0:41 - Buns, in Damon's arms.
- •• 0:51 - Left breast, while in shower talking to Boopsie.

Doom Asylum (1987) . . . . Tina
- •• 0:19 - Topless pulling up her top while yelling at kids below.

Firehouse (1987) . . . . Bubbles
Wildest Dreams (1987). . . . . Stella
- ••• 0:22 - Topless wearing panties in bedroom on bed with Bobby.
- • 1:10 - Brief topless fighting on floor with two other women.

Alexa (1988). . . . . Marshall
- • 0:01 - Topless a couple of times taking blue dress off and putting it on again. Long shot.

New York's Finest (1988). . . . . .Joy Sugarman
- 0:04 - Brief topless with a bunch of hookers.
- 0:36 - Topless with her two friends doing push ups on the floor.
- •• 1:02 - Topless making love on top of a guy talking about diamonds.

Cleo/Leo (1989) . . . . Sally
- ••• 0:08 - Topless getting dress pulled off by Leo.

Deadly Embrace (1989). . . . . .Dede Magnolia

Galactic Gigolo (1989) . . . . Dr. Ruth Pepper
a.k.a. Club Earth

Party Incorporated (1989) . . . . .Betty
- 0:07 - Topless on desk with Dickie. Long shot.
- •• 1:08 - Topless in bed with Weston when Marilyn Chambers comes in.

Little Devils (1991). . . . .

Collinson, Madeleine

Identical twin sister of Mary Collinson.
Films:

Come Back Peter (1971; British) . . . .

The Love Machine (1971) . . . . .Sandy
- •• 1:22 - Topless in shower with Robin and her sister when Dyan Cannon discovers them all together. Can't tell who is who.

Twins of Evil (1971) . . . . Freida Gelhorn
- •• 1:07 - Right breast, then brief topless undoing dress, then full frontal nudity after turning into a vampire in bedroom.

Magazines:

Playboy (Oct 1970). . . . . Playmate

Playboy (Dec 1972). . . . . Sex Stars of 1972
- •• 211: Topless.

Playboy (Jan 1979) . . . . 25 Beautiful Years
- ••• 161: Topless lying on bed.

Collinson, Mary

Identical twin sister of Madeleine Collinson.
Films:

Come Back Peter (1971; British) . . . .

The Love Machine (1971) . . . . Debbie
- •• 1:22 - Topless in shower with Robin and her sister when Dyan Cannon discovers them all together. Can't tell who is who.

Twins of Evil (1971). . . . . Maria Gelhorn

Magazines:

Playboy (Oct 1970). . . . . Playmate

Playboy (Dec 1972). . . . . Sex Stars of 1972
- •• 211: Topless.

Playboy (Jan 1979) . . . . 25 Beautiful Years
- ••• 161: Topless lying on bed.

Colpitts-Cameron, Cissie

a.k.a. Cisse Cameron.
Films:

Beyond the Valley of the Dolls (1970). . . . .
Russ Meyer Film. (Not available on video tape.)

Billy Jack (1971) . . . . Miss Eyelashes

The Happy Hooker Goes to Washington (1977)
. . . . Miss Goodbody
- 0:29 - Very brief topless when her top pops open during the senate hearing.

Porky's II: The Next Day (1983; Canadian)
. . . . .Graveyard Gloria/Sandy Le Toi
   0:26 - Buns in G-string at carnival.
- •• 0:39 - Topless and buns in G-string, stripping for Pee Wee at cemetery.
- •• 0:40 - More topless, pretending to die.
- •• 0:42 - Topless, being carried by Meat.

TV:

The Ted Knight Show (1978) . . . . Graziella

Condon, Iris

Films:

In Search of the Perfect 10 (1986)
. . . . Perfect Girl #6/Jackie
(Shot on video tape.)
- ••• 0:37 - Topless (she's the blonde) playing Twister with Rebecca Lynn. Buns in G-string.

Party Plane (1988) . . . . Renee
- 0:29 - Buns, in white lingerie during audition.
- ••• 0:48 - Topless plane doing a strip tease routine.
- ••• 1:02 - Topless on plane mud wrestling with Carol.
- 1:12 - Left breast, covered with mud, holding the Mad Bomber.
- 1:17 - Left breast, then topless in trunk with the Doctor.

Pucker Up and Bark Like a Dog (1989)
. . . . Stretch Woman

Congie, Terry

Films:

Malibu Hot Summer (1981). . . . . .Dit McCoy
a.k.a. Sizzle Beach
(*Sizzle Beach* is the re-released version with Kevin Costner featured on the cover. It is missing all the nude scenes during the opening credits before 0:06.)
- 0:02 - Side view of right breast, while on floor during opening credits.
   0:39 - In bra, taking off her blouse in front of her drama class.
- •• 0:45 - Topless in front of fireplace with Kevin Costner. Side view of right breast.

Shadows Run Black (1986). . . . . Lee Faulkner

Connelly, Jennifer

Films:
Once Upon a Time in America (1984)
.... Young Deborah
(Long version.)
Creepers (1985; Italian)............. Jennifer Corvino
Labyrinth (1986)......................... Sarah
Some Girls (1988)......................Gabriella
The Hot Spot (1990) .... Gloria Harper
    1:01 - In black bra and panties walking out of lake
    with Don Johnson.
    1:26 - Buns, lying next to Irene next to lake. Long
    shot.
    ••• 1:27 - Topless, talking to Irene next to lake. Wow!
Career Opportunities (1991).................Josie
The Rocketeer (1991) ....Jenny Blake

Conrad, Kimberley

Wife of *Playboy* magazine publisher Hugh Hefner.
Video Tapes:
Playboy Video Centerfold: Kimberley Conrad
...........................Playmate of the Year
Playmates of the Year—The '80's .... Playmate
Playboy Video Calendar 1989 (1988) ..... October
    ••• 0:38 - Nude.
Playboy Video Calendar 1990 (1989) ....December
    ••• 1:03 - Nude.
Magazines:
Playboy (Jan 1988) .... Playmate

Contouri, Chantal

Films:
Alvin Rides Again (1974; Australian)
.... Boobs La Touche
    • 1:15 - Very brief lower frontal nudity, putting panties
    on in the car. Brief topless, putting red dress on.
The Day After Halloween (1978; Australian)
.... Madeline
a.k.a. Snapshot

Cooke, Jennifer

Films:
Gimme an "F" (1981) .... Pam Bethlehem
    1:10 - Wearing United States flag pasties frolicking
    with Dr. Spirit. Nice bouncing action.
    1:38 - Still of pasties scene during end credits.
Friday the 13th, Part VI: Jason Lives (1986) ..... Megan
Made for Cable TV:
The Hitchhiker: Man's Best Friend ....Elanor
    (Available on *The Hitchhiker, Volume 4*.)
    • 0:19 - Brief side view topless getting undressed to
    take a shower.
TV:
The Guiding Light (1981-83) .... Morgan Nelson
V: The Series (1984-85)....................Elizabeth

Coolidge, Rita

Singer.
Films:
Pat Garrett and Billy the Kid (1973) ....Maria
    • 1:34 - Brief right breast getting undressed to get into
    bed with Kris Kristofferson.

Cooper, Jeanne

Mother of actors Corbin and Collin Bernsen.
Films:
The Redhead from Wyoming (1952) .... Myra
The Man from the Alamo (1953) .... Kate Lamar
Let No Man Write My Epitaph (1960) ....Fran
The Boston Strangler (1968) ....Cloe
There Was a Crooked Man (1970) ....Prostitute
    • 0:18 - Brief left breast trying to seduce the sheriff,
    Henry Fonda, in a room.
Kansas City Bomber (1972) .... Vivien
The All-American Boy (1973) .... Nola Bealer
TV:
Bracken's World (1970) ....Grace Douglas
The Young and the Restless (1973-)
.... Katherine Chancellor-Sterling

Copley, Teri

Films:
New Year's Evil (1981) .... Teenage Girl
    • 0:48 - Brief right breast in the back of the car with her
    boyfriend at a drive-in movie. Breast is half sticking
    out of her white bra. Dark, hard to see anything.
Down the Drain (1989) ....Kathy Miller
    • 0:04 - Full frontal nudity making love on couch with
    Andrew Stevens. Looks like a body double.
    •• 0:31 - In two piece swimsuit, then body double nude
    doing strip tease for Stevens. Notice body double
    isn't wearing earrings.
    0:33 - Buns, (probably the body double) on top of
    Stevens.
    1:21 - In black bra in motel room when bad guy
    opens her blouse.
Masters of Menace (1990) .... Sunny
Transylvania Twist (1990)................... Marisa
Made for TV Movies:
I Married a Centerfold (1984) ....
In the Line of Duty: The F.B.I. Murders (1988) ....Vickie
TV:
We Got It Made (1983-84)..........Mickey McKenzie
I Had Three Wives (1985)................ Samantha
Magazines:
Playboy (Nov 1990) .... Teri Copley
    ••• 90-99: Nude—very nice!
Playboy (Dec 1990) ....Sex Stars of 1990
    •• 173: Right breast, while leaning against wall.

Corri, Adrienne

Films:
Corridors of Blood (1957; British) . . . . Rachel
Three Men in a Boat (1958) . . . . Clara Willis
Doctor Zhivago (1965) . . . . Amelia
A Clockwork Orange (1971) . . . . Mrs. Alexander
  •• 0:11 - Breasts through cut-outs in her top, then full
    frontal nudity getting raped by Malcolm McDowell
    and his friends.
Revenge of the Pink Panther (1978) . . . Therese Douvier

Costa, Sara

Films:
Weekend Pass (1984) . . . . Tuesday Del Mundo
  ••• 0:07 - Buns in G-string, then topless during strip
    dance routine on stage.
Stripper (1985) . . . . herself
  ••• 0:16 - Topless doing strip dance routine.
  ••• 0:46 - Topless and buns dancing on stage in a G-
    string.
  ••• 1:12 - Topless doing another strip routine.
Hot Bodies (1988) . . . . herself
  ••• 0:00 - Nude, dancing on stage. Long scene. Dancing
    with a big boa snake.
  ••• 0:04 - Topless and buns in G-string.

Courtney, Dori

Films:
Hollywood Hot Tubs 2—Educating Crystal (1989)
  . . . . Hot Tub Girl
  •• 1:00 - Topless stuck in the spa and getting her hair
    freed.
Tango & Cash (1989) . . . . .Dressing Room Girl
  • 1:06 - Topless, sitting in chair looking in the mirror in
    the background. Long shot.
Mob Boss (1990). . . . . Kathryn
  ••• 0:31 - In black bra, talking with Eddie Deezen, then
    topless. Nice close-up. Long scene.
Millenium Countdown (1991). . . . .
Sorority Girls and the Creature from Hell (1991) . . . . . .

Cox, Ashley

Films:
Drive-In (1976) . . . . Mary-Louise
King of the Mountain (1981) . . . . Elaine
Looker (1981). . . . . .Candy
Night Shift (1982). Jenny Lynn
Magazines:
Playboy (Dec 1977). . . . . Playmate

Cox, Courteney

Films:
Down Twisted (1987) . . . . Farah
Masters of the Universe (1987) . . . . .Julie Winston
Cocoon, The Return (1988). . . . . Sara

Blue Desert (1990) . . . . Lisa Roberts
  0:52 - Silhouette of right breast, standing up with
    Steve. Probably a body double. Very, very brief right
    nipple between Steve's arms lying in bed. Dark, hard
    to see.
  •• 0:53 - Left breast, lying in bed under Steve. A little
    hard to see her face, but it sure looks like her to me!
    1:14 - Buns and part of left breast getting towel.
    Looks like a body double.
Curiosity Kills (1990) . . . . Gwen
Mr. Destiny (1990). . . . . .Jewel Jagger
TV:
Misfits of Science (1985-86) . . . . Gloria Dinallo
Family Ties (1987-89). . . . . Lauren Miller
Music Videos:
Dancing in the Dark/Bruce Springsteen
  . . . . .Girl Who Goes Up on Stage

Crampton, Barbara

Films:
Body Double (1984) . . . . Carol Sculley
  •• 0:04 - Brief right breast, while making love in bed
    with another man when her husband walks in.
Fraternity Vacation (1985) . . . . Chrissie
  ••• 0:16 - Topless and buns in bedroom with two guys
    taking off her swimsuit.
Re-Animator (1985) . . . . Megan Halsey
  (Unrated version.)
  •• 0:10 - Brief buns putting panties on, then topless,
    putting bra on after making love with Dan.
  •• 1:09 - Full frontal nudity, lying unconscious on table
    getting strapped down.
  • 1:10 - Topless getting her breasts fondled by a head-
    less body.
  • 1:19 - Topless on the table.
Chopping Mall (1986). Suzie
  •• 0:22 - Brief topless taking off top in furniture store in
    front of her boyfriend on the couch.
From Beyond (1986) . . . . . . Dr. Katherine McMichaels
  •• 0:44 - Brief topless after getting blouse torn off by
    the creature in the laboratory.
  0:51 - Buns getting on top of Jeffrey Combs in black
    leather outfit.
Kidnapped (1986). . . . . .Bonnie
  0:35 - In white bra and panties in hotel room.
  ••• 0:37 - Topless getting tormented by a bad guy in
    bed.
  •• 1:12 - Topless opening her pajamas for David
    Naughton.
  •• 1:14 - Topless in white panties getting dressed.
Puppet Master (1989) . . . . Woman at Carnival
Trancers II (1991). . . . . Sadie Brady
TV:
The Young and the Restless
  . . . . Leanna Randolph Newman
Days of Our Lives (1983) . . . . Trista Evans
Magazines:
Playboy (Dec 1986) . . . .
  ••• 174-179:

Crockett, Karlene

Films:
Charlie Chan & the Curse of the Dragon Queen (1981)
. . . . .Brenda Lupowitz
Eyes of Fire (1983) . . . . Leah
- 0:44 - Brief topless sitting up in the water and scaring Mr. Dalton.
- 1:16 - Topless talking to Dalton who is trapped in a tree. Brief topless again when he pulls the creature out of the tree.
Massive Retaliation (1984) . . . . Marianne Briscoe

Crosby, Cathy Lee

Films:
The Laughing Policeman (1974) . . . . .Kay Butler
Coach (1978). . . . . .Randy
- 0:31 - Very brief side view of left breast when Michael Biehn opens the door while she's putting on her top.
  0:52 - In wet white T-shirt at the beach and in her house with Biehn.
  1:11 - Very, very brief topless in shower room with Biehn. Blurry, hard to see anything.
The Dark (1979) . . . . .Zoe
TV:
That's Incredible (1980-84) . . . . host

Crosby, Denise

Granddaughter of actor/singer Bing Crosby.
Films:
48 Hours (1982) . . . . Sally
  0:47 - Very, very brief side view of half of left breast, while swinging baseball bat at Eddie Murphy.
- 1:24 - Very brief side view of right breast when James Remar pushes her onto bed.
- 1:25 - Very brief topless then very brief side view of right breast attacking Nick Nolte.
The Trail of the Pink Panther (1982) . . . .
Curse of the Pink Panther (1983). . . . . Bruno's Moll
The Man Who Loved Women (1983) . . . . Enid
Desert Hearts (1986). . . . . Pat
Eliminators (1986). . . . . .Nora Hunter
  0:47 - In wet white tank top inside an airplane cockpit that has crashed in the water.
  0:50 - Wet tank top getting out of the plane.
Arizona Heat (1988) . . . . .Jill Andrews
- 1:13 - Brief upper half of left breast in shower with Larry.
Miracle Mile (1989). . . . . Landa
Pet Sematary (1989) . . . . Rachel Creed
Skin Deep (1989) . . . . Angie Smith
TV:
Star Trek: The Next Generation (1987-88)
. . . . Lt. Tasha Yar
Magazines:
Playboy (Mar 1979). . . . . . . A Different Kind of Crosby
••• 99-103: Full frontal nudity.
Playboy (May 1988) . . . . Star Treat
••• 74-79: Nude, photos from the 1979 pictorial.

Crosby, Katja

Films:
It's Alive III: Island of the Alive (1988) . . . .
A Return to Salem's Lot (1988). . . . . Cathy
- •• 0:36 - Topless making love in bed with Joey.
- • 0:48 - Side view of right breast kissing Joey outside next to a stream.

Crosby, Lucinda

Films:
Blue Thunder (1983) . . . . .Bel-Air Woman
The Naked Cage (1985). . . . . Rhonda
Blue Movies (1988) . . . . Randy Moon
- • 0:10 - Topless in hot tub.
- •• 0:11 - Topless shooting porno movie.
- ••• 0:30 - Topless auditioning for Buzz.
- • 0:59 - Topless on desk in porno movie.
Pretty Woman (1990). . . . . Olsen Sister

Cruikshank, Laura

Films:
Ruthless People (1986). . . . .
Buying Time (1987). . . . . Jessica
- •• 0:52 - Topless several times making love with Ron on pool table.

Cser, Nancy

Films:
Joy (1983; French/Canadian) . . . . .unidentified
Perfect Timing (1984) .Lacy
  0:54 - In white lingerie, taking off clothes for Harry and posing.
- ••• 0:56 - Topless getting photographed by Harry.
- • 0:58 - Topless, making love with Harry.
- • 1:01 - Topless.
Separate Vacations (1985) . . . . Stewardess
Head Office (1986) . . . . Dantley's Secretary

Cummins, Juliette

Films:
Friday the 13th, Part V—A New Beginning (1985)
. . . . .Robin
- ••• 1:01 - Topless, wearing panties getting undressed and climbing into bed just before getting killed.
  1:05 - Very brief topless, covered with blood when Reggie discovers her dead.
Psycho III (1986) . . . . Red
- ••• 0:39 - Topless making love with Duke in his motel room, then getting thrown out.
Slumber Party Massacre II (1987) . . . . Sheila
- •• 0:24 - In black bra, then topless in living room during a party with her girlfriends.

Deadly Dreams (1988) . . . . Maggie Kallir
  • 0:25 - Topless on bed, taking off her blouse and kissing Alex.
  ••• 0:55 - Topless and brief buns, making love with Jack in bed.
Magazines:
  Playboy (Nov 1986) . . . . Sex in Cinema 1986
  •• 129: Topless in a photo from *Psycho III*.

Curran, Lynette

Films:
  Alvin Purple (1973; Australian) . . . . . . First Sugar Girl
  •• 0:02 - Brief full frontal nudity when Alvin opens the door.
  Heatwave (1983; Australian) . . . . Evonne
  Bliss (1985; Australian) . . . . Bettina Joy
  The Year My Voice Broke (1987; Australian)
  . . . . .Anne Olson

Currie, Cherie

  Singer.
  Identical twin sister of singer/actress Marie Currie Lukather.
Films:
  Foxes (1980). . . . . Annie
  Parasite (1982) . . . . Dana
  Wavelength (1982) . . . . Iris Longacre
    0:09 - Brief side view of right breast and buns getting out of bed. Dark, don't really see anything.
  The Rosebud Beach Hotel (1985) . . . . Cherie
    1:13 - Singing with her twin sister in braless pink T-shirt on the beach.

Currie, Sondra

Films:
  Policewoman (1974). . . . .
  Jessi's Girls (1976) . . . . .Jessica
  • 0:02 - Nude in water cleaning up, then brief left breast getting dressed.
  • 0:07 - Topless getting raped by four guys. Fairly long scene.
  • 0:37 - Topless kissing Clay under a tree. Hard to see because of the shadows.
  The Last Married Couple in America (1980)
  . . . . Lainy
  •• 1:32 - Topless taking off her clothes in bedroom in front of Natalie Wood, George Segal and her husband.
  The Concrete Jungle (1982) . . . . Katherine
  Street Justice (1988) . . . . Mandy
Magazines:
  Playboy (Nov 1980) . . . . Sex in Cinema 1980
  • 174: Side view of right breast.

Curtin, Jane

Films:
  How to Beat the High Cost of Living (1980)
  . . . . .Elaine
    1:28 - In pink bra, distracting everybody in the mall so her friends can steal money.
  • 1:29 - Close up topless, taking off her bra. Probably a body double.
  O.C. and Stiggs (1987) . . . . Elinore Schwab
Made for TV Movies:
  Common Ground (1990) . . . . Alice McGoff
TV:
  Saturday Night Live (1975-80)
  . . . . .Not Ready For Primetime Player
  Kate and Allie (1984-90) . . . . Allie Lowell
  Working It Out (1990) . . . . Sarah Marshall

Curtis, Allegra

  Daughter of actor Tony Curtis and his second wife, actress Christine Kaufmann.
Films:
  Midnight Cop (1988; German) . . . . . . Monika Carstens
  Guns (1990). . . . . Robyn
Magazines:
  Playboy (Apr 1990) . . . . Brava, Allegra!
  ••• 92-97: Full frontal nudity.

Curtis, Jamie Lee

  Daughter of actor Tony Curtis and actress Janet Leigh.
  Wife of actor Christopher Guest.
Films:
  Halloween (1978) . . . . Laurie
  The Fog (1980) . . . . Elizabeth Solley
  Prom Night (1980) . . . . Kim
  Terror Train (1980; Canadian) . . . . .Alena
  Halloween II (1981) . . . . Laurie
  Road Games (1981) . . . . .Hitch/Pamela
  Trading Places (1983). . . . . .Ophelia
  ••• 1:00 - Topless in black panties after taking red dress off in bathroom while Dan Aykroyd watches.
  ••• 1:09 - Topless and black panties taking off halter top and pants getting into bed with a sick Aykroyd.
  The Adventures of Buckaroo Banzai, Across the 8th Dimension (1984) . . . . Dr. Sandra Banzai
  Grandview, U.S.A. (1984) . . . . . Michelle "Mike" Cody
  ••• 1:00 - Left breast, in bed with C. Thomas Howell.
  Love Letters (1984) . . . . Anna Winter
  ••• 0:31 - Topless in bathtub reading a letter, then topless in bed making love with James Keach.
  • 0:36 - Brief topless in lifeguard station with Keach.
  ••• 0:44 - Brief topless admiring a picture taken of her by Keach.
  ••• 0:46 - Topless and buns in bedroom undressing with Keach.
  • 0:49 - Topless in black and white Polaroid photographs that Keach is taking.
  • 1:07 - Right breast, sticking out of slip, then right breast, while sleeping in bed with Keach.

Terror in the Aisles (1984) . . . . Hostess
Perfect (1985) . . . . Jessie Wilson
    0:14 - No nudity, but doing aerobics in leotards.
    0:26 - More aerobics in leotards.
    0:40 - More aerobics, mentally making love with
    John Travolta while leading the class.
    1:19 - More aerobics when photographer is shooting
    pictures.
    1:32 - In red leotard after the article comes out in
    Rolling Stone.
Tall Tales and Legends: Annie Oakley (1985)
. . . . Annie Oakley
A Man in Love (1987) . . . . Susan Elliot
A Fish Called Wanda (1988) . . . . Wanda
    0:21 - In black bra and panties changing in the bed-
    room talking to Kevin Kline.
    0:35 - In black bra sitting on bed getting undressed.
Blue Steel (1989) . . . . .Megan Turner
    1:27 - Very, very brief buns twice when rolling out of
    bed, trying to get her gun. Dark.
Queens Logic (1991) . . . . Grace
Made for TV Movies:
Death of a Centerfold: The Dorothy Stratten Story
   (1981) . . . . .Dorothy Stratten
She's in the Army Now (1981) . . . .
TV:
Operation Petticoat (1977-78) . . . . . . Lt. Barbara Duran
Anything but Love (1989-) . . . . .Hannah Miller
Magazines:
Playboy (Nov 1983) . . . . Sex in Cinema 1983
••• 151: Topless and right breast photo from *Trading
   Places.*

Cutter, Lise
Films:
Buy & Cell (1989) . . . . .Dr. Ellen Scott
Havana (1990) . . . . .Patty
  • 0:44 - Most of side of left breast with Robert Redford.
    Very, very brief part of right breast while he turns her
    around. Very brief left breast when Redford puts a
    cold glass on her chest. Dark, hard to see.
TV:
Equal Justice . . . . Andrea Kanin

Cyr, Myriam
Films:
Gothic (1986; British) . . . . Claire
  •• 0:53 - Left breast, then topless lying in bed with Gab-
    riel Byrne.
  • 0:55 - Brief left breast lying in bed. Long shot.
  • 1:02 - Topless sitting on pool table opening her top
    for Julian Sands. Special effect with eyes in her nip-
    ples.
  • 1:12 - Buns and brief topless covered with mud.
Frankenstein Unbound (1990) . . . . . Information Officer

D'Abo, Maryam
Cousin of actress Olivia d'Abo.
Films:
Xtro (1982) . . . . .Analise
  ••• 0:25 - Topless making love with her boyfriend on the
    floor in her bedroom.
  •• 0:56 - Brief topless with her boyfriend again.
Until September (1984) . . . . .Nathalie
White Nights (1985) . . . . French Girl Friend
The Living Daylights (1987) . . . . Kara Milovy
Miniseries:
Master of the Game (1984) . . . . Dominique
Made for TV Movies:
Something Is Out There (1988) . . . . Ta'ra
Magazines:
Playboy (Sep 1987) . . . . D'Abo
  ••• 132-139:
Playboy (Dec 1987) . . . . .Sex Stars of 1987
  ••• 154: Right breast, sitting behind cello.

D'Abo, Olivia
Cousin of actress Maryam d'Abo.
Films:
Bolero (1984) . . . . Paloma
  • 0:38 - Nude covered with bubbles taking a bath.
  • 1:05 - Brief topless in the steam room with Bo.
  • 1:32 - Topless in the steam room talking with Bo.
    Hard to see because it's so steamy.
Conan the Destroyer (1984) . . . . Princess Jehnna
Bullies (1985) . . . . Becky Cullen
  •• 0:39 - In wet white T-shirt swimming in river while
    Matt watches.
Dream to Believe (1985; Canadian) . . . . Robin Crew
    0:29 - Working out in training room wearing a sexy
    cotton tank top.
Into the Fire (1988) . . . . Liette
    0:07 - Very, very brief silhouette of left breast in bed
    with Wade.
  •• 0:32 - Topless on bed with Wade. A little bit dark and
    hard to see.
  •• 1:10 - Topless in the bathtub. (Note her panties
    when she gets up.)
TV:
The Wonder Years (1987-) . . . . Karen Arnold

D'Angelo, Beverly
Films:
Annie Hall (1977) . . . . Actress in Rob's TV Show
First Love (1977) . . . . .Shelley
    0:05 - Very, very brief half of left breast when her
    jacket opens up while talking to William Katt.
    0:11 - In white bra and black panties in Katt's bed-
    room.
  • 1:10 - Brief topless taking off her top in bedroom
    with Katt.

The Sentinel (1977) . . . . Sandra
    0:25 - Masturbating in red leotard and tights on
    couch in front of Cristina Raines.
  • 0:33 - Brief topless playing cymbals during Raines'
    nightmare (in B&W).
    1:24 - Brief topless long shot with zombie make up,
    munching on a dead Chris Sarandon.
Hair (1979) . . . . Sheila
  • 0:59 - In white bra and panties, then topless on rock
    near pond. Medium long shot.
 ••• 1:01 - Topless in panties getting out of the pond.
  • 1:38 - Side view of right breast changing clothes in
    car with George.
Coal Miner's Daughter (1980) . . . . Patsy Cline
Honky Tonk Freeway (1981) . . . . Carmen
Paternity (1981) . . . . .Maggie
Finders Keepers (1983) . . . . .Standish Logan
National Lampoon's Vacation (1983)
. . . . .Ellen Griswold
 •• 0:18 - Brief topless taking a shower in the motel.
  • 1:19 - Brief topless taking off shirt and jumping into
    the swimming pool.
Highpoint (1984; Canadian) . . . . Lise Hatcher
National Lampoon's European Vacation (1985)
. . . . .Ellen Griswold
Big Trouble (1986) . . . . Blanche Ricky
Slow Burn (1986) . . . . Laine Fleischer
  • 1:01 - Topless making love with Eric Roberts. Don't
    see her face. Part of lower frontal nudity showing
    tattoo.
Maid to Order (1987) . . . . Stella
Aria (1988; U.S./British) . . . . Gilda
High Spirits (1988) . . . . Sharon
Cold Front (1989; Canadian) . . . . Amanda O'Rourke
National Lampoon's Christmas Vacation (1989)
. . . . .Ellen Griswold
Daddy's Dyin'... Who's Got the Will? (1990) . . . . .Evalita
Pacific Heights (1990) . . . . Ann
  • 0:01 - Sort of topless in reflection on TV screen, then
    right breast, in bed with Michael Keaton.
    0:03 - Very brief buns, turning over on bed when two
    guys burst in to the house.
The Pope Must Die (1991) . . . . .Veronica Dante
TV:
Captains and the Kings (1976) . . . . .Miss Emmy

D'Arbanville, Patti
Films:
Rancho Deluxe (1975) . . . . .Betty Fargo
Big Wednesday (1978) . . . . Sally
The Fifth Floor (1978) . . . . Cathy Burke
The Main Event (1979) . . . . Donna
Time After Time (1979; British) . . . . Shirley
Hog Wild (1980; Canadian) . . . . Angie
Modern Problems (1981) . . . . Darcy
  • 0:48 - Very brief right breast in bed after Chevy
    Chase has telekinetic sex with her.

Bilitis (1982; French) . . . . Bilitis
 ••• 0:25 - Topless copying Melissa undressing.
 •• 0:27 - Topless on tree.
 ••• 0:31 - Full frontal nudity taking off swimsuit with Me-
    lissa.
    0:36 - Buns, cleaning herself in the bathroom.
 •• 0:59 - Topless and buns making love with Melissa.
The Boys Next Door (1985) . . . . .Angie
Real Genius (1985) . . . . Sherry Nugil
Call Me (1988) . . . . Coni
Fresh Horses (1988) . . . . .Jean
TV:
Wiseguy (1989-90) . . . . .Amber Twine
Magazines:
Playboy (May 1977) . . . . Our Lady D'Arbanville
 ••• Full frontal nudity in *Bilitis* photos taken by David
    Hamilton.

Dahms, Gail
Films:
The Silent Partner (1978) . . . . Louise
  • 0:31 - Right breast in bathroom with another guy
    when Elliott Gould surprises them.
The Tomorrow Man (1979) . . . .

Daily, Elizabeth
a.k.a. E. G. Daily.
Films:
The Escape Artist (1982) . . . . .Sandra
One Dark Night (1983) . . . . Leslie
Valley Girl (1983) .Loryn
 •• 0:16 - In bra through open jumpsuit, then brief top-
    less on bed with Tommy.
Wacko (1983) . . . . Bambi
No Small Affair (1984) . . . . .Susan
Streets of Fire (1984) . . . . .Baby Doll
Fandango (1985) . . . . .Judy
Pee Wee's Big Adventure (1985) . . . . Dottie
Loverboy (1989) . . . . .Linda
Magazines:
Playboy (Nov 1983) . . . . Sex in Cinema 1983
 •• 146: Topless.

Dale, Cynthia
Films:
My Bloody Valentine (1981; Canadian) . . . . Patty
Heavenly Bodies (1985) . . . . Samantha Blair
  • 0:30 - Brief topless fantasizing about making love
    with Steve while doing aerobic exercises.
The Boy In Blue (1986; Canadian) . . . . .Margaret
 ••• 1:15 - Topless standing in a loft kissing Nicholas
    Cage.
Moonstruck (1987) . . . . Sheila
Made for Cable Movies:
The Liberators (1987; Disney) . . . . . .Elizabeth Giddings
Made for TV Movies:
Sadie and Son (1987) . . . . Paula Melvin

Dale, Jennifer

Films:
Stone Cold Dead (1979; Canadian). . . . Claudia Grissom
Suzanne (1980; Canadian) . . . . Suzanne
- •• 0:29 - Topless when boyfriend lifts her sweatshirt up when she's sitting on couch doing homework.
- •• 0:53 - Topless with Nicky on the floor.

Your Ticket is No Longer Valid (1982) . . . . . . Laura
- •• 0:27 - In black panties, then topless when her husband fantasizes, then makes love with her.
- 1:23 - Left breast in bed with Montoya, then sitting, waiting for Richard Harris.

Of Unknown Origin (1983; Canadian) . . . . . Lorrie Wells
Separate Vacations (1985) . . . . Sarah Moore
- • 0:17 - Brief right breast in bed with her husband after son accidentally comes into their bedroom.
- 0:20 - In a bra and slip showing the baby sitter the house before leaving.
- •• 1:14 - Topless on the cabin floor with Jeff after having a fight with her husband.
- • 1:19 - Brief right breast, in bed with her husband.

Magazines:
Playboy (Nov 1980) . . . . Sex in Cinema 1980
- • 181: Right breast.

Dalle, Béatrice

Films:
Betty Blue (1986; French). . . . . Betty
- ••• 0:01 - Topless making love in bed with Zorg. Long sequence.
- ••• 0:30 - Nude on bed having sex with boyfriend.
- ••• 1:03 - Nude trying to sleep in living room.
- ••• 1:21 - Topless in white tap pants in hallway.
- ••• 1:29 - Topless lying down with Zorg.
- ••• 1:39 - Topless sitting on bathtub crying & talking.

On a Vole Charlie Spencer! (1987) . . . . Movie Star
Magazines:
Playboy (Nov 1987) . . . . Sex in Cinema 1987
- •• 141: Topless in blue light from *Betty Blue*.

Daly, Jeannie

See: Carol, Jean.

Daly, Tyne

Daughter of actor James Daly.
Wife of actor Georg Stanford Brown.
Films:
John and Mary (1969). Hilary
The Adultress (1973) . . . . Inez
- • 0:21 - Brief side view of right breast in room with Carl. Brief out of focus topless in bed.
- • 0:51 - Topless outside with Hank.
- ••• 0:53 - Topless on a horse with Hank.

The Enforcer (1976) . . . . Kate Moore
Telefon (1977) . . . . Dorothy Putterman
Zoot Suit (1981). . . . . Alice
The Aviator (1984) . . . . Evelyn Stiller

Movers and Shakers (1985) . . . . Nancy Derman
Made for TV Movies:
Intimate Strangers (1977) . . . .
The Last to Go (1991) . . . .
TV:
Cagney & Lacey (1982-88) . . . . Mary Beth Lacey
(Won four Emmy Awards.)

Danner, Blythe

Films:
To Kill a Clown (1971) . . . . Lily Frischer
- • 1:10 - Side view of left breast sitting on bed talking to Alan Alda. Hair covers breast, hard to see. Buns, getting up and running out of the house.

1776 (1972). . . . . Martha Jefferson
Hearts of the West (1975) . . . . Miss Trout
Futureworld (1976) . . . . Tracy Ballard
The Great Santini (1980) . . . . Lillian Meechum
Man, Woman and Child (1983) . . . . Sheila Beckwith
Brighton Beach Memoirs (1986) . . . . Kate
Another Woman (1988). Lydia
Alice (1990). . . . . Dorothy
Mr. & Mrs. Bridge (1990). . . . . Grace
Made for Cable Movies:
Judgement (1990; HBO) . . . . Emmeline Guitry
Made for TV Movies:
Money, Power, Murder (1989) . . . . Jeannie
TV:
Adam's Rib (1973) . . . . Amanda Bonner

Danning, Sybil

a.k.a. Sybille Danninger.
Films:
Bluebeard (1972). . . . . The Prostitute
- • 1:08 - Brief topless kissing Nathalie Delon showing her how to make love to her husband.
- • 1:09 - Brief left breast, lying on the floor with Delon just before Richard Burton kills both of them.

Maiden Quest (1972) . . . . Kriemhild
a.k.a. The Long Swift Sword of Siegfried
Private Screenings.
- • 0:02 - Topless in bath, surrounded by topless blonde servants.
- • 0:04 - Topless in the bath again.
- ••• 0:10 - Nude in tub surrounded by topless servant girls.
- ••• 0:12 - Topless on bed, getting rubbed with ointment by the servant girls.
- •• 0:35 - Topless while in bed with Siegfried.
- • 1:00 - Topless in bed with Siegfried.
- ••• 1:19 - Topless in bed with Siegfried.

Naughty Nymphs (1972; German) . . . . Elizabeth
a.k.a. Passion Pill Swingers
- ••• 0:21 - Nude taking a bath while yelling at her two sisters.
- • 0:30 - Topless and buns throwing Nicholas out of her bedroom.
- •• 0:38 - Full frontal nudity running away from Burt.

Albino (1976) . . . . Sally
a.k.a. Night of the Askari
- 0:19 - Topless, then full frontal nudity getting raped by the Albino and his buddies.

The Loves of a French Pussycat (1976) . . . . . Andrea
••• 0:18 - Topless dancing with her boss, then in bed.
•• 0:24 - Topless and buns in swimming pool.
   0:40 - In sheer white bra and panties doing things around the house. Long sequence.
- 0:46 - Topless in bathtub with a guy.
- 1:03 - Left breast sticking out of bra, then topless.

The Twist (1976) . . . . Jacques' Secretary
•• 1:24 - Brief topless sitting next to Bruce Dern during his daydream.

God's Gun (1977) . . . . Jenny
a.k.a. A Bullet from God
- 1:09 - Right breast popping out of dress with a guy in the barn during flashback.

Cat in the Cage (1978) . . . . Susan Khan
- 0:24 - Brief topless getting slapped around by Ralph.
- 0:25 - Brief left breast several times smoking and talking to Ralph, brief left breast getting up.
•• 0:30 - Full frontal nudity getting out of the pool.
- 0:52 - Black bra and panties undressing and getting into bed with Ralph. Brief left breast and buns.
   1:02 - In white lingerie in bedroom.
   1:10 - In white slip looking out window.
   1:15 - In black slip.
- 1:18 - Very brief right breast several times, struggling with an attacker on the floor.

Kill Castro (1978) . . . . Veronica
a.k.a. Cuba Crossing
Separate Ways (1979) . . . . Mary
Battle Beyond the Stars (1980) . . . . St. Exmin
The Day of the Cobra (1980) . . . . Brenda
- 0:41 - Buns and side view of right breast getting out of bed and putting robe on with Lou. Long shot.

How to Beat the High Cost of Living (1980)
. . . . Charlotte
The Man with Bogart's Face (1980) . . . . Cynthia
Nightkill (1981) . . . . Monika Childs
Daughter of Death (1982) . . . . Susan
a.k.a. Julie Darling
•• 0:36 - Topless in bed with Anthony Franciosa.
- 0:38 - Brief right breast under Franciosa.

S.A.S. San Salvador (1982) . . . . . Countess Alexandra
- 0:07 - Brief left breast, while lying on the couch and kissing Malko.

Chained Heat (1983; U.S./German) . . . . Erika
••• 0:30 - Topless in the shower with Linda Blair.
Hercules (1983) . . . . Arianna
Private Passions (1983) . . . . Katherine
Howling II (1984) . . . . Stirba
- 0:35 - Left breast, then topless with Mariana in bedroom about to have sex with a guy.
- 1:20 - Very brief topless during short clips during the end credits. Same shot repeated about 10 times.

Malibu Express (1984) . . . . Countess Luciana
- 0:13 - Brief topless making love in bed with Cody.

They're Playing with Fire (1984) . . . . Diane Stevens
   0:04 - In two piece swimsuit on boat. Long scene.
••• 0:08 - Topless and buns making love on top of Jay in bed on boat. Nice!
•• 0:10 - Topless and buns getting out of shower, then brief side view of right breast.
   0:43 - In black bra and slip, in boat with Jay.
•• 0:47 - In black bra and slip, at home with Michael, then panties, then topless and buns getting into shower.
••• 1:12 - In white bra and panties in room with Jay then topless.

Jungle Warriors (1985) . . . . Angel
   0:53 - Buns, getting a massage lying face down.
Panther Squad (1986; French/Belgian) . . . . Ilona
Reform School Girls (1986) . . . . Warden Sutter
Young Lady Chatterley II (1986) . . . .
••• 1:02 - Topless in the hut on the table with the Gardener.

Amazon Women on the Moon (1987) . . . . . Queen Lara
Phantom Empire (1987) . . . . The Alien Queen
Talking Walls (1987) . . . . Bathing Beauty
The Tomb (1987) . . . . Jade
Warrior Queen (1987) . . . . Berenice
L.A. Bounty (1989) . . . . Ruger
Made for Cable TV:
The Hitchhiker: Face to Face . . . . Gloria Loring
   (Available on *The Hitchhiker, Volume 4*.)
•• 0:10 - In red bra and panties, then right breast making love with Robert Vaughn.

Magazines:
Playboy (Aug 1983) . . . .
Playboy (Nov 1983) . . . . Sex in Cinema 1983
•• 145: Topless.
Playboy (Dec 1983) . . . . Sex Stars of 1983
••• 210: Full frontal nudity.
Playboy (Dec 1984) . . . . Sex Stars of 1984
- 202: Half of right breast and lower frontal nudity.
Playboy (Dec 1986) . . . . Sex Stars of 86
158:

Danon, Leslie

Films:
Beach Balls (1988) . . . . Kathleen
- 1:06 - In bra, then brief topless in car with Doug.
Marked for Death (1990) . . . . Girl #1

Dante, Crisstyn

Films:
Midnight Crossing (1988)
. . . . Body double for Kim Cattrall
- 0:29 - Brief left breast making love on small boat, body double for Kim Cattrall.
State Park (1988; Canadian) . . . . Blond in Net
- 0:45 - Very, very brief left breast putting swimsuit top back on after being rescued from net by the guy in the bear costume.
Last Call (1990) . . . . Hooker

Danziger, Maia

Films:
High Stakes (1989) . . . . Veronica
Last Exit to Brooklyn (1990). . . . . Mary Black
    0:10 - Out of focus buns and right breast.
    • 0:12 - Very brief topless making love with Harry. Topless after.

Darnell, Vicki

Films:
Senior Week (1987) . . . . Everett's Dream Teacher
  •• 0:03 - Topless during classroom fantasy.
Brain Damage (1988) . . . . .Blonde in Hell Club
Frankenhooker (1990). . . . . Sugar
    • 0:36 - Brief middle part of each breast through slit bra during introduction to Jeffrey.
  •• 0:37 - Breasts, sticking out of black lingerie while getting legs measured.
    • 0:38 - Right breast, while sitting in chair.
    • 0:39 - Topless through slit lingerie three times while folding clothes.
    0:40 - Buns, fighting over drugs.
  ••• 0:41 - Very brief right breast, sitting on bed (on the right) enjoying drugs. Topless dancing with the other girls.

Das, Alisha

Films:
The Slugger's Wife (1985) . . . . Lola
Danger Zone II: Reaper's Revenge (1988) . . . . . Francine
Nightwish (1988) . . . . Kim
  •• 1:09 - Brief topless, then left breast in open dress caressing herself while lying on the ground.
    • 1:10 - Braless under see-through purple dress.

Davidovich, Lolita

a.k.a. Lolita David.
Films:
Class (1983) . . . . 1st Girl (motel)
Recruits (1986) . . . . Susan
The Big Town (1987) . . . . Black Lace Stripper
Blindside (1988; Canadian). . . . . Adele
  •• 0:32 - Topless dancing on stage.
    0:39 - Sort of buns bending over and pointing a gun through her legs in front of mirror.
A New Life (1988). . . . .
Blaze (1989) . . . . Blaze Starr
    0:09 - In bra doing her first strip routine. Very brief side views of left breast under hat.
    0:15 - Strip tease routine in front of Paul Newman. At the end, she takes off bra to reveal pasties.
    0:42 - In black bra and panties with Newman.
  •• 0:48 - Topless on top of Newman, then side view of left breast.
Made for Cable Movies:
Prison Stories, Women on the Inside (1990; HBO)
. . . . Lorretta

Davidson, Eileen

Films:
Goin' All the Way (1981) .BJ
  ••• 0:12 - Topless in the girls' locker room shower. Standing next to Monica.
  ••• 0:22 - Exercising in her bedroom in braless pink T-shirt, then topless talking on the phone to Monica.
House on Sorority Row (1983) . . . . Vicki
  •• 0:16 - Topless and buns in room making love with her boyfriend.
    0:19 - In white bikini top by the pool.
Easy Wheels (1989) . . . . She Wolf
Eternity (1989) . . . . Dahlia/Valerie
    0:33 - In black bra and panties in dressing room. Brief buns standing in bathtub during Jon Voight's flashback.
    • 0:52 - Brief left breast, then topless, in bed with Voight. Don't see face.
TV:
The Young and the Restless . . . . Ashley Abbott
Broken Badges (1990-91). . . . . .Bullet

Davis, Carole

a.k.a. Carol Davis.
Films:
Piranha II: The Spawning (1981; Dutch). . . . .
C.O.D. (1983) . . . . Contessa Bazzini
    • 1:25 - Brief topless in dressing room scene in black panties, garter belt and stockings when she takes off her robe.
    1:29 - In black top during fashion show.
The Princess Academy (1986) . . . . Sonia
Mannequin (1987) . . . . .Roxie
The Shrimp on the Barbie (1990). . . . . .Domonique
    0:58 - Buns, in pool that is visible from inside restaurant. Don't see her face.
    0:58 - In black bra and panties, then topless doing strip tease in front of Bruce. Very dark.
If Looks Could Kill (1991) . . . . .Areola Canasta

Davis, Geena

Ex-wife of actor Jeff Goldblum.
Films:
Tootsie (1982) . . . . April
    0:34 - In white bra and panties in dressing room with Dustin Hoffman.
    0:44 - In white bra and panties exercising in dressing room while Hoffman reads his script.
Transylvania 6-5000 (1985) . . . . .Odette
The Fly (1986) . . . . Veronica Quaife
    0:40 - Brief almost side view of left breast getting out of bed.
The Accidental Tourist (1988). . . . . Muriel
  (Academy Award for Best Supporting Actress.)
Beetlejuice (1988) . . . . Barbara
Earth Girls are Easy (1989) . . . . Valerie
    0:11 - In yellow two piece swimsuit during song and dance number in beauty salon.

0:12 - In frilly pink lingerie waiting at home for her fiance to return.

0:22 - In pink two piece swimsuit doing a lot of different things for a long time. This is probably the greatest swimsuit scene in a PG movie!

Quick Change (1990) . . . . .Phyllis

Thelma and Louise (1991). . . . . .Thelma

Davis, Judy

Films:

High Rolling (1977; Australian) . . . . .Lynn

My Brilliant Career (1979; Australian) . . . . Syblla Melvyn

Winter of Our Dreams (1981) . . . . .Lou

- 0:19 - Brief left breast sticking out of yellow robe in bed with Pete.
- 0:26 - Very brief side view of left breast taking off top to change. Long shot.
- •• 0:48 - Topless taking off top and getting into bed with Bryan Brown, then brief right breast lying down with him.

The Final Option (1982; British) . . . . Frankie

Heatwave (1983; Australian) . . . . Kate

A Passage to India (1984; British) . . . . . . Adela Quested

Kangaroo (1986; Australian) . . . . Harriet Somers

High Tide (1987; Australian) Lilli

Alice (1990) . . . . Vicki

Made for TV Movies:

A Woman Called Golda (1982) . . . .

Davis, Phyllis

Films:

The Last of the Secret Agents? (1966) . . . . .Beautiful Girl

Live a Little, Love a Little (1968) . . . . .2nd Secretary

Beyond the Valley of the Dolls (1970) . . . . . . Susan Lake

Russ Meyer Film. (Not available on video tape.)

Sweet Sugar (1972) . . . . Sugar

(With brown hair.)

- ••• 0:34 - Topless in bed with a guard.
- ••• 0:50 - Topless in the shower with Dolores.
- •• 0:57 - Brief topless in the bathroom.

The Day of the Dolphin (1973) . . . . Secretary

Terminal Island (1973) . . . . Joy Lange

- ••• 0:39 - Topless and buns in a pond, full frontal nudity getting out, then more topless putting blouse on while a guy watches.

Train Ride to Hollywood (1975). . . . .

The Choirboys (1977) . . . . .Foxy/Gina

The Best of Sex and Violence (1981) . . . . . Sugar/Joy

- •• 0:56 - Topless after bath and in bed in scenes from *Sweet Sugar.*
- ••• 0:59 - Topless and buns walking out of lake in scene from *Terminal Island.*

Famous T & A (1982) . . . . Joy/Sugar

(No longer available for purchase, check your video store for rental.)

- ••• 0:02 - Nude in lots of great out-takes from *Terminal Island.* Check this out if you are a Phyllis Davis fan!

- ••• 0:51 - Topless in scenes from *Sweet Sugar.* Includes more out-takes.
- ••• 1:04 - More out-takes from *Sweet Sugar.*

Guns (1990). . . . . Kathryn Hamilton

TV:

Love, American Style (1970-74) . . . . . . repertory player

Vega$ (1978-81) . . . . Beatrice Travis

Davis, Sammi

No relation to the late entertainer Sammy Davis, Jr.

Films:

Hope and Glory (1987; British). . . . . Dawn Rohan

A Prayer for the Dying (1987) . . . . Anna

Consuming Passions (1988; U.S./British) . . . . . . .Felicity

The Lair of the White Worm (1988; British)

. . . . .Mary Trent

The Rainbow (1989) . . . . Winifred Inger

- ••• 0:21 - Topless and buns with Amanda Donohoe undressing, running outside in the rain, jumping into the water, then talking by the fireplace.
- •• 0:30 - Topless and buns posing for a painter.
- • 1:33 - Brief right breast and buns getting out of bed.
- ••• 1:44 - Nude running outside with Donohoe.

Made for Cable Movies:

The Perfect Bride (1991) . . . . Stephanie

Made for TV Movies:

Pack of Lies (1987). . . . . .Julie

Day, Alexandra

Films:

Erotic Images (1983). . . . . Logan's Girlfriend

- •• 0:37 - Topless getting out of bed while Logan talks on the phone to Britt Ekland.

Boarding House (1984) . . . . Girl in Bathroom

Body Double (1984). . . . . .Girl in Bathroom #1

Young Lady Chatterley II (1986)

. . . . Jenny "Maid in Hut"

- ••• 0:06 - Topless in hut on the bed with the Gardener.
- ••• 0:28 - Topless taking bath with Harlee McBride.

Video Tapes:

The Girls of Penthouse (1984)

. . . . Tattoo Woman & Use Me Woman

- ••• 0:34 - Nude, getting tattooed by another woman, then making love with her.
- ••• 0:40 - Nude, dancing and stripping off her clothes down to stockings and garter belt, then on bed. Quick cuts and strobe light make it hard to see.

Day, Catlyn

Films:

Kandyland (1987) . . . . .Diva

- ••• 0:50 - Topless wearing pasties doing strip routine.
- • 1:06 - Brief topless talking on the telephone in dressing room.
- • 1:12 - Brief topless during dance routine.

Wilding, The Children of Violence (1990)

. . . . Officer Breedlove

De La Croix, Raven
Films:
Up! (1976) . . . . Margo Winchester
Russ Meyer film.
Topless.
The Lost Empire (1983) . . . . White Star
••• 1:05 - Topless with a snake after being drugged by the bad guy.
•• 1:07 - Topless lying on a table.
Screwballs (1983) . . . . Miss Anna Tomical
••• 1:08 - Topless during strip routine in nightclub.
Best Chest in the West (1984) . . . . herself
••• 0:34 - Topless doing strip tease routine on stage.
Magazines:
Playboy (Nov 1976) . . . . Sex in Cinema 1976
•• 153: Topless.

De Leeuw, Lisa
Adult film actress.
Films:
Up 'n' Coming (1987) . . . . Altheah Anderson
(R-rated version reviewed, X-rated version available.)
• 0:33 - Very brief topless by the pool when her robe opens.
• 0:48 - Brief topless walking around the house when her robe open.
•• 0:49 - Left breast talking with a guy, then topless walking into the bedroom.

de Light, Venus
Films:
Stripper (1985) . . . . herself
• 0:59 - Brief topless, on stage, blowing fire.
••• 1:07 - Topless and buns in black G-string, doing routine on stage, using fire.
Hot Bodies (1988) . . . . herself
•• 0:22 - Topless, dancing and taking off dress.
••• 0:24 - Nude in large champagne glass prop.
••• 0:27 - Nude dancing on stage.
••• 0:47 - Topless and buns in G-string stripping in nurse uniform.
••• 0:49 - Topless and buns on hospital gurney.
••• 0:52 - Topless and buns dancing with a dummy prop.

De Liso, Debra
Films:
The Slumber Party Massacre (1982) . . . . Kim
• 0:08 - Very brief topless getting soap from Trish in the shower.
•• 0:29 - In beige bra and panties, then topless putting on a U.S.A. shirt while changing with the other girls.
Iced (1988) . . . . Trina
• 0:11 - In a bra, then brief nude making love with Cory in hotel room.
Dr. Caligari (1989) . . . . Grace Butter

De Lorenzo, Anneka
Real name is Marjorie Thoreson.
Films:
The Centerfold Girls (1974) . . . . Pam
Caligula (1980) . . . .
(X-rated, 147 minute version.)
••• 1:16 - Nude, making love with Lori Wagner. Long scene.
Magazines:
Penthouse (Sep 1973) . . . . Pet

De Medeiros, Maria
Films:
La Lectrice (1989; French) . . . . Silent Nurse
a.k.a. The Reader
Henry & June (1990) . . . . Anais Nin
• 0:50 - Brief right breast, popping out of dress top.
•• 0:52 - Topless lying in bed with Richard E. Grant.
•• 1:13 - Topless in bed with Fred Ward, buns getting out. Right breast standing by the window.
••• 1:31 - Topless in bed with Brigitte Lahaie.
1:37 - Nude under sheer black patterned dress.
•• 1:43 - Close up of right breast as Ward plays with her.
•• 2:01 - Left breast, then topless after taking off her top in bed with Uma Thurman.
Magazines:
Playboy (Nov 1991) . . . . Sex in Cinema 1991
•• 145: Topless, lying in bed with Richard E. Grant. From *Henry & June*.

De Mornay, Rebecca
Films:
Risky Business (1983) . . . . Lana
• 0:28 - Brief nude standing by the window with Tom Cruise.
Runaway Train (1985) . . . . Sara
The Slugger's Wife (1985) . . . . Debby Palmer
The Trip to Bountiful (1986) . . . . Thelma
And God Created Woman (1988) . . . . Robin
(Unrated version.)
•• 0:06 - Brief Left breast and buns in gymnasium with Vincent Spano. Brief right breast making love.
• 0:53 - Brief buns and topless in the shower when Spano sees her.
•• 1:02 - Brief left breast with Langella on the floor.
••• 1:12 - Topless making love with Spano in a museum.
Feds (1988) . . . . Elizabeth De Witt
Dealers (1989) . . . . Anna Schuman
0:59 - In black bra, making love with Daniel.
Backdraft (1991) . . . . Helen McCaffrey
Made for Cable Movies:
By Dawn's Early Light (1990; HBO) . . . . . Cindy Moreau
Made for TV Movies:
An Inconvenient Woman (1991) . . . . Flo March

De Moss, Darcy
Films:
Gimme an "F" (1981) . . . . One of the "Ducks"
Hardbodies (1984) . . . . Dede
••• 0:55 - Topless in the back seat of the limousine with
Rounder.
Friday the 13th, Part VI: Jason Lives (1986) . . . . . . .Nikki
Reform School Girls (1986) . . . . .Knox
Can't Buy Me Love (1987) . . . . .Patty
0:46 - In black bra and patterned panties in locker
room.
Return to Horror High (1987) . . . . Sheri Haines
• 0:21 - Very brief left breast when her sweater gets lifted up while she's on some guy's back.
Night Life (1989) . . . . .Roberta Woods
Living to Die (1990) . . . . Maggie Sams
0:11 - Taking off clothes to white bra, panties, garter
belt and stockings in hotel room with a customer.
• 0:32 - Buns, getting out of spa while Wings Hauser
watches without her knowing.
0:33 - Buns, in long shot when Hauser fantasizes
about dancing with her.
••• 0:56 - In black bra, then topless and buns making
love with Hauser.
• 1:20 - Topless in mirror taking off black top for the
bad guy.

De Prume, Cathryn
Films:
Deadtime Stories (1987) . . . . Goldi-lox
•• 1:08 - Topless taking a shower, quick cuts.
Five Corners (1988) . . . . Brita
Bloodhounds of Broadway (1989) . . . . .Showgirl
Navy SEALS (1990) . . . . Bartender

De Rossi, Barbara
Films:
Hearts and Armour (1983) . . . . Bradamante
•• 1:05 - Topless while sleeping with Ruggero.
La Cicala (The Cricket) (1983) . . . . Saveria
•• 0:39 - Nude swimming under waterfall with Clio
Goldsmith.
•• 0:43 - Topless undressing in room with Goldsmith.
• 0:57 - Brief right breast changing into dress in room.
• 1:05 - In wet white lingerie in waterfall with a guy,
then in a wet dress.
1:26 - Very brief buns in bed with Anthony Franciosa.
•• 1:28 - Topless in bathroom with Franciosa.
• 1:36 - Brief right breast making love with trucker.
Made for Cable Movies:
Mussolini and I (1985; HBO) . . . .
Blood Ties (1986; Italian; Showtime) . . . . .Luisa
• 0:58 - Brief topless on couch when bad guy rips her
clothes off.

De Vasquez, Devin
Star Search Winner 1986 – Spokesmodel.
Films:
Can't Buy Me Love (1987) .Iris
House II: The Second Story (1987) . . . . The Virgin
Guns (1990) . . . . Cash
• 1:12 - Brief side of right breast and buns undressing
for bath.
Video Tapes:
Playboy Video Magazine, Volume 8 . . . . . Playmate
Playmate Playoffs . . . . Playmate
Playboy Video Calendar 1988 (1987) . . . . . Playmate
Magazines:
Playboy (Oct 1981)
. . . . Girls of the Southeastern Conference, Part II
144: Topless. She was attending Louisiana State Uni-
versity.
Playboy (Jun 1985) . . . . Playmate
Playboy (Nov 1986) . . . . .Revvin' Devin
••• 80-87: Nude.

Dean, Felicity
Films:
Crossed Swords (1978) . . . . .Lady Jane
Success is the Best Revenge (1984; British) . . . .
Steaming (1985; British) . . . . Dawn
•• 1:12 - Topless painting on herself.
The Whistle Blower (1987; British)
. . . . .Cynthia Goodburn

Deane, Lezlie
Films:
976-EVIL (1988) . . . . Suzie
• 0:34 - Brief right breast in open leather jacket, making love on top of Spike. Brief topless several times
getting off him.
•• 0:37 - Brief topless opening jacket after putting on
underwear.
Girlfriend from Hell (1989) . . . . .Diane

Deats, Danyi
Films:
The Allnighter (1987) . . . . Junkie
River's Edge (1987) . . . . .Jamie
• 0:03 - Topless, dead lying next to river with her killer.
(All the shots of her topless in this film aren't exciting
unless you like looking at dead bodies).
• 0:15 - Close up topless, then full frontal nudity when
Crispin Glover pokes her with a stick.
0:16 - Full frontal nudity when the three boys leave.
0:22 - Full frontal nudity when all the kids come to
see her body. (She's starting to look very discolored).
0:24 - Right breast when everybody leaves.
0:30 - Right breast when they come to dump her
body in the river.

DeBell, Kristine
Adult films:
Alice in Wonderland (1977) . . . . Alice
Films:
Meatballs (1979; Canadian) . . . . .A.L.
The Big Brawl (1980) .Nancy
T.A.G.: The Assassination Game (1982) . . . . .Nancy
Club Life (1987) . . . . Fern
Magazines:
Playboy (Nov 1976) . . . . Sex in Cinema 1976
• 152: Left breast.

Delaney, Kim
Films:
That Was Then... This Is Now (1985). . . . .Cathy Carlson
Campus Man (1987). . . . . Dayna Thomas
Hunter's Blood (1987). . . . . Melanie
The Drifter (1988) . . . . .Julia Robbins
• 0:11 - Brief topless making love with Miles O'Keeffe on motel floor.
•• 0:21 - Topless in bed talking with Timothy Bottoms.
Made for TV Movies:
Cracked Up (1987) . . . . Jackie
Something Is Out There (1988). . . . . Mandy
TV:
All My Children . . . . Jenny Gardner
Tour of Duty (1988-89). . . . . Alex Devilin

Delon, Nathalie
Films:
When Eight Bells Toll (1971; British) . . . . Charlotte
Bluebeard (1972) . . . . Erika
• 1:03 - Topless in bed, showing Richard Burton her breasts.
• 1:09 - Brief right breast lying on the floor with Sybil Danning just before Richard Burton kills both of them.
The Godson (1972; Italian/French) . . . . . . Jan Lagrange
The Romantic Englishwoman (1975; British/French)
. . . . Miranda

Delora, Jennifer
Films:
Robot Holocaust (1986) . . . . Nyla
Sexpot (1986). . . . . .Barbara
••• 0:28 - In bra, then topless with her two sisters when their bras pop off. (She's in the middle.)
•• 0:36 - Topless on bed with Gorilla.
• 1:32 - Topless during outtakes of 0:28 scene.
Deranged (1987) . . . . .Maryann
Young Nurses in Love (1987) . . . . Bunny
New York's Finest (1988). . . . . .Loretta Michaels
• 0:02 - Brief topless pretending to be a black hooker.
• 0:04 - Brief topless with a bunch of hookers.
• 0:36 - Topless with her two friends doing push ups on the floor.

Sensations (1988) . . . . Della Randall
• 0:11 - Brief topless talking to Jenny to wake her up.
• 0:13 - Brief topless a couple of times in open robe.
•• 0:38 - Topless making love with a guy on bed.
Bedroom Eyes II (1989) . . . . Gwendolyn
•• 0:04 - Undressing in hotel room with Vinnie. Topless, then making love.
Cleo/Leo (1989). . . . . Bernice
Frankenhooker (1990) . . . . .Angel
• 0:36 - Brief topless during introduction to Jeffrey.
••• 0:41 - Topless dancing in room with the room with the other hookers. (Nice tattoos!)
Bad Girls Dormitory (1991) . . . . Lisa
Deadly Manor (1991). . . . . .Amanda
Fright House (1991). . . . . Dr. Victoria Sedgewick
Phantasy (1991). . . . . Fantasy
Suburban Commando (1991) . . . . Hooker

Dempsey, Sandra
Films:
Video Vixens (1973) .Actress
•• 0:05 - Full frontal nudity, lying down getting make up put on.
The Swinging Cheerleaders (1974) . . . 1st Girl at Tryout

Deneuve, Catherine
Films:
The Umbrellas of Cherbourg (1964)
. . . . .Genevieve Emery
Repulsion (1965; B&W) . . . . Carol
The April Fool's (1969) . . . . .Catherine Gunther
La Grande Bourgeoise (1974; Italian) . . . . . . Linda Murri
Hustle (1975). Nicole Britton
Lovers Like Us (1975) . . . . Nelly
a.k.a. The Savage
• 1:06 - Brief left upper half of left breast in bed with Yves Montand. Dark.
••• 1:09 - Topless sitting up in bed.
The Last Metro (1980) . . . . Marion
Je Vous Aime (1981). Alice
a.k.a. I Love You All
A Choice of Arms (1983; French) . . . . Nicole
The Hunger (1983) .Miriam
• 0:08 - Brief topless taking a shower with David Bowie. Probably a body double, you don't see her face.
Love Song (1985) . . . . Margaux
Scene of the Crime (1987; French). Lili
Magazines:
Playboy (Sep 1963) . . . . Europe's New Sex Sirens
Playboy (Oct 1965) . . . . France's Deneuve Wave
Playboy (Jan 1989). . . . . .Women of the Sixties
• 159: Topless sitting by the window.

Denier, Lydie

Films:
The Nightstalker (1987) . . . . First Victim
••• 0:03 - Topless making love with big guy.
Bulletproof (1988) . . . . Tracy
•• 0:14 - Topless in Gary Busey's bathtub.
0:20 - Brief buns, putting on shirt after getting out of bed. Very, very brief side view of left breast.
Paramedics (1988) . . . . Liette
Red Blooded American Girl (1988) . Rebecca Murrin
••• 0:00 - Topless in bed wearing panties, garter belt and stockings. Buns, rolling over. Long scene.
Blood Relations (1989) . . . . Marie
•• 0:07 - Left breast making love with Thomas on stairway.
• 0:44 - Brief left breast in bed with Thomas' father. Very brief cuts of her topless in B&W.
0:47 - Getting out of swimming pool in a one piece swimsuit.
••• 0:54 - Full frontal nudity undressing for the Grandfather.
Satan's Princess (1989) . . . . Nicole St. James
• 0:27 - Full frontal nudity, getting out of pool.
••• 0:28 - Full frontal nudity, next to bed and in bed with Karen.
••• 0:45 - Topless and buns, making love in bed with Robert Forster.
TV:
Tarzan (1991-) . . . . Jane

Derek, Bo

Real name is Cathleen Collins.
Wife of director John Derek.
Films:
Fantasies (1974) . . . . Anastasia
a.k.a. Once Upon a Love
• 0:03 - Left breast, in bathtub.
•• 0:15 - Topless taking off top, then right breast, in bathtub.
• 0:43 - Topless getting her dress top pulled down.
• 0:59 - Brief topless in the water. Very brief full frontal nudity walking back into the house.
• 1:00 - Buns and left breast several times outside the window.
• 1:17 - Upper left breast, in bathtub again.
Orca, The Killer Whale (1977) . . . . Annie
10 (1979) . . . . Jennifer Hanley
1:18 - In yellow swimsuit running in slow motion towards Dudley Moore in his daydream.
• 1:27 - Brief buns and topless taking off towel and putting on robe when Moore visits her. Long shot, hard to see.
• 1:34 - Brief topless taking off dress trying to seduce Moore. Dark, hard to see.
• 1:35 - Topless, lying in bed. Dark, hard to see.
•• 1:39 - Topless, going to fix the skipping record. Long shot, hard to see.

A **Change of Seasons** (1980) . . . . . Lindsey Routledge
•• 0:00 - Topless in hot tub during the opening credits.
• 0:25 - Side view of left breast in the shower talking to Anthony Hopkins.
Tarzan, The Ape Man (1981) . . . . Jane
••• 0:43 - Nude taking a bath in the ocean, then in a wet white dress.
• 1:35 - Brief topless painted all white.
• 1:45 - Topless washing all the white paint off in the river with Tarzan.
•• 1:47 - Topless during the ending credits playing with Tarzan and the orangutan. (When I saw this film in a movie theater, the entire audience actually stayed to watch the credits!)
Bolero (1984) . . . . Ayre McGillvary
••• 0:19 - Topless making love with Arabian guy covered with honey, messy.
••• 0:58 - Topless making love in bed with the bullfighter.
••• 1:38 - Topless during fantasy love making session with bullfighter in fog.
Ghosts Can't Do It (1989) . . . .
••• 0:26 - In one piece swimsuit on beach, then full frontal nudity taking it off. Brief buns covered with sand on her back. Long scene.
••• 0:32 - Topless, sitting and washing herself. Very brief buns, jumping into tub.
•• 0:48 - Full frontal nudity taking a shower.
• 0:49 - Very, very brief topless and buns jumping into pool. Long shot. Full frontal nudity under water.
0:52 - Very, very brief partial topless pulling a guy into the pool
1:00 - In wet dress, dancing sexily in the rain.
•• 1:12 - Topless behind mosquito net with her boyfriend.
Video Tapes:
Playboy Video Magazine, Volume 1 . . . . herself
Magazines:
Playboy (Mar 1980) . . . . Bo
••• 146-157: Nude.
Playboy (Aug 1980) . . . . Bo Is Back
••• 108-119: Nude in Japanese bath.
Playboy (Sep 1981) . . . . Tarzan
Playboy (Dec 1984) . . . . .Sex Stars of 1984
••• 209: Topless lying in water.
Playboy (Jan 1989) . . . . .Women of the Eighties
••• 255: Full frontal nudity.
Playboy (Nov 1989) . . . . Sex in Cinema 1989
••• 133: Topless in still from *Ghosts Can't Do It*.

Dern, Laura

Daughter of actor Bruce Dern and actress Diane Ladd.
Films:
Ladies and Gentlemen, The Fabulous Stains (1982)
. . . . Jessica McNeil
(Not available on video tape.)
Mask (1985). . . . . .Diana
Smooth Talk (1985) . . . . Connie
Blue Velvet (1986) . . . . Sandy Williams

Fat Man and Little Boy (1989) . . . . . . Kathleen Robinson
Wild at Heart (1990) . . . . Lula
- ••• 0:07 - Topless putting on black halter top.
- •• 0:26 - Left breast, then topless sitting on Nicholas Cage's lap in bed.
- •• 0:35 - Topless wriggling around in bed with Cage.
- • 0:41 - Brief topless several times making love with Cage. Hard to see because it keeps going overexposed. Great moaning, though.

Rambling Rose (1991) . . . . Rose

Derval, Lamya

Films:
The Lonely Guy (1983)
. . . . One of "The Seven Deadly Sins"
Hellhole (1985) . . . . Jacuzzi Girl
- ••• 1:08 - Topless (she's on the right) sniffing glue in closet with another woman.
- ••• 1:12 - Full frontal nudity in Jacuzzi room with Mary Woronov.

Howling IV: The Original Nightmare (1988) . Elanor
- •• 0:32 - Brief left breast, then topless making love with Richard. Nice silhouette on the wall.

Desmond, Donna

Films:
Tender Loving Care (1974) . . . .
The Black Gestapo (1975) . . . . White Whore
Fugitive Girls (1975) . . . .
The Naughty Stewardesses (1978) . . . . Margie
- •• 0:12 - Topless leaning out of the shower.

Detmers, Maruschka

Films:
Devil in the Flesh (1986; French/Italian)
. . . . Giulia Dozza
- • 0:20 - Very brief side view of left breast and buns going past open door way to get a robe.
- ••• 0:27 - Nude, talking to Andrea's dad in his office.
- • 0:55 - Topless putting a robe on. Dark.
- •• 0:57 - Topless and buns in bedroom with Andrea.
- •• 1:09 - Topless in hallway with Andrea.
- 1:19 - Performing fellatio on Andrea. Dark, hard to see.
- ••• 1:22 - Full frontal nudity holding keys for Andrea to see, brief buns.
- 1:42 - Lower frontal nudity dancing in living room in red robe.

Hanna's War (1988) . . . . Hanna Senesh
Magazines:
Playboy (Nov 1986) . . . . Sex in Cinema 1986
- ••• 128: Topless in a photo from *Devil in the Flesh* with Federico Pitzalis.

Devine, Loretta

Films:
Little Nikita (1988) . . . . Verna McLaughlin
- • 1:03 - Very brief left breast in bed after Sidney Poitier jumps out of bed when River Phoenix bursts into their bedroom.

Sticky Fingers (1988) . . . . Diane

Dey, Susan

Films:
Skyjacked (1972) . . . . Elly Brewster
First Love (1977) . . . . Caroline Hedges
- ••• 0:31 - Topless making love in bed with William Katt. Long scene.
- • 0:51 - Topless taking off her top in her bedroom with Katt.

Looker (1981) . . . . Cindy
- 0:28 - In white one piece swimsuit shooting a commercial at the beach.
- • 0:36 - Buns, then brief topless in computer imaging device. Topless in computer monitor.

Echo Park (1986) . . . . Meg "May" Greer
- • 1:17 - Brief glimpse of right breast, while doing a strip tease at a party.

The Trouble with Dick (1986) . . . . Diane
Made for TV Movies:
The Gift of Life (1982) . . . . Jolee Sutton
TV:
The Partridge Family (1970-74) . . . . . . Laurie Partridge
Loves Me, Loves Me Not (1977) . . . . Jane
Emerald Point N.A.S. (1983-84) . . . Celia Mallory Warren
L.A. Law (1986-91) . . . . Dep. D.A. Grace Van Owen
Magazines:
Playboy (Dec 1977) . . . . Sex Stars of 1977
- • 213: Left breast under sheer white gown in a photo from *First Love*.

Di'Lazzaro, Dalila

Films:
Andy Warhol's Frankenstein
(1974; Italian/German/French) . . . . The Girl
- •• 0:09 - Topless lying on platform in the lab.
- • 0:37 - Close up of left breast while the Count cuts her stitches. (Pretty bloody.)
- 0:43 - Topless, covered with blood, strapped to table
- • 0:49 - Topless on table, all wired up.
- • 1:03 - Right breast lying on table. Long shot.
- • 1:05 - More right breast, long shot.
- •• 1:06 - More topless on table, then standing in the lab.
- •• 1:20 - Brief right breast when Otto pulls her top down.
- •• 1:23 - Topless on table again, then walking around. (Scar on chest.) Lower frontal nudity when Otto pulls her bandage down, then more gross topless when he removes her guts.

The Last Romantic Lover (1978) . . . .
Creepers (1985; Italian) . . . .

Miss Right (1987) . . . .
Magazines:
Playboy (Jan 1990) . . . .
••• 104: Polaroid collage taken by Andy Worhol.

Dickinson, Angie

Films:
Rio Bravo (1959) . . . . Feathers
Ocean's Eleven (1960) . . . . Beatrice Ocean
Cast a Giant Shadow (1966) . . . . .Emma Marcus
The Chase (1966) . . . . Ruby Calder
Point Blank (1967) . . . . .Chris
　　0:46 - In white slip when John Vernon opens her
　　dress.
　　• 0:51 - Topless in background putting dress on. Kind
　　of a long shot.
Pretty Maids All in a Row (1971) . . . . Miss Smith
Buns.
Big Bad Mama (1974) . . . . Wilma McClatchie
　　0:38 - Buns, making love in bed with Tom Skerritt.
　••• 0:48 - Topless in bed with William Shatner.
　••• 1:18 - Topless and brief full frontal nudity putting a
　　shawl and then a dress on.
Dressed to Kill (1980) . . . . Kate Miller
　　• 0:01 - Brief side view behind shower door. Long shot,
　　hard to see.
　　0:02 - Frontal nude scene in shower is a body double,
　　Victoria Lynn Johnson.
　　0:24 - Brief buns getting out of bed after coming
　　home from museum with a stranger.
Charlie Chan & the Curse of the Dragon Queen (1981)
. . . . Dragon Queen
Death Hunt (1981) . . . . .Vanessa
Big Bad Mama II (1987) . . . . Wilma McClatchie
　•• 0:52 - Topless (probably a body double) in bed with
　　Robert Culp. You don't see her face with the body.
Miniseries:
Hollywood Wives (1988) . . . . Sadie La Salle
Made for TV Movies:
Once Upon a Texas Train (1988) . . . . .Maggie
TV:
Police Woman (1974-78)
. . . . Sgt. Suzanne "Pepper" Anderson
Pearl (1978) . . . . .Midge
Cassie and Company (1982) . . . . Cassie Holland

Dickinson, Janice

Model.
Films:
Exposed (1983) . . . . .Model
Magazines:
Playboy (Mar 1988) . . . . Going Wild with a Model
••• 70-77: Full frontal nudity.

Dietrich, Cindi

Films:
The Man Who Loved Women (1983) . . . . Darla
Out of Control (1984) .Robin
　• 0:29 - Topless taking off her red top. Long shot.
St. Elmo's Fire (1985) . . . . Flirt

Digard, Uschi

a.k.a Uschi Digart or Ursula Digard.
Films:
The Beauties and the Beast . . . . Mary
Nude by lake.
Cherry, Harry & Raquel (1969) . . . . .Soul
The Scavengers (1969) . . . .
Supervixens (1973) . . . . SuperSoul
Russ Meyer film.
Truck Stop Women (1974) . . . . . . Truck Stop Woman
　•• 0:18 - Topless getting arrested in the parking lot by
　　the police officer, then buns and topless getting
　　frisked in a room.
Fantasm (1976; Australian) . . . .
Kentucky Fried Movie (1977) . . . .Woman in Shower
　•• 0:09 - Topless getting breasts massaged in the show-
　　er, then squished breasts against the shower door.
Superchick (1978) . . . . .Mayday
　••• 0:42 - Buns and topless getting whipped acting dur-
　　ing the making of a film, then talking to three peo-
　　ple.
Beneath the Valley of the Ultravixens (1979)
. . . . SuperSoul
The Best of Sex and Violence (1981) . . . .
Truck Stop Woman
　• 0:47 - Topless getting chased by policeman in park-
　　ing lot in scene from *Truck Stop Women*.
Famous T & A (1982) . . . . Truck Stop Woman
(No longer available for purchase, check your video
store for rental.)
　•• 0:44 - Topless scenes from *Harry, Cherry & Raquel* and
　　Truck Stop Women.

Dillon, Melinda

Films:
Bound For Glory (1976) . . . . .Mary Guthrie
Close Encounters of the Third Kind (1977)
. . . . .Jillian Guiler
Slap Shot (1977) . . . . .Suzanne
　••• 0:30 - Right breast, lying in bed with Paul Newman,
　　then topless sitting up and talking. Nice, long scene.
F.I.S.T. (1978) . . . . Anna Zerinkas
Absence of Malice (1981) . . . . Teresa
A Christmas Story (1983) . . . . Mrs. Parker
Songwriter (1984) . . . . Honey Carder
Harry and the Hendersons (1987) . . . Nancy Henderson
Spontaneous Combustion (1989) . . . . Nina
Staying Together (1989) . . . . Eileen McDermott

Dockery, Erika

a.k.a. Ericka Dockray.
Films:
Basic Training (1984). . . . . .Salesgirl 2
• 0:00 - Brief topless standing behind the desk.
Hardbodies (1984) . . . . .Hardbody in Car

Dollarhide, April Dawn

Films:
Party Favors (1987). . . . .
(Shot on video tape.)
Caged Fury (1989) . . . . Rhonda Wallace
0:33 - In white bra in open blouse on couch with Jack
Carter.
•• 0:41 - Topless undressing to enter prison with other
topless women.

Dombasle, Arielle

Films:
Tess (1979; French/British) . . . . .Mercy Chant
The Story of "O" Continues (1981; French)
. . . . Nathalie
a.k.a. *Les Fruits de la Passion*
• 0:17 - Brief left breast, lying on her stomach in bed
with Klaus Kinski.
••• 0:40 - Full frontal nudity on bed, making love in front
of O.
• 1:00 - Very, very brief left breast, while grabbing her
blouse out of Kinski's hands.
Le Beau Mariage (1982; French) . . . . .Clarisse
Pauline at the Beach (1983; French). . . . . . . Marion
• 0:24 - Brief topless lying in bed with a guy when her
cousin looks in the window.
•• 0:43 - Brief topless in house kissing Henri, while he
takes her white dress off.
•• 0:59 - Topless walking down the stairs in a white bikini bottom while putting a white blouse on.
The Boss' Wife (1986) . . . . Mrs. Louise Roalvang
• 1:01 - Brief topless getting a massage by the swimming pool.
••• 1:07 - Topless trying to seduce Daniel Stern.
•• 1:14 - Brief topless in Stern's shower.
Twisted Obsession (1990) . . . . Marion Derain
Miniseries:
Lace II (1985) . . . . .Maxine
Magazines:
Playboy (Dec 1983). . . . . Sex Stars of 1983
•• 209: Topless.

Donnelly, Patrice

Films:
Personal Best (1982) . . . . Tory Skinner
•• 0:16 - Full frontal nudity after making love with Mariel Hemingway.
•• 0:30 - Full frontal nudity in steam room.
1:06 - Topless in shower.
American Anthem (1987) . . . . Danielle

Donohoe, Amanda

Films:
Castaway (1986) . . . . .Lucy Irvine
(Topless a lot, only the best are listed.)
•• 0:32 - Nude on beach after helicopter leaves.
•• 0:48 - Full frontal nudity lying on her back on the
rocks at the beach.
••• 0:51 - Topless on rock when Reed takes a blue sheet
off her, then catching a shark.
••• 0:54 - Nude yelling at Reed at the campsite, then
walking around looking for him.
••• 1:01 - Topless getting seafood out of a tide pool.
••• 1:03 - Topless lying down at night talking with Reed
in the moonlight.
••• 1:18 - Topless taking off bathing suit top after the visitors leave, then arguing with Reed.
••• 1:22 - Topless talking to Reed.
Foreign Body (1986; British) . . . . .Susan
0:37 - Undressing in her bedroom down to lingerie.
Very brief side view of right breast, then brief left
breast putting blouse on.
•• 0:40 - Topless opening her blouse for Ram.
The Lair of the White Worm (1988; British)
. . . . Lady Sylvia Marsh
(Wears short black hair in this film.)
• 0:52 - Nude, opening a tanning table and turning
over.
• 0:57 - Brief left breast licking the blood off a phallic-
looking thing.
• 1:19 - Brief topless jumping out to attack Angus,
then walking around her underground lair (her
body is painted for the rest of the film).
• 1:22 - Topless walking up steps with a large phallic
thing strapped to her body.
The Rainbow (1989) . . . . Winifred Inger
••• 0:21 - Nude with Sammi Davis undressing, running
outside in the rain, jumping into the water, then
talking by the fireplace.
••• 0:43 - Full frontal nudity taking off nightgown and
getting into bed with Davis, then right breast.
••• 1:44 - Nude running outside with Davis.
TV:
L.A. Law (1991-) . . . . C. J. Lamb
Magazines:
Playboy (Nov 1987) . . . . Sex in Cinema 1987
•• 144-145: Full frontal nudity from *Castaway*.

Doody, Alison

Films:
A Prayer for the Dying (1987) . . . . .Siobhan
Taffin (1988; U.S./British) . . . . .Charlotte
• 0:14 - Very, very brief side view of right breast when
Pierce Brosnan rips her blouse open. Long shot, hard
to see.
Indiana Jones and the Last Crusade (1989)
. . . . Dr. Elsa Schneider

Doss, Terri Lynn

Films:
Lethal Weapon (1987). . . . . Girl in Shower #2
Die Hard (1988) . . . . Girl at Airport
Video Tapes:
Playboy Video Calendar 1989 (1988) . . . . . . .March
••• 0:09 - Nude.
Glamour Through Your Lens—Outdoor Techniques
(1989). . . . . herself
 0:07 - Buns in blue swimsuit bottom in wet yellow
 top in the pool.
 0:47 - In black bra, panties, garter belt and stockings
 standing outside. Most of her buns.
Playboy's Sexy Lingerie II (1990) . . . .
Magazines:
Playboy (Jul 1988). Playmate
102:

Douglass, Robyn

Films:
Breaking Away (1979). . . . . Katherine
Partners (1982) . . . . .Jill
 •• 1:00 - Brief topless taking off her top and getting into
 bed with Ryan O'Neil.
The Lonely Guy (1983). . . . . Danielle
 • 0:05 - Upper half of right breast in sheer nightgown
 in bed with Raoul while talking to Steve Martin.
 Great nightgown!
 0:33 - In sheer beige negligee lying on couch talking
 to Martin on the phone.
 • 1:03 - Very, very brief peek at left nipple when she
 flashes it for Martin so he'll let her into his party.
Romantic Comedy (1983). . . . . Kate
Made for TV Movies:
Her Life as a Man (1984). . . . .
TV:
Houston Knights . . . . Lt. Joanne Beaumont
Battlestar Galactica (1980) . . . . .Jamie Hamilton
Magazines:
Playboy (Dec 1974). . . . . cover girl
 • Half of left breast.
Playboy (Jul 1975). . . . . A Long Look At Legs
Playboy (Jan 1980) . . . . World of Playboy
 • 11: Right breast wearing corset and white stockings.
 Small photo.

Down, Lesley-Anne

Films:
From Beyond the Grave (1973). . . . . . Rosemary Seaton
The Pink Panther Strikes Again (1976). . . . . .Olga
The Betsy (1978) . . . . Lady Bobby Ayres
 • 0:38 - Brief left breast with Tommy Lee Jones.
 • 0:57 - Very brief left breast in bed with Jones.
The Great Train Robbery (1979) . . . . Miriam
Hanover Street (1979). . . . . Margaret Sallinger
 • 0:22 - In bra and slip, then brief topless in bedroom
 with Harrison Ford.
Rough Cut (1980; British) . . . . Gillian Bramley

Sphinx (1981) . . . . Erica Baron
Nomads (1986) . . . . Flax
Scenes from the Goldmine (1987) . . . . .Herself
Miniseries:
North and South (1985) . . . . Madeline Fabray
North and South, Book II (1986) . . . . . Madeline Fabray
TV:
Upstairs, Downstairs . . . .
Magazines:
Playboy (Dec 1979) . . . . .Sex Stars of 1979
 •• 254: Topless.
Playboy (May 1985). . . . . Grapevine
217: B&W.

Drake, Gabrielle

Films:
The Man Outside (1968; British) . . . . B.E.A. Girl
There's a Girl in My Soup (1970)
. . . . Julia Halford-Smythe
 • 0:09 - In beige bra with Peter Sellers, brief left breast
 in bed with him. Might be a body double.
Connecting Rooms (1971; British) . . . . .Jean
TV:
UFO (1970) . . . . Lieutenant Gay Ellis

Drake, Marciee

Films:
Jackson County Jail (1976)
. . . . Candy (David's Girlfriend)
 • 0:04 - Brief topless wrapping towel around herself, In
 front of Howard Hessman. Long shot.
The Toolbox Murders (1978). . . . . Debbie
 •• 0:09 - In wet blouse, then topless taking it off and
 putting a dry one on.

Drake, Michele

Films:
American Gigolo (1980). . . . . 1st Girl on Balcony
 • 0:03 - Topless on the balcony while Richard Gere and
 Lauren Hutton talk.
History of the World, Part I (1981) . . . .
Magazines:
Playboy (May 1979). . . . . Playmate

Drescher, Fran

Films:
Doctor Detroit (1983) . . . . Karen Blittstein
The Rosebud Beach Hotel (1985). . . . . .Linda
The Big Picture (1989) . . . . .Polo Habel
Cadillac Man (1990) . . . . Joy Munchack
 • 0:07 - Very brief right breast several times while in
 bed with Robin Williams.
Made for Cable TV:
Dream On: The Second Greatest Story Ever Told
 (1991; HBO). . . . . Kathleen
TV:
Princesses (1991-) . . . .

Drew, Linzi
Films:
An American Werewolf in London (1981)
. . . . Brenda Bristols
- 1:26 - Side view of left breast in porno movie while David Naughton talks to his friend, Jack.
- 1:27 - Brief topless in movie talking on the phone.

Emmanuelle in Soho (1981) . . . . Showgirl
Topless on stage.

Salome's Last Dance (1987) . . . . 1st Slave
(Appears with 2 other slaves–can't tell who is who.)
- •• 0:08 - Topless in black costume around a cage.
- •• 0:52 - Topless during dance number.

Aria (1988; U.S./British) . . . . Girl
- 1:09 - Topless on operating table after car accident. Hair is all covered with bandages.
- •• 1:10 - Topless getting shocked to start her heart.

The Lair of the White Worm (1988; British)
. . . . Maid/Nun

Driggs, Deborah
Films:
Total Exposure (1991) . . . . Kathy
- ••• 0:08 - Topless dancing in front of Jeff Conaway, then making love in bed with him. Long scene.
- 0:22 - Brief side view topless in B&W photos that Conaway looks at.
- 0:24 - Brief buns in black G-string and side of right breast changing clothes in locker room.
- •• 0:25 - Topless and buns, trying to beat up Season Hubley.

Video Tapes:
Playboy Video Calendar 1991 (1990) . . . . . October
- ••• 0:40 - Nude.

Playboy Video Centerfold: Deborah Driggs & Karen Foster (1990) . . . . Playmate
- ••• 0:02 - Doing a strip tease, other dancing, some in bed. Nude.

Playboy's Sexy Lingerie II (1990) . . . .
Magazines:
Playboy (Mar 1990). . . . . Playmate

Duffek, Patty
Films:
Hard Ticket to Hawaii (1987) . . . . Patticakes
- •• 0:48 - Topless talking to Michelle after swimming.

Picasso Trigger (1989). . . . . Patticakes
- •• 1:04 - Topless taking a Jacuzzi bath.

Savage Beach (1989) . . . . Patticakes
- 0:06 - Topless in spa with Lisa London, Dona Speir and Hope Marie Carlton.
- •• 0:50 - Topless changing clothes.

Video Tapes:
Playmate Playoffs . . . . Playmate
Magazines:
Playboy (May 1984) . . . . Playmate
102-115:

Duffy, Julia
Films:
Battle Beyond the Stars (1980). . . . . Mol
Cutter's Way (1981) . . . . Young Girl
a.k.a. Cutter and Bone
Night Warning (1982) . . . . Julie Linden
0:44 - Upper half of left breast.
- 0:46 - Brief topless when her boyfriend pulls the sheets down.
- •• 0:47 - Brief topless when Susan Tyrrell opens the bedroom door.

Wacko (1983) . . . . Mary Graves
Miniseries:
Blue and the Gray (1982). . . . . Mary Hale
Made for TV Movies:
Menu for Murder (1990) . . . . Susan Henshaw
TV:
Newhart (1983-90) . . . . Stephanie Vanderkellen
Wizards and Warriors (1983) . . . . Princess Ariel
Baby Talk (1991) . . . . Maggie

Duke, Patty
a.k.a. Patty Duke Astin.
Films:
4D Man (1959) . . . . Marjorie Sullivan
The Miracle Worker (1962; B&W). . . . . Helen Keller
Valley of the Dolls (1967) . . . . Neely O'Hara
By Design (1982; Canadian). . . . . Helen
- •• 0:49 - Left breast, lying in bed.
- •• 1:05 - Brief left breast sitting on bed.
- 1:06 - Brief left breast, then brief right breast lying in bed with the photographer.

Something Special (1987) . . . . Mrs. Doris Niceman
Miniseries:
Captains and the Kings (1976)
. . . . Bernadette Hennessey Armagh
Made for TV Movies:
The Miracle Worker (1979). . . . . Anne Sullivan
Everybody's Baby: The Rescue of Jessica McClure (1989)
Absolute Strangers (1991) . . . . Judge Ray
TV:
The Patty Duke Show (1963-66) . . . Patty & Cathy Lane
It Takes Two (1982-83). . . . . Molly Quinn
Hail to the Chief (1985) . . . . . . President Julia Mansfield

Dumas, Sandrine
a.k.a. Sandra Dumas.
Films:
Twice a Woman (1979). . . . . Sylvia
- 0:06 - Topless, kneeling on the bed, then more brief topless in bed with Bibi Andersson.
- ••• 0:47 - Brief right breast, then topless in bed with Andersson. Long scene.
- 1:15 - Left breast, lying in bed with Anthony Perkins. Long shot.
- ••• 1:23 - Topless with Andersson.

Aria (1988; U.S./British) . . . .
Valmont (1989) . . . . Martine

Dunaway, Faye

Films:
Bonnie and Clyde (1967) . . . . Bonnie Parker
The Thomas Crown Affair (1968) . . . . . . Vicky Anderson
The Arrangement (1969) . . . . Gwen
    0:25 - Brief buns in various scenes at the beach with
    Kirk Douglas.
Little Big Man (1970) . . . . .Mrs. Pendrake
The Three Musketeers (1973) . . . . Milady
Chinatown (1974) . . . . .Evelyn
    • 1:26 - Very brief right breast, in bed talking to Jack
      Nicholson.
    • 1:28 - Very brief right breast in bed talking to Nichol-
      son. Very brief flash of right breast under robe when
      she gets up to leave the bedroom.
The Towering Inferno (1974) . . . . .Susan Franklin
The Four Musketeers (1975) . . . . Milady
Three Days of the Condor (1975) . . . . Kathy Hale
Network (1976) . . . . .Diana Christensen
(Academy Award for Best Actress.)
    • 1:10 - Brief left breast twice, taking off clothes in
      room with William Holden.
Voyage of the Damned (1976) . . . . Denise Kreisler
Eyes of Laura Mars (1978) . . . . Laura Mars
The Champ (1979) . . . . Annie
The First Deadly Sin (1980) . . . . Barbara Delaney
Mommie Dearest (1981) . . . . Joan Crawford
The Wicked Lady (1983; British) . . . . . . Barbara Skelton
Ordeal by Innocence (1984) . . . . Rachel Argyle
Supergirl (1984; British) . . . . .Selena
Barfly (1987) . . . . .Wanda Wilcox
    • 0:58 - Brief upper half of breasts in bathtub talking to
      Mickey Rourke.
Midnight Crossing (1988) . . . . Helen Barton
A Handmaid's Tale (1990) . . . . Serena Joy
The Two Jakes (1990) . . . . Evelyn Mulwray
TV:
Ladies of the Night (1986) . . . . Lil Hutton

Dunlap, Dawn

Films:
Laura (1979) . . . . Laura
a.k.a. Shattered Innocence
    • 0:20 - Brief side view of left breast and buns talking
      to Maud Adams, then brief side view of right breast
      putting on robe.
    ••• 0:23 - Nude, dancing while being photographed.
    ••• 1:15 - Nude, letting Paul feel her so he can sculpt her,
      then making love with him.
    1:22 - Buns, putting on panties talking to Maud Ad-
      ams.
Forbidden World (1982) . . . . Tracy Baxter
    • 0:27 - Brief topless getting ready for bed.
    ••• 0:37 - Nude in steam bath.
    •• 0:54 - Topless in shower with June Chadwick.
Night Shift (1982) . . . . .Maxine

Heartbreaker (1983) . . . . .Kim
    • 0:49 - Topless putting on dress in bedroom.
    0:51 - Very, very brief right breast in open dress dur-
      ing rape attempt. Dark.
    •• 1:02 - Left breast, lying on bed with her boyfriend.
      Long scene.
Barbarian Queen (1985) . . . . Taramis
    • 0:00 - Topless, in the woods getting raped.

Dupree, Christine

a.k.a. Christine Dupré.
Films:
Armed and Dangerous (1986) . . . . . . Peep Show Girl
    • 0:58 - Very, very brief topless shots behind glass
      dancing in front of John Candy and Eugene Levy.
Magazines:
Penthouse (Sep 1985) .Pet

Dusenberry, Ann

Films:
Jaws II (1978) . . . . Tina Wilcox
Heart Beat (1979) . . . . Stevie
    •• 0:41 - Full frontal nudity frolicking in bathtub with
      Nick Nolte.
Cutter's Way (1981) . . . . .Valerie Duran
a.k.a. Cutter and Bone
Basic Training (1984) . . . . Melinda Griffin
    ••• 1:13 - Topless in Russian guy's bedroom.
Lies (1984; British) . . . . .Robyn Wallace
    •• 0:10 - Topless opening the shower curtain in front of
      her boyfriend.
    • 0:11 - Right breast while kissing her boyfriend.
The Men's Club (1986) . . . . Page
    •• 1:05 - Topless lying in bed after making love with Roy
      Scheider.
TV:
Little Women (1979) . . . . Amy March Laurence
The Family Tree (1983) . . . . .Molly Nichols Tanner
Life with Lucy (1986-87) . . . . Margo McGibbon

Duvall, Shelley

Films:
Brewster McCloud (1970) . . . . .Suzanne
McCabe and Mrs. Miller (1971) . . . . .Ida Coyle
Thieves Like Us (1974) . . . . Keechie
Nashville (1975) . . . . L.A. Jane
Buffalo Bill and the Indians (1976) . . . . . .Mrs. Cleveland
Annie Hall (1977) . . . . .Pam
Three Women (1977) . . . . Millie
Popeye (1980) . . . . Olive Oyl
The Shining (1980) . . . . Wendy Torrance
Time Bandits (1981; British) . . . . .Pansy
Roxanne (1987) . . . . Dixie
Magazines:
Playboy (Nov 1975) . . . . Sex in Cinema 1975
    ••• 188: Topless photo.

Dziubinska, Anulka

a.k.a. Anulka.
Films:
Vampyres (1974) . . . . Miriam
  • 0:00 - Brief full frontal nudity in bed with Fran, kissing each other before getting shot.
  • 0:43 - Topless taking a shower with Fran.
  ••• 0:58 - Topless and buns in bed with Fran, drinking Ted's blood. Brief lower frontal nudity.
Lisztomania (1975; British). . . . . Lola Montez
  •• 0:08 - Topless sitting on Roger Daltrey's lap, kissing him. Nice close up.
  • 0:21 - Topless, backstage with Daltrey after the concert.
  • 0:39 - Topless, wearing pasties, during Daltrey's nightmare/song and dance number.
Magazines:
Playboy (May 1973) . . . . Playmate

Easterbrook, Leslie

Films:
Just Tell Me What You Want (1980) . . . . . Hospital Nurse
Police Academy (1984) . . . . Callahan
Police Academy II: Their First Assignment (1985)
. . . . Callahan
Private Resort (1985) . . . . Bobbie Sue
  •• 0:14 - Very brief buns taking off swimsuit, then topless under sheer white nightgown.
Police Academy III: Back in Training (1986) . . . . Callahan
Police Academy 4: Citizens on Patrol (1987)
. . . . Callahan
  0:35 - In wet T-shirt in swimming pool pretending to be a drowning victim for the class.
Police Academy 5: Assignment Miami Beach (1988)
. . . . Callahan
Police Academy 6: City Under Siege (1989)
. . . . Callahan
Made for TV Movies:
The Taking of Flight 847: The Uli Derickson Story (1988)
. . . . Audrey
TV:
Laverne & Shirley (1980-83) . . . . Rhonda Lee

Easton, Jackie

a.k.a. Jacki Easton.
Films:
Hardbodies (1984) . . . . Girl in dressing room
  •• 0:27 - Topless taking off dress to try on swimsuit.
  •• 0:40 - Topless with other topless girls posing for photographs taken by Rounder. She's wearing a white skirt.
School Spirit (1985) . . . . Hogette

Eastwood, Jayne

Films:
My Pleasure Is My Business (1974) . . . . Isabella
  • 1:16 - Topless in bed trying to get His Excellency's attention.
  •• 1:28 - Topless sitting up in bed with blonde guy.
One Man (1979; Canadian) . . . . Alicia Brady
Night Friend (1987; Canadian) . . . . . . Rita the Bag Lady
Candy Mountain (1988; Swiss/Canadian/French)
. . . . Lucille
Cold Comfort (1988) . . . . Mrs. Brocket
Hostile Takeover (1988; Canadian) . . . . Mrs. Talmage
a.k.a. Office Party

Eccles, Aimée

Films:
Group Marriage (1972) . . . . Chris
  0:15 - Buns, getting into bed.
  • 1:15 - Brief side view of left breast and buns getting into the shower.
Ulzana's Raid (1972) . . . . McIntosh's Indian Woman
Paradise Alley (1978) . . . . Susan
The Concrete Jungle (1982) . . . . Spider
Lovelines (1984) . . . . Nisei

Eden, Simone

Video Tapes:
Playboy Video Calendar 1990 (1989) . . . . . . .August
  ••• 0:40 - Nude.
Playboy's Wet and Wild (1989) . . . .
Playmates at Play (1990) . . . . Gotta Dance
Magazines:
Playboy (Feb 1989) . . . . Playmate

Edmondson, Donna

Video Tapes:
Playboy Video Centerfold: Donna Edmondson
. . . . Playmate of the Year
Playmates of the Year—The '80's . . . . Playmate
Playboy Video Calendar 1988 (1987) . . . . . Playmate
Playboy's Wet and Wild (1989) . . . .
Playmates at Play (1990) . . . . Gotta Dance
Magazines:
Playboy (Nov 1986) . . . . Playmate

Edwards, Barbara

Films:
Malibu Express (1984) .May
  •• 0:10 - Topless taking a shower with Kimberly McArthur on the boat.
  •• 1:05 - Topless serving Cody coffee while he talks on the telephone.
Terminal Entry (1986) . . . . Lady Electric
  ••• 0:05 - Topless taking a shower and getting a towel during video game scene.

Another Chance (1989) . . . . .Diana the Temptress
••• 0:38 - Topless in trailer with Johnny.
Video Tapes:
Playboy Video Magazine, Volume 4 . . . . . Playmate
Playmates of the Year—The '80's . . . . Playmate
Playboy's Playmate Review 3 (1985). . . . . Playmate
Playboy Video Calendar 1987 (1986) . . . . Playmate
Playboy's Sexy Lingerie (1988). . . . .
Playboy's Wet and Wild (1989) . . . .
Playboy Video Centerfold: Kerri Kendall (1990)
. . . . Playmate
••• 0:37 - Nude.
Magazines:
Playboy (Sep 1983). . . . . Playmate
Playboy (Jun 1984) . . . . .Playmate of the Year
134-147:

Edwards, Ella

Films:
Sweet Sugar (1972) .Simone
• 0:58 - Topless in bed with Mojo.
Detroit 9000 (1973) . . . . Helen
Mr. Ricco (1975) . . . . Sally

Ege, Julie

Films:
On Her Majesty's Secret Sevice (1969; British)
. . . . .Scandanavian Girl
Creatures the World Forgot (1971; British)
. . . . Nala, The Girl
0:56 - Very brief topless several times (it looks like a
stunt double) fighting in cave with The Dumb Girl.
Hard to see.
• 1:32 - Very, very brief half of right breast when fight-
ing a snake that is wrapped around her face.
The Mutations (1973; British) . . . . .Hedi
a.k.a. Freakmaker
Topless in bathtub.

Eggar, Samantha

Films:
The Collector (1965). . . . . Miranda Grey
Doctor Dolittle (1967). . . . . .Emma
A Name for Evil (1973) . . . . .Joanna Blake
• 0:42 - Very brief topless turning over in bed with
Robert Culp. Dark, hard to see.
The Uncanny (1977; British) . . . . Edina
The Brood (1979) . . . . Nola Carveth
Curtains (1983; Canadian) . . . . . . Samantha Sherwood
Made for Cable Movies:
A Ghost in Monte Carlo (1990). . . . .
TV:
Anna and the King (1972). . . . . .Anna Owens

Egger, Jolanda

Video Tapes:
Playmates at Play (1990)
. . . . Bareback, Making Waves
Magazines:
Playboy (Jun 1983). Playmate

Eichhorn, Lisa

Films:
The Europeans (1979; British) . . . . Gertrude Wentworth
Yanks (1979) .Jean Moreton
• 1:48 - Brief topless in bed when Richard Gere rolls off
her.
Why Would I Lie? (1980) . . . . Kay
Cutter's Way (1981) . . . . .Maureen "Mo" Cutter
a.k.a. Cutter and Bone
• 1:07 - Brief right breast, wearing bathrobe, lying on
lounge chair while Jeff Bridges looks at her.
The Weather in the Streets (1983; British) . . . . . . .Olivia
Wild Rose (1984) . . . . June Lorich
Opposing Force (1986) . . . . .Lieutenant Casey
a.k.a. Hell Camp
• 0:17 - Wet T-shirt after going through river.
••• 0:33 - Topless getting sprayed with water and dusted
with white powder.
•• 1:03 - Topless after getting raped by Anthony Zerbe
in his office, while another officer watches.
Grim Prairie Tales (1990) . . . . Maureen
Moon 44 (1990) . . . . .Terry Morgan

Eilber, Janet

Films:
Whose Life Is It, Anyway? (1981) . . . . Patty
•• 0:30 - Nude, ballet dancing during B&W dream se-
quence.
• 1:13 - Very brief side of left breast when her back is
turned while changing clothes.
Romantic Comedy (1983) . . . . Allison
Hard to Hold (1984). . . . . Diana Lawson
TV:
Two Marriages (1983-84) . . . . Nancy Armstrong
The Best Times (1985) . . . . .Joanne Braithwaite

Ekberg, Anita

Films:
Back from Eternity (1956; B&W) . . . . Rena
Hollywood or Bust (1956) . . . . .Herself
War and Peace (1956; U.S./Italian). . . . . .Helene
La Dolce Vita (1960; Italian/B&W) . . . . .Sylvia
Boccaccio 70 (1962; Italian). . . . . Anita
Four for Texas (1963). . . . . .Elya Carlson
Woman Times Seven (1967). . . . . Claudie
Made for TV Movies:
S.H.E. (1979) . . . .
Magazines:
Playboy (Jan 1989) . . . . Women of the Fifties
•• 118: B&W photo sitting on the floor.

71

Ekland, Britt
Films:
After the Fox (1966) . . . . Gina Romantiea
The Bobo (1967). . . . . .Olimpia Segura
The Night They Raided Minsky's (1968)
. . . . Rachel Schpitendavel
Topless.
The Cannibals (1969) . . . . Antigone
Stiletto (1969). . . . . .Illeana
What the Peeper Saw (1972) . . . . Elise
    0:38 - Sort of side view of left breast in bed. Don't re-
    ally see anything.
The Wicker Man (1973; British) . . . . Willow
••• 0:58 - Topless in bed knocking on the wall, then
    more topless and buns getting up and walking
    around the bedroom. Long scene.
The Man with the Golden Gun (1974; British)
. . . . .Mary Goodnight
Endless Night (1977) . . . . Greta
• 1:21 - Brief topless several times with Michael.
Slavers (1977) . . . . .Anna
Topless.
Sex on the Run (1979; German/French/Italian)
. . . . .Countess Trivulsi
a.k.a. Some Like It Cool
a.k.a. Casanova and Co.
• 0:44 - Left breast while making love in bed with Tony
    Curtis (don't see her face).
The Monster Club (1981) . . . . .Lintom's Mother
Erotic Images (1983) . . . . .Julie Todd
• 0:16 - Brief side view of left breast in bed with Glenn.
••• 0:29 - In bra, then topless in bed with Glenn.
    0:33 - In bra, in open robe looking at herself in the
    mirror.
    1:27 - In black bra, talking to Sonny.
Love Scenes (1984). . . . . Annie
Moon in Scorpio (1987) . . . . Linda
Beverly Hills Vamp (1989) . . . . Madam Cassandra
Scandal (1989) . . . . Mariella Novotny
(Unrated version.)
•• 0:31 - Topless lying on table with John Hurt.
• 0:51 - Right breast talking with Hurt and Christine.
Magazines:
Playboy (May 1989) .Scandal
• 87-88: Left and right breasts.

Eleniak, Erika
Films:
E.T. The Extraterrestrial (1982) . . . . .Pretty Girl
The Blob (1988) . . . . Vicki De Soto
Made for TV Movies:
Baywatch (1989). . . . . Shauni
TV:
Charles in Charge (1988) . . . . Stephanie
Baywatch (1989-90) . . . . Shauni McLain
Baywatch (1991-) . . . . Shauni McLain

Video Tapes:
Playboy Video Centerfold: Fawna MacLaren
(1988) . . . . .Playmate
••• 0:07 - In studio, nude.
Playboy Video Calendar 1991 (1990). . . . . . . .May
••• 0:18 - Nude.
Magazines:
Playboy (Jul 1989) . . . . Playmate
98:
Playboy (Dec 1989) . . . . Holy Sex Stars of 1989!
••• 181: Topless, reclining.
Playboy (Aug 1990) . . . . Beauty on the Beach
••• 68-75: Nude.
Playboy (Dec 1990) . . . . .Sex Stars of 1990
••• 173: Full frontal nudity, leaning back against wall.

Elian, Yona
Films:
The Jerusalem File (1972; U.S./Israel) . . . . Raschel
The Last Winter (1983) . . . . .Maya
•• 0:48 - Topless taking off her robe to get into pool.
    0:49 - Buns, lying on marble slab with Kathleen
    Quinlan.

Elise, Esther
See: Alise, Esther.

Elvira
Real name is Cassandra Peterson.
Films:
The Working Girls (1973) . . . . .Katya
    0:18 - Dancing in a G-string on stage in a club.
••• 0:20 - Topless, dancing on stage.
The Best of Sex and Violence (1981) . . . . .Katya
•• 0:40 - Brief topless dancing on stage in scene from
    Working Girls.
Famous T & A (1982) . . . . .Katya
(No longer available for purchase, check your video
store for rental.)
••• 0:28 - Topless scene from *Working Girls.*
Stroker Ace (1983) . . . . Woman with Lugs
Pee Wee's Big Adventure (1985). . . . . Biker Mama
Echo Park (1986) . . . . Sheri
Allan Quartermain and the Lost City of Gold (1987)
. . . . .Sorais
Elvira, Mistress of the Dark (1988) . . . . .Elvira
    0:31 - Getting undressed into black lingerie in her
    bedroom while being watched from outside the
    window.
    1:31 - *Very* skillfully twirling two tassels on the tips of
    her bra.

Errickson, Krista

Films:
Little Darlings (1980) . . . . Cinder
The First Time (1981) . . . . Dana
a.k.a. Doin' It
Mortal Passions (1989) . . . . Emily
•• 0:08 - Brief topless in bed with Darcy, while tied to the bed. Topless getting untied and rolling over.
• 0:11 - Very brief right breast, rolling back on top of Darcy.
••• 0:40 - Topless after dropping her sheet for Burke, then making love with him.
••• 0:46 - Topless getting into bed with her husband.
TV:
Hello, Larry (1979-80) . . . . .Diane Adler

Estores, Lourdes

Video Tapes:
Playmate Playoffs . . . . Playmate
Playboy's Playmate Review (1982) . . . . . . Playmate
••• 0:56 - At the beach, under water, outside near river. Nude.
Magazines:
Playboy (Jun 1982) . . . . Playmate

Evans, Linda

Films:
Beach Blanket Bingo (1965) . . . . .Sugar Kane
Those Calloways (1965) . . . . .Bridie Mellot
The Klansman (1974) . . . . Nancy Poteet
The Avalanche Express (1979). . . . . Elsa Lang
Tom Horn (1980) . . . . .Glendoline Kimmel
Miniseries:
North and South, Book II (1986). . . . . Rose Sinclair
Made for TV Movies:
The Last Frontier (1986) . . . . Kate
TV:
Big Valley (1965-69) . . . . Audra Barkley
Hunter (1977). . . . . Marty Shaw
Dynasty (1981-89) . . . . Krystle Jennings Carrington
Magazines:
Playboy (Jul 1971). . . . . Blooming Beauty
Playboy (Dec 1981). . . . . Sex Stars of 1981
••• 241: Topless.
Playboy (Jan 1989) . . . . .Women of the Seventies
••• 216: Topless sitting in water.

Evenson, Kim

Films:
The Big Bet (1985). . . . . Beth
•• 0:36 - Right breast, sitting on couch with Chris.
•• 0:45 - Brief topless, twice, taking off swimsuit top.
•• 0:54 - Brief topless three times in elevator when Chris pulls her sweater up.
•• 1:06 - Nude when Chris fantasizes about her being in the video tape that he's watching. Long shot.

••• 1:19 - In white bra and panties, then nude while undressing for Chris.
Porky's Revenge (1985; Canadian) . . . . .Inga
•• 0:02 - Right breast, while opening her graduation gown during Pee Wee's dream.
•• 1:27 - Topless showing Pee Wee that she doesn't have any clothes under her graduation gown.
Kidnapped (1986) . . . . Debbie
• 0:25 - Right breast in bed talking on the phone. Long shot, hard to see.
0:30 - In blue nightgown in room.
••• 1:28 - Topless getting her arm prepared for a drug injection. Long scene.
••• 1:30 - Topless acting in a movie. Long shot, then close up. Wearing a G-string.
Kandyland (1987) . . . . Joni
0:26 - In purple bra and white panties practicing dancing on stage.
••• 0:31 - Topless doing first dance routine.
•• 0:45 - Brief topless during another routine with bubbles floating around.
Video Tapes:
Playmate Playoffs . . . . Playmate
Playboy's Wet and Wild (1989). . . . .
Playboy Video Centerfold: Kerri Kendall (1990)
. . . . Playmate
••• 0:35 - Nude.
Playmates at Play (1990) . . . . Flights of Fancy
Magazines:
Playboy (Sep 1984) . . . . Playmate

Fabian, Ava

Films:
Dragnet (1987) . . . . Baitmate
Terminal Exposure (1988) . . . . Bruce's Girl
To Die For (1988). . . . . .Franny
Limit Up (1989) . . . . .Sasha
Ski School (1990). Victoria
••• 0:53 - In white bra and panties, then topless making love with Johnny.
Video Tapes:
Playboy Video Magazine, Volume 12 . . . . Playmate
Playmate Playoffs . . . . Playmate
Playboy's Sexy Lingerie (1988) . . . .
Playboy Video Calendar 1990 (1989). . . . . July
••• 0:34 - Nude.
Playboy's Wet and Wild (1989). . . . .
Playboy's Sexy Lingerie II (1990) . . . .
Playmates at Play (1990) . . . . Gotta Dance
Magazines:
Playboy (Aug 1986) . . . . Playmate
86:

Fairchild, June

Films:
Pretty Maids All in a Row (1971)
. . . . Sonya "Sonny" Swingle
Drive, He Said (1972) . . . . Sylvie
- 0:16 - Buns and brief topless walking around in the dark while Gabriel shines a flashlight on her.
- 1:01 - Topless, then brief nude getting dressed while Gabriel goes crazy and starts trashing a house.
Top of the Heap (1972) . . . . Balloon Thrower
Detroit 9000 (1973) . . . . .Barbara
Your Three Minutes Are Up (1973) . . . . Sandi
Thunderbolt and Lightfoot (1974) . . . . Gloria
- 0:20 - Very brief right breast getting dressed in the bathroom after making love with Clint Eastwood.
The Student Body (1975) . . . . Mitzi Mashall
- 0:15 - Brief topless and buns, running and jumping into the pool during party. Brief long shot topless, while in the pool.
- • 0:21 - Topless getting into bed.

Fairchild, Morgan

Films:
The Seduction (1982) . . . . Jamie
- 0:02 - Brief topless under water, swimming in pool.
- 0:05 - Very brief left breast, getting out of the pool to answer the telephone.
  0:13 - In white bra changing clothes while listening to telephone answering machine.
  0:50 - In white lingerie in her bathroom while Andrew Stevens watches from inside the closet.
- • 0:51 - Topless pinning her hair up for her bath, then brief left breast in bathtub covered with bubbles.
- 1:21 - Topless getting into bed. Kind of dark, hard to see anything.
Pee Wee's Big Adventure (1985) . . . . "Dottie"
Campus Man (1987) . . . . .Katherine Van Buren
Deadly Illusion (1987) . . . . . Jane Mallory/Sharon Burton
Midnight Cop (1988; German) . . . . .Lisa
  0:23 - In white panties with her dress pulled up in restroom with Alex.
Phantom of the Mall: Eric's Revenge (1988)
. . . . .Karen Wilton
Mob Boss (1990). . . . . Gina
Made for Cable Movies:
The Haunting of Sarah Hardy (1989; USA) . . . .
Miniseries:
79 Park Avenue (1977) . . . .
North and South (1985) . . . . Burdetta Halloran
North and South, Book II (1986) . . . . . Burdetta Halloran
Made for TV Movies:
Initiation of Sarah (1978) . . . .
How to Murder a Millionaire (1990) . . . . Loretta
Menu for Murder (1990). . . . . Paula Preston
TV:
Search for Tomorrow (1971) . . . .
Dallas (1978) . . . . Jenna Wade
Flamingo Road (1981-82) . . . Constance Weldon Carlyle

Paper Dolls (1984) . . . . Racine
Falcon Crest (1985-86). . . . . .Jordan Roberts
Magazines:
Playboy (Apr 1982) . . . . Grapevine
- 254: B&W photo, in bathtub. Upper half of right breast.

Faithful, Marianne

Singer.
Former girlfriend of *Rolling Stones* singer Mick Jagger.
Films:
Girl on a Motorcycle (1968; French/British)
. . . . .Rebecca
a.k.a. Naked Under Leather
- • 0:05 - Nude, getting out of bed, walking to the door.
- 0:38 - Brief side view of left breast putting nightgown on.
- 1:23 - Brief topless while lying down and talking with Alain Delon.
- 1:30 - Very brief right breast a couple of times making love with Delon.
Hamlet (1969; British) . . . . Ophelia
Assault on Agathon (1976). . . . . .Helen Rochefort

Falana, Lola

Singer.
Films:
The Liberation of L. B. Jones (1970) . . . . . . .Emma Jones
  0:19 - Very brief topless walking by the doorway in the bathroom. Very long shot, don't really see anything.
The Klansman (1974). . . . . Loretta Sykes
Lady Cocoa (1974). . . . . Coco
- 0:45 - Left breast lying on bed, pulling up yellow towel. Long shot, hard to see.
- • • 1:23 - Topless on boat with a guy.
Mad About You (1990) . . . . Casey's Secretary
TV:
The New Bill Cosby Show (1972-73) . . . . .regular
Ben Vereen... Comin' At Ya (1975) . . . . .regular

Fallender, Deborah

Films:
Monty Python's Jabberwocky (1977) . . .The Princess
- 0:56 - Buns and brief full frontal nudity in bath when Michael Palin accidentally enters the room.
  0:57 - Topless under sheer white robe.
Best Defense (1984). .Toni
Stitches (1985). . . . . Nurse

Farinelli, Patty

Video Tapes:
Playboy's Playmate Review (1982) . . . . Playmate
- • • 0:11 - Full frontal nudity during library photo shoot and by swimming pool.
Magazines:
Playboy (Dec 1981) . . . . Playmate

Faro, Caroline

Films:
Rendez-Vous (1986; French). . . . . Juliette
  • 0:22 - Buns, walking up stairs, then full frontal nudity
    on second floor during play. Buns, hugging Romeo
    and falling back into a net.
Sincerely Charlotte (1986; French)
. . . . Irene the Baby Sitter

Farrow, Mia

Sister of actress Tisa Farrow.
Daughter of actress Maureen O'Sullivan.
Films:
Rosemary's Baby (1968) . . . . . Rosemary Woodhouse
  • 0:10 - Brief left breast in room in new apartment on
    floor with John Cassavetes. Hard to see anything.
  • 0:43 - Brief close up of her breasts while she's sitting
    on a boat during a nightmare.
  •• 0:44 - Buns walking on boat, then breasts during im-
    pregnation scene with the devil.
Secret Ceremony (1968). . . . . Cenci
See No Evil (1971) . . . . Sarah
The Great Gatsby (1974). . . . . Daisy Buchanan
Avalanche (1978) . . . . Caroline Brace
Death on the Nile (1978; British)
. . . . Jacqueline de Bellefort
A Wedding (1978) . . . . Buffy Brenner
  ••• 1:10 - Topless posing in front of a painting, while
    wearing a wedding veil..
Hurricane (1979) . . . . Charlotte Bruckner
  • 0:39 - Brief left breast in open dress top while crawl-
    ing under bushes at the beach.
A Midsummer Night's Sex Comedy (1982). . . . . . . Ariel
Broadway Danny Rose (1984) . . . . .Tina Vitale
Supergirl (1984; British) . . . . .Alura
Zelig (1984) . . . . .Dr. Fletcher
The Purple Rose of Cairo (1985) . . . . Cecelia
Hannah and Her Sisters (1986) . . . . Hannah
Radio Days (1987). . . . . Sally White
New York Stories (1989) . . . . .Lisa
Alice (1990) . . . . .Alice
TV:
Peyton Place (1964-66)
. . . . .Allison MacKenzie/Harrington

Farrow, Tisa

Sister of actress Mia Farrow.
Daughter of actress Maureen O'Sullivan.
Films:
Some Call It Loving (1972) . . . . .Jennifer
  ••• 1:17 - Topless in bed with Troy.
Fingers (1978). . . . . Carol
Winter Kills (1979) . . . . Nurse Two
Zombie (1980) . . . . .Anne Bolles
Search and Destroy (1981) . . . . Kate
Magazines:
Playboy (Jul 1973). .Tisa
  •• 87: Topless.

Faulkner, Sally

Films:
Vampyres (1974) . . . . .Harriet
  • 1:14 - Side of left breast, partial buns, then right
    breast while making love with John in the trailer.
  •• 1:22 - Full frontal nudity getting her clothes ripped
    off by Fran and Miriam in the wine cellar before be-
    ing killed.
Alien Prey (1984; British) . . . . .Josephine
  • 0:32 - Very, very brief left breast taking off top.
    0:36 - Buns, in bed with Glory Annen.
  • 0:37 - Topless on her back in bed with Annen.

Favier, Sophie

Films:
Frank and I (1983). . . . . Maud
  • 0:16 - Nude, undressing then topless lying in bed
    with Charles.
  • 0:40 - Brief topless in bed with Charles.
Cheech and Chong's The Corsican Brothers (1984)
. . . . Lovely

Fawcett, Farrah

Ex-wife of actor Lee Majors.
Films:
Myra Breckinridge (1970) . . . .
Logan's Run (1976) . . . . Holly
Sunburn (1979) . . . . Ellie
Saturn 3 (1980) . . . . .Alex
  •• 0:17 - Brief right breast taking off towel and running
    to Kirk Douglas after taking a shower.
The Cannonball Run (1981) . . . . Pamela
Extremities (1986) . . . . .Marjorie
  • 0:37 - Brief side view of right breast when Joe pulls
    down her top in the kitchen. Can't see her face, but
    reportedly her.
Double Exposure: The Story of Margaret Bourke-White
  (1989) . . . . .Margaret Bourke-White
    0:39 - Most of side of left breast, while sitting in bed
    giving Frederic Forrest a shave.
See You in the Morning (1989) . . . . Jo Livingston
Made for TV Movies:
The Burning Bed (1984). . . . .
The Red Light Sting (1984) . . . .
Between Two Women (1986). . . . .
Poor Little Rich Girl: The Barbara Hutton Story (1987)
. . . . Barbara Hutton
Small Sacrifices (1989) . . . . .Diane Downs
TV:
Harry-O (1974-76) . . . . .Next door neighbor
Charlie's Angels (1976-77) . . . . .Jill Munroe
Good Sports (1991-) . . . . Gayle Roberts

Fenech, Edwige

Films:

Sex with a Smile (1976; Italian) . . . . Dream Girl
  •• 0:03 - Topless tied to bed with two holes cut in her
    red dress top.
    0:09 - Buns, in jail cell in court when the guy pulls her
    panties down with his sword.
  •• 0:13 - Brief topless in bed with Dracula taking off her
    top and hugging him.
  • 0:16 - Topless in bathtub. Long shot.
Phantom of Death (1988) . . . .

Fenn, Sherilyn

Films:

Out of Control (1984) . . . . .Katie
    0:19 - In wet white T-shirt in pond with the other
    girls.
The Wild Life (1984) . . . . Penny Hallin
Just One of the Guys (1986) . . . . Sandy
Thrashin' (1986) . . . . Velvet
The Wraith (1986). . . . . .Keri
Zombie High (1987) . . . . Suzi
Two Moon Junction (1988) . . . . April
  (Blonde hair throughout the film.)
  ••• 0:07 - Topless taking a shower in the country club
    shower room.
  •• 0:27 - Brief topless on the floor kissing Perry.
  •• 0:42 - Topless in gas station restroom changing cam-
    isole tops with Kristy McNichol.
  • 0:54 - Brief topless making love with Perry in a motel
    room.
  ••• 1:24 - Nude at Two Moon Junction making love with
    Perry. Very hot!
  • 1:40 - Brief left breast and buns in the shower with
    Perry.
Crime Zone (1989) . . . . Helen
    0:16 - In black lingerie and stockings in bedroom.
  •• 0:23 - Topless wearing black panties making love
    with Bone. Dark, long shot.
Meridian (1989) . . . . Catherine
  a.k.a. Kiss of the Beast
  •• 0:23 - White bra and panties, getting clothes taken
    off by Lawrence. Then topless.
  ••• 0:28 - Topless in bed with Oliver.
  •• 0:51 - Topless getting her blouse ripped open lying
    in bed.
    1:11 - Briefly in white panties and bra putting red
    dress on.
True Blood (1989) . . . . Jennifer Scott
  • 1:22 - Very brief right breast in closet trying to stab
    Spider with a piece of mirror.
Backstreet Dreams (1990) . . . . Lucy
  • 0:00 - Right breast while sleeping in bed with Dean.
    Medium long shot.
Wild at Heart (1990) . . . . .Girl in Accident
Made for TV Movies:
Dillinger (1991). . . . . Billie Frechette

TV:
TV 101 (1988-89) . . . .
Twin Peaks (1990-91). . . . . Audrey Horne
Magazines:
Playboy (Dec 1990) . . . . Fenn-tastic!
  ••• 82-91: Topless photos, some are B&W.

Ferguson, Kate

Films:

Break of Day (1977; Australian) . . . . .Jean
Spaced Out (1980; British). . . . . Skipper
  • 1:07 - Brief topless making love with Willy in bed. Lit
    with red light.
The Pirate Movie (1982; Australian) . . . . Edith

Ferrare, Ashley

Films:

Revenge of the Ninja (1983) . . . . Cathy
    0:33 - In white lingerie sitting on couch with Dave.
  • 0:48 - Brief topless getting attacked by the Sumo Ser-
    vant in the bedroom.
    1:13 - In wet white tank top talking on the phone.
Cyclone (1986) . . . . Carla Hastings
  0:04 - Working out at health club with Heather Tho-
    mas.

Ferrare, Cristina

Former model.
Ex-wife of ex-car maker John De Lorean.
Spokeswoman for *Ultra Slim-Fast*.
Films:

Mary, Mary, Bloody Mary (1975) . . . . Mary
  •• 0:07 - Brief topless making love with some guy on
    the couch just before she kills him.
  ••• 0:41 - Topless when Greta helps pull down Ferrare's
    top to take a bath.
    1:12 - Bun and brief silhouette of left breast getting
    out of bed and getting dressed.
TV:
Incredible Sunday (1988-89) . . . . co-host

Ferratti, Rebecca

Films:

Cheerleader Camp (1988) . . . . Theresa Salazar
  a.k.a. Bloody Pom Poms
Silent Assassins (1988) . . . . .Miss Amy
Gor (1989). . . . . Talena
How I Got Into College (1989). . . . Game Show Hostess
Video Tapes:
Playboy Video Calendar 1989 (1988). . . . . . . .June
  ••• 0:21 - Nude.
Playboy's Wet and Wild (1989). . . . .
Playmates at Play (1990) . . . . Gotta Dance
Magazines:
Playboy (Jun 1986). Playmate

Ferreol, Andrea

Films:

Submission (1976; Italian) . . . . .Juliet
•• 0:43 - Topless in room with Franco Nero and Elaine.
Sex on the Run (1979; German/French/Italian) . . . .
a.k.a. Some Like It Cool
a.k.a. Casanova and Co.
La Nuit de Varennes (1983; French/Italian)
. . . . .Madame Adelaide Gagnon
Letters to an Unknown Lover (1985) . . . . Julia
A Zed and Two Noughts (1985; British) . . . Alba Bewick

Ferris, Irena

Films:

Covergirl (1982; Canadian). . . . . .Kit Paget
•• 0:19 - Brief topless taking off robe and getting into
bathtub with Dee.
• 0:43 - Very brief right breast sticking out of nightgown.
• 0:46 - Upper half of left breast during modeling session.
• 0:47 - Topless in mirror in dressing room.
0:49 - Brief topless getting attacked by Joel.
• 0:53 - Brief left breast, putting another blouse on.
• 0:53 - Brief left breast, putting on blouse.

TV:
Cover Up (1984-85) . . . . Billie

Feuer, Debra

Films:

Moment by Moment (1978). . . . . Stacie
To Live and Die in L.A. (1985) . . . . Bianca Torres
• 1:17 - Brief topless on video tape being played back
on TV in empty house, hard to see anything.
Homeboy (1988) . . . . .Ruby
Night Angel (1989) . . . . .Kirstle
• 0:46 - Brief side of left breast. Dark.

Ficatier, Carol

Video Tapes:
Playboy Video Calendar 1987 (1986) . . . . Playmate
Playmates at Play (1990) . . . . Making Waves
Magazines:
Playboy (Dec 1985). . . . . Playmate

Fiedler, Bea

Films:

Island of 1000 Delights . . . . Julia
•• 0:25 - Full frontal nudity washing herself in bathtub,
then nude taking off her towel for Michael.
•• 0:27 - Topless lying on floor after making love, then
buns walking to chair.
•• 0:46 - Full frontal nudity taking off her dress and kissing Howard.
•• 0:50 - Topless in white bikini bottoms coming out of
the water to greet Howard.

••• 1:06 - Topless sitting in the sand near the beach,
then nude talking with Sylvia.
••• 1:17 - Right breast (great close up) making love with
Sylvia.
••• 1:18 - Topless above Sylvia.
Hot Chili (1985) . . . . .The Music Teacher
•• 0:08 - Topless playing the cello while being fondled
by Ricky.
0:29 - Buns, playing the violin.
•• 0:34 - Nude during fight in restaurant with Chi Chi.
Hard to see because of the flashing light.
••• 0:36 - Topless lying on inflatable lounge in pool,
playing a flute.
••• 0:43 - Left breast playing a tuba.
••• 1:01 - Topless and buns dancing in front of Mr.
Lieberman.
• 1:07 - Buns, then right breast dancing with Stanley.

Field, Sally

Films:

Stay Hungry (1976) . . . . .Mary Kay Farnsworth
0:27 - Buns, then very, very brief side view of left
breast jumping back into bed. Very fast, everything
is a blur, hard to see anything.
Heroes (1977) . . . . .Carol
Smokey and the Bandit (1977). . . . . Carrie
The End (1978) . . . . .Mary Ellen
Hooper (1978). . . . . Gwen
Beyond the Poseidon Adventure (1979)
. . . . .Celeste Whitman
Norma Rae (1979) . . . . Norma Rae
(Academy Award for Best Actress.)
0:11 - In white bra in motel room with George.
Absence of Malice (1981). . . . . Megan Carter
Back Roads (1981) .Amy Post
Kiss Me Goodbye (1982) . . . . .Kay Villano
Places in the Heart (1984) . . . . Edna Spalding
(Academy Award for Best Actress.)
Murphy's Romance (1985) . . . . .Emma Moriarity
Punchline (1988) . . . . Lilah Krytsick
Surrender (1988) . . . . Daisy Morgan
0:06 - In black slip getting up out of bed and wash-
ing up in the bathroom.
Steel Magnolias (1989) . . . . .M'Lynn Eatenton
Not Without My Daughter (1991) . . . .Betty Mahmoody
Soapdish (1991) . . . . .Celeste Talbert
Made for TV Movies:
Sybil (1976) . . . . Sybil
(Emmy Award for Best Actress in a Drama Special.)
TV:
Gidget (1965-66) . . . . Francine "Gidget" Lawrence
The Flying Nun (1967-70) . . . . .Sister Bertrille
Alias Smith and Jones (1971-73). . . . . . Clementine Hale
Girl with Something Extra (1973-74) . . . . . . Sally Burton

Fiorentino, Linda
Films:
After Hours (1985)........................Kiki
    0:11 - In black bra and skirt doing paper maché.
  •• 0:19 - Topless taking off bra in doorway while Griffin
    Dunne watches.
Gotcha! (1985) .... Sasha
  •• 0:53 - Brief topless getting searched at customs.
Visionquest (1985) ....Carla
The Moderns (1988) ....Rachel Stone
  • 0:40 - Topless sitting in bathtub while John Lone
    shaves her armpits.
  • 0:41 - Right breast while turning over onto stomach
    in bathtub.
  •• 1:18 - Topless getting out of tub while covered with
    bubbles to kiss Keith Carradine.
Queens Logic (1991).........................Carla
Made for Cable Movies:
The Neon Empire (1989).................... Lucy

Flanagan, Fionnula
Films:
Ulysses (1967; U.S./British) .... Gerty MacDowell
Sinful Davey (1969; British).............. Penelope
Crossover (1980; Canadian) ....Abadaba
  a.k.a. Mr. Patman
  • 0:27 - Brief topless opening her robe and flashing
    James Coburn.
P.K. and the Kid (1982) ....
James Joyce's Women (1983) ....Molly Bloom
  • 0:48 - Brief topless getting out of bed.
  ••• 0:56 - Topless getting back into bed.
  ••• 1:02 - Full frontal nudity masturbating in bed talking
    to herself. Very long scene—9 minutes!
Reflections (1984; British) .... Charlotte Lawless
Youngblood (1986)....................Miss McGill
Miniseries:
Rich Man, Poor Man (1976) ....Clothilde
Made for TV Movies:
Mary White (1977) ....
Young Love, First Love (1979).............. Audrey
The Ewok Adventure (1984) .... Catarine
A Winner Never Quits (1986) .... Mrs. Wyshner
TV:
How the West was Won (1978-79) . Aunt Molly Culhane

Fluegel, Darlanne
Films:
Eyes of Laura Mars (1978).................... Lulu
Battle Beyond the Stars (1980) .... Sador
The Last Fight (1983) .... Sally
Once Upon a Time in America (1984)........... Eve
To Live and Die in L.A. (1985) ....Ruth Lanier
  •• 0:44 - Brief topless and buns, in bed when William
    Petersen comes home.
  1:29 - In stockings on couch with Petersen.
  • 1:50 - Very brief topless on bed with Petersen in a
    flashback.

Running Scared (1986) .... Anna Costanzo
Tough Guys (1986) .... Skye Foster
  • 0:47 - Very brief side view of right breast, leaning
    over to kiss Kirk Douglas.
Border Heat (1988) ....Peggy Martin
  0:23 - In black bra straddling Ryan in the bedroom.
Bulletproof (1988) .... Devon Shepard
Freeway (1988) .... Sarah "Sunny" Harper
  • 0:27 - In bra in bathroom taking a pill, then very, very
    brief right breast, getting into bed.
  • 0:28 - Brief left breast putting on robe and getting
    out of bed.
Lock Up (1989) .... Melissa
Project: Alien (1990)........... "Bird" McNamara
  • 0:18 - Buns, getting out of bed and putting on a ki-
    mono.
TV:
Crime Story (1986-89) .... Julie Torello
Hunter (1990-91).................. Joanne Malinski
Magazines:
Playboy (Aug 1978) .... "Eyes" Has It
  •• 96: Left breast.
  • 99: Topless in bed.

Fonda, Bridget
Daughter of actor Peter Fonda.
Granddaughter of actor Henry Fonda.
Films:
You Can't Hurry Love (1984) .... Peggy
Aria (1988; U.S./British) ....Girl Lover
  •• 0:59 - Brief right breast, then topless lying down on
    bed in hotel room in Las Vegas.
  •• 1:02 - Topless in the bathtub with her boyfriend.
Scandal (1989)................. Mandy Rice-Davis
  (Unrated version.)
  • 0:20 - Brief topless dressed as an Indian dancing
    while Christine tries to upstage her.
  0:54 - In white lingerie, then lower frontal nudity in
    sheer nightgown in room with a guy.
  1:05 - Brief buns walking back into bedroom. Long
    shot.
Shag (1989)....................... Melaina Buller
Frankenstein Unbound (1990) .... Mary
The Godfather, Part III (1990)......... Grace Hamilton
Strapless (1990) .... Amy Hempel
Doc Hollywood (1991)..........................

Fonda, Jane
Daughter of actor Henry Fonda.
Sister of actor Peter Fonda.
Has done a lot of exercise video tapes.
Films:
Period of Adjustment (1962) .... Isabel Haverstick
Joy House (1964)........................Melinda
Cat Ballou (1965)..................... Cat Ballou
The Chase (1966)................... Anna Reeves
The Game is Over (1966)............. Renee Saccard
Barefoot in the Park (1967) ....Corrie Bratter

Barbarella (1968; French/Italian) . . . . Barbarella
•• 0:04 - Topless getting out of space suit during open-
ing credits in zero gravity. Hard to see because the
frame is squeezed so the lettering will fit.
They Shoot Horses, Don't They? (1969) . . . . Gloria
Klute (1971) . . . . Bree Daniel
(Academy Award for Best Actress.)
• 0:27 - Side view of left and right breasts stripping in
the old man's office.
A Doll's House (1973) . . . . Nora
Steelyard Blues (1973) . . . . Iris Caine
The Blue Bird (1976) . . . . Night
Fun with Dick and Jane (1977) . . . . .Jane Harper
Julia (1977) . . . . Lillian Hellman
California Suite (1978) . . . . Hannah Warren
Comes a Horseman (1978) . . . . Ella
Coming Home (1978) . . . . .Sally Hyde
(Academy Award for Best Actress.)
•• 1:26 - Making love in bed with Jon Voight. Topless
only when her face is visible. Buns and brief left
breast when you don't see a face is a body double.
The China Syndrome (1979) . . . . Kimberly Wells
The Electric Horseman (1979) . . . . Hallie
9 to 5 (1980) . . . . Judy Bernly
On Golden Pond (1981) . . . . Chelsea Thayer Wayne
Rollover (1981) . . . . Lee Winters
Agnes of God (1985). . . . . Dr. Martha Livingston
The Morning After (1986) . . . . Alex Sternbergen
• 1:08 - Brief topless making love with Jeff Bridges.
Old Gringo (1989) . . . . Harriet Winslow
• 1.24 - Side of left breast undressing in front of Jimmy
Smits. Sort of brief right breast lying in bed, hugging
him.
Stanley and Iris (1990) . . . . Iris King
Made for TV Movies:
The Dollmaker (1984). . . . .
(Emmy Award for Best Actress.)

Fontaine, Alisha

Films:
The Gang that Couldn't Shoot Straight (1971)
. . . . Jelly's Girl
The Gambler (1974) . . . . Howie's Girl
French Quarter (1978)
. . . . Gertrude "Trudy" Dix/Christine Delaplane
• 0:12 - Dancing on stage for the first time. Buns in G-
string. Topless in large black pasties.
• 0:47 - Brief left breast several times, posing for Mr.
Beloq.
• 0:49 - Left breast again.
•• 1:13 - Topless during auction.
•• 1:18 - Brief topless, then buns making love with Tom,
then topless again.
•• 1:26 - Brief topless getting her top pulled down during party.
• 1:31 - Brief topless getting tied down during voodoo
ceremony.
•• 1:32 - More topless tied down during ceremony.

Ford, Anitra

Films:
The Big Bird Cage (1972) . . . . Terry
• 0:15 - Left breast and buns taking shower. Brief lower
frontal nudity after putting shirt on when leaving.
0:19 - Brief lower frontal nudity turing around.
• 0:44 - Brief left breast during gang rape.
1:14 - Brief left breast in gaping dress. Dark.
Invasion of the Bee Girls (1973) . . . . Dr. Susan Harris
••• 0:47 - Topless and buns undressing in front of a guy
in front of a fire.
Stacey (1973) . . . . Tish
•• 0:13 - Topless in bed making love with Frank.
Dead People (1974). . . . . Laura
The Longest Yard (1974) . . . . Melissa
0:01 - Topless under see-though red nightgown with
Burt Reynolds.

Ford, Maria

Films:
Dance of the Damned (1988) . . . . Teacher
• 0:11 - Brief topless during dance routine in club
wearing black panties, garter belt and stockings.
Stripped to Kill II (1988) . . . . Shady
•• 0:21 - Topless, dancing on table in front of the detective. Buns, walking away.
• 0:40 - Brief upper half of left breast in the alley with
the detective.
•• 0:52 - Topless and buns during dance routine.
Haunting of Morella (1990) . . . . .Diane
The Rain Killer (1990). . . . . Satin
•• 0:29 - Nude, dancing on stage in club. Backlit too
much.
••• 0:37 - Topless in bedroom with Jordan, taking off her
clothes, getting tied to bed. Long scene.
• 0:41 - Topless lying on her back on bed, dead.
• 0:48 - Same scene from 0:41 when Rosewall looks at
B&W police photo.
Naked Obsession (1991). . . . .
Magazines:
Playboy (Nov 1988) . . . . Sex in Cinema 1988
••• 137: Full frontal nudity standing in front of a pole.

Foreman, Deborah

a.k.a. Debby Lynn Foreman.
Films:
I'm Dancing as Fast as I Can (1981) . . . . Cindy
Valley Girl (1983) . . . . Julie
Real Genius (1985). . . . . .Susan
3:15—The Moment of Truth (1986)
. . . . Sherry Havilland
0:26 - Very brief blurry buns and side view of left
breast jumping out of bed when her parents come
home. Long shot, hard to see anything.
April Fool's Day (1986). . . . . Muffy/Buffy
Destroyer (1988) . . . . Susan Malone
Waxwork (1988) . . . . .Sarah

Forte, Valentina

Films:
Cut and Run (1985) . . . . .Ana
••• 0:29 - Brief left breast being made love to in bed.
Then topless sitting up in bed and left side view and
buns taking a shower.
Inferno in Diretta (1985; Italian) . . . .

Fossey, Brigitte

Films:
Forbidden Games (1953; French) . . . . Paulette
Going Places (1974; French). . . . . Young Mother
••• 0:32 - In bra, then topless in open blouse on the train
when she lets Pierrot suck the milk out of her
breasts.
Blue Country (1977; French). . . . . .Louise
The Man Who Loved Women (1977; French)
. . . . Benevieve Bigey
Quintet (1979) . . . . Vivia
La Boum (1980; French) . . . . Francoise
Chanel Solitaire (1981) . . . . .Adrienne
Enigma (1982) . . . . Karen
Cinema Paradiso (1988; Italian/French). . . . . Elena

Foster, Jodie

Films:
Kansas City Bomber (1972). . . . . .Rita
Napolean and Samantha (1972) . . . . Samantha
One Little Indian (1973) . . . . Martha
Tom Sawyer (1973). . . . . .Becky Thatcher
Alice Doesn't Live Here Anymore (1975) . . . . Audrey
Bugsy Malone (1976) . . . . .Tallulah
Echoes of Summer (1976). . . . . .Deirdre Striden
Taxi Driver (1976). . . . . Iris Steensman
Candleshoe (1977) . . . . Casey
Freaky Friday (1977) . . . . Annabel Andrews
Carny (1980) . . . . Donna
Foxes (1980). . . . . Jeanie
O'Hara's Wife (1982). . . . . .Barbara O'Hara
The Hotel New Hampshire (1984). . . . . Franny
Siesta (1987). . . . . .Nancy
0:47 - In a black slip combing Ellen Barkin's hair.
0:50 - In a slip again in bedroom with Barkin.
The Accused (1988) . . . . Sarah Tobias
(Academy Award for Best Actress.)
• 1:27 - Brief topless a few times during rape scene on
pinball machine by Dan and Bob.
Five Corners (1988). . . . . Linda
Silence of the Lambs (1990) . . . . Clarice Starling
Made for Cable Movies:
The Blood of Others (1984; HBO) . . . .
Made for TV Movies:
The Little Girl Who Lives Down the Lane
(1976; Canadian) . . . .
TV:
Bob & Carol & Ted & Alice (1973)
. . . . .Elizabeth Henderson
Paper Moon (1974-75) . . . . Addie Pray

Foster, Karen

Video Tapes:
Playboy Video Calendar 1991 (1990). . . . . . . March
**Playboy Video Centerfold: Deborah Driggs &
Karen Foster** (1990) . . . . Playmate
••• 0:24 - Baton twirling, outside on bed, other miscella-
neous things. Nude.
Playboy's Sexy Lingerie II (1990) . . . .
Magazines:
Playboy (Oct 1989) . . . . Playmate

Foster, Lisa Raines

a.k.a. Lisa Foster or Lisa Raines.
Films:
Fanny Hill (1981; British) . . . . Fanny Hill
•• 0:09 - Nude, getting into bathtub, then drying herself off.
• 0:10 - Full frontal nudity getting into bed.
••• 0:12 - Full frontal nudity making love with Phoebe in
bed.
••• 0:30 - Nude, making love in bed with Charles.
•• 0:49 - Topless, whipping her lover, Mr. H., in bed.
•• 0:53 - Nude getting into bed with William while Hannah watches through the keyhole.
••• 1:26 - Nude, getting out of bed, then running down
the stairs to open the door for Charles.
Spring Fever (1983; Canadian). . . . . Lena
The Blade Master (1984) . . . .
a.k.a. Ator, The Invincible
Made for Cable TV:
The Hitchhiker: Killer . . . . Patty
• 0:02 - Very brief topless standing in the bathtub just
before getting shot.
• 0:23 - Very brief topless again in Jenny Seagrove's
flashback.
Magazines:
Playboy (Nov 1983) . . . . Sex in Cinema 1983
•• 145: Topless.

Foster, Meg

Films:
Thumb Tripping (1972) . . . . Shay
• 1:19 - Very, very brief topless leaning back in field
with Jack. Long shot.
• 1:20 - Topless at night. Face is turned away from the
camera.
Welcome to Arrow Beach (1973) . . . Robbin Stanley
a.k.a. Tender Flesh
0:12 - Buns and brief side view of right breast getting
undressed to skinny dip in the ocean.
•• 0:40 - Topless getting out of bed.
A Different Story (1979) . . . . Stella
0:12 - In white bra and panties exercising and changing clothes in her bedroom.
•• 0:53 - Topless sitting on Perry King, rubbing cake all
over each other on bed.
• 0:59 - Brief buns and side view of right breast, while
getting into bed with King.

Carny (1980) . . . . Greta
Ticket to Heaven (1981; Canadian) . . . . Ingrid
The Osterman Weekend (1983) . . . . Ali Tanner
    0:14 - Very, very brief tip of right breast after getting
    nightgown out of closet.
The Emerald Forest (1985) . . . . Jean Markham
Masters of the Universe (1987) . . . . .Evil-Lyn
The Wind (1987). . . . . Sian Anderson
They Live (1988). . . . . .Holly
Leviathan (1989). . . . . Martin
Relentless (1989). . . . . Carol Dietz
Stepfather 2 (1989). . . . . Carol Grayland
Tripwire (1989) . . . . Julia
Backstab (1990) . . . . .Sara Rudnick
Blind Fury (1990) . . . . Lynn Devereaux
Jezebel's Kiss (1990) . . . . .Amanda Faberson
Diplomatic Immunity (1991). . . . . .Gerta Hermann
Made for Cable TV:
The Hitchhiker: The Martyr . . . .
TV:
Sunshine (1975) . . . . .Nora
Cagney & Lacey (1982) . . . . Chris Cagney

Fox, Samantha

Former British "Page 3 Girl."
Singer - "Touch Me."
Not to be confused with the adult film actress with the
    same name.
Magazines:
Penthouse (Jun 1987). . . . .
Playboy (Dec 1988). . . . . Sex Stars of 1988
••• 185: Topless.
Playboy (Feb 1989). . . . . The Year in Sex
••• 142: Topless.

Fox, Samantha

Adult film actress.
Not to be confused with the British singer with the same
    name.
a.k.a. Stacia Micula.
Adult Films:
Babylon Pink (1979) . . . .
Films:
C.O.D. (1983). . . . . Female Reporter
In Love (1983) . . . .
Simply Irresistible (1983) . . . . Arlene Brooks
    (R-rated version. *Irresistable* is the X-rated version.)
    • 1:20 - In see-through white nightgown, then brief
      peeks at right breast when nightgown gapes open.
Delivery Boys (1984) . . . . Woman in Tuxedo
Streetwalkin' (1985) . . . . Topless Dancer
Sex Appeal (1986) . . . . Sheila
••• 1:14 - In black lingerie, then topless and buns in
    black G-string with Rhonda. Long scene.
Slammer Girls (1987). . . . . Mosquito
•• 0:17 - Topless in the shower hassling Melody with
    Tank.
Warrior Queen (1987). . . . . Philomena

Fox, Vivica

Films:
Born on the Fourth of July (1989) . . . . Hooker
    • 0:50 - Brief right breast, while taking off bra on top
      of patient in hospital. Dark.
TV:
Generations (1990-) . . . . .Maya Daniels

Franklin, Diane

Films:
Amityville II: The Possession (1982)
. . . . .Patricia Montelli
    • 0:41 - Half of right breast sitting on bed talking to her
      brother.
The Last American Virgin (1982) . . . . .Karen
••• 1:06 - Topless in room above the bleachers with Jas-
    on.
•• 1:17 - Topless and almost lower frontal nudity taking
    off her panties in the clinic.
Better Off Dead (1985) . . . . .Monique Junet
Second Time Lucky (1986). . . . . Eve
    0:07 - In white bra and panties in frat house bed-
    room taking her dress off because it's wet.
•• 0:13 - Topless a lot during first sequence in the Gar-
    den of Eden with Adam.
••• 0:28 - Brief full frontal nudity running to Adam after
    trying an apple.
    • 0:41 - Left breast taking top of dress down.
••• 1:01 - Topless, opening her blouse in defiance, while
    standing in front of a firing squad.
Terrorvision (1986). . . . . Suzy Putterman
Bill and Ted's Excellent Adventure (1989)
. . . . Princess Joanna
How I Got Into College (1989) . . . . .Sharon Browne
Made for TV Movies:
Deadly Lessons (1983) . . . . Stephanie

Franklin, Pamela

Films:
The Prime of Miss Jean Brodie (1969) . . . . . . Sandy
•• 1:21 - Topless posing as a model for Teddy's paint-
    ing. Brief right breast, kissing him. Long shot of
    buns, while getting dressed.
The Legend of Hell House (1973; British) Florence Tanner
Food of the Gods (1976) . . . . .Lorna
The Witching (1983). . . . . Lori
a.k.a. Necromancy
•• 0:38 - Topless lying in bed during nightmare.
    0:46 - Partial right breast, tied to a stake. Flames from
    fire are in the way.
    • 1:07 - Brief topless putting on black robe.
    • 1:17 - Brief topless in several quick cuts.

Frazier, Sheila

Films:
Superfly (1972). . . . . Georgia
•• 0:40 - Topless and buns, making love in the bathtub with Superfly.
California Suite (1978) . . . . Bettina Panama
Two of a Kind (1983) . . . . Reporter
Made for TV Movies:
Three the Hard Way (1974). . . . . .Wendy Kane
The Lazarus Syndrome (1976). . . . . Gloria St. Clair

Frederick, Vicki

Films:
All That Jazz (1979). . . . . Menage Partner
...All the Marbles (1981). . . . . Iris
a.k.a. The California Dolls
• 1:03 - Brief side view of left breast crying in the shower after fighting with Peter Falk.
Body Rock (1984) . . . . Claire
A Chorus Line (1985) . . . . Sheila
Stewardess School (1987) . . . . Miss Grummet
Made for Cable TV:
Dream On: Doing the Bossa Nova (1990; HBO)
. . . . Valerie

Freeman, Lindsay

Films:
Young Lady Chatterley (1977). . . Sybil (light-duty maid)
Fairytales (1979). . . . . .Jill
•• 0:24 - Nude on hill with Jack.

Gabrielle, Monique

Adult Films:
Bad Girls IV . . . . Sandy
(Credits have her listed as Luana Chass.)
••• 0:15 - Left breast, then topless in bed masturbating while Ron Jeremy peeks from window.
••• 1:24 - Nude, making love (non-explicitly) with Jerry Butler.
Films:
Night Shift (1982) . . . . Tessie
• 0:56 - Brief topless on college guy's shoulders during party in the morgue.
Black Venus (1983). Ingrid
••• 0:03 - Nude in Sailor Room at the bordello.
••• 1:01 - Topless and buns, taking off clothes for Madame Lilli's customers.
Chained Heat (1983; U.S./German) . . . . Debbie
••• 0:08 - Nude, stripping for the Warden in his office.
••• 0:09 - Nude, getting into the spa with the Warden.
Bachelor Party (1984) . . . . .Tracey
•• 1:11 - Full frontal nudity in the hotel bedroom with Tom Hanks as his bachelor party gift.
Hard to Hold (1984) .Wife #1
Love Scenes (1984). . . . . Uncredited
••• 1:11 - Full frontal nudity making love with Rick on bed.

The Big Bet (1985) . . . . Fantasy Girl in Elevator
••• 0:51 - In purple bra, then eventually nude in elevator with Chris.
Hot Moves (1985) . . . . Babs
• 0:29 - Nude on the nude beach.
•• 1:07 - Topless on and behind the sofa with Barry trying to get her top off.
The Rosebud Beach Hotel (1985) . . . . Lisa
•• 0:22 - Topless and buns undressing in hotel room with two other girls. She's on the right.
•• 0:44 - Topless taking off her red top in basement with two other girls and two guys.
• 0:56 - In black see-through nightie in hotel room with Peter Scolari.
Emmanuelle 5 (1986) . . . . .Emmanuelle
Penthouse Love Stories (1986)
. . . . Monique and AC/DC Lover
••• 0:01 - Nude in bedroom entertaining herself. A must for Monique fans!
••• 0:18 - Nude making love with another woman.
Screen Test (1986). . . . . Roxanne
•• 0:06 - Topless taking off clothes in back room in front of a young boy.
••• 0:42 - Nude, with Michelle Bauer, seducing a boy in his day dream.
•• 1:20 - Topless taking off her top for a guy.
Weekend Warriors (1986) . . . . Showgirl on plane
• 0:51 - Brief topless taking off top with other showgirls.
Young Lady Chatterley II (1986). . . . . Eunice
•• 0:15 - Topless in the woods with the Gardener.
••• 0:43 - Topless in bed with Virgil.
Amazon Women on the Moon (1987)
. . . . .Taryn Steele
••• 0:05 - Nude during Penthouse Video sketch. Long sequence of her nude in unlikely places.
Deathstalker II (1987)
. . . . Reena the Seer/Princess Evie
• 0:57 - Brief topless getting dress torn off by guards.
••• 1:01 - Topless making love with Deathstalker.
• 1:24 - Topless, laughing during the blooper scenes during the end credits.
Up 'n' Coming (1987) . . . . Boat Girl #1
(R-rated version reviewed, X-rated version available.)
• 0:39 - Topless wearing white shorts on boat. Long shot.
• 0:40 - More brief nude shots on the boat.
Not of This Earth (1988). . . . . Agnes
The Return of the Swamp Thing (1988) . . Miss Poinsettia
Silk 2 (1989). . . . . Jenny "Silk" Sleighton
••• 0:27 - Topless, then full frontal nudity taking a shower while killer stalks around outside.
0:28 - Very, very brief blurry right breast in open robe when she's on the sofa during fight.
• 0:29 - Brief topless doing a round house kick on the bad guy. Right breast several times during the fight.
••• 0:55 - Topless taking off her blouse and making love on bed. Too much diffusion!
Transylvania Twist (1990) . . . . Patty (Patricia)

976-EVIL, Part 2 (1991) . . . .
Angel Eyes (1991) . . . .
Evil Toons (1991) . . . .
Scream Queen Hot Tub Party (1991). . . . .
Tower of Terror (1991) . . . .
Made for Cable TV:
Dream On: 555-HELL (1990; HBO) . . . . . . Scuba Lady
•• 0:07 - Topless wearing a scuba mask and bikini bottom when she opens the door.
Video Tapes:
Red Hot Rock (1984) . . . . .Lab Girl
••• 0:06 - Topless and brief buns dancing after throwing off lab coat during "Lovelite" by O'Bryan.
Magazines:
Playboy (Nov 1982) . . . . Sex in Cinema 1982
•• 163: Topless still from *Night Shift*.
Penthouse (Dec 1982) . . . . Pet
105-123:
Playboy (Jul 1989). . . . . B-Movie Bimbos
••• 131: Full frontal nudity sitting on a car/helicopter.

Gainsbourg, Charlotte

Films:
Kung Fu Master (1989; French). . . . . Lucy
a.k.a. Le Petit Amour
The Little Thief (1989; French) . . . . . . Janine Castang
a.k.a. La Petite Voleuse
•• 0:41 - Topless twice, taking off blouse in bedroom with Michel.

Galik, Denise

Films:
The Happy Hooker (1975). . . . . .Cynthia
California Suite (1978) . . . . .Bunny
Humanoids from the Deep (1980) . . . . .Linda Beale
Melvin and Howard (1980) . . . . .Lucy
Partners (1982) . . . . .Clara
Get Crazy (1983) . . . .
Eye of the Tiger (1986) . . . . .Christie
Made for Cable TV:
The Hitchhiker: Dead Heat . . . . Arielle
•• 0:20 - Topless taking off blouse and standing up with Cal in the barn, then right breast lying down in the hay with him.

Gallardo, Silvana

Films:
Death Wish II (1982) . . . . Rosario
• 0:11 - Buns, on bed getting raped by gang. Brief topless on bed and floor.
• 0:13 - Nude, trying to get to the phone. Very brief full frontal nudity, lying on her back on the floor after getting hit.
Made for Cable Movies:
Prison Stories, Women on the Inside (1990; HBO)
. . . . Mercedes

Gamba, Veronica

Films:
A Night in Heaven (1983) . . . . Tammy
Video Tapes:
Playboy's Playmate Review 2 (1984) . . . . . Playmate
Magazines:
Playboy (Nov 1983) . . . . Playmate

Gannes, Gayle

Films:
The Prey (1980) . . . . Gail
• 0:36 - Brief topless putting T-shirt on before the creature attacks her.
Hot Moves (1985) . . . . Jamie
•• 1:09 - Topless in bed with Joey.

Ganzel, Teresa

Films:
The Toy (1982) . . . . Fancy Bates
C.O.D. (1983) . . . . Lisa Foster
• 0:46 - Right breast hanging out of dress while dancing at disco with Zack.
• 1:25 - Brief side view of left breast taking off purple robe in dressing room scene. Then in white bra talking to Albert.
1:29 - In white bra during fashion show.
Made for TV Movies:
Rest In Peace, Mrs. Columbo (1990) . . . . . Dede Perkins

Garber, Terri

Films:
Toy Soldiers (1983) . . . . .Amy
• 0:18 - Brief right breast taking off her tank top when the army guys force her. Her head is down.
Miniseries:
North and South (1985) . . . . Ashton Main
North and South, Book II (1986) . . . . Ashton Main
TV:
Dynasty . . . . Leslie
Mr. Smith (1983) . . . . Dr. Judy Tyson

Garr, Teri

Films:
Head (1968). . . . . Testy True
The Conversation (1974) .Amy
Young Frankenstein (1974; B&W) . . . . .Inga
Won Ton Ton, The Dog Who Saved Hollywood (1976)
. . . . Fluffy Peters
Close Encounters of the Third Kind (1977)
. . . . .Ronnie Neary
Oh God! (1977). . . . . Bobbie Landers
The Black Stallion (1979) . . . . Alec's Mother
Honky Tonk Freeway (1981). . . . . .Ericka
The Escape Artist (1982). . . . . Arlene

One from the Heart (1982). . . . . .Frannie
•• 0:09 - Brief topless getting out of the shower.
   0:10 - In a bra, getting dressed in bedroom.
•• 0:40 - Side view of right breast changing in. bedroom while Frederic Forrest watches.
••• 1:20 - Brief topless in bed when standing up after
   Forrest drops in though the roof while she's in bed
   with Raul Julia.
Tootsie (1982). . . . . Sandy
The Black Stallion Returns (1983) . . . . Alec's Mother
Mr. Mom (1983). . . . . Caroline
The Sting II (1983) . . . . Veronica
Firstborn (1984) . . . . Wendy
After Hours (1985) . . . . Julie
Miracles (1986). . . . . Jean Briggs
Full Moon in Blue Water (1988) . . . . .Louise
   0:50 - Walking around in Gene Hackman's bar in a
   bra while changing blouses and talking to him.
Let It Ride (1989) . . . . Pam
Out Cold (1989). . . . . Sunny Cannald
Short Time (1990). . . . . Carolyn Simpson
Waiting for the Light (1991) . . . .
Made for Cable Movies:
To Catch a King (1984; HBO) . . . .
Made for TV Movies:
Fresno (1986) . . . . Talon Kensington
Pack of Lies (1987) . . . .
TV:
The Sonny and Cher Comedy Hour (1973-74) . . regular
Girl with Something Extra (1973-74). . . . . Amber
Burns and Schreiber Comedy Hour (1973) . . . . . regular
The Sonny Comedy Revue (1974). . . . . regular
Good & Evil (1991-). Denise

Gastoni, Lisa
Films:
Female Friends (1958; British) . . . . Marny Friend
Three Men in a Boat (1958) . . . . . Primrose Porterhouse
Gidget Goes to Rome (1963) . . . . Anna Cellini
Submission (1976; Italian) . . . . Elaine
   0:28 - Lower frontal nudity on the floor behind the
   counter with Franco Nero.
• 0:30 - Left breast, while talking on the phone with
   her husband while Nero fondles her.
•• 0:32 - Topless and buns, making love on bed with
   Nero. Slightly out of focus.
•• 0:33 - Topless getting out of bed.
••• 0:43 - Topless in room with Juliet and Nero. Long
   scene.
••• 0:45 - More topless on the floor yelling at Nero.
   0:54 - Brief lower frontal nudity in slip, sitting on
   floor with Nero.
••• 0:57 - Left breast, while wearing slip, walking in front
   of pharmacy. Then full frontal nudity while wearing
   only stockings. Long scene.
•• 1:00 - Topless in pharmacy with Nero.
•• 1:28 - Topless when Nero cuts her slip open. Nice
   close up.
•• 1:29 - Topless getting up out of bed.

Gauthier, Connie
Films:
18 Again! (1988) . . . . .Artist's Model
•• 0:29 - Very brief topless, then buns taking her robe
   off during art class.
Magazines:
Penthouse (Jun 1987) . . . . .Pet

Gavin, Erica
Films:
Vixen (1968) . . . . Vixen Palmer
Caged Heat (1974) . . . . .Jacqueline Wilson
   a.k.a. Renegade Girls
• 0:08 - Buns, getting strip searched before entering
   prison.
•• 0:25 - Topless in shower scene.
• 0:30 - Brief side view of left breast in another shower
   scene.

Gavin, Mary
See: Samples, Candy.

Gaybis, Anne
Films:
Fairytales (1979) . . . . Snow White
••• 0:21 - Nude in room with the seven little dwarfs sing-
   ing and dancing.
10 Violent Women (1982) . . . . .Vickie
The Lost Empire (1983) . . . .
The Witching (1983) . . . . Spirit
   a.k.a. Necromancy
Hollywood Zap! (1986) . . . . Debbie

Geeson, Judy
Films:
Berserk (1967; British) . . . . .Angela Rivers
To Sir, with Love (1967; British) . . . . Pamela Dare
Hammerhead (1968) . . . . Sue Trenton
Here We Go Round the Mulberry Bush
   (1968; British) . . . . Mary Gloucester
   Nude, swimming.
The Executioner (1970; British) . . . . .Polly Bendel
10 Rillington Place (1971; British). . . . . Beryl Evans
Fear in the Night (1972; British). . . . . Peggy Heller
   a.k.a. Dynasty of Fear
Brannigan (1975; British) . . . . Jennifer Thatcher
Carry on England (1976; British) . . . . . .Sgt. Tilly Willing
The Eagle Has Landed (1977; British)
   . . . . Pamela Verecker
Horror Planet (1980; British). . . . . Sandy
   a.k.a. Inseminoid
•• 0:31 - Brief topless on the operating table.
• 0:37 - Same scene during brief flashback.

Geffner, Deborah

Films:

All That Jazz (1979) . . . . .Victoria
- 0:17 - Brief topless taking off her blouse and walking up the stairs while Roy Scheider watches. A little out of focus.

Star 80 (1983). . . . . Billie

Exterminator 2 (1984). . . . . Caroline

Magazines:

Playboy (Mar 1980). . . . . All That Fosse
- 177: Topless sitting on couch.

Gemser, Laura

a.k.a. Moira Chen.

Films:

Emmanuelle, The Joys of a Woman (1975)
. . . . Massage Woman

Black Emanuelle (1976). . . . . .Emanuelle
- 0:00 - Brief topless daydreaming on airplane.
- 0:19 - Left breast in car kissing a guy at night.
- 0:27 - Topless in shower with a guy.
- 0:30 - Full frontal nudity making love with a guy in bed.
- 0:37 - Topless taking pictures with Karin Schubert.
- 0:41 - Full frontal nudity lying on bed dreaming about the day's events while masturbating, then full frontal nudity walking around.
- 0:49 - Topless in studio with Johnny.
- 0:52 - Full frontal nudity by the pool kissing Gloria.
- 0:52 - Brief right breast making love on the side of the road.
- 1:00 - Nude, taking a shower, then answering the phone.
- 1:04 - Topless on boat after almost drowning.
- 1:08 - Full frontal nudity dancing with African tribe, then making love with the leader.
- 1:14 - Full frontal nudity taking off clothes by waterfall with Johnny.
- 1:23 - Topless making love with the field hockey team on a train.

Emanuelle in Bangkok (1977) . . . . .Emanuelle
- 0:07 - Topless making love with a guy.
- 0:12 - Full frontal nudity changing in hotel room.
- 0:17 - Full frontal nudity getting a bath, then massaged by another woman.
- 0:35 - Topless during orgy scene.
- 0:53 - Topless in room with a woman, then taking a shower.
- 1:01 - Topless in tent with a guy and woman.
- 1:08 - Full frontal nudity dancing in a group of guys.
- 1:16 - Full frontal nudity taking a bath with a woman.
- 1:18 - Topless on bed making love with a guy.

Emanuelle's Amazon Adventure (1977) . .Emanuelle
- 0:17 - Brief left breast in flashback sequence in bed with a man.
- 0:21 - Brief topless making love in bed.

- 0:25 - Brief topless in the water with a blonde woman.
- 1:10 - Full frontal nudity painting her body.
- 1:11 - Brief topless in boat.
- 1:13 - Nude walking out of the water trying to save Isabelle.
- 1:14 - Brief topless getting into the boat with Isabelle.

Two Super Cops (1978; Italian) . . . . Susy Lee

Bushido Blade (1979; British/U.S.) . . . . .Tomoe
- 1:08 - Brief right breast taking off her top in bedroom with Captain Hawk.

Emanuelle the Seductress (1979; Greek) . Emanuelle
- 0:01 - Full frontal nudity lying in bed with Mario.
- 0:02 - Brief topless riding horse on the beach.
- 0:42 - Topless making love then full frontal nudity getting dressed with Tommy.
- 0:48 - Topless undressing in bedroom, then in white panties, then nude talking to Alona.
- 0:54 - Topless walking around in a skirt.
- 1:02 - Topless outside taking a shower, then on lounge chair making love with Tommy.

The Best of Sex and Violence (1981) . . . . Emanuelle
- 0:23 - Side of left breast while getting clothes taken off by a guy. Long shot. Scene from *Emanuelle Around the World.*

Ator, The Fighting Eagle (1982) . . . . Indun

Famous T & A (1982) . . . . Emanuelle
(No longer available for purchase, check your video store for rental.)
- 0:55 - Topless scenes from *Emanuelle Around the World.*

Endgame (1983) . . . . Lilith
- 1:10 - Brief topless a couple of times getting blouse ripped open by a gross looking guy.

Caged Women (1984; French/Italian) Emmanuelle/Laura
a.k.a. Women's Prison Massacre

Metamorphosis (1989). . . . . .Prostitute
- 0:37 - Very brief topless several times in Peter's flashback.
- 0:43 - Very brief topless in flashback again.

Quest for the Mighty Sword (1989) . . . . Grimilde

Magazines:

Playboy (May 1979). . . . . Foreign Sex Stars
- 170-171: Nude.

George, Susan

Films:

The Looking Glass War (1970; British) . . . . .Susan

Die Screaming Marianne (1972). . . . . .Marianne

Straw Dogs (1972) . . . . .Amy
- 0:32 - Topless taking off sweater, tossing it down to Dustin Hoffman, then looking out the door at the workers.
- 1:00 - Topless on couch getting raped by one of the construction workers.

Dirty Mary, Crazy Larry (1974) . . . . Mary

Mandingo (1975) . . . . Blanche
  • 1:36 - Brief topless in bed with Ken Norton.
Out of Season (1975; British) . . . . Joanna
Small Town in Texas (1976). . . . . Mary Lee
Tintorera (1977). . . . . .Gabriella
  • 0:42 - Very brief topless waking up Steve.
Enter the Ninja (1981) . . . . Mary-Ann Landers
Venom (1982; British). .Louise
The Jigsaw Man (1984). . . . . .Penny
House Where Evil Dwells (1985) . . . . Laura
  ••• 0:21 - Topless in bed making love with Edward Al-
     bert.
  •• 0:59 - Topless making love again.
Lightning, The White Stallion (1986). . . . Madame Rene
Made for TV Movies:
Jack the Ripper (1988). . . . . Catherine
Magazines:
Playboy (Nov 1972) . . . . Sex in Cinema 1972
  •• 160: Topless on couch from *The Straw Dogs*.
Playboy (Dec 1972). . . . . Sex Stars of 1972
  •• 208: Topless.

Gershon, Gina

Films:
3:15—The Moment of Truth (1986) . . . .
  One of the Cobrettes
Sweet Revenge (1987). . . . . K.C.
  • 0:41 - Brief topless in water under a waterfall with
     Lee.
Cocktail (1988). . . . . Coral
  • 0:31 - Very, very brief right breast romping around in
     bed with Tom Cruise.
Red Heat (1988) . . . . .Cat Manzetti

Gibb, Cynthia

Films:
Salvador (1986) . . . . Cathy Moore
Youngblood (1986) . . . . Jessie Chadwick
  • 0:50 - Brief topless and buns making love with Rob
     Lowe in his room.
Jack's Back (1987) . . . . Chris Moscari
     1:00 - Getting undressed in white camisole and pant-
     ies while someone watches her from outside.
     1:30 - Running around the house in a white slip try-
     ing to get away from the killer.
Malone (1987) . . . . Jo Barlow
Modern Girls (1987) . . . . .Cece
Short Circuit 2 (1988). . . . . .Sandy Banatoni
Death Warrant (1990). . . . . Amanda Beckett
     0:52 - In bra, undressing for prison guards.
Made for TV Movies:
The Karen Carpenter Story (1989). . . . . Karen Carpenter
When We Were Young (1989). . . . . Ellen
TV:
Search for Tomorrow (1981-83) . . . . .Suzi Wyatt Martin
Fame (1983-86) . . . . Holly Laird

Giblin, Belinda

Films:
Jock Petersen (1974; Australian) . . . . . . Moira Winton
  a.k.a. Petersen
  •• 0:21 - Left breast several times, under a cover with
     Jock, then buns when cover is removed.
End Play (1975; Australian) . . . . .Margret Gifford
Demolition (1977) . . . .
The Empty Beach (1985) . . . . Marion Singer

Gibson, Greta

Films:
Warlords (1988) . . . . .Harem Girl
  •• 1:05 - Topless in tent with the other harem girls.
     Holding a snake.
  •• 1:09 - Topless again.
Beverly Hills Vamp (1989) . . . . Screen Test Starlet
  •• 0:53 - Topless and brief buns in G-string lying on Mr.
     Pendleton's desk.

Giftos, Elaine

Films:
Gas-s-s! (1970). . . . . .Cilla
On a Clear Day, You Can See Forever (1970) . . . . Muriel
The Student Nurses (1970) . . . . .Sharon
  a.k.a. Young LA Nurses
  • 1:14 - Brief topless undressing and getting into bed
     with terminally ill boy. Dark, hard to see.
Everything You Wanted to Know About Sex, But We're
  (1972) . . . . .Mrs. Ross
The Wrestler (1974) . . . . Debbie
Paternity (1981) . . . . Woman in Bar
Angel (1983) . . . . Patricia Allen
The Trouble with Dick (1986). . . . . Sheila

Gilbert, Melissa

Older sister of actress Sara Gilbert.
Films:
Sylvester (1985). . . . . .Charlie
  • 0:23 - Very, very brief topless struggling with a guy
     in truck cab. Seen through a dirty windshield.
  •• 0:24 - Very brief left breast after Richard Farnsworth
     runs down the stairs to help her. Seen from the open
     door of the truck.
Ice House (1988) . . . . Kay
     0:51 - Making love with another guy while her real-
     life husband watches while he's tied up.
Made for TV Movies:
The Miracle Worker (1979). . . . . .Helen Keller
The Diary of Anne Frank (1980) . . . . Anne Frank
Donor (1990). . . . .
Joshua's Heart (1990) . . . .
TV:
Little House on the Prairie (1974-83)
  . . . . Laura Ingalls Wilder

Gilbert, Pamela

Films:

Cyclone (1986) . . . . uncredited Shower Girl
   0:06 - Buns and topless brunette in the showers.
   Long shot.
Evil Spawn (1987). . . . . Elaine Talbot
••• 0:46 - Nude taking off black lingerie and going
   swimming in pool. Hubba, hubba!
••• 0:49 - Topless in the pool, then full frontal nudity
   getting out.
Demonwarp (1988) . . . . Carrie Austin
••• 0:20 - In bra, then topless in bed with Jack.
••• 0:22 - Right breast, then topless lying in bed, making
   love with Jack.
•• 1:23 - Topless, strapped to table.
 • 1:24 - Topless several more times on the table.
•• 1:25 - Topless getting up and getting dressed.

Gildersleeve, Linda

Films:

Beach Bunnies (1977) . . . .
Cinderella (1977) . . . . Farm Girl (redhead)
••• 0:21 - Topless and buns with her brunette sister in
   their house making love with the guy who is looking
   for Cinderella.
 •• 1:24 - Full frontal nudity with her sister again when
   the Prince goes around to try and find Cinderella.
The Happy Hooker Goes to Washington (1977)
   . . . . Honeymoon Wife
 • 0:35 - Brief topless in a diner during the filming of a
   commercial.

Gillingham, Kim

Films:

Valet Girls (1987) . . . . Madonna Wannabe
Corporate Affairs (1990). . . . . Ginny Malmquist
 • 1:09 - Topless, climbing out of cubicle.

Girling, Cindy

Films:

Left for Dead (1978) . . . . Pauline Corte
•• 0:19 - Nude, taking off shirt in bedroom.
Daughter of Death (1982) . . . . Irene
a.k.a. Julie Darling
 •• 0:12 - Topless in bathtub and getting out.
Hostile Takeover (1988; Canadian) . . . . . . Mrs. Gayford
a.k.a. Office Party

Glazowski, Liz

Films:

The Happy Hooker Goes Hollywood (1980) . . . . Liz
Magazines:
Playboy (Apr 1980) . . . . Playmate

Glenn, Charisse

Films:

Bad Influence (1990) . . . . Stylish Eurasian Woman
••• 1:26 - Topless and partial lower frontal nudity making love on Rob Lowe.
 • 1:28 - Very brief left breast in bed with the blonde
   woman.
Magazines:
Playboy (Nov 1990) . . . . Sex in Cinema 1990
 • 146: Left breast.

Go, Jade

Films:

Big Trouble in Little China (1986)
   . . . . Chinese Girl in White Tiger
The Last Emperor (1987) . . . . Ar Mo
 • 0:10 - Right breast in open top after breast feeding
   the young Pu Yi.
 • 0:20 - Right breast in open top telling Pu Yi a story.
 • 0:29 - Right breast in open top breast feeding an older Pu Yi. Long shot.

Goldsmith, Clio

Films:

Honey (1980; Italian) . . . . Annie
•• 0:05 - Nude kneeling in a room.
•• 0:20 - Nude getting into the bathtub.
•• 0:42 - Nude getting changed.
••• 0:44 - Nude while hiding under the bed.
•• 0:58 - Nude getting disciplined, taking off clothes,
   then kneeling.
The Gift (1982; French) . . . . Barbara
•• 0:39 - Brief topless several times in the bathroom,
   then right breast in bathtub.
 • 0:49 - Topless lying in bed sleeping.
   0:51 - Very brief left breast turning over in bed.
 • 0:52 - Brief right breast then buns, reaching for
   phone while lying in bed.
   1:16 - Very brief left breast getting out of bed. Dark,
   hard to see.
The Heat of Desire (1982; French) . . . . Carol
a.k.a. Plein Sud
 • 0:09 - Topless and buns, getting out of bed in train
   to look out the window. Dark.
 • 0:12 - Brief topless in bathroom mirror when Serge
   peeks in.
•• 0:19 - Full frontal nudity in the bathtub.
•• 0:20 - Nude, sitting on the floor with Serge's head in
   her lap.
•• 0:21 - Buns, lying face down on floor. Very brief topless. A little dark. Then topless sitting up and drinking out of bottle.
 • 0:22 - Right breast, in gaping robe sitting on floor
   with Serge.
 • 0:24 - Partial left breast consoling Serge in bed.
 • 0:25 - Topless sitting on chair on balcony, then walking inside. Dark.

- 0:56 - Topless walking from bathroom and getting into bed. Dark.
- 0:57 - Brief right breast, while on couch with Guy Marchand.
- • 0:58 - Topless getting dressed while Serge is yelling.

La Cicala (The Cricket) (1983) . . . . Cicala
- • 0:26 - Nude when Wilma brings her in to get Anthony Franciosa excited again.
- • 0:39 - Nude swimming under waterfall with Barbara de Rossi.
- • • 0:43 - Full frontal nudity undressing in room with de Rossi.

Miss Right (1987) . . . .

Golino, Valeria

Films:
Blind Date (1984) . . . . Girl in Bikini
(Not the same 1987 *Blind Date* with Bruce Willis.)
Detective School Dropouts (1986) . . . . Caterina
Big Top Pee Wee (1988) . . . . Gina Piccolapupula
Rain Man (1988). . . . . Suzanna
- 0:35 - Very brief left breast four times and very, very brief right breast once with open blouse fighting with Tom Cruise after getting out of the bathtub.

Torrents of Spring (1990) . . . . Gemma
Hot Shots (1991) . . . .

Gonzalez, Cordelia

Films:
Homeboy (1988) . . . . .Cuban Boxer's Wife
Born on the Fourth of July (1989) . . . . . .Maria Elena
- • • 1:43 - Topless in black panties, then full frontal nudity in bed with Tom Cruise.

Goodfellow, Joan

Films:
Lolly-Madonna XXX (1973). . . . . .Sister Gutshall
Buster and Billie (1974) . . . . Billie
0:33 - Brief topless in truck with Jan-Michael Vincent. Dark, hard to see.
- 1:06 - Buns, then brief topless in the woods with Vincent.
- 1:25 - Brief left breast getting raped by jerks.

Sunburn (1979) . . . . Joanna
A Flash of Green (1984) . . . . .Mitchie

Gorcey, Elizabeth

Films:
Teen Wolf (1985) . . . . Tina
The Trouble with Dick (1986) . . . . Haley
- 0:13 - Very brief left breast in gaping T-shirt while she lies on bed, plays with a toy and laughs.
0:26 - Lower half of buns under robe on sofa with Dick.
0:27 - Half of right breast on top of Dick in bed.

Iced (1988). . . . . Diane

Graham, Sherri

Films:
Bad Girls from Mars (1990) . . . . .Swimmer
- • 0:22 - Very brief topless diving into, then climbing out of pool.

Mob Boss (1990) . . . . Bar Girl
- • 0:46 - Topless and buns, dancing on stage. Medium long shot.

Grant, Faye

Films:
Internal Affairs (1990) . . . . Penny
- 0:50 - Right breast, while straddling Richard Gere while she talks on the telephone.

Made for Cable TV:
Tales From the Crypt: Spoiled (1991; HBO) . . . . . . Janet
Miniseries:
V (1983) . . . . Dr. Julie Parrish
V: The Final Battle (1984). . . . . Dr. Julie Parrish
Made for TV Movies:
Omen IV: The Awakening (1991) . . . . .Karen York
TV:
Greatest American Hero (1981-83). . . . . . .Rhonda Blake
V: The Series (1984-85) . . . . Dr. Julie Parrish

Grant, Lee

Mother of actress Dinah Manoff.
Films:
In the Heat of the Night (1967) . . . . .Mrs. Leslie Colbert
Valley of the Dolls (1967) . . . . .Miriam
Marooned (1969) . . . . Celia Pruett
The Landlord (1970) . . . . .Mrs. Enders
There Was a Crooked Man (1970) . . . . .Mrs. Bullard
Plaza Suite (1971) . . . . .Norma Hubley
Portnoy's Complaint (1972). . . . . Sophie Portnoy
Shampoo (1975) . . . . Felicia
- 0:03 - Brief topless in bed sitting up and putting bra on talking to Warren Beatty. Long shot, hard to see.

Airport '77 (1977) . . . . Karen Wallace
Damien, Omen II (1978) . . . . .Ann Thorn
The Mafu Cage (1978). Ellen
a.k.a. My Sister, My Love
When Ya Comin' Back Red Ryder (1979)
. . . . Clarisse Ethridge
(Not available on video tape.)
Little Miss Marker (1980) . . . . The Judge
Charlie Chan & the Curse of the Dragon Queen (1981)
. . . . Mrs. Lupowitz
Visiting Hours (1982; Canadian). . . . . . . .Deborah Ballin
Teachers (1984). . . . . Dr. Burke
The Big Town (1987) . . . . Ferguson Edwards
Defending Your Life (1991) . . . . Lena Foster
Miniseries:
Backstairs at the White House (1979) . . . Grace Coolidge
TV:
Peyton Place (1965-66) . . . . Stella Chernak
Fay (1975-76) . . . . Fay Stewart

Gray, Andee

Films:
Sno-Line (1984) . . . . Ruth Lyle
9 1/2 Ninjas (1990) . . . . Lisa Thorne
•• 1:02 - Topless making love with Joe in the rain.
• 1:19 - Brief topless during flashback.

Gray, Julie

Films:
Stryker (1983; Philippines) . . . . Laurenz
School Spirit (1985) . . . . Kendall
Dr. Alien (1989) . . . . Karla
a.k.a. I Was a Teenage Sex Mutant
••• 0:44 - In white bra, then topless in Janitor's room with Wesley.

Greenberg, Sandy

Video Tapes:
Playmates at Play (1990) . . . . Easy Rider
Magazines:
Playboy (Jun 1987) . . . . Playmate

Grier, Pam

Cousin of actor/former football player Rosey Grier.
Films:
Beyond the Valley of the Dolls (1970)
. . . . Black Party Goer
Russ Meyer Film. (Not available on video tape.)
The Big Doll House (1971) . . . . Grear
• 0:28 - Very brief most of right breast rolling over in bed.
•• 0:32 - Topless getting her back washed by Collier. Arms in the way a little bit.
• 0:44 - Left breast covered with mud sticking out of her top after wrestling with Alcott.
The Big Bird Cage (1972) . . . . Blossom
Twilight People (1972) . . . . The Panther Woman
Coffy (1973) . . . . Coffy
• 0:05 - Upper half of right breast in bed with a guy.
0:19 - Buns, walking past the fireplace, seen through a fish tank.
•• 0:25 - Topless in open dress getting attacked by two masked burglars.
••• 0:38 - Buns and topless undressing in bedroom. Wow!
• 0:42 - Brief right breast when breast pops out of dress while she's leaning over. Dark, hard to see.
0:49 - In black bra and panties in open dress with a guy in the bedroom.
Naked Warriors (1973) . . . . Mamawi
a.k.a. The Arena
•• 0:08 - Brief left breast, then lower frontal nudity and side view of right breast getting washed down in court yard.
••• 0:52 - Topless getting oiled up for a battle. Wow!
Scream, Blacula, Scream (1973) . . . . Lisa Fortier
Foxy Brown (1974) . . . . Foxy Brown

Bucktown (1975) . . . . Aretha
Friday Foster (1975) . . . . Friday Foster
Sheba, Baby (1975) . . . . Sheba Shayne
• 0:26 - Side view of left breast, lying in bed with Brick.
Drum (1976) . . . . Regine
• 0:58 - Very brief topless getting undressed and into bed with Maxwell.
Greased Lightning (1977) . . . . Mary Jones
Fort Apache, The Bronx (1981) . . . . Charlotte
Something Wicked this Way Comes (1983) . Dust Witch
Tough Enough (1983) . . . . Mura
On the Edge (1985) . . . . Cora
(Unrated version—not the R-rated version.)
0:18 - In leotards, leading an aerobics dance class.
•• 0:42 - Topless in the mirror, then full frontal nudity making love with Bruce Dern standing up. Then brief left breast. A little dark.
Stand Alone (1985) . . . . Catherine
Vindicator (1986; Canadian) . . . . Hunter
a.k.a. Frankenstein '88
The Allnighter (1987) . . . . Sgt. MacLeish
Above the Law (1988) . . . . Delores "Jacks" Jackson
Class of 1999 (1990) . . . . Ms. Connors
Magazines:
Playboy (Nov 1972) . . . . Sex in Cinema 1972
•• 162: Topless, sitting on Thalmus Rasulala.
Playboy (Nov 1973) . . . . Sex in Cinema 1973
•• 154: Topless and buns.
Playboy (Dec 1973) . . . . Sex Stars of 1973
• 205: Left breast.

Griffeth, Simone

Films:
Death Race 2000 (1975) . . . . Annie Smith
• 0:32 - Side view of left breast, while holding David Carradine. Dark, hard to see.
••• 0:56 - Topless and buns getting undressed and lying on bed with Carradine.
Hot Target (1985) . . . . Christine Webber
•• 0:09 - Topless taking off top for shower, then topless and brief frontal nudity taking shower.
••• 0:19 - Topless in bed after making love with Steve Marachuck.
•• 0:21 - Buns, getting out of bed and walking to bathroom.
•• 0:23 - Topless in bed with Marachuck again.
• 0:34 - Topless in the woods with Marachuck while cricket match goes on.
The Patriot (1986) . . . . Sean
•• 0:46 - Brief topless lying in bed, making love with Ryder.
TV:
Ladies' Man (1980-81) . . . . Gretchen
Bret Maverick (1982) . . . . Jasmine DuBois
Amanda's (1983) . . . . Arlene Cartwright

Griffith, Melanie

Daughter of actress Tippi Hedren.
Wife of actor Don Johnson.
Sister of actress Tracy Griffith.
Films:
Smile (1974) . . . . Karen Love
    0:07 - Brief glimpse at panties, bending over to pick up dropped box.
- 0:34 - Very, very brief side view of right breast in dressing room, just before passing behind a rack of clothes.
- 0:47 - Very brief side view of right breast, then side view of left breast when Little Bob is outside taking pictures.
- 0:48 - Very brief topless as Polaroid photograph that Little Bob took develops.
- 1:51 - Topless in the same Polaroid in the policeman's sun visor.

Night Moves (1975) . . . . Delly Grastner
- 0:42 - Brief topless changing tops outside while talking with Gene Hackman.
- 0:46 - Nude, saying "hi" from under water beneath a glass bottom boat.
- 0:47 - Brief side view of right breast getting out of the water.

The Drowning Pool (1976) . . . . Schuuler Devereaux
Joyride (1977) . . . . Susie
- 0:05 - Topless in back of station wagon with Robert Carradine, hard to see anything.
- •• 0:59 - Brief topless in spa with everybody.
- 1:11 - Brief topless in shower with Desi Arnaz, Jr.

One on One (1977) . . . . Hitchhiker
Roar (1981). . . . . Melanie
Body Double (1984) . . . . Holly Body
- •• 0:20 - Topless in brunette wig dancing around in bedroom while Craig Wasson watches through a telescope.
- 0:28 - Topless in bedroom again while Wasson and the Indian welding on the satellite dish watch.
- •• 1:12 - Topless and buns on TV that Wasson is watching.
- •• 1:13 - Topless and buns on TV after Wasson buys the video tape.
- 1:19 - Brief buns in black leather outfit in bathroom during filming of movie.
- 1:20 - Brief buns again in the black leather outfit.

Fear City (1984) . . . . Loretta
    0:04 - Buns, in blue G-string, dancing on stage.
- •• 0:07 - Topless, dancing on stage.
- ••• 0:23 - Topless dancing on stage wearing a red G-string.

Something Wild (1986). . . . ."Lulu"/Audrey Hankel
- ••• 0:16 - Strips to topless in bed with Jeff Daniels.
- 0:25 - Topless and buns standing in the window.

Cherry 2000 (1988) . . . . E. Johnson
    0:19 - Topless in a shadow on the wall while changing clothes.
The Milagro Beanfield War (1988). . . . . . . Flossie Devine

Stormy Monday (1988) . . . . Kate
    0:03 - Buns and side of right breast, behind shower door. Don't see anything because of the glass.
- 1:11 - Very brief left breast, while making love in bed with Brendan.

Working Girl (1989) . . . . Tess McGill
    0:08 - In bra, panties, garter belt and stockings in front of a mirror.
    0:32 - In black bra, garter belt and stockings trying on clothes.
    0:43 - In black bra, garter belt and stockings getting out of bed.
    1:15 - In white bra, taking off her blouse with Harrison Ford.
- 1:18 - Very, very brief right breast turning over in bed with Ford.
- 1:20 - Topless, vacuuming. Long shot seen from the other end of the hall.

The Bonfire of the Vanities (1990) . . . . Maria Ruskin
In the Spirit (1990). . . . . Lureen
Pacific Heights (1990) . . . . Patty Parker
Paradise (1991) . . . .
Made for Cable Movies:
Women & Men: Stories of Seduction (1990; HBO)
 . . . . Hadley
Made for TV Movies:
She's in the Army Now (1981) . . . .
TV:
Once an Eagle (1976-77) . . . . Jinny Massengale
Carter Country (1978-79) . . . . Tracy Quinn
Magazines:
Playboy (Oct 1976) . . . . Fast Starter
- •• 100-103: Nude.

Playboy (Jan 1986). . . . . Double Take
- •• 94-103: Topless and buns in photos with Don Johnson in photos that were taken in 1976.

Griffith, Tracy

Sister of actress Melanie Griffith.
Films:
Fear City (1984). . . . . Sandra Cook
The Good Mother (1988) . . . . Babe
- 0:06 - Brief topless opening her blouse to show a young Anna what it's like being pregnant.

Fast Food (1989) . . . . Samantha
Sleepaway Camp III: Teenage Wasteland (1989)
 . . . . Marcia Holland
The First Power (1990). . . . . Tess Seaton

Grubel, Ilona

Films:
Jonathan (1973; German) . . . . Eleanore
Target (1985). . . . . Carla
- 1:12 - Brief topless in bed with Matt Dillon.

Guerin, Florence

Films:
Black Venus (1983). . . . . Louise
- •• 0:45 - Nude talking, then making love with Venus in bed.
- ••• 1:16 - Nude frolicking on the beach with Venus.
- ••• 1:18 - Nude in bedroom getting out of wet clothes with Venus.
- • 1:21 - Buns in bed with Jacques and Venus.

Bizarre (1986; Italian) . . . . Laurie
- •• 0:03 - Topless on bed with Guido. Lower frontal nudity while he molests her with a pistol.
- ••• 0:18 - Nude after taking off her clothes in hotel room with a guy. Nice.
- ••• 0:30 - Full frontal nudity making love with Edward in the water.
- • 0:34 - Brief side of right breast, taking off robe in bathroom with Edward. (He's made himself up to look like a woman.)
- ••• 0:36 - Topless in white panties making love with Edward.
- •• 0:40 - Topless and brief lower frontal nudity in Guido's office with him.
- ••• 0:45 - Nude, playing outside with Edward, then making love with his toe.
- •• 0:47 - Topless getting out of bed and putting a blouse on.
- •• 0:49 - Topless with Edward when Guido comes in.
- • 1:11 - Topless sitting in chair talking to Edward.
- • 1:20 - Lower frontal nudity, putting the phone down there.
- • 1:28 - Buns and lower frontal nudity on bed when Guido rips her clothes off and rapes her.

Guerra, Blanca

Films:
Falcon's Gold (1982). . . . .
a.k.a. Robbers of the Sacred Mountain
Erendira (1983; Brazilian) . . . . Ulysses' Mother
Separate Vacations (1985) . . . . Alicia
- • 0:56 - Topless on the bed with David Naughton when she turns out to be a hooker.

Walker (1988) . . . . Yrena
Santa Sangre (1990; Italian/Spanish). . . . . .Concha

Guerrero, Evelyn

Films:
Wild Wheels (1969). . . . . Sissy
Trackdown (1976). . . . . Social Worker
The Toolbox Murders (1978). . . . . Maria
Fairytales (1979). . . . . .S & M Dancer
- •• 0:38 - Topless wearing masks with two other blonde S&M Dancers.
- •• 0:56 - Full frontal nudity dancing with the other S&M Dancers again.

Cheech & Chong's Next Movie (1980)
. . . . .Welfare Office Worker

Cheech & Chong's Nice Dreams (1981) . . . . .Donna
- • 0:43 - Brief left breast sticking out of her spandex outfit, sitting down at table in restaurant.
  0:56 - In burgundy lingerie in her apartment with Cheech Marin.

Things are Tough all Over (1982) . . . . .Donna
Magazines:
Playboy (Sep 1980) . . . . Lights, Camera, Chaos!
- ••• 103: Nude.

Guerri, Ruth

Video Tapes:
Playboy's Playmate Review 2 (1984) . . . . . Playmate
Playmates at Play (1990) . . . . . Thrill Seeker, Bareback
Magazines:
Playboy (Jul 1983) . . . . Playmate

Gunden, Scarlett

Films:
Island of 1000 Delights. . . . . Francine
- ••• 0:02 - Topless on beach dancing with Ching. Upper half of buns sitting down.
  0:20 - Dancing braless in sheer brown dress.
- •• 0:44 - Full frontal nudity getting tortured by Ming.
- • 1:16 - Topless on beach after Ching rescues her.

Melody in Love (1978) . . . . .Angela
- ••• 0:17 - Full frontal nudity taking off dress and dancing in front of statue.
- ••• 0:50 - Nude with a guy on a boat.
- •• 0:53 - Topless on another boat with Octavio.
- •• 0:59 - Buns and topless in bed talking to Rachel.
- •• 1:12 - Full frontal nudity getting a tan on boat with Rachel.
- • 1:14 - Topless making love in bed with Rachel and Octavio.

Guthrie, Lynne

Films:
Night Call Nurses (1972) . . . . Cynthia
a.k.a. Young LA Nurses 2
- • 0:00 - Topless on hospital roof taking off robe and standing on edge just before jumping off.

The Working Girls (1973) . . . . Jill
- ••• 0:43 - Topless, dancing on stage at club.
- •• 0:48 - Topless in swimming pool with Nick.

Tears of Happiness (1974) . . . . Lisa

Gutteridge, Lucy

Films:
Top Secret (1984) . . . . Hillary
The Trouble with Spies (1984) . . . . Mona Smith
Tusks (1990). . . . . Micah Hill
- •• 0:23 - Topless in tub taking a bath.

Made for Cable TV:
The Hitchhiker: In the Name of Love . . . . Jackie
- • 0:08 - Topless on bed talking to herself about Billy after unzipping and opening the top of her dress.
- •• 0:17 - Topless making love with Greg Evigan.
  0:21 - Topless in black and white photos that accidentally fall out of envelope.

Miniseries:
Little Gloria...Happy At Last! (1982) . . . .
Till We Meet Again (1989). . . . . Eve

Made for TV Movies:
The Woman He Loved (1988) . . . . Thelma

Hackett, Joan
Films:
The Group (1966). . . . . Dottie Renfrew
Will Penny (1968) . . . . Catherine Allen
Support Your Local Sheriff! (1969). . . . . . . Prudy Perkins
The Terminal Man (1974) . . . . Dr. Janet Ross
One Trick Pony (1980) . . . . Lonnie Fox
- ••• 1:21 - Nude getting out of bed and getting dressed while talking to Paul Simon.
Flicks (1981) . . . . Capt. Grace
Only When I Laugh (1981) . . . . Toby
The Escape Artist (1982) . . . . Aunt Sybil

Made for TV Movies:
Paper Dolls (1982) . . . .

TV:
The Defenders (1961-62) . . . . Joan Miller
Another Day (1978) . . . . Ginny Gardner

Haddon, Dayle
Films:
Paperback Hero (1973; Canadian). . . . . Joanna
  0:31 - Lower half of buns, under T-shirt while standing behind a bar with Keir Dullea.
The World's Greatest Athlete (1973) . . . . Jane
Sex with a Smile (1976; Italian) . . . . The Girl
- •• 0:23 - Topless, covered with bubbles in the bathtub.
- • 0:43 - Buns, taking off robe to take a shower, then brief topless with Marty Feldman.
Spermula (1976). . . . . Spermula
The Last Romantic Lover (1978) . . . .
  0:56 - Topless.
The French Woman (1979) . . . . .Elizabeth
  a.k.a. Madame Claude
- • 0:15 - Very, very brief topless in dressing room.
- •• 0:49 - Topless on bed with Madame Claude.
- • 0:55 - Topless kissing Pierre, then buns while lying on the floor.
  1:10 - In two piece swimsuit on sailboat.
- • 1:11 - Left breast, then buns at the beach with Frederick.
North Dallas Forty (1979) . . . . Charlotte
Cyborg (1989) . . . . Pearl Prophet

Made for Cable Movies:
Bedroom Eyes (1985; Canadian; HBO) . . . . Alixe
  1:06 - Getting undressed in tap pants and white camisole top while Harry watches in the mirror.

Made for Cable TV:
The Hitchhiker: Ghost Writer . . . . .Debby Hunt
(Available on *The Hitchhiker, Volume 3*.)
  0:05 - In black slip kissing Barry Bostwick.
- • 0:14 - Topless and buns, getting into hot tub with Willem DaFoe before trying to drown him.

Magazines:
Playboy (Apr 1973) . . . . Disney's Latest Hit
- ••• 147-153: Topless and buns.
Playboy (Dec 1973) . . . . .Sex Stars of 1973
- •• 209: Topless.

Hahn, Gisela
She's now a Producer.
Films:
They Call Me Trinity (1971; Italian) . . . . .Sarah
Julia (1974; German) .Miriam
- •• 0:12 - Topless tanning herself outside.
- • 1:14 - Brief topless sitting in the rain.

Hahn, Jessica
The woman in the TV evangelist Jim Bakker scandal.
Music Videos:
Wild Thing/Sam Kinison. . . . . The Girl
Magazines:
Playboy (Nov 1987) . . . . . . Jessica, On Her Own Terms
- ••• 90-99: Topless.
Playboy (Dec 1987) . . . . .Sex Stars of 1987
- ••• 157: Topless.
Playboy (Feb 1988) . . . . The Year in Sex
- ••• 128: Topless wearing a hat.
Playboy (Sep 1988) . . . . Jessica
- ••• 118-127: Nude.
Playboy (Dec 1988) . . . . .Sex Stars of 1988
- ••• 188: Topless.
Playboy (Jan 1989). . . . . .Women of the Eighties
- ••• 257: Full frontal nudity.
Playboy (Feb 1989) . . . . The Year in Sex
  137: Left breast.

Hajek, Gwendolyn
Films:
Traxx (1988) . . . . Playmate
Magazines:
Playboy (Sep 1987) . . . . Playmate
  98:

Hallier, Lori
Films:
My Bloody Valentine (1981; Canadian) . . . .
Warning Sign (1985). Reporter
Higher Education (1987; Canadian) . . . Nicole Hubert
  • 0:44 - Right breast, twice, while making love with
    Andy in bed.

Halligan, Erin
Films:
I'm Dancing as Fast as I Can (1981) . . . . Denise
Joysticks (1983) . . . . Sandy
  •• 1:08 - Right breast, then topless in bed with Jefferson
    surrounded by candles.

Hamilton, Jane
a.k.a. Adult film actress Veronica Hart.
Films:
Delivery Boys (1984) . . . . Art Snob
R.S.V.P. (1984). . . . . Mrs. Ellen Edwards
Sex Appeal (1986) . . . . Monica
  ••• 0:58 - Topless dancing on the bed with Tony in his
    apartment. Long scene.
Sexpot (1986) . . . . Beth
  ••• 0:28 - In bra, then topless with her two sisters when
    their bras pop off. (She's on the right.)
  • 1:32 - Topless during outtakes of 0:28 scene.
If Looks Could Kill (1987) . . . . .Mary Beth
Slammer Girls (1987) . . . . Miss Crabapples
Student Affairs (1987) . . . . Veronica
  •• 0:48 - Topless changing in dressing room, showing
    herself off to a guy.
  • 0:51 - Brief topless in a school room during a movie.
  •• 0:56 - In black lingerie outfit, then topless in bed-
    room while she tape records everything.
Wildest Dreams (1987) . . . . Ruth Delaney
Wimps (1987) . . . . Tracy
  • 0:40 - Lifting up her sweater and shaking her breasts
    in the back of the car with Francis. Too dark to see
    anything.
  •• 0:44 - Topless and buns taking off sweater in a res-
    taurant.
Young Nurses in Love (1987) . . . . Franchesca
  •• 1:05 - Topless on top of a guy on a gurney.
New York's Finest (1988). . . . . .Bunny
Sensations (1988) . . . . Tippy
Bedroom Eyes II (1989) . . . . .JoBeth McKenna
  • 0:50 - Topless knifing Linda Blair, then fighting with
    Wings Hauser.
Cleo/Leo (1989) . . . . Cleo Clock
  •• 0:13 - Nude undressing in front of three guys.
  • 0:21 - Topless changing in dressing room.
  ••• 0:22 - Topless changing in dressing room with the
    Store Clerk.
  0:40 - In bra and panties.
  •• 1:07 - Left breast and lower frontal nudity making
    love with Bob on bed.
Enrapture (1989). . . . . Annie

Hamilton, Linda
Films:
T.A.G.: The Assassination Game (1982) . . . . .Susan
Children of the Corn (1984). . . . . .Vicky Baxter
The Terminator (1984). . . . . Sarah Connor
  •• 1:18 - Brief topless about four times making love on
    top of Michael Biehn in motel room.
Black Moon Rising (1986) . . . . Nina
  • 0:50 - Brief left breast, making love in bed with Tom-
    my Lee Jones.
King Kong Lives! (1986). . . . . Amy Franklin
  • 0:47 - Very, very brief right breast getting out of
    sleeping bag after camping out near King Kong.
Mr. Destiny (1990). . . . . .Ellen Burrows
Terminator 2: Judgement Day (1991). . . . Sarah Connor
Made for TV Movies:
Rape and Marriage: The Rideout Case (1980). . . . .
Secrets of a Mother and Daughter (1983) . . . .
Secret Weapons (1985) . . . .
Club Med (1986). . . . . .Kate
Go Toward the Light (1988). . . . . Claire Madison
TV:
Secrets of Midland Heights (1980-81) . . . . . .Lisa Rogers
King's Crossing (1982). . . . . Lauren Hollister
Beauty and the Beast (1987-90). . . . . Catherine

Hamilton, Suzanna
Films:
Tess (1979; French/British). . . . . Izz
Brimstone and Treacle (1982; British) . . Patricia Bates
  •• 0:47 - Topless in bed when Sting opens her blouse
    and fondles her.
  •• 1:18 - Topless in bed when Sting fondles her again.
  • 1:20 - Brief lower frontal nudity writhing around on
    the bed after Denholm Elliott comes downstairs.
1984 (1984) . . . . Julia
  •• 0:38 - Full frontal nudity taking off her clothes in the
    woods with John Hurt.
  ••• 0:52 - Nude in secret room standing and drinking
    and talking to Hurt. Long scene.
  • 1:11 - Side view of left breast kneeling down.
  •• 1:12 - Topless after picture falls off the wall.
Wetherby (1985; British) . . . . Karen Creasy
  0:42 - In white lingerie top and bottom.
  1:03 - In white lingerie getting into bed and lying
    down.
  1:06 - In white lingerie, fighting with John.

Hammond, Barbara
Films:
Angel III: The Final Chapter (1988)
  . . . . Video Girl #2
  • 0:34 - Topless (on the right) on video monitor during
    audition tape talking with her roommate.
Vampire at Midnight (1988) . . . . Kelly
  •• 0:07 - Topless and buns, getting out of the shower
    and drying herself off.
  • 0:16 - Left breast, dead, in Victor's car trunk. Bloody.

Hannah, Daryl
Films:
The Final Terror (1981) . . . . Wendy
Blade Runner (1982) . . . . Pris
Summer Lovers (1982) . . . . .Cathy Featherstone
  • 0:07 - Very brief topless getting out of bed.
    0:17 - In a two piece swimsuit.
    0:54 - Buns, lying on rock with Valerie Quennessen
    watching Michael dive off a rock.
    0:56 - In a swimsuit again.
    • 1:03 - Brief right breast sweeping the balcony.
The Pope of Greenwich Village (1984) . . . . Diane
Reckless (1984). . . . . Tracey Prescott
    0:48 - In a white bra fighting in gymnasium with
    Johnny then in pool area in bra and panties.
  ••• 0:52 - Topless in furnace room of school making love
    with Johnny. Lit with red light.
Splash (1984) . . . . Madison
  • 0:27 - Brief right breast, swimmming under water,
    entering the sunken ship.
  • 0:28 - Buns, walking around the Statue of Liberty.
  • 1:26 - Brief right, then left breast in tank when Eu-
    gene Levy looks at her.
  • 1:44 - Brief right breast, under water when frogman
    grabs her from behind.
Clan of the Cave Bear (1985) . . . . Ayla
Legal Eagles (1986). . . . . Chelsea Deardon
Roxanne (1987) . . . . .Roxanne Kowalski
Wall Street (1987). . . . . Darian Taylor
High Spirits (1988) . . . . .Mary Plunkett
Steel Magnolias (1989) . . . . Annelle Dupuy Desoto
Crazy People (1990) . . . . Kathy
Made for TV Movies:
Paper Dolls (1982) . . . . .Taryn Blake

Harden, Marcia Gay
Films:
Miller's Crossing (1990) . . . . Verna
Late for Dinner (1991) . . . .
Made for Cable Movies:
Fever (1991; HBO). . . . . Lacy
  • 0:18 - Brief topless making love in bed with Sam
    Neill.
  •• 1:31 - In bra in bed with bad guy, then topless when
    he opens her bra. Kind of dark.

Hargitay, Mariska
Films:
Jocks (1986) . . . . .Nicole
Welcome to 18 (1986). Joey
  • 0:26 - Buns, taking a shower when video camera is
    taping her.
    0:43 - Watching herself on the videotape playback.

Harper, Jessica
Films:
Phantom of the Paradise (1974) . . . . .Phoenix
Love and Death (1975) . . . . .Natasha
Inserts (1976). . . . . Cathy Cake
  ••• 1:15 - Topless in garter belt and stockings, lying in
    bed for Richard Dreyfus. Long scene.
Suspiria (1977; Italian) . . . . Susy Banyon
The Evictors (1979) . . . . Ruth
Stardust Memories (1980; B&W) . . . . Violinist
Pennies from Heaven (1981) . . . . .Joan
  • 0:43 - Brief topless in open nightgown.
Shock Treatment (1981). . . . . Janet Majors
My Favorite Year (1982). . . . . K.C. Downing
The Imagemaker (1985). . . . . Cynthia
The Blue Iguana (1988) . . . . Cora
TV:
Studs Lonigan (1979). . . . . .Loretta
Little Women (1979) . . . . Jo March

Harrell, Georgia
Films:
Incoming Freshman (1979) . . . . Student
The First Turn-On! (1983) . . . . .Michelle Farmer
  ••• 1:17 - Topless and brief buns in cave with everybody
    during orgy scene.
The Gig (1985) . . . . The Blonde

Harrington, Tabitha
Films:
Crossover (1980; Canadian). . . . . .Montgomery
 a.k.a. Mr. Patman
  • 0:11 - Brief right breast, then brief full frontal nudity
    lying in bed, then struggling with James Coburn in
    her room. Wearing white makeup on her face.
  •• 0:29 - Nude walking in to room to talk with Coburn,
    then topless and brief buns leaving.
Star 80 (1983) . . . . .Blonde

Harris, Lee Anne
Identical twin sister of actress Lynette Harris.
a.k.a. Leigh Harris.
Films:
I, the Jury (1982) . . . . .1st twin
  ••• 0:48 - Topless on bed talking to Armand Assante.
  • 0:52 - Full frontal nudity on bed wearing red wig,
    talking to the maniac.
Sorceress (1982) . . . . Mira
  ••• 0:11 - Topless (on the left) greeting the creature with
    her sister. Upper half of buns, getting dressed.
  •• 0:29 - Topless (she's the second one) undressing with
    her sister in front of Erlick and Baldar.
Magazines:
Playboy (Mar 1981) . . . . My Sister, My Self
  ••• 152-155: Topless and buns.
Playboy (Mar 1982) . . . . Aye, Barbara
  • 152: Topless in small photos from *I, the Jury.*

Harris, Lynette

Identical twin sister of actress Leigh Harris.
Films:
I, the Jury (1982) .2nd twin
••• 0:48 - Topless on bed talking to Armand Assante.
• 0:52 - Full frontal nudity on bed wearing red wig, talking to the maniac.
Sorceress (1982). . . . . .Mara
••• 0:11 - Topless (on the right) greeting the creature with her sister.
••• 0:29 - Topless (she's the first one) undressing with her sister in front of Erlick and Baldar.
Magazines:
Playboy (Mar 1981). . . . . My Sister, My Self
••• 152-155: Topless and buns.
Playboy (Mar 1982). . . . . Aye, Barbara
• 152: Topless in small photos from *I, the Jury*.

Harris, Moira

Films:
The Fanatasist (1986; Irish) . . . . Patricia Teeling
• 1:24 - Brief topless and buns climbing onto couch for the weird photographer.
• 1:28 - Brief right breast leaning over to kiss the photographer.
• 1:31 - Very brief side view of left breast in bathtub.
One More Saturday Night (1986) . . . . .Peggy

Harrison, Jenilee

Films:
Tank (1984) . . . . Sarah
Curse III: Bloody Sacrifice (1990)
. . . . Elizabeth Armstrong
••• 0:43 - Topless sitting in bathtub. Almost side of right breast when wrapping a towel around herself.
TV:
Three's Company (1980-82) . . . . Cindy Snow
Dallas (1984-86) . . . . .Jamie Ewing Barnes

Harrold, Kathryn

Films:
Nightwing (1979). . . . . Anne Dillon
The Hunter (1980) . . . . Dotty
Modern Romance (1981) . . . . Mary Harvard
• 0:46 - Very brief topless and buns taking off robe and getting into bed with Albert Brooks.
1:05 - In pink lingerie opening her blouse to undo her skirt while talking to Brooks.
Pursuit of D.B. Cooper (1981). . . . . Hannah
The Sender (1982) . . . . .Gail Farmer
Yes, Giorgio (1982) . . . . Pamela Taylor
Heartbreakers (1984) . . . . Cyd
0:02 - In black bra and panties changing clothes in Peter Coyote's studio.
Into the Night (1985) . . . . .Christie
Raw Deal (1986). . . . . .Monique

Made for Cable Movies:
Best Legs in the 8th Grade (1984; HBO). . . . .
Dead Solid Perfect (1988; HBO). . . . . .Beverly T. Lee
Rainbow Drive (1990; Showtime). . . . . Christine
Made for TV Movies:
Man Against the Mob (1988). . . . . Marilyn Butler
TV:
MacGruder & Loud (1985) . . . . . Jenny Loud McGruder
Capital News (1990) . . . . Mary Ward
I'll Fly Away (1991-) . . . .

Harry, Deborah

Lead singer of the rock group *Blondie*.
Films:
Union City (1980) . . . . .Lillian
Videodrome (1983; Canadian) . . . . Nicki Brand
•• 0:16 - Topless rolling over on the floor when James Woods is piercing her ear with a pin.
0:22 - In black bra, sitting on couch with James Woods.
Forever Lulu (1987) . . . . .Lulu
Hairspray (1988) . . . . Velma
Satisfaction (1988). . . . . .Tina
Shown on TV as "Girls of Summer."
Tales From the Darkside, The Movie (1990) . . . . . . Betty

Hart, La Gena

Films:
Weekend Warriors (1986). . . . . Debbie (car hop)
Million Dollar Mystery (1987). . . . . Hope
Born to Race (1988). Jenny
Made for Cable TV:
The Hitchhiker: Last Scene . . . . Leda
(Available on *The Hitchhiker, Volume 2*.)
•• 0:01 - Topless making love with a guy in bed.

Hart, Roxanne

Films:
The Bell Jar (1979) . . . .
The Verdict (1982) . . . . Sally Doneghy
Oh God, You Devil! (1984). . . . . Wendy Shelton
Old Enough (1984) . . . . Carla
The Tender Age (1984) .Sara
1:01 - In bed in a camisole and tap pants talking to John Savage.
Highlander (1986). . . . . .Brenda Wyatt
• 1:30 - Brief topless making love with Christopher Lambert. Dark, hard to see.
The Pulse (1988) . . . . Ellen
Once Around (1990) . . . . Gail Bella
Made for Cable Movies:
The Last Innocent Man (1987; HBO). . . . .
••• 1:06 - Topless in bed making love, then sitting up and arguing with Ed Harris in his apartment.
Made for TV Movies:
Samaritan: The Mitch Snyder Story (1986). . . . .

Hart, Veronica

See: Hamilton, Jane.

Hartman, Lisa

Films:
Deadly Blessing (1981) . . . . Faith
  1:31 - Brief left breast after getting hit with a rock by
  Maren Jensen. (It doesn't look like a real chest, prob-
  ably wearing a special-effect appliance over her
  breasts.)
Where the Boys Are '84 (1984) . . . . Jennie
Made for TV Movies:
Just Tell Me You Love Me (1978) . . . .
Full Exposure: The Sex Tapes (1989) . . . . . Sarah Dutton
Bare Essentials (1991) . . . .
TV:
Tabitha (1977-78) . . . . Tabitha Stephens
Knots Landing (1982-83) . . . . Ciji Dunne
High Performance (1983) . . . . Kate Flannery

Hassett, Marilyn

Films:
The Other Side of the Mountain (1975) . . . . Jill Kinmont
Two-Minute Warning (1976). . . . . Lucy
The Other Side of the Mountain, Part II (1978)
. . . . Jill Kinmont
The Bell Jar (1979) . . . . Esther Greenwood
  • 0:10 - In bra, then brief topless in bed with Buddy.
  Dark, hard to see.
  •• 1:09 - Topless taking off her clothes and throwing
  them out the window while yelling.
Massive Retaliation (1984) . . . . Louis Fredericks
Messenger of Death (1988). . . . . Josephine
Twenty Dollar Star (1991) . . . .
Made for Cable TV:
The Hitchhiker: Man of Her Dreams . . . . . . Jill McGinnis

Hawn, Goldie

Wife of actor Kurt Russell.
Films:
The One and Only, Genuine, Original Family Band
  (1967). . . . . Giggly Girl
Cactus Flower (1969) . . . . Toni Simmons
There's a Girl in My Soup (1970) . . . . Marion
  • 0:37 - Buns and very brief right side view of her body
  getting out of bed and walking to a closet to get a
  robe. Long shot.
Butterflies Are Free (1972). Jill
Dollars (1972). . . . . Dawn Divine
The Girl from Petrovka (1974). . . . . Oktyabrina
  1:30 - Very, very brief topless in bed with Hal Hol-
  brook. Don't really see anything—it lasts for about
  one frame.
The Sugarland Express (1974). . . . . Lou Jean Poplin
Shampoo (1975). . . . . Jill
The Duchess and the Dirtwater Fox (1976)
. . . . Amanda Quaid

Foul Play (1978). . . . . Gloria Mundy
Lovers and Liars (1979) . . . . Anita
Private Benjamin (1980). . . . . Judy Benjamin
Seems Like Old Times (1980) . . . . Glenda
Best Friends (1982) . . . . Paula McCullen
  • 0:18 - Very, very brief side view of right breast get-
  ting into the shower with Burt Reynolds.
  • 1:14 - Upper half of left breast in the shower, twice.
Protocol (1984) . . . . Sunny
Swing Shift (1984) . . . . Kay Walsh
Wildcats (1986). . . . . Molly
  • 0:30 - Brief topless in bathtub.
Overboard (1987) . . . . Joanna Slayton/Annie
  0:07 - Buns, wearing a revealing swimsuit that shows
  most of her derriere to Kurt Russell.
Bird on a Wire (1990). . . . . Marianne Graves
  • 0:31 - Buns, in open dress climbing up ladder with
  Mel Gibson.
  • 1:18 - Very brief top of right breast rolling over on
  top of Gibson in bed. Don't see her face.
Deceived (1991) . . . .
TV:
Good Morning, World (1967-68) . . . . Sandy Kramer
Rowan And Martin's Laugh-In (1968-70) . . . . regular

Hay, Alexandra

Films:
Guess Who's Coming to Dinner? (1967) . . . . . . Car Hop
How Sweet It Is (1968). . . . . Gloria
Skidoo (1968) . . . . Darlene Banks
The Model Shop (1969). . . . . Gloria
1,000 Convicts and a Woman (1971; British)
. . . . Angela Thorne
The Love Machine (1971). . . . . Tina St. Claire
  • 0:34 - Brief topless in bed with Robin.
  • 0:38 - Brief topless coming around the corner putting blue bathrobe on.
How to Seduce a Woman (1973) . . . . Nell Brinkman
  • 1:05 - Brief right breast in mirror taking off black
  dress.
  ••• 1:06 - Topless posing for pictures. Long scene.
  • 1:47 - Topless during flashback. Lots of diffusion.
How Come Nobody's on our Side? (1976) . . . . . Brigitte
One Man Jury (1978). Tessie

Hayden, Jane

Films:
Confessions of a Pop Performer (1975; British) . . . .
Emily (1976; British) . . . . Rachel
  •• 1:09 - Topless in bed with Billy.

Hayden, Linda

Films:
Baby Love (1969) . . . . Luci
    0:32 - Buns, standing in room when Nick sneaks in.
    0:34 - Very brief right breast, white throwing doll at Robert.
    • 0:39 - Topless in mirror taking a bath. Long shot. Brief left breast hidden by steam.
    • 0:52 - Brief topless taking off her top to show Nick while sunbathing.
    1:25 - Brief topless calling Robert. Long shot.
    1:27 - Very brief topless sitting up while talking to Robert.
    • 1:28 - Topless in open robe struggling with Robert.
Blood on Satan's Claw (1971; British) . . . . Angel
Confessions of a Window Cleaner (1974; British)
. . . . Elizabeth
The House on Straw Hill (1976; British)
. . . . Linda Hindstatt
    • 0:28 - Topless getting undressed in her room.
    ••• 0:47 - Topless, masturbating in bed.
    •• 1:06 - Right breast, in bed with Fiona Richmond.

Haynes, Linda

Films:
The Drowning Pool (1976) . . . . Gretchen
Rolling Thunder (1977) . . . . Linda Forchet
Brubaker (1980) . . . . Carol
    • 1:03 - Topless getting dressed with Huey in bedroom when Robert Redford comes in.
Human Experiments (1980) . . . . Rachel Foster

Heasley, Marla

Films:
Born to Race (1988) . . . . Andrea Lombardo
    • 0:52 - Buns, outside at night while kissing Joseph Bottoms.
The Marrying Man (1991) . . . . Sheila

Heatherton, Joey

Singer.
Films:
Bluebeard (1972) . . . . Anne
    • 0:25 - Topless under black see-through nightie while Richard Burton photographs her. Very brief right breast.
    ••• 1:46 - Brief topless opening her dress top to taunt Richard Burton.
The Happy Hooker Goes to Washington (1977)
. . . . Xaviera Hollander
Cry Baby (1990) . . . . Milton's Mother
TV:
Dean Martin Presents the Golddiggers (1968) . . . regular
Joey & Dad (1975) . . . . co-host
Magazines:
Playboy (Dec 1972) . . . . Sex Stars of 1972
    •• 214: Topless.

Helmcamp, Charlotte J.

a.k.a. Charlotte Kemp.
Films:
Posed for Murder (1988) . . . . Laura Shea
    • 0:00 - Topless in photos during opening credits.
    ••• 0:22 - Posing for photos in sheer green teddy, then topless in sailor's cap, then great topless shots wearing just a G-string.
    0:31 - Very brief right breast in photo on desk.
    0:44 - In black one piece swimsuit.
    ••• 0:52 - Topless in bed making love with her boyfriend.
Frankenhooker (1990) . . . . Honey
    •• 0:26 - Topless yanking down her top outside of Jeffrey's car window.
Repossessed (1990) . . . . Incredible Girl
Video Tapes:
Playboy Video Magazine, Volume 3 . . . . . Playmate
Playboy's Playmate Review 3 (1985) . . . . . Playmate
Magazines:
Playboy (Dec 1982) . . . . Playmate

Hemingway, Margaux

Model.
Older sister of actress Mariel Hemingway.
Granddaughter of writer Ernest Hemingway.
Films:
Lipstick (1976) . . . . Chris McCormick
    •• 0:10 - Brief topless opening the shower door to answer the telephone.
    •• 0:19 - Brief topless during rape attempt, including close-up of side view of left breast.
    0:24 - Buns, lying on bed while rapist runs a knife up her leg and back while she's tied to the bed.
    •• 0:25 - Brief topless getting out of bed.
Killer Fish (1979; Italian/Brazilian) . . . . Gabrielle
They Call Me Bruce? (1982) . . . . Karmen
Over the Brooklyn Bridge (1983) . . . . Elizabeth
Inner Sanctum (1991) . . . .
Does some topless scenes herself, Michelle Bauer body doubles some others.
Magazines:
Playboy (May 1990) . . . . Papa's Girl
    ••• 126-135: Nude.
Playboy (Dec 1990) . . . . Sex Stars of 1990
    •• 175: Left breast, lying in bed.

Hemingway, Mariel

Younger sister of actress Margaux Hemingway.
Granddaughter of writer Ernest Hemingway.
Films:
Lipstick (1976) . . . . Kathy McCormick
Manhattan (1979; B&W) . . . . Tracy
Personal Best (1982) . . . . Chris Cahill
(Before breast enlargement.)
    •• 0:16 - Brief lower frontal nudity getting examined by Patrice Donnelly, then topless after making love.
    •• 0:30 - Topless in the steam room talking with the other women.

Star 80 (1983) . . . . .Dorothy Stratten
   (After breast enlargement.)
   •• 0:00 - Topless in still photos during opening credits.
   • 0:02 - Topless lying on bed in Paul's flashbacks.
   ••• 0:22 - Topless during Polaroid photo session with
      Paul
   • 0:25 - Topless during professional photography ses-
      sion. Long shot.
   • 0:36 - Brief topless during photo session.
   • 0:57 - Right breast, in centerfold photo on wall.
   • 1:04 - Upper half of breasts, in bathtub.
   • 1:05 - Brief topless in photo shoot flashback.
   • 1:17 - Brief topless during layout flashbacks.
   • 1:20 - Very brief topless in photos on the wall.
   •• 1:33 - Topless undressing before getting killed by
      Paul. More brief topless layout flashbacks.
Creator (1985) . . . . Meli
   0:38 - Brief topless cooling herself off by pulling up
      T-shirt in front of a fan.
   • 1:10 - Brief topless flashing David Ogden Stiers dur-
      ing football game to distract him.
The Mean Season (1985) . . . . Christine Connelly
   •• 0:15 - Topless taking a shower.
Superman IV: The Quest for Peace (1987)
   . . . . Lacy Warfield
Suicide Club (1988) . . . . Sasha Michaels
Sunset (1988) . . . . Cheryl King
Delirious (1991) . . . . .Janet
Made for Cable Movies:
Steal the Sky (1988; HBO). . . . . Helen Mason
   Topless, but too dark to see anything.
Magazines:
Playboy (Apr 1982) . . . . Personal Best
   • 104-109: Topless in stills from the film, buns doing
      the splits.
Playboy (Jan 1984) . . . . Star 80
Playboy (Jan 1989) . . . . Women of the Eighties
   ••• 248: Topless.

Hendry, Gloria

Films:
Live and Let Die (1973; British) . . . . .Rosie
Black Belt Jones (1974) . . . . Sidney
Savage Sisters (1974) . . . . .Lynn Jackson
Bare Knuckles (1984) . . . . Barbara Darrow
Magazines:
Playboy (Jul 1973). . . . . Sainted Bond
   • 147-149: Topless and buns.
Playboy (Dec 1973). . . . . Sex Stars of 1973
   •• 204: Full frontal nudity.

Henner, Marilu

Films:
Between the Lines (1977) . . . . Danielle
   0:27 - Dancing on stage wearing pasties.
Bloodbrothers (1978) . . . . Annette
Hammett (1982). . . . . .Kit Conger/Sue Alabama

The Man Who Loved Women (1983)
   . . . . Agnes Chapman
   •• 0:18 - Brief topless in bed with Burt Reynolds.
Cannonball Run II (1984). . . . . Betty
Johnny Dangerously (1984) Lil
Perfect (1985) . . . . .Sally
   0:13 - Working out on exercise machine.
Rustler's Rhapsody (1985) . . . . Miss Tracy
L.A. Story (1991) . . . . Trudi
Made for Cable Movies:
Love with a Perfect Stranger (1986; Showtime) . . . .
Made for Cable TV:
Chains of Gold (1991; Showtime) . . . . .Jackie
TV:
Taxi (1978-83) . . . . Elaine Nardo
Evening Shade (1990-) . . . . Ava

Henry, Laura

Films:
Heavenly Bodies (1985) . . . . Debbie
   • 0:46 - Brief topless making love while her boyfriend,
      Jack, watches TV.
Separate Vacations (1985) . . . . Nancy

Hensley, Pamela

Films:
There Was a Crooked Man (1970) . . . . Edwina
   • 0:12 - Very brief left breast lying on pool table with a
      guy.
Doc Savage: The Man of Bronze (1975) . . . . Mona
Rollerball (1975). . . . . .Mackie
Buck Rogers in the 25th Century (1979)
   . . . . .Princess Ardala
Double Exposure (1983) . . . . Sergeant Fontain
TV:
Marcus Welby, M.D. (1975-76) . . . . .Janet Blake
Kingston: Confidential (1977) . . . . Beth Kelly
Buck Rogers (1979-80). . . . . .Princess Ardala
240 Robert (1981) . . . . Deputy Sandy Harper
Matt Houston (1982-85) . . . . .C. J. Parsons

Herred, Brandy

Films:
Some Call It Loving (1972) . . . . .Cheerleader
   ••• 1:12 - Nude dancing in a club doing a strip tease
      dance in a cheerleader outfit.
The Arousers (1973). . . . .

Herrin, Kymberly

Films:
Ghostbusters (1984) . . . . .Dream Ghost
Romancing the Stone (1984) . . . . Angelina
   0:00 - In wet white blouse in Western setting as Kath-
      leen Turner types her story.
Roadhouse (1989) . . . . Party Girl

Video Tapes:
Playmate Playoffs . . . . Playmate
Magazines:
Playboy (Mar 1981). . . . . Playmate
120-132:

Herring, Laura
Films:
Silent Night, Deadly Night III: Better Watch Out!
(1989). . . . . .Jerri
••• 0:48 - Topless in bathtub with her boyfriend Chris.
The Forbidden Dance (1990) . . . . Nisa

Hershey, Barbara
a.k.a. Barbara Seagull.
Films:
Last Summer (1969). Sandy
Topless in boat. Topless during rape.
The Baby Maker (1970). . . . . Tish
• 0:14 - Side view of left breast taking off dress and diving into the pool. Long shot and dark. Buns in water.
0:23 - Left breast (out of focus) under sheet in bed.
The Liberation of L. B. Jones (1970). . . . . Nella Mundine
Boxcar Bertha (1972) . . . . Bertha Thompson
•• 0:10 - Topless making love with David Carradine in a
railroad boxcar, then brief buns walking around
when the train starts moving.
• 0:52 - Nude, side view in house with David Carradine.
0:54 - Buns, putting on dress after hearing a gun
shot.
Diamonds (1975) . . . . Sally
The Stunt Man (1980) . . . . Nina
• 1:29 - Buns and side view of left breast in bed in a
movie within a movie while everybody is watching
in a screening room.
Americana (1981) . . . . Girl
Take This Job and Shove It (1981) . . . . J. M. Halstead
The Entity (1983) . . . . Carla Moran
• 0:33 - Topless and buns getting undressed before
taking a bath. Don't see her face.
0:59 - "Topless" during special effect when The Entity fondles her breasts with invisible fingers.
• 1:32 - "Topless" again getting raped by The Entity
while Alex Rocco watches helplessly.
The Right Stuff (1983). . . . . Glennis Yeager
The Natural (1984) . . . . .Harriet Bird
Hannah and Her Sisters (1986) . . . . .Lee
Tin Men (1986). . . . . .Nora
Beaches (1988) . . . . Hillary Whitney Essex
The Last Temptation of Christ (1988)
. . . . Mary Magdelene
• 0:16 - Brief buns behind curtain. Brief right breast
making love, then brief topless.
0:17 - Buns, while sleeping.
•• 0:20 - Topless, tempting Jesus.
• 2:12 - Brief tip of left breast, lying on the ground.
• 2:13 - Left breast while caressing her pregnant belly.

Shy People (1988) . . . . Ruth
A World Apart (1988). . . . . Diana Roth
Defenseless (1991). . . . . .T. K. Katwuller
Made for Cable Movies:
Paris Trout (1991; Showtime). . . . . Hanna Trout
Made for TV Movies:
A Killing in a Small Town (1990). . . . . . .Candy Morrison
TV:
The Monroes (1966-67). . . . . Kathy Monroe
From Here to Eternity (1980) . . . . Karen Holmes
Magazines:
Playboy (Aug 1972) . . . . Boxcar Bertha
•• 82-85: Nude with David Carradine.
Playboy (Nov 1972) . . . . Sex in Cinema 1972
161: Buns.
Playboy (Dec 1972) . . . . .Sex Stars of 1972
••• 208: Topless.

Hetrick, Jennifer
a.k.a. Jenni Hetrick.
Films:
Squeeze Play (1979) . . . . Samantha
a.k.a. Jenni Hetrick.
•• 0:00 - Topless in bed after making love.
• 0:26 - Right breast, brief topless with Wes on the
floor.
0:37 - In bra, in bedroom with Wes.
Made for TV Movies:
Absolute Strangers (1991) . . . . Nancy Klein
TV:
L.A. Law . . . . Connie Hammond
UNSUB (1989). . . . .

Hey, Virginia
Films:
The Road Warrior (1981) . . . . .Warrior Woman
Castaway (1986) . . . . Janice
The Living Daylights (1987)
. . . . Rubavitch (Colonel Pushkin's girlfriend)
• 1:10 - Brief side view of left breast when James Bond
uses her to distract bodyguard.
Obsession: A Taste For Fear (1987). . . . . .Diane
• 0:04 - Buns and very brief side view of right breast
dropping towel to take a shower.
•• 0:14 - Brief right breast in bed when sheet falls down.
• 0:38 - Topless lying down, wearing a mask, while
talking to a girl.
••• 1:03 - Topless waking up in bed.
••• 1:17 - Topless in hallway with Valerie.
• 1:19 - Brief lower frontal nudity and right breast in
bed with Valerie, then buns in bed.
••• 1:20 - Topless getting dressed, walking and running
around the house when Valerie gets killed.
• 1:26 - Topless tied up in chair.
Magazines:
Playboy (Sep 1982) . . . . .Warrior Women
162-163: Nude.

Heywood, Anne

Films:
Checkpoint (1957; British) . . . . Gabriela
The Fox (1967) . . . . .March
The Lady of Monza (1970; Italian) . . . . Virginia de Leyva
Trader Horn (1973) . . . . .Nicole
The Shaming (1979) . . . . Evelyn Wyckoff
  a.k.a. Good Luck, Miss Wyckoff
  a.k.a. The Sin
  ••• 0:49 - Right breast, then topless in open blouse after
  being raped by Rafe in her classroom.
  0:52 - Topless on classroom floor, making love with
  Rafe.
What Waits Below (1986) . . . . Frida Shelley

Hicks, Catherine

Films:
Death Valley (1982) . . . . Sally
Better Late Than Never (1983) . . . . Sable
Garbo Talks (1984) . . . . Jane
The Razor's Edge (1984) . . . . Isabel
  • 0:43 - Brief upper half of left breast, in bed after see-
  ing a cockroach.
Fever Pitch (1985) . . . . Flo
  • 0:11 - Brief left breast, while sitting on bed in hotel
  room talking with Ryan O'Neal.
Peggy Sue Got Married (1986) . . . . Carol Heath
Star Trek IV: The Voyage Home (1986) . . . .Gillian Taylor
Like Father, Like Son (1987) . . . . Dr. Amy Larkin
Child's Play (1988) . . . . Karen Barclay
Souvenir (1988) . . . . Tina Boyer
Daddy's Little Girl (1989) . . . .
Running Against Time (1990) . . . .
Made for Cable Movies:
Laguna Heat (1987; HBO) . . . . .Jane Algernon
  •• 0:50 - Topless and buns, running around the beach
  with Harry Hamlin.
  •• 1:05 - Brief topless in bed making love with Harry
  Hamlin, having her head hit the headboard.
TV:
The Bad News Bears (1979-80) . . . . . .Dr. Emily Rappant
Tucker's Witch (1982-83) . . . . .Amanda Tucker

Higgins, Clare

Films:
1919 (1984; British) . . . . .Young Sophie
Hellraiser (1987). . . . . Julia
  • 0:17 - Very, very brief left breast and buns making
  love with Frank.
  1:10 - In white bra in bedroom putting necklace on.
Hellraiser II—Hellbound (1988) . . . . Julia
  • 0:20 - Very, very brief right breast, lying in bed with
  Frank. Scene from *Hellraiser.*

Higginson, Jane

Films:
Danger Zone II: Reaper's Revenge (1988)
  . . . . .Donna
  •• 0:17 - Topless unconscious on sofa while the bad
  guys take Polaroid photos of her.
  • 0:18 - Brief topless in the photo that Wade looks at.
  • 0:22 - Brief left breast adjusting her blouse outside.
  Long shot.
  • 0:34 - Left breast in another Polaroid photograph.
  0:45 - In black bra, panties and stockings posing on
  motorcycle for photograph.
Slaughterhouse (1988). . . . . .Annie

Hill, Mariana

Films:
Paradise, Hawaiian Style (1966) . . . . Lani
Medium Cool (1969) . . . . Ruth
  • 0:18 - Close-up of breast in bed with John.
  •• 0:36 - Nude, running around the house frolicking
  with John.
El Condor (1971) . . . . Claudine
Thumb Tripping (1972) . . . . Lynn
  • 1:14 - In black bra, then very, very brief left breast
  when Jack comes to cover her up.
  • 1:19 - Topless frolicking in the water with Gary.
  1:20 - In white swimsuit, dancing in bar.
High Plains Drifter (1973). . . . . Callie Travers
Dead People (1974) . . . . Arletty
The Godfather, Part II (1974) . . . . Deanna
The Last Porno Flick (1974) . . . .
Schizoid (1980) . . . . .Julie
  0:58 - Left breast, while making love in bed with
  Klaus Kinski. Dark, hard to see.
Blood Beach (1981) . . . . Catherine

Hilton, Robyn

Films:
Video Vixens (1973) . . . . .Inga
  •• 1:18 - Topless, opening her top in a room full of reporters.
The Last Porno Flick (1974) . . . .

Holcomb, Sarah

Films:
National Lampoon's Animal House (1978)
  . . . . Clorette DePasto
  •• 0:56 - Brief topless lying on bed after passing out in
  Tom Hulce's bed during toga party.
Walk Proud (1979) . . . . .Sarah Lassiter
Caddyshack (1980) . . . . .Maggie O'Hooligan
Happy Birthday, Gemini (1980) . . . . Judith Hastings

Holden, Marjean
Films:
Stripped to Kill II (1988) . . . . Something Else
   •• 0:17 - Topless during strip dance routine.
Silent Night, Deadly Night 4: Initiation (1990) . . . . Jane

Hollander, Xaviera
Author of "The Happy Hooker."
Films:
My Pleasure Is My Business (1974) . . . . Gabriele
   •• 0:14 - Full frontal nudity in everybody's daydream.
   •• 0:39 - Topless sitting up in bed and putting on a
      blouse.
   •• 0:40 - Topless getting back into bed.
   ••• 0:59 - Topless and buns taking off clothes to go
      swimming in the pool, swimming, then getting out.
   •• 1:09 - Topless, buns and very brief lower frontal nu-
      dity, underwater in indoor pool with Gus.
   • 1:31 - Buns and very brief side view of right breast,
      undressing at party.
Penthouse Love Stories (1986) . . . . herself

Hollitt, Raye
Films:
Skin Deep (1989) . . . . Lonnie
(Check this out if you like muscular women.)
   • 0:26 - Brief side view topless and buns getting un-
      dressed and into bed with John Ritter.
Immortalizer (1990) . . . . Queenie

Holloman, Bridget
Films:
Slumber Party '57 (1976) . . . . Bonnie May
   • 0:10 - Topless with her five girl friends during swim-
      ming pool scene. Hard to tell who is who.
   • 0:26 - Left breast in truck with her cousin Cal.
Evils of the Night (1985) . . . . Heather

Holvöe, Maria
Films:
Willow (1988) . . . . .Cherlindrea
The Last Warrior (1989) . . . . Katherine
   •• 1:24 - Right breast, after the Japanese warrior re-
      moves her dress.
Worth Winning (1989) . . . . Erin Cooper

Horn, Linda
Films:
American Gigolo (1980) . . . . 2nd Girl on Balcony
   • 0:03 - Topless on the balcony while Richard Gere and
      Lauren Hutton talk.
The Great Muppet Caper (1981) . . . .

Howard, Barbara
Films:
Friday the 13th, Part IV—The Final Chapter
   (1984) . . . . .Sara
        0:52 - In white bra and panties putting on a robe in
        the bedroom getting ready for her boyfriend.
   • 1:01 - Buns, through shower door.
Racing with the Moon (1984) . . . . Gatsby Girl
Running Mates (1985) . . . .
Lucky Stiff (1988) . . . . Frances
White Palace (1990) . . . . Sherri Klugman
TV:
Falcon Crest (1985-86) . . . . .Robin Agretti

Howell, Margaret
Films:
Tightrope (1984) .Judy Harper
   • 0:44 - Brief left breast viewed from above in a room
      with Clint Eastwood.
Girls Just Want to Have Fun (1985) . . . . Mrs. Glenn

Hubley, Season
Ex-wife of actor Kurt Russell.
Films:
Hardcore (1979) . . . . Niki
   • 0:27 - Topless acting in a porno movie.
   ••• 1:05 - Full frontal nudity talking to George C. Scott
      in a booth. Panties mysteriously appear later on.
Vice Squad (1982) . . . . Princess
        0:34 - In black bra in Ramrod's apartment.
        0:57 - Buns, getting out of bed after making love
        with a John.
        1:25 - In black bra, tied up by Ramrod.
Pretty Kill (1987) . . . . Heather Todd
Total Exposure (1991) . . . . .Andi Robinson
        0:07 - Buns, getting into hot tub. Probably a body
        double.
Made for Cable TV:
The Hitchhiker: Cabin Fever . . . . .Miranda
        0:12 - In white bra, under cabin with Rick.
Made for TV Movies:
She Lives (1973) . . . .
The Three Wishes of Billy Grier (1984) . . . . Phyllis
Shakedown on Sunset Strip (1988)
        . . . . Officer Audre Davis
Child in the Night (1990) . . . . Valerie Winfield
Vestige of Honor (1990) . . . . Marilyn
TV:
Kung Fu (1974-75) . . . . Margit McLean
Family (1976-77) .Salina Magee

Hughes, Sharon

Films:

Chained Heat (1983; U.S./German) . . . . Val
•• 0:30 - Brief topless in the shower with Linda Blair.
•• 0:51 - Buns, in lingerie, stripping for a guy.
•• 1:04 - Topless in the spa with the Warden.
The Man Who Loved Women (1983) . . . . Nurse
Hard to Hold (1984) . . . . Wife
The Last Horror Film (1984) . . . . Stripper
American Justice (1986) . . . . Valerie
A Fine Mess (1986) . . . . Tina
Grotesque (1987) . . . .

Hughes, Wendy

Films:

Jock Petersen (1974; Australian). . . . . Patricia Kent
a.k.a. Petersen
••• 0:12 - Topless in her office with Tony.
• 0:13 - Topless making love with Tony on the floor.
•• 0:44 - Nude running around the beach with Tony.
•• 0:50 - Nude in bed making love with Tony.
• 1:24 - Full frontal nudity when Tony rapes her in her
office.
Newsfront (1978; Australian) . . . . Amy McKenzie
My Brilliant Career (1979; Australian) . . . . . . Aunt Helen
Lonely Hearts (1983; Australian) . . . . Patricia
• 1:05 - Brief topless getting out of bed and putting a
dress on. Dark, hard to see.
Careful, He Might Hear You (1984; Australian)
. . . . .Vanessa
An Indecent Obsession (1985) . . . . . Honour Langtry
0:32 - Possibly Wendy topless, could be Sue because
Luce is fantasizing about Wendy while making love
with Sue. Dark, long shot, hard to see.
•• 1:10 - Left breast, making love in bed with Wilson.
My First Wife (1985) . . . . Helen
1:00 - Brief topless and lower frontal nudity under
water during husband's dream. Don't see her face.
•• 1:08 - In bra, then topless on the floor with her husband.
•• 1:10 - Topless in bed lying down, then fighting with
her husband. A little dark.
Happy New Year (1987) . . . . Carolyn Benedict
Warm Nights on a Slow Moving Train (1987) . . The Girl
1:23 - Very, very brief silhouette of right breast getting back into bed after killing a man.
Echoes of Paradise (1989) . . . . Maria
Made for Cable Movies:
The Heist (1989; HBO) . . . . Susan
• 0:52 - Very brief side view of right breast making love
in bed with Pierce Brosnan.
Made for TV Movies:
Donor (1990) . . . . Dr. Farrell

Hull, Dianne

Films:

The Arrangement (1969) . . . . Ellen
The Magic Garden of Stanley Sweetheart (1970)
. . . . Cathy
Hot Summer Week (1973; Canadian) . . . .
Man on a Swing (1974) . . . . Maggie Dawson
Aloha, Bobby and Rose (1975) . . . . Rose
The Fifth Floor (1978) . . . . Kelly McIntyre
•• 0:29 - Topless and buns in shower while Carl watch-
es, then brief full frontal nudity running out of the
shower.
•• 1:09 - Topless in whirlpool bath getting visited by
Carl again, then raped.
You Better Watch Out (1980) . . . . Jackie Stadling
The New Adventures of Pippi Longstocking (1988)
. . . . Mrs. Settigren

Hunt, Marsha A.

Films:

The Sender (1982) . . . . Nurse Jo
Howling II (1984) . . . . Mariana
•• 0:33 - Topless in bedroom with Sybil Danning and a
guy.

Hunter, Heather

Adult film actress.

Films:

Frankenhooker (1990) . . . . Chartreuse
• 0:36 - Brief topless during introduction to Jeffrey.
• 0:37 - Brief topless bending over behind Sugar.
••• 0:41 - Brief topless and buns, running in front of bed.
A little blurry. Then topless and buns dancing with
the other girls.
• 0:43 - Topless dodging flying leg with Sugar.
•• 0:44 - Topless, crawling on the floor.

Hunter, Kaki

Films:

Roadie (1980) . . . . Lola Bouiliabase
Willie and Phil (1980) . . . . Patti Sutherland
Porky's (1981; Canadian) . . . . .Wendy
• 1:02 - Brief full frontal nudity, then brief topless in the
shower scene.
Whose Life Is It, Anyway? (1981) . . . . Mary Jo
Porky's II: The Next Day (1983; Canadian) . . . . . .Wendy
Just the Way You Are (1984) . . . . Lisa
Porky's Revenge (1985; Canadian) . . . . .Wendy
1:22 - In white bra and panties taking off her clothes
to jump off a bridge.

Hunter, Neith

Films:

Born in East L.A. (1987) . . . . Marcie
Near Dark (1987) . . . . Lady in Car
Fright Night, Part 2 (1988) . . . . Young Admirer

Silent Night, Deadly Night 4: Initiation (1990)
. . . . Kim
- 0:03 - Brief topless several times in bed with Hank.
- 0:47 - Brief topless during occult ceremony when a worm comes out of her mouth.
- 1:05 - Right breast, while lying on floor. Long shot.
  1:06 - Topless, covered with gunk, transforming into a worm.
- 1:07 - Very brief side of right breast, while sitting up.

Hunter, Rachel

Wife of singer Rod Stewart.
Sports Illustrated swimsuit model.
Video Tapes:
Sports Illustrated's 25th Anniversary Swimsuit Video (1989) . . . . herself
(The version shown on HBO left out two music video segments at the end. If you like buns, definitely watch the video tape!)
- 0:03 - Right breast in see-through black swimsuit with white stars on it.
Sports Illustrated Super Shape-Up Program: Body Sculpting (1990) . . . . herself

Huntly, Leslie

Films:
The Naked Cage (1985) . . . . Peaches
Back to School (1986) . . . . Coed #1
- • 0:14 - Brief topless in the shower room when Rodney Dangerfield first arrives on campus.
Demon of Paradise (1987) . . . . Gobby
- • 0:51 - Topless taking off her top on a boat, then swimming in the ocean.
Stewardess School (1987) . . . . Alison Hanover
- • 0:46 - Topless, doing a strip tease on a table at a party at her house.
Satan's Princess (1989) . . . . Karen Rhodes
- • • 0:27 - Topless sitting on bed and in bed with Nicole.

Huppert, Isabelle

Films:
Going Places (1974; French). . . . . .Jacqueline
- 1:53 - Brief upper half of left breast making love with Jean-Claude.
The Lacemaker (1977) . . . . Beatrice
Heaven's Gate (1980). . . . . .Ella
- • 1:10 - Nude running around the house and in bed with Kris Kristofferson.
- • • 1:18 - Nude, taking a bath in the river and getting out.
- 2:24 - Very brief left breast getting raped.
Loulou (1980; French) .Nelly
- 0:06 - Very, very brief topless leaning over in bed.
- 0:18 - Brief topless getting out of bed.
- 0:27 - Brief topless turning over in bed.
- • 0:36 - Topless lying in bed talking on phone. Mostly right breast.

- 0:40 - Lower frontal nudity and buns taking off panties and getting into bed.
- • 0:59 - Left breast in bed with André, then topless taking him to the bathroom.
Clean Slate (1981) . . . .
La Truit (The Trout) (1982) . . . . Frederique
Entre Nous (1983; French). . . . . Helen Webber
a.k.a. Coup de Foudre
- 1:01 - Brief topless in shower room talking about her breasts with Miou-Miou.
My Best Friend's Girl (1984; French)
. . . . .Vivian Arthund
a.k.a. La Femme du Mon Ami
- 0:40 - Brief left breast peeking out of bathrobe walking around in living room.
  1:00 - Buns, making love with Thierry Lhermitte while his friend watches.
Sincerely Charlotte (1986; French) . . . . . . .Charlotte
  0:20 - Brief topless in bathtub. Long shot.
  1:07 - Very brief left breast changing into red dress in the back seat of the car.
- • 1:15 - Topless in bed with Mathieu. Kind of dark.
The Bedroom Window (1987) . . . . .Sylvia Wentworth
- • 0:06 - Briefly nude while looking out the window at attempted rape.
Story of Women (1988; French) . . . . Marie Latour

Hurley, Elizabeth

Films:
Aria (1988; U.S./British) . . . . .Marietta
- 0:46 - Brief topless, turning around while singing.
  0:47 - Buns.
Rowing with the Wind (1988) . . . . Clair Clairmont

Hushaw, Katherine

Video Tapes:
Playboy Video Calendar 1988 (1987). . . . . Playmate
Playboy's Wet and Wild (1989). . . . .
Magazines:
Playboy (Oct 1986) . . . . Playmate

Hussey, Olivia

Films:
Romeo and Juliet (1968) . . . . Juliet
- 1:37 - Very brief topless rolling over and getting out of bed with Romeo.
The Man with Bogart's Face (1980) . . . . .Elsa Borsht
Virus (1980; Japanese) . . . . Marit
Escape 2000 (1981). . . . . Chris
Made for Cable Movies:
Psycho IV: The Beginning (1990; Showtime)
. . . . Norma Bates
- • 0:49 - Topless in motel room mirror while young Norman, watches through peephole.
Made for TV Movies:
Ivanhoe (1982) . . . . .Rebecca
Stephen King's "It" (1990) . . . . Audra

Huston, Anjelica

Daughter of actor/director John Huston.
Films:
Hamlet (1969; British). . . . . Court Lady
A Walk with Love and Death (1969) . . . . . .Lady Claudia
The Last Tycoon (1976). . . . . .Edna
Swashbuckler (1976). . . . . Woman of Dark Visage
The Postman Always Rings Twice (1981)
. . . . Madge
   • 1:30 - Brief side view left breast sitting in trailer with
     Jack Nicholson.
Frances (1982) . . . . . Hospital Sequence: Mental Patient
Ice Pirates (1984) . . . . .Maida
This is Spinal Tap (1984) . . . . Polly Deutsch
Prizzi's Honor (1985). . . . . .Maerose Prizzi
The Dead (1987). . . . . Gretta Conroy
Gardens of Stone (1987). . . . . Samantha Davis
Enemies, A Love Story (1989) . . . . Tamara
The Witches (1989). . . . . . . Grand High Witch/Eva Ernst
The Grifters (1990) . . . . .Lilly Dillon
Miniseries:
Lonesome Dove (1989). . . . . Clara Allen

Hutchinson, Tracey E.

Films:
The Wild Life (1984) . . . . .Poker Girl #2
   • 1:23 - Brief topless in a room full of guys and girls
     playing strip poker when Lea Thompson looks in.
Into the Night (1985) . . . . Federal Agent
Masterblaster (1986). . . . . .Lisa
••• 0:57 - Topless taking a shower (wearing panties).
Amazon Women on the Moon (1987). . . . . Floozie
   1:18 - Brief right breast hitting balloon while Carrie
   Fisher talks to a guy. This sketch is in B&W and appears after the first batch of credits.

Hutton, Lauren

Films:
Little Fauss and Big Halsy (1970). . . . . Rita Nebraska
The Gambler (1974) . . . . Billie
Gator (1976). . . . . Aggie Maybank
Viva Knievel (1977) . . . . Kate Morgan
Welcome to L.A. (1977). . . . . .Nora Bruce
   • 0:56 - Very brief, obscured glimpse of left breast un-
     der red light in photo darkroom.
A Wedding (1978) . . . . Florence Farmer
American Gigolo (1980) . . . . Michelle
   • 0:37 - Left breast, making love with Richard Gere in
     bed in his apartment.
Paternity (1981) .Jenny Lufton
Zorro, The Gay Blade (1981). . . . . Charlotte
Lassiter (1984) . . . . Kari Von Fursten
   • 0:18 - Brief topless over-the-shoulder shot making
     love with a guy on the bed just before killing him.
Once Bitten (1985) . . . . Countess
Malone (1987) . . . . Jamie
Made for Cable Movies:
Fear (1991; Showtime) . . . . .Jessica

The Rhinemann Exchange (1977) . . .Leslie Hawkewood
Paper Dolls (1984) . . . . Colette Ferrier
Magazines:
Penthouse (Sep 1986)
. . . . .The Secret Nudes of Lauren Hutton
••• 158-169: 1962 B&W photos.

Hyde, Kimberly

Films:
The Last Picture Show (1971; B&W)
. . . . Annie-Annie Martin
•• 0:36 - Full frontal nudity, getting out of pool to meet
     Randy Quaid and Cybill Shepherd.
   • 0:37 - Topless several times, sitting at edge of pool
     with Bobby.
   • 0:38 - More topless, sitting on edge of pool in back-
     ground.
Video Vixens (1973) . . . . Claudine

Hyser, Joyce

Ex-girlfriend of singer Bruce Springsteen.
Films:
They All Laughed (1981) . . . . .Sylvia
Staying Alive (1983). . . . . Linda
Valley Girl (1983) . . . . Joyce
This is Spinal Tap (1984) . . . . Belinda
Just One of the Guys (1986). . . . . Terry Griffith
   0:10 - In two piece swimsuit by the pool with her
   boyfriend.
•• 1:27 - Brief topless opening her blouse to prove that
     she is really a girl.
Wedding Band (1989) . . . . Karla Thompson

Iman

Model.
Films:
The Human Factor (1979) . . . . .Sarah
Exposed (1983) . . . . Model
Out of Africa (1985). . . . . Mariammo
No Way Out (1987) . . . . Nina Beka
Surrender (1988) . . . . Hedy
L.A. Story (1991) . . . . Cynthia
Made for Cable Movies:
Lies of the Twins (1991) . . . . Elle
Magazines:
Playboy (Jan 1986). . . . . Beauty and the Beasts
••• 146-155: Topless.

Inch, Jennifer

Films:
Frank and I (1983). . . . . Frank/Frances
   0:10 - Brief buns, getting pants pulled down for a
   spanking.
••• 0:22 - Nude getting undressed and walking to the
     bed.

- 0:24 - Brief nude when Charles pulls the sheets off her.
  0:32 - Brief buns, getting spanked by two older women.
- ••• 0:38 - Full frontal nudity getting out of bed and walking to Charles at the piano.
- •• 0:45 - Full frontal nudity lying on her side by the fireplace. Dark, hard to see.
- •• 1:09 - Brief topless making love with Charles on the floor.
- ••• 1:11 - Nude taking off her clothes and walking toward Charles at the piano.
Higher Education (1987; Canadian) . . . . . Gladys/Glitter
Soft Touch (1987). . . . . Tracy Anderson
(Shown on *The Playboy Channel* as *Birds in Paradise*.)
- • 0:01 - Full frontal nudity during the opening credits.
- • 0:02 - Topless with her two girlfriends during the opening credits.
- ••• 0:17 - Topless exercising on the floor, walking around the room, the lying on bed. Long scene.
- • 0:20 - Full frontal nudity getting out of bed.
- •• 0:23 - Topless in bed.
- ••• 0:50 - Topless sunbathing on boat with Carrie.
- •• 1:01 - Full frontal nudity, sitting on towel, watching Carrie.
- • 1:02 - Full frontal nudity, waving to a dolphin.
- •• 1:04 - Topless at night by campfire with Carrie.
- ••• 1:05 - Brief left breast, then topless putting on skirt and walking around the island.
- •• 1:13 - Topless in hut with island guy.
- •• 1:19 - Topless in stills during the end credits.
Soft Touch II (1987) . . . . Tracy Anderson
Seen on The Playboy Channel as "Birds in Paradise."
- • 0:01 - Topless during opening credits.
- • 0:02 - Topless with her two girlfriends during opening credits.
- •• 0:14 - Topless dancing in Harry's bar by herself.
- • 0:27 - Full frontal nudity on stage at Harry's after robbers tell her to strip.
- • 0:29 - Side of left breast tied to Neill on bed.
- • 0:31 - Topless tied up when Ashley and Carrie discover her.
- •• 0:52 - Full frontal nudity during strip poker game, then covered with whipped cream.
- • 0:57 - Full frontal nudity getting out of bed.
State Park (1988; Canadian). . . . . Linnie
- • 0:34 - Brief right breast, undoing swimsuit top while sunbathing.
- • 0:39 - Brief topless, taking off swimsuit top while cutting Raymond's hair.
Physical Evidence (1989). . . . . Waitress

Ingersoll, Amy
Films:
Knightriders (1981) . . . . Linet
- • 0:00 - Very brief left breast, while lying down, then sitting up in woods next to Ed Harris.
Splash (1984) . . . . Reporter

Innes, Alexandra
Films:
Perfect Timing (1984) . . . . Salina
- •• 1:06 - Right breast and buns, posing for Harry.
Joshua Then and Now (1985; Canadian) . . . . Joanna

Isaacs, Susan
Films:
Deadly Passion (1985) . . . . Trixie
- •• 0:02 - Topless sitting up in bed talking to Brent Huff.
She's Out of Control (1989) . . . . Receptionist
The War of the Roses (1989) . . . . . Auctioneer's Assistant

Jackson, Glenda
Films:
The Music Lovers (1971) . . . . Nina Milyukova
Full frontal nudity after stripping in railway carriage.
Sunday, Bloody Sunday (1971) . . . . Alex Greville
Women in Love (1971) . . . . Gudrun Brangwen
(Academy Award for Best Actress.)
- ••• 1:20 - Topless taking off her blouse on the bed with Oliver Reed watching her, then making love.
- •• 1:49 - Brief left breast making love with Reed in bed again.
A Touch of Class (1972) . . . . Vicki Allessio
(Academy Award for Best Actress.)
The Nelson Affair (1973) . . . . Lady Emma Hamilton
The Romantic Englishwoman (1975; British/French)
. . . . Elizabeth
- • 0:30 - Brief full frontal nudity outside, taking robe off in front of Michael Caine.
- • 0:31 - Buns, walking back into the house.
- • 1:08 - Side view of right breast sitting at edge of poll talking to Thomas.
- • 1:45 - Very, very brief topless in bed talking with Thomas.
The Incredible Sarah (1976) . . . . Sarah Bernhardt
Nasty Habits (1977) . . . . Alexandra
The Class of Miss MacMichael (1978)
. . . . Conor MacMichael
House Calls (1978). . . . . Ann Atkinson
Stevie (1978) . . . . Stevie Smith
Lost and Found (1979). . . . . Tricia
Hopscotch (1980) . . . . Isobel von Schmidt
Return of the Soldier (1983; British) . . . . Margaret
Turtle Diary (1986; British) . . . . Naerea Duncan
Beyond Therapy (1987) . . . . Charlotte
Salome's Last Dance (1987) . . . . Herodias/Lady Alice
The Rainbow (1989) . . . . Anna Brangwen
Magazines:
Playboy (Dec 1973) . . . . Sex Stars of 1973
- • 206: Right breast in see-through blouse.
Playboy (Nov 1976) . . . . Sex in Cinema 1976
- • 146: Topless sitting by the pool in a photo from *The Romantic Englishwoman*.

Jackson, Jennifer Lyn

Video Tapes:
Playboy Video Calendar 1990 (1989)
.... September
••• 0:46 - Nude.
Magazines:
Playboy (Apr 1989) .... Playmate

Jackson, La Toya

Singer.
Member of the singing Jackson clan.
Magazines:
Playboy (Mar 1989)............. Don't Tell Michael
••• 122-133: Topless and buns.
Playboy (Dec 1989)......... Holy Sex Stars of 1989!
••• 185: Topless in bed.
Playboy (Nov 1991) .... Free at Last
••• 82-91: Topless and buns.

Jackson, Victoria

Films:
Baby Boom (1987) .... Eve, the Nanny
Casual Sex? (1988)..................... Melissa
    0:30 - Brief buns lying down with Lea Thompson at
    a nude beach.
    0:33 - Brief buns wrapping a towel around herself
    just before getting a massage. Long shot, hard to
    see.
    1:06 - Brief buns getting out of bed.
Family Business (1989) .... Christine
UHF (1989)................................ Teri
I Love You to Death (1990) .... Lacey
TV:
Saturday Night Live (1986-) .... regular

Jacobs, Emma

Films:
The Stud (1978; British) .... Alexandra
  •• 0:44 - In bra, then topless taking bra off in bedroom.
  • 0:48 - Close up of breasts making love with Tony in
   his dark apartment.
  • 1:14 - Topless in bed with Tony, yelling at him.
Lifeforce (1985)................... Crew Member

Jagger, Bianca

Ex-wife of singer Mick Jagger.
Films:
The American Success Company (1979)... Corinne
  •• 0:35 - Topless under see-through black top while sit-
   ting on bed.
The Cannonball Run (1981) .... Sheik's Sister
C.H.U.D. II (1989)............................

Jahan, Marine

Films:
Flashdance (1983)
.... uncredited Dance Double for Jennifer Beals
Streets of Fire (1984) .... "Torchie's" Dancer
    0:28 - Buns in G-string dancing in club.
    0:34 - More dancing.
  • 0:35 - Very brief right breast under body stocking,
   then almost topless under stocking when taking off
   T-shirt.
Video Tapes:
Freedanse with Marine Jahan .... herself

Janssen, Marlene

Films:
School Spirit (1985) .... Sleeping Princess
  •• 0:42 - Topless and buns, sleeping when old guy goes
   invisible to peek at her.
Video Tapes:
Playboy's Playmate Review 2 (1984) ..... Playmate
Playmates at Play (1990) .... Flights of Fancy
Magazines:
Playboy (Nov 1982) .... Playmate

Jasaé

Films:
Cave Girl (1985)............. Locker Room Student
  •• 0:05 - Topless with four other girls in the girls' locker
   room undressing, then running after Rex. She's sitting on a bench, wearing red and white panties.
Roadhouse (1989) .... Strip Joint Girl
Bad Girls from Mars (1990) .... Terry
  ••• 0:03 - Topless taking off her top.
  •• 0:05 - More topless going into dressing room.
Mob Boss (1990) .... Bar Girl
  •• 0:46 - Topless serving drinks to the guys at the table.

Jemison, Anna

See: Monticelli, Anna-Maria.

Jennings, Claudia

Films:
The Love Machine (1971) .... Darlene
Group Marriage (1972) .... Elaine
  ••• 1:02 - Topless under mosquito net in bed with Phil.
   Long scene.
Unholy Rollers (1972)..................... Karen
40 Carats (1973) .... Gabriella
Gator Bait (1973) .... Desiree
  • 0:06 - Brief left and right breasts during boat chase
   sequence.
Truck Stop Women (1974)................. Rose
  • 0:27 - Brief topless taking off blouse.
   0:48 - Brief side view of right breast in mirror.
  • 1:10 - Brief topless wrapping and unwrapping a towel around herself.

The Man Who Fell to Earth (1976; British)
. . . . uncredited Girl by the Pool
(Uncensored version.)
- • 1:42 - Topless, standing by the pool and kissing Bernie Casey.
The Great Texas Dynamite Chase (1977)
. . . . Candy Morgan
Moonshine County Express (1977) . . . . . Betty Hammer
Death Sport (1978) . . . . Deneer
Impulsion (1978) . . . .
The Best of Sex and Violence (1981). . . . . Rose
- •• 0:46 - Topless taking off her blouse in scene from *Truck Stop Women*.
Famous T & A (1982) . . . . Rose
(No longer available for purchase, check your video store for rental.)
- •• 0:26 - Topless scenes from *Single Girls* and *Truck Stop Women*.

Magazines:
Playboy (Nov 1969) . . . . Playmate
Playboy (Nov 1972) . . . . Sex in Cinema 1972
- • 166: Topless in photo from *The Unholy Rollers*.
Playboy (Dec 1972). . . . . Sex Stars of 1972
- •• 211: Topless.
Playboy (Dec 1973). . . . . Sex Stars of 1973
- •• 208: Full frontal nudity.
Playboy (Jan 1979) . . . . 25 Beautiful Years
- ••• 162: Topless.
Playboy (Sep 1979) . . . . Claudia Recaptured
- ••• 118-123: Topless.
Playboy (Jan 1989) . . . . Women of the Seventies
- ••• 217: Topless.

Jennings, Julia
Films:
Teachers (1984) . . . . The Blonde
- •• 0:05 - Brief left breast, while sitting up in bed with Nick Nolte.
Dragnet (1987). . . . . Sylvia Wiss

Jenrette, Rita
Ex-wife of former U.S. Representative John Jenrette, who was convicted in 1980 in the FBI's Abscam probe. Now using her maiden name of Rita Carpenter.
Films:
Zombie Island Massacre (1984). . . . . Sandy
- ••• 0:01 - Topless taking a shower while Joe sneaks up on her. Topless in bed with Joe.
- •• 0:10 - Brief right breast with open blouse, in boat with Joe. Left breast with him on the couch.
The Malibu Bikini Shop (1985) . . . . Aunt Ida
End of the Line (1987) . . . . Sharon
Magazines:
Playboy (Apr 1981)
. . . . The Liberation of a Congressional Wife
- ••• 116-125: Full frontal nudity.
Playboy (May 1984) . . . . Hello, Young Lovers
- •• 128-129: Right breast.

Jensen, Maren
Films:
Beyond the Reef (1981) . . . . .Diana
(Not available on video tape.)
Deadly Blessing (1981). . . . . Martha
- •• 0:27 - Topless and buns changing into a nightgown while a creepy guy watches through the window.
  0:52 - Buns, getting into the bathtub. Kind of steamy and hard to see.
- • 0:56 - Brief topless in bathtub with snake. (Notice that she gets into the tub naked, but is wearing black panties in the water).
TV:
Battlestar Galactica (1978-79) . . . . .Athena

Jillson, Joyce
Astrologer.
Films:
Slumber Party '57 (1976). . . . . .Gladys
The Happy Hooker Goes to Washington (1977)
. . . . herself
Superchick (1978) . . . . Tara B. True/Superchick
- • 0:03 - Brief upper half of right breast leaning back in bathtub.
- •• 0:06 - Topless in bed throwing cards up.
- • 0:16 - Brief topless under net on boat with Johnny.
- • 0:29 - Brief right breast several times in airplane restroom with a Marine.
  1:12 - Buns, frolicking in the ocean with Johnny. Don't see her face.
- • 1:27 - Close up of breasts (probably body double) when sweater pops open.

Johari, Azizi
Films:
Body and Soul (1981) . . . . Pussy Willow
- ••• 0:31 - Topless sitting on bed with Leon Isaac Kennedy, then left breast lying in bed.
Magazines:
Playboy (Jun 1975). . . . . Playmate

Johns, Tracy Camilla
Films:
She's Gotta Have It (1987; B&W) . . . . . . Nola Darling
- •• 0:06 - Topless lying down in bed with Jamie.
- •• 0:58 - Topless on floor with Greer.
- •• 1:15 - Topless making love with Mars.
- ••• 1:41 - Topless in bed masturbating.
Mo' Better Blues (1990) . . . . Club Patron
New Jack City (1991) . . . . Unigua
  0:40 - Buns, while dancing in red bra, panties, garter belt and stockings.
- • 0:53 - Buns and right breast in bed with Nino.

Johnson, Anne-Marie

Films:
Hollywood Shuffle (1987) .Lydia
I'm Gonna Git You Sucka (1988) . . . .
Robot Jox (1990) . . . . Athena
•• 0:35 - Buns, walking to the showers after talking to Achilles and Tex.
Miniseries:
Jackie Collins' Lucky/Chances (1990). . . . .
TV:
Double Trouble (1984-85). . . . . Aileen Lewis
In the Heat of the Night (1988). . . . . Althea Tibbs

Johnson, Deborah Nicholle

a.k.a. Debi Johnson.
Video Tapes:
Playmate Playoffs . . . . Playmate
Playmates at Play (1990) . . . . .Hardbodies
Magazines:
Playboy (Oct 1984) . . . . Playmate

Johnson, Jill

Films:
Party Favors (1987) . . . . Trixie
(Shot on video tape.)
•• 0:04 - Topless in dressing room, taking off blue dress and putting on red swimsuit.
••• 0:35 - Topless in doctors office taking off her clothes.
••• 1:03 - Topless doing strip routine in cowgirl costume. More topless after.
• 1:16 - Topless taking off swimsuit next to pool during final credits.
Wildest Dreams (1987) . . . . .Rachel Richards
•• 0:51 - Topless on bed underneath Bobby in a net.
• 1:10 - Brief topless during fight with two other women.
Party Plane (1988) . . . . .Laurie
••• 0:06 - Topless and buns changing clothes and getting into spa with her two girlfriends. (She's wearing a black swimsuit bottom.)
••• 0:11 - Topless getting out of spa.
•• 0:16 - Topless in pool after being pushed in and her swimsuit top comes off.
•• 0:20 - In bra and panties, then topless on plane doing a strip tease.
Taking Care of Business (1990) . . . . . . .Tennis Court Girl

Johnson, Michelle

Films:
Blame It on Rio (1984) . . . . Jennifer Lyons
•• 0:19 - Topless on the beach greeting Michael Caine and Joseph Bologna with Demi Moore, then brief topless in the ocean.
• 0:26 - Topless taking her clothes off for Caine on the beach. Dark, hard to see.
•• 0:27 - Topless seducing Caine. Dark, hard to see.

••• 0:56 - Full frontal nudity taking off robe and sitting on bed to take a Polaroid picture of herself.
• 0:57 - Very brief topless in the Polaroid photo showing it to Caine.
• 1:02 - Brief topless taking off her top in front of Caine while her dad rests on the sofa.
Gung Ho (1985) . . . . Heather
Beaks The Movie (1987) . . . . Vanessa
• 0:26 - Brief topless covered with bubbles after taking a bath. Don't see her face.
• 0:31 - Brief topless covered with bubbles after getting out of bathtub with Christopher Atkins. Don't see her face.
Slipping into Darkness (1987) . . . . .Carlyle
The Jigsaw Murders (1988) . . . . Kathy DaVonzo
0:51 - Posing in leotards in dance studio.
1:07 - Posing in lingerie on bed.
1:20 - In light blue dance outfit.
1:27 - Posing in blue swimsuit.
Waxwork (1988) . . . . China
Genuine Risk (1989) . . . . Girl
0:27 - In black bra in room with Henry.
0:29 - In bra in open top coming out of the bathroom.
• 0:43 - On bed in black bra and panties with Henry. Left breast peeking out of the top of her bra.
Made for Cable TV:
Tales From the Crypt: Split Second (1991; HBO)
. . . . .Liz Kelly-Dixon
••• 0:15 - Topless, offering her towel to Ted for him to dry her off.
0:19 - In bra and panties with Ted at night.
TV:
Werewolf (1987) . . . .

Johnson, Sandy

Films:
Two-Minute Warning (1976) . . . . Button's Wife
Gas Pump Girls (1978) . . . .
Halloween (1978) . . . . Judith Meyers
0:06 - Very brief topless covered with blood on floor after Michael stabs her to death.
H.O.T.S. (1979) . . . . Stephanie
•• 0:27 - Topless on balcony in red bikini bottoms.
•• 1:34 - Topless during football game during huddle with all the other girls.
Magazines:
Playboy (Jun 1974). . . . . Playmate

Johnson, Sunny

Films:
National Lampoon's Animal House (1978)
. . . . Otter's Co-Ed
Dr. Heckyl and Mr. Hype (1980). . . . . Coral Careen
Where the Buffalo Roam (1980) . . . .
The Night the Lights Went Out in Georgia (1981)
. . . . .Wendy

Flashdance (1983) . . . . Jennie Szabo
- 1:28 - Topless on stage with other strippers.

Made for TV Movies:
The Red Light Sting (1984) . . . .

Johnson, Victoria Lynn

Films:
Dressed to Kill (1980) . . . . Body Double
- •• 0:02 - Frontal nudity in the shower body doubling for Angie Dickinson.

Video Tapes:
The Girls of Penthouse (1984) . . . . Centerfold
- ••• 0:43 - Nude during photo session with Bob Guccione.

Magazines:
Penthouse (Aug 1976) . . . . Pet
91-103:
Penthouse (Nov 1977) . . . . Pet of the Year
75-90:

Joi, Marilyn

Films:
The Happy Hooker Goes to Washington (1977)
. . . . Sheila
- 0:09 - Left breast while on a couch.
- 0:47 - Brief topless during car demonstration.
- •• 1:14 - Topless in military guy's office.

Kentucky Fried Movie (1977) . . . . Cleopatra
- 1:11 - Topless in bed with Schwartz.

Ilsa, Harem Keeper of the Oil Sheiks (1978) . . . . . . Velvet
Nurse Sherri (1978). . . . .
C.O.D. (1983). . . . . Debbie Winter
- •• 1:16 - Topless during photo session.
- 1:25 - Brief topless taking off robe wearing red garter belt during dressing room scene.
  1:26 - In red bra, while talking to Albert.
  1:30 - In red bra during fashion show.

Satan's Princess (1989) . . . . Hooker

Jones, Charlene

Films:
Unholy Rollers (1972) . . . . Beverly
The Woman Hunt (1975; U.S./Philippines) . . . .
Hard to Hold (1984) . . . . Wife
Avenging Angel (1985) . . . . Hooker
Perfect (1985). . . . . Shotsy
- 0:17 - Topless stripping on stage in a club. Buns in G-string.

Jones, Grace

Films:
Conan the Destroyer (1984) . . . . Zula
Deadly Vengeance (1985) . . . . Slick's Girlfriend
Although the copyright on the movie states 1985, it looks more like the 1970's.
- ••• 0:06 - Right breast, then topless in bed with Slick.

- •• 0:13 - Left breast, when Slick sits up in bed, then full frontal nudity after he gets up.

A View to a Kill (1985) . . . . May Day
Vamp (1986) . . . . .Katrina
0:23 - Topless under wire bra, dancing on stage. Body is painted, so it's difficult to see.
Straight to Hell (1987; British) . . . . Sonya

Magazines:
Playboy (Apr 1979) . . . .
Playboy (Jan 1985). . . . .
101: Small color photo.
Playboy (Jul 1985) . . . . Amazing Grace
- 82-87: Topless band buns in B&W photos of her and Dolph Lundgren.

Jones, Josephine Jaqueline

a.k.a. J. J. Jones.
Former Miss Bahamas.

Films:
Black Venus (1983) . . . . Venus
- •• 0:05 - Topless in Jungle Room.
- ••• 0:11 - Nude, in bedroom, posing for Armand while he sketches.
- 0:14 - Topless and buns making love with Armand in bed.
- •• 0:17 - Nude, posing for Armand while he models in clay, then on the bed, kissing him.
- 0:21 - Brief nude getting dressed.
- ••• 0:38 - Nude, making love in bed with Karin Schubert.
  0:45 - Nude, talking and then making love in bed with Louise.
- •• 0:50 - Topless when Pierre brings everybody in to see her.
- •• 0:57 - Topless in silhouette while Armand fantasizes about his statue coming to life.
- ••• 1:04 - Nude.
- ••• 1:07 - Nude with the two diplomats on the bed.
- ••• 1:16 - Nude frolicking on the beach with Louise.
- ••• 1:18 - Topless in bedroom getting out of wet clothes with Louise.
- •• 1:21 - Topless in bed with Jacques.
- •• 1:24 - Full frontal nudity getting out of bed.

Love Circles Around the World (1984) . . . . . Brigid
- •• 0:18 - Topless, then nude running around her apartment chasing Jack.
- 0:30 - Topless, making love with Count Crispa in his hotel room.

Warrior Queen (1987) . . . . Chloe
- ••• 0:20 - Topless making love with Vespa.

Jones, Marilyn

Films:
Support Your Local Sheriff! (1969) . . . . Bordello Girl
The Scenic Route (1978) . . . . Lena
Meteor (1979). . . . . Stunt

The Men's Club (1986). . . . . Allison
    •• 1:21 - Topless wearing gold panties standing in bed-
        room talking to Harvey Keitel.
TV:
    Secrets of Midland Heights (1980-81) . . . . Holly Wheeler
    King's Crossing (1982) . . . . Carey Hollister

Jones, Rachel
Films:
Dracula's Widow (1988) . . . . Jenny
    Brief left breast, then brief topless lying in the bathtub,
    getting stabbed by Sylvia Kristel.
Fresh Horses (1988) . . . . Bobo

Jones, Rebunkah
Films:
Frankenstein General Hospital (1988)
    . . . . Elizabeth Rice
    •• 1:05 - Topless in the office letting Mark Blankfield ex-
        amine her back.
Hide and Go Shriek (1988) . . . .

Jourdan, Catherine
Films:
Girl on a Motorcycle (1968; French/British). . . Catherine
    a.k.a. Naked Under Leather
The Godson (1972; Italian/French) . . . . . . Hatcheck Girl
Aphrodite (1982; German/French) . . . . Valerie
    • 0:34 - Brief upper half of breasts in bathtub.

Joyner, Michelle
Films:
Grim Prairie Tales (1990) . . . . Jenny
    • 0:36 - Very brief right breast, then left breast while
        making love with Marc McClure. Kind of dark.
I Love You to Death (1990) . . . . Donna Joy

Julian, Janet
Films:
Humongous (1982; Canadian) . . . . Sandy Ralston
Fear City (1984) . . . . .Ruby
Choke Canyon (1986). . . . . .Vanessa Pilgrim
King of New York (1990). . . . . .Jennifer
    • 0:26 - Very brief left breast, standing in subway car
        kissing Christopher Walken. Don't see her face.

Kafkaloff, Kim
a.k.a Adult film actress Sheri St. Clair or Sheri St. Cloud.
Films:
Sex Appeal (1986) . . . . Stephanie
    •• 0:29 - Buns, in G-string in Tony's bachelor pad. Top-
        less dancing and on bed.
Slammer Girls (1987). Ginny
    • 0:23 - Brief topless changing clothes under table in
        the prison cafeteria.

Kaitan, Elizabeth
a.k.a. Elizabeth Cayton.
Films:
Silent Night, Deadly Night, Part 2 (1986). . . . . Jennifer
    0:58 - Most of right breast, then buns, kissing Ricky.
Slavegirls from Beyond Infinity (1987) . . . . . . Daria
    (Wearing skimpy two piece loincloth outfit during most
    of the movie.)
    ••• 0:38 - Topless undressing and jumping into bed with
        Rik.
Assault of the Killer Bimbos (1988) . . . . .Lulu
    •• 0:41 - Brief topless during desert musical sequence,
        opening her blouse, then taking off her shorts, then
        putting on a light blue dress. Don't see her face.
Friday the 13th, Part VII: The New Blood (1988)
    . . . . .Robin
    • 0:53 - Brief left breast in bed making love with a guy.
    • 0:55 - Brief topless sitting up in bed after making love
        and the sheet falls down.
    •• 1:00 - Brief topless again sitting up in bed and put-
        ting a shirt on over her head.
Nightwish (1988) . . . . Donna
    • 0:04 - In wet T-shirt, then brief topless taking it off
        during experiment. Long shot.
Twins (1988) . . . . Secretary
Dr. Alien (1989) . . . . .Waitress
    a.k.a. I Was a Teenage Sex Mutant
Under the Boardwalk (1989) . . . . .Donna
Aftershock (1990) . . . . Sabina
Lockdown (1990). . . . . Monica Taylor
Roller Blade Warriors (1990). . . . .
The Girl I Want (1991) . . . .
Vice Academy, Part 3 (1991) . . . .

Kallianiotes, Helena
Films:
The Baby Maker (1970) . . . . .Wanda
    • 1:30 - Brief topless when Barbara Hershey sees her in
        bed with Tad.
Five Easy Pieces (1970). . . . . Palm Apodaca
Kansas City Bomber (1972) . . . . .Jackie Burdette
Shanks (1974) . . . . Mata Hari
The Drowning Pool (1976). . . . . Elaine Reaves
The Passover Plot (1976) . . . . .Visionary Woman
Stay Hungry (1976) . . . . Anita

Kaminsky, Dana
Films:
Hot Resort (1984) . . . . Melanie
    •• 1:02 - Topless taking off her white dress in a boat.
Irreconcilable Differences (1984) . Woman in Dress Shop

Kane, Carol
Films:
Carnal Knowledge (1971) . . . . Jennifer
Desperate Characters (1971) . . . . Young Girl
    (Not available on video tape.)

The Last Detail (1973) . . . . Young Whore
  • 1:02 - Brief topless sitting on bed talking with Randy Quaid. Her hair is in the way, hard to see.
Dog Day Afternoon (1975) . . . . Jenny
Hester Street (1975) . . . . Gitl
Annie Hall (1977) . . . . Allison
The World's Greatest Lover (1977) . . . . Annie
The Mafu Cage (1978) . . . . Cissy
  a.k.a. My Sister, My Love
  0:08 - Very brief tip of left breast in the bathtub.
When a Stranger Calls (1979) . . . . Jill Johnson
Norman Loves Rose (1982; Australian) . . . .
Over the Brooklyn Bridge (1983). . . . . Cheryl
Racing with the Moon (1984). . . . . Annie
Transylvania 6-5000 (1985). . . . . Lupi
Jumpin' Jack Flash (1986) . . . . .Cynthia
Ishtar (1987). . . . . Carol
The Princess Bride (1987) . . . . Valerie
License to Drive (1988). Mom
Scrooged (1988). . . . . . . The Ghost of Christmas Present
Sticky Fingers (1988). . . . . Kitty
The Lemon Sisters (1990) . . . . Franki D'Angelo
My Blue Heaven (1990). . . . . Shaldeen
TV:
Taxi (1981-83) . . . . Simka Gravas
All Is Forgiven (1986) . . . . Nicolette Bingham
American Dreamer (1990). . . . . .Lillian Abernathy

Kaprisky, Valerie

Films:
  Aphrodite (1982; German/French) . . . . Pauline
  ••• 0:12 - Nude, washing herself off in front of a two-way mirror while a man on the other side watches.
  Breathless (1983) . . . . .Monica Poiccard
  0:23 - Brief side view of left breast in her apartment. Long shot, hard to see anything.
  ••• 0:47 - Topless in her apartment with Richard Gere kissing.
  •• 0:52 - Brief full frontal nudity standing in the shower when Gere opens the door, afterwards, buns in bed.
  •• 0:53 - Topless, holding up two dresses for Gere to pick from, then topless putting the black dress on.
  • 1:23 - Topless behind a movie screen with Gere. Lit with red light.
  L'Annee Des Meduses (1987; French) . . . . .Chris
  •• 0:06 - Topless pulling down swimsuit at the beach.
  ••• 0:24 - Full frontal nudity while taking off dress with older man.
  ••• 0:42 - Topless walking around the beach talking to everybody.
  • 0:46 - Topless on the beach taking a shower.
  ••• 1:02 - Topless on the beach with her mom.
  ••• 1:37 - Nude dancing on the boat for Romain.
  •• 1:42 - Topless walking from the beach to the bar.
  •• 1:43 - Topless in swimming pool.
Magazines:
  Playboy (Dec 1983) . . . . Sex Stars of 1983
  •• 209: Topless.

Kapture, Mitzi

Films:
  Private Road (1987) . . . . .Helen Milshaw
  0:50 - Wearing a white bra during a strip-spin-the-bottle game.
  •• 1:29 - Topless, making love in bed with Greg Evigan.
Angel III: The Final Chapter (1988). . . . . Molly Stewart
  Lethal Persuit (1989) . . . . Debra J.
  •• 0:32 - Topless in motel shower, then getting out. (You can see the top of her swimsuit bottom.)
  0:47 - In wet tank top talking with Warren.
Liberty & Bash (1989) .Sarah
  0:45 - Very briefly sitting up in bed in a semi-transparent yellow sheet.

Karlatos, Olga

Films:
  Wifemistress (1977; Italian)
  . . . . Miss Paula Pagano, M.D.
  •• 0:42 - Topless undressing in room with Laura Antonelli. Right breast and part of left breast lying in bed with Marcello Mastroianni.
  • 0:46 - Brief topless in bed with Mastroianni and Clara.
  Zombie (1980). Mrs. Menard
  • 0:40 - Topless and buns taking a shower.
  Once Upon a Time in America (1984)
  . . . . .Woman in the Puppet Theatre
  (Long version.)
  •• 0:11 - Right breast twice when bad guy pokes at her nipple with a gun.

Karman, Janice

Films:
Switchblade Sisters (1975) . . . .
  Slumber Party '57 (1976). . . . . Hank
  •• 1:06 - Topless, sitting watching Smitty and David make love in the stable.

Karr, Marcia

Films:
The Concrete Jungle (1982) . . . . Marcy
  Chained Heat (1983; U.S./German). . . . . .Twinks
  ••• 0:30 - Topless, getting soaped up by Edy Williams in the shower.
  • 0:37 - Brief topless, taking off her top in bed with Edy Williams at night.
  •• 0:40 - Topless in cell getting raped by the guard.
Savage Streets (1985) . . . . Stevie
  Killer Workout (1987) . . . . Rhonda
  a.k.a. Aerobi-Cide
  1:03 - Topless, opening her jacket to show the policeman her scars. Unappealing.
  1:12 - Topless in locker room, killing a guy. Covered with the special effects scars.

Kasdorf, Lenore

Films:
Dark Horse (1984). . . . . Alice
Missing in Action (1984). . . . . Ann
 • 0:41 - Very brief topless when Chuck Norris sneaks
   back in room and jumps into bed with her.
L.A. Bounty (1989) . . . . Kelly Rhodes
Made for Cable Movies:
Dinner At Eight (1989) . . . . Lucy
TV:
The Guiding Light . . . . Rita Stapleton

Katon, Rosanne

Films:
The Swinging Cheerleaders (1974) . . . . Lisa
 •• 0:25 - Topless taking off her blouse in her teacher's
   office. Half of right breast while he talks on the
   phone.
Chesty Anderson, U.S. Navy (1975) . . . . Cocoa
Fox Fire (1976) . . . .
Coach (1978). . . . . Sue
 • 0:10 - Very brief topless flashing her breasts along
   with three of her girlfriends for their four boyfriends.
Motel Hell (1980) . . . . Suzi
Body and Soul (1981) . . . . Melody
 • 0:04 - Left breast several times making love in restroom with Leon Isaac Kennedy.
Lunch Wagon (1981) . . . . Shannon
 • 0:01 - Brief topless getting dressed.
 • 0:04 - Brief side view of left breast changing tops in
   room in gas station with Pamela Bryant while a guy
   watches through key hole.
 •• 0:10 - Topless changing again in gas station.
Zapped! (1982). . . . . Donna
Bachelor Party (1984) . . . . Bridal Shower Hooker
Harem (1985; French). . . . . Judy
Magazines:
Playboy (Sep 1978). . . . . Playmate
Playboy (Jul 1981). . . . . Body and Soulmates
 •• 148: Left breast.
Playboy (Jun 1991) . . . . Funny Girls
 ••• 97: Full frontal nudity in lingerie.

Kaye, Caren

Films:
Checkmate (1973) . . . . Alex
The Lords of Flatbush (1974). . . . . .Wedding Guest
Looking for Mr. Goodbar (1977) . . . . .Rhoda
Kill Castro (1978) . . . . Tracy
 a.k.a. Cuba Crossing
Some Kind of Hero (1982) . . . . Sheila
My Tutor (1983) . . . . Terry Green
 •• 0:25 - Topless walking into swimming pool.
 •• 0:52 - Topless in the pool with Matt Lattanzi.
 ••• 0:55 - Right breast, lying in bed making love with
   Lattanzi.
Satan's Princess (1989) . . . . Leah
Teen Witch (1989) . . . . Margaret

TV:
The Betty White Show (1977-78) . . . . Tracy Garrett
Blansky's Beauties (1977) . . . . Bambi Benton
Who's Watching the Kids? (1978). . . . . . . Stacy Turner
It's Your Move (1984-85) . . . . Eileen Burton
Empire (1984) . . . . Meredith

Kaye-Mason, Clarissa

Films:
Age of Consent (1969; Australian) . . . . Meg
 • 0:05 - Brief topless, crawling on the bed to watch TV.
Adam's Women (1972; Australian) . . . . Matron
The Good Wife (1987; Australian) . . . . Mrs. Jackson
 a.k.a. The Umbrella Woman

Keaton, Camille

Films:
I Spit on Your Grave (1978) . . . . Jennifer
 (Uncut, unrated version.)
 • 0:05 - Topless undressing to go skinny dipping in
   lake.
 •• 0:23 - Left breast sticking out of bathing suit top,
   then topless after top is ripped off. Right breast several times.
 • 0:25 - Topless, getting raped by the jerks.
 • 0:27 - Buns and brief full frontal nudity, crawling
   away from the jerks.
 • 0:29 - Nude, walking through the woods.
 • 0:32 - Topless, getting raped again.
 • 0:36 - Topless and buns after rape.
 • 0:38 - Buns, walking to house.
 • 0:40 - Buns and lower frontal nudity in the house.
 • 0:41 - More topless and buns on the floor.
 • 0:45 - Nude, very dirty after all she's gone through.
 • 0:51 - Full frontal nudity while lying on the floor.
 • 0:52 - Side of left breast while in bathtub.
 •• 1:13 - Full frontal nudity seducing Matthew before
   killing him.
 ••• 1:23 - Full frontal nudity in front of mirror, then getting into bathtub. Long scene.
Raw Force (1981). . . . . .Girl in Toilet
 •• 0:28 - Topless in bathroom with a guy.
 •• 0:29 - Topless in bathroom again with the guy.
 • 0:31 - Topless in bathroom again when he rips her
   pants off.
The Concrete Jungle (1982). . . . . Rita
 • 0:41 - In black bra, then topless getting raped by
   Stone. Brief lower frontal nudity sitting up afterwards.

Keaton, Diane

Films:
Lovers and Other Strangers (1970). . . . . .Joan
The Godfather (1972) . . . . .Kay Adams
Play It Again Sam (1972) . . . . Linda Christie
Sleeper (1973). . . . . Luna
The Godfather, Part II (1974) . . . . .Kay Adams

Love and Death (1975) . . . . Sonja
Harry and Walter Go to New York (1976)
. . . . Lissa Chestnut
I Will, I Will... For Now (1976) . . . . Katie Bingham
Annie Hall (1977) . . . . Annie Hall
(Academy Award for Best Actress.)
Looking for Mr. Goodbar (1977) . . . . Theresa
•• 0:11 - Right breast in bed making love with her
teacher, Martin, then putting blouse on.
• 0:31 - Brief left breast over the shoulder when the
Doctor playfully kisses her breast.
•• 1:04 - Brief topless smoking in bed in the morning,
then more topless after Richard Gere leaves.
••• 1:17 - Topless making love with Gere after doing a lot
of cocaine.
• 1:31 - Brief topless in the bathtub when James brings
her a glass of wine.
2:00 - Getting out of bed in a bra.
•• 2:02 - Topless during rape by Tom Berenger, before
he kills her. Hard to see because of strobe lights.
Interiors (1978) . . . . Renata
Manhattan (1979; B&W) . . . . Mary Wilke
Reds (1981) . . . . Louise Bryant
Shoot the Moon (1982) . . . . Faith Dunlap
The Little Drummer Girl (1984) . . . . Charlie
Mrs. Soffel (1984) . . . . Kate Soffel
Crimes of the Heart (1986) . . . . Lenny Magrath
Baby Boom (1987) . . . . J.C. Wiatt
The Good Mother (1988) . . . . Anna
The Godfather, Part III (1990) . . . . Kay Adams
The Lemon Sisters (1990) . . . . Eloise Hamer

Keller, Marthe

Films:
And Now My Love (1974; French)
. . . . Sarah/Her Mother/Her Grandmother
Marathon Man (1976) . . . . Elsa
•• 0:42 - Topless lying on the floor after Dustin Hoffman
rolls off her.
Black Sunday (1977) . . . . Dahlia
Bobby Deerfield (1977) . . . . Lillian
The Formula (1980) . . . . Lisa
The Amateur (1982) . . . . Elisabeth
Wagner (1983; British) . . . . Mathilde Wesedonck
Red Kiss (1985; French) . . . . Bronka
Femmes de Persone (1986; French) . . . . Cecile
Dark Eyes (1987; Italian/Russian) . . . . Tina
Made for Cable Movies:
The Nightmare Years (1989) . . . . Tess
Young Catherine (1991) . . . . Johanna

Kellerman, Sally

Films:
The Boston Strangler (1968) . . . . Dianne Cluny
The April Fool's (1969) . . . . Phyllis Brubaker
Brewster McCloud (1970) . . . . Louise
Topless in fountain.

M*A*S*H (1970) . . . . . . Margaret "Hot Lips" Houlihan
• 0:42 - Very, very brief left breast opening her blouse
for Frank in her tent.
• 1:11 - Very, very brief buns and side view of right
breast during shower prank. Long shot, hard to see.
• 1:54 - Very brief topless in a slightly different angle of
the shower prank during the credits.
Last of the Red Hot Lovers (1972) . . . . . . Elaine Navazio
Reflection of Fear (1973) . . . . Anne
Rafferty and the Gold Dust Twins (1975)
. . . . Mac Beachwood
The Big Bus (1976) . . . . Sybil Crane
Welcome to L.A. (1977) . . . . Ann Goode
A Little Romance (1979) . . . . Kay King
Foxes (1980) . . . . Mary
Serial (1980) . . . . Martha
••• 0:03 - Topless sitting on the floor with a guy.
Fatal Attraction (1981; Canadian) . . . . . Michelle Keys
a.k.a. Head On
• 0:46 - Brief topless in building making out with a
guy. Dark, hard to see.
1:19 - Brief half of left breast, after struggling with a
guy.
You Can't Hurry Love (1984) . . . . Kelly Bones
Moving Violations (1985) . . . . . Judge Nedra Henderson
Back to School (1986) . . . . Diane
That's Life! (1986) . . . . Holly Parrish
Meatballs III (1987) . . . . Roxy Du Jour
Three for the Road (1987) . . . . Blanche
Made for TV Movies:
Secret Weapons (1985) . . . .
TV:
Centennial (1978-79) . . . . Lise Bockweiss
Magazines:
Playboy (Dec 1980) . . . . Sex Stars of 1980
•• 243: Topless.

Kelley, Sheila

Films:
Some Girls (1988) . . . . Irenka
• 0:13 - Topless and buns getting something at the
end of the hall while Michael watches. Long shot,
hard to see.
• 1:01 - Topless in window while Michael watches
from outside. Long shot, hard to see.
1:17 - In black slip seducing Michael after funeral.
Breaking In (1989) . . . . Carrie
Mortal Passions (1989) . . . . Adele
Staying Together (1989) . . . . Beth Harper
Where the Heart Is (1990) . . . . Sheryl
Pure Luck (1991) . . . .
Made for TV Movies:
The Fulfillment of Mary Gray (1989) . . . . Kate
TV:
L.A. Law . . . . Gwen

113

Kelly, Debra

a.k.a. Candy Moore.
Films:
Tomboy and the Champ (1961) . . . . Tommy Joe
The Night of the Grizzly (1966). . . . . Meg
Lunch Wagon (1981) . . . . Diedra
•• 0:53 - Topless under sheer robe, then topless on
couch with Arnie.
Hot Resort (1984) . . . . .Liza
Prizzi's Honor (1985). . . . . .Bride at Mexican Chapel
TV:
The Lucy Show (1962-65). . . . . Chris Carmichael

Kelly, Paula

Films:
Sweet Charity (1969). . . . . Helene
The Andromeda Strain (1971). . . . . Nurse
Cool Breeze (1972). . . . . Mrs. Harris
Top of the Heap (1972). . . . . .Singer
Trouble Man (1973) . . . . Cleo
Uptown Saturday Night (1974). . . . . .Leggy Peggy
Jo Jo Dancer, Your Life Is Calling (1986). . . . . . Satin Doll
0:26 - Doing a strip tease in the night club wearing
gold pasties and a gold G-string.
Miniseries:
Chiefs (1983) . . . . .Liz Watts
TV:
Night Court (1984). . . . . .Liz Williams
Magazines:
Playboy (Aug 1969) . . . . Sweet Paula
Debut of pubic hair in *Playboy* magazine.
Playboy (Jul 1972). . . . . .Too Much
••• 138: Topless.
••• 140-141: Topless.
Playboy (Nov 1972) . . . . Sex in Cinema 1972
•• 163: Topless in photo from *Top of the Heap.*
Playboy (Jan 1979) . . . . 25 Beautiful Years
•• 160-161: Topless strobe photo from Aug 1969.
Playboy (Jan 1989) . . . . Women of the Sixties
•• 160-161: Topless strobe photo from Aug 1969.

Kelly, Sharon

a.k.a. Adult film actress Colleen Brennan.
Films:
The Beauties and the Beast. . . . .
Nude, being carried into a cave by the beast.
Supervixens (1973). . . . . SuperCherry
Russ Meyer film.
Alice Goodbody (1974) . . . .
Gosh (1974) . . . .
Carnal Madness (1975). . . . .
Hustle (1975) . . . . Gloria Hollinger
• 0:12 - Brief topless several times getting rolled out of
freezer, dead.
• 1:03 - In pasties, dancing behind curtain when Gloria's father imagines the dancer is Gloria.
• 1:42 - In black lingerie, brief buns and side views of
breast in bed in film.

Shampoo (1975) . . . . Painted Lady
• 1:17 - Brief topless covered with tattoos all over her
body during party. Lit with strobe light.
Slammer Girls (1987) . . . . Professor
• 0:23 - Brief topless changing clothes under table in
the prison cafeteria.
•• 0:35 - Topless squishing breasts against the window
during prison visiting hours.
•• 0:37 - Topless with an inflatable male doll.

Kemp, Charlotte

See: Helmcamp, Charlotte J.

Kendall, Kerri

Video Tapes:
Playboy Video Centerfold: Kerri Kendall (1990)
. . . . Playmate
••• 0:00 - Nude throughout.
Magazines:
Playboy (Sep 1990) . . . . Playmate

Kennedy, Sheila

Films:
The First Turn-On! (1983) . . . . Dreamgirl
• 0:52 - In red two piece swimsuit, then topless when
the top falls down during Danny's daydream.
• 0:59 - Right breast in bed with Danny.
Spring Break (1983; Canadian). . . . . Carla
•• 0:49 - Topless during wet T-shirt contest.
Ellie (1984) . . . . Ellie May
•• 0:29 - Full frontal nudity posing for Billy while he
takes pictures of her just before he falls over a cliff.
0:38 - In white bra and panties, in barn loft with
Frank.
0:58 - In white bra and panties struggling to get
away from Edward Albert.
• 1:16 - In bra and panties taking off dress with Art.
Topless taking off bra and throwing them on antlers.
Brief topless many times while frolicking around.
Magazines:
Penthouse (Dec 1981). . . . . .Pet
97-133:
Penthouse (Dec 1983). . . . . Pet of the Year
115-129:
Penthouse (Oct 1987). . . . . Sheila Revisited
52-61:

Kensit, Patsy

Singer in the group *Eighth Wonder.*
Films:
Oh, Alfie! (1975; British). . . . . Penny
a.k.a. Alfie Darling
Hanover Street (1979) . . . . .Sarah Sallinger
Absolute Beginners (1986; British) . . . . Suzette
Chicago Joe and the Showgirl (1989; British)
. . . . Joyce Cook

Lethal Weapon 2 (1989) . . . . Rika Van Den Haas
  •• 1:15 - Right breast lying in bed with Mel Gibson.
  •• 1:19 - Topless in bed with Gibson.
Blue Tornado (1990) . . . .
Bullseyel (1991) . . . .

Kenton, Linda
Films:
Hot Resort (1984) . . . . Mrs. Geraldine Miller
  • 0:11 - Very brief right breast, while in back of car with
    a guy.
  • 0:16 - Right breast, while passed out in closet with a
    bunch of guys.
  • 0:24 - Brief upper half of right breast, while on boat
    with a guy.
  • 0:46 - Brief topless in Volkswagen.
  • 0:51 - Brief topless in bathtub with Bronson Pinchot.
  • 1:24 - Brief topless making love on a table while cov-
    ered with food.
Magazines:
Penthouse (May 1983) . . . . Pet

Kernohan, Roxanne
Films:
Angel III: The Final Chapter (1988) . . . . . . White Hooker
Critters 2: The Main Course (1988) . . . . Lee
  •• 0:37 - Brief topless after transforming from an alien
    into a Playboy Playmate.
Fatal Pulse (1988) . . . .
Not of This Earth (1988) . . . . Lead Hooker
  ••• 0:41 - Topless in cellar with Paul just before getting
    killed with two other hookers. Wearing a blue top.
Phoenix the Warrior (1988) . . . . Meda
Tango & Cash (1989) . . . . .Dressing Room Girl
  • 1:06 - Brief topless in dressing room with three other
    girls. She's the second one in the middle.
Scream Queen Hot Tub Party (1991) . . . .
Magazines:
Playboy (Jul 1989) . . . . B-Movie Bimbos
  ••• 136: Topless straddling a car wearing an open bath-
    Ing sult.

Kerr, Deborah
Films:
The Gypsy Moths (1969) . . . . .Elizabeth Brandon
(Not available on video tape.)

Kerr, E. Katherine
Films:
Reuben, Reuben (1983) . . . . Lucille Haxby
  • 0:51 - Brief left breast in bedroom, undressing in
    front of Tom Conti.
Silkwood (1984) . . . . Gilda Schultz
Children of a Lesser God (1986) . . . . Mary Lee Ochs

Kerridge, Linda
Films:
Fade to Black (1980) . . . . Marilyn
  • 0:44 - Topless in the shower.
Strangers Kiss (1984) . . . . Shirley
Surf II (1984) . . . . Sparkle
Down Twisted (1987) . . . . Soames
Alien from L.A. (1988) . . . . Roeyis Freki/Auntie Pearl
Magazines:
Playboy (Dec 1980) . . . . Double Take
  ••• 218-227: Full frontal nudity.

Kersh, Kathy
Films:
Americanization of Emily (1964) . . . .
Gemini Affair (1974) . . . . Jessica
    0:10 - In white bra and black panties changing in
      front of Marta Kristen.
  •• 0:11 - Nude getting into bed with Kristen.
  • 0:12 - Brief topless turning over onto her stomach in
    bed.
  •• 0:17 - Nude, standing up in bed and jumping off.
  ••• 0:57 - Nude in bed with Kristen.
  •• 1:04 - Left breast sitting up in bed after Kristen
    leaves.

Kerwin, Maureen
Films:
The Destructors (1974; British) . . . . Lucianne
Laura (1979) . . . . Martine
  a.k.a. Shattered Innocence
  • 0:03 - Brief full frontal nudity getting out of bed and
    putting white bathrobe on.

Kesner, Jillian
Films:
The Student Body (1975) . . . . Carrie Rafferty
  •• 0:29 - Left breast, making out with Carter in the car.
Firecracker (1981) . . . . Susanne Carter
Raw Force (1981) . . . . .Cookie Winchell
Moon In Scorpio (1987) . . . . .Claire
  •• 0:39 - Topless sitting on deck of boat with bathing
    suit top down.
Beverly Hills Vamp (1989) . . . . Claudia
    0:06 - In white lingerie riding a guy like a horse.
    0:33 - In white slip with Brock.
    0:42 - Almost topless in bed with Brock. Too dark to
      see anything.
    1:09 - In white nightgown attacking Russell in bed
      with Debra Lamb and Michelle Bauer.
    1:17 - In white nightgown, getting killed as a vam-
      pire by Kyle.
Naked Force (1991) . . . .
TV:
Co-ed Fever (1979) . . . . Melba

Kidder, Margot

Films:
Gaily Gaily (1969). . . . . Adeline
Quackser Fortune has a Cousin in the Bronx
(1970; Irish) . . . . Zazel
•• 1:03 - Topless undressing on a chair, then brief right,
then breasts when Gene Wilder kisses her.
• 1:05 - Side view of left breast, then buns, getting out
of bed.
Sisters (1973) . . . . Danielle Breton
• 0:11 - Very brief left breast, undressing while walking
down hallway. Long shot.
• 0:14 - Topless opening her robe on couch for her
new boyfriend. Shadows make it hard to see.
Gravey Train (1974). . . . . Margie
The Reincarnation of Peter Proud (1975)
. . . . Marcia Curtis
• 1:29 - Brief topless sitting in bathtub masturbating
while remembering getting raped by husband.
Superman (1978) . . . . Lois Lane
The Amityville Horror (1979). . . . . Kathleen Lutz
Superman II (1980). . . . . Lois Lane
Willie and Phil (1980) . . . . Jeanette Sutherland
Heartaches (1981; Canadian) . . . . Rita Harris
Topless.
Some Kind of Hero (1982) . . . . Toni
0:52 - In white corset making love with Richard Pryor
on the floor.
0:56 - In bra with robe standing outside the door
talking to Pryor.
Trenchcoat (1983). . . . . Mickey Raymond
Little Treasure (1985) . . . . Margo
0:53 - Stripping in bar, doesn't show anything.
1:13 - Nude dancing by swimming pool. Long shot,
don't see anything.
Keeping Track (1988) . . . . Mickey Tremaine
Made for Cable Movies:
Glitter Dome (1985; HBO) . . . . Willie
1:04 - Topless on balcony after making love with
James Garner the night before. Long shot, hard to
see anything.
Made for Cable TV:
The Hitchhiker: Night Shift . . . . Jane Reynolds
(Available on *The Hitchhiker, Volume 2*.)
• 0:13 - In a white corset, then brief left breast over the
shoulder shot.
TV:
Nichols (1971-72). . . . . Ruth
Magazines:
Playboy (Mar 1975). . . . . Margot
••• 86-93: Full frontal nudity.

Kidman, Nicole

Wife of actor Tom Cruise.
Films:
BMX Bandits (1984; Australian). . . . . Judy
Dead Calm (1989) . . . . Rae Ingram
• 0:59 - Brief buns and topless with the attacker.

Days of Thunder (1990) . . . . Dr. Claire Lewicki
Made for Cable Movies:
Bangkok Hilton (1990) . . . .

Kiel, Sue

Films:
Red Heat (1987; U.S./German) . . . . Hedda
• 0:56 - Brief topless in shower room scene (third girl
behind Linda Blair). Long shot, hard to see.
Straight to Hell (1987; British) . . . . Leticia
Survivor (1987) . . . . The Woman
••• 0:33 - Right breast, then topless and buns making
love with Survivor in hammock. Long scene.

Kiger, Susan Lynn

Adult Films:
Deadly Love (1974) . . . .
a.k.a. Hot Nasties
First Playboy Playmate to do an adult film *before* she became a Playmate. Nude with snake and nude performing fellatio.
Films:
H.O.T.S. (1979). . . . . Honey Shayne
• 0:00 - Topless in shower room with the other girls.
•• 0:33 - Topless in pool making love with Doug.
• 1:33 - Topless in football game.
Seven (1979) . . . . Jennie
Angels Brigade (1980) . . . .
The Happy Hooker Goes Hollywood (1980) . . Susie
• 0:42 - Topless, singing "Happy Birthday" to a guy
tied up on the bed.
••• 0:43 - Topless, wearing a red garter belt playing pool
with K.C. Winkler.
The Return (1980) . . . .
Death Screams (1982) . . . .
Magazines:
Playboy (Jan 1977). . . . . Playmate
Playboy (Dec 1979) . . . . Sex Stars of 1979
••• 258: Full frontal nudity.

King, Tracey Ann

Films:
Hammer (1972) . . . . The Black Magic Woman
The Naughty Stewardesses (1978) . . . . Barbara
•• 0:56 - Topless dancing by the pool in front of everybody.

Kingsley, Danitza

Films:
You Can't Hurry Love (1984) . . . . Tracey
Amazons (1986) . . . . Tshingi
••• 0:30 - Topless and buns quite a few times with Col-
ungo out of and in bed.
Jack's Back (1987) . . . . Denise Johnson
South of Reno (1987). Louise
Verne Miller (1988) . . . . German Drink Girl

Kinmont, Kathleen

Wife of actor Lorenzo Lamas.

Films:

Hardbodies (1984) . . . . Pretty Skater

Fraternity Vacation (1985) . . . . Marianne

••• 0:16 - Topless and buns taking off her swimsuit in bedroom with two guys.

Winners Take All (1987) . . . . Party Girl #5

Halloween 4: The Return of Michael Meyers (1988) Kelly

0:51 - In bra and panties in front of the fireplace with Brady.

Phoenix the Warrior (1988) . . . . Phoenix

Bride of Re-Animator (1989) . . . . . . Gloria/The Bride

• 0:58 - Brief topless several times with her top pulled down to defibrillate her heart.

1:17 - Topless under gauze. Her body has gruesome looking special effects appliances all over it.

1:22 - More topless under gauze.

1:24 - More topless. Pretty unappealing.

1:27 - Brief buns, when turning around after ripping out her own heart.

Midnight (1989) . . . . .Party

Rush Week (1989) . . . . Julie Ann McGuffin

• 0:07 - Brief topless several times during modeling session. Buns in G-string getting dressed. Long shot.

SnakeEater II: The Drug Buster (1990)

. . . . Detective Lisa Forester

The Art of Dying (1991) . . . . .Holly

• 0:28 - Brief left breast, making love with Wings Hauser in the kitchen. Brief topless when he pours milk on her.

•• 0:33 - Topless in bathtub with Hauser. Intercut with Janet getting stabbed.

Night of the Warrior (1991) . . . .

Magazines:

Playboy (Nov 1991) . . . . Sex in Cinema 1991

• 144: Topless under sheer dress, but has the gruesome looking special effects on. From *Bride of Re-Animator.*

Kinnaman, Melanie

Films:

Friday the 13th, Part V—A New Beginning (1985)

. . . . .Pam Roberts

1:08 - In wet white blouse coming back into the house from the rain.

Thunder Alley (1985) . . . . .Star

• 0:52 - Brief topless under water in pool talking to a guy.

• 1:14 - Topless and buns making love on bed and getting out.

Kinski, Nastassja

Films:

To the Devil, a Daughter (1976) . . . .Catherine Beddows

Full frontal nudity at the end of the film.

Virgin Campus (1976). . . . .

Stay As You Are (1978) . . . .

For Your Love Only (1979) . . . .

Tess (1979; French/British) . . . . Tess Durbeyfield

• 0:47 - Brief left breast, opening blouse in field to feed her baby.

Boarding School (1980; Italian) . . . . Deborah

• 1:32 - Topless making love with a guy.

Cat People (1982) . . . . .Irena Gollier

••• 1:03 - Nude at night, walking around outside chasing a rabbit.

•• 1:35 - Topless taking off blouse, walking up the stairs and getting into bed.

• 1:37 - Brief right breast, lying in bed with John Heard.

•• 1:38 - Topless getting out of bed and walking to the bathroom.

•• 1:40 - Brief buns, getting back into bed. Topless in bed.

•• 1:47 - Full frontal nudity, walking around in the cabin at night.

• 1:49 - Topless, tied to the bed by Heard.

One from the Heart (1982) . . . . .Leila

• 1:13 - Brief topless in open blouse when she leans forward after walking on a ball.

Exposed (1983) . . . . .Elizabeth Carlson

•• 0:54 - Topless in bed with Rudolf Nureyev.

The Moon in the Gutter (1983; French/Italian). . .Loretta

The Hotel New Hampshire (1984) . . . . . . Susie the Bear

Paris, Texas (1984; French/German). . . . . .Jane

Unfaithfully Yours (1984) . . . . .Daniella Eastman

• 0:37 - Topless and buns in the shower.

Harem (1985; French) . . . . .Diane

• 0:14 - Topless getting into swimming pool.

•• 1:04 - Topless in motel room with Ben Kingsley.

Maria's Lovers (1985) . . . . Maria Bosic

0:59 - In a black bra.

• 1:12 - Brief right breast, while looking at herself in the mirror.

Revolution (1986) . . . . Daisy McConnahay

Magdelena (1988) . . . . Magdalena

Torrents of Spring (1990). . . . . .Maria

Kirkland, Sally

Films:

Going Home (1971). . . . . Ann Graham

The Sting (1973) . . . . .Crystal

The Way We Were (1973). . . . . Pony Dunbar

Big Bad Mama (1974). . . . . Barney's Woman

•• 0:13 - Topless and buns waiting for Barney then throwing shoe at Billy Jean.

Crazy Mama (1975). .Ella Mae

A Star is Born (1976) . . . . Photographer

Tracks (1977) . . . . uncredited

Private Benjamin (1980). . . . . .Helga

Double Exposure (1983). . . . . Hooker

•• 0:26 - Topless in alley getting killed.

Fatal Games (1984) . . . . Diane Paine

Love Letters (1984) . . . . Hippie

Anna (1987) . . . . Anna

•• 0:28 - Topless in the bathtub talking to Daniel.

Talking Walls (1987) . . . . Hooker
Cold Feet (1989) . . . . Maureen Linoleum
(In tight fitting spandex dresses during most of the film.)
  • 0:56 - In black bra and panties taking off her dress in
    bedroom with Keith Carradine. Brief right breast
    pulling bra down.
  • 0:58 - Brief side view of right breast sitting up in bed
    talking to Carradine.
High Stakes (1989). . . . . Melanie "Bambi" Rose
  • 0:01 - In two piece costume, doing a strip tease rou-
    tine on stage. Buns in G-string, then very, very brief
    topless flashing her breasts.
    1:11 - In black bra cutting her hair in front of a mir-
    ror.
Paint It Black (1989) . . . . Marion Easton
    0:05 - Most of left breast, while sitting in bed talking
    to Rick Rossovich.
Best of the Best (1990) . . . .
Revenge (1990) . . . . Rock Star
Bullseye! (1991) . . . .
Made for TV Movies:
The Haunted (1991) . . . . .Janet

Kitaen, Tawny

Wife of singer David Coverdale of the rock group *White-snake.*
Films:
Bachelor Party (1984) . . . . Debbie Thompson
**The Perils of Gwendoline in the Land of the Yik
Yak** (1984; French) . . . . Gwendoline
  ••• 0:36 - Topless in the rain in the forest, taking off her
    top. More topless with Willard.
  •• 0:52 - Buns, walking around with Willard in cos-
    tumes.
  • 0:55 - Buns, falling into jail cell, then in jail cell in cos-
    tume.
  • 0:57 - Buns, rescuing Beth in torture chamber.
  •• 1:01 - Topless in S&M costume in front of mirrors.
  • 1:04 - Brief topless escaping from chains.
  • 1:07 - Buns, in costume while riding chariot and next
    to wall.
  • 1:09 - Buns, standing up.
  •• 1:11 - Buns, in costume during fight. Wearing green
    ribbon.
  •• 1:18 - Topless making love with Willard.
Crystal Heart (1987) . . . . Alley Daniels
  •• 0:46 - Topless and buns "making love" with Lee Cur-
    reri through the glass.
  •• 0:50 - Nude, crashing through glass shower door,
    covered with blood during her nightmare.
  • 1:14 - Brief topless making love with Curreri in and
    falling out of bed.
Happy Hour (1987). . . . . Misty Roberts
Instant Justice (1987) .Virginia
Witchboard (1987) . . . . Linda
  • 1:26 - Topless, nude, brief full frontal nudity stuck in
    the shower and breaking the glass doors to get out.
Made for Cable Movies:
The Glory Years (1987; HBO) . . . .

TV:
Santa Barbara (1989-90) . . . . Lisa
Video Tapes:
Whitesnake—Trilogy (1987) . . . . The Girl
  • 0:10 - (2 min., 17 sec. into "Here I Go Again.") Very
    brief right breast, leaning out of car.
    0:18 - Most of her buns, while kissing David Cover-
    dale in out-take from "Is This Love."

Klenck, Margaret

Films:
Hard Choices (1986) . . . . .Laura
  •• 1:10 - Left breast, then topless making love with
    Bobby. Nice close up shot.
  • 1:11 - Very brief half of left breast and lower frontal
    nudity getting back into bed. Long shot.
Loose Cannons (1990) . . . . Eva Braun
TV:
One Life to Live .Edwina Lewis

Koizumi, Ariane

See: Ariane.

Kong, Venice

Films:
Beverly Hills Cop II (1987) . . . . Playmate
Video Tapes:
Playboy's Wet and Wild (1989). . . . .
Playboy Video Centerfold: Kerri Kendall (1990)
  . . . . Playmate
  ••• 0:41 - Full frontal nudity.
Playmates at Play (1990) . . . . Making Waves
Magazines:
Playboy (Sep 1985) . . . . Playmate

Konopski, Sharry

Video Tapes:
Playboy Video Calendar 1989 (1988). . . . . April
  ••• 0:13 - Nude.
Playboy's Wet and Wild (1989). . . . .
Magazines:
Playboy (Aug 1987) . . . . Playmate

Koscina, Sylva

Films:
Hercules (1959; Italian) . . . . Iole
The Secret War of Harry Frigg (1969)
  . . . . Countess di Montefiore
The Slasher (1975) . . . . Barbara
  •• 0:17 - Left breast lying down getting a massage.
  •• 1:18 - Topless undressing and putting a robe on at
    her lover's house. Left breast after getting stabbed.

Sex on the Run (1979; German/French/Italian)
. . . . Jelsamina
a.k.a. Some Like It Cool
a.k.a. Casanova and Co.
- ••• 0:28 - Topless and brief buns dropping her top for Tony Curtis, then walking around with the "other" Tony Curtis.
- •• 1:20 - Topless talking to her husband.

Kossack, Christine

Films:
Three Men and a Baby (1987). . . . . . .One of Jack's Girls
The Brain (1988). . . . . Vivian
- •• 0:24 - Topless on monitor, then topless in person during Jim's fantasy.
- •• 1:11 - Topless again in the basement during Jim's hallucination.

Kotero, Patty "Apollonia"

See: Apollonia.

Kozak, Harley Jane

Films:
House on Sorority Row (1983) . . . . Diane
Clean and Sober (1988) . . . . Ralston Receptionist
When Harry Met Sally... (1989). . . . . Helen
Aracnophobia (1990) . . . . Molly Jennings
Side Out (1990). . . . . .Kate Jacobs
- • 0:53 - Brief left breast, the out of focus left breast in bed with Peter Horton.
TV:
Santa Barbara . . . . Mary Duvall

Kozak, Heidi

Films:
Slumber Party Massacre II (1987) . . . . Sally
Friday the 13th, Part VII: The New Blood (1988)
. . . . Sandra
- • 0:36 - Buns taking off clothes to go skinny dipping. Brief topless under water just before getting killed by Jason.

Krige, Alice

Films:
Chariots of Fire (1981) . . . . Sybil Gordon
Ghost Story (1981). . . . . Alma/Eva
- • 0:41 - Brief topless making love in bedroom with Craig Wasson.
- •• 0:44 - Topless in bathtub with Wasson.
- •• 0:46 - Topless sitting up in bed.
- ••• 0:49 - Buns, then topless standing on balcony turning and walking to bedroom talking to Wasson.
King David (1985) . . . . .Bathsheba
- •• 1:16 - Full frontal nudity getting a bath outside at dusk while Richard Gere watches.
Barfly (1987). . . . . Tully

Haunted Summer (1988) . . . . Mary Godwin
See You in the Morning (1989) . . . . Beth Goodwin
Made for Cable Movies:
Baja Oklahoma (1988; HBO) . . . . .Patsy Cline

Kriss, Katherine

Films:
American Flyers (1985) .Vera
Hot Chili (1985). . . . . .Allison Baxter
- ••• 0:56 - Topless getting out of the pool talking to Ricky.
- • 1:09 - Buns and side view of left breast lying down and kissing Ricky.
Student Confidential (1987). . . . . Elaine's Friend

Kristel, Sylvia

Films:
Emmanuelle (1974). . . . . .Emmanuelle
- • 0:11 - Topless making love with her husband under a mosquito net in bed.
- ••• 0:26 - Topless making love on an airplane.
- •• 0:35 - Topless with blonde woman in squash court after playing squash.
- ••• 1:03 - Topless after taking off clothes in locker room with another woman to get ready for squash.
Julia (1974; German) . . . . .Julia
0:23 - Brief topless in the lake.
- •• 0:25 - Topless on deck in the lake.
- • 0:28 - Brief topless changing clothes at night. Long shot.
- •• 0:34 - Topless on boat with two boys.
- •• 0:42 - Topless taking off her towel.
- • 1:12 - Topless on tennis court with Patrick.
Emmanuelle, The Joys of a Woman (1975)
. . . . .Emmanuelle
- • 0:18 - Topless making love with her husband in bedroom.
- •• 0:22 - Topless, then full frontal nudity, undressing in bedroom, then making love with her husband.
- ••• 0:32 - Topless with acupuncture needles stuck in her. More topless masturbating while fantasizing about Christopher.
- • 0:53 - Right breast, while making love with polo player in locker room.
- ••• 0:58 - Nude, getting massaged by another woman.
- ••• 1:14 - Right breast in bedroom in open dress, then topless with Jean in bed. Flashback of her with three guys in a bordello.
Goodbye Emmanuelle (1977) . . . . .Emmanuelle
- •• 0:03 - Full frontal nudity in bath and getting out.
- •• 0:04 - Full frontal nudity taking off dress.
- ••• 0:06 - Full frontal nudity in bed with Angelique.
- •• 0:26 - Topless with photographer in old house.
0:42 - Brief side view of right breast, in bed with Jean.
- ••• 1:03 - Full frontal nudity on beach with movie director.
- •• 1:06 - Full frontal nudity lying on beach sleeping.
- •• 1:28 - Side view of left breast lying on beach with Gregory while dreaming.

Airport '79: The Concorde (1979) . . . . Isabelle
Tigers in Lipstick (1979) . . . . The Girl
   0:04 - Topless in photograph on the sand.
   0:06 - Braless in sheer nightgown lying in bed.
  •• 0:09 - Topless lying in bed with The Arab.
  • 0:16 - Lying in bed in red lingerie, then left breast for
     awhile.
Lady Chatterley's Lover (1981; French/British)
. . . . Constance Chatterley
  •• 0:25 - Nude in front of mirror.
  • 0:59 - Brief topless with the Gardener.
  • 1:04 - Brief topless.
  ••• 1:16 - Nude in bedroom with the Gardener.
Private Lessons (1981). . . . . Mallow
  • 0:20 - Very brief topless sitting up next to the pool
     when the sprinklers go on.
  •• 0:24 - Topless and buns, stripping for Billy. Some
     shots might be a body double.
  •• 0:51 - Topless in bed when she "dies" with Howard
     Hessman.
  • 1:28 - Topless making love with Billy. Some shots
     might be a body double.
Private School (1983) . . . . Ms. Copuletta
   0:57 - In wet white dress after falling in the pool.
Emmanuelle IV (1984) . . . . Sylvia
  •• 0:00 - Topless in photos during opening credits.
The Big Bet (1985) . . . . Michelle
  • 0:07 - Left breast in open nightgown while Chris tries
     to fix her sink.
  •• 0:20 - Topless dressing while Chris watches through
     binoculars.
  •• 0:28 - Topless undressing while Chris watches
     through binoculars.
  ••• 0:40 - Topless getting out of the shower and drying
     herself off.
  • 1:00 - Topless getting into bed while Chris watches
     through binoculars.
  ••• 1:13 - Topless in bedroom with Chris, then making
     love.
Mata Hari (1985) . . . . Mata Hari
  ••• 0:11 - Topless making love with a guy on a train.
  • 0:31 - Topless standing by window after making love
     with the soldier.
  • 0:35 - Topless making love in empty house by the
     fireplace.
  •• 0:52 - Topless masturbating in bed wearing black
     stockings.
  •• 1:02 - Topless having a sword fight with another top-
     less woman.
  •• 1:03 - Topless in bed smoking opium and making
     love with two women.
Red Heat (1987; U.S./German) . . . . Sofia
   0:23 - In red lingerie.
  •• 0:56 - Topless in shower room scene.
  • 1:01 - Brief topless raping Linda Blair.
Dracula's Widow (1988) . . . . .Vanessa
Hot Blood (1989; Spanish) . . . . Sylvia
  • 0:44 - Buns, getting molested by Dom Luis.

Magazines:
  Playboy (Dec 1976) . . . . .Sex Stars of 1976
  •• 187: Topless drinking from champagne bottle.
  Playboy (Dec 1977) . . . . .Sex Stars of 1977
  •• 212: Topless with Jeff Bridges.
  Playboy (Dec 1984) . . . . .Sex Stars of 1984
  • 205: Left breast, lying on chair.

Kristen, Marta

Films:
  Terminal Island (1973) . . . . .Lee Phillips
  Gemini Affair (1974). .Julie
  ••• 0:32 - Topless wearing beige panties talking with Jes-
     sica in the bathroom.
  • 0:56 - Very, very brief left breast and lower frontal nu-
     dity standing next to bed with a guy. Very brief left
     breast in bed with him.
  ••• 0:59 - Topless and buns making love in bed with Jes-
     sica. Wowzers!
  Once (1974) . . . . Humanity
  (Not available on video tape.)
  Battle Beyond the Stars (1980). . . . . Lux
TV:
  Lost in Space (1965-68) . . . . .Judy Robinson

Lahaie, Brigitte

Films:
  Friendly Favors (1983) .Greta
  a.k.a. Six Swedes on a Pump
  Private Screenings.
  •• 0:02 - Full frontal nudity riding a guy in bed. (She's
     wearing a necklace.)
  ••• 0:39 - Full frontal nudity on "exercise bike."
  ••• 0:46 - Full frontal nudity taking off clothes and run-
     ning outside with the other girls. Nice slow motion
     shots.
  •• 0:53 - Topless, making love with Kerstin.
  ••• 1:01 - Full frontal nudity in room with the Italian.
  ••• 1:15 - Full frontal nudity in room with guy from the
     band.
  Henry & June (1990) . . . . Harry's Whore
  •• 0:23 - Brief buns and topless under sheer white dress
     going up stairs with Fred Ward.
  •• 1:22 - Topless in sheer white dress again. Nude un-
     der dress walking up stairs.
  ••• 1:23 - Topless and buns making love with another
     woman while Anais and Hugo watch.
  • 1:31 - Topless in bed with Anais. Intercut with Uma
     Thurman, so hard to tell who is who.

Laine, Karen

Films:
  Pretty in Pink (1986) . . . . .Girl at Prom
Made for Cable Movies:
  Baja Oklahoma (1988; HBO). . . . . .Girl at Drive-In
  • 0:04 - Left breast, in truck with a jerk guy. Dark, hard
     to see anything.

Lamarr, Hedy

First instance of celebrity nudity in film.

Films:

Ecstasy (1932; B&W) . . . . The Wife
- 0:25 - Brief topless starting to run after a horse in a field.
- 0:26 - Long shot running through the woods, side view naked, then brief topless hiding behind a tree.

Ziegfield Girl (1941; B&W) . . . . Sandra Kolter
Dishonored Lady (1947; B&W) . . . . . Madeleine Damien
Samson and Delilah (1949; B&W) . . . . Delilah

Lamb, Debra

Films:

Stripped to Kill (1987) . . . . Amateur Dancer
B.O.R.N. (1988) . . . . Sue
Deathrow Game Show (1988) . . . . . Shanna Shallow
••• 0:23 - Topless dancing in white G-string and garter belt during the show.
Stripped to Kill II (1988) . . . . Mantra
•• 0:04 - Topless during strip dance routine.
••• 0:42 - Topless in black lingerie during strip dance routine.
W. B., Blue and the Bean (1988) . . . . . . .Motel Clerk
a.k.a. Bail Out
- 0:42 - Full frontal nudity opening door in motel to talk to David Hasselhoff.
Warlords (1988) . . . . Harem Girl
••• 0:14 - Topless, getting her blouse ripped off by a bad guy, then kidnapped.
••• 0:17 - Topless shackled to another girl.
Beverly Hills Vamp (1989) . . . . .Jessica
0:33 - In black slip, with Russell.
••• 0:36 - Topless and buns in red G-string posing for Russell while he photographs her.
••• 0:41 - More topless posing on bed.
1:09 - In white nightgown attacking Russell in bed with Michelle Bauer and Jillian Kesner.
1:19 - In white nightgown, getting killed as a vampire by Kyle.
Out Cold (1989) . . . . Panetti's Dancer
- 1:04 - Brief topless dancer in G-string on stage. Don't see her face.
Satan's Princess (1989) . . . . Fire Eater/Dancer
•• 0:23 - Topless in G-string doing a fire dance in club.
- 0:25 - Topless, doing more dancing. Long shot.
Invisible Maniac (1990) . . . . .Betty
- 0:21 - Buns and very brief side view of right breast in the shower with the other girls.
••• 0:43 - In bra, then topless and buns standing on the left in the locker room with the other girls.
- 0:44 - Buns and brief topless in the shower with the other girls.
•• 0:56 - In bra, then topless getting killed by Dr. Smith.
- 0:58 - Brief topless, dead, discovered by April and Joan.

Mob Boss (1990). . . . . Janise
Evil Spirits (1991) . . . .

Made for Cable TV:
Dream On: And Your Little Dog, Too (1991; HBO)
. . . . Snake Lady
Magazines:
Playboy (Jul 1991) . . . . Grapevine
••• 174: In boots, lying on the floor. B&W.

Landon, Laurene

Girlfriend of Christian Brando (Marlon Brando's son).

Films:

...All the Marbles (1981) .Molly
a.k.a. The California Dolls
I, the Jury (1982) . . . . .Velda
Hundra (1983) . . . . Hundra
- 0:29 - Very brief topless, several times, riding her horse in the surf. Partial buns. Blurry.
Yellow Hair and the Fortress of Gold (1984)
. . . . Yellow Hair
America 3000 (1986) . . . . Vena
Armed Response (1986) . . . . Deborah
It's Alive III: Island of the Alive (1988) . . . . .Sally
Maniac Cop (1988) . . . . Theresa
Wicked Stepmother (1989) . . . . Vanilla
Maniac Cop 2 (1990) . . . . Teresa Mallory

Landry, Karen

Films:

The Personals (1982) . . . . Adrienne
Patti Rocks (1988). . . . . .Patti
0:48 - Buns, walking from bathroom to bedroom and shutting the door. Long shot.
- 0:48 - Very brief right breast in shower with Billy.
•• 1:04 - Topless in bed with Eddie while Billy is out in the living room.

Landry, Tamara

Films:

R.S.V.P. (1984) . . . . Vicky
•• 0:43 - Topless sitting in van taking top off.
•• 0:48 - Topless making love in the van with two guys.
Tango & Cash (1989) . . . . Girl in Bar
Mob Boss (1990) . . . .

Lands, Wendy

Films:

One Night Only (1984; Canadian) . . . . .Jane
•• 0:36 - Topless taking a bath while Jamie watches through keyhole.
•• 0:38 - Brief left breast in open robe.
- 1:15 - Brief topless in bed with policeman.
Busted Up (1986). . . . . .Drayton's Date

Lane, Diane

Wife of actor Christopher Lambert.

Films:

A Little Romance (1979) . . . . Lauren
Touched by Love (1980) . . . . Karen
Ladies and Gentlemen, The Fabulous Stains
(1982) . . . . .Corinne Burns
(Not available on video tape.)
Six Pack (1982) . . . . Breezy
The Outsiders (1983) . . . . Cherry Valance
Rumble Fish (1983; B&W). . . . . .Patty
The Cotton Club (1984) . . . . .Vera Cicero
Streets of Fire (1984). . . . . Ellen Aim
The Big Town (1987) . . . . Lorry Dane
 0:51 - Doing a strip routine in the club wearing a G-
 string and pasties while Matt Dillon watches.
••• 1:17 - Topless making love on bed with Dillon.
 1:27 - Brief left breast wearing pasties walking into
 dressing room while Dillon plays craps.
Lady Beware (1987). . . . . Katya Yarno
 0:10 - Walking around in her apartment in a red silk
 teddy getting ready for bed.
 0:14 - Lying down in white semi-transparent pajamas after fantasizing.
 0:24 - In black bra in apartment.
••• 0:46 - Topless in her apartment and in bed making
 love with Mack.
•• 0:52 - Brief topless during Jack's flashback when he is
 in the store.
•• 0:59 - Brief side view topless in bed with Mack again
 during another of Jack's flashbacks.
 • 1:02 - Very brief topless in bed with Mack.
 1:06 - Brief topless lying in bed behind thin curtain
 in another of Jack's flashbacks.
Priceless Beauty (1989; Italian) . . . . China/Anna
•• 0:34 - Topless in bed with Christopher Lambert.
 • 0:35 - Brief left breast, then side of right breast on
 top of Lambert.
Vital Signs (1989). . . . . Gina Wyler
••• 1:11 - In white bra, then topless making love with
 Michael in the basement.

Made for Cable Movies:

Descending Angel (1990; HBO) . . . . Irina Stroia
 • 0:01 - Brief right breast making love with Eric Roberts
 on train during opening credits.
•• 0:44 - In white camisole top with Roberts, then topless lying in bed with him.

Miniseries:

Lonesome Dove (1989). . . . . Lorena Wood

Lane, Krista

See: Lynn, Rebecca.

Lane, Nikki

Films:

Death of a Soldier (1985) . . . . Stripper in bar
•• 0:49 - Nude, dancing on stage.
The Big Hurt (1987) . . . .

Lange, Jessica

Films:

King Kong (1976) . . . . Dwan
 1:20 - Almost topless when King Kong is playing with
 her in his hand. Hand covers nipple of left breast.
All That Jazz (1979) . . . . Angelique
How to Beat the High Cost of Living (1980). . . . . Louise
The Postman Always Rings Twice (1981)
 . . . . Cora Papadakis
 0:17 - Making love with Jack Nicholson on the kitch-
 en table. No nudity, but still exciting.
 0:18 - Pubic hair peeking out of right side of her
 panties when Nicholson grabs her crotch.
 • 1:03 - Very, very brief topless, then very, very brief
 right breast twice, when Nicholson rips her dress
 down to simulate a car accident.
 1:26 - Brief lower frontal nudity when Nicholson
 starts crawling up over her in bed.
Frances (1982) . . . . Frances Farmer
 • 0:41 - Very brief upper half of left breast lying on bed
 and throwing a newspaper.
 • 0:50 - Brief full frontal nudity covered with bubbles
 standing up in bathtub and wrapping a towel
 around herself. Long shot, hard to see.
 • 1:01 - Brief buns and right breast running into the
 bathroom when the police bust in. Very, very brief
 full frontal nudity, then buns closing the bathroom
 door. Reportedly her, even though you don't see her
 face clearly.
Tootsie (1982) . . . . .Julie Nichols
(Academy Award for Best Supporting Actress.)
Country (1984) . . . . .Jewell Ivy
Sweet Dreams (1985). . . . . .Patsy Kline
Crimes of the Heart (1986) . . . . Meg Magrath
Everybody's All-American (1988) . . . . Babs
 0:32 - Brief topless in sheer nightgown in bedroom
 with Dennis Quaid.
 • 0:54 - Buns and very, very brief side view of left
 breast by the campfire by the lake with Timothy
 Hutton at night. Might be a body double.
Far North (1988) . . . . .Kate

Made for Cable Movies:

Cat on a Hot Tin Roof (1985; HBO) . . . .

Langencamp, Heather

Films:

Nickel Mountain (1985) . . . . .Callie
••• 0:24 - Topless in bed lying with Willard.
 • 0:29 - Side view of left breast and brief topless falling
 on bed with Willard.
 0:29 - In white panties, peeking out the window.
A Nightmare on Elm Street (1985) . . . Nancy Thompson
A Nightmare on Elm Street 3: The Dream Warriors
(1987) . . . . Nancy Thompson

TV:

Just the Ten of Us (1989-90). . . . . .Marie

Langenfeld, Sarah
Films:
Blood Link (1983)......................Christine
- •• 1:01 - Topless in bed taking off her top in bed with Craig.
- • 1:04 - Topless in bed with Keith.

The Act (1984) .... Leslie

Langlois, Lisa
Films:
Blood Relatives (1978; French/Canadian) ....Muriel
Happy Birthday to Me (1980) .... Amelia
Class of 1984 (1982).......................Patsy
The Man Who Wasn't There (1983) ...Cindy Worth
- •• 0:58 - Nude running away from two policemen after turning visible.
- ••• 1:08 - Topless in white panties dancing in her apartment with an invisible Steve Guttenberg.
  1:47 - Very, very brief upper half of left breast throwing bouquet at wedding.

The Nest (1987) .... Elizabeth Johnson
Mind Field (1990) .... Sarah Paradis

Langrick, Margaret
Films:
My American Cousin (1985; Canadian)........Sandy
Harry and the Hendersons (1987).... Sarah Henderson
Cold Comfort (1988) ....Dolores
- •• 0.16 - In tank top and panties, then topless undressing in front of Stephen.
- • 0:19 - Very brief side of left breast and buns getting robe.
- •• 0.41 - Doing strip tease in front of her dad and Stephen. In black bra and panties, then topless.
- • 0:42 - Very brief topless jumping into bed.

Martha, Ruth & Edie (1988; Canadian) ..... Young Edie
American Boyfriends (1990) .... Sandy Wilcox

Lankford, Kim
Films:
Malibu Beach (1978) .... Dina
  0:32 - Buns, running into the ocean.
- • 0:34 - Brief right breast getting out of the ocean.
- • 1:16 - Right breast on beach at night with boyfriend.
- • 1:19 - Brief topless at top of the stairs.
- •• 1:20 - Brief topless when her parent's come home.
- • 1:21 - Topless in bed with her boyfriend.

The Octagon (1980) ....Nancy
Cameron's Closet (1989)............. Dory Lansing
Made for Cable TV:
The Hitchhiker: A Time for Rifles ... Rae Bridgeman
- ••• 0:03 - Topless on the pool table making love with a guy.

Dream On: Premarital Ex (1990; HBO) .... Hannah
TV:
The Waverly Wonders (1978) .... Connie Rafkin
Knots Landing (1979-83) ....Ginger Ward

Large, Bonnie
Films:
The Happy Hooker Goes to Washington (1977)
.... Carolyn (Model)
- • 0:06 - Topless during photo shoot.

Magazines:
Playboy (Mar 1973) .... Playmate

Lasseter, Vicki
Video Tapes:
Playboy's Playmate Review (1982)....... Playmate
- ••• 0:43 - In office, in the woods. Full frontal nudity.

Magazines:
Playboy (Feb 1981) .... Playmate

Laure, Carole
Films:
Get Out Your Handkerchiefs (1978)....... Solange
- •• 0:21 - Topless sitting in bed listening to her boyfriend talk.
- •• 0:31 - Topless sitting in bed knitting.
- • 0:41 - Upper half of left breast in bed.
- •• 0:47 - Left breast sitting in bed while the three guys talk.
- • 1:08 - Brief right breast when the little boy peeks at her while she sleeps.
  1:10 - Lower frontal nudity while he looks at her some more.
- ••• 1:17 - Full frontal nudity taking off nightgown while sitting on bed for the little boy.

Victory (1981) .... Renee
Heartbreakers (1984) .... Liliane
- • 0:56 - Brief topless making love in car with Nick Mancuso. Dark, hard to see.
- • 1:25 - In sheer black dress, then brief right breast making love in art gallery with Peter Coyote.

The Surrogate (1984; Canadian).... Anouk Vanderlin
- • 0:48 - Very brief topless when Frank rips her blouse open in his apartment.

Sweet Country (1985)..................... Eva
- •• 0:31 - Topless changing in apartment while Randy Quaid watches.
- • 0:43 - Nude in auditorium with other women prisoners.
- ••• 1:13 - Nude in bed with Quaid.

Magazines:
Playboy (Nov 1979)........... Sex in Cinema 1979
- •• 181: Topless.

Laurin, Marie
Films:
The Lonely Guy (1983)
.... One of "The Seven Deadly Sins"
Creature (1985)................. Susan Delambre
- •• 0:41 - Topless and brief buns with blood on her shoulders, getting Jon to take his helmet off.

Talking Walls (1987)........................Jeanne

Made for Cable TV:
The Hitchhiker: Petty Thieves. . . . . Pearl
- •• 0:09 - Topless making love with Steve Railsback on the couch.
- •• 0:15 - Topless playing with a doll in the bathtub, then buns, standing up and wrapping herself with a towel.
- 0:18 - In black bra, then topless undressing in front of John Colicos.

Law, Barbara
Films:
The Surrogate (1984; Canadian) . . . . . .Maggie Simpson
Made for Cable Movies:
Bedroom Eyes (1985; Canadian; HBO) . . . . Jobeth
- • 0:02 - Topless taking off clothes while Harry watches through the window.
- •• 0:07 - Topless and buns, kissing a woman.
- • 0:14 - Topless during Harry's flashback when he talks to the psychiatrist.
- •• 0:23 - Topless and buns dancing in bedroom.
- • 0:57 - Topless with Mary, kissing on floor.
- 1:17 - In beige bra, panties, garter belt and stockings in bed with Harry.
- • 1:23 - Brief topless on top of Harry.

Lawrence, Suzanne Remey
Films:
Delivery Boys (1984) . . . . Nurse
0:34 - In bra and panties after doing a strip tease with another nurse while dancing in front of a boy who is lying on an operating table.
R.S.V.P. (1984) . . . . Stripper
- •• 0:56 - Topless dancing in a radio station in front of a D.J.

Le Brock, Kelly
Spokeswoman for Pantene cosmetics.
Wife of actor Steven Seagal.
Films:
The Woman in Red (1984) . . . . Charlotte
0:02 - Wearing the red dress, dancing over the air vent in the car garage while Gene Wilder watches.
- • 1:13 - Brief right breast, getting into bed. Too far to see anything.
1:15 - Brief lower frontal nudity getting out of bed when her husband comes home. Very brief left breast, but it's blurry and hard to see.
Weird Science (1985) . . . . .Lisa
0:12 - In blue underwear and white top baring her midriff for the two boys when she is first created.
1:29 - In blue leotard and grey tube top gym clothes to teach boy's gym class.
Hard to Kill (1990) . . . . Andy Stewart

LeBeau, Becky
a.k.a. Darlene Beaumont.
Films:
Joysticks (1983) . . . . Liza
Hollywood Hot Tubs (1984) . . . . Veronica
- •• 0:49 - Topless changing in the locker room with other girl soccer players while Jeff watches.
- • 0:54 - Topless in hot tub with the other girls and Shawn.
Centerfold Screen Test (1985) . . . . herself
0:14 - In wet white T-shirt, auditioning in pool.
School Spirit (1985) . . . . .Hogette
Back to School (1986) . . . . . . .Bubbles, the Hot Tub Girl
Best Chest in the West II (1986) . . . . herself
- ••• 0:46 - Dancing in red two piece swimsuit. Buns, then topless.
- •• 0:55 - Buns and topless after winning semi-finals.
Takin' It All Off (1987) . . . . .Becky
- •• 0:16 - Topless and brief full frontal nudity getting introduced to Allison.
- ••• 0:23 - In black bra and panties, then nude doing a strip routine outside.
- • 0:35 - Brief full frontal nudity pushing Elliot into the pool.
- • 0:36 - Brief topless in studio with Allison again.
- • 0:36 - Brief left breast in dance studio with Allison.
- •• 1:23 - Nude, dancing with all the other women on stage.
The Underachievers (1987) . . . . Ginger Bronsky
- ••• 0:40 - Topless in swimming pool playing with an inflatable alligator after her exercise class has left.
Not of This Earth (1988) . . . . Happy Birthday Girl
- ••• 0:47 - Topless doing a Happy Birthday stripper-gram for the old guy.
Ninja Academy (1990) . . . . Nudist
- •• 0:26 - Nude, carrying plate, then going to swing at nudist colony. Then playing volleyball (she's the first one to hit the ball).
Transylvania Twist (1990) . . . . Rita
Music Videos:
California Girls/David Lee Roth
. . . . .Girl Squeezing Suntan Lotion Bottle
Video Tapes:
Soft Bodies (1988). . . . . herself
- ••• 0:01 - In two piece swimsuit, then topless in swimming pool.
- •• 0:08 - On bed during photo session in various lingerie, then topless and buns in G-string.
- ••• 0:16 - In bra and panties, then topless on bed.
Soft Bodies Invitational (1990) . . . . herself
0:00 - Buns, under short skirt playing tennis with Nina Alexander.
- ••• 0:15 - Topless posing with Alexander in photo session.
- •• 0:24 - In two piece swimsuit, then topless arguing with Alexander about who has better breasts.
- ••• 0:38 - In red bra and panties outside on brides, then topless.
- ••• 0:44 - Topless and buns in G-string in spa.

Soft Bodies: Curves Ahead (1991) . . . . herself
    0:00 - Buns in G-string, playing Frisbee with Kylie Rose.
   ••• 0:32 - Topless in pool with Tamara. Buns and partial lower frontal nudity. Long scene.
   ••• 0:36 - Topless posing for photographs in various outfits.
   ••• 0:41 - On balcony in two piece swimsuit, then topless and buns taking an outdoor shower. Long scene.
   ••• 0:45 - Topless and buns in G-string, posing on bed for photo session in various lingerie. Long scene.
   ••• 0:51 - In two piece swimsuit outside at night in spa. Topless and buns in G-string. Long scene.
Magazines:
Playboy (Feb 1989) .Grapevine
  • 166: Left breast sticking out from under T-shirt in B&W photo.
Playboy (Jul 1989) . . . . B-Movie Bimbos
  ••• 139: Full frontal nudity standing in a car filled with bubbles wearing pink stockings and a garter belt.

Lee, Adriane
Films:
Breeders (1986) . . . . Alec
  •• 0:49 - Topless, undressing while talking on the phone.
  • 1:07 - Brief topless, covered with goop, in the alien nest.
  • 1:08 - Brief topless in nest behind Frances Raines.
  • 1:09 - Brief topless behind Raines again.
  • 1:11 - Topless, lying back in the goop, then long shot topless.
Mutant Hunt (1987) . . . . Amber Dawn
Necropolis (1987) . . . . Cult Member

Lee, Cynthia
Films:
New York Nights (1983) . . . . The Porn Star
  •• 1:15 - Topless in the steam room talking to the prostitute.
  ••• 1:26 - Topless in office with the financier making love on his desk.
Hot Resort (1984) . . . . Alice
  • 1:08 - Topless in the bathtub.

Lee, Joie
Sister of actor/director Spike Lee.
Films:
She's Gotta Have It (1987; B&W) . . . .Clorinda Bradford
School Daze (1988). . . . . Lizzie Life
Do the Right Thing (1989) . . . . Jade
Mo' Better Blues (1990) . . . . Indigo Downes
  •• 1:06 - Right breast while in bed with Bleek.
  • 1:08 - Very, very brief right breast while pounding the bed and yelling at Bleek.

Lee, Kaaren
Films:
The Right Stuff (1983) . . . . Young Widow
Roadhouse 66 (1984) . . . . Jesse Duran
  •• 1:00 - Topless, taking off her top to go skinny dipping with Willem Dafoe. Dark.
St. Elmo's Fire (1985) . . . . .Welfare Woman
Remote Control (1987) . . . . Patricia

Lee, Luann
Films:
Terminal Exposure (1988) . . . . Bruce's Girl
Video Tapes:
Playboy Video Centerfold: Luann Lee. . . . Playmate
Playboy Video Calendar 1988 (1987). . . . . Playmate
Playboy's Wet and Wild (1989). . . . .
Magazines:
Playboy (Jan 1987). Playmate

Lee, Pat
Films:
Porky's (1981; Canadian) . . . . Stripper
  • 0:33 - Brief topless dancing on stage at Porky's showing her breasts to Pee Wee.
Starman (1984) . . . . Bracero Wife
And God Created Woman (1988). . . . . .Inmate
(Unrated version.)
Young Guns (1988) . . . . Janey

Lee, Robin
a.k.a. Robbie Lee.
Films:
Big Bad Mama (1974) . . . . Polly McClatchie
  • 0:09 - Brief left breast in open dress in car when cops try to pull her car over.
    0:22 - Polly in see through slip on stage with her sister and a stripper.
  • 0:32 - Brief topless running around the bedroom chasing her sister.
Switchblade Sisters (1975) . . . .

Lee, Tamara
Former adult film actress.
Video Tapes:
Soft Bodies: Curves Ahead (1991) . . . . herself
  ••• 0:23 - In lingerie on chair, then topless during photo session. Brief lower frontal nudity under sheer lingerie. Long scene.
  ••• 0:31 - In chair by pool. Topless and partial lower frontal nudity.

Lee-Hsu, Diana

Films:
License to Kill (1989)........................Loti
Video Tapes:
Playboy Video Calendar 1989 (1988) ..... February
••• 0:05 - Nude.
Playmates at Play (1990) ....Gotta Dance
Magazines:
Playboy (May 1988) .... Playmate
98:
Playboy (Aug 1989) ....License to Thrill
••• 126-131: Nude.

Légerè, Phoebe

Singer.
Films:
Mondo New York (1987) ....Singer
  0:01 - On stage, singing "Marilyn Monroe." Buns
  and most of lower frontal nudity while writhing on
  stage in a mini-skirt.
The Toxic Avenger: Part II (1988) .... Claire
  • 0:31 - Brief right breast, while caressing herself while
  making out with the Toxic Avenger.
King of New York (1990)...........Bordello Woman
The Toxic Avenger III: The Last Temptation of Toxie
  (1990).................................. Claire
Magazines:
Playboy (Jun 1988) ....Mondo Phoebe
•• 70-77: Nude.
Playboy (Nov 1988) .... Sex in Cinema 1988
  • 138: Left breast, lying on bed, getting a hug from
  the Toxic Avenger.
Playboy (Dec 1988).............. Sex Stars of 1988
  • 184: Right breast, popping out of top.

Leigh, Barbara

Films:
The Student Nurses (1970)..............Priscilla
a.k.a. Young LA Nurses
  ••• 0:43 - Topless on the beach with Les. Long scene.
The Christian Licorice Store (1971) ....Starlet
Pretty Maids All in a Row (1971) .... Jean McDrew
Frenzy (1972; British) ....Brenda Blaney
Junior Bonner (1972) .... Charmagne
Terminal Island (1973) ....Bunny Campbell
  ••• 0:22 - Topless and buns undressing in room while
  Bobbie watches from the bed.
Boss Nigger (1974).................... Miss Pruitt
Seven (1979)............................ Alexa
Mistress of the Apes (1981).....................
Famous T & A (1982) ....Bunny Campbell
  (No longer available for purchase, check your video
  store for rental.)
  ••• 0:45 - Topless scene from *Terminal Island*. Includes
  additional takes that weren't used.
Miniseries:
The Search for the Nile (1972) ... Isabel Arundel Burton

Magazines:
Playboy (May 1973)..................... Indian
••• 149-155: Topless.
Playboy (Jan 1977)................Natural Leigh
••• 85-91: B&W photos. Full frontal nudity.

Leigh, Carrie

Former girlfriend of *Playboy* publisher Hugh Hefner.
Films:
A Fine Mess (1986) .... Second Extra
Beverly Hills Cop II (1987) ....Herself
Blood Relations (1989)...........Thomas' Girlfriend
Magazines:
Playboy (Jul 1986) ....Carrie Leigh
••• 114-125: Nude.
Playboy (Aug 1988) ....The Great Palimony Caper
•• 64: Left breast and lower frontal nudity, B&W.
Playboy (Dec 1988) ....Sex Stars of 1988
••• 188: Full frontal nudity.
Playboy (Feb 1989) .... The Year in Sex
•• 143: Topless in B&W photo.

Leigh, Jennifer Jason

Daughter of the late actor Vic Morrow.
Films:
Eyes of a Stranger (1981)................. Tracy
  • 1:15 - Very brief topless lying in bed getting attacked
  by rapist.
  •• 1:19 - Left breast, cleaning herself in bathroom.
Fast Times at Ridgemont High (1982)
  .... Stacy Hamilton
  • 0:18 - Left breast, making out with Ron in a dugout.
  ••• 1:00 - Topless in poolside dressing room.
Wrong is Right (1982) ....Young Girl
Easy Money (1983) .... Allison Capuletti
Grandview, U.S.A. (1984)........... Candy Webster
Flesh + Blood (1985).................... Agnes
  • 0:45 - Brief right breast being held down.
  •• 1:05 - Full frontal nudity getting into the bath with
  Rutger Hauer and making love.
  ••• 1:16 - Full frontal nudity getting out of bed with
  Hauer and walking to the window.
  ••• 1:35 - Nude throwing clothes into the fire.
The Hitcher (1986)...................... Nash
The Men's Club (1986) .... Teensy
Sister Sister (1987) .... Lucy Bonnard
  •• 0:01 - Topless making love during a dream.
  0:52 - In lingerie talking with Eric Stoltz.
  •• 0:53 - Left breast, making love with Stoltz in her bedroom.
  • 0:58 - Topless in bathtub surrounded by candles.
Under Cover (1987)................Tanille Lareoux
Heart of Midnight (1988) .... Carol
  • 0:27 - Very brief side view of right breast reaching for
  soap in the shower.
The Big Picture (1989) .... Lydia Johnson

Last Exit to Brooklyn (1990). . . . . Tralata
- •• 1:28 - Topless, opening her blouse in bar after getting drunk.
- • 1:33 - Topless getting drug out of car, placed on mattress, then basically raped by a long line of guys. Long, painful-to-watch scene.
- • 1:35 - Topless lying on mattress when Spook comes to save her.

Miami Blues (1990) . . . . Susie Waggoner
  0:07 - Very brief upper half of right breast, while changing clothes behind Alec Baldwin.
- ••• 0:10 - Topless in panties, taking off red dress and getting into bed.
  0:24 - Very, very brief half of right breast while taking a bath. Long shot.
- • 0:33 - Topless making love with Baldwin in the kitchen.

Backdraft (1991) . . . . Jennifer Vaitkus
Made for Cable Movies:
Buried Alive (1990) . . . . Joanna
Made for TV Movies:
Girls of the White Orchid (1983) . . . .
The Killing of Randy Webster (1985) . . . .

Leighton, Roberta

Films:
Barracuda (1978) . . . .
Stripes (1981) . . . . .Anita
- • 0:07 - Topless, wearing blue panties, while putting her shirt on and talking to Bill Murray.

Covergirl (1982; Canadian). . . . . .Dee Anderson
  0:16 - Almost topless making love dressed like a nun.
TV:
The Young and the Restless (1978-86) . . Dr. Casey Reed

Lemmons, Kasi

Films:
School Daze (1988). . . . . .Perry
Vampire's Kiss (1989) . . . . Jackie
- •• 0:05 - In black bra and panties, then topless in living room with Nicholas Cage.

Silence of the Lambs (1990) . . . .
Made for Cable Movies:
The Court-Martial of Jackie Robinson (1990) . . . . Rachel
Made for TV Movies:
The Lakeside Killer (1979) . . . . Hostage

Lenska, Rula

Films:
Confessions of a Pop Performer (1975; British) . . . .
Oh, Alfie! (1975; British) . . . . .Louise
  a.k.a. Alfie Darling
- •• 0:12 - Topless, then left breast in bed after making love with Alfie.

Undercovers Hero (1975) . . . . Grenier Girl
The Deadly Females (1976). . . . . .Luisa

Lentini, Susan

Films:
Action Jackson (1988) . . . . VW Driver
Roadhouse (1989) . . . . .Bandstand Babe
Made for Cable TV:
Dream On: Sex and the Single Parent (1990; HBO)
. . . . .Ms. Brodsky
  0:04 - In white bra and panties in front of class while Jeremy fantasizes about her.
- •• 0:10 - Topless twice talking to Martin while he fantasizes about her.

Lenz, Kay

Ex-wife of actor/singer David Cassidy.
Films:
Breezy (1974). . . . . Breezy
  Topless and nude.
White Line Fever (1975) . . . . .Jerri Hummer
The Great Scout and Cathouse Thursday (1976)
. . . . Thursday
Moving Violation (1979) . . . . .Cam Johnson
The Passage (1979; British) . . . . .Leah Bergson
  Topless.
Fast Walking (1981) . . . . .Moke
- • 0:26 - Brief topless closing the door after pulling James Woods into the room.
  0:42 - Caressing herself under her dress while in prison visiting room, talking to George.
- ••• 1:27 - Topless getting hosed down and dried off outside by James Woods.
- • 1:32 - Brief left breast, making love with Woods.

House (1986). . . . . Sandy Sinclair
Death Wish 4: The Crackdown (1987) . . .Karen Sheldon
Stripped to Kill (1987) . . . . .Cody Sheehan
- •• 0:23 - Topless dancing on stage.
- ••• 0:47 - Topless dancing in white lingerie.

Fear (1988) . . . . Sharon Haden
Headhunters (1988). . . . . Katherine Hall
Physical Evidence (1989) . . . . .Deborah Quinn
Streets (1989) . . . . Sergeant
Made for Cable Movies:
Hitler's Daughter (1990). . . . .
Miniseries:
Rich Man, Poor Man (1976). . . . . Kate Jordache
Made for TV Movies:
Initiation of Sarah (1978) . . . .
Sanctuary of Fear (1979) . . . .
TV:
Rich Man, Poor Man—Book II (1976-77)
. . . . Kate Jordache
Magazines:
Playboy (Nov 1982) . . . . Sex in Cinema 1982
- ••• 161: Topless photo from *Fast Walking*.

Leo, Melissa

Films:
Always (1984) . . . . Peggy
Streetwalkin' (1985) . . . . Cookie
   •• 0:15 - Topless, stripping and taking off her top for a customer.
   • 0:18 - Brief right breast, having sex with her pimp on the floor.
Deadtime Stories (1987) . . . . Judith "Mama" Baer
A Time of Destiny (1988) . . . . Josie
TV:
Young Riders (1989-90) . . . . Emma Shannon

Lesniak, Emilia

Films:
Fear City (1984) . . . . Bibi
   •• 0:16 - Topless, dancing at the Metropole club.
   •• 1:00 - Topless, dancing on the stage.
9 Deaths of the Ninja (1985). . . . . Jennifer Barnes
Hollywood Vice Squad (1986). . . . . Linda

Levin, Rachel

Films:
Gaby, A True Story (1987). . . . . Gaby
   • 0:56 - Right breast, then topless on the floor making love with another handicapped boy, Fernando.
White Palace (1990) . . . . Rachel

Lewis, Charlotte

Films:
The Golden Child (1986) . . . . Kee Nang
Pirates (1986; French). . . . . Dolores
Dial Help (1988) . . . . Jenny Cooper
   1:06 - Black panties and bare back dressing in black corset top and stockings. Yowza!
   •• 1:09 - Brief right breast while rolling around in the bathtub.
Tripwire (1989). . . . . Trudy
Made for TV Movies:
Bare Essentials (1991) . . . . Tarita

Lewis, Fiona

Films:
The Fearless Vampire Killers (1967) . . . . Maid
Dr. Phibes Rises Again (1972) . . . . Diana
Lisztomania (1975; British). . . . . Countess Marie
   •• 0:00 - Topless in bed getting breasts kissed by Roger Daltrey to the beat of a metronome.
   • 0:01 - Brief topless swinging a chandelier to Daltrey.
   •• 0:03 - Brief topless and buns running from chair (long shot). Brief topless catching a candle on the bed.
   •• 0:04 - Brief left breast when her dress top is cut down. Left breast, sitting inside a piano with Daltrey.

Drum (1976). . . . . Augusta Chauvet
   ••• 0:57 - Topless taking a bath, getting out, then having Pam Grier dry her off.
Tintorera (1977). . . . . Patricia
   0:20 - Side view of left breast in silhouette. Long shot, hard to see. Nude swimming under water just before getting eaten by a shark. Don't see her face.
The Fury (1978). . . . . Dr. Susan Charles
Dead Kids (1981). . . . . Gwen Parkinson
   a.k.a. Strange Behavior
Strange Invaders (1983). . . . . Waitress/Avon Lady
Innerspace (1987) . . . . Dr. Margaret Canker
Magazines:
Playboy (Dec 1976) . . . . Sex Stars of 1976
   ••• 186: Full frontal nudity.

Lightstone, Marilyn

Films:
Lies My Father Told Me (1975; Canadian)
   . . . . Annie Herman
In Praise of Older Women (1978; Canadian) . . . Klari
   • 0:45 - Left breast, twice, on floor with Tom Berenger before being discovered by Karen Black.
Spasms (1983; Canadian) . . . . Dr. Rothman
The Surrogate (1984; Canadian) . . . . Dr. Harriet Forman
Made for TV Movies:
Anne of Green Gables (1985; Canadian) . . . .

Lindeland, Liv

Films:
Picasso Trigger (1989) . . . . Inga
Guns (1990). . . . . Ace
Magazines:
Playboy (Jan 1971). . . . . Playmate
Playboy (Dec 1972) . . . . Sex Stars of 1972
   216:

Lindemulder, Janine

Films:
Spring Fever USA (1988) . . . . Heather Lipton
   •• 0:14 - Taking off her stockings, then brief topless undressing for bath, then taking a bath.
Caged Fury (1989). . . . . Lulu
   0:14 - Dancing in bar in black bra and G-string.
   • 0:16 - Brief topless dancing in front of Erik Estrada.
Magazines:
Penthouse (Dec 1987). Pet
Penthouse (Sep 1990) . . . . Tony and Janine
   •• 82-91: Nude with a guy.
Penthouse (Mar 1991). . . . . Robo-Pet
   ••• 42-51: Nude, partially covered with silver paint.

Linden, Jennie
Films:
Nightmare (1963; British) . . . . .Janet
Dr. Who and the Daleks (1965; British) . . . . .Barbara
A Severed Head (1971; British) . . . . Georgie Hands
    0:02 - Buns, rolling over on the floor with Ian Holm.
Women in Love (1971) . . . . Ursula Bragwen
    • 0:38 - Brief topless skinny dipping in the river with
       Glenda Jackson.
    • 1:11 - Brief topless in a field with Alan Bates. Scene is
       shown sideways.
Hedda (1975; British) . . . . Mrs. Elvsted
Old Dracula (1975; British) . . . . Angela

Lindley, Gisele
Films:
Forbidden Zone (1980; B&W) . . . . The Princess
  ••• 0:21 - Topless in jail cell.
  ••• 0:39 - Topless turning a table around.
  •• 0:45 - Topless bending over, making love with a frog.
  •• 0:51 - Topless in a cave.
  •• 0:53 - More topless scenes.
  •• 1:06 - Even more topless scenes.
S.O.B. (1981) . . . .

Little, Michele
Films:
Out of the Blue (1982) . . . .
Radioactive Dreams (1984) . . . . Rusty Mars
My Demon Lover (1987) . . . . Denny
Out of Bounds (1987) . . . . Crystal
Sweet Revenge (1987) . . . . Lee
    • 0.41 - Brief topless in water under a waterfall with
       K.C.
Appointment with Fear (1988) . . . . Carol

Lizer, Kari
Films:
Smokey Bites the Dust (1981) . . . . Cindy
Private School (1983) . . . . Rita
    • 0:30 - Very brief left breast popping out of cheerlead-
       er's outfit along with the Coach.
Gotchal (1985) . . . . Muffy
TV:
Sunday Dinner (1991) . . . .

Lloyd, Emily
Films:
Wish You Were Here (1987) . . . . Lynda
    • 0:43 - Buns, singing in the alley and lifting up her
       skirt to moon an older neighbor woman.
Chicago Joe and the Showgirl (1989; British)
  . . . . Betty Jones
Cookie (1989) . . . . .Carmella "Cookie" Voltecki
In Country (1989) . . . . Samantha Hughes

Lloyd, Sue
Films:
Happy Housewives . . . . The Blonde
Revenge of the Pink Panther (1978)
  . . . . Claude Russo/Claudine Russo
The Stud (1978; British) . . . . Vanessa
    • 1:04 - Topless in the swimming pool with Joan Col-
      lins and Tony.
The Bitch (1979; British) . . . . Vanessa Grant
    • 1:12 - Side view of left breast and topless in the
      swimming pool.
Rough Cut (1980; British) . . . .

Locke, Sondra
Films:
The Heart is a Lonely Hunter (1968) . . . . Mick Kelley
Willard (1971) . . . . .Joan
Suzanne (1973) . . . . .Suzanne
  a.k.a. The Second Coming of Suzanne
  Suzanne has nudity in it, *The Second Coming of Suzanne*
  has the nudity cut out.
  •• 0:27 - Topless sitting, looking at a guy. Brief left
      breast several times lying down.
  ••• 0:29 - Topless lying down.
The Outlaw Josey Wales (1976) . . . . .Laura Lee
  •• 1:20 - Briefly nude in rape scene.
Death Game, The Seducers (1977) . . . . Jackson
  a.k.a. Mrs. Manning's Weekend
    0:16 - Buns and brief right breast in spa with Colleen
      Camp trying to get George in with them.
    • 0:48 - Brief topless running around the room trying
      to keep George away from the telephone.
The Gauntlet (1977) . . . . Gus Mally
  •• 1:10 - Brief right breast, then topless getting raped
      by two biker guys in a box car while Clint is tied up.
Every Which Way But Loose (1978) . .Lynn Halsey Taylor
Any Which Way You Can (1980) . . . . .Lynne
Bronco Billy (1980) . . . . .Antoinette
Sudden Impact (1983) . . . . Jennifer Spencer
Ratboy (1986) . . . . .Nikki Morrison

Lockhart, Anne
Daughter of actress June Lockhart.
Films:
Joyride (1977) . . . . Cindy
  •• 0:59 - Brief topless in the spa with everybody.
  ••• 1:00 - Topless, standing in the kitchen kissing Desi
      Arnaz Jr.
The Young Warriors (1983; U.S./Canadian) . . . . Lucy
  •• 0:42 - Topless and buns making love with Kevin on
      the bed. Looks like a body double.
Troll (1986) . . . . Young Eunice St. Clair
Dark Tower (1987) . . . . .Elaine
Big Bad John (1989) . . . . .Lady Police Officer
Made for TV Movies:
Just Tell Me You Love Me (1978) . . . .
TV:
Battlestar Galactica (1979) . . . . Sheeba

Locklin, Loryn

Films:
Catch Me... If You Can (1989) . . . . Melissa
   0:18 - In blue one-piece swimsuit by the pool.
   1:32 - In bra trying to get policeman's attention.
   Very, very brief side of right breast turing around.
   Looks like she's wearing flesh-colored pasties.
Taking Care of Business (1990) . . . . Jewel
   • 0:42 - Buns and very brief side view, twice, seen
   through door, changing by the pool. Then in black
   two piece swimsuit.
Made for TV Movies:
Shoot First: A Cop's Vengeance (1991) . . . . Lea

Lombardi, Leigh

Films:
The Wild Life (1984) . . . . Stewardess
Murphy's Law (1986) . . . . Stewardess
A Tiger's Tale (1988) . . . . Marcia
Moontrap (1989) . . . . .Mera
   •• 1:08 - Topless with Walter Koenig in moon tent.

Lomez, Céline

Films:
The Far Shore (1976) . . . . Eulalia Turner
Plague (1978; Canadian). . . . .
a.k.a. The Gemini Strain
The Silent Partner (1978) . . . . Elaine
   • 1:05 - Side view of left breast, then topless, then
   buns with Elliott Gould.
The Kiss (1988) . . . . Aunt Irene

London, Lisa

Films:
H.O.T.S. (1979) . . . . Jennie O'Hara
   • 1:22 - Topless changing clothes by the closet while a
   crook watches her.
   • 1:33 - Topless playing football.
The Happy Hooker Goes Hollywood (1980) . . . . . Laurie
Sudden Impact (1983). . . . . .Young Hooker
   •• 1:04 - Topless in bathroom, walking to Nick in the
   bed.
The Naked Cage (1985). . . . . .Abbey
   •• 0:22 - Topless in S&M costume with Angel Tompkins.
   •• 0:38 - Left breast making out in bed with Angel
   Tompkins.
Private Resort (1985). .Alice
   0:51 - In beige bra and panties several times with Ben
   and Jack while she's drunk.
Savage Beach (1989) . . . . Rocky
   • 0:06 - Topless in spa with Patty Duffek, Dona Speir
   and Hope Marie Carlton.
   •• 0:50 - Topless changing clothes.
Guns (1990) . . . . Rocky

Dream On: The Charlotte Letter (1991; HBO)
   . . . . Candy Striper #2
   • 0:06 - Topless several times, acting in adult film that
   Martin is watching on TV. (She's first to take her outfit off.)

Long, Shannon

Video Tapes:
Playboy Video Calendar 1990 (1989). . . . November
   ••• 0:57 - Nude.
Magazines:
Playboy (Oct 1988) . . . . Playmate

Long, Shelley

Films:
A Small Circle of Friends (1980) . . . . Alice
Night Shift (1982) . . . . Belinda Keaton
   0:20 - In black teddy and robe talking to Henry Win-
   kler in the hallway.
   0:37 - In panties, socks and tank top cooking break-
   fast in Winkler's kitchen.
Hello Again! (1987). . . . . Lucy Chadman
   • 0:58 - Brief buns, in hospital gown, walking down
   hallway.
Outrageous Fortune (1987) . . . . Lauren Ames
Troop Beverly Hills (1989) . . . . Phyllis Nefler
Don't Tell Her It's Me (1990) . . . . .Lizzie Potts
TV:
Cheers (1982-87). . . . . Diane Chambers

Lopez, Maria Isabel

Films:
Silip (1985) . . . . Tonya
Mission Manila (1989) . . . . Jessie
   • 0:22 - Brief right breast several times in bed while
   Harry threatens her with knife.

Lords, Traci

Infamous under age adult film actress. Unfortunately, all
of the adult films she was in before she was 18 years old
are now illegal. The only legal adult film she did is *Traci,
I Love You.*
Films:
Not of This Earth (1988) . . . . Nadine
   •• 0:25 - Buns and side view of left breast drying herself
   off with a towel while talking to Jeremy.
   0:27 - In blue swimsuit by swimming pool.
   •• 0:42 - Topless in bed making love with Harry.
   0:46 - Walking around the house in white lingerie.
Fast Food (1989) . . . . Dixie Love
   1:20 - In black bra in storage room with Auggie.
Cry Baby (1990). . . . . .Wanda
Shock 'Em Dead (1990) . . . . Lindsay Roberts
Raw Nerve (1991) . . . .

Video Tapes:
Warm Up with Traci Lords . . . . Exercise Video Tape
Red Hot Rock (1984) . . . . .Miss Georgia
  •• 0:41 - Topless several times in open-front swimsuit
       during beauty pageant during "Gimme Gimme
       Good Lovin'" by Helix.
  •• 0:42 - Topless on stage wearing black outfit with
       mask, smashing a large avocado during the same
       song.
Magazines:
Penthouse (Sep 1984) . . . . Pet
  ••• 97-115: Nude.

Loren, Sophia

Films:
Two Nights with Cleopatra (1954; Italian/B&W)
. . . . Cleopatra/Nisca
  (It seems that her nude scenes have been cut for the vid-
  eo tape version.)
Boy on a Dolphin (1957) . . . . Phaedra
  Wet blouse.
Era Lui, Si, Si (1957) . . . .
The Pride and the Passion (1957) . . . . Juana
Desire Under the Elms (1958) . . . . Anna Cabot
Houseboat (1958) . . . . .Cinzia Zaccardi
A Breath of Scandal (1960) . . . . Princess Olympia
Heller in Pink Tights (1960) . . . . .Angela Rossini
Two Women (1960; Italian) . . . . Cesira
  (Academy Award for Best Actress.)
El Cid (1961) . . . . .Chimene
Boccaccio 70 (1962; Italian) . . . . .Zoe
The Fall of the Roman Empire (1964) . . . . .Lucilla
Yesterday, Today and Tomorrow (1964; Italian)
. . . . Adelina
Arabesque (1966) . . . . .Yasmin Azir
Man of La Mancha (1972) . . . . Dulcinea/Aldonza
Angela (1977; Canadian) . . . . Angela
The Cassandra Crossing (1977; British) . . . . . . .Jennifer
A Special Day (1977) . . . . Antonietta
Brass Target (1978) . . . . .Mara
Firepower (1979) . . . . .Adele Tasca
Magazines:
Playboy (Jan 1989) . . . . .Women of the Fifties
  • 120: B&W photo from *Era Lui, Si, Si.*

Loring, Lisa

Films:
Iced (1988) . . . . Jeanette
  • 0:46 - Brief left breast in bathtub.
  • 0:53 - Buns and brief right breast in bathtub with
       Alex.
  •• 1:05 - Brief lower frontal nudity and buns getting
       into hot tub. Topless in hot tub just before getting
       electrocuted.
  •• 1:13 - Full frontal nudity lying dead in the hot tub.
  • 1:18 - Brief full frontal nudity lying dead in the hot
       tub again.

Death Feud (1989) . . . . Roxey
  0:06 - Dancing in club with feathery pasties. Later,
       wearing the same thing under a sheer negligee.
  0:41 - Dancing again with the same pasties.
  1:20 - Dancing with red tassel pasties.
TV:
The Addams Family (1964-66)
. . . . Wednesday Thursday Addams

Lorraine, Nita

Films:
Happy Housewives . . . . Jenny Elgin
  • 0:31 - Brief side view of left breast and buns in barn
       chasing after Bob.
  • 0:32 - Brief topless in open dress talking to police-
       man.
The Viking Queen (1967) . . . . .Nubian Girl-Slave
All Neat in Black Stockings (1969) . . . . Jolasta

Louise, Helli

Films:
Happy Housewives . . . . Newsagent's Daughter
  •• 0:16 - Topless with Mrs. Wain and Bob in the bath-
       tub.
Confessions of a Pop Performer (1975; British) . . . .

Love, Lucretia

Films:
Battle of the Amazons (1973) . . . . Eraglia
Naked Warriors (1973) . . . . .Deidre
  a.k.a. The Arena
  • 0:07 - Brief topless getting clothes torn off by guards.
  •• 0:08 - Brief nude getting washed down in court yard.
  1:08 - Brief buns, bent over riding a horse.
The Tormented (1978; Italian) . . . .
Dr. Heckyl and Mr. Hype (1980) . . . . Debra Kate

Love, Patti

Films:
Butley (1974; British) . . . . Female Student
That'll Be the Day (1974; British) . . . . . . Sandra's Friend
Terror (1979; British) . . . .
The Long Good Friday (1980; British) . . . . Carol
Steaming (1985; British) . . . . .Josie
  • 0:08 - Frontal nudity, getting undressed.
  • 0:45 - Brief topless.
  • 1:30 - Topless, jumping around in the pool.

Love, Suzanna
Films:
Cocaine Cowboys (1979) . . . . Lucy
    1:02 - Undressing to see-through bra and panties.
Devonsville Terror (1983) . . . . Jenny
Olivia (1983) . . . . Olivia
a.k.a. A Taste of Sin
  •• 0:34 - Buns and topless making love with Mike.
  •• 0:58 - Topless and buns making love with Mike in the
    shower.
  • 1:08 - Very brief full frontal nudity getting into bed
    with Richard. Dark, long shot.
  •• 1:09 - Buns, lying in bed. Dark. Full frontal nudity
    getting out of bed and going to the bathroom.

Lovelace, Linda
Adult Films:
Deep Throat (1972) . . . .
  Nude, etc.
Films:
Linda Lovelace for President (1975). . . . .
Magazines:
Playboy (Apr 1973) . . . . Say "Ah!"
  •• 95: Topless.
Playboy (Dec 1973). . . . . Sex Stars of 1973
  • 200: Topless.
Playboy (Jan 1989) . . . . Women of the Seventies
  •• 214: Topless.

Lowell, Carey
Films:
Dangerously Close (1986). . . . . Julie
Down Twisted (1987) . . . . Maxine
Me & Him (1988; West German) . . . . . Janet Landerson
License to Kill (1989). . . . . Pam Bouvier
The Guardian (1990) . . . . Kate
  •• 0:37 - Right breast twice, in bed with Phil.

Lowry, Lynn
Films:
Sugar Cookies (1973). . . . . Alta/Julie
  ••• 0:03 - Brief topless falling out of hammock, then top-
    less on couch with Max, then nude. Long scene.
    (Brunette wig as Alta.)
    0:13 - Brief right breast in B & W photo.
  • 0:14 - Left breast on autopsy table.
  •• 0:20 - Topless in movie.
  •• 0:52 - Topless taking off clothes for Mary Woronov.
    Topless on bed. (Blonde as Julie.)
  ••• 1:00 - Topless and buns with Woronov in bedroom,
    nude while wrestling with her.
  • 1:04 - Topless with Woronov in bathtub.
  ••• 1:06 - Nude in bed with Woronov. Long scene.
  • 1:11 - Right breast outside displaying herself to Max.
  • 1:16 - Right breast, then topless making love with
    Woronov.
  ••• 1:20 - Nude with Woronov and Max. Long scene.

They Came From Within (1975; Canadian) . . . .Forsythe
Fighting Mad (1976) . . . . .Lorene
Cat People (1982) . . . . Ruthie
  • 0:16 - In black bra in Malcolm McDowell's hotel
    room, then brief topless when bra pops open after
    crawling down the stairs.

Lumley, Joanna
Films:
Games That Lovers Play (1970). . . . . Fanny
  Private Screenings.
  •• 0:17 - Nude, getting out of bed and putting on robe.
  • 0:50 - Right breast, while in bed with Jonathan.
  •• 1:18 - Topless sitting in bed, talking on the phone.
  •• 1:29 - Brief topless several times in bed with Con-
    stance and a guy. Topless after and during the end
    credits.
Shirley Valentine (1989) . . . . .Marjorie
TV:
The New Avengers (1976) . . . . .Purdy

Lunghi, Cherie
Films:
Excalibur (1981; British). . . . . .Guenevere
  • 1:25 - Brief topless in the forest kissing Lancelot.
King David (1985) . . . . .Michal
  •• 0:28 - Topless lying in bed with Richard Gere. (Her
    hair is in the way a little bit.)
Letters to an Unknown Lover (1985) . . . . .Helene
  0:40 - In white slip in her bedroom.
Parker (1985; British) . . . .
The Mission (1986; British). . . . . .Carlotta
To Kill a Priest (1988) . . . . Halina
Miniseries:
Master of the Game (1984) . . .Margaret Van der Merwe

Lussier, Sheila
Films:
Bits and Pieces (1985) . . . . .Tanya
  •• 0:07 - In bra, tied down by Arthur, then brief topless
    a couple of times as he cuts her bra off before he kills
    her. Brief right breast several times with blood on
    her.
My Chauffeur (1986) . . . . Party Girl

Luu, Tuy Ann
a.k.a. Thuy An Luu.
Films:
Diva (1982; French) . . . . .Alba
  • 0:13 - Topless in B&W photos when record store
    clerk asks to see her portfolio.
  • 0:15 - More of the B&W photos on the wall.
    1:27 - Very brief upper half of left breast taking off
    top, seen through window. Long shot.
Off Limits (1988). . . . . Lanh
  •• 0:48 - Topless dancing on stage in a nightclub.

Lynch, Kelly

Films:
Portfolio (1983). . . . . Elite Model
Light of Day (1987). . . . . Elaine
Cocktail (1988) . . . . Kerry Coughlin
    0:45 - Buns, wearing a two piece swimsuit at the
    beach.
    1:01 - Buns, in string bikini swimsuit on boat with
    Tom Cruise and Bryan Brown.
Drugstore Cowboy (1989) . . . . .Dianne Hughes
    0:17 - In black bra and pants in living room with Matt
    Dillon.
Roadhouse (1989) . . . . Doc
  •• 1:04 - Topless and buns getting out of bed with a
    sheet wrapped around her.
Warm Summer Rain (1989) . . . . Kate
  • 0:03 - Brief topless and side view of buns in B&W ly-
    ing on floor during suicide attempt. Quick cuts top-
    less getting shocked to start her heart.
  •• 0:23 - Full frontal nudity when Guy gets off her in
    bed.
  •• 0:24 - Side view of right breast in bed, then topless.
  ••• 0:58 - Buns then topless, getting washed by Guy on
    the table.
  ••• 1:07 - Brief buns making love. Quick cuts full frontal
    nudity spinning around. Side view of left breast with
    Guy.
  ••• 1:09 - Nude picking up belongings and running out
    of burning house with Guy.
Desperate Hours (1990) . . . . .Nancy Breyers
  • 0:10 - Brief topless, walking on sidewalk with Mickey
    Rourke when her breasts pop out of her suit.
  • 1:19 - Brief topless, getting wired with a hidden mi-
    crophone in bathroom.
Made for Cable TV:
The Hitchhiker: The Joker . . . . Theresa/Melissa
    0:11 - Very, very brief left breast in storage room with
    Alan when a masked Timothy Bottoms ties them to-
    gether.
Magazines:
Playboy (Nov 1989) . . . . Sex in Cinema 1989
  • 137: Upper half of left breast from *Roadhouse*.

Lynley, Carol

Films:
The Light in the Forest (1958). . . . . Shenandoe Hastings
The Poseidon Adventure (1972) . . . . .Nonny Parry
Son of Blob (1972) . . . .
The Four Deuces (1975) . . . . Wendy
Flood! (1976) . . . .
The Cat and The Canary (1978) . . . . . . .Anabelle West
Dark Tower (1987) . . . . Tilly
Blackout (1989) . . . . Esther Boyle
  •• 1:01 - Brief topless leaning against the wall while
    someone touches her left breast.
Howling VI—The Freaks (1990). . . . . . .Miss Eddington
TV:
The Immortal (1970-71) . . . . Sylvia

Lynn, Rebecca

a.k.a. Adult film actress Cameron or Krista Lane.
Films:
Free Ride (1986) . . . . Nude Girl #2
  • 0:25 - Brief buns taking a shower with another girl.
In Search of the Perfect 10 (1986)
. . . . .Perfect Girl #7/Ellen
(Shot on video tape.)
  ••• 0:37 - Topless (she's the redhead) playing Twister
    with Iris Condon. Buns in G-string.
Sensations (1988) . . . . Jenny Hunter
  • 0:11 - Topless, sleeping on couch.
  •• 0:23 - Topless talking on the telephone.
  •• 1:09 - Topless making love in bed with Brian.
Thrilled to Death (1988) . . . . Elaine Jackson
  • 0:01 - Topless twice when Baxter opens her blouse.
  •• 0:31 - Topless in locker room talking to Nan.

Lyons, Susan

Films:
The Good Wife (1987; Australian) . . . . . . Mrs. Fielding
a.k.a. The Umbrella Woman
  • 1:22 - Very brief topless coming in from the balcony.
...Almost (1990; Australian) . . . . .Caroline

MacDonald, Wendy

Films:
Dark Side of the Moon (1989). . . . . .Alex
  • 0:54 - In bra, then brief topless having it torn off.
    Don't see her face.
Living to Die (1990). . . . . Rookie Policewoman
Blood Money (1991) . . . . .Susan
Magazines:
Playboy (Oct 1990) . . . . Grapevine
  • 183: Buns in stocking/garter belt. B&W.

MacGraw, Ali

Films:
Goodbye, Columbus (1969) . . . . .Brenda
  • 0:50 - Very brief side view of left breast, taking off
    dress before running and jumping into a swimming
    pool. Brief right breast jumping into pool.
  • 1:11 - Very brief side view of right breast in bed with
    Richard Benjamin. Brief buns, getting out of bed and
    walking to the bathroom.
Love Story (1970) . . . . Jenny Cavilleri
The Getaway (1972) . . . . Carol McCoy
    0:16 - In wet white blouse after jumping in pond
    with Steve McQueen.
  • 0:19 - Very brief left breast lying back in bed kissing
    McQueen.
Convoy (1978). . . . . Melissa
Players (1979) . . . . Nicole
Just Tell Me What You Want (1980). . .Bones Burton
  •• 0:16 - Topless getting dressed in her bedroom.
  •• 1:26 - Brief topless in bathroom getting ready to take
    a shower.

MacKenzie, Jan

Films:

Gator Bait II—Cajun Justice (1988) . . . . . . Angelique
    0:13 - Most of right breast while kissing her husband.
    0:29 - Most of right breast while in bed.
  •• 0:34 - Buns and side view of left breast, taking a bath
    outside. Brief topless a couple of times while the bad
    guys watch.
  • 0:41 - Brief side view of left breast taking off towel in
    front of the bad guys.
    1:05 - Brief buns occasionally when her blouse flaps
    up during boat chase.
The American Angels, Baptism of Blood (1989)
. . . . Luscious Lisa
    0:07 - Buns in G-string on stage in club. More buns
    getting lathered up for wrestling match.
  • 0:11 - Topless and buns when a customer takes her
    top off. She's covered with shaving cream.
  •• 0:12 - Topless taking a shower when Diamond Dave
    looks in to talk to her.
  • 0:56 - Right breast in wrestling ring with Dave.

Mackenzie, Patch

Films:

Goodbye, Norma Jean (1975) . . . . Ruth Latimer
Serial (1980) . . . . Stella
  • 0:59 - Brief topless in mirror in swinger's club with
    Martin Mull.
Graduation Day (1981) . . . . Anne Ramstead
It's Alive III: Island of the Alive (1988) . . . . Robbins

MacLaine, Shirley

Films:

The Trouble with Harry (1955) . . . . Jennifer Rogers
Around the World in 80 Days (1956) . . . . Princess Houda
Hot Spell (1958; B&W) . . . . Virginia Duval
Some Came Running (1958) . . . . Ginny Moorhead
The Apartment (1960; B&W) . . . . Fran Kubelik
Can-Can (1960) . . . . Simone Pistache
All In a Night's Work (1961) . . . . Katie Robbins
Irma La Douce (1963) . . . . Irma La Douce
Gambit (1966) . . . . Nicole
Woman Times Seven (1967) . . . . Paulette
Sweet Charity (1969) . . . . Charity Hope Valentine
Two Mules for Sister Sara (1970) . . . . Sara
Desperate Characters (1971) . . . . Sophie
  (Not available on video tape.)
  Topless in bed with Kenneth Mars.
The Turning Point (1977) . . . . DeeDee
Being There (1979) . . . . Eve Rand
A Change of Seasons (1980) . . . . Karen Evans
Loving Couples (1980) . . . . Evelyn
Terms of Endearment (1983) . . . . . Aurora Greenway
  (Academy Award for Best Actress.)
    1:00 - Very, very brief right breast wrestling with Jack
    Nicholson in the ocean when she finally frees his
    hand from her breast. One frame. Hard to see, but
    for the sake of thoroughness....

Cannonball Run II (1984) . . . . Veronica
Madame Sousatzka (1988) . . . . Madame Sousatzka
Steel Magnolias (1989) . . . . Ouiser Boudreaux
Postcards from the Edge (1990) . . . . Doris Mann
Waiting for the Light (1991) . . . .
Video Tapes:
Shirley MacLaine's Inner Workout (1989) . . . . Herself
Magazines:
Playboy (Nov 1972) . . . . Sex in Cinema
  • 159: Topless lying in bed with Kenneth Mars. Small
    photo, hard to tell it's her.

MacLaren, Fawna

Video Tapes:

Playboy Video Centerfold: Fawna MacLaren
  (1988) . . . . 35th Anniversary Playmate
  ••• 0:11 - In front of brick wall. In studio, in bed. Nude.
Playboy Video Calendar 1990 (1989) . . . . . . January
  ••• 0:01 - Nude.
Playboy's Sexy Lingerie II (1990) . . . .
Playmates at Play (1990) . . . . Gotta Dance
Magazines:
Playboy (Jan 1989) . . . . Playmate

Macpherson, Elle

Sports Illustrated magazine swimsuit model. Cover girl in
1986, 1987 and 1988.
Spokesmodel for *Biotherm* cosmetics.
Films:
Alice (1990) . . . . Model
Video Tapes:
Sports Illustrated's 25th Anniversary Swimsuit
  Video (1989) . . . . herself
  (The version shown on HBO left out two music video
  segments at the end. If you like buns, definitely watch
  the video tape!)
    0:22 - In wet yellow tank top and orange bikini bot-
    toms at the beach.
  • 0:23 - Very, very brief lower topless readjusting the
    yellow tank top.
Sports Illustrated Super Shape-Up Program: Stretch and
  Strengthen (1990) . . . . Herself
Magazines:
GQ (Jan 1991) . . . . A Man and an Elle of a Woman
  • 118-127: Wearing a blue fishnet top, a wet white
    swimsuit and just a swimsuit bottom (hair gets in the
    way a bit).

Madigan, Amy

Films:

Love Child (1982) . . . . Terry Jean Moore
  • 0:08 - Brief side view of right breast and buns taking
    a shower in jail while the guards watch.
  •• 0:53 - Brief topless and buns, making love with Beau
    Bridges in a room at the women's prison.
Love Letters (1984) . . . . Wendy
Places in the Heart (1984) . . . . Viola Kelsey

Streets of Fire (1984). McCoy
Alamo Bay (1985). . . . . Glory
•• 0:28 - Topless lying in motel bed with Ed Harris.
•• 0:30 - Topless sitting up in the bed.
0:40 - Walking in parking lot in a wet T-shirt.
Twice in a Lifetime (1985). . . . . Sunny Sobel
Nowhere to Hide (1987) . . . . Barbara Cutter
• 1:04 - Brief side view of right breast taking off towel
to get dressed in cabin. Long shot, hard to see.
The Prince of Pennsylvania (1988) . . . Carla Headlee
• 0:37 - Left breast and buns getting out of bed with
Keanu Reeves and putting on a robe.
Field of Dreams (1989). . . . . Annie
Uncle Buck (1989). . . . . Chanice Kobolowski
Miniseries:
The Day After (1983) . . . . Alison
Made for TV Movies:
Roe vs. Wade (1989). . . . . Sarah Weddington
Lucky Day (1991) . . . . Kari Campbell

Madonna

Full name is Madonna Louise Cicconi.
Singer.
Ex-wife of actor Sean Penn.
Films:
A Certain Sacrifice (1981). . . . . Bruna
(Very grainy film, done before she got famous.)
••• 0:22 - Topless during weird rape/love scene with one
guy and two girls.
• 0:40 - Brief right breast in open top lying on floor after getting attacked by guy in back of restaurant.
• 0:57 - Brief topless during love making scene, then
getting smeared with blood.
Desperately Seeking Susan (1985). . . . . Susan
0:09 - Briefly in black bra taking off her blouse in bus
station restroom.
1:16 - In black bra getting out of pool and lying
down on lounge chair.
Visionquest (1985) . . . . Nightclub singer
Shanghai Surprise (1986) . . . . Gloria Tatlock
Who's That Girl? (1987) . . . . Nikki Finn
Bloodhounds of Broadway (1989). . Hortense Hathaway
Dick Tracy (1990) . . . . Breathless Mahoney
0:20 - Topless under sheer black gown, talking to
Warren Beatty.
Truth or Dare (1991) . . . . herself
Video Tapes:
Madonna: The Immaculate Collection (1990)
. . . . Miscellaneous Personalities
• 0:18 - (2 min., 10 sec. into "Papa Don't Preach.")
Very, very brief left breast in black strapless outfit
when she throws her head back. (After the daughter
character she plays walks up the subway stairs.)
0:18 - (1 min., 36 sec. into "Papa Don't Preach.")
Very, very brief upper half of right breast after first
head throwback in black strapless outfit. Long shot.
0:50 - (1 min., 6 sec. into "Vogue.") Wearing sheer
black blouse. Also at (1:18 and 1:33).

Magazines:
Penthouse (Sep 1985) . . . . pictorial
• 150-161: B&W photos, need to shave her armpits!
Playboy (Sep 1985) . . . . pictorial
• 119-131: B&W photos, need to shave her armpits!
Playboy (Dec 1986) . . . . Sex Stars of 86
Playboy (Jan 1989). . . . . Women of the Eighties
•• 247: Topless B&W photo.
Vanity Fair (Apr 1990). . . . . White Heat
•• 144: Left breast in B&W photo taken by Helmut
Newton. She's standing on a table, opening her
vest.
Playboy (Dec 1990) . . . . Sex Stars of 1990
•• 171: In sheer top from "Vogue" music video.
Vanity Fair (Apr 1991) . . . . The Misfit
•• 167: Topless under sheer sheet. Other Marilyn Mon-
roe-like photographs.
Penthouse (Sep 1991)
. . . . Truth or Bare, Madonna: The Lost Nudes
••• 179-183: B&W photos taken by Jere Threndgill in
spring of 1979.

Madsen, Virginia

Sister of actor Michael Madsen.
Films:
Class (1983) . . . . Lisa
•• 0:20 - Brief left breast when Andrew McCarthy acci-
dentally rips her blouse open at the girl's school.
Dune (1984) . . . . Princess Irulan
Electric Dreams (1984). . . . . Madeline
Creator (1985). . . . . Barbara
0:53 - Walking on beach in a blue one piece swimsuit
with Vincent Spano.
••• 0:58 - Nude in shower with Spano.
Fire With Fire (1986) . . . . Lisa
Modern Girls (1987) . . . . Kelly
Slam Dance (1987) . . . . Yolanda Caldwell
Zombie High (1987) . . . . Andrea
Hot to Trot (1988) . . . . Allison Rowe
Heart of Dixie (1989) . . . . Delia
The Hot Spot (1990) . . . . Dolly Harshaw
• 0:41 - Side view of left breast while sitting on bed
talking to Don Johnson.
• 0:47 - Tip of right breast when Johnson kisses it.
•• 1:16 - Buns, undressing for a swim outside at night.
Topless hanging on rope.
• 1:18 - Buns, getting out of water with Johnson. Long
shot.
• 1:21 - Left breast when robe gapes open while sitting
up.
1:23 - Brief lower frontal nudity and buns in open
robe after jumping off tower at night.
1:24 - Topless at bottom of hill with Johnson. Long
shot.
1:45 - Nude, very, very briefly running out of house.
Very blurry, could be anybody.

Made for Cable Movies:
Mussolini and I (1985; HBO) . . . . Claretta Petacci
Long Gone (1987; HBO) . . . . Dixie Lee Boxx
    0:05 - Buns, sleeping on bed face down in bedroom
    with William L. Petersen and a young kid.
Gotham (1988; Showtime) . . . . Rachel Carlyle
a.k.a. The Dead Can't Lie
  • 0:50 - Brief topless in the shower when Tommy Lee
    Jones comes over to her apartment, then topless ly-
    ing on the floor.
  •• 1:12 - Topless, dead, in the freezer when Jones
    comes back to her apartment, then brief topless on
    the bed.
  • 1:18 - Topless in the bathtub under water.
Third Degree Burn (1989; HBO) . . . . Anne Scholes
Ironclads (1991) . . . . Betty Stuart
Made for Cable TV:
The Hitchhiker: Perfect Order . . . . Christina
    0:11 - In black lingerie being photographed by the
    photographer in his studio.
  •• 0:14 - Brief topless changing clothes while Simon
    watches her on video monitor.
    0:16 - Topless getting into water in Simon's studio.
    Her body is covered with white makeup.

Magnuson, Ann
Films:
The Hunger (1983) . . . . . . Young Woman from Disco
  • 0:05 - Brief topless in kitchen with David Bowie just
    before he kills her.
Perfect Strangers (1984) . . . . Maida
Desperately Seeking Susan (1985) . . . . Cigarette Girl
Making Mr. Right (1987) . . . . Frankie Stone
Mondo New York (1987) . . . . Poetry Reader
A Night in the Life of Jimmy Reardon (1987)
. . . . Joyce Fickett
    1:01 - Right leg in stocking and garter belt kissing
    River Phoenix in the library of her house.
Tequila Sunrise (1988) . . . . Shaleen
Checking Out (1989) . . . . Connie Hagen
Heavy Petting (1989) . . . herself/Television Spokesmodel
Love at Large (1990) . . . . Doris
TV:
Anything but Love (1989-) . . . . Catherine Hughes

Malin, Kym
Films:
Joysticks (1983) . . . . Lola
  • 0:03 - Topless with Alva showing a nerd their breasts
    by pulling their blouses open.
  ••• 0:18 - Topless during strip-video game with Jeffer-
    son, then in bed with him.
  • 0:57 - Topless during fantasy sequence, lit with red
    lights, hard to see anything.
  • 1:02 - Brief topless in slide show in courtroom.
Mike's Murder (1984) . . . . Beautiful Girl #1

Weird Science (1985) . . . . Girl Playing Piano
  • 0:55 - Brief topless several times as her clothes get
    torn off by the strong wind and she gets sucked up
    and out of the chimney.
Die Hard (1988) . . . . Hostage
Picasso Trigger (1989) . . . . Kym
  •• 1:04 - Topless taking a shower.
Roadhouse (1989) . . . . Party Girl
Guns (1990) . . . . Kym
    0:27 - Oil wrestling with Hugs.
  ••• 0:28 - Showering (in back) while talking to Hugs (in
    front).
Video Tapes:
Playboy's Playmate Review (1982) . . . . Playmate
  ••• 0:37 - In bar, on empty stage. Nude.
Magazines:
Playboy (May 1982) . . . . Playmate
Playboy (Nov 1983) . . . . Sex in Cinema 1983
  • 147: Right breast in photo from *Joysticks*.

Mandel, Suzy
Films:
Confessions of a Driving Instructor (1976; British) . . . . .
Playbirds (1978; British) . . . . Lena
  •• 0:12 - Nude stripping in Playbird office.
Blonde Ambition (1980; British) . . . .

Mani, Karen
Films:
Alley Cat (1982) . . . . Billie
  • 0:01 - Brief topless in panties taking night gown off
    during opening credits.
    0:17 - In two piece swimsuit sitting by the pool.
  ••• 0:38 - Brief side view of right breast and buns getting
    into the shower. Full frontal nudity in the shower.
  ••• 0:48 - Topless in women's prison shower room
    scene. Long scene.
Avenging Angel (1985) . . . . Janie Soon Lee
  ••• 0:06 - Nude taking a shower, right breast in mirror
    drying herself off, then in bra getting dressed.

Manion, Cindy
Films:
Blow Out (1981) . . . . Dancing Coed
Preppies (1984) . . . . Jo
  • 0:11 - Brief topless changing into waitress costumes
    with her two friends.
  • 0:44 - Topless during party with the three preppie
    guys.
The Toxic Avenger (1985) . . . . Julie
    0:14 - In white, two piece swimsuit in locker room.

Mansfield, Jayne
Films:
Pete Kelly's Blues (1955) . . . . Cigarette Girl
Underwater! (1955) . . . .
The Girl Can't Help It (1957) . . . . Jerri Jordan

Promises, Promises (1963; B&W) . . . . . Sandy Brooks
0:02 - Bubble bath scene.
••• 0:04 - Topless drying herself off with a towel. Same shot also at 0:48.
••• 0:06 - Topless in bed. Same shot also at 0:08, 0:39 and 0:40.
••• 0:59 - Buns, kneeling next to bathtub, right breast in bathtub, then topless drying herself off.
A Guide for the Married Man (1967). . Technical Advisor
The Wild, Wild World of Jayne Mansfield (1968; B&W) . . . . Topless.

TV:
Down You Go (1956) . . . . regular panelist
Video Tapes:
Playboy Video Centerfold: Dutch Twins (1989) . . . . herself
••• 0:39 - Topless in color and B&W shots from *Promises, Promises.*
Magazines:
Playboy (Feb 1955) . . . . Playmate
Playboy (Jan 1979) . . . . 25 Beautiful Years
•• 154: Topless lying on a pink bed.

Marceau, Sophie

Films:
La Boum (1980; French) Vic
L'Amour Braque (1985; French) . . . .
Police (1986; French). . . . . Noria

Margolin, Janet

Films:
David and Lisa (1962; B&W) . . . . Lisa
Bus Riley's Back in Town (1965). . . . . Judy
Take the Money and Run (1969) . . . . Louise
The Last Embrace (1979) . . . . Ellie "Eva" Fabian
• 1:10 - Brief topless in bathtub with Bernie, before strangling him.
•• 1:14 - Right breast, while reaching for the phone in bed with Roy Scheider.
• 1:20 - Left breast in photo that Schelder is looking at with a magnifying glass (it's supposed to be her grandmother).
1:22 - Almost topless in the shower talking to Scheider.
Distant Thunder (1988). . . . . Barbara Lambert
Ghostbusters II (1989). . . . . The Prosecutor
TV:
Lanigan's Rabbi (1977) . . . . Miriam Small

Margot, Sandra

Films:
Caged Fury (1989) .Crazy Daisy
1:13 - Buns in G-string and bra dancing for some men.
•• 1:15 - Topless taking off bra.
The Sleeping Car (1990) . . . . 19-Year Old Girl

Marie, Jeanne

Films:
If Looks Could Kill (1987) . . . . Jeannie Burns
•• 0:06 - Topless taking off her robe and kissing George.
Student Affairs (1987) . . . . Robin Ready
• 0:35 - Brief topless wearing black panties in bed trying to seduce a guy.
••• 0:41 - Topless making love with another guy, while banging her back against the wall.
• 0:44 - Very brief topless in VW with a nerd.
• 1:09 - Very brief topless falling out of a trailer home filled with water.
Wildest Dreams (1987). . . . . Isabelle
•• 0:35 - Topless in panties in bedroom with Bobby.
Wimps (1987) . . . . Janice
•• 0:20 - Topless in bed taking off top with Charles.
Young Nurses in Love (1987) . . . . . . Nurse Ellis Smith
• 0:31 - Brief side view of left breast in mirror with Dr. Riley.
•• 1:09 - Topless in panties, getting into bed with Dr. Riley.

Marino, Bonnie

Video Tapes:
Playboy Video Calendar 1991 (1990). . . . . . . .June
••• 0:22 - Nude.
Magazines:
Playboy (Jun 1990). . . . . Playmate

Markov, Margaret

Films:
The Hot Box (1972). . . . . .Lynn Forrest
• 0:12 - Topless when bad guy cuts her swimsuit top open.
•• 0:16 - Topless in stream consoling Bunny.
• 0:21 - Topless in the furthest hammock from camera. Long shot.
••• 0:45 - Topless bathing in stream with the other girls.
Black Mama, White Mama (1973; U.S./Philippines) . . . . Karen Brent
Naked Warriors (1973). . . . . Bodicia
a.k.a. The Arena
• 0:07 - Brief topless getting clothes torn off by guards.
• 0:13 - Topless getting her dress ripped off, then raped during party.
• 0:19 - Brief left breast, on floor making love, then right breast and buns.
0:45 - In sheer white dress consoling Septimus, then walking around.
• 0:52 - Brief topless sitting down, listening to Cornelia.

Marsillach, Blanca
Films:
Flesh + Blood (1985) . . . . .Clara
•• 0:11 - Full frontal nudity on bed having convulsions after getting hit on the head with a sword.
Collector's Item (1988) . . . . .Jacqueline
•• 0:52 - In white bra cleaning up Tony Musante in bed, then topless.
1:04 - Lower frontal nudity while watching Musante and Laura Antonelli making love in bed.
• 1:18 - Topless getting dressed. A little dark.
•• 1:22 - Topless changing clothes in bedroom while Antonelli talks to her.
Dangerous Obsession (1990; Italian). . . . . . . .Jessica
• 0:02 - Left breast, getting fondled by Johnny in recording studio. Lower frontal nudity when he pulls down her panties.
•• 0:05 - Topless opening her blouse while Johnny plays his saxophone.
• 0:17 - Lower frontal nudity on the stairs with Johnny, then brief topless.
• 0:29 - Brief topless in video tape on T.V.
•• 0:40 - Topless changing blouses.
••• 0:56 - Full frontal nudity masturbating while looking at pictures of Johnny. Buns, then more full frontal nudity getting video taped.
••• 0:58 - Topless in bed with a gun. Nude walking around the house. Long scene.
• 1:05 - Brief topless on beach, burying a dog.
• 1:06 - Brief full frontal nudity during video taping session.
•• 1:07 - Topless cleaning up Dr. Simpson.
••• 1:13 - Topless taking chains off Dr. Simpson, then lying in bed. Full frontal nudity making love with him.

Marsillach, Cristina
Films:
Every Time We Say Goodbye (1986) . . . . Sarah
1:00 - In white slip in her bedroom.
1:03 - In white slip again.
•• 1:09 - Right breast, then brief topless lying in bed with Tom Hanks.
Collector's Item (1988) . . . . .Young Marie
•• 0:12 - Right breast in elevator with Tony Musante.
•• 0:36 - Topless in open blouse, then full frontal nudity in hut with Musante.

Martin, Danielle
a.k.a. Adult film actress Danielle.
Films:
My Therapist (1983) . . . . Francine
Shot on video tape.
•• 0:29 - In bra, garter belt, stockings and panties, then topless in room with Rip.
Video Tapes:
The Girls of Penthouse (1984)
. . . . .Bad to the Bone Woman
••• 0:07 - Nude, taking off her leather outfit.

Martin, Pamela Sue
Films:
Buster and Billie (1974) . . . .
The Lady in Red (1979) . . . . Polly Franklin
• 0:07 - Right breast, while in bedroom with a guy clutching her clothes.
••• 0:20 - Topless in jail with a group of women prisoners waiting to be examined by a nurse.
Flicks (1981). . . . . Liz
Torchlight (1984). . . . . .Lillian Gregory
Made for TV Movies:
Human Feelings (1978) . . . .
TV:
The Nancy Drew Mysteries (1977-78) . . . . Nancy Drew
The Hardy Boys Mysteries (1977-78) . . . . . Nancy Drew
Dynasty (1981-84). . . . . .Fallon Carrington Colby
Magazines:
Playboy (Jul 1978) . . . . Nancy Drew Grows Up
•• 87-91: Sort of topless.

Mason, Marsha
Ex-wife of playwright Neil Simon.
Films:
Blume in Love (1973) . . . . Arlene
• 0:22 - Side view of right breast, then brief topless lying in bed with George Segal.
• 0:35 - Very brief right breast reaching over the bed.
•• 0:54 - Brief topless twice, reaching over to get a pillow while talking to Segal.
Cinderella Liberty (1973). . . . . Maggie Paul
0:09 - Brief panties shot leaning over pool table when James Caan watches.
•• 0:17 - Side view of left breast in room with Caan. Brief right breast sitting down on bed.
••• 0:38 - Topless sitting up in bed, yelling at Caan.
• 0:54 - Very brief left breast turning over in bed and sitting up.
Audrey Rose (1977) . . . . .Janice Templeton
The Goodbye Girl (1977). . . . . Paula McFadden
The Cheap Detective (1978) . . . . Georgia Merkle
Chapter Two (1979). . . . . Jennie MacLaine
Promises in the Dark (1979) . . . . . . Dr. Alexandra Kenda
Only When I Laugh (1981). . . . . Georgia
Max Dugan Returns (1983) . . . . Nora
Heartbreak Ridge (1986) . . . . .Aggie
Drop Dead Fred (1991) . . . .
Made for Cable Movies:
Dinner At Eight (1989). . . . . .Millicent Jordan
The Image (1990) . . . . .Jean Cromwell
• 0:08 - Two brief side views of left breast standing in bathroom after Albert Finney gets out of the shower.
TV:
Sibs (1991-) . . . .

Massey, Anna
Films:
Peeping Tom (1960; British) . . . . .Helen Stephens
Frenzy (1972; British). . . . . Babs Milligan
•• 0:45 - Topless getting out of bed and then buns, walking to the bathroom. Most probably a body double.
Sweet William (1980; British) . . . . .Edna
Five Days One Summer (1982) . . . . .Jennifer Pierce
Foreign Body (1986; British) . . . . Miss Furze
Mountains of the Moon (1989). . . . . Mrs. Arundell
The Tall Guy (1990) . . . . .Mary

Mastrantonio, Mary Elizabeth
Films:
Scarface (1983). . . . . Gina
• 2:36 - (0:39 into tape 2) Very, very brief left breast when she gets shot and her nightgown opens up when she gets hit.
The Color of Money (1986). . . . . Carmen
• 0:41 - Brief topless in bathroom mirror drying herself off while Paul Newman talks to Tom Cruise. Long shot, hard to see.
Slam Dance (1987) . . . . .Helen Drood
The January Man (1988) . . . . Bernadette Flynn
• 0:40 - Topless in bed with Kevin Kline. Side view of left breast squished against Kline.
••• 0:42 - Topless after Kline gets out of bed. Brief shot, but very nice!
The Abyss (1989) . . . . .Lindsey Brigman
• 1:41 - Topless during C.P.R. scene.
Class Action (1991). . . . . Margaret Ward
Robin Hood: Prince of Thieves (1991) . . . . Marian
Made for Cable Movies:
Mussolini and I (1985; HBO) . . . . . Edda Mussolini Ciano

Mathias, Darian
Films:
My Chauffeur (1986) .Dolly
Blue Movies (1988). Kathy
• 0:35 - Very brief topless twice acting for the first time in a porno film.

Mathis, Samantha
Films:
Pump Up the Volume (1990) . . . . Nora Diniro
•• 1:13 - Topless taking off sweater on patio with Christian Slater.
Made for TV Movies:
83 Hours 'til Dawn (1990). . . . . .Julie Burdock
Extreme Close-Up (1990) . . . .
To My Daughter (1990) . . . .
TV:
Aaron's Way (1988). . . . . Roseanne Miller

Matlin, Marlee
Films:
Children of a Lesser God (1986) . . . . .Sarah
(Academy Award for Best Actress.)
0:44 - Brief buns under water in swimming pool. Don't see her face.
0:47 - Part of left breast hugging William Hurt seen from under water.
Walker (1988) .Ellen Martin
Made for TV Movies:
Bridge to Silence (1988). . . . .
TV:
Reasonable Doubts (1991-). . . . .

Matthews, Lisa
Video Tapes:
Playboy Video Calendar 1991 (1990). . . .September
Playboy's Sexy Lingerie II (1990) . . . .
Magazines:
Playboy (Apr 1990) . . . . Playmate
Playboy (Jun 1991). . . . . Playmate of the Year
••• 144-155: Nude.

Mattson, Robin
Films:
Namu, The Killer Whale (1966) . . . . .Lisa Rand
Bonnie's Kids (1973) . . . . Myra
• 0:05 - Brief side view of right breast changing in bedroom while two men watch from outside.
••• 0:07 - Topless washing herself in the bathroom.
Candy Stripe Nurses (1974) . . . . Dianne
•• 0:22 - Nude in gym with the basketball player.
••• 0:40 - Nude in bed with the basketball player.
Return to Macon County (1975) . . . . .Junell
Wolf Lake (1978). . . . . .Linda
a.k.a. Survive the Night at Wolf Lake
• 0:54 - Brief full frontal nudity during rape in cabin. Dark.
• 0:55 - Brief topless afterwards.
Take Two (1988) . . . . Susan Bentley
0:21 - Exercising in yellow outfit while Frank Stallone plays music.
•• 0:25 - Brief topless taking a shower.
0:26 - Showing Grant Goodeve her new two piece swimsuit.
••• 0:29 - Topless in bed with Goodeve.
••• 0:45 - Right breast in shower, then topless getting into bed.
• 0:47 - Brief topless getting out of bed and putting an overcoat on.
0:51 - One piece swimsuit by the swimming pool.
1:12 - In two piece swimsuit at the beach.
••• 1:28 - Topless taking a shower after shooting Goodeve in bed.
Made for TV Movies:
False Witness (1989) . . . . .Jody

TV:
The Guiding Light (1976-77) . . . . Hope Bauer
General Hospital (1980-83) . . . . . Heather Grant Webber
Ryan's Hope (1984) . . . . Delia Reid
Santa Barbara (1985-) . . . . Gina Capwell Timmons

May, Mathilda

a.k.a. Mathilda May Haim.
Daughter of French playwright Victor Haim.
Films:
Dream One (1984; British/French) . . . . Alice
Letters to an Unknown Lover (1985) . . . . Agnes
• 0:43 - Upper half of breasts in bathtub when Gervais opens the door.
••• 0:58 - Buns and topless taking off her robe in Gervais' room.
Lifeforce (1985) . . . . Space Girl
• 0:08 - Full frontal nudity in glass case upside down.
• 0:13 - Topless, lying down in space shuttle. Blue light.
••• 0:16 - Topless sitting up in lab to suck the life out of military guard. Brief full frontal nudity.
•• 0:17 - Topless again in the lab.
•• 0:19 - Topless walking around, then buns.
••• 0:20 - Topless walking down the stairs. Brief nude fighting with the guards.
•• 0:44 - Topless with Steve Railsback in red light during his nightmare.
• 1:10 - Brief topless in space shuttle with Railsback.

Mayne, Belinda

Films:
Krull (1983) . . . . Vella
Don't Open 'Till Christmas (1984; British) . . . . Kate
Lassiter (1984) . . . . Helen Boardman
••• 0:06 - In bra then topless letting Tom Selleck undress her while her husband is in the other room.
Fatal Beauty (1987) . . . . Traci

Mayo-Chandler, Karen

Films:
Beverly Hills Cop (1984) . . . . Maitland Receptionist
Explorers (1986) . . . . Starkiller's Girl Friend
Hamburger—The Motion Picture (1986)
. . . . Dr. Victoria Gotbottom
• 0:03 - Brief topless in her office trying to help, then seduce Russell.
Out of the Dark (1988) . . . . .Barbara
• 0:16 - Brief topless pulling red dress down wearing black stocking in Kevin's studio.
••• 0:17 - Topless and buns posing during photo shoot.
Stripped to Kill II (1988) . . . . Cassandra
0:06 - Black bra and panties in dressing room.
•• 0:18 - Topless taking off her top for a customer.
Take Two (1988) . . . . Dorothy
•• 1:17 - Brief topless on bed when her gold dress is pulled down a bit.

Death Feud (1989) . . . . Anne
0:26 - In lingerie with a customer.
•• 0:36 - In white lingerie, then topless several times outside taking off robe.
Magazines:
Playboy (Dec 1989) . . . . The Joker Was Wild
••• 94-103: Nude.

Mayor, Cari

Films:
Spring Fever USA (1988) . . . . Girl on Campus
Summer Job (1989) . . . . Donna
• 0:10 - Brief topless twice, taking off her top before and after Herman comes into the room.

Mayron, Melanie

Films:
Harry and Tonto (1974) . . . . Ginger
(She's a lot heavier in this film than she is now.)
• 0:57 - Very brief topless in motel room with Art Carney taking off her towel and putting on blouse. Long shot, hard to see.
Car Wash (1976) . . . . Marsha
The Great Smokey Roadblock (1976) . . . . Lulu
You Light Up My Life (1977) . . . . Annie Gerrara
Girlfriends (1978) . . . . Susan Weinblatt
(She's still a bit overweight.)
• 0:14 - Buns, very brief lower frontal nudity and brief left breast getting dressed in bathroom.
Heartbeeps (1981) . . . . .Susan
Missing (1982) . . . . Terry Simon
The Boss' Wife (1986) . . . . Janet Keefer
Sticky Fingers (1988) . . . . Lolly
Checking Out (1989) . . . . Jenny Macklin
My Blue Heaven (1990) . . . . Crystal
Made for TV Movies:
Hustling (1975) . . . . Dee Dee
Playing for Time (1980) . . . .
(Lost a lot of weight.)
0:11 - Brief side view of left breast getting her hair cut. She's behind Vanessa Redgrave. You can't really see anything.
TV:
thirtysomething (1987-91) . . . . Melissa Steadman

McArthur, Kimberly

Films:
Young Doctors in Love (1982) . . . . Jyll Omato
•• 0:58 - Topless in front of Dabney Coleman after taking off her Santa Claus outfit in his study.
Easy Money (1983) . . . . Ginger Jones
•• 0:47 - Topless sunbathing in the backyard when seen by Rodney Dangerfield.
Malibu Express (1984) .Faye
•• 0:10 - Topless taking a shower on the boat with Barbara Edwards.
Slumber Party Massacre II (1987) . . . . .Amy

TV:
　　Santa Barbara (1988-90) . . . . Kelly
Video Tapes:
　　Playmate Playoffs . . . . Playmate
　　Playboy's Playmate Review (1982) . . . . . . Playmate
　　••• 0:19 - In sauna, taking a shower, in front of fireplace.
　　　　Nude.
Magazines:
　　Playboy (Jan 1982) . . . . Playmate

McBride, Harlee

Films:
　　Young Lady Chatterley (1977) . . . Cynthia Chatterley
　　•• 0:19 - Nude masturbating in front of mirror.
　　••• 0:41 - Nude in bathtub while maid washes her.
　　••• 0:52 - Nude in car while the chauffeur is driving.
　　••• 1:03 - Nude in the garden with the sprinklers on
　　　　making love with the Gardener.
　　House Calls (1978) . . . .
　　Young Lady Chatterley II (1986) . Cynthia Chatterley
　　•• 0:20 - Topless getting a massage with Elanor.
　　••• 0:28 - Topless taking a bath with Jenny.
　　••• 0:35 - Topless in library seducing Virgil.
　　••• 0:50 - Topless in back of the car with the Count.
　　••• 0:58 - Topless in the garden with Robert.
Magazines:
　　Playboy (Dec 1977). . . . . Sex Stars of 1977
　　••• 217: Full frontal nudity lying on bed.

McBroom, Dirga

Films:
　　Flashdance (1983). . . . . Heels
　　The Rosebud Beach Hotel (1985). . . . . .Bellhop
　　• 0:49 - Buns, then topless, standing with the other
　　　　bell hops, outfitted with military attire. (She's the
　　　　one at the far end, furthest from the camera.)
　　Vendetta (1986) . . . . Widow

McClellan, Michelle

See: Bauer, Michelle.

McCormick, Maureen

Films:
　　Take Down (1978) . . . . Brooke Cooper
　　The Idolmaker (1980) . . . . Ellen Fields
　　Texas Lightning (1980) .Fay
　　　　1:04 - Very brief upper half of right breast popping
　　　　out of slip while struggling on bed with two jerks.
　　　　Long shot, hard to see.
　　Return to Horror High (1987) . . . . Officer Tyler
TV:
　　The Brady Bunch (1969-74) . . . . Marcia Brady

McCullough, Julie

Films:
　　Big Bad Mama II (1987) . . . . Polly McClatchie
　　•• 0:12 - Topless with Danielle Brisebois playing in a
　　　　pond underneath a waterfall.
　　•• 0:36 - In lingerie, then topless sitting on Jordan who
　　　　is tied up in bed.
　　The Blob (1988). . . . . Susie
TV:
　　Growing Pains (1989-) . . . . .Julie
Video Tapes:
　　Playboy Video Calendar 1987 (1986). . . . . Playmate
　　Playboy Video Calendar 1988 (1987). . . . . Playmate
Magazines:
　　Playboy (Feb 1986) . . . . Playmate
　　　　84:
　　Playboy (Oct 1989) . . . . .Julie McCullough
　　••• 74-79: Nude.
　　Playboy (Dec 1989) . . . . Holy Sex Stars of 1989!
　　•• 181: Left breast, while sitting in a chair.

McCurry, Natalie

Films:
　　Dead-End Drive-In (1986; Australian) . . . . . . .Carmen
　　•• 0:19 - Topless in red car with Ned Manning.
Made for TV Movies:
　　Danger Down Under (1988) . . . . .Katherine Dillingham

McDaniel, Donna

Films:
　　Angel (1983) . . . . .Crystal
　　• 0:19 - Brief topless, dead in bed when the killer pulls
　　　　the covers down.
　　Hollywood Hot Tubs (1984) . . . . Leslie Maynard

McDermott, Colleen

Films:
　　Paradise Motel (1985) . . . . Debbie
　　•• 0:24 - Topless in motel room with Mic, when Sam
　　　　lets them use a room.
　　Demonwarp (1988). Cindy
　　•• 0:23 - Topless and buns drying herself off after taking
　　　　a shower.
　　• 0:24 - Very brief lower frontal nudity, under her tow-
　　　　el, trying to run up the stairs.

McDonough, Mary

Films:
　　Mortuary (1981) . . . . .Christie Parson
　　(All scenes with nudity are probably a body double.)
　　　　0:15 - Buns and very brief topless making love with
　　　　her boyfriend on the floor. Long shot, hard to see.
　　　　1:06 - Full frontal nudity on table in the morgue,
　　　　dead.
TV:
　　The Waltons (1972-81) . . . . Erin Walton

McEnroe, Annie
Films:
The Hand (1981). . . . . Stella Roche
•• 0:51 - Topless undressing for Michael Caine.
Warlords of the 21st Century (1982). . . . . Carlie
a.k.a. Battletruck
The Survivors (1983). Doreen
Howling II...Your Sister is a Werewolf (1984) . . . . . Jenny
Purple Hearts (1984) . . . . Hallaway
•• 1:23 - Brief topless coming out of the bathroom sur-
prising Ken Wahl and Cheryl Ladd.
True Stories (1986) . . . . Kay Culver
Wall Street (1987). . . . . Muffie Livingston
Beetlejuice (1988). . . . . Jane Butterfield
Cop (1988). . . . . Amy Cranfield
Magazines:
Playboy (Nov 1981) . . . . Sex in Cinema 1981
•• 172: Topless.

McGavin, Graem
Films:
Angel (1983). . . . . Lana
•• 0:31 - Topless standing in hotel bathroom talking to
her John.
My Tutor (1983) . . . . Sylvia
••• 0:21 - In white bra, then topless in back seat of a car
in a parking lot with Matt Lattanzi.
Weekend Pass (1984) . . . . Tawny Ryatt

McGillis, Kelly
Films:
Reuben, Reuben (1983) . . . . Geneva Spofford
Witness (1985) . . . . Rachel
••• 1:18 - Topless taking off her top to take a bath while
Harrison Ford watches.
Top Gun (1986) . . . . Charlie
Made in Heaven (1987) . . . Annie Packert/Ally Chandler
Unsettled Land (1987) . . . . Anda
The Accused (1988) . . . . Kathryn Murphy
The House on Carroll Street (1988). . . . . Emily
• 0:39 - Brief topless reclining into the water in the
bathtub.
Winter People (1989) . . . . Collie Wright
Cat Chaser (1991). . . . .
Full frontal nudity.

McGovern, Elizabeth
Films:
Ordinary People (1980). . . . . Jeanine
Ragtime (1981). . . . . Evelyn Nesbit
••• 0:52 - Topless in living room sitting on couch and ar-
guing with a lawyer. Very long scene.
Lovesick (1983). Chloe Allen

Once Upon a Time in America (1984) . . . . Deborah
(Long version.)
• 2:33 - (0:32 into tape 2) Brief glimpses of left breast
when Robert De Niro tries to rape her in the back
seat of a car.
Racing with the Moon (1984). . . . . . . Caddie Winger
• 0:45 - Upper half of breast in pond with Sean Penn.
The Bedroom Window (1987) . . . . Denise
1:25 - Topless silhouette on shower curtain when
Steve Guttenberg peeks in the bathroom.
She's Having a Baby (1988) . . . . Kristy
Johnny Handsome (1989). . . . . Donna McCarty
•• 0:47 - Right breast in bed with Mickey Rourke.
A Handmaid's Tale (1990) . . . . Moira
A Shock to the System (1990) . . . . Stella Anderson
Made for Cable Movies:
Women & Men: Stories of Seduction (1990; HBO)
. . . . Vicki
0:18 - In white lingerie in train car with Beau Bridges.
••• 0:22 - Topless when Bridges takes her top off when
she lies back in bed.

McGregor, Angela Punch
Films:
The Island (1980) . . . . Beth
•• 0:45 - Topless taking off poncho to make love with
Michael Caine in hut after rubbing stuff on him.
0:50 - Braless under poncho walking towards Caine.
We of the Never Never (1983) . . . . Jeannie
A Test of Love (1984; Australian) . . . . . Jessica Hathaway

McIntaggart, Peggy
Video Tapes:
Playboy Video Centerfold: Peggy McIntagart
. . . . Playmate
Playboy Video Calendar 1991 (1990). . . . . February
••• 0:05 - Nude.
Playmates at Play (1990) . . . . Gotta Dance
Magazines:
Playboy (Jan 1990). . . . . Playmate

McIntosh, Valerie
Films:
Weekend Pass (1984). Etta
The Naked Cage (1985) . . . . Ruby
••• 0:24 - Topless and buns in infirmary, then getting at-
tacked by Smiley. Brief lower frontal nudity.
• 0:28 - Topless, hanging by rope dead.
Quicksilver (1986) . . . . Hooker

McIssac, Marianne
Films:
In Praise of Older Women (1978; Canadian) . . Julika
•• 0:23 - Topless and buns, getting into bed with Tom
Berenger.
TV:
The Baxters (1980-81) . . . . Allison Baxter

McNeil, Kate

a.k.a. Kathryn McNeil.
Films:
Beach House (1982) . . . .
House on Sorority Row (1983) . . . . Katherine
Monkey Shines: An Experiment in Fear (1988)
. . . . Melanie Parker
• 1:07 - Brief upper half of right breast, making love
with Allan. Dark, hard to see anything.
TV:
As the World Turns . . . . Karen Haines-Stenbeck
WIOU (1990-91) . . . . Taylor Young

McNichol, Kristy

Films:
The End (1978). Julie Lawson
Little Darlings (1980) . . . . Angel
The Night the Lights Went Out in Georgia (1981)
. . . . Amanda Child
Only When I Laugh (1981) . . . . Polly
The Pirate Movie (1982; Australian). . . . . .Mabel
White Dog (1982) . . . . Julie Sawyer
Brief topless when blouse gapes open.
Just the Way You Are (1984) . . . . Susan
• 0:50 - Very brief left breast showing her friend that
she's not too hot because there is nothing under her
white coat. Medium long shot.
You Can't Hurry Love (1984). . . . . .Rhonda
Dream Lover (1986). . . . . Kathy Gardner
• 0:17 - Very, very brief right breast getting out of bed,
then walking around in a white top and underwear.
0:21 - Walking around in the white top again. Same
scene used in flashbacks at 0:34, 0:46 and 0:54.
Two Moon Junction (1988). . . . . Patti Jean
•• 0:42 - Topless in gas station restroom changing camisole tops with Sherilyn Fenn.
The Forgotten One (1989) . . . . Barbara Stupple
0:06 - Jogging in braless pink top, then talking to Terry O'Quinn.
1:33 - In pink top lying in bed.
Made for TV Movies:
Like Mom, Like Me (1978) . . . .
TV:
Empty Nest . . . . Barbara Weston
Apple's Way (1974-75) . . . . Patricia Apple
Family (1976-80) . . . . Letitia "Buddy" Lawrence

McQuade, Kris

Films:
Alvin Purple (1973; Australian). . . . . Samantha
••• 0:21 - Topless and buns, painting each other's bodies
with Alvin.
Alvin Rides Again (1974; Australian) . . . . Mandy
••• 0:48 - Full frontal nudity, taking off red dress and get-
ting into bed with Alvin. More topless lying in bed.
Long scene.
Lonely Hearts (1983; Australian) . . . . .Rosemarie
The Coca-Cola Kid (1985; Australian) . . . . Juliana

McVeigh, Rose

a.k.a. Rosemary McVeigh.
Films:
A Night in Heaven (1983) . . . . Alison
Porky's Revenge (1985; Canadian) . . . . . Miss Webster
••• 0:39 - In black bra, panties, garter belt and stockings
then topless in her apartment with Mr. Dobish while
Pee Wee and his friends secretly watch.

Medak, Karen

Films:
A Girl to Kill For (1989) . . . . Sue
••• 0:17 - Topless showering at the beach after surfing
with Chuck.
0:38 - In bra lying on desk in office with Chuck.
•• 1:08 - Topless in spa when Chuck takes her shirt off.
Then miscellaneous shots making love.
The Marrying Man (1991) . . . . Sherry

Mejias, Isabelle

Films:
Daughter of Death (1982) . . . . .Julie
a.k.a. Julie Darling
Bay Boy (1985; Canadian) . . . . Mary McNeil
•• 1:28 - Brief topless in her bedroom with Kiefer Suth-
erland, then brief topless in bed with him.
Higher Education (1987; Canadian) . . . . . Carrie Hanson
Meatballs III (1987) . . . . .Wendy
Fall From Innocence (1988) . . . .
State Park (1988; Canadian). . . . . Marsha
Made for TV Movies:
Special People (1984). . . . . .Julie

Melato, Mariangela

Films:
Love and Anarchy (1974; Italian) . . . . Salome
The Nada Gang (1974; French/Italian). . . . . Cash
The Seduction of Mimi (1974; Italian) . . . .
Swept Away (1975; Italian) . . . . .Raffaela Lenzetti
*a.k.a. Swept Away...by an unusual destiny in the blue sea
of august*
•• 1:10 - Topless on the sand when Giancarlo Giannini
catches her and makes love with her.
Moses (1976; British/Italian). . . . . Princess Bithia
Flash Gordon (1980) . . . . Kala
So Fine (1981) . . . . Lira
Summer Night (1987; Italian) . . . . Signora Bolk
•• 0:26 - Topless behind gauze net over bed making
love with a German guy.
•• 1:02 - Topless on the bed making love with the prisoner.
•• 1:09 - Topless again.
••• 1:13 - Buns, walking out of the ocean, then topless
with wet hair.

Mell, Marisa

Films:
5 Sinners (1961) . . . . Liliane
French Dressing (1964) . . . . Francoise Fayol
Casanova '70 (1965; Italian) . . . . Thelma
City of Fear (1965) . . . . Ilona
Masquerade (1965) . . . . Sophie
Objective 500 Million (1966) . . . . Yo
Secret Agent Super Dragon (1966) . . . . . . Charity Farrell
Anyone Can Play (1968; Italian) . . . . Paola
Danger: Diabolik (1968) . . . . Eva Kant
Mahogany (1975) . . . . Carlotta Gavin
Sex on the Run (1979; German/French/Italian)
. . . . Francesca
a.k.a. Some Like It Cool
a.k.a. Casanova and Co.
   • 0:52 - Very, very brief left breast getting out of bed
      with Tony Curtis.
      1:12 - Braless in white nightgown.
Quest for the Mighty Sword (1989) . . . . Nephele
Magazines:
Playboy (Mar 1977) . . . . Comeback for Casanova
   •• 89: Topless in water.

Menzies, Heather

Wife of actor Robert Urich.
Films:
The Sound of Music (1965) . . . . Louisa
Hawaii (1966) . . . . Mercy Bromley
How Sweet It Is (1968) . . . . Tour Girl
Hail, Hero! (1969) . . . . Molly Adams
Outside In (1972) . . . . Chris
Sssssssss (1973) . . . . Kristine Stoner
   a.k.a. Ssssnake
Piranha (1978) . . . . Maggie McKeown
Endangered Species (1982) . . . . Susan
TV:
Logan's Run (1977-78) . . . . Jessica
Magazines:
Playboy (Aug 1973) . . . . Tender Trapp
   ••• 81-85: Nude.

Meredith, Penny

Films:
Happy Housewives . . . . Margaretta
   • 0:02 - Brief right breast talking on the telephone
      while Bob makes love with her.
   •• 0:19 - Topless standing up in bathtub talking to Bob.
   • 0:34 - In sheer black lingerie.
   • 1:05 - Brief topless pulling her top down when inter-
      rupted by the policeman at the window.
The Flesh & Blood Show (1974; British) . . . .

Meyer, Bess

Films:
One More Saturday Night (1986) . . . . Tobi
   • 1:02 - Brief topless in bed with Tom Davis.
She's Out of Control (1989) . . . . Cheryl
TV:
Parenthood (1990) . . . . Julie

Michaels, Lorraine

Films:
Star 80 (1983) . . . . Paul's Party Guest
Malibu Express (1984) . . . . Liza Chamberlin
   ••• 0:23 - Topless in the shower making love with Shane,
      while camera photographs them.
B.O.R.N. (1988) . . . . Dr. Black
Magazines:
Playboy (Apr 1981) . . . . Playmate

Michaelsen, Helle

Video Tapes:
Playboy Video Calendar 1991 (1990) . . . . April
   ••• 0:14 - Nude.
Magazines:
Playboy (Aug 1988) . . . . Playmate

Michan, Cherie

Films:
Wrong is Right (1982) . . . . Erika
Fever Pitch (1985) . . . . Rose O'Sharon
Made for Cable TV:
**Dream On: The Name of the Game is Five-Card
   Stud** (1991; HBO) . . . . Alison
   ••• 0:16 - In black bra, then topless, literally losing her
      shirt during poker game.
      0:17 - Very brief nipple seen through her folded
      arms.

Michelle, Ann

Films:
Haunted (1974) . . . .
Young Lady Chatterley (1977) . . . . . . Gwen (roommate)
French Quarter (1978)
   . . . . . "Coke Eye" Laura/Policewoman in French Hotel
   • 0:42 - Right breast, when Josie wakes her up.
   ••• 0:43 - Topless in bed, caressing Josie's breasts.
   •• 0:58 - Topless during voodoo ceremony. Close ups of
      breasts with snake.
   • 1:19 - Brief topless, sitting in bed.
   ••• 1:20 - More topless sitting in bed, talking to a cus-
      tomer. Long scene.

Michelle, Shelley
Films:
In the Cold of the Night (1989) . . . . Model 3
Overexposed (1990)
. . . . body double for Catherine Oxenberg
•• 0:54 - Left breast several times, buns when taking off
panties, lower frontal nudity while in bed with Hank.
Wearing a wig with wavy hair.
Pretty Woman (1990) . . . . body double for Julia Roberts
(Body double for Julia Roberts *only* at the begining of the
film when she is getting dressed.)
0:04 - In black panties and bra, waking up and getting dressed.

Micula, Stacia
See: Fox, Samantha.

Mierisch, Susan
Films:
Cave Girl (1985) . . . . Locker Room Student
•• 0:05 - Topless with four other girls in the girls' locker
room undressing, then running after Rex. She's
blonde, wearing red panties and a necklace.
Neon Maniacs (1985) . . . . Young Lover
• 0:07 - Very brief upper half of right breast while kissing her boyfriend at night.

Miles, Sarah
Films:
The Servant (1963) . . . . Vera
Those Magnificent Men in their Flying Machines (1965)
. . . . Patricia Rawnsley
Blow-Up (1966; British/Italian) . . . . Patricia
Ryan's Daughter (1970) . . . . Rosy Ryan
Lady Caroline Lamb (1973) . . . . . Lady Caroline Lamb
The Man Who Loved Cat Dancing (1973)
. . . . Catherine Crocker
Topless.
The Sailor Who Fell From Grace with the Sea
(1976). . . . . Anne Osborne
• 0:18 - Topless sitting at the vanity getting dressed
while her son watches through peephole.
•• 0:23 - Topless, fantasizing about her husband.
•• 0:42 - Nude, making love with Kris Kristofferson.
• 1:15 - Brief right breast, in bed with Kristofferson.
The Big Sleep (1978; British) . . . . . Charlotte Sternwood
Venom (1982; British) . . . . Dr. Marion Stowe
Ordeal by Innocence (1984) . . . . Mary Durrant
Steaming (1985; British) . . . . Sarah
•• 0:23 - Topless getting into pool with Vanessa
Redgrave.
•• 0:49 - Topless getting undressed.
•• 1:31 - Nude lying down next to pool.
Hope and Glory (1987; British) . . . . Grace Rohan
White Mischief (1988). Alice
Made for Cable Movies:
A Ghost in Monte Carlo (1990) . . . .

Magazines:
Playboy (Jul 1976)
. . . . Kris and Sarah & The Soul of Sarah
••• 122-129: Nude.
Playboy (Dec 1976) . . . . .Sex Stars of 1976
••• 181: Full frontal nudity standing on bed with Kris
Kristofferson.
Playboy (Jan 1989). . . . . Women of the Seventies
•• 213: Topless in bed with Kris Kristofferson.

Miles, Sylvia
Films:
The Sentinel (1977). . . . . Gerde
• 0:33 - Brief left breast, three times, standing behind
Beverly D'Angelo. Right breast, ripping dress of
Christina Raines. B&W dream.
1:23 - Brief topless, three times, with D'Angelo made
up to look like zombies, munching on a dead Chris
Sarandon.
1:27 - Very brief right breast during big zombie
scene.
• 1:28 - Brief topless when the zombies start dying.
The Funhouse (1981). . . . . Madame Zena
Wall Street (1987) . . . . .Realtor
Crossing Delancey (1988) . . . . . . Hannah Mandelbaum
Spike of Bensonhurst (1988) . . . . Congresswoman
She-Devil (1989) .Mrs. Fisher

Milford, Penelope
Films:
Man on a Swing (1974) . . . . Evelyn Moore
Coming Home (1978) . . . . Viola Munson
• 1:19 - Doing strip tease in room with Jane Fonda and
two guys. Sort of right breast peeking out between
her arms when she changes her mind.
The Last Word (1979) . . . . Denise Travis
Endless Love (1981) . . . . Ingrid
Take This Job and Shove It (1981) . . . . . . Lenore Meade
Blood Link (1983) . . . . Julie Warren
•• 0:22 - Topless in bed with Craig. Very brief left breast
grabbing pillow.
•• 1:24 - In black bra in greenhouse with Keith, then
topless, then brief right breast.
••• 1:35 - Topless in bedroom with Keith.
The Golden Seal (1983) . . . . Tania Lee
Heathers (1989) . . . . Pauline Fleming
Made for Cable TV:
The Hitchhiker: Man at the Window
. . . . .Diane Hampton
•• 0:09 - Topless in white panties making love with her
husband on the couch.
Made for TV Movies:
The Burning Bed (1984). . . . .

Milhench, Ann
Films:
Blood Debts (1983)........................Lisa
Sloane (1984) .... Janice Thursby
•• 0:02 - Topless and buns getting out of shower and being held by kidnappers.

Miller, Ginger
Video Tapes:
Boxing Babes (1991)...................... herself
Magazines:
Penthouse (Sep 1986) .... Pet

Miller, Marjorie
See: Poremba, Jean.

Miller, Sherrie
Films:
Goin' All the Way (1981) ....Candy
0:47 - Brief right breast getting out of bubble bath.
•• 0:49 - Topless with Artie during his fantasy.
Separate Vacations (1985)................... Sandy

Millian, Andra
Films:
Stacy's Knights (1983)..................... Stacy
Nightfall (1988) ....Anna
• 0:12 - Very brief topless making love with David Birney.
• 0:41 - Very brief topless making love in front of a fire.
0:58 - Same scene in a flashback while the guy is talking to another woman.

Mills, Donna
Films:
Play Misty for Me (1971)................. Tobie
• 1:10 - Brief side view of right breast hugging Clint Eastwood in a pond near a waterfall. Long shot, hard to see.
Murph the Surf (1975) .... Ginny Eaton
Fire! (1977)....................................
Made for TV Movies:
Bunco (1977) ....
Doctor's Private Lives (1978).....................
TV:
The Good Life (1971-72)................ Jane Miller
Knots Landing (1980-89) ....
Abby Ewing Sumner Cunningham
Magazines:
Playboy (Nov 1989) .... Oh! Donna
• 82-87: Buns in photos taken around 1966.

Mills, Hayley
Daughter of actor Sir John Mills.
Sister of actress Juliet Mills.
Films:
Tiger Bay (1959; British/B&W) .... Gillie
Pollyanna (1960) ....Pollyanna
Whistle Down the Wind (1961; British) .. Kathy Bostock
In Search of the Castaways (1962) .... Mary grant
The Chalk Garden (1964)................... Laurel
The Moon-Spinners (1964) .... Nikky Ferris
The Parent Trap (1964)
.... Sharon McKendirck/Susan Evers
That Darn Cat (1965)................. Patti Randall
The Trouble with Angels (1966) .... Mary Clancy
Deadly Strangers (1974; British)............. Belle
1:02 - Buns in bathtub when her uncle watches her.
1:05 - In black bra, garter belt and panties while Steven fantasizes as he sees her through a keyhole.
••• 1:13 - In white bra and panties while Steven watches through keyhole, then topless taking off bra and reading a newspaper.
1:15 - In white bra, getting dressed.
Endless Night (1977) .... Ellie
Appointment with Death (1988) ....Miss Quinton
Miniseries:
The Flame Trees of Thika (1982)............... Tilly
Made for TV Movies:
The Parent Trap II (1986) ....

Mills, Juliet
Daughter of actor Sir John Mills.
Sister of actress Hayley Mills.
Films:
The Rare Breed (1966) .... Hilary Price
Avanti! (1973) .... Pamela Piggott
(Not available on video tape. Shown on *The Arts and Entertainment Channel* periodically. Scenes are listed as 0:00 since I can't time correctly with the commercials.)
0:00 - Buns, climbing out of the water onto a rock.
• 0:00 - Side view of right breast lying on rock talking to Jack Lemmon.
••• 0:00 - Brief topless waving to fishermen on a passing boat.
0:00 - Brief buns putting something up in the closet in Jack Lemmon's hotel room.
Beyond the Door (1975; Italian/U.S.).......... Jessica
Miniseries:
Till We Meet Again (1989) ....Vivianne
TV:
Nanny and the Professor (1970-71) .... Phoebe Figalilly
Magazines:
Playboy (Nov 1973) .... Sex in Cinema 1973
•• 153: Topless in photo from *Avanti*.

Mimieux, Yvette

Films:
Where the Boys Are (1960) . . . . Melanie
Diamond Head (1962) . . . . Sloan Howland
The Four Horsemen of the Apocalypse (1962)
. . . . Chi-Chi Desnoyers
Three in the Attic (1968). . . . . .Tobey Clinton
Jackson County Jail (1976) . . . . Dinah Hunter
  • 0:39 - Topless in jail cell getting raped by policeman.
The Black Hole (1979). . . . . Dr. Kate McGraw
The Time Machine (1980). . . . . Weena
Made for TV Movies:
Perry Mason: The Case of the Desperate Deception
  (1990). . . . . Danielle Altmann
TV:
The Most Deadly Game (1970-71) . . . . . .Vanessa Smith
Berrengers (1985). . . . . .Shane Bradley

Minnick, Dani

Films:
The Sleeping Car (1990). . . . . Joanne
Made for Cable TV:
Tales From the Crypt: The Man Who was Death
  (1989; HBO) . . . . Cynthia Baldwin
  • 0:17 - Very brief side view of right breast in shower.

Miou-Miou

Films:
Going Places (1974; French). . . . . .Marie-Ange
  ••• 0:14 - Topless sitting in bed, filing her nails. Full fron-
    tal nudity standing up and getting dressed.
  •• 0:48 - Topless in bed with Pierrot and Jean-Claude.
  • 0:51 - Left breast under Pierrot.
  ••• 0:52 - Buns in bed when Jean-Claude rolls off her. Full
    frontal nudity sitting up with the two guys in bed.
  •• 1:21 - Brief topless opening the door. Topless and
    panties walking in after the two guys.
  • 1:27 - Partial left breast taking off dress and walking
    into house.
    1:28 - Very brief topless closing the shutters.
  •• 1:31 - Full frontal nudity in open dress running after
    the two guys. Long shot. Full frontal nudity putting
    her wet dress on.
  • 1:41 - Topless in back of car. Dark.
The Genius (1976; Italian/German/French) . . . . Lucy
Jonah—Who Will be 25 in the Year 2000
  (1976; Swiss). . . . . Marie
Memories of a French Whore (1979) . . . .
My Other Husband (1981; French) . . . .
Entre Nous (1983; French) . . . . Madeleine
  a.k.a. Coup de Foudre
Dog Day (1984; French) . . . . .Jessica
La Lectrice (1989; French) . . . . Constance/Marie
  a.k.a. The Reader
    1:06 - Making love with a guy while reading to him
    in bed.

• 1:18 - Full frontal nudity lying in bed. Close-up pan
    shot from lower frontal nudity, then left breast, then
    right breast.
• 1:20 - Very brief right breast, then lower frontal nu-
    dity getting dressed.
Magazines:
Playboy (Nov 1990) . . . . Sex in Cinema 1990
  •• 144: Topless in still from *Going Places*.

Miracle, Irene

Films:
Midnight Express (1978; British) . . . . .Susan
  •• 1:39 - Topless in prison visiting booth showing her
    breasts to Brad Davis so he can masturbate.
Inferno (1980; Italian) . . . . Rose Elliot
In the Shadow of Kilimanjaro (1985) . . . . . Lee Ringtree
    0:18 - Brief breasts in bed with Timothy Bottoms.
    Kind of hard to see anything because it's dark.
The Last Days of Philip Banter (1987). . .Elizabeth Banter
Puppet Master (1989) . . . . Dana Hadley
Watchers II (1990) . . . . Sarah Ferguson
    0:28 - In pink leotard, going into aerobics studio.
  ••• 0:40 - Side view in black bra, then topless a few times
    in the bathtub.
Made for TV Movies:
Shattered Dreams (1990). . . . . .Elaine
Magazines:
Playboy (Nov 1978) . . . . Sex in Cinema 1978
  •• 183: Topless still from *Midnight Express*.

Mirren, Helen

Films:
A Midsummer Night's Dream (1968) . . . . Hermia
Age of Consent (1969; Australian) . . . . Cora
  • 0:48 - Topless several times in the mirror. Brief lower
    frontal nudity, kneeling on the floor.
  •• 0:55 - Brief topless and buns quite a few time, snor-
    keling under water.
  ••• 1:20 - Topless and half of buns, posing in the water
    for James Mason. Then getting out.
Savage Messiah (1972; British) . . . . Gosh Smith-Boyle
  0:40 & 1:13.
O Lucky Man! (1973; British) . . . . Patricia Burgess
Caligula (1980) . . . . Caesonia
  (X-rated, 147 minute version.)
    1:02 - Side view of buns with Malcolm McDowell
  • 1:13 - Brief topless several times getting out of bed
    to run after McDowell. Dark.
    1:15 - Very brief left breast taking off her dress to dry
    McDowell off.
The Fiendish Plot of Dr. Fu Manchu (1980) . . Alice Rage
Hussy (1980; British) . . . . .Beaty
  •• 0:22 - Left breast, then side of right breast lying in
    bed with John Shea.
  ••• 0:29 - Nude, making love in bed with Shea.
  •• 0:31 - Full frontal nudity in bathtub.
The Long Good Friday (1980; British). . . . . Victoria

Excalibur (1981; British) . . . . Morgana
   • 1:31 - Side view of left breast under a fishnet outfit climbing into bed.
2010 (1984) . . . . Tanya Kirbuk
Cal (1984; Irish) . . . . Marcella
   1:18 - In a white bra and slip.
   •• 1:20 - Brief frontal nudity taking off clothes and getting into bed with Cal in his cottage, then right breast making love.
White Knights (1985) . . . . Galina Ivanova
The Mosquito Coast (1986) . . . . Mother
Pascali's Island (1988; British) . . . . Lydia Neuman
   • 1:00 - Left breast, lying in bed with Charles Dance. Long shot.
Red King, White Knight (1989) . . . . .Anna
When the Whales Came (1989) . . . . . .Clemmie Jenkins
The Cook, The Thief, His Wife & Her Lover (1990)
  . . . . Georgina Spica
   0:22 - In black bra in restroom performing fellatio on Michael.
   •• 0:32 - In lingerie undressing, then lower frontal nudity, buns and left breast in kitchen with Michael.
   • 0:42 - Buns and right breast, while making love with Michael again.
   •• 0:57 - Topless sitting and talking with Michael.
   1:01 - Buns, kneeling on table.
   • 1:05 - Brief topless, while leaning back on table with Michael.
   1:07 - Lower frontal nudity opening her coat for Michael.
   • 1:11 - Buns and topless in kitchen.
   ••• 1:14 - Buns, getting into meat truck. Full frontal nudity in truck and walking around with Michael.
The Comfort of Strangers (1991) . . . . Caroline
Made for TV Movies:
Mystery! Cause Célèbre (1991) . . . .Alma Rattenbury
   •• 0:27 - Topless in bed when Bowman pulls down the sheets in bed.
   • 0:28 - Brief topless and buns putting slip on.
Magazines:
Playboy (Nov 1990) . . . . Sex in Cinema 1990
   • 147: Topless and buns.

Misch Owens, Laura

Films:
French Quarter (1978) . . . . "Ice Box" Josie/Girl on Bus
   • 0:41 - Topless under sheer white nightgown.
   ••• 0:43 - Full frontal nudity taking off nightgown, wearing garter belt. Getting into bed with Laura.
Magazines:
Playboy (Feb 1975) . . . . Playmate

Moffat, Kitty

Films:
The Beast Within (1982) . . . . .Amanda Platt
   •• 0:06 - Topless, getting her dress torn off by the beast while she is unconscious. Don't see her face, could be a body double.
TV:
Boone (1983-84) . . . . .Susannah Sawyer

Molina, Angela

Films:
That Obscure Object of Desire
   (1977; French/Spanish) . . . . Conchita
   • 0:53 - Brief topless in bathroom.
   •• 1:20 - Nude dancing in front of a group of tourists.
   • 1:29 - Brief topless, taunting Fernando Rey.
The Sabina (1979; Spanish/Swedish) . . . . Pepa
The Eyes, The Mouth (1983; Italian/French) . . . . . Vanda
Demons in the Garden (1984; Spanish) . . . . Angela
Camorra (1986; Italian) . . . . Annunziata
Streets of Gold (1986) . . . . Elena

Moncure, Lisa

Films:
Moving (1988) . . . . Nina Franklin
Lisa (1989) . . . . Sarah
Corporate Affairs (1990) . . . . Carolyn Bean
   • 1:07 - Very, very brief left breast, while kicking Douglas out of cubicle.

Monique

See: Gabrielle, Monique.

Monroe, Marilyn

Films:
Love Happy (1949) . . . . Grunion's Client
All About Eve (1950) . . . . Miss Casswell
Gentlemen Prefer Blondes (1953) . . . . Lorelei
How to Marry a Millionaire (1953) . . . . .Pola
There's no Business like Show Business (1954) . . . . Vicky
Bus Stop (1956) . . . . Cherie
The Seven Year Itch (1957) . . . . The Girl
Some Like it Hot (1959; B&W) . . . . . . .Sugar Kane Kowa
The Misfits (1961) . . . . Roslyn Taber
   0:33 - Almost left breast twice stretching and sitting up in bed.
   0:39 - In two piece swimsuit running out of the lake.
Magazines:
Playboy (Dec 1953) . . . . . . .Sweetheart of the Month Premiere issue of *Playboy* magazine.
Playboy (Jan 1979) . . . . 25 Beautiful Years
   •• 152: Topless in pose from premiere issue.
Playboy (Jan 1987) . . . . Marilyn Remembered 88-95:
Playboy (Jan 1989) . . . . Women of the Fifties
   •• 114: Topless in pose from premiere issue.

Montgomery, Julie

Films:
Girls Night Out (1984) . . . .
a.k.a. Scared to Death
Revenge of the Nerds (1984) . . . . .Betty
  •• 0:49 - Frontal nudity getting ready for a shower.
    1:10 - Topless in the pie pan.
Up the Creek (1984) . . . . .Lisa
The Kindred (1987) . . . . Cindy Russell
South of Reno (1987) . . . . Susan
  • 1:22 - Brief topless kissing Martin. Dark, hard to see.
    1:25 - In motel room wearing black top and panties,
    then pink spandex top with the panties.
Stewardess School (1987) . . . . Pimmie Polk
Made for TV Movies:
Earth-Star Voyager (1988) . . . . Dr. Sally Arthur

Monticelli, Anna-Maria

a.k.a. Anna Jemison.
Films:
Smash Palace (1981; New Zealand) . . . . . Jacqui Shaw
    0:21 - Silhouette of right breast changing while sit-
    ting on the edge of the bed.
  ••• 0:39 - Topless in bed after arguing, then making up
    with Bruno Lawrence.
Heatwave (1983; Australian) . . . . .Victoria
My First Wife (1985) . . . . .Hillary
Nomads (1986) . . . . Niki
  • 0:57 - Left breast, making love in bed with Pierce
    Brosnan. Dark, hard to see anything.

Moore, Candy

See: Kelly, Debra.

Moore, Christine

Films:
Alexa (1988) . . . . Alexa
    0:04 - In red slip in bedroom.
    0:06 - In black bra, on bed with Tommy.
    0:11 - In black lingerie talking on phone in bed.
  •• 0:24 - Topless lying in bed with Anthony while remi-
    niscing.
  •• 1:08 - Topless in bed with Anthony again.
Thrilled to Death (1988) . . . . Nan Christie
    0:31 - In bra in women's locker room.
  ••• 0:38 - Topless in office with Mr. Dance just before kill-
    ing him.

Moore, Demi

Wife of actor Bruce Willis.
Films:
Parasite (1982) . . . . .Patricia Welles
Blame It on Rio (1984) . . . . Nicole Hollis
  • 0:19 - Very brief right breast turning around to greet
    Michael Caine and Joseph Bologna.

No Small Affair (1984) .Laura
  • 1:34 - Very, very brief side view of left breast in bed
    with Jon Cryer.
St. Elmo's Fire (1985) . . . . .Jules
About Last Night... (1986) . . . . Debbie
    0:32 - In white bra getting dressed.
  • 0:34 - Brief upper half of right breast in the bathtub
    with Rob Lowe.
    0:35 - In white bra getting dressed.
  • 0:50 - Side view of right breast, then very brief top-
    less.
  ••• 0:51 - Buns and topless in bed with Lowe, arching
    her back, then lying in bed when he rolls off her.
  •• 0:52 - Topless and buns in kitchen with Lowe.
One Crazy Summer (1986) . . . . Cassandra
Wisdom (1986) . . . . .Karen
The Seventh Sign (1988) . . . . .Abby Quinn
  • 1:03 - Brief topless, taking off bathrobe to take a
    bath. She's about 8 months pregnant, so she's pret-
    ty big.
We're No Angels (1989) . . . . .Molly
  • 0:18 - One long shot, then two brief side views of left
    breast when Robert De Niro watches from outside.
    Reflections in the window make it hard to see.
Ghost (1990) . . . . Molly Jensen
Mortal Thoughts (1991) . . . . .Cynthia Kellogg
Nothing But Trouble (1991) . . . .

Moore, Jeanie

Films:
Vampire at Midnight (1988) . . . . .Amalia
  •• 0:32 - Topless getting up to run an errand.
Wild Man (1988) .Lady at Pool
Dream Trap (1989) . . . . .Blondee
After Dark, My Sweet (1990) . . . . Nanny
The Final Alliance (1990) . . . . Carrie
  • 1:03 - Brief topless getting into bed with David Has-
    selhoff, then brief right breast twice in bed with him.
    A little dark.

Moore, Melissa

Films:
Caged Fury (1989) . . . . Gloria
Scream Dream (1989) . . . . Jamie Summers
  ••• 0:39 - Topless in black panties in room with Derrick.
    Then straddling him.
  •• 0:58 - Topless in dressing room pulling her top down
    during transformation into monster.
Invisible Maniac (1990) . . . . Bunny
  • 0:21 - Buns in shower with the other girls.
  ••• 0:43 - In bra, then topless sitting with yellow towel
    in locker room with the other girls.
  • 0:44 - Topless in shower with the other girls.
  ••• 1:09 - In bra, then topless making out in Principal's
    Office with Chet. Long scene.
Repossessed (1990) . . . . Bimbo Student
  •• 0:05 - Topless pulling her top down in classroom in
    front of Leslie Nielsen.

Vampire Cop (1990). . . . . Melanie Roberts
••• 0:46 - Topless in bed with the Vampire Cop.
•• 0:51 - Right breast, sitting in bed talking with Hans.
• 1:21 - Right breast, in bed on the phone during end
    credits.
Vice Academy, Part 2 (1990) . . . . Glaze
Into the Sun (1991). . . . .
The Killing Zone (1991) . . . .
Nightie Nightmare (1991) . . . .
Poker Night (1991) . . . .
Soul Mates (1991). . . . .
Tower of Terror (1991) . . . .
Magazines:
Playboy (Jul 1991). . . . . The Height Report
••• 140-141: Full frontal nudity on bed.

Moore, Terry

Ex-wife of the late billionaire Howard Hughes.
Films:
Mighty Joe Young (1949; B&W) . . . . Jill Young
Come Back, Little Sheba (1952; B&W)
. . . . Marie Buckholder
Daddy Long Legs (1955). . . . . Linda
Double Exposure (1983) . . . . Married Woman
Hellhole (1985). . . . . .Sidnee Hammond
TV:
tvEmpire (1962-63). . . . . Constance Garret
Magazines:
Playboy (Aug 1984) . . . . The Merriest Widow
••• 130-139: Topless and buns. 55 years old.
Playboy (Dec 1984). . . . . Sex Stars of 1984
••• 208: Topless.
Playboy (Jan 1989) . . . . Women of the Eighties
••• 254: Topless.

Moran, Sharon

Films:
If Looks Could Kill (1987) . . . . .Madonna Maid
•• 0:17 - Full frontal nudity after Laura leaves the apart-
    ment.
Young Nurses in Love (1987) . . . . Bambi/Bibi

More, Camilla

Identical twin sister of actress Carey More.
Films:
Friday the 13th, Part IV—The Final Chapter
(1984). . . . . Tina
• 0:26 - Very brief topless in the lake jumping up with
    her twin sister to show they are skinny dipping.
• 0:48 - Left breast, in bed with Crispin Glover.
Dark Side of the Moon (1989). . . . . Lesli
The Serpent of Death (1989) . . . . Rene
•• 0:15 - Brief topless in bed with Jeff Fahey.
•• 1:22 - Brief left breast while in bed, then topless and
    buns, getting out of bed (in mirror).

More, Carey

Identical twin sister of actress Camilla More.
Films:
Friday the 13th, Part IV—The Final Chapter
(1984) . . . . .Terri
• 0:26 - Very brief topless in the lake jumping up with
    her twin sister to show they are skinny dipping.
Once Bitten (1985) . . . . Moll Flanders Vampire

Morgan, Alexandra

Films:
The First Nudie Musical (1979) . . . . Mary La Rue
• 0:54 - Topless, singing and dancing during dancing
    dildo routine.
••• 1:04 - Full frontal nudity in bed trying to do a take.
    1:07 - Topless in bed with a guy with a continuous
    erection.
•• 1:17 - Topless in bed in another scene.
The Happy Hooker Goes Hollywood (1980) . . . . . . .Max
Erotic Images (1983). . . . . .Emily Stewart
•• 0:57 - In black lingerie, then topless on the living
    room floor with Glenn.
• 1:05 - Topless in bed, making love with Glenn.
••• 1:12 - Topless in the kitchen with Glenn.
•• 1:21 - Right breast, on couch with Glenn.
Spellbinder (1988). . . . . Pamela

Morgan, Cindy

Films:
Caddyshack (1980) . . . . .Lacey Underall
0:50 - Very, very brief side view of left breast sliding
    into the swimming pool. Very blurry.
•• 0:58 - Topless in bed with Danny three times.
Tron (1982) . . . . Lora/Yori
TV:
Bring 'Em Back Alive (1982-83) . . . . Gloria Marlowe

Morgan, Debbi

Films:
Mandingo (1975). . . . . .Dite
• 0:17 - Topless in bed talking to Perry King.
Miniseries:
Roots: The Next Generation (1979) . . . Elizabeth Harvey
Made for TV Movies:
The Jesse Owens Story (1984) . . . .
TV:
All My Children . . . . Angie Hubbard
Behind the Screen (1981-82) . . . . Lynette Porter
Generations (1990-) . . . . Chantal Marshall

Morgan, Shelly Taylor

Films:
The Sword and the Sorcerer (1982) . . . . Bar-Bra
• 0:54 - Brief topless when Lee Horsley crashes
    through the window and almost lands on her.
My Tutor (1983). . . . . Louisa

Scarface (1983) . . . . Woman at the Babylon Club
Malibu Express (1984) . . . . Anita Chamberlain
- • 0:22 - Topless doing exercises on the floor.
- •• 0:26 - Topless making love with Shane in bed while being video taped. Then right breast while standing by door.
TV:
General Hospital . . . . Lorena Sharpe

Moritz, Louisa
Films:
Death Race 2000 (1975) . . . . Myra
- • 0:28 - Topless and buns getting a massage and talking to David Carradine.
One Flew Over the Cuckoo's Nest (1975) . . . . Rose
The Happy Hooker Goes to Washington (1977)
. . . . Natalie Naussbaum
Loose Shoes (1977) . . . . Margie
Lunch Wagon (1981) . . . . Sunshine
- • 0:37 - Topless in spa.
True Confessions (1981) . . . . Whore
The Last American Virgin (1982) . . . . Carmela
- ••• 0:42 - Topless and buns in her bedroom with Rick.
Chained Heat (1983; U.S./German) . . . . Bubbles
Hot Chili (1985) . . . . Chi Chi
0:06 - Brief buns turning around in white apron after talking with the boys.
- •• 0:34 - Nude during fight in restaurant with the Music Teacher. Hard to see because of the flashing light.
Jungle Warriors (1985) . . . . Laura McCashin

Moro, Alicia
Films:
The Exterminators of the Year 3000 (1985; Italian)
. . . . Trash
Slugs (1988; Spanish) . . . . Maureen Watson
Hot Blood (1989; Spanish) . . . . Alicia
- • 0:00 - Buns and lower frontal nudity in stable with Ricardo. Long shot.
- • 0:06 - In bra and panties with Julio, then buns and topless. Looks like a body double because hair doesn't match.

Morris, Anita
Films:
The Happy Hooker (1975) . . . . . . Linda Jo/Mary Smith
- • 0:59 - Topless lying on table while a customer puts ice cream all over her.
- • 1:24 - Topless covered with whipped cream getting it sprayed off with champagne by another customer.
So Fine (1981) . . . . So Fine Dancer
The Hotel New Hampshire (1984) . . . . Ronda Ray
Maria's Lovers (1985) . . . . Mrs. Wynic
Absolute Beginners (1986; British) . . . . Dido Lament
Blue City (1986) . . . . Molvina Kerch
Ruthless People (1986) . . . . Carol
18 Again! (1988) . . . . Madeline

Aria (1988; U.S./British) . . . . Phoebe
Bloodhounds of Broadway (1989) . . . . . Missouri Martin
Made for Cable TV:
Tales From the Crypt: Spoiled (1991; HBO) . . . . Fuschia
TV:
Berrengers (1985) . . . . Babs Berrenger

Morris, Kim
Video Tapes:
Playboy Video Calendar 1988 (1987) . . . . . Playmate
Playboy's Wet and Wild (1989) . . . .
Magazines:
Playboy (Mar 1986) . . . . Playmate

Mulford, Nancy
Films:
Any Man's Death (1989) . . . . Tara
Act of Piracy (1990) . . . . Laura Warner
- • 0:11 - Very brief left breast under Gary Busey in bed. Dark, hard to see.
0:12 - In white lingerie, walking around on the boat shooting everybody.
- • 0:34 - Brief, upper half of left breast, in bed with Ray Sharkey.
0:35 - In white nightgown.

Mullen, Patty
Films:
Doom Asylum (1987) . . . . Judy LaRue/Kiki LaRue
In red two piece swimsuit a lot.
Frankenhooker (1990) . . . . Elizabeth
- •• 1:01 - Topless and buns in garter belt and stockings, in room with a customer.
Magazines:
Penthouse (Aug 1986) . . . . Pet
Penthouse (Jan 1988) . . . . Pet of the Year
125-139:

Müller, Lillian
a.k.a. Liliane Mueller or Yulis Ruvaal.
Films:
Sex on the Run (1979; German/French/Italian)
. . . . Angela
a.k.a. Some Like It Cool
a.k.a. Casanova and Co.
- ••• 0:15 - Second woman (blonde) to take off her clothes with the other two women, nude. Long scene.
Best Defense (1984) . . . . French Singer
Magazines:
Playboy (Aug 1975) . . . . Playmate
Playboy (Nov 1977) . . . . Sex in Cinema 77
- •• 166: Topless.

Munro, Caroline
Films:
Captain Kronos, Vampire Hunter (1972; British) . . .Carla
    0:24 - "Nude" scene in the barn with Kronos. Dark,
    strategically placed shadows hide everything.
    0:51 - In barn again, but now she has strategically
    placed hair hiding everything.
The Golden Voyage of Sinbad (1974; British)
. . . . Margiana
    0:51 - Very brief right nipple, sticking out of top
    when Sinbad carries her from the boat to the shore.
    Long shot.
The Spy Who Loved Me (1977; British) . . . . Naomi
Starcrash (1979; Italian) . . . . Stella Star
The Last Horror Film (1984) . . . . .Jana Bates
Slaughter High (1986) . . . . Carol
    0:19 - Walking around her house in lingerie and a
    robe.

Murakoshi, Suzen
Films:
Wall Street (1987) . . . . Girl in Bed
    • 0:13 - Brief full frontal nudity getting out of bed and
    walking past the camera in Charlie Sheen's bedroom
    (slightly out of focus).
Quick Change (1990) . . . . Hostage

Muti, Ornella
Films:
Summer Affair (1979) . . . . .Lisa
    • 0:44 - Topless silhouette in cave by the water.
    • 1:00 - Brief topless getting chased around in the
    grass and by the beach.
Flash Gordon (1980) . . . . Princess Aura
Love and Money (1980) . . . . Catherine Stockheinz
    0:31 - In bra and panties in bedroom with Ray Shar-
    key getting dressed.
Famous T & A (1982) . . . . .Lisa
    (No longer available for purchase, check your video
    store for rental.)
    • 0:07 - Brief topless in scenes from *Summer Affair*.
Tales of Ordinary Madness (1983) . . . . Cass
Swann in Love (1984; French/German)
. . . . Odette de Crècy
    •• 1:15 - Brief left breast, making love with Jeremy
    Irons.
    ••• 1:28 - Topless sitting on bed talking to Irons.
Made for Cable TV:
The Hitchhiker: True Believer. . . . .
    (Available on *The Hitchhiker, Volume 3*.)

Nankervis, Debbie
Films:
Alvin Purple (1973; Australian). . . . . Girl in Blue Movie
    •• 1:04 - Nude, running after Alvin in bedroom.
Libido (1973; Australian). . . . . First Girl
Alvin Rides Again (1974; Australian) . . Woman Cricketer

Naples, Toni
Films:
Doctor Detroit (1983) . . . . .Dream Girl
Chopping Mall (1986) . . . . Bathing Beauty
Deathstalker II (1987) . . . . Sultana
    • 0:55 - Brief topless in strobe lights making love with
    the bad guy. Hard to see because of blinking lights.
    Might be a body double, don't see her face.
Transylvania Twist (1990) . . . . Maxine

Napoli, Susan
a.k.a. Stephanie Ryan.
Susan Napoli is her real name.
Films:
Wildest Dreams (1987). . . . . .Punk #4
    • 0:21 - Brief left breast, leaning backwards on couch
    with her boyfriend.
Frankenhooker (1990) . . . . Anise
    • 0:42 - Brief left breast on bed with Amber, taking off
    her top. Brief topless after Angel explodes.
    • 0:43 - Topless, kneeling on bed screaming before ex-
    ploding.
Street Hunter (1990) . . . . Eddie's Girl
    •• 0:40 - Topless in bed with Eddie (she's on the left,
    wearing white panties).
Magazines:
Penthouse (Feb 1986) .Pet

Nassar, Deborah Ann
a.k.a. Debbie Nassar.
Films:
Stripped to Kill (1987) . . . . Dazzle
    ••• 0:07 - Topless wearing a G-string dancing on stage
    with a motorcycle prop.
Dance of the Damned (1988) . . . . .La Donna
    • 0:07 - Brief topless during dance routine in club.

Natividad, Francesca "Kitten"
Vital statistics: 5' 3" tall, 116 pounds, 44-25-35.
Adult Films:
Bad Girls IV . . . .
    •• 0:26 - Topless in back of pizza truck.
Titillation (1982) . . . .
    Topless.
Films:
Up! (1976). . . . . .Greek Chorus
    Russ Meyer film.
Beneath the Valley of the Ultravixens (1979)
. . . . Lavonia & Lola Langusta
The Lady in Red (1979) . . . . . . .uncredited Partygoer
    • 0:39 - Brief topless outside during party.
An Evening with Kitten (1983) . . . . herself
    •• 0:02 - Topless busting out of her blouse.
    •• 0:09 - Topless in miniature city scene.
    • 0:11 - Brief topless on stage.
    • 0:20 - Left breast, in bed with a vampire.

••• 0:21 - Topless and buns in G-string during dance in large champagne glass prop. Long scene.
••• 0:24 - Topless on beach in mermaid costume with little shell pasties.
••• 0:25 - Topless in the glass again.
•• 0:28 - Topless in and out of glass.
•• 0:29 - Brief topless during end credits.

My Tutor (1983) . . . . Anna Maria
••• 0:10 - Topless in room with Matt Lattanzi, then lying in bed.

Doin' Time (1984). . . . . Tassle

Takin' It Off (1984) . . . . Betty Bigones
•• 0:01 - Topless dancing on stage.
••• 0:04 - Topless and buns dancing on stage.
•• 0:29 - Topless in the Doctor's office.
••• 0:32 - Nude dancing in the Psychiatrists' office.
••• 0:39 - Nude in bed with a guy during fantasy sequence playing with vegetables and fruits.
•• 0:49 - Topless in bed covered with popcorn.
• 0:51 - Nude doing a dance routine in the library.
••• 1:09 - Nude splashing around in a clear plastic bathtub on stage.
•• 1:20 - Nude at a fat farm dancing.
•• 1:24 - Nude running in the woods in slow motion.

The Wild Life (1984) . . . . Stripper #2
••• 0:50 - Topless doing strip routine in a bar just before a fight breaks out.

Night Patrol (1985) . . . . Hippie Woman
•• 1:01 - Topless in kitchen with Pat Paulsen, the other police officer and her hippie boyfriend.

Takin' It All Off (1987) . . . . Betty Bigones
••• 0:12 - Nude, washing herself in the shower.
•• 0:39 - Nude, on stage in a giant glass, then topless backstage in her dressing room.
•• 0:42 - Topless in flashbacks from *Takin' It Off.*
0:46 - Topless in group in the studio.
••• 0:53 - Nude, dancing on the deck outside. Some nice slow motion shots.
•• 1:16 - Topless on stage in club.
••• 1:23 - Nude, dancing with all the other women on stage.

The Tomb (1987) . . . . Stripper
••• 0:19 - Topless and buns in G-string dancing on stage.
• 0:21 - Brief topless again.

Another 48 Hrs. (1990) . . . . Girl in Movie
• 1:04 - Brief topless on movie screen when two motorcycles crash through it.

Buford's Beach Bunnies (1991) . . . .

The Girl I Want (1991) . . . .

Magazines:
Playboy (Nov 1982) . . . . Sex in Cinema 1982
••• 160: Topless.
Playboy (Nov 1990) . . . . Sex in Cinema 1990
•• 138: Topless in still from *Another 48 Hrs.*

Neal, Christy
Films:
Coming Together (1978) . . . . Vicky Hughes
a.k.a. A Matter of Love
0:12 - In bra and panties, in bedroom with Frank.
• 0:30 - Brief right breast in shower with Angie.
• 0:37 - Topless and buns making love standing up in front of sliding glass door with Frank. Quick cuts.
• 0:49 - Brief topless again during flashbacks.
•• 0:57 - Topless with Angie and Richard.
• 1:05 - Topless on beach with Angie. Long shot.

Take Down (1978) . . . . Suzette Smith

Negoda, Natalya
Films:
Little Vera (1988; U.S.S.R.) . . . . Vera
0:15 - Very brief topless and buns getting dressed. Dark, hard to see.
••• 0:50 - Topless making love with Sergei.
•• 1:05 - Topless taking off her dress in the kitchen.

Magazines:
Playboy (May 1989) . . . . That Glasnost Girl
••• 140-149: Topless.
Playboy (Nov 1989) . . . . Sex in Cinema 1989
•• 131: Topless in out-of-focus still from *Little Vera.*
Playboy (Dec 1989) . . . . Holy Sex Stars of 1989!
••• 184: Topless.

Neidhardt, Elke
Films:
Alvin Purple (1973; Australian)
. . . . Woman in Blue Movie
•• 1:07 - In red bra, then full frontal nudity in bedroom with Alvin during showing of film.

Libido (1973; Australian) . . . . Penelope

Inside Looking Out (1977; Australian) . . . . Marianne

Nelligan, Kate
Films:
The Romantic Englishwoman (1975; British/French)
. . . . Isabel

Dracula (1979). . . . . Lucy

Crossover (1980; Canadian). . . . . Peabody
a.k.a. Mr. Patman

Eye of the Needle (1981) . . . . Lucy
•• 0:52 - Brief left breast, while drying herself off in the bathroom when Donald Sutherland accidentally sees her.
1:15 - Top half of buns, making love in bed with Sutherland.
• 1:26 - Topless making love in bed with Sutherland after he killed her husband. Dark, hard to see.

Without a Trace (1983) . . . . Susan Selky

Eleni (1985) . . . . Eleni

Made for Cable Movies:
Control (1987; HBO) . . . .

Made for TV Movies:
  Therese Raquin (1981) . . . .
  Kojak: The Price of Justice (1987) . . . . Kitty

Nero, Toni

Films:
  Silent Night, Deadly Night (1984) . . . . Pamela
    • 0:30 - Brief right breast twice just before Billy gets
       stabbed during fantasy scene.
    • 0:42 - Topless in stock room when Andy attacks her.
    • 0:44 - Topless in stock room struggling with Billy,
       then getting killed by him.
  Silent Night, Deadly Night, Part 2 (1986) . . Pamela
    •• 0:22 - Topless in back of toy store in flashback from
       Silent Night, Deadly Night.

Newmar, Julie

Films:
  Mackenna's Gold (1969) . . . . Hesh-ke
    1:09 - Brief topless and buns under water. Long
       shots, hard to see anything. Not clear because of all
       the dirty water. Brief buns, getting out of the pond.
  Love Scenes (1984) . . . . Belinda
  Streetwalkin' (1985) . . . . Queen Bee
  Deep Space (1988) . . . . Lady Elaine
  Ghosts Can't Do It (1989) . . . .
TV:
  Batman (1966-67) . . . . The Catwoman

Nicholas, Angela

Films:
  Psychos in Love (1987) . . . . Diane
  Wildest Dreams (1987) . . . . Claudia
    •• 1:01 - Topless typing on computer doing Bobby's
       book keeping.
  Galactic Gigolo (1989) . . . . Peggy Sue Peggy
  a.k.a. Club Earth
Magazines:
  Penthouse (Aug 1985) . . . . Pet

Nielsen, Brigitte

Ex-wife of actor Sylvester Stallone.
Films:
  Red Sonja (1985) . . . . Red Sonja
    • 0:01 - Half of right nipple through torn outfit, while
       sitting up.
  Rocky IV (1985) . . . . Ludmilla
  Cobra (1986) . . . . Ingrid
  Beverly Hills Cop II (1987) . . . . Karla Fry
  Bye Bye Baby (1989) . . . . Lisa
    • 0:20 - Brief side view of right breast, while lying on a
       guy in bed. Nice buns shot also.
  Domino (1989) . . . . Domino
    • 0:05 - Right breast, lying down next to swimming
       pool, topless getting out.
    ••• 1:04 - Right breast, caressing herself in a white linge-
       rie body suit, wearing a black wig.

976-EVIL, Part 2 (1991) . . . .
Made for TV Movies:
  Murder by Moonlight (1989) . . . .
Magazines:
  Playboy (Aug 1986) . . . . Brigitte
    •• 70-77: Topless.
  Playboy (Dec 1987) . . . . Gitte the Great
    ••• 80-93: Nice.
  Playboy (Feb 1988) . . . . The Year in Sex
    ••• 129: Topless at the beach.
  Playboy (Dec 1988) . . . . Sex Stars of 1988
    • 187: Buns and side view of right breast.
  Playboy (Jan 1989) . . . . Women of the Eighties
    •• 251: Topless.

Niemi, Lisa

Wife of actor Patrick Swayze.
Films:
  Slam Dance (1987) . . . . Ms. Schell
    ••• 0:54 - Nude in Tom Hulce's apartment.
    • 1:00 - Topless, dead, lying on the floor in Hulce's
       apartment.
  She's Having a Baby (1988) . . . . Model
  Steel Dawn (1988) . . . . Kasha
TV:
  Super Force (1990) . . . . Carla Frost

Nirvana, Yana

Films:
  Cinderella (1977) . . . . Drucella
    • 0:02 - Topless taking off clothes with her sister Mari-
       bella to let Cinderella wash.
    • 0:06 - Brief topless sitting up in bed with Maribella.
  Club Life (1987) . . . . Butchette
  He's My Girl (1987) . . . . Olga
  Another 48 Hrs. (1990) . . . . CHP Officer
TV:
  The Last Precinct (1986) . . . . Sgt. Martha Haggerty

Noel, Monique

Video Tapes:
  Playboy's Wet and Wild (1989) . . . .
Magazines:
  Playboy (May 1989) . . . . Playmate

North, Noelle

Films:
  Report to the Commissioner (1975) . . . . Samantha
  Slumber Party '57 (1976) . . . . Angie
    •• 0:37 - Buns, then topless in bed with a party guest of
       her parents.
  Sweater Girls (1978) . . . .
  Jekyll & Hyde...Together Again (1982) . . . . Student

North, Sheree

Films:
Lawman (1971). . . . . .Laura Shelby
(Not available on video tape.)

Norton-Taylor, Judy

TV:
The Waltons (1972-81) . . . . . .Mary Ellen Walton Willard
Video Tapes:
Playboy Video Magazine, Volume 10. . . . . . herself
Magazines:
Playboy (Aug 1985). . . . . .The Punch in Judy
••• 77-81: Frontal nudity.

Novak, Lenka

Films:
Terror on Tape. . . . . Suzy
Topless scene from *Vampire Hookers*.
Kentucky Fried Movie (1977) . . . . . . Linda Chambers
• 0:09 - Topless sitting on a couch with two other girls.
Coach (1978). . . . . .Marilyn
• 0:10 - Very brief topless flashing her breasts along
with her girlfriends for their boyfriends.
Vampire Hookers (1979) . . . . Suzy
0:22 - In sheer green dress getting into coffin.
0:33 - In sheer green dress again.
0:45 - In sheer green dress again.
•• 0:51 - Topless in bed during the orgy with the guy
and the other two Vampire Hookers.

Nychols, Darcy

Films:
Mugsy's Girls (1985) . . . . Madame Antoinette
Slammer Girls (1987). . . . . Tank
• 0:17 - Topless ripping blouse open while hassling
Melody.

Nygren, Mia

Films:
Emmanuelle IV (1984) . . . . Emmanuelle IV
0:13 - Buns, lying on table after plastic surgery.
••• 0:15 - Full frontal nudity walking around looking at
her new self in the mirror.
• 0:20 - Brief topless a couple of times making love on
top of a guy getting coached by Sylvia Kristel in
dream-like sequence.
•• 0:22 - Full frontal nudity taking off blouse in front of
Dona.
0:25 - Almost making love with a guy in bar.
••• 0:30 - Nude undressing in front of Maria.
•• 0:39 - Full frontal nudity taking her dress off and getting covered with a white sheet.
••• 0:40 - Full frontal nudity lying down and then putting dress back on.
•• 0:45 - Full frontal nudity during levitation trick.
0:49 - Right bra cup reclining on bed.

• 0:52 - Brief topless in stable.
••• 0:54 - Topless taking off black dress in chair. Brief
lower frontal nudity.
0:57 - Brief lower frontal nudity putting on white
panties.
• 1:00 - Brief topless when Susanna takes her dress off.
• 1:03 - Brief right breast making love on ground with
a boy.
••• 1:07 - Topless walking on beach.
• 1:09 - Topless with Dona. Dark.
Plaza Real (1988) . . . .
Magazines:
Playboy (Dec 1984) . . . . .Sex Stars of 1984
• 204: Right breast.

O'Brien, Maureen

Films:
She'll be Wearing Pink Pyjamas (1985; British)
. . . . .Joan
• 0:46 - Brief topless making love in bed with Tom.
Dark.
Zina (1985; British) . . . .

O'Connell, Natalie

Films:
Breeders (1986) . . . . .Donna
• 0:02 - Very brief left breast, getting her blouse ripped
by creature.
•• 0:44 - Topless, sitting up in hospital bed, then buns,
walking down the hall.
••• 0:47 - More topless and buns, walking around outside.
• 1:10 - Brief topless, standing up in the alien nest.
I Was a Teenage T.V. Terrorist (1987)
. . . . .Woman on Audition Line

O'Connell, Taaffe

Films:
Galaxy of Terror (1981) . . . . .Damelia
•• 0:42 - Topless getting raped by a giant alien slug.
Nice and slimy.
0:46 - Buns, covered with slime being discovered by
her crew mates.
Caged Fury (1984). . . . . Honey
•• 0:17 - Topless on bed with a guard. Mostly left
breast.
0:40 - Very, very brief tip of left breast peeking out
between arms in shower.
• 1:06 - Very brief topless getting blouse ripped open
by a guard in the train.
Hot Chili (1985). . . . . Brigitte
••• 0:21 - Topless lying on the bed. Shot with lots of diffusion.
• 0:30 - Brief topless playing the drums.
• 1:11 - Brief topless in bed making love with Ernie,
next to her drunk husband.

Not of This Earth (1988) . . . . Damelia
  • 0:04 - Brief topless and buns from *Galaxy of Terror*
    during the opening credits.
TV:
Blansky's Beauties (1977) . . . . Hillary S. Prentiss

O'Connor, Glynnis

Films:
Ode to Billy Joe (1976) . . . . Bobby Lee Hartley
California Dreaming (1978) . . . . Corky
  •• 0:11 - Topless pulling her top over her head when
    T.T. is using the bathroom.
    1:12 - In white bra, in bed with T.T.
  ••• 1:14 - Topless in bed with T.T.
Those Lips, Those Eyes (1980) . . . . Ramona
  • 0:37 - Left breast in car with Tom Hulce. Dark, hard
    to see.
  •• 1:12 - Topless and buns on bed with Tom Hulce.
    Dark.
Night Crossing (1981) . . . . Petra Wetzel
Melanie (1982) . . . . Melanie
  • 0:08 - Very brief right breast, while turning over in
    bed next to Don Johnson.
  •• 0:09 - Topless, while sitting up and putting on a T-
    shirt, then getting out of bed.
Made for TV Movies:
The Boy in the Plastic Bubble (1976) . . . . Gina
TV:
Sons and Daughters (1974) . . . . Anita Cramer

O'Grady, Lani

Films:
Massacre at Central High (1976) . . . . Jane
  ••• 1:09 - Topless walking out of a tent and getting back
    into it with Rainbeaux Smith and Robert Carradine.
TV:
The Headmaster (1970-71) . . . . Judy
Eight is Enough (1977-81) . . . . Mary Bradford

O'Neal, Tatum

Wife of tennis player John McEnroe.
Daughter of actor Ryan O'Neal.
Films:
Paper Moon (1973) . . . . Addie Loggins
The Bad News Bears (1976) . . . . Manda Whurlizer
International Velvet (1978) . . . . Sarah Brown
Circle of Two (1980) . . . . Sarah Norton
  •• 0:56 - Topless standing behind a chair in Richard Bur-
    ton's studio talking to him.
Little Darlings (1980) . . . . Ferris
  • 0:35 - Very, very brief half of left nipple, sticking out
    of swimsuit top when she comes up for air after fall-
    ing into the pool to get Armand Assante's attention.
Certain Fury (1985) . . . . Scarlet
Magazines:
Playboy (Nov 1982) . . . . Sex in Cinema 1982
  •• 165: Topless photo from *Circle of Two*.

O'Neill, Remy

Films:
Angel of H.E.A.T. (1981) . . . . Andrea Shockley
  a.k.a. The Protectors, Book I
  •• 0:43 - Topless, wearing a blue swimsuit, wrestling in
    the mud with Mary Woronov.
Erotic Images (1983) . . . . Vickie Coleman
  ••• 0:04 - Topless sitting in chaise lounge talking to Britt
    Ekland about sex survey. Long scene.
  • 0:06 - Topless in bed with Marvin. Brief lower frontal
    nudity.
  •• 0:07 - Brief left breast in spa with TV repairman, then
    brief topless.
Hollywood Hot Tubs (1984) . . . . Pam Landers
  • 1:00 - Brief right breast in hot tub with Jeff.
Return to Horror High (1987) . . . . Esther Molvania
To Die For (1988) . . . . Jane
Hollywood Hot Tubs 2—Educating Crystal (1989)
  . . . . Pam Landers
    0:57 - Swinging tassels on the tips of her belly danc-
    ing top.
The Forbidden Dance (1990) . . . . Robin

O'Reilly, Erin

Films:
How Sweet It Is (1968) . . . . Tour Girl
Little Fauss and Big Halsy (1970) . . . . Sylvene McFall
T. R. Baskin (1971) . . . . Kathy
Blume in Love (1973) . . . . Cindy
  • 0:40 - Topless and buns, getting out of bed with
    George Segal.
Busting (1974) . . . . Doris

O'Reilly, Kathryn

Films:
Jack's Back (1987) . . . . Hooker
Puppet Master (1989) . . . . Carissa Stamford
  • 0:41 - Left breast in bathtub, covered with bubbles.
  • 0:43 - Brief left breast getting out of tub. Nipple cov-
    ered with bubbles.
    0:50 - Riding on Frank in bed. Don't see anything,
    but still exciting. Very brief buns under sheer night-
    gown when she gets off Frank.
    1:11 - Right breast under sheer black nightgown,
    dead sitting at the table. Blood on her face.

O'Shea, Missy

Films:
Blow Out (1981) . . . . Dancing Coed
    0:00 - Dancing in sheer nightgown while a campus
    guard watches from outside the window.
New York Nights (1983) . . . . The Model
    0:30 - In white bra in restroom making love with the
    photographer.
  •• 0:37 - in black bra, panties, garter belt and stockings
    then topless taking off bra and getting into bed.

•• 0:40 - Topless on floor when the photographer throws her on the floor and rips her bra off.
••• 0:41 - Full frontal nudity putting bathrobe on.
• 0:44 - Topless standing in front of a mirror with short black hair and a moustache getting dressed to look like a guy.

O'Toole, Annette

Films:
Smile (1974) . . . . Doria Houston
   0:34 - In white bra and panties in dressing room.
   1:06 - In white bra and slip talking to Joan Prather in bedroom.
One on One (1977) . . . . .Janet Hays
King of the Gypsies (1978) . . . . Sharon
Foolin' Around (1980). . . . . Susan
48 Hours (1982) . . . . Elaine
Cat People (1982). . . . . .Alice Perrin
 ••• 1:30 - In a bra, then topless undressing in locker room.
  • 1:31 - Some topless shots of her in the pool. Distorted because of the water.
  • 1:33 - Brief right breast, after getting out of the pool.
Superman III (1983) . . . . .Lana Lang
Cross My Heart (1987). . . . . Kathy
   0:44 - In pink bra standing in bedroom with Martin Short.
 •• 0:46 - Left breast, in bed with Short.
 •• 0:48 - Topless in bed when Short heads under the covers.
 •• 0:49 - Brief topless again getting her purse.
  • 1:05 - Brief topless and buns, dressing after Short finds out about her daughter.
Love at Large (1990). . . . . Mrs. King
Made for Cable Movies:
Best Legs in the 8th Grade (1984; HBO) . . . .
Miniseries:
The Kennedys of Massachusetts (1990). . Rose Fitzgerald
Made for TV Movies:
Love for Rent (1979). . . . .
Stand by Your Man (1981) . . . .
The Dreamer of Oz (1990) . . . . Maud
Stephen King's "It" (1990) . . . . Beverly Marsh
Magazines:
Playboy (Nov 1982) . . . . Sex in Cinema 1982
   166: Buns, in a photo from *48 Hours*, but scene is not on video tape.

Obregon, Ana

Films:
Bolero (1984) . . . . Catalina Terry
  • 1:32 - Brief topless making love with Robert.
Killing Machine (1986) . . . . .Liza

Ohana, Claudia

Films:
Erendira (1983; Brazilian). . . . . .Erendira
  • 0:14 - Topless getting fondled by a guy against her will.
 •• 0:26 - Topless lying in bed sweating and crying after having to have sex with an army of men.
••• 1:04 - Topless lying in bed sleeping.
   1:08 - Brief topless getting out of bed. Long shot, hard to see.
 •• 1:24 - Topless and buns on bed with Ulysses.
Priceless Beauty (1989; Italian) . . . . Lisa
Magazines:
Playboy (Oct 1984) . . . . The Girls from Brazil
 •• 88-89: Nude.
Playboy (Dec 1984) . . . . .Sex Stars of 1984
 •• 205: Left breast, leaning on table.

Olin, Lena

Films:
Fanny and Alexander (1983; Swedish/French/German) .
After the Rehearsal (1984; Swedish) . . . . .Anna Egerman
The Unbearable Lightness of Being (1988)
 . . . . .Sabina
 •• 0:03 - Topless in bed with Tomas looking at themselves in a mirror.
   0:17 - In black bra and panties looking at herself in a mirror on the floor.
   1:21 - In black bra, panties, garter belt and stockings.
 •• 1:29 - Topless and buns while Tereza photographs her. Long shots, hard to see.
  • 1:43 - Very brief left breast, in bed with Tomas.
   2:32 - Brief topless in B&W photo found in a drawer by Tomas.
Enemies, A Love Story (1989) . . . . Masha
 •• 0:16 - In white bra, then brief topless several times in bed with Ron Silver. Topless again after making love and starting to make love again.
Havana (1990). .Bobby Duran

Oliver, Leslie

Films:
The Student Teachers (1973) . . . .
Thunderbolt and Lightfoot (1974). . . . . . . Teenager
 •• 1:16 - Brief topless in bed when robbers break in and George Kennedy watches her.

Oliver, Pita

Films:
Deadly Companion (1979). . . . . .Lorraine
  • 0:14 - Very brief left breast, then very brief topless sitting up in bed during Michael Sarrazin's daydream. Dark.
   1:32 - Brief full frontal nudity, dead on bed when Susan Clark comes into the bedroom.
Prom Night (1980) . . . . Vicki
 •• 0:35 - Brief buns, mooning Mr. Sykes.

Ono, Yoko

Wife of the late singer John Lennon.
Films:
Imagine: John Lennon (1988) . . . . Herself
• 0:43 - Nude in B&W photos from John Lennon's
White Album.
0:57 - Brief full frontal nudity from album cover again
during an interview.
1:27 - Almost topless in bed with Lennon.

Otis, Carré

Model.
Films:
Wild Orchid (1990) . . . . Emily Reed
•• 0:51 - Left breast in mirror looking at herself while
getting dressed.
••• 1:01 - Topless when a guy takes off her dress while
Mickey Rourke watches.
••• 1:02 - Right breast, then topless on the floor with Jerome.
• 1:31 - Brief topless in flashback with Jerome.
• 1:42 - Topless opening her blouse for Rourke.
••• 1:44 - Nude making love with Rourke. Nice and
sweaty.
Magazines:
Playboy (Jun 1990) . . . . Wild Orchid
••• 83-87: Nude in photos from *Wild Orchid.*
Playboy (Nov 1990) . . . . Sex in Cinema 1990
•• 146: Topless in still from *Wild Orchid.*

Owens, Susie

Films:
They Bite (1991) . . . .
Video Tapes:
Playboy Video Calendar 1989 (1988) . . . . . . August
••• 0:29 - Nude.
Playboy's Wet and Wild (1989) . . . .
Playmates at Play (1990) . . . . Gotta Dance
Magazines:
Playboy (Mar 1988). . . . . Playmate

Pacula, Joanna

Films:
Gorky Park (1983) . . . . Irina
•• 1:20 - Brief topless in bed making love with William
Hurt.
Not Quite Paradise (1986; British). . . . . .Gila
a.k.a. Not Quite Jerusalem
• 1:04 - Left breast, lying in bed with Sam Robards.
Death Before Dishonor (1987) . . . . Elli
The Kiss (1988) . . . . Felice
•• 0:49 - Side view topless making love with a guy. Intercut with Meredith Salenger seeing a model of a
body spurt blood.
• 0:57 - Topless covered with body paint doing a ceremony in a hotel room.

•• 1:24 - Brief right breast, while making love with a
guy on bed while Salenger is asleep in the other
room.
Sweet Lies (1989). . . . . Joëlle
Marked for Death (1990) . . . . Leslie
Made for Cable Movies:
36 Hours (1989). . . . .
Breaking Point (1989) . . . . Nurse
TV:
E.A.R.T.H. Force (1990) . . . . Diana Randall

Pai, Sue Francis

a.k.a. Suzie Pai.
Films:
Big Trouble in Little China (1986). . . . . Miao Yin
Jakarta (1988) . . . . .Esha
• 1:01 - Brief right breast, while making love in the
courtyard with Falco.
1:13 - Brief side of right breast while kissing Falco.
•• 1:13 - Side view of right breast, then brief topless
twice, making love under a mosquito net with Falco.
Hard to see her face clearly.
Magazines:
Penthouse (Jan 1981) .Pet
87-105:

Paige, Kym

Video Tapes:
Playboy Video Calendar 1988 (1987). . . . . Playmate
Playmates at Play (1990) . . . . Hoops
Magazines:
Playboy (May 1987). . . . . Playmate

Paine, Bonnie

Films:
Ninja Academy (1990) . . . . Nudist
• 0:26 - Brief buns and topless playing volleyball.
(She's the second blonde on the far side of the net
who misses the ball.)
Twisted Justice (1990) . . . . Hooker
•• 0:11 - Topless in black panties and stockings, getting
photographed.

Paine, Heidi

Films:
In Search of the Perfect 10 (1986) . . . Perfect Girl #8
(Shot on video tape.)
••• 0:45 - Brief topless pulling down her top outside of
car.
Wildest Dreams (1987). . . . . Dancee
• 0:23 - Topless in the arms of a gladiator in Bobby's
bedroom.
New York's Finest (1988) . . . . Carley Pointer
• 0:04 - Brief topless with a bunch of hookers.
• 0:36 - Topless with her two friends doing push ups
on the floor.
Roadhouse (1989) . . . . Party Girl

Skin Deep (1989) . . . . Tina
  • 0:01 - Brief side view topless sitting on John Ritter's lap while Denise Crosby watches.
Alien Seed (1991) . . . .
Demon Sword (1991) . . . .

Pallenberg, Anita

Films:
A Degree of Murder (1967) . . . . Marie
Barbarella (1968; French/Italian) . . . . . The Black Queen
Candy (1968) . . . . Nurse Bullock
Performance (1970) . . . . .Pherber
  • 0:44 - Side view of left breast, in bed with Mick Jagger.
  ••• 0:47 - Topless and buns, in bathtub with Lucy and Jagger.
  • 0:50 - Buns, injecting herself with drugs.
  •• 1:20 - Right breast, while lying on the floor. Then topless and buns, in bed with Chas.

Pallett, Lori Deann

Films:
Summer's Games (1987) . . . . .Torch Carrier
  • 0:00 - Half topless running in short T-shirt carrying torch.
  •• 0:04 - Topless opening her swimsuit top after contest. (2nd place winner.)
Screwball Hotel (1988) . . . . .Candy
  ••• 0:26 Topless in the shower while Herbie is accidentally in there with her.
Magazines:
Penthouse (Jun 1989) . . . .
  15 51;

Palme, Beatrice

Films:
Foxtrap (1986) . . . . Marianna
  •• 0:41 - Brief breasts and buns in bed with Fred Williamson, then more breasts making love.
Cinema Paradiso (1988; Italian/French) . . . .

Palmer, Gretchen

Films:
The Malibu Bikini Shop (1985) . . . . .Woman
Crossroads (1986) . . . . Beautiful Girl/Dancer
Red Heat (1988) . . . . Hooker
  • 1:20 - Topless and buns in hotel during shoot out.
When Harry Met Sally... (1989) . . . . Stewardess

Palmer, Jaclyn

Films:
Party Plane (1988) . . . . .Suzie
  ••• 0:06 - Topless and buns changing clothes and getting into spa with her two girlfriends. (She's the dark haired one.)
  ••• 0:11 - Topless again, getting out of spa.

  ••• 0:23 - In bra, then topless doing strip tease routine on plane.
  •• 0:35 - Topless doing another routine on the plane.
Roadhouse (1989) . . . . .Party Girl

Paluzzi, Lucianna

Films:
Muscle Beach Party (1964) . . . . .Julie
Thunderball (1965; British) . . . . Fiona Volpe
39 Women (1969) . . . .
Black Gunn (1972) . . . . .Toni
Manhunt (1973) . . . . Eva
  a.k.a. The Italian Connection.
The Klansman (1974) . . . . Trixie
The Sensuous Nurse (1979) . . . .
  •• 0:20 - Topless in room, ripping off her clothes and reluctantly making love with Benito.

Papanicolas, Tanya

Films:
Vamp (1986) . . . . .Waitress
Blood Diner (1987) . . . . Sheetar & Bitsy
  • 0:15 - Brief topless as photographer during topless aerobics photo shoot.
  • 0:24 - Topless, dead on operating table, then dead, standing up.

Parkins, Barbara

Films:
Valley of the Dolls (1967) . . . . .Anne Welles
The Mephisto Waltz (1971) . . . . Roxanne
  • 1:26 - Left breast, while kissing Alan Alda during witchcraft sequence.
Asylum (1972; British) . . . . .Bonnie
Christina (1974) . . . . Christina
Shout at the Devil (1976; British) . . . . Rosa
Bear Island (1980; British/Canadian) . . . . . Judith Ruben
Made for Cable Movies:
To Catch a King (1984; HBO) . . . .
TV:
Peyton Place (1964-69)
  . . . . Betty Anderson/Harrington/Cord
Captains and the Kings (1976) . . . . .Martinique
Magazines:
Playboy (Dec 1977) . . . . .Sex Stars of 1977
  • 215: Left breast standing looking out the window.

Parton, Julie

  a.k.a. Adult film actress Nina Alexander.
  Cousin of singer/actress Dolly Parton.
Films:
Erotic Images (1983) . . . . Marvin's Nurse
  0:08 - Brief topless in office with Marvin. Dark, hard to see.
The Rosebud Beach Hotel (1985) . . . . Bellhop
  •• 0:49 - Buns, then topless, standing in line. Second from the camera.

Penthouse Love Stories (1986). . . . Loveboat Woman
- ••• 0:51 - In white bra and panties in bed. Nude masturbating while the other girls watch. Nice, long, sweaty scene.

Video Tapes:
Soft Bodies Invitational (1990) . . . . . Nina Alexander
- 0:00 - Buns, under short skirt, playing tennis with Becky LeBeau.
- ••• 0:03 - In lingerie during photo session, then topless and buns in G-string. Long scene.
- ••• 0:15 - Topless posing with LeBeau.
- ••• 0:18 - Outside in dress, then undressing to two piece swimsuit, then topless. Long scene.
- 0:24 - In two piece swimsuit, then topless arguing with LeBeau about who has better breasts.
- ••• 0:28 - In two piece swimsuit, then topless by the pool.

Pascal, Olivia

Films:
Island of 1000 Delights . . . . Peggy
- •• 0:16 - Topless, tied up while being tortured by two guys. Upper half lower frontal nudity.
- •• 0:23 - Full frontal nudity lying in bed, then buns running out the door. Full frontal nudity running up stairs, nude hiding in bedroom.
- 0:33 - In braless black dress.
- ••• 0:57 - Nude, taking off her clothes in shower with Michael.
- • 1:26 - Brief topless running on the beach with Michael.

The Joy of Flying . . . . Maria
- •• 0:39 - Topless wearing panties, in bedroom with George, then nude.
- •• 0:46 - Nude with George in bathroom.

Vanessa (1977) . . . . .Vanessa
- ••• 0:08 - Nude undressing, taking a bath and getting washed by Jackie. Long scene.
- ••• 0:16 - Buns, then full frontal nudity getting a massage.
- • 0:26 - Topless getting fitted for new clothes.
- • 0:47 - Full frontal nudity when Adrian rips her clothes off.
- ••• 0:56 - Full frontal nudity on beach with Jackie.
- ••• 1:05 - Nude making love with Jackie in bed. Nice close up of left breast.
- •• 1:19 - Full frontal nudity lying on the table.
- •• 1:27 - Topless in white panties, garter belt and stockings shackled up by Kenneth.

Sex on the Run (1979; German/French/Italian)
. . . . .Convent Girl
a.k.a. Some Like It Cool
a.k.a. Casanova and Co.
- ••• 0:15 - First woman (brunette) to take off her clothes with the other two women, full frontal nudity. Long scene.

C.O.D. (1983). . . . . Holly Fox
- 1:30 - In white top during fashion show.

Paul, Alexandra

Films:
American Nightmare (1981; Canadian)
. . . . .Isabelle Blake/Tanya Kelly
- ••• 0:02 - Left breast while smoking in bed. Topless before getting killed. Long scene.

Christine (1983). . . . . .Leigh
Just the Way You Are (1984). . . . . .Bobbie
American Flyers (1985) . . . . .Becky
- • 0:50 - Very brief right breast, then very brief half of left breast changing tops with David Grant. Brief side view of right breast. Dark.
- •• 1:13 - Brief topless in white panties getting into bed with David Grant.

8 Million Ways to Die (1986). . . . . Sunny
- •• 0:24 - Full frontal nudity, standing in bathroom while Jeff Bridges watches.

Dragnet (1987) . . . . Connie Swail
Harlequin Romance: Out of the Shadows (1988)
. . . . Jan Lindsey

Made for Cable TV:
The Hitchhiker: Minuteman . . . . .Julie
- •• 0:04 - Brief left breast in car with husband, then brief topless flashing the couple on the motorcycle.

Made for TV Movies:
Paper Dolls (1982) . . . . Laurie
The Laker Girls (1990) . . . . Heidi/Jenny

Paul, Nancy

Films:
Sheena (1984) . . . . Betsy Ames
Gulag (1985) . . . . .Susan
- •• 0:42 - Buns, then topless taking a shower while David Keith daydreams while he's on a train.

Paul, Sue

Films:
All That Jazz (1979) . . . . Stacy
- • 1:18 - Brief right breast in bed with Roy Scheider at the hospital.

Magazines:
Playboy (Mar 1980) . . . . .All That Fosse
- • 176: Right breast, kneeling on all fours.

Payne, Julie

Films:
The Lonely Guy (1983) . . . . Rental Agent
Private School (1983) . . . . .Coach Whelan
- • 0:30 - Very brief left breast popping out of cheerleader's outfit along with Rita.

Fraternity Vacation (1985) . . . . Naomi Tvedt
Jumpin' Jack Flash (1986)
. . . . Receptionist at Elizabeth Arden
Just Between Friends (1986). . . . . .Karen

Peabody, Dixie Lee

Films:
Bury Me an Angel (1972) . . . . Dag
     0:11 - Very brief silhouette of left breast getting into
     bed.
  • 0:13 - Very brief right breast getting back into bed.
  ••• 0:41 - Nude, skinny dipping in river and getting out.
  • 1:16 - Topless making love in bed with Dan Hagger-
     ty. Lit with red light.
Night Call Nurses (1972) . . . . Robin
a.k.a. Young LA Nurses 2
  •• 0:35 - Topless taking off clothes in encounter group.
  • 0:39 - Brief topless in Barbara's flashback.

Peake, Teri Lynn

a.k.a. Terri Lenée Peake.
Films:
In Search of the Perfect 10 (1986) . . Perfect Girl #9
  (Shot on video tape.)
  ••• 0:47 - Buns and topless taking a shower.
Murphy's Law (1986) . . . .
Boys Night Out (1987) . . . . Maid
  ••• 0:25 - Buns in G-string, then topless doing a strip
     routine. Long scene.
Night of the Living Babes (1987) . . . . Vesuvia
  ••• 0:25 - Topless and buns in G-string, dancing in front
     of Chuck and Buck. Long scene.
Summer's Games (1987) . . . . Penthouse Girl
Wet Water T's (1987) . . . . herself
  ••• 0:13 - Topless and buns, dancing on stage in white
     G-string, in a contest.
  •• 0:36 - Topless again during judging.
  •• 0:39 - Topless during semi-finals.
  ••• 0:40 - Topless dancing with the other women.
  ••• 0:43 - Topless dancing during finals.
  •• 0:46 - Topless during final judging.
Magazines:
Penthouse (Oct 1987) . . . . Pet
  77-93:

Pearce, Adrienne

Films:
Lethal Woman (1988) . . . . Trudy
Purgatory (1988) . . . . Janine
  •• 0:51 - Brief topless in shower scene with Kirsten.
American Ninja 3: Blood Hunt (1989) Minister's Secretary

Pearce, Jacqueline

Films:
How to Get Ahead in Advertising (1988) . . . . Maud
White Mischief (1988) . . . . Idina
  •• 0:07 - Topless standing up in the bathtub while sev-
     eral men watch.
TV:
Blake's 7 . . . . Servalan

Peckinpaugh, Barbara

a.k.a. Adult film actress Susanna Britton.
Films:
Erotic Images (1983) . . . . Cheerleader
  • 0:07 - Topless dancing in an office with another
     cheerleader.
The Witching (1983) . . . . Jennie
a.k.a. Necromancy
  ••• 0:02 - Topless and buns in open gown during occult
     ceremony. Brief full frontal nudity holding a doll up.
Basic Training (1984) . . . . Salesgirl 1
  • 0:00 - Topless on desk with another salesgirl.
Best Chest in the West (1984) . . . . Chrissy
  ••• 0:28 - In two piece swimsuit, then topless and buns.
Body Double (1984) . . . . Girl #2 (Holly Does Hollywood)
Penthouse Love Stories (1986) . . Therapist's Assistant
  ••• 0:45 - Nude, making love in Therapist's office, with
     the patient.
Roller Blade (1986) . . . . Bod Sister
  •• 0:33 - Topless during ceremony. Cut on her throat is
     unappealing.
  ••• 0:35 - Full frontal nudity after dip in hot tub with the
     other two Bod Sisters. (She's the first to leave.)
  •• 0:40 - Nude, on skates with the other two Bod Sis-
     ters. (She's in the middle.)

Pedriana, Lesa

Video Tapes:
Playmates at Play (1990)
  . . . . Thrill Seeker, Flights of Fancy
Magazines:
Playboy (Apr 1984) . . . . Playmate

Peña, Elizabeth

Films:
Times Square (1980) . . . . Disco Hostess
Crossover Dreams (1985) . . . . Liz
Down and Out in Beverly Hills (1986) . . . . Carmen
*batteries not included (1987) . . . . Marisa
La Bamba (1987) . . . . Rosie Morales
  • 0:06 - Brief side view of right breast taking a shower
     outside when two young boys watch her from a wa-
     ter tower. Long shot, hard to see.
Blue Steel (1989) . . . . Tracy Perez
Jacob's Ladder (1990) . . . . Jezzie
  • 0:14 - Side view of right breast taking off robe and
     getting into shower with Tim Robbins.
  ••• 0:16 - Topless several times opening dress and put-
     ting pants on. Then in black bra.
  •• 0:31 - Very, very brief topless in bed with Robbins,
     then left breast a lot. Dark.
Made for TV Movies:
Shannon's Deal (1989) . . . . Lucy
TV:
Tough Cookies (1986) . . . . Officer Connie Rivera
I Married Dora (1987-88) . . . . Dora
Shannon's Deal (1991) . . . . Lucy

Pendlebury, Anne

Films:
Alvin Purple (1973; Australian). . . . . .Woman with Pin
•• 0:48 - Right breast and lower frontal nudity, lying in
bed, talking with Alvin.
Jock Petersen (1974; Australian) . . . . .Peggy
a.k.a. Petersen

Penhaligon, Susan

Films:
Soldier of Orange (1977; Dutch). . . . . Susan
• 1:34 - Brief topless kissing her boyfriend when Rutger
Hauer sees them through the window. Medium long
shot.
••• 1:36 - Topless in bed with her boyfriend and Hauer.
The Uncanny (1977; British) . . . . .Janet

Perkins, Elizabeth

Films:
About Last Night... (1986) . . . . Joan
From the Hip (1987) . . . . Jo Ann
Big (1988). . . . . Susan
Sweet Hearts Dance (1988). . . . . .Adie Nims
Avalon (1990) . . . . Ann
Love at Large (1990). . . . . Stella Wynkowski
The Doctor (1991) . . . . .June Ellis
he said, she said (1991). . . . . Lorie Bryer
• 1:15 - Brief topless getting into the shower with
Kevin Bacon.

Perle, Rebecca

Films:
Bachelor Party (1984) . . . . Screaming Woman
Tightrope (1984) .Becky Jacklin
Savage Streets (1985) . . . . .Cindy Clark
0:24 - In bra and panties, fighting with Brenda in the
locker room.
•• 0:53 - Brief topless in biology class getting her top
torn off by Linda Blair.
Stitches (1985) .Bambi Belinka
•• 0:34 - Topless during female medical student's class
where they examine each other.
Heartbreak Ridge (1986) . . . . Student in Shower
• 1:48 - Very brief topless getting out of shower when
the Marines rescue the students.
Not of This Earth (1988) . . . . Alien Girl
0:53 - In black swimsuit wearing sunglasses.

Perrine, Valerie

Films:
Slaughterhouse Five (1972) . . . . . Montana Wildhack
• 0:39 - Topless in *Playboy* magazine as a Playmate.
• 0:43 - Topless getting into the bathtub.
••• 1:27 - Topless in a dome with Michael Sacks.

The Last American Hero (1973) . . . . Marge
a.k.a. Hard Driver
Lenny (1974; B&W) . . . . Honey Bruce
0:04 - Doing a strip tease on stage down to pasties
and buns in a G-string. No nudity, but still nice.
••• 0:14 - Topless in bed when Dustin Hoffman pulls the
sheet off her then makes love.
•• 0:17 - Topless sitting on the floor in a room full of
flowers when Hoffman comes in.
0:24 - Left breast wearing pastie doing dance in
flashback.
• 0:43 - Right breast with Kathryn Witt.
Mr. Billion (1977). . . . . Rosi Jones
Superman (1978). . . . . Eve
The Electric Horseman (1979) . . . . .Charlotta Steele
The Magician of Lublin (1979) . . . . .Zeftel
Can't Stop the Music (1980) . . . . . . Samantha Simpson
Agency (1981; Canadian). . . . . Brenda Wilcox
The Border (1982) . . . . Marcy
Water (1986; British) . . . . Pamela
Maid to Order (1987) . . . . Georgette Starkey
TV:
Leo and Liz in Beverly Hills (1986) . . . . .Liz Green
Magazines:
Playboy (May 1972). Valerie
••• 103-107: Nice.
Playboy (Dec 1972) . . . . .Sex Stars of 1972
•• 210: Topless.
Playboy (Nov 1973) . . . . Sex in Cinema
•• 151: Right breast.
Playboy (Dec 1977) . . . . .Sex Stars of 1977
• 211: Left breast.
Playboy (Aug 1981) . . . . Viva Valeriel
•• 152-159: Topless.
Playboy (Nov 1981) . . . . Sex in Cinema 1981
•• 165: Topless.
Playboy (Jan 1989) . . . . .Women of the Eighties
•• 251: Topless.

Persson, Carina

Video Tapes:
Playboy's Playmate Review 2 (1984) . . . . . Playmate
Playmates at Play (1990)
. . . . .Thrill Seeker, Free Wheeling
Magazines:
Playboy (Aug 1983) . . . . Playmate

Pescia, Lisa

Films:
Tough Guys (1986) . . . . Customer #1
Body Chemistry (1990). . . . . .Claire
••• 0:18 - Topless making love with Marc Singer standing up, then at foot of bed.
0:35 - In purple bra in van with Singer.
0:55 - Buns, standing in hallway. Long shot.

Peters, Lorraine

Films:
More Deadly than the Male (1961) . . . . Rita
The Wicker Man (1973; British) . . . . Girl on Grave
  • 0:22 - Side view of right breast sitting on grave, crying. Dark, long shot, hard to see.
The Innocent (1985; British) . . . .

Peterson, Cassandra

See: Elvira.

Pettet, Joanna

Films:
The Group (1966) . . . . Kay Strong
Casino Royale (1967; British) . . . . Mata Bond
The Night of the Generals (1967; British/French)
  . . . . Ulrike von Seidlitz-Gaber
Robbery (1967; British) . . . . Kate Clifton
Blue (1968) . . . . Joanne Morton
The Best House in London (1969; British)
  . . . . Josephine Pacefoot
Welcome to Arrow Beach (1973) . . . . Grace Henry
  a.k.a. Tender Flesh
The Evil (1977) . . . . Caroline
Double Exposure (1983) . . . . Mindy Jordache
  •• 0:55 - Topless, making love in bed with Adrian.
Sweet Country (1985) . . . . Monica
Miniseries:
Captains and the Kings (1976) . . . Katherine Hennessey
TV:
Knots Landing (1983) . . . . Janet Baines

Pettijohn, Angelique

a.k.a. Heaven St. John.
Adult Films:
Body Talk (1982) . . . . Cassie
  Topless and more!
Titillation (1982) . . . . Brenda Weeks
  Topless and more!
Films:
Clambake (1967) . . . . Gloria
Childish Things (1969) . . . . Angelique
The Curious Female (1969) . . . . Susan
Heaven with a Gun (1969) . . . . Emily
The Mad Doctor of Blood Island (1969; Philippines/U.S.)
  . . . . Sheila Willard
Tell Me That You Love Me, Junie Moon (1970) . . Melissa
The G.I. Executioner (1971) . . . . Bonnie
  •• 0:16 - Doing a strip routine on stage. Buns in G-string, very brief side view of right breast, then topless at end.
  •• 0:40 - Topless, lying asleep in bed.
  ••• 0:58 - Topless and buns, undressing in front of Dave, getting into bed, fighting an attacker and getting shot. Long scene.
  • 1:14 - Topless, lying shot in rope net.

The Lost Empire (1983) . . . . Whiplash
  0:29 - In a sexy, black leather outfit fighting in prison with Heather.
Bio-Hazard (1984) . . . . Lisa Martyn
  •• 0:30 - Partial left breast on couch with Mitchell. In beige bra and panties talking on telephone, breast almost falling out of bra.
  ••• 1:15 - Left breast, on couch with Mitchell, in out-take scene during the end credits.
  • 1:16 - Upper half of left breast on couch again during a different take.
Repo Man (1984) . . . . Repo Wife No. 2
Takin' It Off (1984) . . . . Anita Little
TV:
Star Trek: The Gamesters of Triskelion . . . . Shahna

Pfeiffer, Michelle

Sister of actress DeDee Pfeiffer.
Films:
Falling in Love Again (1980) . . . . Sue Wellington
The Hollywood Knights (1980) . . . . Suzi Q.
Charlie Chan & the Curse of the Dragon Queen (1981)
  . . . . Cordelia Farrington III
Grease 2 (1982) . . . . Stephanie Zinone
Scarface (1983) . . . . Elvira
Into the Night (1985) . . . . Diana
  • 0:27 - Buns and very brief side nudity in her brother's apartment getting dressed. Long shot, hard to see.
Ladyhawke (1985) . . . . Isabeau
Sweet Liberty (1986) . . . . Faith Healey
Amazon Women on the Moon (1987) . . Brenda Landers
The Witches of Eastwick (1987) . . . . . . Sukie Ridgemont
Dangerous Liaisons (1988) . . . . Madame de Tourvel
Married to the Mob (1988) . . . . Angela de Marco
Tequila Sunrise (1988) . . . . Jo Ann
  1:14 - Upside down reflection in water getting on top of Mel Gibson. Can't tell it's her. Only see silhouette. Probably wearing a body suit. Brief buns, holding onto Gibson when he pulls a sheet over their heads. Blurry.
The Fabulous Baker Boys (1989) . . . . Susie Diamond
The Russia House (1990) . . . . Katya
Made for TV Movies:
Natica Jacks . . . . Natica Jackson
The Children Nobody Wanted (1980) . . . . Jennifer
TV:
Delta House (1979) . . . . Bombshell

Pflanzer, Krista

Films:
Cheerleader Camp (1988) . . . .
  a.k.a. Bloody Pom Poms
Magazines:
Penthouse (Jul 1986) . . . . Pet
Penthouse (Jun 1991) . . . . Krista Revisited
  ••• 40-45: Nude.

Picard, Nicole

Films:
Deadtime Stories (1987) . . .Rachel (Red Riding Hood)
• 0:48 - Very brief right breast in shack with boyfriend.
Dangerous Love (1988). Jane

Pickett, Cindy

Films:
Night Games (1980). . . . . Valerie St. John
•• 0:05 - Brief topless getting scared by her husband in
the shower.
• 0:45 - Buns and topless by and in the swimming pool
with Joanna Cassidy.
0:46 - Topless in sheer blue dress during fantasy sequence with Cassidy.
•• 0:48 - Brief full frontal nudity getting out of the pool,
then topless lying down with Cassidy.
1:03 - Dancing at night in a see through nightgown.
••• 1:14 - Full frontal nudity standing up in bathtub,
then topless during fantasy with a guy in gold.
•• 1:18 - Topless getting out of pool at night.
••• 1:24 - Topless sitting up in bed and stretching.
Ferris Bueller's Day Off (1986). . . . . Katie Bueller
The Men's Club (1986) . . . . Hannah
Hot to Trot (1988). . . . . Victoria Peyton
Deepstar Six (1989) . . . . Diane Norris
Made for TV Movies:
Into the Homeland (1987) . . . .
Plymouth (1991). . . . . Addy
TV:
The Guiding Light (1976-80) . . . . . . Jackie Scott Marler
Call to Glory (1984-85). . . . . Vanessa Sarnac
St. Elsewhere (1986-88) . . . . .Dr. Carol Novino
Magazines:
Playboy (Nov 1979) . . . . Sex in Cinema 1979
• 175: Topless, small photo, hard to see.
Playboy (Dec 1980). . . . . Sex Stars of 1980
•• 244: Topless.

Pisier, Marie-France

Films:
Love at Twenty (1963; French/Italian/Japan) . . . . Colette
Trans-Europ-Express (1968; French) . . . . Eva
Stolen Kisses (1969; French) . . . . .Colette Tazzi
Cousin, Cousine (1975; French) . . . . .Karine
Other Side of Midnight (1977) . . . . Noëlle Page
• 0:10 - Very brief topless in bed with Lanchon.
0:28 - Buns, in bed with John Beck. Medium long
shot.
0:45 - In white bra, in dressing room talking to Henri.
0:50 - Topless in bathtub, giving herself an abortion
with a coat hanger. Painful to watch!
•• 1:11 - Topless wearing white slip in room getting
dressed in front of Henri.
••• 1:17 - Full frontal nudity in front of fireplace with Armand, rubbing herself with oil, then making love
with ice cubes. Very nice!

• 1:35 - Full frontal nudity taking off dress for Constan-
tin in his room.
The Bronte Sisters (1979; French). . . . . .Charlotte
French Postcards (1979). . . . . .Madame Tessier
•• 0:16 - In white bra, then topless in dressing room
while a guy watches without her knowing.
Love on the Run (1979) . . . . Colette
Chanel Solitaire (1981). . . . . Gabrielle Chanel
Miss Right (1987) . . . . Bebe
•• 0:07 - Topless in open top dress when the reporter
discovers her in a dressing room behind a curtain.
Miniseries:
Scruples (1980) . . . . Valentine O'Neill

Pitt, Ingrid

Films:
Where Eagles Dare (1969) . . . . Heidi
The House That Dripped Blood (1970). . . . . Carla
Vampire Lovers (1970; British) . . . . . Marcilla/Carmilla
•• 0:32 - Topless and buns in the bathtub and reflection
in the mirror talking to Emma.
The Wicker Man (1973; British) . . . . Librarian
•• 1:11 - Brief topless in bathtub seen by Edward Wood-
ward.
Transmutations (1986). . . . . Pepperdine
Hanna's War (1988) . . . . Margit

Plato, Dana

Films:
Return to Bogey Creek (1977) . . . .
TV:
Diff'rent Strokes (1978-84). . . . . . .Kimberly Drummond
Magazines:
Playboy (Jun 1989). . . . . Diff'rent Dana
• 78-83: Lower nudity and wearing a pink see-through
bra.

Player Jarreau, Susan

a.k.a. Susie Player.
Films:
Invasion of the Bee Girls (1973) . . . . Girl
Malibu Beach (1978). . . . . .Sally
• 0:28 - Side view of left breast with boyfriend at night
on the beach. Long shot.
0:32 - Buns, running into the ocean with her two
male friends.
0:33 - Brief side view of left breast in water. Long
shot.
• 0:34 - Brief topless in the ocean, then topless by the
fire getting dressed.

Podewell, Cathy

Films:
Night of the Demons (1987) . . . . .Judy
0:06 - Brief buns, changing clothes while talking on
the phone.
0:07 - In white bra taking off her sweater.

Made for TV Movies:
Earth Angel (1991) . . . . Angela
TV:
Dallas (1989-91) . . . . .Cally Ewing

Poremba, Jean

a.k.a. Adult film actress Candie Evans.
a.k.a. Marjorie Miller.
Films:
You Can't Hurry Love (1984) . . . . . . .Model in Back
- 0:05 - Topless posing in the backyard getting photographed.
-- 0:48 - Nude in backyard again getting photographed.
Night of the Living Babes (1987)
. . . . .Mondo Zombie Girl Darlene
--- 0:12 - Topless wearing dark purple wig and long gloves, with the other Mondo Zombie Girls.
--- 0:16 - More topless and buns in bed with Buck.
- 0:50 - Topless on the couch with the other Zombie Girls.
- 0:52 - Topless on the couch again.
Party Favors (1987) . . . . Bobbi
(Shot on video tape.)
-- 0:04 - Topless in dressing room, taking off red top and putting on black one.
- 0:23 - Brief topless when blouse pops off while delivering pizza.
--- 0:27 - Topless and buns in G-string doing a strip routine outside.
- 0:31 - Brief topless flapping her blouse to cool off.
--- 1:04 - Topless doing a strip routine in a little girl outfit. Buns, in G-string. More topless after.
- 1:16 - Nude taking off swimsuit next to pool during final credits.
Takin' It All Off (1987) . . . . Allison
0:36 - In pink bra and G-string.
--- 0:49 - In white lingerie, then topless, then nude dancing.
--- 0:58 - Topless, dancing outside when she hears the music.
--- 0:59 - Nude dancing in a park.
-- 1:01 - Nude dancing in a laundromat.
--- 1:03 - Nude dancing in a restaurant.
--- 1:07 - Nude in shower with Adam.
-- 1:13 - Topless dancing for the music in a studio.
--- 1:23 - Nude dancing with all the other women on stage.

Potter, Madeleine

Films:
The Bostonians (1984) . . . . Verena Tarrant
Suicide Club (1988) . . . . .Nancy
Bloodhounds of Broadway (1989) . . . . .Widow Mary
Slaves of New York (1989) . . . . Daria
- 1:14 - Topless making love with Stash on chair. Mostly see left breast. Dark.

Potts, Annie

Films:
Corvette Summer (1978) . . . . Vanessa
- 0:51 - Silhouette of right breast in van with Mark Hamill. Out of focus topless washing herself in the van while talking to him. Don't really see anything.
King of the Gypsies (1978) . . . . Persa
Heartaches (1981; Canadian) . . . . Bonnie Howard
Crimes of Passion (1984) . . . . Amy Grady
Ghostbusters (1984) . . . . Janine Melnitz
Jumpin' Jack Flash (1986) . . . . .Liz Carlson
Pretty in Pink (1986) . . . . .Iona
Pass the Ammo (1988) . . . . .Darla Potter
Ghostbusters II (1989) . . . . Janine Melnitz
Who's Harry Crumb? (1989) . . . . Helen Downing
0:55 - In sheer black bra lying in bed with Jeffrey Jones.
1:00 - More in the same bra in photograph that Jones is looking at.
Texasville (1990) . . . . Karla
TV:
Goodtime Girls (1980) . . . . .Edith Bedelmeyer
Designing Women (1986-) . . . . Mary Jo Shively

Power, Deborah

Films:
Emmanuelle IV (1984) .Maria
1:09 - Buns, lying down getting a massage from Mia Nygren.
Glamour (1985; French) . . . .

Power, Taryn

Daughter of actor Tyrone Power.
Films:
Sinbad and the Eye of the Tiger (1977; U.S./British)
. . . . Dione
1:16 - Very brief buns, skinny dipping in pond with Jane Seymour. Long shot, but still pretty amazing for a G-rated film.
1:18 - Very brief partial side view of right breast, running away from the troglodyte.
Tracks (1977) . . . . Stephanie
- 0:32 - Brief side view of right breast changing in her room on the train. Don't see her face.
- 1:15 - Brief left breast making love with Dennis Hopper in a field.
Made for TV Movies:
The Count of Monte Cristo (1975) . . . .

Powers, Beverly

Films:
Kissin' Cousins (1964) .Trudy
More Dead than Alive (1968) . . . . .Sheree
Angel in My Pocket (1969) . . . . Charlene de Gaulle
J. W. Coop (1971) . . . . Dora Mae

Invasion of the Bee Girls (1973) . . . Harriet Williams
- 1:14 - In white bra and panties, then right breast and buns taking off her clothes for her husband.

Powers, Stephanie
Films:
Crescendo (1972; British) . . . . Susan
(Not available on video tape.)

Prather, Joan
Films:
Single Girls (1973) . . . .
Big Bad Mama (1974) . . . . Jane Kingston
- • 1:15 - Topless and buns in the bathroom with Tom Skerritt.
Smile (1974) . . . . Robin
0:47 - Brief buns in dressing room, taking off pants while Little Bob is outside taking pictures. (She's wearing a pink ribbon in her hair.)
Rabbit Test (1978) . . . . Segoynia
The Best of Sex and Violence (1981) . . . . . . Herself
- • 0:38 - Topless getting her breasts squeezed by an attacker. Dark.
Famous T & A (1982) . . . . herself
(No longer available for purchase, check your video store for rental.)
- 0:49 - Brief topless in scene from *Single Girls*.
Made for TV Movies:
The Deerslayer (1978) . . . .
TV:
Executive Suite (1976-77) . . . . Glory Dalessio
Eight is Enough (1979-81) . . . . Janet Bradford

Prentiss, Paula
Films:
Where the Boys Are (1960) . . . . Tuggle Carpenter
Man's Favorite Sport? (1964) . . . . Abigail Page
The World of Henry Orient (1964) . . . . Stella
In Harm's Way (1965; B&W) . . . . Bev
What's New, Pussycat? (1965; U.S./French) . . . . Liz
Catch-22 (1970) . . . . Nurse Duckett
- 0:22 - Full frontal nudity in water throwing her dress to Alan Arkin who is swimming in the water during his dream. Long shot, over exposed, hard to see.
Move (1970) . . . . Dolly Jaffe
Last of the Red Hot Lovers (1972) . . . . . . Bobbi Michele
The Parallax View (1974) . . . . Lee Carter
The Stepford Wives (1975) . . . . Bobby
The Black Marble (1980) . . . . . Sgt. Natalie Zimmerman
Buddy Buddy (1981) . . . . Celia Clooney
Saturday the 14th (1981) . . . . Mary
TV:
He & She (1967-68) . . . . Paula Hollister

Preston, Kelly
a.k.a. Kelly Palzis.
Wife of actor John Travolta.
Films:
10 to Midnight (1983) . . . . Doreen
Christine (1983) . . . . Roseanne
Metalstorm: The Destruction of Jared-Syn (1983)
. . . . Dhyana
Mischief (1985) . . . . Marilyn McCauley
- • • 0:56 - In a bra, then topless making love with Doug McKeon in her bedroom.
Secret Admirer (1985) . . . . . . Deborah Anne Fimple
- • • 0:53 - Brief topless in car with C. Thomas Howell.
- 1:17 - Very brief topless in and out of bed.
52 Pick-Up (1986) . . . . Cini
- 0:09 - Brief buns in film made by blackmailers.
- 0:36 - Topless on video tape made by kidnappers.
SpaceCamp (1986) . . . . Tish
Amazon Women on the Moon (1987) . . . . Violet
Love at Stake (1988) . . . . Sara Lee
Spellbinder (1988) . . . . Miranda Reed
- • • • 0:19 - Topless in bed making love with Timothy Daly. 1:26 - Dancing around in a sheer white gown with nothing underneath during cult ceremony at the beach.
A Tiger's Tale (1988) . . . . Shirley
- • • 0:03 - Topless in the car, letting C. Thomas Howell open her blouse and look at her breasts.
Twins (1988) . . . . Marnie Mason
The Experts (1989) . . . . Bonnie
Made for Cable Movies:
The Perfect Bride (1991) . . . . Laura
Made for Cable TV:
Tales From the Crypt: The Switch (1990; HBO) . . . Linda
0:19 - In red, one piece swimsuit at the beach with a young Carlton.
TV:
For Love and Honor (1983) . . . . Mary Lee

Primeaux, Suzanne
Films:
Stripper (1985) . . . . herself
- • • 0:03 - Topless dancing on stage, kneeling on her left knee. Very brief buns in G-string.
Traxx (1988) . . . . Hooker #1
- • • 0:37 - Topless, dancing on stage while wearing a mask.

Principal, Victoria
Films:
The Life and Times of Judge Roy Bean (1972)
. . . . Marie Elena
The Naked Ape (1972) . . . . Cathy
(Not available on video tape.)
Topless.
Earthquake (1974) . . . . Rosa
I Will, I Will... For Now (1976) . . . . Jackie Martin
Vigilante Force (1976) . . . . Linda

Made for TV Movies:
Naked Lie (1989) . . . . .Joanne Dawson
Don't Touch My Daughter (1991). . . . .
TV:
Dallas (1978-89) . . . . Pamela Barnes Ewing
Magazines:
Playboy (Dec 1972). . . . . Sex Stars of 1972
••• 210: Left breast.
Playboy (Sep 1973) . . . . . The Naked Ape & "Ape" Girl
••• 161-167: Topless and buns.
Playboy (Dec 1973). . . . . Sex Stars of 1973
• 210: Right breast.
Playboy (Dec 1976). . . . . Sex Stars of 1976
••• 183: Topless and in black panties lying down.

Prophet, Melissa

Films:
Players (1979). . . . . Ann
Van Nuys Blvd. (1979) . . . . Cameille
Looker (1981). . . . . Commercial Script Girl
Time Walker (1982). .Jennie
• 0:27 - Brief topless putting bra on while a guy watch-
es from outside the window.
1:17 - Very, very brief right breast in shower when
the mummy comes to get the crystal.
Fatal Games (1984) . . . . Nancy Wilson
• 0:14 - Buns and side view of left breast in shower
with other girls. Long shot. (she's wearing a white
towel on her head.)
Invasion U.S.A. (1985). . . . . McGuirre
Action Jackson (1988) . . . . .Newscaster
GoodFellas (1990). . . . . Angie
Magazines:
Playboy (May 1987) . . . . .Diary of a Hollywood Starlet
••• 86-93: Full frontal nudity.

Props, Renee

a.k.a. Babette Props.
Films:
Weird Science (1985) . . . . One of The Weenies
Free Ride (1986). . . . . Kathy
• 0:13 - Brief topless in the shower while Dan watches.
TV:
As the World Turns . . . . .Ellie Snyder

Purl, Linda

Films:
Crazy Mama (1975) . . . . Cheryl
0:05 - In pink, two piece swimsuit at the beach.
• 0:52 - Very brief buns, then brief topless when Snake
and Donny Most keep opening the door after she
has taken a shower. Long shot, hard to see.
The High Country (1980; Canadian) . . . . Kathy
1:03 - Brief buns taking a shower in the waterfall.
Visiting Hours (1982; Canadian) . . . . Sheila Munroe
Viper (1988) . . . . Laura Macalla
Web of Deceit (1991) . . . .

Made for TV Movies:
Pleasures (1986). . . . .
TV:
Happy Days (1974-75) . . . . Gloria
Matlock (1986-89). . . . . Charlene Matlock
Under Cover (1991). . . . . Kate Del'Amico

Quennessen, Valerie

Films:
French Postcards (1979). . . . . .Toni
Like a Turtle on Its Back (1981; French) . . . . . .Nietzsche
Conan the Barbarian (1982). . . . . .The Princess
Summer Lovers (1982) . . . . .Lina
• 0:12 - Topless on balcony.
••• 0:19 - Nude on the beach with Michael.
• 0:23 - Brief topless in a cave with Michael.
•• 0:30 - Topless lying on the floor with Michael.
0:54 - Buns, lying on a rock with Daryl Hannah
watching Michael dive off a rock.
• 1:03 - Left breast in bed.
•• 1:05 - Topless dancing on the balcony.
1:09 - Topless on the beach.

Quick, Diana

Films:
The Big Sleep (1978; British) . . . . .Mona Grant
1919 (1984; British). . . . . Anna
Ordeal by Innocence (1984) . . . . Gwenda Vaughn
The Misadventures of Mr. Wilt (1990) . . . . .Sally
Miniseries:
Brideshead Revisited (1981; British) . . . . . .Julia Flyte
0:18 - (Part 10 on TV or Book 5 on video tape.) Several quick peeks at partial right breast in mirror,
while lying under Jeremy Irons in bed.
•• 0:19 - Left breast, in bed lying on top of Jeremy Irons
after making love with him.

Quigley, Linnea

Films:
Fairytales (1979) . . . . .Dream Girl
•• 1:07 - Topless waking up after being kissed by The
Prince.
Nightstalker (1979) . . . .
Stone Cold Dead (1979; Canadian) . . . .
Summer Camp (1979). . . . .
Cheech & Chong's Nice Dreams (1981)
. . . . Blondie Group #2
Don't Go Near the Park (1981) . . . .
Graduation Day (1981). . . . . .Dolores
•• 0:36 - Topless by the piano in classroom with Mr.
Roberts unbuttoning her blouse.
The Young Warriors (1983; U.S./Canadian) . . .Ginger
• 0:05 - Nude in and getting out of bed in bedroom.
The Black Room (1984) . . . . Milly
Fatal Games (1984) . . . . .Athelete

Silent Night, Deadly Night (1984) . . . . Denise
••• 0:52 - Topless on pool table with Tommy, then putting on shorts and walking around the house. More topless, impaled on antlers.

The Return of the Living Dead (1985) . . . . . . Trash
••• 0:05 - Topless and buns, strip tease and dancing in cemetery. (Lower frontal nudity is covered with some kind of make-up appliance).
• 1:08 - Topless, walking out of the cemetery to eat someone.

Savage Streets (1985) . . . . Heather
• 0:28 - Topless getting raped by the jerks.

Silent Night, Deadly Night, Part 2 (1986) . . Denise
••• 0:26 - Topless on pool table and getting dressed flashback from *Silent Night, Deadly Night*.

Creepozoids (1987) . . . . Blanca
•• 0:15 - Topless taking off her top to take a shower.
•• 0:16 - Right breast, while standing in shower with Butch.
• 0:24 - Right breast several times while sleeping in bed with Butch.

Night of the Demons (1987) . . . . Suzanne
•• 0:52 - Topless twice, opening her dress top while acting weird. Pushes a tube of lipstick into her left breast. (Don't try this at home kids!)
0:56 - Lower frontal nudity, lifting her skirt up for Jay.

Nightmare Sisters (1987) . . . . Melody
(This is the best video tape for viewing all three "Scream Queens.")
••• 0:39 - Topless standing in panties with Mickey and Marci after transforming from nerds to sexy women.
••• 0:40 - Topless in the kitchen with Mickey and Marci.
••• 0:44 - Topless in the bathtub with Mickey and Marci. Excellent, long scene.
••• 0:46 - Topless in the bathtub. Nice close up.
••• 0:48 - Still more topless in the bathtub.
••• 0:55 - Topless dancing and singing in front of Kevin. Long scene.
•• 0:57 - Topless on the couch with Bud.

Treasure of the Moon Goddess (1987) . . . .
American Rampage (1988) . . . .

Hollywood Chainsaw Hookers (1988) . . . . Samantha
•• 0:32 - Topless, dancing on stage.
• 1:02 - Topless, (but her body is painted) dancing in a ceremony.

A Nightmare on Elm Street 4: The Dream Master (1988) . . . . Soul from Freddy's Chest
• 1:23 - Brief topless twice, trying to get out of Freddy's body. Don't see her face clearly.

Sorority Babes in the Slimeball Bowl-O-Rama (1988)
. . . . Spider

Vice Academy (1988) . . . . Didi
••• 0:45 - Topless making love with Chuck while he's handcuffed.

Assault of the Party Nerds (1989) . . . . Bambi
••• 0:25 - Topless straddling Cliff in bed.

Deadly Embrace (1989) . . . . Michelle Arno
•• 0:15 - In white lingerie, then topless and buns during Chris' fantasy.
•• 0:34 - Topless and buns caressing herself.
•• 0:43 - Topless again.
0:46 - Brief topless.
•• 0:50 - Topless and buns undressing.
••• 0:58 - Topless in bed on top of Chris, then making love.
• 1:02 - Topless and buns on top of Chris while Charlotte watches on T.V.
1:11 - Topless in Chris' fantasy.
• 1:12 - Topless and buns in playback of video tape.

Dr. Alien (1989) . . . . Rocker Chick #2
a.k.a. I Was a Teenage Sex Mutant
••• 0:21 - Topless in white outfit during dream sequence with two other rocker chicks.

Murder Weapon (1989) . . . . Dawn
• 0:08 - Buns and very brief side of left breast walking into shower. Long shot.
•• 0:40 - Topless taking off her top in car.
•• 0:48 - Topless and buns taking off her top in bedroom.
••• 0:50 - Topless in bed on top of a guy. Excellent long scene. Brief buns, getting out of bed.

Robot Ninja (1989) . . . . Miss Barbeau

Witchtrap (1989) . . . . Ginger O'Shey
••• 0:34 - Nude taking off robe and getting into the shower.
•• 0:36 - Topless just before getting killed when the shower head goes into her neck.

Vice Academy, Part 2 (1990) . . . . Didi
•• 1:04 - Buns in G-string, then topless dancing with Ginger Lynn Allen on stage at club.

Virgin High (1990) . . . . Kathleen
•• 0:24 - Topless, nonchalantly making love on top of Derrick.
•• 0:55 - Brief topless several times on top of Derrick, then topless.
• 1:21 - Topless in photo during party.

Blood Church (1991) . . . .
A Psycho in Texas (1991) . . . .
Sex Bomb (1991) . . . .

Magazines:
Playboy (Jan 1985) . . . . The Girls of Rock 'n' Roll
Playboy (Nov 1988) . . . . Sex in Cinema 1988
•• 137: Topless with tattoos across her breasts holding a chainsaw.
Playboy (Jul 1989) . . . . B-Movie Bimbos
••• 134: Full frontal nudity leaning on a car wearing stockings and an orange garter belt.

Quinlan, Kathleen

Films:
Lifeguard (1975) . . . . Wendy
I Never Promised You a Rose Garden (1977)
. . . . Deborah
- 0:27 - Topless changing in a mental hospital room with the orderly.
- 0:52 - Brief topless riding a horse in a hallucination sequence. Blurry, hard to see. Then close up of left breast (could be anyone's).
The Promise (1979) . . . . Nancy/Marie
The Runner Stumbles (1979) . . . . Sister Rita
Hanky Panky (1982) . . . . Janet Dunn
The Last Winter (1983) . . . . Joyce
- •• 0:48 - Brief side view of left breast taking off her robe and diving into pool Very brief buns.
  0:49 - Buns, lying on marble slab, talking with Maya.
  0:50 - Very brief right breast sitting up. Long shot, hard to see.
Twilight Zone—The Movie (1983) . . . . Helen
Warning Sign (1985) . . . . Joanie Morse
Man Outside (1987) . . . . Grace Freemont
Wild Thing (1987) . . . . Jane
Clara's Heart (1988) . . . . Leona Hart
Sunset (1988) . . . . Nancy Shoemaker
The Doors (1991) . . . .
Made for Cable Movies:
Blackout (1985) . . . . Chris
  0:26 - Brief side view of left breast making love in bed. Dark, hard to see.
Trapped (1989) . . . .

Rabett, Catherine

Films:
The Living Daylights (1987) . . . .
Maurice (1987; British) . . . . Pippa Durham
Frankenstein Unbound (1990) . . . . Elizabeth
  1:10 - Very brief left breast lying dead after getting shot by Frankenstein. Unappealing looking because of all the gruesome makeup.

Rae, Taija

Adult film actress.
Films:
Delivery Boys (1984) . . . . Nurse
  0:34 - In bra and panties after doing a strip tease with another nurse while dancing in front of a boy who is lying on an operating table.
Sex Appeal (1986) . . . . Rhonda
- •• 1:14 - In black lingerie, then topless in black push-up teddy with Sheila.

Raines, Cristina

a.k.a. Tina Herazo.
Films:
Hex (1973) . . . . Oriole
Stacey (1973) . . . . Pamela

Nashville (1975) . . . . Mary
Russian Roulette (1975) . . . . Bogna Kirchoff
The Duellists (1977) . . . . Adele
The Sentinel (1977) . . . . Alison Parker
- 0:18 - Briefly in sheer beige bra, putting her blouse on.
- 0:33 - Very, very brief left breast immediately after Sylvia Miles rips her dress off. B&W dream sequence.
Touched by Love (1980) . . . . Amy
North Shore (1987) . . . . Rick's Mother
TV:
Centennial (1978-79) . . . . Lucinda
Flamingo Road (1981-82) . . . . Lane Ballou

Raines, Frances

Films:
The Mutilator (1983) . . . .
Topless by the pool.
Breeders (1986) . . . . Karinsa Marshall
- ••• 0:12 - Nude stretching and exercising in photo studio.
- 0:16 - Brief full frontal nudity, getting attacked by the creature.
- ••• 0:53 - Topless and buns, taking off her blouse and walking down the hall and into the basement. Long scene.
- 1:07 - Very brief right breast in the alien nest with the other women.
- 1:10 - Brief topless standing up.

Raines, Lisa

See: Foster, Lisa Raines.

Rains, Gianna

Films:
Firehouse (1987) . . . . Barrett Hopkins
- ••• 0:33 - Topless taking a shower, then drying herself just before the fire alarm goes off.
- •• 0:56 - Topless making love with the reporter on the roof of a building.
Homeboy (1988) . . . . Phyllis

Rampling, Charlotte

Films:
Rotten to the Core (1965; British) . . . . Sara
Georgy Girl (1966; British/B&W) . . . . Meredith
The Long Duel (1967; British) . . . . Jane Stafford
The Damned (1969; German) . . . . . Elizabeth Thallman
Three (1969; British) . . . . Marty
Asylum (1972; British) . . . . Barbara
Corky (1972) . . . . Corky's Wife
Henry VIII and His Six Wives (1972; British)
. . . . Anne Boleyn
'Tis a Pity She's a Whore (1972; Italian) . . Annabella
Topless.

Caravan to Vaccares (1974; British/French)...... Lila
Brief buns standing at window, then brief full frontal nudity getting back into bed.

The Night Porter (1974; Italian/U.S.)..........Lucia
•• 0:11 - Side nudity being filmed with a movie camera
in the concentration camp line.
• 0:13 - Nude running around a room while a Nazi
taunts her by shooting his gun near her.
••• 1:12 - Topless doing a song and dance number wearing pants, suspenders and a Nazi hat. Long scene.

Zardoz (1974; British)................. Consuella
• 1:44 - Very brief right breast feeding her baby in time
lapse scene at the end of the film.

Farewell, My Lovely (1975; British)......... Velma

Foxtrot (1976; Mexican/Swiss)............... Julia

Orca, The Killer Whale (1977)........ Rachel Bedford

The Purple Taxi (1977; French/Italian/Irish)... Sharon

Stardust Memories (1980; B&W).............Dorrie

The Verdict (1982)...................... Laura

Angel Heart (1987)..........Margaret Krusemark
• 1:10 - Brief left breast dead on the floor, covered with
blood.
• 1:46 - Very brief left breast during flashback of the
dead-on-the-floor-covered-with-blood scene.

Mascara (1987).......................Gaby Hart

D.O.A. (1988)...................Mrs. Fitzwaring

Magazines:

Playboy (Nov 1972)........... Sex in Cinema 1972
• 167: Topless lying down in bed in a photo from *'Tis
a Pity She's a Whore*.

Playboy (Mar 1974)..................... Zardoz
• 142: Buns and side view of left breast.

Playboy (Dec 1977)............. Sex Stars of 1977
•• 213: Right breast and half of lower frontal nudity
standing against fireplace.

Randall, Anne

Films:

The Split (1968)...................... Negli's Girl

The Model Shop (1969)................. 2nd Model

Hell's Bloody Devils (1970)............... Amanda

The Christian Licorice Store (1971)........ Texas Girl

A Time for Dying (1971)............. Nellie Winters

Get to Know Your Rabbit (1972)......... Stewardess

Stacey (1973).................... Stacey Hansen
••• 0:01 - Topless taking off her driving jump suit.
••• 0:12 - Topless changing clothes.
••• 0:39 - Topless in bed with Bob.

Westworld (1973).....................Servant Girl

TV:

Hee Haw (1972-73)...................... regular

Magazines:

Playboy (May 1967).................... Playmate

Playboy (Dec 1973).............. Sex Stars of 1973
• 208: Left breast.

Randolph, Windsor Taylor

a.k.a. Ty Randolph.
a.k.a. Adult film actress Lisa Berenger.

Films:

Body Double (1984).................... Mindy
••• 1:50 - Topless in the shower during filming of movie
with Craig Wasson made up as a vampire.

Amazons (1986).........................Dyala
•• 0:22 - Topless skinny dipping then getting dressed
with Tashi.
•• 0:24 - Brief topless getting her top opened by bad
guys then fighting them.

Penitentiary III (1987)......................Sugar

Caged Fury (1989).............Warden Sybil Thorn
•• 0:55 - Topless and buns undressing for bath, then in
the bathtub.

Deadly Embrace (1989)........Charlotte Morland
0:19 - In yellow one piece swimsuit by the pool with
Chris.
0:27 - In wet, white T-shirt in the kitchen with Chris.
•• 0:28 - Topless taking off her top. Mostly side view of
left breast.
• 0:29 - More left breast, while in bed with Chris.
••• 0:30 - Topless, making love in bed with Chris.
• 1:10 - Brief right breast, on T.V. when she replays video tape for Linnea Quigley.

Rattray, Heather

Films:

Across the Great Divide (1976)............... Holly

The Further Adventures of the Wilderness Family -
(1978)......................... Jenny Robinson

The Sea Gypsies (1978)................... Courtney

Mountain Family Robinson (1979)............Jenny

Basket Case 2 (1989).....................Susan
• 1:20 - Brief right breast twice when white blouse
gapes open in bedroom with Duane. Special effect
scar on her stomach makes it a little unappealing
looking.

TV:

As the World Turns (1990-)............. Lily Walsh

Ray, Ola

Films:

Body and Soul (1981)................. Hooker #1
• 0:54 - Brief topless sitting on top of Leon Isaac
Kennedy in bed with two other hookers.

48 Hours (1982)................. Vroman's Dancers

Night Shift (1982)........................ Dawn

10 to Midnight (1983)..................... Ola
•• 1:27 - Buns, then topless in the shower.

Fear City (1984)................... Honey Powers

The Nightstalker (1987)..................Sable Fox

Music Videos:

Thriller/Michael Jackson (1983)........ His Girlfriend

Magazines:
Playboy (Jun 1980) . . . . Playmate
144:
Playboy (Jul 1981). . . . . Body and Soulmates
• 148: Right breast.
Playboy (Dec 1984). . . . . Sex Stars of 1984
••• 206: Topless.

Raymond, Candy

Films:
Alvin Rides Again (1974; Australian) . . . . Girl in Office
• 0:05 - Lower frontal nudity and buns, in office with
Alvin.
Don's Party (1976; Australian). . . . . Kerry
Monkey Grip (1983; Australian) . . . . Lillian

Reams, Cynthia

Films:
10 to Midnight (1983). . . . . Hooker
••• 1:25 - Topless in hotel room with killer when he tries
to elude Charles Bronson.
Radioactive Dreams (1984) . . . . .Buster Heavy

Redgrave, Lynn

Daughter of actor Sir Michael Redgrave.
Sister of actress Vanessa Redgrave.
Spokeswoman for Weight Watchers products.
Films:
Georgy Girl (1966; British/B&W). . . . . .Georgy
The Virgin Soldiers (1969). . . . . .Phillipa Raskin
The Happy Hooker (1975). . . . . Xaviera Hollander
(Before Weight Watchers.)
0:43 - In black bra and panties doing a strip tease
routine in a board room while Tom Poston watches.
Morgan Stewart's Coming Home (1987)
. . . . Nancy Stewart
Getting It Right (1989) . . . . Joan
•• 0:46 - Brief right breast, then brief topless on couch
seducing Gavin. Longer right breast shot when
wrestling with him.
Midnight (1989) . . . . Midnight
Made for TV Movies:
What Ever Happened to Baby Jane? (1991)
. . . . .Jane Hudson
TV:
Centennial (1978-79)
. . . . .Charlotte Buckland Lloyd Seccombe
House Calls (1979-81). . . . . .Ann Anderson
Teachers Only (1982-83). . . . . .Diana Swanson
Chicken Soup (1989) . . . . .Maddie
Magazines:
Playboy (Nov 1989) . . . . Sex in Cinema 1989
• 131: Right breast lying in sofa in a still from *Getting
It Right.*

Redgrave, Vanessa

Daughter of actor Sir Michael Redgrave.
Sister of actress Lynn Redgrave.
Films:
Blow-Up (1966; British/Italian). . . . . .Jane
Camelot (1967) . . . . .Guenevere
Isadora (1968; British) . . . . Isadora Duncan
0:47 - Brief glimpses of topless and buns dancing
around in her boyfriend's house at night. Hard to see
anything.
• 2:19 - Very brief topless dancing on stage after com-
ing back from Russia.
The Sea Gull (1968) . . . . Nina
Murder on the Orient Express (1974; British) . . . . . Mary
Out of Season (1975; British) . . . . .Ann
The Seven-Per-Cent Solution (1976) . . . . Lola Deveraux
Julia (1977) . . . . .Julia
Agatha (1979) . . . . Agatha Christie
Yanks (1979) . . . . .Helen
• 1:25 - Brief side of left breast and buns, taking off
robe and getting into bed.
Bear Island (1980; British/Canadian) . . . . Hedi Lindquist
Wagner (1983; British). . . . . Cosima
The Bostonians (1984) . . . . Olive Chancellor
Steaming (1985; British) . . . . Nancy
• 1:32 - Buns and brief side view of right breast getting
into pool.
Wetherby (1985; British) . . . . .Jean Travers
Prick Up Your Ears (1987; British) . . . . Peggy Ramsay
Consuming Passions (1988; U.S./British) . . . .Mrs. Garza
0:40 - Almost side view of left breast making love
with a guy on her bed.
The Ballad of the Sad Cafe (1991) . . . .
Made for Cable Movies:
Young Catherine (1991). . . . . .Empress
Made for TV Movies:
Playing for Time (1980) . . . . Fania Fenelon
0:11 - Very brief buns sitting down to get her hair
cut.
A Man for All Seasons (1988) . . . . Lady Alice
What Ever Happened to Baby Jane? (1991)
. . . . Blanche Hudson

Redman, Amanda

Films:
Richard's Things (1980) . . . . .Josie
•• 0:51 - Topless, lying in bed talking to Liv Ullman.
Give My Regards to Broad Street (1984; British)
. . . . .Office Receptionist
For Queen and Country (1989; British) . . . . Stacey

Reed, Penelope

Films:
Amazons (1986) . . . . Tashi
•• 0:22 - Topless and buns undressing to go skinny dipping. More topless getting dressed.
• 0:24 - Brief topless getting top opened by bad guys.
Far Out Man (1990). . . . . Stewardess

Reed, Tracy
Films:
...All the Marbles (1981) . . . . Diane
a.k.a. The California Dolls
Running Scared (1986) . . . . .Maryann
 • 0:18 - Brief buns.
 • 1:30 - Very brief topless in bed with Gregory Hines.
Made for TV Movies:
Death of a Centerfold: The Dorothy Stratten Story
 (1981). . . . . .Mindy
TV:
Knots Landing . . . . Charlotte Anderson
Love, American Style (1969-70) . . . . . . repertory player
Barefoot in the Park (1970-71) . . . . .Corie Bratter

Regan, Mary
Films:
Heart of the Stag (1983; New Zealand)
 . . . . .Cathy Jackson
 • 0:03 - Brief right breast twice, very brief lower frontal
   nudity in bed with her father.
 •• 1:06 - Topless in bed, ripping her blouse open while
   yelling at her father.
Midnight Dancer (1987; Australian) . . . . Crystal
a.k.a. Belinda
 •• 0:29 - Topless in dressing room, undressing and rubbing makeup on herself.
 •• 0:56 - In bra, then topless in panties, changing
   clothes and getting into bed.
The Year My Voice Broke (1987; Australian)
 . . . . Miss McColl
Out of the Body (1988; Australian) . . . . . . Marry Mason
Fever (1989; Australian) . . . . .Leanne Welles

Regard, Suzanne M.
Films:
48 Hours (1982) . . . . Cowgirl Dancer
 0:39 - Dancer in red-neck bar wearing silver star pasties.
Malibu Express (1984). . . . . Sexy Sally
 • 0:50 - Brief topless talking on the telephone.
 •• 1:06 - Topless talking on the telephone.

Reidy, Gabrielle
Films:
Educating Rita (1983; British) . . . . .Barbara
The Fanatasist (1986; Irish) . . . . .Kathy O'Malley
 • 0:03 - Topless getting attacked in a room.

Relph, Emma
Films:
Eureka (1983; British) . . . . Mary (blue dress)
 • 1:17 - Brief topless during African voodoo ceremony.
The Witches (1989). . . . . Millie

Renet, Sinitta
Films:
Shock Treatment (1981). . . . .
Foreign Body (1986; British) . . . . . .Lovely Indian Girl
 • 0:06 - Buns, then topless in bedroom.

Reyes, Pia
Video Tapes:
Playboy's Sexy Lingerie (1988) . . . .
Playboy Video Calendar 1990 (1989). . . . . . . .June
 ••• 0:28 - Nude.
Magazines:
Playboy (Nov 1988) . . . . Playmate

Rialson, Candice
Films:
Candy Stripe Nurses (1974) . . . . Sandy
 •• 0:05 - Topless in hospital linen closet with a guy.
 •• 0:08 - Topless smoking and writing in bathtub.
 • 0:14 - Topless in hospital bed.
Pets (1974). . . . . .Bonnie
 •• 0:26 - Topless dancing in field while Dan is watching
   her while he's tied up.
 ••• 0:33 - Topless making love on top of Dan while he's
   still tied up.
 0:35 - Running through woods in braless orange top.
 •• 0:40 - Topless getting into bath at Geraldine's house.
 • 0:45 - Topless posing for Geraldine.
 0:54 - In black and red lingerie outfit getting ready
 for bed.
 ••• 1:02 - Topless taking off lingerie in bed with Ron,
   then making love with him.
 1:34 - Almost topless, getting whipped by Vincent.
The Eiger Sanction (1975) . . . . Art Student
Summer School Teachers (1975). . . . . . . Conklin T.
 • 0:14 - Breasts and buns when Mr. Lacy fantasizes
   about what she looks like. Don't see her face, but it
   looks like her.
 ••• 0:38 - Topless outside with other teacher, kissing on
   the ground.
Hollywood Boulevard (1976). . . . .Candy Wednesday
 •• 0:29 - Topless getting her blouse ripped off by actors
   during a film.
 ••• 0:32 - Topless sunbathing with Bobbi and Jill.
 •• 0:45 - Brief topless in the films she's watching at the
   drive-in. Same as 0:29.
Chatterbox (1977) . . . . Penny
 •• 0:01 - Left breast, in bed with Ted, then topless getting out of bed.
 0:10 - In white bra wrestling on couch with another
 woman.
 ••• 0:15 - Side view of right breast then topless during
   demonstration on stage.
 ••• 0:26 - Topless in bed talking on phone.
 0:32 - In open dress letting her "chatterbox" sing
 during talk show. Something covers pubic area.
 •• 0:35 - Topless during photo shoot.

•• 0:38 - Topless again for more photos while opening a red coat.
•• 0:43 - Topless in bed with Ted.
••• 0:55 - Topless taking off white dress, walking up the stairs and opening the door.
•• 1:09 - Topless opening her raincoat for Ted.
Moonshine County Express (1977) . . . . .Mayella
Stunts (1977) . . . . .Judy Blake
Winter Kills (1979) . . . . Second Blonde Girl

Richarde, Tessa
Films:
The Beach Girls (1982) . . . . Doreen
Cat People (1982). . . . . Billie
•• 1:00 - Topless in bed with Malcolm McDowell trying to get him excited.
The Last American Virgin (1982). . . . . Brenda
•• 0:15 - Brief topless walking into the living room when Gary's parents come home.
Young Doctors in Love (1982). . . . . Rocco's Wife

Richards, Kim
Films:
Escape to Witch Mountain (1975). . . . . Tia
Assault on Precinct 13 (1976) . . . . Kathy
No Deposit, No Return (1976) . . . . Tracy
Special Delivery (1976) . . . . Juliette
The Car (1977) . . . . Lynn Marie
Return from Witch Mountain (1978). . . . . Tia
Meatballs, Part II (1984) . . . . Cheryl
Tuff Turf (1984) . . . . Frankie Croyden
1:07 - In black lingerie getting dressed.
• 1:29 - Brief topless supposedly of a body double (Fiona Morris) in bedroom with James Spader but I have heard from a very reliable source that it really was her.
TV:
Nanny and the Professor (1970-71) . . Prudence Everett
Here We Go Again (1973) . . . . Jan
James at 15 (1977-78). . . . . Sandy Hunter
Hello, Larry (1979-80). . . . . Ruthie Adler

Richardson, Joely
Daughter of actress Vanessa Redgrave and director Tony Richardson.
Sister of actress Natasha Richardson.
Films:
The Hotel New Hampshire (1984). . . . . Waitress
Wetherby (1985; British). . . . . Young Jean Travers
•• 1:10 - Topless in room with Jim when he takes off her coat.
Drowning by Numbers (1988; British)
. . . . Cissie Colpitts 3
Magazines:
Playboy (Nov 1991) . . . . Sex in Cinema 1991
•• 146: Topless on sofa. From *Drowning by Numbers*.

Richardson, Natasha
Daughter of actress Vanessa Redgrave and director Tony Richardson.
Sister of actress Joely Richardson.
Films:
Gothic (1986; British). . . . . Mary
A Month in the Country (1988; British) . . . . Alice Keach
Patty Hearst (1989) . . . . Patricia Hearst
•• 0:13 - Topless, blindfolded in the bathtub while talking to a woman member of the S.L.A.
A Handmaid's Tale (1990) . . . . .Kate
•• 0:30 - Topless twice at the window getting some fresh air.
• 0:59 - Topless making love with Aidan Quinn.
••• 1:00 - Topless after Quinn rolls off her.
The Comfort of Strangers (1991) . . . . Mary
••• 0:45 - Topless sleeping in bed. Long shot. Then closer topless after waking up. Long scene.
•• 1:05 - Topless making love with Colin. Lit with blue light.
•• 1:06 - Right breast, lying in bed with Colin. Lit with blue light.

Richardson, Rickey
Films:
Bloody Trail (1972) . . . . .Miriam
1:01 - Peek at left breast in torn blouse.
• 1:05 - Right breast while sleeping, dark, hard to see.
The Hot Box (1972). . . . . Ellie St. George
•• 0:16 - Topless cleaning herself off in stream and getting out.
• 0:21 - Topless sleeping in hammocks. (She's the second one from the front.)
• 0:26 - Topless getting accosted by the People's Army guys.
••• 0:43 - Full frontal nudity making love with Flavio.
••• 0:45 - Topless in stream bathing with the other three girls.
• 1:01 - Topless taking off top in front of soldiers.

Richmond, Fiona
Films:
The House on Straw Hill (1976; British). . . . .Suzanne
••• 0:05 - Buns and topless undressing and getting into bed and making love with Udo Kier.
•• 0:56 - In black bra, then topless undressing in front of Kier.
••• 1:00 - Topless in bedroom, then making love with Kier.
1:03 - Brief buns, lying on Linda's bed.
1:05 - Buns, lying on Linda's bed.
•• 1:06 - Right breast, in bed with Linda.
•• 1:07 - Topless in bed with Linda.
• 1:09 - Buns and side of left breast getting up from bed.
• 1:11 - Full frontal nudity, getting stabbed in the bathroom. Covered with blood.

Fiona (1978; British). . . . . Fiona Richmond
  •• 0:23 - Topless on boat with a blonde woman rubbing
      oil on her.
  •• 0:27 - In a bra, then frontal nudity stripping in a guy's
      office for an audition.
  •• 0:35 - Topless, then frontal nudity lying down during
      photo session.
  • 0:51 - Topless walking around her apartment in
      boots.
  •• 1:00 - Topless with old guy ripping each other's
      clothes off.
  •• 1:08 - Frontal nudity taking off clothes for a shower.
History of the World, Part I (1981). . . . . Queen

Richmond, Laura

Video Tapes:
  Playboy's Sexy Lingerie (1988). . . . .
  Playboy Video Calendar 1990 (1989) . . . . . February
  ••• 0:07 - Nude.
  Playboy Video Centerfold: Kerri Kendall (1990)
  . . . . Playmate
  ••• 0:39 - Nude.
Magazines:
  Playboy (Sep 1988). . . . . Playmate

Richter, Debi

Miss California 1975.
Films:
  Hometown, U.S.A. (1979). . . . . .Dolly
  Swap Meet (1979) . . . . Susan
  Gorp (1980) . . . . .Barbara
  Hot Moves (1985). . . . . .Heidi
    • 0:29 - Topless on nude beach.
    ••• 1:09 - Topless in bed with Michael.
  Square Dance (1987) . . . . Gwen
    a.k.a. Home is Where the Heart Is
  Winners Take All (1987). . . . . Cindy Wickes
      0:25 - In bra, in bed with motorcycle racer.
  Promised Land (1988). . . . . Pammie
  The Banker (1989) . . . . Melanie
  Cyborg (1989). . . . . .Nady Simmons
      0:28 - Buns, after taking off clothes and running into
      the ocean.
    • 0:30 - Brief left breast by the fire showing herself to
      Jean-Claude Van Damme.
TV:
  Aspen (1977) . . . . Angela Morelli
  All Is Forgiven (1986) . . . . .Sherry Levy

Richters, Christine

Video Tapes:
  Playmates at Play (1990) . . . . Free Wheeling
Magazines:
  Playboy (May 1986) . . . . Playmate

Richwine, Maria

Films:
  The Buddy Holly Story (1978) . . . . . . .Maria Elena Holly
  Hamburger—The Motion Picture (1986)
  . . . . Conchita
  •• 0:49 - Topless trying to seduce Russell in a room.

Rio, Nicole

Films:
  The Zero Boys (1985). . . . . Sue
  Sorority House Massacre (1987) . . . . Tracy
  •• 0:20 - In a sheer bra changing clothes with two other
      girls in a bedroom.
  •• 0:49 - Topless in a tepee with her boyfriend, Craig,
      just before getting killed.
  The Visitants (1987) . . . .
  Terminal Exposure (1988) . . . . Hostage Girl

Rixon, Cheryl

Films:
  Swap Meet (1979). .Annie
  Used Cars (1980) . . . . .Margaret
  •• 0:29 - Topless after getting her dress torn off during
      a used car commercial.
Magazines:
  Penthouse (Dec 1977). .Pet
  127-139:
  Penthouse (Nov 1979). . . . . Pet of the Year
  158-169:

Roberts, Julia

Films:
  Blood Red (1988). . . . . .Maria Collogero
  Mystic Pizza (1988) . . . . Daisy Araujo
  Satisfaction (1988). . . . . .Daryle Shane
      Shown on TV as "Girls of Summer."
  Steel Magnolias (1989) . . . . .Shelby Eatenton
  Flatliners (1990). . . . . Rachel Mannus
  Pretty Woman (1990). . . . . .Vivian Ward
      (Shelley Michelle, the body double for Julia Roberts, only
      did the *opening* scenes when Roberts is supposed to be
      getting dressed in her sexy outfit—*not* for the nude
      scene at 1:30.)
    • 1:30 - Very, very brief tip of left breast, then right
      breast, then left breast seen through head board, in
      bed with Gere. It's her—look especially at the verti-
      cal vein that pops out in the middle of her forehead
      whenever her blood pressure goes up.
  Dying Young (1991). . . . .
  Sleeping with the Enemy (1991) . . . . Laura Burney
Made for Cable Movies:
  Baja Oklahoma (1988; HBO) . . . . Candy

Roberts, Luanne

Films:
The Dark Side of Tomorrow (1970) . . . . .Producer's Wife
Weekend with the Babysitter (1970) . . . . . Mona Carlton
Welcome Home, Soldier Boys (1972) . . . . .Charlene
Thunderbolt and Lightfoot (1974)
. . . . .Suburban Housewife
• 0:57 - Brief full frontal nudity standing behind a sliding glass door tempting Jeff Bridges.

Roberts, Mariwin

Films:
Cinderella (1977) . . . . .Trapper's Daughter
••• 0:11 - Frontal nudity getting a bath outside by her blonde sister. Long scene.
Fairytales (1979). . . . . Elevator Operator
• 0:20 - Brief full frontal nudity in the elevator.
•• 0:23 - Topless again, closer shot.
Magazines:
Penthouse (Apr 1978). Pet
91-103:

Roberts, Tanya

Films:
Forced Entry (1975) . . . . Nancy Ulman
0:57 - In white bra and panties walking around the house.
The Yum-Yum Girls (1976) . . . . April
California Dreaming (1978). . . . . Stephanie
Fingers (1978). . . . . Julie
0:33 - In red two piece swimsuit talking on a pay phone while Harvey Keitel talks with her.
Racquet (1979) . . . . .Bambi
The Tourist Trap (1979). . . . . Becky
The Beastmaster (1982) . . . . Kiri
••• 0:35 - Topless in a pond while Marc Singer watches, then topless getting out of the water when his pet ferrets steal her towel.
Hearts and Armour (1983) . . . . Angelica
Sheena (1984). . . . . Sheena
••• 0:19 - Nude taking a shower under a waterfall.
••• 0:54 - Nude taking a bath in a pond while Ted Wass watches.
A View to a Kill (1985). . . . . Stacey Sutton
Purgatory (1988) . . . . Carly Arnold
• 0:29 - Nude, getting into the shower.
• 0:42 - Very brief topless in bed with the Warden.
0:43 - In white lingerie in whorehouse.
•• 0:57 - Left breast, then brief topless in bed talking to Tommy.
Night Eyes (1990). .Nikki
(Unrated version.)
0:18 - In white one piece swimsuit by the pool.
• 0:20 - Side view of left breast getting dressed while sitting on bed.
0:25 - In white lingerie, making love in bed with Michael.

0:30 - Repeat of last scene on TV when Andrew Stevens brings the video tape home to watch.
0:55 - Making love with Stevens. Don't see anything, but still steamy. Bubble covered left breast in tub with Stevens.
••• 1:09 - Topless giving Stevens a massage, then making love. Nice! Buns and left breast in the shower making love.
• 1:27 - Buns, making love with Stevens in a chair.
Twisted Justice (1990) . . . . Secretary
Inner Sanctum (1991). . . . .
Second Nature (1991) . . . .
Made for Cable Movies:
Body Slam (1989; HBO). . . . .
TV:
Charlie's Angels (1980-81) . . . . Julie Rogers
Magazines:
Playboy (Oct 1982) . . . .
••• Nice.
Playboy (Nov 1982) . . . . Sex in Cinema 1982
••• 161: Topless from *The Beastmaster.*
Playboy (Jan 1989). . . . . .Women of the Eighties
•• 251: Topless.
Playboy (Nov 1991) . . . . Sex in Cinema 1991
• 144: Side view of left breast, straddling Andrew Stevens. From *Night Eyes.*

Roberts, Teal

Films:
Fatal Games (1984). . . . . Lynn Fox
••• 0:08 - Topless on bed and floor when Frank takes her clothes off, more topless in shower.
•• 0:21 - Topless in sauna with Sue.
Hardbodies (1984) . . . . Kristi Kelly
•• 0:03 - Topless in bed after making love with Scotty, then putting her sweater on.
••• 0:47 - Topless standing in front of closet mirrors talking about breasts with Kimberly.
••• 0:56 - Topless making love with Scotty on the beach.
•• 1:22 - Topless on fancy car bed with Scotty.
Beverly Hills Cop II (1987) . . . . Stripper
•• 0:45 - Topless and buns, wearing G-string at the 385 North Club.

Robertson, Kimmy

Films:
The Last American Virgin (1982) . . . . Rose
Bad Manners (1989) . . . . Sarah Fitzpatrick
•• 0:38 - Topless and buns taking off robe and getting into the shower when Mouse takes a picture of her.
1:16 - In white bra when Piper rips her blouse open while she's tied up on the piano.
1:18 - Briefly on piano again.
Honey, I Shrunk the Kids (1989). . . . . . . Gloria Forrester
Trust Me (1989) . . . . Party Gal
TV:
Twin Peaks (1990-91). Lucy

Rohmer, Patrice
Films:
The Harrad Summer (1974) . . . . Marcia
Hustle (1975) . . . . Linda (Dancer)
  • 1:03 - In pasties, dancing on stage behind beaded curtain. Buns in G-string.
Jackson County Jail (1976) . . . . Cassie Anne
Revenge of the Cheerleaders (1976) . . . . Sesame
  • 0:28 - Brief topless and buns in the boys shower room.
Small Town in Texas (1976) . . . . Trudy

Rojo, Helena
Films:
Aguirre: Wrath of God (1972; West German) . . . . . Inez
Mary, Mary, Bloody Mary (1975) . . . . Greta
  • 0:42 - Buns and brief topless getting into bathtub with Cristina Ferrare.
Foxtrot (1976; Mexican/Swiss) . . . . Alexandra

Romanelli, Carla
Films:
Steppenwolf (1974) . . . . Maria
  ••• 0:59 - Topless sitting on bed with John Huston. Long scene.
The Sensuous Nurse (1979) . . . . Tosca
  •• 0:06 - Topless, then nude standing in the winery, then running around.
  •• 0:41 - Nude, in basement, playing army, then making love with bearded guy.
The Lonely Lady (1983) . . . . Carla Maria Peroni
  •• 1:10 - Brief topless taking off her top to make love with Pia Zadora while a guy watches.
A Very Moral Night (1985; Hungarian) . . . .

Rome, Sydne
Films:
Diary of Forbidden Dreams (1973; Italian)
. . . . The Girl
  ••• 0:06 - Brief topless taking off torn T-shirt in a room, then topless sitting on edge of bed.
  ••• 0:09 - Nude getting out of shower, drying herself off and getting dressed.
  • 0:20 - Brief side view of right breast, while talking to Marcello Mastroianni in her room.
  •• 0:22 - Brief topless putting shirt on.
  •• 1:28 - Topless outside on stairs fighting for her shirt.
  • 1:30 - Brief buns and topless climbing onto truck.
Sex with a Smile (1976; Italian)
. . . . "A Dog's Day" segment
The Twist (1976) . . . . Nathalie
Just a Gigolo (1979; German) . . . . Cilly
Looping (1981) . . . .
Magazines:
Playboy (Nov 1980) . . . . Sex in Cinema 1980
  •• 178: Topless.

Rose, Gabrielle
Films:
The Journey of Natty Gann (1985) . . . . . Exercise Matron
Family Viewing (1987; Canadian) . . . . Sandra
  • 0:27 - Brief left breast, lying down with Stan. Seen on TV that Van watches.
  • 0:29 - Same 0:27 scene again.
The Stepfather (1987) . . . . Dorothy
Speaking Parts (1989; Canadian) . . . . Clara
  •• 0:41 - Right breast, on TV monitor, masturbating with Lance. Then topless getting dressed.

Rose, Jamie
Films:
Just Before Dawn (1980) . . . . Megan
  0:33 - Topless in pond. Long shot.
  • 0:34 - Brief topless in pond, closer shot.
  •• 0:36 - Brief upper half of left breast, then brief topless several times splashing in the water.
  • 0:37 - Topless getting out of the water.
Heartbreakers (1984) . . . . Libby
  ••• 0:09 - Topless in bed talking with Nick Mancuso and Peter Coyote.
Tightrope (1984) . . . . Melanie Silber
  0:07 - Buns, lying face down on bed, dead.
Rebel Love (1985) . . . . Columbine Cromwell
Playroom (1989) . . . . Marcy
Made for TV Movies:
Voices Within: The Lives of Truddi Chase (1990)
. . . . Truddi's Mother
TV:
Falcon Crest (1981-83) . . . . Victoria Gioberti Hogan
Lady Blue (1985-86) . . . . Detective Katy Mahoney
St. Elsewhere (1986-88) . . . . Dr. Susan Birch

Rose, Laurie
Films:
The Hot Box (1972) . . . . Sue
  •• 0:16 - Topless cleaning herself off in stream and getting out.
  •• 0:21 - Topless sleeping in hammocks. (She's the first one from the front.)
  • 0:26 - Topless getting accosted by the People's Army guys.
  ••• 0:45 - Topless in stream bathing with the other three girls.
  • 0:58 - Full frontal nudity getting raped by Major Dubay.
The Roommates (1973) . . . . Brea
The Working Girls (1973) . . . . Denise
Policewoman (1974) . . . .
The Woman Hunt (1975; U.S./Philippines) . . . .
The Wizard of Speed & Time (1988) . . . .

Rose, Sherrie Ann
Films:
After School (1987) . . . . First Tribe Member
Spring Fever USA (1988) . . . . .Vinyl Vixen #1
Summer Job (1989) . . . . Kathy Shields
    0:25 - In bed wearing white bra and panties talking
    to Bruce. Long scene.
    0:52 - Buns, walking around in swimsuit and jacket.
  •• 0:53 - Topless taking off swimsuit top kneeling by the
    phone, then brief buns standing up.
    1:15 - In yellow two piece swimsuit walking on the
    beach.
  •• 1:24 - Brief topless taking off her yellow top on the
    beach talking to Bruce.
A Climate for Killing (1990) . . . . .Rita Paris
  •• 1:30 - Topless in bed while Wayne recollects his
    crime to John Beck.
Magazines:
Playboy (Apr 1989) . . . . The Girls of Spring Break
  ••• 74: Topless lying down, wearing a bikini bottom.

Ross, Annie
Films:
Straight on Till Morning (1974). . . . . .Liza
Oh, Alfie! (1975; British) . . . . Claire
a.k.a. Alfie Darling
  •• 1:34 - Topless on top of Alfie in open black dress
    while he's lying injured in bed.
Yanks (1979) .Red Cross Lady
Superman III (1983) . . . . Vera Webster
Witchery (1988) . . . . Rose Brooks
Basket Case 2 (1989). . . . . .Granny Ruth

Ross, Katherine
Films:
The Graduate (1967) . . . . Elaine Robinson
Butch Cassidy and the Sundance Kid (1969) . . Etta Place
Tell Them Willie Boy is Here (1969) . . . . Lola
    0:22 - Very, very brief breast sitting up with Robert
    Blake. Topless getting up when guy with rifle dis-
    turbs her and Blake. Buns, getting dressed. Long
    shot, dark, hard to see.
They Only Kill Their Masters (1972) . . . . Kate
  (Not available on video tape.)
The Betsy (1978). . . . . Sally Hardeman
The Legacy (1979; British). . . . . .Maggie Walsh
The Final Countdown (1980) . . . . Laurel Scott
Wrong is Right (1982). . . . . .Sally Blake
A Climate for Killing (1990). . . . . Grace Hines
The Shadow Riders (1991) . . . . Kate Connery
Made for TV Movies:
Secrets of a Mother and Daughter (1983) . . . .

Ross, Ruthy
Films:
The Centerfold Girls (1974). . . . . .Glory
  ••• 0:49 - Topless and buns posing for photographer
    outside with Charly.
Magazines:
Playboy (Jun 1973). . . . . .Playmate

Ross, Shana
Films:
Penthouse Love Stories (1986) . . . . AC/DC Lover
  ••• 0:17 - Full frontal nudity in bedroom with Monique
    Gabrielle.
Magazines:
Penthouse (Aug 1983). .Pet

Rossellini, Isabella
Daughter of actress Ingrid Bergman.
Spokesmodel for Lancôme cosmetics.
Films:
A Matter of Time (1976; Italian/U.S.) . . . . Sister Pia
White Nights (1985) . . . . Darya Greenwood
Blue Velvet (1986). . . . . .Dorothy
  • 1:08 - Brief topless in apartment.
  • 1:40 - Nude, standing bruised on porch.
Siesta (1987) . . . . .Marie
Tough Guys Don't Dance (1987) . . . . Madeleine
Cousins (1989). . . . . Marie Hardy
Wild at Heart (1990) .Perdita
Made for Cable Movies:
Lies of the Twins (1991) . . . . Rachel

Routledge, Alison
Films:
The Quiet Earth (1985; New Zealand) . . . . . . .Joanne
    0:49 - Brief buns, after making breakfast for Zac.
  •• 1:24 - Topless in guard tower making love with Api.
Bridge to Nowhere (1986; New Zealand) . . . . Lise

Rowan, Gay
Films:
The Girl in Blue (1973; Canadian). . . . . .Bonnie
a.k.a. U-turn
  • 0:06 - Left breast, in bed with Scott.
  • 0:31 - Brief topless in bathtub.
  • 0:48 - Right breast, in shower talking to Scott. Brief
    topless (long shot) on balcony throwing water
    down at him.
  • 1:21 - Brief right breast and buns getting out of bed
    and running out of the room.
Sudden Fury (1975) . . . . Janet
S.O.B. (1981). . . . .
Second Thoughts (1983) . . . . .Annie

Rowe, Misty

Films:

The Hitchhikers (1971) . . . . .Maggie
- 0:00 - Brief side view of left breast getting dressed.
- 0:17 - Very brief topless getting dress ripped open, then raped in van.
- 0:48 - Brief right breast while getting dressed.
- 1:09 - Left breast, making love with Benson.
- 1:10 - Brief topless taking a bath in tub.
- 1:13 - Very brief right breast in car with another victim.

Goodbye, Norma Jean (1975) . . . . .Norma Jean Baker
- 0:02 - In white bra putting makeup on.
- •• 0:08 - In white bra and panties, then topless.
- 0:14 - Brief topless in bed getting raped.
- 0:31 - Very, very brief silhouette of right breast, in bed with Rob.
- ••• 0:59 - Topless during shooting of stag film, then in B&W when some people watch the film.
- 1:14 - In white bra and panties undressing.

Loose Shoes (1977). .Louise
The Man with Bogart's Face (1980). . . . . Duchess
National Lampoon's Class Reunion (1982)
. . . . .Cindy Shears
- 0:37 - Very brief topless running around school stage in Hawaiian hula dance outfit.

Double Exposure (1983) . . . . .Bambi
Meatballs, Part II (1984) . . . . .Fanny
Made for TV Movies:
When Things Were Rotten (1975) . . . . . . .Maid Marion
TV:
Hee Haw (1972-) . . . . regular
Happy Days (1974-75) . . . . Wendy
When Things Were Rotten (1975) . . . . . . .Maid Marion
Hee Haw Honeys (1978-79) . . . . .Misty Honey
Joe's World (1979-80) . . . . .Judy Wilson
Magazines:
Playboy (Nov 1976) . . . . Misty
- ••• 104-107: Nude.

Royce, Roselyn

Films:

Cheech & Chong's Nice Dreams (1981)
. . . . Beach Girl #3
- 0:29 - Brief topless on the beach with two other girls. Long shot, unsteady, hard to see.

Malibu Hot Summer (1981) . . . . Cheryl Rielly
a.k.a. Sizzle Beach
(*Sizzle Beach* is the re-released version with Kevin Costner featured on the cover. It is missing all the nude scenes during the opening credits before 0:06.)
- •• 0:15 - On exercise bike, then topless getting into bed.
- ••• 0:16 - Topless sitting up in bed, buns going to closet to get dressed to go jogging.
- 0:26 - In pink two piece swimsuit running to answer the phone.
- •• 0:52 - Topless on boat with Brent.

Off the Wall (1982). . . . . .Buxom Blonde
- 0:35 - Left breast kissing an inmate in visiting room while the guards watch.
- •• 0:51 - Left breast again, kissing inmate through bars while the guards watch.

Rubens, Mary Beth

Films:

Prom Night (1980) . . . . Kelly
- 0:59 - Very brief right breast making out with Drew in the locker room.
- 1:02 - Brief upper half of breasts, standing up to put dress on. Dark.

Firebird 2015 AD (1981) . . . .
Perfect Timing (1984) . . . . .Judy
- 0:04 - In a bra, then topless in bedroom with Joe.
- •• 0:05 - Nude, walking to kitchen, then talking with Harry.
- 0:08 - Left breast seen through the camera's view finder.
- 0:10 - Nude, getting dressed in bedroom.
- 0:49 - In red bra and panties.
- •• 0:50 - Nude, in bed with Joe.
- ••• 1:00 - Nude, discovering Joe's hidden video camera, then going downstairs.

TV:
E.N.G. (1989-90) . . . . Bobby

Ruiz, Mia M.

Films:

Witchcraft II: The Temptress (1989) . . . . . .Michelle
- 0:27 - Brief topless several times making love with a guy on the floor during William's hallucination.

Demon Wind (1990) . . . .
Wild at Heart (1990)
. . . . Mr. Reindeer's Resident Valet #1
- •• 0:32 - Topless standing next to Mr. Reindeer on the right, holding a tray. Long scene.

Russell, Betsy

Films:

Private School (1983) . . . . .Jordan Leigh-Jensen
(Blonde hair.)
- 0:02 - Taking a shower behind a frosted door.
- 0:04 - Very, very brief right breast and buns when Bubba takes her towel off through window.
- ••• 0:19 - Topless riding a horse after Kathleen Wilhoite steals her blouse.
- 0:35 - In jogging outfit stripping down to black bra and panties, brief upper half of buns.
- 1:15 - In white bra and panties, in room with Bubba.
- 1:24 - Upper half of buns flashing with the rest of the girls during graduation ceremony.

Out of Control (1984) . . . . .Chrissie
(Brunette hair.)
    0:19 - In white corset and panties in the pond.
  •• 0:29 - Topless taking off her top while playing Strip
    Spin the Bottle.
    0:30 - Buns, taking off her panties.
Avenging Angel (1985) . . . . Angel/Molly Stewart
Tomboy (1985) . . . . Tomasina "Tommy" Boyd
  •• 0:44 - In wet T-shirt, then brief topless after landing
    in the water with her motorcycle.
  •• 0:59 - Topless making love with the race car driver in
    an exercise room.
Cheerleader Camp (1988). . . . . Alison Wentworth
a.k.a. Bloody Pom Poms

Russell, Karen

Films:
  Vice Academy (1988) . . . . .Shawnee
  •• 0:09 - Topless exposing herself to Duane to disarm
    him.
  •• 1:13 - Topless pulling her top down to distract a bad
    guy.
  Dr. Alien (1989) . . . . Coed #2
  a.k.a. I Was a Teenage Sex Mutant
  ••• 0:53 - Topless taking off her top (she's on the right)
    in the women's locker room before another coed
    takes her's off in front of Wesley.
  Easy Wheels (1989) . . . . .Candy
  Hell High (1989) . . . . .Teen Girl
  •• 0:04 - Topless in shack with Teen Boy while little girl
    watches through a hole in the wall.
  Murder Weapon (1989) . . . . Amy
  ••• 0:05 - Topless in bed with a guy after taking off her
    swimsuit top, then making love on top of him. Long
    scene.
  • 0:34 - Brief topless in shower.
    0:58 - In black bra and panties in bedroom.
  Dick Tracy (1990) . . . . Dancer
  Havana (1990) . . . . Dancer #2
  Mob Boss (1990). . . . . .Mary
  Wilding, The Children of Violence (1990) . . . Cathy
  •• 0:20 - Topless in bedroom when Wings Hauser pulls
    her lingerie down.
  The Girl I Want (1991) . . . .

Russell, Theresa

Wife of director Ken Russell.
Films:
  Straight Time (1978) . . . . Jenny Mercer
  ••• 1:00 - Left breast, while in bed with Dustin Hoffman.
    Don't see her face.
  Bad Timing: A Sensual Obsession (1980)
  . . . . Milena Flaherty
    0:14 - Buns and topless under short, sheer blouse.
    0:17 - Almost brief right breast in bed during Art Gar-
    funkel's flashback. Very brief left breast kneeling on
    bed with him.

  • 0:31 - Full frontal nudity in bed with Garfunkel. Inter-
    cut with tracheotomy footage. Kind of gross.
  •• 0:32 - Right breast, while sitting in bed talking to
    Garfunkel.
  • 0:41 - Brief topless several times on operating table.
  • 0:55 - Full frontal nudity making love on stairwell
    with Garfunkel. Quick cuts.
  • 0:56 - Brief topless twice after stairwell episode while
    throwing a fit.
  •• 1:45 - In bra, then topless passed out on bed while
    Garfunkel cuts her clothes off. Brief full frontal nudi-
    ty.
  •• 1:48 - More topless cuts while Garfunkel makes love
    to her while she's unconscious from drug overdose.
  Eureka (1983; British) . . . . Tracy
    0:38 - In lingerie talking to Rutger Hauer.
  • 0:40 - Right breast, lying in bed with Hauer.
  • 1:04 - Very brief left breast in bed with Hauer, then
    brief lower frontal nudity and brief buns when Gene
    Hackman bursts into the room.
  •• 1:09 - Topless on a boat with Hauer.
  • 1:41 - Left breast peeking out from under black top
    while lying in bed.
  ••• 1:59 - Full frontal nudity kicking off sheets in the bed.
  The Razor's Edge (1984). . . . . .Sophie
  Insignificance (1985) .Actress
  Black Widow (1987) . . . . Catherine
  • 0:28 - Briefly nude, making love in cabin.
  •• 1:18 - Nude in pool with Paul.
  Aria (1988; U.S./British) . . . . King Zog
  Track 29 (1988; British) . . . . .Linda Henry
  Impulse (1989). . . . . .Lottie
  •• 0:37 - Left breast, making love with Stan in bed.
  Physical Evidence (1989) . . . . Jenny Hudson
  Whore (1991) . . . .
Magazines:
  Playboy (Nov 1980) . . . . Sex in Cinema 1980
  • 181: Topless.
  Playboy (Nov 1983) . . . . Sex in Cinema 1983
  • 145: Topless.

Ruval, Yulis

See: Müller, Lillian.

Ryan, Meg

Films:
  Rich and Famous (1981) . . . . .Debbie at 18 years
  Armed and Dangerous (1986) . . . . . Maggie Cavanaugh
  Top Gun (1986) . . . . Carole
  Innerspace (1987) . . . . Lydia
  D.O.A. (1988) . . . . .Sydney Fuller
  The Presidio (1988) . . . . Donna
  Promised Land (1988) . . . . Beverly
  • 0:22 - Very brief side view of left breast in bed with
    Kiefer Sutherland.
  When Harry Met Sally... (1989) . . . . Sally Albright
  Joe vs. the Volcano (1990) . . . . . DeDe/Angelica/Patricia
  The Doors (1991). . . . . Pamela Courson

TV:
One of the Boys (1982). . . . . Jane
Wildside (1985). Cally Oaks

Ryan, Stephanie
See: Napoli, Susan.

Sachs, Adrianne
Films:
Two to Tango (1988) . . . . Cecilia Lorca
•• 0:29 - Side of left breast and buns in bedroom with
Lucky Lara. More left breast while Dan Stroud
watches through camera.
•• 0:59 - Topless and buns in bed with Dan Stroud.
In the Cold of the Night (1989) . . . . Kimberly Shawn
••• 0:52 - Buns and topless in shower, then making love
with Scott. Long, erotic scene.
• 0:59 - Brief topless in outdoor spa.
•• 1:06 - Topless making love on Scott's lap in bed.
Best of the Best (1990) . . . . Kelly

Sägebrecht, Marianne
Films:
Sugarbaby (1985; German). . . . . Sugarbaby
The Bagdad Café (1988) . . . . Jasmin
(Check this out if you like full-figured women.)
•• 1:09 - Right breast slowly lowering her top, posing
while Jack Palance paints.
•• 1:12 - More topless posing for Palance.
Moon Over Parador (1988). . . . . Magor
The War of the Roses (1989) . . . . Susan
Rosalie Goes Shopping (1990) . . . . . Rosalie Greenspace
Magazines:
Playboy (Nov 1988) . . . . Sex in Cinema 1988
• 136: Topless from *Bagdad Café.*

Sahagun, Elena
Films:
Caged Fury (1989) . . . . Tracy Collins
0:54 - In bra when Buck holds her hostage.
•• 1:01 - Left breast while taking a shower.
Corporate Affairs (1990) . . . . Stacy
Marked for Death (1990) . . . . Carmen
Naked Obsession (1991) . . . .
Magazines:
Playboy (Nov 1991) . . . . Sex in Cinema 1991
••• 143: Topless, wearing white mask, in scene from *Na-
ked Obsession.* (Incorrectly identified as Maria Ford.)

Salem, Pamela
Films:
The Bitch (1979; British) . . . . Lynn
•• 0:46 - Topless in bed making love with a guy after
playing at a casino.
After Darkness (1985) . . . . Elizabeth Huninger
Salome (1986) . . . . Herodias

Samples, Candy
Adult film actress.
a.k.a. Mary Gavin.
Films:
Fantasm (1976; Australian). . . . .
Up! (1976) . . . . The Headsperson
Russ Meyer film.
Superchick (1978) . . . . Lady on Boat
••• 0:08 - Topless in bed with Johnny on boat.
Beneath the Valley of the Ultravixens (1979)
. . . . The Very Big Blonde
Best Chest in the West (1984). . . . . herself
••• 0:54 - Topless dancing on stripping and dancing on
stage with Pat McCormick.

Sanda, Dominique
Films:
First Love (1970; German/Swiss) . . . . Sinaida
The Conformist (1971; Italian/French) . . Anna Quadri
The Garden of the Finzi-Continis
(1971; Italian/German). . . . . Micol
0:24 - In braless wet white T-shirt after getting
caught in a rainstorm.
• 1:12 - Topless sitting on a bed after turning a light on
so the guy standing outside can see her.
Without Apparent Motive (1972; French). . Sandra Forest
Impossible Object (1973; French). . . . . Nathalie
a.k.a. Story of a Love Story
The Makintosh Man (1973; British) . . . .
Conversation Piece (1974; Italian/French) . . . . . Mother
Steppenwolf (1974) . . . . Hermine
1:40 - Brief lower frontal nudity, sleeping with a guy.
• 1:41 - Very brief left breast, waking up and rolling
over to hug John Huston.
1900 (1976; Italian) . . . . Ada
•• 2:12 - (0:05 into tape 2.) Full frontal nudity under
thin fabric dancing with Robert De Niro for photographer.
Damnation Alley (1977). . . . . Janice
The Inheritance (1978; Italian) . . . . Irene
•• 0:18 - Full frontal nudity getting undressed and lying
on the bed with her new husband.
••• 0:37 - Full frontal nudity lying in bed with her lover.
• 1:19 - Very brief right breast, while undoing top for
Anthony Quinn.
••• 1:22 - Left breast, lying in bed. Full frontal nudity
jumping out of bed after realizing that Quinn is
dead.
Cabo Blanco (1982). . . . . Marie Claire Allesandri
Beyond Good and Evil
(1984; Italian/German/French). . . Lou-Andreas-Salome
Magazines:
Playboy (Mar 1972) . . . . Magnifique Dominique
••• 87-89: Nice.
Playboy (Nov 1972) . . . . Sex in Cinema
• 159: Topless.
Playboy (Dec 1972) . . . . Sex Stars of 1972
•• 207: Left breast.

Playboy (Nov 1973) . . . . Sex in Cinema
 • 158: Left breast.
Playboy (Dec 1973) . . . . Sex Stars of 1973
 •• 211: Left breast.
Playboy (Nov 1978) . . . . Sex in Cinema 1978
 • 184: Right breast.

Sandlund, Debra

Films:
Tough Guys Don't Dance (1987) . . . . . . Patty Lareine
 •• 1:24 - Topless ripping her blouse off to kiss the po-
  liceman after they have killed and buried another
  woman.
Murder by Numbers (1990) . . . . Leslie
TV:
Full House (1990) . . . . Cindy

Sandrelli, Stefania

Films:
Seduced and Abandoned (1964; Italian)
 . . . . Agnese Ascalone
The Conformist (1971; Italian/French) . . . . Giulia
1900 (1976; Italian) . . . . Anita Foschi
The Key (1983; Italian) . . . . Teresa
 (Nude a lot. Only the best are listed.)
 ••• 0:31 - Nude when Nino examines her while she's
  passed out. Long scene.
 •• 0:42 - Full frontal nudity in bathtub while Nino peeks
  in over the door.
 •• 1:04 - In lingerie, then topless and buns, undressing
  sexily in front of Nino.
 •• 1:16 - Left breast, sticking out of nightgown so Nino
  can suck on it.
 ••• 1:19 - Topless and buns making love in bed with Laszlo.
 •• 1:21 - Topless and buns getting up and cleaning herself.
 •• 1:28 - Topless sitting in bed talking to Nino.
 ••• 1:30 - Nude, getting on top of Nino in bed.

Sands, Peggy

Films:
Into the Night (1985) . . . . Shameless Woman
 • 0:43 - Topless putting dress on after coming out of
  men's restroom stall after a man leaves the stall first.
Beverly Hills Cop II (1987) . . . . Stripper
 • 0:48 - Very brief topless, dancing at the 385 North
  Club.
Phoenix the Warrior (1988) . . . . Keela
Far Out Man (1990) . . . . Misty
Lady Avenger (1991) . . . .
Millenium Countdown (1991) . . . .

Sara, Mia

Films:
Ferris Bueller's Day Off (1986) . . . . Slone Peterson
Legend (1986) Lili
Apprentice to Murder (1987) . . . . Alice
 • 0:29 - Left side view topless making love with Chad
  Lowe.
Queenie (1987) . . . . Queenie Kelly/Dawn Avalon
Shadows in the Storm (1988) . . . . Melanie
 0:51 - Standing in bathtub all covered with bubbles
  talking to Ned Beatty.
Any Man's Death (1989) . . . . Gerlind
 • 0:50 - Brief right nipple when John Savage undoes
  her top. Don't see her face.
A Climate for Killing (1990) . . . . Elise Shipp
Miniseries:
Till We Meet Again (1989) . . . . Delphine

Sarandon, Susan

Ex-wife of actor Chris Sarandon.
Films:
Joe (1970) . . . . Melissa Compton
 • 0:02 - Topless and very brief lower frontal nudity tak-
  ing off clothes and getting into bathtub with Frank.
Lady Liberty (1972; Italian/French) . . . . Sally
The Front Page (1974) . . . . Peggy
The Great Waldo Pepper (1975) . . . . Mary Beth
The Rocky Horror Picture Show (1975; British)
 . . . . Janet Weiss
The Great Smokey Roadblock (1976) . . . . Ginny
Other Side of Midnight (1977) . . . Catherine Douglas
 • 1:10 - Topless in bedroom with John Beck. Long
  shot, then right breast while lying in bed.
  2.18 - In wet white nightgown running around outside during a storm.
King of the Gypsies (1978) . . . . Rose
 • 0:49 - Brief right breast during fight with Judd Hirsch.
Pretty Baby (1978) . . . . Hattie
 0:12 - Feeding a baby with her left breast, while sitting by the window in the kitchen.
 • 0:24 - Brief side view, taking a bath.
 ••• 0:39 - Topless on the couch when Keith Carradine
  photographs her.
Something Short of Paradise (1979) . . . . Madeleine Ross
Loving Couples (1980) . . . . Stephanie
Atlantic City (1981; U.S./Canadian) . . . . Sally
 •• 0:50 - Left breast cleaning herself with lemon juice
  while Burt Lancaster watches through window.
The Tempest (1982) . . . . Aretha
 0:58 - In braless white tank top washing clothes with
  Molly Ringwald in the ocean.
 1:53 - In wet white T-shirt on balcony during rainstorm with Jason Robards and Raul Julia.
 1:55 - In wet white T-shirt on the beach.
 • 1:57 - Brief right, then left breasts in open T-shirt saving someone in the water.

The Hunger (1983). . . . . Sarah Roberts
••• 0:59 - In a wine stained white T-shirt, then topless during love scene with Catherine Deneuve.
The Buddy System (1984). . . . . Emily
Compromising Positions (1985) . . . . .Judith Singer
The Witches of Eastwick (1987). . . . . Jane Spofford
Bull Durham (1988) . . . . Annie Savoy
    1:39 - Brief right breast peeking out from under her dress after crawling on the kitchen floor to get a match.
The January Man (1988) . . . . .Christine Starkey
Sweet Hearts Dance (1988). . . . . .Sandra Boon
    1:23 - Almost a left breast in bathroom mirror changing clothes.
    1:25 - Very, very brief left breast under white bathrobe arguing with Don Johnson in the bathroom.
White Palace (1990) . . . . Nora Baker
••• 0:28 - Topless on top of James Spader. Great shots of right breast.
• 0:38 - Topless on bed with Spader.
Thelma and Louise (1991). . . . . .Louise
Made for Cable Movies:
Mussolini and I (1985; HBO) . . . .

Saunders, Pamela

Video Tapes:
Playboy Video Magazine, Volume 11. . . . Playmate
Playboy Video Calendar 1987 (1986) . . . . Playmate
Playmates at Play (1990) . . . . .Bareback
Magazines:
Playboy (Nov 1985) . . . . Playmate

Saura, Marina

Films:
Flesh + Blood (1985) . . . . Polly
• 0:59 - Brief left breast during feast in the castle.
• 1:09 - Topless on balcony of the castle with everybody during the day.
Crystal Heart (1987) . . . . Justine

Savoy, Theresa Ann

Films:
La Bambina (1976; Italian) . . . .
Caligula (1980). . . . . .Drusilla
(X-rated, 147 minute version.)
•• 0:01 - Nude, running around in the forest with Malcolm McDowell.
• 0:05 - Buns, rolling in bed with McDowell. Very brief topless getting out of bed.
• 0:26 - Left breast several times in bed.
• 0:46 - Brief right breast in bed with McDowell again.
• 1:15 - Left breast with McDowell and Helen Mirren.
• 1:22 - Very brief left breast getting up in open dress.
•• 1:45 - Full frontal nudity, then buns when dead and McDowell tries to revive her.

Scacchi, Greta

Films:
Heat and Dust (1982) . . . . .Olivia Rivers
•• 1:25 - Buns, lying in bed under a mosquito net with Douglas, then topless rolling over.
Burke and Wills (1985; Australian) . . . . . .Julia Matthews
The Coca-Cola Kid (1985; Australian) . . . . .Terri
••• 0:49 - Nude taking a shower with her daughter.
•• 1:20 - Brief topless wearing a Santa Claus outfit while in bed with Eric Roberts.
The Ebony Tower (1985) . . . . .Mouse
• 0:38 - Topless having a picnic.
• 0:43 - Brief nude walking into the lake.
Good Morning, Babylon (1987; Italian/French)
. . . . Edna
•• 1:05 - Topless in the woods making love with Vincent Spano.
A Man in Love (1987) . . . . Jane Steiner
••• 0:31 - Topless with Peter Coyote.
•• 1:04 - Buns and left breast in bed with Coyote.
    1:10 - Brief side view topless, putting black dress on.
• 1:24 - Brief topless in bed.
White Mischief (1988) . . . . .Diana Broughton
•• 0:16 - Topless taking a bath while an old man watches through a peephole in the wall.
•• 0:24 - Brief topless in bedroom with her husband.
•• 0:29 - Brief topless taking off bathing suit top in the ocean in front of Charles Dance.
•• 0:30 - Topless lying in bed talking to Dance.
Presumed Innocent (1990) . . . . . . Carolyn Polhemus
• 0:46 - Left breast, while making love on desk with Harrison Ford.
• 0:53 - Buns, lying in bed on top of Ford.
Magazines:
Playboy (Nov 1988) . . . . Sex in Cinema 1988
•• 141: Topless in bathtub in a photo from *White Mischief.*

Scarabelli, Michele

Films:
Covergirl (1982; Canadian) . . . . Snow Queen
Perfect Timing (1984) . . . . .Charlotte
•• 1:11 - Brief buns, then topless in bed with Harry.
• 1:18 - Topless in bed with Harry during the music video.
SnakeEater II: The Drug Buster (1990) . . . . . . .Dr. Pierce
Made for Cable Movies:
Age-Old Friends (1989; HBO). . . . . Nurse Wilson
Made for Cable TV:
The Hitchhiker: Face to Face . . . . Dr. Ensman
(Available on *The Hitchhiker, Volume 4.*)
••• 0:07 - Topless in Robert Vaughn's office.
TV:
Alien Nation (1989-90) . . . . Susan Francisco

Schneider, Maria
Films:
Last Tango In Paris (1972) . . . . Jeanne
(X-rated, letterbox version.)
- • 0:15 - Lower frontal nudity and very brief buns, rolling on the floor.
- • 0:44 - Topless in jeans, walking around the apartment.
- •• 0:53 - Left breast, lying down, walking to Marlon Brando, then topless.
- ••• 0:55 - Topless, kneeling while talking to Brando.
- • 0:56 - Side of left breast.
- • 0:57 - Topless, rolling off the bed, onto the floor.
- •• 1:01 - Right breast, in bathroom. Topless in mirror.
- • 1:03 - Brief topless in bathroom with Brando while she puts on makeup.
- ••• 1:04 - Nude, in bathroom with Brando, then sitting on counter.
- • 1:27 - Brief lower frontal nudity, pulling up her dress in elevator.
- • 1:30 - Topless in bathtub with Brando.
- ••• 1:32 - Nude, standing up in bathtub while Brando washes her. More topless, getting out. Long scene.
La Baby Sitter (1975; French/Italian/German) . . Michele
The Passenger (1975; Italian) . . . . Girl
Memories of a French Whore (1979) . . . .
A Woman Called Eva (1979) . . . .
Mamma Dracula (1980; Belgian/French) . . Nancy Hawaii
Magazines:
Playboy (Feb 1973) . . . . Two to "Tango" & Maria
- ••• 132-137: Nude.
Playboy (Nov 1973) . . . . Sex in Cinema 1974
- •• 159: Topless.
Playboy (Dec 1973) . . . . Sex Stars of 1973
- •• 211: Half of right breast.

Schneider, Romy
Films:
Vengeance... One by One . . . .
     0:02 - In black slip getting dressed.
     0:28 - Very brief left breast when a soldier rips her bra open during struggle.
     1:14 - In black lingerie in her husband's flashback.
Boccaccio 70 (1962; Italian) . . . . . . "The Job" Segment
     1:18 - In white slip talking on the phone.
What's New, Pussycat? (1965; U.S./French)
   . . . . Carole Werner
Dirty Hands (1975; French) . . . . Julie
- • 0:01 - Buns and right breast getting a tan, lying on the grass after a man's kite lands on her.
- •• 0:09 - Side view of right breast, while lying in bed with a man, then topless.
- • 1:04 - Topless lying on floor, then brief topless sitting up and looking at something on the table.
Bloodline (1979) .Helene Martin
Magazines:
Playboy (Dec 1976) . . . . Sex Stars of 1976
- •• 186: Topless lying down, hard to recognize it's her.

Schoelen, Jill
Films:
D.C. Cab (1983) . . . . .Claudette
Hot Moves (1985) . . . . Julie Ann
That Was Then... This Is Now (1985) . . .Angela Shepard
Thunder Alley (1985) . . . . Beth
The Stepfather (1987) . . . . Stephanie Maine
- •• 1:16 - Buns and brief side of right breast getting into the shower. Topless in the shower.
Curse II: The Bite (1988) . . . . .Lisa Snipes
Cutting Class (1988) . . . . Paula Carson
     1:01 - Side view of left breast taking off robe. Long shot. Almost topless turing around.
     1:03 - Very, very brief topless in mirror when putting robe on. (Out of focus.)
Phantom of the Opera (1989) . . . . Christine
Popcorn (1991) . . . . Maggie
Made for TV Movies:
Shattered Spirits (1986) . . . . Allison

Schubert, Karin
Films:
Bluebeard (1972) . . . . .Greta
- • 1:43 - Brief topless, spinning around, unwrapping herself from a red towel for Richard Burton.
Till Marriage Do Us Part (1974; Italian) . . . . Evelyn
Black Emanuelle (1976) . . . . Anne Danielli
- • 0:06 - Brief topless adjusting a guy's tie.
- ••• 0:14 - Topless making love in gas station with the gas station attendant.
- ••• 0:37 - Nude, running in the jungle while Laura Gemser takes pictures of her.
- • 0:40 - Topless, kissing Gemser.
- • 0:44 - Right breast, making love with Johnny in bed.
Black Venus (1983) . . . . .Marie
- •• 0:38 - Nude in bed with Venus, making love.
Panther Squad (1986; French/Belgian) . . . . Barbara

Schygulla, Hanna
Films:
The Marriage of Maria Braun (1979; German)
   . . . . .Maria Braun
Berlin Alexanderplatz (1983; West German) . . . .
La Nuit de Varennes (1983; French/Italian)
   . . . . Countess Sophie de la Borde
A Love in Germany (1984; French/German)
   . . . . Pauline Kropp
The Delta Force (1986) . . . . Ingrid
Forever Lulu (1987) . . . . .Elaine
- • 1:03 - Brief topless in and getting out of bubble bath.
Dead Again (1991) . . . .

Scoggins, Tracy
Films:
Toy Soldiers (1983) . . . . .Monique
In Dangerous Company (1988) . . . . .Evelyn
    0:12 - In a white bra, making love with a guy.
    0:42 - Very, very brief half of left breast in bed with
    Blake. Then, very, very brief left breast getting out of
    bed. Blurry, hard to see.
    0:58 - Brief upper half of left breast taking a bath.
    Long shot, hard to see.
The Gumshoe Kid (1990) . . . . .Rita Benson
    0:33 - In two piece white swimsuit. Nice bun shot
    while Jay Underwood hides in the closet.
  ••• 1:10 - Side view of left breast in the shower with Un-
    derwood. Excellent slow motion topless shot while
    turning around. Brief side view of right breast in bed
    afterwards.
The Raven Red Kiss-Off (1990) . . . . .Vala Vuvalle
Watchers II (1990) . . . . .Barbara White
TV:
Renegades (1983) . . . . Tracy
Hawaiian Heat (1984) . . . . Irene Gorley
The Colbys (1985-88) . . . . .Monica Colby
Video Tapes:
Tracy Scoggins' Tough Stuff Workout . . . . herself

Scott, Susie
Films:
Student Confidential (1987) . . . . Susan Bishop
  • 0:02 - Lying in bed covered with a gold sheet. Sort of
    right breast through her hair.
  •• 1:26 - Full frontal nudity standing in front of Greg.
Video Tapes:
Playboy's Playmate Review 3 (1985) . . . . . Playmate
Playmates at Play (1990) . . . . Making Waves
Magazines:
Playboy (May 1983) . . . . Playmate

Seagrove, Jenny
Films:
Nate and Hayes (1983) . . . . Sophia
Appointment with Death (1988) . . . . Dr. Sarah King
Harlequin Romance: Magic Moments (1989)
. . . . Melanie James
The Guardian (1990) . . . . Camilla
  ••• 0:21 - Side view of left breast in bathtub with the
    baby. Right breast, then topless.
    0:23 - Buns, drying herself off. Long shot.
  •• 0:38 - Topless, mostly left breast on top of Phil. Don't
    see her face, probably a body double.
    0:46 - Buns, skinny dipping. Long shot.
  •• 0:47 - Topless healing her wound by a tree. Side view
    of right breast.
  • 1:18 - Very brief topless under sheer gown in forest
    just before getting hit by a Jeep.
    1:24 - Very briefly topless scaring Carey Lowell. Body
    is painted all over.
Bullseye! (1991) . . . .

Miniseries:
A Woman of Substance (1984) . . . . . . Young Emma Hart
Made for TV Movies:
In Like Flynn (1985) . . . .

Senit, Laurie
Films:
Body and Soul (1981) . . . . Hooker #3
  • 0:54 - Brief topless lying next to Leon Isaac Kennedy
    in bed with two other hookers.
Doctor Detroit (1983) . . . . .Dream Girl
The Witching (1983) . . . . .Witches Coven
  a.k.a. Necromancy
R.S.V.P. (1984) . . . . Sherry Worth
  •• 1:00 - Topless in the shower with Harry Reems.
  •• 1:06 - Topless again.

Sennet, Susan
Films:
Big Bad Mama (1974) . . . . Billy Jean
  •• 0:49 - Topless and buns with Tom Skerritt.
  •• 0:51 - Topless and buns in bed with Skerritt.
Tidal Wave (1975; U.S./Japanese) . . . .
TV:
Ozzie's Girls (1973) . . . . .Susie Hamilton

Serna, Assumpta
Films:
Lola (1986) . . . . Silvia
Matador (1986; Spanish) . . . . .Maria Cardinal
  • 0:03 - Topless taking off wrap and making love with
    a guy just before she kills him.
  ••• 1:38 - Topless on floor with Diego. Long shot, hard
    to see. Topless in front of the fire.
  • 1:41 - Brief topless making love with Diego.
  • 1:43 - Topless lying on floor dead.
Wild Orchid (1990) . . . . Hanna
  ••• 0:39 - Topless at the beach and in the limousine. Very
    erotic.
Magazines:
Playboy (Jun 1990) . . . . .Wild Orchid
  •• 84: Topless in photos from *Wild Orchid*.

Severance, Joan
Films:
No Holds Barred (1989) . . . . .Samantha Moore
See No Evil, Hear No Evil (1989) . . . . Eve
  •• 1:08 - Topless in and leaning out of the shower while
    Gene Wilder tries to get her bag.
Worth Winning (1989) . . . . Lizbette
Bird on a Wire (1990) . . . . Rachel Varnay
Second Nature (1991) . . . .

Made for Cable Movies:
Another Pair of Aces (1991) . . . . Susan Davis
(Video tape includes nude scenes not shown on cable
TV.)
•• 1:00 - Brief topless several times, making love with
Kris Kristofferson in bed.
TV:
Wiseguy (1989). Susan Profitt
Magazines:
Playboy (Jan 1990) . . . . Texas Twister
••• 84-95: Nude.

Seymour, Jane

Her eyes are different colors—one is green and the other
brown.
Films:
Young Winston (1972; British). . . . . . .Pamela Plowden
Live and Let Die (1973; British) . . . . Solitaire
Sinbad and the Eye of the Tiger (1977; U.S./British)
. . . . Farah
1:16 - Very brief buns, skinny dipping in pond with
Taryn Power. Long shot, but still pretty amazing for
a G-rated film.
1:17 - Very brief partial right breast (arm covers most
of it) screaming when scared by the troglodyte.
Oh, Heavenly Dog! (1980) . . . . .Jackie Howard
Somewhere in Time (1980). . . . . Elise McKenna
Lassiter (1984) . . . . Sara
0:10 - Buns and brief side view of right breast lying
on stomach on bed with Tom Selleck.
Head Office (1986) . . . . Jane
The Tunnel (1987) . . . . Maria
• 0:29 - Very brief left breast in bed with Peter Weller
when the sheet is pulled down.
•• 0:44 - Brief right beast getting dressed, throwing off
her robe.
Made for Cable Movies:
Jamaica Inn (1982) . . . . .Mary Yellan
1:47 - (0:14 into volume 2) Braless under a wet white
dress changing clothes in a stagecoach.
Miniseries:
Captains and the Kings (1976) . . . . . .Chisholm Armagh
Seventh Avenue (1977). . . . . .Eva Meyers
East of Eden (1981). . . . . Cathy/Kate Ames
War and Remembrance (1988) . . . . Natalie Jastrow
Made for TV Movies:
The Story of David (1976). . . . . .Bathsheba
Battlestar Gallactica (1978) . . . . Serina
The Dallas Cowboy Cheerleaders (1979). . . . .
The Scarlet Pimpernel (1982) . . . .
The Sun Also Rises (1984) . . . . .Lady Brett
Jack the Ripper (1988). . . . . .Emma
The Richest Man in the World: The Story of Aristot
(1988). . . . . Maria Callas
The Woman He Loved (1988) . . . . Wallis Simpson

Seymour, Stephanie

Sports Illustrated swimsuit model.
Video Tapes:
Sports Illustrated's 25th Anniversary Swimsuit Video
(1989) . . . . .herself
(The version shown on HBO left out two music video
segments at the end. If you like buns, definitely watch
the video tape!)
Magazines:
Playboy (Mar 1991) . . . . Stephanie
••• 112-123: Topless and buns.

Shapiro, Hilary

See: Shepard, Hilary.

Sharkey, Rebecca

See: Wood-Sharkey, Rebecca.

Sharpe, Cornelia

Films:
Kansas City Bomber (1972) . . . . Tammy O'Brien
Serpico (1973) . . . . Leslie
•• 0:41 - Topless in bathtub with Al Pacino.
Busting (1974). . . . . .Jackie
Open Season (1974; U.S./Spanish). . . . . Nancy
The Reincarnation of Peter Proud (1975)
. . . . Nora Hayes
•• 0:03 - Topless in bed with Michael Sarrazin, then
buns when getting out of bed.
The Next Man (1976) . . . . .Nicole Scott
a.k.a. Double Hit
Venom (1982; British) . . . . .Ruth Hopkins
Made for TV Movies:
S.H.E. (1979) . . . .

Shattuck, Shari

Films:
Portfolio (1983) . . . . Elite Model
The Naked Cage (1985) . . . . .Michelle
•• 0:42 - Buns and topless in shower, then getting
slashed by Rita during a dream.
•• 1:00 - Left breast getting attacked by Smiley in jail
cell, then fighting back.
1:28 - In panties, during fight with Rita.
Hot Child in the City (1987). . . . . Abby
Arena (1988) . . . . .Jade
1:06 - Upper half of buns sitting up in bed. Brief half
of right breast, getting up while wearing robe.
The Uninvited (1988). . . . . .Suzanne

The Spring (1989) . . . . .Dyanne
  • 0:00 - Nude, several times, swimming under the water. Shot from under water.
  • 0:50 - Topless and buns, swimming under water.
  •• 0:51 - Topless, getting out of the water.
  •• 0:59 - Brief topless, turning over in bed with Dack Rambo.
  • 1:05 - Standing up in wet lingerie, then swimming under water.
Mad About You (1990) . . . . Renee
Made for TV Movies:
The Laker Girls (1990) . . . . Libby

Shaver, Helen
Films:
Shoot (1976; Canadian) . . . . .Paula Lissitzen
The Supreme Kid (1976; Canadian) . . . . .Girl
Outrageous! (1977; Canadian) . . . . Jo
High-Ballin' (1978) . . . . Pickup
In Praise of Older Women (1978; Canadian)
  . . . . Ann MacDonald
  ••• 1:40 - Blue bra and panties, then topless with Tom Berenger.
  ••• 1:42 - Nude lying in bed with Berenger, then getting out and getting dressed.
Starship Invasions (1978; Canadian) . . . . .Betty
The Amityville Horror (1979). . . . . .Carolyn
Gas (1981; Canadian) .Rhonda
Harry Tracy (1982; Canadian) . . . . .Catherine
The Osterman Weekend (1983) . . .Virginia Tremayne
  •• 0:24 - Topless in an open blouse yelling at her husband in the bedroom.
  • 0:41 - Topless in the swimming pool when everyone watches on the TV.
Best Defense (1984) . . . . Claire Lewis
The Color of Money (1986). . . . . .Janelle
Desert Hearts (1986) . . . . .Vivian Bell
  • 1:05 - Brief topless in bed in hotel room.
  ••• 1:09 - Topless making love in bed with Patricia Charboneau.
The Believers (1987) . . . . Jessica Halliday
  • 0:38 - Brief glimpse of right breast while lying in bed with Martin Sheen.
  1:17 - Buns, getting out of bed.
Innocent Victim (1988) . . . . Benet Archdale
  • 1:05 - Very brief side of left breast on top of a guy in bed.
Made for Cable Movies:
The Park is Mine (1985; HBO) . . . . .Valery Weaver
  • 0:46 - Very brief topless undressing then very, very brief left breast catching clothes from Tommy Lee Jones.
Made for TV Movies:
Mothers, Daughters and Lovers (1989) . . . .
Rest In Peace, Mrs. Columbo (1990) . . . . . Vivian Dimitri
TV:
United States (1980) . . . . Libby Chapin
Jessica Novak (1981) . . . . Jessica Novak
WIOU (1990-91) . . . . .Kelby Robinson

Magazines:
Playboy (Oct 1978) . . . . . . Observing "Older Women"
  •• 193-194: Topless and buns.
Playboy (Nov 1978) . . . . Sex in Cinema 1978
  •• 185: Full frontal nudity on bed.

Shaw, Fiona
Films:
Mountains of the Moon (1989) . . . . .Isabel
  •• 0:33 - Topless and very brief lower frontal nudity letting Patrick Bergin wax the hair off her legs.
  •• 1:43 - Topless in bed after Bergin returns from Africa.
My Left Foot (1989; British) . . . . .Dr. Eileen Cole
Three Men and a Little Lady (1990) . . . . Miss Lomax

Shaw, Linda
Adult film actress.
Films:
Body Double (1984) . . . . Linda Shaw
  • 1:11 - Left breast on TV monitor..

Shaw, Tina
Films:
The Secrets of Love—Three Rakish Tales (1986)
  . . . . The Weaver's Wife
  ••• 0:10 - Topless in bed with Luke.
  ••• 0:17 - Topless in the barn.
Salome's Last Dance (1987) . . . . .2nd Slave
  (Appears with 2 other slaves–can't tell who is who.)
  •• 0:08 - Topless in black costume around a cage.
  •• 0:52 - Topless during dance number.
The Lair of the White Worm (1988; British) . . Maid/Nun
Taffin (1988; U.S./British) . . . . Lola the Stripper
  •• 1:04 - Topless doing routine in a club.

Shayne, Linda
Films:
Humanoids from the Deep (1980) . . . . Miss Salmon
  • 1:06 - Topless after getting bathing suit ripped off by a humanoid.
The Lost Empire (1983) . . . . Cindy Blake
Screwballs (1983) . . . . Bootsie Goodhead
  ••• 0:43 - Right breast, while in back of van at drive-in theater, then topless.
Big Bad Mama II (1987) . . . . .Bank Teller
Out of Bounds (1987) . . . . .Chris Cage
Daddy's Boys (1988) . . . . .Nanette

Shé, Elizabeth
Films:
Howling V (1989) . . . . Mary Lou Summers
  • 0:33 - Buns and side view of right breast getting into pool with Donovan.
  • 0:36 - Very brief full frontal nudity climbing out of pool with Donovan.
Howling VI—The Freaks (1990) . . . . Mary Lou Summers

Shea, Katt

a.k.a. Kathleen M. Shea or Katt Shea Ruben.
Actress turned Director.
Films:
The Cannonball Run (1981) . . . . Starting Girl
My Tutor (1983) . . . . Mud Wrestler
  • 0:48 - Brief topless when a guy rips her dress off.
Scarface (1983). . . . . Woman at the Babylon Club
Cannonball Run II (1984) . . . .
Hollywood Hot Tubs (1984) . . . . Dee-Dee
  • 0:21 - Topless with her boyfriend while Shawn is
    working on the hot tub.
Preppies (1984) . . . . Margot
  ••• 0:20 - Topless teasing Richard through the glass door
    of her house.
    0:54 - In bra and panties with Trini, practicing sexual
    positions on the bed.
  • 1:07 - Brief topless after taking off bra in bed.
R.S.V.P. (1984). . . . . Rhonda Rivers
  • 0:31 - Side view of left breast, making love in bed
    with Jonathan.
Barbarian Queen (1985) . . . . Estrild
  • 0:31 - Brief topless getting top torn off by guards.
The Destroyers (1985). . . . . Audrey
Psycho III (1986). . . . . .Patsy

Shear, Rhonda

Films:
Basic Training (1984). . . . . Debbie
  •• 0:07 - Topless making love with Mark.
    0:15 - In bra, making love on Mark's desk.
Doin' Time (1984). .Adrianne
Spaceballs (1987) . . . . Woman in Diner
Made for Cable TV:
Up All Night (1991- ;USA) . . . . host
Magazines:
Playboy (Jun 1991) . . . . Funny Girls
  ••• 92: Full frontal nudity.

Sheedy, Ally

Films:
Bad Boys (1983) . . . . J. C. Walenski
  • 0:12 - Very, very brief left breast kneeling on floor
    next to bed when Sean Penn leaves. A little blurry
    and a long shot.
Wargames (1983) . . . . .Jennifer
The Breakfast Club (1985). . . . . Allison Reynolds
St. Elmo's Fire (1985) . . . . Leslie
Blue City (1986) .Annie Rayford
    0:44 - Very very brief left breast lying on bed reach-
    ing her arm around Judd Nelson while kissing him.
    Dark and blurry.
Short Circuit (1986) . . . . Stephanie Speck
Maid to Order (1987) . . . . .Jessie Montgomery
    0:40 - Buns, taking off dress and diving into the pool.
    Long shot and dark. Don't see her face.
    0:42 - Buns, walking with a towel around her hair.
    Another long shot and you don't see her face.

Heart of Dixie (1989) . . . . Maggie
Betsy's Wedding (1990) . . . . Connie Hopper
Only the Lonely (1991) . . . . Theresa
Made for Cable Movies:
Fear (1991; Showtime). . . . . .K.C.

Sheen, Jacqueline

Video Tapes:
Playboy Video Calendar 1991 (1990). . . . December
  ••• 0:49 - Nude.
Magazines:
Playboy (Jul 1990) . . . . Playmate

Shepard, Hilary

a.k.a. Hilary Shapiro.
Films:
Soup for One (1982) . . . .
Radioactive Dreams (1984) . . . . .Biker Leader
Weekend Pass (1984) . . . . .Cindy Hazard
  •• 1:05 - In red bra, then topless taking off bra.
  • 1:07 - Buns and topless getting into bathtub.
Private Resort (1985) . . . . Shirley
  ••• 0:36 - Topless, then buns, taking off her dress in front
    of Ben.
Tough Guys (1986) . . . . Sandy
Hunk (1987) . . . . Alexis Cash
Lucky Stiff (1988). . . . . Cissy
Peace Maker (1990) . . . . Dori Caisson
    1:08 - Brief upper half of buns, taking off shirt and
    getting into shower. Brief side view of upper half of
    left breast, twice while making love with Townsend.
Made for Cable TV:
Dream On: The First Episode (1990; HBO) . . . . . .Date 2

Shepard, Jewel

Films:
Raw Force (1981). . . . . Drunk Sexpot
  • 0:31 - Topless in black swimsuit, when a guy adjusts
    her straps and it falls open.
Zapped! (1982) . . . . uncredited Girl in Car
  • 0:39 - Brief topless after red and white top pops off
    when Scott Baio uses his Telekinesis on her.
My Tutor (1983) . . . . Girl in Phone Booth
  • 0:40 - Brief left breast in car when Matt Lattanzi fan-
    tasizes about making love with her.
Christina (1984) . . . . Christina
Hollywood Hot Tubs (1984) . . . . Crystal Landers
  (Not topless, but bouncing around a lot in short, braless
  T-shirts.)
The Return of the Living Dead (1985) . . . . .Casey
Party Camp (1987) . . . . .Dyanne Stein
  ••• 0:57 - In white bra and panties, then topless playing
    strip poker with the boys.
Scenes from the Goldmine (1987) . . . . Dana
The Underachievers (1987) . . . . .Sci-Fi Teacher
  • 0:27 - Topless ripping off her Star Trek uniform when
    someone enters her classroom. Dark, hard to see.

Going Undercover (1988; British) . . . . Peaches
Hollywood Hot Tubs 2—Educating Crystal (1989)
Crystal Landers
    0:38 - In white slip during Gary's fantasy.
    • 1:12 - Brief left breast, while lying down, kissing
    Gary.
Naked Force (1991) . . . .

Shepherd, Cybill
Films:
The Last Picture Show (1971; B&W) . . . .Jacy Farrow
  •• 0:37 - Undressing on diving board. Very brief left
    breast falling onto diving board. Brief topless tossing
    bra aside.
  • 0:38 - Brief left breast jumping into the water.
  ••• 1:05 - Topless and buns in motel room with Jeff
    Bridges.
The Heartbreak Kid (1972) . . . . Kelly Corcoran
Daisy Miller (1974) . . . . Annie P. "Daisy" Miller
Special Delivery (1976) . . . . .Mary Jane
Taxi Driver (1976) . . . . Betsy
The Lady Vanishes (1979; British) . . . . Amanda Kelly
The Return (1980). Daughter
Chances Are (1989) . . . . Corrine Jeffries
    1:11 - In white bra and tap pants getting dressed.
    1:22 - In bra with Robert Downey Jr. and Ryan
    O'Neal in living room.
Alice (1990) . . . . Nancy Brill
Texasville (1990). . . . . .Jacy Farrow
Made for Cable Movies:
Which Way Home (1991) . . . . .Karen Parsons
Made for TV Movies:
Moonlighting (1985) . . . . .Maddie Hayes
TV:
The Yellow Rose (1983-84) . . . . Colleen Champion
Moonlighting (1985-89) . . . . .Maddie Hayes
Magazines:
Playboy (Nov 1972) . . . . Sex in Cinema
  • 170: B&W topless.
Playboy (Dec 1972). . . . . Sex Stars of 1972
  •• 208: B&W topless.

Sheppard, Delia
Films:
Witchcraft II: The Temptress (1989). . . . . . .Dolores
  •• 1:20 - Brief topless several times with William.
Rocky V (1990) . . . . Karen
The Adventures of Ford Fairlane (1991). . . . . . . Pussycat
Naked Force (1991) . . . .
Sex Bomb (1991) . . . .
Magazines:
Penthouse (Apr 1988). Pet
Playboy (Nov 1990) . . . . Sex in Cinema 1990
  •• 143: Right breast, in still from *Witchcraft, Part II.*
Playboy (Dec 1990). . . . . Sex Stars of 1990
  •• 177: Buns.

Sheridan, Nicollette
Wife of actor Harry Hamlin.
Films:
The Sure Thing (1985) . . . . The Sure Thing
Made for Cable Movies:
Deceptions (1990; Showtime) . . . . . Adrienne Erickson
  • 0:35 - Very, very brief silhouette of breasts hugging
    Hamlin when camera tilts down from her head to
    her buns.
Miniseries:
Jackie Collins' Lucky/Chances (1990) . . . . .Lucky
TV:
Knots Landing (1990-) . . . . .Paige Matheson

Sherman, Geraldine
Films:
Interlude (1968). . . . . .Natalie
Poor Cow (1968) . . . . Trixie
Take a Girl Like You (1970). . . . . Anna
There's a Girl in My Soup (1970) . . . . .Caroline
  •• 0:43 - Topless in bed, then getting out after Goldie
    Hawn splashes water on her.
Get Carter (1971) . . . . Girl in Cafe
Cry of the Penguins (1972) . . . . Penny

Sherwood, Robin
Films:
The Tourist Trap (1979) . . . . .Eileen
Hero at Large (1980) . . . .
Serial (1980) . . . . Woman
Death Wish II (1982). . . . . Carol Kersey
  • 0:15 - Topless after getting raped by gang member
    in their hideout.
The Love Butcher (1982) . . . . Sheila

Shields, Brooke
Films:
Alice, Sweet Alice (1977) . . . . .Karen
King of the Gypsies (1978). . . . . Tita
Pretty Baby (1978) .Violet
  (She was only 11–12 years old at this time so there isn't
  really a whole lot to see here!)
  • 0:57 - Topless and buns taking a bath.
  • 1:26 - Topless posing on couch for Keith Carradine.
  • 1:28 - Buns, getting thrown out of the room, then
    trying to get back in.
Tilt (1978) . . . . .Tilt
Just You and Me, Kid (1979). . . . . .Kate
Wanda Nevada (1979) . . . . Wanda Nevada
Blue Lagoon (1980) . . . . Emmeline
  (Nudity is a body double, Kathy Trout.)
    0:27 - Nude swimming underwater after growing up
    from little children.
    0:43 - More underwater swimming.
    1:00 - Topless body double lying on a rock.
    1:09 - Right breast of body double in hammock.
    1:24 - Body double breast feeding the baby.

Endless Love (1981) . . . . Jade
    0:37 - Body double, side view of right breast in bed with David.
    1:08 - Body double very brief left breast, in bed with another guy during David's dream.
Sahara (1984) . . . . Dale
    0:51 - In a wet T-shirt taking a shower under a water fall.
Speed Zone (1989) . . . . Stewardess
Backstreet Dreams (1990) . . . . Stephanie "Stevie" Bloom

Shirley, Aleisa

Films:
Sweet Sixteen (1982) . . . . Melissa Morgan
  • 0:16 - Side view of body, nude, taking a shower.
  • 1:11 - Topless undressing to go skinny dipping with Hank. Dark, hard to see.
  • 1:13 - Topless, getting out of the water.
Made for Cable TV:
The Hitchhiker: Shattered Vows . . . . Pamela
  • 0:08 - Topless and buns in bathroom with Jeff.
    0:12 - In bedroom wearing white lingerie.
  •• 0:18 - In bed wearing black bra, panties, garter belt and stockings, then topless.

Shoop, Pamela Susan

Films:
Empire of the Ants (1977) . . . . Coreen Bradford
One Man Jury (1978) . . . . Wendy
Halloween II (1981) . . . . Karen
  ••• 0:48 - Topless getting into the whirlpool bath with Budd in the hospital.
Made for TV Movies:
The Dallas Cowboy Cheerleaders (1979) . . . .

Shower, Kathy

Films:
Double Exposure (1983) . . . . Mudwrestler #1
Commando Squad (1987) . . . . Kat Withers
The Further Adventures of Tennessee Buck (1987)
. . . . Barbara Manchester
    0:22 - In white lingerie in her hut getting dressed.
  ••• 0:57 - Topless getting rubbed with oil by the cannibal women. Nice close up shots.
  •• 1:02 - Topless in a hut with the Chief of the tribe.
Frankenstein General Hospital (1988)
. . . . Dr. Alice Singleton
    0:35 - In white lingerie outfit pacing in her office.
  • 1:15 - Brief topless running out of her office after the monster, putting her lab coat on.
Out on Bail (1988) . . . . Sally Anne
  • 1:01 - Brief topless in shower with Robert Ginty.
Bedroom Eyes II (1989) . . . . Carolyn Ross
  •• 0:22 - Topless in the studio fighting with her lover.
    0:58 - In lingerie in bed with Hauser, then in bathroom.

TV:
Santa Barbara (1987-90) . . . .
Video Tapes:
Playboy Video Magazine, Volume 9 . . . . . Playmate
Playmates of the Year—The '80's . . . . Playmate
Playboy Video Calendar 1987 (1986) . . . . . Playmate
Magazines:
Playboy (May 1985) . . . . Playmate
Playboy (Dec 1986) . . . . Sex Stars of 86
  156:
Playboy (May 1988) . . . . Kathy Goes Hollywood
  ••• 130-137: Nude.
Playboy (Jan 1989) . . . . Women of the Eighties
  ••• 254: Full frontal nudity.

Shue, Elizabeth

Films:
The Karate Kid (1984) . . . . Ali
Link (1986) . . . . Jane Chase
  • 0:50 - Brief right breast and buns, side view of a body double, standing in bathroom getting ready to take a bath while Link watches.
Adventures in Babysitting (1987) . . . . Chris Parker
Cocktail (1988) . . . . Jordan Mooney
    0:52 - Side view of left breast standing up in waterfall with Tom Cruise when she takes off her swimsuit top.
Back to the Future, Part II (1989) . . . . Jennifer
Back to the Future, Part III (1990) . . . . Jennifer
The Marrying Man (1991) . . . . Adele Horner
Soapdish (1991) . . . . Lori
Made for TV Movies:
Call to Glory (1984) . . . . Jackie Sarnac
TV:
Call to Glory (1984-85) . . . . Jackie Sarnac

Shugart, Renee

Films:
Spring Fever USA (1988) . . . . Beach Beauty
Summer Job (1989) . . . . Karen
    0:15 - In lingerie reading a magazine.
  • 0:42 - Topless taking off her top. Long shot, dark.
  • 0:45 - In white lingerie, standing on stairs, then very brief left breast flashing.

Siani, Sabrina

Films:
Ator, The Fighting Eagle (1982) . . . . Roon
    0:44 - Topless bathing in stream. This is such a long shot, you can't see anything, much less tell it's her.
2020 Texas Gladiators (1983; Italian) . . . . Maida
  •• 0:07 - Left breast, in open white dress after gang rape.
  • 0:34 - Topless during rape.
The Throne of Fire (1983; Italian) . . . . . Princess Belkaren

Silver, Cindy
Films:
Gimme an "F" (1981) . . . . One of the "Ducks"
Hardbodies (1984) . . . . .Kimberly
•• 0:07 - Brief topless on beach when a dog steals her
  bikini top.
••• 0:47 - Topless standing in front of closet mirrors talking about breasts with Kristi.

Simmons, Allene
Films:
Porky's (1981; Canadian) . . . . Jackie
• 1:02 - Topless in the shower scene.
Time Walker (1982). . . . . Nurse
R.S.V.P. (1984). . . . . .Patty De Fois Gras
•• 0:13 - Topless taking off red top behind the bar with
  the bartender.
•• 0:38 - Topless in bed with Mr. Edwards, then buns
  running to hide in the closet.
•• 0:41 - Frontal nudity in room with Mr. Anderson.
••• 0:51 - Topless talking to Toby in the hallway trying to
  get help for the Governor.

Simms Wiegers, Ona
Films:
Enrapture (1989) . . . . .Chase Webb
•• 0:13 - In red bra, panties, garter belt and stockings.
  Buns in G-string, then topless undressing when she
  doesn't know Keith is watching.
•• 0:17 - Topless when Keith fantasizes about her while
  he's making love with Martha.
•• 0:21 - Topless in back of limousine with a lucky guy.
••• 1:08 - Full frontal nudity making love on top of Keith
  in bed.
The Art of Dying (1991) . . . . .Frances Warner

Singer, Lori
Sister of actor Marc Singer.
Films:
Footloose (1984). . . . . Ariel
The Falcon and the Snowman (1985) . . . . .Lana
The Man With One Red Shoe (1985). . . . . Maddy
Trouble in Mind (1986) . . . . Georgia
• 1:01 - Very brief left breast, in bed with Kris Kristof-
  ferson.
Summer Heat (1987) . . . . .Roxy
•• 0:36 - Topless in bed with Jack. Kind of dark and hard
  to see.
Made in U.S.A. (1988) . . . . Annie
• 0:26 - Brief left breast and very brief lower frontal nudity in the back of a convertible with Dar at night.
  0:44 - In white, braless tank top talking to a used car
  salesman.
Warlock (1990) . . . . Kassandra

Storm and Sorrow (1990) . . . . Molly Higgins
TV:
Fame (1982-83) . . . . .Julie Miller

Sirtis, Marina
Films:
The Wicked Lady (1983; British) . . . . . . Jackson's Girl
••• 1:06 - Full frontal nudity in and getting out of bed
  when Faye Dunaway discovers her in bed with Alan
  Bates.
••• 1:20 - Topless getting whipped by Dunaway during
  their fight during Bates' hanging.
Blind Date (1984) . . . . Hooker
(Not the same 1987 *Blind Date* with Bruce Willis.)
••• 0:21 - Topless walking to and lying in bed just before
  taxi driver kills her.
Death Wish III (1985) . . . . .Maria
• 0:42 - Topless getting blouse ripped open next to a
  car by the bad guys.
• 0:43 - More topless on mattress at the bad guy's
  hangout.
TV:
Star Trek: The Next Generation (1987-)
. . . . Counselor Deanna Troi

Sissons, Kimber
Films:
You Can't Hurry Love (1984) . . . . .Brenda
  0:48 - Partial side of right breast in open shirt, bend-
  ing over to pick up her bra off the coffee table.
Phantom of the Mall: Eric's Revenge (1988) . . . . . . Suzie
The Adventures of Ford Fairlane (1991) . . . . . . .Pussycat
Made for Cable TV:
Dream On: The Charlotte Letter (1991; HBO)
. . . . Candy Striper #3
•• 0:06 - Topless several times, getting examined by a
  doctor while acting in adult film that Martin is
  watching on TV. (She's the blonde one.)

Skinner, Anita
Films:
Girlfriends (1978). . . . . Anne Munroe
Sole Survivor (1982) . . . . .Denise Watson
• 0:29 - Very, very brief right breast in bed with Dr. Richardson. Brief side view of right breast when he
  jumps out of bed.
  1:13 - In bra, zipping up pants.

Skinner, Rainee
Films:
Rebel (1985; Australian) . . . . Prostitute in bed
• 0:37 - Brief topless sitting up in bed.
Kiss the Night (1988). . . . .
Pandemonium (1988) . . . .

Skye, Ione

a.k.a. Ione Skye Leitch.
Films:
A Night in the Life of Jimmy Reardon (1987)
. . . . .Denise Hunter
River's Edge (1987) . . . . .Clarissa
Stranded (1987) . . . . Deirdre Clark
The Rachel Papers (1989) . . . . Rachel
- •• 0:58 - Topless getting undressed and into bed with
  Charles. Long shot, then topless in bed.
- ••• 1:03 - Brief topless in three scenes. From above in
  bathtub, in bed and in bathtub again.
- •• 1:04 - Left breast, making love sitting up with
  Charles.
- • 1:06 - Brief topless sitting up in bathtub.
- • 1:08 - Brief topless long shot getting dressed in
  Charles' room.
- • 1:28 - Brief topless kissing Charles in bed during his
  flashback.

Say Anything (1989) . . . . Diane Court
Made for Cable TV:
Nightmare Classics: Carmilla (1989; HBO) . . . . . . Marie

Slater, Helen

Films:
Supergirl (1984; British) . . . . .Linda Lee/Supergirl
The Legend of Billie Jean (1985) . . . . Billie Jean
0:06 - Brief wet T-shirt getting out of pond.
Ruthless People (1986) . . . . Sandy Kessler
The Secret of My Success (1987) . . . . Christy
Happy Together (1988) . . . . . . Alexandra "Alex" Page
- •• 0:17 - Brief right breast changing clothes while talking to Patrick Dempsey. Unfortunately, she has a
  goofy expression on her face.
  0:57 - In red lingerie tempting Dempsey. Later, panties under panty hose when Dempsey pulls her dress
  up while she's on roller skates.
  1:07 - Very brief panties under panty hose again
  straddling Dempsey in the hallway.
  1:14 - Panties under white stockings while changing
  in the closet.

Sticky Fingers (1988) . . . . Hattie
City Slickers (1991) . . . .
TV:
Capital News (1990) . . . . .Anne McKenna

Slater, Suzanne

a.k.a. Suzee Slater.
Films:
Savage Streets (1985) . . . . uncredited
- •• 0:09 - Topless being held by jerks when they yank her
  tube top down.

Chopping Mall (1986) . . . . Leslie
- •• 0:28 - Brief topless in bed showing breasts to Mike.
  0:31 - Walking around the mall in panties and a
  blouse.

Take Two (1988) . . . . .Sherrie
- •• 0:11 - Topless in office talking with Grant Goodeve,
  wearing panties, garter belt and stockings.
- • 1:00 - Topless undressing to get into hot tub wearing
  black underwear bottom.

The Big Picture (1989) . . . . Stewardess
Cartel (1990) . . . . Nancy
0:28 - In red two piece swimsuit modeling on motor-
cycle.
0:35 - Brief bra and panties on bed during struggle.
- • 0:36 - Topless during brutal rape/murder scene.

Magazines:
Playboy (Jul 1989) . . . . B-Movie Bimbos
- •• 137: Full frontal nudity lying on a car wearing a gir-
  dle and stockings.

Smith, Cheryl

a.k.a. Rainbeaux Smith.
Films:
Video Vixens (1973) . . . . .Twinkle Twat Girl
- ••• 0:24 - Full frontal nudity doing a commercial, sitting
  next to pool.

Caged Heat (1974) .Lauelle
a.k.a. Renegade Girls
- • 0:04 - Brief left breast, dreaming in her jail cell that a
  guy is caressing her through the bars.
- •• 0:25 - Topless in the shower scene.
- •• 0:50 - Brief nude in the solitary cell.

The Swinging Cheerleaders (1974) . . . . . . .Andrea
- •• 0:12 - Topless taking off her bra and putting sheer
  blouse on.
- • 0:17 - Left breast, several times, sitting in bed with
  Ross.

Farewell, My Lovely (1975; British) . . . . .Doris
- • 0:56 - Frontal nudity in bedroom in a bordello with
  another guy before getting beaten by the madam.

Drum (1976) . . . . Sophie Maxwell
- •• 0:54 - Topless in the stable trying to get Yaphet Kotto
  to make love with her.

Massacre at Central High (1976) . . . . Mary
- • 0:27 - Brief topless in a classroom getting attacked by
  some guys.
- ••• 1:09 - Nude walking around on a mountain side with
  Robert Carradine and Lani O'Grady.

Revenge of the Cheerleaders (1976) . . . . . . Heather
- • 0:00 - Brief topless changing tops in back of car.
  (Blonde on the far right.)
  0:28 - Buns, in shower room scene.
  0:36 - Full frontal nudity, but covered with bubbles.

Slumber Party '57 (1976) . . . . Sherry
Cinderella (1977) . . . . Cinderella
- •• 0:03 - Topless dancing and singing.
- ••• 0:30 - Frontal nudity getting "washed" by her sisters
  for the Royal Ball.
- •• 0:34 - Topless in the forest during a dream.
- ••• 0:41 - Topless taking a bath. Frontal nudity drying
  herself off.
- • 1:16 - Brief topless with the Prince.

- 1:30 - Brief left breast after making love with the Prince to prove it was her.
- 1:34 - Brief side view of left breast making love in the Prince's carriage.

Laserblast (1978). . . . . Kathy
The Best of Sex and Violence (1981). . . . .Cinderella
- 0:14 - Topless taking a bath in scene from *Cinderella*.

Parasite (1982) . . . . Captive Girl
- • 0:08 - Topless tied by wrists in kitchen.
- • 0:12 - Topless knocking gun out of guy's hands standing behind fence.

Smith, Crystal

Films:
Hot Dog... The Movie (1984) . . . . .Motel Clerk
- • 0:10 - Nude getting out of spa and going to the front desk to sign people in.

Magazines:
Playboy (Sep 1971). . . . . Playmate

Smith, Donna

Video Tapes:
Playmate Playoffs . . . . Playmate
Playboy Video Calendar 1987 (1986) . . . . Playmate
Playmates at Play (1990) . . . . .Hoops

Magazines:
Playboy (Mar 1985). . . . . Playmate

Smith, Julie Kristen

Films:
Pretty Smart (1986). . . . . Samantha Falconwright
- • 0:26 - Topless in bed.
- • 0:40 - Topless in bed.
- • 0:52 - Topless sitting in lounge by the pool.

Angel III: The Final Chapter (1988). . . . . . .Darlene
- • • 0:40 - Topless during caveman shoot with a brunette girl.
- • • 0:44 - Topless again dancing in caveman shoot.

Smith, Linda

Films:
Hardcore (1979) . . . . Hope (Mistress Victoria)
The Beastmaster (1982) . . . . .Kiri's Friend
- • 0:35 - Topless in a pond with Tanya Roberts.

Smith, Madeline

Films:
Vampire Lovers (1970; British). . . . . .Emma
- • 0:32 - Topless trying on a dress in the bedroom after Carmilla has taken a bath.
- • 0:49 - Topless in bed, getting her top pulled down by Carmilla.

Live and Let Die (1973; British) . . . . Miss Caruso
Bawdy Adventures of Tom Jones (1976) . . . . Sophia

TV:
Doctor in the House (1970-73) . . . . Nurse

Smith, Maggie

Films:
The Prime of Miss Jean Brodie (1969). . . . . . Jean Brodie
(Academy Award for Best Actress.)
California Suite (1978) . . . . .Diana Barrie
- • 1:05 - Very brief side of left breast, putting night-gown on over her head.

Quartet (1981; British/French) . . . . Lois
Lily in Love (1985) . . . . Lily Wynn
A Private Function (1985). . . . . Joyce Chilvers
A Room with a View (1986; British) . . .Charlotte Bartlett
The Lonely Passion of Judith Hearne (1988)
. . . . Judith Hearne

Smith, Martha

Films:
National Lampoon's Animal House (1978)
. . . . Babs Jansen
Blood Link (1983) . . . . Hedwig
- • • 0:41 - Topless, wearing black panties while in bed with Keith.
- • 0:50 - Topless getting slapped around by Keith.
- • • • 0:51 - Topless sitting up in bed when Craig and Keith meet each other for the first time.
- • 1:13 - Topless, wearing red panties, in bed with Kei-th.

TV:
Scarecrow and Mrs. King (1983-88)
. . . . .Francine Desmond

Magazines:
Playboy (Jul 1973) . . . . Playmate

Smith, Rainbeaux

See: Smith, Cheryl.

Smith, Savannah

Films:
Five Days from Home (1978) . . . . Georgie Haskin
North Dallas Forty (1979) . . . . .Joanne
- • 0:27 - Very brief topless in bed tossing around with Nick Nolte.

The Long Riders (1980) . . . . Zee

Snodgress, Carrie

Films:
Diary of a Mad Housewife (1970). . . . . . .Tina Balser
- • • • 0:01 - Topless taking off nightgown and getting dressed, putting on white bra while Richard Ben-jamin talks to her.
  0:36 - Buns and brief side view of left breast, while kissing Frank Langella.
- • 0:41 - Very brief topless lying on floor when Langella pulls the blanket up.
- • 0:54 - Topless lying in bed with Langella.
  1:03 - In white bra and panties getting dressed in Langella's apartment.

1:10 - In white bra and panties in Langella's apartment again.
- ••• 1:21 - Topless in the shower with Langella, then drying herself off.

The Fury (1978) . . . . .Hester
Homework (1982). . . . . .Dr. Delingua
Trick or Treats (1982) . . . . Joan
A Night in Heaven (1983) . . . . Mrs. Johnson
Pale Rider (1985). . . . . Sarah Wheeler
Murphy's Law (1986) . . . . Joan Freeman

Snyder, Susan Marie

Films:

Sleepaway Camp II: Unhappy Campers (1988)
. . . . .Mare
- • 0:08 - Brief topless lifting up her T-shirt.
- • 0:24 - Brief topless flashing in boy's cabin.
- • 0:33 - Topless in Polaroid photograph that Angela confiscates from the boys.

TV:

Santa Barbara . . . . Laken Capwell
As the World Turns . . . . .Julie Wendall

Snyder, Suzanne

Films:

The Oasis (1984). . . . . .Jennifer
Remo Williams: The Adventure Begins (1985)
. . . . Nurse/Soap Opera
Weird Science (1985) . . . . Deb
Night of the Creeps (1986) . . . . .Lisa
Pretty Kill (1987). . . . . Franci/Stella/Paul
Killer Klowns from Outer Space (1988) . . . . Debbie
The Night Before (1988) .Lisa
Retribution (1988) . . . . Angel
  0:50 - Very, very brief blurry left breast getting up in bed with George after his nightmare.
The Return of the Living Dead II (1988) . . . . Brenda
Femme Fatale (1990) . . . . Andrea
- ••• 0:08 - Topless, nonchalantly taking off her top and posing for Billy Zane's painting. (She sometimes has a bag over her head.)
- •• 0:46 - Topless posing again with the bag on and off her head.

Socas, Maria

Films:

The Warrior and the Sorceress (1984) . . . . Naja
(Topless in every scene she's in.)
- ••• 0:15 - Topless wearing robe and bikini bottoms in room with Zeg. Sort of brief buns, leaving the room.
- •• 0:22 - Topless standing by a wagon at night.
- •• 0:27 - Topless in room with David Carradine. Dark. Most of buns when leaving the room.
- •• 0:31 - Topless and buns climbing down wall.
- • 0:34 - Brief topless, then left breast with rope around her neck at the well.
- • 0:44 - Topless when Carradine rescues her.

- • 0:47 - Topless walking around outside.
- • 0:57 - More topless outside.
- • 1:00 - Topless watching a guy pound a sword.
- • 1:05 - Topless under a tent after Carradine uses the sword. Long shot.
- • 1:09 - Topless during big fight scene.
- • 1:14 - Topless next to well. Long shot.

Deathstalker II (1987). . . . .
  0:50 - In see-through nightgown after telling Deathstalker she is going to marry him.
Hollywood Boulevard II (1989) . . . . Amazon Queen

Solari, Suzanne

Films:

Roller Blade (1986) . . . . Sister Sharon Cross
  0:04 - Buns, in G-string, lying in bed.
- • 1:21 - Brief upper half of right breast, taking off suit. Buns in G-string.
Hell Comes to Frogtown (1987). . . . . Runaway Girl

Soles, P.J.

P.J. stands for Pamela Jane.
Ex-wife of actor Dennis Quaid.

Films:

Carrie (1976) . . . . .Norma
Halloween (1978) . . . . Lynda
- • 1:04 - Brief right breast, sitting up in bed after making love in bed with Bob.
- • 1:07 - Brief topless getting strangled by Michael in the bedroom.
Breaking Away (1979) . . . . Suzy
Old Boyfriends (1979) . . . . Sandy
Rock 'n' Roll High School (1979) . . . . Riff Randell
Private Benjamin (1980). . . . . Private Wanda Winter
Stripes (1981) . . . . .Stella
Sweet Dreams (1985) . . . . .Wanda
B.O.R.N. (1988) . . . . Liz
Alienator (1990) . . . . .Tara

Magazines:

Playboy (Nov 1981) . . . . Sex in Cinema 1981
- •• 166: Topless.

Somers, Kristi

Films:

Rumble Fish (1983; B&W) . . . .
Hardbodies (1984) . . . . .Michelle
- •• 0:53 - Nude, dancing on the beach while Ashley plays the guitar and sings.
Girls Just Want to Have Fun (1985). . . . . .Rikki
Mugsy's Girls (1985) . . . . Laurie
- • 0:15 - Brief topless several times while mud wrestling.
- •• 0:29 - Topless and buns in bathtub on bus.
- • 0:34 - Brief topless holding up sign to get truck driver to stop.
Savage Streets (1985) . . . . Valerie
  0:24 - In bra and panties in the locker room.

Tomboy (1985) . . . . Seville Ritz
•• 0:14 - Topless taking a shower while talking to Betsy Russell.
• 0:53 - Brief topless stripping at a party.
Hell Comes to Frogtown (1987) . . . . Arabella
Return to Horror High (1987) . . . . Ginny McCall

Somers, Suzanne
Films:
American Graffiti (1973) . . . . . . The Blonde in the T-bird
Magnum Force (1973) . . . . uncredited Pool Girl
•• 0:26 - In blue swimsuit getting into a swimming pool, brief topless a couple of times before getting shot, brief topless floating dead.
Yesterday's Hero (1979; British) . . . . Cloudy Martin
Nothing Personal (1980; Canadian) . . . . Abigail
1:07 - In wet T-shirt sitting with her feet in a pond talking with Donald Sutherland.
Miniseries:
Hollywood Wives (1988) . . . . Gina Germaine
TV:
Three's Company (1977-81) . . . . Chrissy Snow
She's the Sheriff (1987-90) . . . . .Hildy
Step by Step (1991-) . . . .
Magazines:
Playboy (Feb 1980) . . . Suzanne Somers' Playmate Test
•• 136-145: Old photos taken before she was famous. Nude.
Playboy (Dec 1984) . . . . Suzanne Take Two
••• 120-129: New photos. Topless and buns.

Sommer, Elke
Films:
Sweet Ecstasy (1962; B&W) . . . . Elke
Nude.
A Shot in the Dark (1964) . . . . Maria Gambrelli
Boy, Did I Get a Wrong Number (1966) . . . . Didi
The Corrupt Ones (1966) . . . . Lily
The Oscar (1966) . . . . Kay Bergdahl
The House of Exorcism (1975) . . . .
Topless.
Ten Little Indians (1975) . . . . Vera
Left for Dead (1978) . . . . Magdalene Krushcen
•• 0:38 - Left breast, while posing for photographer.
• 0:39 - Very brief left breast in B&W photo.
0:58 - Buns and topless when police officers lift her up to put plastic under her. Covered with blood, can't see her face.
• 1:09 - Very brief left breast in B&W photo.
The Prisoner of Zenda (1979) . . . . The Countess
Lily in Love (1985) . . . . Alicia Brown
Magazines:
Playboy (Sep 1970) . . . .
Playboy (Jan 1979) . . . . 25 Beautiful Years
•• 159: Topless getting into a pool.
Playboy (Jan 1989) . . . . Women of the Seventies
•• 217: Topless getting into pool.

Sommerfield, Diane
Films:
Love in a Taxi (1980) . . . . Carine
Back Roads (1981) . . . . Liz
The Nightstalker (1987) . . . . .Lonnie Roberts
• 0:35 - Side view of right breast lying dead in morgue.

Sorenson, Heidi
Films:
History of the World, Part I (1981) . . . .
Fright Night (1985) . . . . Hooker
Spies Like Us (1985) . . . . .Fitz-Hume's Supervisor
Roxanne (1987) . . . . .Trudy
Magazines:
Playboy (Jul 1981) . . . . Playmate
120:

Soutendijk, Reneé
Films:
Spetters (1980; Dutch) . . . . Fientje
•• 1:12 - Topless making love in trailer with Jeff.
The Girl with the Red Hair (1983; Dutch) . . . . . . .Hannie
The Cold Room (1984) Lili
The Fourth Man (1984; Dutch) . . . . Christine
••• 0:27 - Full frontal nudity removing robe, brief buns in bed, side view left breast, then topless in bed with Gerard.
• 0:32 - Brief left breast in bed with Gerard after he hallucinates and she cuts his penis off.
••• 0:53 - Left breast, then right breast in red dress when Gerard opens her dress.
• 1:11 - Topless making love with Herman while Gerard watches through keyhole.
Grave Secrets (1990) . . . . Iris Norwood
Eve of Destruction (1991) . . Dr. Eve Simmons/Eve VIII
Made for Cable Movies:
Murderers Among Us: The Simon Wiesenthal Story (1989; HBO) . . . . .Cyla
Made for Cable TV:
The Hitchhiker: Murderous Feelings . . . Sara Kendal
••• 0:04 - In bra, then topless with stockings and a garter belt on couch with a guy.
• 0:18 - Right breast when mysterious attacker surprises her from behind.

Spacek, Sissy
Films:
Prime Cut (1972) . . . . Poppy
• 0:25 - Brief side view of left breast lying in hay, then buns when Gene Hackman lifts her up to show to Lee Marvin.
••• 0:30 - Topless sitting in bed, then getting up to try on a dress while Marvin watches.
0:32 - Close up of breasts though sheer black dress in a restaurant.
Badlands (1973) . . . . Holly
Ginger in the Morning (1973) . . . . .Ginger

Carrie (1976) . . . . Carrie White
- •• 0:02 - Nude, taking a shower, then having her first menstrual period in the girls' locker room.
- • 1:25 - Brief topless taking a bath to wash all the pig blood off her after the dance.

Three Women (1977) . . . . Pinky Rose
Welcome to L.A. (1977) . . . . Linda Murray
- •• 0:51 - Brief topless after bringing presents into Keith Carradine's bedroom.

Heart Beat (1979) . . . . Carolyn Cassady
Coal Miner's Daughter (1980) . . . . Loretta Lynn
(Academy Award for Best Actress.)
Raggedy Man (1981) . . . . Nita
0:43 - Side view of left breast washing herself off while two guys peep from outside window. Long shot, don't really see anything.

Missing (1982) . . . . Beth Horman
The River (1984) . . . . Mae Garvey
Marie (1986) . . . . Marie Ragghianti
'night Mother (1986) . . . . Jessie Cates
Violets Are Blue (1986) . . . . Gussie Sawyer
The Long Walk Home (1990) . . . . . . Miriam Thompson

Speir, Dona L.

Films:
Doin' Time (1984) . . . . Card Holder
Dragnet (1987) . . . . Baitmate
Hard Ticket to Hawaii (1987) . . . . Donna
- • 0:01 - Topless on boat kissing her boyfriend, Rowdy.
- ••• 0:23 - Topless in the spa with Hope Marie Carlton looking at diamonds they found.
- ••• 1:04 - Topless and buns with Rowdy after watching a video tape.
- •• 1:33 - Topless during the end credits.

Picasso Trigger (1989) . . . . Donna
0:17 - In white lingerie on boat with Hope Marie Carlton.
- ••• 0:49 - Topless and buns standing, then making love in bed.

Savage Beach (1989) . . . . Dona
0:06 - Almost topless in spa with the three other women.
- • 0:32 - Topless changing clothes in airplane with Hope Marie Carlton.
- •• 0:48 - Nude, going for a swim on the beach with Carlton.

Guns (1990) . . . . Donna Hamilton
- ••• 1:00 - Topless and buns in black G-string getting dressed in locker room. Then in black lingerie.

Video Tapes:
Playmate Playoffs . . . . Playmate
Playboy Video Calendar 1987 (1986) . . . . Playmate
Glamour Through Your Lens—Outdoor Techniques
(1989) . . . . herself
0:22 - Posing by Corvette in shorts and a top.
0:35 - In white two piece swimsuit on lounge chair by the pool.

Playboy's Wet and Wild (1989) . . . .
Magazines:
Playboy (Mar 1984) . . . . Playmate

Spelvin, Georgina

Adult flim actress.
Films:
Police Academy III: Back in Training (1986)
. . . . The Hooker

Spradling, Charlie

a.k.a. Charlie.
Films:
The Blob (1988) . . . . Co-ed
Meridian (1989) . . . . Gina
a.k.a. Kiss of the Beast
- •• 0:22 - Topless getting her blouse torn off by Lawrence while lying on the table.
- ••• 0:28 - Topless standing next to fireplace, then topless on the couch. Hot!

Twice Dead (1989) . . . . Tina
- •• 1:11 - Topless taking off jacket next to bed.
- ••• 1:14 - Topless making love with her boyfriend in bed.
- • 1:18 - Brief topless dead in bed.

Puppet Master II (1990) . . . . Wanda
- •• 1:04 - Topless getting out of bed and adjusting her panties.

Ski School (1990) . . . . Paulette
Wild at Heart (1990) . . . . Irma
- •• 0:40 - Brief topless in bed during flashback.

Sprinkle, Annie

Adult flim actress.
Films:
Mondo New York (1987) . . . . Model/Performer
- • 0:17 - Nude, painted body with other models during "Rapping & Rocking" segment.

Wimps (1987) . . . . Head Stripper
- •• 1:12 - Topless on stage with two other strippers, teasing Francis.

Young Nurses in Love (1987) . . . . Twin Falls
- •• 0:23 - Topless getting measured by Dr. Spencer.

St. George, Cathy

Films:
Star 80 (1983) . . . . Playboy Mansion Guest
Video Tapes:
Playboy's Playmate Review 2 (1984) . . . . . Playmate
Playboy's Wet and Wild (1989) . . . .
Magazines:
Playboy (Aug 1982) . . . . Playmate

St. Jon, Ashley

Films:

Takin' It Off (1984) . . . . Sin
••• 0:20 - Topless and buns doing two dance routines on stage.
•• 0:53 - Nude, stripping and dancing in the library.

Weekend Pass (1984) . . . . Xylene B-12
•• 0:13 - Topless dancing on stage.

The Wild Life (1984) . . . . Stripper #1
••• 0:47 - Topless and brief buns doing strip tease routine in front of Christopher Penn and his friends.

Centerfold Screen Test (1985) . . . . herself
••• 0:32 - Topless and buns in G-string, taking off her fur coat while auditioning in a car.

Staley, Lora

Films:

American Nightmare (1981; Canadian)
. . . . Louise Harmon
•• 0:44 - Topless and buns in G-string dancing on stage.
••• 0:54 - Topless making love in bed with Eric.
• 0:59 - Brief right breast, then topless auditioning in TV studio.

Thief (1981) . . . . Paula

Staller, Ilona

a.k.a. Adult film actress Cicciolina.
Was elected to a seat on the Italian Parliament in 1987.

Films:

Inhibition . . . . Anna
••• 0:08 - Nude taking a shower with Carol.
• 0:43 - Brief full frontal nudity getting out of swimming pool.
••• 0:55 - Topless making love in the water with Robert.
••• 1:00 - Full frontal nudity getting disciplined by Carol.

Magazines:

Playboy (Feb 1988) . . . . The Year in Sex
••• 134: Full frontal nudity.

Playboy (Feb 1991) . . . . The Year in Sex
• Left breast, making the "victory" sign with her left hand.

Stark, Koo

Former girlfriend of Prince Andrew of England in 1982, before he met and married "Fergie."
Special Stills Photographer in the film *Aria.*

Films:

Justine . . . . Justine
•• 0:09 - Topless getting fondled by a nun.
• 0:16 - Topless getting attacked by a nun.
• 0:57 - Topless in open dress getting attacked by old guy.
••• 1:00 - Topless getting bathed, then lower frontal nudity.
• 1:28 - Right breast and buns taking off clothes, then brief full frontal nudity getting dressed again.
• 1:32 - Topless getting thrown in to the water.

The Rocky Horror Picture Show (1975; British)
. . . . Bridesmaid

Emily (1976; British) . . . . Emily
•• 0:08 - Topless, lying in bed caressing herself while fantasizing about James.
••• 0:30 - Topless in studio posing for Augustine, then kissing her.
••• 0:42 - Buns and topless taking a shower after posing for Augustine.
•• 0:56 - Left breast, under a tree with James.
• 1:16 - Topless in the woods seducing Rupert.

Cruel Passion (1978) . . . .

Electric Dreams (1984) . . . . Girl in Soap Opera

Stavin, Mary

Films:

Octopussy (1983; British) . . . . Octopussy Girl
A View to a Kill (1985) . . . . Kimberley Jones
House (1986) . . . . Tanya
Open House (1987) . . . . Katie Thatcher

Howling V (1989) . . . . Anna
•• 1:09 - Topless three times drying herself off while Richard watches in the mirror. Possible body double.

Steenburgen, Mary

Wife of actor Malcolm McDowell.

Films:

Goin' South (1978) . . . . Julia Tate
Time After Time (1979; British) . . . . Amy Robbins

Melvin and Howard (1980) . . . . Lynda Dummar
•• 0:31 - Topless and buns, ripping off barmaid outfit and walking out the door.

Ragtime (1981) . . . . Mother
A Midsummer Night's Sex Comedy (1982) . . . . . Adrian
Cross Creek (1983) . . . . Marjorie Kinnan Rawlings
Romantic Comedy (1983) . . . . Phoebe
Dead of Winter (1987)
. . . . Julie Rose/Katie McGovern/Evelyn
End of the Line (1987) . . . . Rose Pickett
Miss Firecracker (1989) . . . . Elain
Parenthood (1989). . . . . Karen Buckman
Back to the Future, Part III (1990) . . . . Clara Clayton

Made for TV Movies:

One Magic Christmas (1985; U.S./Canadian)
. . . . Ginny Grainger
The Attic—The Hiding of Anne Frank (1988) . Miep Gies

Stefanelli, Simonetta

Films:

The Godfather (1972) . . . . Apollonia
•• 1:50 - Topless in bedroom on honeymoon night.

Three Brothers (1982; Italian) . . . . . Young Donato's Wife

Magazines:

Playboy (Nov 1972) . . . . Sex in Cinema 1972
• 161: Left breast, grainy photo from *The Godfather.*

Playboy (Mar 1974) . . . . . . The Don's Daughter-In-Law
••• 97-99: Topless.

Stein, Pamela J.

Video Tapes:
Playboy Video Calendar 1989 (1988) . . . September
••• 0:33 - Nude.
Magazines:
Playboy (Nov 1987) . . . . Playmate

Stensgaard, Yutte

Real name is Jytte Stensgaard.
Films:
Lust for a Vampire (1970; British) . . . . Mircalla
••• 0:19 - Topless, three times, getting a massage from another school girl.
0:22 - Very, very brief full frontal nudity while diving into the water. Long shot, don't see anything.
•• 0:53 - Topless outside with Lestrange. Left breast when lying down.
• 0:58 - Topless during Lestrange's dream.
Scream and Scream Again (1970; British) . . . . Erika
The Buttercup Chain (1971; British) . . . .

Stephenson, Pamela

Films:
Stand Up Virgin Soldiers (1976) . . . . Nurse
Topless and brief buns after removing clothes and getting into bed.
History of the World, Part I (1981)
. . . . Mademoiselle Rimbaud
The Secret Policeman's Other Ball (1982; British) . . . . .
Scandalous (1983) . . . . Fiona Maxwell Sayle
Superman III (1983) . . . . Lorelei Ambrosia
Bloodbath at the House of Death (1985; British)
. . . . Barbara Coyle
• 0:50 - Very brief topless getting clothes ripped off by an unseen being.
TV:
Saturday Night Live (1984-85) . . . . regular

Stern, Ellen

Films:
The Duchess and the Dirtwater Fox (1976) . . . .
Jessi's Girls (1976) . . . . Kana
••• 1:10 - Left breast, then topless in bed with a guy.

Stevens, Brinke

Films:
The Slumber Party Massacre (1982) . . . . Linda
•• 0:07 - Buns, then topless taking a shower during girls locker room scene.
Sole Survivor (1982) . . . . Jennifer
•• 0:15 - In bra playing cards, then topless.
The Man Who Wasn't There (1983) . . . . . Nymphet
• 0:45 - Buns and brief topless in the girls' shower, when she gets shampoo from an invisible Steve Guttenberg.

Private School (1983) . . . . Uncredited School Girl
•• 0:42 - Brief topless and buns in shower room scene. She's the brunette wearing a pony tail who passes in front of the chalkboard.
The Witching (1983) . . . . Black Sabbath Member
a.k.a. Necromancy
Body Double (1984) . . . . Girl in Bathroom #3
• 1:12 - Topless sitting in chair in adult film preview that Craig Wasson watches on TV.
Psycho III (1986) . . . . . body double for Diana Scarwid
•• 0:30 - Brief topless and buns getting ready to take a shower, body doubling for Diana Scarwid.
Nightmare Sisters (1987) . . . . Marci
(This is the best video tape for viewing all three "Scream Queens.")
••• 0:39 - Topless standing in panties with Melody and Mickey after transforming from nerds to sexy women.
••• 0:40 - Topless in the kitchen with Melody and Mickey.
••• 0:44 - Nude in the bathtub with Melody and Mickey. Excellent, long scene.
••• 0:47 - Topless in the bathtub. Nice close up.
••• 0:48 - Still more buns and topless in the bathtub.
Slavegirls from Beyond Infinity (1987) . . . . . . Shala
0:29 - Chained up wearing black lingerie.
• 0:31 - Brief side view of left breast on table. Nice pan from her feet to her head while she's lying face down.
Grandmother's House (1988) . . . . Woman
The Jigsaw Murders (1988) . . . . Stripper #1
• 0:28 - Very, very brief topless posing for photographer in white bra and panties when camera passes between her and the other stripper.
Sorority Babes in the Slimeball Bowl-O-Rama
(1988) . . . . Taffy
0:07 - In panties getting spanked with Michelle Bauer.
••• 0:12 - Nude showering off whipped cream in bathtub while talking to a topless Michelle Bauer. Excellent long scene!
Warlords (1988) . . . . Dow's Wife
Murder Weapon (1989) . . . . Girl in Shower on TV
• 1:00 - Brief left breast on TV that the guys are watching. Scene from *Nightmare Sisters*.
Bad Girls from Mars (1990) . . . . Myra
• 0:11 - Brief side of left breast, then topless getting massaged on diving board.
Mob Boss (1990) . . . . Sara
Transylvania Twist (1990) . . . . Betty Lou
Naked Force (1991) . . . .
Scream Queen Hot Tub Party (1991) . . . .
Video Tapes:
The Girls of Penthouse (1984) . . . . Ghost Town Woman
Red Hot Rock (1984) . . . . Miss Utah
• 0:41 - Brief topless several times in open-front swimsuit during beauty pageant during "Gimme Gimme Good Lovin'" by Helix.

Stevens, Connie

Films:

Scorchy (1971) . . . . Jackie Parker
- •• 0:23 - Open blouse, revealing left bra cup while talking on the telephone. Brief topless swimming in the
  water after taking off bathing suit top.
- •• 0:52 - Side view left breast, taking a shower.
- ••• 0:56 - Brief right breast making love in bed with Greg
  Evigan. Topless getting tied to the bed by the
  thieves. Kind of a long shot and a little dark and hard
  to see.
- • 1:00 - Brief topless getting covered with a sheet by
  the good guy.

Grease 2 (1982) . . . . Miss Mason
Back to the Beach (1987) . . . . Connie
Tapeheads (1988) . . . . June Tager

Miniseries:

Scruples (1980) . . . . Maggie McGregor

Made for TV Movies:

The Littlest Angel (1969) . . . .
Playmates (1972) . . . .
Love's Savage Fury (1979) . . . .

TV:

Hawaiian Eye (1959-63) . . . . .Cricket Blake
Wendy and Me (1964-65) . . . . Wendy Conway

Stevens, Stella

Mother of actor Andrew Stevens.

Films:

Li'l Abner (1959) . . . . .Appasionata von Climax
Girls! Girls! Girls! (1962) . . . . Robin Gantner
The Nutty Professor (1963) . . . . Stella Purdy
The Ballad of Cable Hogue (1970) . . . . .Hildy
  1:12 - Buns changing into nightgown in bedroom.
- • 1:14 - Brief top half of breasts in outdoor tub, then
  buns running into cabin when stagecoach arrives.

The Poseidon Adventure (1972) . . . . .Linda Rogo
Slaughter (1972) . . . . Ann
- •• 0:47 - Left breast, several times in bed with Jim
  Brown.
- • 0:55 - Left breast, making love in bed with Brown
  again. Dark.
- • 0:57 - Brief right breast, in bed afterwards. Close up
  shot.
- ••• 1:14 - Buns and topless taking a shower and getting
  out. This is her best nude scene.

Arnold (1973) . . . . Karen
The Manitou (1977) . . . . Amelia Crusoe
Chained Heat (1983; U.S./German) . . . . Taylor
The Longshot (1986) . . . . .Nicki
Down the Drain (1989) . . . . Sophia
  0:45 - In black lingerie yelling at Dino in the bathroom.
Last Call (1990) . . . . .Betty
  0:52 - Very brief left nipple popping out of black lingerie top while making love with Jason on a pool table.

Made for TV Movies:

Man Against the Mob (1988) . . . . Joey Day

TV:

Santa Barbara . . . . .Phyllis Blake
Ben Casey (1965) .Jane Hancock
Flamingo Road (1981-82) . . . . Lute-Mae Sanders

Magazines:

Playboy (Jan 1960) . . . . Playmate
Playboy (Dec 1973) . . . . .Sex Stars of 1973
- • 210: Topless behind plants.
Playboy (Jan 1989) . . . . .Women of the Sixties
  161: Half of left breast behind pink material.

Stevenson, Judy

Films:

Alvin Rides Again (1974; Australian) . . . . . Housewife
- •• 0:01 - Full frontal nudity, dropping her towel while
  Alvin washes her window.
Cathy's Child (1979; Australian) Lil

Stewart, Alexandra

Films:

Goodbye Emmanuelle (1977) . . . . .Dorothee
The Uncanny (1977; British) . . . . Mrs. Blake
In Praise of Older Women (1978; Canadian) . . Paula
- •• 1:21 - Topless in bed with Tom Berenger.
- •• 1:23 - Nude, in and out of bed with Berenger.
The Last Chase (1980) .Eudora
Agency (1981; Canadian) . . . . Mimi
Chanel Solitaire (1981) . . . .
Under the Cherry Moon (1986; B&W) . . . . .Mrs. Sharon

Made for Cable TV:

The Hitchhiker: Shattered Vows . . . .Jackie Winslow
- • 0:04 - In white bra and panties, then side view topless making love in bed with Jeff.

Magazines:

Playboy (Oct 1978) . . . . . . Observing "Older Women"
- • 193-194: Topless.

Stewart, Liz

Video Tapes:

Playmate Playoffs . . . . Playmate
Playboy's Wet and Wild (1989) . . . .

Magazines:

Playboy (Jul 1984) . . . . Playmate

Stone, Dee Wallace

See: Wallace Stone, Dee.

Stone, Sharon

Films:

Stardust Memories (1980; B&W)
 . . . . .Blonde on Passing Train
Deadly Blessing (1981) . . . . Lana

Irreconcilable Differences (1984) . . . Blake Chandler
•• 0:56 - Topless lowering her blouse in front of Ryan
   O'Neal during film test.
King Solomon's Mines (1985) . . . . .Jessica
Allan Quartermain and the Lost City of Gold (1987)
. . . . Jesse Huston
Cold Steel (1987) . . . . Kathy Conners
   • 0:33 - Brief left breast making love in bed with Brad
     Davis. Dark, hard to see. Brief topless turning over
     after making love.
Police Academy 4: Citizens on Patrol (1987)
. . . . Claire Matson
Above the Law (1988). . . . . Sara Toscani
Action Jackson (1988) . . . . .Patrice Dellaplane
•• 0:34 - Topless in a steam room. Hard to see because
   of all the steam.
   • 0:56 - Brief right breast, dead, on the bed when po-
     lice view her body.
Blood and Sand (1989; Spanish) . . . . .Doña Sol
   0:57 - Very brief upper half of right breast, making
   love on table with Juan.
•• 0:58 - Left breast, making love in bed with Juan.
   Don't see her face well.
••• 1:04 - Topless quite a few times, making love with
   Juan in the woods.
Total Recall (1990) . . . . .Lori
he said, she said (1991). . . . . Linda
Scissors (1991) . . . .
Miniseries:
War and Remembrance (1988) . . . . Janice Henry
TV:
Bay City Blues (1983) . . . . .Cathy St. Marie
Magazines:
Playboy (Jul 1990). . . . . .Dishing with Sharon
••• 118-127: Topless in B&W photos.

Stoner, Sherri

Story editor for Steven Spielberg.
She was used as the animator's model for Ariel in Disney's
The Little Mermaid and Belle in Disney's *Beauty and the
Beast.*
Films:
Impulse (1984) . . . . Young Girl
Lovelines (1984) . . . . Suzy
Reform School Girls (1986). . . . . .Lisa
   • 1:03 - Very brief topless and buns, lying on stomach
     in the restroom, getting branded by bad girls.

Stowe, Madeline

Films:
Stakeout (1987) . . . . Maira McGuire
   0:43 - Buns and brief side view of right breast getting
   a towel after taking a shower while Richard Dreyfus
   watches her.
Tropical Snow (1989). . . . . Marina
   • 0:05 - Very brief side view of left breast putting red
     dress on.

• 0:11 - Buns, lying in bed. Very brief right breast sitting up. (I wish they could have panned the camera
  to the right!)
•• 0:24 - Topless in mirror putting red dress on.
   0:32 - Buns, lying on top of Tavo in bed.
   • 0:54 - Brief topless making love in the water with
     Tavo. Then buns, lying on the beach (long shot.)
   1:22 - Long shot side view of right breast in water
   with Tavo.
Worth Winning (1989). . . . . Veronica Briskow
Closet Land (1990) . . . . The Author
Revenge (1990) . . . . .Miryea
   0:44 - Side view of buns when Kevin Costner pulls up
   her dress to make love with her.
   0:52 - In white slip talking to Costner in bedroom.
   • 1:00 - Buns, making love with Costner in jeep. Very
     brief topless coming out of the water.
   • 1:07 - Very brief topless when Costner is getting beat
     up.
The Two Jakes (1990). . . . . Lillian Bodine
   0:23 - Very brief buns, when Jack Nicholson lifts her
   slip up in bed.
TV:
The Gangster Chronicles (1981). . . . . Ruth Lasker

Strain, Julie

Films:
Double Impact (1991). . . . .
Video Tapes:
Penthouse Centerfold—Julie Strain (1991). . . . .Pet
Magazines:
Playboy (May 1991) . . . . Grapevine
•• 183: Left breast.
Penthouse (Jun 1991) . . . . .Pet
••• 71-85: Nude.
Playboy (Jul 1991) . . . . .The Height Report
••• 134-135: Full frontal nudity.

Strasberg, Susan

Daughter of acting teacher Lee Strasberg.
Films:
The Trip (1967) . . . . Sally Groves
The Brotherhood (1968) . . . . Emma Ginetta
Psych-Out (1968). . . . . .Jennie Davis
The Manitou (1977). . . . . Karen Tandy
   1:33 - Topless, fighting the creature in bed. Really
   bad special effects. Too dark to see anything.
Rollercoaster (1977). . . . . .Fran
In Praise of Older Women (1978; Canadian) .Bobbie
•• 1:03 - Left breast, while making love in bed with Tom
   Berenger.
••• 1:04 - Topless in bed after Berenger rolls off her.
Bloody Birthday (1980) . . . . Miss Davis
Sweet Sixteen (1982). . . . . Joanne Morgan
The Delta Force (1986) . . . . Debra Levine
TV:
The Marriage (1954) . . . . Emily Marriott
Toma (1973-74). . . . . Patty Toma

Stratten, Dorothy
Films:
Americathon (1979) . . . .
Autumn Born (1979) . . . . Tara
    0:03 - In dressing room in beige bra, panties, garter belt and stockings changing clothes. Long, close-up lingering shots.
    0:16 - Unconscious in beige lingerie, then conscious, walking around the room.
    0:21 - In bra and panties getting her rear end whipped while tied to the bed.
  •• 0:26 - Left breast taking bath, then right breast getting up, then topless dressing.
  • 0:30 - Side view of left breast, then topless climbing back into bed.
    0:35 - In beige bra and panties in the shower with her captor.
    0:43 - Quick cuts of various scenes.
  ••• 0:46 - In white bra and panties, side view of left breast and buns, then topless in bathtub. Long scene.
  • 0:50 - Side view of left breast and buns getting undressed. Nice buns shot. Right breast lying down in chair.
  • 1:03 - Brief topless shots during flashbacks.
Skatetown, U.S.A. (1979) . . . .
Galaxina (1980) . . . . Galaxina
They All Laughed (1981) . . . . Dolores Martin
Video Tapes:
Dorothy Stratten, The Untold Story . . . . . . Herself
Playboy Video Magazine, Volume 4 . . . . . Playmate
Playmates of the Year—The '80's . . . . Playmate
Magazines:
Playboy (Aug 1979) . . . . Playmate
Playboy (Dec 1979) . . . . Sex Stars of 1979
  ••• 258: Topless.
Playboy (Jun 1980) . . . . Playmate of the Year
  ••• 168-179: Nude.
Playboy (Jan 1989) . . . . Women of the Eighties
  219: Full frontal nudity.

Streep, Meryl
Films:
Julia (1977) . . . . Anne Marie
The Deer Hunter (1978) . . . . Linda
Kramer vs. Kramer (1979) . . . . Joanna Kramer
Manhattan (1979; B&W) . . . . Jill
The Seduction of Joe Tynan (1979) . . . . . . Karen Traynor
The French Lieutenant's Woman (1981) . . . . Sarah/Anna
Sophie's Choice (1982) . . . . Sophie
  (Academy Award for Best Actress.)
Still of the Night (1982) . . . . Brooke Reynolds
  0:22 - Side view of right breast and buns taking off robe for the massage guy. Long shot, don't see her face.
Falling In Love (1984) . . . . Molly Gilmore

Silkwood (1984) . . . . Karen Silkwood
  • 0:24 - Very brief glimpse of upper half of left breast when she flashes it in nuclear reactor office.
Out of Africa (1985) . . . . Karen Blixen
Plenty (1985) . . . . Susan
Heartburn (1986) . . . . Rachel
Ironweed (1987) . . . . Helen
A Cry in the Dark (1988) . . . . Lindy Chamberlain
  1:44 - Brief side view of right breast in jail being examined by two female guards. Don't see her face, probably a body double.
She-Devil (1989) . . . . Mary Fisher
Postcards from the Edge (1990) . . . . Suzanne Vale
Defending Your Life (1991) . . . . Julia
Miniseries:
Holocaust (1978) . . . . Inga Helms Weiss

Stromeir, Tara
a.k.a. Tara Strohmeier.
Films:
Truck Turner (1974) . . . . Turnpike
Hollywood Boulevard (1976) . . . . Jill McBain
  •• 0:00 - Topless getting out of van and standing with film crew.
  • 0:31 - Silhouette of breasts, making love with P.G.
  ••• 0:32 - Topless sunbathing with Bobbi and Candy.
  ••• 0:33 - Topless acting for film on hammock. Long scene.
Kentucky Fried Movie (1977) . . . . Girl
  •• 1:16 - In bra, then topless making love on couch with her boyfriend while people on the TV news watch them.
Malibu Beach (1978) . . . . Glorianna
  • 0:08 - Topless kissing her boyfriend at the beach when someone steals her towel.
Made for TV Movies:
The Lakeside Killer (1979) . . . . Janie

Strong, Brenda
Films:
Weekend Warriors (1986) . . . . Danny El Dubois
  • 0:44 - Topless, lit from the side, standing in the dark.
Spaceballs (1987) . . . . Nurse

Struthers, Sally
Films:
Five Easy Pieces (1970) . . . . Betty
  0:15 - In a bra sitting on a couch in the living room with Jack Nicholson and another man and a woman.
  • 0:33 - Brief topless a couple of times making love with Nicholson. Lots of great moaning, but hard to see anything.
The Getaway (1972) . . . . Fran Clinton
  1:15 - In black bra getting out of bed and leaning over injured bad guy to get something.
Made for TV Movies:
Intimate Strangers (1977) . . . .

TV:
The Tim Conway Comedy Hour (1970) . . . . regular
The Summer Smother's Show (1970) . . . . regular
All In the Family (1971-78) . . . . .Gloria Bunker Stivic
Gloria (1982-83) . . . . .Gloria Bunker Stivic
9 to 5 (1986-88) . . . . Marsha Shrimpton

Stuart, Cassie

Films:
Ordeal by Innocence (1984) . . . . . . .Maureen Clegg
•• 1:14 - Topless in bed talking to Donald Sutherland.
Slayground (1984; British) . . . . Fran
Stealing Heaven (1988) . . . . Petronilla

Stubbs, Imogen

Films:
Deadline (1988) . . . . Lady Romy-Burton
0:42 - Doing handstands in a bikini top.
• 0:44 - Brief left breast, while getting out of bed with
John Hurt. Full frontal nudity turning toward bed,
brief topless getting back into bed.
A Summer Story (1988) . . . . Megan David
•• 0:36 - Left breast several times, then right breast
while making love with Frank in barn.
0:41 - Very, very brief buns, frolicking in pond at
night with Frank.
1:03 - Very brief silhouette of left breast during
Frank's flashback sequence.
Erik the Viking (1989) . . . . Aud
True Colors (1991) . . . . •
Made for Cable Movies:
Fellow Traveller (1989; HBO) . . . . . . .Sarah Aitchison
• 0:54 - Topless in bed with Asa. Very, very brief right
breast when he rolls off her.

Sukowa, Barbara

Films:
Berlin Alexanderplatz (1983; West German) . . . .
The Sicilian (1987) . . . . . . Camilia Duchess of Crotone
(Director's uncut version.)
•• 0:05 - Buns and brief topless taking a bath, three
times.
• 0:07 - Brief right breast reading Time magazine. Full
frontal nudity in the mirror standing up in the tub.
• 0:08 - Brief right breast standing at the window
watching Christopher Lambert steal a horse.
••• 1:01 - In bra, then topless in bedroom with Lambert.
More topless, then nude. Long scene.

Sullivan, Sheila

Films:
Hickey and Boggs (1972) . . . . Edith Boggs
A Name for Evil (1973) . . . . .Luanna Baxter
• 0:51 - Full frontal nudity dancing in the bar.
• 0:54 - Topless while Robert Culp makes love with her.
• 0:56 - Topless getting dressed.
• 1:17 - Nude, skinny dipping with Culp.

Sutton, Lori

Films:
History of the World, Part I (1981) . . . .
Looker (1981) . . . . .Reston Girl
Fast Times at Ridgemont High (1982) . . . . Playmate
Malibu Express (1984) . . . . Beverly
••• 0:54 - Topless and buns, making love in bed with
Cody.
Up the Creek (1984) . . . . Cute Girl
• 0:40 - Brief topless pulling up her T-shirt to get the
crowd excited while cheerleading the crowd.
Night Patrol (1985) . . . . Edith Hutton
••• 0:47 - In white bra, panties, garter belt and stockings, then topless three times taking off bra in bedroom with the Police officer.

Swanson, Brenda

Films:
Dangerous Love (1988) . . . . .Felicity
Skin Deep (1989) . . . . .Emily
Steel and Lace (1990) . . . . Miss Fairweather
•• 0:58 - Topless in lunchroom, opening her blouse in
front of one of the bad guys on the table.

Swanson, Jackie

Films:
Lethal Weapon (1987) . . . . .Amanda Huntsacker
•• 0:01 - Brief topless standing on balcony rail getting
ready to jump.
It's Alive III: Island of the Alive (1988) . . . .
Perfect Victim (1988) . . . . Carrie Marks

Sykes, Brenda

Films:
The Baby Maker (1970) . . . . .Francis
Getting Straight (1970) . . . . Luan
The Liberation of L. B. Jones (1970) . . . . .Jelly
Honky (1971) . . . . Shella Smith
••• 0:42 - Topless with her boyfriend, making love on the
floor.
• 1:22 - Brief topless several times getting raped by
two guys.
Pretty Maids All in a Row (1971) . . . . . . .Pamela Wilcox
Skin Game (1971) . . . . .Naomi
Black Gunn (1972) . . . . Judith
• 0:45 - Brief side view of right breast, while getting
out of bed with Jim Brown.
Cleopatra Jones (1973) . . . . .Tiffany
Mandingo (1975) . . . . Ellen
• 0:58 - Topless in bed with Perry King.
Drum (1976) . . . . Calinda
• 0:19 - Topless standing next to bed with Ken Norton.
TV:
Ozzie's Girls (1973) . . . . . . Brenda (Jennifer) MacKenzie
Executive Suite (1976-77) . . . . .Summer Johnson

Magazines:
Playboy (Oct 1972) . . . . Brown, Black and White
  • 88: Almost topless.
Playboy (Nov 1972) . . . . Sex in Cinema 1972
  • 162: Left breast, in a photo from *Black Gunn*.

Taggart, Sharon

Films:
The Last Picture Show (1971; B&W)
. . . . Charlene Duggs
  •• 0:11 - In bra, then topless making out in truck with
    Timothy Bottoms.
The Harrad Experiment (1973) . . . . Barbara

Tallman, Patricia

Films:
Knightriders (1981) . . . . Julie
  • 0:46 - Brief topless in the bushes in moonlight talking
    to her boyfriend while a truck driver watches.
Monkey Shines: An Experiment in Fear (1988)
. . . . Party Guest and Stunts
After Midnight (1989) . . . . Stunt Player
Roadhouse (1989) . . . . Bandstand Babe
Night of the Living Dead (1990) . . . . Barbara

Tamerlis, Zoe

a.k.a. Zoë Tamerlaine.
Films:
Ms. 45 (1980) . . . . Thana
Special Effects (1984) . . . . Amelia/Elaine
    0:01 - Side view of right breast, wearing pasties dur-
      ing photo session.
  • 0:16 - Brief topless sitting by pool with Eric Bogozian.
  •• 0:19 - Topless getting into bed and in bed with
    Bogozian.
  • 0:22 - Topless, dead in spa while Bogozian washes
    her off.
    0:44 - Brief topless in moviola that Bogozian watch-
      es.
  •• 1:12 - Topless making love on bed with Keefe.
  • 1:17 - Topless getting into bed during filming of
    movie. Brief topless during Bogozian's flashbacks.
    1:20 - More left breast shots on moviola getting
      strangled.
  ••• 1:33 - Topless with Bogozian when he takes her dress
    off.
  • 1:35 - Topless sitting on bed kissing Bogozian. More
    topless and more flashbacks.
  • 1:40 - Brief topless during struggle. Dark.
Heavy Petting (1989) . . . . herself/Writer, Actress

Tate, Sharon

Wife of director Roman Polanski.
Victim of the Manson Family murders in 1969.
Films:

The Fearless Vampire Killers (1967) . . . Sarah Shagal
  • 0:24 - Very, very brief topless struggling in bathtub
    with vampire. Hard to see.
Valley of the Dolls (1967) . . . . Jennifer North
Ciao Frederico! (1971) . . . .
TV:
The Beverly Hillbillies (1963-65) . . . . Janet Trego
Magazines:
Playboy (Jan 1989) . . . . Women of the Sixties
  • 160: Side view of right breast, taking a bubble bath.

Taylor, Elizabeth

Films:
Psychotic (1975; Italian) . . . .
a.k.a. *Driver's Seat*
    0:03 - In sheer beige bra in changing room.
    0:34 - In sheer white slip walking around.

Taylor, Kimberly

Films:
Bedroom Eyes II (1989) . . . . .Michelle
Cleo/Leo (1989) . . . . .Store Clerk
  ••• 0:22 - Topless in white panties, changing in dressing
    room with Jane Hamilton. Very nice!
Party Incorporated (1989) . . . . Felicia
  •• 0:26 - Topless shaking her breasts trying an outfit on.
  ••• 0:39 - Topless and buns in G-string in the bar with
    the guys.
Frankenhooker (1990) . . . . Amber
  • 0:36 - Brief left breast in green top during introduc-
    tion to Jeffrey.
  •• 0:37 - Brief topless during exam by Jeffrey. Then top-
    less getting breasts measured with calipers.
  • 0:41 - Brief right breast, twice, enjoying drugs.
  •• 0:42 - Topless, getting off bed and onto another bed
    with Anise.
  • 0:43 - Topless kneeling in bed screaming before ex-
    ploding.
Magazines:
Penthouse (Dec 1988) . . . . .Pet

Taylor-Young, Leigh

Films:
I Love You, Alice B. Toklas (1968) . . . . Nancy
The Big Bounce (1969) . . . . Nancy Barker
  (Not available on video tape.)
The Adventurers (1970) . . . . Amparo
The Buttercup Chain (1971; British) . . . . Manny
The Horsemen (1971) . . . . Zereh
Soylent Green (1973) . . . . Shirl
Can't Stop the Music (1980) . . . . Claudia Walters
Looker (1981) . . . . Jennifer Long
Jagged Edge (1985) . . . . Virginia Howell
Secret Admirer (1985) . . . . Elizabeth Fimple
Honeymoon Academy (1990) . . . . Mrs. Doris Kent
TV:
Dallas . . . . Kimberly Cryder

Tenison, Reneé

Video Tapes:
Playboy Video Centerfold: Reneé Tenison
. . . . Playmate of the Year
Playboy Video Calendar 1991 (1990) . . . . . . August
••• 0:31 - Nude.
Magazines:
Playboy (Nov 1989) . . . . Playmate

Tennant, Victoria

Wife of comedian/actor Steve Martin.
Films:
The Ragman's Daughter (1974; British) . . . Doris Randall
Horror Planet (1980; British) . . . . Barbara
  a.k.a. Inseminoid
All of Me (1984) . . . . Terry Hoskins
The Holcroft Covenant (1985) . . . . Helden Tennyson
Flowers in the Attic (1987) . . . . Mother
Best Seller (1988) . . . . Roberta Gillian
Whispers (1989) . . . . Hilary Thomas
  • 0:43 - Buns and side of right breast getting into bath-
    tub. Long shot, looks like a body double (the pony-
    tail in her hair changes position).
  • 0:44 - Buns and brief topless running down the
    stairs. Looks like the same body double.
A Handmaid's Tale (1990) . . . . Aunt Lydia
L.A. Story (1991) . . . . Sara

Terashita, Jill

Films:
The Big Bet (1985) . . . . Koko
Terminal Entry (1986) . . . . Gwen
Night of the Demons (1987) . . . . Frannie
  •• 0:57 - Topless making love with her boyfriend in a
    coffin.
Sleepaway Camp III: Teenage Wasteland (1989)
. . . . Arab
  •• 0:16 - Topless putting sweatshirt on.
Why Me? (1990) . . . . Hostess

Texter, Gilda

Films:
Angels Hard as They Come (1971) . . . . Astrid
  • 0:26 - Brief topless several times when bad guys try
    to rape her. Dark.
Vanishing Point (1971) . . . . Nude Rider
  • 1:17 - Topless riding motorcycle.
  ••• 1:19 - Topless riding motorcycle and walking around
    without wearing any clothes. Long scene.

Thackray, Gail

Films:
In Search of the Perfect 10 (1986) . . Perfect Girl #5
(Shot on video tape.)
  ••• 0:31 - Topless and buns trying on all sorts of lingerie
    in dressing room.

Party Favors (1987) . . . . Nicole
(Shot on video tape.)
  • 0:04 - Topless in dressing room with the other three
    girls changing into blue swimsuit.
  • 0:11 - Brief left breast in the swimsuit during dance
    practice.
  • 0:12 - Topless during dance practice.
  • 0:17 - More topless during dance practice.
  •• 0:42 - Topless doing strip routine at anniversary par-
    ty. Great buns in G-string shots.
  ••• 1:01 - Topless and buns in G-string after stripping
    from cheerleader outfit. Lots of bouncing breast
    shots. Mingling with the men afterwards.
  • 1:16 - Nude by the swimming pool during the final
    credits.
Takin' It All Off (1987) . . . . Hannah
Death Feud (1989) . . . . Harry's Girl Friend
  •• 1:12 - Topless on bed with Harry.
  1:16 - In black lingerie on boat with Harry.

Theel, Lynn

Films:
Fyre (1979) . . . .
Humanoids from the Deep (1980) . . . . Peggy Larsen
  • 0:30 - Brief topless getting raped on the beach by a
    humanoid.
  • 0:51 - Brief topless, dead, lying on the beach all cov-
    ered with seaweed.
Without Warning (1980) . . . . Beth
Hollywood Boulevard II (1989) . . . . Ann Gregory

Thelen, Jodi

Films:
Four Friends (1981) . . . . Georgia
  •• 0:17 - Left breast in open blouse three times with her
    three male friends.
  0:58 - In pink bra taking off her blouse.
The Black Stallion Returns (1983) . . . . Tabari
Twilight Time (1983) . . . . Lena
Made for TV Movies:
Follow Your Heart (1990) . . . . Cecile

Theodore, Sondra

Video Tapes:
Playboy's Wet and Wild (1989) . . . .
Magazines:
Playboy (Jul 1977) . . . . Playmate

Thomas, Betty

Films:
Jackson County Jail (1976) . . . . Waitress
Tunnelvision (1976) . . . .
Loose Shoes (1977) . . . . Biker Chick #1
  • 0:02 - Brief right breast dancing on the table during
    the *Skateboarders from Hell* sketch.

Used Cars (1980) . . . . .Bunny
　　0:37 - Dancing on top of a car next to Kurt Russell
　　wearing pasties to attract customers (wearing a bru-
　　nette wig).
Homework (1982). . . . .
Troop Beverly Hills (1989) . . . . Velda Plendor
TV:
Hill Street Blues (1981-87). . . . . Lucy Bates

Thomas, Heather
Films:
Zappedl (1982). .Jane Mitchell
　　0:20 - Brief open sweater, wearing a bra when Scott
　　Baio uses telekinesis to open it.
　　1:28 - Body double, very, very brief topless in photo
　　that Willie Aames gives to Robby.
　　1:29 - Body double brief topless when Baio drops her
　　dress during the dance.
Cyclone (1986). .Teri Marshall
Deathstone (1986) . . . .
Red Blooded American Girl (1988) . . . . Paula Bukowsky
　　1:19 - Lower half of right breast when Andrew
　　Stevens is on top of her. Very, very brief silhouette of
　　right breast. Probably a body double.
TV:
Co-ed Fever (1979). . . . . Sandi
The Fall Guy (1981-86) . . . . .Jodi Banks
The Ultimate Challenge (1991-) . . . . Co-Host

Thompson, Cynthia Ann
Films:
Cave Girl (1985) . . . . .Eba
•• 1:04 - Topless making love with Rex.
Tomboy (1985) . . . . Amanda
　• 0:23 - Brief right breast getting out of car in auto re-
　　pair shop.
　•• 1:02 - Topless delivering drinks to two guys in the
　　swimming pool.
Not of This Earth (1988) . . . . Third Hooker (black dress)

Thompson, Emma
Wife of actor/director Kenneth Branagh.
Films:
Henry V (1989) . . . . .Princess Katherine
The Tall Guy (1990) . . . . Kate
••• 0:33 - Very brief right breast, brief buns, then topless
　　during funny love making scene with Jeff Goldblum.
Dead Again (1991) . . . . Margaret Strauss/Jane Doe

Thompson, Lea
Films:
All The Right Moves (1983) . . . . .Lisa
••• 1:00 - Topless, getting undressed and into bed with
　　Tom Cruise in his bedroom.
Jaws 3 (1983) . . . . .Kelly Ann Bukowski

Red Dawn (1984). . . . . Erica
The Wild Life (1984). . . . . Anita
　　0:38 - In bra and panties putting body stocking on.
Back to the Future (1985) . . . . . . Lorraine Baines-McFly
Howard the Duck (1986) . . . . Beverly Switzler
SpaceCamp (1986) . . . . Kathryn
Some Kind of Wonderful (1987). . . . . . . Amanda Jones
Casual Sex? (1988) . . . . .Stacy
　　0:27 - Buns, lying down at nude beach with Victoria
　　Jackson.
　　0:30 - Buns at the beach. Pan shot from her feet to
　　her head.
Going Undercover (1988; British)
　. . . . . .Marigold De La Hunt
The Wizard of Loneliness (1988). . . . . Sybil
Back to the Future, Part II (1989)
　. . . . . Lorraine Baines-McFly
Back to the Future, Part III (1990)
　. . . . . Maggie McFly/Lorraine McFly
Made for Cable TV:
Tales From the Crypt: Only Sin Deep (1989; HBO)
　. . . . . .Sylvia

Thompson, Victoria
Films:
The Harrad Experiment (1973). . . . . Beth Hillyer
　　0:08 - Buns, in the bathroom while talking to Harry.
　• 0:10 - Brief topless getting into bed.
　•• 0:21 - Topless in nude encounter group.
　• 0:41 - Topless getting into the swimming pool with
　　Don Johnson and Laurie Walters.
　　0:49 - Buns, getting dressed after making love with
　　Johnson.
The Harrad Summer (1974). . . . . Beth Hillyer
　• 0:53 - Buns and brief topless running down hallway.
　　0:59 - Buns on inflatable lounge in the pool.
　　1:00 - Buns, lying face down on lounge chair.
Famous T & A (1982) . . . . Beth Hillyer
(No longer available for purchase, check your video
　store for rental.)
　• 1:07 - Brief topless scene from *The Harrad Experi-
　　ment*.

Thorne, Dyanne
Films:
Ilsa, She Wolf of the S.S. (1974) . . . . .Ilsa
　•• 0:00 - Buns, then topless making love in bed.
　••• 0:01 - Topless taking a shower.
　•• 0:29 - Buns and topless in bed with the American.
　•• 0:49 - In bra, then topless undressing. Right breast
　　while lying in bed.
Ilsa, Harem Keeper of the Oil Sheiks (1978) . . . .Ilsa
Ilsa, The Wicked Warden (1980). . . . . .Ilsa
Hellhole (1985) . . . . Chrysta

Thornton, Sigrid

Films:

The Day After Halloween (1978; Australian) . Angela
a.k.a. Snapshot
- • 0:04 - Very brief topless in ad photos on wall.
- •• 0:19 - Topless during modeling session at the beach.
- ••• 0:21 - More topless at the beach.
- •• 0:37 - Topless in magazine ad several times.
- • 0:43 - Brief right breast in magazine ad.
- • 0:46 - Topless in ad again.
- • 1:18 - Entering room covered with the ad.
  1:20 - In beige bra in room with weirdo guy.
The Man from Snowy River (1982; Australian). . . .Jessica
Slate, Wyn & Me (1987; Australian) . . . . . Blanche/Max
The Lighthorsemen (1988; Australian). . . . . .Anne
Return to Snowy River (1988) . . . . .Jessica
TV:
Paradise (1989-90) . . . . Amelia Lawson
Guns of Paradise (1991-) . . . . Amelia Lawson

Thulin, Ingrid

Films:
Brink of Life (1957; Swedish/B&W) . . . . Cecila
Wild Strawberries (1957; Swedish/B&W)
. . . . Marianne Borg
The Magician (1959; B&W). . . . . Manda Aman
The Four Horsemen of the Apocalypse (1962)
. . . . Marguerite Laurier
The Winter Light (1963; Swedish/B&W)
. . . . Marta Lundberg
Hour of the Wolf (1968; Swedish) . . . . .Veronica Vogler
The Damned (1969; German). . .Sophie Von Essenbeck
- •• 1:23 - Topless in bed with Frederick. Long scene for
  a 1969 film.
- • 2:03 - Left breast in bed with Martin (her son in the
  film).
Cries and Whispers (1972; Swedish) . . . . .Karin
Moses (1976; British/Italian) . . . . Miriam
After the Rehearsal (1984; Swedish) . . . . .Rakel

Thurman, Uma

Films:
Kiss Daddy Goodnight (1987) . . . . Laura
Dangerous Liaisons (1988) . . . . . . Cécile de Volanges
- ••• 0:59 - Topless taking off her nightgown in her bed-
  room with John Malkovich.
Johnny Be Good (1988) . . . . Georgia Elkans
The Adventures of Baron Munchausen (1989)
. . . . .Venus/Rose
  1:14 - Brief upper half of right breast when the flying
  ladies wrap her with the flowing cloth.
Henry & June (1990). . . . . June Miller
Where the Heart Is (1990) . . . . Daphne McBain
- • 0:08 - Topless during art film, but her entire body is
  artfully painted to match the background paintings.
  The second segment.
  0:40 - More topless with body painted posing for her
  sister. Long shot.

1:16 - In slide of painting taken at 0:40.
1:43 - Same painting from 0:40 during the end cred-
its.
Made for TV Movies:
Robin Hood (1991) . . . . Maid Marian
Magazines:
Playboy (Dec 1990) . . . . .Sex Stars of 1990
- • 179: Left breast, while kneeling. B&W.

Ticotin, Rachel

Films:
Fort Apache, The Bronx (1981). . . . . Isabelle
- • 1:25 - Brief upper half of breasts in bathtub while
  Paul Newman pours bubble bath in.
Critical Condition (1987) . . . . Rachel
Total Recall (1990) . . . . .Melina
Made for Cable Movies:
Prison Stories, Women on the Inside (1990; HBO) . . . Iris
  0:07 - Brief buns, squatting while getting strip
  searched in jail. Don't see her face.
Made for TV Movies:
Spies, Lies & Naked Thighs (1988). . . . . .Sonia
TV:
For Love and Honor (1983) . . . . Cpl. Grace Pavlik
Ohara (1987-88) . . . . Teresa Storm

Tilly, Meg

Sister of actress Jennifer Tilly.
Films:
Fame (1980) . . . . Principal Dancer
Tex (1982). . . . . Jamie Collins
The Big Chill (1983). . . . . Chloé
One Dark Night (1983) . . . . .Julie
Psycho II (1983) . . . . Mary
  0:35 - Buns and very brief topless of body double,
  getting out of the shower while Anthony Perkins
  watches through a peep hole.
Impulse (1984) . . . . Jenny
  0:58 - In wet red swimsuit in photograph, then top-
  less in B&W photograph (don't see her face) when
  Tim Matheson looks at photos.
Agnes of God (1985) . . . . Sister Agnes
Off Beat (1986) . . . . Rachel Wareham
Masquerade (1988) . . . . Olivia Lawrence
  0:55 - In pink nightgown in bedroom.
The Girl in a Swing (1989) . . . . Karin Foster
- •• 0:44 - In white bra, then topless and buns.
- •• 0:50 - Nude, swimming under water.
- ••• 1:14 - Topless sitting on swing, then making love.
  1:18 - In white bra, sitting in front of a mirror.
- ••• 1:44 - Topless at the beach.
Valmont (1989) . . . . Tourvel
The Two Jakes (1990). . . . . Kitty Berman
Made for Cable TV:
Nightmare Classics: Carmilla (1989; HBO) . . . . .Carmilla
Made for TV Movies:
In the Best Interest of the Child (1990). . Jennifer Colton

Tippo, Patti
Films:
10 to Midnight (1983). . . . . Party Girl
  •• 0:52 - Topless, making love with a guy in the laundry
    room at a party when Andrew Stevens surprises
    them.
Omega Syndrome (1986) . . . . Sally
Sid and Nancy (1986; British) .Tanned and Sultry Blonde
Brain Dead (1989). . . . . Resident

Tolan, Kathleen
Films:
Death Wish (1974). . . . . Carol Toby
  • 0:09 - Brief topless and buns getting raped by three
    punks.
The Line (1982) . . . .
The Rosary Murders (1987). . . . . Sister Ann Vania

Tolo, Marilu
Films:
The Oldest Profession (1967) . . "Anticipation" sequence
    1:23 - Brief side view of left breast walking to the
    bathroom. Shown as a negative image, so it's hard
    to see.
Confessions of a Police Captain (1971) . .Serena Li Puma
Bluebeard (1972) . . . . Brigitt
  • 1:25 - Topless in sheer blue blouse arguing with Ri-
    chard Burton.
  •• 1:27 - Topless getting whipped by Burton.
Beyond Fear (1975). .Nicole
The Greek Tycoon (1978) . . . . Sophia Matalas
Magazines:
Playboy (Nov 1978) . . . . Sex in Cinema 1978
  • 184: Upper half of left breast.

Tomasino, Jeana
Films:
History of the World, Part I (1981). . . . .
Looker (1981). . . . . Suzy
The Beach Girls (1982) . . . . .Ducky
  •• 0:12 - Topless and buns, lying on the beach with Gin-
    ger, while a guy looks through a telescope.
  ••• 0:54 - Topless on a sailboat with a guy.
  • 0:55 - Brief topless on the beach after being "saved"
    after falling off the boat.
  •• 1:12 - Topless in sauna with Ginger and an older guy.
10 to Midnight (1983) . . . . Karen
    0:26 - In white lingerie changing in bedroom while
    the killer watches from inside the closet.
Double Exposure (1983) . . . . Renee
  • 0:20 - Very brief glimpse of left breast under water in
    swimming pool.
Up the Creek (1984) . . . . Molly
Magazines:
Playboy (Nov 1980) . . . . Playmate

Tompkins, Angel
Films:
Hang Your Hat on the Wind (1969) . . . . Fran Harper
I Love My Wife (1970) . . . . Helene Donnelly
Prime Cut (1972). Clarabelle
  • 1:03 - Very brief left breast sitting up in bed to talk to
    Lee Marvin.
    1:04 - Very brief back side view of left breast jumping
    out of bed.
The Don is Dead (1973). . . . . Ruby
How to Seduce a Woman (1973) . . . . Pamela
    1:28 - In bra and panties for a long time getting a
    massage in bedroom.
The Teacher (1974) . . . . .Diane Marshall
  ••• 0:09 - Topless on a boat taking off her swimsuit.
  ••• 0:12 - More topless on the boat getting a suntan.
  ••• 0:36 - Topless taking off her top in bedroom, then
    buns and topless taking a shower.
  • 0:41 - Brief right breast lying back on bed.
  •• 0:43 - Brief topless opening her bathrobe for Jay
    North.
  •• 0:47 - Side view of right breast lying on bed, then
    right breast from above.
  •• 0:52 - Topless in boat after making love.
Walking Tall, Part II (1975) . . . . .Marganne Stilson
The Farmer (1977). . . . . Betty
The Bees (1978). . . . . Sandra Miller
One Man Jury (1978). . . . . Kitty
Alligator (1980) .News Reporter
The Naked Cage (1985) . . . . Diane Wallace
  •• 0:22 - In lingerie, then topless with Abbey.
  • 0:38 - Brief right breast, in bed with Abbey.
Dangerously Close (1986) . . . . Mrs. Waters
Murphy's Law (1986) .Jan
  • 0:19 - Topless doing a strip routine on stage while
    Charles Bronson watches.
  • 0:27 - Brief topless doing another routine.
Amazon Women on the Moon (1987) . . . . . . .First Lady
    1:00 - In white nightgown, then black bra, panties,
    garter belt and stockings.
A Tiger's Tale (1988). . . . . La Vonne
Crack House (1989) . . . . Mother
Relentless (1989). . . . . .Carmen
Made for Cable TV:
The Hitchhiker: Homebodies . . . . Janet O'Mell
TV:
Search (1972-73). . . . . .Gloria Harding
Magazines:
Playboy (Feb 1972) .Angel
  ••• 87-91: Lots of photos of her in a river.
Playboy (Jun 1972). . . . . Prime Cut
  ••• 123: Topless.
Playboy (Dec 1972) . . . . .Sex Stars of 1972
  ••• 210: Full frontal nudity.
Playboy (Dec 1973) . . . . .Sex Stars of 1973
  •• 209: Full frontal nudity.

Toothman, Lisa

Films:
Hard Rock Zombies (1985) . . . .
Witchcraft III: The Kiss of Death (1991). . Charlotte
   •• 1:02 - Buns and topless in shower with Louis while
      William has a bad dream.
   •• 1:12 - Left breast on bed with Louis, against her will.

Torek, Denise

Films:
New York's Finest (1988). . . . . Hooker #2
Sensations (1988). . . . . Phone Girl #2
   • 0:23 - Topless talking on the phone sex line.

Tough, Kelly

Video Tapes:
Playboy's Playmate Review (1982) . . . . . . Playmate
   ••• 0:27 - Camping, in bedroom setting. Nude.
Playmates at Play (1990) . . . . Making Waves
Magazines:
Playboy (Oct 1981) . . . . Playmate

Townsend, K.C.

Films:
Husbands (1970) . . . . Barmaid
All That Jazz (1979) . . . . Stripper
   • 0:21 - Topless backstage getting Joey excited before
      he goes on stage. Lit by red light.
Below the Belt (1980) . . . . Thalia

Travis, Nancy

Films:
Three Men and a Baby (1987). . . . . Sylvia
Married to the Mob (1988) . . . . .Karen Lutnig
   • 0:15 - Buns and brief side view of right breast, with
      Tony in hotel room. Brief topless in the bathtub.
Air America (1990) . . . . Corinne Landreaux
Internal Affairs (1990) . . . . .Kathleen Avila
   • 0:38 - Side view of left breast when Raymond opens
      the shower door to talk to her.
Loose Cannons (1990) . . . . Riva
Three Men and a Little Lady (1990) . . . . Sylvia

Travis, Stacey

Films:
Deadly Dreams (1988) . . . . .Librarian
Phantasm II (1988) . . . . Jeri
Dr. Hackenstein (1989) . . . . Melanie Victor
Hardware (1990) . . . . .Jill
   • 0:21 - Almost topless in shower. Brief left breast in
      bed with Moses. Lit with blue light.
   0:38 - Brief topless in bedroom seen by a guy
      through telescope. Infrared-looking effect.

Treas, Terri

Films:
The Nest (1987). . . . . .Dr. Morgan Hubbard
Deathstalker III: The Warriors From Hell (1988)
   . . . . .Camlearde
The Terror Within (1988) . . . . .Linda
The Fabulous Baker Boys (1989). . . . . Girl in Bed
   • 0:00 - Brief upper half of right breast when sheet falls
      down when she leans over in bed.
Frankenstein Unbound (1990) . . . . .Computer Voice
TV:
Seven Brides for Seven Brothers (1982-83)
   . . . . Hannah McFadden
Alien Nation (1989-90) . . . . Cathy Frankel

Trickey, Paula

Films:
Maniac Cop 2 (1990). . . . . Cheryl
   •• 0:41 - In orange two piece swimsuit on stage, then
      topless and buns in G-string.
Made for Cable TV:
Dream On: Futile Attraction (1991; HBO) . . . Janice
   •• 0:02 - Topless sitting in bed with Martin.

Tristan, Dorothy

Films:
Klute (1971). . . . . .Arlyn Page
Scarecrow (1973). . . . . .Coley
Man on a Swing (1974) . . . . Janet
Swashbuckler (1976) . . . . Alice
California Dreaming (1978). . . . . .Fay
   0:05 - In braless white top, jogging on the beach
      with Glynnis O'Connor.
   • 0:20 - Brief topless changing clothes while a group of
      boys peek through a hole in the wall.

Truchon, Isabelle

Films:
Backstab (1990). . . . . Jennifer
   •• 0:08 - In bra, then topless in back seat of car with
      James Brolin.
   • 0:16 - Buns, black panties and stockings while on the
      floor with Brolin. Brief right breast.
   • 0:18 - Brief buns in front of fireplace. Side view of
      right breast. Buns, while walking into the other
      room.
If Looks Could Kill (1991) . . . . 1st Class Stewardess

Turner, Janine

Films:
Young Doctors in Love (1982). . . . . cameo
Tai-Pan (1986) . . . . Shevaun
Monkey Shines: An Experiment in Fear (1988)
. . . . Linda Aikman
    0:01 - Side view of buns, lying in bed when Jason Be-
    ghe wakes up. Don't really see anything.
Steel Magnolias (1989) . . . . Nancy Beth Marmillion
TV:
General Hospital (1982) . . . . Laura Templeton
Northern Exposure (1990-) . . . . Maggie O'Connell

Turner, Kathleen

Films:
Body Heat (1981) . . . . Maddy Walker
  • 0:22 - Brief side view of left breast in bed with Wil-
    liam Hurt.
  •• 0:24 - Topless in a shack with Hurt.
    0:32 - Buns, getting dressed. Long shot, hard to see.
  • 0:54 - Brief left breast in bathtub. Long shot, hard to
    see.
The Man with Two Brains (1983) . Dolores Benedict
  • 0:08 - Right breast when Steve Martin is operating
    on her in the operating room.
    0:22 - In sheer lingerie in bedroom with Steve Mar-
    tin, teasing him and driving him crazy.
  • 0:36 - Buns, in hotel room with a guy about to
    squeeze her buns when Steve Martin walks in.
Crimes of Passion (1984) . . Joanna Crane/China Blue
  ••• 0:45 - Topless, wearing black panties and stockings,
    lying in bed with Bobby.
  • 1:00 - Right breast in back of a limousine with a rich
    couple.
    1:22 - In blue bra and panties.
  • 1:27 - Right breast in bed with Bobby.
Romancing the Stone (1984) . . . . Joan Wilder
The Jewel of the Nile (1985) . . . . Joan Wilder
Prizzi's Honor (1985) . . . . Irene Walker
  • 0:30 - Very brief left breast making love with Jack
    Nicholson on bed.
Peggy Sue Got Married (1986) . . . . Peggy Sue
Julia and Julia (1987; Italian) . . . . Julia
(This movie was shot using a high-definition video sys-
tem and then transferred to film.)
  ••• 0:32 - Topless making love in bed with her husband.
  ••• 1:08 - Topless, then right breast making love in bed
    with Sting.
The Accidental Tourist (1988) . . . . Sarah
Switching Channels (1988) . . . . Christy
The War of the Roses (1989) . . . . Barbara Rose
    0:06 - In braless white blouse walking around on the
    sidewalk with Michael Douglas.
V. I. Warshawski (1991) . . . . V. I. Warshawski
Made for Cable Movies:
A Breed Apart (1984; HBO) . . . . Stella Clayton
  •• 1:12 - Topless in bed with Rutger Hauer, then left
    breast.

Tweed, Shannon

Films:
Of Unknown Origin (1983; Canadian) . . Meg Hughes
  • 0:00 - Brief side view of right breast taking a shower.
Hot Dog... The Movie (1984) . . . . Sylvia Fonda
  ••• 0:42 - Topless getting undressed, then making love
    in bed and in hot tub with Harkin.
The Surrogate (1984; Canadian) . . . . Lee Wake
  ••• 0:03 - Topless taking a Jacuzzi bath.
  • 0:42 - Brief topless changing in bedroom, then in bra
    getting dressed. Long shot.
  ••• 1:02 - Topless in sauna talking with Frank. Long
    scene.
Meatballs III (1987) . . . . The Love Goddess
Steele Justice (1987). . . . . Angela
Cannibal Women in the Avocado Jungle of Death (1988)
. . . . Dr. Margot Hunt
Lethal Woman (1988). Tory
  ••• 1:04 - Topless at the beach with Derek. Brief buns in
    white bikini bottom.
In the Cold of the Night (1989) . . . . Lena
  • 0:02 - Right breast while making love with Scott.
Night Visitor (1989) . . . . Lisa Grace
Last Call (1990) . . . . Cindy/Audrey
  • 0:12 - In black body stocking, dancing on stage. Top-
    less and buns in G-string underneath.
  •• 0:29 - Right breast, on the floor with William Katt.
  •• 0:39 - Brief buns, rotating in chair with Katt. Topless
    leaning against column.
  • 0:40 - Topless on stair railing.
  • 1:01 - Left breast, while leaning against column and
    kissing Katt.
  • 1:02 - Left breast in bed with Katt.
  ••• 1:05 - Topless making love on roof with Katt.
Twisted Justice (1990) . . . . Hinkle
Night Eyes, Part 2 (1991) . . . .
Made for Cable TV:
The Hitchhiker: Doctor's Orders . . . . Dr. Rita de Roy
    0:15 - In black bra, panties, garter belt and stockings.
TV:
Falcon Crest (1982-83). . . . . Diana Hunter
Fly By Night (1991) . . . . Sally "Slick" Monroe
Video Tapes:
Playboy Video Magazine, Volume 1 . . . . . Playmate
Playmates of the Year—The '80's . . . . Playmate
Playboy's Playmate Review (1982) . . . . Playmate
  ••• 0:47 - In bed, in photo shoot by a table, by a piano,
    in bathtub.
Magazines:
Playboy (Nov 1981) . . . . Playmate
Playboy (Nov 1983) . . . . Sex in Cinema 1983
  •• 146: Topless.
Playboy (Jan 1989) . . . . Women of the Eighties
  • 249: Full frontal nudity, lying in bed. B&W photo.
Playboy (May 1991) . . . . Boss Tweeds
  ••• 144-153: Nude, with her sister, Tracy Tweed.

Twomey, Anne

Films:
Refuge (1981) . . . .
The Imagemaker (1985) . . . . Molly Grainger
    0:11 - Very, very brief topless reading newspaper in bedroom (wearing flesh colored tape over her nipples). Then in white bra and panties talking to a guy in bed.
    1:04 - In bra and skirt undressing in front of Michael Nouri.
Deadly Friend (1986) . . . . Jeannie Conway
Last Rites (1988) . . . . .Zena Pace
Made for TV Movies:
Bump in the Night (1991). . . . . Sarah

Tyrrell, Susan

Likes to only show one breast in nude scenes!
Films:
The Steagle (1971). . . . . .Louise
   • 0:48 - Brief left breast twice, lying on bed with Richard Benjamin.
Fat City (1972) . . . . .Oma
The Killer Inside Me (1975) . . . . Joyce Lakeland
Andy Warhol's Bad (1977; Italian) . . . . Mary Aiken
I Never Promised You a Rose Garden (1977) . . . . Lee
Islands in the Stream (1977) Lil
Loose Shoes (1977). . . . . Boobies
Forbidden Zone (1980; B&W) . . . . Queen Doris
  •• 0:19 - Left breast sticking out of dress, sitting on big dice with Herve Villechaize.
  •• 1:02 - Left breast sticking out of dress after fighting with the Ex-Queen.
Fast Walking (1981) . . . . Evie
Night Warning (1982) . . . . Cheryl Roberts
  • 0:17 - Left breast, sticking out of dress just before she stabs the TV repairman.
Angel (1983). . . . . Selly Mosler
Avenging Angel (1985) . . . . Selly Mosler
Flesh + Blood (1985) . . . . .Celine
  • 1:35 - Right breast sticking out of her dress when everybody throws their clothes into the fire.
The Offspring (1986) . . . . Beth Chandler
The Underachievers (1987) . . . . Mrs. Grant
Big Top Pee Wee (1988) . . . . Midge Montana
Far From Home (1989) . . . . .Agnes Reed
  • 0:29 - Very, very brief right breast in bathtub getting electrocuted.
Cry Baby (1990) . . . . Ramona
Made for TV Movies:
Sidney Sheldon's Windmill of the Gods (1988) . . .Neusa
TV:
Open All Night (1981-82) . . . . Gretchen Feester

Tyson, Cathy

Films:
Mona Lisa (1987). . . . . Simone
Business as Usual (1988; British). . . . .
The Serpent and the Rainbow (1988)
    . . . . Dr. Marielle Duchamp
  • 0:41 - Brief topless making love with Dennis. Probably a body double, don't see her face.

Udenio, Fabiana

Films:
Hardbodies 2 (1986) . . . . .Cleo/Princess
Bride of Re-Animator (1989). . . . . . . .Francesca Danelli
    0:45 - Most of her left breast in bed with Dan. His hand covers it most of the time.
Robocop 2 (1990) . . . . Sunblock Woman
Diplomatic Immunity (1991). . . . . Teresa
  •• 1:06 - Topless in panties, on the floor with her hands tied behind her back when Klaus rips her blouse open to photograph her.

Udy, Claudia

Films:
American Nightmare (1981; Canadian). . . . .Andrea
  ••• 0:08 - Buns, then topless dancing on stage.
   • 0:22 - Buns getting into bathtub. Topless during struggle with killer.
Joy (1983; French/Canadian). . . . . .Joy
  •• 0:11 - Nude, undressing, getting into bath then into and out of bed.
  ••• 0:14 - Nude in bed with Marc.
  ••• 0:31 - In swimsuits, posing for photos, then full frontal nudity.
  •• 0:54 - Topless sitting with Bruce at encounter group.
  • 1:04 - Buns and topless getting into bathtub.
Out of Control (1984). . . . . .Tina
    0:19 - In leopard skin pattern bra and panties.
  • 0:28 - In leopard bra and panties playing Strip Spin the Bottle, then very brief topless taking off her top. Long shot.
  • 0:47 - Brief left breast getting raped by bad guy on the boat.
  • 0:54 - Brief left breast, then right breast making love with Cowboy.
Savage Dawn (1984). . . . .
Night Force (1986) . . . . Christy Hanson
  •• 0:07 - Topless making love in the stable with Steve during her engagement party.
  ••• 0:10 - Nude, fantasizing in the shower.
The Pink Chiquitas (1986; Canadian) . . . . .Helen
Dragonard (1988) . . . . .Arabella
  •• 1:11 - Topless dressed as Cleopatra dancing a routine in front of a bunch of guys.
Edge of Sanity (1988). Liza
Any Man's Death (1989) . . . . .Laura
Thieves of Fortune (1989) . . . . Marissa

Udy, Helene

Films:
Pick-Up Summer (1979; Canadian) . . . . Suzy
   0:34 - Very, very brief topless when the boys spray
   her and she jumps up.
My Bloody Valentine (1981; Canadian) . . . . Sylvia
The Dead Zone (1983) . . . . Weizak's Mother
One Night Only (1984; Canadian) . . . . Suzanne
   • 0:50 - Buns and right breast in bed talking with a
     guy.
   • 1:12 - Over the shoulder, brief left breast on top of a
     guy in bed.
The Hollywood Detective (1989). . . . .

Vaccaro, Brenda

Films:
Midnight Cowboy (1969) . . . . Shirley
   •• 1:28 - Brief topless in bed with Jon Voight.
I Love My Wife (1970). . . . . Jody Burrows
Once is Not Enough (1975) . . . . Linda
Airport '77 (1977). . . . . Eve Clayton
House by the Lake (1977; Canadian). . . . . Diane
  Topless.
The First Deadly Sin (1980) . . . . Monica Gilbert
Chanel Solitaire (1981) . . . .
Zorro, The Gay Blade (1981). . . . . Florinda
Supergirl (1984; British) . . . . Bianca
Water (1986; British). Bianca
Heart of Midnight (1988) . . . . .Betty
Edgar Allan Poe's "The Masque of the Red Death"
  (1990). . . . .
Made for TV Movies:
Paper Dolls (1982) .Julia Blake
TV:
Sara (1976). . . . . .Sara Yarnell
Dear Detective (1979)
  . . . . .Detective Sergeant Kate Hudson

Vaccaro, Tracy

Films:
The Man Who Loved Women (1983) . . . . Legs
Magazines:
Playboy (Oct 1983) . . . . Playmate

Valen, Nancy

Films:
The Heavenly Kid (1985). . . . . Melissa
Porky's Revenge (1985; Canadian) . . . . Ginger
The Big Picture (1989) . . . . .Young Sharon
Listen to Me (1989) . . . . .Mia
   • 0:06 - Very, very brief left breast in bed with Garson
    when Kirk Cameron first meets him.
Loverboy (1989) .Jenny Gordon
TV:
Hull High (1990). . . . . Donna Breedlove

van Breeschooten, Karin

Identical twin sister of Miryam van Breeschooten.
Video Tapes:
Playboy Video Calendar 1990 (1989). . . . . .October
  ••• 0:51 - Nude.
Playboy Video Centerfold: Dutch Twins (1989)
  . . . . Playmate
Magazines:
Playboy (Sep 1989) . . . . Playmate

van Breeschooten, Miryam

Identical twin sister of Karin van Breeschooten.
Video Tapes:
Playboy Video Calendar 1990 (1989). . . . . .October
  ••• 0:51 - Nude.
Playboy Video Centerfold: Dutch Twins (1989)
  . . . . Playmate
Magazines:
Playboy (Sep 1989) . . . . Playmate

Van De Ven, Monique

Films:
Turkish Delight (1974; Dutch) . . . . Olga
  •• 0:24 - Topless when Rutger Hauer opens her blouse,
    then nude on the bed.
  •• 0:27 - Topless, waking up in bed.
  ••• 0:33 - Topless on bed with Hauer, then nude getting
    up to fix flowers.
   0:42 - Buns, with Hauer at the beach.
  •• 0:46 - Topless modeling for Hauer, then brief nude
    running around outside.
  •• 0:54 - Topless in bed with open blouse with flowers.
  • 1:04 - In wet T-shirt in the rain with Hauer, then brief
    topless coming down the stairs.
Katie's Passion (1978; Dutch). . . . . .Katy
   0:38 - Brief buns when guy rips her panties off.
  •• 0:45 - Topless in hospital when a group of doctors
    examine her.
   0:50 - Left breast a couple of times talking to a doc-
    tor. Brief buns sitting down.
   1:12 - Buns, getting into bed.
  ••• 1:18 - Nude burning all her old clothes and getting
    into bathtub.
The Assault (1986; Dutch)
  . . . . .Truus Coster/Saskia de Graaff
Amsterdamned (1988; Dutch) . . . . .Laura
Paint It Black (1989). . . . . .Kyla Leif

Van Doren, Mamie

Films:
Running Wild (1955) . . . . Irma Bean
High School Confidential (1958; B&W) . . Gwen Dulaine
Teacher's Pet (1958; B&W). . . . . .Peggy De Fore
Sex Kittens Go to College (1960) . . . . Dr. Mathilda West
Three Nuts in Search of a Bolt (1964). . . . .Saxie Symbol
Free Ride (1986). . . . . .Debbie Stockwell

Magazines:
   Playboy (Jan 1989) . . . . Women of the Sixties
      • 156: Topless under sheer yellow dress in photo from
      1964.

Van Kamp, Merete
Films:
   The Osterman Weekend (1983) . . . . . Zuna Brickman
      •• 0:01 - Topless and brief buns in bed on a TV monitor,
      then topless getting injected by two intruders.
      • 0:35 - Brief topless on video again while Rutger Hau-
      er watches in the kitchen on TV.
      • 1:30 - Topless again on video during TV show.
   You Can't Hurry Love (1984). . . . . .Monique
   Lethal Woman (1988) . . . . .Diana/Christine
Miniseries:
   Princess Daisy (1983) . . . . Daisy
TV:
   Dallas (1985-86) . . . . Grace

Van Patten, Joyce
Films:
   Housewife (1972) . . . . Bernadette
      • 0:46 - Topless and buns on pool table getting at-
      tacked by Yaphet Kotto. Probably a body double,
      don't see her face.
         1:04 - Most of left breast getting on top of Kotto. In
         side view, you can see black tape over her nipple.
      • 1:05 - Brief side of right breast under Kotto's arm sev-
      eral times after she falls on the floor with him.
   The Falcon and the Snowman (1985) . . . . . . Mrs. Boyce
   St. Elmo's Fire (1985) . . . . Mrs. Beamish
   Blind Date (1987) . . . . .Nadia's Mother
   Monkey Shines: An Experiment in Fear (1988)
      . . . . Dorothy Mann
   Trust Me (1989) . . . . Nettie Brown
TV:
   The Good Guys (1968-70) . . . . Claudia Gramus

Van Vooren, Monique
Films:
   Tarzan and the She-Devil (1953) . . . . Lyra
   Gigi (1958). . . . . .Showgirl
   Ash Wednesday (1973) . . . . .German Woman
   Sugar Cookies (1973) . . . . Helene
   Andy Warhol's Frankenstein
      (1974; Italian/German/French) . . . . Katherine
      •• 0:47 - Topless in bed with Nicholas. Brief lower fron-
      tal nudity twice when he rolls on top of her.
      • 1:21 - Left breast letting Sascha, the creature, caress
      her breast.
      • 1:26 - Topless, dead, when her breasts pop out of her
      blouse.
   Wall Street (1987) . . . .

Vander Woude, Teresa
Films:
   Killer Workout (1987) .Jaimy
      a.k.a. Aerobi-Cide
      •• 0:43 - Topless in locker room with Tommy during his
      nightmare.
   Night Visitor (1989) . . . . Kelly Fremont

Vanity
Singer.
a.k.a. D. D. Winters.
Real name is Denise Matthews.
Films:
   Tanya's Island (1980; Canadian) . . . . .Tanya
      0:04 - Very brief topless and buns covered with paint
      during B&W segment.
      ••• 0:07 - Nude caressing herself and dancing during the
      opening credits.
      •• 0:09 - Nude making love on the beach.
      0:11 - Brief right breast, while talking to Lobo.
      •• 0:19 - Brief topless on the beach with Lobo, then
      more topless while yelling at him.
      • 0:28 - Mostly topless in flimsy halter top exploring a
      cave.
      • 0:33 - Full frontal nudity undressing in tent.
      • 0:35 - Left breast sleeping. Dark, hard to see.
      0:37 - Buns while sleeping.
      • 0:40 - Topless superimposed over another scene.
      0:48 - Brief buns swimming in the ocean.
      •• 0:51 - Full frontal nudity walking out of the ocean
      and getting dressed.
      • 0:53 - Brief topless in open blouse.
      •• 1:08 - Topless in middle of compound when Lobo
      rapes her in front of Blue.
      • 1:16 - Full frontal nudity running through the jungle
      in slow motion. Brief buns.
   Terror Train (1980; Canadian) . . . . Merry
   The Best of Sex and Violence (1981) . . . . .Tanya
      • 0:24 - Buns and topless in various scenes from *Tan-
      ya's Island.*
   Famous T & A (1982) . . . . .Tanya
      (No longer available for purchase, check your video
      store for rental.)
      • 1:02 - Topless scenes from *Tanya's Island.*
   The Last Dragon (1985). . . . . .Laura
   52 Pick-Up (1986) . . . . Doreen
      ••• 0:50 - Topless, stripping in room while Roy Scheider
      takes Polaroid pictures.
   Never Too Young to Die (1986). . . . . .Donja Deering
      0:25 - In white bra in the kitchen with John Stamos
      while he tends to her wounded arm.
      • 1:04 - Wearing a bikini swimsuit, putting on suntan
      lotion. Brief topless in quick cuts making love with
      John in a cabin bedroom.
   Deadly Illusion (1987) . . . . .Rina
   Action Jackson (1988) . . . . Sydney Ash
      •• 0:29 - Topless in bed with Craig T. Nelson.

Made for Cable Movies:
Memories of Murder (1990; Lifetime) . . . . Carmen
Magazines:
Playboy (Jan 1985) . . . . The Girls of Rock 'n' Roll
106:
Playboy (May 1985) . . . .
83-87:
Playboy (Sep 1986) . . . . Playboy Gallery
129: Photo taken Jan 1981
Playboy (Apr 1988) . . . . Vanity
••• 68-79: Nude.
Playboy (Dec 1988) . . . . Sex Stars of 1988
••• 185: Topless.
Playboy (Jan 1989) . . . . Women of the Eighties
•• 256: Right breast.
Playboy (Oct 1989) . . . . Grapevine
• 175: Upper half topless in B&W photo.

Vargas, Valentina
Films:
The Name of the Rose (1986) . . . . The Girl
••• 0:46 - Topless and buns making love with Christian
Slater in the monastery kitchen.
The Big Blue (1988) . . . . Bonita

Vasquez, Roberta
Films:
Easy Wheels (1989) . . . . Tondalco
Picasso Trigger (1989) . . . . Pantera
Street Asylum (1989) . . . . Kristen
Guns (1990) . . . . Nicole Justin
•• 0:50 - Right breast while making love on motorcycle
with her boyfriend.
The Rookie (1990) . . . . Heather Torres
Video Tapes:
Playmate Playoffs . . . . Playmate
Playboy Video Calendar 1987 (1986) . . . . Playmate
Playboy's Wet and Wild (1989) . . . .
Playmates at Play (1990) . . . . Hardbodies
Magazines:
Playboy (Nov 1984) . . . . Playmate

Vaughn, Linda Rhys
Video Tapes:
Playboy's Playmate Review (1982) . . . . . . Playmate
••• 1:06 - On horseback. Next to stream. Nude.
Playmates at Play (1990) . . . . Bareback
Magazines:
Playboy (Apr 1982) . . . . Playmate

Vega, Isela
Films:
Bring Me the Head of Alfredo Garcia (1974) . . Elita
• 0:25 - Brief right breast a couple of times, then brief
topless in bed with Warren Oaks.
••• 0:44 - Topless when Kris Kristofferson rips her top off.
Long scene.

•• 0:52 - Topless sitting in shower with wet hair.
•• 1:49 - Still from shower scene during credits.
Drum (1976) . . . . Marianna
• 0:04 - Topless in bed with the maid, Rachel.
•• 0:22 - Brief topless standing next to the bed with
Maxwell.
The Streets of L.A. (1979) . . . .
Barbarosa (1982) . . . . Josephina
Magazines:
Playboy (Jul 1974) . . . . Viva Vega
Nude scenes from *Bring Me the Head of Alfredo Garcia.*
Playboy (Nov 1976) . . . . Sex in Cinema 1976
•• 155: Topless.

Venora, Diane
Films:
Wolfen (1981) . . . . Rebecca Neff
The Cotton Club (1984) . . . . Gloria Swanson
Terminal Choice (1985; Canadian) . . . . Anna
0:44 - In lingerie, talking to Frank.
• 0:48 - Brief left breast, making love in bed with
Frank. Don't see her face.
F/X (1986) . . . . Ellen
0:37 - Walking around her apartment in a white slip.
Bird (1988) . . . . Chan Richardson Parker

Venus, Brenda
Films:
The Eiger Sanction (1975) . . . . George
• 0:50 - Very brief topless opening her blouse to get
Clint Eastwood to climb up a hill.
• 1:06 - Topless taking off her clothes in Eastwood's
room, just before she tries to kill him. Dark, hard to
see.
Swashbuckler (1976) . . . . Bath Attendant
48 Hours (1982) . . . . Hooker
Magazines:
Playboy (Jul 1986) . . . . Henry's Venus
•• 72-79: B&W photos. Full frontal nudity with lots of
diffusion.

Verkaik, Petra
Video Tapes:
Playboy Video Calendar 1991 (1990) . . . . November
••• 0:45 - Nude.
Playboy's Sexy Lingerie II (1990) . . . .
Magazines:
Playboy (Dec 1989) . . . . Playmate

Vernon, Kate
Daughter of actor John Vernon.
Films:
Chained Heat (1983; U.S./German) . . . . Cellmate
Alphabet City (1984) . . . . Angie
Roadhouse 66 (1984) . . . . Melissa Duran
• 1:03 - Brief topless in back of car with Judge Rein-
hold. Dark.

Pretty in Pink (1986) . . . . .Benny
The Last Days of Philip Banter (1987) . . . . Brent
Hostile Takeover (1988; Canadian) . . . . Sally
  a.k.a. Office Party
  • 0:35 - Very brief, left breast undressing in office with
    John Warner. Dark.
  •• 0:39 - Right breast, turning over in her sleep, then
    playing with the chain.
Made for TV Movies:
Daughters of Privilege (1990) . . . . Diana

Veronica, Christina

a.k.a. Christina Veronique.
Films:
  Sexpot (1986) . . . . .Betty
  ••• 0:28 - In bra, then topless with her two sisters when
    their bras pop off. (She's on the left.)
  •• 0:46 - Topless taking off her top in boat with Gorilla.
  • 0:54 - Topless lying on the grass with Gorilla.
  • 1:28 - Topless during outtakes of 0:28 scene.
  Thrilled to Death (1988) . . . . .Satin
  •• 0:33 - Topless talking to Cliff during porno film
    shoot.
  Girlfriend from Hell (1989) . . . . Dancer
  ••• 1:17 - Topless dancing on stage in club.
  Party Incorporated (1989) . . . . .Christina
  ••• 0:52 - Buns and topless dancing in front of every-
    body at party.
Roadhouse (1989). . . . . .Strip Joint Girl
A Woman Obsessed (1989) . . . . Crystal the Maid
Corporate Affairs (1990) . . . . .Tanning Woman
  0:47 - Side of right breast, getting tanned.

Verrell, Cec

Films:
  Runaway (1984) . . . . Hooker
  •• 0:44 - Topless in hotel bathroom while Tom Selleck
    sneaks into her room.
Hollywood Vice Squad (1986) . . . . Judy
Silk (1986) . . . . Jenny Sleighton
  Hell Comes to Frogtown (1987) . . . . .Centinella
  •• 0:19 - Topless taking off her blouse and getting into
    sleeping bag with Roddy Piper. Brief topless again
    after he throws her off him.

Veruschka

Ballet dancer.
Films:
  Blow-Up (1966; British/Italian). . . . . .Veruschka
  The Bride (1985) . . . . Countess
Magazines:
  Playboy (Jan 1989) . . . . Women of the Seventies
  •• 214: Topless wearing body paint.

Vetri, Victoria

a.k.a. *Playboy* Playmate Angela Dorian.
Films:
  Group Marriage (1972) .Jan
  ••• 0:28 - Buns and topless getting into bed with Dennis,
    Sander and Chris. More topless sitting in bed. Long
    scene.
  • 1:19 - Brief side view of right breast in lifeguard
    booth.
  Invasion of the Bee Girls (1973) . . . . .Julie Zorn
  • 0:30 - Brief topless getting molested by jerks.
  ••• 1:19 - Topless in the bee transformer, then brief buns
    getting rescued.
Made for TV Movies:
  Night Chase (1970) . . . .
Magazines:
  Playboy (Sep 1967) . . . . Playmate
  Used alternate name of Angela Dorian for the centerfold.
  Playmate of the Year 1968.
  Playboy (Nov 1972) . . . . Sex in Cinema 1972
  • 166: Topless in a photo from *Group Marriage*. Small
    photo, hard to see anything.

Vickers, Vicki

a.k.a. Adult film actress Raven.
Films:
  Penthouse Love Stories (1986)
  . . . . Snapshot and Loveboat Woman
  ••• 0:37 - Nude, taking pictures of herself.
  •• 0:51 - Topless on hammock watching Julie Parton.
  •• 0:55 - Left breast, twice while lying on hammock.
Angel Eyes (1991) . . . .
Video Tapes:
  The Girls of Penthouse (1984) . . . . .The Locket
  ••• 0:17 - Topless, then nude, making love.

Vogel, Darlene

Films:
  Back to the Future, Part II (1989) . . . . Spike
  Ski School (1990). . . . . Lori
  • 1:03 - Topless in bed with Johnny.

Vold, Ingrid

Films:
  Side Roads (1988) . . . . .Bonnie Velasco
  • 0:29 - Brief topless in motel room, getting undressed
    and carried into bed by Joe.
  0:30 - In white lingerie, talking with Joe. Long scene.
  0:56 - In white bra and panties, changing clothes.
  • 1:45 - Brief topless in mirror, getting out of bed.
Communion (1989) . . . . uncredited Magician's Assistant
  Angel of Passion (1991) . . . . Vanessa
  • 1:01 - Brief topless posing on the couch for the pho-
    tographer.

213

Von Palleske, Heidi
Films:
Dead Ringers (1988) . . . . Cary
  • 0:45 - Brief left breast sticking out of bathrobe talking
    to Jeremy Irons in the bathroom.
Renegades (1989) . . . . Hooker in Bar

Voorhees, Deborah
a.k.a. Debisue Voorhees.
Films:
Avenging Angel (1985) . . . . Roxie
Friday the 13th, Part V—A New Beginning (1985)
. . . . Tina
  ••• 0:41 - Topless after making love with Eddie, then ly-
    ing down and relaxing just before getting killed.
  • 0:43 - Buns and brief left breast when Eddie turns her
    over and discovers her dead.
Appointment with Fear (1988) . . . . Ruth
  • 0:21 - Very, very brief side view of left breast taking
    off bra to go swimming, then very brief topless get-
    ting out of the pool.

Vorgan, Gigi
Films:
Hardcore (1979) . . . . Teenage Girl
  • 0:32 - Topless on sofa in Peter Boyle's apartment.
Children of a Lesser God (1986) . . . . Announcer
Rain Man (1988) . . . . Voice-Over Actress
Red Heat (1988) . . . . Audrey
Vital Signs (1989) . . . . Nell

Wagner, Lindsay
Films:
Two People (1973) . . . . Deidre McCluskey
  (Not available on video tape.)

Wagner, Lori
Films:
Caligula (1980) . . . .
  (X-rated, 147 minute version.)
  ••• 1:16 - Nude, making love with Anneka Di Lorenzo.
    Long scene.
UHF (1989) . . . . Mud Wrestler
Magazines:
Penthouse (Feb 1991) . . . . Lori–Caligula Revisited
  •• Nude in recent photos and Caligula photos.

Wahl, Corinne
See: Alphen, Corinne.

Walker, Arnetia
Films:
The Wizard of Speed & Time (1988) . . . .
Scenes from the Class Struggle in Beverly Hills
  (1989) . . . . To-Bel
  • 0:37 - Topless making love with Frank on the sofa.
  •• 1:10 - Topless in bed waking up with Howard.
  ••• 1:23 - Topless making love on top of Ed Begley, Jr. on
    the floor.
Made for Cable Movies:
Cast a Deadly Spell (1991; HBO) . . . . Hipolite Kropolkin

Walker, Kathryn
Films:
Midnight Dancer (1987; Australian) . . . . Kathy
  a.k.a. Belinda
Dangerous Game (1988; Australian) . . . . Kathryn
  • 1:19 - Very, very brief topless when her black top is
    pulled up while struggling with Murphy.

Wallace Stone, Dee
a.k.a. Dee Wallace.
Wife of actor Christopher Stone.
Films:
The Hills Have Eyes (1977) . . . . Lynne Wood
10 (1979) . . . . Mary Lewis
The Howling (1981) . . . . Karen White
E.T. The Extraterrestrial (1982) . . . . Mary
Cujo (1983) . . . . Donna
Secret Admirer (1985) . . . . Connie Ryan
Critters (1986) . . . . Helen Brown
Shadow Play (1986) . . . . Morgan Hanna
  • 1:06 - Brief topless making love with Ron Kuhlman.
    Kind of dark and hard to see.
The Christmas Visitor (1987) . . . . Elizabeth
Club Life (1987) . . . . Tilly Francesca
I'm Dangerous Tonight (1990) . . . . Wanda
Popcorn (1991) . . . . Suzanne
Made for TV Movies:
Sins of Innocence (1986) . . . . Vicki McGary
Addicted to his Love (1988) . . . . Betty Ann Brennan
Stranger on My Land (1988) . . . . Annie
TV:
Together We Stand (1986) . . . . Lori Randall

Walter, Jessica
Films:
Lilith (1964; B&W) . . . . Laura
Grand Prix (1966) . . . . Pat
The Group (1966) . . . . Libby MacAusland
Play Misty for Me (1971) . . . . Evelyn
  • 0:13 - Very brief right breast in bed with Clint East-
    wood. Lit with blue light. Hard to see anything.
The Flamingo Kid (1984) . . . . Phyllis Brody
Miniseries:
Wheels (1978) . . . . Ursula
Bare Essence (1983) . . . . Ava Marshall

TV:
For the People (1965) . . . . Phyllis Koster
Amy Prentiss (1974-75). . . . . Amy Prentiss
All That Glitters (1977) . . . . Joan Hamlyn

Walters, Julie
Films:
Educating Rita (1983; British) . . . . Rita
She'll be Wearing Pink Pyjamas (1985; British)
. . . . Fran
- ••• 0:07 - Full frontal nudity taking a shower with the other women. Long scene.
- •• 0:58 - Nude, undressing and going skinny dipping in mountain lake, then getting out. Nice bun shot walking into the lake.
Personal Services (1987) . . . . Cynthia Payne
- • 0:21 - Very brief side view of left breast, while reaching to turn off radio in the bathtub. Her face is covered with cream.
Prick Up Your Ears (1987; British) . . . . Elise Orton
Buster (1988) . . . . June

Walters, Laurie
Films:
The Harrad Experiment (1973) . . . . Sheila Grove
- • 0:29 - Topless in white panties with Don Johnson.
- • 0:40 - Nude taking off blue dress and getting into the swimming pool with Johnson.
The Harrad Summer (1974) . . . . Sheila Grove
0:02 - Topless undressing in bathroom. Long shot, out of focus.
- •• 1:00 - Topless lying face up getting a tan on lounge chair, then buns getting up and pushing Harry into the pool.
Famous T & A (1982) . . . . Sheila Grove
(No longer available for purchase, check your video store for rental.)
- • 1:08 - Topless scene from *The Harrad Experiment*.
- • 1:11 - Full frontal nude scene from *The Harrad Experiment*.
Made for TV Movies:
Eight is Enough: A Family Reunion (1987)
. . . . Joannie Bradford
TV:
Eight is Enough (1977-81) . . . . Joannie Bradford

Waltrip, Kim
Films:
Pretty Smart (1986). . . . . . . Sara Gentry (the teacher)
- •• 0:53 - Topless sunbathing with her students.
Nights in White Satin (1987) . . . . Stevie Hughes
0:37 - In white wig, bra, panties, garter belt and stocking during photo session.
0:39 - Brief side view of left breast in black slip during photo session.
- • 0:53 - Topless in bathtub with Walker. Out of focus, hard to see.

Ward, Pamela
Films:
Hellhole (1985) . . . . Tina
School Spirit (1985) . . . . Girl in Sorority Room
- ••• 0:15 - Buns, then topless while Billy is invisible. More topless with other women in shower room.

Ward, Rachel
Wife of actor Bryan Brown.
Films:
Night School (1980) . . . . Elanor
- • 0:24 - In sheer white bra and panties, taking off clothes to take a shower. Topless taking off bra. Hard to see because she's behind a shower curtain.
0:28 - Buns, when her boyfriend rubs red paint all over her in the shower.
The Final Terror (1981). . . . . Margaret
Sharky's Machine (1981) . . . . Dominoe
Dead Men Don't Wear Plaid (1982) . . . . . . Juliet Forrest
Against All Odds (1984) . . . . Jessie Wyler
0:49 - Very brief buns lying down with Jeff Bridges.
0:50 - Wet white dress in water. Long shot, don't see anything.
1:01 - The sweaty temple scene. Erotic, but you don't really see anything.
The Good Wife (1987; Australian) . . . . Marge Hills
a.k.a. The Umbrella Woman
Hotel Colonial (1988). . . . . Irene Costa
How to Get Ahead in Advertising (1988) . . . . Julia
After Dark, My Sweet (1990) . . . . Fay Anderson
- • 1:22 - Very, very brief half of right breast under Jason Patric in bed when he moves slightly.
Made for Cable Movies:
Fortress (1985; HBO) . . . . Sally Jones
- • 0:38 - Swimming in a sheer bra underwater.
Miniseries:
The Thorn Birds (1983) . . . . Meggie Cleary
Made for TV Movies:
And the Sea Will Tell (1991) . . . . Jennifer Jenkins
Magazines:
Playboy (Mar 1984) . . . . Roving Eye
- ••• 203: Topless in photos that weren't used in *Night School*.

Warner, Julie
Films:
Flatliners (1990). . . . . One of Joe's Women
Doc Hollywood (1991) . . . . Lou

Warren, Jennifer
Films:
Night Moves (1975) . . . . Paula
- •• 0:56 - Topless in bed with Gene Hackman.
- • 0:57 - Right breast after making love in bed with Hackman.
Another Man, Another Chance (1977; U.S./French)
. . . . Mary

Slap Shot (1977). . . . . .Francine Dunlop
Ice Castles (1979) . . . . .Deborah Macland
TV:
Paper Dolls (1984) . . . . .Dinah Caswell

Wasa, Maxine

Films:
L.A. Bounty (1989). . . . . .Model
  • 0:07 - Right breast while posing for Wings Hauser while he paints. Left breast, getting up. Long shot.
  • 0:26 - Left breast while posing on couch for Hauser.
  •• 0:38 - Topless lying on couch again.
Savage Beach (1989) . . . . Sexy Beauty
  ••• 0:08 - Side view of left breast, in pool with Shane, then topless getting out of pool.
  ••• 0:10 - Topless while Shane talks on the phone.
Made for Cable TV:
Dream On: The First Episode (1990; HBO)
  . . . . Andrea Kelly
Video Tapes:
Playboy's Wet and Wild (1989) . . . .
Magazines:
Playboy (Nov 1989) . . . . Sex in Cinema 1989
  •• 134: Side view of left breast from *Savage Beach*.

Watkins, Michelle

Films:
Terms of Endearment (1983). . . . . .Woman
The Outing (1987) .Faylene
  • 0:12 - Topless taking off her top, standing by the edge of the swimming pool, then running topless through the house with panties on.

Watson, Alberta

Films:
In Praise of Older Women (1978; Canadian) . . .Mitzi
  •• 0:51 - Topless sitting in chair talking with Tom Berenger, then more topless lying in bed. Long scene.
Power Play (1978; Canadian) . . . . Donna
  0:21 - Brief topless lying on table getting shocked through her nipples.
Stone Cold Dead (1979; Canadian). . . . . . . Olivia Page
The Soldier (1982) . . . . Susan Goodman
The Keep (1983). . . . . .Eva Cuza
  • 0:59 - Very brief topless making love with Scott Glenn, then brief lower frontal nudity.
White of the Eye (1988) . . . . .Ann Mason

Way, Renee

Films:
The Newlydeads (1988) . . . .
Party Plane (1988). . . . . .Andy
  ••• 0:01 - Topless taking off her blouse to fix the plane.
  ••• 0:06 - Topless sitting on edge of spa.
  ••• 0:11 - Topless again, getting out of spa.
  • 0:12 - Brief topless dropping her towel while talking to Tim.

Wayne, April

Former model for Ujena Swimwear (*Swimwear Illustrated* magazine).
Films:
Moon in Scorpio (1987) . . . . .Isabel
  • 0:32 - Brief right breast in bed with a guy.
  • 0:35 - Brief topless putting bathing suit on in a bathroom on a boat when a guy opens the door.
Party Camp (1987) . . . . .Nurse Brenda

Wayne, Carol

Films:
The Party (1968) .June Warren
Scavenger Hunt (1979) . . . . Nurse
Savannah Smiles (1983). . . . . Doreen
Heartbreakers (1984). . . . . Candy
  0:22 - In black wig and bra posing for Peter Coyote in his studio.
  ••• 0:41 - In white bra and panties, then brief topless in the mirror stripping in front of Coyote and Nick Mancuso. Then brief topless lying in bed with Coyote.
Surf II (1984) . . . . Mrs. O'Finlay
TV:
The Tonight Show . . . . .regular
Magazines:
Playboy (Feb 1984) . . . . .101 Nights with Johnny
  ••• 56-61: Full frontal nudity.

Weatherly, Shawn

Miss South Carolina 1980.
Miss U.S.A. 1980.
Miss Universe 1980.
Films:
Cannonball Run II (1984). . . . . .Dean's Girl
Police Academy III: Back in Training (1986)
  . . . . .Cadet Adams
Shadowzone (1989). . . . . .Dr. Kidwell
Thieves of Fortune (1989) . . . . Peter
  • 1:09 - Brief topless several times, taking a shower (while wearing beard and moustache disguise).
  ••• 1:21 - Topless in white panties distracting tribe so she can get away.
TV:
Baywatch (1988-90). .Jil Riley

Weaver, Jacki

Films:
Alvin Purple (1973; Australian) . . . . Second Sugar Girl
  •• 0:33 - Brief full frontal nudity, lying in bean bag chair.
Jock Petersen (1974; Australian) . . . . . . Susie Petersen
  a.k.a. Petersen
  ••• 0:01 - Full frontal nudity lying in bed with Jock.
Picnic at Hanging Rock (1975) . . . . .Minnie
The Removalists (1975) . . . . Marilyn Carter
Caddie (1976) . . . . .Josie
Squizzy Taylor (1984). . . . . Dolly

Weaver, Sigourney

Films:

Annie Hall (1977) . . . . Alvy's Date Outside Theatre
Alien (1979) . . . . Ripley
Eyewitness (1981) . . . . Tony Sokolow
Deal of the Century (1983) . . . . Mrs. De Voto
The Year of Living Dangerously (1983; Australian)
. . . . Jill Bryant
Ghostbusters (1984) . . . . Dana Barrett
Aliens (1986). . . . . Ripley
Half Moon Street (1986) . . . . Lauren Slaughter
- • 0:05 - Brief topless in the bathtub.
- •• 0:11 - Brief topless in the bathtub again.
- • 0:18 - Brief buns and side view of right breast putting on makeup in front of the mirror. Wearing a black garter belt and stockings.
- ••• 0:39 - Topless riding exercise bike while being photographed, then brief topless getting out of the shower.
  0:46 - Very, very brief topless wearing a sheer black blouse with no bra during daydream sequence.
- • 0:50 - Brief topless in bed with Michael Caine, then left breast.
  1:16 - In braless, wet, white blouse in bathroom after knocking a guy out.
One Woman or Two (1986; French) . . . . Jessica
a.k.a. Une Femme Ou Deux
  1:30 - In braless white blouse.
- •• 1:31 - Very brief side view of left breast in bed with Gerard Depardieu.
Gorillas in the Mist (1988) . . . . Dian Fossey
Ghostbusters II (1989). . . . . Dana Barrett
Working Girl (1989) . . . . Katherine Parker
  1:22 - In white lingerie, sitting in bed, then talking to Harrison Ford.

Webb, Chloe

Films:

Sid and Nancy (1986; British) . . . . Nancy
- • 0:21 - Left breast, under Sid's arm in bed with him. Covered up, hard to see.
- •• 0:44 - Topless in bed after making love, then arguing with Sid.
Twins (1988). . . . . Linda Mason
Heart Condition (1990). . . . . Crystal
Queens Logic (1991). Patricia
Made for TV Movies:
Lucky Day (1991) . . . . Allison Campbell
TV:
Thicke of the Night (1983) . . . . regular
China Beach (1989) . . . . Laurette

Weber, Sharon Clark

See: Clark, Sharon.

Weigel, Teri

The first *Playboy* Playmate to star in adult films *after* she became a Playmate.

Adult Films:

The Barlow Affairs (1991) . . . .
Lingerie Busters (1991) . . . .
Starr (1991) . . . .
Wicked (1991) . . . .
Films:
Cheerleader Camp (1988) . . . . Pam Bently
a.k.a. Bloody Pom Poms
Glitch (1988) . . . . Lydia
  0:41 - In pink bathing suit talking to blonde guy.
- • 0:54 - Very brief side view of right breast in bathtub with dark haired guy.
Return of the Killer Tomatoes (1988) . . . Matt's Playmate
The Banker (1989) . . . . Jaynie
- ••• 0:02 - Taking off dress, then in lingerie, then topless making love with Osbourne in bed. More topless after.
Far From Home (1989) . . . . Woman in Trailer
- •• 0:16 - Topless making love when Drew Barrymore peeks in window.
Night Visitor (1989) . . . . Victim in Cellar
- • 0:50 - Brief out of focus topless changing tops in the cellar.
- • 0:55 - Right breast, during ceremony. Very brief topless just before being stabbed.
Savage Beach (1989). . . . . Anjelica
- ••• 0:33 - Topless taking off black teddy and getting into bed to make love.
- •• 0:47 - Topless making love in the back seat of car.
Marked for Death (1990). . . . . Sexy Girl #2
- • 0:39 - Brief topless on bed with Jimmy when Steven Seagal bursts into the room. (She's the brunette.)
Predator 2 (1990) . . . . Columbian Girl
- • 0:22 - Brief topless making love on bed. More topless several times being held on the floor, brief full frontal nudity getting up when the Predator starts his attack.
Video Tapes:
Playboy Video Centerfold: Teri Weigel. . . Playmate
Playboy Video Calendar 1988 (1987). . . . . Playmate
Playboy's Wet and Wild (1989). . . . .
Playboy's Sexy Lingerie II (1990) . . . .
Magazines:
Playboy (Apr 1986) . . . . Playmate

Weiss, Roberta

Films:

Autumn Born (1979) . . . . Melissa
  0:07 - Buns, wearing panties and bending over desk to get whipped.
Cross Country (1983; Canadian) . . . . Alma Jean
- •• 0:59 - Topless on bed with two other people.

217

The Dead Zone (1983) . . . . Alma Frechette
• 0:49 - Briefly in beige bra, then brief topless when the killer rips her blouse open during Christopher Walken's vision.
Abducted (1986; Canadian) . . . . Renee
Made for Cable TV:
The Hitchhiker: And If We Dream . . Rosanne Lucas
(Available on *The Hitchhiker, Volume 3*.)
•• 0:11 - Topless and buns in barn making love with Stephen Collins.
•• 0:17 - Topless in dream classroom with Collins.
• 0:23 - Brief topless in bed after second dream with Collins.

Welch, Lisa
Films:
Revenge of the Nerds (1984) . . . . Suzy
Magazines:
Playboy (Sep 1980) . . . . Playmate
118:

Welch, Tahnee
Daughter of actress Raquel Welch.
Films:
Cocoon (1985) . . . . Kitty
1:01 - Buns walking into swimming pool.
Lethal Obsession (1987) . . . . Daniela Santini
0:14 - Buns, putting on robe after talking to John on the phone.
• 0:15 - Half of left breast, taking off coat to hug John in the kitchen.
0:16 - Sort of left breast, in bed with John. Too dark to see anything.
1:16 - Buns, getting an injection.
Cocoon, The Return (1988). . . . . Kitty
TV:
Falcon Crest (1987-89) . . . . Shannon

Weller, Mary Louise
Films:
The Evil (1977) . . . . Laurie Belden
National Lampoon's Animal House (1978)
. . . . Mandy Pepperidge
••• 0:38 - In white bra, then topless in bedroom while John Belushi watches on a ladder through the window.
The Bell Jar (1979) . . . . Doreen
Blood Tide (1982). . . . . Sherry
Forced Vengeance (1982) . . . . Claire Bonner
Q (1982). . . . . Mrs. Pauley

Welles, Gwen
Films:
A Safe Place (1971). . . . . Bari
Hit (1973). Sherry Nielson
California Split (1974) . . . . Susan Peters

Nashville (1975). Sueleen Gay
•• 2:09 - In bra singing to a room full of men, then topless doing a strip tease, buns walking up the steps and out of the room.
Between the Lines (1977) . . . . Laura
•• 0:32 - Buns and topless drying off with a towel in front of a mirror.
Desert Hearts (1986) . . . . Gwen
The Men's Club (1986) . . . . Redhead
Sticky Fingers (1988) . . . . Marcie
Magazines:
Playboy (Nov 1972) . . . . . . Variation of a Vadim Theme
••• 111-115: Full frontal nudity.
Playboy (May 1975). . . . . .The Splendor of Gwen
••• 96-99: Full frontal nudity.

Welles, Terri
Films:
Looker (1981) . . . . Lisa
• 0:02 - Brief topless getting photographed for operation. In black bra and panties in her apartment a lot.
Video Tapes:
Playmates of the Year—The '80's . . . . Playmate
Magazines:
Playboy (Dec 1980) . . . . Playmate
Playboy (Jun 1981). . . . . Playmate of the Year
162-173:

Wells, Jennifer
a.k.a. Jennifer Welles.
Films:
Sugar Cookies (1973) . . . . Max's Secretary
• 0:28 - Topless in red panties in Max's office while he talks on the phone, then lower frontal nudity.
•• 0:56 - Full frontal nudity getting dressed.
The Groove Tube (1974). . . . . The Geritan Girl
•• 0:21 - Dancing nude around her husband, Chevy Chase.

Wells, Victoria
Films:
Cheech & Chong's Nice Dreams (1981)
. . . . .Beach Girl #1
• 0:29 - Brief topless on the beach with two other girls. Long shot, unsteady, hard to see.
Losin' It (1982). . . . .

Wesley, Shannon
a.k.a. Adult film actress Savannah.
Films:
Invisible Maniac (1990) . . . . Vicky
• 0:21 - Buns and very, very brief side of left breast in the shower with the other girls.
• 0:33 - Right breast covered with bubbles.
••• 0:43 - In bra, then topless and lots of buns in locker room with the other girls.

•• 0:44 - Buns and left breast in the shower with the other girls.
••• 1:04 - Undressing in locker room in white bra and panties, then topless. More topless taking a shower and getting electrocuted.

Whitaker, Christina

Films:
The Naked Cage (1985) . . . . Rita
••• 0:08 - Topless in bed with Willy.
• 0:55 - Brief topless in gaping sweatshirt during fight with Sheila.
1:28 - Panties during fight with Shari Shattuck.
1:29 - Sort of left breast in gaping dress.
Assault of the Killer Bimbos (1988) . . . . Peaches
Stormquest (1988) . . . .
Vampire at Midnight (1988) . . . . Ingrid

Whitcraft, Elizabeth

Films:
Birdy (1985) . . . . Rosanne
Angel Heart (1987) . . . . Connie
(Blonde hair.)
•• 0:33 - Topless in bed talking with Mickey Rourke while taking off her clothes.
Working Girl (1989) . . . . Doreen DiMucci
(Brunette hair.)
•• 0:29 - Topless on bed on Alec Baldwin when Melanie Griffith opens the door and discovers them.
GoodFellas (1990) . . . . Tommy's Girlfriend at Copa

White, Sheila

Films:
Here We Go Round the Mulberry Bush (1968; British)
. . . . Paula
Oliver! (1968; British) . . . . Bet
Confessions of a Window Cleaner (1974; British). . .Rosie
Confessions of a Pop Performer (1975; British) . . . .Rosie
Oh, Alfie! (1975; British) . . . . Norma
a.k.a. Alfie Darling
Miniseries:
I, Claudius—Episode 12, A God in Colchester
(1976; British) . . . . Lady Messalina
Available on video tape in *I, Claudius–Volume 6.*
•• 0:00 - Left breast, in bed with Mnester.
• 0:02 - Buns, getting out of bed and putting on a sheer dress.
• 0:18 - Right breast, in bed with Silius.
••• 0:29 - Topless in bed with Silius.

White, Vanna

Films:
Gypsy Angels . . . .
(Unreleased film.)
Graduation Day (1981) . . . . .Doris
Looker (1981) . . . . Reston Girl

Made for TV Movies:
The Goddess of Love (1988) . . . . Venus
TV:
Wheel of Fortune (1982-) . . . . Hostess
Video Tapes:
Vanna White—Get Slim, Stay Slim . . . . .Herself
Magazines:
Playboy (May 1987). . . . . Vanna
••• 134-143: In sheer lingerie from catalog she did before *Wheel of Fortune.*
Playboy (Dec 1987) . . . . .Sex Stars of 1987
••• 150: In sheer black lingerie.
Playboy (Dec 1988) . . . . .Sex Stars of 1988
•• 183: Right breast under lingerie.

Whitfield, Lynn

Films:
Doctor Detroit (1983) . . . . Thelma
Silverado (1985). . . . . Ray
The Slugger's Wife (1985) . . . . .Tina Alvarado
Dead Aim (1987) . . . . Sheila Freeman
Jaws: the Revenge (1987). . . . . Louisa
Made for Cable Movies:
The Josephine Baker Story (1991; HBO)
. . . . Josephine Baker
• 0:00 - Topless dancing during opening credits. Slow motion.
•• 0:13 - Topless taking off her dress top for the French painter.
••• 0:14 - Topless in the mirror and dancing with the painter after making love. Nice. Dancer doing splits looks like a body double.
0:16 - Brief buns, in wet dress, getting out of swimming pool.
••• 0:31 - Topless on stage doing the Banana Dance.
••• 0:33 - Topless some more, doing the Banana Dance.
• 2:02 - Brief topless dancing during flashback.
Miniseries:
Women of Brewster Place (1989) . . . . Ciel
Made for TV Movies:
Triumph of the Heart: The Ricky Bell Story (1991)
. . . . Natala
TV:
Equal Justice (1991-) . . . . Maggie Mayfield
Magazines:
Playboy (Apr 1991) . . . . Grapevine
••• 170: Topless in B&W photo from *The Josephine Baker Story.*

Whitlow, Jill

Films:
Porky's (1981; Canadian) . . . . Mindy
Mask (1985). . . . . .Annie Marie
Weird Science (1985) . . . . Perfume Salesgirl
Night of the Creeps (1986) . . . . Cynthia Cronenberg
0:31 - In bra and panties taking off sweater.
• 0:33 - Brief topless putting nightgown on over her head in her bedroom.

Thunder Run (1986) . . . . Kim
Twice Dead (1989) . . . . Robin/Myrna
   0:27 - In white slip, getting ready for bed, then walking around the house.

Whitman, Kari

Films:
Masterblaster (1986) . . . . .Jennifer
Phantom of the Mall: Eric's Revenge (1988)
. . . . Melody Austin
  •• 0:25 - Topless in bed about five times with Peter.
   Don't see her face.
Men at Work (1990) . . . . Judy

Whitton, Margaret

Films:
Love Child (1982) . . . . Jacki Steinberg
9 1/2 Weeks (1986) . . . . Molly
The Best of Times (1986) . . . . Darla
Ironweed (1987) . . . . Katrina
  •• 1:19 - Full frontal nudity leaving the house and walk-
   ing down steps while young Francis brushes a horse.
The Secret of My Success (1987) . . . . . .Vera Prescott
  • 0:31 - Very brief topless taking off swimsuit top in
   swimming pool with Michael J. Fox.
Little Monsters (1989) . . . .
Major League (1989) . . . . Rachel Phelps
Made for TV Movies:
The Summer My Father Grew Up (1991) . . . . . . Naomi
TV:
Hometown (1985) . . . . Barbara Donnelly
Fine Romance (1989) . . . . .Louisa
Good & Evil (1991-) . . . . Genny

Widdoes, Kathleen

Films:
The Group (1966) . . . . .Helena Davidson
Petulia (1968; U.S./British) . . . . .Wilma
The Sea Gull (1968) . . . . Masha
The Mephisto Waltz (1971) . . . . Maggie West
Savages (1972) . . . . Leslie
I'm Dancing as Fast as I Can (1981) . . . . . . Dr. Rawlings
The End of August (1982) . . . . Adele
Without a Trace (1983) . . . . Ms. Hauser
TV:
As the World Turns . . . . Emma Snyder
Magazines:
Playboy (Mar 1972) . . . . Savages
  • 142: Topless.
  • 145: Topless.

Wiesmeier, Lynda

Films:
Joysticks (1983) . . . . .Candy
Private School (1983) . . . . School Girl
  ••• 0:42 - Nude in shower room scene. First blonde in
   shower on the left.

Malibu Express (1984) . . . . June Khnockers
  •• 0:04 - Topless in locker room taking jumpsuit off.
  • 1:16 - Topless leaning out of racing car window while
   a helicopter chases her and Cody.
Preppies (1984) . . . . .Trini
  0:54 - In bra and panties, practicing sexual positions
   on beds with Margot.
  ••• 1:06 - Topless on bed with Mark.
R.S.V.P. (1984) . . . . Jennifer Edwards
  •• 0:11 - Topless diving into the pool while Toby fantasizes about her being nude.
  • 0:19 - Topless in kitchen when Toby fantasizes about
   her again.
  ••• 1:21 - Nude getting out of the pool and kissing Toby,
   when she really is nude.
Wheels of Fire (1984) . . . . Harley
  a.k.a. Desert Warrior
Avenging Angel (1985) . . . . Debbie
Real Genius (1985) . . . . Chris' Girl at Party
Evil Town (1987) . . . . Dianne
  ••• 0:09 - Topless on top of Tony outside while camping.
  •• 0:11 - Right breast while making out with boyfriend
   outside. Topless getting up.
  • 0:13 - Topless in open blouse running from bad guy.
   Nice bouncing action.
  •• 0:15 - Topless getting captured by bad guys.
  •• 0:17 - Topless getting out of car and brought into the
   house.
  •• 0:23 - Topless tied up in chair.
Video Tapes:
Playboy Video Magazine, Volume 2 . . . . . Playmate
Playboy's Playmate Review (1982) . . . . Playmate
  ••• 1:17 - Undressing and taking a shower. Wow! In ballet studio. Nude.
Red Hot Rock (1984) . . . . Girl in Shower
  • 0:01 - Brief upper half of buns, then topless taking off
   bra while a guy peeks into the locker room during
   "Girls" by Dwight Tilley.
  • 0:02 - Brief full frontal nudity in the shower. (On the
   left.)
Playboy's Wet and Wild (1989) . . . .
Playmates at Play (1990) . . . . Hardbodies
Magazines:
Playboy (Jul 1982) . . . . Playmate

Wild, Sandra

Video Tapes:
Playboy's Wet and Wild (1989) . . . .
Playboy's Sexy Lingerie II (1990) . . . .
Magazines:
Playboy (Aug 1991) . . . . California Dreamin'
  •• 136: Side view of right breast, bending over.

Wildsmith, Dawn

Ex-wife of director Fred Olen Ray.
Films:
Armed Response (1986) . . . . Thug
Cyclone (1986) . . . . Henna

Star Slammer—The Escape (1986) . . . . Muffin
Surf Nazis Must Die (1986) . . . . Eva
• 0:25 - Topless being fondled at the beach wearing a wet suit by Adolf. Mostly right breast.
Commando Squad (1987) . . . . Consuela
Evil Spawn (1987) . . . . .Evelyn
Phantom Empire (1987) . . . . Eddy Colchilde
The Tomb (1987) . . . . Anna Conda
••• 0:54 - Topless taking off robe in room with Michelle Bauer, then getting pushed onto a bed full of snakes.
B.O.R.N. (1988) . . . . .Singer
Deep Space (1988) . . . . .Janice
Hollywood Chainsaw Hookers (1988) . . . . Samantha
It's Alive III: Island of the Alive (1988) . . . .
Warlords (1988) . . . . Danny
Beverly Hills Vamp (1989) . . . . .Sherry Santa Monica
Alienator (1990) . . . . Caroline
Demon Sword (1991) . . . .

Wilkes, Donna

Films:
Schizoid (1980) . . . . Allison Foles
0:12 - Topless taking off her bra in bathroom while Klaus Kinski watches. Buns, getting into the shower. Out of focus shots.
•• 0:13 - Side view topless getting into the shower.
Angel (1983) . . . . Angel/Molly
Grotesque (1987) . . . . Kathy
TV:
Hello, Larry (1979) . . . . .Diane Adler

Wilkinson, June

Films:
The Immoral Mr. Teas (1959) . . . . uncredited torso
Russ Meyer film.
Sno-Line (1984) . . . . Audrey
Talking Walls (1987) . . . . Blonde
• 0:13 - Brief left breast, in car room, getting green towel yanked off.
0:14 - Very, very brief left breast in car room again. Dark.
•• 1:08 - Brief topless, getting green towel taken off.
Keaton's Cop (1990) . . . . Archie "Big Mama" Gish
Magazines:
Playboy (Jan 1989) . . . . .Women of the Fifties
••• 116: Topless, wearing a gold bikini bottom.

Williams, Barbara

Films:
Thief of Hearts (1984) . . . . Mickey Davis
(Special Home Video Version.)
• 0:16 - Right breast in bathtub when her husband comes in and tries to read her diary.
••• 0:53 - Topless making love with Steven Bauer.
Jo Jo Dancer, Your Life Is Calling (1986) . . . . Dawn
Tiger Warsaw (1988) . . . . Karen
Watchers (1988) . . . . .Nora

Williams, Edy

Films:
The Secret Life of an American Wife (1968)
. . . . Susie Steinberg
0:32 - In blonde wig wearing black bra and panties getting into bed.
1:15 - In black bra and panties again coming out of bedroom into the hallway.
Beyond the Valley of the Dolls (1970). . . . Ashley St. Ives
Russ Meyer Film. (Not available on video tape.)
The Seven Minutes (1971) . . . . Faye Osborn
Dr. Minx (1975) . . . .
Topless.
The Best of Sex and Violence (1981) . . . . . . .Herself
•• 0:46 - Topless in various scenes from *Dr. Minx*.
Famous T & A (1982) . . . . herself
(No longer available for purchase, check your video store for rental.)
•• 0:39 - Topless scenes from *Dr. Minx*.
Chained Heat (1983; U.S./German) . . . . Paula
•• 0:30 - Full frontal nudity in the shower, soaping up Twinks.
•• 0:36 - Topless at night in bed with Twinks.
Hollywood Hot Tubs (1984) . . . . Desiree
••• 0:26 - Topless, trying to seduce Shawn while he works on a hot tub.
1:26 - In black lingerie outfit in the hallway.
• 1:30 - Partial topless with breasts sticking out of her bra while she sits by hot tub with Jeff.
•• 1:32 - Topless in hot tub room with Shawn.
• 1:38 - Topless again in the hot tub lobby.
Hellhole (1985) . . . . .Vera
••• 0:22 - Topless on bed posing for Silk.
••• 0:24 - Topless in white panties in shower, then fighting with another woman.
••• 1:03 - Topless in mud bath with another woman. Long scene.
Mankillers (1987) . . . . Sergeant Roberts
Rented Lips (1988) . . . . .Heather Darling
• 0:22 - Topless in bed, getting fondled by Robert Downey, Jr. during porno movie shoot.
Bad Manners (1989) . . . . .Mrs. Slatt
Dr. Alien (1989) . . . . .Buckmeister
a.k.a. I Was a Teenage Sex Mutant
••• 0:54 - Topless taking off her top in the women's locker room in front of Wesley.
Bad Girls from Mars (1990) . . . . Emanuelle
•• 0:17 - Topless several times changing in back of convertible car.
••• 0:23 - Topless changing out of wet dress.
••• 0:30 - Topless taking off blouse to get into spa.
• 0:32 - Topless in back of Porsche and getting out.
••• 0:35 - Topless in store, signing autograph for robber.
• 0:47 - Topless taking off her top again.
••• 0:58 - Topless in T.J.'s office. More topless when wrestling with Martine.
• 1:05 - Topless tied up.
• 1:07 - Topless again.
•• 1:17 - Topless taking off her outfit during outtakes.

Magazines:
   Playboy (Mar 1973) . . . . All About Edy
   ••• 135-141: Nude.
   Playboy (Jan 1978) . . . . The Year in Sex
   •• 201: Nude in swimming pool.
   Playboy (Nov 1989) . . . . Sex in Cinema 1989
   ••• 134: Topless still from *Bad Girls From Mars*.

Williams, JoBeth

Films:
   Kramer vs. Kramer (1979) . . . . Phyllis Bernard
      • 0:45 - Buns and brief topless in the hallway meeting
         Dustin Hoffman's son.
   The Dogs of War (1980; British) . . . . Jessie
   Stir Crazy (1980) . . . . Meredith
   Endangered Species (1982) . . . . Harriet Purdue
   Poltergeist (1982) . . . . Diane Freeling
   The Big Chill (1983) . . . . Karen
   American Dreamer (1984) . . . . Cathy Palmer
   Teachers (1984) . . . . Lisa
      • 1:39 - Brief topless taking off clothes and running
         down school hallway yelling at Nick Nolte.
   Desert Bloom (1986) . . . . Lily
   Poltergeist II: The Other Side (1986) . . . . Diane Freeling
   Memories of Me (1988) . . . . Lisa McConnell
   Welcome Home (1989) . . . . Sarah
   Dutch (1991) . . . .
   Switch (1991) . . . .
Miniseries:
   The Day After (1983) . . . . Nancy
Made for TV Movies:
   Adam (1983) . . . .
   Baby M (1988) . . . . Mary Beth Whitehead
   My Name is Bill W. (1989) . . . . Lois Wilson
   Child in the Night (1990) . . . . Dr. Jackie Hollis
TV:
   Somerset (1975) . . . . Carrie Wheeler
   The Guiding Light (1977-81) . . . . Brandy Shelooe

Williams, Vanessa

   Dethroned Miss America 1984.
   Singer.
   Not the same Vanessa Williams in *New Jack City*.
Films:
   Under the Gun (1989) . . . . Samantha Richards
   Another You (1991) . . . .
   Harley Davidson & The Marlboro Man (1991) . . . .
Made for TV Movies:
   Full Exposure: The Sex Tapes (1989) . . . . Valentine
Magazines:
   Penthouse (Sep 1984) . Here She Comes, Miss America
   ••• 66-75: B&W nude photos.
   Penthouse (Nov 1984) . . . . Tom Chaipel interview
   ••• 85-89: More B&W nude photos.

Williams, Wendy O.

   Lead singer of *The Plasmatics*.
Adult Films:
   Candy Goes to Hollywood (1979) . . . .
Films:
   Reform School Girls (1986) . . . . Charlie
      •• 0:26 - Topless talking to two girls in the shower.
   Pucker Up and Bark Like a Dog (1989) . . . . Butch
Magazines:
   Playboy (Oct 1986) . . . . Oh, Wendy O.!
      •• 70-75: Topless.

Wilson, Ajita

Films:
   The Joy of Flying . . . . Madame Gaballi
      •• 1:20 - Full frontal nudity undressing for George.
      •• 1:23 - Topless, making love on top of George.
      • 1:25 - Left breast, while in bed with George.
   Love Lust and Ecstasy . . . . Sara
      •• 0:02 - Nude taking a shower and getting into bed
         with an old guy.
      •• 0:04 - Nude making love with a young guy.
      •• 0:17 - Topless in bathtub, then making love on bed.
      •• 0:22 - Topless making love in a swimming pool, in a
         river, by a tree.
      •• 0:26 - Nude getting undressed and taking a shower.
      •• 0:35 - Full frontal nudity changing clothes.
      ••• 0:54 - Full frontal nudity making love in bed.
   Catherine Cherie (1982) . . . . Dancer/Miss Ajita
      • 0:23 - Topless and buns dancing in club. Covered
         with paint. Long shot.
      0:24 - Brief buns, greeting Carlo after the show.
      •• 0:43 - Full frontal nudity in room with Carlo.
   A Man for Sale (1982) . . . . Dancer/Model
      • 0:02 - Topless several times posing for photographer
         with another model.
      • 0:26 - Topless and buns, dancing in an erotic ballet
         show.
   Savage Island (1985) . . . . Marie

Wilson, Alisa

Films:
   The Terror on Alcatraz (1986) . . . . Clarissa
      • 1:14 - Brief topless opening her blouse to distract
         Frank, so she can get away from him.
   Loverboy (1989) . . . . Nurse Darlene

Wilson, Cheryl-Ann

Films:
   Terminal Choice (1985; Canadian) . . . . Nurse Fields
   Cellar Dweller (1987) . . . . Lisa
      •• 0:59 - Brief right breast, then topless taking a shower.
TV:
   Days of Our Lives . . . .

Wilson, Sheree J.

Films:
Fraternity Vacation (1985) . . . . Ashley Taylor
    0:43 - In white leotard at aerobics class.
   • 0:47 - Topless and buns of her body double in the
    bedroom (Roberta Whitewood) when the guys pho-
    tograph her with a telephoto lens.
    1:01 - In white leotard exercising in living room with
    Leigh McCloskey.
Crimewave (1986) . . . .
Miniseries:
Kane and Able. . . . .
TV:
Our Family Honor (1985-86). . . . . .Rita Danzig
Dallas (1987-91) . . . . April

Winchester, Maude

Films:
Birdy (1985) . . . . Doris Robinson
  •• 1:32 - Topless in car letting Mathew Modine feel her.
Brain Dead (1989). . . . . .Crazy Anna

Windsor, Romy

Films:
Thief of Hearts (1984). . . . . .Nicole
  (Special Home Video Version.)
  ••• 0:12 - Full frontal nudity with Steven Bauer getting
    dressed.
Howling IV: The Original Nightmare (1988) . . . . . Marie
Big Bad John (1989) . . . . .Marie Mitchelle
Edgar Allan Poe's "The House of Usher" (1990). . . Molly

Winger, Debra

Films:
Slumber Party '57 (1976) . . . . Debbie
  • 0:10 - Topless with her five girl friends during swim-
    ming pool scene. Hard to tell who is who.
  ••• 0:53 - Topless three times, lying down, making out
    with Bud.
Thank God It's Friday (1978). . . . . .Jennifer
French Postcards (1979) . . . . Melanie
Urban Cowboy (1980) . . . . Sissy
Cannery Row (1982). . . . . Suzy
An Officer and a Gentleman (1982) . . Paula Pokrifki
  ••• 1:05 - Brief side view of right breast, then topless
    making love with Richard Gere in a motel.
Terms of Endearment (1983). . Emma Greenway Horton
Mike's Murder (1984) . . . . .Betty
  • 0:26 - Brief left breast in bathtub.
Legal Eagles (1986). . . . . Laura Kelly
Black Widow (1987) . . . . Alexandra
Betrayed (1988) . . . . Katie Phillips/Cathy Weaver
Everybody Wins (1990) . . . . Angela Crispini
    0:50 - Side view of left breast, lying on Nick Nolte in
    bed. Long shot.

The Sheltering Sky (1990) . . . . Kit Moresby
  0:13 - Upper half of lower frontal nudity in open robe
    when John Malkovich caresses her stomach.
  0:24 - Buns, getting out of bed.
  • 0:41 - Very brief topless grabbing sheets and getting
    out of bed with Tunner.
  1:58 - Lower frontal nudity and sort of buns, getting
    undressed with Belqassim.
TV:
Wonder Woman . . . . Drusilla/Wonder Girl

Winkler, K.C.

Films:
H.O.T.S. (1979) . . . . Cynthia
  • 0:27 - Topless in blue bikini bottom on balcony.
  •• 0:31 - Topless in van making love, then arguing with
    John.
The Happy Hooker Goes Hollywood (1980)
 . . . . .Amber
  •• 0:41 - Topless in cowboy outfit on bed with a guy.
  ••• 0:43 - Topless, wearing a blue garter belt playing
    pool with Susan Kiger.
Night Shift (1982) . . . . Cheryl
Armed and Dangerous (1986) . . . . Vicki
TV:
High Rollers . . . . hostess
Magazines:
Playboy (Jan 1979) . . . . .The Great Playmate Hunt
  ••• 190: Full frontal nudity.
Playboy (Oct 1985) . . . . Grapevine
  • 241: In swimsuit, showing left breast. B&W.
Playboy (Mar 1986) . . . . Grapevine
  • 176: In wet swimsuit. B&W.
Playboy (Sep 1989) . . . . Body by Winkler
  ••• 82-87: Nude.

Winningham, Mare

Films:
One Trick Pony (1980) . . . . McDeena Dandridge
  •• 0:14 - Topless in the bathtub with Paul Simon, smok-
    ing a cigarette. Long scene.
Threshold (1983; Canadian) . . . . .Carol Severance
  • 0:56 - Brief full frontal nudity, lying on operating ta-
    ble, then side view of left breast getting prepped for
    surgery.
St. Elmo's Fire (1985) .Wendy
Nobody's Fool (1986) . . . . .Pat
Made in Heaven (1987) . . . . Brenda Carlucci
Shy People (1988) . . . . Candy
Miracle Mile (1989) . . . . .Julie Peters
Turner & Hooch (1989) . . . . Emily Carson
Miniseries:
The Thorn Birds (1983) . . . . Justine O'Neill
Made for TV Movies:
Helen Keller: The Miracle Continues (1984) . . . .
Magazines:
Playboy (Nov 1981) . . . . Sex in Cinema 1981
  •• 170: Topless in bathtub from *One Trick Pony*.

Winters, D.D.
See: Vanity.

Witt, Kathryn
Films:
Lenny (1974; B&W) . . . . Girl
• 0:43 - Right breast with Valerie Perrine while Dustin Hoffman watches.
Looker (1981) . . . . Tina Cassidy
0:17 - In beige lingerie undressing in her room.
Star 80 (1983) . . . . Robin
Cocaine Wars (1986) . . . . .Janet
• 0:36 - Brief topless and buns making love in bed with John Schneider.
Demon of Paradise (1987) . . . . Annie
TV:
Flying High (1978-79) . . . . .Pam Bellagio

Witter, Karen
Films:
Dangerously Close (1986) . . . . Betsy
The Perfect Match (1987) . . . . Tammy
Hero and the Terror (1988) . . . . Ginger
Out of the Dark (1988) . . . . Jo Ann
Paramedics (1988) . . . . .Danger Girl
0:03 - In white bra and panties in bedroom with a heart attack victim while the paramedics try to save him.
0:07 - In wet blouse after getting in a car crash with a guy in the fountain.
Silent Assassins (1988) . . . . Sushi Bar Girl
The Vineyard (1988) . . . .
Another Chance (1989) . . . . Nancy Burton
• 0:44 - Brief side view of right breast and buns getting out of bed.
0:45 - In two piece swimsuit.
Edgar Allan Poe's "Buried Alive" (1989) . . . . .Janet
Midnight (1989) . . . . Missy Angel
• 0:32 - In bed with Mickey. Nice squished breasts against him, but only a very brief side view of left breast.
0:48 - In two piece swimsuit, going into the pool.
0:58 - In nightgown, walking around with lots of makeup on her face.
Popcorn (1991) . . . . Joy
TV:
One Life to Live (1990-) . . . . Tina Lord Roberts
Video Tapes:
Playboy's Playmate Review (1982) . . . . . . Playmate
••• 0:00 - Deep sea fishing, sunbathing on sailboat. Nude.
Playmates at Play (1990) . . . . Making Waves
Magazines:
Playboy (Mar 1982) . . . . Playmate

Wolf, Rita
Films:
My Beautiful Laundrette (1985; British) . . . . . . Tania
•• 0:15 - Topless holding blouse up, showing off her breasts outside window to Omar.
Slipstream (1990) . . . . Maya

Wood, Cyndi
Films:
Apocalypse Now (1979) . . . . Playmate
Van Nuys Blvd. (1979) . . . . Moon
Magazines:
Playboy (Feb 1973) . . . . Playmate

Wood, Jane
Films:
The Ragman's Daughter (1974; British)
. . . . Older Tony's Wife
Lassiter (1984) . . . . Mary Becker
She'll be Wearing Pink Pyjamas (1985; British)
. . . . .Jude
• 0:07 - Nude, shaving her legs in the women's shower room.
Blood Red Roses (1986; Scottish) . . . .

Wood, Janet
Films:
Angels Hard as They Come (1971) . . . . Vicki
•• 1:09 - Topless taking off her top, dancing with Clean Sheila at the biker's party.
•• 1:16 - Topless outside when the General rips her blouse open.
Terror House (1972) . . . . Pamela
The Centerfold Girls (1974) . . . . .Linda
•• 0:14 - Topless putting on robe, getting out of bed.
Slumber Party '57 (1976) . . . . Smitty
• 0:10 - Topless with her five girl friends during swimming pool scene. Hard to tell who is who.
•• 1:06 - Left breast, then topless in stable with David while his sister watches.

Wood, Lana
Sister of the late actress Natalie Wood.
Films:
The Searchers (1956) . . . . Debbie as a Child
Diamonds are Forever (1971) . . . . .Plenty O'Toole
A Place Called Today (1972) . . . . . . Carolyn Scheider
••• 0:40 - Side view of left breast, then topless lying down talking to Ron.
Demon Rage (1981) . . . .
a.k.a. Dark Eyes
Topless in bed.
TV:
The Long Hot Summer (1965-66) . . . . Eula Harker
Peyton Place (1966-67) . . . . Sandy Webber
Capitol (1983) . . . . Fran Bruke

Magazines:
Playboy (Apr 1971) . . . .
Playboy (Nov 1972) . . . . Sex in Cinema
  159: Hard to see anything.
Playboy (Sep 1987) . . . . .25 Years of James Bond
••• 128: Topless.

Wood, Laurie
Video Tapes:
Playboy Video Calendar 1990 (1989) . . . . April
••• 0:18 - Nude.
Magazines:
Playboy (Mar 1989). . . . . Playmate

Wood-Sharkey, Rebecca
a.k.a. Rebecca Sharkey.
Films:
Friday the 13th, Part V—A New Beginning (1985)
. . . . Lana
  • 0:33 - Brief topless opening her dress while changing
    to go out with Billy.
Mask (1985) . . . . Angel

Woodell, Pat
Films:
The Big Doll House (1971) . . . . Bodine
  • 0:27 - Brief topless hung by wrists and whipped by a
    guard. Hair covers most of her breasts.
The Roommates (1973). . . . . Heather
The Woman Hunt (1975; U.S./Philippines) . . . .
TV:
Petticoat Junction (1963-65) . . . . . . Bobby Jo Bradley

Woods, Connie
Films:
Night of the Living Babes (1987). . . . . Lulu
  • 0:46 - Topless and buns in lingerie, in a cell with
    Buck.
  ••• 0:48 - More topless in cell with Buck.
  • 0:50 - Topless getting rescued with Michelle Bauer.
The Forbidden Dance (1990) . . . . Trish
Made for Cable TV:
Dream On: Futile Attraction (1991; HBO). . .Darlene
  •• 0:03 - Topless dressed as a cheerleader on top of
    Martin in bed.

Woronov, Mary
Films:
Sugar Cookies (1973). . . . . Camila
  ••• 0:10 - Topless in bathtub, then wearing white pant-
    ies exercising topless on the floor. Long scene.
  • 1:04 - Topless with Julie in the bathtub.
  • 1:07 - Brief topless, then left breast, making love with
    Julie.
  • 1:17 - Brief right breast when Lynn Lowry yanks her
    dress up.

Silent Night, Bloody Night (1974) . . . . .Diane
Death Race 2000 (1975). . . . . Calamity Jane
  • 0:27 - Brief topless arguing with Matilda the Hun.
Hollywood Boulevard (1976) . . . . Mary McQueen
Jackson County Jail (1976) . . . . Pearl
Mr. Billion (1977) . . . . .Actress
The Lady in Red (1979) . . . . .Woman Bankrobber
Rock 'n' Roll High School (1979) . . . . Evelyn Togar
Angel of H.E.A.T. (1981). . . . . .Samantha Vitesse
  a.k.a. The Protectors, Book I
  ••• 0:11 - Frontal nudity changing clothes on a boat
    dock after getting out of the lake.
  •• 0:43 - Topless wrestling in the mud after wearing
    white bathing suit.
Heartbeeps (1981). . . . . Party House Owner
Eating Raoul (1982) . . . . Mary Bland
  ••• 0:46 - Topless on the couch struggling with Ed Beg-
    ley, Jr. More topless while Raoul counts money on
    her stomach. Long scene.
  • 0:53 - Buns and side view of right breast in hospital
    room with Raoul. A little dark.
Get Crazy (1983) . . . .
Night of the Comet (1984) . . . . Carol
Hellhole (1985) . . . . Dr. Fletcher
Chopping Mall (1986) . . . . Mary Bland
Nomads (1986) . . . . Dancing Mary
Let It Ride (1989) . . . . .Quinella
Scenes from the Class Struggle in Beverly Hills
  (1989) . . . . .Lizabeth
  ••• 1:06 - In black lingerie, then topless in bedroom,
    then in bed with Juan.
Dick Tracy (1990). . . . . .Welfare Person
Rock 'n' Roll High School Forever (1990) . .Doctor Vadar
Warlock (1990) . . . . .Channeller
Watchers II (1990) . . . . Dr. Glatman

Wren, Clare
Films:
Season of Fear (1989). . . . . Sarah Drummond
  0:23 - Topless in bed with Mick. Long shot, hard to
    see.
  0:25 - Brief silhouette, behind shower door.
  • 0:42 - Side view of left breast, on top of Mick. Very,
    very brief left breast, turning over when they hear a
    noise outside.
Steel and Lace (1990) . . . . Gally
TV:
Young Riders (1991-) . . . . Rachel

Wright, Amy
Films:
The Deer Hunter (1978). . . . . Bridesmaid
Girlfriends (1978) . . . . Ceil
  • 0:42 - Brief topless getting out of bed to talk to Mel-
    anie Mayron.
The Amityville Horror (1979) . . . . .Jackie
Breaking Away (1979) . . . . Nancy
Heartland (1980) . . . . Clara

Inside Moves (1980) . . . . Ann
Stardust Memories (1980; B&W) . . . . Shelley
The Accidental Tourist (1988) . . . . Rose Leary
Crossing Delancey (1988) . . . . Ricki

Wright, Jenny

Films:

Pink Floyd The Wall (1982) . . . . . . .American Groupie
••• 0:41 - Topless backstage in back of a truck doing a
strip tease dance in front of some people.
World According to Garp (1982) . . . . Curbie
•• 0:33 - Brief topless behind the bushes with Robin
Williams giving him "something to write about."
The Wild Life (1984) . . . . Eileen
•• 0:22 - In bra and panties, then topless changing in
her bedroom while Christopher Penn watches from
the window.
St. Elmo's Fire (1985) . . . . .Felicia
Near Dark (1987) . . . . Mae
Out of Bounds (1987) . . . . Dizz
The Chocolate War (1988) . . . . Lisa
Valentino Returns (1988) . . . . .Sylvia Fuller
A Shock to the System (1990) . . . . . . Melanie O'Connor
Young Guns II (1990) . . . . Jane Greathouse
• 1:07 - Buns, taking off her clothes, getting on a horse
and riding away. Hair covers breasts.
• 1:38 - Buns, walking down stairs during epilogue.
Queens Logic (1991) . . . . Asha
TV:
Capital News (1990) . . . . Doreen Duncan

Wright, Robin

Films:

Hollywood Vice Squad (1986) . . . . .Lori
The Princess Bride (1987) . . . . Buttercup
State of Grace (1990) . . . . .Kathleen
•• 0:38 - Topless making love standing up with Sean
Penn in the hall. Dark.
1:01 - In bra on bed with Penn, than walking around
while talking to him.
• 1:58 - Brief side of right breast taking off towel and
putting on blouse.
Denial (1991) . . . .
TV:
Santa Barbara . . . . Kelly Capwell

Wright, Sylvia

Films:

Bloody Birthday (1980) . . . .
Terror on Tour (1980) . . . . Carol
Malibu Hot Summer (1981) . . . . .Actress at Party
a.k.a. Sizzle Beach
(*Sizzle Beach* is the re-released version with Kevin Costner featured on the cover. It is missing all the nude
scenes during the opening credits before 0:06.)
•• 0:01 - Nude, standing up during opening credits.

••• 1:07 - Topless fixing her hair in front of mirror, then
full frontal nudity talking to Howard.
• 1:09 - Topless on top of Howard.

Wyss, Amanda

Films:

Fast Times at Ridgemont High (1982) . . . . Lisa
Better Off Dead (1985) . . . . Beth Truss
A Nightmare on Elm Street (1985) . . . . .Tina Gray
Silverado (1985) . . . . Phoebe
Deadly Innocents (1988) . . . . Andy/Angela
•• 0:12 - Topless, taking off T-shirt and putting on lin-
gerie.
••• 1:29 - Right breast, twice, with Andrew Stevens.
Powwow Highway (1988; U.S./British) . . . Rabbit Layton
To Die For (1988) . . . . .Celia Kett
Black Magic Woman (1990) . . . . .Diane Abbott

Yates, Cassie

Films:

The Evil (1977) . . . . Mary
Rolling Thunder (1977) . . . . Candy
Convoy (1978) . . . . .Violet
• 0:21 - Very brief left breast, while in truck sleeper
with Kris Kristofferson.
F.I.S.T. (1978) . . . . .Molly
FM (1978) . . . . Laura Coe
The Osterman Weekend (1983) . . . . . Betty Cardone
•• 0:48 - Topless getting into bed with Chris Sarandon
while Rutger Hauer watches on TV.
• 0:51 - Right breast, making love with Sarandon.
Unfaithfully Yours (1984) . . . . Carla Robbins
Made for TV Movies:
Of Mice and Men (1981) . . . .
St. Helens (1981) . . . .
Listen To Your Heart (1983) . . . .
TV:
Rich Man, Poor Man—Book II (1976-77) . .Annie Adams
Nobody's Perfect (1980) . . .Detective Jennifer Dempsey
Detective in the House (1985) . . . . Diane Wyman

York, Susannah

Films:

Tunes of Glory (1960) . . . . Morag Sinclair
Tom Jones (1963) . . . . .Sophie
A Man for All Seasons (1966) . . . . Margaret More
The Killing of Sister George (1968) .Alice McNaught
0:19 - Topless under sheer blue nightgown.
0:59 - In black bra and panties.
1:45 - In black bra and panties getting undressed.
•• 2:07 - (0:09 into tape 2) Topless lying in bed with another woman.
Images (1972) . . . . .Cathryn
• 0:59 - Brief lower frontal nudity, then right breast lying on the bed.
1:38 - Brief buns in the shower.
X, Y and Zee (1972) . . . . Stella

That Lucky Touch (1975). . . . . Julia Richardson
The Adventures of Eliza Fraser (1976; Australian)
. . . . Elisa Fraser
   • 1:10 - Brief topless twice during ceremony. Paint on
     her face while running from hut.
The Silent Partner (1978) . . . . Julie
   • 0:38 - Very brief right breast pulling her dress back
     up with Elliott Gould.
Superman (1978) . . . . Lara
The Shout (1979) . . . . Rachel Fielding
   •• 0:53 - Brief topless changing from a bathrobe to a
     blouse in bedroom.
   • 1:02 - Brief nude in upstairs room getting ready to
     make love with Alan Bates.
     1:05 - Brief buns, standing at end of hallway.
     1:09 - In white slip inside and outside house.
     1:11 - Topless in bathtub with John Hurt.
   • 1:18 - Brief topless getting up from bed with Bates.
     Long shot, hard to see anything.
The Awakening (1980) . . . . Jane Turner
Falling in Love Again (1980) . . . . Sue Lewis
Pretty Kill (1987). . . . . Toni
A Summer Story (1988) . . . . Mrs. Narracrombe

Young, Karen

Films:
Handgun (1983; British) . . . . Kathleen Sullivan
a.k.a. Deep in the Heart
Brief buns and topless when rapist forces her to remove
her clothes.
Almost You (1984) . . . . Lisa Willoughby
     1:00 - Partial left breast while kissing Griffin Dunne in
     bed.
Birdy (1985) . . . . Hannah Rourke
9 1/2 Weeks (1986). . . . . Sue
Heat (1987) . . . . Holly
Jaws: the Revenge (1987) . . . . Carla Brody
Torch Song Trilogy (1988). . . . . Laurel
Criminal Law (1989) . . . . Ellen Falkner
   • 1:21 - Very brief buns, then brief topless in bed with
     Ben.
Night Game (1989) . . . . Roxy
     0:02 - In white slip with Roy Scheider.
   • 0:06 - Right breast, while in bed with Scheider after
     he answers the phone.
Made for TV Movies:
The Summer My Father Grew Up (1991) . . . . Chandelle

Young, Robbin

Films:
For Your Eyes Only (1981). . . . . Flower Shop Girl
Night Shift (1982). . . . . Nancy
Magazines:
Playboy (Jun 1981) . . . . For Your Eyes Only
   ••• 126-127: Topless (won a contest to appear in the
     film and in *Playboy* magazine).
Playboy (Dec 1981). . . . . Sex Stars of 1981
   ••• 244: Frontal nudity.

Young, Sean

Films:
Jane Austen in Manhattan (1980). . . . . Ariadne
Stripes (1981) . . . . Louise Cooper
Blade Runner (1982) . . . . Rachael
Young Doctors in Love (1982) . . . . . Dr. Stephanie Brody
     0:48 - In white panties and camisole top in the sur-
     gery room with Michael McKean.
Dune (1984) . . . . Chani
Baby... Secret of the Lost Legend (1985)
. . . . Susan Matthew-Loomis
No Way Out (1987) . . . . Susan Atwell
     0:11 - In black stockings, garter belt & corset in love
     scene in back of limousine with Kevin Costner.
   ••• 0:13 - Side view of left breast, then brief right breast,
     going into Nina's apartment with Costner.
     0:21 - In bed in pink lingerie and a robe talking on
     telephone when Costner is in Manila.
     0:31 - In corset and stockings with garter belt in
     bathroom talking to Costner.
Wall Street (1987) . . . . Kate Gekko
The Boost (1989). . . . . Linda Brown
     0:16 - Very, very brief topless jumping into the swim-
     ming pool with James Woods. Very, very brief side
     view of right breast getting out of the pool, sitting
     on edge, then getting pulled back in.
   •• 0:17 - Left breast, while in pool talking to Woods.
     0:48 - Brief topless under water in spa with Woods.
Cousins (1989). Tish Kozinski
Fire Birds (1990) . . . . Billie Lee Guthrie
a.k.a. Wings of the Apache
   • 0:52 - Very, very brief right breast twice in bed with
     Nicholas Cage.
A Kiss Before Dying (1991). . . . .

Zabou

Films:
**The Perils of Gwendoline in the Land of the Yik
Yak** (1984; French) . . . . Beth
   •• 0:36 - Topless in the rain in the forest, taking off her
     blouse.
   •• 0:57 - Topless in torture chamber getting rescued by
     Tawny Kitaen.
   •• 1:04 - Topless after Kitaen escapes.
   • 1:11 - Buns, in costume during fight.
One Woman or Two (1986; French). . . . . . Constance
a.k.a. Une Femme Ou Deux
   •• 0:28 - Brief topless pulling up her blouse for Gerard
     Depardieu.
C'est La Vie (1990; French) . . . . Bella

Zadora, Pia
Singer.
Films:
Santa Claus Conquers the Martians (1964) . . . . . Girmar
Butterfly (1982) . . . . .Kady
    0:15 - Silhouette changing while Stacey Keach
    watches.
  •• 0:33 - Topless and buns getting into the bath.
  ••• 0:35 - Topless in bathtub when Stacey Keach is giv-
    ing her a bath.
The Lonely Lady (1983) . . . . JeniLee Randall
  • 0:12 - Brief topless getting raped by Joe, after getting
    out of the pool.
  •• 0:22 - Brief topless, then left breast, while making
    love with Walter.
  •• 0:28 - Side view topless lying in bed with Walter.
  •• 0:44 - Buns and side view of left breast taking a
    shower.
  • 0:46 - Very brief right breast, in bed with George.
  •• 1:05 - Left breast, then brief topless making love with
    Vinnie.
Voyage of the Rock Aliens (1985) . . . . DeeDee
a.k.a. When the Rains Begin to Fall
Hairspray (1988) . . . . .The Beatnik Chick
Magazines:
Penthouse (Oct 1983) . . . . Pia
  103-119:
Playboy (Nov 1983) . . . . Sex in Cinema 1983
  •• 144: Frontal nudity.

Zane, Lisa
Films:
Gross Anatomy (1989) .Luann
Pucker Up and Bark Like a Dog (1989)
. . . . Taylor Phillips
  •• 0:52 - Topless in shower with Max. Left breast, while
    in bed.
Bad Influence (1990) . . . . Claire
  • 0:39 - Brief topless on video tape seen on TV at party.
Femme Fatale (1990) . . . . .Cynthia
Freddy's Dead: The Final Nightmare (1991) . . . .

Zann, Lenore
Films:
Happy Birthday to Me (1980) . . . . .Maggie
American Nightmare (1981; Canadian) . . . . Tina
  ••• 0:25 - Topless and buns dancing on stage.
  •• 1:05 - Topless and buns dancing on stage again.
Visiting Hours (1982; Canadian) . . . . .Lisa
  0:39 - In panties with Michael Ironside.
One Night Only (1984; Canadian) . . . . .Anne
  •• 0:20 - Topless getting dressed in bedroom with
    Jamie.
  • 1:04 - Right breast in bedroom with Jamie.
  ••• 1:19 - Topless and buns making love with Jamie.
Def-Con 4 (1985) . . . . J. J.
Pretty Kill (1987) . . . . Carrie

Zinszer, Pamela
Films:
The Happy Hooker Goes to Washington (1977)
. . . . .Linda
  • 1:19 - Brief topless in raincoat flashing in front of
    congressional panel.
Magazines:
Playboy (Mar 1974) . . . . Playmate

Zucker, Miriam
Films:
Wildest Dreams (1987). . . . . Customer
New York's Finest (1988) . . . . Mrs. Rush
Sensations (1988) . . . . Cookie Woman
  • 0:06 - Topless on couch making love with a guy
    while Jenny and Brian watch.
A Woman Obsessed (1989) . . . . Betsy

Zuniga, Daphne
Films:
The Initiation (1984) . . . . Kelly Terry
The Sure Thing (1985) . . . . .Alison Bradbury
Visionquest (1985) . . . . .Margie Epstein
Modern Girls (1987) . . . . Margo
Spaceballs (1987). . . . . Princess Vespa
Last Rites (1988) . . . . .Angela
  • 0:04 - Very brief topless running into the bathroom
    to escape from being shot. Covered with blood,
    don't see her face. Very brief right breast reaching
    for a bathrobe. Don't really see anything.
  0:40 - Buns, behind a shower door.
  0:50 - Buns, getting out of bed and standing in front
    of Tom Berenger.
The Fly II (1989). . . . . Beth
Gross Anatomy (1989) . . . . .Laurie Rorbach
Staying Together (1989) . . . . Beverly Young
  •• 0:56 - Buns, lying in bed with Kit. Nice, long buns
    scene.

Actors

Aames, Willie

Films:
Scavenger Hunt (1979) . . . . Kenny Stevens
Paradise (1981). . . . . David
 0:42 - Buns, walking into the ocean with a fishing
 net. Dark, hard to see anything.
 •• 1:12 - Frontal nudity swimming with Phoebe Cates
 under water.
Zapped! (1982). . . . . Peyton
Made for TV Movies:
An Eight is Enough Wedding (1989) . . . . .Tommy
TV:
Swiss Family Robinson (1975-76) . . . . . . Fred Robinson
We'll Get By (1975). . . . . .Kenny Platt
Eight is Enough (1977-81) . . . . .Tommy Bradford
We're Movin' (1982). host
Charles in Charge (1984-85). . . . . Buddy Lembeck

Abele, Jim

Films:
Student Affairs (1987) . . . . .Andrew Armstrong
 • 1:07 - Buns, when his friends play a practical joke on
 him in the shower.
Wimps (1987). . . . . .Charles Conrad

Abraham, Ken

Films:
Creepozoids (1987) . . . . Butch
 •• 0:16 - Side view of buns, standing in shower with
 Linnea Quigley.
Vice Academy (1988) . . . . Dwayne
Deadly Embrace (1989) . . . . .Chris Thompson
 •• 0:17 - Buns, taking a shower.
 • 1:01 - Brief buns, making love on top of Linnea Quigley.

Agterberg, Toon

Films:
Spetters (1980; Dutch) . . . . .Hans
 ••• 0:35 - Frontal nudity, measuring and comparing his
 manlihood with his friends in the auto shop.
 • 1:21 - Buns, getting gang raped by gay guy he has
 been stealing money from.

Albert, Edward

Son of actor Eddie Albert.
Films:
Butterflies Are Free (1972). . . . . Don
Forty Carats (1973). . . . . Peter Latham
The Domino Principle (1977) . . . . Ross Pine
The Purple Taxi (1977; French/Italian/Irish) . . . . . . Jerry
The Greek Tycoon (1978) . . . . Nico Tomasis
Galaxy of Terror (1981). . . . . Cabren
Ellie (1984) . . . . Tom

House Where Evil Dwells (1985) . . . . Ted
 • 1:00 - Very brief, upper half of buns, making love
 with Susan George on the floor.
Getting Even (1986). . . . . .Taggar
The Underachievers (1987) . . . .
The Rescue (1988) . . . . Commander Merrill
Miniseries:
The Last Convertible (1979). . . . . .Ron Dalrymple
TV:
The Yellow Rose (1983-84). . . . . Quisto Champion
Falcon Crest (1986-89). . . . . Jeff Wainwright

Alden, John

Films:
The Young Warriors (1983; U.S./Canadian). . . . Jorge
 • 0:16 - Dropping his pants in a room during pledge
 at fraternity.
Making the Grade (1984). . . . . Egbert Williamson

Alin, Jeff

Films:
Coming Together (1978) . . . . Frank Hughes
a.k.a. A Matter of Love
 • 1:05 - Buns, putting pants on with Richard.

Altamura, John

Films:
Young Nurses in Love (1987) . . . .
New York's Finest (1988) . . . . .Brian Morrison
The Toxic Avenger: Part II (1988) . . . . Toxic Avenger
The Marilyn Diaries (1990) . . . . .Frankie
Private Screenings.
 • 0:13 - Buns, in hall after Marilyn Chambers takes his
 sheet away.
The Toxic Avenger III: The Last Temptation of Toxie
 (1990) . . . . Toxic Avenger

Amer, Nicholas

Miniseries:
I, Claudius—Episode 12, A God in Colchester
 (1976; British) . . . . .Mnester
Available on video tape in *I, Claudius—Volume 6.*
 • 0:04 - Brief buns, in bed with Lady Messalina.

Anderson, Marc

Films:
Coming Together (1978) . . . . .Richard Duncan
a.k.a. A Matter of Love
 •• 0:13 - Buns kneeling and kissing Angie, then more
 buns making love.
 • 0:58 - Buns, making love with Vicky.
 • 1:05 - Buns, putting pants on with Frank.

Andrews, Anthony

Films:
Under the Volcano (1984). . . . . Hugh Firmin
The Second Victory (1986) . . . . Major Hanlon
Hanna's War (1988) . . . . . Squadron Leader McCormick
The Lighthorsemen (1988; Australian)
. . . . Major Meinertzhagen

Miniseries:
Brideshead Revisited (1981; British) . . Sebastian Flyte
•• 0:17 - (Part 3 on TV or Book 2 on video tape.) Buns,
standing on roof with Jeremy Irons after talking with
Cordelia.

Made for TV Movies:
The Scarlet Pimpernel (1982) . . . .
Bluegrass (1988) . . . . Fitzgerald

Anglade, Jean-Hughes

Films:
Betty Blue (1986; French). . . . . Zorg
••• 0:09 - Frontal nudity.
•• 1:03 - Nude trying to sleep in living room.
•• 1:39 - Frontal nudity walking to the bathroom.
•• 1:45 - Frontal nudity talking on the telephone.
La Femme Nikita (1991; French) . . . . Marco

Anthony, Corwyn

Films:
Student Confidential (1987). . . . . Greg
• 1:26 - Buns, getting into bed with Susan.

Antin, Steve

Films:
The Last American Virgin (1982) . . . . Rick
Sweet Sixteen (1982) . . . . Hank Burke
The Goonies (1985) . . . . Troy
Penitentiary III (1987) . . . . Roscoe
The Accused (1988) . . . . Bob Joiner
• 1:29 - Buns, raping Jodi Foster on the pinball ma-
chine.

Arkin, Alan

Films:
The Russians are Coming, The Russians are Coming
(1966). . . . . Rozanov
Wait Until Dark (1967) . . . . Boat
Woman Times Seven (1967) . . . . Fred
The Heart is a Lonely Hunter (1968) . . . . John Singer
Catch-22 (1970) . . . . Captain Yossarian
• 0:52 - Buns, standing wearing only his hat, talking to
Dreedle. Don't see his face.
Last of the Red Hot Lovers (1972) . . . . Barneau Cashman
Freebie and the Bean (1974) . . . . Bean
Hearts of the West (1975) . . . . Kessler
Rafferty and the Gold Dust Twins (1975). . . . . . . Rafferty
The Seven-Per-Cent Solution (1976) . . . . Sigmund Freud
The In-Laws (1979) . . . . Sheldon Kornpett

Simon (1980). . . . . Simon Mendelssohn
Chu Chu and the Philly Flash (1981) . . . . Flash
Improper Channels (1981; Canadian) . . . . Jeffrey
Bad Medicine (1985) . . . . Dr. Madera
Joshua Then and Now (1985; Canadian)
. . . . Reuben Shapiro
Big Trouble (1986) . . . . Leonard Hoffman
Coupe de Ville (1990) . . . . Fred Libner
Edward Scissorhands (1990). . . . . Bill
Havana (1990). . . . . Joe Volpi
The Rocketeer (1991). . . . . Peevy

Ashby, Linden

Films:
Night Angel (1989) . . . . Craig
• 1:22 - Buns, kneeling down to pick up picture. Don't
see his face.

Atkins, Christopher

Films:
Blue Lagoon (1980). . . . . Richard
•• 0:27 - Nude swimming underwater after growing up
from little children.
• 0:29 - Buns, underwater.
•• 1:03 - Nude swimming under water.
• 1:05 - Buns, kissing Brooke Shields.
•• 1:09 - Very brief frontal nudity in water slide with
Shields.
The Pirate Movie (1982; Australian) . . . . Frederic
A Night in Heaven (1983) . . . . Rick
• 1:03 - Very brief frontal nudity when he pulls down
his pants in hotel room with Leslie Ann Warren.
• 1:15 - Brief buns on boat with Leslie Ann Warren's
angry husband.
Beaks The Movie (1987). . . . . Peter
Listen to Me (1989) . . . . Bruce Arlington
TV:
Dallas (1983-84) . . . . Peter Richards
Rock 'n' Roll Summer Action (1985). . . . . host
Magazines:
Playboy (Nov 1980) . . . . Sex in Cinema 1980
•• 183: Frontal nudity.

Babb, Roger

Films:
Working Girls (1987) . . . . Paul
• 1:18 - Frontal nudity with Molly.

Bacon, Kevin

Films:
Animal House (1978) . . . . Chip Diller
Friday the 13th (1980) . . . . Jack
• 0:39 - Close up of buns when Marci squeezes them.
Only When I Laugh (1981). . . . . Don
Diner (1982) . . . . Fenwick
Forty Deuce (1982) . . . . Rickey
Footloose (1984) . . . . Ren

Enormous Changes at the Last Minute (1985)
.... Dennis
Quicksilver (1986)...................... Jack Casey
End of the Line (1987) .... Everett
White Water Summer (1987) Vic
She's Having a Baby (1988)..... Jefferson "Jake" Briggs
The Big Picture (1989) .... Nick Chapman
Criminal Law (1989) .... Martin Thiel
Tremors (1989) ....Valentine McKee
Flatliners (1990) .... David Labraccio
he said, she said (1991)................ Dan Hanson
Queens Logic (1991)...................... Dennis
TV:
The Guiding Light ....Tim Werner

Baggetta, Vincent
Films:
Two-Minute Warning (1976)............. Ted Shelley
The Man Who Wasn't There (1983) .... Riley
• 0:23 - Buns, lying on the floor after fighting with the other guys.
TV:
Chicago Story (1982) ....Lou Pellegrino

Bahner, Blake
Films:
Sensations (1988)....................Brian Ingles
•• 0:10 - Very, very brief lower frontal nudity pushing the covers off the bed, then buns getting out of bed.
Caged Fury (1989) .... Buck Lewis
Lethal Pursuit (1989)..................... Warren

Baio, Scott
Films:
Bugsy Malone (1976) ....Bugsy Malone
Skatetown, U.S.A. (1979) .... Richie
Foxes (1980)........................... Brad
Zapped! (1982)........................ Barney
I Love N.Y. (1987) .... Mario Colone
• 1:19 - Brief, upper half of buns, getting out of bed. Dark, hard to see.
TV:
Happy Days (1977-84) .... Charles "Chachi" Arcola
Blansky's Beauties (1977) ....Anthony DeLuca
Who's Watching the Kids? (1978)
.... Frankie "The Fox" Vitola
Joanie Loves Chachi (1982-83) .... Chachi Arcola
Charles in Charge (1984-85)............... Charles

Baker, Scott
Films:
Delivery Boys (1984) .... Snooty Man
Cleo/Leo (1989) ....Leo Blockman
• 0:09 - Very brief buns after getting his butt kicked.

Baldwin, William
Brother of actor Alec Baldwin.
Films:
Flatliners (1990)...................... Joe Hurley
Backdraft (1991)................Brian McCaffrey
Brief buns in the shower with Jason Gedrick.

Ball, Rod
Films:
Porky's (1981; Canadian) .... Steve
• 0:18 - Brief frontal nudity sitting on bench in the cabin.
• 0:21 - Very brief frontal nudity, following Meat out the front door of the cabin, then buns, in front of the house.
Porky's II: The Next Day (1983; Canadian) .... Steve
Rhinestone (1984) .... Heckler

Banderas, Antonio
Films:
Matador (1986; Spanish) ....Angel
Women on the Verge of a Nervous Breakdown (1988; Spanish) .... Carlos
Tie Me Up! Tie Me Down! (1990; Spanish) .... Ricky
• 1:17 - Buns in mirror on ceiling, making love with Victoria Abril. Long shot.

Barbareschi, Luca
Films:
Bye Bye Baby (1989) ....Paulo
• 0:20 - Brief buns, on top of Brigitte Nielsen in bed.

Barro, Cesare
Films:
My Father's Wife (1981; Italian) .... Claudio
• 0:52 - Buns, bringing Patricia champagne.

Bates, Alan
Films:
Whistle Down the Wind (1961; British)
.... Arthur Blakey, The Man
Zorba the Greek (1963; B&W) ....Basil
Georgy Girl (1966; British/B&W) ....Jos
King of Hearts (1966; French/Italian)
.... Private Charles Plumpick
Women in Love (1971) .... Rupert
• 0:25 - Buns and brief frontal nudity walking around the woods rubbing himself with everything.
• 0:50 - Buns, making love with Ursula after a boy and girl drown in the river.
••• 0:54 - Nude fighting with Oliver Reed In a room in front of a fireplace. Long scene.
An Unmarried Woman (1978) ....Saul
The Rose (1979)........................ Rudge
The Shout (1979)................ Charles Crossly

Quartet (1981; British/French) . . . . .H.J. Heidler
Return of the Soldier (1983; British) . . . . .Chris
The Wicked Lady (1983; British) . . . . .Jerry Jackson
Duet for One (1987) . . . . .David Cornwallis
A Prayer for the Dying (1987) . . . . .Jack Meehan
We Think the World of You (1988; British) . . . . Frank
Club Extinction (1990) . . . . .Dr. Marsfeldt
Hamlet (1990) . . . . King Claudius
Made for TV Movies:
Pack of Lies (1987) . . . . .Stewart

Bean, Sean

Films:
How to Get Ahead in Advertising (1988) . . . . Carry Frisk
Stormy Monday (1988) . . . . Brendan
  •• 0:37 - Buns, putting on his underwear while Melanie Griffith watches.

Beatty, Warren

Brother of actress/author Shirley MacLaine.
Films:
Splendor in the Grass (1961). . . . . Bud Stamper
Lilith (1964; B&W) . . . . .Vincent Bruce
Bonnie and Clyde (1967) . . . . Clyde
McCabe and Mrs. Miller (1971) . . . . . John McCabe
Dollars (1972). . . . . .Joe Collins
The Parallax View (1974). . . . . Joe
The Fortune (1975). . . . . Nicky
Shampoo (1975). . . . . .George
  • 0:42 - Upper half of buns with pants a little bit down in the bathroom with Julie Christie.
  • 1:24 - Buns, making love with Christie when Goldie Hawn discovers them. Long shot, hard to see.
Heaven Can Wait (1978). . . . . .Joe Pendleton
Reds (1981) . . . . .John Reed
Ishtar (1987). Lyle Rogers
Dick Tracy (1990) . . . . .Dick Tracy
TV:
The Many Loves of Dobie Gillis (1959-60)
. . . . Milton Armitage

Beghe, Jason

Films:
Compromising Positions (1985) . . . . .Cupcake
Monkey Shines: An Experiment in Fear (1988)
. . . . .Allan Mann
  • 0:01 - Side view of buns while on the floor, stretching to go running.
Made for TV Movies:
Man Against the Mob: The Chinatown Murders (1989) Sammy

Begley, Ed, Jr.

Films:
Blue Collar (1978). . . . . .Bobby Joe
Hardcore (1979). . . . . Soldier
Private Lessons (1981). . . . . .Jack Travis

Cat People (1982) . . . . .Joe Creigh
Eating Raoul (1982) . . . . .Hippie
Young Doctors in Love (1982) . . . Young Simon's Father
Get Crazy (1983) .Colin
Protocol (1984) .Hassler
Streets of Fire (1984) . . . . Ben Gunn
Transylvania 6-5000 (1985) . . . . Gil Turner
Amazon Women on the Moon (1987) . . . . . . Griffin
  • 0:54 - Buns, walking around as the Son of the Invisible Man. This section is in B&W.
The Accidental Tourist (1988). . . . . Charles
Scenes from the Class Struggle in Beverly Hills (1989) . . Peter
Made for TV Movies:
A Shining Season (1979) . . . .
Spies, Lies & Naked Thighs (1988). . . . .
In the Best Interest of the Child (1990)
. . . . Howard Feldon
TV:
Roll Out (1973-74). . . . . .Lt. Robert W. Chapman
St. Elsewhere (1982-88) . . . . Dr. Victor Erlich
Parenthood (1990). . . . . Gil Buckman

Belle, Ekkhardt

Films:
Julia (1974; German) . . . . .Patrick
  • 1:01 - Very brief buns in bed with Terry.

Beltran, Robert

Films:
Zoot Suit (1981) .Lowrider
Eating Raoul (1982) . . . . .Raoul
Lone Wolf McQuade (1983). . . . . Kayo
Night of the Comet (1984) . . . . .Hector
Gaby, A True Story (1987) . . . . .Luis
Scenes from the Class Struggle in Beverly Hills
  (1989) . . . . .Juan
  • 1:34 - Brief buns, when his shorts are pulled down by Frank.
To Die Standing (1991) . . . .
Made for TV Movies:
The Chase (1991). . . . . Mike Silva

Benben, Brian

Films:
Clean and Sober (1988). . . . . .Martin Laux
I Come in Peace (1990) . . . . Laurence Smith
Made for Cable TV:
Dream On: Doing the Bossa Nova (1990; HBO)
. . . . Martin Tupper
  • 0:07 - Brief lower half of buns making love on photocopier with Vicki Frederick.
TV:
The Gangster Chronicles (1981). . . . . . . .Michael Lasker
Kay O'Brien (1986) . . . . Dr. Mark Doyle

Benjamin, Richard

Actor turned director.
Husband of actress Paula Prentiss.
Films:
Goodbye, Columbus (1969) . . . . Neil
  • 1:11 - Brief buns, walking into the bathroom. Very,
    very brief frontal nudity. Blurry, hard to see any-
    thing.
Catch-22 (1970) . . . . Major Danby
Diary of a Mad Housewife (1970) . . . . . . Jonathan Balser
The Marriage of a Young Stockbroker (1971)
  . . . . William Alren
The Steagle (1971) . . . . Harold Weiss
Portnoy's Complaint (1972) . . . . Alexander Portnoy
The Last of Sheila (1973) . . . . Tom
Westworld (1973) . . . . Peter Martin
Sunshine Boys (1975) . . . . Ben Clark
House Calls (1978) . . . . Dr. Norman Solomon
Love at First Bite (1979) . . . . Dr. Jeff Rosenberg
Scavenger Hunt (1979) . . . . Stuart
First Family (1980) . . . . . Press Secretary Bunthorne
How to Beat the High Cost of Living (1980) . . . . . Albert
The Last Married Couple in America (1980)
  . . . . Marv Cooper
Saturday the 14th (1981) . . . . John
TV:
He & She (1967-68) . . . . Dick Hollister
Quark (1978) . . . . Adam Quark

Benson, Robby

Films:
Lucky Lady (1973) . . . . Billy Webber
Ode to Billy Joe (1976) . . . . Billy Joe McAllister
One on One (1977) . . . . Henry Steele
The Chosen (1978; Italian/British) . . . . . Danny Saunders
The End (1978) . . . . The Priest
Ice Castles (1979) . . . . Nick Peterson
Walk Proud (1979) . . . . Emilio
Tribute (1980; Canadian) . . . . Jud Templeton
Running Brave (1983; Canadian) . . . . Billy Mills
Harry and Son (1984) . . . . Howard
Modern Love (1990) . . . . Greg Frank
  •• 0:35 - Brief buns running out of room after finding
    out he's going to be a father.
    0:36 - Long shot of buns, standing on roof of house
    yelling the good news to the world.
TV:
Tough Cookies . . . . Det. Cliff Brady

Berenger, Tom

Films:
Looking for Mr. Goodbar (1977) . . . . Gary
The Sentinel (1977) . . . . Man at End
In Praise of Older Women (1978; Canadian)
  . . . . Andras Vayda
  • 0:32 - Buns, in bed with Karen Black (seen in mirror).
    Long shot.
  •• 1:04 - Buns, rolling off Susan Strasberg. Kind of dark.

  •• 1:07 - Very brief lower frontal nudity three times,
    standing up and picking up Strasberg.
  • 1:20 - Very brief frontal nudity turning over in bed
    waiting for Alexandra Stewart.
  • 1:23 - Very, very brief blurry frontal nudity turning
    over in bed after getting mad at Alexandra Stewart.
  ••• 1:42 - Buns, undressing with Helen Shaver. Very brief
    balls.
Butch and Sundance: The Early Days (1979)
  . . . . Butch Cassidy
The Dogs of War (1980; British) . . . . Drew
The Big Chill (1983) . . . . Sam
Eddie and the Cruisers (1983) . . . . Frank
Fear City (1984) . . . . Matt Rossi
Rustler's Rhapsody (1985) . . . . Rex O'Herlihan
Platoon (1986) . . . . Barnes
Someone to Watch Over Me (1987) . . . . . . Mike Keagan
Betrayed (1988) . . . . Gary Simmons
Last Rites (1988) . . . . Michael
Shoot to Kill (1988) . . . . Jonathan Knox
Born on the Fourth of July (1989)
  . . . . Recruiting Sergeant
Major League (1989) . . . . Jake Taylor
Love at Large (1990) . . . . Harry Dobbs
The Field (1991) . . . .
Made for Cable TV:
Dream On: The Second Greatest Story Ever Told
  (1991; HBO) . . . . Nick Spencer
TV:
One Life to Live . . . . Tim Siegel

Berger, Helmut

Films:
The Damned (1969; German)
  . . . . Martin Von Essenbeck
  • 2:03 - Buns, walking up to his mother and ripping
    her dress off. Dark, don't see his face.
Dorian Gray (1970) . . . . Dorian Gray
The Garden of the Finzi-Continis (1971; Italian/German)
  Alberto
Ash Wednesday (1973) . . . . Erich
Ludwig (1973; Italian) . . . . Ludwig
Conversation Piece (1974; Italian/French) . . . . . Konrad
The Romantic Englishwoman (1975; British/French)
  . . . . Thomas
  • 1:08 - Upper half of buns, sitting at edge of pool talk-
    ing to Glenda Jackson.
Code Name: Emerald (1985) . . . . Ernst Ritter
The Godfather, Part III (1990) . . . . . . Frederick Keinszig

Berling, Peter

Films:
Aguirre: Wrath of God (1972; West German)
  . . . . Don Fernando de Guzman
Julia (1974; German) . . . . Alex Lovener
  0:12 - Brief buns, playing the piano outside on the
    dock.

The Marriage of Maria Braun (1979; German)
.... Bronski
Fitzcarraldo (1982) .... Opera Manager

Bernsen, Collin

Son of actress Jeanne Cooper.
Brother of actor Corbin Bernsen.
Films:
Dangerous Love (1988).................. Brooks
Mr. Destiny (1990) ....Tom Robertson
Puppet Master II (1990) .... Michael
•• 1:10 - Buns, while putting out fire on the bed.

Bernsen, Corbin

Son of actress Jeanne Cooper.
Brother of actor Collin Bernsen.
Husband of actress Amanda Pays.
Films:
S.O.B. (1981) ....
Hello Again! (1987)............... Jason Chadman
Bert Rigby, You're a Fool (1989) .... Jim Shirley
Disorganized Crime (1989).............Frank Salazar
Major League (1989) ....Roger Dorn
• 0:58 - Brief buns running in locker room to cover
himself with a towel when Rachel comes in to talk to
the team.
Made for Cable Movies:
Dead on the Money (1991)......................
Made for TV Movies:
Three the Hard Way (1974)...................Boy
Line of Fire: The Morris Dees Story (1991)
.... Morris Dees
TV:
L.A. Law (1986-) .... Arnie Becker

Biehn, Michael

Films:
Coach (1978)........................... Jack
• 1:11 - Upper half of buns in shower with Cathy Lee
Crosby.
Hogwild (1980; Canadian) ....Tim
The Fan (1981) .... Douglas Breen
The Lords of Discipline (1983)...........Alexander
The Terminator (1984) ....Kyle Reese
• 0:06 - Side view of buns after arriving from the fu-
ture. Brief buns running down the alley. A little dark.
Aliens (1986)....................... Corporal Hicks
In a Shallow Grave (1988)........... Garnet Montrose
The Seventh Sign (1988)............. Russell Quinn
The Abyss (1989) ....Lieutenant Coffey
Navy SEALS (1990) .... Curran

Blake, Robert

Films:
PT 109 (1963) .... "Bucky" Harris
This Property is Condemned (1966)........... Sidney
In Cold Blood (1967; B&W) .... Perry Smith
Tell Them Willie Boy is Here (1969) .... Willie
0:22 - Sort of buns when Katherine Ross lies down
with him. Very, very brief lower frontal nudity seen
through spread legs (one frame). More buns. Long
shot, hard to see.
Electra Glide in Blue (1973) .... John Wintergreen
Busting (1974)........................... Farrell
Coast to Coast (1980) .... Charlie Callahan
TV:
Baretta (1975-78).............Detective Tony Baretta
Hell Town (1985)................Father Noah Rivers

Blundell, Graeme

Films:
Alvin Purple (1973; Australian) ....Alvin Purple
•• 0:21 - Brief nude, painting each other's bodies with
Samantha.
•• 0:22 - Buns and brief frontal nudity in bedroom with
the Kinky Lady.
• 0:25 - Brief buns with Mrs. Warren—who turns out to
be a man.
• 0:26 - Very brief frontal nudity running out of room,
then buns going down the stairs.
••• 0:33 - Nude, undressing and taking a shower. Shot
at fast speed.
•• 1:04 - Nude, running away from the girl during
showing of movie.
• 1:21 - Buns, getting chased by a group of women
down the street.
Alvin Rides Again (1974; Australian) ....Alvin Purple
• 0:06 - Buns, running out of the office after he's awakened. Blurry.
Don's Party (1976; Australian) .... Simon
The Year My Voice Broke (1987; Australian)
.... Nils Olson

Bogosian, Eric

Films:
Special Effects (1984)....................Neville
• 0:21 - Buns, while fighting with Zoe Tamerlis in bed.
Medium long shot.
Talk Radio (1988)................ Barry Champlain
Sex, Drugs, Rock & Roll (1991) ....

Bonanno, Louis

Films:
Sex Appeal (1986)......................... Tony
Night of the Living Babes (1987) .... Buck
Student Affairs (1987) .... Louie Balducci
Wimps (1987) ....Francis
• 1:13 - Buns, running into a restaurant kitchen.

Bond, Steve
Films:
Massacre at Central High (1976) . . . . Craig
H.O.T.S. (1979) . . . . John
- 0:32 - Buns, trapped in van with K. C. Winkler.
The Prey (1980) . . . . Joel
Magdelena (1988) . . . . Joseph Mohr
To Die For (1988) . . . . Tom
TV:
Santa Barbara . . . . Mack Blake
General Hospital (1983-86) . . . . Jimmy Lee Holt

Bondy, Christopher
Made for Cable Movies:
Deadly Survailance (1991; Showtime) . . . . . . Nickels
- 0:31 - Buns, dropping his towel to run after Michael.

Boorman, Charley
Son of British director John Boorman.
Films:
Dream One (1984; British/French) . . . . Cunegond
The Emerald Forest (1985) . . . . Tommy
- 0:23 - Brief buns, running through camp.
- 0:24 - Brief buns running from waterfall and diving into pond.
- 0:30 - Buns, during ceremony.
- 0:45 - Buns, running away from the Fierce People with his dad.
- 1:02 - Buns running on the rocks, then bun in hut.
- •• 1:31 - Buns climbing up the building.
- 1:35 - Buns running down the hall to save Kachiri.

Boretski, Paul
Films:
Spacehunter: Adventures in the Forbidden Zone (1983) . . . . Jarrett
Perfect Timing (1984) . . . . Joe
- •• 0:11 - Brief frontal nudity and buns, rolling over on the bed.
- 0:29 - Frontal nudity on the roof in the snow with Bonnie.
- 0:35 - Buns, on bed getting slapped on the behind.
- 0:50 - Buns, in bed with Judy.
- •• 1:03 - Brief frontal nudity on TV with Judy while he and Bonnie watch.

Bottoms, Joseph
Brother of actors Sam and Timothy Bottoms.
Films:
The Dove (1974; British) . . . . Robin Lee Graham
Crime and Passion (1976) . . . . Larry
High Rolling (1977; Australian) . . . . Texas
The Black Hole (1979) . . . . Lieutenant Charles Pizer
Cloud Dancer (1980) . . . . Tom Loomis
Surfacing (1980) . . . . Joe
- 0:23 - Buns, in bed with Kathleen Beller.

King of the Mountain (1981) . . . . Buddy
Blind Date (1984) . . . . Jonathon Ratcliffe
(Not the same 1987 *Blind Date* with Bruce Willis.)
Born to Race (1988) . . . . Al Pagura
- 0:55 - Brief buns taking off bathrobe on deck and jumping into the lake.
Miniseries:
Holocaust (1978) . . . . Rudi Weiss

Bottoms, Sam
Brother of actors Joseph and Timothy Bottoms.
Films:
The Last Picture Show (1971; B&W) . . . . Billy
- 0:41 - Brief buns, after falling out of car with Jimmy Sue.
Class of '44 (1973) . . . . Marty
The Outlaw Josey Wales (1976) . . . . Jamie
Apocalypse Now (1979) . . . . Lance
Bronco Billy (1980) . . . . Leonard
Prime Risk (1985) . . . . Bill Yeoman

Bottoms, Timothy
Brother of actors Joseph and Sam Bottoms.
Films:
Johnny Got His Gun (1971) . . . . Joe Bonham
The Last Picture Show (1971; B&W) . . . Sonny Crawford
The Paper Chase (1973) . . . . Hart
The White Dawn (1974) . . . . Daggett
Small Town in Texas (1976) . . . . Poke
Rollercoaster (1977) . . . . Young Man
The Other Side of the Mountain, Part II (1978)
. . . . John Boothe
Hurricane (1979) . . . . Jack Sanford
The High Country (1900, Canadian) . . . . Jim
- 1:19 - Buns, walking into the pond with Linda Purl.
- 1:24 - Buns, pulling underwear on after getting out of sleeping bag.
Hambone and Hillie (1984) . . . . Michael
Invaders from Mars (1986) . . . . George Gardner
What Waits Below (1986) . . . . Maj. Stevens
The Drifter (1988) . . . . Arthur
Istanbul (1990) . . . . Frank
Texasville (1990) . . . . Sonny
Miniseries:
East of Eden (1981) . . . . Adam Trask

Bowen, Michael
Films:
Forbidden World (1982) . . . . Jimmy Swift
Valley Girl (1983) . . . . Tommy
Night of the Comet (1984) . . . . Larry
The Wild Life (1984) . . . . Vince
The Check is in the Mail (1986) . . . . Gary Jackson
Echo Park (1986) . . . . August
Iron Eagle (1986) . . . . Knotcher
Mortal Passions (1989) . . . . Burke
- 0:42 - Brief buns, on top of Adele.

Bowie, David

Singer.
Films:
The Man Who Fell to Earth (1976; British)
. . . . Thomas Jerome Newton
(Uncensored version.)
    0:58 - Brief buns, turning over in bed with Candy
    Clark.
    1:56 - Frontal nudity and brief buns in bed with
    Clark. Don't see his face.
Just a Gigolo (1979; German) . . . . Paul
The Hunger (1983) . . . . John
Merry Christmas, Mr. Lawrence (1983; Japanese/British)
. . . . Celliers
Yellowbeard (1983). .Henson
Into the Night (1985) . . . . Colin Morris
Absolute Beginners (1986; British). . . . . Vendice Partners
Labyrinth (1986). . . . . .Jareth
The Last Temptation of Christ (1988) . . . . Pontius Pilate
Made for Cable TV:
Dream On: The Second Greatest Story Ever Told
(1991; HBO) . . . . .Sir Roland Moorecock

Boyle, Lance

Films:
Maiden Quest (1972). . . . . Siegfried
a.k.a. The Long Swift Sword of Siegfried
Private Screenings.
  •• 0:24 - Buns, during orgy scene.

Boyle, Peter

Films:
Medium Cool (1969) . . . . Gun Clinic Manager
Diary of a Mad Housewife (1970)
. . . .-. Man in Group Therapy Session
Joe (1970). . . . . Joe Curran
T. R. Baskin (1971) . . . . Jack Mitchell
The Candidate (1972). Lucas
Kid Blue (1973). Preacher Bob
Steelyard Blues (1973) . . . . Eagle Throneberry
Young Frankenstein (1974; B&W) . . . . Monster
Swashbuckler (1976). . . . . Lord Durant
Taxi Driver (1976) . . . . Wizard
F.I.S.T. (1978) . . . . Max Graham
Beyond the Poseidon Adventure (1979)
. . . . Frank Massetti
Hardcore (1979) . . . . Andy Mast
North Dallas Forty (1979) . . . . Emmett
Where the Buffalo Roam (1980) . . . . .Lazlo
Outland (1981). . . . . Sheppard
Hammett (1982). Jimmy Ryan
Yellowbeard (1983). . . . . Moon
Johnny Dangerously (1984) . . . . Dundee
The Dream Team (1989) . . . . Jack
  •• 0:05 - Buns, getting up out of chair.
Men of Respect (1990) . . . . Duffy

Made for Cable Movies:
The Tragedy of Flight 103: The Inside Story (1990; HBO)
. . . . .Fred Ford
Miniseries:
From Here to Eternity (1979) . . . . Fatso Judson
TV:
Joe Bash (1986) . . . . Officer Joe Bash

Branagh, Kenneth

Director.
Husband of actress Emma Thompson.
Films:
High Season (1988; British) . . . . Rich Lamb
  • 0:56 - Buns, putting a wrap around Jacqueline Bisset
    after they fool around in the water.
A Month in the Country (1988; British) . . . . Moon
Henry V (1989) . . . . King Henry V
Dead Again (1991). . . . . . . Roman Strauss/Mike Church

Brando, Marlon

Films:
A Streetcar Named Desire (1951; B&W)
. . . . Stanley Kowalski
On the Waterfront (1954; B&W) . . . . Terry Malloy
(Academy Award for Best Actor.)
The Nightcomers (1971; British) . . . . Peter Quint
  0:30 - Looks like you can see something between his
  legs, but most of his midsection is hidden by bed
  post.
The Godfather (1972) . . . . .Don Vito Corleone
(Academy Award for Best Actor.)
Last Tango In Paris (1972). . . . . .Paul
(X-rated, letterbox version.)
  • 1:59 - Brief buns, pulling his pants down to moon a
    woman at a dance.
The Missouri Breaks (1976) . . . . Lee Clayton
A Dry White Season (1989) . . . . .Ian McKenzie
The Freshman (1990). . . . . .Carmine Sabatini

Brannan, Gavin

Films:
Private Passions (1983) . . . . Mark
  • 1:19 - Buns, lying in bed on top of Sybil Danning.

Bridges, Jeff

Son of actor Lloyd Bridges.
Brother of actor Beau Bridges.
Films:
The Last Picture Show (1971; B&W). . . . .Duane Jackson
Fat City (1972). . . . . Ernie
The Last American Hero (1973) . . . . . . .Elroy Jackson, Jr.
a.k.a. Hard Driver
Thunderbolt and Lightfoot (1974) . . . . Lightfoot
Hearts of the West (1975) . . . . .Lewis Tater
Rancho Deluxe (1975) . . . . Jack McKee
King Kong (1976) . . . . Jack Prescott
Stay Hungry (1976) . . . . Craig Blake

The American Success Company (1979) . . . . Harry
Winter Kills (1979). . . . . .Nick Kegan
  •• 0:50 - Buns, getting dressed after making love with
    Belinda Bauer.
Heaven's Gate (1980) . . . . John
Cutter's Way (1981) . . . . Richard Bone
  a.k.a. Cutter and Bone
Kiss Me Goodbye (1982). . . . . Rupert Baines
Tron (1982). . . . . Flynn/Clu
Against All Odds (1984) . . . . .Terry Brogan
Starman (1984). . . . . Starman
Jagged Edge (1985) . . . . Jack Forester
8 Million Ways to Die (1986). . . . . . . .Matthew Scudder
The Morning After (1986). . . . . .Turner
Nadine (1987) . . . . Vernon Hightower
Tucker: The Man and His Dream (1988)
  . . . . Preston Tucker
The Fabulous Baker Boys (1989) . . . . Jack Baker
See You in the Morning (1989). . . . . .Larry
Texasville (1990). . . . . Duane

Brockette, Gary

Films:
The Last Picture Show (1971; B&W)
  . . . . Bobby Sheen
  • 0:36 - Upper frontal nudity and buns, getting out of
    pool and greeting Randy Quaid and Cybill Shep-
    herd. More buns, getting back into the pool.
Ice Pirates (1984) . . . . Percy the Robot
The Philadelphia Experiment (1984)
  . . . . .Adjutant/Andrews
Mac and Me (1988) . . . . Doctor

Brosnan, Pierce

Films:
The Long Good Friday (1980; British) . . . . First Irishman
Nomads (1986) . . . . .Pommler
  • 0:56 - Buns, taking his pants off by the window. Kind
    of dark, hard to see.
The Fourth Protocol (1987; British) . . . . .Petrofsky
The Deceivers (1988) . . . . William Savage
Taffin (1988; U.S./British) . . . . Mark Taffin
Mister Johnson (1991). . . . . Harry Rudbeck
Made for Cable Movies:
The Heist (1989; HBO) . . . . Bobby Skinner
Miniseries:
James Clavell's Noble House (1988) . . . . Dunross
TV:
Remington Steele (1982-86) . . . . Remington Steele

Brown, Bryan

Husband of actress Rachel Ward.
Films:
Breaker Morant (1979; Australian)
  . . . . Lt. Peter Handcock
Cathy's Child (1979; Australian) . . . . Nicko

Winter of Our Dreams (1981) . . . . Reb
  • 0:48 - Brief buns falling into bed with Judy Davis.
The Empty Beach (1985) . . . . Cliff Hardy
Parker (1985; British) . . . .
Rebel (1985; Australian) . . . . Tiger Kelly
F/X (1986) . . . . .Rollie Tyler
Tai-Pan (1986) . . . . Dirk Struan/"Tai-Pan"
The Good Wife (1987; Australian) . . . . Sonny Hills
  a.k.a. The Umbrella Woman
Cocktail (1988) . . . . Doug Coughlin
Gorillas in the Mist (1988) . . . . Bob Campbell
FX 2 (1991) . . . . .Rollie Tyler
Miniseries:
The Thorn Birds (1983) . . . .

Brown, Clancy

Films:
Bad Boys (1983). . . . . Viking Lofgren
The Adventures of Buckaroo Banzai, Across the 8th
  Dimension (1984) . . . . Rawhide
The Bride (1985) . . . . .Viktor
Thunder Alley (1985) . . . . .Weasel
Highlander (1986) . . . . .Kuragan
Extreme Prejudice (1987) . . . . Sgt. Larry McRose
Shoot to Kill (1988) . . . . Steve
Blue Steel (1989). . . . . .Nick Mann
  • 1:27 - Upper half of buns lying on the bathroom
    floor. Don't see his face, so it could be anybody.
Season of Fear (1989) . . . . Ward St. Clair
Made for Cable Movies:
Cast a Deadly Spell (1991; HBO) . . . . .Harry Borden
Made for TV Movies:
Love, Lies and Murder (1991) . . . . David Brown

Brown, Dwier

Films:
House (1986). . . . . .Lieutenant
Field of Dreams (1989). . . . . John Kinsella
The Guardian (1990) . . . . Phil
    0:37 - Soft of buns, in bed with Carey Lowell. Don't
    see his face.

Brown, Murray

Films:
Vampyres (1974). . . . . Ted
  •• 0:22 - Buns, making love in bed with Fran.
  • 0:56 - Buns, falling into bed.

Brown, Woody

Films:
The Accused (1988). Danny
  • 1:28 - Buns, raping Jodi Foster on the pinball ma-
    chine.
Off Limits (1988) . . . . .Co-Pilot
The Rain Killer (1990). . . . . .Jordan Rosewall
  ••• 0:39 - Buns, getting into bed, kneeling next to bed,
    then getting into bed with Satin. Long scene.

TV:
Flamingo Road (1981-82) . . . . Skipper Weldon
The Facts of Live (1983-84) . . . . Cliff

Bullington, Perry
Films:
Chatterbox (1977) . . . . Ted
• 0:02 - Buns, stumbling around the room.

Bumiller, William
Films:
Last Resort (1985) . . . . Etienne
Overexposed (1990) . . . . Hank
• 0:54 - Brief buns, taking off his pants to get into bed
with Catherine Oxenberg.

Burton, Jeff
Films:
Planet of the Apes (1968) . . . . Dodge
• 0:26 - Very brief buns taking off clothes to go skinny
dipping. (Guy on the right.)
Sweet Charity (1969) . . . . Policeman

Butcher, Glenn
Films:
Young Einstein (1989; Australian)
. . . . Ernest Rutherford
• 0:56 - Buns standing in front of sink when Marie
comes to rescue Einstein. (He's the one on the left.)

Byrd, Tom
Films:
Twilight Zone—The Movie (1983) . . . . G.I.
Out Cold (1989) . . . . Mr. Holstrom
• 0:10 - Brief frontal nudity getting out of bed with Teri
Garr when her husband comes home.
Young Guns II (1990) . . . . Pit Inmate
TV:
Boone (1983-84) . . . . Boone Sawyer

Byrne, Gabriel
Husband of actress Ellen Barkin.
Films:
Excalibur (1981; British) . . . . Uther
The Keep (1983) . . . . Kaempffer
Wagner (1983; British) . . . . Karl Ritter
Defense of the Realm (1986; British) . . . . . . Nick Mullen
Gothic (1986; British) . . . . Byron
Hello Again! (1987) . . . . Kevin Scanlon
Julia and Julia (1987; Italian) . . . . Paolo
(This movie was shot using a high-definition video sys-
tem and then transferred to film.)
Lionheart (1987) . . . . The Black Prince

Siesta (1987) . . . . Augustine
1:28 - Brief buns and frontal nudity, getting out of
bed. Long shot, hard to see.
A Soldier's Tale (1988; New Zealand) . . . . Saul
Miller's Crossing (1990) . . . . Tom Reagan
Made for Cable Movies:
Mussolini and I (1985; HBO) . . . . Vittorio Mussolini

Cadman, Josh
Films:
Goin' All the Way (1981) . . . . Bronk
• 1:05 - Buns, in the shower talking to Boom Boom.
Pennies from Heaven (1981) . . . .
Angel (1983) . . . . Spike

Cage, Nicholas
Films:
Rumble Fish (1983; B&W) . . . . Smokey
Valley Girl (1983) . . . . Randy
The Cotton Club (1984) . . . . Vincent Dwyer
Racing with the Moon (1984) . . . . Nicky
Birdy (1985) . . . . Al Columbato
The Boy in Blue (1986; Canadian) . . . . Ned Hanlan
Peggy Sue Got Married (1986) . . . . Charlie Bodell
Moonstruck (1987) . . . . Ronny Cammareri
Raising Arizona (1987) . . . . H.I. McDonnough
Vampire's Kiss (1989) . . . . Peter Loew
Fire Birds (1990) . . . . Jake Preston
a.k.a. Wings of the Apache
Wild at Heart (1990) . . . . Sailor
Zandalee (1991) . . . . Johnny Collins
•• 0:30 - Buns, making love in bed with Zandalee.

Calderon, Paul
Films:
Band of the Hand (1986) . . . . Tito
Sticky Fingers (1988) . . . . Speed
Sea of Love (1989) . . . . Serafino
King of New York (1990) . . . . Joey Dalesio
Q & A (1990) . . . . Roger Montalvo
• 1:50 - Brief buns, on floor of boat, getting strangled
by Nick Nolte.

Cali, Joseph
Films:
Saturday Night Fever (1977) . . . . Joey
(R-rated version.)
Voices (1979) . . . . Pinky
The Competition (1980) . . . . Jerry Di Salvo
The Lonely Lady (1983) . . . . Vincent Dacosta
• 1:05 - Buns, near pool table and walking around the
house with Pia Zadora.
TV:
Flatbush (1979) . . . . Presto Prestopopolos
Today's F.B.I. (1981-82) . . . . Nick Frazier

Callow, Simon
Films:
Amadeus (1984) . . . . Emanuel Schikaneder
The Good Father (1986) . . . . Mark Varner
A Room with a View (1986; British)
. . . . The Reverend Mr. Beebe
- • 1:04 - Frontal nudity taking off clothes and jumping into pond.
- ••• 1:05 - Nude running around with Freddy and George in the woods. Lots of frontal nudity.
Maurice (1987; British) . . . . Mr. Ducie
Manifesto (1988) . . . . Police Chief Hunt
Mr. & Mrs. Bridge (1990) . . . . Dr. Sauer
Postcards from the Edge (1990) . . . . Simon Asquith

Campbell, Nicholas
Films:
Certain Fury (1985) . . . . Sniffer
- • 0:36 - Buns, getting undressed to rape Irene Cara.

Carradine, David
Son of actor John Carradine.
Brother of actors Keith and Robert Carradine.
Films:
Macho Callahan (1970). . . . . . Colonel David Mountford
Boxcar Bertha (1972) . . . . Big Bill Shelly
- • 0:54 - Buns, putting pants on after hearing a gun shot.
Mean Streets (1973) . . . . Drunk
Death Race 2000 (1975) . . . . Frankenstein
Bound For Glory (1976) . . . . Woody Guthrie
Cannonball (1976; U.S./Hong Kong)
. . . . "Cannonball" Buckman
Gray Lady Down (1977) . . . . Captain Gates
The Serpent's Egg (1977) . . . . Abel Rosenberg
Thunder and Lightning (1977) . . . . Harley Thomas
Death Sport (1978). . . . . Kaz Oshay
Circle of Iron (1979) . . . . Chang-Sha
Cloud Dancer (1980) . . . . Brad Randolph
Americana (1981) . . . . Soldier
Q (1982). . . . . Detective Shepard
Lone Wolf McQuade (1983) . . . . Rawley
On the Line (1984; Spanish) . . . . .Bryant
- • 0:11 - Buns, lying on a table, getting a massage by three women.
The Warrior and the Sorceress (1984) . . . . Kain
Armed Response (1986) . . . . Jim Roth
P.O.W.: The Escape (1986) . . . . Colonel Cooper
Warlords (1988) . . . . Dow
Crime Zone (1989) . . . . Jason
Tropical Snow (1989) . . . . Oskar
Bird on a Wire (1990) . . . . Eugene
Martial Law (1991) . . . . Dalton Rhodes
Made for Cable Movies:
Deadly Survailance (1991; Showtime). . . . . . Lieutenant
Miniseries:
North and South (1985) . . . . Justin LaMotte
North and South, Book II (1986). . . . . . . Justin LaMotte

Made for TV Movies:
A Winner Never Quits (1986) . . . . .Pete Gray
TV:
Shane (1966) . . . . Shane
Kung Fu (1972-75). . . . . Kwai Chang Caine

Carradine, Keith
Son of actor John Carradine.
Brother of actors David and Robert Carradine.
Films:
McCabe and Mrs. Miller (1971) . . . . .Cowboy
Hex (1973). . . . . .Whizzer
Nashville (1975). . . . . .Tom Frank
- • 0:47 - Buns, sitting on floor after getting out of bed.
Lumiere (1976; French) . . . . David Foster
The Duellists (1977). . . . . .D'Hubert
Welcome to L.A. (1977) . . . . Carroll Barber
Pretty Baby (1978). Bellocq
An Almost Perfect Affair (1979) . . . . Hal
Old Boyfriends (1979) . . . . .Wayne
Southern Comfort (1981). . . . . Spencer
Choose Me (1984). . . . . .Mickey
Maria's Lovers (1985) . . . . Clarence Butts
The Inquiry (1986) . . . . Titus Valerius
Trouble in Mind (1986) . . . . .Coop
Backfire (1987). . . . . Clinton James
The Moderns (1988) . . . . Nick Hart
- •• 1:17 - Buns, walking into bathroom with Linda Fiorentino.
Cold Feet (1989) . . . . Monte
Daddy's Dyin'... Who's Got the Will? (1990) . . Clarence
The Ballad of the Sad Cafe (1991) . . . .
Made for Cable Movies:
Judgement (1990; HBO) . . . . Perre Guitry
Payoff (1991; Showtime) . . . . . Peter "Mac" MacAlister
- • 0:01 - Sort of buns, in shower, seen from above, looking down.
Miniseries:
Chiefs (1983) . . . . Foxy Funderburke
Made for TV Movies:
A Rumor of War (1980) . . . .

Carrier, Gene
Video Tapes:
The Girls of Penthouse (1984)
. . . . Ghost Town Cowboy
- ••• 0:31 - Frontal nudity with Jody Swafford. Buns, carrying her to couch and making love.

Case, Robert
Films:
Hot Blood (1989; Spanish). . . . . Ricardo
- •• 1:20 - Buns, with Alicia in stable.

Casey, Bernie
Former football player.
Films:
Black Gunn (1972) . . . . Seth
Boxcar Bertha (1972) . . . . Von Morton
Cleopatra Jones (1973) . . . . Reuben
The Man Who Fell to Earth (1976; British). . . . Peters
(Uncensored version.)
   • 1:42 - Buns, getting out of swimming pool during a
    black and white dream sequence.
Sharky's Machine (1981). Arch
Never Say Never Again (1983) . . . . Felix Leiter
Revenge of the Nerds (1984) . . . . U. N. Jefferson
Spies Like Us (1985) . . . . Colonel Rhombus
Backfire (1987) . . . . Clinton James
Steele Justice (1987) . . . . Reese
I'm Gonna Git You Sucka (1988). . . . . John Slade
Bill and Ted's Excellent Adventure (1989) . . . . . Mr. Ryan
Another 48 Hrs. (1990). . . . . Kirkland Smith
Made for Cable TV:
Chains of Gold (1991; Showtime). . . . . Sgt. Palco
Made for TV Movies:
Brian's Song (1971). . . . .
Love is Not Enough (1978) . . . .
Ring of Passion (1978) . . . . Joe Louis
TV:
Harris and Company (1979) . . . . Mike Harris
Bay City Blues (1983) . . . . Ozzie Peoples

Casey, Lawrence
Films:
The Student Nurses (1970) . . . . Dr. Jim Casper
a.k.a. Young LA Nurses
   •• 0:52 - Buns, walking to Karen Carlson to talk.
The Great Waldo Pepper (1975) . . . . German Star
Borderline (1980) . . . . Andy Davis
TV:
The Rat Patrol (1966-68). . . . . . . Private Mark Hitchcock

Castillo, Eduardo
Films:
Gnaw: Food of the Gods II (1988; Canadian)
. . . . Carlos
   • 0:46 - Buns, walking through bushes to take a lead.
    More buns, running away from the giant rats.

Cazenove, Christopher
Films:
There's a Girl in My Soup (1970). . . . . Nigel
East of Elephant Rock (1976; British) . . . .
Eye of the Needle (1981) . . . . David
Heat and Dust (1982) . . . . Douglas Rivers
   •• 1:25 - Buns lying in bed with Greta Scacchi under a
    mosquito net.
Until September (1984) . . . . Philip
Mata Hari (1985) . . . . Captain Karl Von Byerling
Three Men and a Little Lady (1990) . . . . Edward

Ceinos, Jose Antonio
Films:
Black Venus (1983) . . . . Armand
   • 0:14 - Buns, making love with Venus in bed.

Chapman, Graham
Films:
Monty Python and the Holy Grail (1974; British)
. . . . King Arthur
Monty Python's Life of Brian (1979)
. . . . Brian Called Brian
   ••• 1:03 - Buns before opening window, frontal nudity
    opening window and being surprised by his flock of
    followers, buns putting clothes on. Funniest frontal
    nude scene.
The Secret Policeman's Other Ball (1982; British) . . . . . .
Monty Python's the Meaning of Life (1983; British) . . . .
Yellowbeard (1983) . . . . Yellowbeard
The Secret Policeman's Private Parts (1984) . . . .
TV:
Monty Python's Flying Circus . . . . .regular
The Big Show (1980) .regular

Clay, Nicholas
Films:
Excalibur (1981; British). . . . . .Lancelot
   •• 1:13 - Buns, fighting with himself in a suit of armor.
   • 1:31 - Brief buns, running into the woods after wak-
    ing up. Long shot, hard to see.
Lady Chatterley's Lover (1981; French/British)
. . . . Oliver Mellors (The Gardener)
   ••• 0:21 - Nude, washing himself while Sylvia Kristel
    watches from the trees.
Evil Under the Sun (1982) . . . . Patrick Redfern
Lionheart (1987) . . . . Charles de Montfort
Made for TV Movies:
Poor Little Rich Girl: The Barbara Hutton Story (1987)
. . . . Prince Alexis Mdivani

Clementi, Pierre
Films:
The Conformist (1971; Italian/French) . . . Nino Seminara
Steppenwolf (1974) . . . . Pablo
   • 1:40 - Very brief frontal nudity, sleeping on floor with
    Dominique Sanda.
Quartet (1981; British/French) . . . . Theo
Exposed (1983) Vic

Coates, Kim
Films:
The Boy in Blue (1986; Canadian) . . . McCoy Man No. 2
Red Blooded American Girl (1988). . . . . Dennis
   • 0:01 - Buns, giving Rebecca a glass in bed.
   • 0:30 - Very brief buns, getting into bathtub.
Cold Front (1989; Canadian) . . . . Mantha

Cochran, Ian

Films:
Bolero (1984) . . . . Robert Stewart
- 1:26 - Buns, making love with Catalina.

Coleman, Dabney

Films:
This Property is Condemned (1966) . . . . Salesman
I Love My Wife (1970). . . . . Frank Donnelly
Cinderella Liberty (1973). . . . . .Executive Officer
The Dove (1974; British) . . . . Charles Huntley
The Towering Inferno (1974) . . . . . . Assistant Fire Chief
Bite the Bullet (1975) . . . . Jack Parker
The Other Side of the Mountain (1975) . . .Dave McCoy
Midway (1976) . . . . .Captain Murray Arnold
Rolling Thunder (1977). . . . . Maxwell
Viva Knievel (1977) . . . . Ralph Thompson
How to Beat the High Cost of Living (1980)
. . . . Jack Heintzel
Melvin and Howard (1980). . . . . .Judge Keith Hayes
Nothing Personal (1980; Canadian) . . . . Tom Dickerson
Modern Problems (1981) . . . . .Mark
- ••• 1:09 - Buns, taking off towel in front of Patti
  D'Arbanville.
On Golden Pond (1981) . . . . Bill Ray
Tootsie (1982). . . . . .Ron
Young Doctors in Love (1982). . . . . . . .Dr. Joseph Prang
Wargames (1983) .McKittrick
Cloak and Dagger (1984) . . . . . . Jack Flack/Hal Osborne
Short Time (1990). . . . . Burt Simpson
Where the Heart Is (1990). . . . . Stewart McBain
Made for TV Movies:
Baby M (1988) . . . . Skoloff
TV:
That Girl (1966-67). . . . . Dr. Leon Bessemer
Mary Hartman, Mary Hartman (1975-78)
. . . . Merle Jeeter
Apple Pie (1978). . . . . .Fast Eddie Murtaugh
Buffalo Bill (1983-84) . . . . Bill Bittinger
The Slap Maxwell Story (1987-88) . . . . . . Slap Maxwell
Drexell's Class (1991-) . . . . .Otis Drexell

Coleman, Warren

Films:
Young Einstein (1989; Australian) . . .Lunatic Professor
- 0:55 - Buns in Lunatic Asylum taking a shower.
- 0:56 - More buns standing in front of sink when
  Marie comes to rescue Einstein. (He's the one on the
  right.)
- 0:58 - Brief buns crowding into the shower stall with
  the other Asylum people.

Colomby, Scott

Films:
Caddyshack (1980). .Tony
Porky's (1981; Canadian) . . . . Brian Schwartz
Porky's II: The Next Day (1983; Canadian) . . . . . . .Brian

TV:
Sons and Daughters (1974) . . . . Stash
Szysznyk (1977-78) . . . . .Tony La Placa

Conaway, Jeff

Films:
The Eagle Has Landed (1977; British) . . . .
I Never Promised You a Rose Garden (1977)
. . . . .Lactamaeon
Grease (1978) . . . . .Kenickie
Covergirl (1982; Canadian) . . . . T. C. Sloane
- •• 0:43 - Very brief lower frontal nudity getting out of
  bed.
The Patriot (1986) .Mitchell
The Sleeping Car (1990) . . . . Bud Sorenson
Total Exposure (1991) . . . . Peter Keynes
TV:
Taxi (1978-83). . . . . Bobby Wheeler
Wizards and Warriors (1983) . . . . .Prince Erik Greystone
Berrengers (1985) . . . . John Higgins

Conlon, Tim

Films:
Prom Night III (1989) .Alex
- 0:15 - Brief buns and very brief balls when the flag
  he's wearing falls off.

Cooper, Terence

Films:
Casino Royale (1967; British) . . . . Cooper
Heart of the Stag (1983; New Zealand)
. . . . .Robert Jackson
- 0:03 - Buns, making love in bed on top of his daugh-
  ter. Don't see his face.
The Shrimp on the Barbie (1990). . . . . .Ian Hobart

Corbo, Robert

Films:
Last Rites (1988) . . . . Gino
- 0:03 - Buns and frontal nudity in a room with
  Daphne Zuniga just before getting caught by another woman and shot.

Corri, Nick

Films:
Gotcha! (1985) . . . . Manolo
A Nightmare on Elm Street (1985). . . . . .Rod Lane
Lawless Land (1988). . . . .
Slaves of New York (1989) . . . . Marley Mantello
Tropical Snow (1989) . . . . Tavo
- •• 0:11 - Buns in bed with Madeline Stowe.
- •• 0:44 - Buns, standing naked in police station.
Predator 2 (1990) .Detective

Costner, Kevin

Films:
Chasing Dreams (1981) . . . .
Malibu Hot Summer (1981) . . . . John Logan
a.k.a. Sizzle Beach
(*Sizzle Beach* is the re-released version with Kevin Costner featured on the cover. It is missing all the nude scenes during the opening credits before 0:06.)
Night Shift (1982). .Frat Boy #1
Stacy's Knights (1983). . . . . .Will
Table for Five (1983) . . . . Newlywed
Testament (1983) . . . . Phil Pitkin
American Flyers (1985) . . . . Marcus
Fandango (1985) . . . . .Gardner Barnes
Silverado (1985) . . . . Jake
Shadows Run Black (1986) . . . . Jimmy Scott
No Way Out (1987) . . . . Lt. Cmdr. Tom Farrell
The Untouchables (1987) . . . . Eliot Ness
Bull Durham (1988) . . . . .Crash Davis
Field of Dreams (1989) . . . . .Ray Kinsella
The Gunrunner (1989) . . . . Ted Beaubien
Dances with Wolves (1990) . . . . Lt. John Dunbar
•• 0:37 - Brief buns, washing his clothes in the pond.
••• 0:40 - Buns, standing by himself after scaring away Kicking Bird.
Revenge (1990). . . . . Cochran
•• 1:14 - Brief buns getting out of bed and wrapping a sheet around himself.
Robin Hood: Prince of Thieves (1991) . Robin of Locksley

Cramer, Grant

Films:
New Year's Evil (1981). . . . . .Derek Sullivan
Hardbodies (1984) . . . . .Scotty
• 0:03 - Brief buns, getting out of bed after making love with Kristi.
Killer Klowns from Outer Space (1988) . . . . .Mike
Made for TV Movies:
An Inconvenient Woman (1991) . . . . .Lonny

Crawford, Johnny

Films:
The Restless Ones (1965) . . . . David Winton
Village of the Giants (1965). . . . . Horsey
El Dorado (1967) . . . . Luke MacDonald
The Naked Ape (1972). . . . . Lee
(Not available on video tape.)
Frontal nudity.
The Great Texas Dynamite Chase (1977). . . . . Slim
Tilt (1978). . . . . Mickey
TV:
The Rifleman (1958-63) . . . . Mark McCain
Magazines:
Playboy (Dec 1973). . . . . Sex Stars of 1973
•• 211: Frontal nudity.

Crew, Carl

Films:
Blood Diner (1987) . . . . George Tutman
• 1:02 - Buns, mooning Sheeba through the passenger window of a van.

Cruise, Tom

Husband of Nicole Kidman.
Ex-husband of Mimi Rogers.
Films:
Endless Love (1981) . . . . Billy
Taps (1981) . . . . David Shawn
Losin' It (1982). . . . . .Woody
All The Right Moves (1983) . . . . Stef
•• 1:00 - Very brief frontal nudity getting undressed in his bedroom with Lea Thompson.
The Outsiders (1983) . . . . Steve Randle
Risky Business (1983) . . . . Joel
The Color of Money (1986) . . . . Vincent
Legend (1986). . . . . Jack
Top Gun (1986) . . . . Maverick
Cocktail (1988) . . . . .Brian Hanagan
Rain Man (1988) . . . . .Charlie Babbitt
Born on the Fourth of July (1989) . . . . . . Ron Kovic
• 0:47 - Very brief buns, sort of, in bed at hospital when his rear end is sticking through the bottom of a bed.
Days of Thunder (1990) . . . . Cole Trickle

Culp, Robert

Films:
PT 109 (1963) . . . . .Ens. "Barney" Ross
Bob & Carol & Ted & Alice (1969). . . . . Bob
Hickey and Boggs (1972) . . . . .Frank Boggs
A Name for Evil (1973) . . . . John Blake
•• 0:52 - Frontal nudity running through the woods with a woman.
• 1:07 - Buns, going skinny dipping. Lots of bun shots underwater.
The Great Scout and Cathouse Thursday (1976)
. . . . Jack Colby
Goldengirl (1979) . . . . .Esselton
Turk 182 (1985). . . . . Mayor Tyler
Big Bad Mama II (1987). . . . . Daryl Pearson
Pucker Up and Bark Like a Dog (1989). . . . . .Gregor
Silent Night, Deadly Night III: Better Watch Out! (1989) Lt. Connely
Made for TV Movies:
Columbo Goes to College (1990). . . . . Jordan Rowe
TV:
I Spy (1965-68) .Kelly Robinson
Greatest American Hero (1981-83). . . . . Bill Maxwell
Magazines:
Playboy (Mar 1973) . . . . "Evil" Doings
•• 148: Side view naked.

Cvetkovic, Svetozar

Films:
Montenegro (1981; British/Swedish) . . . . Montenegro
••• 1:07 - Frontal nudity taking a shower while Susan Anspach watches.
Manifesto (1988) . . . . Rudi

Dacus, Don

Films:
Hair (1979) . . . . Woof
• 0:57 - Buns, taking off clothes and diving into pond with Treat Williams and Hud.

Dafoe, Willem

Films:
Roadhouse 66 (1984) . . . . Johnny Harte
•• 1:02 - Buns, standing up while kissing Jesse.
The Last Temptation of Christ (1988) . . . . . . Jesus Christ
Mississippi Burning (1988) . . . . Alan Ward
Off Limits (1988) . . . . Bud McGriff
Born on the Fourth of July (1989) . . . . Charlie
Triumph of the Spirit (1989) . . . . Salamo Arouch
Cry Baby (1990) . . . . Hateful Guard
Wild at Heart (1990) . . . . Bobby Peru
Flight of the Intruder (1991) . . . . Cole

Daltrey, Roger

Singer with *The Who* and on his own.
Films:
Lisztomania (1975; British) . . . . Franz Liszt
• 0:01 - Brief buns standing on bed tying a sheet to make some pants. Dark, don't see his face.
Tommy (1975; British) . . . . Tommy
The Kids are Alright (1979; British) . . . .
The Legacy (1979; British) . . . . Clive
McVicar (1980; British) . . . . Tom McVicar
If Looks Could Kill (1991) . . . . Blade

Damian, Leo

Films:
The Last Temptation of Christ (1988) . . Person in Crowd
Ghosts Can't Do It (1989) . . . .
• 1:31 - Brief, lower buns sliding down stack of hay. Long shot.

Daniels, Jeff

Films:
Ragtime (1981) . . . . O'Donnell
Terms of Endearment (1983) . . . . Flap Horton
The Purple Rose of Cairo (1985)
. . . . Tom Baxter/Gil Shepherd
Heartburn (1986) . . . . Richard
Marie (1986) . . . . Eddie Sisk

Something Wild (1986) . . . . Charles Driggs
•• 0:16 - Buns, lying in bed after making love with Melanie Griffith.
The House on Carroll Street (1988) . . . . Cochran
Sweet Hearts Dance (1988) . . . . Sam Manners
Checking Out (1989) . . . . Ray Macklin
Aracnophobia (1990) . . . . Dr. Ross Jennings

Daughton, James

Films:
Malibu Beach (1978) . . . . Bobby
• 0:32 - Buns, running into the ocean with his friends.
National Lampoon's Animal House (1978)
. . . . Greg Marmalard
The Beach Girls (1982) . . . . Scott
• 0:33 - Buns and very brief frontal nudity taking off clothes and running into the ocean.
Blind Date (1984) . . . . David
(Not the same 1987 *Blind Date* with Bruce Willis.)
House of the Rising Sun (1987) . . . .
Girlfriend from Hell (1989) . . . . David

Daveau, Alan

Films:
Screwballs (1983) . . . . Howie Bates
• 1:00 - Buns, after losing at strip bowling.

Davies, Stephen

Films:
Inserts (1976) . . . . Rex
•• 0:31 - Buns and balls, on bed with Veronica Cartwright, making a porno movie for Richard Dreyfus.
Heart Beat (1979) . . . . Bob Bendix
The Razor's Edge (1984) . . . . Malcolm
The Nest (1987) . . . . Homer
Corporate Affairs (1990) . . . . Ukranian #2
Made for Cable Movies:
Philip Marlowe, Private Eye: Finger Man (1983; HBO) . .

Davis, Brad

Films:
Midnight Express (1978; British) . . . . Billy Hayes
• 0:12 - Buns, standing naked in front of guards after getting caught trying to smuggle drugs.
A Small Circle of Friends (1980) . . . . Leo DaVinci
•• 1:22 - Brief buns, dropping his pants with several other guys for Army draft inspection.
Chariots of Fire (1981) . . . . Jackson Scholz
Querelle (1982) . . . . Querella
Cold Steel (1987) . . . . Johnny Modine
Rosalie Goes Shopping (1990) . . . . Liebling Ray
Made for Cable Movies:
Blood Ties (1986; Italian; Showtime) . . . .
Miniseries:
Roots (1977) . . . . Ol' George Johnson
Chiefs (1983) . . . . Chief Sonny Butts

Davis, Mac

Singer.
Films:
North Dallas Forty (1979) . . . . Maxwell
   • 0:53 - Brief buns getting a can of Coke in the locker
   room.
Cheaper to Keep Her (1980) . . . . Bill Dekkar
The Sting II (1983) . . . . Hooker
TV:
The Mac Davis Show (1974-76) . . . . Host

Day-Lewis, Daniel

Films:
Gandhi (1982) . . . . Colin
The Bounty (1984) . . . . Fryer
My Beautiful Laundrette (1985; British) . . . . Johnny
A Room with a View (1986; British) . . . . Cecil Vyse
Stars and Bars (1988) . . . . Henderson Bores
   •• 1:21 - Brief buns, trying to open the window. Very,
   very brief frontal nudity when he throws the statue
   out the window. Blurry and dark. More buns, climb-
   ing out the window and into a trash dumpster.
The Unbearable Lightness of Being (1988) . . . . Thomas
My Left Foot (1989; British) . . . . Christy Brown
   (Academy Award for Best Actor.)

De La Brosse, Simon

Films:
Pauline at the Beach (1983; French) . . . . Sylvain
The Little Thief (1989; French) . . . . Raoul
   a.k.a. La Petite Voleuse
   • 1:07 - Very brief buns and frontal nudity jumping
   into bed (seen in mirror).
Strike it Rich (1990) . . . . Philippe

De Lint, Derek

Films:
Soldier of Orange (1977; Dutch) . . . . Alex
Mata Hari (1985) . . . . Handsome Traveler
The Assault (1986; Dutch) . . . . Anton Steenwijk
Mascara (1987) . . . . Chris Brine
Stealing Heaven (1988) . . . . Abelard
   ••• 0:47 - Brief frontal nudity taking off his shirt. Then
   buns, in bed making love with Kim Thomson.
   1:07 - Brief side view of buns under Kim. Long shot.
The Unbearable Lightness of Being (1988) . . . . . . Franz

De Niro, Robert

Films:
Bloody Mama (1970) . . . . Lloyd Barker
Mean Streets (1973) . . . . Johnny Boy
The Godfather, Part II (1974) . . . . Vito Corleone
1900 (1976; Italian) . . . . Alfredo Berlinghieri
   • 1:59 - Very brief buns making love with Dominique
   Sanda in the hay. Don't see his face.
The Last Tycoon (1976) . . . . Monroe Stahr

Taxi Driver (1976) . . . . Travis Bickle
New York, New York (1977) . . . . Jimmy Doyle
The Deer Hunter (1978) . . . . Michael
   •• 0:50 - Nude, running in street, then more nude by
   basketball court. Brief frontal nudity getting covered
   by Christopher Walken's jacket. Long shot.
Raging Bull (1980) . . . . Jake La Motta
   (Academy Award for Best Actor.)
True Confessions (1981) . . . . Des Spellacy
King of Comedy (1983) . . . . Rupert Pupkin
Falling In Love (1984) . . . . Frank Raftis
Once Upon a Time in America (1984) . . . . Noodles
   (Long version.)
Brazil (1985; British) . . . . Tuttle
The Mission (1986; British) . . . . Mendoza
Angel Heart (1987) . . . . Louis Cyphre
The Untouchables (1987) . . . . Al Capone
Midnight Run (1988) . . . . Jack Walsh
Jackknife (1989) . . . . Joseph "Megs" Megessey
We're No Angels (1989) . . . . Ned
GoodFellas (1990) . . . . James Conway
Stanley and Iris (1990) . . . . Stanley Everett Cox
Awakenings (1991) . . . . Leonard Lowe
Backdraft (1991) . . . . Donald Rimgale
Guilty by Suspicion (1991) . . . . David Merrill

Dempsey, Patrick

Films:
Can't Buy Me Love (1987) . . . . Ronald Miller
Meatballs III (1987) . . . . Rudy
   •• 0:19 - Buns, in the shower when first being visited by
   Sally Kellerman.
Happy Together (1988) . . . Christopher "Chris" Wooden
Some Girls (1988) . . . . Michael
   • 0:34 - Brief frontal nudity, then buns running all
   around the house chasing Jennifer Connelly.
Loverboy (1989) . . . . Randy Bodek
Mobsters (1991) . . . . Meyer Lansky
TV:
Fast Times (1986) . . . . Mike Damone

Denney, David

Films:
Under Cover (1987) . . . . Hassie Pearl
   • 0:43 - Brief buns walking around boy's locker room
   wearing his jock strap.

Depardieu, Gérard

Films:
Going Places (1974; French) . . . . Jean-Claude
   • 0:42 - Upper half of buns and pubic hair talking to
   Pierrot.
   •• 0:49 - Buns in bed, then more buns making love to
   Miou-Miou. Nice up and down action.
   • 0:50 - Brief buns switching places with Pierrot.
   • 0:51 - Brief frontal nudity getting out of bed. Dark,
   hard to see. Subtitles get in the way.

1900 (1976; Italian) . . . . Olmo Dalco
- • 1:36 - Brief frontal nudity sitting at table with Robert De Niro. Again when walking into the bedroom.
- ••• 1:40 - Nude getting out of bed after the girl has a seizure.

Get Out Your Handkerchiefs (1978). . . . . Raoul
The Last Metro (1980) . . . . Bernard Granger
Loulou (1980; French) . . . . Loulou
- • 0:07 - Brief buns, getting out of bed after it breaks. Dark.
- •• 0:36 - Buns, lying in bed with Isabelle Huppert.

The Moon in the Gutter (1983; French/Italian) . . Gerard
Return of Martin Guerre (1983; French) . . Martin Guerre
Jean de Florette (1986; French). . . . . Jean Cadoret
Police (1986; French) . . . . Mangin
Camille Claudel (1989; French). . . . . Auguste Rodin
Cyrano De Bergerac (1990). . . . . . . Cyrano De Bergerac
Green Card (1990) . . . . Georges
Too Beautiful for You (1990; French) . . . . Bernard

Depp, Johnny

Films:
A Nightmare on Elm Street (1985) . . . . Glen Lantz
Private Resort (1985) . . . . Jack
- •• 0:12 - Buns, in hotel room with Leslie Easterbrook.

Platoon (1986) . . . . Lerner
Cry Baby (1990) . . . . Cry-Baby
Edward Scissorhands (1990) . . . . . Edward Scissorhands
TV:
21 Jump Street (1987-90) . . . . Tommy Hanson

Dern, Bruce

Father of actress Laura Dern.
Ex-husband of actress Diane Ladd.
Films:
Marnie (1964). . . . . Sailor
Hush...Hush, Sweet Charlotte (1965; B&W) . . . . John Mayhew
The Wild Angels (1966). . . . . Loser (Joey Kerns)
Rebel Rousers (1967). . . . . J. J.
The St. Valentine's Day Massacre (1967) . . . . . John May
The Trip (1967). John, Guru
Waterhole 3 (1967). Deputy
Support Your Local Sheriff! (1969). . . . . Joe Danby
Bloody Mama (1970) . . . . Kevin Kirkman
Silent Running (1971). . . . . Lowell
The Cowboys (1972). . . . . Long Hair
The Great Gatsby (1974). . . . . Tom Buchanan
The Laughing Policeman (1974) . . . . Leo Larsen
The Twist (1976). William
- •• 0:45 - Buns, taking off his clothes and walking onto stage during a play. Long shot.

Black Sunday (1977) . . . . Lander
Coming Home (1978) . . . . Captain Bob Hyde
- •• 2:03 - Buns, taking off his clothes at the beach and running into the ocean.

The Driver (1978) . . . . The Detective

Tattoo (1981). . . . . Karl Kinski
- •• 1:36 - Buns, while making love with Maud Adams before she kills him.

Harry Tracy (1982; Canadian). . . . . Harry Tracy
That Championship Season (1982) . . . George Sitkoswki
On the Edge (1985). . . . . Wes
(Unrated version—not the R-rated version.)
- • 0:52 - Brief buns, seen from below while floating in a pond.

1969 (1988). . . . . Cliff
World Gone Wild (1988) . . . . Ethan
The ' burbs (1989). . . . . Mark Rumsfield
After Dark, My Sweet (1990) . . . . Uncle Bud
Made for Cable Movies:
The Court-Martial of Jackie Robinson (1990) . Ed Higgins
Made for TV Movies:
Toughlove (1985) . . . .
TV:
Stoney Burke (1962-63) . . . . E. J. Stocker

Desarthe, Gerard

Films:
A Love in Germany (1984; French/German) Karl Wyler
- • 0:28 - Buns, lying in bed with Maria.

Dewaere, Patrick

Films:
Going Places (1974; French) . . . . Pierrot
- • 0:42 - Upper half of buns starting to leave the room. Surgical tape on his buns.
- •• 0:48 - Buns in bed with Marie-Ange.
- • 0:50 - Brief buns, switching places with Jean-Claude. 1:41 - Sort of buns, making love in back seat of car. Dark.
- • 1:42 - Buns, getting out of car and pulling up his pants.

Catherine & Co. (1975; French). . . . . Francois
Beau Pere (1981; French). . . . . Remi
The Heat of Desire (1982; French) . . . . . . Serge Laine
a.k.a. Plein Sud
- • 0:17 - Buns, getting out of bed and going into Carol's "house" that she has made out of sheets. 0:20 - Pubic hair, while lying on his back.
- • 0:21 - Side view of buns, on the floor with Carol. 0:57 - Brief side view of buns, getting out of bed and putting on pants.
- • 1:02 - Buns, getting into bed with Carol. Very, very brief frontal nudity hidden by subtitles.
- • 1:14 - Buns, taking off pants and getting into bed.

Diehl, John

Films:
Stripes (1981) . . . . Cruiser
Angel (1983) . . . . Crystal
- • 0:35 - Buns, washing blood off himself. Dark, hard to see. Long scene.

D.C. Cab (1983) . . . . Kidnapper

Joysticks (1983). . . . . .Arnie
National Lampoon's Vacation (1983)
. . . . Assistant Mechanic
City Limits (1984) . . . . Whitey
A Climate for Killing (1990). . . . . Wayne Paris
TV:
Miami Vice (1984-89) . . . . Detective Larry Zito

Dimone, Jerry

Films:
Tomboy (1985) . . . . Randy Star
•• 0:59 - Buns, making love with Betsy Russell in the exercise room.

Dorison, Zag

Films:
Deadly Innocents (1988) . . . . Crazy Norm
• 0:04 - Buns, standing on top of van and mooning the paramedics.

Douglas, Kirk

Father of actor Michael Douglas.
Films:
Out of the Past (1947; B&W) . . . . Whit Sterling
Champion (1949; B&W) . . . . Midge Kelly
A Letter to Three Wives (1949; B&W) . . . George Phipps
The Glass Menagerie (1950; B&W) . . . . . . Jim O'Connor
Along the Great Divide (1951; B&W) . . . . . Len Merrick
The Big Carnival (1951; B&W) . . . . Charles Tatum
Detective Story (1951; B&W) . . . . Jim McLeod
The Big Sky (1952; B&W) . . . . .Deakins
20,000 Leagues Under the Sea (1954) . . . . . . Ned Land
Man without a Star (1955) . . . . Dempsey Rae
Ulysses (1955; Italian) . . . . Ulysses
Gunfight at the O.K. Corral (1957)
. . . . .John H. "Doc" Holliday
Paths of Glory (1957; B&W) . . . . Colonel Dax
The Vikings (1958) . . . . .Einar
Last Train from Gun Hill (1959) . . . . Matt Morgan
Spartacus (1960). . . . . Spartacus
Seven Days in May (1964; B&W) . . . .
   Colonel Martin "Jiggs" Casey
In Harm's Way (1965; B&W) . . . . .Paul Eddington
Cast a Giant Shadow (1966) . . . .Colonel Mickey Marcus
The Way West (1967) . . . . . . .Senator William J. Tadlock
The Brotherhood (1968) . . . . Frank Ginetta
The Arrangement (1969) . . . . .Eddie and Evangelos
There Was a Crooked Man (1970). . .Paris Pitman, Jr.
• 0:11 - Brief upper half of buns leaving bedroom wearing only his gun belt.
•• 1:09 - Brief buns and balls, jumping into a barrel to take a bath in prison.
A Gunfight (1971). . . . . Will Tenneray
Once is Not Enough (1975) . . . . Mike Wayne
The Chosen (1978; Italian/British) . . . . Caine
The Fury (1978) .Peter Sandza

Holocaust 2000 (1978) . . . . Robert Caine
•• 0:52 - Buns, during nightmare sequence. Long shots, hard to tell it's him.
The Villain (1979). . . . . Cactus Jack
The Final Countdown (1980) . .Captain Matthew Yelland
Saturn 3 (1980) . . . . Adam
• 0:57 - Brief buns fighting with Harvey Keitel, more brief buns sitting down in bed with Farrah Fawcett.
The Man from Snowy River (1982; Australian)
. . . . Spur/Harrison
Eddie Macon's Run (1983) . . . . .Marazack
Tough Guys (1986) . . . . .Archie Long
• 1:36 - Buns, standing on moving train, mooning Charles Durning.
Made for TV Movies:
Drawl (1984) . . . .

Douglas, Michael

Son of actor Kirk Douglas.
Films:
Napolean and Samantha (1972) . . . . .Danny
Coma (1978) . . . . Dr. Mark Bellows
The China Syndrome (1979) . . . . .Richard Adams
Running (1979) . . . . Michael Andropolis
It's My Turn (1980) . . . . Ben Lewin
The Star Chamber (1983). . . . . Steven Hardin
Romancing the Stone (1984). . . . . Jack Colton
A Chorus Line (1985) . . . . Zack
The Jewel of the Nile (1985). . . . . Jack Colton
Fatal Attraction (1987) . . . . .Dan Gallagher
•• 0:16 - Brief buns pulling his pants down to make love with Glenn Close on the kitchen sink.
• 0:17 - Very brief buns falling into bed with Close.
• 0:22 - Brief buns, taking a shower.
Wall Street (1987) . . . . .Gordon Gekko
   (Academy Award for Best Actor.)
Black Rain (1989) . . . . Nick Conklin
The War of the Roses (1989) . . . . Oliver Rose
   1:36 - Almost buns, cleaning himself in the bidet.
TV:
The Streets of San Francisco (1972-76)
. . . . Inspector Steve Keller

Downey, Robert, Jr.

Films:
Baby, It's You (1983) . . . . Stewart
Firstborn (1984). . . . . Lee
Tuff Turf (1984) . . . . Jimmy Parker
Weird Science (1985). . . . . Ian
Back to School (1986) . . . . .Derek
Less than Zero (1987) .Julian
   1:22 - Very brief blurry buns in bedroom with another guy when Andrew McCarthy discovers them.
The Pick-Up Artist (1987) . . . . Jack Jericho
1969 (1988). . . . . .Ralph
Johnny Be Good (1988) . . . . .Leo Wiggins

Rented Lips (1988) . . . . Wolf Dangler
- 0:01 - Buns, wearing fishnet shorts in S&M outfit during porno movie shoot.
- 0:22 - Buns, through shorts again during playback of the film.

Chances Are (1989) . . . . .Alex Finch
Air America (1990) . . . . .Billy Covington
Too Much Sun (1990). . . . .
Soapdish (1991) . . . . David

TV:
Saturday Night Live (1985-86) . . . . regular

Dukes, David

Films:
The Strawberry Statement (1970) . . . . .Guard
The Wild Party (1975). . . . . .James Morrison
A Little Romance (1979) . . . . George De Marco
The First Deadly Sin (1980). . . . . Daniel Blank
Without a Trace (1983) . . . . Graham Selky
The Men's Club (1986) . . . . .Phillip
See You in the Morning (1989) . . . . .Peter
A Handmaid's Tale (1990) . . . . Doctor

Made for Cable Movies:
Cat on a Hot Tin Roof (1985; HBO). . . . .
The Josephine Baker Story (1991; HBO) . . . . Jo Bouillon

Made for Cable TV:
The Hitchhiker: Remembering Melody . . . . . . .Ted
- 0:05 - Buns, taking a shower.

Miniseries:
Beacon Hill (1975) . . . . Robert Lasslter
79 Park Avenue (1977) . . . . .Mike Koshko
The Winds of War (1983) . . . . Leslie Slote

Dye, Cameron

Films:
Valley Girl (1983) . . . . Fred
Body Rock (1984) . . . . E-Z
The Joy of Sex (1984) . . . . Alan Holt
The Last Starfighter (1984) . . . . .Andy
Fraternity Vacation (1985). . . . . Joe Gillespie
Heated Vengeance (1987). . . . .
Scenes from the Goldmine (1987). . . . . . . Niles Dresden
Stranded (1987) . . . . Lt. Scott
Out of the Dark (1988) . . . . Kevin Silver/Bobo
- 0:32 - Brief buns when Kristi yanks his underwear down while he is throwing a basketball. Don't see his face.

Men at Work (1990) . . . . .Lurinski

Earhar, Kirt

Films:
Summer Job (1989) . . . . Tom
- 0:30 - Buns in black G-string bikini when his swim trunks get ripped off.
- 0:43 - Buns in G-string underwear getting out of bed and going to the bathroom.

Eastwood, Clint

Former Mayor of Carmel, California.
Films:
For a Few Dollars More (1965; Italian)
. . . . The Man With No Name
A Fistful of Dollars (1967; Italian)
. . . . The Man With No Name
The Good, The Bad, and The Ugly
(1967; Italian/Spanish) .Joe
Coogan's Bluff (1968) . . . . Coogan
Hang 'em High (1968). . . . . Jed Cooper
Where Eagles Dare (1969) . . .Lieutenant Morris Schaffer
Kelly's Heroes (1970) . . . . Kelly
Two Mules for Sister Sara (1970) . . . . .Hogan
The Beguiled (1971) . . . . John McBurney
Dirty Harry (1971) . . . . .Harry Callahan
Play Misty for Me (1971) . . . . Dave Garland
Joe Kidd (1972) . . . . .Joe Kidd
High Plains Drifter (1973). . . . . The Stranger
Magnum Force (1973). . . . . .Harry Callahan
Thunderbolt and Lightfoot (1974)
. . . . John "Thunderbolt" Doherty
The Eiger Sanction (1975) . . . . Jonathan Hemlock
The Enforcer (1976) . . . . .Harry Callahan
The Outlaw Josey Wales (1976) . . . . Josey Wales
The Gauntlet (1977) . . . . Ben Shockley
Every Which Way But Loose (1978) . . . . . . Philo Beddoe
Escape from Alcatraz (1979). . . . . Frank Morris
0:07 - Buns, walking down jail hallway with two guards, don't see his face, so probably a body double.
Any Which Way You Can (1980) . . . . Philo Beddoe
Bronco Billy (1980) . . . . Bronco Billy
Firefox (1982) . . . . .Mitchell Gant
Honkytonk Man (1982) . . . . .Red Stovall
Sudden Impact (1983). . . . . .Harry Callahan
City Heat (1984) . . . . Lieutenant Speer
Tightrope (1984). . . . . Wes Block
- 0:33 - Buns, on the bed on top of Becky. Slow pan, red light, covered with sweat.
Pale Rider (1985) . . . . Preacher
Heartbreak Ridge (1986) . . . . Highway
The Dead Pool (1988) . . . . .Harry Callahan
Pink Cadillac (1989). . . . . Tommy Nowak
The Rookie (1990) . . . . Nick Pulovski
White Hunter Black Heart (1990) . . . . John Wilson

TV:
Rawhide (1959-66) . . . . Rowdy Yates

Edwards, Anthony

Films:
Fast Times at Ridgemont High (1982) . . . . . Stoner Bud
Heart Like a Wheel (1983)
. . . . John Muldowney, Age 15-23
Revenge of the Nerds (1984) . . . . Gilbert
Gotcha! (1985) . . . . .Jonathan Moore
The Sure Thing (1985). .Lance
Top Gun (1986). . . . . Lt. Nick Bradshaw

How I Got Into College (1989) . . . . .Kip Hammet
Downtown (1990) . . . . .Alex Kearney
• 0:19 - Buns, outside after getting his police uniform ripped off.

TV:

It Takes Two (1982-83) . . . . Andy Quinn

Eek-A-Mouse

Films:

New Jack City (1991) . . . . .Fat Smitty
• 0:15 - Buns, when Nino holds a gun to his head and makes him walk nude outside.

Elwes, Cary

Films:

Another Country (1984; British) . . . . .Harcourt
Oxford Blues (1984) . . . . .Lionel
The Bride (1985). . . . . .Josef
Lady Jane (1987; British) . . . . .Guilford Dudley
• 1:19 - Brief buns, getting out of bed.
The Princess Bride (1987) . . . . Westley the Farmboy
Glory (1989). Cabot Forbes
Days of Thunder (1990) . . . . Russ Wheeler

Estevez, Emilio

Son of actor Martin Sheen.
Brother of actor Charlie Sheen.

Films:

Tex (1982) . . . . Johnny Collins
Nightmares (1983) . . . . J. J.
The Outsiders (1983) . . . . .Two-Bit Matthews
Repo Man (1984) . . . . .Otto
The Breakfast Club (1985). . . . . Andrew Clark
St. Elmo's Fire (1985) . . . . Kirbo
That Was Then... This Is Now (1985). . . . .Mark Jennings
Maximum Overdrive (1986) . . . . .Bill Robinson
Wisdom (1986). John Wisdom
Stakeout (1987) . . . . Bill Reimers
Young Guns (1988). . .William H. Bonney (Billy the Kid)
• 1:19 - Brief buns standing up in the bathtub.
Men at Work (1990) . . . . .James St. James
Young Guns II (1990)
. . . . .William H. Bonney (Billy the Kid)
•• 1:00 - Buns, getting up out of bed, putting his pants on.

Everett, Rupert

Films:

Dance with a Stranger (1985; British) . . . . David Blakely
Duet for One (1987) . . . . Constantine Kassanis
Hearts of Fire (1987) . . . . James Colt
The Right Hand Man (1987) . . . . Harry Ironminster
The Comfort of Strangers (1991) . . . . Colin
•• 0:47 - Buns, walking around the room, looking for his clothes.
• 1:05 - Buns, making love with Natasha Richardson on bed. Lit with blue light.

Fahey, Jeff

Films:

Psycho III (1986) . . . . Duane
Backfire (1987) . . . . Donnie
• 0:22 - Brief, partial buns taking a shower, then very brief, out of focus frontal nudity in shower when blood starts to gush out of the shower head.
Split Decisions (1988) . . . . .Ray McGuinn
Impulse (1989) . . . . .Stan
The Serpent of Death (1989) . . . . Jake Bonner
True Blood (1989) . . . . Raymond Trueblood
Curiosity Kills (1990) . . . . Matthew
The Last of the Finest (1990) . . . . Rick Rodrigues
White Hunter Black Heart (1990) . . . . Pete Verrill
Body Parts (1991) . . . .

Falconeti, Sonny

Films:

Angel of Passion (1991). . . . . Will
• 0:22 - Buns frolicking in the surf with Carol while wearing a G-string.

Falk, Peter

Films:

Penelope (1966) . . . . Lieutenant Bixbee
Anzio (1968; Italian). . . . . Corporal Rabinoff
Husbands (1970) . . . . Archie
Woman Under the Influence (1974). . . . .Nick Longhetti
Murder by Death (1976) . . . . Sam Diamond
The Brink's Job (1978) . . . . Tony Pino
The Cheap Detective (1978) . . . . Lou Peckinpaugh
The In-Laws (1979) . . . . .Vince Ricardo
...All the Marbles (1981) . . . . .Harry
a.k.a. The California Dolls
The Great Muppet Caper (1981) . . . .
Big Trouble (1986). . . . . .Steve Rickey
Cookie (1989) . . . . Dominick "Dino" Capisco
In the Spirit (1990) . . . . .Roger Flan
•• 0:17 - Buns, three times while standing up, a little embarrassed, talking to Crystal.

TV:

The Untouchables (1959-63) . . . . .Nate Selko
Columbo (1971-77). . . . . Lieutenant Columbo

Farmer, Gary

Films:

Police Academy (1984) . . . . Sidewalk Store Owner
Powwow Highway (1988; U.S./British) . .Philbert Bono
•• 1:00 - Buns, in bedroom getting out of bed to wake up Buddy.
Renegades (1989) . . . . George

Made for TV Movies:

Plymouth (1991) . . . . Todd

Ferris, Larry

Films:

Penthouse Love Stories (1986). . . . . . . Ecstacize Man
- •• 0:32 - Frontal nudity and buns with a woman in the shower.

Field, Todd

Films:

Back to Back (1990). . . . . Todd Brand
- •• 0:33 - Buns, walking to and jumping into swimming pool. Don't see his face.

TV:

Take Five (1987) . . . . Kevin Davis

Finney, Albert

Films:

Under the Volcano (1984). . . . . Geoffrey Firmin
- ••• 0:49 - Buns and brief frontal nudity in bathroom with Jacqueline Bisset and Anthony Andrews when they try to give him a shower.
- •• 0:52 - Buns and very brief frontal nudity, putting on his underwear.

Orphans (1987) . . . . Harold
Miller's Crossing (1990) . . . . Leo

Firth, Peter

Films:

Equus (1977). . . . . Alan Strang
- • 1:19 - Frontal nudity standing in a field with a horse.
- ••• 2:00 - Nude in loft above the horses in orange light with Jenny Agutter. Long scene.

Joseph Andrews (1977; British/French) . Joseph Andrews
Tess (1979; French/British) . . . . Angel Clare
When Ya Comin' Back Red Ryder (1979)
. . . . Stephen Ryder
(Not available on video tape.)
Lifeforce (1985). . . . . Caine
Letter to Brezhnev (1986; British) . . . . Peter
Innocent Victim (1988) . . . . Terence
The Hunt for Red October (1990) . . . . Ivan Putin

Fitzpatrick, Bob

Films:

If Looks Could Kill (1987) . . . . Doorman
- ••• 0:18 - Buns, undressing and getting into bed with the maid.

Fletcher, Dexter

Films:

Bugsy Malone (1976) . . . . Baby Face
The Elephant Man (1980; B&W) . . . . Bytes' Boy
The Bounty (1984) . . . . Ellison
Revolution (1986) . . . . Ned Dobb
Lionheart (1987) . . . . Michael

The Rachel Papers (1989) . . . . Charles Highway
- • 0:58 - Very brief buns, jumping into bed with Ione Skye.

Twisted Obsession (1990) . . . . Malcolm Greene

Flower, George "Buck"

Films:

Video Vixens (1973) . . . . Rex Boorski
- •• 0:52 - Frontal nudity taking off his pants, then buns in bed with actress during filming of a movie. In B&W.

Flicks (1981). . . . .
Code Name Zebra (1987) . . . . Bundy
Party Favors (1987) . . . . Pop
(Shot on video tape.)
Berserker (1988). . . . .
Cheerleader Camp (1988) . . . . Pop
a.k.a. Bloody Pom Poms
Mac and Me (1988). . . . . Security Guard
Sorority Babes in the Slimeball Bowl-O-Rama (1988)
. . . . Janitor
They Live (1988) . . . . Drifter

Forster, Robert

Films:

Justine (1969) . . . . Narouz
Medium Cool (1969) . . . . John
- •• 0:36 - Nude, running around the house frolicking with Ruth.

The Don is Dead (1973) . . . . Frank
Avalanche (1978) . . . . Nick Thorne
The Black Hole (1979) . . . . Capt. Dan Holland
Hollywood Harry (1985). . . . . Harry Petry
The Delta Force (1986) . . . . Abdul
The Banker (1989) . . . . Dan
Satan's Princess (1989) . . . . Lou Cherney
Diplomatic Immunity (1991) . . . . Stonebridge

TV:

Banyon (1972-73) . . . . Miles C. Banyon
Nakia (1974) . . . . Deputy Nakia Parker
Once a Hero (1979) . . . . Gumshoe

Fox, James

Films:

The Chase (1966). . . . . Jason "Jake" Rogers
Thoroughly Modern Millie (1967) . . . . Jimmy Smith
Isadora (1968; British) . . . . Gordon Craig
Performance (1970) . . . . Chas
- • 0:00 - Very brief frontal nudity and buns making love with a woman. Don't see his face.
- • 0:02 - Buns, getting up next to his girlfriend.
- • 0:24 - Brief buns, getting roughed up by bad guys.

Greystoke: The Legend of Tarzan, Lord of the Apes
(1984) . . . . Lord Eskar
A Passage to India (1984; British) . . . . . . Richard Fielding
Absolute Beginners (1986; British) . . . Henley of Mayfair
The Whistle Blower (1987; British) . . . . Lord

Frey, Sam
Films:
Nea (A Young Emmanuelle) (1978; French). . . . .
The Little Drummer Girl (1984). . . . . Khalil
Black Widow (1987) . . . . Paul
•• 1:18 - Buns, walking into swimming pool.
Miniseries:
War and Remembrance (1988) . . . . .Rabinovitz

Friels, Colin
Films:
Monkey Grip (1983; Australian) . . . . Javo
Kangaroo (1986; Australian) . . . . .Richard Somers
•• 1:08 - Buns, running into the ocean.
• 1:09 - Frontal nudity walking towards Judy Davis.
Long shot, hard to see anything.
Malcolm (1986; Australian). . . . . .Malcolm
High Tide (1987; Australian) . . . . .Mick
Warm Nights on a Slow Moving Train (1987) . .The Man
Ground Zero (1988; Australian) . . . . . . .Harvey Denton
Darkman (1990). . . . . Louis Strack, Jr.

Gallagher, Peter
Films:
The Idolmaker (1980) . . . . Cesare
Summer Lovers (1982) . . . . Michael Pappas
• 0:22 - Buns, running into the water after Valerie
Quennessen.
• 0:54 - Frontal nudity getting ready to dive off a rock
while Daryl Hannah and Quennessen watch. Long
shot, hard to see anything.
Dreamchild (1986; British) . . . . Jack Dolan
Late for Dinner (1991) . . . . Bob Freeman
Made for TV Movies:
Skag (1980) . . . . John Skagska

Ganios, Tony
Films:
The Wanderers (1979). . . . . .Peppy
Back Roads (1981) . . . . .Bartini
Continental Divide (1981). . . . . .Possum
Porky's (1981; Canadian) . . . . .Meat
•• 0:21 - Brief buns, running out of the cabin during
practical joke.
Porky's Revenge (1985; Canadian) . . . . .Meat
•• 0:16 - Buns, getting out of swimming pool (the fifth
guy getting out). More buns running around.
Die Hard 2 (1990). . . . . Baker

Garcia, Andres
Films:
Tintorera (1977). . . . . Miguel
• 0:41 - Very brief frontal nudity in boat kitchen with
Susan George and Steve.
•• 0:42 - Nude, picking up George and throwing her
overboard.

Garfunkel, Art
Films:
Catch-22 (1970) . . . . Captain Nately
Carnal Knowledge (1971) . . . . Sandy
Bad Timing: A Sensual Obsession (1980)
. . . . Alex Linden
• 0:55 - Buns, making love with Theresa Russell on
stairwell. Don't see his face.
• 0:57 - Buns (Sort of see his balls through his legs), on
top of Russell when visited by Harvey Keitel.
1:48 - Side view of buns while in bed with an unconscious Russell.

Garrison, Bob
Films:
Hollywood Hot Tubs 2—Educating Crystal (1989)
. . . . Billy "Derrick" Dare
• 0:53 - Buns, running up to hot dog stand.

Gedrick, Jason
Films:
Massive Retaliation (1984) . . . . Eric Briscoe
The Heavenly Kid (1985) . . . . Lenny
•• 0:31 - Brief buns, in clothing store when Bobby mag-
ically dresses him in better looking clothes.
Iron Eagle (1986). . . . . .Doug
Born on the Fourth of July (1989). . . . . Martinez
Backdraft (1991). . . . . .Tim Krizminski
Brief buns in the shower with William Baldwin.

Gere, Richard
Films:
Looking for Mr. Goodbar (1977) . . . . Tony
•• 1:00 - Buns, on Diane Keaton's floor doing push-ups,
then running around in his jock strap.
Yanks (1979) . . . . Matt
American Gigolo (1980). . . . . .Julian
•• 0:39 - Buns and frontal nudity, but a long shot, so it's
hard to see anything.
An Officer and a Gentleman (1982) . . . . . . .Zack Mayo
Beyond the Limit (1983) . . . . .Dr. Eduardo Plarr
• 0:21 - Buns.
Breathless (1983) . . . . Jesse
•• 0:11 - Frontal nudity dancing and singing in the
shower. Hard to see because of the steam.
•• 0:52 - Buns, taking his pants off to get into the shower with Valerie Kaprisky, then more buns in bed. Very
brief frontal nudity. Dark, hard to see.
• 0:53 - Very, very brief top of frontal nudity popping
up when Kaprisky gets out of bed.
The Cotton Club (1984). . . . . .Dixie Dwyer
King David (1985) . . . . .David
No Mercy (1986) . . . . Eddie Jilletie
Power (1986). . . . . Pete St. John
Miles From Home (1988) . . . . .Frank Roberts
Internal Affairs (1990) . . . . .Dennis Peck
Pretty Woman (1990). . . . . .Edward Lewis

Gibson, Mel

Films:
Mad Max (1979). . . . . Max
Tim (1979) . . . . Tim Melville
Gallipoli (1981). . . . . .Frank Dunne
•• 1:18 - Buns, running into the water. (He's the guy on the left.)
The Road Warrior (1981). . . . . Max
The Year of Living Dangerously (1983; Australian)
. . . . .Guy Hamilton
The Bounty (1984) . . . . Fletcher Christian
Mrs. Soffel (1984) . . . . Ed Biddle
The River (1984) . . . . Tom Garvey
Mad Max Beyond Thunderdome (1985). . . . . Max
Lethal Weapon (1987). . . . . .Martin Riggs
••• 0:06 - Buns, getting out of bed and walking to the refrigerator.
Tequila Sunrise (1988). . . . . McKussie
Lethal Weapon 2 (1989) . . . . .Martin Riggs
Air America (1990) . . . . .Gene Ryack
Bird on a Wire (1990) . . . . Rick Jarmin
•• 1:01 - Brief close-up of buns when Rachel operates on his gunshot wound. Don't see his face, but it is him.
Hamlet (1990) . . . . Hamlet

Glenn, Scott

Films:
The Baby Maker (1970). . . . . .Tad
• 1:30 - Buns in bed with Charlotte.
Angels Hard as They Come (1971) . . . . .Long John
Hex (1973) . . . . Jimbang
Nashville (1975) . . . . .Glenn Kelly
Fighting Mad (1976). . . . . Charlie
Apocalypse Now (1979) . . . . Civilian
More American Graffiti (1979) . . . . Newt
Urban Cowboy (1980) . . . . Wes
The Challenge (1982) . . . . Rich
Personal Best (1982) . . . . Terry Tingloff
The Keep (1983). . . . . Glaeken Trismegestus
The Right Stuff (1983). . . . . Alan Shepard
Silverado (1985) . . . . Emmett
Wild Geese II (1985) . . . . John Haddad
Off Limits (1988). . . . . Colonel Dexter Armstrong
Verne Miller (1988). . . . . Verne Miller
Miss Firecracker (1989) . . . . Mac Sam
The Hunt for Red October (1990) . . . . Bart Mancuso
Silence of the Lambs (1990) . . . .
Backdraft (1991). . . . . .John Adcox
Made for Cable Movies:
Women & Men 2: Three Short Stories (1991; HBO)
. . . . Henry

Goldan, Wolf

Films:
Melody in Love (1978). . . . . .Octavio
• 1:14 - Buns, while making love in bed with Rachel and Angela.

Goldblum, Jeff

Ex-husband of actress Geena Davis.
Films:
California Split (1974) . . . . Lloyd Harris
Death Wish (1974) . . . . Freak 1
• 0:10 - Brief buns standing with pants down in living room raping Carol with his two punk friends.
Nashville (1975). . . . . Tricycle Man
Special Delivery (1976) . . . . Snake
St. Ives (1976) . . . . .Hood
Annie Hall (1977). . . . . Party Guest
Between the Lines (1977). . . . . .Max
The Sentinel (1977) .Jack
Invasion of the Body Snatchers (1978) . . . . . Jack Bellicec
Remember My Name (1978) . . . . .Mr. Nadd
Thank God It's Friday (1978) . . . . Tony
The Big Chill (1983) . . . . Michael
The Right Stuff (1983) . . . . Recruiter
Threshold (1983; Canadian). . . . . .Aldo Gehring
The Adventures of Buckaroo Banzai, Across the 8th Dimension (1984) . . . . New Jersey
Into the Night (1985). . . . . Ed Okin
Silverado (1985). . . . . .Slick
Transylvania 6-5000 (1985) . . . . Jack Harrison
The Fly (1986) . . . . Seth Brundle
Beyond Therapy (1987) . . . . .Bruce
Vibes (1988). . . . . Nick Deezy
Earth Girls are Easy (1989) . . . . .Mac
The Tall Guy (1990) . . . . .Dexter King
0:34 - Brief right cheek of buns, rolling around on the floor with Kate. Don't see his face.
Twisted Obsession (1990) . . . . Daniel Gillis
TV:
Tenspeed and Brown Shoe (1980)
. . . . Lionel "Brown Shoe" Whitney

Gonzales, Joe

Films:
Brain Damage (1988) . . . . .Guy in Shower
• 0:54 - Buns, taking a shower.

Goodeve, Grant

Films:
License to Drive (1988) . . . . .Mr. Nice Guy
Take Two (1988) . . . . Barry Griffith/Frank Bentley
• 0:31 - Buns, in bed with Robin Mattson.
••• 0:46 - Buns, getting into bed with Mattson again.
Made for TV Movies:
An Eight is Enough Wedding (1989). . . . . .David
TV:
Eight is Enough (1977-81) . . . . David Bradford
Dynasty (1983) .Chris Deegan
Northern Exposure (1990-) . . . . Rick

Graham, Gary
Films:
The Hollywood Knights (1980) . . . . Jimmy Shine
The Last Warrior (1989) . . . . Gibb
• 0:07 - Brief buns, taking off his towel when he sees a
ship.
Robot Jox (1990) . . . . Achilles
• 0:32 - Very brief buns, getting dressed in his room
while talking to Athena.
TV:
Alien Nation (1989-90) . . . . Det. Matthew Sikes

Grant, David
Films:
French Postcards (1979) . . . . Alex
Happy Birthday, Gemini (1980). . . . . Randy Hastings
The End of August (1982) . . . . Robert
American Flyers (1985) . . . . David
• 0:05 - Brief buns and very, very brief frontal nudity
taking off shorts and walking to bathroom.
Bat 21 (1988) . . . . Ross Carver

Grant, Richard E.
Films:
Withnail and I (1987; British). . . . . Withnail
How to Get Ahead in Advertising (1988). . . Bagley
• 0:19 - Brief buns wearing apron in kitchen all cov-
ered with food. Brief buns again talking with Rachel
Ward at top of stairs.
Mountains of the Moon (1989). . . . . Oliphant
Henry & June (1990). . . . . Hugo
Warlock (1990) . . . . Redferne
L.A. Story (1991). . . . . Roland

Graves, Rupert
Films:
A Room with a View (1986; British)
. . . . Freddy Honeychurch
••• 1:05 - Nude running around with Mr. Beebe and
George in the woods. Lots of frontal nudity.
Maurice (1987; British) . . . . Alec Scudder
A Handful of Dust (1988) . . . . John Beaver

Greenquist, Brad
Films:
The Bedroom Window (1987) . . . . Henderson
• 0:35 - Buns, turning off the light while Steve Guttenberg spies on him.

Greenwood, Bruce
Films:
Bear Island (1980; British/Canadian) . . . . Technician
Wild Orchid (1990) . . . . Jermone McFarland
•• 1:02 - Buns, in room with Carré Otis.

St. Elsewhere (1986-88) . . . . Dr. Seth Griffin

Gregory, Andre
Films:
My Dinner with Andre (1981) . . . . Andre
Author! Author! (1982) . . . . J.J.
Protocol (1984) . . . . Nawaf Al Kabeer
The Mosquito Coast (1986) . . . . Mr. Spellgood
Street Smart (1987) . . . . Ted Avery
The Last Temptation of Christ (1988) . . . John the Baptist
Some Girls (1988) . . . . Mr. D'Arc
• 1:24 - Buns, standing in the study looking at a book.
Very brief frontal nudity when he turns around to sit
at his desk.
The Bonfire of the Vanities (1990) . . . . . . Aubrey Buffing

Guest, Christopher
Husband of actress Jamie Lee Curtis.
Films:
The Hospital (1971) . . . . Resident
The Hot Rock (1972) . . . . Policeman
Death Wish (1974) . . . . Patrolman Reilly
The Fortune (1975) . . . . Boy Lover
Girlfriends (1978) . . . . Eric
• 1:04 - Buns, running after Melanie Mayron in her
apartment, then hugging her.
The Last Word (1979) . . . . Roger
The Long Riders (1980) . . . . Charlie Ford
Heartbeeps (1981) . . . . Calvin
This is Spinal Tap (1984) . . . . Nigel Tufnel
Little Shop of Horrors (1986) . . . . 1st Customer
Beyond Therapy (1987) . . . . Bob
Sticky Fingers (1988) . . . . Sam
TV:
Saturday Night Live (1984-85) . . . . regular

Gunner, Robert
Films:
Planet of the Apes (1968) . . . . Landon
• 0:26 - Very brief buns taking off clothes to go skinny
dipping. (Guy on the left.)

Guttenberg, Steve
Films:
The Chicken Chronicles (1977) . . . . David Kessler
Can't Stop the Music (1980) . . . . Jack Morell
Diner (1982) . . . . Eddie
The Man Who Wasn't There (1983) . . . Sam Cooper
••• 0:54 - Buns, dropping his pants in office with three
other men.
• 1:46 - Brief buns, while kissing Cindy during their
wedding ceremony.
Police Academy (1984) . . . . Carey Mahoney
Bad Medicine (1985) . . . . Jeff Marx
Cocoon (1985) . . . . Jack Bonner

Police Academy II: Their First Assignment (1985)
. . . . Carey Mahoney
Police Academy III: Back in Training (1986)
. . . . Carey Mahoney
Short Circuit (1986) . . . . Newton Crosby
Amazon Women on the Moon (1987). . . . . . Jerry Stone
The Bedroom Window (1987) . . . . Terry Lambert
  •• 0:05 - Buns, getting out of bed and walking to the
    bathroom.
Police Academy 4: Citizens on Patrol (1987)
. . . . Carey Mahoney
Three Men and a Baby (1987). . . . . Michael
Cocoon, The Return (1988). . . . . Jack Bonner
High Spirits (1988) . . . . Jack
Surrender (1988) . . . . Marty
Don't Tell Her It's Me (1990). . . . . Gus Kubicek
Three Men and a Little Lady (1990) . . . . Michael
Miniseries:
The Day After (1983) . . . . Stephen
TV:
Billy (1979). . . . . Billy Fisher
No Soap, Radio (1982) . . . . Roger

Haggerty, Dan

Films:
The Tender Warrior (1971) . . . . Cal
Bury Me an Angel (1972) . . . . .Ken
  • 1:17 - Brief buns, making love with Dag in bed. Lit
    with red light. Kind of a long shot, don't see his face
    very well.
Hex (1973) . . . . Brother Billy
The Life and Times of Grizzly Adams (1974)
. . . . James Capen Adams
King of the Mountain (1981) . . . . Rick
Abducted (1986; Canadian) . . . . Joe
Elves (1989) . . . . Mike McGavin
Inheritor (1990) . . . . .Dr. Berquist
TV:
The Life and Times of Grizzly Adams (1977-78)
. . . . James "Grizzly" Adams

Hall, Michael Keyes

Films:
Blackout (1989) . . . . Alan Boyle
  • 1:19 - Buns and balls viewed from the rear while
    stabbing Richard in bed.

Hamilton, Neil

Films:
The Tall Guy (1990) . . . . Naked George
  •• 0:04 - Buns, walking around apartment talking to Jeff
    Goldblum. Brief frontal nudity (out of focus).
  • 0:06 - More buns, when getting introduced to Gold-
    blum.
  • 1:22 - Brief buns, during end credits.

Hamlin, Harry

Husband of actress Nicollette Sheridan.
Films:
Movie Movie (1978) . . . . Joey Popchik
Clash of the Titans (1981) . . . . Perseus
King of the Mountain (1981) . . . . Steve
Making Love (1982) . . . . Bart
Blue Skies Again (1983) . . . . Sandy
Made for Cable Movies:
Laguna Heat (1987; HBO). . . . . .Tom Shephard
  • 0:50 - Buns, walking into the ocean with Catherine
    Hicks.
Dinner At Eight (1989) . . . . Larry Renault
Deceptions (1990; Showtime) . . . . .Nick Gentry
Miniseries:
Master of the Game (1984) . . . . Tony Blackwell
Made for TV Movies:
Deadly Intentions...Again? (1991) . . . . . Charles Raynor
TV:
Studs Lonigan (1979). . . . . Studs Lonigan
L.A. Law (1986-91) . . . . Michael Kuzak

Haney, Daryl

Films:
Daddy's Boys (1988) . . . . Jimmy
  • 0:17 - Buns, getting undressed in room with Christie.

Harris, Ed

Films:
Borderline (1980). . . . . .Hotchkiss
Knightriders (1981) . . . . Billy Davis
  • 0:01 - Buns, kneeling in the woods. Long shot, hard
    to see.
  • 1:51 - Upper half of buns, standing in a pond doing
    something with a stick.
Creepshow (1982). . . . . Hank
The Right Stuff (1983) . . . . John Glenn
Under Fire (1983). . . . . .Gates
A Flash of Green (1984) . . . . .Jimmy Wing
Places in the Heart (1984) . . . . Wayne Lomax
Swing Shift (1984) . . . . Jack Walsh
  • 0:03 - Very brief frontal nudity when he sits down in
    chair wearing a towel around his waist.
Alamo Bay (1985) . . . . Shang
Code Name: Emerald (1985) . . . . Gus Lang
Sweet Dreams (1985). . . . . .Charlie Dick
To Kill a Priest (1988) . . . . Stefan
Walker (1988) . . . . .William Walker
The Abyss (1989). . . . . Virgil "Bud" Brigman
Jacknife (1989). . . . . Dave
State of Grace (1990). . . . . .Frankie
Made for Cable Movies:
The Last Innocent Man (1987; HBO) . . . .
Paris Trout (1991; Showtime) . . . . .Harry Seagraves

Harris, Jim
Films:
Squeeze Play (1979)...................... Wes
•• 0:39 - Buns, tied up in a room while people walking by look in through open door.
Waitress! (1982) .... Jerry

Harris, Richard
Films:
The Bible (1966)........................... Cain
Hawaii (1966).................... Rafer Hoxworth
Camelot (1967)....................... King Arthur
Cromwell (1970; British)................ Cromwell
A Man Called Horse (1970)........ Lord John Morgan
The Molly Maguires (1970).. James McParlan/McKenna
99 and 44/100% Dead (1974) ....Harry Crown
Juggernaut (1974; British).................... Fallon
Return of a Man Called Horse (1976) .... John Morgan
Robin and Marian (1976)................ King Richard
The Cassandra Crossing (1977; British) ....Chamberlain
Orca, The Killer Whale (1977)........ Captain Nolan
The Wild Geese (1978; British) ....Rafer Janders
The Last Word (1979) ....Danny Travis
Tarzan, The Ape Man (1981)................. Parker
Your Ticket is No Longer Valid (1982) ...... Jason
• 1:19 - Buns, taking off robe and sitting on the floor.
Triumphs of a Man Called Horse (1983; U.S./Mexican)
............................Man Called Horse
Highpoint (1984; Canadian)............Louis Kinney
Martin's Day (1985; Canadian) ....Martin Steckert
Wetherby (1985; British)................ Sir Thomas
The Field (1991) ....Bull McCabe

Hartman, Billy
Films:
Slaughter High (1986).................... Frank
• 1:00 - Brief buns in bed with Stella.

Hasselhoff, David
Husband of actress Pamela Bach.
Ex-husband of actress Catherine Hickland.
Films:
Revenge of the Cheerleaders (1976)....... Boner
• 0:28 - Buns in shower room scene.
••• 0:30 - Frontal nudity in shower room scene while soaping Gail.
Starcrash (1979; Italian) ....Simon
W. B., Blue and the Bean (1988) .... White Bread
a.k.a. Bail Out
Witchery (1988) .... Gary
The Final Alliance (1990)................ Will Colton
Made for TV Movies:
The Cartier Affair (1985) ....
Knight Rider 2000 (1991) ....Michael Knight
TV:
The Young and the Restless .... Snapper
Knight Rider (1982-86) ....Michael Knight

Baywatch (1989-90).............. Mitch Bucannon
Baywatch (1991-)................ Mitch Bucannon

Hauer, Rutger
Films:
Turkish Delight (1974; Dutch) .... Erik
••• 0:01 - Brief nude walking around his apartment talking to a woman he has just picked up.
• 0:04 - Buns, in bed (covered with a sheet), then very brief frontal nudity throwing another girl out.
•• 0:36 - Frontal nudity getting up to answer the door with flowers.
•• 1:12 - Frontal nudity lying in bed depressed.
•• 1:16 - Buns, making love with Olga in bed.
Soldier of Orange (1977; Dutch) .... Erik Lanshoff
Katie's Passion (1978; Dutch).............. Dandy
• 1:12 - Buns seen through torn pants while he is kneeling on the floor.
•• 1:15 - Brief frontal nudity getting out of bed.
Spetters (1980; Dutch).................. Witkamp
Chanel Solitaire (1981)........... Etienne De Balsan
Nighthawks (1981) .... Wulfgar
Blade Runner (1982) ....Roy Batty
Eureka (1983; British)........ Claude Maillot Van Horn
The Osterman Weekend (1983) ....John Tanner
Flesh + Blood (1985)................... Martin
• 1:35 - Buns, in a jock strap running up stairs after everybody throws their clothes into the fire.
Ladyhawke (1985) ....Etienne of Navarre
The Hitcher (1986)...................John Ryder
Wanted: Dead or Alive (1987) .... Nick Randall
The Blood of Heroes (1989) .... Sallow
Bloodhounds of Broadway (1989) ....The Brain
Blind Fury (1990)..................... Nick Parker
Made for Cable Movies:
A Breed Apart (1984; HBO) .... Jim Malden

Hauser, Wings
Films:
Homework (1982) .... Red Dog
Vice Squad (1982) .... Ramrod
Deadly Force (1983)............... Stoney Cooper
A Soldier's Story (1984)................ Lt. Byrd
3:15—The Moment of Truth (1986)..... Mr. Havilland
Jo Jo Dancer, Your Life Is Calling (1986) .... Cliff
Tough Guys Don't Dance (1987) .... Regency
The Wind (1987) .... Phil
The Carpenter (1988) .... Ed
Dead Man Walking (1988)..............John Luger
Bedroom Eyes II (1989) .... Harry Ross
L.A. Bounty (1989)................... Cavanaugh
Street Asylum (1989) ....Sgt. Arliss Ryder
Living to Die (1990).............. Nick Carpenter
The Art of Dying (1991)................... Jack
•• 0:28 - Buns, standing in kitchen making love with Kathleen Kinmont.
Blood Money (1991) .... Jack

Hayes, Alan

Films:

Friday the 13th, Part IV—The Final Chapter
(1984)................................ Paul
  • 0:26 - Brief buns, swinging on a rope jumping into
    the lake.
Neon Maniacs (1985) .... Steven

Heard, John

Films:

Between the Lines (1977)................ Harry
  •• 1:17 - Buns, putting his pants on.
First Love (1977)...................... David
Chilly Scenes of Winter (1979) .... Charles
Heart Beat (1979) .... Jack Kerouac
Cutter's Way (1981) .... Alex Cutter
  a.k.a. Cutter and Bone
Cat People (1982)................... Oliver Yates
  • 1:37 - Very brief side view of buns, taking off his
    pants and sitting on bed next to Nastassja Kinski.
  •• 1:50 - Buns, making love with Nastassja Kinski in bed
    in a cabin.
C.H.U.D. (1984) .... George Cooper
After Hours (1985) .... Bartender
Heaven Help Us (1985)............. Brother Timothy
The Trip to Bountiful (1986) .... Ludie Watts
Beaches (1988)........................ John Pierce
Big (1988)............................ Paul
The Milagro Beanfield War (1988)....... Charlie Bloom
The End of Innocence (1989) .... Dean
Home Alone (1990) .... Peter
Made for TV Movies:
Necessity (1988)....................... Charlie
Cross of Fire (1989)............... Steve Stephenson

Hehn, Sascha

Films:

Melody in Love (1978)................... Alain
  •• 1:08 - Buns with Melody outside. Very brief erect pe-
    nis under covers.
  • 1:16 - Buns, twice while making love with Melody
    near an erupting volcano.

Herrier, Mark

Films:

Tank (1984) .... Elliot
Porky's Revenge (1985; Canadian) .... Billy
  •• 0:16 - Buns, getting out of swimming pool (the sec-
    ond guy getting out). More buns running around.

Hershberger, Gary

Films:

Paradise Motel (1985)..................... Sam
  •• 0:33 - Buns, running away from the Coach's house.

Heston, Charlton

Films:

The Ten Commandments (1956) .... Moses
Ben-Hur (1959) .... Judah Ben-Hur
  (Academy Award for Best Actor.)
El Cid (1961) .... Rodrigo Diaz de Bivar/El Cid
Planet of the Apes (1968) .... George Taylor
  • 0:26 - Buns, seen through a waterfall and while walk-
    ing on rocks. Long shots.
  • 1:04 - Buns standing in middle of the room when the
    apes tear his loin cloth off.
The Omega Man (1971) .... Neville
Soylent Green (1973)............... Detective Thorn
The Three Musketeers (1973)....... Cardinal Richelieu
Airport 1975 (1974)............... Alan Murdock
Earthquake (1974)....................... Graff
Midway (1976) .... Captain Matt Garth
Gray Lady Down (1977)........ Capt. Paul Blanchard
Almost an Angel (1990)................... Moses
TV:
The Colbys (1985-86) .... Jason Colby

Hewitt, Martin

Films:

Endless Love (1981) .... David
  • 0:22 - Buns when seen in front of fireplace in living
    room with Brooke Shields. Long shot.
  • 0:27 - Very brief buns in bedroom when Shields clos-
    es the door. Another long shot.
  •• 0:28 - Buns, jumping into bed with Shields.
  • 0:38 - Buns, lying on top of Shields in bed.
Yellowbeard (1983) .... Dan
Out of Control (1984) .... Keith
Killer Party (1986) .... Blake
Alien Predator (1987).................. Michael
Carnal Crimes (1991)......................
TV:
The Family Tree (1983) .... Sam Benjamin

Hewlett, David

Films:

Where the Heart Is (1990)............... Jimmy
  • 0:56 - Buns, walking around the hall in an angel cos-
    tume.

Hindley, Tommy

Films:

Silent Night, Deadly Night 4: Initiation (1990)
.... Hank
  • 0:03 - Brief buns, carrying Kim onto bed.

Hinton, Darby

Films:

Son of Flubber (1963) .... Second Hobgoblin
Without Warning (1980) .... Randy
Firecracker (1981) .... Chuck Donner

257

Malibu Express (1984) . . . . Cody Abilene
• 0:08 - Brief buns, taking a shower on his boat.
TV:
Daniel Boone (1964-70) . . . . Israel Boone

Hoffman, Dustin

Films:
The Graduate (1967) . . . . Ben Braddock
John and Mary (1969). John
Midnight Cowboy (1969) . . . . Ratso
Little Big Man (1970) . . . . Jack Crabb
Straw Dogs (1972) . . . . David
Papillon (1973) . . . . Louis Dega
Lenny (1974; B&W) . . . . Lenny Bruce
All the President's Men (1976) . . . . Carl Bernstein
Marathon Man (1976). . . . . Babe
•• 1:09 - Buns, getting out of the bathtub and putting
some pajamas on while someone lurks outside the
bathroom.
Straight Time (1978). . . . . Max Dembo
0:38 - Very, very brief tip of penis in jail shower scene
after getting sprayed by guard. Don't really see any-
thing.
Agatha (1979). . . . . Wally Stanton
Kramer vs. Kramer (1979) . . . . Ted Kramer
(Academy Award for Best Actor.)
Tootsie (1982). . . . . Michael
Ishtar (1987). Chuck Clarke
Rain Man (1988). . . . . Raymond Babbitt
(Academy Award for Best Actor.)
Family Business (1989) . . . . Vito
Dick Tracy (1990) . . . . Mumbles

Hoffman, Thom

Films:
The Fourth Man (1984; Dutch) . . . . Herman
• 1:00 - Frontal nudity on cross when Gerard pulls his
red trunks down. Long shot.
•• 1:10 - Nude in bathroom when Gerard comes in.
••• 1:11 - Buns making love on bed with Christine while
Gerard watches through keyhole.

Holbrook, Hal

Husband of actress Dixie Carter.
Films:
Wild in the Streets (1968) . . . . Senator John Fergus
The People Next Door (1970) . . . . David Hoffman
Magnum Force (1973) . . . . Lieutenant Briggs
The Girl from Petrovka (1974). . . . . Joe
• 0:40 - Brief buns, getting out of bed, putting on a
robe and talking to Goldie Hawn.
Midway (1976) . . . . Commander Joseph Rochefort
The Fog (1980). . . . . Malone
The Kidnapping of the President (1980; Canadian)
. . . . President Adam Scott
Creepshow (1982) . . . . Henry Northrup
The Star Chamber (1983) . . . . Benjamin Caulfield

Wall Street (1987) . . . . Lou Mannheim
The Unholy (1988). . . . . Archbishop Mosley
Miniseries:
Blue and the Gray (1982). . . President Abraham Lincoln
Made for TV Movies:
A Killing in a Small Town (1990). . . . . Dr. Beardsley
TV:
The Senator (1970-71). . . . . Senator Hayes Stowe

Hooten, Peter

Films:
Fantasies (1974) . . . . Damir
a.k.a. Once Upon a Love
• 1:06 - Buns, dropping his towel in front of Bo Derek.
Long shot, don't see his face.
• 1:18 - Buns again. Same shot from 1:06.
The Student Body (1975). . . . . Carter Blalock
Orca, The Killer Whale (1977) . . . . Paul
The Soldier (1982) . . . .

Hopper, Dennis

Films:
Rebel Without a Cause (1955) . . . . Goon
Giant (1956) . . . . Jordan Benedict III
The Trip (1967) . . . . Max
Easy Rider (1969). . . . . Billy
Mad Dog Morgan (1976). . . . . Daniel Morgan
The American Friend (1977). . . . . Ripley
Tracks (1977) . . . . Sgt. Jack Falen
•• 0:58 - Frontal nudity running through the train. Long
scene.
King of the Mountain (1981) . . . . Cal
The Osterman Weekend (1983) . . . . . Richard Tremayne
Rumble Fish (1983; B&W) . . . . Father
My Science Project (1985) . . . . Bob Roberts
Blue Velvet (1986) . . . . Frank Booth
Hoosiers (1986) . . . . Shooter
Running Out of Luck (1986). . . . . Video Director
The Texas Chainsaw Massacre 2 (1986)
. . . . Lieutenant "Lefty" Enright
Black Widow (1987). . . . . Ben
River's Edge (1987) . . . . Feck
Straight to Hell (1987; British) . . . . I.G. Farben
Riders of the Storm (1988). . . . . Captain
Chattahoochee (1990) . . . . Walker Benson
• 0:32 - Brief buns, leaving the shower room after talk-
ing to Gary Oldman.
Flashback (1990) . . . . Huey Walker
Made for Cable Movies:
Doublecrossed (1991; HBO). . . . . Barry Seal
Paris Trout (1991; Showtime). . . . . Paris Trout
Magazines:
Playboy (Dec 1976) . . . . The Year in Sex 1976
•• 141: Frontal nudity running through train.

Howard, Adam Coleman

Films:
Quiet Cool (1986). . . . . .Joshua Greer
Slaves of New York (1989) . . . . Stash
• 1:15 - Buns, putting on his pants and silhouette of penis. Dark, hard to see.
No Secrets (1991). . . . .

Howard, Alan

Films:
Americanization of Emily (1964) . . . . Port Ensign
Little Big Man (1970) . . . . Adolescent Jack Crabb
Oxford Blues (1984) . . . . .Simon
The Cook, The Thief, His Wife & Her Lover (1990)
Michael
•• 0:32 - Buns, then brief frontal nudity with Helen Mirren.
• 0:42 - Buns, on top of Mirren.
• 1:11 - Buns, with Mirren in kitchen.
••• 1:14 - Buns, getting into meat truck. Frontal nudity getting hosed off and walking around with Mirren.

Howell, C. Thomas

Husband of actress Rae Dawn Chong.
Films:
The Outsiders (1983) . . . . .Ponyboy Curtis
Grandview, U.S.A. (1984) . . . . Tim Pearson
Red Dawn (1984) . . . . Robert
Tank (1984) . . . . Billy
Secret Admirer (1985). . . . . Michael Ryan
The Hitcher (1986) . . . . .Jim Halsey
Soul Man (1986). . . . . Mark Watson
A Tiger's Tale (1988) . . . . Bubber Drumm
• 0:38 - Upper half of buns getting undressed in bedroom while Ann-Margret changes in the bathroom.
The Return of the Musketeers (1989) . . . . Raoul
Curiosity Kills (1990). . . . . Cat Thomas
Far Out Man (1990) . . . . .Himself
Side Out (1990) . . . . Monroe Clark
Made for TV Movies:
Into the Homeland (1987) . . . .
TV:
Two Marriages (1983-84) . . . . Scott Morgan

Howes, Dougie

Films:
Salome's Last Dance (1987) . . . . .Phoney Salome
• 1:05 - Very brief frontal nudity at the end of a dance routine when you think he's a female Salome.

Howman, Karl

Films:
The House on Straw Hill (1976; British)
. . . . Small Youth
•• 0:36 - Buns, raping Linda Hayden in a field, while his friend holds a gun.

Huff, Brent

Films:
Coach (1978). . . . . Keith
The Perils of Gwendoline in the Land of the Yik Yak (1984; French) . . . . .Willard
• 0:51 - Brief buns, in G-string while wearing costume.
•• 0:52 - Buns, in G-string, walking around with Tawny Kitaen in costumes.
•• 0:54 - More buns, after the women realize he's a man.
••• 0:56 - Buns, in jail while wearing only the G-string.
Deadly Passion (1985) . . . . Sam Black
Stormquest (1988). . . . . Zar

Hughes, Brendan

Films:
Return to Horror High (1987). . . . . Steven Blake
Stranded (1987). . . . . Prince
To Die For (1988). . . . . Vlad Tepish
• 1:13 - Buns, making love with Kate.
Howling VI—The Freaks (1990) . . . . .Ian

Hurt, John

Films:
10 Rillington Place (1971; British). . .Timothy John Evans
The Ghoul (1975) . . . . .Tom
East of Elephant Rock (1976; British) . . . .
The Disappearance (1977). . . . .
Midnight Express (1978; British) . . . . .Max
Alien (1979). . . . . Kane
The Shout (1979). . . . . .Anthony Fielding
The Elephant Man (1980; B&W) . . . . John Merrick
Heaven's Gate (1980). . . . . .Irvine
History of the World, Part I (1981) . . . . Jesus
Night Crossing (1981) . . . . Peter Strelzyks
Partners (1982) . . . . .Kerwin
The Osterman Weekend (1983) . . . Lawrence Fassett
• 0:01 - Buns, getting out of bed and walking to the shower.
1984 (1984) . . . . .Winston Smith
• 1:11 - Buns, walking from the bed to the window next to Suzanna Hamilton.
Champions (1984). . . . . Bob Champion
The Hit (1984) . . . . .Braddock
Jake Speed (1986) . . . . .Sid
From the Hip (1987) . . . . Douglas Benoit
Aria (1988; U.S./British) . . . . .The Actor
Deadline (1988). . . . . .Granville Jones
White Mischief (1988) . . . . Colville
Scandal (1989). . . . . Stephen Ward
(Unrated version.)
Frankenstein Unbound (1990) . . . . Buchanan
The Field (1991). . . . .
King Ralph (1991) . . . .

Hurt, William
Films:
Altered States (1980) . . . . Eddie Jessup
    0:46 - Brief pubic hair twice when Charles Haid and
    Bob Balaban help him out of isolation tank.
  • 0:54 - Very brief buns, standing in the shower when
    he starts transforming. More buns standing near
    door and walking to bed.
Body Heat (1981) . . . . Ned Racine
Eyewitness (1981) . . . . Daryll Deever
The Big Chill (1983) . . . . Nick
Gorky Park (1983) . . . . Arkady Renko
Kiss of the Spider Woman (1985; U.S./Brazilian)
 . . . . Luis Molina
  (Academy Award for Best Actor.)
Children of a Lesser God (1986) . . . . James Leeds
Broadcast News (1987) . . . . Tom Grunik
  •• 0:59 - Brief buns getting up from bed after making
    love with Jennifer. Shadow of semi-erect penis on
    the wall when she notices it.
The Accidental Tourist (1988) . . . . Macon
A Time of Destiny (1988) . . . . Martin
Alice (1990) . . . . Doug
I Love You to Death (1990) . . . . Harlan
The Doctor (1991) . . . . Dr. Jack McKee

Hutton, Timothy
Films:
Made in Heaven (1987) . . . . . Mike Shea/Elmo Barnett
  •• 0:08 - Buns, standing in a room when he first gets to
    heaven.
Everybody's All-American (1988) . . . . Donnie
A Time of Destiny (1988) . . . . Jack McKenna
Q & A (1990) . . . . Al Rielly
Torrents of Spring (1990) . . . . Dimitri Sanin

Ipalé, Aharon
Films:
Too Hot To Handle (1975) . . . . . Dominco de la Torres
  • 0:39 - Buns, in bed with Cheri Caffaro. Dark, hard to
    see.
The Final Option (1982; British) . . . . Malek
One Man Out (1988) . . . . The General
Made for TV Movies:
The Great Pretender (1991) . . . . Bratso

Irons, Jeremy
Films:
Nijinsky (1980; British) . . . . Mikhail Fokine
The French Lieutenant's Woman (1981) . . Charles/Mike
Moonlighting (1982; British) . . . . Nowak
Betrayal (1983; British) . . . . Jerry
Swann in Love (1984; French/German) . . Charles Swann
The Mission (1986; British) . . . . Gabriel
Reversal of Fortune (1990) . . . . Claus von Bülow
  (Academy Award for Best Actor.)

Miniseries:
Brideshead Revisited (1981; British) . . Charles Ryder
  •• 0:17 - (Part 3 on TV or Book 2 on video tape.) Buns,
    standing on roof with Anthony Andrews after talk-
    ing with Cordelia.

Jagger, Mick
Singer with *The Rolling Stones.*
Husband of model/actress Jerry Hall.
Films:
Performance (1970) . . . . Turner
  0:48 - Side view of buns, getting out of bathtub.
Burden of Dreams (1982) . . . .
Running Out of Luck (1986) . . . . Himself
  • 0:42 - Brief buns in mirror in room with Rae Dawn
    Chong lying in bed. Another buns long shot in bed
    on top of Chong.

Janssen, David
Films:
To Hell and Back (1955) . . . . Lieutenant Lee
The Green Berets (1968) . . . . George Beckworth
The Shoes of a Fisherman (1968) . . . . George Faber
Marooned (1969) . . . . Ted Dougherty
Macho Callahan (1970) . . . . . . Diego "Macho" Callahan
Once is Not Enough (1975) . . . . Tom Colt
  • 1:22 - Buns, taking off clothes and walking to the
    bathroom.
Two-Minute Warning (1976) . . . . Steve
Golden Rendezvous (1977) . . . . Charles Conway
Inchon (1981) . . . . David Feld
TV:
Richard Diamond, Private Detective (1957-60)
 . . . . Richard Diamond
The Fugitive (1963-67) . . . . Dr. Richard Kimble
O'Hara, U.S. Treasury (1971-72) . . . . Jim O'Hara
Harry-O (1974-76) . . . . Harry Orwell
Centennial (1978-79) . . . . Paul Garrett

Jenkins, John
Films:
Patti Rocks (1988) . . . . Eddie
  • 1:07 - Buns, making love with Patti in bed.

Jeter, Michael
Films:
Hair (1979) . . . . Woodrow Sheldon
  • 1:06 - Buns in front of Army guys.
Ragtime (1981) . . . .
Soup for One (1982) . . . .
The Money Pit (1986) . . . . Arnie
Dead Bang (1989) . . . . Dr. Krantz
Tango & Cash (1989) . . . . Skinner

Johnson, Don

Husband of actress Melanie Griffith.

Films:

The Magic Garden of Stanley Sweetheart (1970)
. . . . Stanley Sweetheart
Zachariah (1971) . . . . .Matthew
The Harrad Experiment (1973) . . . . Stanley Cole
•• 0:18 - Brief frontal nudity after getting out of the
shower while Laurie Walters watches.
Return to Macon County (1975) . . . . Harley McKay
A Boy and His Dog (1976). Vic
Melanie (1982) . . . . Carl
Miami Vice (1984). . . . . Sonny Crockett
Cease Fire (1985) . . . . Tim Murphy
Sweet Hearts Dance (1988). . . . . Wiley Boon
Dead Bang (1989). . . . . Detective Jerry Beck
The Hot Spot (1990) . . . . Harry Madox
•• 0:41 - Brief buns, pulling up his underwear, talking to
Virginia Madsen.
• 1:17 - Buns, undressing to go swimming with Mads-
en.
• 1:18 - Buns, getting out of the water. Long shot.
Harley Davidson & The Marlboro Man (1991)
. . . . Marlboro
Paradise (1991). . . . .

Made for TV Movies:

Beulah Land (1980). . . . .
The Revenge of the Stepford Wives (1980) . . . .

TV:

From Here to Eternity (1980) . . . Jefferson Davis Prewitt
Miami Vice (1984-89) . . . . Sonny Crockett

Johnson, Joseph Alan

Films:

Berserker (1988) . . . .
Iced (1988) . . . . Alex
• 0:46 - Brief buns in bathtub reminiscing about mak-
ing love with a girl.

Jones, Griff Rhys

Films:

The Misadventures of Mr. Wilt (1990) . . Henry Wilt
• 0:34 - Sort of buns, while naked and tied to inflatable
doll.
• 0:36 - More buns, up on balcony. Long shot.

Jones, Sam J.

Films:

10 (1979) . . . . David Hanley
Flash Gordon (1980). . . . . Flash Gordon
My Chauffeur (1986) . . . . Battle
•• 0:44 - Buns, running around the park naked.
Jane and the Lost City (1987; British) . . . . "Jungle" Jack
Silent Assassins (1988). . . . . Sam Kettle
One Man Force (1989) . . . . Pete

Under the Gun (1989). . . . . Braxton
• 0:41 - Brief buns, taking a shower at Vanessa Williams
place. Don't see his face.
Driving Force (1990) . . . . Steve

TV:

Code Red (1981-82) . . . . Chris Rorchek
Highwayman (1987-88). . . . . .Highwayman

Jones, Tommy Lee

Films:

Jackson County Jail (1976) . . . . Coley Blake
Rolling Thunder (1977) . . . . Johnny Vohden
The Betsy (1978) . . . . Angelo Perino
Eyes of Laura Mars (1978) . . . . John Neville
Coal Miner's Daughter (1980) .Doolittle "Mooney" Lynn
Back Roads (1981) . . . . .Elmore Pratt
The Executioner's Song (1982) . . . . . . Gary Gillmore
(European Version.)
•• 0:48 - Buns, walking to kitchen after hitting Rosanna
Arquette.
Nate and Hayes (1983) . . . . .Captain Bully Hayes
The River Rat (1984) . . . . Billy
Black Moon Rising (1986) . . . . .Quint
Stormy Monday (1988) . . . . .Cosmo
Fire Birds (1990). Brad Little
a.k.a. Wings of the Apache

Made for Cable Movies:

Cat on a Hot Tin Roof (1985; HBO) . . . .
The Park is Mine (1985; HBO) . . . . Mitch
Gotham (1988; Showtime). . . . . Eddie Mallard
a.k.a. The Dead Can't Lie
• 0:50 - Buns, walking over to Virginia Madsen. Dark,
hard to see anything.

Miniseries:

Lonesome Dove (1989) . . . . Woodrow F. Call

Made for TV Movies:

Stranger on My Land (1988) . . . .

TV:

One Life to Live . . . . .Dr. Mark Toland

Jones, Tyronne Granderson

Films:

Angel III: The Final Chapter (1988) . . . . . .L.A. Pimp
•• 0:32 - Buns, standing in alley after Angel pushes him
out of the car.
Twins (1988) . . . . .Mover #2
Harlem Nights (1989) . . . . Crapshooter

Julia, Raul

Films:

Panic in Needle Park (1971). . . . . Marco
The Gumball Rally (1976). . . . . Franco
Eyes of Laura Mars (1978) . . . . .Michael Reisler
The Escape Artist (1982). . . . . .Stu Quinones

One from the Heart (1982). . . . . .Ray
- 1:20 - Very brief buns getting out of bed with Teri Garr when Frederic Forrest crashes through the ceiling.

The Tempest (1982) . . . . Kalibanos
Compromising Positions (1985) . . . . David Suarez
Kiss of the Spider Woman (1985; U.S./Brazilian)
. . . . Valentin
The Morning After (1986). . . . . Joaquin Manero
Moon Over Parador (1988). . . . . . . Roberto Strausmann
Tequila Sunrise (1988). . . . . Escalante
Trading Hearts (1988). .Vinnie
Frankenstein Unbound (1990). . . . . . Victor Frankenstein
Presumed Innocent (1990) . . . . Sandy Stern
The Rookie (1990). . . . . Strom

Juliano, Al

Films:
True Love (1989). . . . . Male Stripper
- 0:43 - Buns in G-string dancing on stage in a club.

Kantor, Richard

Films:
Baby, It's You (1983) . . . . Curtis
Out of Control (1984) . . . . Gary
- 0:29 - Buns, pulling his underwear down during a game of strip spin the bottle.

TV:
Finder of Lost Loves (1984-85) . . . . Brian Fletcher

Katt, William

Films:
Carrie (1976) . . . . Tommy Ross
First Love (1977). Elgin Smith
Big Wednesday (1978) . . . . Jack
Baby... Secret of the Lost Legend (1985)
. . . . George Loomis
House (1986) . . . . Roger Cobb
White Ghost (1988) . . . . .Steve Shepard
Last Call (1990). . . . . .Paul Avery
- ••• 0:29 - Buns, on floor with Shannon Tweed.
- 0:41 - Brief buns, getting up from bed and putting his pants on.
- 1:02 - Brief buns, in bed with Tweed.

TV:
Greatest American Hero (1981-83) . . . . . . Ralph Hanley

Kay, Norman

Films:
Lonely Hearts (1983; Australian) . . . . .Peter
- 1:03 - Buns, getting out of bed. Very brief frontal nudity.

Man of Flowers (1984; Australian). . . . . .Charles Bremer

Keitel, Harvey

Films:
Who's That Knocking at My Door? (1968) . . . . .J.R.
Mean Streets (1973) .Charlie
Alice Doesn't Live Here Anymore (1975) . . . . Ben
Buffalo Bill and the Indians (1976) . . . . Ed
Mother, Jugs & Speed (1976). . . . . Speed
Taxi Driver (1976) . . . . .Sport
The Duellists (1977). .Feraud
Welcome to L.A. (1977) . . . . Ken Hood
Blue Collar (1978) . . . . .Jerry
Eagle's Wing (1978; British) . . . . Henry
Fingers (1978) . . . . Jimmy Angelelli
Bad Timing: A Sensual Obsession (1980)
. . . . Inspector Netusil
Death Watch (1980) . . . . Roddy
Saturn 3 (1980) . . . . Benson
The Border (1982) . . . . .Cal
Exposed (1983) . . . . Rivas
La Nuit de Varennes (1983; French/Italian)
. . . . Thomas Paine
Dream One (1984; British/French) . . . . Mr. Legend
Falling In Love (1984) . . . . .Ed Lasky
Camorra (1986; Italian) . . . . Frankie Acquasanta
The Inquiry (1986). . . . . .Pontius Pilate
The Men's Club (1986) . . . . Sully
- 1:22 - Buns, getting up off the bed to talk to Allison.

Off Beat (1986) . . . . Bank Robber
Wise Guys (1986). . . . . .Bobby Dilea
The Pick-Up Artist (1987) . . . . .Alonzo
Blindside (1988; Canadian) . . . . .Gruber
The January Man (1988) . . . . .Frank Starkey
The Last Temptation of Christ (1988). . . . . .Judas
GoodFellas (1990) . . . . J. R.
The Two Jakes (1990). . . . . Jake Berman
Thelma and Louise (1991) . . . .

Keith, David

Films:
The Rose (1979). . . . . Mal
Brubaker (1980). . . . . .Larry Lee Bullen
The Great Santini (1980) . . . . Red Pettus
Back Roads (1981) . . . . .Mason
Take This Job and Shove It (1981) . . . . Harry Meade
An Officer and a Gentleman (1982). . . . . Sid Worley
Independence Day (1983) . . . . .Jack Parker
The Lords of Discipline (1983) . . . . Will
Firestarter (1984) . . . . Andrew McGee
Gulag (1985) . . . . Mickey Almon
- •• 1:26 - Buns, standing outside with Malcolm McDowell in the snow being hassled by guards.

Heartbreak Hotel (1988) . . . . Elvis Presley
White of the Eye (1988) . . . . .Paul White
Made for TV Movies:
Friendly Fire (1978) . . . .
TV:
Co-ed Fever (1979) . . . . Tuck
Flesh and Blood (1991-) . . . . .Arlo Weed

Keller, Todd

Films:
Penthouse Love Stories (1986). . Service Station Man
•• 0:11 - Brief frontal nudity in bedroom with a woman.

Kerwin, Brian

Films:
Hometown, U.S.A. (1979). . . . . T.J. Swackhammer
Murphy's Romance (1985) . . . . Bobbie Jack Moriarity
•• 0:55 - Brief buns walking into the bathroom.
Nickel Mountain (1985) . . . . George
King Kong Lives! (1986) . . . . Hank Mitchell
Torch Song Trilogy (1988). . . . . .Ed
Miniseries:
Blue and the Gray (1982) . . . . .Malachi Hale
Made for TV Movies:
Bluegrass (1988). . . . . .Dancy
Switched at Birth (1991) . . . . Bob Mays
TV:
Lobo (1979-81). . . . . Deputy Birdwell Hawkins
The Chisholms (1979). . . . . Gideon Chisholm

Kime, Jeffrey

Films:
Quartet (1981; British/French) . . . . James
•• 0:49 - Nude, posing with two women for the por-
nographer.
Joy (1983; French/Canadian). . . . . .Helmut
The State of Things (1983) . . . . .Mark

King, Perry

Films:
Slaughterhouse Five (1972). . . . . Robert Pigrim
The Lords of Flatbush (1974). . . . . Chico
Mandingo (1975) . . . . Hammond
•• 0:17 - Frontal nudity walking to bed to make love
with Dite.
The Wild Party (1975). . . . . .Dale Sword
Lipstick (1976) . . . . Steve Edison
Andy Warhol's Bad (1977; Italian) . . . . L-T
The Choirboys (1977). . . . . Slate
A Different Story (1979) . . . . Albert
• 1:33 - Buns, through shower door, then brief buns
getting out of the shower to talk to Meg Foster.
Search and Destroy (1981) . . . . Kip Moore
Class of 1984 (1982). .Andy
Switch (1991) .Steve Brooks
Miniseries:
Captains and the Kings (1976) . . . . Rory Armagh
Aspen (1977) . . . . Lee Bishop
The Last Convertible (1979) . . . . Russ Currier
Made for TV Movies:
Love's Savage Fury (1979). . . . .
Danielle Steel's "Kaleidoscope" (1990) . . John Chapman
TV:
The Quest (1982) . . . . .Dan Underwood
Riptide (1984-86) . . . . Cody Allen

Kingsley, Ben

Films:
Gandhi (1982) . . . . Mahatma Gandhi
(Academy Award for Best Actor.)
Betrayal (1983; British). . . . . .Robert
Harem (1985; French) . . . . Selim
Turtle Diary (1986; British). . . . . .William Snow
Maurice (1987; British). . . . . .Lasker Jones
Pascali's Island (1988; British). . . . . Basil Pascali
Without a Clue (1988) . . . . .Dr. Watson
Slipstream (1990). . . . . Avatar
Made for Cable Movies:
**Murderers Among Us: The Simon Wiesenthal
Story** (1989; HBO) . . . . Simon Wiesenthal
•• 0:27 - Buns and brief frontal nudity standing in and
leaving a line in a concentration camp.

Kirby, Bruno

a.k.a. B. Kirby, Jr.
Films:
The Harrad Experiment (1973) . . . . . . Harry Schacht
• 0:41 - Brief frontal nudity, getting into the swimming
pool with Beth, Don Johnson and Laurie Walters.
Between the Lines (1977). . . . . .David
Borderline (1980). . . . . Jimmy Fante
Where the Buffalo Roam (1980) . . . . Marty Lewis
Modern Romance (1981). . . . . .Jay
This is Spinal Tap (1984) . . . . Tommy Pischedda
Birdy (1985). . . . . Renaldi
Bert Rigby, You're a Fool (1989). . . . . . . .Kyle DeForest
We're No Angels (1989). . . . . Deputy
When Harry Met Sally... (1989) . . . . Jess
City Slickers (1991) . . . . Ed
TV:
The Super (1972). . . . . Anthony Girelli

Kirby, Michael

Films:
My Pleasure is My Business (1974) . . . . Gus
• 0:41 - Brief buns while making love with Xaviera Hol-
lander.
Bugsy Malone (1976). . . . . .Angelo
In Praise of Older Women (1978; Canadian). . . . .
The Silent Partner (1978) . . . . Packard
Meatballs (1979; Canadian) . . . . Eddy
Crossover (1980; Canadian) . . . . .Dr. Turley
a.k.a. Mr. Patman
Agency (1981; Canadian). . . . . Peters

Kleemann, Gunter

Films:
I Spit on Your Grave (1978) . . . . Andy
(Uncut, unrated version.)
• 0:33 - Buns, raping Jennifer.

Kline, Kevin

Husband of actress Phoebe Cates.

Films:

Sophie's Choice (1982) . . . . .Nathan Landau
The Big Chill (1983) . . . . Harold
The Pirates of Penzance (1983) . . . . Pirate King
Violets Are Blue (1986) . . . . Henry Squires
  • 1:02 - Brief buns, standing up and putting on his
  shorts, on island with Sissy Spacek.
A Fish Called Wanda (1988) . . . . Otto
The January Man (1988) . . . . Nick Starkey
I Love You to Death (1990) . . . . Joey
  • 0:10 - Buns, wearing an apron walking from the bed-
  room in Victoria Jackson's apartment.
Soapdish (1991) . . . . .Jeffrey

Knight, Wyatt

Films:

Porky's (1981; Canadian) . . . . Tommy Turner
Porky's Revenge (1985; Canadian) . . . Tommy Turner
  •• 0:16 - Buns, getting out of swimming pool (the first
  guy getting out). More buns running around.
  • 0:54 - Buns, getting his underwear pulled down
  while trying to escape from a motel room from Balbricker.

Kologie, Ron

Films:

Iced (1988) . . . . Carl
  • 0:39 - Buns, in bathroom snorting cocaine.

Kotto, Yaphet

Films:

The Liberation of L. B. Jones (1970). . .Sonny Boy Mosby
Man and Boy (1971) . . . . Nate Hodges
Across 110th Street (1972) . . . . Det. Lt. Pople
Housewife (1972) . . . . .Bone
Live and Let Die (1973; British) . . . . .Kananga
Truck Turner (1974) . . . . Blue
Drum (1976) . . . . Blaise
  • 1:02 - Buns, getting hung upside down in barn and
  spanked along with Ken Norton.
Blue Collar (1978) . . . . Smokey
Alien (1979) . . . . .Parker
Brubaker (1980) . . . . Dickie Coombes
The Star Chamber (1983) . . . . Det. Harry Lowes
Warning Sign (1985) . . . . .Major Connolly
Eye of the Tiger (1986) . . . . .J. B. Deveraux
Pretty Kill (1987) . . . . Harris
The Jigsaw Murders (1988) . . . . .Dr. Fillmore
Midnight Run (1988) . . . . Alonzo Mosely
Tripwire (1989) . . . . Lee Pitt

Made for Cable Movies:

The Park is Mine (1985; HBO) . . . . Eubanks

Made for TV Movies:

For Love and Honor (1983)
  . . . . Platoon Sgt. James "China" Bell

Krabbé, Jeroen

Films:

Soldier of Orange (1977; Dutch) . . . . Gus
Spetters (1980; Dutch) . . . . Henkhof
The Fourth Man (1984; Dutch) . . . . .Gerard
  ••• 0:03 - Frontal nudity getting out of bed and walking
  down the stairs.
  •• 0:26 - Frontal nudity drying himself off and getting
  into bed.
  • 0:33 - Buns, getting out of bed.

Kristofferson, Kris

Films:

Blume in Love (1973) . . . . Elmo
Pat Garrett and Billy the Kid (1973) . . . Billy the Kid
  • 0:37 - Buns, getting into bed with a girl after Harry
  Dean Stanton gets out. Long shot, hard to see.
Bring Me the Head of Alfredo Garcia (1974) . . . . . . Paco
Alice Doesn't Live Here Anymore (1975) . . . . . . .David
The Sailor Who Fell From Grace with the Sea (1976)
  . . . . .Jim Cameron
A Star is Born (1976) .Johnny
Vigilante Force (1976) . . . . .Aaron Arnold
Semi-Tough (1977) . . . . Shake Tiller
Convoy (1978) . . . . Rubber Duck
Heaven's Gate (1980) . . . . Averill
Rollover (1981) .Hub Smith
Flashpoint (1984) . . . . Logan
Songwriter (1984) . . . . .Blackie Buck
Trouble in Mind (1986) . . . . .Hawk
Big Top Pee Wee (1988) . . . . Mace Montana
Welcome Home (1989) . . . . .Jake
Millennium (1990) . . . . .Bill Smith

Made for Cable Movies:

The Tracker (1988; HBO) . . . . .Noble Adams
Another Pair of Aces (1991) . . . . Capt. Elvin Metcalf
  (Video tape includes nude scenes not shown on cable
  TV.)

Magazines:

Playboy (Jul 1976) . . . . Kris and Sarah
  •• 126: Buns, in bed with Sarah Miles.

Kuhlman, Ron

Films:

To Be or Not To Be (1983) . . . . Polish Flyer
Splash (1984) . . . . Man with Date
Omega Syndrome (1986) . . . .
Shadow Play (1986) . . . . .John Crown
  • 1:06 - Buns, standing and holding Dee Wallace in his
  arms.

Made for TV Movies:

The Brady Brides (1981) . . . . Phillip Covington III

Lackey, Skip
Films:
Once Bitten (1985). . . . . Russ
- 1:11 - Brief buns in the school showers trying to see if Mark got bitten by a vampire.

Lafayette, John
Films:
The Shaming (1979) . . . . Rafe
a.k.a. Good Luck, Miss Wyckoff
a.k.a. The Sin
- •• 0:43 - Very brief frontal nudity, taking off his jumpsuit in classroom with Anne Heywood.
- • 0:52 - Buns, making love on top of Heywood.

Lambert, Christopher
Husband of actress Diane Lane.
Films:
Greystoke: The Legend of Tarzan, Lord of the Apes (1984). . . . . John Clayton/Tarzan
Subway (1985; French). . . . . Fred
Highlander (1986) . . . . Conner MacLeod
- • 1:30 - Buns making love with Roxanne Hart.
The Sicilian (1987) . . . . Salvatore Giullano
(Director's uncut version.)
- •• 1:02 - Buns, when the Duchess yanks his underwear down. Don't see his face, but probably him.
Priceless Beauty (1989; Italian) . . . . Monroe
Why Me? (1990). . . . . Gus Cardinale

Lamden, Derek
Films:
Baby Love (1969) . . . . Nick
1:29 - Brief buns in shower when Luci opens the door.

Lang, Perry
Films:
Teen Lust (1978). . . . . Terry
- • 0:01 - Buns in jock strap getting his pants pulled down while he does pull ups.
1941 (1979) . . . . Dennis
Alligator (1980). . . . . Kelly
The Big Red One (1980) . . . . Kaiser
The Hearse (1980). . . . . Paul
Body and Soul (1981) . . . . Charles Golphin
O'Hara's Wife (1982). . . . . Rob O'Hara
T.A.G.: The Assassination Game (1982) . . . . Frank
Spring Break (1983; Canadian) . . . . Adam
- • 0:27 - Brief buns opening his towel in the shower, mooning his three friends.
Sahara (1984) . . . . Andy
Jocks (1986) . . . . Jeff
Jacob's Ladder (1990) . . . . Jacob's Assailant
TV:
Bay City Blues (1983) . . . . Frenchy Nuckles

Lattanzi, Matt
Husband of singer/actress Olivia Newton-John.
Films:
Rich and Famous (1981). . . . . The Boy, Jim
- ••• 1:10 - Buns, making love with Jacqueline Bisset.
Grease 2 (1982). . . . .
My Tutor (1983). . . . . Bobby Chrystal
That's Life! (1986) . . . . Larry Bartlet
Roxanne (1987) . . . . Trent
Catch Me... If You Can (1989). . . . . Dylan

Laughlin, John
Films:
An Officer and a Gentleman (1982) . . . . Troy
Crimes of Passion (1984) . . . . Bobby Grady
- • 0:58 - Buns, getting dressed after having sex with Kathleen Turner. (Viewed through peep hole by Anthony Perkins.)
Footloose (1984) . . . . Woody
The Hills Have Eyes, Part II (1985) . . . . Hulk
Space Rage (1987). . . . . Walker
Midnight Crossing (1988) . . . . Jeffrey Schubb
TV:
The White Shadow (1980-81) . . . . Paddy Falahey

Lawrence, Bruno
Films:
Smash Palace (1981; New Zealand) . . . . Al Shaw
- ••• 0:39 - Buns in bed after arguing, then making up with Jacqui.
Treasure of the Yankee Zephyr (1981) . . . . Barker
Warlords of the 21st Century (1982) . . . . Willie
a.k.a. Battletruck
Heart of the Stag (1983; New Zealand) . . . . Peter Daley
Utu (1984; New Zealand) . . . . Williamson
An Indecent Obsession (1985) . . . . Matt Sawyer
The Quiet Earth (1985; New Zealand) . . . Zac Hobson
- •• 0:02 - Brief frontal nudity lying on the bed.
- •• 0:04 - Brief nude getting back into bed.
- • 0:33 - Very brief frontal nudity jumping out of the ocean. Blurry, hard to see anything.
- •• 1:01 - Frontal nudity during flashback lying in bed.
Rikky & Pete (1988; Australian) . . . . Sonny

Layne, Scott
Films:
Vice Academy, Part 2 (1990). . . . . Petrolino
- • 0:49 - Buns, in men's locker room twice when Linnea Quigley and Ginger Lynn Allen come in.

Lee, Mark
Films:
Gallipoli (1981) . . . . Archy Hamilton
- •• 1:18 - Buns, running into the water with Mel Gibson. (Mark is the guy on the right.)
Emma's War (1986) . . . . John Davidson

Legein, Marc
Films:
The Secrets of Love—Three Rakish Tales (1986)
.... Luke
• 0:18 - Buns, in the hay with the Weaver's wife.
• 0:24 - More buns.

Leguizamo, John
Films:
Casualties of War (1989).................... Diaz
• 0:53 - Buns, pulling his pants down to rape Oahn.
Die Hard 2 (1990)........................ Burke
Revenge (1990) ....Ignacio

Leinert, Mike
Films:
Easy Wheels (1989) ....Meatball
• 0:52 - Brief buns, putting his pants on.

Lemmon, Jack
Films:
It Should Happen to You (1954; B&W) .. Pete Sheppard
Mister Roberts (1955) ......Ens. Frank Thurlowe Pulver
Fire Down Below (1957) ....Tony
Some Like it Hot (1959; B&W) .... Jerry/Daphne
The Apartment (1960; B&W) .... C. C. Baxter
The Wackiest Ship in the Army (1961)...Lt. Rip Crandall
Days of Wine and Roses (1962; B&W)............ Joe
Irma La Douce (1963)..................... Nestor
Good Neighbor Sam (1964) ....Sam Bissel
The Great Race (1965) .... Professor Fate
The Fortune Cookie (1966; B&W) .... Harry Hinkle
The Odd Couple (1968) ....Felix Ungar
The April Fool's (1969) .... Howard Brubaker
The Out of Towners (1970).........George Kellerman
Avanti! (1973)................ Wendell Armbruster
(Not available on video tape. Shown on *The Arts and En-
tertainment Channel* periodically. Scenes are listed as
0:00 since I can't time correctly with the commercials.)
• 0:00 - Buns, standing up in bathtub talking to Juliet
Mills.
Save the Tiger (1973) .... Harry Stoner
The Front Page (1974) .... Hildy Johnson
The Prisoner of Second Avenue (1975) ....Mel
Airport '77 (1977)................... Don Gallagher
The China Syndrome (1979)............. Jack Godell
Tribute (1980; Canadian) ....Scottie Templeton
Buddy Buddy (1981)................ Victor Clooney
Missing (1982) .... Ed Horman
Mass Appeal (1984) ....Father Farley
Macaroni (1985; Italian) .... Robert Traven
That's Life! (1986)................. Harvey Fairchild
TV:
That Wonderful Guy (1949-50).............. Harold
Toni Twin Time (1950) .... host
Ad Libbers (1951)........................ regular
Heaven for Betsy (1952) .... Pete Bell

Lennon, John
Late singer with *The Beatles* and on his own.
Films:
A Hard Day's Night (1964; British) .... John
Help! (1965; British)........................ John
How I Won the War (1967) .... Gripweed
Imagine: John Lennon (1988) .... Himself
• 0:43 - Nude in B&W photos from his White Album.
0:57 - Brief frontal nudity of album cover again dur-
ing interview.

Lester, Jeff
Films:
In the Cold of the Night (1989) ....Scott Bruin
• 0:05 - Very brief buns, rolling over to strangle Shan-
non Tweed.
TV:
Once a Hero (1979) .... Captain Justice/Brad Steele
Walking Tall (1981) .... Deputy Grady Spooner

Levine, Mark
Films:
Spring Fever USA (1988) ....Duke Dork
• 1:17 - Buns, twice, in boat hallway with his skinny
brother after being tricked.

Levy, Eugene
Films:
Going Beserk (1983) ....Sal di Pasquale
National Lampoon's Vacation (1983) .....Car Salesman
Splash (1984)....................Walter Kornbluth
Armed and Dangerous (1986)....... Norman Kane
• 1:02 - Cheeks of his buns through the back of leather
pants while dressed in drag with John Candy to es-
cape from the bad cops.
Club Paradise (1986) .... Barry Steinberg
TV:
Second City TV Comedy (1977-81) ....Earl Camembert
SCTV Network 90 (1981-83) ....regular

Lhermitte, Thierry
Films:
Next Year if All Goes Well (1983; French) ......Maxime
My Best Friend's Gir (1984) ....Pascal Saulnier
My New Partner (1984; French)............Francois
Until September (1984) ....Xavier de la Pérouse
•• 0:43 - Buns, after making love with Karen Allen.
0:53 - Almost frontal nudity getting out of bathtub.

Liebman, Ron
Films:
Where's Poppa? (1970) ....Sidney Hocheiser
• 0:45 - Buns running across the street, then in front of
door in hall, then brief buns leaving George Segal's
apartment.

The Hot Rock (1972). . . . . Murch
Slaughterhouse Five (1972). . . . . Paul Lazzaro
Your Three Minutes Are Up (1973) . . . . .Mike
Won Ton Ton, The Dog Who Saved Hollywood (1976) .
  Rudy Montague
Norma Rae (1979) . . . . .Reuben
Zorro, The Gay Blade (1981). . . . . .Esteban
Romantic Comedy (1983). . . . . .Leo
Phar Lap (1984; Australian) . . . . Dave Davis
TV:
Kaz (1978-79). . . . . Martin "Kaz" Kazinsky

Lindon, Vincent
Films:
Half Moon Street (1986). . . . . .Sonny
  • 1:04 - Buns, getting out of bed with Sigourney Weaver.

Lipton, Robert
Films:
Blue (1968). . . . . Antonio
Bullitt (1968). . . . . First Aide
Tell Them Willie Boy is Here (1969) . . . . . . .Newcombe
Lethal Woman (1988) . . . . Major Derek Johnson
  • 1:05 - Brief buns in the water on the beach with Shannon Tweed.
TV:
The Survivors (1969-70) . . . . Tom

Lithgow, John
Films:
Obsession (1976) . . . . Robert La Salle
The Big Fix (1978). . . . . Sam Sebastian
Rich Kids (1979) . . . . Paul Philips
Blow Out (1981). . . . . Burke
World According to Garp (1982). . . . . .Roberta
Terms of Endearment (1983). . . . . Sam Burns
Twilight Zone—The Movie (1983). . . Airplane Passenger
2010 (1984) . . . . Walter Curnow
The Adventures of Buckaroo Banzai, Across the 8th
  Dimension (1984) . . . . Dr. Emilio Lizardo/John Whorfin
Footloose (1984). . . . . .Reverend Moore
Santa Claus (1985) . . . . .Bozo
Harry and the Hendersons (1987) . . . George Henderson
The Manhattan Project (1987) . . . . . . John Mathewson
Distant Thunder (1988). . . . . .Mark Lambert
Out Cold (1989) . . . . .Dave Geary
Memphis Belle (1990). . . . . Colonel Bruce Derringer
Made for Cable Movies:
Glitter Dome (1985; HBO) . . . .
Traveling Man (1989; HBO). . . . .
  • 0:48 - Brief buns, trying to get the VCR away from Mona in her living room.
Miniseries:
The Day After (1983) . . . .
Made for TV Movies:
The Boys (1991) . . . . Artie Margulies

Lloyd, Christopher
Films:
Goin' South (1978) . . . . .Towfield
The Lady in Red (1979) . . . . Frognose
Schizoid (1980) . . . . Gilbert
Mr. Mom (1983) . . . . Larry
To Be or Not To Be (1983) . . . . .Capt. Schultz
The Adventures of Buckaroo Banzai, Across the 8th
  Dimension (1984) . . . . John Bigboote
Star Trek III: The Search for Spock (1984). . . . . . . Kruge
Back to the Future (1985) . . . . .Dr. Emmett Brown
Clue (1985) . . . . .Professor Plum
Miracles (1986) . . . . .Harry
Walk Like a Man (1987) . . . . .Reggie
Eight Men Out (1988) . . . . Bill Burns
Track 29 (1988; British) . . . . Henry Henry
  • 0:34 - Very brief side view of his buns lying in the hospital getting spanked by Sandra Bernhard.
Who Framed Roger Rabbit (1988) . . . . Judge Doom
Back to the Future, Part II (1989) . . . .Dr. Emmett Brown
The Dream Team (1989) . . . . Henry
Back to the Future, Part III (1990). . . .Dr. Emmett Brown
Why Me? (1990) . . . . .Bruno Daley
Suburban Commando (1991) . . . .
TV:
Taxi (1979-83) . . . . "Reverend Jim" Ignatowski

Lowe, Rob
Films:
Class (1983) . . . . Skip
The Outsiders (1983) . . . . Sodapop
The Hotel New Hampshire (1984) . . . . John
Oxford Blues (1984). . . . . Nick Di Angelo
St. Elmo's Fire (1985) . . . . Billy
About Last Night... (1986). . . . . Danny
  •• 0:52 - Buns and almost frontal nudity when he opens the refrigerator with Demi Moore.
Youngblood (1986) . . . . Dean Youngblood
  ••• 0:16 - Buns, standing in hallway in jockstrap and walking around while Cindy Gibb watches.
Square Dance (1987). .Rory
a.k.a. Home is Where the Heart Is
Illegally Yours (1988) . . . . Richard Dice
Masquerade (1988). . . . . .Tim Whalen
  ••• 0:04 - Buns, getting up from bed with Kim Cattrall.
  •• 0:30 - Buns, making love with Meg Tilly in bed.
Bad Influence (1990) . . . . .Alex
  ••• 1:27 - Buns, going into the bathroom.
TV:
A New Kind of Family (1979-80) . . . . Tony Flanagan
Video Tapes:
Rob Lowe's Home Video (1989) . . . . .himself
  Nude. A little bit hard to tell if it's him (it's a copy of a copy of a copy...) Rob's video tape of his sexual tryst with two teenage girls can be purchased from *Midnight Blue*. The address is located at the end of this book.

Lundgren, Dolph

Films:
A View to a Kill (1985) . . . . Venz
Masters of the Universe (1987) . . . . He-Man
The Punisher (1989) . . . . Frank Castle
• 0:06 - Upper half of buns, kneeling in his underground hideout. Don't see his face.
• 1:23 - Same shot at 00:06 used again.
Red Scorpion (1989) . . . . Lt. Nikolai
I Come in Peace (1990) . . . . Jack Caine
Showdown in Little Tokyo (1991) . . . .

Luther, Michael

Films:
Malibu Beach (1978) . . . . Paul
• 0:32 - Buns, running into the ocean with his friends.

Lynch, John

Films:
Cal (1984; Irish) . . . . Cal
• 1:20 - Buns, getting into bed with Helen Mirren.

Maccanti, Roberto

Films:
1900 (1976; Italian) . . . . Olmo as a Child
• 0:53 - Frontal nudity undressing and showing the young Alfredo his penis.

MacGowran, Jack

Films:
Age of Consent (1969; Australian) . . . . .Nat Kelly
• 1:01 - Brief buns, running into the ocean when Miss Marley sees him.
•• 1:02 - Buns, running away from her to the cabin while holding a dog to cover up his private parts.

MacLachlan, Kyle

Films:
Dune (1984) . . . . Paul Atreides/Maudib
Blue Velvet (1986) . . . . .Jeffrey
•• 0:41 - Buns and very brief frontal nudity running to closet in Isabella Rossellini's apartment.
The Hidden (1987) . . . . Lloyd Gallagher
Don't Tell Her It's Me (1990) . . . . Trout
The Doors (1991) . . . .
TV:
Twin Peaks (1990-91) . . . . Dale Cooper

Madsen, Michael

Brother of actress Virginia Madsen.
Films:
Wargames (1983) . . . . Steve
The Natural (1984) . . . . Bump Bailey
Racing with the Moon (1984) . . . . Frank
Thelma and Louise (1991) . . . .

Made for Cable TV:
The Hitchhiker: Man at the Window
. . . . .John Hampton
•• 0:09 - Buns, making love with his wife on the couch.
TV:
Our Family Honor (1985-86) . . . . .Augie Danzig

Maiden, Tony

Films:
Spaced Out (1980; British) . . . . Willy
• 0:38 - Buns, getting examined by Cosia.

Malkovich, John

Films:
The Killing Fields (1984) . . . . .Al
Places in the Heart (1984) . . . . Mr. Will
Eleni (1985) . . . . .Nick
The Glass Menagerie (1987) . . . . .Tom
Making Mr. Right (1987) . . . . .Dr. Jeff Peters/Ulysses
The Sheltering Sky (1990) . . . . Port
••• 0:32 - Frontal nudity and half of buns, getting out of bed and opening door.
Queens Logic (1991) . . . . .Eliot

March, John

Films:
Moon 44 (1990) . . . . Moose Haggerty
• 0:43 - Brief buns in shower room. (Sort of see frontal nudity through grating in the shower divider.)

Marchand, Guy

Films:
Cousin, Cousine (1975; French) . . . . Pascal
Loulou (1980; French) . . . . André
•• 0:59 - Buns, getting out of bed with Isabelle Huppert.
The Heat of Desire (1982; French) . . . . .Max
a.k.a. Plein Sud
Entre Nous (1983; French) . . . . .Michel
a.k.a. Coup de Foudre

Margotta, Michael

Films:
The Strawberry Statement (1970) . . . . Swatch
Drive, He Said (1972) . . . . Gabriel
•• 1:21 - Running nude across the grass and up some stairs, then trashing a biology room at the university.
Times Square (1980) . . . . .Jo Jo
Can She Bake a Cherry Pie? (1983) . . . . Larry
Made for TV Movies:
She Lives (1973) . . . . .Al

Marin, Richard "Cheech"

Films:
Up in Smoke (1978) . . . . .Pedro De Pacas
Cheech & Chong's Next Movie (1980) . . . . .Himself
Cheech & Chong's Nice Dreams (1981). . . . .Himself
 • 0:57 - Brief buns climbing over railing to escape Donna's husband, Animal.
Things are Tough all Over (1982) . . . . . .Mr. Slyman
 • 0:21 - Buns in the laundromat dryer.
Still Smokin' (1983). . . . . .Himself
Yellowbeard (1983). . . . . .El Segundo
The Corsican Brothers (1984) . . . .
After Hours (1985) . . . . Neil
Echo Park (1986). . . . . Sid
Born in East L.A. (1987). . . . . Rudy Robles
Rude Awakening (1989) . . . . .Zeus
The Shrimp on the Barbie (1990) . . . . . . .Carlos Muñoz

Marinaro, Ed

Films:
Fingers (1978). . . . . .Gino
Dead Aim (1987) . . . . .Malcolm "Mace" Douglas
 • 0:52 - Buns, in bed making love with Amber. Dark, hard to see.
Queens Logic (1991). . . . . Jack
Made for TV Movies:
Menu for Murder (1990). . . . . Det. Russo
TV:
Laverne & Shirley (1980-81) . . . . Sonny St. Jacques
Hill Street Blues (1981-87). . . . . Officer Joe Coffey

Markle, Stephen

Films:
Ticket to Heaven (1981; Canadian) . . . . .Karl
Perfect Timing (1984) . . . . Harry
 • 0:58 - Buns, making love with Lacy.

Marotte, Carl

Films:
Pick-Up Summer (1979; Canadian) . . . . Steve
 • 0:18 - Side view of buns, hanging a B.A. out passenger window at Rod.
Gas (1981; Canadian). . . . . .Bobby
My Bloody Valentine (1981; Canadian) . . . . .Dave

Marshall, David Anthony

Films:
Another 48 Hrs. (1990) . . . . .Willie Hickok
 • 0:57 - Buns, putting pants on after getting out of bed.

Martinez, Nacho

Films:
Matador (1986; Spanish) . . . . .Diego Montes
 ••• 0:29 - Buns making love with Eva in bed.

Masterson, Sean

Made for Cable TV:
**Dream On: The Name of the Game is Five-Card
 Stud** (1991; HBO) . . . . Carter
 • 0:17 - Brief buns, after losing his clothes during poker game.
 •• 0:18 - Buns again getting up from the table.

Mathers, James

Films:
Aria (1988; U.S./British) . . . . Boy Lover
 • 1:00 - Brief dark outline of frontal nudity in hotel room with his girlfriend.
 • 1:02 - Frontal nudity under water in the bathtub with his girlfriend.

Matheson, Tim

Films:
Magnum Force (1973). . . . . Sweet
Almost Summer (1978) . . . . Kevin Hawkins
Animal House (1978) . . . . Eric "Otter" Stratton
 • 0:08 - Buns, changing clothes in his bedroom while talking to Boone.
1941 (1979). . . . . Birkhead
A Little Sex (1982) . . . . Michael Donovan
To Be or Not To Be (1983) . . . . Lieutenant Sobinski
The House of God (1984). . . . . .Dr. Basch
 (Not available on video tape.)
Impulse (1984). . . . . Stuart
 • 0:17 - Buns, getting out of bed with Meg Tilly.
Up the Creek (1984) . . . . .Bob McGraw
Fletch (1985) . . . . .Alan Stanwyk
Speed Zone (1989) . . . . Jack
Drop Dead Fred (1991) . . . .
Made for Cable Movies:
Buried Alive (1990) . . . . Clint
Made for TV Movies:
The Quest (1976). . . . . Quentin Beaudine
Listen To Your Heart (1983) . . . .
Joshua's Heart (1990). . . . .
Stephen King's "Sometimes They Come Back" (1991)
 . . . . .Jim Norman
TV:
Window on Main Street (1961-62). . . . . . Roddy Miller
The Virginian (1969-70). . . . . Jim Horn
Bonanza (1972-73) . . . . .Griff King
Tucker's Witch (1982-83) . . . . Rick Tucker
Just in Time (1988). . . . .

Maury, Derrel

Films:
Massacre at Central High (1976) . . . . .David
 • 0:32 - Buns, romping around in the ocean with Kimberly Beck. Dark, long shot. Hard to see anything.
TV:
Apple Pie (1978) . . . . Junior Hollyhock
Joanie Loves Chachi (1982-83). . . . . Mario

Mazmanian, Marius
Films:
Video Vixens (1973) . . . . Psychiatrist
•• 0:42 - Buns and balls from behind, frolicking on couch with his patient. In B&W.

McCarthy, Andrew
Films:
Class (1983) . . . . Jonathan
Heaven Help Us (1985) . . . . Michael Dunn
Brief buns by the swimming pool.
St. Elmo's Fire (1985) . . . . Kevin
Pretty in Pink (1986) . . . . Blane McDonough
Less than Zero (1987) . . . . Clay
• 0:03 - Very brief buns getting out of bed to answer the phone.
Mannequin (1987) . . . . Jonathan Switcher
Fresh Horses (1988) . . . . Matt Larkin
Kansas (1988) . . . . Wade Corey
Weekend at Bernie's (1989) . . . . Larry Wilson
Club Extinction (1990) . . . . The Assassin

McCleery, Gary
Films:
Hard Choices (1986) . . . . Bobby
•• 1:11 - Buns, making love on top of Laura.

McDonald, Joshua
Films:
Eleven Days, Eleven Nights (1988; Italian) . . Michael
a.k.a. Top Model
• 0:33 - Buns, when Sarah removes his underwear.

McDowell, Malcolm
Husband of actress Mary Steenburgen.
Films:
If... (1969) . . . . Mick Travers
Long Ago Tomorrow (1970) . . . . Bruce Pritchard
A Clockwork Orange (1971) . . . . Alex
• 0:27 - Very brief nude having sex with two women in his bedroom. Shot at fast speed.
0:52 - Upper half of frontal nudity getting admitted to jail.
O Lucky Man! (1973; British) . . . . Mick Travis
Voyage of the Damned (1976) . . . . Max Gunter
Time After Time (1979; British) . . . . Herbert G. Wells
Caligula (1980) . . . . Caligula
(X-rated, 147 minute version.)
• 0:05 - Buns, rolling around in bed with Drusilla.
• 0:36 - Brief buns, taking ring off of Peter O'Toole.
• 0:46 - Very brief buns running to bed.
0:51 - Buns, putting Drusilla down in bed.
• 1:14 - Nude walking around outside in the rain. Dark, long shot.
2:23 - Very brief buns under his white robe.

Cat People (1982) . . . . Paul Gollier
• 1:06 - Side view of buns, lying on the bathroom floor. Partial lower frontal nudity when he gets up.
Blue Thunder (1983) . . . . Cochrane
Get Crazy (1983) . . . . Reggie
Gulag (1985) . . . . Englishman
•• 1:26 - Buns, standing outside with David Keith in the snow being hassled by guards.
The Caller (1989) . . . .
Class of 1999 (1990) . . . . Dr. Miles Langford
Disturbed (1990) . . . . Dr. Derek Russell
Jezebel's Kiss (1990) . . . . Benjamin J. Faberson
•• 1:12 - Buns, making love with Jezebel.
Moon 44 (1990) . . . . Major Lee

McGann, Paul
Films:
Withnail and I (1987; British) . . . . Marwood
Innocent Victim (1988) . . . . Barry
The Rainbow (1989) . . . . Anton Skrebensky
•• 1:30 - Buns, opening a bottle of wine in room with Sammi Davis.
• 1:44 - Very brief frontal nudity and buns running up a hill with Amanda Donohoe.

McGill, Bruce
Films:
National Lampoon's Animal House (1978) . . . . . . D-Day
The Hand (1981) . . . . Brian Ferguson
Tough Enough (1983) . . . . Tony Fallon
Silkwood (1984) . . . . Mace Hurley
No Mercy (1986) . . . . Lt. Hall
Wildcats (1986) . . . . Dan Darwill
Out Cold (1989) . . . . Ernie Cannald
•• 0:12 - Frontal nudity, opening the shower door, talking to Teri Garr. Brief buns, putting on underwear.
Made for TV Movies:
Shoot First: A Cop's Vengeance (1991) . . . . Shifton
TV:
Delta House (1979) . . . . D-Day

McKeon, Doug
Films:
Turnaround . . . . Ben
Uncle Joe Shannon (1978) . . . . Robbie
Night Crossing (1981) . . . . Frank Strelzyks
On Golden Pond (1981) . . . . Billy Ray
Mischief (1985) . . . . Jonathan
• 0:56 - Brief buns, putting on his underwear after making love with Kelly Preston.
TV:
Centennial (1978-79) . . . . Philip Wendell
Big Shamus, Little Shamus (1979) . . . . Max Sutter

McNichol, Peter

Films:

Dragonslayer (1981) . . . . Galen
- 0:27 - Very brief buns diving into pond. Sort of frontal nudity swimming under water. Hard to see because the water is so murky.

Meadows, Stephen

Films:

Night Eyes (1990) . . . . Michael Vincent
(Unrated version.)
- 0:27 - Buns and balls in bed with Tanya Roberts while Andrew Stevens watches on monitor.

Metrano, Art

Films:

Cheaper to Keep Her (1980) . . . . Tony Turino
History of the World, Part I (1981). . . . Leonardo da Vinci
Police Academy II: Their First Assignment (1985)
. . . . Lt. Mauser
- 0:39 - Buns, in the locker room after the guys put epoxy resin in his shampoo.
Police Academy III: Back in Training (1986)
. . . . Commandant Mauser

Mitchell, Mark

Films:

The Outing (1987) . . . . Mike Daley
- 1:08 - Buns when his friend gets killed, then very brief frontal nudity sitting up.

Modine, Matthew

Films:

Baby, It's You (1983) . . . . Steve
Private School (1983) . . . . Jim
Streamers (1983) . . . . Billy
The Hotel New Hampshire (1984). . . . . Chip Dove
Mrs. Soffel (1984) . . . . Jack Biddle
Birdy (1985) . . . . Birdy
- 1:25 - Buns, squatting on the end of his bed, thinking he's a bird.
- 1:29 - Buns, sitting on the bed. Longer shot.
- •• 1:33 - Buns, walking around naked in his bedroom.
- 1:42 - Buns, waking up when Nicholas Cage comes into his bedroom.
Visionquest (1985) . . . . Louden Swain
- 1:29 - Very brief buns taking off underwear to get weighed for wrestling match.
Full Metal Jacket (1987) . . . . Private Joker
Orphans (1987) . . . . Treat
Married to the Mob (1988) . . . . Mike Downey
Gross Anatomy (1989) . . . . Joe Slovac
Memphis Belle (1990) . . . . Dennis
Pacific Heights (1990) . . . . Drake Goodman

Moir, Richard

Films:

In Search of Anna (1978; Australian) . . . . Tony
Chain Reactions (1980; Australian)
. . . . Junior Constable Pillott
Heatwave (1983; Australian) . . . . Steven
An Indecent Obsession (1985) . . . . Luce Daggett
- 0:31 - Buns at the beach with his pals. Don't see his face.

Monahan, Dan

Films:

Only When I Laugh (1981) . . . . Jason
Porky's (1981; Canadian) . . . . Pee Wee
- 0:22 - Buns, running down the road at night. Long shot.
Porky's II: The Next Day (1983; Canadian)
. . . . Pee Wee
- 0:39 - Buns at cemetery with Graveyard Gloria, then upper half of lower frontal nudity when he's holding her.
- 0:40 - Upper half of lower frontal nudity when he drops Gloria.
- 0:42 - Nude, trying to hide Steve.
- ••• 0:44 - Nude when guys with shotguns shoot at him.
Up the Creek (1984) . . . . Max
Porky's Revenge (1985; Canadian) . . . . Pee Wee
- •• 0:02 - Buns, when his graduation gown gets accidentally torn off during a dream.
- •• 0:16 - Buns, getting out of swimming pool (the fourth guy getting out). More buns running around.
- •• 1:27 - Buns, getting his graduation gown torn off.
From the Hip (1987) . . . . Larry
The Prince of Pennsylvania (1988) . . Tommy Rutherford

Montgomery, Chad

Films:

Nightmare at Shadow Woods (1983) . . . . . . Gregg
a.k.a. Blood Rage
- 0:52 - Brief buns, making love with Andrea on diving board just before getting killed.

Moore, Dudley

Films:

The Wrong Box (1966; British) . . . . John Finsbury
30 is a Dangerous Age, Cynthia (1968; British)
. . . . Rupert Street
Bedazzled (1968; British) . . . . Stanley Moon
Foul Play (1978) . . . . Stanley Tibbets
10 (1979) . . . . George Webber
- 0:47 - Buns, at neighbor's party just before Julie Andrews sees him through a telescope.
Wholly Moses (1980) . . . . Harvey/Herschel
Arthur (1981) . . . . Arthur Bach
Six Weeks (1982) . . . . Patrick Dalton
Lovesick (1983) . . . . Saul Benjamin
Romantic Comedy (1983) . . . . Jason

Best Defense (1984) . . . . Wylie Cooper
Micki & Maude (1984) . . . . Rob Salinger
Unfaithfully Yours (1984). . . . . Claude Eastman
Santa Claus (1985) . . . . Patch
Like Father, Like Son (1987) . . . . Dr. Jack Hammond
Arthur 2 On the Rocks (1988) . . . . Arthur Bach
Crazy People (1990) . . . . Emory

Moore, Kenny
Films:
Personal Best (1982) . . . . Denny Stiles
 •• 1:31 - Nude, getting out of bed and walking to the
   bathroom.

Moore, Michael J.
Films:
Border Heat (1988) . . . . J. C. Ryan
 • 0:14 - Buns, taking off his clothes and getting into
   spa with Darlanne Fluegel.

Moreno, Jaime
Films:
Amor Ciego (1980; Mexican) . . . . .Daniel
 ••• 0:51 - Frontal nudity standing up from bed, then
   buns when Apollonia hugs him.
 • 0:53 - Buns, making love in bed with Apollonia.

Morrow, Rob
Films:
Private Resort (1985) .Ben
 • 0:36 - Brief buns standing with Hillary Shapiro worshiping Baba Rama.
 •• 0:39 - Buns getting caught naked by Mrs. Rawlins,
   then more buns, running through the halls.
TV:
Northern Exposure (1990-) . . . . .Joel Fleischman

Moses, Mark
Films:
Someone to Watch Over Me (1987) . . . . . Win Hockings
Born on the Fourth of July (1989) . . . Optimistic Doctor
Made for Cable Movies:
The Tracker (1988; HBO) . . . . Tom Adams
 •• 0:35 - Buns, getting out of the river after washing
   himself, then getting hassled by some bandits.

Moss, Robert
Films:
Spring Fever USA (1988) . . . . Dick Dork
 • 1:17 - Buns, twice, in boat hallway with his heavy
   brother after being tricked.

Mulcahy, Jack
Films:
Porky's (1981; Canadian) . . . . .Frank Bell
 • 0:21 - Very brief frontal nudity, getting up from
   bench. Then buns in front of the cabin.
Porky's II: The Next Day (1983; Canadian) . . . .Frank Bell

Mulkey, Chris
Films:
Loose Ends (1975) . . . . Billy Regis
The Long Riders (1980) . . . .
48 Hours (1982). . . . . .Cop
First Blood (1982) . . . . Ward
Timerider (1983) . . . . Daniels
Heartbreak Hotel (1988) . . . . Steve Ayres
Patti Rocks (1988). . . . . Billy
 •• 0:24 - Nude in restroom with Eddie, undressing and
   putting on underwear.

Nassi, Joe
Films:
Sorority House Massacre (1987) . . . . Craig
 • 0:50 - Buns, running away from the killer that has
   just killed his girlfriend Tracy in a tepee.

Naughton, David
Films:
Separate Ways (1979) . . . . Jerry Lansing
Midnight Madness (1980) . . . . Adam
An American Werewolf in London (1981)
 . . . . David Kessler
 • 0:24 - Very brief buns running naked through the
   woods.
 • 0:58 - Buns, during his transformation into a were-
   wolf.
 •• 1:09 - Brief frontal nudity and buns waking up in wolf
   cage at the zoo. Long shot, hard to see anything.
   More buns, running around the zoo.
Hot Dog... The Movie (1984). . . . . .Dan
Not for Publication (1984) . . . . Barry
Separate Vacations (1985) . . . . .Richard Moore
The Boy in Blue (1986; Canadian) . . . . Bill
Kidnapped (1986) . . . . .Vince McCarthy
Overexposed (1990) . . . . Phillip
The Sleeping Car (1990) . . . . Jason McCree
Steel and Lace (1990) . . . . .Dunn
Made for TV Movies:
The Goddess of Love (1988) . . . . Ted
TV:
Makin' It (1979). Billy Manucci
At Ease (1983) . . . . P.F.C. Tony Baker
My Sister Sam (1986-89) . . . . Jack

Nazario, Al

Films:

Incoming Freshman (1979). . . . . Mooner
- 0:44 - Buns, mooning Professor Bilbo during his day-dream.
- 0:56 - Buns again during Bilbo's daydream.
- 1:19 - Buns, during end credits.

Neeson, Liam

Films:

Excalibur (1981; British) . . . . .Gawain
Krull (1983). . . . . Kegan
The Bounty (1984) . . . . .Churchill
The Innocent (1985; British) . . . .
The Mission (1986; British) . . . . Fielding
Duet for One (1987). . . . . Totter
- 1:07 - Buns, behind shower door, getting out of shower. Very, very brief buns, falling into bed when robe flies up. Long shot.
Next of Kin (1989) . . . . Briar
Darkman (1990) . . . . Peyton Westlake/Darkman

Neidorf, David

Films:

Bull Durham (1988) . . . . .Bobby
Born on the Fourth of July (1989) . . . . Patient
Made for Cable Movies:

Rainbow Drive (1990; Showtime) . . . .Bernie Maxwell
- 1:16 - Buns, in shower room when Peter Weller is in-terrogating him.

Nelson, Bob

Films:

Sorceress (1982). . . . . .Erlick
- 0:43 - Brief buns, just before being put to death.
- •• 0:45 - Buns, getting massaged.
The Falcon and the Snowman (1985) . . . . FBI Agent
Miracles (1986). . . . . .Sargeant Levit

Nero, Franco

Films:

Submission (1976; Italian) . . . . Armond
- 0:32 - Brief side view of buns when making love with Lisa on the bed.
Die Hard 2 (1990). . . . . Esperanza

Nicholson, Jack

Films:

The Little Shop of Horrors (1960; B&W) . . .Wilbur Force
Studs Lonigan (1960; B&W) . . . . Weary Reilly
The Raven (1963) . . . . Rexford Bedlo
The Terror (1963) . . . . .Lt. Andre Duvalier
Ride in the Whirlwind (1965) . . . . Wes
Rebel Rousers (1967). . . . . .Bunny
Easy Rider (1969) . . . . George Hanson

Five Easy Pieces (1970). . . . . Robert Dupea
On a Clear Day, You Can See Forever (1970) Tad Pringle
Carnal Knowledge (1971) . . . . .Jonathan
A Safe Place (1971) . . . . Mitch
The Last Detail (1973) . . . . .Buddusky
Chinatown (1974). . . . . .J.J.
- 1:28 - Very brief buns, putting pants on getting out of bed after making love with Faye Dunaway.
One Flew Over the Cuckoo's Nest (1975)
. . . . .R. P. McMurphy
(Academy Award for Best Actor.)
The Passenger (1975; Italian) . . . . .David Locke
Tommy (1975; British) . . . . Specialist
The Last Tycoon (1976) . . . . Brimmer
The Missouri Breaks (1976) . . . . Tom Logan
The Shooting (1976) . . . . Billy Spear
Goin' South (1978) . . . . Henry Moon
The Shining (1980) . . . . .Jack Torrance
The Postman Always Rings Twice (1981) . . . .
Frank Chambers
- 1:25 - Buns, lying across the bed.
Reds (1981) . . . . Eugene O'Neill
The Border (1982) . . . . .Charlie
Terms of Endearment (1983) . . . . Garrett Breedlove
Prizzi's Honor (1985) . . . . .Charley Partanna
2:05 - Buns, sort of. Viewed from above while he takes a shower. Hard to see anything.
Heartburn (1986). . . . . Mark
Ironweed (1987) . . . . Francis Phelan
The Witches of Eastwick (1987) . . . . . . Daryl Van Horne
Batman (1989). . . . . Jack Napier/The Joker
The Two Jakes (1990). . . . . .Jake Gittes

Nock, Thomas

Films:

Alpine Fire (1985; Swiss) . . . . Bob
- 0:08 - Brief buns, outside taking a bath.

Nolan, Tom

Films:

Fast Times at Ridgemont High (1982) . . . .Dennis Taylor
Up the Creek (1984) .Whitney
School Spirit (1985) . . . . Billy Batson
- 0:17 - Buns in open hospital smock. More buns while running up stairs.
TV:

Jessie (1984). . . . . Officer Hubbell

Nolte, Nick

Films:

Return to Macon County (1975) . . . . Bo Hollinger
The Deep (1977) . . . . .David Sanders
Who'll Stop the Rain? (1978) . . . . Ray
Heart Beat (1979) . . . . .Neal Cassady
North Dallas Forty (1979) . . . . .Phillip Elliott
- 0:49 - Brief buns, pulling down underwear to get into whirlpool bath in locker room.

48 Hours (1982) . . . . Jack Cates
Cannery Row (1982) . . . . Doc
Under Fire (1983) . . . . Russel Price
Teachers (1984) . . . . Alex
Down and Out in Beverly Hills (1986). . . Jerry Baskin
• 0:28 - Buns, changing out of wet clothes on patio.
• 1:37 - Brief buns, changing out of Santa Claus outfit.
Weeds (1987) . . . . Lee Umstetter
•• 0:51 - Buns, getting out of bed and putting his pants on.
New York Stories (1989) . . . . Lionel Dobie
Three Fugitives (1989) . . . . Daniel Lucas
Another 48 Hrs. (1990) . . . . Jack Cates
Everybody Wins (1990) . . . . Tom O'Toole
Q & A (1990) . . . . Mike Brennan
Miniseries:
Rich Man, Poor Man (1976) . . . . Tom Jordache

Norton, Ken

Former boxer.
Films:
Mandingo (1975) . . . . Mede
•• 1:36 - Buns, standing in bed with Susan George. More buns making love with her.
Drum (1976) . . . . Drum
• 1:02 - Buns, getting hung upside down in barn and spanked along with Yaphet Kotto.
Mugsy's Girls (1985) . . . . Branscombe
TV:
The Gong Show (1976-80) . . . . Panelist

Nouri, Michael

Films:
Flashdance (1983) . . . . Nick Hurley
The Imagemaker (1985) . . . . Roger Blackwell
Thieves of Fortune (1989) . . . . Juan Luis
• 0:57 - Buns, taking a shower outside. Long shot.
Project: Alien (1990) . . . . Jeff Milker
Total Exposure (1991) . . . . Dave Murphy
Miniseries:
Beacon Hill (1975) . . . . Giorgia Bellonci
The Last Convertible (1979) . . . . . Jean R.G.R. des Barres
TV:
The Gangster Chronicles (1981)
. . . . Charles "Lucky" Luciano
Bay City Blues (1983) . . . . Joe Rohner
Downtown (1986-87) . . . . Detective John Forney

Nureyev, Rudolf

Ballet dancer.
Films:
Valentino (1977; British) . . . . Rudolph Valentino
Exposed (1983) . . . . Daniel Jelline
••• 0:54 - Buns, in bed with Nastassja Kinski.

O'Keeffe, Miles

Films:
Tarzan, The Ape Man (1981) . . . . Tarzan
• 0:45 - Sort of buns, under loin cloth in the surf. Lots of other semi-bun shots in the loin cloth throughout the rest of the film.
1:09 - Buns, in loin cloth at side of lake with Bo Derek.
• 1:48 - Buns, in loin cloth wrestling with orangutan during end credits.
Ator, The Fighting Eagle (1982) . . . . Ator
The Blade Master (1984) . . . .
a.k.a. Ator, The Invincible
Sword of the Valiant (1984; British) . . . . Gawain
Campus Man (1987) . . . . Cactus Jack
Iron Warrior (1987) . . . . Ator
The Drifter (1988) . . . . Trey
• 0:11 - Brief upper half of buns on the motel floor with Kim Delaney.
Waxwork (1988) . . . . Count Dracula
Liberty & Bash (1989) . . . . Liberty

O'Neal, Ryan

Father of actress Tatum O'Neal.
Films:
Love Story (1970) . . . . Oliver Barret IV
What's Up Doc? (1972) . . . . Professor Howard Bannister
Paper Moon (1973) . . . . Moses Pray
The Thief Who Came to Dinner (1973) . . . . Webster
Barry Lyndon (1975; British) . . . . Barry Lyndon
The Driver (1978) . . . . The Driver
Oliver's Story (1978) . . . . Oliver Barret IV
The Main Event (1979) . . . . Eddie "Kid Natural" Scanlon
Green Ice (1981; British) . . . . Wiley
So Fine (1981) . . . . Bobby
Partners (1982) . . . . Benson
•• 0:48 - Buns, in Indian outfit for photo session with Robyn Douglass. Don't see his face.
Irreconcilable Differences (1984) . . . . Albert Brodsky
Fever Pitch (1985) . . . . Taggart
Tough Guys Don't Dance (1987) . . . . Tim Madden
Chances Are (1989) . . . . Philip Train
TV:
Good Sports . . . . Bobby Tannen
tvEmpire (1962-63) . . . . Tal Garret
Peyton Place (1964-69) . . . . Rodney Harrington

O'Quinn, Terry

a.k.a. Terrance O'Quinn.
Films:
Heaven's Gate (1980) . . . . Captain Minardi
Without a Trace (1983) . . . . Parent
Mrs. Soffel (1984) . . . . Buck McGovern
Places in the Heart (1984) . . . . Buddy Kelsey
Mischief (1985) . . . . Claude Harbrough
Stephen King's "Silver Bullet" (1985) . . Sheriff Joe Haller
SpaceCamp (1986) . . . . Launch Director
Black Widow (1987) . . . . Bruce

The Stepfather (1987) . . . . Jerry Blake
••• 0:02 - Buns, getting undressed, frontal nudity in mirror as he gets into the shower.
Young Guns (1988) . . . . Alex McSween
The Forgotten One (1989) . . . .
• 1:11 - Brief buns turning over in bed with Evelyn.
Pin (1989) . . . . Dr. Linden
Stepfather 2 (1989) . . . . The Stepfather
Blind Fury (1990) . . . . Frank Devereaux
The Rocketeer (1991) . . . . Howard Hughes
Made for TV Movies:
Danielle Steel's "Kaleidoscope" (1990) . . . . Henry
The Last to Go (1991) . . . . Daniel
Shoot First: A Cop's Vengeance (1991) . . . Sgt. Nicholas

O'Reilly, Cyril

Films:
Porky's (1981; Canadian) . . . . Tim
• 0:21 - Very, very brief frontal nudity, getting up from bench. Then buns, in front of the cabin.
Porky's II: The Next Day (1983; Canadian) . . . . Tim
Purple Hearts (1984) . . . . Zuma
Dance of the Damned (1988) . . . . Vampire
Navy SEALS (1990) . . . . Rexer

O, George

Films:
Summer Job (1989) . . . . Herman
• 0:17 - Buns getting his underwear torn off by five angry women then running back to his room.
Popcorn (1991) . . . . 1st Hood
Made for Cable TV:
Chains of Gold (1991; Showtime) . . . . Corner Man

Occhipinti, Andrea

Films:
Bolero (1984) . . . . Angel the Bullfighter
•• 0:57 - Buns, lying in bed with Bo Derek, then making love with her.
Conquest (1984; Italian) . . . . Ilias
A Blade in the Dark (1986; Italian) . . . . Bruno

Olandt, Ken

Films:
April Fool's Day (1986) . . . . Rob
Summer School (1987) . . . . Larry
•• 0:48 - Brief buns wearing a red G-string in a male stripper club.
Made for TV Movies:
The Laker Girls (1990) . . . . Rick

Oldman, Gary

Films:
Sid and Nancy (1986; British) . . . . Sid Vicious
Prick Up Your Ears (1987; British) . . . . Joe Orton

Track 29 (1988; British) . . . . Martin
• 1:24 - Buns, holding onto Christopher Lloyd and stabbing him.
We Think the World of You (1988; British)
. . . . Johnny Burney
Criminal Law (1989) . . . . Ben Chase
• 1:21 - Very, very brief blurry frontal nudity in bed with Ellen.
Chattahoochee (1990) . . . . Emmett Foley
• 1:17 - Brief buns, standing while guards search his clothes. Very, very brief frontal nudity turning around to get a high-pressure enema. Long shot, don't really see anything.
State of Grace (1990) . . . . Jackie

Oliviero, Silvio

Films:
Graveyard Shift (1987) . . . . Stephen Tsepes
• 0:09 - Buns, climbing into his coffin.
Nightstick (1987) . . . . Ismael
Psycho Girls (1987) . . . .
The Understudy: Graveyard Shift II (1988) . . . . . . Baisez

Ontkean, Michael

Films:
The Peace Killers (1971) . . . . Jeff
Necromancy (1972) . . . . Frank Brandon
Hot Summer Week (1973; Canadian) . . . .
Slap Shot (1977) . . . . Ned Braden
•• 1:56 - Brief buns skating off the hockey rink carrying a trophy wearing his jock strap.
Voices (1979) . . . . Drew Rothman
Willie and Phil (1980) . . . . Willie
Making Love (1982) . . . . Zack
The Witching (1983) . . . . Frank
a.k.a. Necromancy
Just the Way You Are (1984) . . . . Peter
The Allnighter (1987) . . . . Mickey Leroi
Maid to Order (1987) . . . . Nick McGuire
Clara's Heart (1988) . . . . Bill Hart
Street Justice (1988) . . . . Curt Flynn
Cold Front (1989; Canadian) . . . . Derek McKenzie
Postcards from the Edge (1990) . . . . Robert Murch
Made for Cable Movies:
The Blood of Others (1984; HBO) . . . .
TV:
The Rookies (1972-74) . . . . Officer Willie Gillis
Twin Peaks (1990-91) . . . . Harry S. Truman

Pace, Richard

Films:
I Spit on Your Grave (1978) . . . . Matthew
(Uncut, unrated version.)
• 0:42 - Buns, undressing in the house to rape Jennifer.
1:15 - Silhouette of penis while getting hung (by the neck) by Jennifer.

Packer, David

Films:
You Can't Hurry Love (1984) . . . . Eddie
  • 0:59 - Buns, in store taking his pants off while people
    watch him from the sidewalk.
Trust Me (1989) . . . . Sam Brown
Crazy People (1990) . . . . Mark Olander
Miniseries:
V: The Final Battle (1984) . . . . Daniel Bernstein
TV:
The Best Times (1985). . . . . Niel "Trout" Troutman
What's Alan Watching? (1989) . . . . Jeff

Pankow, John

Films:
The Hunger (1983) . . . . 1st Phone Booth Youth
To Live and Die in L.A. (1985) . . . . John Vukovich
  • 1:06 - Buns, changing in the locker room.
*batteries not included (1987) . . . . Kovacs
The Secret of My Success (1987). . . . . Fred Melrose
Monkey Shines: An Experiment in Fear (1988)
. . . . Geoffrey Fisher
Talk Radio (1988) . . . . Dietz
Mortal Thoughts (1991) . . . .

Parker, Jameson

Films:
The Bell Jar (1979) . . . . Buddy
  • 0:09 - Frontal nudity silhouette standing in bedroom
    with Marilyn Hassett, then buns. Dark, hard to see.
A Small Circle of Friends (1980) . . . . Nick Baxter
White Dog (1982). . . . . Roland Gray
American Justice (1986) . . . . Dave Buchanon
Prince of Darkness (1987) . . . . Brian
TV:
Simon & Simon (1981-89)
. . . . Andrew Jackson (A.J.) Simon

Pasdar, Adrian

Films:
Streets of Gold (1986). . . . . Timmy Boyle
Near Dark (1987) . . . . Caleb
Made in U.S.A. (1988) . . . . Dar
  • 0:12 - Buns, walking to sit down at the laundromat
    when he washes all his clothes with Christopher
    Penn.
Vital Signs (1989) . . . . Michael Chatham
  1:11 - Upper half of buns, with his pants partially
    down in basement with Diane Lane.
Torn Apart (1990) . . . . Ben Arnon

Patric, Jason

Son of actor/author Jason Miller.
Grandson of actor/comedian Jackie Gleason.
Films:
Solarbabies (1986) . . . . Jason

The Lost Boys (1987) . . . . Michael
After Dark, My Sweet (1990) . . Kevin "Collie" Collins
  •• 1:19 - Buns, taking off pants and getting into bed
    with Rachel Ward. More brief buns on top of her.
Frankenstein Unbound (1990) . . . . Lord Byron
Denial (1991). . . . .
Made for TV Movies:
Toughlove (1985) . . . .

Patrick, Randal

Made for Cable Movies:
By Dawn's Early Light (1990; HBO) . . . . O'Toole
  • 0:14 - Brief buns in shower room getting dressed
    during red alert.

Patterson, Jimmy

Films:
The Young Warriors (1983; U.S./Canadian)
. . . . "Ice Test" Monty
  • 0:14 - Buns, dropping pants and sitting on a block of
    ice during pledge at fraternity.

Paxton, Bill

Films:
Mortuary (1981) . . . . Paul Andrews
Stripes (1981) . . . .
Impulse (1984) . . . . Eddie
Streets of Fire (1984) . . . . Clyde
The Terminator (1984). . . . . Punk Leader
Commando (1985) . . . . Intercept Officer
Weird Science (1985) . . . . Chet
  •• 0:30 - Buns taking off towel to give to his younger
    brother in the kitchen.
Aliens (1986) . . . . Private Hudson
Near Dark (1987). . . . . Severen
Pass the Ammo (1988). Jesse
Brain Dead (1989) . . . . Jim Reston
Next of Kin (1989). . . . . Gerald Gates
Back to Back (1990). . . . . Bo Brand
The Last of the Finest (1990) . . . . Howard "Hojo" Jones
Navy SEALS (1990) . . . . Dane
Predator 2 (1990) . . . . Jerry
Slipstream (1990). . . . . Matt Owens
Made for TV Movies:
Deadly Lessons (1983) . . . .

Peck, Brian

Films:
The Last American Virgin (1982) . . . . Victor
  • 0:20 - Buns, during penis measurement in boy's lock-
    er room. Don't see his face.

Penn, Christopher

Brother of actor Sean Penn.
Films:
All The Right Moves (1983) . . . . Brian

Rumble Fish (1983; B&W). B.J.
Footloose (1984). . . . . Willard
The Wild Life (1984) . . . . Tom Drake
Pale Rider (1985). . . . . .Josh LaHood
At Close Range (1986) . . . . Tommy Whitewood
Made in U.S.A. (1988) . . . . Tuck
- 0:12 - Buns, walking to sit down at the laundromat when he washes all his clothes with Adrian Pasdar.

Penn, Sean

Ex-husband of singer/actress Madonna.
Brother of actor Christopher Penn.
Films:
Taps (1981). . . . . .Alex Dwyer
Fast Times at Ridgemont High (1982) . . . . . . .Jeff Spicoli
Bad Boys (1983) . . . . Mick O'Brien
- 0:10 - Brief buns getting up off the floor with Ally Sheedy.
- 0:46 - Buns taking a shower.
Crackers (1984). . . . . Dillard
Racing with the Moon (1984) . . . Henry "Hopper" Nash
The Falcon and the Snowman (1985) . . . . . Daulton Lee
At Close Range (1986) . . . . Brad Whitewood, Jr.
Shanghai Surprise (1986) . . . . Glendon Wasey
Colors (1988) . . . . Danny McGavin
Judgment in Berlin (1988). . . . . Gunther X
Casualties of War (1989) . . . . Sergeant Meserve
We're No Angels (1989) . . . . Jim
State of Grace (1990) . . . . .Terry

Pepe, Paul

Films:
Saturday Night Fever (1977) . . . . Double J.
(R-rated version.)
- 0:22 - Buns, while making love in back seat of car with a girl.

Peter, Jens

Films:
Wild Orchid (1990) . . . . .Voleyball Player
- 1:29 - Bun, in room with Jacqueline Bisset and Carré Otis.

Petersen, William L.

Films:
Thief (1981) . . . . Katz & Jammer Bartender
To Live and Die in L.A. (1985) . . . . . Richard Chance
- 0:44 - Brief frontal nudity, but hard to see anything because it's dark.
Manhunter (1986) . . . . Will Graham
Cousins (1989) . . . . Tom Hardy
Young Guns II (1990) . . . . Pat Garrett
Made for Cable Movies:
Long Gone (1987; HBO) . . . . Cecil "Stud" Cantrell

Phelps, Matthew

Films:
Dreamaniac (1987) . . . . Foster
Nightmare Sisters (1987). . . . . .J.J.
(This is the best video tape for viewing all three "Scream Queens.")
- •• 0:53 - Buns, taking off his pants and getting into bed with Michelle Bauer.

Pitzalis, Fredrico

Films:
Devil in the Flesh (1986; French/Italian) . . . . .Andrea
- 0:57 - Brief buns in bed with Maruschka Detmers.
- 1:19 - Frontal nudity when Detmers performs fellatio on him. Dark, hard to see.

Placido, Donato

Films:
Caligula (1980) . . . . .Proculus
(X-rated, 147 minute version.)
- 1:11 - Frontal nudity taking his robe off for Malcolm McDowell. Buns, getting raped by McDowell's fist.

Prescott, Robert

Films:
The Lords of Discipline (1983) . . . .
Bachelor Party (1984). . . . . Richard Chance
- 1:18 - Buns, after being hung out the window by sheets by Tom Hanks and his friends.
The Joy of Sex (1984). . . . . Tom Pittman
Real Genius (1985). . . . . Kent

Price, Alan

Films:
O Lucky Man! (1973; British) . . . .
Oh, Alfie! (1975; British) . . . . Alfie Elkins
a.k.a. Alfie Darling
- •• 0:14 - Buns washing himself off in the kitchen while talking to Louise's husband.

Pryor, Richard

Comedian.
Films:
Lady Sings the Blues (1972) . . . . .Piano Man
Some Call It Loving (1972). . . . . .Jeff
Uptown Saturday Night (1974)
. . . . Sharpe Eye Washington
Car Wash (1976) . . . . Daddy Rich
Silver Streak (1976) . . . . Grover Muldoon
Greased Lightning (1977) . . . . Wendell Scott
Which Way Is Up? (1977). . . . . Leroy Jones/Rufus Jones/ Rev. Thomas
Blue Collar (1978) . . . . Zeke
The Wiz (1978) . . . . The Wiz
Richard Pryor—Live in Concert (1979) . . . . Himself

Stir Crazy (1980) . . . . Harry Monroe
Wholly Moses (1980) . . . . Pharaoh
Bustin' Loose (1981) . . . . Joe Braxton
Richard Pryor Live on the Sunset Strip (1982) . . . Himself
Some Kind of Hero (1982) . . . . Eddie Keller
The Toy (1982) . . . . Jack Brown
Richard Pryor—Here and Now (1983) . . . . Himself
Superman III (1983) . . . . Gus Gorman
Brewster's Millions (1985) . . . . . . Montgomery Brewster
Richard Pryor—Live and Smokin' (1985) . . . . . . Himself
Jo Jo Dancer, Your Life Is Calling (1986)
. . . . Jo Jo Dancer/Alter Ego
  •• 0:06 - Buns, walking naked out of the hospital wait-
    ing for the limousine.
Moving (1988) . . . . Arlo Pear
Harlem Nights (1989) . . . . Sugar Ray
See No Evil, Hear No Evil (1989) . . . . Wally
Another You (1991) . . . . Eddie
TV:
The Richard Pryor Show (1977) . . . . Host

Purcell, James

Films:
S.O.B. (1981) . . . .
Where Are the Children? (1986) . . . . Robin Legler
Bad Dreams (1988) . . . . Paramedic
Playroom (1989) . . . . Paul
  •• 0:25 - Buns, making love with Jamie Rose on a chair.

Quaid, Dennis

Brother of actor Randy Quaid.
Films:
9/30/55 (1977) . . . . Frank
Our Winning Season (1978) . . . . Paul Morelli
Seniors (1978) . . . . Alan
Breaking Away (1979) . . . . Mike
Gorp (1980) . . . . Mad Grossman
The Long Riders (1980) . . . . Ed Miller
All Night Long (1981) . . . . Freddie Dupler
Caveman (1981) . . . . Lar
The Night the Lights Went Out in Georgia (1981) . . . . .
  Travis Child
Jaws 3 (1983) . . . . Mike Brody
The Right Stuff (1983) . . . . Gordon Cooper
Tough Enough (1983) . . . . Art Long
Dreamscape (1984) . . . . Alex Gardner
Enemy Mine (1985) . . . . Davidge
The Big Easy (1987) . . . . Remy McSwain
  • 0:24 - Brief buns when Ellen Barkin pulls his under-
    wear down in bed.
  ••• 0:51 - Buns, putting underwear on after getting out
    of bed after talking on the telephone.
Innerspace (1987) . . . . Tuck Pendleton
  •• 0:08 - Buns, standing naked in the street as taxi
    drives off with his towel. Kind of a long shot.
Suspect (1987) . . . . Eddie Sanger
D.O.A. (1988) . . . . Dexter Cornell
Everybody's All-American (1988) . . . . Gavin

Great Balls of Fire (1989) . . . . Jerry Lee Lewis
Come See the Paradise (1990) . . . . Jack McGurn
Postcards from the Edge (1990) . . . . Jack Falkner
  1:03 - Side view of buns, leaning out of the shower,
    talking to Meryl Streep.

Quaid, Randy

Brother of actor Dennis Quaid.
Films:
The Last Picture Show (1971; B&W) . . Lester Marlow
  • 0:38 - Very brief frontal nudity jumping into pool af-
    ter Cybill Shepherd jumps in.
The Last Detail (1973) . . . . Meadows
Lolly-Madonna XXX (1973) . . . . Finch Feather
Paper Moon (1973) . . . . Leroy
Bound For Glory (1976) . . . . Luther Johnson
The Missouri Breaks (1976) . . . . Little Tod
The Choirboys (1977) . . . . Proust
Midnight Express (1978; British) . . . . Jimmy Booth
Foxes (1980) . . . . Jay
The Long Riders (1980) . . . . Clell Miller
Heartbeeps (1981) . . . . Charlie
National Lampoon's Vacation (1983) . . . . . Cousin Eddie
The Wild Life (1984) . . . . Charlie
The Wraith (1986) . . . . Sheriff Loomis
Bloodhounds of Broadway (1989) . . . . Feet Samuels
National Lampoon's Christmas Vacation (1989)
. . . . Cousin Eddie
Out Cold (1989) . . . . Lester Atlas
Days of Thunder (1990) . . . . Tim Daland
Quick Change (1990) . . . . Loomis
TV:
Saturday Night Live (1985-86) . . . . regular
Davis Rules (1990-) . . . . Dwight

Quill, Tom

Films:
Staying Together (1989) . . . . Brian McDermott
  • 0:03 - Brief buns getting out of bed with Stockard
    Channing. Hard to see because of the reflections in
    the window.

Quinn, Aidan

Films:
Reckless (1984) . . . . Johnny Rourke
  • 1:03 - Very brief frontal nudity and buns running into
    Daryl Hannah's brother's room when her parents
    come home early.
  • 1:12 - Side view nude, taking a shower.
Desperately Seeking Susan (1985) . . . . Dez
The Mission (1986; British) . . . . Felipe
Stakeout (1987) . . . . Richard "Stick" Montgomery
Crusoe (1989) . . . . Crusoe
Avalon (1990) . . . . Jules Krichinsky
A Handmaid's Tale (1990) . . . . Nick
The Lemon Sisters (1990) . . . . Frankie McGuinness

Lies of the Twins (1991) . . . . Jonathan & James McEwan

Railsback, Steve

Films:
The Visitors (1972) . . . . Mike Nickerson
Angela (1977; Canadian) . . . . Jean
The Stunt Man (1980). . . . . Cameron
Escape 2000 (1981) . . . . Paul
The Golden Seal (1983) . . . . Jim Lee
Torchlight (1984) . . . . Jake Gregory
Lifeforce (1985) . . . . Carlsen
   • 1:26 - Buns, standing with Mathilda May after he
   stabs her with the sword. Surrounded by special ef-
   fects.
Armed and Dangerous (1986). . . . . The Cowboy
The Blue Monkey (1987). . . . . Detective Jim Bishop
Scenes from the Goldmine (1987). . . . . Harry Spiros
The Wind (1987). . . . . Kesner
The Assassin (1989). . . . . Hank Wright
Scissors (1991) . . . .
Made for TV Movies:
Helter Skelter (1976). . . . . Charles Manson
Good Cops, Bad Cops (1990) . . . . Jimmy Donnelly

Rano, Corey

Films:
Predator 2 (1990). . . . . Ramon Vega
   • 0:23 - Buns, hanging upside down several times.
   • 0:26 - Nude, hanging upside down, dead.

Reckert, Winston

Films:
Your Ticket Is No Longer Valid (1982)
   . . . . Antonio Montoya
   • 1:24 - Buns, in bed with Jennifer Dale.

Reed, Mathew

Films:
Perfect (1985). . . . . Roger
   • 1:01 - Buns, dancing in a jock strap at Chippendale's.

Reed, Oliver

Films:
The Curse of the Werewolf (1961). . . . . Leon
Oliver! (1968; British) . . . . Bill Sikes
Women in Love (1971) . . . . Gerald Crich
   ••• 0:54 - Nude, fighting with Alan Bates in a room in
   front of a fireplace. Long scene.
The Three Musketeers (1973) . . . . Althos
Blood in the Streets (1974; French/Italian) . Vito Cipriani
The Four Musketeers (1975) . . . . Athos
Ten Little Indians (1975) . . . . Hugh
Tommy (1975; British) . . . . Frank Hobbs
Burnt Offerings (1976) . . . . Ben

The Great Scout and Cathouse Thursday (1976)
   . . . . Joe Knox
The Big Sleep (1978; British) . . . . Eddie Mars
The Class of Miss MacMichael (1978). . . Terence Sutton
The Prince and the Pauper (1978) . . . . . . Miles Hendon
   a.k.a. Crossed Swords
The Brood (1979). Dr. Raglan
Dr. Heckyl and Mr. Hype (1980). . . Dr. Heckyl/Mr. Hype
Condorman (1981) . . . . Krokov
Venom (1982; British) . . . . Dave
Spasms (1983; Canadian). . . . . Suzanne Kincaid
The Sting II (1983). . . . . Doyle Lonnegan
Black Arrow (1984) . . . . Sir Daniel Brackley
Castaway (1986) . . . . Gerald Kingsland
   •• 1:46 - Nude, doing things around the hut during the
   storm.
Dragonard (1988) . . . . Captain Shanks
The Return of the Musketeers (1989). . . . . Athos
Skeleton Coast (1989) . . . . Captain Simpson
Edgar Allan Poe's "The House of Usher" (1990)
   . . . . Roderick Usher
The Pit and the Pendulum (1991) . . . . The Cardinal
Made for TV Movies:
The Lady and the Highwayman (1989) . . Sir Philip Gage

Regehr, Duncan

Films:
The Monster Squad (1987) . . . . Count Dracula
The Banker (1989) . . . . Osbourne
   • 0:03 - Buns, getting out of bed with Teri Weigel.
   Don't see his face.
Gore Vidal's Billy the Kid (1989) . . . . Pat Garrett
TV:
Wizards and Warriors (1983) . . . . . Prince Dirk Blackpool

Reinhold, Judge

Films:
Stripes (1981) . . . . Elmo
Fast Times at Ridgemont High (1982) . . . Brad Hamilton
The Lords of Discipline (1983) . . . . Macabbee
Beverly Hills Cop (1984). . . . . . Detective Billy Rosewood
Gremlins (1984). . . . . Gerald
Roadhouse 66 (1984). . . . . Beckman Hallsgood, Jr.
Head Office (1986) . . . . Jack Issel
Off Beat (1986) . . . . Joe Gower
Ruthless People (1986). . . . . Ken Kessler
Beverly Hills Cop II (1987) . . . . Detective Billy Rosewood
Rosalie Goes Shopping (1990) . . . . Priest
Zandalee (1991) . . . . Thierry Martin
   ••• 0:21 - Buns in bed with Zandalee.
   • 0:23 - Upper half of buns, standing by the window.

Reves, Robbie

Films:
Shadowzone (1989) . . . . James
   0:16 - Frontal nudity long shot.
   • 0:26 - Frontal nudity lying under plastic bubble.

Reynolds, Burt

Husband of actress Loni Anderson.
Films:
Operation C.I.A. (1965; B&W) . . . . Mark Andrews
Shark! (1969) . . . . Caine
a.k.a. Maneaters!
Deliverance (1972) . . . . Lewis
Fuzz (1972). . . . . Detective Steve Carella
The Man Who Loved Cat Dancing (1973) . . . Jay Grobart
White Lightning (1973). . . . . Gator McKlusky
The Longest Yard (1974) . . . . Paul Crewe
Hustle (1975) . . . . Lieutenant Phil Gaines
Gator (1976). . . . . Gator McKlusky
Semi-Tough (1977). . . . . Billy Clyde Puckett
Smokey and the Bandit (1977) . . . . .Bandit
The End (1978). . . . . Sonny Lawson
Hooper (1978) . . . . Sonny Hooper
Starting Over (1979). . . . . .Phil Potter
Rough Cut (1980; British) . . . . Jack Rhodes
Smokey and the Bandit II (1980). . . . . .Bandit
The Cannonball Run (1981) . . . . J. J. McClure
Paternity (1981) . . . . .Buddy Evans
Sharky's Machine (1981). . . . . Sharky
Best Friends (1982) . . . . .Richard Babson
The Best Little Whorehouse in Texas (1982) . . . . Ed Earl
The Man Who Loved Women (1983)
. . . . David Fowler
 •• 1:25 - Brief buns, chiseling a statue after making love
   with Julie Andrews.
Smokey and the Bandit III (1983) . . . . . .The Real Bandit
Stroker Ace (1983) . . . . Stroker Ace
Cannonball Run II (1984) . . . . J. J. McClure
City Heat (1984). . . . . Mike Murphy
Stick (1985) . . . . Stick
Heat (1987) . . . . Mex
Malone (1987) . . . . Richard Malone
Rent-a-Cop (1988) . . . . .Church
Breaking In (1989) . . . . .Ernie Mullins
Physical Evidence (1989). . . . . Joe Paris
Modern Love (1990) . . . . Colonel Parker
TV:
Riverboat (1959-60) . . . . .Ben Frazer
Gunsmoke (1962-65) . . . . Quint Asper
Hawk (1966). . . . . .Lt. John Hawk
Dan August (1970-71) . . . . Det. Lt. Dan August
B. L. Stryker (1989-90) . . . . B. L. Stryker
Evening Shade (1990-). . . . . Wood Newton
Magazines:
Cosmopolitan (Apr 1972) . . . . Centerfold

Rios, Javier

Films:
Q & A (1990) . . . . Boat Lover
 • 1:44 - Brief buns, on boat, getting pulled out of bed
   by Nick Nolte.

Robbins, Tim

Films:
Toy Soldiers (1983) . . . . Bean
No Small Affair (1984) . . . . .Nelson
Fraternity Vacation (1985) . . . . . .Larry "Mother" Tucker
The Sure Thing (1985) . . . . Gary Cooper
Howard the Duck (1986) . . . . Phil Blumburtt
Bull Durham (1988) . . . Ebby Calvin "Nuke" La Loosh
 • 0:03 - Buns, in locker room making love with Millie
   when the coach sees them.
Five Corners (1988) . . . . .Harry
Tapeheads (1988) . . . . Josh Tager
Erik the Viking (1989) . . . . Erik
Miss Firecracker (1989) . . . . Delmount Williams
Cadillac Man (1990) . . . . Larry
Jacob's Ladder (1990). . . . . Jacob Singer
 •• 0:40 - Buns, twice in bathroom getting ready for ice
   bath.

Roberts, Eric

Films:
King of the Gypsies (1978). . . . . Dave
Raggedy Man (1981) . . . . Teddy
Star 80 (1983) . . . . Paul Snider
 • 1:39 - Buns, lying dead on floor, covered with blood
   after shooting Dorothy, then himself.
The Pope of Greenwich Village (1984) . . . . Paulie
The Coca-Cola Kid (1985; Australian). . . . . Becker
Nobody's Fool (1986) . . . . Riley
Slow Burn (1986). . . . . .Jacob Asch
Rude Awakening (1989). . . . . .Fred
Made for Cable Movies:
Descending Angel (1990; HBO) . . . . .Michael Rossi

Robinson, David

Films:
Revenge of the Cheerleaders (1976) . . . . Jordan
 • 0:13 - Buns when Tish plays with him while she's under the counter.
Mephisto (1981; German) . . . .

Ross, Chelchie

Films:
On the Right Track (1981) . . . . Customer
One More Saturday Night (1986) . . . . . Dad Lundahl
 • 0:39 - Buns, squished against the car window in back
   seat with Moira Harris.
The Untouchables (1987). . . . . Reporter
Above the Law (1988) . . . . Nelson Fox
Made for Cable Movies:
Rainbow Drive (1990; Showtime). . . . . Tom Cutter

Ross, Willie

Films:
The Cook, The Thief, His Wife & Her Lover (1990)
. . . . Roy
> 0:03 - Buns, on ground covered with dog feces getting urinated on by Albert. (Talk about a bad day!)
> • 0:07 - Buns, kneeling on ground while dogs walk around.
> • 0:09 - Buns, standing up.

Strike it Rich (1990). . . . . Man at Theater

Rossi, Leo

Films:
Grand Theft Auto (1977). Sal
Halloween II (1981) . . . . Budd
> • 0:48 - Buns, getting out of the whirlpool bath to check the water temperature.

Heart Like a Wheel (1983). . . . . Jack Muldowney
River's Edge (1987) . . . . Jim
The Accused (1988) . . . . Cliff "Scorpion" Albrect
Leonard, Part 6 (1988) . . . . Chef
Relentless (1989). Sam Dietz
Maniac Cop 2 (1990) .Turkell
Too Much Sun (1990). . . . .
TV:
Partners in Crime (1984). . . . . .Lt. Ed Vronsky
Tour of Duty (1988-90). . . . . Jake Bridger

Rossovich, Rick

Films:
The Lords of Discipline (1983). . . . . Pig
Streets of Fire (1984). . . . . Officer Cooley
The Terminator (1984) . . . . Matt
Warning Sign (1985). . . . . Bob
The Morning After (1986). . . . . Detective
Top Gun (1986) . . . . .Ron Kerner
Roxanne (1987) . . . . .Chris McDonell
Spellbinder (1988) . . . . .Derek Clayton
Paint It Black (1989) . . . . Jonathan Dunbar
> • 0:48 - Upper half of buns getting out of bed with Julie Carmen.

Navy SEALS (1990) . . . . Leary
Made for Cable TV:
Tales From the Crypt: The Switch (1990; HBO)
. . . . Hans
> •• 0:23 - Buns standing in front of mirror after being transformed into a younger Carlton.

Made for TV Movies:
Deadly Lessons (1983) . . . .
TV:
MacGruder & Loud (1985) . . . . Geller
Sons and Daughters (1990-91) . . . . Spud Lincoln

Rowlatt, Michael

Films:
Spaced Out (1980; British). . . . . Cliff
> • 0:42 - Buns, getting out of bed trying to get away from Partha.

Rubbo, Joe

Films:
The Last American Virgin (1982) . . . . .David
> • 0:45 - Buns, in bed making love with Carmilla while his buddies watch through the key hole.

Hot Chili (1985). . . . . .Arney
> • 0:24 - Brief buns getting whipped by Brigitte.

Russell, Kurt

Husband of actress Goldie Hawn.
Films:
The Horse in the Gray Flannel Suit (1968)
. . . . .Ronnie Gardner
The Computer Wore Tennis Shoes (1969) . . . . . .Dexter
The Barefoot Executive (1971) . . . . Steven Post
Fool's Parade (1971). . . . . Johnny Jesus
Now You See Him, Now You Don't (1972). .Dexter Riley
Charley & the Angel (1973). . . . . .Ray Ferris
Superdad (1973) . . . . Bart
The Strongest Man in the World (1975). . . . . . . .Dexter
Used Cars (1980) . . . . Rudy Russo
> • 1:04 - Very brief buns putting on red underwear.

Escape from New York (1981) . . . . Snake Pliskin
The Thing (1982). . . . . MacReady
Silkwood (1984). . . . . Drew Stephens
Swing Shift (1984). . . . . .Lucky Lockhart
The Mean Season (1985) . . . . Malcolm Anderson
The Best of Times (1986) . . . . Reno Hightower
Big Trouble in Little China (1986). . . . . Jack Burton
Overboard (1987) . . . . Dean Proffitt
Tequila Sunrise (1988) . . . . Lt. Nick Frescia
Tango & Cash (1989) . . . . Cash
> •• 0:31 - Brief buns walking into the prison shower room with Sylvester Stallone.

Winter People (1989). . . . . Wayland Jackson
Backdraft (1991) . . . . Stephen McCaffrey
Made for TV Movies:
The Quest (1976). . . . . Morgan

Rust, Richard

Films:
The Student Nurses (1970) . . . . .Les
a.k.a. Young LA Nurses
> • 0:43 - Buns, lying in sand with Barbara Leigh.

The Last Movie (1971) . . . . Pisco
Kid Blue (1973) . . . . Train Robber
The Great Gundown (1976). . . . . .Joe Riles

Rydell, Christopher
Films:
Gotchal (1985) . . . . Bob Jensen
Mask (1985) . . . . .High School Student
The Sure Thing (1985) . . . . Charlie
The Check is in the Mail (1986). . . . . . . Drunken Sailor
Blood and Sand (1989; Spanish) . . . . Juan
   • 0:15 - Buns, running away after fighting bull. Dark, long shot.
   •• 0:18 - Buns, between shower curtain when Sharon Stone watches.
   • 1:05 - Buns, on top of Stone. Long shot.
How I Got Into College (1989) . . . . Oliver
Listen to Me (1989) . . . . Tom Lloynd
Under the Boardwalk (1989). . . . . Tripper
Side Out (1990) .Wiley Hunter

Sadler, William
Films:
Die Hard 2 (1990). . . . . Colonel Stuart
   •• 0:02 - Buns, exercising in hotel room before leaving for the airport.
Hard to Kill (1990) . . . . .Vernon Trent
The Hot Spot (1990). . . . . .Frank Sutton

Sador, Daniel
Films:
Sugar Cookies (1973) . . . . .Gus
   0:37 - Buns in bed with Dola, then running around.

Sands, Julian
Films:
The Killing Fields (1984) . . . . Swain
Oxford Blues (1984) . . . . Colin
The Doctor and the Devils (1985) . . . . Dr. Murray
Gothic (1986; British) . . . . Shelley
   •• 0:17 - Buns, standing on roof in the rain.
A Room with a View (1986; British) . George Emerson
   ••• 1:05 - Nude running around with Freddy and Mr. Beebe in the woods. Lots of frontal nudity.
Siesta (1987). . . . . Kit
Vibes (1988) . . . . Dr. Harrison Steele
Aracnophobia (1990) . . . . Dr. James Atherton
Warlock (1990) . . . . Warlock
Magazines:
Playboy (Nov 1986) . . . . Sex in Cinema 1986
   • 128: Buns, in photo from *A Room with a View*. Kind of blurry.

Sanville, Michael
Films:
The First Turn-On! (1983) . . . . Mitch
   • 1:18 - Buns, in cave orgy scene on top of Annie.

Sarandon, Chris
Ex-husband of actress Susan Sarandon.
Films:
Dog Day Afternoon (1975) . . . . Leon
Lipstick (1976). . . . . Gordon Stuart
   •• 0:50 - Buns, standing in his studio talking to Margaux Hemingway on the telephone.
The Sentinel (1977) . . . . .Michael Lerman
Cuba (1979) . . . . Juan Polido
The Osterman Weekend (1983) . . . . . . .Joseph Cardone
Protocol (1984) . . . . Michael Ransome
Fright Night (1985) . . . . Jerry Dandridge
The Princess Bride (1987). . . . . Prince Humperdinck
Child's Play (1988) . . . . Mike Norris
Slaves of New York (1989) . . . . .Victor Okrent
Whispers (1989). . . . . .Detective Tony
Made for TV Movies:
Mayflower Madam (1987) . . . .

Savage, John
Films:
The Killing Kind (1973) . . . . Terry Lambert
   • 0:00 - Upper half of buns when other guys pull his shorts down during rape of girl.
   •• 0:58 - Buns in shower when Mrs. Lambert opens the curtains to take a picture.
The Deer Hunter (1978). . . . . Steven
The Beat (1986). . . . . Frank Ellsworth
Do the Right Thing (1989). . . . . Clifton

Schneider, John
Films:
Eddie Macon's Run (1983) . . . . Eddie Macon
   • 0:15 - Brief left side view of buns when beginning to cross the stream. Dark, hard to see.
Cocaine Wars (1986) . . . . Cliff
The Curse (1987). . . . . Carl Willis
Ministry of Vengeance (1989) . . . . .David Miller
Speed Zone (1989) . . . . .Cannonballer
TV:
The Dukes of Hazzard (1979-85) . . . . Bo Duke

Schott, Bob
Films:
The Working Girls (1973) . . . . Roger
   • 0:07 - Buns, getting out of bed to meet Honey.
Force Five (1981) . . . . Carl

Schwarzenegger, Arnold
Husband of Kennedy clan member/news reporter Maria Shriver.
Films:
Hercules in New York (1970) . . . . Hercules
   a.k.a. Hercules Goes Bananas
The Long Goodbye (1973). . . . . Hoods
Stay Hungry (1976) . . . . .Joe Santo

Pumping Iron (1977) . . . .
The Villain (1979) . . . . Handsome Stranger
Conan the Barbarian (1982) . . . . Conan
Conan the Destroyer (1984) . . . . Conan
The Terminator (1984) . . . . The Terminator
  ••• 0:03 - Buns, kneeling by garbage truck, walking to look at the city and walking toward the three punks at night.
Commando (1985) . . . . Matrix
Red Sonja (1985) . . . . Kalidor
Raw Deal (1986) . . . . Mark Kaminsky
Predator (1987) . . . . Major Dutch Schaefer
The Running Man (1987) . . . . Ben Richards
Red Heat (1988) . . . . Ivan Danko
  •• 0:02 - Buns in the sauna and outside fighting in the snow.
Twins (1988) . . . . Julius Benedict
Kindergarten Cop (1990) . . . . Kimble
Total Recall (1990) . . . . Doug Quaid
Terminator 2: Judgement Day (1991) . . . The Terminator
Made for TV Movies:
The Jayne Mansfield Story (1980) . . . .

Scorpio, Bernie

Identical twin brother of Lennie Scorpio.
Films:
Video Vixens (1973) . . . . Turnip Twin
  ••• 1:05 - Frontal nudity standing next to his identical twin brother after their trial.

Scorpio, Lennie

Identical twin brother of Bernie Scorpio.
Films:
Video Vixens (1973) . . . . Turnip Twin
  •• 1:03 - Frontal nudity, then buns on top of victim in bed.
  ••• 1:05 - Frontal nudity standing next to his identical twin brother after their trial.

Scuddamore, Simon

Films:
Slaughter High (1986) . . . . Marty
  • 0:05 - Nude in girl's shower room when his class-mates pull a prank on him.

Segado, Alberto

Films:
Two to Tango (1988) . . . . Lucky Lara
  • 0:29 - Buns on top of Adrienne Sachs, making love with her in bed.

Selby, David

Films:
Night of Dark Shadows (1971)
  . . . . Quentin/Charles Collins
Up the Sandbox (1972) . . . . Paul Reynolds

The Girl In Blue (1973; Canadian) . . . . Scott
  a.k.a. U-turn
  • 0:10 - Brief buns getting out of bed and putting on pants. Dark.
  0:44 - Left half of buns in shower.
  •• 1:14 - Buns, walking into the bathroom.
Super Cops (1974) . . . . Bob Hantz
Rich Kids (1979) . . . . Steve Sloan
Raise the Titanic (1980; British) . . . . . Dr. Gene Seagram
Rich and Famous (1981) . . . . Doug Blake
TV:
Flamingo Road (1981-82) . . . . Michael Tyrone
Falcon Crest (1982-86) . . . . Richard Channing

Selleck, Tom

Films:
The Seven Minutes (1971) . . . . Phil Sanford
Terminal Island (1973) . . . . Dr. Norman Milford
Coma (1978) . . . . Sean
High Road to China (1983) . . . . O'Malley
Lassiter (1984) . . . . Lassiter
  • 1:00 - Buns, getting out of bed after making love with Lauren Hutton.
Runaway (1984) . . . . Ramsay
Three Men and a Baby (1987) . . . . Peter
Her Alibi (1989) . . . . Phil Blackwood
An Innocent Man (1989) . . . . Jimmy Rainwood
Quigley Down Under (1990) . . . . Matthew Quigley
Three Men and a Little Lady (1990) . . . . Peter
The Shadow Riders (1991) . . . .
Miniseries:
The Sacketts (1979) . . . .
Made for TV Movies:
Bunco (1977) . . . .
TV:
The Rockford Files (1979-80) . . . . Lance White
Magnum P.I. (1980-88) . . . . Thomas Magnum

Serbedzija, Rade

Films:
Hanna's War (1988) . . . . Captain Ivan
Manifesto (1988) . . . . Emile
  • 0:18 - Buns, under sheet and getting out of bed.

Serna, Pepe

Films:
The Student Nurses (1970) . . . . Luis
  a.k.a. Young LA Nurses
Group Marriage (1972) . . . . Ramon
The New Centurions (1972) . . . . Young Mexican
The Day of the Locust (1975) . . . . Miguel
  • 2:01 - Buns on top of Karen Black, then buns jumping out of bed.
Car Wash (1976) . . . . Chuco
Swashbuckler (1976) . . . . Street Entertainer
The Jerk (1979) . . . . Punk #1
Walk Proud (1979) . . . . Cesar

Honeysuckle Rose (1980) . . . . Rooster
Inside Moves (1980) . . . . Herrada
Vice Squad (1982). . . . . Pete Mendez
Deal of the Century (1983) . . . . Vardis
Heartbreaker (1983) . . . . Loco
Scarface (1983). . . . . Angel
The Adventures of Buckaroo Banzai, Across the 8th
   Dimension (1984) . . . . Reno Nevada
Red Dawn (1984) . . . . Aardvark's Father
Fandango (1985) . . . . Gas Station Mechanic
Out of Bounds (1987) . . . . Murano
Postcards from the Edge (1990) . . . . Raoul
The Rookie (1990). . . . . Lt. Ray Garcia

Shane, Michael

Films:
Savage Beach (1989) . . . . Shane Abeline
  •• 0:08 - Buns, getting out of pool.

Shannon, George

Films:
Sugar Cookies (1973). . . . . Max
  •• 0:14 - Buns, on top of Mary Woronov in bed.

Sharkey, Ray

Films:
The Lords of Flatbush (1974). . . . . Student
Trackdown (1976). . . . . Flash
Stunts (1977) . . . . Pauley
Paradise Alley (1978). Legs
Who'll Stop the Rain? (1978) . . . . Smitty
Heart Beat (1979) . . . . Ira
The Idolmaker (1980) . . . . Vince Vacarddi
Love and Money (1980) . . . . Byron Levin
Willie and Phil (1980) . . . . Phil
Some Kind of Hero (1982) . . . . Vinnie
Body Rock (1984) . . . . Terrence
Hellhole (1985). . . . . Silk
Wise Guys (1986) . . . . Marco
Scenes from the Class Struggle in Beverly Hills
  (1989) . . . . Frank
  • 1:10 - Brief buns sleeping in bed with Zandra.
Act of Piracy (1990). . . . . Jack Wilcox
  • 0:33 - Brief side view of buns on top of Laura in bed.
  •• 0:35 - Brief buns, getting out of bed and putting on
    robe.
The Rain Killer (1990) . . . . Vince Capra
TV:
Man in the Family (1991-) . . . . Sal

Shea, John

Films:
Hussy (1980; British) . . . . Emory
  •• 0:29 - Buns making love with Helen Mirren in bed.
    Half of lower frontal nudity when she rolls off him.
Missing (1982) . . . . Charles Horman
Windy City (1984). . . . . Danny Morgan

Unsettled Land (1987) . . . .
A New Life (1988) . . . . Doc
Magic Moments (1989) . . . . Troy Gardner

Sheen, Martin

Father of actors Emilio Estevez and Charlie Sheen.
Films:
Rage (1972). Major Holliford
Badlands (1973). . . . . Kit
The Cassandra Crossing (1977; British) . . . . Navarro
Eagle's Wing (1978; British) . . . . Pike
Apocalypse Now (1979) . . . . Captain Willard
  • 0:07 - Brief buns, in bedroom after opening door for
    military guys.
The Final Countdown (1980) . . . . Warren Lasky
Enigma (1982). . . . . Alex Holbeck
Gandhi (1982) . . . . Walker
That Championship Season (1982) . . . . Tom Daley
The Dead Zone (1983). . . . . Greg Stillson
Man, Woman and Child (1983) . . . . Bob Beckwith
Firestarter (1984) . . . . Capt. Hollister
The Believers (1987). . . . . Dr. Cal Jamison
Wall Street (1987) . . . . Carl Fox
Cold Front (1989; Canadian) . . . . John Hyde
The Maid (1990) . . . . Anthony Wayne
Cadence (1991). . . . .
Made for Cable Movies:
The Guardian (1984; HBO) . . . .
Made for TV Movies:
The Little Girl Who Lives Down the Lane
  (1976; Canadian) . . . . Frank Hallet
Samaritan: The Mitch Snyder Story (1986). . . . .

Sheffer, Craig

Films:
Voyage of the Rock Aliens (1985). . . . . Frankie
  a.k.a. When the Rains Begin to Fall
Fire With Fire (1986) . . . . Joe Flsk
Split Decisions (1988) . . . . Eddie McGuinn
Blue Desert (1990). . . . . Randall Atkins
Instant Karma (1990). . . . . Zane Smith
  • 1:15 - Brief buns on top of Penelope. Don't see his
    face.
Night Breed (1990) . . . . Boone
TV:
The Hamptons (1983) . . . . Brian Chadway

Shellen, Steve

Films:
Gimme an "F" (1981) . . . . Tommy Hamilton
  0:56 - Dancing in his underwear in the boy's shower
    room while the girls peek in at him.
  • 0:57 - Brief upper half of buns.
Burglar (1987) . . . . Christopher Marshall
  • 0:26 - Buns, in front of closet that Whoopi Goldberg
    is hiding in. Don't see his face, but probably him.
Modern Girls (1987) . . . . Brad

The Stepfather (1987) . . . . Jim Ogilvie
Talking Walls (1987) . . . . Paul Barton
  •• 0:58 - Buns, taking off his clothes and running down
     railroad tracks.
American Gothic (1988) . . . . Paul
Casual Sex? (1988) . . . . Nick
Murder One (1988; Canadian) . . . . Wayne Coleman
Damned River (1990) . . . . Ray
Made for Cable TV:
The Hitchhiker: Love Sounds. . . . . Kerry
  •• 0:15 - Brief buns, making love in the house with
     Belinda Bauer.
  •• 0:22 - Buns, making love in the boat with Bauer.
Tales From the Crypt: Lover Come Hack To Me
(1989; HBO) . . . . Charles
  • 0:10 - Buns, getting undressed with his newlywed
    wife in a strange house.

Shirin, Moti
Films:
The Little Drummer Girl (1984) . . . . Michel
  •• 1:07 - Nude, in a prison cell when Diane Keaton
    looks at his scars.
Unsettled Land (1987) . . . . Salim

Sibbit, John
Films:
Love Circles Around the World (1984) . . . . Jack
  • 0:06 - Very brief frontal nudity pulling his underwear
    down and getting into bed.
  •• 0:19 - Buns, trying to run away from Brigid after she
    yanks his underwear off.

Siegel, David
Films:
Private Passions (1983) . . . . Tonl
  • 0:29 - Buns, with Laura. Don't see his face.

Singer, Marc
Brother of actress Lori Singer.
Films:
Go Tell the Spartans (1978) . . . . Captain Al Olivetti
The Beastmaster (1982) . . . . Dar
If You Could See What I Hear (1982) . . . . . . Tom Sullivan
Born to Race (1988) . . . . Kenny Landruff
In the Cold of the Night (1989) . . . . Ken Strom
Body Chemistry (1990) . . . . Dr. Tom Redding
  • 0:18 - Buns, standing up in hallway holding Claire
    while making love. Long shot.
A Man Called Serge (1990) . . . . Von Kraut
Watchers II (1990) . . . . Paul Ferguson
Miniseries:
  V (1983) . . . . Mike Donovan
  V: The Final Battle (1984) . . . . Mike Donovan
TV:
  V: The Series (1984-85) . . . . Mike Donovan
  Dallas (1986-87) . . . . Matt Cantrell

Skarsgard, Stellan
Films:
The Unbearable Lightness of Being (1988)
. . . . The Engineer
  • 2:18 - Buns, making love with Tereza in his apart-
    ment.

Slater, Christian
Films:
The Legend of Billie Jean (1985) . . . . Binx
The Name of the Rose (1986) . . . . Adso of Melk
  • 0:48 - Buns, making love with The Girl in the monas-
    tery kitchen.
Tucker: The Man and His Dream (1988) . . . . Junior
Gleaming the Cube (1989) . . . . Brian Kelly
Heathers (1989) . . . . J.D.
The Wizard (1989) . . . . Nick Woods
Pump Up the Volume (1990) . . . . Mark Hunter
Tales From the Darkside, The Movie (1990) . . . . . . Andy
Young Guns II (1990) . . . . Arkansas Dave Rudbaugh
Mobsters (1991) . . . . Lucky Luciano
Robin Hood: Prince of Thieves (1991) . . . . . Will Scarlett

Sloane, Lance
Films:
The Big Bet (1985) . . . . Chris
  •• 0:38 - Buns, taking off robe and getting into bed
    with Angela Roberts after visiting Mrs. Roberts.
  •• 0:52 - Buns, on elevator floor with Monique Gabrielle
    during his daydream.
  • 1:07 - Buns, getting into tub with Kimberly Evenson
    during video tape fantasy. Long shot.

Smith, Charlie Martin
Films:
The Culpepper Cattle Co. (1972) . . . . Tim Slater
Fuzz (1972) . . . . Baby
American Graffiti (1973) . . . . Terry the Toad
Pat Garrett and Billy the Kid (1973) . . . . Bowdre
Rafferty and the Gold Dust Twins (1975) . . . . Alan
No Deposit, No Return (1976) . . . . Longnecker
The Buddy Holly Story (1978) . . . . Ray Bob
More American Graffiti (1979) . . . . Terry the Toad
Herbie Goes Bananas (1980) . . . . D. J.
Never Cry Wolf (1983) . . . . Tyler
  • 0:32 - Buns warming himself and drying his clothes
    after falling through the ice.
  • 1:18 - Very brief frontal nudity running and jumping
    off a rock into the pond.
  • 1:20 - Buns running in meadow with the caribou.
  • 1:23 - Brief silhouette of lower frontal nudity while
    scampering up a hill. More buns when chasing the
    caribou.
Starman (1984) . . . . Shermin
The Untouchables (1987) . . . . Oscar Wallace
The Hot Spot (1990) . . . . Lon Gulick

Smits, Jimmy

Films:
Running Scared (1986) . . . . Julio Gonzales
Terror on the Blacktop (1987) . . . . Bo
Old Gringo (1989) . . . . Arroyo
  • 1:26 - Half of his buns on bed with Jane Fonda. Long shot, don't see his face.
Vital Signs (1989) . . . . Dr. David Redding
TV:
L.A. Law (1986-) . . . . Victor Sifuentes

Spader, James

Films:
Tuff Turf (1984) . . . . Morgan Hiller
Pretty in Pink (1986) . . . . Steff McKee
Baby Boom (1987) . . . . Ken Arrenberg
Jack's Back (1987) . . . . John/Rick Wesford
Mannequin (1987) . . . . Richards
The Rachel Papers (1989) . . . . De Forest
sex, lies and videotape (1989) . . . . Graham Dalton
Bad Influence (1990) . . . . Michael Boll
White Palace (1990) . . . . Max Baron
  •• 0:38 - Buns, taking off clothes and getting into bed with Susan Sarandon. Don't see his face.
True Colors (1991) . . . . Tim
TV:
The Family Tree (1983) . . . . Jake Nichols

Spanjer, Maarten

Films:
Spetters (1980; Dutch) . . . . Jeff
  ••• 0:35 - Frontal nudity, measuring and comparing his manlihood with his friends in the auto shop.
  • 1:12 - Buns climbing into bed in trailer with Reneé Soutendijk.

Spano, Joe

Films:
American Graffiti (1973) Vic
Roadie (1980) . . . . Ace
Terminal Choice (1985; Canadian) . . . . Frank Holt
  ••• 0:34 - Buns, taking off towel and getting dressed in locker room while talking to Anna.
  • 0:49 - Buns, making love in bed with Anna. Long shot, don't see his face.
Made for Cable Movies:
Fever (1991; HBO) . . . . Junkman
Made for TV Movies:
The Girl Who Came Between Them (1990) . . . . Jim
TV:
Hill Street Blues (1981-87) . . . . Henry Goldblume

Spano, Vincent

Films:
Over the Edge (1979) . . . . Mark
Baby, It's You (1983) . . . . Sheik

The Black Stallion Returns (1983) . . . . Raj
Rumble Fish (1983; B&W) . . . . Steve
Alphabet City (1984) . . . . Johnny
Creator (1985) . . . . Boris
  • 0:28 - Brief buns, in shower room with David Ogden Stiers after working out in a gym.
  • 0:57 - Brief buns, before taking a shower.
Maria's Lovers (1985) . . . . Al Griselli
Good Morning, Babylon (1987; Italian/French)
  . . . . Nicola Bonnano
Made for Cable Movies:
Blood Ties (1986; Italian; Showtime) . . . .

Spechtenhauser, Robert Egon

Films:
Bizarre (1986; Italian) . . . . Edward
  • 0:29 - Partial buns, taking a shower when Laurie peeks in at him.
  • 0:31 - Brief buns, on top of Laurie in the water.
  ••• 0:36 - Buns, on bed with Laurie. (He's made up to look like a woman.)

Springfield, Rick

Singer.
Films:
Hard to Hold (1984) . . . . James Roberts
  • 0:06 - Buns, running down the hall getting chased by a bunch of young girls.
  •• 0:15 - Buns, lying in bed sleeping.
Made for TV Movies:
Battlestar Gallactica (1978) . . . . Lieutenant Zac

Stallone, Sylvester

Ex-husband of actress Brigitte Nielsen.
Adult Films:
The Italian Stallion (1970) . . . . Stud
  X-rated film that Stallone did before he got famous. Originally called *A Party at Kitty and Stud's*. Re-titled and re-released in 1985. He has lots of nude scenes in this film.
Films:
The Lords of Flatbush (1974) . . . . Stanley Rosiello
Capone (1975) . . . . Frank Nitti
  (Not available on video tape.)
Death Race 2000 (1975) . . . . . Machine Gun Joe Viterbo
Farewell, My Lovely (1975; British) . . . . Kelly/Jonnie
Cannonball (1976; U.S./Hong Kong) . . . .
Rocky (1976) . . . . Rocky Balboa
F.I.S.T. (1978) . . . . Johnny Kouak
Paradise Alley (1978) . . . . Cosmo Carboni
Rocky II (1979) . . . . Rocky Balboa
Nighthawks (1981) . . . . Deke De Silva
Victory (1981) . . . . Robert Hatch
First Blood (1982) . . . . Rambo
Rocky III (1982) . . . . Rocky Balboa
Rhinestone (1984) . . . . Nick
Rambo: First Blood, Part II (1985) . . . . Rambo

Rocky IV (1985). Rocky Balboa
Cobra (1986) . . . . Marion Cobretti
Over the Top (1987) . . . . Lincoln Hawk
Lock Up (1989) . . . . Frank
Tango & Cash (1989) . . . . .Ray Tango
  •• 0:31 - Brief buns walking into the prison shower room with Kurt Russell.
Rocky V (1990) . . . . Rocky Balboa
Oscar (1991). . . . .
Made for Cable TV:
Dream On: The Second Greatest Story Ever Told (1991; HBO) . . . . himself

Stern, Daniel
Films:
Breaking Away (1979) . . . . Cyril
Starting Over (1979). . . . . Student 2
It's My Turn (1980) . . . . Cooperman
A Small Circle of Friends (1980). . . . . Crazy Kid
  • 1:22 - Brief buns, dropping his pants with several other guys for Army draft inspection.
Stardust Memories (1980; B&W). . . . . Actor
Honky Tonk Freeway (1981) . . . .
I'm Dancing as Fast as I Can (1981) . . . . Jim
Diner (1982) . . . . Shrevie
Blue Thunder (1983). . . . . Lymangood
Get Crazy (1983) . . . . Neil
C.H.U.D. (1984) . . . . The Reverend
Key Exchange (1985) . . . . Michael
The Boss' Wife (1986) . . . . Joel Keefer
Born in East L.A. (1987). . . . . Jimmy
D.O.A. (1988). . . . . Hal Petersham
The Milagro Beanfield War (1988). . . . . .Herbie Platt
Coupe de Ville (1990) . . . . Marvin Libner
Home Alone (1990) . . . . .Marv
My Blue Heaven (1990). . . . . Will Stubbs
City Slickers (1991) . . . . .Phil
Made for Cable Movies:
The Court-Martial of Jackie Robinson (1990)
. . . . William Cline
TV:
Hometown (1985) . . . . Joey Nathan

Stevens, Andrew
Son of actress Stella Stevens.
Films:
Massacre at Central High (1976). . . . . .Mark
Vigilante Force (1976). . . . . Paul Sinton
The Boys in Company C (1978) . . . . .Billy Ray Pike
The Fury (1978) . . . . Robin Sandza
Death Hunt (1981) . . . . .Alvin
The Seduction (1982) . . . . Derek
10 to Midnight (1983) . . . . Paul McAnn
Deadly Innocents (1988). . . . . Bob Appling
Red Blooded American Girl (1988)
. . . . Owen Augustus Urban III
The Terror Within (1988). . . . . .David
Down the Drain (1989). . . . . Victor Scalia

Night Eyes (1990) . . . . Will
(Unrated version.)
  ••• 1:11 - Buns in the shower.
  ••• 1:26 - Side view of buns with Tanya Roberts seen through a window.
TV:
Code Red (1981-82) . . . . .Ted Rorchek
Emerald Point N.A.S. (1983-84)
. . . . .Lieutenant Glenn Matthews

Sting
Singer with *The Police* and on his own.
Films:
Quadrophenia (1979; British). . . . . .The Ace Face
Brimstone and Treacle (1982; British) . . Martin Taylor
  • 1:19 - Buns, making love with Suzanna Hamilton on her bed. Dark, hard to see.
Dune (1984) . . . . .Feyd Rautha
The Bride (1985) . . . . Frankenstein
Plenty (1985). . . . . Mick
Julia and Julia (1987; Italian). . . . . Daniel
(This movie was shot using a high-definition video system and then transferred to film.)
  •• 1:11 - Buns, sleeping in bed when Kathleen Turner leaves. Don't see his face very well.
Stormy Monday (1988) . . . . Finney

Stockwell, John
Films:
So Fine (1981) . . . . .Jim
Losin' It (1982). . . . . Spider
Christine (1983). . . . . .Dennis
Eddie and the Cruisers (1983) . . . . Keith
City Limits (1984) . . . . Lee
My Science Project (1985) . . . . Michael Harlan
Dangerously Close (1986) . . . . Randy McDevill
  • 0:33 - Brief buns in steamy locker room.
Top Gun (1986). . . . . Cougar
Miniseries:
North and South (1985) . . . . Billy Hazard

Stokes, Barry
Films:
Happy Housewives. . . . . Bob
  • 0:31 - Brief buns, running away from Mrs. Elgin and her daughter in the barn.
Spaced Out (1980; British). . . . . Oliver
  • 0:54 - Buns, undressing to get in bed with Prudence.
Alien Prey (1984; British). . . . . .Anders
  •• 1:19 - Buns, getting on top of Glory Annen in bed.

Stoltz, Eric
Films:
Fast Times at Ridgemont High (1982) . . . . . Stoner Bud
Surf II (1984) . . . . Chuck
The Wild Life (1984). . . . . .Bill Conrad
Code Name: Emerald (1985) . . . . Andy Wheeler

Mask (1985) . . . . Rocky Dennis
The New Kids (1985) .Mark
Lionheart (1987). . . . . .Robert Nerra
Sister Sister (1987) . . . . Matt Rutledge
Some Kind of Wonderful (1987) . . . . .Keith Nelson
Haunted Summer (1988). . . . . .Percy Shelley
   ••• 0:09 - Nude, under the waterfall and walking around
     in the river. Long scene.
Manifesto (1988) . . . . Christopher
   • 1:16 - Buns, helping Camilla unroll Emile in the rug.
The Fly II (1989) . . . . Martin
Say Anything (1989) . . . . Vahlere
Memphis Belle (1990). . . . . Danny Daily
Made for TV Movies:
Paper Dolls (1982) . . . . Steve

Stone, Christopher
Husband of actress Dee Wallace Stone.
Films:
The Grasshopper (1970) . . . . .Jay Rigney
    0:26 - Buns through shower door when Jacqueline
     Bisset comes in to join him.
   • 1:17 - Brief buns lying in bed talking to Bisset.
The Howling (1981). . . . . R. William "Bill" Neill
   • 0:48 - Brief buns, rolling over while making love with
     Elizabeth Brooks in front of a campfire.
Cujo (1983) . . . . Steve
The Annihilators (1985). . . . . Bill Esker
Miniseries:
Blue and the Gray (1982) . . . . .Major Fairbairn
TV:
The Interns (1970-71) . . . . Dr. Pooch Hardin
Spencer's Pilots (1976) . . . . Cass Garrett
Harper Valley P.T.A. (1981-82). . . . . .Tom Meechum
Dallas (1984) . . . . Dave Stratton

Street, Elliot
Films:
Honky (1971) . . . .
Welcome Home, Soldier Boys (1972) . . . . Fat Back
The Harrad Experiment (1973) . . . . Wilson
   •• 0:44 - Frontal nudity taking off clothes and getting
     into the swimming pool.

Sutherland, Donald
Films:
Die, Die, My Darling (1965) . . . . Joseph
Dr. Terror's House of Horrors (1965) . . . . . . .Bob Carroll
The Dirty Dozen (1967) . . . . Vernon Pinkley
Kelly's Heroes (1970). . . . . Oddball
M*A*S*H (1970) . . . . .Hawkeye Pierce
Start the Revolution Without Me (1970)
  . . . . .Charles Coupe/Pierre De Sisi
Johnny Got His Gun (1971). . . . . .Jesus Christ
Klute (1971) . . . . .John Klute
Don't Look Now (1973). . . . . .John Baxter
   • 0:27 - Buns, in the bathroom with Julie Christie.

Steelyard Blues (1973) . . . . .Jesse Veldini
The Day of the Locust (1975). . . . . .Homer
1900 (1976; Italian) . . . . Attila
The Disappearance (1977). . . . . .Jay
The Eagle Has Landed (1977; British) . . . . . . Liam Devlin
Kentucky Fried Movie (1977) . . . . Clumsy
Animal House (1978) . . . . Dave Jennings
   • 1:22 - Buns, reaching up in kitchen to get something
     when his sweater goes up. Out of focus.
Invasion of the Body Snatchers (1978)
  . . . . Matthew Bennell
The Great Train Robbery (1979). . . . . Agan
Murder by Decree (1979). . . . . Robert Lees
Bear Island (1980; British/Canadian) . . . . Frank Lansing
Nothing Personal (1980; Canadian)
  . . . . Professor Roger Keller
Ordinary People (1980) . . . . Calvin
Eye of the Needle (1981) . . . . .Faber
Max Dugan Returns (1983) . . . . Brian
Threshold (1983; Canadian). . . . . Dr. Vrain
Crackers (1984) . . . . .Weslake
Ordeal by Innocence (1984) . . . . .Arthur Calgary
Heaven Help Us (1985) . . . . Brother Thadeus
Revolution (1986) . . . . Sergeant Major Peasy
The Rosary Murders (1987) . . . . Father Koesler
Lock Up (1989) . . . . .Warden Drumgoole
Lost Angels (1989). . . . . Dr. Charles Loftis
Backdraft (1991) . . . . Ronald Bartel

Swayze, Patrick
Films:
Skatetown, U.S.A. (1979). . . . . Ace
The Outsiders (1983) . . . . Darrel
Uncommon Valor (1983) . . . . Scott
Grandview, U.S.A. (1984). . . . . . . Ernie "Slam" Webster
Red Dawn (1984). . . . . .Jed
Youngblood (1986) . . . . Derek Sutton
Dirty Dancing (1987). . . . . Johnny Castle
Steel Dawn (1988) . . . . Nomad
Tiger Warsaw (1988) . . . . .Chuck "Tiger" Warsaw
Next of Kin (1989). . . . . Truman Gates
Roadhouse (1989) .Dalton
   ••• 0:30 - Brief buns getting out of bed while Kathleen
     Wilhoite watches.
Ghost (1990) . . . . Sam Wheat
Point Break (1991) . . . . .Bodhi
Miniseries:
North and South (1985) . . . . Orry Main
North and South, Book II (1986) . . . . Orry Main
TV:
Renegades (1983) . . . . Bandit

Tabor, Erin
Films:
I Spit on Your Grave (1978) . . . . .Johnny
  (Uncut, unrated version.)
   • 0:25 - Buns, undressing to rape Jennifer.
   • 1:20 - Buns, undressing at gun point.

Taylor, Zach
Films:
Group Marriage (1972) . . . . .Phil
   •• 0:43 - Buns, walking on beach with Jan.

Tepper, William
Films:
Drive, He Said (1972) . . . . Hector
Breathless (1983) . . . . Paul
Miss Right (1987) . . . . Terry Bartell
   • 0:47 - Buns, jumping out of bed with Karen Black
     when the bed catches fire.

Terrell, John Canada
Films:
Recruits (1986) . . . . Winston
She's Gotta Have It (1987; B&W) . . . . . . Greer Childs
   • 0:59 - Buns, making love with Nola Darling.
Rooftops (1989) . . . . Junkie Cop
Def by Temptation (1990) . . . . Bartender #1
   •• 0:09 - Nude, running through house trying to get
     away from The Temptress.
The Return of Superfly (1990) . . . . . . .Detective Loomey

Terry, Nigel
Films:
The Lion in the Winter (1968; British) . . . . . .Prince John
Excalibur (1981; British) . . . . .King Arthur
Deja Vu (1984) . . . . .Michel/Greg
   • 1:17 - Very brief buns, jumping out of bed when Ja-
     clyn Smith tries to kill him with a knife.
Sylvia (1985; New Zealand) . . . . Aden Morris

Thompson, Jack
Films:
Libido (1973; Australian). .Ken
Jock Petersen (1974; Australian). . . . . . .Tony Petersen
   a.k.a. Petersen
   ••• 0:13 - Buns, making love with Wendy Hughes on the
     floor.
   ••• 0:20 - Frontal nudity under tarp with Moira during
     protest.
   • 0:22 - Buns in bed with Suzy.
   •• 0:44 - Nude running around the beach with Hughes.
   •• 0:50 - Frontal nudity undressing, then buns lying in
     bed.
Mad Dog Morgan (1976) . . . . Detective Manwaring
Breaker Morant (1979; Australian). . . Major J. F. Thomas
The Earthling (1980) . . . . Ross Daley
The Man from Snowy River (1982; Australian). . . Clancy
Merry Christmas, Mr. Lawrence (1983; Japanese/British)
   . . . . Hicksley-Ellis
Sunday Too Far Away (1983; Australian) . . . . Foley
Burke and Wills (1985; Australian) . .Robert O'Hara Burke
Flesh + Blood (1985). . . . . .Hawkwood
Ground Zero (1988; Australian) . . . . Trebilcock

Thomsen, Kevin
Films:
Cleo/Leo (1989). Bob Miller
   • 1:07 - Brief frontal nudity, then buns making love
     with Jane Hamilton on bed.
Enrapture (1989) . . . . Keith

Tierney, Aidan
Films:
Family Viewing (1987; Canadian) . . . . Van
   •• 0:26 - Brief buns, getting up out of bed and putting
     on his underwear.

Torgl, Mark
Films:
The First Turn-On! (1983). . . . . .Dwayne
   1:02 - Buns, dropping his pants for Michelle.

Torn, Rip
Films:
Payday (1972) . . . . Maury Dann
   • 1:21 - Brief buns getting up out of bed.
Slaughter (1972) . . . . .Hoffo
The Man Who Fell to Earth (1976; British)
   . . . . .Nathan Bryce
Coma (1978) . . . . .Dr. George
The Seduction of Joe Tynan (1979) . . . Senator Kittner
Heartland (1980) . . . . .Clyde
One Trick Pony (1980) . . . . Walter Fox
The Beastmaster (1982) . . . . .Maax
Cross Creek (1983) . . . . .Marsh Turner
Flashpoint (1984). . . . . .Sheriff Wells
Summer Rental (1985) . . . . .Scully
Beer (1986) . . . . Buzz Beckerman
Extreme Prejudice (1987). . . . . . . Sheriff Hank Pearson
Defending Your Life (1991) . . . . Bob Diamond
Made for Cable Movies:
Another Pair of Aces (1991) . . . . Capt. Jack Parsons

Tovatt, Patrick
Films:
On the Nickel (1980) . . . .
Ellie (1984) . . . . .Art
   • 1:19 - Brief blurry buns while falling down the stairs.

Tubb, Barry
Films:
The Legend of Billie Jean (1985). . . . . Hubie
Mask (1985). . . . . .Dewey
Top Gun (1986) . . . . Henry Ruth
Valentino Returns (1988). . . . . .Wayne Gibbs
   •• 1:15 - Buns, fighting two other guys after skinny dip-
     ping with Jenny Wright at night. Very, very brief,
     blurry frontal nudity after getting hit and rolling into
     the water.

Warm Summer Rain (1989) . . . . Guy
- •• 0:23 - Lower frontal nudity getting off Kelly Lynch in bed.
- 0:25 - Side view of buns dreaming in bed.
- •• 0:58 - Frontal nudity kneeling on floor and behind the table while washing Lynch.
- • 1:00 - Buns while getting washed by Lynch.
- • 1:07 - Brief buns making love with Lynch. Quick cuts.
- ••• 1:09 - Nude picking up belongings and running out of burning house with Lynch.

TV:
Bay City Blues (1983) . . . . .Mickey Wagner

Tyson, Richard

Films:
Three O'Clock High (1987) . . . . .Buddy Revell
Two Moon Junction (1988) . . . . .Perry
- • 0:58 - Very, very brief buns wrestling with April in a motel room. Dark, hard to see.
Kindergarten Cop (1990) . . . . .Crisp

TV:
Hardball (1989-90) . . . .

Underwood, Jay

Films:
The Boy Who Could Fly (1986) . . . . .Eric
The Invisible Kid (1988) . . . . Grover Dunn
- • 0:27 - Brief buns running around the school halls after becoming visible with his friend, Milton.
Uncle Buck (1989) . . . . Bug
The Gumshoe Kid (1990) . . . . .Jeff Sherman

Valentine, Scott

Films:
Deadtime Stories (1987) . . . . .Peter
- • 0:19 - Buns, getting out of bath.
My Demon Lover (1987). Kaz
Made for Cable Movies:
After the Shock (1990) . . . . .Shannon
TV:
Family Ties (1985-89) . . . . Nick Moore

Van Damme, Jean-Claude

Films:
No Retreat, No Surrender (1986) . . . . . Ivan the Russian
Bloodsport (1987) . . . . Frank
- •• 0:50 - Brief buns putting underwear on after spending the night with Janice.
Cyborg (1989) . . . . .Gibson Rickenbacker
Kick Boxer (1989) . . . . .Kurt Sloane
Death Warrant (1990). . . . . .Louis Burke
Lionheart (1990) . . . . .Lyon
- ••• 0:47 - Buns, putting on robe after getting out of bed.
Double Impact (1991). . . . . Chad/Alec

Van Hetenryck, Kevin

Films:
Basket Case (1982) . . . . .Duane Bradley
- •• 1:21 - Frontal nudity, twice, running around at night.
Basket Case 2 (1989) .Duane
- • 0:34 - Buns standing in front of mirror looking at his large scar on the side of his body.

Van Hoffman, Brant

Films:
Police Academy (1984) . . . . .Kyle Blankes
The Further Adventures of Tennessee Buck (1987)
. . . . .Ken Manchester
- • 0:38 - Brief buns, behind a mosquito net making love with his disinterested wife.

Van Tongeren, Hans

Films:
Spetters (1980; Dutch) . . . . Ron Hartman
- ••• 0:35 - Frontal nudity, measuring and comparing his manlihood with his friends in the auto shop.
Summer Lovers (1982). . . . . Jan Tolin

Ventura, Clyde

Films:
Bury Me an Angel (1972). . . . . Bernie
Gator Bait (1973) . . . .
Terminal Island (1973) . . . . .Dillon
- •• 0:42 - Buns, taking off pants with Phyllis Davis, then covered with honey and bees, then running to jump into a pond.
Serial (1980) . . . . Donald

Villard, Tom

Films:
Parasite (1982). . . . . Zeke
Surf II (1984) . . . . Jacko O'Finlay
Heartbreak Ridge (1986) . . . . Profile
The Trouble with Dick (1986) . . . . .Dick Kendred
0:30 - Side view of buns, leaving Haley's room.
- • 0:58 - Buns from under his shirt, getting out of bed to open the door.
Weekend Warriors (1986). . . . . .Mort Seblinsky
TV:
We Got It Made (1983-84). . . . . .Jay Bostwick

Vincent, Jan-Michael

Films:
Going Home (1971). . . . . Jimmy Graham
The Mechanic (1972). . . . . Steve McKenna
The World's Greatest Athlete (1973). . . . . .Nanu
Buster and Billie (1974) . . . . Buster Lane
- ••• 1:06 - Frontal nudity taking off his underwear and walking to Billie. Buns, in slow motion, swinging into the water.

Bite the Bullet (1975) . . . . Carbo
White Line Fever (1975) . . . . Carrol Jo Hummer
Baby Blue Marine (1976). . . . . Marion Hedgepeth
Vigilante Force (1976). . . . . Ben Arnold
Damnation Alley (1977) . . . . Tanner
Big Wednesday (1978) . . . . Matt
Hooper (1978) . . . . Ski
Defiance (1980) . . . . Tommy
The Return (1980). Deputy
Hard Country (1981) . . . . Kyle Richardson
Born in East L.A. (1987). . . . . McCalister
Enemy Territory (1987) . . . . Parker
Deadly Embrace (1989). . . . . Stewart Morland
Alienator (1990) . . . . Commander
Demonstone (1990) . . . . Andrew Buck
Raw Nerve (1991). . . . .
Xtro 2, The Second Encounter (1991). . . . .
Miniseries:
The Winds of War (1983) . . . . Byron Henry
TV:
The Survivors (1969-70) . . . . Jeffrey Hastings
Airwolf (1984-86) . . . . Stringfellow Hawke

Voight, Jon
Films:
Midnight Cowboy (1969) . . . . Joe Buck
  • 0:20 - Very brief buns, walking into bedroom and jumping into bed with Cass.
  • 1:28 - Buns, in bed with Brenda Vaccaro.
Catch-22 (1970) . . . . Milo Minderbinder
Deliverance (1972) . . . . Ed
The All-American Boy (1973). . . . . Vic Bealer
Conrack (1974). Pat Conroy
The Odessa File (1974; British) . . . . Peter Miller
Coming Home (1978). . . . . Luke Martin
  (Academy Award for Best Actor.)
The Champ (1979) . . . . Bill
Table for Five (1983) . . . . J. P. Tannen
Runaway Train (1985) . . . . Manny
Desert Bloom (1986). Jack

Vu-An, Eric
Films:
The Sheltering Sky (1990) . . . . Belqassim
  • 1:59 - Buns, rolling over in bed with Debra Winger. Long shot, don't see his face.

Walsh, M. Emmet
Films:
Slap Shot (1977). . . . . Dickie Dunn
Straight Time (1978) . . . . Earl Frank
  • 0:47 - Buns, handcuffed to fence in the middle of the road with his pants down.
The Jerk (1979) . . . . Madman

Fast Walking (1981) . . . . Sgt. George Sager
  • 0:59 - Frontal nudity standing in the doorway of Evie's mobile home yelling at James Woods after he interrupts Walsh making love with Evie.
Blade Runner (1982) . . . . Bryant
Scandalous (1983). . . . . Simon Reynolds
Blood Simple (1984) . . . . Private Detective
Missing in Action (1984) . . . . Tuck
Fletch (1985) . . . . Dr. Dolan
Back to School (1986) . . . . Coach Turnbull
The Best of Times (1986) . . . . Charlie
Critters (1986). . . . . Harv
Wildcats (1986) . . . . Coes
Harry and the Hendersons (1987) . . . . George, Sr.
The Milagro Beanfield War (1988) . . . . Governor
Sunset (1988) . . . . Chief Dibner
Catch Me... If You Can (1989) . . . . . . Johnny Phatmun
Red Scorpion (1989) . . . . Dewey Ferguson
Chattahoochee (1990). . . . . Morris
Narrow Margin (1990). . . . . . . Sergeant Dominick Benti
Miniseries:
The Right of the People (1986) . . . . Mayor
Brotherhood of the Rose (1989). . . . . Hardy
Made for TV Movies:
Love & Lies (1990). . . . . Clyde Wilson
TV:
The Sandy Duncan Show (1972) . . . . Alex Lembeck
Dear Detective (1979) . . . . Capt. Gorcey
East of Eden (1981) . . . . Sheriff Quinn
UNSUB (1989). . . . . Ned

Ward, Fred
Films:
Escape from Alcatraz (1979). . . . . John Anglin
Southern Comfort (1981). . . . . Reece
The Right Stuff (1983) . . . . Gus Grissom
Timerider (1983) . . . . Lyle Swann
Uncommon Valor (1983) . . . . Wilkes
Silkwood (1984). Morgan
Swing Shift (1984) . . . . Biscuits Toohey
Remo Williams: The Adventure Begins (1985)
  . . . . Remo Williams
Secret Admirer (1985) . . . . Lou Fimple
Off Limits (1988) . . . . Dix
The Prince of Pennsylvania (1988) . . . . Gary
Henry & June (1990) . . . . Henry Miller
  ••• 1:39 - Buns, twice, making love with Maria de Madeiros.
Miami Blues (1990) . . . . Sergeant Hoke Moseley
Made for Cable Movies:
Cast a Deadly Spell (1991; HBO) . . . . H. Phillip Lovecraft

Ward, Wally
Films:
Weird Science (1985). . . . . A Weenie
Thunder Run (1986). Paul
The Chocolate War (1988) . . . . Archie

The Invisible Kid (1988) . . . . Milton McClane
  • 0:27 - Brief buns running around the school halls af-
    ter becoming visible with his friend, Grover.
TV:
Fast Times (1986) . . . . Mark Ratner

Warden, Jack

Films:
You're in the Army Now (1951) . . . . Morse
The Man Who Loved Cat Dancing (1973) . . . . . . Dawes
Shampoo (1975) . . . . Lester Carr
All the President's Men (1976) . . . . Harry Rosenfeld
Death on the Nile (1978; British) . . . . Dr. Bessner
Heaven Can Wait (1978) . . . . Max Corkle
...and Justice for All (1979) . . . . Judge Rayford
Being There (1979) . . . . President Bobby
Beyond the Poseidon Adventure (1979)
  . . . . Harold Meredith
The Champ (1979) . . . . Jackie
Used Cars (1980) . . . . Roy L. Fuchs/Luke Fuchs
Chu Chu and the Philly Flash (1981) . . . . . . Commander
The Great Muppet Caper (1981) . . . .
So Fine (1981) . . . . Jack
The Verdict (1982) . . . . Mickey Morrissey
Crackers (1984) . . . . Garvey
Problem Child (1990) . . . . Big Ben
  • 1:07 - Buns, on TV in bar, mooning into the camera
    when he doesn't know it is on. (Yes, it is him.)
TV:
The Bad News Bears (1979-80) . . . . . Morris Buttermaker
Crazy Like a Fox (1984-86) . . . . Harry Fox

Warren, Mike

Films:
Butterflies Are Free (1972) . . . . Roy
Drive, He Said (1972) . . . . Easly Jefferson
  • 0:09 - Buns and very brief frontal nudity in the show-
    er room with the other basketball players.
Cleopatra Jones (1973) . . . . Andy
Fast Break (1979) . . . . Preacher
TV:
Sierra (1974) . . . . Ranger P.J. Lewis
Paris (1979-80) . . . . Willie Miller
Hill Street Blues (1981-87) . . . . Officer Bobby Hill

Wasson, Craig

Films:
Rollercoaster (1977) . . . . Hippie
The Boys in Company C (1978) . . . . Dave Bisbee
Go Tell the Spartans (1978) . . Corporal Stephen Courcey
Carny (1980) . . . . Mickey
Schizoid (1980) . . . . Doug
Four Friends (1981) . . . . Danilo Prozor

Ghost Story (1981) . . . . Don/David
  •• 0:08 - Brief frontal nudity falling out the window,
    then buns, landing next to the pool.
  • 0:41 - Buns, making love with Alice Krige in bed-
    room.
Second Thoughts (1983) . . . . Will
Body Double (1984) . . . . Jake
The Men's Club (1986) . . . . Paul
A Nightmare on Elm Street 3: The Dream Warriors
  (1987) . . . . Dr. Neil Goldman
Made for TV Movies:
Skag (1980) . . . . David Skagska
Why Me? (1984) . . . .
TV:
Phyllis (1977) . . . . Mark Valenti

Waters, John

Films:
The Adventures of Eliza Fraser (1976; Australian)
  . . . . Dave Bracefell
  • 0:27 - Side view of buns, undressing and getting into
    bed.
  •• 0:29 - Naked, walking around outside. Buns, stand-
    ing in doorway.
  •• 0:32 - Brief pubic hair, then buns while getting off
    bed to hide under it.
  0:34 - Upper half of buns in bed on top of Susannah
    York.
  •• 0:38 - Buns, jumping on York, then getting pushed
    out the door.

Waterston, Sam

Films:
The Great Gatsby (1974) . . . . Nick Carraway
Rancho Deluxe (1975) . . . . Cecil Colson
Capricorn One (1978) . . . . Peter Willis
Eagle's Wing (1978; British) . . . . White Bull
Interiors (1978) . . . . Mike
Heaven's Gate (1980) . . . . Canton
Hopscotch (1980) . . . . Cutter
Sweet William (1980; British) . . . . William
  • 0:27 - Buns, seen through a window in the door,
    standing on balcony with Jenny Agutter.
The Killing Fields (1984) . . . . Sydney Schanberg
Warning Sign (1985) . . . . Cal Morse
Just Between Friends (1986) . . . . Harry Crandall
September (1987) . . . . Peter
Welcome Home (1989) . . . . Woody
Made for Cable Movies:
Finnegan Begin Again (1985) . . . .
The Nightmare Years (1989) . . . . William
Miniseries:
Q.E.D. (1982) . . . . Quentin E. Deverill
TV:
I'll Fly Away (1991-) . . . .

Waybill, John "Fee"

Lead singer of *The Tubes*.

Films:

Ladies and Gentlemen, The Fabulous Stains (1982)
. . . . Lou Corpse
(Not available on video tape.)

Video Tapes:

Red Hot Rock (1984) . . . . himself
••• 0:13 - Nude, getting dressed in locker room during
"Sports Fans" by The Tubes.
• 0:29 - Buns, in G-string S&M outfit during "Mondo
Bondage" by The Tubes.

Weaving, Hugo

Films:

The Right Hand Man (1987) . . . . Ned Devine
...Almost (1990; Australian) . . . . Jake
0:52 - Very brief out of focus buns when he drops his
pants in front of Rosanna Arquette. Don't see his
face. Note in the very next scene, he's wearing underwear!

Wehe, Oliver

Films:

Erendira (1983; Brazilian) . . . . Ulysses
• 1:24 - Buns, getting into bed with Erendira.

Weller, Peter

Films:

Just Tell Me What You Want (1980) . . . Steven Routledge
Shoot the Moon (1982) . . . . Frank Henderson
Of Unknown Origin (1983; Canadian) . . . . Bart Hughes
The Adventures of Buckaroo Banzai, Across the 8th
Dimension (1984) . . . . Buckaroo Banzai
Firstborn (1984) . . . . Sam
Robocop (1987) . . . . Alex Murphy/Robocop
The Tunnel (1987) . . . . Juan Pablo
Shakedown (1988) . . . . Roland Dalton
Leviathan (1989). . . . . William Beck
Robocop 2 (1990). . . . . Alex Murphy/Robocop
Cat Chaser (1991) . . . .

Made for Cable Movies:

Apology (1986; HBO) . . . . Rad Hungare
• 1:04 - Brief buns, putting pants on, getting out of
bed to chase after intruder at night.
Rainbow Drive (1990; Showtime) . . . . . . Mike Gallagher
Women & Men: Stories of Seduction (1990; HBO)
. . . . Hobie

Welsh, Kenneth

Films:

Covergirl (1982; Canadian). . . . . . .Harrison Chandler
• 1:23 - Brief buns, seen on video tape used to get him
in trouble. Long shot.
Of Unknown Origin (1983; Canadian) . . . . James
Falling In Love (1984) . . . . Doctor

Heartburn (1986). . . . . .Dr. Appel
The House on Carroll Street (1988) . . . . Hackett
Physical Evidence (1989) . . . . .Harry Norton
The Freshman (1990). . . . . .Dwight Armstrong

Weston, Jack

Films:

Fuzz (1972) . . . . Detective Meyer Meyer
Gator (1976) . . . . Irving Greenfield
The Ritz (1976) . . . . Gaetano Proclo
Cuba (1979) . . . . .Gutman
Can't Stop the Music (1980) . . . . Benny Murray
Four Seasons (1981) . . . . Danny Zimmer
• 0:48 - Brief buns in water while skinny dipping with
Rita Moreno.
High Road to China (1983) . . . . .Struts
Dirty Dancing (1987). . . . . Max Kellerman
Ishtar (1987) .Marty Freed
Short Circuit 2 (1988) . . . . Oscar Baldwin

Whiting, Leonard

Films:

Romeo and Juliet (1968) . . . . .Romeo
•• 1:34 - Buns, in bed with Juliet, then getting out to
stretch. Long scene.

Wilby, James

Films:

Maurice (1987; British). . . . . Maurice Hall
A Handful of Dust (1988). . . . . .Tony Last
A Summer Story (1988) . . . . Frank Ashton
• 0:08 - Buns, in creek with Mr. Garten while skinny
dipping

Wilder, Gene

Films:

The Producers (1968). . . . . .Leo Bloom
Quackser Fortune has a Cousin in the Bronx (1970; Irish)
. . . . Quackser Fortune
Start the Revolution Without Me (1970)
. . . . .Claude Coupe/Philippe De Sisi
Willy Wonka and the Chocolate Factory (1971)
. . . . .Willy Wonka
Blazing Saddles (1974). .Jim
The Little Prince (1974; British) . . . . .The Fox
Young Frankenstein (1974; B&W) . . . . .Dr. Frankenstein
The Adventure of Sherlock Holmes' Smarter Brother
(1975) . . . . Sigerson Holmes
Silver Streak (1976) . . . . George Caldwell
The World's Greatest Lover (1977) . . . . . .Rudy Valentine
The Frisco Kid (1979). . . . . Avram Belinsky
Stir Crazy (1980) . . . . Skip Donahue
Hanky Panky (1982). . . . . Michael Jordon
The Woman in Red (1984). . . . . .Theodore Pierce
• 1:15 - Side view of buns getting back into bed with
Kelly Le Brock after getting out to take his under-
wear off the lamp.

Haunted Honeymoon (1986) . . . . Larry Abbot
See No Evil, Hear No Evil (1989) . . . . .Dave
Funny About Love (1990) . . . . .Duffy Bergman
Another You (1991) . . . . George Washington

Williams, Jason
Films:
Time Walker (1982). . . . . Jeff
Down and Out in Beverly Hills (1986) . . . . Lance
Danger Zone II: Reaper's Revenge (1988) . . . Wade
•• 0:06 - Buns, getting out of bed and putting pants on.
Vampire at Midnight (1988) . . . . Detective Roger Sutter

Williams, Treat
Films:
The Ritz (1976) . . . . Michael Brick
The Eagle Has Landed (1977; British)
. . . . .Captain Happy Clark
1941 (1979) . . . . Sitarski
Hair (1979) . . . . Berger
• 0:57 - Buns, taking off clothes and diving into pond
with Hud and Woof.
Why Would I Lie? (1980). . . . . .Cletus
Prince of the City (1981) . . . . .Daniel Ciello
Pursuit of D.B. Cooper (1981) . . . . Meade
Flashpoint (1984) . . . . .Ernie
•• 0:03 - Buns, putting on pants in locker room while
talking to Kris Kristofferson.
Once Upon a Time in America (1984)
. . . . Jimmy O'Donnell
(Long version.)
Smooth Talk (1985) . . . . Arnold Friend
The Men's Club (1986) . . . . .Terry
Dead Heat (1988). . . . . .Roger Mortis
Heart of Dixie (1989) .Hoyt
Sweet Lies (1989) . . . . .Peter
0:52 - Side view of buns in bed with Joanna Pacula.
Very, very brief, blurry frontal nudity getting out of
bed. Don't really see anything.
Made for Cable Movies:
Third Degree Burn (1989; HBO) . . . . . . Scott Weston
• 0:43 - Brief buns taking off his robe with Virginia
Madsen in his bedroom.
TV:
Eddie Dodd (1991-) . . . . Eddie Dodd

Wilson, Lambert
Films:
Chanel Solitaire (1981) . . . .
Sahara (1984) . . . . .Jaffar
Red Kiss (1985; French). . . . . .Stephane
Rendez-Vous (1986; French). . . . . Quentin
• 0:22 - Very brief buns, falling with Juliet onto net dur-
ing play.

Wilson, Robert Brian
Films:
Silent Night, Deadly Night (1984) . . . . . . Billy at 18
• 0:30 - Sort of buns in bed with Pamela.

Wilson, Roger
Films:
Porky's (1981; Canadian) . . . . .Mickey
Thunder Alley (1985) . . . . Richie
Second Time Lucky (1986) . . . . Adam Smith
•• 0:13 - Buns, in the Garden of Eden.
•• 0:30 - Buns, standing out in the rain.
TV:
Seven Brides for Seven Brothers (1982-83)
. . . . Daniel McFadden

Winchester, Jeff
Films:
Olivia (1983) . . . . Richard
a.k.a. A Taste of Sin
• 1:17 - Buns, getting stuffed into trunk by Olivia.
Dark.

Winn, David
Films:
My Therapist (1983) . . . . .Mike Jenner
Shot on video tape.
•• 0:19 - Buns, making love with Marilyn Chambers in
bed.

Woltz, Randy
Films:
The Young Warriors (1983; U.S./Canadian)
. . . . "Brick Test" Frank
• 0:16 - Dropping his pants in a room during pledge
at fraternity.

Wood, Timothy
Films:
Love Circles Around the World (1984) . . . . Michael
•• 1:29 - Frontal nudity, lying in bed with Jill after making love while video taping it.

Woods, James
Films:
Hickey and Boggs (1972). . . . . .Lt. Wyatt
The Visitors (1972). . . . . .Bill Schmidt
The Way We Were (1973). . . . . Frankie McVeigh
The Gambler (1974) . . . . .Bank Officer
Distance (1975) . . . . Larry
Night Moves (1975). . . . . .Quentin
The Choirboys (1977) . . . . Bloomguard
The Onion Field (1979) . . . . Gregory Powell
•• 1:33 - Buns, taking a shower in the prison.
The Black Marble (1980) . . . . .Fiddler

Eyewitness (1981) . . . . Aldo
Fast Walking (1981) . . . . Fast-Walking Miniver
Split Image (1982) . . . . Prattt
Videodrome (1983; Canadian) . . . . Max Renn
Against All Odds (1984) . . . . Jake Wise
Once Upon a Time in America (1984) . . . . Max
   (Long version.)
Cat's Eye (1985) . . . . .Morrison
Joshua Then and Now (1985; Canadian)
   . . . . Joshua Shapiro
Salvador (1986) . . . . Richard Boyle
Best Seller (1988) . . . . Cleve
Cop (1988). . . . . .Lloyd Hopkins
The Boost (1989) . . . . Lenny Brown
Immediate Family (1989) . . . . Michael Spector
True Believer (1989) . . . . Eddie Dodd
The Hard Way (1991) . . . . .John Moss
Made for Cable Movies:
Women & Men: Stories of Seduction (1990; HBO)
   . . . . Robert
Miniseries:
Holocaust (1978) . . . . Karl Weiss
Made for TV Movies:
My Name is Bill W. (1989). . . . . .Bill Wilson
The Boys (1991) . . . . .Walter Farmer

Woods, Michael
Films:
Lady Beware (1987). . . . . Jack Price
   •• 0:43 - Buns, lying down in Diane Lane's bed.
TV:
Bare Essence (1983) . . . . .Sean Benedict
Our Family Honor (1985-86). . . . . . . Jerry Cole (Danzig)
Capital News (1990) . . . . Clay Gibson

Wright, Dorsey
Films:
Hair (1979) . . . . Hud
   • 0:57 - Buns, taking off clothes and diving into pond
      with Treat Williams and Woof.
Ragtime (1981). . . . .
The Hotel New Hampshire (1984). . . . . Junior Jones

Youngs, Jim
Films:
The Wanderers (1979). . . . . .Buddy
Footloose (1984). . . . . .Chuck
Out of Control (1984) . . . . Cowboy
   • 0:54 - Buns making love with Claudia Udy.
Hot Shot (1986) . . . .
Nobody's Fool (1986) . . . . Billy
Youngblood (1986). . . . . Kelly Youngblood
You Talkin' To Me (1987) . . . . Bronson Green

Yurasek, John
Films:
Less than Zero (1987). . . . . Naked Man
   • 1:22 - Brief buns standing up when Andrew Mc-
      Carthy discovers him with Robert Downey, Jr.

Zane, Billy
Films:
Back to the Future (1985) . . . . Match
Critters (1986) . . . . .Steve Elliot
Back to the Future, Part II (1989) . . . . Match
Dead Calm (1989) . . . . Hughie Warriner
   • 1:01 - Buns, walking around on the boat.
Femme Fatale (1990). . . . . .Elijah Hooper
Memphis Belle (1990) . . . . "Val" Valentine
Made for TV Movies:
The Case of the Hillside Stranglers (1989)
   . . . . Kenneth Bianchi
TV:
Twin Peaks (1990-91). . . . . John Justice Wheeler

Zelnicker, Michael
Films:
Pick-Up Summer (1979; Canadian). . . . . Greg
   • 0:04 - Brief buns, hanging a B.A. out the back win-
      dow of the van.
Hog Wild (1980; Canadian) . . . . .Pete
Touch and Go (1984). . . . . McDonald
Bird (1988) . . . . .Red Rodney

Titles

10 (1979)
Julie Andrews . . . . Sam
Bo Derek. . . . . Jennifer Hanley
    1:18 - In yellow swimsuit running in slow motion to-
    wards Dudley Moore in his daydream.
    • 1:27 - Brief buns and topless taking off towel and
    putting on robe when Moore visits her. Long shot,
    hard to see.
    • 1:34 - Brief topless taking off dress trying to seduce
    Moore. Dark, hard to see.
    • 1:35 - Topless, lying in bed. Dark, hard to see.
    •• 1:39 - Topless, going to fix the skipping record. Long
    shot, hard to see.
Sam J. Jones . . . . David Hanley
Dudley Moore. . . . . George Webber
    • 0:47 - Buns, at neighbor's party just before Julie An-
    drews sees him through a telescope.
Dee Wallace Stone . . . . Mary Lewis

10 to Midnight (1983)
Kelly Preston . . . . Doreen
Ola Ray. . . . . Ola
    •• 1:27 - Buns, then topless in the shower.
Cynthia Reams . . . . Hooker
    ••• 1:25 - Topless in hotel room with killer when he tries
    to elude Charles Bronson.
Andrew Stevens . . . . Paul McAnn
Patti Tippo . . . . Party Girl
    •• 0:52 - Topless, making love with a guy in the laundry
    room at a party when Andrew Stevens surprises
    them.
Jeana Tomasino. . . . . Karen
    0:26 - In white lingerie changing in bedroom while
    the killer watches from inside the closet.

18 Again! (1988)
Connie Gauthier . . . . Artist's Model
    •• 0:29 - Very brief topless, then buns taking her robe
    off during art class.
Anita Morris . . . . Madeline

1900 (1976; Italian)
Robert De Niro . . . . Alfredo Berlinghieri
    • 1:59 - Very brief buns making love with Dominique
    Sanda in the hay. Don't see his face.
Gérard Depardieu . . . . Olmo Dalco
    • 1:36 - Brief frontal nudity sitting at table with Robert
    De Niro. Again when walking into the bedroom.
    ••• 1:40 - Nude getting out of bed after the girl has a sei-
    zure.
Roberto Maccanti . . . . Olmo as a Child
    • 0:53 - Frontal nudity undressing and showing the
    young Alfredo his penis.
Dominique Sanda. . . . . .Ada
    •• 2:12 - (0:05 into tape 2.) Full frontal nudity under
    thin fabric dancing with Robert De Niro for photog-
    rapher.
Stefania Sandrelli. . . . . Anita Foschi
Donald Sutherland .Attila

1984 (1984)
Suzanna Hamilton . . . . .Julia
    •• 0:38 - Full frontal nudity taking off her clothes in the
    woods with John Hurt.
    ••• 0:52 - Nude in secret room standing and drinking
    and talking to Hurt. Long scene.
    • 1:11 - Side view of left breast kneeling down.
    •• 1:12 - Topless after picture falls off the view screen on
    the wall.
John Hurt. .Winston Smith
    • 1:11 - Buns, walking from the bed to the window
    next to Suzanna Hamilton.

2020 Texas Gladiators (1983; Italian)
Sabrina Siani . . . . Maida
    •• 0:07 - Left breast, in open white dress after gang
    rape.
    • 0:34 - Topless during rape.

48 Hours (1982)
Greta Blackburn . . . . Lisa
    •• 0:13 - Topless and buns in bathroom in hotel room
    with James Remar.
Denise Crosby . . . . .Sally
    0:47 - Very, very brief side view of half of left breast,
    while swinging baseball bat at Eddie Murphy.
    • 1:24 - Very brief side view of right breast when James
    Remar pushes her onto bed.
    • 1:25 - Very brief topless then very brief side view of
    right breast attacking Nick Nolte.
Chris Mulkey . . . . .Cop
Nick Nolte . . . . Jack Cates
Annette O'Toole. . . . . .Elaine
Ola Ray . . . . Vroman's Dancers
Suzanne M. Regard . . . . Cowgirl Dancer
    0:39 - Dancer in red-neck bar wearing silver star past-
    ies.
Brenda Venus. . . . . Hooker

52 Pick-Up (1986)
Ann-Margret . . . . Barbara Mitchell
Vanity . . . . Doreen
    ••• 0:50 - Topless, stripping in room while Roy Scheider
    takes Polaroid pictures.
Kelly Preston . . . . Cini
    • 0:09 - Brief buns in film made by blackmailers.
    • 0:36 - Topless on video tape made by kidnappers.

8 Million Ways to Die (1986)
Rosanna Arquette. .Sarah
    1:00 - In a bra in Jeff Bridges' apartment.
Jeff Bridges . . . . Matthew Scudder
Alexandra Paul. . . . . Sunny
    •• 0:24 - Full frontal nudity, standing in bathroom while
    Jeff Bridges watches.

9 1/2 Ninjas (1990)
Andee Gray . . . . Lisa Thorne
    •• 1:02 - Topless making love with Joe in the rain.
    • 1:19 - Brief topless during flashback.

9 1/2 Weeks *(1986)*
Kim Basinger. . . . . .Elizabeth
- 0:27 - Blindfolded while Mickey Rourke plays with an ice cube on her. Brief right breast.
  0:36 - Masturbating while watching slides of art.
  0:41 - Playing with food at the refrigerator with Rourke. Messy, but erotic.
- 0:54 - Very brief left breast rolling over in bed.
  0:58 - Making love with Rourke in clock tower.
- ••• 1:11 - In wet lingerie, then topless making love in a wet stairwell with Rourke.
  1:19 - Doing a sexy dance for Rourke in a white slip.
  1:22 - Buns, showing off to Rourke on building.
Margaret Whitton . . . . Molly
Karen Young . . . . Sue

About Last Night... *(1986)*
Rob Lowe . . . . Danny
- •• 0:52 - Buns and almost frontal nudity when he opens the refrigerator with Demi Moore.
Demi Moore . . . . Debbie
  0:32 - In white bra getting dressed.
- 0:34 - Brief upper half of right breast in the bathtub with Rob Lowe.
  0:35 - In white bra getting dressed.
- 0:50 - Side view of right breast, then very brief topless.
- ••• 0:51 - Buns and topless in bed with Lowe, arching her back, then lying in bed when he rolls off her.
- •• 0:52 - Topless and buns in kitchen with Lowe.
Elizabeth Perkins . . . . Joan

The Abyss *(1989)*
Michael Biehn . . . . Lieutenant Coffey
Ed Harris . . . . Virgil "Bud" Brigman
Mary Elizabeth Mastrantonio. . . . . .Lindsey Brigman
- 1:41 - Topless during C.P.R. scene.

The Accused *(1988)*
Steve Antin . . . . .Bob Joiner
- 1:29 - Buns, raping Jodi Foster on the pinball machine.
Woody Brown . . . . Danny
- 1:28 - Buns, raping Jodi Foster on the pinball machine.
Jodie Foster . . . . .Sarah Tobias
- 1:27 - Brief topless a few times during rape scene on pinball machine by Dan and Bob.
Kelly McGillis. Kathryn Murphy
Leo Rossi . . . . Cliff "Scorpion" Albrect

Act of Piracy *(1990)*
Belinda Bauer . . . . .Sandy Andrews
Nancy Mulford . . . . Laura Warner
- 0:11 - Very brief left breast under Gary Busey in bed. Dark, hard to see.
  0:12 - In white lingerie, walking around on the boat shooting everybody.
- 0:34 - Brief, upper half of left breast, in bed with Ray Sharkey.
  0:35 - In white nightgown. ·

Ray Sharkey . . . . Jack Wilcox
- 0:33 - Brief side view of buns on top of Laura in bed.
- •• 0:35 - Brief buns, getting out of bed and putting on robe.

Action Jackson *(1988)*
Vanity . . . . Sydney Ash
- •• 0:29 - Topless in bed with Craig T. Nelson.
Susan Lentini . . . . VW Driver
Melissa Prophet . . . . Newscaster
Sharon Stone . . . . Patrice Dellaplane
- •• 0:34 - Topless in a steam room. Hard to see because of all the steam.
- 0:56 - Brief right breast, dead, on the bed when police view her body.

The Adultress *(1973)*
Tyne Daly. . . . . .Inez
- 0:21 - Brief side view of right breast in room with Carl. Brief out of focus topless in bed.
- •• 0:51 - Topless outside with Hank.
- ••• 0:53 - Topless on a horse with Hank.

The Adventures of Eliza Fraser *(1976; Australian)*
Abigail . . . . Buxom Girl
- 0:01 - Topless when Martin pulls the sheets off her.
John Waters . . . . Dave Bracefell
- 0:27 - Side view of buns, undressing and getting into bed.
- •• 0:29 - Naked, walking around outside. Buns, standing in doorway.
- •• 0:32 - Brief pubic hair, then buns while getting off bed to hide under it.
  0:34 - Upper half of buns in bed on top of Susannah York.
- •• 0:38 - Buns, jumping on York, then getting pushed out the door.
Susannah York . . . . .Elisa Fraser
- 1:10 - Brief topless twice during ceremony. Paint on her face while running from hut.

After Dark, My Sweet *(1990)*
Bruce Dern. . . . . Uncle Bud
Jeanie Moore . . . . Nanny
Jason Patric . . . . .Kevin "Collie" Collins
- •• 1:19 - Buns, taking off pants and getting into bed with Rachel Ward. More brief buns on top of her.
Rachel Ward. . . . . .Fay Anderson
- 1:22 - Very, very brief half of right breast under Jason Patric in bed when he moves slightly.

After Hours *(1985)*
Rosanna Arquette. . . . . Marcy
  0:48 - In bed, dead, in panties. Arm covers breasts.
Linda Fiorentino. . . . . Kiki
  0:11 - In black bra and skirt doing paper maché.
- •• 0:19 - Topless taking off bra in doorway while Griffin Dunne watches.
Teri Garr. . . . . .Julie
John Heard. . . . . Bartender
Richard "Cheech" Marin . . . . .Neil

After School (1987)
Renee Coleman . . . . September Lane
- •• 0:35 - Topless and buns getting into bathtub. Almost lower frontal nudity.

Sherrie Ann Rose . . . . First Tribe Member

Age of Consent (1969; Australian)
Clarissa Kaye-Mason . . . . Meg
- • 0:05 - Brief topless, crawling on the bed to watch TV.

Jack MacGowran . . . . Nat Kelly
- • 1:01 - Brief buns, running into the ocean when Miss Marley sees him.
- •• 1:02 - Buns, running away from her to the cabin while holding a dog to cover up his private parts.

Helen Mirren . . . . Cora
- • 0:48 - Topless several times in the mirror. Brief lower frontal nudity, kneeling on the floor.
- •• 0:55 - Brief topless and buns quite a few time, snorkeling under water.
- ••• 1:20 - Topless and half of buns, posing in the water for James Mason. Then getting out.

Alamo Bay (1985)
Ed Harris . . . . Shang
Amy Madigan . . . . Glory
- •• 0:28 - Topless lying in motel bed with Ed Harris.
- •• 0:30 - Topless sitting up in the bed.
- 0:40 - Walking in parking lot in a wet T-shirt.

Albino (1976)
a.k.a. Night of the Askari
Sybil Danning . . . . Sally
- • 0:19 - Topless, then full frontal nudity getting raped by the Albino and his buddies.

Alexa (1988)
Ruth Corrine Collins . . . . Marshall
- • 0:01 - Topless a couple of times taking blue dress off and putting it on again. Long shot.

Christine Moore . . . . Alexa
- 0:04 - In red slip in bedroom.
- 0:06 - In black bra, on bed with Tommy.
- 0:11 - In black lingerie talking on phone in bed.
- •• 0:24 - Topless lying in bed with Anthony while reminiscing.
- •• 1:08 - Topless in bed with Anthony again.

Alien Prey (1984; British)
Glory Annen . . . . Jessica
- • 0:22 - Topless unbuttoning blouse to sunbathe.
- •• 0:34 - Topless taking off top, getting into bed with Josephine, then making love with her.
- 0:36 - Buns, rolling on top of Josephine.
- ••• 0:38 - More topless when Josephine is playing with her.
- 0:39 - More buns in bed. Long shot.
- • 0:46 - Left breast and buns standing up in bathtub.
- •• 1:05 - Topless getting out of bed and putting a dress on.
- •• 1:19 - Topless in bed with Anders. Brief buns when he rips her panties off.

Sally Faulkner . . . . Josephine
- • 0:32 - Very, very brief left breast taking off top.
- 0:36 - Buns, in bed with Glory Annen.
- • 0:37 - Topless on her back in bed with Annen.

Barry Stokes . . . . Anders
- •• 1:19 - Buns, getting on top of Glory Annen in bed.

All That Jazz (1979)
Leah Ayres-Hamilton . . . . Nurse Capobianco
Sandahl Bergman . . . . Sandra
- •• 0:52 - Topless dancing on scaffolding during a dance routine.

Vicki Frederick . . . . Menage Partner
Deborah Geffner . . . . Victoria
- • 0:17 - Brief topless taking off her blouse and walking up the stairs while Roy Scheider watches. A little out of focus.

Jessica Lange . . . . Angelique
John Lithgow . . . . Lucas Sergeant
Sue Paul . . . . Stacy
- • 1:18 - Brief right breast in bed with Roy Scheider at the hospital.

K.C. Townsend . . . . Stripper
- • 0:21 - Topless backstage getting Joey excited before he goes on stage. Lit by red light.

...All the Marbles (1981)
a.k.a. The California Dolls
Angela Aames . . . . Louise
- •• 0:20 - Topless in Peter Falk's motel room talking with Iris, then sitting on the bed.

Peter Falk . . . . Harry
Vicki Frederick . . . . Iris
- • 1:03 - Brief side view of left breast crying in the shower after fighting with Peter Falk.

Laurene Landon . . . . Molly
Tracy Reed . . . . Diane

All The Right Moves (1983)
Tom Cruise . . . . Stef
- •• 1:00 - Very brief frontal nudity getting undressed in his bedroom with Lea Thompson.

Christopher Penn . . . . Brian
Lea Thompson . . . . Lisa
- ••• 1:00 - Topless, getting undressed and into bed with Tom Cruise in his bedroom.

Alley Cat (1982)
Karen Mani . . . . Billie
- • 0:01 - Brief topless in panties taking night gown off during opening credits.
- 0:17 - In two piece swimsuit sitting by the pool.
- ••• 0:38 - Brief side view of right breast and buns getting into the shower. Full frontal nudity in the shower.
- ••• 0:48 - Topless in women's prison shower room scene. Long scene.

...Almost (1990; Australian)
Rosanna Arquette . . . . Wendy
Susan Lyons . . . . Caroline

Hugo Weaving . . . . Jake
    0:52 - Very brief out of focus buns when he drops his pants in front of Rosanna Arquette. Don't see his face. Note in the very next scene, he's wearing underwear!

Alpine Fire (1985; Swiss)

Thomas Nock . . . . Bob
   • 0:08 - Brief buns, outside taking a bath.

Altered States (1980)

Blair Brown . . . . Emily Jessup
   • 0:10 - Brief left breast making love with William Hurt in red light from an electric heater.
   •• 0:34 - Topless lying on her stomach during Hurt's mushroom induced hallucination.
   1:39 - Buns, sitting in hallway with Hurt after the transformations go away.
William Hurt . . . . Eddie Jessup
   0:46 - Brief pubic hair twice when Charles Haid and Bob Balaban help him out of isolation tank.
   • 0:54 - Very brief buns, standing in the shower when he starts transforming. More buns standing near door and walking to bed.

Alvin Purple (1973; Australian)

Abigail . . . . Girl in See-Through
   0:01 - On bus in see-through top. Hard to see anything.
Graeme Blundell . . . . Alvin Purple
   •• 0:21 - Brief nude, painting each other's bodies with Samantha.
   •• 0:22 - Buns and brief frontal nudity in bedroom with the Kinky Lady.
   • 0:25 - Brief buns with Mrs. Warren—who turns out to be a man.
   • 0:26 - Very brief frontal nudity running out of room, then buns going down the stairs.
   ••• 0:33 - Nude, undressing and taking a shower. Shot at fast speed.
   •• 1:04 - Nude, running away from the girl during showing of movie.
   • 1:21 - Buns, getting chased by a group of women down the street.
Lynette Curran . . . . First Sugar Girl
   •• 0:02 - Brief full frontal nudity when Alvin opens the door.
Kris McQuade . . . . Samantha
   ••• 0:21 - Topless and buns, painting each other's bodies with Alvin.
Debbie Nankervis . . . . Girl in Blue Movie
   •• 1:04 - Nude, running after Alvin in bedroom during showing of movie.
Elke Neidhardt . . . . Woman in Blue Movie
   •• 1:07 - In red bra, then full frontal nudity in bedroom with Alvin during showing of film.
Anne Pendlebury . . . . Woman with Pin
   •• 0:48 - Right breast and lower frontal nudity, lying in bed, talking with Alvin.
Jacki Weaver . . . . Second Sugar Girl
   •• 0:33 - Brief full frontal nudity, lying in bean bag chair.

Alvin Rides Again (1974; Australian)

Abigail . . . . Mae
   ••• 0:12 - Topless in store with Alvin.
Graeme Blundell . . . . Alvin Purple
   • 0:06 - Buns, running out of the office after he's awakened. Blurry.
Chantal Contouri . . . . Boobs La Touche
   • 1:15 - Very brief lower frontal nudity, putting panties on in the car. Brief topless, putting red dress on.
Kris McQuade . . . . Mandy
   ••• 0:48 - Full frontal nudity, taking off red dress and getting into bed with Alvin. More topless lying in bed. Long scene.
Debbie Nankervis . . . . Woman Cricketer
Candy Raymond . . . . Girl in Office
   • 0:05 - Lower frontal nudity and buns, in office with Alvin.
Judy Stevenson . . . . Housewife
   •• 0:01 - Full frontal nudity, dropping her towel while Alvin washes her window.

Amazon Women on the Moon (1987)

Corinne Alphen . . . . Shari
   ••• 1:13 - In black bra, then topless on TV while Ray watches.
Rosanna Arquette . . . . Karen
Belinda Balaski . . . . Bernice Pitnik
Ed Begley, Jr. . . . . Griffin
   • 0:54 - Buns, walking around as the Son of the Invisible Man. This section is in B&W.
Lana Clarkson . . . . Alpha Beta
Sybil Danning . . . . Queen Lara
Monique Gabrielle . . . . Taryn Steele
   ••• 0:05 - Nude during Penthouse Video sketch. Long sequence of her nude in unlikely places.
Steve Guttenberg . . . . Jerry Stone
Tracey E. Hutchinson . . . . Floozie
   1:18 - Brief right breast hitting balloon while Carrie Fisher talks to a guy. This sketch is in B&W and appears after the first batch of credits.
Michelle Pfeiffer . . . . Brenda Landers
Kelly Preston . . . . Violet
Angel Tompkins . . . . First Lady
   1:00 - In white nightgown, then black bra, panties, garter belt and stockings.

Amazons (1986)

Danitza Kingsley . . . . Tshingi
   ••• 0:30 - Topless and buns quite a few times with Colungo out of and in bed.
Windsor Taylor Randolph . . . . Dyala
   •• 0:22 - Topless skinny dipping then getting dressed with Tashi.
   •• 0:24 - Brief topless getting her top opened by bad guys then fighting them.
Penelope Reed . . . . Tashi
   •• 0:22 - Topless and buns undressing to go skinny dipping. More topless getting dressed.
   • 0:24 - Brief topless getting top opened by bad guys.

The Ambassador *(1984)*
Ellen Burstyn . . . . Alex Hacker
- ••• 0:06 - Topless opening her robe to greet her lover.
- ••• 0:07 - Brief topless making love in bed.
- ••• 0:29 - Topless in a movie while her husband, Robert Mitchum, watches.

The American Angels, Baptism of Blood *(1989)*
Jan MacKenzie. .Luscious Lisa
- 0:07 - Buns in G-string on stage in club. More buns getting lathered up for wrestling match.
- • 0:11 - Topless and buns when a customer takes her top off. She's covered with shaving cream.
- •• 0:12 - Topless taking a shower when Diamond Dave looks in to talk to her.
- • 0:56 - Right breast in wrestling ring with Dave.

American Flyers *(1985)*
Rae Dawn Chong . . . . Sarah
Kevin Costner . . . . Marcus
David Grant . . . . David
- • 0:05 - Brief buns and very, very brief frontal nudity taking off shorts and walking to bathroom.
Katherine Kriss. . . . . Vera
Alexandra Paul . . . . Becky
- • 0:50 - Very brief right breast, then very brief half of left breast changing tops with David Grant. Brief side view of right breast. Dark.
- •• 1:13 - Brief topless in white panties getting into bed with David Grant.

American Gigolo *(1980)*
Michele Drake. . . . . 1st Girl on Balcony
- • 0:03 - Topless on the balcony while Richard Gere and Lauren Hutton talk.
Richard Gere. . . . . Julian
- •• 0:39 - Buns and frontal nudity, but a long shot, so it's hard to see anything.
Linda Horn . . . . 2nd Girl on Balcony
- • 0:03 - Topless on the balcony while Richard Gere and Lauren Hutton talk.
Lauren Hutton. . . . . Michelle
- • 0:37 - Left breast, making love with Richard Gere in bed in his apartment.

American Nightmare *(1981; Canadian)*
Alexandra Paul . . . . Isabelle Blake/Tanya Kelly
- ••• 0:02 - Left breast while smoking in bed. Topless before getting killed. Long scene.
Lora Staley . . . . Louise Harmon
- •• 0:44 - Topless and buns in G-string dancing on stage.
- ••• 0:54 - Topless making love in bed with Eric.
- • 0:59 - Brief right breast, then topless auditioning in TV studio.
Claudia Udy . . . . Andrea
- ••• 0:08 - Buns, then topless dancing on stage.
- • 0:22 - Buns getting into bathtub. Topless during struggle with killer.
Lenore Zann . . . . Tina
- ••• 0:25 - Topless and buns dancing on stage.
- •• 1:05 - Topless and buns dancing on stage again.

The American Success Company *(1979)*
Belinda Bauer. . . . . .Sarah
Jeff Bridges. . . . . .Harry
Bianca Jagger. . . . . Corinne
- • 0:35 - Topless under see-through black top while sitting on bed.

An American Werewolf in London *(1981)*
Jenny Agutter. . . . . .Alex Price
- • 0:41 - Brief right breast in bed with David Naughton. Dark, hard to see.
Linzi Drew . . . . .Brenda Bristols
- • 1:26 - Side view of left breast in porno movie while David Naughton talks to his friend, Jack.
- • 1:27 - Brief topless in movie talking on the phone.
David Naughton . . . . David Kessler
- • 0:24 - Very brief buns running naked through the woods.
- • 0:58 - Buns, during his transformation into a werewolf.
- •• 1:09 - Brief frontal nudity and buns waking up in wolf cage at the zoo. Long shot, hard to see anything. More buns, running around the zoo.

Amityville II: The Possession *(1982)*
Diane Franklin . . . . .Patricia Montelli
- • 0:41 - Half of right breast sitting on bed talking to her brother.

Amor Ciego *(1980; Mexican)*
Apollonia . . . . Patty
- • 0:32 - Topless getting out of hammock.
- ••• 0:52 - Right breast, standing up, then topless kissing Daniel. More topless in bed.
- ••• 0:59 - Buns, making love in bed, then topless afterwards.
- •• 1:11 - Topless, taking off her towel and putting Daniel's hand on her left breast.
- •• 1:15 - Topless, turning over, then lying in bed.
Jaime Moreno . . . . Daniel
- ••• 0:51 - Frontal nudity standing up from bed, then buns when Apollonia hugs him.
- • 0:53 - Buns, making love in bed with Apollonia.

And God Created Woman *(1988)*
(Unrated version.)
Rebecca De Mornay. .Robin
- •• 0:06 - Brief Left breast and buns in gymnasium with Vincent Spano. Brief right breast making love.
- • 0:53 - Brief buns and topless in the shower when Spano sees her.
- •• 1:02 - Brief left breast with Langella on the floor.
- ••• 1:12 - Topless making love with Spano in a museum.
Pat Lee. . . . . .Inmate

...and God created woman *(1957; French)*
Brigitte Bardot . . . . .Juliette
- • 0:40 - Very brief side view of right breast getting out of bed.

Andy Warhol's Frankenstein
(1974; Italian/German/French)

Dalila Di'Lazzaro . . . . The Girl
- •• 0:09 - Topless lying on platform in the lab.
- • 0:37 - Close up of left breast while the Count cuts her stitches. (Pretty bloody.)
  0:43 - Topless, covered with blood, strapped to table
- • 0:49 - Topless on table, all wired up.
- • 1:03 - Right breast lying on table. Long shot.
- • 1:05 - More right breast, long shot.
- •• 1:06 - More topless on table, then standing in the lab.
- •• 1:20 - Brief right breast when Otto pulls her top down.
- •• 1:23 - Topless on table again, then walking around. (Scar on chest.) Lower frontal nudity when Otto pulls her bandage down, then more gross topless when he removes her guts.

Monique Van Vooren . . . . Katherine
- •• 0:47 - Topless in bed with Nicholas. Brief lower frontal nudity twice when he rolls on top of her.
- • 1:21 - Left breast letting Sascha, the creature, caress her breast
- • 1:26 - Topless, dead, when her breasts pop out of her blouse.

Angel *(1983)*

Josh Cadman. . . . . Spike
John Diehl. . . . . Crystal
- • 0:35 - Buns, washing blood off himself. Dark, hard to see. Long scene.

Elaine Giftos . . . . .Patricia Allen
Donna McDaniel. . . . . Crystal
- • 0:19 - Brief topless, dead in bed when the killer pulls the covers down.

Graem McGavin . . . . Lana
- •• 0:31 - Topless standing in hotel bathroom talking to her John.

Susan Tyrrell . . . . Selly Mosler
Donna Wilkes . . . . Angel/Molly

Angel Heart *(1987)*

Lisa Bonet . . . . Epiphany Proudfoot
- ••• 1:27 - Topless in bed with Mickey Rourke. It gets kind of bloody.
- • 1:32 - Topless in bathtub.
- • 1:48 - Topless in bed, dead.

Robert De Niro . . . . Louis Cyphre
Charlotte Rampling. . . . . Margaret Krusemark
- • 1:10 - Brief left breast dead on the floor, covered with blood.
- • 1:46 - Very brief left breast during flashback of the dead-on-the-floor-covered-with-blood scene.

Elizabeth Whitcraft . . . . Connie
- •• 0:33 - Topless in bed talking with Mickey Rourke while taking off her clothes.

Angel III: The Final Chapter *(1988)*

Maud Adams. . . . . Nadine
Laura Albert . . . . Nude Dancer

- • 0:00 - Brief topless dancing in a casino. Wearing red G-string.
- • 0:01 - Brief topless dancing in background.
- • 0:06 - Side view of left breast and buns yelling at Molly for taking her picture.

Barbara Hammond. . . . . .Video Girl #2
- • 0:34 - Topless (on the right) on video monitor during audition tape talking with her roommate.

Tyronne Granderson Jones . . . . .L.A. Pimp
- •• 0:32 - Buns, standing in alley after Angel pushes him out of the car.

Mitzi Kapture . . . . Molly Stewart
Roxanne Kernohan. . . . . White Hooker
Julie Kristen Smith . . . . Darlene
- ••• 0:40 - Topless during caveman shoot with a brunette girl.
- ••• 0:44 - Topless again dancing in caveman shoot.

Angel of H.E.A.T. *(1981)*
a.k.a. The Protectors, Book I

Marilyn Chambers . . . . Angel Harmony
- •• 0:15 - Full frontal nudity making love with an intruder on the bed.
- • 0:17 - Topless in a bathtub.
- •• 0:40 - Topless in a hotel room with a short guy.
- • 0:52 - Topless getting out of a wet suit.
- •• 1:01 - Topless sitting on floor with some robots.
- • 1:29 - Topless in bed with Mark.

Remy O'Neill . . . . Andrea Shockley
- •• 0:43 - Topless, wearing a blue swimsuit, wrestling in the mud with Mary Woronov.

Mary Woronov. . . . . .Samantha Vitesse
- ••• 0:11 - Frontal nudity changing clothes on a boat dock after getting out of the lake.
- •• 0:43 - Topless wrestling in the mud after wearing white bathing suit.

Angel of Passion *(1991)*

Sonny Falconeti . . . . Will
- • 0:22 - Buns frolicking in the surf with Carol while wearing a G-string.

Ingrid Vold. . . . . Vanessa
- • 1:01 - Brief topless posing on the couch for the photographer.

Angels Hard as They Come *(1971)*

Scott Glenn . . . . Long John
Gilda Texter . . . . .Astrid
- • 0:26 - Brief topless several times when bad guys try to rape her. Dark.

Janet Wood . . . . Vicki
- •• 1:09 - Topless taking off her top, dancing with Clean Sheila at the biker's party.
- •• 1:16 - Topless outside when the General rips her blouse open.

Animal House *(1978)*

Kevin Bacon. . . . . Chip Diller
Tim Matheson . . . . Eric "Otter" Stratton
- • 0:08 - Buns, changing clothes in his bedroom while talking to Boone.

Donald Sutherland . . . . .Dave Jennings
- 1:22 - Buns, reaching up in kitchen to get something when his sweater goes up. Out of focus.

Anna *(1987)*
Sally Kirkland. . . . . .Anna
- •• 0:28 - Topless in the bathtub talking to Daniel.

Another 48 Hrs. *(1990)*
Bernie Casey . . . . Kirkland Smith
David Anthony Marshall . . . . .Willie Hickok
- 0:57 - Buns, putting pants on after getting out of bed.

Francesca "Kitten" Natividad. . . . . .Girl in Movie
- 1:04 - Brief topless on movie screen when two motorcycles crash through it.

Yana Nirvana. . . . . CHP Officer
Nick Nolte. . . . . .Jack Cates

Another Chance *(1989)*
Vanessa Angel . . . . Jacky Johanssen
- 0:26 - Sort of topless under water in spa. Hard to see because of the bubbles.

Leslee Bremmer. . . . . Girl in Womanizer's Meeting
Barbara Edwards . . . . .Diana the Temptress
- ••• 0:38 - Topless in trailer with Johnny.

Karen Witter . . . . Nancy Burton
- 0:44 - Brief side view of right breast and buns getting out of bed.
  0:45 - In two piece swimsuit.

Another Pair of Aces *(1991; Made for Cable Movie)*
(Video tape includes nude scenes not shown on cable TV.)
Kris Kristofferson . . . . Capt. Elvin Metcalf
Joan Severance . . . . Susan Davis
- •• 1:00 - Brief topless several times, making love with Kris Kristofferson in bed.

Rip Torn . . . . Capt. Jack Parsons

Any Man's Death *(1989)*
Nancy Mulford . . . . Tara
Mia Sara . . . . Gerlind
- 0:50 - Brief right nipple when John Savage undoes her top. Don't see her face.

Claudia Udy . . . . Laura

Aphrodite *(1982; German/French)*
Catherine Jourdan. . . . . Valerie
- 0:34 - Brief upper half of breasts in bathtub.

Valerie Kaprisky . . . . Pauline
- ••• 0:12 - Nude, washing herself off in front of a two-way mirror while a man on the other side watches.

Apocalypse Now *(1979)*
Sam Bottoms . . . . Lance
Colleen Camp . . . . Playmate
Linda Carpenter . . . . Playmate
Scott Glenn. . . . . Civilian
Martin Sheen . . . . .Captain Willard
- 0:07 - Brief buns, in bedroom after opening door.

Cyndi Wood . . . . Playmate

Apology *(1986; Made for Cable Movie)*
Peter Weller . . . . Rad Hungare
- 1:04 - Brief buns, putting pants on, getting out of bed to chase after intruder at night.

Appointment with Fear *(1988)*
Michele Little . . . . Carol
Deborah Voorhees . . . . Ruth
- 0:21 - Very, very brief side view of left breast taking off bra to go swimming, then very brief topless getting out of the pool.

Apprentice to Murder *(1987)*
Mia Sara. . . . . Alice
- 0:29 - Left side view topless making love with Chad Lowe.

Aria *(1988; U.S./British)*
Beverly D'Angelo . . . . .Gilda
Linzi Drew . . . . Girl
- 1:09 - Topless on operating table after car accident. Hair is all covered with bandages.
- •• 1:10 - Topless getting shocked to start her heart.

Sandrine Dumas. . . . .
Bridget Fonda . . . . .Girl Lover
- •• 0:59 - Brief right breast, then topless lying down on bed in hotel room in Las Vegas.
- •• 1:02 - Topless in the bathtub with her boyfriend.

Elizabeth Hurley .Marietta
- 0:46 - Brief topless, turning around while singing to a guy.
  0:47 - Buns.

John Hurt. . . . . .The Actor
James Mathers . . . . Boy Lover
- 1:00 - Brief dark outline of frontal nudity in hotel room with his girlfriend.
- 1:02 - Frontal nudity under water in the bathtub with his girlfriend.

Anita Morris . . . . Phoebe
Theresa Russell . . . . King Zog

Arizona Heat *(1988)*
Denise Crosby . . . . Jill Andrews
- 1:13 - Brief upper half of left breast in shower with Larry.

Armed and Dangerous *(1986)*
Christine Dupree . . . . Peep Show Girl
- 0:58 - Very, very brief topless shots behind glass dancing in front of John Candy and Eugene Levy.

Eugene Levy. . . . . Norman Kane
- 1:02 - Cheeks of his buns through the back of leather pants while dressed in drag with John Candy to escape from the bad cops.

Steve Railsback. The Cowboy
Meg Ryan . . . . Maggie Cavanaugh
K.C. Winkler. . . . . Vicki

Armed Response (1986)

Michelle Bauer . . . . Stripper
- 0:41 - Topless, dancing on stage.

Bobbie Bresee . . . . .Anna
David Carradine . . . . Jim Roth
Laurene Landon . . . . Deborah
Dawn Wildsmith . . . . Thug

The Art of Dying (1991)

Wings Hauser . . . . Jack
- •• 0:28 - Buns, standing in kitchen making love with Kathleen Kinmont.

Kathleen Kinmont . . . . .Holly
- • 0:28 - Brief left breast, making love with Wings Hauser in the kitchen. Brief topless when he pours milk on her.
- •• 0:33 - Topless in bathtub with Hauser. Intercut with Janet getting stabbed.

Ona Simms Wiegers . . . . .Frances Warner

Assault of the Killer Bimbos (1988)

Elizabeth Kaitan. . . . . Lulu
- •• 0:41 - Brief topless during desert musical sequence, opening her blouse, then taking off her shorts, then putting on a light blue dress. Don't see her face.

Christina Whitaker. . . . . Peaches

Assault of the Party Nerds (1989)

Michelle Bauer . . . . Muffin
- • 0:16 - Side view of left breast kissing Bud.
- ••• 0:20 - Topless lying in bed seen from Bud's point of view, then sitting up by herself.
- • 1:15 - Brief right breast, then topless in bed with Scott.

Linnea Quigley . . . . .Bambi
- ••• 0:25 - Topless straddling Cliff in bed.

Atlantic City (1981; U.S./Canadian)

Susan Sarandon . . . . Sally
- •• 0:50 - Left breast cleaning herself with lemon juice while Burt Lancaster watches through window.

Autumn Born (1979)

Dorothy Stratten. . . . . Tara
- 0:03 - In dressing room in beige bra, panties, garter belt and stockings changing clothes. Long, close-up lingering shots.
- 0:16 - Unconscious in beige lingerie, then conscious, walking around the room.
- 0:21 - In bra and panties getting her rear end whipped while tied to the bed.
- •• 0:26 - Left breast taking bath, then right breast getting up, then topless dressing.
- • 0:30 - Side view of left breast, then topless climbing back into bed.
- 0:35 - In beige bra and panties in the shower with her captor.
- 0:43 - Quick cuts of various scenes.
- ••• 0:46 - In white bra and panties, side view of left breast and buns, then topless in bathtub. Long scene.

- 0:50 - Side view of left breast and buns getting undressed. Nice buns shot. Right breast lying down in chair.
- 1:03 - Brief topless shots during flashbacks.

Roberta Weiss. . . . . Melissa
0:07 - Buns, wearing panties and bending over desk to get whipped.

Avanti! (1973)

(Not available on video tape. Shown on *The Arts and Entertainment Channel* periodically. Scenes are listed as 0:00 since I can't time correctly with the commercials.)

Jack Lemmon . . . . .Wendell Armbruster
- • 0:00 - Buns, standing up in bathtub talking to Juliet Mills.

Juliet Mills . . . . Pamela Piggott
0:00 - Buns, climbing out of the water onto a rock.
- • 0:00 - Side view of right breast lying on rock talking to Jack Lemmon.
- ••• 0:00 - Brief topless waving to fishermen on a passing boat.
0:00 - Brief buns putting something up in the closet in Jack Lemmon's hotel room.

Avenging Angel (1985)

Laura Burkett . . . . .Blonde Hooker
Charlene Jones. . . . . Hooker
Karen Mani . . . . .Janie Soon Lee
- ••• 0:06 - Nude taking a shower, right breast in mirror drying herself off, then in bra getting dressed.

Betsy Russell. . . . . Angel/Molly Stewart
Susan Tyrrell. . . . . Selly Mosler
Deborah Voorhees . . . . .Roxie
Lynda Wiesmeier . . . . Debbie

Baby Love (1969)

Linda Hayden. . . . . Luci
0:32 - Buns, standing in room when Nick sneaks in.
0:34 - Very brief right breast, white throwing doll at Robert.
- • 0:39 - Topless in mirror taking a bath. Long shot. Brief left breast hidden by steam.
- • 0:52 - Brief topless taking off her top to show Nick while sunbathing.
1:25 - Brief topless calling Robert from window. Long shot.
1:27 - Very brief topless sitting up while talking to Robert.
- • 1:28 - Topless in open robe struggling with Robert.

Derek Lamden . . . . .Nick
1:29 - Brief buns in shower when Luci opens the door.

The Baby Maker (1970)

Scott Glenn . . . . Tad
- • 1:30 - Buns in bed with Charlotte.

Barbara Hershey. . . . . Tish
- • 0:14 - Side view of left breast taking off dress and diving into the pool. Long shot and dark. Buns in water.
0:23 - Left breast (out of focus) under sheet in bed.

Helena Kallianiotes . . . . Wanda
- 1:30 - Brief topless when Barbara Hershey sees her in bed with Tad.

Brenda Sykes. . . . . Francis

Baby, It's You (1983)
Rosanna Arquette . . . . Jill
- •• 1:17 - Left breast, making love in bed with Vincent Spano.

Robert Downey, Jr. . . . . .Stewart
Richard Kantor . . . . Curtis
Matthew Modine . . . . Steve
Vincent Spano. . . . . Sheik

Bachelor Party (1984)
Angela Aames . . . . .Mrs. Klupner
Monique Gabrielle . . . . Tracey
- •• 1:11 - Full frontal nudity in the hotel bedroom with Tom Hanks as his bachelor party gift.

Rosanne Katon . . . . Bridal Shower Hooker
Tawny Kitaen . . . . Debbie Thompson
Rebecca Perle . . . . Screaming Woman
Robert Prescott . . . . Richard Chance
- 1:18 - Buns, after being hung out the window by sheets by Tom Hanks and his friends.

Back to Back (1990)
Apollonia. . . . . .Jesse Duro
Susan Anspach . . . . Madeline Hix
Todd Field . . . . Todd Brand
- •• 0:33 - Buns, walking to and jumping into swimming pool. Don't see his face.

Bill Paxton. . . . . Bo Brand

Back to School (1986)
Adrienne Barbeau . . . . Vanessa
Robert Downey, Jr. . . . . Derek
Leslie Huntly . . . . Coed #1
- •• 0:14 - Brief topless in the shower room when Rodney Dangerfield first arrives on campus.

Sally Kellerman . . . . Diane
Becky LeBeau . . . . Bubbles, the Hot Tub Girl
M. Emmet Walsh. . . . . .Coach Turnbull

Backfire (1987)
Karen Allen . . . . .Mara
- 0:48 - Lots of buns, then brief topless with Keith Carradine in the bedroom.
- 1:00 - Brief topless in the shower.

Keith Carradine. Clinton James
Bernie Casey . . . . Clinton James
Jeff Fahey . . . . Donnie
- 0:22 - Brief, partial buns taking a shower, then very brief, out of focus frontal nudity in shower when blood starts to gush out of the shower head.

Backstab (1990)
June Chadwick . . . . Mrs. Caroline Chambers
Meg Foster . . . . .Sara Rudnick
Isabelle Truchon . . . . .Jennifer
- •• 0:08 - In bra, then topless in back seat of car with James Brolin.

- 0:16 - Buns, black panties and stockings while on the floor with Brolin. Brief right breast.
- 0:18 - Brief buns in front of fireplace. Side view of right breast. Buns, while walking into the other room.

Backstreet Dreams (1990)
Maria Celedonio. Maria M.
Sherilyn Fenn . . . . Lucy
- 0:00 - Right breast while sleeping in bed with Dean. Medium long shot.

Brooke Shields . . . . Stephanie "Stevie" Bloom

Bad Boys (1983)
Clancy Brown. . . . . .Viking Lofgren
Sean Penn . . . . Mick O'Brien
- 0:10 - Brief buns getting up off the floor with Ally Sheedy.
- •• 0:46 - Buns taking a shower.

Ally Sheedy . . . . .J. C. Walenski
- 0:12 - Very, very brief left breast kneeling on floor next to bed when Sean Penn leaves. A little blurry and a long shot.

Bad Girls from Mars (1990)
Jasaé . . . . Terry
- ••• 0:03 - Topless taking off her top.
- ••• 0:05 - More topless going into dressing room.

Dana Bentley . . . . Martine
- •• 0:28 - Topless taking off her blouse in office.
- •• 0:59 - Topless several times wrestling with Edy Williams.

Sherri Graham . . . . .Swimmer
- •• 0:22 - Very brief topless diving into, then climbing out of pool.

Brinke Stevens . . . . .Myra
- 0:11 - Brief side of left breast, then topless getting massaged on diving board.

Edy Williams. . . . . Emanuelle
- •• 0:17 - Topless several times changing in back of convertible car.
- ••• 0:23 - Topless changing out of wet dress in bathroom.
- ••• 0:30 - Topless taking off blouse to get into spa.
- 0:32 - Topless in back of Porsche and getting out.
- ••• 0:35 - Topless in store, signing autograph for robber.
- 0:47 - Topless taking off her top again.
- ••• 0:58 - Topless in T.J.'s office. More topless when wrestling with Martine.
- 1:05 - Topless tied up.
- 1:07 - Topless again.
- •• 1:17 - Topless taking off her outfit during outtakes.

Bad Influence (1990)
Charisse Glenn. . . . . .Stylish Eurasian Woman
- ••• 1:26 - Topless and partial lower frontal nudity making love on Rob Lowe.
- 1:28 - Very brief left breast in bed with the blonde woman.

Rob Lowe. . . . . .Alex
- ••• 1:27 - Buns, going into the bathroom.

307

James Spader . . . . Michael Boll
Lisa Zane. . . . . Claire
  • 0:39 - Brief topless on video tape seen on TV at party.

Bad Manners (1989)
Karen Black . . . . Mrs. Fitzpatrick
Kimmy Robertson . . . . Sarah Fitzpatrick
  •• 0:38 - Topless and buns taking off robe and getting
    into the shower when Mouse takes a picture of her.
    1:16 - In white bra when Piper rips her blouse open
    while she's tied up on the piano.
    1:18 - Briefly on piano again.
Edy Williams . . . . Mrs. Slatt

Bad Timing: A Sensual Obsession (1980)
Art Garfunkel. . . . . .Alex Linden
  • 0:55 - Buns, making love with Theresa Russell on
    stairwell. Don't see his face.
  • 0:57 - Buns (Sort of see his balls through his legs), on
    top of Russell when visited by Harvey Keitel.
    1:48 - Side view of buns while in bed with an uncon-
    scious Russell.
Harvey Keitel .Inspector Netusil
Theresa Russell . . . . .Milena Flaherty
    0:14 - Buns and topless under short, sheer blouse.
    0:17 - Almost brief right breast In bed during Art Gar-
    funkel's flashback. Very brief left breast kneeling on
    bed with him.
  • 0:31 - Full frontal nudity in bed with Garfunkel. Inter-
    cut with tracheotomy footage. Kind of gross.
  •• 0:32 - Right breast, while sitting in bed talking to
    Garfunkel.
  • 0:41 - Brief topless several times on operating table.
  • 0:55 - Full frontal nudity making love on stairwell
    with Garfunkel. Quick cuts.
  • 0:56 - Brief topless twice after stairwell episode while
    throwing a fit.
  •• 1:45 - In bra, then topless passed out on bed while
    Garfunkel cuts her clothes off. Brief full frontal nudi-
    ty.
  •• 1:48 - More topless cuts while Garfunkel makes love
    to her while she's unconscious from an overdose of
    drugs.

The Bagdad Café (1988)
Marianne Sägebrecht . . . . Jasmin
  •• 1:09 - Right breast slowly lowering her top, posing
    while Jack Palance paints.
  •• 1:12 - More topless posing for Palance.

Baja Oklahoma (1988; Made for Cable Movie)
Alice Krige. . . . . Patsy Cline
Karen Laine . . . . Girl at Drive-In
  • 0:04 - Left breast, in truck with a jerk guy. Dark, hard
    to see anything.
Julia Roberts . . . . .Candy

The Ballad of Cable Hogue (1970)
Stella Stevens . . . . Hildy
    1:12 - Buns changing into nightgown in bedroom.
  • 1:14 - Brief top half of breasts in outdoor tub, then
    buns running into cabin when stagecoach arrives.

The Banker (1989)
Robert Forster . . . . .Dan
Duncan Regehr . . . . Osbourne
  • 0:03 - Buns, getting out of bed with Teri Weigel.
    Don't see his face.
Debi Richter . . . . .Melanie
Teri Weigel . . . . Jaynie
  ••• 0:02 - Taking off dress, then in lingerie, then topless
    making love with Osbourne in bed. More topless af-
    ter.

Barbarella (1968; French/Italian)
Jane Fonda. . . . . Barbarella
  •• 0:04 - Topless getting out of space suit during open-
    ing credits in zero gravity. Hard to see because the
    frame is squeezed so the lettering will fit.
Anita Pallenberg. . . . . The Black Queen

Barbarian Queen (1985)
Lana Clarkson. . . . . Amethea
  •• 0:38 - Brief topless during attempted rape.
  ••• 0:48 - Topless being tortured with metal hand then
    raped by torturer.
Dawn Dunlap. . . . . Taramis
  • 0:00 - Topless, in the woods getting raped.
Katt Shea . . . . Estrild
  • 0:31 - Brief topless getting top torn off by guards.

Barfly (1987)
Faye Dunaway . . . . Wanda Wilcox
  • 0:58 - Brief upper half of breasts in bathtub talking to
    Mickey Rourke.
Alice Krige . . . . Tully

Basic Training (1984)
Angela Aames . . . . Cheryl
  • 0:19 - Brief topless in bathtub.
Erika Dockery . . . . Salesgirl 2
  • 0:00 - Brief topless standing behind the desk.
Ann Dusenberry . . . . Melinda Griffin
  ••• 1:13 - Topless in Russian guy's bedroom.
Barbara Peckinpaugh . . . . Salesgirl 1
  • 0:00 - Topless on desk with another salesgirl.
Rhonda Shear. . . . . Debbie
  •• 0:07 - Topless making love with Mark.
    0:15 - In bra, making love on Mark's desk.

Basket Case (1982)
Kevin Van Hetenryck . . . . .Duane Bradley
  •• 1:21 - Frontal nudity, twice, running around at night.

Basket Case 2 (1989)

Heather Rattray . . . . Susan
- • 1:20 - Brief right breast twice when white blouse gapes open in bedroom with Duane. Special effect scar on her stomach makes it a little unappealing looking.

Annie Ross . . . . Granny Ruth
Kevin Van Hetenryck . . . . Duane
- • 0:34 - Buns standing in front of mirror looking at his large scar on the side of his body.

Bay Boy (1985; Canadian)

Isabelle Mejias . . . . .Mary McNeil
- •• 1:28 - Brief topless in her bedroom with Kiefer Sutherland, then brief topless in bed with him.

Beach Balls (1988)

Leslie Danon . . . . .Kathleen
- • 1:06 - In bra, then brief topless in car with Doug.

The Beach Girls (1982)

Debra Blee . . . . Sarah
- ••• 1:22 - Brief topless opening her swimsuit top on the beach.

Corinne Bohrer . . . . .Champagne Girl
James Daughton . . . . .Scott
- • 0:33 - Buns and very brief frontal nudity taking off clothes and running into the ocean.

Tessa Richarde . . . . .Doreen
Jeana Tomasino . . . . .Ducky
- •• 0:12 - Topless and buns, lying on the beach with Ginger, while a guy looks through a telescope.
- ••• 0:54 - Topless on a sailboat with a guy.
- • 0:55 - Brief topless on the beach after being "saved" after falling off the boat.
- •• 1:12 - Topless in sauna with Ginger and an older guy.

Beaks The Movie (1987)

Christopher Atkins . . . . .Peter
Michelle Johnson . . . . Vanessa
- • 0:26 - Brief topless covered with bubbles after taking a bath. Don't see her face.
- • 0:31 - Brief topless covered with bubbles after getting out of bathtub with Christopher Atkins. Don't see her face.

The Beast Within (1982)

Bibi Besch . . . . Caroline MacCleary
- •• 0:06 - Topless, getting her blouse torn off by the beast while she is unconscious. Dark, hard to see her face.

Kitty Moffat . . . . Amanda Platt
- •• 0:06 - Topless, getting her dress torn off by the beast while she is unconscious. Don't see her face, could be a body double.

The Beastmaster (1982)

Tanya Roberts . . . . Kiri
- ••• 0:35 - Topless in a pond while Marc Singer watches, then topless getting out of the water when his pet ferrets steal her towel.

Marc Singer . . . . .Dar

Linda Smith . . . . .Kiri's Friend
- • 0:35 - Topless in a pond with Tanya Roberts.

Rip Torn . . . . .Maax

Bedroom Eyes
(1985; Made for Cable Movie; Canadian)

Dayle Haddon . . . . Alixe
- 1:06 - Getting undressed in tap pants and white camisole top while Harry watches in the mirror.

Barbara Law . . . . .Jobeth
- • 0:02 - Topless taking off clothes while Harry watches through the window.
- •• 0:07 - Topless and buns, kissing a woman.
- • 0:14 - Topless during Harry's flashback when he talks to the psychiatrist.
- •• 0:23 - Topless and buns dancing in bedroom.
- •• 0:57 - Topless with Mary, kissing on floor.
- 1:17 - In beige bra, panties, garter belt and stockings in bed with Harry.
- • 1:23 - Brief topless on top of Harry.

Bedroom Eyes II (1989)

Linda Blair . . . . Sophie Stevens
- 0:31 - Buns, in bed with Wings Hauser.
- • 0:33 - Brief left breast under bubbles in the bathtub. Don't see her face.

Jennifer Delora . . . . Gwendolyn
- •• 0:04 - Undressing in hotel room with Vinnie. Topless, then making love.

Jane Hamilton . . . . .JoBeth McKenna
- • 0:50 - Topless knifing Linda Blair, then fighting with Wings Hauser.

Wings Hauser . . . . Harry Ross
Kathy Shower . . . . Carolyn Ross
- •• 0:22 - Topless in the artist's studio fighting with her lover while Wings Hauser watches through the window.
- 0:58 - In lingerie in bed with Hauser, then in bathroom.

Kimberly Taylor . . . . .Michelle

The Bedroom Window (1987)

Brad Greenquist . . . . .Henderson
- • 0:35 - Buns, turning off the light while Steve Guttenberg spies on him.

Steve Guttenberg . . . . Terry Lambert
- •• 0:05 - Buns, getting out of bed and walking to the bathroom.

Isabelle Huppert . . . . Sylvia Wentworth
- •• 0:06 - Briefly nude while looking out the window at attempted rape.

Elizabeth McGovern . . . . .Denise
- 1:25 - Topless silhouette on shower curtain when Steve Guttenberg peeks in the bathroom.

The Believers (1987)

Helen Shaver . . . . .Jessica Halliday
- • 0:38 - Brief glimpse of right breast while lying in bed with Martin Sheen.
- 1:17 - Buns, getting out of bed.

Martin Sheen . . . . Dr. Cal Jamison

The Bell Jar (1979)
Roxanne Hart . . . .
Marilyn Hassett . . . . Esther Greenwood
- • 0:10 - In bra, then brief topless in bed with Buddy. Dark, hard to see.
- •• 1:09 - Topless taking off her clothes and throwing them out the window while yelling.
Jameson Parker . . . . .Buddy
- • 0:09 - Frontal nudity silhouette standing in bedroom with Marilyn Hassett, then buns. Dark, hard to see.
Mary Louise Weller . . . . .Doreen

Best Chest in the West (1984)
Michelle Bauer . . . . Michelle
- ••• 0:24 - In two piece swimsuit, then topless and buns.
Leslee Bremmer. . . . . Leslee
- ••• 0:29 - In black, two piece swimsuit, then topless and buns.
- • 0:32 - More topless during judging and winning the 2nd round.
Raven De La Croix. . . . . herself
- ••• 0:34 - Topless doing strip tease routine on stage.
Barbara Peckinpaugh. . . . . Chrissy
- ••• 0:28 - In two piece swimsuit, then topless and buns.
Candy Samples . . . . herself
- ••• 0:54 - Topless dancing on stripping and dancing on stage with Pat McCormick.

Best Chest in the West II (1986)
Leslee Bremmer. . . . . herself
- 0:49 - Dancing in pink top. Buns, in G-string.
Becky LeBeau . . . . herself
- ••• 0:46 - Dancing in red two piece swimsuit. Buns, then topless.
- •• 0:55 - Buns and topless after winning semi-finals.

Best Friends (1982)
Goldie Hawn. .Paula McCullen
- • 0:18 - Very, very brief side view of right breast getting into the shower with Burt Reynolds.
- • 1:14 - Upper half of left breast in the shower, twice.
Burt Reynolds . . . . .Richard Babson

The Best of Sex and Violence (1981)
Elvira. . . . . Katya
- •• 0:40 - Brief topless dancing on stage in scene from Working Girls.
Vanity. . . . . Tanya
- • 0:24 - Buns and topless in various scenes from Tanya's Island.
Angela Aames . . . . Little Bo Peep
- • 0:18 - Brief topless in scene from Fairytales.
- • 0:20 - Brief right breast in scene from Fairytales.
Phyllis Davis . . . . Sugar/Joy
- •• 0:56 - Topless after bath and in bed in scenes from Sweet Sugar.
- ••• 0:59 - Topless and buns walking out of lake in scene from Terminal Island.
Uschi Digard . . . . .Truck Stop Woman
- • 0:47 - Topless getting chased by policeman in parking lot in scene from Truck Stop Women.

Laura Gemser. . . . . Emanuelle
- • 0:23 - Side of left breast while getting clothes taken off by a guy. Long shot. Scene from Emanuelle Around the World.
Claudia Jennings . . . . Rose
- •• 0:46 - Topless taking off her blouse in scene from Truck Stop Women.
Joan Prather. . . . . .Herself
- •• 0:38 - Topless getting her breasts squeezed by an attacker. Dark.
Cheryl Smith . . . . Cinderella
- • 0:14 - Topless taking a bath in scene from Cinderella.
Edy Williams. . . . . .Herself
- •• 0:46 - Topless in various scenes from Dr. Minx.

The Betsy (1978)
Jane Alexander . . . . Alicia Hardeman
Kathleen Beller. . . . . Betsy Hardeman
- ••• 0:12 - Brief nude getting into swimming pool.
- •• 1:14 - Topless in bed with Tommy Lee Jones.
Lesley-Anne Down . . . . Lady Bobby Ayres
- • 0:38 - Brief left breast with Tommy Lee Jones.
- • 0:57 - Very brief left breast in bed with Jones.
Tommy Lee Jones. . . . . Angelo Perino
Katherine Ross . . . . Sally Hardeman

Betty Blue (1986; French)
Jean-Hughes Anglade. Zorg
- ••• 0:09 - Frontal nudity.
- •• 1:03 - Nude trying to sleep in living room.
- •• 1:39 - Frontal nudity walking to the bathroom.
- •• 1:45 - Frontal nudity talking on the telephone.
Béatrice Dalle. . . . . Betty
- ••• 0:01 - Topless making love in bed with Zorg. Long sequence.
- ••• 0:30 - Nude on bed having sex with boyfriend.
- ••• 1:03 - Nude trying to sleep in living room.
- ••• 1:21 - Topless in white tap pants in hallway.
- ••• 1:29 - Topless lying down with Zorg.
- ••• 1:39 - Topless sitting on bathtub crying & talking.

Between the Lines (1977)
Jeff Goldblum. . . . . .Max
John Heard. . . . . Harry
- •• 1:17 - Buns, putting his pants on.
Marilu Henner . . . . .Danielle
- 0:27 - Dancing on stage wearing pasties.
Bruno Kirby . . . . .David
Gwen Welles . . . . .Laura
- •• 0:32 - Buns and topless drying off with a towel in front of a mirror.

Beverly Hills Cop II (1987)
Venice Kong. . . . . .Playmate
Carrie Leigh . . . . .Herself
Brigitte Nielsen. . . . . Karla Fry
Judge Reinhold. . . . . .Detective Billy Rosewood
Teal Roberts. . . . . Stripper
- •• 0:45 - Topless and buns, wearing G-string at the 385 North Club.

Peggy Sands . . . . Stripper
- 0:48 - Very brief topless, dancing at the 385 North Club.

Beverly Hills Vamp (1989)
Michelle Bauer . . . . Kristina
- 0:12 - Buns and brief side view of right breast in bed biting a guy.
0:33 - In red slip, with Kyle.
- • 0:38 - Topless trying to get into Kyle's pants.
1:09 - In black lingerie attacking Russell in bed with Debra Lamb and Jillian Kesner.
1:19 - In black lingerie enticing Mr. Pendleton into bedroom.
1:22 - In black lingerie, getting killed as a vampire by Kyle.
Britt Ekland . . . . Madam Cassandra
Greta Gibson. . . . . Screen Test Starlet
- •• 0:53 - Topless and brief buns in G-string lying on Mr. Pendleton's desk.
Jillian Kesner . . . . .Claudia
0:06 - In white lingerie riding a guy like a horse.
0:33 - In white slip with Brock.
0:42 - Almost topless in bed with Brock. Too dark to see anything.
1:09 - In white nightgown attacking Russell in bed with Debra Lamb and Michelle Bauer.
1:17 - In white nightgown, getting killed as a vampire by Kyle.
Debra Lamb . . . . .Jessica
0:33 - In black slip, with Russell.
- ••• 0:36 - Topless and buns in red G-string posing for Russell while he photographs her.
- ••• 0:41 - More topless posing on bed.
1:09 - In white nightgown attacking Russell in bed with Michelle Bauer and Jillian Kesner.
1:19 - In white nightgown, getting killed as a vampire by Kyle.
Dawn Wildsmith . . . . .Sherry Santa Monica

Beyond the Limit (1983)
Elpidia Carrillo. . . . . .Clara
- •• 0:31 - Topless making love with Richard Gere. Long scene.
- •• 1:08 - Topless talking to Gere. Another long scene.
Richard Gere. . . . . Dr. Eduardo Plarr
- 0:21 - Buns.

Big Bad Mama (1974)
Angie Dickinson . . . . Wilma McClatchie
0:38 - Buns, making love in bed with Tom Skerritt.
- ••• 0:48 - Topless in bed with William Shatner.
- ••• 1:18 - Topless and brief full frontal nudity putting a shawl and then a dress on.
Sally Kirkland. . . . . .Barney's Woman
- •• 0:13 - Topless and buns waiting for Barney then throwing shoe at Billy Jean.
Robin Lee . . . . .Polly McClatchie
- 0:09 - Brief left breast in open dress in car when cops try to pull her car over.

0:22 - Polly in see-through slip on stage with her sister and a stripper.
- 0:32 - Brief topless running around the bedroom chasing her sister.
Joan Prather . . . . Jane Kingston
- •• 1:15 - Topless and buns in the bathroom with Tom Skerritt.
Susan Sennet . . . . Billy Jean
- 0:49 - Topless and buns with Tom Skerritt.
- 0:51 - Topless and buns in bed with Skerritt.

Big Bad Mama II (1987)
Danielle Brisebois . . . . Billy Jean McClatchie
- ••• 0:12 - Topless with Julie McCullough playing in a pond underneath a waterfall.
0:36 - In a white slip standing at the door talking to McCullough, then talking to Angie Dickinson.
Robert Culp . . . . Daryl Pearson
Angie Dickinson . . . . .Wilma McClatchie
- •• 0:52 - Topless (probably a body double) in bed with Robert Culp. You don't see her face with the body.
Julie McCullough . . . . Polly McClatchie
- •• 0:12 - Topless with Danielle Brisebois playing in a pond underneath a waterfall.
- •• 0:36 - In lingerie, then topless sitting on Jordan who is tied up in bed.
Linda Shayne . . . . .Bank Teller

The Big Bet (1985)
Stephanie Blake . . . . Mrs. Roberts
- ••• 0:04 - Topless sitting on bed, then making love with Chris.
- •• 0:37 - Nude on bed with Chris. Shot at fast speed, he runs between bedrooms.
- •• 0:59 - Full frontal nudity in bed again. Shot at fast speed.
Elizabeth Cochrell . . . . Sister in Stag Film
- ••• 1:05 - Topless and buns, undressing and getting into bathtub in a video tape that Chris is watching.
- •• 1:08 - Topless again on video tape, when Chris watches it on TV at home.
Kim Evenson . . . . Beth
- •• 0:36 - Right breast, sitting on couch with Chris.
- •• 0:45 - Brief topless, twice, taking off swimsuit top.
- •• 0:54 - Brief topless three times in elevator when Chris pulls her sweater up.
- •• 1:06 - Nude when Chris fantasizes about her being in the video tape that he's watching. Long shot.
- ••• 1:19 - In white bra and panties, then nude while undressing for Chris.
Monique Gabrielle . . . . Fantasy Girl in Elevator
- ••• 0:51 - In purple bra, then eventually nude in elevator with Chris.
Sylvia Kristel . . . . .Michelle
- 0:07 - Left breast in open nightgown while Chris tries to fix her sink.
- •• 0:20 - Topless dressing while Chris watches through binoculars.
- •• 0:28 - Topless undressing while Chris watches through binoculars.

••• 0:40 - Topless getting out of the shower and drying herself off.

• 1:00 - Topless getting into bed while Chris watches through binoculars.

••• 1:13 - Topless in bedroom with Chris, then making love.

Lance Sloane. . . . . Chris

•• 0:38 - Buns, taking off robe and getting into bed with Angela Roberts after visiting Mrs. Roberts.

•• 0:52 - Buns, on elevator floor with Monique Gabrielle during his daydream.

• 1:07 - Buns, getting into tub with Kimberly Evenson during video tape fantasy. Long shot.

Jill Terashita. . . . . Koko

The Big Bird Cage (1972)

Teda Bracci. . . . . Bull Jones

•• 0:15 - Topless in front of the guard, Rocco.

• 0:51 - Very brief right breast, then left breast during fight with Pam Grier. Brief left breast standing up in rice paddy.

Anitra Ford. . . . . Terry

• 0:15 - Left breast and buns taking shower. Brief lower frontal nudity after putting shirt on when leaving.

0:19 - Brief lower frontal nudity turing around.

• 0:44 - Brief left breast during gang rape.

1:14 - Brief left breast in gaping dress. Dark.

Pam Grier . . . . Blossom

The Big Chill (1983)

Tom Berenger. . . . . Sam

Glenn Close . . . . Sara

• 0:27 - Topless sitting down in the shower crying.

Jeff Goldblum . . . . Michael

William Hurt . . . . Nick

Kevin Kline . . . . Harold

Meg Tilly. . . . . Chloé

JoBeth Williams . . . . Karen

The Big Doll House (1971)

Roberta Collins . . . . Alcott

••• 0:33 - Topless in shower. Seen through blurry window by prison worker, Fred. Blurry, but nice.

• 0:34 - Brief left breast, while opening her blouse for Fred.

Pam Grier . . . . Grear

• 0:28 - Very brief most of right breast rolling over in bed.

•• 0:32 - Topless getting her back washed by Collier. Arms in the way a little bit.

• 0:44 - Left breast covered with mud sticking out of her top after wrestling with Alcott.

Pat Woodell . . . . Bodine

• 0:27 - Brief topless hung by wrists and whipped by a guard. Hair covers most of her breasts.

The Big Easy (1987)

Ellen Barkin . . . . Anne Osborne

0:21 - White panties in lifted up dress in bed with Dennis Quaid.

0:32 - Brief buns jumping up in kitchen after pinching a guy who she thinks is Quaid.

Dennis Quaid. . . . . Remy McSwain

• 0:24 - Brief buns when Ellen Barkin pulls his underwear down in bed.

••• 0:51 - Buns, putting underwear on after getting out of bed after talking on the telephone.

The Big Sleep (1978; British)

Candy Clark . . . . Camilla Sternwood

••• 0:18 - Topless, sitting in a chair when Robert Mitchum comes in after a guy is murdered.

• 0:30 - Brief topless in photo that Mitchum is looking at.

0:38 - Topless in the photos again. Out of focus.

•• 0:39 - Topless sitting in chair during recollection of the murder.

•• 1:03 - Very brief full frontal nudity in bed, throwing open the sheets for Mitchum.

1:05 - Very, very brief buns, getting up out of bed.

Joan Collins . . . . Agnes Lozelle

Sarah Miles . . . . Charlotte Sternwood

Diana Quick. . . . . Mona Grant

Oliver Reed . . . . Eddie Mars

The Big Town (1987)

Suzy Amis . . . . Aggie Donaldson

Lolita Davidovich . . . . Black Lace Stripper

Lee Grant. . . . . Ferguson Edwards

Diane Lane. . . . . Lorry Dane

0:51 - Doing a strip routine in the club wearing a G-string and pasties while Matt Dillon watches.

••• 1:17 - Topless making love on bed with Dillon in hotel room.

1:27 - Brief left breast wearing pasties walking into dressing room while Dillon plays craps.

Bilitis (1982; French)

Patti D'Arbanville . . . . Bilitis

••• 0:25 - Topless copying Melissa undressing.

•• 0:27 - Topless on tree.

••• 0:31 - Full frontal nudity taking off swimsuit with Melissa.

0:36 - Buns, cleaning herself in the bathroom.

•• 0:59 - Topless and buns making love with Melissa.

Bio-Hazard (1984)

Angelique Pettijohn . . . . Lisa Martyn

•• 0:30 - Partial left breast on couch with Mitchell. In beige bra and panties talking on telephone, breast almost falling out of bra.

••• 1:15 - Left breast, on couch with Mitchell, in out-take scene during the end credits.

• 1:16 - Upper half of left breast on couch again during a different take.

Bird on a Wire *(1990)*

David Carradine . . . . Eugene
Mel Gibson . . . . Rick Jarmin
- •• 1:01 - Brief close-up of buns when Rachel operates on his gunshot wound. Don't see his face, but it is him.

Goldie Hawn .Marianne Graves
- • 0:31 - Buns, in open dress climbing up ladder with Mel Gibson.
- • 1:18 - Very brief top of right breast rolling over on top of Gibson in bed. Don't see her face.

Joan Severance . . . . Rachel Varnay

Birdy *(1985)*

Sandra Beall . . . . Shirley
Nicholas Cage . . . . .Al Columbato
Bruno Kirby . . . . .Renaldi
Matthew Modine . . . . .Birdy
- • 1:25 - Buns, squatting on the end of his bed, thinking he's a bird.
- • 1:29 - Buns, sitting on the bed. Longer shot.
- •• 1:33 - Buns, walking around naked in his bedroom.
- • 1:42 - Buns, waking up when Nicholas Cage comes into his bedroom.

Elizabeth Whitcraft . . . . Rosanne
Maude Winchester . . . . .Doris Robinson
- •• 1:32 - Topless in car letting Mathew Modine feel her.

Karen Young . . . . .Hannah Rourke

The Bitch *(1979; British)*

Joan Collins . . . . Fontaine Khaled
- 0:01 - In long slip getting out of bed and putting a bathrobe on.
- • 0:03 - Brief topless in the shower with a guy.
- •• 0:24 - Brief topless taking black corset off for the chauffeur in the bedroom, then buns getting out of bed and walking to the bathroom.
- 0:39 - Making love in bed wearing a blue slip.
- • 1:01 - Left breast after making love in bed.

Sue Lloyd . . . . .Vanessa Grant
- • 1:12 - Side view of left breast and topless in the swimming pool.

Pamela Salem . . . . Lynn
- •• 0:46 - Topless in bed making love with a guy after playing at a casino.

Bits and Pieces *(1985)*

Sandy Brooke . . . . .Mrs. Talbot
- ••• 1:03 - Topless in bathtub washing herself before the killer drowns her. Very brief right breast when struggling.
- • 1:09 - Brief topless under water in bathtub, dead.

Tally Chanel . . . . .Jennifer
- 0:58 - In the woods with the killer, seen briefly in bra and panties before and after being killed.

Sheila Lussier . . . . Tanya
- •• 0:07 - In bra, tied down by Arthur, then brief topless a couple of times as he cuts her bra off before he kills her. Brief right breast several times with blood on her.

Bizarre *(1986; Italian)*

Florence Guerin . . . . Laurie
- •• 0:03 - Topless on bed with Guido. Lower frontal nudity while he molests her with a pistol.
- ••• 0:18 - Nude after taking off her clothes in hotel room with a guy. Nice.
- ••• 0:30 - Full frontal nudity making love with Edward in the water.
- • 0:34 - Brief side of right breast, taking off robe in bathroom with Edward. (He's made himself up to look like a woman.)
- ••• 0:36 - Topless in white panties making love with Edward.
- •• 0:40 - Topless and brief lower frontal nudity in Guido's office with him.
- ••• 0:45 - Nude, playing outside with Edward, then making love with his toe.
- •• 0:47 - Topless getting out of bed and putting a blouse on.
- •• 0:49 - Topless with Edward when Guido comes in.
- • 1:11 - Topless sitting in chair talking to Edward.
- • 1:20 - Lower frontal nudity, putting the phone down there.
- • 1:28 - Buns and lower frontal nudity on bed when Guido rips her clothes off and rapes her.

Robert Egon Spechtenhauser . . . . Edward
- • 0:29 - Partial buns, taking a shower when Laurie peeks in at him.
- • 0:31 - Brief buns, on top of Laurie in the water.
- ••• 0:36 - Buns, on bed with Laurie. (He's made up to look like a woman.)

Black Emanuelle *(1976)*

Laura Gemser . . . . Emanuelle
- • 0:00 - Brief topless daydreaming on airplane.
- • 0:19 - Left breast in car kissing a guy at night.
- •• 0:27 - Topless in shower with a guy.
- ••• 0:30 - Full frontal nudity making love with a guy in bed.
- ••• 0:37 - Topless taking pictures with Karin Schubert.
- •• 0:41 - Full frontal nudity lying on bed dreaming about the day's events while masturbating, then full frontal nudity walking around.
- •• 0:49 - Topless in studio with Johnny.
- ••• 0:52 - Full frontal nudity by the pool kissing Gloria.
- • 0:52 - Brief right breast making love on the side of the road.
- •• 1:00 - Nude, taking a shower, then answering the phone.
- •• 1:04 - Topless on boat after almost drowning.
- •• 1:08 - Full frontal nudity dancing with African tribe, then making love with the leader.
- •• 1:14 - Full frontal nudity taking off clothes by waterfall with Johnny.
- •• 1:23 - Topless making love with the field hockey team on a train.

Karin Schubert .Anne Danielli
- • 0:06 - Brief topless adjusting a guy's tie.
- ••• 0:14 - Topless making love in gas station with the gas station attendant.

••• 0:37 - Nude, running in the jungle while Laura Gemser takes pictures of her.
• 0:40 - Topless, kissing Gemser.
• 0:44 - Right breast, making love with Johnny in bed.

Black Moon Rising (1986)
Linda Hamilton . . . . Nina
• 0:50 - Brief left breast, making love in bed with Tommy Lee Jones.
Tommy Lee Jones . . . . Quint

Black Rainbow (1989; British)
Rosanna Arquette . . . . Martha Travis
0:48 - In black bra, panties, garter belt and stockings in while talking to Tom Hulce.
••• 0:50 - Topless in bed with Hulce, then walking to bathroom.

Black Venus (1983)
Jose Antonio Ceinos . . . . Armand
• 0:14 - Buns, making love with Venus in bed.
Monique Gabrielle . . . . Ingrid
••• 0:03 - Nude in Sailor Room at the bordello.
••• 1:01 - Topless and buns, taking off clothes for Madame Lilli's customers.
Florence Guerin . . . . .Louise
•• 0:45 - Nude talking, then making love with Venus in bed.
••• 1:16 - Nude frolicking on the beach with Venus.
••• 1:18 - Nude in bedroom getting out of wet clothes with Venus.
• 1:21 - Buns in bed with Jacques and Venus.
Josephine Jaqueline Jones . . . . Venus
•• 0:05 - Topless in Jungle Room.
••• 0:11 - Nude, in bedroom, posing for Armand while he sketches.
• 0:14 - Topless and buns making love with Armand in bed.
•• 0:17 - Nude, posing for Armand while he models in clay, then on the bed, kissing him.
• 0:21 - Brief nude getting dressed.
••• 0:38 - Nude, making love in bed with Karin Schubert.
0:45 - Nude, talking and then making love in bed with Louise.
•• 0:50 - Topless when Pierre brings everybody in to see her.
•• 0:57 - Topless in silhouette while Armand fantasizes about his statue coming to life.
••• 1:04 - Nude.
••• 1:07 - Nude with the two diplomats on the bed.
••• 1:16 - Nude frolicking on the beach with Louise.
••• 1:18 - Topless in bedroom getting out of wet clothes with Louise.
•• 1:21 - Topless in bed with Jacques.
•• 1:24 - Full frontal nudity getting out of bed.
Karin Schubert . . . . Marie
•• 0:38 - Nude in bed with Venus, making love.

Black Widow (1987)
Sam Frey . . . . .Paul
•• 1:18 - Buns, walking into swimming pool.
Dennis Hopper . . . . Ben
Terry O'Quinn . . . . .Bruce
Theresa Russell . . . . Catherine
• 0:28 - Briefly nude, making love in cabin.
•• 1:18 - Nude in pool with Paul.
Debra Winger . . . . Alexandra

Blackout (1989)
Michael Keyes Hall . . . . Alan Boyle
• 1:19 - Buns and balls viewed from the rear while stabbing Richard in bed.
Carol Lynley . . . . .Esther Boyle
•• 1:01 - Brief topless leaning against the wall while someone touches her left breast.

Blade Runner (1982)
Joanna Cassidy . . . . Zhora
•• 0:54 - Topless getting dressed after taking a shower while talking with Harrison Ford.
Daryl Hannah . . . . Pris
Rutger Hauer . . . . .Roy Batty
M. Emmet Walsh . . . . Bryant
Sean Young . . . . Rachael

Blame It on Rio (1984)
Michelle Johnson . . . . Jennifer Lyons
•• 0:19 - Topless on the beach greeting Michael Caine and Joseph Bologna with Demi Moore, then brief topless in the ocean.
• 0:26 - Topless taking her clothes off for Caine on the beach. Dark, hard to see.
•• 0:27 - Topless seducing Caine. Dark, hard to see.
••• 0:56 - Full frontal nudity taking off robe and sitting on bed to take a Polaroid picture of herself.
• 0:57 - Very brief topless in the Polaroid photo showing it to Caine.
• 1:02 - Brief topless taking off her top in front of Caine while her dad rests on the sofa.
Demi Moore . . . . Nicole Hollis
• 0:19 - Very brief right breast turning around to greet Michael Caine and Joseph Bologna.

Blaze (1989)
Lolita Davidovich . . . . Blaze Starr
0:09 - In bra doing her first strip routine. Very brief side views of left breast under hat.
0:15 - Strip tease routine in front of Paul Newman. At the end, she takes off bra to reveal pasties.
0:42 - In black bra and panties with Newman.
•• 0:48 - Topless on top of Newman, then side view of left breast.

Blind Date (1984)
(Not the same 1987 *Blind Date* with Bruce Willis.)
Kirstie Alley . . . . Claire Parker
• 0:12 - Brief topless making love in bed with Joseph Bottoms. Dark, hard to see anything.
Joseph Bottoms . . . . Jonathon Ratcliffe

Lana Clarkson . . . . Rachel
- • 0:52 - Brief topless rolling over in bed when Joseph Bottoms sneaks in. Dark, hard to see.
  1:11 - In two piece swimsuit during a modeling assignment.
  1:18 - In two piece swimsuit by pool.
James Daughton . . . . David
Valeria Golino . . . . Girl in Bikini
Marina Sirtis . . . . Hooker
- ••• 0:21 - Topless walking to and lying in bed just before taxi driver kills her.

Blindside (1988; Canadian)
Lolita Davidovich . . . . Adele
- •• 0:32 - Topless dancing on stage.
  0:39 - Sort of buns bending over and pointing a gun through her legs in front of mirror.
Harvey Keitel . . . . Gruber

Blood and Sand (1989; Spanish)
Christopher Rydell . . . . Juan
- • 0:15 - Buns, running away after fighting bull. Dark, long shot.
- •• 0:18 - Buns, between shower curtain when Sharon Stone watches.
- • 1:05 - Buns, on top of Stone. Long shot.
Sharon Stone . . . . .Doña Sol
  0:57 - Very brief upper half of right breast, making love on table with Juan.
- •• 0:58 - Left breast, making love in bed with Juan. Don't see her face well.
- ••• 1:04 - Topless quite a few times, making love with Juan in the woods.

Blood Diner (1987)
Cynthia Baker . . . . Cindy
- ••• 0:44 - Nude outside by fire with her boyfriend, then fighting a guy with an axe.
Carl Crew . . . . George Tutman
- • 1:02 - Buns, mooning Sheeba through the passenger window of a van.
Tanya Papanicolas . . . . Sheetar & Bitsy
- • 0:15 - Brief topless as photographer during topless aerobics photo shoot.
- • 0:24 - Topless, dead on operating table, then dead, standing up.

Blood Link (1983)
Sarah Langenfeld . . . . .Christine
- •• 1:01 - Topless in bed taking off her top in bed with Craig.
- • 1:04 - Topless in bed with Keith.
Penelope Milford . . . . Julie Warren
- •• 0:22 - Topless in bed with Craig. Very brief left breast grabbing pillow.
- •• 1:24 - In black bra in greenhouse with Keith, then topless, then brief right breast.
- ••• 1:35 - Topless in bedroom with Keith.

Martha Smith . . . . Hedwig
- •• 0:41 - Topless, wearing black panties while in bed with Keith.
- • 0:50 - Topless getting slapped around by Keith.
- ••• 0:51 - Topless sitting up in bed when Craig and Keith meet each other for the first time.
- • 1:13 - Topless, wearing red panties, in bed with Keith.

Blood Relations (1989)
Lydie Denier . . . . .Marie
- •• 0:07 - Left breast making love with Thomas on stairway.
- • 0:44 - Brief left breast in bed with Thomas' father. Very brief cuts of her topless in B&W.
  0:47 - Getting out of swimming pool in a one piece swimsuit.
- ••• 0:54 - Full frontal nudity undressing for the Grandfather.
Carrie Leigh . . . . Thomas' Girlfriend

Blood Ties (1986; Made for Cable Movie; Italian)
Maria Conchita Alonso . . . . .Caterina
- •• 0:35 - Brief topless when Vincent Spano rips her dress off.
Brad Davis . . . .
Barbara De Rossi . . . . Luisa
- • 0:58 - Brief topless on couch when bad guy rips her clothes off.
Vincent Spano . . . .

Bloodbath at the House of Death (1985; British)
Pamela Stephenson . . . . Barbara Coyle
- • 0:50 - Very brief topless getting clothes ripped off by an unseen being.

Bloodsport (1987)
Leah Ayres-Hamilton . . . . Janice
Jean-Claude Van Damme . . . . Frank
- •• 0:50 - Brief buns putting underwear on after spending the night with Janice.

Bloodstone (1988)
Laura Albert . . . . Kim Chi
- • 0:05 - Very brief side view of left breast turning around in pool to look at a guy.

Bloody Birthday (1980)
Julie Brown . . . . Beverly
- ••• 0:13 - Dancing in red bra, then topless while two boys peek through hole in the wall, then buns. Nice, long scene.
  0:48 - In bedroom wearing red bra.
  1:03 - In bedroom again in the red bra.
Susan Strasberg . . . . Miss Davis
Sylvia Wright . . . .

Bloody Trail (1972)
Rickey Richardson . . . . .Miriam
  1:01 - Peek at left breast in torn blouse.
- • 1:05 - Right breast while sleeping, dark, hard to see.

Blow Out (1981)

Nancy Allen . . . . Sally
  • 0:58 - Brief upper half of right breast with the sheet pulled up in B&W photograph that John Travolta examines.
John Lithgow . . . . Burke
Cindy Manion . . . . Dancing Coed
Missy O'Shea . . . . Dancing Coed
  0:00 - Dancing in sheer nightgown while a campus guard watches from outside the window.

Blue Desert (1990)

Courteney Cox . . . . Lisa Roberts
  0:52 - Silhouette of right breast, standing up with Steve. Probably a body double. Very, very brief right nipple between Steve's arms lying in bed. Dark, hard to see.
  •• 0:53 - Left breast, lying in bed under Steve. A little hard to see her face, but it sure looks like her to me!
  1:14 - Buns and part of left breast getting towel. Looks like a body double.
Craig Sheffer . . . . Randall Atkins

Blue Lagoon (1980)

Christopher Atkins . . . . Richard
  •• 0:27 - Nude swimming underwater after growing up from little children.
  • 0:29 - Buns, underwater.
  •• 1:03 - Nude swimming under water.
  • 1:05 - Buns, kissing Brooke Shields.
  •• 1:09 - Very brief frontal nudity in water slide with Shields.
Brooke Shields. . . . . Emmeline
  0:27 - Nude swimming underwater after growing up from little children.
  0:43 - More underwater swimming.
  1:00 - Topless body double lying on a rock.
  1:09 - Right breast of body double in hammock.
  1:24 - Body double breast feeding the baby.

Blue Movies (1988)

Vickie Benson . . . .
Lucinda Crosby . . . . Randy Moon
  • 0:10 - Topless in hot tub.
  •• 0:11 - Topless shooting porno movie.
  ••• 0:30 - Topless auditioning for Buzz.
  • 0:59 - Topless on desk in porno movie.
Darian Mathias . . . . Kathy
  • 0:35 - Very brief topless twice acting for the first time in a porno film.

Blue Steel (1989)

Clancy Brown . . . . Nick Mann
  • 1:27 - Upper half of buns lying on the bathroom floor. Don't see his face, so it could be anybody.
Jamie Lee Curtis . . . . Megan Turner
  1:27 - Very, very brief buns twice when rolling out of bed, trying to get her gun. Dark.
Elizabeth Peña . . . . Tracy Perez

Blue Velvet (1986)

Laura Dern . . . . Sandy Williams
Dennis Hopper . . . . Frank Booth
Kyle MacLachlan . . . . Jeffrey
  •• 0:41 - Buns and very brief frontal nudity running to closet in Isabella Rossellini's apartment.
Isabella Rossellini . . . . Dorothy
  • 1:08 - Brief topless in apartment.
  • 1:40 - Nude, standing bruised on porch.

Bluebeard (1972)

Agostina Belli . . . . Caroline
  • 1:31 - Brief left breast lying on grass getting a tan.
  •• 1:32 - Topless taking off clothes and lying on the couch.
Sybil Danning . . . . The Prostitute
  • 1:08 - Brief topless kissing Nathalie Delon showing her how to make love to her husband.
  • 1:09 - Brief left breast, lying on the floor with Delon just before Richard Burton kills both of them.
Nathalie Delon . . . . Erika
  • 1:03 - Topless in bed, showing Richard Burton her breasts.
  • 1:09 - Brief right breast lying on the floor with Sybil Danning just before Richard Burton kills both of them.
Joey Heatherton . . . . Anne
  • 0:25 - Topless under black see-through nightie while Richard Burton photographs her. Very brief right breast.
  ••• 1:46 - Brief topless opening her dress top to taunt Richard Burton.
Karin Schubert . . . . Greta
  • 1:43 - Brief topless, spinning around, unwrapping herself from a red towel for Richard Burton.
Marilu Tolo . . . . Brigitt
  • 1:25 - Topless in sheer blue blouse arguing with Richard Burton.
  •• 1:27 - Topless getting whipped by Burton.

Blume in Love (1973)

Susan Anspach . . . . Nina Blume
Kris Kristofferson . . . . Elmo
Marsha Mason . . . . Arlene
  • 0:22 - Side view of right breast, then brief topless lying in bed with George Segal.
  • 0:35 - Very brief right breast reaching over the bed.
  •• 0:54 - Brief topless twice, reaching over to get a pillow while talking to Segal.
Erin O'Reilly . . . . Cindy
  • 0:40 - Topless and buns, getting out of bed with George Segal.

Boarding School (1980; Italian)

Nastassja Kinski . . . . Deborah
  • 1:32 - Topless making love with a guy.

Bobbie Jo and the Outlaw (1976)

Belinda Balaski . . . . Essie Beaumont
  • 0:29 - Topless in pond with Marjoe Gortner and Lynda Carter.

Lynda Carter . . . . Bobbie Jo Baker
- •• 0:17 - Brief left breast making love with Marjoe Gortner.
- •• 0:27 - Brief left breast making love with Gortner again.
- • 0:29 - Very brief breasts in pond with Gortner experimenting with mushrooms.

Body and Soul (1981)

Azizi Johari . . . . Pussy Willow
- ••• 0:31 - Topless sitting on bed with Leon Isaac Kennedy, then left breast lying in bed.

Rosanne Katon . . . . Melody
- • 0:04 - Left breast several times making love in restroom with Leon Isaac Kennedy.

Perry Lang . . . . Charles Golphin
Ola Ray . . . . Hooker #1
- • 0:54 - Brief topless sitting on top of Leon Isaac Kennedy in bed with two other hookers.

Laurie Senit . . . . Hooker #3
- • 0:54 - Brief topless lying next to Leon Isaac Kennedy in bed with two other hookers.

Body Chemistry (1990)

Lisa Pescia . . . . Claire
- ••• 0:18 - Topless making love with Marc Singer standing up, then at foot of bed.
  0:35 - In purple bra in van with Singer.
  0:55 - Buns, standing in hallway. Long shot.

Marc Singer . . . . Dr. Tom Redding
- • 0:18 - Buns, standing up in hallway holding Claire while making love. Long shot.

Body Double (1984)

Barbara Crampton . . . . Carol Sculley
- •• 0:04 - Brief right breast, while making love in bed with another man when her husband walks in.

Alexandra Day . . . . Girl in Bathroom #1
Melanie Griffith . . . . Holly Body
- •• 0:20 - Topless in brunette wig dancing around in bedroom while Craig Wasson watches through a telescope.
- • 0:28 - Topless in bedroom again while Wasson and the Indian welding on the satellite dish watch.
- •• 1:12 - Topless and buns on TV that Wasson is watching.
- •• 1:13 - Topless and buns on TV after Wasson buys the video tape.
- • 1:19 - Brief buns in black leather outfit in bathroom during filming of movie.
- • 1:20 - Brief buns again in the black leather outfit.

Barbara Peckinpaugh. . . Girl #2 (Holly Does Hollywood)
Windsor Taylor Randolph . . . . Mindy
- ••• 1:50 - Topless in the shower during filming of movie with Craig Wasson made up as a vampire.

Linda Shaw . . . . Linda Shaw
- • 1:11 - Left breast in monitor while Craig Wasson watches TV.

Brinke Stevens . . . . Girl in Bathroom #3
- • 1:12 - Topless sitting in chair in adult film preview that Craig Wasson watches on TV.

Craig Wasson . . . . Jake

Body Heat (1981)

William Hurt . . . . Ned Racine
Kathleen Turner . . . . Maddy Walker
- • 0:22 - Brief side view of left breast in bed with William Hurt.
- •• 0:24 - Topless in a shack with Hurt.
  0:32 - Buns, getting dressed. Long shot, hard to see.
- • 0:54 - Brief left breast in bathtub. Long shot, hard to see.

Bolero (1984)

Ian Cochran . . . . Robert Stewart
- • 1:26 - Buns, making love with Catalina.

Olivia D'Abo . . . . Paloma
- • 0:38 - Nude covered with bubbles taking a bath.
- • 1:05 - Brief topless in the steam room with Bo.
- • 1:32 - Topless in the steam room talking with Bo. Hard to see because it's so steamy.

Bo Derek . . . . Ayre McGillvary
- ••• 0:19 - Topless making love with Arabian guy covered with honey, messy.
- ••• 0:58 - Topless making love in bed with the bullfighter.
- ••• 1:38 - Topless during fantasy love making session with bullfighter in fog.

Ana Obregon . . . . Catalina Terry
- • 1:32 - Brief topless making love with Robert.

Andrea Occhipinti . . . . Angel the Bullfighter
- •• 0:57 - Buns, lying in bed with Bo Derek, then making love with her.

Bonnie's Kids (1973)

Tiffany Bolling . . . . Ellie
- •• 0:21 - Topless, modeling in office.
- • 1:16 - Brief right breast making love in bed.

Robin Mattson . . . . Myra
- • 0:05 - Brief side view of right breast changing in bedroom while two men watch from outside.
- ••• 0:07 - Topless washing herself in the bathroom.

The Boost (1989)

James Woods . . . . Lenny Brown
Sean Young . . . . Linda Brown
  0:16 - Very, very brief topless jumping into the swimming pool with James Woods. Very, very brief side view of right breast getting out of the pool, sitting on edge, then getting pulled back in.
- •• 0:17 - Left breast, while in pool talking to Woods.
  0:48 - Brief topless under water in spa with Woods.

The Border (1982)

Elpidia Carrillo . . . . Maria
- • 1:19 - Right breast, opening her blouse in shack with Jack Nicholson.

Harvey Keitel . . . . Cal

Jack Nicholson . . . . Charlie
Valerie Perrine. . . . . .Marcy

Border Heat (1988)
Darlanne Fluegel. . . . . Peggy Martin
    0:23 - In black bra straddling Ryan in the bedroom.
Michael J. Moore. . . . . J. C. Ryan
   • 0:14 - Buns, taking off his clothes and getting into
    spa with Darlanne Fluegel.

Born on the Fourth of July (1989)
Tom Berenger. . . . . Recruiting Sergeant
Tom Cruise . . . . .Ron Kovic
   • 0:47 - Very brief buns, sort of, in bed at hospital
    when his rear end is sticking through the bottom of
    a bed.
Willem Dafoe . . . . Charlie
Vivica Fox . . . . Hooker
   • 0:50 - Brief right breast, while taking off bra on top
    of patient in hospital. Dark.
Jason Gedrick . . . . .Martinez
Cordelia Gonzalez. . . . . .Maria Elena
  ••• 1:43 - Topless in black panties, then full frontal nudi-
    ty in bed with Tom Cruise.
Mark Moses . . . . Optomistic Doctor
David Neidorf . . . . Patient

Born to Race (1988)
Joseph Bottoms. . . . . Al Pagura
   • 0:55 - Brief buns taking off bathrobe on deck and
    jumping into the lake.
La Gena Hart. . . . . Jenny
Marla Heasley . . . . .Andrea Lombardo
   • 0:52 - Buns, outside at night while kissing Joseph
    Bottoms.
Marc Singer . . . . Kenny Landruff

The Boss' Wife (1986)
Arielle Dombasle. . . . . Mrs. Louise Roalvang
   • 1:01 - Brief topless getting a massage by the swim-
    ming pool.
  ••• 1:07 - Topless trying to seduce Daniel Stern at her
    place.
  •• 1:14 - Brief topless in Stern's shower.
Melanie Mayron . . . . Janet Keefer
Daniel Stern . . . . Joel Keefer

Boxcar Bertha (1972)
David Carradine . . . . Big Bill Shelly
   • 0:54 - Buns, putting pants on after hearing a gun
    shot.
Bernie Casey. . . . . Von Morton
Barbara Hershey . . . . .Bertha Thompson
  •• 0:10 - Topless making love with David Carradine in a
    railroad boxcar, then brief buns walking around
    when the train starts moving.
   • 0:52 - Nude, side view in house with David Carra-
    dine.
    0:54 - Buns, putting on dress after hearing a gun
    shot.

A Boy and His Dog (1976)
Suzanne Benton. .Quilla June
  •• 0:29 - Nude, getting dressed while Don Johnson
    watches.
   • 0:45 - Right breast lying down with Johnson after
    making love with him.
Don Johnson Vic

The Boy in Blue (1986; Canadian)
Melody Anderson. . . . . Dulcie
    0:07 - Brief cleavage making love with Nicholas
    Cage, then very brief top half of right breast when a
    policeman scares her.
Nicholas Cage . . . . .Ned Hanlan
Kim Coates. .McCoy Man No. 2
Cynthia Dale . . . . Margaret
  ••• 1:15 - Topless standing in a loft kissing Nicholas
    Cage.
David Naughton . . . . .Bill

Boys Night Out (1987)
Teri Lynn Peake . . . . Maid
  ••• 0:25 - Buns in G-string, then topless doing a strip
    routine. Long scene.

The Brain (1988)
Christine Kossack . . . . Vivian
  •• 0:24 - Topless on monitor, then topless in person
    during Jim's fantasy.
  •• 1:11 - Topless again in the basement during Jim's
    hallucination.

Brain Damage (1988)
Vicki Darnell. . . . . Blonde in Hell Club
Joe Gonzales . . . . .Guy in Shower
   • 0:54 - Buns, taking a shower.

Breathless (1983)
Richard Gere . . . . Jesse
  •• 0:11 - Frontal nudity dancing and singing in the
    shower. Hard to see because of the steam.
  •• 0:52 - Buns, taking his pants off to get into the show-
    er with Valerie Kaprisky, then more buns in bed. Very
    brief frontal nudity. Dark, hard to see.
   • 0:53 - Very, very brief top of frontal nudity popping
    up when Kaprisky gets out of bed.
Valerie Kaprisky . . . . Monica Poiccard
    0:23 - Brief side view of left breast in her apartment.
    Long shot, hard to see anything.
  ••• 0:47 - Topless in her apartment with Richard Gere
    kissing.
  •• 0:52 - Brief full frontal nudity standing in the shower
    when Gere opens the door, afterwards, buns in bed.
  •• 0:53 - Topless, holding up two dresses for Gere to
    pick from, then topless putting the black dress on.
   • 1:23 - Topless behind a movie screen with Gere. Lit
    with red light.
William Tepper. . . . . .Paul

A Breed Apart (1984; Made for Cable Movie)

Jane Bentzen . . . . Reporter
- ••• 0:55 - Left breast in bed with Powers Booth, then full frontal nudity getting out of bed and putting her clothes on.

Rutger Hauer . . . . Jim Malden

Kathleen Turner . . . . Stella Clayton
- •• 1:12 - Topless in bed with Rutger Hauer, then left breast.

Breeders (1986)

LeeAnne Baker . . . . Kathleen
- ••• 0:28 - Nude, undressing from her nurse outfit in the kitchen, then taking a shower.
- • 0:59 - Brief topless in alien nest. (She's the blonde in front.)
- •• 1:08 - Topless in alien nest.
- ••• 1:09 - Topless in alien nest again. (Behind Alec.)
- • 1:11 - Topless behind Alec again. Then long shot when nest is electrocuted. (On the left.)

Amy Brentano . . . . Gail
- • 0:59 - Long shot of buns, getting into the next.
- • 1:07 - Topless in nest, throwing her head back.
- •• 1:08 - Brief topless, writhing around in the nest, then topless, arching her back.
- • 1:11 - Topless, long shot, just before the nest is destroyed.

Adriane Lee . . . . Alec
- •• 0:49 - Topless, undressing while talking on the phone.
- • 1:07 - Brief topless, covered with goop, in the alien nest.
- • 1:08 - Brief topless in nest behind Frances Raines.
- • 1:09 - Brief topless behind Raines again.
- • 1:11 - Topless, lying back in the goop, then long shot topless.

Natalie O'Connell . . . . Donna
- • 0:02 - Very brief left breast, getting her blouse ripped by creature.
- •• 0:44 - Topless, sitting up in hospital bed, then buns, walking down the hall.
- ••• 0:47 - More topless and buns, walking around outside.
- • 1:10 - Brief topless, standing up in the alien nest.

Frances Raines . . . . Karinsa Marshall
- ••• 0:12 - Nude stretching and exercising in photo studio.
- • 0:16 - Brief full frontal nudity, getting attacked by the creature.
- ••• 0:53 - Topless and buns, taking off her blouse and walking down the hall and into the basement. Long scene.
- • 1:07 - Very brief right breast in the alien nest with the other women.
- • 1:10 - Brief topless standing up.

Bride of Re-Animator (1989)

Kathleen Kinmont . . . . Gloria/The Bride
- • 0:58 - Brief topless several times with her top pulled down to defibrillate her heart.
- 1:17 - Topless under gauze. Her body has gruesome looking special effects appliances all over it.
- 1:22 - More topless under gauze.
- 1:24 - More topless. Pretty unappealing.
- 1:27 - Brief buns, when turning around after ripping out her own heart.

Fabiana Udenio . . . . Francesca Danelli
- 0:45 - Most of her left breast in bed with Dan. His hand covers it most of the time.

Brimstone and Treacle (1982; British)

Sting . . . . Martin Taylor
- • 1:19 - Buns, making love with Suzanna Hamilton on her bed. Dark, hard to see.

Suzanna Hamilton . . . . Patricia Bates
- •• 0:47 - Topless in bed when Sting opens her blouse and fondles her.
- •• 1:18 - Topless in bed when Sting fondles her again.
- • 1:20 - Brief lower frontal nudity writhing around on the bed after Denholm Elliott comes downstairs.

Bring Me the Head of Alfredo Garcia (1974)

Kris Kristofferson . . . . Paco

Isela Vega . . . . Elita
- • 0:25 - Brief right breast a couple of times, then brief topless in bed with Warren Oaks.
- ••• 0:44 - Topless when Kris Kristofferson rips her top off. Long scene.
- •• 0:52 - Topless sitting in shower with wet hair.
- •• 1:49 - Still from shower scene during credits.

Broadcast News (1987)

Lois Chiles . . . . Jennifer Mack

William Hurt . . . . Tom Grunik
- •• 0:59 - Brief buns getting up from bed after making love with Jennifer. Shadow of semi-erect penis on the wall when she notices it.

Brubaker (1980)

Jane Alexander . . . . Lillian

Linda Haynes . . . . Carol
- • 1:03 - Topless getting dressed with Huey in bedroom when Robert Redford comes in.

David Keith . . . . Larry Lee Bullen

Yaphet Kotto . . . . Dickie Coombes

Bull Durham (1988)

Kevin Costner . . . . Crash Davis

David Neidorf . . . . Bobby

Tim Robbins . . . . Ebby Calvin "Nuke" La Loosh
- • 0:03 - Buns, in locker room making love with Millie when the coach sees them.

Susan Sarandon . . . . Annie Savoy
- 1:39 - Brief right breast peeking out from under her dress after crawling on the kitchen floor to get a match.

Bulletproof (1988)
Lydie Denier . . . . Tracy
•• 0:14 - Topless in Gary Busey's bathtub.
0:20 - Brief buns, putting on shirt after getting out of
bed. Very, very brief side view of left breast.
Darlanne Fluegel . . . . Devon Shepard

Bullies (1985)
Olivia D'Abo . . . . Becky Cullen
•• 0:39 - In wet white T-shirt swimming in river while
Matt watches.

Burglar (1987)
Steve Shellen. . . . . Christopher Marshall
• 0:26 - Buns, in front of closet that Whoopi Goldberg
is hiding in. Don't see his face, but probably him.

Bury Me an Angel (1972)
Dan Haggerty . . . . Ken
• 1:17 - Brief buns, making love with Dag in bed. Lit
with red light. Kind of a long shot, don't see his face
very well.
Dixie Lee Peabody. . . . . Dag
0:11 - Very brief silhouette of left breast getting into
bed.
• 0:13 - Very brief right breast getting back into bed.
••• 0:41 - Nude, skinny dipping in river and getting out.
• 1:16 - Topless making love in bed with Dan Haggerty. Lit with red light.
Clyde Ventura . . . . Bernie

Bushido Blade (1979; British/U.S.)
Laura Gemser . . . . Tomoe
• 1:08 - Brief right breast taking off her top in bedroom
with Captain Hawk.

Buster and Billie (1974)
Joan Goodfellow . . . . Billie
0:33 - Brief topless in truck with Jan-Michael Vincent.
Dark, hard to see.
• 1:06 - Buns, then brief topless in the woods with Vincent.
• 1:25 - Brief left breast getting raped by jerks.
Pamela Sue Martin . . . .
Jan-Michael Vincent . . . . Buster Lane
••• 1:06 - Frontal nudity taking off his underwear and
walking to Billie. Buns, in slow motion, swinging
into the water.

Butterfly (1982)
Pia Zadora. . . . . Kady
0:15 - Silhouette changing while Stacey Keach
watches.
•• 0:33 - Topless and buns getting into the bath.
••• 0:35 - Topless in bathtub when Stacey Keach is giving her a bath.

Buying Time (1987)
Laura Cruikshank. . . . . Jessica
•• 0:52 - Topless several times making love with Ron on
pool table.

By Dawn's Early Light (1990; Made for Cable Movie)
Rebecca De Mornay . . . . Cindy Moreau
Randal Patrick . . . . O'Toole
• 0:14 - Brief buns in shower room getting dressed
during red alert.

By Design (1982; Canadian)
Sara Botsford . . . . Angie
• 0:23 - Full frontal nudity in the ocean. Long shot,
hard to see anything.
• 1:08 - Brief side view of left breast making love in bed
while talking on the phone.
Patty Duke . . . . Helen
•• 0:49 - Left breast, lying in bed.
•• 1:05 - Brief left breast sitting on bed.
• 1:06 - Brief left breast, then brief right breast lying in
bed with the photographer.

Bye Bye Baby (1989)
Carol Alt. . . . . Sandra
0:09 - Part of right breast, while in the shower.
0:22 - Wearing a white bra, while taking off her
blouse in the doctor's office.
Luca Barbareschi . . . . Paulo
• 0:20 - Brief buns, on top of Brigitte Nielsen in bed.
Brigitte Nielsen. . . . . Lisa
• 0:20 - Brief side view of right breast, while lying on a
guy in bed. Nice buns shot also.

C.O.D. (1983)
Corinne Alphen . . . . Cheryl Westwood
• 0:21 - Brief topless changing clothes in dressing
room while talking to Zacks.
• 1:25 - Brief topless taking off her blouse in dressing
room scene.
1:26 - In green bra, talking to Albert.
1:28 - In green bra during fashion show.
Carole Davis. . . . . Contessa Bazzini
• 1:25 - Brief topless in dressing room scene in black
panties, garter belt and stockings when she takes off
her robe.
1:29 - In black top during fashion show.
Samantha Fox . . . . Female Reporter
Teresa Ganzel. . . . . Lisa Foster
• 0:46 - Right breast hanging out of dress while dancing at disco with Zack.
• 1:25 - Brief side view of left breast taking off purple
robe in dressing room scene. Then in white bra talking to Albert.
1:29 - In white bra during fashion show.
Marilyn Joi . . . . Debbie Winter
•• 1:16 - Topless during photo session.
• 1:25 - Brief topless taking off robe wearing red garter
belt during dressing room scene.
1:26 - In red bra, while talking to Albert.
1:30 - In red bra during fashion show.
Olivia Pascal . . . . Holly Fox
1:30 - In white top during fashion show.

Caddyshack (1980)
Scott Colomby . . . . .Tony
Sarah Holcomb . . . . Maggie O'Hooligan
Cindy Morgan. Lacey Underall
    0:50 - Very, very brief side view of left breast sliding into the swimming pool. Very blurry.
    •• 0:58 - Topless in bed with Danny three times.

Cadillac Man (1990)
Fran Drescher . . . . .Joy Munchack
    • 0:07 - Very brief right breast several times while in bed with Robin Williams.
Tim Robbins . . . . .Larry

Caged Fury (1984)
Taaffe O'Connell. . . . . .Honey
    •• 0:17 - Topless on bed with a guard. Mostly left breast.
    0:40 - Very, very brief tip of left breast peeking out between arms in shower.
    • 1:06 - Very brief topless getting blouse ripped open by a guard in the train.

Caged Fury (1989)
Blake Bahner. . . . . Buck Lewis
April Dawn Dollarhide. . . . . Rhonda Wallace
    0:33 - In white bra in open blouse on couch with Jack Carter.
    •• 0:41 - Topless undressing to enter prison with other topless women.
Janine Lindemulder. . . . . Lulu
    0:11 - Dancing in bar in black bra and G-string.
    • 0:16 - Brief topless dancing in front of Erik Estrada.
Sandra Margot . . . . .Crazy Daisy
    1:13 - Buns in G-string and bra dancing for some men.
    •• 1:15 - Topless taking off bra.
Melissa Moore. . . . . Gloria
Windsor Taylor Randolph . . . . Warden Sybil Thorn
    •• 0:55 - Topless and buns undressing for bath, then in the bathtub.
Elena Sahagun . . . . .Tracy Collins
    0:54 - In bra when Buck holds her hostage.
    •• 1:01 - Left breast while taking a shower.

Caged Heat (1974)
a.k.a. Renegade Girls
Roberta Collins . . . . Belle
    • 0:11 - Very brief topless getting blouse ripped open by Juanita.
    ••• 1:01 - Topless while the prison doctor has her drugged so he can take pictures of her.
Erica Gavin . . . . Jacqueline Wilson
    • 0:08 - Buns, getting strip searched before entering prison.
    •• 0:25 - Topless in shower scene.
    • 0:30 - Brief side view of left breast in another shower scene.

Cheryl Smith . . . . .Lauelle
    • 0:04 - Brief left breast, dreaming in her jail cell that a guy is caressing her through the bars.
    •• 0:25 - Topless in the shower scene.
    •• 0:50 - Brief nude in the solitary cell.

Cal (1984; Irish)
John Lynch. . . . . .Cal
    • 1:20 - Buns, getting into bed with Helen Mirren.
Helen Mirren . . . . Marcella
    1:18 - In a white bra and slip.
    •• 1:20 - Brief frontal nudity taking off clothes and getting into bed with Cal in his cottage, then right breast making love.

California Dreaming (1978)
Kirsten Baker . . . . .Karen
Glynnis O'Connor . . . . Corky
    •• 0:11 - Topless pulling her top over her head when T.T. is using the bathroom.
    1:12 - In white bra, in bed with T.T.
    ••• 1:14 - Topless in bed with T.T.
Tanya Roberts . . . . Stephanie
Dorothy Tristan . . . . Fay
    0:05 - In braless white top, jogging on the beach with Glynnis O'Connor.
    • 0:20 - Brief topless changing clothes while a group of boys peek through a hole in the wall.

California Suite (1978)
Jane Fonda. . . . . Hannah Warren
Sheila Frazier . . . . Bettina Panama
Denise Galik. . . . . Bunny
Maggie Smith . . . . .Diana Barrie
    • 1:05 - Very brief side of left breast, putting nightgown on over her head.

Caligula (1980)
(X-rated, 147 minute version.)
Anneka De Lorenzo . . . .
    ••• 1:16 - Nude, making love with Lori Wagner. Long scene.
Malcolm McDowell .Caligula
    • 0:05 - Buns, rolling around in bed with Drusilla.
    • 0:36 - Brief buns, taking ring off of Peter O'Toole.
    • 0:46 - Very brief buns running to bed.
    0:51 - Buns, putting Drusilla down in bed.
    • 1:14 - Nude walking around outside in the rain. Dark, long shot.
    2:23 - Very brief buns under his white robe.
Helen Mirren . . . . Caesonia
    1:02 - Side view of buns with Malcolm McDowell
    • 1:13 - Brief topless several times getting out of bed to run after McDowell. Dark.
    1:15 - Very brief left breast taking off her dress to dry McDowell off.
Donato Placido . . . . .Proculus
    • 1:11 - Frontal nudity taking his robe off for Malcolm McDowell. Buns, getting raped by McDowell's fist.

Theresa Ann Savoy . . . . .Drusilla
- •• 0:01 - Nude, running around in the forest with Malcolm McDowell.
- • 0:05 - Buns, rolling in bed with McDowell. Very brief topless getting out of bed.
- • 0:26 - Left breast several times in bed.
- • 0:46 - Brief right breast in bed with McDowell again.
- • 1:15 - Left breast with McDowell and Helen Mirren.
- • 1:22 - Very brief left breast getting up in open dress.
- •• 1:45 - Full frontal nudity, then buns when dead and McDowell tries to revive her.

Lori Wagner . . . .
- ••• 1:16 - Nude, making love with Anneka Di Lorenzo. Long scene.

Call Me (1988)
Patricia Charbonneau . . . . .Anna
- •• 1:18 - Brief left breast making love in bed with a guy, then topless putting blouse on and getting out of bed.

Patti D'Arbanville . . . . Coni

Can She Bake a Cherry Pie? (1983)
Karen Black. . . . . .Zee
- 0:40 - Sort of left breast squished against a guy, while kissing him in bed.
- • 1:02 - Very brief upper half of left breast in bed when she reaches up to touch her hair.

Michael Margotta . . . . Larry

Candy Stripe Nurses (1974)
Robin Mattson . . . . Dianne
- •• 0:22 - Nude in gym with the basketball player.
- ••• 0:40 - Nude in bed with the basketball player.

Candice Rialson. . . . . Sandy
- •• 0:05 - Topless in hospital linen closet with a guy.
- •• 0:08 - Topless smoking and writing in bathtub.
- • 0:14 - Topless in hospital bed.

Carnal Knowledge (1971)
Ann-Margret. . . . . Bobbie
- •• 0:48 - Topless and buns making love in bed with Jack Nicholson, then getting out of bed and into shower with Jack.
- • 1:07 - Brief side view of left breast putting a bra on in the bedroom.

Candice Bergen. . . . . Susan
Art Garfunkel. . . . . Sandy
Carol Kane . . . . .Jennifer
Jack Nicholson . . . . Jonathan

Carrie (1976)
Nancy Allen .Chris Hargenson
- •• 0:01 - Nude, in slow motion in girls' locker room behind Amy Irving.

William Katt . . . . .Tommy Ross
P.J. Soles . . . . Norma

Sissy Spacek. . . . . Carrie White
- •• 0:02 - Nude, taking a shower, then having her first menstrual period in the girls' locker room.
- • 1:25 - Brief topless taking a bath to wash all the pig blood off her after the dance.

Cartel (1990)
Suzanne Slater . . . . Nancy
- 0:28 - In red two piece swimsuit modeling on motorcycle.
- 0:35 - Brief bra and panties on bed during struggle.
- • 0:36 - Topless during brutal rape/murder scene.

Castaway (1986)
Amanda Donohoe .Lucy Irvine
- •• 0:32 - Nude on beach after helicopter leaves.
- •• 0:48 - Full frontal nudity lying on her back on the rocks at the beach.
- ••• 0:51 - Topless on rock when Reed takes a blue sheet off her, then catching a shark.
- ••• 0:54 - Nude yelling at Reed at the campsite, then walking around looking for him.
- ••• 1:01 - Topless getting seafood out of a tide pool.
- •• 1:03 - Topless lying down at night talking with Reed in the moonlight.
- ••• 1:18 - Topless taking off bathing suit top after the visitors leave, then arguing with Reed.
- ••• 1:22 - Topless talking to Reed.

Virginia Hey . . . . Janice
Oliver Reed . . . . Gerald Kingsland
- •• 1:46 - Nude, doing things around the hut during the storm.

Casualties of War (1989)
John Leguizamo. . . . . .Diaz
- • 0:53 - Buns, pulling his pants down to rape Oahn.

Sean Penn . . . . Sergeant Meserve

Cat in the Cage (1978)
Colleen Camp . . . . .Gilda Riener
- • 0:36 - Very brief left breast twice, while making love in bed with Bruce.

Sybil Danning . . . . Susan Khan
- • 0:24 - Brief topless getting slapped around by Ralph.
- • 0:25 - Brief left breast several times smoking and talking to Ralph, brief left breast getting up.
- •• 0:30 - Full frontal nudity getting out of the pool.
- • 0:52 - Black bra and panties undressing and getting into bed with Ralph. Brief left breast and buns.
- 1:02 - In white lingerie in bedroom.
- 1:10 - In white slip looking out window.
- 1:15 - In black slip.
- • 1:18 - Very brief right breast several times, struggling with an attacker on the floor.

Cat People (1982)
Ed Begley, Jr. . . . . Joe Creigh
John Heard . . . . Oliver Yates
- • 1:37 - Very brief side view of buns, taking off his pants and sitting on bed next to Nastassja Kinski.
- •• 1:50 - Buns, making love with Nastassja Kinski in bed in a cabin.

Nastassja Kinski . . . . Irena Gollier
- ••• 1:03 - Nude at night, walking around outside chasing a rabbit.
- •• 1:35 - Topless taking off blouse, walking up the stairs and getting into bed.
- • 1:37 - Brief right breast, lying in bed with John Heard.
- •• 1:38 - Topless getting out of bed and walking to the bathroom.
- •• 1:40 - Brief buns, getting back into bed. Topless in bed.
- •• 1:47 - Full frontal nudity, walking around in the cabin at night.
- • 1:49 - Topless, tied to the bed by Heard.

Lynn Lowry . . . . Ruthie
- • 0:16 - In black bra in Malcolm McDowell's hotel room, then brief topless when bra pops open after crawling down the stairs.

Malcolm McDowell . . . . Paul Gollier
- • 1:06 - Side view of buns, lying on the bathroom floor. Partial lower frontal nudity when he gets up.

Annette O'Toole . . . . Alice Perrin
- ••• 1:30 - In a bra, then topless undressing in locker room.
- • 1:31 - Some topless shots of her in the pool. Distorted because of the water.
- • 1:33 - Brief right breast, after getting out of the pool.

Tessa Richarde . . . . Billie
- •• 1:00 - Topless in bed with Malcolm McDowell trying to get him excited.

Catch-22 (1970)
Alan Arkin . . . . Captain Yossarian
- • 0:52 - Buns, standing wearing only his hat, talking to Dreedle. Don't see his face.

Richard Benjamin . . . . Major Danby
Suzanne Benton . . . . Dreedle's WAC
Olimpia Carlisi . . . . Luciana
- • 1:04 - Topless lying in bed talking with Alan Arkin.

Art Garfunkel . . . . Captain Nately
Paula Prentiss . . . . Nurse Duckett
- • 0:22 - Full frontal nudity in water throwing her dress to Alan Arkin who is swimming in the water during his dream. Long shot, over exposed, hard to see.

Jon Voight . . . . Milo Minderbinder

Catherine & Co. (1975; French)
Jane Birkin . . . . Catherine
- • 0:07 - Topless, standing up in the bathtub to open the door for another woman.
- •• 0:09 - Side view of left breast, while taking off her blouse in bed.

- ••• 0:10 - Topless, sitting up and turning the light on, smoking a cigarette.
- •• 0:17 - Right breast, while making love in bed.
- •• 0:24 - Topless taking off her dress, then buns jumping into bed.
- •• 0:36 - Buns and left breast posing for a painter.
- • 0:45 - Topless taking off dress, walking around the house. Left breast, inviting the neighbor in.

Patrick Dewaere . . . . Francois

Catherine Cherie (1982)
Ajita Wilson . . . . Dancer/Miss Ajita
- • 0:23 - Topless and buns dancing in club. Covered with paint. Long shot.
  0:24 - Brief buns, greeting Carlo after the show.
- •• 0:43 - Full frontal nudity in room with Carlo.

Cave Girl (1985)
Jasaé . . . . Locker Room Student
- •• 0:05 - Topless with four other girls in the girls' locker room undressing, then running after Rex. She's sitting on a bench, wearing red and white panties.

Michelle Bauer . . . . Locker Room Student
- •• 0:05 - Topless with four other girls in the girls' locker room undressing, then running after Rex. She's the first to take her top off, wearing white panties, running and carrying a tennis racket.

Susan Mierisch . . . . Locker Room Student
- •• 0:05 - Topless with four other girls in the girls' locker room undressing, then running after Rex. She's blonde, wearing red panties and a necklace.

Cynthia Ann Thompson . . . . Eba
- •• 1:04 - Topless making love with Rex.

Cellar Dweller (1987)
Pamela Bellwood . . . . Amanda
Cheryl-Ann Wilson . . . . Lisa
- •• 0:59 - Brief right breast, then topless taking a shower.

The Centerfold Girls (1974)
Jennifer Ashley . . . . Charly
- • 0:34 - Topless taking off blouse while changing clothes.
- •• 0:49 - Topless and buns posing for photographer outside with Glory.

Jaime Lyn Bauer . . . . Jackie
- •• 0:04 - Topless getting out of bed and walking around the house.
- ••• 0:14 - Topless getting undressed in the bathroom.
- •• 0:15 - Brief topless and buns putting on robe and getting out of bed, three times.

Tiffany Bolling . . . . Vera
- • 1:02 - Brief topless in photograph.
- ••• 1:12 - Topless in the shower.
- • 1:21 - Brief topless in motel bed getting raped by two guys after they drug her beer.

Teda Bracci . . . . Rita
- • 0:18 - Topless taking off her clothes in the living room in front of everybody.

Kitty Carl . . . . Sandi
  •• 0:45 - Topless taking off her top while sitting on the bed with Perry.
    0:51 - Topless on the beach, dead. Long shot, hard to see.
Anneka De Lorenzo . . . . Pam
Ruthy Ross . . . . Glory
  ••• 0:49 - Topless and buns posing for photographer outside with Charly.
Janet Wood . . . . Linda
  •• 0:14 - Topless putting on robe and getting out of bed.

Centerfold Screen Test *(1985)*
Leslee Bremmer . . . . herself
    0:22 - Topless under fishnet top. (Practically see-through top.)
  •• 0:24 - Dancing, wearing the fishnet top and black G-string.
  ••• 0:28 - Closer shot, dancing, while wearing the top.
Becky LeBeau . . . . herself
    0:14 - In wet white T-shirt, auditioning in pool.
Ashley St. Jon . . . . herself
  ••• 0:32 - Topless and buns in G-string, taking off her fur coat while auditioning in a car.

Centerfold Screen Test, Take 2 *(1986)*
Michelle Bauer . . . . Marsha
  ••• 0:12 - Topless taking off her dress for Mr. Johnson. Then full frontal nudity. Nice, long scene.

Certain Fury *(1985)*
Nicholas Campbell . . . . Sniffer
  • 0:36 - Buns, getting undressed to rape Irene Cara.
Irene Cara . . . . Tracy
    0:32 - Getting undressed to take a shower.
  • 0:36 - Topless behind shower door while Sniffer comes into the bathroom. Brief topless in quick cuts when he tries to rape her.
Tatum O'Neal . . . . Scarlet

A Certain Sacrifice *(1981)*
Madonna . . . . Bruna
  ••• 0:22 - Topless during weird rape/love scene with one guy and two girls.
  • 0:40 - Brief right breast in open top lying on floor after getting attacked by guy in back of restaurant.
  • 0:57 - Brief topless during love making scene, then getting smeared with blood.

Chained Heat *(1983; U.S./German)*
Jennifer Ashley . . . . Grinder
Greta Blackburn . . . . Lulu
Linda Blair . . . . Carol
  ••• 0:30 - Topless in the shower.
  •• 0:56 - In bra, then topless in the Warden's office when he rapes her.
Christina Cardan . . . . Miss King
Sybil Danning . . . . Erika
  ••• 0:30 - Topless in the shower with Linda Blair.

Monique Gabrielle . . . . Debbie
  ••• 0:08 - Nude, stripping for the Warden in his office.
  ••• 0:09 - Nude, getting into the spa with the Warden.
Sharon Hughes . . . . Val
  •• 0:30 - Brief topless in the shower with Linda Blair.
  •• 0:51 - Buns, in lingerie, stripping for a guy.
  •• 1:04 - Topless in the spa with the Warden.
Marcia Karr . . . . Twinks
  ••• 0:30 - Topless, getting soaped up by Edy Williams in the shower.
  • 0:37 - Brief topless, taking off her top in bed with Edy Williams at night.
  •• 0:40 - Topless in cell getting raped by the guard.
Louisa Moritz . . . . Bubbles
Stella Stevens . . . . Taylor
Kate Vernon . . . . Cellmate
Edy Williams . . . . Paula
  •• 0:30 - Full frontal nudity in the shower, soaping up Twinks.
  •• 0:36 - Topless at night in bed with Twinks.

The Challenge *(1982)*
Donna Kei Benz . . . . Akiko
  • 1:23 - Topless making love with Scott Glenn in motel room. Could be a body double. Dark, hard to see anything.
Scott Glenn . . . . Rich

A Change of Seasons *(1980)*
Bo Derek . . . . Lindsey Routledge
  •• 0:00 - Topless in hot tub during the opening credits.
  • 0:25 - Side view of left breast in the shower talking to Anthony Hopkins.
Shirley MacLaine . . . . Karen Evans

Chattahoochee *(1990)*
Dennis Hopper . . . . Walker Benson
  • 0:32 - Brief buns, leaving the shower room after talking to Gary Oldman.
Gary Oldman . . . . Emmett Foley
  • 1:17 - Brief buns, standing while guards search his clothes. Very, very brief frontal nudity turning around to get a high-pressure enema. Long shot, don't really see anything.
M. Emmet Walsh . . . . Morris

Chatterbox *(1977)*
Perry Bullington . . . . Ted
  • 0:02 - Buns, stumbling around the room.
Candice Rialson . . . . Penny
  •• 0:01 - Left breast, in bed with Ted, then topless getting out of bed.
    0:10 - In white bra wrestling on couch with another woman.
  ••• 0:15 - Side view of right breast then topless during demonstration on stage.
  ••• 0:26 - Topless in bed talking on phone.
    0:32 - In open dress letting her "chatterbox" sing during talk show. Something covers pubic area.
  •• 0:35 - Topless during photo shoot.

•• 0:38 - Topless again for more photos while opening a red coat.

•• 0:43 - Topless in bed with Ted.

••• 0:55 - Topless taking off white dress, walking up the stairs and opening the door.

•• 1:09 - Topless opening her raincoat for Ted.

Cheech & Chong's Nice Dreams (1981)

Evelyn Guerrero . . . . Donna

• 0:43 - Brief left breast sticking out of her spandex outfit, sitting down at table in restaurant.

0:56 - In burgundy lingerie in her apartment with Cheech Marin.

Richard "Cheech" Marin . . . . Himself

• 0:57 - Brief buns climbing over railing to escape Donna's husband, Animal.

Linnea Quigley . . . . Blondie Group #2

Roselyn Royce . . . . Beach Girl #3

• 0:29 - Brief topless on the beach with two other girls. Long shot, unsteady, hard to see.

Victoria Wells . . . . Beach Girl #1

• 0:29 - Brief topless on the beach with two other girls. Long shot, unsteady, hard to see.

Chinatown (1974)

Faye Dunaway. . . . . .Evelyn

• 1:26 - Very brief right breast, in bed talking to Jack Nicholson.

• 1:28 - Very brief right breast in bed talking to Nicholson. Very brief flash of right breast under robe when she gets up to leave the bedroom.

Jack Nicholson . . . . .J.J.

• 1:28 - Very brief buns, putting pants on getting out of bed after making love with Faye Dunaway.

Chopping Mall (1986)

Angela Aames . . . . Miss Vanders

Barbara Crampton . . . . .Suzie

•• 0:22 - Brief topless taking off top in furniture store in front of her boyfriend on the couch.

Toni Naples. . . . . Bathing Beauty

Suzanne Slater . . . . Leslie

•• 0:28 - Brief topless in bed showing breasts to Mike.

0:31 - Walking around the mall in panties and a blouse.

Mary Woronov . . . . .Mary Bland

Cinderella (1977)

Linda Gildersleeve . . . . Farm Girl (redhead)

••• 0:21 - Topless and buns with her brunette sister in their house making love with the guy who is looking for Cinderella.

•• 1:24 - Full frontal nudity with her sister again when the Prince goes around to try and find Cinderella.

Yana Nirvana. . . . . Drucella

• 0:02 - Topless taking off clothes with her sister Maribella to let Cinderella wash.

• 0:06 - Brief topless sitting up in bed with Maribella.

Mariwin Roberts . . . . .Trapper's Daughter

••• 0:11 - Frontal nudity getting a bath outside by her blonde sister. Long scene.

Cheryl Smith . . . . Cinderella

•• 0:03 - Topless dancing and singing.

••• 0:30 - Frontal nudity getting "washed" by her sisters for the Royal Ball.

•• 0:34 - Topless in the forest during a dream.

••• 0:41 - Topless taking a bath. Frontal nudity drying herself off.

• 1:16 - Brief topless with the Prince.

• 1:30 - Brief left breast after making love with the Prince to prove it was her.

• 1:34 - Brief side view of left breast making love in the Prince's carriage.

Cinderella Liberty (1973)

Dabney Coleman . . . . Executive Officer

Marsha Mason . . . . Maggie Paul

0:09 - Brief panties shot leaning over pool table when James Caan watches.

•• 0:17 - Side view of left breast in room with Caan. Brief right breast sitting down on bed.

••• 0:38 - Topless sitting up in bed, yelling at Caan.

• 0:54 - Very brief left breast turning over in bed and sitting up.

Circle of Two (1980)

Tatum O'Neal . . . . .Sarah Norton

•• 0:56 - Topless standing behind a chair in Richard Burton's studio talking to him.

City Limits (1984)

Kim Cattrall . . . . Wickings

•• 1:02 - Right breast, while sitting up in bed with a piece of paper stuck to her.

Rae Dawn Chong. . . . . .Yogi

John Diehl . . . . .Whitey

John Stockwell . . . . Lee

Class (1983)

Jacqueline Bisset. . . . . Ellen

Candace Collins . . . . Buxom Girl

Lolita Davidovich . . . . 1st Girl (motel)

Rob Lowe. . . . . Skip

Virginia Madsen . . . . Lisa

•• 0:20 - Brief left breast when Andrew McCarthy accidentally rips her blouse open at the girl's school.

Andrew McCarthy . . . . .Jonathan

Class of Nuke 'Em High (1986)

Janelle Brady . . . . .Chrissy

•• 0:26 - Topless sitting on bed in the attic with Warren.

• 0:31 - Brief topless scene from 0:26 superimposed over Warren's nightmare.

Cleo/Leo (1989)

Ginger Lynn Allen . . . . .Karen

••• 0:39 - Full frontal nudity getting out of the shower, getting dried with a towel by Jane Hamilton, then in nightgown.

••• 0:57 - Full frontal nudity getting out of the shower and dried off again.

Scott Baker. . . . . Leo Blockman

• 0:09 - Very brief buns after getting his butt kicked.

Ruth Corrine Collins . . . . Sally
••• 0:08 - Topless getting dress pulled off by Leo.
Jennifer Delora . . . . Bernice
Jane Hamilton . . . . Cleo Clock
  •• 0:13 - Nude undressing in front of three guys.
  • 0:21 - Topless changing in dressing room.
  ••• 0:22 - Topless changing in dressing room with the
     Store Clerk.
     0:40 - In bra and panties.
  •• 1:07 - Left breast and lower frontal nudity making
     love with Bob on bed.
Kimberly Taylor . . . . Store Clerk
  ••• 0:22 - Topless in white panties, changing in dressing
     room with Jane Hamilton. Very nice!
Kevin Thomsen . . . . Bob Miller
  • 1:07 - Brief frontal nudity, then buns making love
     with Jane Hamilton on bed.

A Climate for Killing (1990)
John Diehl . . . . Wayne Paris
Sherrie Ann Rose . . . . Rita Paris
  •• 1:30 - Topless in bed while Wayne recollects his
     crime to John Beck.
Katherine Ross . . . . Grace Hines
Mia Sara . . . . Elise Shipp

A Clockwork Orange (1971)
Adrienne Corri . . . . Mrs. Alexander
  •• 0:11 - Breasts through cut-outs in her top, then full
     frontal nudity getting raped by Malcolm McDowell
     and his friends.
Malcolm McDowell . . . . Alex
  • 0:27 - Very brief nude having sex with two women in
     his bedroom. Shot at fast speed.
     0:52 - Upper half of frontal nudity getting admitted
     to jail.

Club Extinction (1990)
Alan Bates . . . . Dr. Marsfeldt
Jennifer Beals . . . . Sonja Vogler
  • 1:16 - Brief side of left breast rolling over in bed with
     Hartmann. Don't see her face, but probably her.
  •• 1:17 - Brief topless in bed with Hartmann when he
     kisses her right breast, then brief right breast.
Andrew McCarthy . . . . The Assassin

Coach (1978)
Michael Biehn . . . . Jack
  • 1:11 - Upper half of buns in shower with Cathy Lee
     Crosby.
Cathy Lee Crosby . . . . Randy
  • 0:31 - Very brief side view of left breast when Michael
     Biehn opens the door while she's putting on her top.
     0:52 - In wet white T-shirt at the beach and in her
     house with Biehn.
     1:11 - Very, very brief topless in shower room with
     Biehn. Blurry, hard to see anything.
Brent Huff . . . . Keith

Rosanne Katon . . . . Sue
  • 0:10 - Very brief topless flashing her breasts along
     with three of her girlfriends for their four boyfriends.
Lenka Novak . . . . Marilyn
  • 0:10 - Very brief topless flashing her breasts along
     with her girlfriends for their boyfriends.

The Coca-Cola Kid (1985; Australian)
Kris McQuade . . . . Juliana
Eric Roberts . . . . Becker
Greta Scacchi . . . . Terri
  ••• 0:49 - Nude taking a shower with her daughter.
  •• 1:20 - Brief topless wearing a Santa Claus outfit while
     in bed with Eric Roberts.

Cocaine Wars (1986)
John Schneider . . . . Cliff
Kathryn Witt . . . . Janet
  • 0:36 - Brief topless and buns making love in bed with
     John Schneider.

Cocktail (1988)
Bryan Brown . . . . Doug Coughlin
Tom Cruise . . . . Brian Hanagan
Gina Gershon . . . . Coral
  • 0:31 - Very, very brief right breast romping around in
     bed with Tom Cruise.
Kelly Lynch . . . . Kerry Coughlin
     0:45 - Buns, wearing a two piece swimsuit at the
     beach.
     1:01 - Buns, in string bikini swimsuit on boat with
     Tom Cruise and Bryan Brown.
Elizabeth Shue . . . . Jordan Mooney
     0:52 - Side view of left breast standing up in waterfall
     with Tom Cruise when she takes off her swimsuit
     top.

Coffy (1973)
Pam Grier . . . . Coffy
  • 0:05 - Upper half of right breast in bed with a guy.
     0:19 - Buns, walking past the fireplace, seen through
     a fish tank.
  •• 0:25 - Topless in open dress getting attacked by two
     masked burglars.
  ••• 0:38 - Buns and topless undressing in bedroom.
     Wow!
  • 0:42 - Brief right breast when breast pops out of
     dress while she's leaning over. Dark, hard to see.
     0:49 - In black bra and panties in open dress with a
     guy in the bedroom.

Cold Comfort (1988)
Jayne Eastwood . . . . Mrs. Brocket
Margaret Langrick . . . . Dolores
  •• 0:16 - In tank top and panties, then topless undress-
     ing in front of Stephen.
  • 0:19 - Very brief side of left breast and buns getting
     robe.
  •• 0:41 - Doing strip tease in front of her dad and
     Stephen. In black bra and panties, then topless.
  • 0:42 - Very brief topless jumping into bed.

Cold Feet (1989)
Keith Carradine . . . . Monte
Sally Kirkland . . . . Maureen Linoleum
- • 0:56 - In black bra and panties taking off her dress in bedroom with Keith Carradine. Brief right breast pulling bra down.
- • 0:58 - Brief side view of right breast sitting up in bed talking to Carradine.

Cold Steel (1987)
Brad Davis . . . . Johnny Modine
Sharon Stone . . . . Kathy Conners
- • 0:33 - Brief left breast making love in bed with Brad Davis. Dark, hard to see. Brief topless turning over after making love.

Collector's Item (1988)
Laura Antonelli . . . . Marie Colbert
    0:18 - In white lingerie with Tony Musante.
- • 0:20 - Lower frontal nudity, then right breast making love with Musante. Dark.
    0:37 - In black bra, garter belt and stockings in open robe undressing for Musante.
    0:41 - In the same lingerie again dropping robe and getting dressed.
Blanca Marsillach . . . . Jacqueline
- •• 0:52 - In white bra cleaning up Tony Musante in bed, then topless.
    1:04 - Lower frontal nudity while watching Musante and Laura Antonelli making love in bed.
- • 1:18 - Topless getting dressed. A little dark.
- •• 1:22 - Topless changing clothes in bedroom while Antonelli talks to her.
Cristina Marsillach . . . . Young Marie
- •• 0:12 - Right breast in elevator with Tony Musante.
- •• 0:36 - Topless in open blouse, then full frontal nudity in hut with Musante.

The Color of Money (1986)
Tom Cruise . . . . Vincent
Mary Elizabeth Mastrantonio . . . . Carmen
- • 0:41 - Brief topless in bathroom mirror drying herself off while Paul Newman talks to Tom Cruise. Long shot, hard to see.
Helen Shaver . . . . Janelle

Colors (1988)
Maria Conchita Alonso . . . . Louisa Gomez
- ••• 0:48 - Topless making love in bed with Sean Penn.
Sean Penn . . . . Danny McGavin

The Comfort of Strangers (1991)
Rupert Everett . . . . Colin
- •• 0:47 - Buns, walking around the room, looking for his clothes.
- • 1:05 - Buns, making love with Natasha Richardson on bed. Lit with blue light.
Helen Mirren . . . . Caroline

Natasha Richardson . . . . Mary
- ••• 0:45 - Topless sleeping in bed. Long shot. Then closer topless after waking up. Long scene.
- •• 1:05 - Topless making love with Colin. Lit with blue light.
- •• 1:06 - Right breast, lying in bed with Colin. Lit with blue light.

Coming Home (1978)
Bruce Dern . . . . Captain Bob Hyde
- •• 2:03 - Buns, taking off his clothes at the beach and running into the ocean.
Jane Fonda . . . . Sally Hyde
- •• 1:26 - Making love in bed with Jon Voight. Topless only when her face is visible. Buns and brief left breast when you don't see a face is a body double.
Penelope Milford . . . . Viola Munson
- • 1:19 - Doing strip tease in room with Jane Fonda and two guys. Sort of right breast peeking out between her arms when she changes her mind.
Jon Voight . . . . Luke Martin

Coming Together (1978)
a.k.a. A Matter of Love
Jeff Alin . . . . Frank Hughes
- • 1:05 - Buns, putting pants on with Richard.
Marc Anderson . . . . Richard Duncan
- •• 0:13 - Buns kneeling and kissing Angie, then more buns making love.
- • 0:58 - Buns, making love with Vicky.
- • 1:05 - Buns, putting pants on with Frank.
Christy Neal . . . . Vicky Hughes
    0:12 - In bra and panties, in bedroom with Frank.
- • 0:30 - Brief right breast in shower with Angie.
- • 0:37 - Topless and buns making love standing up in front of sliding glass door with Frank. Quick cuts.
- • 0:49 - Brief topless again during flashbacks.
- •• 0:57 - Topless with Angie and Richard.
- • 1:05 - Topless on beach with Angie. Long shot.

Commando (1985)
Ava Cadell . . . . Girl in Bed
- • 0:46 - Very brief topless three times in bed when Arnold Schwarzenegger knocks a guy through the motel door into her room.
Rae Dawn Chong . . . . Cindy
Bill Paxton . . . . Intercept Officer
Arnold Schwarzenegger . . . . Matrix

Con el Corazón en la Mano (1988; Mexican)
Maria Conchita Alonso . . . .
- • 0:38 - Very, very brief right breast, turning over in bed with her husband.
- • 0:39 - Topless several times, taking a bath.
- •• 1:15 - Topless ripping off her dress. Long shot, side view, standing while kissing a guy.

Conan the Barbarian (1982)
Sandahl Bergman . . . . Valeria
•• 0:49 - Brief left breast making love with Arnold
   Schwarzenegger.
Valerie Quennessen. . . . . The Princess
Arnold Schwarzenegger . . . . Conan

The Concrete Jungle (1982)
Greta Blackburn . . . . Lady in Bar
Sondra Currie . . . . Katherine
Aimée Eccles . . . . .Spider
Marcia Karr . . . . .Marcy
Camille Keaton . . . . .Rita
• 0:41 - In black bra, then topless getting raped by
  Stone. Brief lower frontal nudity sitting up after-
  wards.

Convoy (1978)
Kris Kristofferson .Rubber Duck
Ali MacGraw . . . . Melissa
Cassie Yates. . . . . Violet
• 0:21 - Very brief left breast, while in truck sleeper
  with Kris Kristofferson.

The Cook, The Thief, His Wife & Her Lover (1990)
Alan Howard . . . . Michael
•• 0:32 - Buns, then brief frontal nudity with Helen Mirren.
• 0:42 - Buns, on top of Mirren.
• 1:11 - Buns, with Mirren in kitchen.
••• 1:14 - Buns, getting into meat truck. Frontal nudity
  getting hosed off and walking around with Mirren.
Helen Mirren. . . . . .Georgina Spica
0:22 - In black bra in restroom performing fellatio on
  Michael.
•• 0:32 - In lingerie undressing, then lower frontal nudity, buns and left breast in kitchen with Michael.
• 0:42 - Buns and right breast, while making love with
  Michael again.
•• 0:57 - Topless sitting and talking with Michael.
1:01 - Buns, kneeling on table.
• 1:05 - Brief topless, while leaning back on table with
  Michael.
1:07 - Lower frontal nudity opening her coat for
  Michael.
• 1:11 - Buns and topless in kitchen.
••• 1:14 - Buns, getting into meat truck. Full frontal nudity in truck and walking around with Michael.
Willie Ross. . . . . .Roy
0:03 - Buns, on ground covered with dog feces get-
  ting urinated on by Albert. (Talk about a bad day!)
• 0:07 - Buns, kneeling on ground while dogs walk
  around.
• 0:09 - Buns, standing up.

Cool Blue (1990)
Judie Aronson . . . . Cathy
•• 1:03 - Topless in bed on top of Woody Harrelson.

Corporate Affairs (1990)
Stephen Davies . . . . .Ukranian #2
Kim Gillingham . . . . .Ginny Malmquist
• 1:09 - Topless, climbing out of cubicle.
Lisa Moncure . . . . .Carolyn Bean
• 1:07 - Very, very brief left breast, while kicking Dou-
  glas out of cubicle.
Elena Sahagun . . . . Stacy
Christina Veronica . . . . Tanning Woman
0:47 - Side of right breast, getting tanned.

Corvette Summer (1978)
Annie Potts. . . . . Vanessa
• 0:51 - Silhouette of right breast in van with Mark
  Hamill. Out of focus topless washing herself in the
  van while talking to him. Don't really see anything.

Cousin, Cousine (1975; French)
Marie-Christine Barrault . . . . Marthe
•• 1:05 - Topless in bed with her lover, cutting his nails.
• 1:07 - Brief side view of right breast, while giving him
  a bath.
••• 1:16 - Topless with penciled tattoos all over her body.
1:33 - Braless in see-through white blouse saying
  "good bye" to everybody.
Guy Marchand . . . . Pascal
Marie-France Pisier . . . . Karine

Covergirl (1982; Canadian)
Jeff Conaway . . . . T. C. Sloane
•• 0:43 - Very brief lower frontal nudity getting out of
  bed.
Irena Ferris . . . . Kit Paget
•• 0:19 - Brief topless taking off robe and getting into
  bathtub with Dee.
• 0:43 - Very brief right breast sticking out of nightgown.
• 0:46 - Upper half of left breast during modeling session.
• 0:47 - Topless in mirror in dressing room.
0:49 - Brief topless getting attacked by Joel.
• 0:53 - Brief left breast, putting another blouse on.
• 0:53 - Brief left breast, putting on blouse.
Roberta Leighton . . . . Dee Anderson
0:16 - Almost topless making love dressed like a nun.
Michele Scarabelli . . . . Snow Queen
Kenneth Welsh. . . . . Harrison Chandler
• 1:23 - Brief buns, seen on video tape used to get him
  in trouble. Long shot.

Crazy Mama (1975)
Sally Kirkland . . . . .Ella Mae
Linda Purl. . . . . Cheryl
0:05 - In pink, two piece swimsuit at the beach.
• 0:52 - Very brief buns, then brief topless when Snake
  and Donny Most keep opening the door after she
  has taken a shower. Long shot, hard to see.

Creator (1985)
Mariel Hemingway . . . . Meli
　　0:38 - Brief topless cooling herself off by pulling up
　　T-shirt in front of a fan.
　• 1:10 - Brief topless flashing David Ogden Stiers dur-
　　ing football game to distract him.
Virginia Madsen . . . . .Barbara
　　0:53 - Walking on beach in a blue one piece swimsuit
　　with Vincent Spano.
　••• 0:58 - Nude in shower with Spano.
Vincent Spano. . . . . .Boris
　• 0:28 - Brief buns, in shower room with David Ogden
　　Stiers after working out in a gym.
　• 0:57 - Brief buns, before taking a shower.

Creature (1985)
Marie Laurin . . . . Susan Delambre
　•• 0:41 - Topless and brief buns with blood on her
　　shoulders, getting Jon to take his helmet off.

Creatures the World Forgot (1971; British)
Julie Ege . . . . Nala, The Girl
　　0:56 - Very brief topless several times (it looks like a
　　stunt double) fighting in cave with The Dumb Girl.
　　Hard to see.
　• 1:32 - Very, very brief half of right breast when fight-
　　ing a snake that is wrapped around her face.

Creepozoids (1987)
Ken Abraham . . . . Butch
　•• 0:16 - Side view of buns, standing in shower with
　　Linnea Quigley.
Linnea Quigley . . . . Blanca
　•• 0:15 - Topless taking off her top to take a shower.
　•• 0:16 - Right breast, while standing in shower with
　　Butch.
　• 0:24 - Right breast several times while sleeping in
　　bed with Butch.

Creepshow 2 (1987)
Lois Chiles. .Annie Lansing
　•• 0:59 - Brief topless getting out of boyfriend's bed,
　　then getting dressed.

Crime Zone (1989)
David Carradine . . . . Jason
Sherilyn Fenn . . . . Helen
　　0:16 - In black lingerie and stockings in bedroom.
　•• 0:23 - Topless wearing black panties making love
　　with Bone. Dark, long shot.

Crimes of Passion (1984)
John Laughlin . . . . Bobby Grady
　• 0:58 - Buns, getting dressed after having sex with
　　Kathleen Turner. (Viewed through peep hole by An-
　　thony Perkins.)
Annie Potts . . . . .Amy Grady
Kathleen Turner . . . . Joanna Crane/China Blue
　••• 0:45 - Topless, wearing black panties and stockings,
　　lying in bed with Bobby.
　• 1:00 - Right breast in back of a limousine with a rich
　　couple.

　　1:22 - In blue bra and panties.
　• 1:27 - Right breast in bed with Bobby.

Criminal Law (1989)
Kevin Bacon . . . . .Martin Thiel
Gary Oldman . . . . Ben Chase
　• 1:21 - Very, very brief blurry frontal nudity in bed
　　with Ellen.
Karen Young . . . . Ellen Falkner
　• 1:21 - Very brief buns, then brief topless in bed with
　　Ben.

Critters 2: The Main Course (1988)
Roxanne Kernohan. . . . . Lee
　•• 0:37 - Brief topless after transforming from an alien
　　into a Playboy Playmate.

Cross Country (1983; Canadian)
Nina Axelrod . . . . Lois Hayes
　　0:28 - Brief buns and sort of topless, getting fondled
　　by Richard.
　　1:05 - Very, very brief topless fighting outside the
　　motel in the rain with Johnny.
Roberta Weiss. . . . . Alma Jean
　•• 0:59 - Topless on bed with two other people.

Cross My Heart (1987)
Annette O'Toole. . . . . .Kathy
　　0:44 - In pink bra standing in bedroom with Martin
　　Short.
　•• 0:46 - Left breast, in bed with Short.
　•• 0:48 - Topless in bed when Short heads under the
　　covers.
　•• 0:49 - Brief topless again getting her purse.
　• 1:05 - Brief topless and buns, dressing after Short
　　finds out about her daughter.

Crossover (1980; Canadian)
a.k.a. Mr. Patman
Flonnula Flanagan . . . . Abadaba
　• 0:27 - Brief topless opening her robe and flashing
　　James Coburn.
Tabitha Harrington. . . . . .Montgomery
　• 0:11 - Brief right breast, then brief full frontal nudity
　　lying in bed, then struggling with James Coburn in
　　her room. Wearing white makeup on her face.
　•• 0:29 - Nude walking in to room to talk with Coburn,
　　then topless and brief buns leaving.
Michael Kirby. . . . . Dr. Turley
Kate Nelligan . . . . Peabody

Crystal Heart (1987)
Tawny Kitaen . . . . Alley Daniels
　•• 0:46 - Topless and buns "making love" with Lee Cur-
　　reri through the glass.
　•• 0:50 - Nude, crashing through glass shower door,
　　covered with blood during her nightmare.
　• 1:14 - Brief topless making love with Curreri in and
　　falling out of bed.
Marina Saura . . . . Justine

Curse III: Bloody Sacrifice *(1990)*
Jenilee Harrison . . . . Elizabeth Armstrong
••• 0:43 - Topless sitting in bathtub. Almost side of right
breast when wrapping a towel around herself.

Cut and Run *(1985)*
Karen Black . . . . .Karin
Lisa Blount . . . . .Fran Hudson
Valentina Forte . . . . .Ana
••• 0:29 - Brief left breast being made love to in bed.
Then topless sitting up in bed and left side view and
buns taking a shower.

Cutter's Way *(1981)*
a.k.a. Cutter and Bone
Jeff Bridges . . . . Richard Bone
Julia Duffy . . . . Young Girl
Ann Dusenberry . . . . Valerie Duran
Lisa Eichhorn . . . . Maureen "Mo" Cutter
• 1:07 - Brief right breast, wearing bathrobe, lying on
lounge chair while Jeff Bridges looks at her.
John Heard . . . . .Alex Cutter

Cyborg *(1989)*
Dayle Haddon . . . . Pearl Prophet
Debi Richter . . . . .Nady Simmons
0:28 - Buns, after taking off clothes and running into
the ocean.
• 0:30 - Brief left breast by the fire showing herself to
Jean-Claude Van Damme.
Jean-Claude Van Damme . . . . .Gibson Rickenbacker

Cyclone *(1986)*
Michelle Bauer . . . . .uncredited Shower Girl
• 0:06 - Very brief buns and side of left breast walking
around in locker room. (Passes several times in front
of camera.)
Martine Beswicke . . . . Waters
Ashley Ferrare . . . . .Carla Hastings
0:04 - Working out at health club with Heather Tho-
mas.
Pamela Gilbert . . . . .uncredited Shower Girl
0:06 - Buns and topless brunette in the showers.
Long shot.
Heather Thomas .Teri Marshall
Dawn Wildsmith . . . . Henna

Daddy's Boys *(1988)*
Laura Burkett . . . . .Christie
••• 0:17 - Topless in room with Jimmy.
•• 0:20 - Left breast, while making love with Jimmy in
bed again.
• 0:21 - Brief topless during Jimmy's nightmare.
• 0:43 - Brief topless in bed again, then getting
dressed.
• 0:53 - Brief topless in bed consoling Jimmy.
• 1:11 - Left breast, while in bed with Jimmy.
Daryl Haney . . . . .Jimmy
• 0:17 - Buns, getting undressed in room with Christie.
Linda Shayne. . . . . Nanette

The Damned *(1969; German)*
Helmut Berger . . . . Martin Von Essenbeck
• 2:03 - Buns, walking up to his mother and ripping
her dress off. Dark, don't see his face.
Charlotte Rampling . . . . Elizabeth Thallman
Ingrid Thulin . . . . Sophie Von Essenbeck
•• 1:23 - Topless in bed with Frederick. Long scene for
a 1969 film.
• 2:03 - Left breast in bed with Martin (her son in the
film).

Damned River *(1990)*
Lisa Aliff . . . . Anne
0:28 - Silhouette topless undressing in tent.
• 0:32 - Very, very brief top of right breast in open
blouse, then half of right breast in wet blouse washing her hair.
• 0:50 - Very brief topless struggling with Ray when he
rips her top open. Don't see her face.
Steve Shellen . . . . Ray

Dance of the Damned *(1988)*
Starr Andreeff. . . . . .Jodi
•• 0:03 - Topless dancing in black bikini bottoms on
stage in a club.
1:06 - In black bra, panties, garter belt and stockings
dancing in bar just for the vampire.
•• 1:08 - Topless in the bar with the vampire.
Maria Ford . . . . .Teacher
• 0:11 - Brief topless during dance routine in club
wearing black panties, garter belt and stockings.
Deborah Ann Nassar . . . . .La Donna
• 0:07 - Brief topless during dance routine in club.
Cyril O'Reilly . . . . .Vampire

Dances with Wolves *(1990)*
Kevin Costner. . . . . .Lt. John Dunbar
•• 0:37 - Brief buns, washing his clothes in the pond.
••• 0:40 - Buns, standing by himself after scaring away
Kicking Bird.
Mary McDonough . . . . .Stands with a Fist

Danger Zone II: Reaper's Revenge *(1988)*
Stephanie Blake . . . . .Tattooed Topless Dancer
••• 0:47 - Dancing on stage in bikini bottoms.
Alisha Das . . . . Francine
Jane Higginson. . . . . .Donna
•• 0:17 - Topless unconscious on sofa while the bad
guys take Polaroid photos of her.
• 0:18 - Brief topless in the photo that Wade looks at.
• 0:22 - Brief left breast adjusting her blouse outside.
Long shot.
• 0:34 - Left breast in another Polaroid photograph.
0:45 - In black bra, panties and stockings posing on
motorcycle for photograph.
Jason Williams . . . . .Wade
•• 0:06 - Buns, getting out of bed and putting pants on.

Dangerous Game *(1988; Australian)*
Kathryn Walker . . . . Kathryn
- 1:19 - Very, very brief topless when her black top is pulled up while struggling with Murphy.

Dangerous Liaisons *(1988)*
Glenn Close . . . . Marquise de Merteuil
Michelle Pfeiffer . . . . Madame de Tourvel
Uma Thurman. . . . . Cécile de Volanges
- ••• 0:59 - Topless taking off her nightgown in her bedroom with John Malkovich.

Dangerous Love *(1988)*
Teri Austin. . . . . Dominique
Brenda Bakke . . . . .Chris
Collin Bernsen. . . . . Brooks
Eloise Broady. . . . . Bree
- ••• 0:06 - Topless changing into lingerie in the mirror.
Nicole Picard. . . . . Jane
Brenda Swanson . . . . Felicity

Dangerous Obsession *(1990; Italian)*
Corrine Clery. . . . . Carol Simpson
- 0:14 - Right breast sticking out of lingerie while lying in bed.
- •• 0:36 - Full frontal nudity lying in bed waiting for her husband, then with him, then getting out of bed.
Blanca Marsillach .Jessica
- 0:02 - Left breast, getting fondled by Johnny in recording studio. Lower frontal nudity when he pulls down her panties.
- •• 0:05 - Topless opening her blouse while Johnny plays his saxophone.
- 0:17 - Lower frontal nudity on the stairs with Johnny, then brief topless.
- 0:29 - Brief topless in video tape on T.V.
- •• 0:40 - Topless changing blouses.
- ••• 0:56 - Full frontal nudity masturbating while looking at pictures of Johnny. Buns, then more full frontal nudity getting video taped.
- ••• 0:58 - Topless in bed with a gun. Nude walking around the house. Long scene.
- 1:05 - Brief topless on beach, burying a dog.
- 1:06 - Brief full frontal nudity during video taping session.
- •• 1:07 - Topless cleaning up Dr. Simpson.
- ••• 1:13 - Topless taking chains off Dr. Simpson, then lying in bed. Full frontal nudity making love with him.

Dangerously Close *(1986)*
Carey Lowell. . . . . Julie
John Stockwell . . . . .Randy McDevill
- 0:33 - Brief buns in steamy locker room.
Angel Tompkins . . . . Mrs. Waters
Karen Witter . . . . Betsy

Dark Side of the Moon *(1989)*
Wendy MacDonald. . . . . Alex
- 0:54 - In bra, then brief topless having it torn off. Don't see her face.
Camilla More . . . . Lesli

Daughter of Death *(1982)*
a.k.a. Julie Darling
Sybil Danning . . . . .Susan
- •• 0:36 - Topless in bed with Anthony Franciosa.
- 0:38 - Brief right breast under Franciosa.
Cindy Girling . . . . Irene
- •• 0:12 - Topless in bathtub and getting out.
Isabelle Mejias . . . . .Julie

The Day After Halloween *(1978; Australian)*
a.k.a. Snapshot
Chantal Contouri .Madeline
Sigrid Thornton . . . . .Angela
- 0:04 - Very brief topless in ad photos on wall.
- •• 0:19 - Topless during modeling session at the beach.
- ••• 0:21 - More topless at the beach.
- •• 0:37 - Topless in magazine ad several times.
- 0:43 - Brief right breast in magazine ad.
- 0:46 - Topless in ad again.
- 1:18 - Entering room covered with the ad.
- 1:20 - In beige bra in room with weirdo guy.

The Day of the Cobra *(1980)*
Sybil Danning . . . . .Brenda
- 0:41 - Buns and side view of right breast getting out of bed and putting robe on with Lou. Long shot.

The Day of the Locust *(1975)*
Karen Black . . . . .Faye
Pepe Serna. . . . . .Miguel
- 2:01 - Buns on top of Karen Black, then buns jumping out of bed.
Donald Sutherland. . . . . .Homer

Dead Aim *(1987)*
Ed Marinaro. . . . . Malcolm "Mace" Douglas
- 0:52 - Buns, in bed making love with Amber. Dark, hard to see.
Lynn Whitfield . . . . Sheila Freeman

Dead and Buried *(1981)*
Melody Anderson. . . . . Janet
Lisa Blount. . . . . .Girl on the Beach
- 0:06 - Brief topless on the beach getting her picture taken by a photographer.

Dead Calm *(1989)*
Nicole Kidman. Rae Ingram
- 0:59 - Brief buns and topless with the attacker.
Billy Zane. . . . . Hughie Warriner
- 1:01 - Buns, walking around on the boat.

Dead Ringers *(1988)*
Genevieve Bujold. . . . . .Claire Niveau
- •• 0:49 - Very brief right breast in bed with Jeremy Irons, then brief topless reaching for pills and water. Dark, hard to see.
Heidi Von Palleske . . . . Cary
- 0:45 - Brief left breast sticking out of bathrobe talking to Jeremy Irons in the bathroom.

Dead Solid Perfect *(1988; Made for Cable Movie)*
Corinne Bohrer . . . . Janie Rimmer
••• 0:31 - Nude, getting out of bed to get some ice for Randy Quaid. Nice scene!
Kathryn Harrold . . . . Beverly T. Lee

The Dead Zone *(1983)*
Brooke Adams. . . . . Sarah Bracknell
Martin Sheen . . . . Greg Stillson
Helene Udy. . . . . Weizak's Mother
Roberta Weiss . . . . Alma Frechette
• 0:49 - Briefly in beige bra, then brief topless when the killer rips her blouse open during Christopher Walken's vision.

Dead-End Drive-In *(1986; Australian)*
Natalie McCurry . . . . Carmen
•• 0:19 - Topless in red car with Ned Manning.

Deadline *(1988)*
John Hurt . . . . Granville Jones
Imogen Stubbs . . . . Lady Romy-Burton
0:42 - Doing handstands in a bikini top.
• 0:44 - Brief left breast, while getting out of bed with John Hurt. Full frontal nudity turning toward bed, brief topless getting back into bed.

Deadly Blessing *(1981)*
Lisa Hartman. . . . . Faith
1:31 - Brief left breast after getting hit with a rock by Maren Jensen. (It doesn't look like a real chest, probably wearing a special-effect appliance over her breasts.)
Maren Jensen . . . . Martha
•• 0:27 - Topless and buns changing into a nightgown while a creepy guy watches through the window.
0:52 - Buns, getting into the bathtub. Kind of steamy and hard to see.
• 0:56 - Brief topless in bathtub with snake. (Notice that she gets into the tub naked, but is wearing black panties in the water).
Sharon Stone . . . . Lana

Deadly Companion *(1979)*
Susan Clark. . . . . Paula West
• 0:19 - Brief left breast, while consoling Michael Sarrazin in bed, then brief side view of left breast.
• 0:20 - Brief topless sitting up in bed.
Pita Oliver. . . . . Lorraine
• 0:14 - Very brief left breast, then very brief topless sitting up in bed during Michael Sarrazin's daydream. Dark.
1:32 - Brief full frontal nudity, dead on bed when Susan Clark comes into the bedroom.

Deadly Dreams *(1988)*
Juliette Cummins. . . . . Maggie Kallir
• 0:25 - Topless on bed, taking off her blouse and kissing Alex.
••• 0:55 - Topless and brief buns, making love with Jack in bed.
Stacey Travis . . . . Librarian

Deadly Embrace *(1989)*
Ken Abraham . . . . Chris Thompson
•• 0:17 - Buns, taking a shower.
• 1:01 - Brief buns, making love on top of Linnea Quigley.
Michelle Bauer. . . . . Female Spirit of Sex
•• 0:22 - Topless caressing herself during fantasy sequence.
••• 0:28 - Topless taking off tube top and caressing herself.
••• 0:40 - Topless and buns kissing blonde guy. Nice close up of him kissing her breasts.
• 0:42 - Side of left breast lying down with the guy.
• 1:03 - Buns and side of right breast with the guy.
Ruth Corrine Collins . . . . Dede Magnolia
Linnea Quigley. Michelle Arno
•• 0:15 - In white lingerie, then topless and buns during Chris' fantasy.
•• 0:34 - Topless and buns caressing herself.
•• 0:43 - Topless again.
0:46 - Brief topless.
•• 0:50 - Topless and buns undressing.
••• 0:58 - Topless in bed on top of Chris, then making love.
• 1:02 - Topless and buns on top of Chris while Charlotte watches on T.V.
1:11 - Topless in Chris' fantasy.
• 1:12 - Topless and buns in playback of video tape.
Windsor Taylor Randolph . . . . Charlotte Morland
0:19 - In yellow one piece swimsuit by the pool with Chris.
0:27 - In wet, white T-shirt in the kitchen with Chris.
•• 0:28 - Topless taking off her top. Mostly side view of left breast.
• 0:29 - More left breast, while in bed with Chris.
••• 0:30 - Topless, making love in bed with Chris.
• 1:10 - Brief right breast, on T.V. when she replays video tape for Linnea Quigley.
Jan-Michael Vincent . . . . Stewart Morland

Deadly Innocents *(1988)*
Zag Dorison. . . . . Crazy Norm
• 0:04 - Buns, standing on top of van and mooning the paramedics.
Andrew Stevens . . . . Bob Appling
Amanda Wyss . . . . Andy/Angela
•• 0:12 - Topless, taking off T-shirt and putting on lingerie.
••• 1:29 - Right breast, twice, with Andrew Stevens.

Deadly Passion *(1985)*
Ingrid Boulting. . . . . Martha Greenwood
• 0:46 - Brief buns taking off clothes and jumping into pool. Long shot.
•• 0:47 - Topless getting out of pool and kissing Brent Huff. Right breast in bed.
• 0:54 - Topless in whirlpool bath with Huff.
••• 1:02 - Topless, wearing white panties and massaging herself in front of a mirror.

•• 1:31 - Topless taking off clothes and jumping into bed with Huff.

Brent Huff . . . . Sam Black

Susan Isaacs . . . . Trixie

•• 0:02 - Topless sitting up in bed talking to Brent Huff.

Deadly Strangers (1974; British)

Hayley Mills . . . . Belle

1:02 - Buns in bathtub when her uncle watches her.

1:05 - In black bra, garter belt and panties while Steven fantasizes as he sees her through a keyhole.

••• 1:13 - In white bra and panties while Steven watches through keyhole, then topless taking off bra and reading a newspaper.

1:15 - In white bra, getting dressed.

Deadly Survailance (1991; Made for Cable Movie)

Susan Almgren . . . . Rachel

0:00 - Very, very brief right breast getting dressed. Don't see her face. B&W.

• 0:12 - Topless in the shower. Long shot.

•• 0:34 - Topless in the shower with Nickels.

••• 0:54 - Buns, in black panties and bra, then topless in room with Michael Ironside.

Christopher Bondy . . . . Nickels

• 0:31 - Buns, dropping his towel to run after Michael.

David Carradine . . . . Lieutenant

Deadly Vengeance (1985)

Althought the copyright on the movie states 1985, it looks more like the 1970's.

Grace Jones . . . . Slick's Girlfriend

••• 0:06 - Right breast, then topless in bed with Slick.

•• 0:13 - Left breast, when Slick sits up in bed, then full frontal nudity after he gets up.

Deadtime Stories (1987)

Cathryn De Prume . . . . Goldi-lox

•• 1:08 - Topless taking a shower, quick cuts.

Melissa Leo . . . . Judith "Mama" Baer

Nicole Picard . . . . Rachel (Red Riding Hood)

• 0:48 - Very brief right breast in shack with boyfriend.

Scott Valentine . . . . Peter

• 0:19 - Buns, getting out of bath.

Death Feud (1989)

Greta Blackburn . . . . Jenny

0:29 - In sexy black dress talking to Frank Stallone.

1:04 - In black lingerie on couch.

Lisa Loring . . . . Roxey

0:06 - Dancing in club with feathery pasties. Later, wearing the same thing under a sheer negligee.

0:41 - Dancing again with the same pasties.

1:20 - Dancing with red tassel pasties.

Karen Mayo-Chandler . . . . Anne

0:26 - In lingerie with a customer.

•• 0:36 - In white lingerie, then topless several times outside taking off robe.

Gail Thackray . . . . Harry's Girl Friend

•• 1:12 - Topless on bed with Harry.

1:16 - In black lingerie on boat with Harry.

Death Game, The Seducers (1977)

a.k.a. Mrs. Manning's Weekend

Colleen Camp . . . . Donna

0:16 - Buns, in spa with Sondra Locke trying to get George in with them.

• 0:47 - Brief topless jumping up and down on the bed while George is tied up.

•• 1:16 - Topless behind stained glass door taunting George. Hard to see.

Sondra Locke . . . . Jackson

0:16 - Buns and brief right breast in spa with Colleen Camp trying to get George in with them.

• 0:48 - Brief topless running around the room trying to keep George away from the telephone.

Death of a Soldier (1985)

Nikki Lane . . . . Stripper in bar

•• 0:49 - Nude, dancing on stage.

Death Race 2000 (1975)

David Carradine . . . . Frankenstein

Roberta Collins . . . . Matilda the Hun

•• 0:27 - Topless being interviewed and arguing with Calamity Jane.

Simone Griffeth . . . . Annie Smith

• 0:32 - Side view of left breast, while holding David Carradine. Dark, hard to see.

••• 0:56 - Topless and buns getting undressed and lying on bed with Carradine.

Louisa Moritz . . . . Myra

• 0:28 - Topless and buns getting a massage and talking to David Carradine.

Sylvester Stallone . . . . Machine Gun Joe Viterbo

Mary Woronov . . . . Calamity Jane

• 0:27 - Brief topless arguing with Matilda the Hun.

Death Wish (1974)

Jeff Goldblum . . . . Freak 1

• 0:10 - Brief buns standing with pants down in living room raping Carol with his two punk friends.

Christopher Guest . . . . Patrolman Reilly

Kathleen Tolan . . . . Carol Toby

• 0:09 - Brief topless and buns getting raped by three punks.

Death Wish II (1982)

Roberta Collins . . . . Woman at Party

Silvana Gallardo . . . . Rosario

• 0:11 - Buns, on bed getting raped by gang. Brief topless on bed and floor.

• 0:13 - Nude, trying to get to the phone. Very brief full frontal nudity, lying on her back on the floor after getting hit.

Robin Sherwood . . . . Carol Kersey

• 0:15 - Topless after getting raped by gang member in their hideout.

Death Wish III (1985)
Marina Sirtis . . . . Maria
- 0:42 - Topless getting blouse ripped open next to a car by the bad guys.
- 0:43 - More topless on mattress at the bad guy's hangout.

Deathrow Game Show (1988)
Esther Alise . . . . Groupie
- •• 0:08 - Topless in bed with Chuck.

Debra Lamb . . . . Shanna Shallow
- ••• 0:23 - Topless dancing in white G-string and garter belt during the show.

Deathstalker (1983)
Barbi Benton. . . . . Codille
- •• 0:39 - Topless struggling while chained up and everybody is fighting.
- 0:47 - Right breast, struggling on the bed with Deathstalker.

Lana Clarkson . . . . Kaira
- •• 0:26 - Topless when her cape opens, while talking to Deathstalker and Oghris.
- ••• 0:29 - Topless lying down by the fire when Deathstalker comes to make love with her.
- 0:49 - Brief topless with gaping cape, sword fighting with a guard.

Deathstalker II (1987)
Monique Gabrielle . . . . Reena the Seer/Princess Evie
- 0:57 - Brief topless getting dress torn off by guards.
- ••• 1:01 - Topless making love with Deathstalker.
- 1:24 - Topless, laughing during the blooper scenes during the end credits.

Toni Naples. . . . . Sultana
- 0:55 - Brief topless in strobe lights making love with the bad guy. Hard to see because of blinking lights. Might be a body double, don't see her face.

Maria Socas. . . . .
- 0:50 - In see-through nightgown after telling Deathstalker she is going to marry him.

Deceptions (1990; Made for Cable Movie)
Harry Hamlin . . . . Nick Gentry

Nicollette Sheridan . . . . Adrienne Erickson
- 0:35 - Very, very brief silhouette of breasts hugging Hamlin when camera tilts down from her head to her buns.

The Deep (1977)
Jacqueline Bisset . . . . Gail Berke
- ••• 0:01 - Scuba diving underwater in a wet T-shirt.
- 0:08 - More wet T-shirt, getting out of water, onto boat.

Nick Nolte. .David Sanders

The Deer Hunter (1978)
Robert De Niro . . . . Michael
- •• 0:50 - Nude, running in street, then more nude by basketball court. Brief frontal nudity getting covered by Christopher Walken's jacket. Long shot.

John Savage . . . . Steven

Meryl Streep . . . . Linda

Amy Wright . . . . Bridesmaid

Def by Temptation (1990)
John Canada Terrell . . . . Bartender #1
- •• 0:09 - Nude, running through house trying to get away from The Temptress.

Deja Vu (1984)
Claire Bloom . . . .

Nigel Terry. Michel/Greg
- 1:17 - Very brief buns, jumping out of bed when Jaclyn Smith tries to kill him with a knife.

Delta Fox (1977)
Priscilla Barnes . . . . .Karen
- 0:36 - Left breast undressing in room for David. Very dark, hard to see.
- 0:38 - Very brief topless struggling with a bad guy and getting slammed against the wall.
- 0:39 - Very brief blurry left breast running in front of the fireplace.
- 0:40 - Topless sneaking out of house. Brief topless getting into Porsche.
- 0:49 - Brief right breast reclining onto bed with David. Side view of left breast several times while making love.
- 1:29 - Very brief side view of left breast in David's flashback.

Demon of Paradise (1987)
Leslie Huntly. . . . . .Gobby
- •• 0:51 - Topless taking off her top on a boat, then swimming in the ocean.

Kathryn Witt. . . . . .Annie

Demon Seed (1977)
Julie Christie. . . . . .Susan Harris
- 0:25 - Side view of left breast, getting out of bed.
- •• 0:30 - Topless and buns getting out of the shower while the computer watches with its camera.

Demonwarp (1988)
Michelle Bauer . . . . Betsy
- •• 0:41 - Topless, taking off her T-shirt to get a tan.
- •• 0:43 - Left breast, lying down, then brief topless getting up when the creature attacks.
- •• 0:47 - Topless putting blood-stained T-shirt back on.
- •• 1:19 - Topless, strapped to table, getting ready to be sacrificed.
- 1:22 - Topless on stretcher, dead.

Pamela Gilbert . . . . Carrie Austin
- ••• 0:20 - In bra, then topless in bed with Jack.
- ••• 0:22 - Right breast, then topless lying in bed, making love with Jack.
- •• 1:23 - Topless, strapped to table.
- 1:24 - Topless several more times on the table.
- •• 1:25 - Topless getting up and getting dressed.

Colleen McDermott . . . . Cindy
- •• 0:23 - Topless and buns drying herself off after taking a shower.

- 0:24 - Very brief lower frontal nudity, under her towel, trying to run up the stairs.

Descending Angel (1990; Made for Cable Movie)
Diane Lane . . . . Irina Stroia
- 0:01 - Brief right breast making love with Eric Roberts on train during opening credits.
- 0:44 - In white camisole top with Roberts, then topless lying in bed with him.

Eric Roberts . . . . Michael Rossi

Desert Hearts (1986)
Patricia Charbonneau . . . . Cay Rivvers
- 1:09 - Brief topless making love in bed with Helen Shaver.

Denise Crosby . . . . Pat
Helen Shaver . . . . Vivian Bell
- 1:05 - Brief topless in bed in hotel room.
- 1:09 - Topless making love in bed with Patricia Charboneau.

Gwen Welles . . . . Gwen

Desperate Hours (1990)
Kelly Lynch . . . . Nancy Breyers
- 0:10 - Brief topless, walking on sidewalk with Mickey Rourke when her breasts pop out of her suit.
- 1:19 - Brief topless, getting wired with a hidden microphone in bathroom.

Desperately Seeking Susan (1985)
Madonna . . . . Susan
    0:09 - Briefly in black bra taking off her blouse in bus station restroom.
    1:16 - In black bra getting out of pool and lying down on lounge chair.

Rosanna Arquette . . . . Roberta Glass
- 0:46 - Topless getting dressed when Aidan Quinn sees her through the fish tank. Long shot, hard to see.

Anne Carlisle . . . . Victoria
Ann Magnuson . . . . Cigarette Girl
Aidan Quinn . . . . Dez

Devil in the Flesh (1986; French/Italian)
Maruschka Detmers . . . . Giulia Dozza
- 0:20 - Very brief side view of left breast and buns going past open door way to get a robe.
- 0:27 - Nude, talking to Andrea's dad in his office.
- 0:55 - Topless putting a robe on. Dark.
- 0:57 - Topless and buns in bedroom with Andrea.
- 1:09 - Topless in hallway with Andrea.
    1:19 - Performing fellatio on Andrea. Dark, hard to see.
- 1:22 - Full frontal nudity holding keys for Andrea to see, brief buns.
    1:42 - Lower frontal nudity dancing in living room in red robe.

Fredrico Pitzalis . . . . Andrea
- 0:57 - Brief buns in bed with Maruschka Detmers.
- 1:19 - Frontal nudity when Detmers performs fellatio on him. Dark, hard to see.

Dial Help (1988)
Charlotte Lewis . . . . Jenny Cooper
    1:06 - Black panties and bare back dressing in black corset top and stockings. Yowza!
- 1:09 - Brief right breast while rolling around in the bathtub.

Diary of a Mad Housewife (1970)
Richard Benjamin . . . . Jonathan Balser
Peter Boyle . . . . Man in Group Therapy Session
Carrie Snodgress . . . . Tina Balser
- 0:01 - Topless taking off nightgown and getting dressed, putting on white bra while Richard Benjamin talks to her.
    0:36 - Buns and brief side view of left breast, while kissing Frank Langella.
- 0:41 - Very brief topless lying on floor when Langella pulls the blanket up.
- 0:54 - Topless lying in bed with Langella.
    1:03 - In white bra and panties getting dressed in Langella's apartment.
    1:10 - In white bra and panties in Langella's apartment again.
- 1:21 - Topless in the shower with Langella, then drying herself off.

Diary of Forbidden Dreams (1973; Italian)
Sydne Rome . . . . The Girl
- 0:06 - Brief topless taking off torn T-shirt in a room, then topless sitting on edge of bed.
- 0:09 - Nude getting out of shower, drying herself off and getting dressed.
- 0:20 - Brief side view of right breast, while talking to Marcello Mastroianni in her room.
- 0:22 - Brief topless putting shirt on.
- 1:28 - Topless outside on stairs fighting for her shirt.
- 1:30 - Brief buns and topless climbing onto truck.

Die Hard (1988)
Cheryl Baker . . . . Woman with Man
- 0:22 - Brief topless in office with a guy when the terrorists first break into the building.

Bonnie Bedelia . . . . Holly McClane
Terri Lynn Doss . . . . Girl at Airport
Kym Malin . . . . Hostage

Die Hard 2 (1990)
Bonnie Bedelia . . . . Holly McClane
Tony Ganios . . . . Baker
John Leguizamo . . . . Burke
Franco Nero . . . . Esperanza
William Sadler . . . . Colonel Stuart
- 0:02 - Buns, exercising in hotel room before leaving for the airport.

A Different Story (1979)
Linda Carpenter . . . . Chastity
- 1:33 - Very brief topless in shower, shutting the door when Meg Foster discovers her with Perry King.

Meg Foster . . . . Stella
    0:12 - In white bra and panties exercising and chang-
    ing clothes in her bedroom.
  •• 0:53 - Topless sitting on Perry King, rubbing cake all
    over each other on bed.
  • 0:59 - Brief buns and side view of right breast, while
    getting into bed with King.
Perry King . . . . Albert
  • 1:33 - Buns, through shower door, then brief buns
    getting out of the shower to talk to Meg Foster.

Diplomatic Immunity (1991)
Robert Forster . . . . Stonebridge
Meg Foster . . . . .Gerta Hermann
Fabiana Udenio . . . . .Teresa
  •• 1:06 - Topless in panties, on the floor with her hands
    tied behind her back when Klaus rips her blouse
    open to photograph her.

Dirty Hands (1975; French)
Romy Schneider . . . . Julie
  • 0:01 - Buns and right breast getting a tan, lying on
    the grass after a man's kite lands on her.
  •• 0:09 - Side view of right breast, while lying in bed
    with a man, then topless.
  • 1:04 - Topless lying on floor, then brief topless sitting
    up and looking at something on the table.

Diva (1982; French)
Tuy Ann Luu . . . . Alba
  • 0:13 - Topless in B&W photos when record store
    clerk asks to see her portfolio.
  • 0:15 - More of the B&W photos on the wall.
    1:27 - Very brief upper half of left breast taking off
    top, seen through window. Long shot.

The Divine Nymph (1977; Italian)
Laura Antonelli . . . . Manoela Roderighi
  •• 0:10 - Full frontal nudity reclining in chair.
  • 0:18 - Right breast in open blouse sitting in bed. Pu-
    bic hair while getting up.

Domino (1989)
Brigitte Nielsen . . . . Domino
  • 0:05 - Right breast, lying down next to swimming
    pool, topless getting out.
  ••• 1:04 - Right breast, caressing herself in a white linge-
    rie body suit, wearing a black wig.

Don't Look Now (1973)
Julie Christie . . . . Laura Baxter
  • 0:27 - Brief topless in bathroom with Donald Suther-
    land.
  •• 0:30 - Topless making love with Sutherland in bed.
Donald Sutherland . . . . .John Baxter
  • 0:27 - Buns, in the bathroom with Julie Christie.

Dona Flor and Her Two Husbands (1978; Brazilian)
Sonia Braga . . . . .Flor
  • 0:13 - Buns and brief topless with her husband.
  •• 0:15 - Topless lying on the bed.
    0:17 - Buns, getting out of bed.

  ••• 0:54 - Topless making love on the bed with her hus-
    band.
  •• 0:57 - Topless lying on the bed.
  ••• 1:41 - Topless kissing her first husband.

Doom Asylum (1987)
Ruth Corrine Collins . . . . .Tina
  •• 0:19 - Topless pulling up her top while yelling at kids
    below.
Patty Mullen . . . . Judy LaRue/Kiki LaRue

Double Exposure (1983)
Pamela Hensley . . . . Sergeant Fontain
Sally Kirkland . . . . Hooker
  •• 0:26 - Topless in alley getting killed.
Terry Moore . . . . Married Woman
Joanna Pettet . . . . Mindy Jordache
  •• 0:55 - Topless, making love in bed with Adrian.
Misty Rowe . . . . Bambi
Kathy Shower . . . . Mudwrestler #1
Jeana Tomasino . . . . Renee
  • 0:20 - Very brief glimpse of left breast under water in
    swimming pool.

Down and Out in Beverly Hills (1986)
Nick Nolte . . . . Jerry Baskin
  • 0:28 - Buns, changing out of wet clothes on patio.
  • 1:37 - Brief buns, changing out of Santa Claus outfit.
Elizabeth Peña . . . . .Carmen
Jason Williams . . . . .Lance

Down the Drain (1989)
Teri Copley . . . . .Kathy Miller
  • 0:04 - Full frontal nudity making love on couch with
    Andrew Stevens. Looks like a body double.
  •• 0:31 - In two piece swimsuit, then body double nude
    doing strip tease for Stevens. Notice body double
    isn't wearing earrings.
    0:33 - Buns, (probably the body double) on top of
    Stevens.
    1:21 - In black bra in motel room when bad guy
    opens her blouse.
Andrew Stevens . . . . Victor Scalia
Stella Stevens . . . . Sophia
    0:45 - In black lingerie yelling at Dino in the bath-
    room.

Downtown (1990)
Anthony Edwards . . . . Alex Kearney
  • 0:19 - Buns, outside after getting his police uniform
    ripped off.

Dr. Alien (1989)
a.k.a. I Was a Teenage Sex Mutant
Laura Albert . . . . .Rocker Chick #3
  ••• 0:21 - Topless in black outfit during dream sequence
    with two other rocker chicks.
Ginger Lynn Allen . . . . .Rocker Chick #1
  ••• 0:21 - Topless in red panties during dream sequence
    with two other rocker chicks.

Michelle Bauer . . . . Coed #1
••• 0:53 - Topless taking off her top (she's on the left) in
the women's locker room after another coed takes
hers off in front of Wesley.
Julie Gray . . . . Karla
••• 0:44 - In white bra, then topless in Janitor's room
with Wesley.
Elizabeth Kaitan. . . . . Waitress
Linnea Quigley . . . . Rocker Chick #2
••• 0:21 - Topless in white outfit during dream sequence
with two other rocker chicks.
Karen Russell. . . . . Coed #2
••• 0:53 - Topless taking off her top (she's on the right)
in the women's locker room before another coed
takes her's off in front of Wesley.
Edy Williams . . . . Buckmeister
••• 0:54 - Topless taking off her top in the women's locker room in front of Wesley.

Dr. Caligari (1989)
Laura Albert . . . . Mrs. Van Houten
••• 0:05 - Topless taking off yellow towel, then sitting in
bathtub.
•• 0:07 - Lying down, making love with guy wearing a
mask.
••• 0:10 - Topless taking orange bra off, then lying back
and playing with herself.
•• 0:11 - More topless, lying on the floor.
•• 0:12 - More topless, lying on the floor again.
• 0:30 - Brief left breast with big tongue.
Catherine Case . . . . Patient with Extra Hormones
Debra De Liso . . . . Grace Butter

Dragonard (1988)
Oliver Reed . . . . .Captain Shanks
Claudia Udy . . . . Arabella
•• 1:11 - Topless dressed as Cleopatra dancing a routine
in front of a bunch of guys.

Dragonslayer (1981)
Caitlin Clarke. . . . . Valerian
0:27 - Body double's very brief side of left breast from
under water.
Peter McNichol. . . . . Galen
• 0:27 - Very brief buns diving into pond. Sort of frontal nudity swimming under water. Hard to see because the water is so murky.

Dream Lover (1986)
Kristy McNichol. . . . . Kathy Gardner
• 0:17 - Very, very brief right breast getting out of bed,
then walking around in a white top and underwear.
0:21 - Walking around in the white top again. Same
scene used in flashbacks at 0:34, 0:46 and 0:54.

The Dream Team (1989)
Peter Boyle . . . . Jack
•• 0:05 - Buns, getting up out of chair.
Christopher Lloyd . . . . .Henry

Dressed to Kill (1980)
Nancy Allen . . . . Liz Blake
1:21 - In black bra, panties and stockings in Michael
Caine's office.
• 1:36 - Topless (from above), buns and brief right
breast in shower.
Angie Dickinson . . . . .Kate Miller
• 0:01 - Brief side view behind shower door. Long shot,
hard to see.
0:02 - Frontal nude scene in shower is a body double,
Victoria Lynn Johnson.
0:24 - Brief buns getting out of bed after coming
home from museum with a stranger.
Victoria Lynn Johnson. . . . . Body Double
•• 0:02 - Frontal nudity in the shower body doubling
for Angie Dickinson.

The Drifter (1988)
Timothy Bottoms . . . . Arthur
Kim Delaney. . . . . Julia Robbins
• 0:11 - Brief topless making love with Miles O'Keeffe
on motel floor.
•• 0:21 - Topless in bed talking with Timothy Bottoms.
Miles O'Keeffe . . . . .Trey
• 0:11 - Brief upper half of buns on the motel floor with
Kim Delaney.

Drive, He Said (1972)
Karen Black . . . . Olive
• 1:05 - Brief topless screaming in the bathtub when
she gets scared when a bird flies in.
1:19 - Brief lower frontal nudity running out of the
house in her bathrobe.
June Fairchild . . . . .Sylvie
• 0:16 - Buns and brief topless walking around in the
dark while Gabriel shines a flashlight on her.
• 1:01 - Topless, then brief nude getting dressed while
Gabriel goes crazy and starts trashing a house.
Michael Margotta . . . . Gabriel
•• 1:21 - Running nude across the grass and up some
stairs, then trashing a biology room at the university.
William Tepper. . . . . .Hector
Mike Warren . . . . Easly Jefferson
• 0:09 - Buns and very brief frontal nudity in the shower room with the other basketball players.

Drum (1976)
Pam Grier. . . . . .Regine
• 0:58 - Very brief topless getting undressed and into
bed with Maxwell.
Yaphet Kotto . . . . .Blaise
• 1:02 - Buns, getting hung upside down in barn and
spanked along with Ken Norton.
Fiona Lewis . . . . Augusta Chauvet
••• 0:57 - Topless taking a bath, getting out, then having
Pam Grier dry her off.
Ken Norton . . . . .Drum
• 1:02 - Buns, getting hung upside down in barn and
spanked along with Yaphet Kotto.

Cheryl Smith . . . . Sophie Maxwell
  •• 0:54 - Topless in the stable trying to get Yaphet Kotto to make love with her.
Brenda Sykes . . . . Calinda
  • 0:19 - Topless standing next to bed with Ken Norton.
Isela Vega . . . . Marianna
  • 0:04 - Topless in bed with the maid, Rachel.
  •• 0:22 - Brief topless standing next to the bed.

Duet for One (1987)
Julie Andrews . . . . Stephanie Anderson
  • 0:28 - Very brief left breast in gaping blouse in bathroom splashing water on her face because she feels sick, then wet T-shirt.
  ••• 1:06 - Topless stretching, lying in bed.
  • 1:07 - Very brief buns and very brief right breast, when she rolls off the bed onto the floor.
  1:30 - In wet white blouse from perspiring after taking an overdose of pills.
Alan Bates . . . . David Cornwallis
Rupert Everett . . . . Constantine Kassanis
Liam Neeson . . . . Totter
  • 1:07 - Buns, behind shower door, getting out of shower. Very, very brief buns, falling into bed when robe flies up. Long shot.

Easy Money (1983)
Sandra Beall . . . . Maid of Honor
Jennifer Jason Leigh . . . . Allison Capuletti
Kimberly McArthur . . . . Ginger Jones
  •• 0:47 - Topless sunbathing in the backyard when seen by Rodney Dangerfield.

Easy Wheels (1989)
Eileen Davidson . . . . She Wolf
Mike Leinert . . . . Meatball
  • 0:52 - Brief buns, putting his pants on.
Karen Russell . . . . Candy
Roberta Vasquez . . . . Tondalco

Eating Raoul (1982)
Ed Begley, Jr. . . . . Hippie
Robert Beltran . . . . Raoul
Mary Woronov . . . . Mary Bland
  ••• 0:46 - Topless on the couch struggling with Ed Begley, Jr. More topless while Raoul counts money on her stomach. Long scene.
  • 0:53 - Buns and side view of right breast in hospital room with Raoul. A little dark.

The Ebony Tower (1985)
Greta Scacchi . . . . Mouse
  • 0:38 - Topless having a picnic.
  • 0:43 - Brief nude walking into the lake.

Echo Park (1986)
Elvira . . . . Sheri
Michael Bowen . . . . August
Susan Dey . . . . Meg "May" Greer
  • 1:17 - Brief glimpse of right breast, while doing a strip tease at a party.
Richard "Cheech" Marin . . . . Sid

Ecstasy (1932; B&W)
Hedy Lamarr . . . . The Wife
  • 0:25 - Brief topless starting to run after a horse in a field.
  • 0:26 - Long shot running through the woods, side view naked, then brief topless hiding behind a tree.

Eddie Macon's Run (1983)
Leah Ayres-Hamilton . . . . Chris
Kirk Douglas . . . . Marazack
John Schneider . . . . Eddie Macon
  • 0:15 - Brief left side view of buns when beginning to cross the stream. Dark, hard to see.

The Eiger Sanction (1975)
Clint Eastwood . . . . Jonathan Hemlock
Candice Rialson . . . . Art Student
Brenda Venus . . . . George
  • 0:50 - Very brief topless opening her blouse to get Clint Eastwood to climb up a hill.
  • 1:06 - Topless taking off her clothes in Eastwood's room, just before she tries to kill him. Dark, hard to see.

Eleven Days, Eleven Nights (1988; Italian)
a.k.a. Top Model
Joshua McDonald . . . . Michael
  • 0:33 - Buns, when Sarah removes his underwear.

Ellie (1984)
Edward Albert . . . . Tom
Sheila Kennedy . . . . Ellie May
  •• 0:29 - Full frontal nudity posing for Billy while he takes pictures of her just before he falls over a cliff.
  0:38 - In white bra and panties, in barn loft with Frank.
  0:58 - In white bra and panties struggling to get away from Edward Albert.
  • 1:16 - In bra and panties taking off dress with Art. Topless taking off bra and throwing them on antlers. Brief topless many times while frolicking around.
Patrick Tovatt . . . . Art
  • 1:19 - Brief blurry buns while falling down the stairs.

Emanuelle in Bangkok (1977)
Laura Gemser . . . . Emanuelle
  •• 0:07 - Topless making love with a guy.
  •• 0:12 - Full frontal nudity changing in hotel room.
  ••• 0:17 - Full frontal nudity getting a bath, then massaged by another woman.
  •• 0:35 - Topless during orgy scene.
  •• 0:53 - Topless in room with a woman, then taking a shower.
  •• 1:01 - Topless in tent with a guy and woman.
  •• 1:08 - Full frontal nudity dancing in a group of guys.
  •• 1:16 - Full frontal nudity taking a bath with a woman.
  •• 1:18 - Topless on bed making love with a guy.

Emanuelle the Seductress *(1979; Greek)*

Laura Gemser . . . . .Emanuelle
- 0:01 - Full frontal nudity lying in bed with Mario.
- 0:02 - Brief topless riding horse on the beach.
- •• 0:42 - Topless making love then full frontal nudity getting dressed with Tommy.
- ••• 0:48 - Topless undressing in bedroom, then in white panties, then nude talking to Alona.
- •• 0:54 - Topless walking around in a skirt.
- •• 1:02 - Topless outside taking a shower, then on lounge chair making love with Tommy.

Emanuelle's Amazon Adventure *(1977)*

Laura Gemser . . . . .Emanuelle
- 0:17 - Brief left breast in flashback sequence in bed with a man.
- 0:21 - Brief topless making love in bed.
- 0:25 - Brief topless in the water with a blonde woman.
- •• 1:10 - Full frontal nudity painting her body.
- 1:11 - Brief topless in boat.
- 1:13 - Nude walking out of the water trying to save Isabelle.
- 1:14 - Brief topless getting into the boat with Isabelle.

Embryo *(1976)*

Barbara Carrera. . . . . .Victoria
     0:36 - Almost topless meeting Rock Hudson for the first time. Hair covers breasts.
     1:09 - In see through top in bedroom with Hudson.
- •• 1:10 - Brief buns and topless in the mirror after making love with Hudson.
- 1:11 - Left breast sticking out of bathrobe.

The Emerald Forest *(1985)*

Tetchie Agbayani . . . . .Caya
- 1:48 - Topless in the river when Kachiri is match making all the couples together.

Charley Boorman . . . . .Tommy
- 0:23 - Brief buns, running through camp.
- 0:24 - Brief buns running from waterfall and diving into pond.
- 0:30 - Buns, during ceremony.
- 0:45 - Buns, running away from the Fierce People with his dad.
- 1:02 - Buns running on the rocks, then bun in hut.
- •• 1:31 - Buns climbing up the building.
- 1:35 - Buns running down the hall to save Kachiri.

Meg Foster . . . . Jean Markham

Emily *(1976; British)*

Jeannie Collings. . . . . Rosalind
- 1:05 - Brief topless on the couch with Gerald while Richard watches.

Jane Hayden . . . . Rachel
- •• 1:09 - Topless in bed with Billy.

Koo Stark . . . . Emily
- •• 0:08 - Topless, lying in bed caressing herself while fantasizing about James.
- ••• 0:30 - Topless in studio posing for Augustine, then kissing her.
- ••• 0:42 - Buns and topless taking a shower after posing for Augustine.
- •• 0:56 - Left breast, under a tree with James.
- 1:16 - Topless in the woods seducing Rupert.

Emmanuelle *(1974)*

Sylvia Kristel . . . . .Emmanuelle
- 0:11 - Topless making love with her husband under a mosquito net in bed.
- ••• 0:26 - Topless making love with a stranger on an airplane.
- •• 0:35 - Topless with blonde woman in squash court after playing squash.
- ••• 1:03 - Topless after taking off clothes in locker room with another woman to get ready for squash.

Emmanuelle IV *(1984)*

Sophie Berger . . . . .Maria
- •• 0:46 - Full frontal nudity putting on robe.
-     0:49 - Buns, taking off robe in front of Mia Nygren.

Sylvia Kristel . . . . Sylvia
- •• 0:00 - Topless in photos during opening credits.

Mia Nygren . . . . .Emmanuelle IV
-     0:13 - Buns, lying on table after plastic surgery.
- ••• 0:15 - Full frontal nudity walking around looking at her new self in the mirror.
- 0:20 - Brief topless a couple of times making love on top of a guy getting coached by Sylvia Kristel in dream-like sequence.
- •• 0:22 - Full frontal nudity taking off blouse in front of Dona.
-     0:25 - Almost making love with a guy in bar.
- ••• 0:30 - Nude undressing in front of Maria.
- •• 0:39 - Full frontal nudity taking her dress off and getting covered with a white sheet.
- ••• 0:40 - Full frontal nudity lying down and then putting dress back on.
- •• 0:45 - Full frontal nudity during levitation trick.
-     0:49 - Right bra cup reclining on bed.
- 0:52 - Brief topless in stable.
- ••• 0:54 - Topless taking off black dress in chair. Brief lower frontal nudity.
-     0:57 - Brief lower frontal nudity putting on white panties.
- 1:00 - Brief topless when Susanna takes her dress off.
- 1:03 - Brief right breast making love on ground with a boy.
- ••• 1:07 - Topless walking on beach.
- 1:09 - Topless with Dona. Dark.

Deborah Power . . . . .Maria
-     1:09 - Buns, lying down getting a massage from Mia Nygren.

Emmanuelle, The Joys of a Woman (1975)

Laura Gemser . . . . Massage Woman
Sylvia Kristel . . . . Emmanuelle
- • 0:18 - Topless making love with her husband in bedroom.
- •• 0:22 - Topless, then full frontal nudity, undressing in bedroom, then making love with her husband.
- ••• 0:32 - Topless with acupuncture needles stuck in her. More topless masturbating while fantasizing about Christopher.
- • 0:53 - Right breast, while making love with polo player in locker room.
- ••• 0:58 - Nude, getting massaged by another woman.
- ••• 1:14 - Right breast in bedroom in open dress, then topless with Jean in bed. Flashback of her with three guys in a bordello.

Endgame (1983)

Laura Gemser . . . . Lilith
- • 1:10 - Brief topless a couple of times getting blouse ripped open by a gross looking guy.

Endless Love (1981)

Tom Cruise . . . . Billy
Martin Hewitt . . . . David
- • 0:22 - Buns when seen in front of fireplace in living room with Brooke Shields. Long shot.
- • 0:27 - Very brief buns in bedroom when Shields closes the door. Another long shot.
- •• 0:28 - Buns, jumping into bed with Shields.
- • 0:38 - Buns, lying on top of Shields in bed.
Penelope Milford. . . . . Ingrid
Brooke Shields. . . . . Jade
0:37 - Body double, side view of right breast in bed with David.
1:08 - Body double very brief left breast, in bed with another guy during David's dream.

Endless Night (1977)

Britt Ekland . . . . Greta
- • 1:21 - Brief topless several times with Michael.
Hayley Mills. . . . . .Ellie

Enemies, A Love Story (1989)

Anjelica Huston. . . . . .Tamara
Lena Olin . . . . Masha
- •• 0:16 - In white bra, then brief topless several times in bed with Ron Silver. Topless again after making love and starting to make love again.

Enrapture (1989)

Deborah Blaisdell . . . . Martha
- ••• 0:10 - Topless undressing in her apartment with Keith.
- •• 0:17 - Left breast, in bed with Keith, then brief topless.
Jane Hamilton. . . . . Annie
Ona Simms Wiegers . . . . .Chase Webb
- •• 0:13 - In red bra, panties, garter belt and stockings. Buns in G-string, then topless undressing when she doesn't know Keith is watching.

- •• 0:17 - Topless when Keith fantasizes about her while he's making love with Martha.
- •• 0:21 - Topless in back of limousine with a lucky guy.
- ••• 1:08 - Full frontal nudity making love on top of Keith in bed.
Kevin Thomsen . . . . Keith

Enter the Dragon (1973)

Ahna Capri. . . . . .Tania
- • 0:47 - Very brief left breast three times in open blouse in bed with John Saxon.

The Entity (1983)

Barbara Hershey. . . . . Carla Moran
- • 0:33 - Topless and buns getting undressed before taking a bath. Don't see her face.
0:59 - "Topless" during special effect when The Entity fondles her breasts with invisible fingers while she sleeps.
- • 1:32 - "Topless" again getting raped by The Entity while Alex Rocco watches helplessly.

Entre Nous (1983; French)

a.k.a. Coup de Foudre
Miou-Miou. . . . . Madeleine
Isabelle Huppert. . . . . Helen Webber
- • 1:01 - Brief topless in shower room talking about her breasts with Miou-Miou.
Guy Marchand. . . . . Michel

Equus (1977)

Jenny Agutter. . . . . .Jill Mason
- ••• 2:00 - Nude in loft above the horses in orange light, then making love with Alan.
Peter Firth . . . . Alan Strang
- • 1:19 - Frontal nudity standing in a field with a horse.
- ••• 2:00 - Nude in loft above the horses in orange light with Jenny Agutter. Long scene.

Erendira (1983; Brazilian)

Blanca Guerra . . . . Ulysses' Mother
Claudia Ohana. . . . . Erendira
- • 0:14 - Topless getting fondled by a guy against her will.
- •• 0:26 - Topless lying in bed sweating and crying after having to have sex with an army of men.
- ••• 1:04 - Topless lying in bed sleeping.
1:08 - Brief topless getting out of bed. Long shot, hard to see.
- •• 1:24 - Topless and buns on bed with Ulysses.
Oliver Wehe. . . . . .Ulysses
- • 1:24 - Buns, getting into bed with Erendira.

Erotic Images (1983)

Alexandra Day . . . . Logan's Girlfriend
- •• 0:37 - Topless getting out of bed while Logan talks on the phone to Britt Ekland.
Britt Ekland . . . . Julie Todd
- • 0:16 - Brief side view of left breast in bed with Glenn.
- ••• 0:29 - In bra, then topless in bed with Glenn.
0:33 - In bra, in open robe looking in the mirror.
1:27 - In black bra, talking to Sonny.

Alexandra Morgan . . . . Emily Stewart
•• 0:57 - In black lingerie, then topless on the living room floor with Glenn.
• 1:05 - Topless in bed, making love with Glenn.
••• 1:12 - Topless in the kitchen with Glenn.
•• 1:21 - Right breast, on couch with Glenn.
Remy O'Neill .Vickie Coleman
••• 0:04 - Topless sitting in chaise lounge talking to Britt Ekland about sex survey. Long scene.
• 0:06 - Topless in bed with Marvin. Brief lower frontal nudity.
•• 0:07 - Brief left breast in spa with TV repairman, then brief topless.
Julie Parton . . . . Marvin's Nurse
0:08 - Brief topless in office with Marvin. Dark, hard to see.
Barbara Peckinpaugh. . . . . Cheerleader
• 0:07 - Topless dancing in an office with another cheerleader.

Eternity (1989)
Eileen Davidson. . . . . .Dahlia/Valerie
0:33 - In black bra and panties in dressing room. Brief buns standing in bathtub during Jon Voight's flashback.
• 0:52 - Brief left breast, then topless, in bed with Voight. Don't see face.

Eureka (1983; British)
Rutger Hauer. . . . . Claude Maillot Van Horn
Emma Relph . . . . Mary (blue dress)
• 1:17 - Brief topless during African voodoo ceremony.
Theresa Russell . . . . Tracy
0:38 - In lingerie talking to Rutger Hauer.
• 0:40 - Right breast, lying in bed with Hauer.
• 1:04 - Very brief left breast in bed with Hauer, then brief lower frontal nudity and brief buns when Gene Hackman bursts into the room.
•• 1:09 - Topless on a boat with Hauer.
• 1:41 - Left breast peeking out from under black top while lying in bed.
••• 1:59 - Full frontal nudity kicking off sheets in the bed.

An Evening with Kitten (1983)
Francesca "Kitten" Natividad. . . . . herself
•• 0:02 - Topless busting out of her blouse.
•• 0:09 - Topless in miniature city scene.
• 0:11 - Brief topless on stage.
• 0:20 - Left breast, in bed with a vampire.
••• 0:21 - Topless and buns in G-string during dance in large champagne glass prop. Long scene.
••• 0:24 - Topless on beach in mermaid costume with little shell pasties.
••• 0:25 - Topless in the glass again.
•• 0:28 - Topless in and out of glass.
•• 0:29 - Brief topless during end credits.

Every Time We Say Goodbye (1986)
Cristina Marsillach. . . . . Sarah
••1:09 - Right breast, then brief topless lying in bed with Tom Hanks.

Everybody's All-American (1988)
Timothy Hutton . . . . Donnie
Jessica Lange . . . . Babs
0:32 - Brief topless in sheer nightgown in bedroom with Dennis Quaid.
• 0:54 - Buns and very, very brief side view of left breast by the campfire by the lake with Timothy Hutton at night. Might be a body double.
Dennis Quaid. . . . . .Gavin

Evil Spawn (1987)
Bobbie Bresee . . . . Lynn Roman
0:14 - Very brief half of right breast in bed with a guy.
0:26 - In red one piece swimsuit.
••• 0:36 - Topless in bathroom looking at herself in the mirror, then taking a shower.
Pamela Gilbert . . . . Elaine Talbot
••• 0:46 - Nude taking off black lingerie and going swimming in pool. Hubba, hubba!
••• 0:49 - Topless in the pool, then full frontal nudity getting out.
Dawn Wildsmith . . . . Evelyn

Evil Town (1987)
Lynda Wiesmeier . . . . Dianne
••• 0:09 - Topless on top of Tony outside while camping.
•• 0:11 - Right breast while making out with boyfriend outside. Topless getting up.
• 0:13 - Topless in open blouse running from bad guy. Nice bouncing action.
•• 0:15 - Topless getting captured by bad guys.
•• 0:17 - Topless getting out of car and brought into the house.
•• 0:23 - Topless tied up in chair.

Excalibur (1981; British)
Katrine Boorman . . . . Igrayne
• 0:14 - Right breast, then topless in front of the fire when Uther tricks her into thinking that he is her husband and makes love to her.
Gabriel Byrne. . . . . .Uther
Nicholas Clay . . . . .Lancelot
•• 1:13 - Buns, fighting with himself in a suit of armor.
• 1:31 - Brief buns, running into the woods after waking up. Long shot, hard to see.
Cherie Lunghi . . . . .Guenevere
• 1:25 - Brief topless in the forest kissing Lancelot.
Helen Mirren . . . . Morgana
• 1:31 - Side view of left breast under a fishnet outfit climbing into bed.
Liam Neeson . . . . Gawain
Nigel Terry. . . . . King Arthur

The Executioner's Song (1982)
(European Version.)
Rosanna Arquette. . . . . Nicole Baker
••• 0:30 - Brief topless in bed, then getting out of bed. Buns, walking to kitchen.
••• 0:41 - Topless in bed with Tommy Lee Jones.
••• 0:48 - Topless on top of Jones making love.

•• 1:36 - Right breast and buns, standing up getting strip searched before visiting Jones in prison.
Tommy Lee Jones . . . . Gary Gillmore
•• 0:48 - Buns, walking to kitchen after hitting Rosanna Arquette.

Exposed (1983)
Iman . . . . .Model
Bibi Andersson . . . . Margaret
Pierre Clementi Vic
Janice Dickinson . . . . .Model
Harvey Keitel. . . . . .Rivas
Nastassja Kinski . . . . Elizabeth Carlson
•• 0:54 - Topless in bed with Rudolf Nureyev.
Rudolf Nureyev .Daniel Jelline
••• 0:54 - Buns, in bed with Nastassja Kinski.

Extreme Prejudice (1987)
Maria Conchita Alonso . . . . Sarita Cisneros
•• 0:27 - Brief topless in the shower while Nick Nolte is in the bathroom talking to her.
Clancy Brown . . . . .Sgt. Larry McRose
Rip Torn .Sheriff Hank Pearson

Extremities (1986)
Farrah Fawcett . . . . Marjorie
• 0:37 - Brief side view of right breast when Joe pulls down her top in the kitchen. Can't see her face, but reportedly her.

Eye of the Needle (1981)
Christopher Cazenove. David
Kate Nelligan . . . . Lucy
•• 0:52 - Brief left breast, while drying herself off in the bathroom when Donald Sutherland accidentally sees her.
1:15 - Top half of buns, making love in bed with Sutherland.
• 1:26 - Topless making love in bed with Sutherland after he killed her husband. Dark, hard to see.
Donald Sutherland . . . . Faber

Eyes of a Stranger (1981)
Jennifer Jason Leigh . . . . Tracy
• 1:15 - Very brief topless lying in bed getting attacked by rapist.
•• 1:19 - Left breast, cleaning herself in bathroom.

Eyes of Fire (1983)
Karlene Crockett . . . . Leah
• 0:44 - Brief topless sitting up in the water and scaring Mr. Dalton.
• 1:16 - Topless talking to Dalton who is trapped in a tree. Brief topless again when he pulls the creature out of the tree.

The Fabulous Baker Boys (1989)
Jeff Bridges . . . . Jack Baker
Michelle Pfeiffer . . . . Susie Diamond
Terri Treas. . . . . Girl in Bed
• 0:00 - Brief upper half of right breast when sheet falls down when she leans over in bed.

Fade to Black (1980)
Linda Kerridge . . . . Marilyn
• 0:44 - Topless in the shower.

Fairytales (1979)
Angela Aames . . . . Little Bo Peep
••• 0:14 - Nude with The Prince in the woods.
Nai Bonet. . . . . Sheherazade
• 0:29 - Buns and very brief left breast doing a belly dance and rubbing oil on herself.
Lindsay Freeman . . . . Jill
•• 0:24 - Nude on hill with Jack.
Anne Gaybis. . . . . .Snow White
••• 0:21 - Nude in room with the seven little dwarfs singing and dancing.
Evelyn Guerrero . . . . S & M Dancer
•• 0:38 - Topless wearing masks with two other blonde S&M Dancers.
•• 0:56 - Full frontal nudity dancing with the other S&M Dancers again.
Linnea Quigley. . . . . .Dream Girl
•• 1:07 - Topless waking up after being kissed by The Prince.
Mariwin Roberts. . . . . Elevator Operator
• 0:20 - Brief full frontal nudity in the elevator.
•• 0:23 - Topless again, closer shot.

Fame (1980)
Irene Cara . . . . Coco
1:16 - In leotard, dancing and talking to Hillary.
• 1:57 - Brief topless during "audition" on a B&W TV monitor.
Meg Tilly . . . . Principal Dancer

Family Viewing (1987; Canadian)
Gabrielle Rose . . . . .Sandra
• 0:27 - Brief left breast, lying down with Stan. Seen on TV that Van watches.
• 0:29 - Same 0:27 scene again.
Aidan Tierney. . . . . Van
•• 0:26 - Brief buns, getting up out of bed and putting on his underwear.

Famous T & A (1982)
(No longer available for purchase, check your video store for rental.)
Elvira . . . . .Katya
••• 0:28 - Topless scene from *Working Girls*.
Vanity . . . . Tanya
• 1:02 - Topless scenes from *Tanya's Island*.
Angela Aames . . . . Little Bo Peep
•• 0:50 - Topless scene from *Fairytales*.
Ursula Andress . . . . herself
••• 0:15 - Full frontal nudity scenes from *Slave of the Cannibal God*.
Brigitte Bardot . . . . .Joan
• 0:25 - Buns, then brief topless in scene from *Ms. Don Juan*.
Jacqueline Bisset. . . . . .Jenny
••• 0:31 - Topless scene from *Secrets*.

Phyllis Davis . . . . Joy/Sugar
••• 0:02 - Nude in lots of great out-takes from *Terminal Island*. Check this out if you are a Phyllis Davis fan!
••• 0:51 - Topless in scenes from *Sweet Sugar*. Includes more out-takes.
••• 1:04 - More out-takes from *Sweet Sugar*.
Uschi Digard . . . . Truck Stop Woman
•• 0:44 - Topless scenes from *Harry, Cherry & Raquel* and *Truck Stop Women*.
Laura Gemser . . . . Emanuelle
••• 0:55 - Topless scenes from *Emanuelle Around the World*.
Claudia Jennings . . . . Rose
•• 0:26 - Topless scenes from *Single Girls* and *Truck Stop Women*.
Barbara Leigh . . . . Bunny Campbell
••• 0:45 - Topless scene from *Terminal Island*. Includes additional takes that weren't used.
Ornella Muti . . . . Lisa
• 0:07 - Brief topless in scenes from *Summer Affair*.
Joan Prather . . . . herself
• 0:49 - Brief topless in scene from *Single Girls*.
Victoria Thompson . . . . Beth Hillyer
• 1:07 - Brief topless scene from *The Harrad Experiment*.
Laurie Walters . . . . Sheila Grove
• 1:08 - Topless scene from *The Harrad Experiment*.
• 1:11 - Full frontal nude scene from *The Harrad Experiment*.
Edy Williams . . . . herself
•• 0:39 - Topless scenes from *Dr. Minx*.

The Fanatasist (1986; Irish)

Moira Harris . . . . Patricia Teeling
• 1:24 - Brief topless and buns climbing onto couch for the weird photographer.
• 1:28 - Brief right breast leaning over to kiss the photographer.
• 1:31 - Very brief side view of left breast in bathtub.
Gabrielle Reidy . . . . Kathy O'Malley
• 0:03 - Topless getting attacked in a room.

Fanny Hill (1981; British)

Lisa Raines Foster . . . . Fanny Hill
•• 0:09 - Nude, getting into bathtub, then drying herself off.
• 0:10 - Full frontal nudity getting into bed.
••• 0:12 - Full frontal nudity making love with Phoebe in bed.
••• 0:30 - Nude, making love in bed with Charles.
•• 0:49 - Topless, whipping her lover, Mr. H., in bed.
•• 0:53 - Nude getting into bed with William while Hannah watches through the keyhole.
••• 1:26 - Nude, getting out of bed, then running down the stairs to open the door for Charles.

Fantasies (1974)

a.k.a. *Once Upon a Love*
Bo Derek . . . . Anastasia
• 0:03 - Left breast, in bathtub.
•• 0:15 - Topless taking off top, then right breast, in bathtub.
• 0:43 - Topless getting her dress top pulled down.
• 0:59 - Brief topless in the water. Very brief full frontal nudity walking back into the house.
• 1:00 - Buns and left breast several times outside the window.
• 1:17 - Upper left breast, in bathtub again.
Peter Hooten . . . . Damir
• 1:06 - Buns, dropping his towel in front of Bo Derek. Long shot, don't see his face.
• 1:18 - Buns again. Same shot from 1:06.

Far From Home (1989)

Susan Tyrrell . . . . Agnes Reed
• 0:29 - Very, very brief right breast in bathtub getting electrocuted.
Teri Weigel . . . . Woman in Trailer
•• 0:16 - Topless making love when Drew Barrymore peeks in window.

Farewell, My Lovely (1975; British)

Charlotte Rampling . . . . Velma
Cheryl Smith . . . . Doris
• 0:56 - Frontal nudity in bedroom in a bordello with another guy before getting beaten by the madam.
Sylvester Stallone . . . . Kelly/Jonnie

Fast Times at Ridgemont High (1982)

Phoebe Cates . . . . Linda Barrett
••• 0:50 - Topless getting out of swimming pool during Judge Reinhold's fantasy.
Lana Clarkson . . . . Mrs. Vargas
Anthony Edwards . . . . Stoner Bud
Jennifer Jason Leigh . . . . Stacy Hamilton
• 0:18 - Left breast, making out with Ron in a dugout.
••• 1:00 - Topless in poolside dressing room.
Tom Nolan . . . . Dennis Taylor
Sean Penn . . . . Jeff Spicoli
Judge Reinhold . . . . Brad Hamilton
Eric Stoltz . . . . Stoner Bud
Lori Sutton . . . . Playmate
Amanda Wyss . . . . Lisa

Fast Walking (1981)

Kay Lenz . . . . Moke
• 0:26 - Brief topless closing the door after pulling James Woods into the room.
0:42 - Caressing herself under her dress while in prison visiting room, talking to George.
••• 1:27 - Topless getting hosed down and dried off outside by James Woods.
• 1:32 - Brief left breast, making love with Woods.
Susan Tyrrell . . . . Evie

M. Emmet Walsh. . . . . Sgt. George Sager
- 0:59 - Frontal nudity standing in the doorway of Evie's mobile home yelling at James Woods after he interrupts Walsh making love with Evie.

James Woods . . . . Fast-Walking Miniver

Fatal Attraction *(1987)*
Anne Archer . . . . Ellen Gallagher
- 0:51 - In white bra, sitting in front of mirror, getting ready for a party.

Glenn Close . . . . .Alex Forrest
- •• 0:17 - Left breast when she opens her top to let Michael Douglas kiss her. Then very brief buns, falling into bed with him.
- • 0:20 - Brief right breast in freight elevator with Douglas.
- ••• 0:32 - Topless in bed talking to Douglas. Long scene, sheet keeps changing positions between cuts.

Michael Douglas . . . . Dan Gallagher
- •• 0:16 - Brief buns pulling his pants down to make love with Glenn Close on the kitchen sink.
- • 0:17 - Very brief buns falling into bed with Close.
- • 0:22 - Brief buns, taking a shower.

Fatal Attraction *(1981; Canadian)*
a.k.a. Head On
Sally Kellerman . . . . Michelle Keys
- • 0:46 - Brief topless in building making out with a guy. Dark, hard to see.
1:19 - Brief half of left breast, after struggling with a guy.

Fatal Games *(1984)*
Angela Bennett . . . . Sue Allen Baines
- •• 0:21 - Full frontal nudity in the sauna with Teal Roberts.
- • 0:23 - Nude, running around the school, trying to get away from the killer. Dark.

Sally Kirkland. . . . . Diane Paine
Melissa Prophet. . . . . Nancy Wilson
- • 0:14 - Buns and side view of left breast in shower with other girls. Long shot. (she's wearing a white towel on her head.)

Linnea Quigley . . . . Athelete
Teal Roberts . . . . .Lynn Fox
- ••• 0:08 - Topless on bed and floor when Frank takes her clothes off, more topless in shower.
- •• 0:21 - Topless in sauna with Sue.

Fatal Mission *(1990)*
Tia Carrere . . . . Mai Chang
- • 0:22 - Side view of right breast while changing tops. Dark.

Fear City *(1984)*
Maria Conchita Alonso . . . . Silver Chavez
Tom Berenger. .Matt Rossi
Rae Dawn Chong . . . . Leila
- ••• 0:26 - Topless and buns, dancing on stage.
- • 0:50 - Brief topless in the hospital getting a shock to get her heart started.

Melanie Griffith . . . . .Loretta
- 0:04 - Buns, in blue G-string, dancing on stage.
- •• 0:07 - Topless, dancing on stage.
- ••• 0:23 - Topless dancing on stage wearing a red G-string.

Tracy Griffith . . . . Sandra Cook
Janet Julian. . . . . Ruby
Emilia Lesniak. . . . . Bibi
- •• 0:16 - Topless, dancing at the Metropole club.
- •• 1:00 - Topless, dancing on the stage.

Ola Ray . . . . Honey Powers

Fearless *(1978)*
Joan Collins . . . . Bridgitte
- • 0:01 - In bra and panties, then brief right breast during opening credits.
- •• 0:41 - Topless after doing a strip tease routine on stage.
- • 1:17 - Undressing in front of Wally in white bra and panties, then right breast.
- • 1:20 - Brief right breast lying dead on couch.

The Fearless Vampire Killers *(1967)*
Fiona Lewis . . . . Maid
Sharon Tate . . . . Sarah Shagal
- • 0:24 - Very, very brief topless struggling in bathtub with vampire. Hard to see.

Felicity *(1978; Australian)*
Glory Annen. . . . . .Felicity
- •• 0:02 - Topless taking off leotard in girl's shower room, then nude taking a shower.
- • 0:05 - Buns, then left breast, then right breast undressing to go skinny dipping.
- •• 0:10 - Topless and buns at night at the girl's dormitory.
- •• 0:15 - Topless undressing in room with Christine.
- • 0:16 - Left breast, while touching herself in bed.
- ••• 0:20 - Lots of lower frontal nudity trying on clothes, bras and panties in dressing room. Brief topless.
- ••• 0:25 - Buns and topless taking a bath. Full frontal nudity when Steve peeks in at her.
- • 0:31 - Brief full frontal nudity losing her virginity on car with Andrew.
- ••• 0:38 - Full frontal nudity in bath with Mei Ling and two other girls. Long scene. Hot!
- ••• 0:58 - Full frontal nudity in bed with Miles.
- ••• 1:13 - Full frontal nudity with Mei Ling making love on bed. Long scene.
- • 1:20 - Left breast, while making love standing up.
- •• 1:21 - Topless and buns making love with Miles.
- •• 1:27 - Nude making love again with Miles.
1:29 - Buns, in the water with Miles.

Fellow Traveller *(1989; Made for Cable Movie)*
Imogen Stubbs. . . . . Sarah Aitchison
- • 0:54 - Topless in bed with Asa. Very, very brief right breast when he rolls off her.

Femme Fatale (1990)

Lisa Blount . . . . Jenny
Suzanne Snyder . . . . Andrea
- ••• 0:08 - Topless, nonchalantly taking off her top and posing for Billy Zane's painting. (She sometimes has a bag over her head.)
- •• 0:46 - Topless posing again with the bag on and off her head.

Billy Zane . . . . Elijah Hooper
Lisa Zane. . . . . .Cynthia

Fever (1991; Made for Cable Movie)

Marcia Gay Harden . . . . Lacy
- • 0:18 - Brief topless making love in bed with Sam Neill.
- •• 1:31 - In bra in bed with bad guy, then topless when he opens her bra. Kind of dark.

Joe Spano . . . . .Junkman

Fever Pitch (1985)

Catherine Hicks. . . . . Flo
- • 0:11 - Brief left breast, while sitting on bed in hotel room talking with Ryan O'Neal.

Cherie Michan . . . . Rose O'Sharon
Ryan O'Neal . . . . .Taggart

The Fifth Floor (1978)

Patti D'Arbanville . . . . Cathy Burke
Dianne Hull. . . . . Kelly McIntyre
- •• 0:29 - Topless and buns in shower while Carl watches, then brief full frontal nudity running out of the shower.
- •• 1:09 - Topless in whirlpool bath getting visited by Carl again, then raped.

The Final Alliance (1990)

David Hasselhoff . . . . Will Colton
Jeanie Moore. . . . . Carrie
- • 1:03 - Brief topless getting into bed with David Hasselhoff, then brief right breast twice in bed with him. A little dark.

Fiona (1978; British)

Fiona Richmond . . . . Fiona Richmond
- •• 0:23 - Topless on boat with a blonde woman rubbing oil on her.
- •• 0:27 - In a bra, then frontal nudity stripping in a guy's office for an audition.
- •• 0:35 - Topless, then frontal nudity lying down during photo session.
- • 0:51 - Topless walking around her apartment.
- •• 1:00 - Topless with old guy ripping each other's clothes off.
- •• 1:08 - Frontal nudity taking off clothes for a shower.

Fire Birds (1990)

a.k.a. Wings of the Apache
Nicholas Cage. . . . . Jake Preston
Tommy Lee Jones . . . . Brad Little
Sean Young. .Billie Lee Guthrie
- • 0:52 - Very, very brief right breast twice in bed with Nicholas Cage.

Firehouse (1987)

Ruth Corrine Collins. Bubbles
Gianna Rains . . . . Barrett Hopkins
- ••• 0:33 - Topless taking a shower, then drying herself just before the fire alarm goes off.
- •• 0:56 - Topless making love with the reporter on the roof of a building.

First Love (1977)

Beverly D'Angelo . . . . .Shelley
0:05 - Very, very brief half of left breast when her jacket opens up while talking to William Katt.
0:11 - In white bra and black panties in Katt's bedroom.
- • 1:10 - Brief topless taking off her top in bedroom with Katt.

Susan Dey . . . . Caroline Hedges
- ••• 0:31 - Topless making love in bed with William Katt. Long scene.
- • 0:51 - Topless taking off her top in her bedroom with Katt.

John Heard. . . . . .David
William Katt . . . . Elgin Smith

The First Nudie Musical (1979)

Leslie Ackerman . . . . Susie
Alexandra Morgan . . . . Mary La Rue
- • 0:54 - Topless, singing and dancing during dancing dildo routine.
- ••• 1:04 - Full frontal nudity in bed trying to do a take.
1:07 - Topless in bed with a guy with a continuous erection.
- •• 1:17 - Topless in bed in another scene.

The First Turn-On! (1983)

Georgia Harrell. . . . . .Michelle Farmer
- ••• 1:17 - Topless and brief buns in cave with everybody during orgy scene.

Sheila Kennedy. . . . . Dreamgirl
- • 0:52 - In red two piece swimsuit, then topless when the top falls down during Danny's daydream.
- • 0:59 - Right breast in bed with Danny.

Michael Sanville . . . . Mitch
- • 1:18 - Buns, in cave orgy scene on top of Annie.

Mark Torgl. . . . . .Dwayne
1:02 - Buns, dropping his pants for Michelle.

Five Easy Pieces (1970)

Susan Anspach. . . . . Catherine Van Oost
Karen Black . . . . Rayette Dipesto
0:48 - In sheer black nightie in bathroom, then walking to bedroom with Jack Nicholson.
Helena Kallianiotes. . . . . Palm Apodaca
Jack Nicholson . . . . Robert Dupea
Sally Struthers . . . . Betty
0:15 - In a bra sitting on a couch in the living room with Jack Nicholson and another man and a woman.
- • 0:33 - Brief topless a couple of times making love with Nicholson. Lots of great moaning, but hard to see anything.

A Flash of Green (1984)
Blair Brown . . . . Catherine "Kat" Hubble
- • 1:30 - Very brief right breast moving around in bed with Ed Harris.

Joan Goodfellow . . . . Mitchie
Ed Harris . . . . Jimmy Wing

Flashdance (1983)
Belinda Bauer . . . . Katie Hurley
Jennifer Beals . . . . Alex
Marine Jahan
. . . . uncredited Dance Double for Jennifer Beals
Sunny Johnson . . . . Jennie Szabo
- • 1:28 - Topless on stage with other strippers.

Dirga McBroom . . . . Heels
Michael Nouri . . . . Nick Hurley

Flashpoint (1984)
Kris Kristofferson . . . . Logan
Rip Torn . . . . Sheriff Wells
Treat Williams . . . . Ernie
- •• 0:03 - Buns, putting on pants in locker room while talking to Kris Kristofferson.

Flesh + Blood (1985)
Nancy Cartwright . . . . Kathleen
- • 0:28 - Brief topless showing Jennifer Jason Leigh how to make love. Long shot.

Rutger Hauer . . . . Martin
- • 1:35 - Buns, in a jock strap running up stairs after everybody throws their clothes into the fire.

Jennifer Jason Leigh . . . . Agnes
- • 0:45 - Brief right breast being held down.
- •• 1:05 - Full frontal nudity getting into the bath with Rutger Hauer and making love.
- ••• 1:16 - Full frontal nudity getting out of bed with Hauer and walking to the window.
- •• 1:35 - Nude throwing clothes into the fire.

Blanca Marsillach . . . . Clara
- •• 0:11 - Full frontal nudity on bed having convulsions after getting hit on the head with a sword.

Marina Saura . . . . Polly
- • 0:59 - Brief left breast during feast in the castle.
- • 1:09 - Topless on balcony of the castle with everybody during the day.

Jack Thompson . . . . Hawkwood
Susan Tyrrell . . . . Celine
- • 1:35 - Right breast sticking out of her dress when everybody throws their clothes into the fire.

The Fly (1986)
Joy Boushel . . . . Tawny
- • 0:54 - Very brief topless viewed from below when Jeff Goldblum pulls her by the arm to get her out of bed.

Geena Davis . . . . Veronica Quaife
0:40 - Brief almost side view of left breast getting out of bed.

Jeff Goldblum . . . . Seth Brundle

Forbidden World (1982)
Michael Bowen . . . . Jimmy Swift
June Chadwick . . . . Dr. Barbara Glaser
- •• 0:29 - Topless in bed making love with Jesse Vint.
- •• 0:54 - Topless taking a shower with Dawn Dunlap.

Dawn Dunlap . . . . Tracy Baxter
- • 0:27 - Brief topless getting ready for bed.
- ••• 0:37 - Nude in steam bath.
- • 0:54 - Topless in shower with June Chadwick.

Forbidden Zone (1980; B&W)
Gisele Lindley . . . . The Princess
- ••• 0:21 - Topless in jail cell.
- ••• 0:39 - Topless turning a table around.
- ••• 0:45 - Topless bending over, making love with a frog.
- •• 0:51 - Topless in a cave.
- •• 0:53 - More topless scenes.
- •• 1:06 - Even more topless scenes.

Susan Tyrrell . . . . Queen Doris
- •• 0:19 - Left breast sticking out of dress, sitting on big dice with Herve Villechaize.
- •• 1:02 - Left breast sticking out of dress after fighting with the Ex-Queen.

Force Ten from Navarone (1978)
Barbara Bach . . . . Maritza
- • 0:32 - Brief topless taking a bath in the German officer's room.

Forced Entry (1975)
Nancy Allen . . . . Hitchhiker
- • 0:44 - Topless and buns tied up by Carl on the beach.

Tanya Roberts . . . . Nancy Ulman
0:57 - In white bra and panties walking around the house.

Foreign Body (1986; British)
Amanda Donohoe . . . . Susan
0:37 - Undressing in her bedroom down to lingerie. Very brief side view of right breast, then brief left breast putting blouse on.
- •• 0:40 - Topless opening her blouse for Ram.

Anna Massey . . . . Miss Furze
Sinitta Renet . . . . Lovely Indian Girl
- • 0:06 - Buns, then topless in bedroom.

Forever Lulu (1987)
Deborah Harry . . . . Lulu
Hanna Schygulla . . . . Elaine
- • 1:03 - Brief topless in and getting out of bubble bath.

The Forgotten One (1989)
Elizabeth Brooks . . . . Carla
Kristy McNichol . . . . Barbara Stupple
0:06 - Jogging in braless pink top, then talking to Terry O'Quinn.
1:33 - In pink top lying in bed.

Terry O'Quinn . . . .
- • 1:11 - Brief buns turning over in bed with Evelyn.

Fort Apache, The Bronx (1981)
Kathleen Beller . . . . .Theresa
Pam Grier . . . . Charlotte
Rachel Ticotin . . . . Isabelle
- 1:25 - Brief upper half of breasts in bathtub while Paul Newman pours bubble bath in.

Fortress (1985; Made for Cable Movie)
Rachel Ward . . . . Sally Jones
- 0:38 - Swimming in a sheer bra underwater.

Four Friends (1981)
Jodi Thelen . . . . Georgia
- •• 0:17 - Left breast in open blouse three times with her three male friends.
0:58 - In pink bra taking off her blouse.
Craig Wasson . . . . Danilo Prozor

Four Seasons (1981)
Bess Armstrong .Ginny Newley
0:26 - In two piece swimsuit on boat putting lotion on herself.
- 0:38 - Brief buns twice skinny dipping in the water with Nick.
0:40 - In one piece swimsuit.
Jack Weston . . . . Danny Zimmer
- 0:48 - Brief buns in water while skinny dipping with Rita Moreno.

The Fourth Man (1984; Dutch)
Thom Hoffman . . . . Herman
- 1:00 - Frontal nudity on cross when Gerard pulls his red trunks down. Long shot.
- •• 1:10 - Nude in bathroom when Gerard comes in.
- ••• 1:11 - Buns making love on bed with Christine while Gerard watches through keyhole.
Jeroen Krabbé . . . . Gerard
- ••• 0:03 - Frontal nudity getting out of bed and walking down the stairs.
- •• 0:26 - Frontal nudity drying himself off and getting into bed.
- 0:33 - Buns, getting out of bed.
Reneé Soutendijk. . . . . .Christine
- ••• 0:27 - Full frontal nudity removing robe, brief buns in bed, side view left breast, then topless in bed with Gerard.
- 0:32 - Brief left breast in bed with Gerard after he hallucinates and she cuts his penis off.
- ••• 0:53 - Left breast, then right breast in red dress when Gerard opens her dress.
- 1:11 - Topless making love with Herman while Gerard watches through keyhole.

The Fourth Protocol (1987; British)
Pierce Brosnan . . . . .Petrofsky
Joanna Cassidy . . . . Vassilieva
- 1:39 - Brief left breast. She's lying dead in Pierce Brosnan's bathtub.
- 1:49 - Same thing, different angle.

Foxtrap (1986)
Beatrice Palme . . . . .Marianna
- •• 0:41 - Brief breasts and buns in bed with Fred Williamson, then more breasts making love.

Frances (1982)
Anjelica Huston . . . . .Hospital Sequence: Mental Patient
Jessica Lange . . . . Frances Farmer
- 0:41 - Very brief upper half of left breast lying on bed and throwing a newspaper.
- 0:50 - Brief full frontal nudity covered with bubbles standing up in bathtub and wrapping a towel around herself. Long shot, hard to see.
- 1:01 - Brief buns and right breast running into the bathroom when the police bust in. Very, very brief full frontal nudity, then buns closing the bathroom door. Reportedly her, even though you don't see her face clearly.

Frank and I (1983)
Sophie Favier . . . . Maud
- 0:16 - Nude, undressing then topless lying in bed with Charles.
- 0:40 - Brief topless in bed with Charles.
Jennifer Inch. . . . . Frank/Frances
0:10 - Brief buns, getting pants pulled down for a spanking.
- ••• 0:22 - Nude getting undressed and walking to the bed.
- 0:24 - Brief nude when Charles pulls the sheets off her.
0:32 - Brief buns, getting spanked by two older women.
- ••• 0:38 - Full frontal nudity getting out of bed and walking to Charles at the piano.
- •• 0:45 - Full frontal nudity lying on her side by the fireplace. Dark, hard to see.
- •• 1:09 - Brief topless making love with Charles on the floor.
- ••• 1:11 - Nude taking off her clothes and walking toward Charles at the piano.

Frankenhooker (1990)
Vicki Darnell. . . . . .Sugar
- 0:36 - Brief middle part of each breast through slit bra during introduction to Jeffrey.
- •• 0:37 - Breasts, sticking out of black lingerie while getting legs measured.
- 0:38 - Right breast, while sitting in chair.
- 0:39 - Topless through slit lingerie three times while folding clothes.
0:40 - Buns, fighting over drugs.
- ••• 0:41 - Very brief right breast, sitting on bed (on the right) enjoying drugs. Topless dancing with the other girls.
Jennifer Delora. . . . . .Angel
- 0:36 - Brief topless during introduction to Jeffrey.
- ••• 0:41 - Topless dancing in room with the room with the other hookers. (Nice tattoos!)

Charlotte J. Helmcamp .Honey
•• 0:26 - Topless yanking down her top outside of Jeffrey's car window.
Heather Hunter . . . . Chartreuse
• 0:36 - Brief topless during introduction to Jeffrey.
• 0:37 - Brief topless bending over behind Sugar.
••• 0:41 - Brief topless and buns, running in front of bed.
A little blurry. Then topless and buns dancing with
the other girls.
• 0:43 - Topless dodging flying leg with Sugar.
•• 0:44 - Topless, crawling on the floor.
Patty Mullen . . . . .Elizabeth
•• 1:01 - Topless and buns in garter belt and stockings,
in room with a customer.
Susan Napoli . . . . Anise
• 0:42 - Brief left breast on bed with Amber, taking off
her top. Brief topless after Angel explodes.
• 0:43 - Topless, kneeling on bed screaming before ex-
ploding.
Kimberly Taylor . . . . Amber
• 0:36 - Brief left breast in green top during introduction to Jeffrey.
•• 0:37 - Brief topless during exam by Jeffrey. Then topless getting breasts measured with calipers.
• 0:41 - Brief right breast, twice, enjoying drugs.
•• 0:42 - Topless, getting off bed and onto another bed
with Anise.
• 0:43 - Topless kneeling in bed screaming before ex-
ploding.

Frankenstein General Hospital *(1988)*
Rebunkah Jones . . . . Elizabeth Rice
•• 1:05 - Topless in the office letting Mark Blankfield examine her back.
Kathy Shower . . . . Dr. Alice Singleton
0:35 - In white lingerie outfit pacing around in her
office.
• 1:15 - Brief topless running out of her office after the
monster, putting her lab coat on.

Frankenstein Unbound *(1990)*
Myriam Cyr .Information Officer
Bridget Fonda . . . . .Mary
John Hurt . . . . Buchanan
Raul Julia . . . . Victor Frankenstein
Jason Patric . . . . Lord Byron
Catherine Rabett . . . . .Elizabeth
1:10 - Very brief left breast lying dead after getting
shot by Frankenstein. Unappealing looking because
of all the gruesome makeup.
Terri Treas . . . . Computer Voice

Fraternity Vacation *(1985)*
Barbara Crampton . . . . .Chrissie
••• 0:16 - Topless and buns in bedroom with two guys
taking off her swimsuit.
Cameron Dye . . . . Joe Gillespie
Kathleen Kinmont . . . . Marianne
••• 0:16 - Topless and buns taking off her swimsuit in
bedroom with two guys.
Julie Payne . . . . Naomi Tvedt

Tim Robbins . . . . .Larry "Mother" Tucker
Sheree J. Wilson . . . . Ashley Taylor
0:43 - In white leotard at aerobics class.
• 0:47 - Topless and buns of her body double in the
bedroom (Roberta Whitewood) when the guys photograph her with a telephoto lens.
1:01 - In white leotard exercising in living room with
Leigh McCloskey.

Free Ride *(1986)*
Tally Chanel . . . . Candy
• 0:57 - Brief topless in bedroom with Dan.
Elizabeth Cochrell . . . . Nude Girl #1
• 0:25 - Brief buns taking a shower with another girl.
Rebecca Lynn . . . . Nude Girl #2
• 0:25 - Brief buns taking a shower with another girl.
Renee Props . . . . .Kathy
• 0:13 - Brief topless in the shower while Dan watches.
Mamie Van Doren . . . . .Debbie Stockwell

Freeway *(1988)*
Darlanne Fluegel . . . . Sarah "Sunny" Harper
• 0:27 - In bra in bathroom taking a pill, then very, very
brief right breast, getting into bed.
• 0:28 - Brief left breast putting on robe and getting
out of bed.

French Postcards *(1979)*
David Grant . . . . .Alex
Marie-France Pisier . . . . .Madame Tessier
•• 0:16 - In white bra, then topless in dressing room
while a guy watches without her knowing.
Valerie Quennessen . . . . .Toni
Debra Winger . . . . Melanie

French Quarter *(1978)*
Lindsay Bloom . . . "Big Butt" Annie/Policewoman in Bar
Susan Clark . . . . Bag Stealer/Sue
Alisha Fontaine
. . . . .Gertrude "Trudy" Dix/Christine Delaplane
• 0:12 - Dancing on stage for the first time. Buns in G-
string. Topless in large black pasties.
• 0:47 - Brief left breast several times, posing for Mr.
Beloq.
• 0:49 - Left breast again.
•• 1:13 - Topless during auction.
•• 1:18 - Brief topless, then buns making love with Tom,
then topless again.
• 1:26 - Brief topless getting her top pulled down.
• 1:31 - Brief topless getting tied down during voodoo
ceremony.
•• 1:32 - More topless tied down during ceremony.
Ann Michelle
. . . . . "Coke Eye" Laura/Policewoman in French Hotel
• 0:42 - Right breast, when Josie wakes her up.
••• 0:43 - Topless in bed, caressing Josie's breasts.
•• 0:58 - Topless during voodoo ceremony. Close ups of
breasts with snake.
• 1:19 - Brief topless, sitting in bed.
••• 1:20 - More topless sitting in bed, talking to a customer. Long scene.

Laura Misch Owens. . . . . "Ice Box" Josie/Girl on Bus
- 0:41 - Topless under sheer white nightgown.
••• 0:43 - Full frontal nudity taking off nightgown, wearing garter belt. Getting into bed with Laura.

The French Woman (1979)
a.k.a. Madame Claude
Dayle Haddon. .Elizabeth
- 0:15 - Very, very brief topless in dressing room.
•• 0:49 - Topless on bed with Madame Claude.
- 0:55 - Topless kissing Pierre, then buns while lying on the floor.
  1:10 - In two piece swimsuit on sailboat.
- 1:11 - Left breast, then buns at the beach with Frederick.

Frenzy (1972; British)
Barbara Leigh .Brenda Blaney
Anna Massey. . . . . Babs Milligan
•• 0:45 - Topless getting out of bed and then buns, walking to the bathroom. Most probably a body double.

Friday the 13th (1980)
Kevin Bacon . . . . Jack
- 0:39 - Close up of buns when Marci squeezes them.

Friday the 13th, Part II (1981)
Kirsten Baker. . . . . .Terry
•• 0:45 - Topless and buns taking off clothes to go skinny dipping.
- 0:47 - Very brief topless jumping up in the water.
- 0:48 - Full frontal nudity and buns getting out of the water. Long shot.

Friday the 13th, Part IV—The Final Chapter (1984)
Judie Aronson . . . . Samantha
- 0:26 - Brief topless and very brief buns taking clothes off to go skinny dipping.
- 0:29 - Brief topless under water pretending to be dead.
•• 0:39 - Topless and brief buns taking off her T-shirt to go skinny dipping at night.
Kimberly Beck. . . . . .Trish
Alan Hayes . . . . Paul
- 0:26 - Brief buns, swinging on a rope jumping into the lake.
Barbara Howard . . . . Sara
  0:52 - In white bra and panties putting on a robe in the bedroom getting ready for her boyfriend.
- 1:01 - Buns, through shower door.
Camilla More . . . . Tina
- 0:26 - Very brief topless in the lake jumping up with her twin sister to show they are skinny dipping.
- 0:48 - Left breast, in bed with Crispin Glover.
Carey More. . . . . Terri
- 0:26 - Very brief topless in the lake jumping up with her twin sister to show they are skinny dipping.

Friday the 13th, Part V—A New Beginning (1985)
Juliette Cummins . . . . .Robin
••• 1:01 - Topless, wearing panties getting undressed and climbing into bed just before getting killed.
  1:05 - Very brief topless, covered with blood when Reggie discovers her dead.
Melanie Kinnaman. . . . . Pam Roberts
  1:08 - In wet white blouse coming back into the house from the rain.
Deborah Voorhees. . . . . .Tina
••• 0:41 - Topless after making love with Eddie, then lying down and relaxing just before getting killed.
- 0:43 - Buns and brief left breast when Eddie turns her over and discovers her dead.
Rebecca Wood-Sharkey . . . . Lana
- 0:33 - Brief topless opening her dress while changing to go out with Billy.

Friday the 13th, Part VII: The New Blood (1988)
Elizabeth Kaitan . . . . .Robin
- 0:53 - Brief left breast in bed making love with a guy.
- 0:55 - Brief topless sitting up in bed after making love and the sheet falls down.
•• 1:00 - Brief topless again sitting up in bed and putting a shirt on over her head.
Heidi Kozak . . . . .Sandra
- 0:36 - Buns taking off clothes to go skinny dipping. Brief topless under water just before getting killed by Jason.

Friendly Favors (1983)
a.k.a. Six Swedes on a Pump
Private Screenings.
Brigitte Lahaie . . . . .Greta
•• 0:02 - Full frontal nudity riding a guy in bed. (She's wearing a necklace.)
••• 0:39 - Full frontal nudity having fun on "exercise bike."
••• 0:46 - Full frontal nudity taking off clothes and running outside with the other girls. Nice slow motion shots.
•• 0:53 - Topless, making love with Kerstin.
••• 1:01 - Full frontal nudity in room with the Italian.
••• 1:15 - Full frontal nudity in room with guy from the band.

From Beyond (1986)
Barbara Crampton . . . . Dr. Katherine McMichaels
•• 0:44 - Brief topless after getting blouse torn off by the creature in the laboratory.
  0:51 - Buns getting on top of Jeffrey Combs in black leather outfit.

The Funhouse (1981)
Elizabeth Berridge . . . . .Amy
•• 0:03 - Brief topless taking off robe to get into the shower, then very brief topless getting out to chase Joey.
Sylvia Miles . . . . .Madame Zena

The Further Adventures of Tennessee Buck (1987)
Kathy Shower . . . . Barbara Manchester
   0:22 - In white lingerie in her hut getting dressed.
  ••• 0:57 - Topless getting rubbed with oil by the cannibal women. Nice close up shots.
  •• 1:02 - Topless in a hut with the Chief of the tribe.
Brant Van Hoffman . . . . Ken Manchester
  • 0:38 - Brief buns, behind a mosquito net making love
  with his disinterested wife.

The G.I. Executioner (1971)
Angelique Pettijohn. Bonnie
  •• 0:16 - Doing a strip routine on stage. Buns in G-
  string, very brief side view of right breast, then topless at end.
  •• 0:40 - Topless, lying asleep in bed.
  ••• 0:58 - Topless and buns, undressing in front of Dave,
  getting into bed, fighting an attacker and getting
  shot. Long scene.
  • 1:14 - Topless, lying shot in rope net.

Gabriela (1984; Brazilian)
Sonia Braga. Gabriela
  •• 0:26 - Topless leaning back out the window making
  love on a table with Marcello Mastroianni.
  ••• 0:27 - Nude, taking a shower outside and cleaning
  herself up.
  • 0:32 - Right breast in bed.
  •• 0:38 - Nude, making love with Mastroianni on the
  kitchen table.
  •• 0:45 - Nude, getting in bed with Mastroianni.
  1:13 - Full frontal nudity, on bed with another man,
  then getting beat up by Mastroianni.
  ••• 1:17 - Nude, changing clothes in the bedroom.
  •• 1:32 - Topless and buns making love outside with
  Mastroianni. Lots of passion!

Gaby, A True Story (1987)
Robert Beltran. . . . . .Luis
Rachel Levin . . . . Gaby
  • 0:56 - Right breast, then topless on the floor making
  love with another handicapped boy, Fernando.

Galaxy of Terror (1981)
Edward Albert. .Cabren
Taaffe O'Connell. Damelia
  •• 0:42 - Topless getting raped by a giant alien slug.
  Nice and slimy.
  0:46 - Buns, covered with slime being discovered by
  her crew mates.

Gallipoli (1981)
Mel Gibson. .Frank Dunne
  •• 1:18 - Buns, running into the water. (He's the guy on
  the left.)
Mark Lee. Archy Hamilton
  •• 1:18 - Buns, running into the water with Mel Gibson.
  (Mark is the guy on the right.)

Games That Lovers Play (1970)
Private Screenings.
Joanna Lumley . . . . Fanny
  •• 0:17 - Nude, getting out of bed and putting on robe.
  • 0:50 - Right breast, while in bed with Jonathan.
  •• 1:18 - Topless sitting in bed, talking on the phone.
  •• 1:29 - Brief topless several times in bed with Constance and a guy. Topless after and during the end
  credits.

The Garden of the Finzi-Continis (1971; Italian/
German)
Helmut Berger . . . . Alberto
Dominique Sanda . . . . .Micol
  0:24 - In braless wet white T-shirt after getting
  caught in a rainstorm.
  • 1:12 - Topless sitting on a bed after turning a light on
  so the guy standing outside can see her.

Gator Bait (1973)
Janit Baldwin . . . .
  •• 0:27 - Topless and buns walking into a pond, then
  getting out and getting dressed.
  • 0:35 - Very brief right breast twice popping out of
  her dress when the bad guys hold her.
  • 0:40 - Brief left breast struggling against two guys on
  the bed.
Claudia Jennings . . . . Desiree
  • 0:06 - Brief left and right breasts during boat chase
  sequence.
Clyde Ventura . . . .

Gator Bait II—Cajun Justice (1988)
Jan MacKenzie . . . . Angelique
  0:13 - Most of right breast while kissing her husband.
  0:29 - Most of right breast while in bed.
  •• 0:34 - Buns and side view of left breast, taking a bath
  outside. Brief topless a couple of times while the bad
  guys watch.
  • 0:41 - Brief side view of left breast taking off towel in
  front of the bad guys.
  1:05 - Brief buns occasionally when her blouse flaps
  up during boat chase.

The Gauntlet (1977)
Clint Eastwood. Ben Shockley
Sondra Locke . . . . Gus Mally
  •• 1:10 - Brief right breast, then topless getting raped
  by two biker guys in a box car while Clint is tied up.

Gemini Affair (1974)
Kathy Kersh . . . . Jessica
  0:10 - In white bra and black panties changing in
  front of Marta Kristen.
  •• 0:11 - Nude getting into bed with Kristen.
  • 0:12 - Brief topless turning over onto her stomach in
  bed.
  •• 0:17 - Nude, standing up in bed and jumping off.
  ••• 0:57 - Nude in bed with Kristen.
  •• 1:04 - Left breast sitting up in bed after Kristen
  leaves.

Marta Kristen . . . . Julie
- ••• 0:32 - Topless wearing beige panties talking with Jessica in the bathroom.
- • 0:56 - Very, very brief left breast and lower frontal nudity standing next to bed with a guy. Very brief left breast in bed with him.
- ••• 0:59 - Topless and buns making love in bed with Jessica. Wowzers!

Genuine Risk (1989)
Michelle Johnson. . . . . Girl
- 0:27 - In black bra in room with Henry.
- 0:29 - In bra in open top coming out of the bathroom.
- • 0:43 - On bed in black bra and panties with Henry. Left breast peeking out of the top of her bra.

Get Out Your Handkerchiefs (1978)
Gérard Depardieu . . . . Raoul
Carole Laure . . . . Solange
- •• 0:21 - Topless sitting in bed listening to her boyfriend talk.
- •• 0:31 - Topless sitting in bed knitting.
- • 0:41 - Upper half of left breast in bed.
- •• 0:47 - Left breast sitting in bed while the three guys talk.
- • 1:08 - Brief right breast when the little boy peeks at her while she sleeps.
- 1:10 - Lower frontal nudity while he looks at her some more.
- ••• 1:17 - Full frontal nudity taking off nightgown while sitting on bed for the little boy.

The Getaway (1972)
Ali MacGraw . . . . Carol McCoy
- 0:16 - In wet white blouse after jumping in pond with Steve McQueen.
- • 0:19 - Very brief left breast lying back in bed kissing McQueen.
Sally Struthers . . . . Fran Clinton
- 1:15 - In black bra getting out of bed and leaning over injured bad guy to get something.

Getting It Right (1989)
Helena Bonham Carter . . . . Minerva Munday
- •• 0:18 - Topless a couple of times in bed talking to Gavin. It's hard to recognize her because she has lots of makeup on her face.
Lynn Redgrave . . . . Joan
- •• 0:46 - Brief right breast, then brief topless on couch seducing Gavin. Longer right breast shot when wrestling with him.

Ghost Story (1981)
Alice Krige. . . . . Alma/Eva
- • 0:41 - Brief topless making love in bedroom with Craig Wasson.
- •• 0:44 - Topless in bathtub with Wasson.
- •• 0:46 - Topless sitting up in bed.
- ••• 0:49 - Buns, then topless standing on balcony turning and walking to bedroom talking to Wasson.

Craig Wasson. . . . . .Don/David
- •• 0:08 - Brief frontal nudity falling out the window, then buns, landing next to the pool.
- • 0:41 - Buns, making love with Alice Krige in bedroom.

Ghosts Can't Do It (1989)
Leo Damian . . . .
- • 1:31 - Brief, lower buns sliding down stack of hay. Long shot.
Bo Derek . . . .
- ••• 0:26 - In one piece swimsuit on beach, then full frontal nudity taking it off. Brief buns covered with sand on her back. Long scene.
- ••• 0:32 - Topless, sitting and washing herself. Very brief buns, jumping into tub.
- •• 0:48 - Full frontal nudity taking a shower.
- • 0:49 - Very, very brief topless and buns jumping into pool. Long shot. Full frontal nudity under water.
- 0:52 - Very, very brief partial topless pulling a guy into the pool
- 1:00 - In wet dress, dancing sexily in the rain.
- •• 1:12 - Topless behind mosquito net with her boyfriend.
Julie Newmar . . . .

The Gift (1982; French)
Clio Goldsmith. . . . . Barbara
- •• 0:39 - Brief topless several times in the bathroom, then right breast in bathtub.
- • 0:49 - Topless lying in bed sleeping.
- 0:51 - Very brief left breast turning over in bed.
- • 0:52 - Brief right breast then buns, reaching for phone while lying in bed.
- 1:16 - Very brief left breast getting out of bed. Dark, hard to see.

Gimme an "F" (1981)
Jennifer Cooke . . . . Pam Bethlehem
- 1:10 - Wearing United States flag pasties frolicking with Dr. Spirit. Nice bouncing action.
- 1:38 - Still of pasties scene during end credits.
Darcy De Moss. . . . . One of the "Ducks"
Steve Shellen . . . . Tommy Hamilton
- 0:56 - Dancing in his underwear in the boy's shower room while the girls peek in at him.
- • 0:57 - Brief upper half of buns.
Cindy Silver . . . . One of the "Ducks"

The Girl from Petrovka (1974)
Goldie Hawn . . . . Oktyabrina
- 1:30 - Very, very brief topless in bed with Hal Holbrook. Don't really see anything—it lasts for about one frame.
Hal Holbrook . . . . .Joe
- • 0:40 - Brief buns, getting out of bed, putting on a robe and talking to Goldie Hawn.

351

The Girl in a Swing (1989)
Meg Tilly . . . . Karin Foster
•• 0:44 - In white bra, then topless and buns.
•• 0:50 - Nude, swimming under water.
••• 1:14 - Topless sitting on swing, then making love.
1:18 - In white bra, sitting in front of a mirror.
••• 1:44 - Topless at the beach.

The Girl in Blue (1973; Canadian)
a.k.a. U-turn
Maud Adams . . . . .Paula/Tracy
• 1:16 - Side view of right breast, while sitting on bed with Scott.
1:19 - In two piece swimsuit getting out of lake.
Gay Rowan . . . . Bonnie
• 0:06 - Left breast, in bed with Scott.
• 0:31 - Brief topless in bathtub.
• 0:48 - Right breast, in shower talking to Scott. Brief topless (long shot) on balcony throwing water down at him.
• 1:21 - Brief right breast and buns getting out of bed and running out of the room.
David Selby . . . . .Scott
• 0:10 - Brief buns getting out of bed and putting on pants. Dark.
0:44 - Left half of buns in shower.
•• 1:14 - Buns, walking into the bathroom.

Girl on a Motorcycle (1968; French/British)
a.k.a. Naked Under Leather
Marianne Faithful . . . . Rebecca
•• 0:05 - Nude, getting out of bed and walking to the door.
• 0:38 - Brief side view of left breast putting nightgown on.
• 1:23 - Brief topless while lying down and talking with Alain Delon.
• 1:30 - Very brief right breast a couple of times making love with Delon.
Catherine Jourdan . . . . Catherine

A Girl to Kill For (1989)
Karen Medak . . . . .Sue
••• 0:17 - Topless showering at the beach after surfing with Chuck.
0:38 - In bra lying on desk in office with Chuck.
•• 1:08 - Topless in spa when Chuck takes her shirt off. Then miscellaneous shots making love.

Girlfriend from Hell (1989)
James Daughton . . . . David
Lezlie Deane . . . . Diane
Christina Veronica . . . . Dancer
••• 1:17 - Topless dancing on stage in club.

Girlfriends (1978)
Christopher Guest . . . . .Eric
• 1:04 - Buns, running after Melanie Mayron in her apartment, then hugging her.

Melanie Mayron . . . . .Susan Weinblatt
• 0:14 - Buns, very brief lower frontal nudity and brief left breast getting dressed in bathroom.
Anita Skinner . . . . Anne Munroe
Amy Wright . . . . Ceil
• 0:42 - Brief topless getting out of bed to talk to Melanie Mayron.

Glitch (1988)
Laura Albert . . . . Topless
• 0:35 - Brief topless auditioning for two guys by taking off her top.
Christina Cardan . . . . Non SAG
• 0:47 - Brief topless in spa taking off her swimsuit top.
Teri Weigel . . . . Lydia
0:41 - In pink bathing suit talking to blonde guy.
• 0:54 - Very brief side view of right breast in bathtub with dark haired guy.

Gnaw: Food of the Gods II (1988; Canadian)
Eduardo Castillo . . . . Carlos
• 0:46 - Buns, walking through bushes to take a lead. More buns, running away from the giant rats.

God's Gun (1977)
a.k.a. A Bullet from God
Sybil Danning . . . . Jenny
• 1:09 - Right breast popping out of dress with a guy in the barn during flashback.
Robert Lipton . . . .

The Godfather (1972)
Marlon Brando . . . . .Don Vito Corleone
Diane Keaton . . . . .Kay Adams
Simonetta Stefanelli . . . . .Apollonia
•• 1:50 - Topless in bedroom on honeymoon night.

Goin' All the Way (1981)
Josh Cadman . . . . .Bronk
• 1:05 - Buns, in the shower talking to Boom Boom.
Gina Calabrese . . . .
•• 0:12 - Left breast, in the girls' locker room shower. Standing on the left.
Eileen Davidson . . . . .BJ
••• 0:12 - Topless in the girls' locker room shower. Standing next to Monica.
••• 0:22 - Exercising in her bedroom in braless pink T-shirt, then topless talking on the phone to Monica.
Sherrie Miller . . . . Candy
0:47 - Brief right breast getting out of bubble bath.
•• 0:49 - Topless with Artie during his fantasy.

Going Places (1974; French)
Miou-Miou . . . . Marie-Ange
••• 0:14 - Topless sitting in bed, filing her nails. Full frontal nudity standing up and getting dressed.
•• 0:48 - Topless in bed with Pierrot and Jean-Claude.
• 0:51 - Left breast under Pierrot.
••• 0:52 - Buns in bed when Jean-Claude rolls off her. Full frontal nudity sitting up with the two guys in bed.
•• 1:21 - Brief topless opening the door. Topless and panties walking in after the two guys.

- 1:27 - Partial left breast taking off dress and walking into house.
  1:28 - Very brief topless closing the shutters.
- •• 1:31 - Full frontal nudity in open dress running after the two guys. Long shot. Full frontal nudity putting her wet dress on.
- 1:41 - Topless in back of car. Dark.

Gérard Depardieu . . . . Jean-Claude
- 0:42 - Upper half of buns and pubic hair talking to Pierrot.
- •• 0:49 - Buns in bed, then more buns making love to Miou-Miou. Nice up and down action.
- 0:50 - Brief buns switching places with Pierrot.
- 0:51 - Brief frontal nudity getting out of bed. Dark, hard to see. Subtitles get in the way.

Patrick Dewaere . . . . Pierrot
- 0:42 - Upper half of buns starting to leave the room. Surgical tape on his buns.
- •• 0:48 - Buns in bed with Marie-Ange.
- 0:50 - Brief buns, switching places with Jean-Claude.
  1:41 - Sort of buns, making love in back seat of car. Dark.
- 1:42 - Buns, getting out of car and pulling up his pants.

Brigitte Fossey . . . . Young Mother
- ••• 0:32 - In bra, then topless in open blouse on the train when she lets Pierrot suck the milk out of her breasts.

Isabelle Huppert . . . . Jacqueline
- 1:53 - Brief upper half of left breast making love with Jean-Claude.

Good Morning, Babylon (1987; Italian/French)
Desiree Becker . . . . Mabel
- 1:06 - Brief topless in the woods making love.

Greta Scacchi . . . . Edna
- •• 1:05 - Topless in the woods making love with Vincent Spano.

Vincent Spano . . . . Nicola Bonnano

The Good Mother (1988)
Tracy Griffith . . . . Babe
- 0:06 - Brief topless opening her blouse to show a young Anna what it's like being pregnant.

Diane Keaton . . . . Anna

The Good Wife (1987; Australian)
a.k.a. The Umbrella Woman
Bryan Brown . . . . Sonny Hills
Clarissa Kaye-Mason . . . . Mrs. Jackson
Susan Lyons . . . . Mrs. Fielding
- 1:22 - Very brief topless coming in from the balcony.

Rachel Ward . . . . Marge Hills

Goodbye Emmanuelle (1977)
Sylvia Kristel . . . . Emmanuelle
- •• 0:03 - Full frontal nudity in bath and getting out.
- •• 0:04 - Full frontal nudity taking off dress.
- ••• 0:06 - Full frontal nudity in bed with Angelique.
- ••• 0:26 - Topless with photographer in old house.
  0:42 - Brief side view of right breast, in bed with Jean.

- ••• 1:03 - Full frontal nudity on beach with movie director.
- •• 1:06 - Full frontal nudity lying on beach sleeping.
- •• 1:28 - Side view of left breast lying on beach with Gregory while dreaming.

Alexandra Stewart . . . . Dorothee

Goodbye, Columbus (1969)
Richard Benjamin . . . . Neil
- 1:11 - Brief buns, walking into the bathroom. Very, very brief frontal nudity. Blurry, hard to see anything.

Ali MacGraw . . . . Brenda
- 0:50 - Very brief side view of left breast, taking off dress before running and jumping into a swimming pool. Brief right breast jumping into pool.
- 1:11 - Very brief side view of right breast in bed with Richard Benjamin. Brief buns, getting out of bed and walking to the bathroom.

Goodbye, Norma Jean (1975)
Patch Mackenzie . . . . Ruth Latimer
Misty Rowe . . . . Norma Jean Baker
  0:02 - In white bra putting makeup on.
- •• 0:08 - In white bra and panties, then topless.
- 0:14 - Brief topless in bed getting raped.
  0:31 - Very, very brief silhouette of right breast, in bed with Rob.
- ••• 0:59 - Topless during shooting of stag film, then in B&W when some people watch the film.
  1:14 - In white bra and panties undressing.

Gorky Park (1983)
William Hurt . . . . Arkady Renko
Joanna Pacula . . . . Irina
- •• 1:20 - Brief topless in bed making love with William Hurt.

Gotcha! (1985)
Nick Corri . . . . Manolo
Anthony Edwards . . . . Jonathan Moore
Linda Fiorentino . . . . Sasha
- •• 0:53 - Brief topless getting searched at customs.

Kari Lizer . . . . Muffy
Christopher Rydell . . . . Bob Jensen

Gotham (1988; Made for Cable Movie)
a.k.a. The Dead Can't Lie
Tommy Lee Jones . . . . Eddie Mallard
- 0:50 - Buns, walking over to Virginia Madsen. Dark, hard to see anything.

Virginia Madsen . . . . Rachel Carlyle
- 0:50 - Brief topless in the shower when Tommy Lee Jones comes over to her apartment, then topless lying on the floor.
- •• 1:12 - Topless, dead, in the freezer when Jones comes back to her apartment, then brief topless on the bed.
- 1:18 - Topless in the bathtub under water.

Gothic (1986; British)
Gabriel Byrne . . . . Byron
Myriam Cyr . . . . Claire
•• 0:53 - Left breast, then topless lying in bed with Gabriel Byrne.
• 0:55 - Brief left breast lying in bed. Long shot.
• 1:02 - Topless sitting on pool table opening her top. Special effect with eyes in her nipples.
• 1:12 - Buns and brief topless covered with mud.
Natasha Richardson. . . . . .Mary
Julian Sands. . . . . Shelley
•• 0:17 - Buns, standing on roof in the rain.

Graduation Day (1981)
Patch Mackenzie. . . . . .Anne Ramstead
Linnea Quigley . . . . .Dolores
•• 0:36 - Topless by the piano in classroom with Mr. Roberts unbuttoning her blouse.
Vanna White. . . . . .Doris

Grandview, U.S.A. (1984)
Jamie Lee Curtis . . . . Michelle "Mike" Cody
••• 1:00 - Left breast, lying in bed with C. Thomas Howell.
C. Thomas Howell. . . . . Tim Pearson
Jennifer Jason Leigh. . . . . .Candy Webster
Patrick Swayze . . . . Ernie "Slam" Webster

The Grasshopper (1970)
Jacqueline Bisset . . . . Christine Adams
0:21 - In flesh colored Las Vegas-style showgirl costume. Dark, hard to see.
0:27 - More showgirl shots.
1:14 - In black two piece swimsuit.
1:16 - Almost left breast while squished against Jay in the shower.
Christopher Stone. .Jay Rigney
0:26 - Buns through shower door when Jacqueline Bisset comes in to join him.
• 1:17 - Brief buns lying in bed talking to Bisset.

Graveyard Shift (1987)
Sugar Bouche .Fabulous Frannie
••• 0:12 - Topless doing a stripper routine on stage.
• 0:24 - Brief topless in the shower.
Kim Cayer. . . . . Suzy
•• 0:06 - In black bra, then brief left breast when vampire rips the bra off.
• 0:53 - Brief topless in junk yard with garter belt, black panties and stockings.
Silvio Oliviero . . . . .Stephen Tsepes
• 0:09 - Buns, climbing into his coffin.

The Grifters (1990)
Annette Bening. Myra Langtry
•• 0:36 - In bra and panties in her apartment, then topless lying in bed "paying" her rent. Kind of dark.
••• 1:06 - Nude, walking down the hall to the bedroom and into bed.
1:30 - Very brief right breast, dead. Long shot.
Anjelica Huston. . . . . .Lilly Dillon

Grim Prairie Tales (1990)
Lisa Eichhorn . . . . Maureen
Michelle Joyner . . . . .Jenny
• 0:36 - Very brief right breast, then left breast while making love with Marc McClure. Kind of dark.

The Groove Tube (1974)
Jennifer Wells . . . . .The Geritan Girl
•• 0:21 - Dancing nude around her husband, Chevy Chase.

Group Marriage (1972)
Aimée Eccles . . . . Chris
0:15 - Buns, getting into bed.
• 1:15 - Brief side view of left breast and buns getting into the shower.
Claudia Jennings . . . . .Elaine
••• 1:02 - Topless under mosquito net in bed with Phil. Long scene.
Pepe Serna. . . . . .Ramon
Zach Taylor . . . . Phil
•• 0:43 - Buns, walking on beach with Jan.
Victoria Vetri . . . . .Jan
••• 0:28 - Buns and topless getting into bed with Dennis, Sander and Chris. More topless sitting in bed. Long scene.
• 1:19 - Brief side view of right breast in lifeguard booth.

The Guardian (1990)
Dwier Brown . . . . Phil
0:37 - Soft of buns, in bed with Carey Lowell. Don't see his face.
Carey Lowell . . . . .Kate
•• 0:37 - Right breast twice, in bed with Phil.
Jenny Seagrove . . . . Camilla
••• 0:21 - Side view of left breast in bathtub with the baby. Right breast, then topless.
0:23 - Buns, drying herself off. Long shot.
•• 0:38 - Topless, mostly left breast on top of Phil. Don't see her face, probably a body double.
0:46 - Buns, skinny dipping. Long shot.
•• 0:47 - Topless healing her wound by a tree. Side view of right breast.
• 1:18 - Very brief topless under sheer gown in forest just before getting hit by a Jeep.
1:24 - Very briefly topless scaring Carey Lowell. Body is painted all over.

Gulag (1985)
David Keith . . . . Mickey Almon
•• 1:26 - Buns, standing outside with Malcolm McDowell in the snow being hassled by guards.
Malcolm McDowell . . . . Englishman
•• 1:26 - Buns, standing outside with David Keith in the snow being hassled by guards.
Nancy Paul. . . . . .Susan
•• 0:42 - Buns, then topless taking a shower while David Keith daydreams while he's on a train.

The Gumshoe Kid (1990)
Tracy Scoggins . . . . .Rita Benson
    0:33 - In two piece white swimsuit. Nice bun shot while Jay Underwood hides in the closet.
- ••• 1:10 - Side view of left breast in the shower with Underwood. Excellent slow motion topless shot while turning around. Brief side view of right breast in bed afterwards.

Jay Underwood . . . . .Jeff Sherman

Guns (1990)
Cynthia Brimhall . . . . Edy Stark
    0:26 - Buns, in G-string singing and dancing at club.
- •• 0:27 - Topless in dressing room.
    0:53 - Buns, in black one piece outfit and stockings, singing in club. Nice legs!

Allegra Curtis . . . . .Robyn
Phyllis Davis . . . . Kathryn Hamilton
Devin De Vasquez . . . . .Cash
- • 1:12 - Brief side of right breast and buns undressing for bath.

Liv Lindeland. . . . . .Ace
Lisa London. . . . . Rocky
Kym Malin . . . . Kym
    0:27 - Oil wrestling with Hugs.
- ••• 0:28 - Showering (in back) while talking to Hugs (in front).

Dona L. Speir . . . . .Donna Hamilton
- ••• 1:00 - Topless and buns in black G-string getting dressed in locker room. Then in black lingerie.

Roberta Vasquez . . . . Nicole Justin
- •• 0:50 - Right breast while making love on motorcycle with her boyfriend.

H.O.T.S. (1979)
Angela Aames . . . . .Boom-Boom Bangs
- • 0:21 - Topless parachuting into pool.
- • 0:39 - Topless in bathtub playing with a seal.
- • 1:33 - Topless playing football.

Lindsay Bloom. . . . . Melody Ragmore
- • 0:28 - Very brief right breast on balcony.
- • 1:34 - Brief topless during football game throwing football as quarterback.

Steve Bond . . . . John
- • 0:32 - Buns, trapped in van with K. C. Winkler.

Pamela Jean Bryant . . . . Teri Lynn
- • 1:33 - Topless during football game.

Sandy Johnson . . . . Stephanie
- •• 0:27 - Topless on balcony in red bikini bottoms.
- •• 1:34 - Topless during football game during huddle with all the other girls.

Susan Lynn Kiger. . . . . Honey Shayne
- • 0:00 - Topless in shower room with the other girls.
- •• 0:33 - Topless in pool making love with Doug.
- • 1:33 - Topless in football game.

Lisa London. Jennie O'Hara
- • 1:22 - Topless changing clothes by the closet while a crook watches her.
- • 1:33 - Topless playing football.

K.C. Winkler . . . . Cynthia
- • 0:27 - Topless in blue bikini bottom on balcony.
- •• 0:31 - Topless in van making love, then arguing with John.

Hair (1979)
Beverly D'Angelo . . . . Sheila
- • 0:59 - In white bra and panties, then topless on rock near pond. Medium long shot.
- ••• 1:01 - Topless in panties getting out of the pond.
- • 1:38 - Side view of right breast changing clothes in car with George.

Don Dacus. . . . . .Woof
- • 0:57 - Buns, taking off clothes and diving into pond with Treat Williams and Hud.

Michael Jeter . . . . .Woodrow Sheldon
- • 1:06 - Buns in front of Army guys.

Treat Williams . . . . Berger
- • 0:57 - Buns, taking off clothes and diving into pond with Hud and Woof.

Dorsey Wright . . . . .Hud
- • 0:57 - Buns, taking off clothes and diving into pond with Treat Williams and Woof.

Half Moon Street (1986)
Vincent Lindon . . . . Sonny
- • 1:04 - Buns, getting out of bed with Sigourney Weaver.

Sigourney Weaver . . . . .Lauren Slaughter
- • 0:05 - Brief topless in the bathtub.
- •• 0:11 - Brief topless in the bathtub again.
- • 0:18 - Brief buns and side view of right breast putting on makeup in front of the mirror. Wearing a black garter belt and stockings.
- ••• 0:39 - Topless riding exercise bike while being photographed, then brief topless getting out of the shower.
    0:46 - Very, very brief topless wearing a sheer black blouse with no bra during daydream sequence.
- • 0:50 - Brief topless in bed with Michael Caine, then left breast.
    1:16 - In braless, wet, white blouse in bathroom after knocking a guy out.

Halloween (1978)
Jamie Lee Curtis . . . . Laurie
Sandy Johnson. . . . . Judith Meyers
    0:06 - Very brief topless covered with blood on floor after Michael stabs her to death.

P.J. Soles . . . . Lynda
- • 1:04 - Brief right breast, sitting up in bed after making love in bed with Bob.
- • 1:07 - Brief topless getting strangled by Michael in the bedroom.

Halloween II (1981)
Jamie Lee Curtis . . . . Laurie
Leo Rossi . . . . Budd
- • 0:48 - Buns, getting out of the whirlpool bath to check the water temperature.

Pamela Susan Shoop . . . . Karen
••• 0:48 - Topless getting into the whirlpool bath with Budd in the hospital.

Hamburger—The Motion Picture (1986)

Debra Blee . . . . Mia Vunk
　0:25 - Briefly in wet dress in the swimming pool.
Randi Brooks. . . . . .Mrs. Vunk
•• 0:52 - Brief topless in helicopter with a guy.
Karen Mayo-Chandler . . . . .Dr. Victoria Gotbottom
• 0:03 - Brief topless in her office trying to help, then seduce Russell.
Maria Richwine . . . . .Conchita
•• 0:49 - Topless trying to seduce Russell in a room.

The Hand (1981)

Annie McEnroe . . . . Stella Roche
•• 0:51 - Topless undressing for Michael Caine.
Bruce McGill . . . . Brian Ferguson

A Handmaid's Tale (1990)

David Dukes . . . . Doctor
Faye Dunaway. . . . . Serena Joy
Elizabeth McGovern . . . . Moira
Aidan Quinn . . . . Nick
Natasha Richardson. . . . . Kate
•• 0:30 - Topless twice at the window getting some fresh air.
• 0:59 - Topless making love with Aidan Quinn.
••• 1:00 - Topless after Quinn rolls off her.
Victoria Tennant . . . . Aunt Lydia

Hanover Street (1979)

Lesley-Anne Down . . . . Margaret Sallinger
• 0:22 - In bra and slip, then brief topless in bedroom with Harrison Ford.
Patsy Kensit. . . . . Sarah Sallinger

The Happy Hooker (1975)

Denise Galik . . . . .Cynthia
Anita Morris . . . . .Linda Jo/Mary Smith
• 0:59 - Topless lying on table while a customer puts ice cream all over her.
• 1:24 - Topless covered with whipped cream getting it sprayed off with champagne by another customer.
Lynn Redgrave . . . . .Xaviera Hollander
0:43 - In black bra and panties doing a strip tease routine in a board room while Tom Poston watches.

The Happy Hooker Goes Hollywood (1980)

Martine Beswicke . . . . .Xaviera Hollander
•• 0:05 - Brief topless in bedroom with Policeman.
••• 0:22 - Brief buns, jumping into the swimming pool, then topless next to the pool with Adam West.
• 0:27 - Topless in bed with West, then topless waking up.
Lindsay Bloom. . . . . .Chris
Tanya Boyd . . . . Sylvie
• 0:39 - Brief topless in jungle room when an older customer accidentally comes in.
Liz Glazowski. . . . . Liz

Susan Lynn Kiger . . . . Susie
• 0:42 - Topless, singing "Happy Birthday" to a guy tied up on the bed.
••• 0:43 - Topless, wearing a red garter belt playing pool with K.C. Winkler.
Lisa London . . . . Laurie
Alexandra Morgan . . . . .Max
K.C. Winkler. . . . . Amber
•• 0:41 - Topless in cowboy outfit on bed with a guy.
••• 0:43 - Topless, wearing a blue garter belt playing pool with Susan Kiger.

The Happy Hooker Goes to Washington (1977)

Dawn Clark . . . . Candy
• 1:18 - Topless, covered with spaghetti in a restaurant.
Cissie Colpitts-Cameron . . . . Miss Goodbody
• 0:29 - Very brief topless when her top pops open during the senate hearing.
Linda Gildersleeve . . . . Honeymoon Wife
• 0:35 - Brief topless in a diner during the filming of a commercial.
Joey Heatherton . . . . Xaviera Hollander
Joyce Jillson . . . . herself
Marilyn Joi . . . . Sheila
• 0:09 - Left breast while on a couch.
• 0:47 - Brief topless during car demonstration.
•• 1:14 - Topless in military guy's office.
Bonnie Large . . . . Carolyn (Model)
• 0:06 - Topless during photo shoot.
Louisa Moritz . . . . Natalie Naussbaum
Pamela Zinszer. . . . . Linda
• 1:19 - Brief topless in raincoat flashing in front of congressional panel.

Happy Housewives (British)

Ava Cadell . . . . Schoolgirl
　0:39 - Buns, getting caught by the Squire and getting spanked.
Jeannie Collings . . . . Mrs. Wain
• 0:16 - Very, very brief right breast with the Newsagent's Daughter and Bob in the bathtub.
Sue Lloyd . . . . The Blonde
Nita Lorraine . . . . Jenny Elgin
• 0:31 - Brief side view of left breast and buns in barn chasing after Bob.
• 0:32 - Brief topless in open dress talking to policeman.
Helli Louise. . . . . Newsagent's Daughter
•• 0:16 - Topless with Mrs. Wain and Bob in the bathtub.
Penny Meredith . . . . Margaretta
• 0:02 - Brief right breast talking on the telephone while Bob makes love with her.
•• 0:19 - Topless standing up in bathtub talking to Bob.
• 0:34 - In sheer black lingerie.
• 1:05 - Brief topless pulling her top down when interrupted by the policeman at the window.

Barry Stokes . . . . Bob
- • 0:31 - Brief buns, running away from Mrs. Elgin and her daughter in the barn.

Happy Together (1988)
Patrick Dempsey . . . . Christopher "Chris" Wooden
Helen Slater . . . . Alexandra "Alex" Page
- •• 0:17 - Brief right breast changing clothes while talking to Patrick Dempsey. Unfortunately, she has a goofy expression on her face.
  0:57 - In red lingerie tempting Dempsey. Later, panties under panty hose when Dempsey pulls her dress up while she's on roller skates.
  1:07 - Very brief panties under panty hose again straddling Dempsey in the hallway.
  1:14 - Panties under white stockings while changing in the closet.

Hard Choices (1986)
Margaret Klenck . . . . Laura
- •• 1:10 - Left breast, then topless making love with Bobby. Nice close up shot.
- • 1:11 - Very brief half of left breast and lower frontal nudity getting back into bed. Long shot.
Gary McCleery . . . . .Bobby
- •• 1:11 - Buns, making love on top of Laura.

Hard Ticket to Hawaii (1987)
Cynthia Brimhall . . . . .Edy
- •• 0:47 - Topless changing out of a dress into a blouse and pants.
- •• 1:33 - Topless during the end credits.
Hope Marie Carlton. Taryn
- •• 0:07 - Topless taking a shower outside while talking to Dona Speir.
- ••• 0:23 - Topless in the spa with Speir looking at diamonds they found.
- ••• 0:40 - Topless and buns on the beach making love with her boyfriend, Jimmy John.
- •• 1:33 - Topless during the end credits.
Patty Duffek . . . . Patticakes
- •• 0:48 - Topless talking to Michelle after swimming.
Dona L. Speir . . . . Donna
- • 0:01 - Topless on boat kissing her boyfriend, Rowdy.
- ••• 0:23 - Topless in the spa with Hope Marie Carlton looking at diamonds they found.
- ••• 1:04 - Topless and buns with Rowdy after watching a video tape.
- •• 1:33 - Topless during the end credits.

Hard to Hold (1984)
Janet Eilber .Diana Lawson
Monique Gabrielle .Wife #1
Sharon Hughes . . . . Wife
Charlene Jones . . . . Wife
Rick Springfield . . . . .James Roberts
- • 0:06 - Buns, running down the hall getting chased by a bunch of young girls.
- •• 0:15 - Buns, lying in bed sleeping.

Hardbodies (1984)
Julie Always . . . . Photo Session Hardbody
- •• 0:40 - Topless with other girls posing topless getting pictures taken by Rounder. She's wearing blue dress with a white belt.
Leslee Bremmer . . . . Photo Session Hardbody
- • 0:02 - Topless in the surf when her friends take off her swimsuit top during the opening credits.
- •• 0:40 - Topless with other topless girls posing for photographs taken by Rounder. She takes off her dress and is wearing a black G-string.
Roberta Collins. . . . . Lana
Grant Cramer. . . . . Scotty
- • 0:03 - Brief buns, getting out of bed after making love with Kristi.
Darcy De Moss. . . . . Dede
- ••• 0:55 - Topless in the back seat of the limousine with Rounder.
Erika Dockery . . . . Hardbody in Car
Jackie Easton . . . . .Girl in dressing room
- •• 0:27 - Topless taking off dress to try on swimsuit.
- •• 0:40 - Topless with other topless girls posing for photographs taken by Rounder. (Wearing a white skirt.)
Kathleen Kinmont . . . . Pretty Skater
Teal Roberts . . . . Kristi Kelly
- •• 0:03 - Topless in bed after making love with Scotty, then putting her sweater on.
- ••• 0:47 - Topless standing in front of closet mirrors talking about breasts with Kimberly.
- ••• 0:56 - Topless making love with Scotty on the beach.
- •• 1:22 - Topless on fancy car bed with Scotty.
Cindy Silver . . . . Kimberly
- •• 0:07 - Brief topless on beach when a dog steals her bikini top.
- ••• 0:47 - Topless standing in front of closet mirrors talking about breasts with Kristi.
Kristi Somers . . . . .Michelle
- •• 0:53 - Nude, dancing on the beach while Ashley plays the guitar and sings.

Hardbodies 2 (1986)
Brenda Bakke . . . . .Morgan
- •• 0:34 - Buns, getting into bathtub, then topless, taking a bath.
Roberta Collins. Lana Logan
Fabiana Udenio . . . . .Cleo/Princess

Hardcore (1979)
Leslie Ackerman . . . . .Felice
- • 0:44 - Topless in porno house with George C. Scott.
Ed Begley, Jr. . . . . .Soldier
Bibi Besch . . . . Mary
Peter Boyle. . . . . .Andy Mast
Season Hubley . . . . Niki
- • 0:27 - Topless acting in a porno movie.
- ••• 1:05 - Full frontal nudity talking to George C. Scott in a booth. Panties mysteriously appear later on.
Linda Smith . . . . .Hope (Mistress Victoria)
Gigi Vorgan . . . . Teenage Girl
- • 0:32 - Topless on sofa in Peter Boyle's apartment.

Hardware *(1990)*
Stacey Travis . . . . Jill
• 0:21 - Almost topless in shower. Brief left breast in bed with Moses. Lit with blue light.
0:38 - Brief topless in bedroom seen by a guy through telescope. Infrared-looking effect.

Harem *(1985; French)*
Rosanne Katon . . . . Judy
Ben Kingsley . . . . Selim
Nastassja Kinski . . . . Diane
• 0:14 - Topless getting into swimming pool.
•• 1:04 - Topless in motel room with Ben Kingsley.

The Harrad Experiment *(1973)*
Don Johnson . . . . Stanley Cole
•• 0:18 - Brief frontal nudity after getting out of the shower while Laurie Walters watches.
Bruno Kirby . . . . Harry Schacht
• 0:41 - Brief frontal nudity, getting into the swimming pool with Beth, Don Johnson and Laurie Walters.
Elliot Street . . . . Wilson
•• 0:44 - Frontal nudity taking off clothes and getting into the swimming pool.
Sharon Taggart . . . . Barbara
Victoria Thompson . . . . Beth Hillyer
0:08 - Buns, in the bathroom while talking to Harry.
• 0:10 - Brief topless getting into bed.
•• 0:21 - Topless in nude encounter group.
• 0:41 - Topless getting into the swimming pool with Don Johnson and Laurie Walters.
0:49 - Buns, getting dressed after making love with Johnson.
Laurie Walters . . . . Sheila Grove
• 0:29 - Topless in white panties with Don Johnson.
• 0:40 - Nude taking off blue dress and getting into the swimming pool with Johnson.

The Harrad Summer *(1974)*
Patrice Rohmer . . . . Marcia
Victoria Thompson . . . . Beth Hillyer
• 0:53 - Buns and brief topless running down hallway.
0:59 - Buns on inflatable lounge in the pool.
1:00 - Buns, lying face down on lounge chair.
Laurie Walters . . . . Sheila Grove
0:02 - Topless undressing in bathroom. Long shot, out of focus.
•• 1:00 - Topless lying face up getting a tan on lounge chair, then buns getting up and pushing Harry into the pool.

Harry and Tonto *(1974)*
Ellen Burstyn . . . . Shirley
Melanie Mayron . . . . Ginger
• 0:57 - Very brief topless in motel room with Art Carney taking off her towel and putting on blouse. Long shot, hard to see.

Haunted Summer *(1988)*
Alice Krige . . . . Mary Godwin
Eric Stoltz . . . . Percy Shelley
••• 0:09 - Nude, under the waterfall and walking around in the river. Long scene.

Havana *(1990)*
Alan Arkin . . . . Joe Volpi
Lise Cutter . . . . Patty
• 0:44 - Most of side of left breast with Robert Redford. Very, very brief part of right breast while he turns her around. Very brief left breast when Redford puts a cold glass on her chest. Dark, hard to see.
Lena Olin . . . . Bobby Duran
Karen Russell . . . . Dancer #2

he said, she said *(1991)*
Kevin Bacon . . . . Dan Hanson
Elizabeth Perkins . . . . Lorie Bryer
• 1:15 - Brief topless getting into the shower with Kevin Bacon.
Sharon Stone . . . . Linda

Heart Beat *(1979)*
Stephen Davies . . . . Bob Bendix
Ann Dusenberry . . . . Stevie
•• 0:41 - Full frontal nudity frolicking in bathtub with Nick Nolte.
John Heard . . . . Jack Kerouac
Nick Nolte . . . . Neal Cassady
Ray Sharkey . . . . Ira
Sissy Spacek . . . . Carolyn Cassady

Heart of Midnight *(1988)*
Jennifer Jason Leigh . . . . Carol
• 0:27 - Very brief side view of right breast reaching for soap in the shower.
Brenda Vaccaro . . . . Betty

Heart of the Stag *(1983; New Zealand)*
Terence Cooper . . . . Robert Jackson
• 0:03 - Buns, making love in bed on top of his daughter. Don't see his face.
Bruno Lawrence . . . . Peter Daley
Mary Regan . . . . Cathy Jackson
• 0:03 - Brief right breast twice, very brief lower frontal nudity in bed with her father.
•• 1:06 - Topless in bed, ripping her blouse open while yelling at her father.

Heartbreak Ridge *(1986)*
Clint Eastwood . . . . Highway
Marsha Mason . . . . Aggie
Rebecca Perle . . . . Student in Shower
• 1:48 - Very brief topless getting out of shower when the Marines rescue the students.
Tom Villard . . . . Profile

Heartbreaker *(1983)*

Apollonia. . . . . Rose
Dawn Dunlap . . . . Kim
- • 0:49 - Topless putting on dress in bedroom.
  0:51 - Very, very brief right breast in open dress during rape attempt. Dark.
- •• 1:02 - Left breast, lying on bed with her boyfriend. Long scene.

Pepe Serna . . . . Loco

Heartbreakers *(1984)*

Kathryn Harrold . . . . Cyd
  0:02 - In black bra and panties changing clothes in Peter Coyote's studio.
Carole Laure . . . . .Liliane
- • 0:56 - Brief topless making love in car with Nick Mancuso. Dark, hard to see.
- • 1:25 - In sheer black dress, then brief right breast making love in art gallery with Peter Coyote.

Jamie Rose. . . . . Libby
- ••• 0:09 - Topless in bed talking with Nick Mancuso and Peter Coyote.

Carol Wayne. . . . . .Candy
  0:22 - In black wig and bra posing for Peter Coyote in his studio.
- ••• 0:41 - In white bra and panties, then brief topless in the mirror stripping in front of Coyote and Nick Mancuso. Then brief topless lying in bed with Coyote.

Hearts and Armour *(1983)*

Barbara De Rossi . . . . Bradamante
- •• 1:05 - Topless while sleeping with Ruggero.

Tanya Roberts . . . . Angelica

Heat and Dust *(1982)*

Christopher Cazenove. . . . . Douglas Rivers
- •• 1:25 - Buns lying in bed with Greta Scacchi under a mosquito net.

Julie Christie . . . . .Anne
Greta Scacchi . . . . Olivia Rivers
- •• 1:25 - Buns, lying in bed under a mosquito net with Douglas, then topless rolling over.

The Heat of Desire *(1982; French)*

a.k.a. Plein Sud
Patrick Dewaere . . . . .Serge Laine
- • 0:17 - Buns, getting out of bed and going into Carol's "house" that she has made out of sheets.
  0:20 - Pubic hair, while lying on his back.
- • 0:21 - Side view of buns, on the floor with Carol.
  0:57 - Brief side view of buns, getting out of bed and putting on pants.
- • 1:02 - Buns, getting into bed with Carol. Very, very brief frontal nudity hidden by subtitles.
- • 1:14 - Buns, taking off pants and getting into bed.

Clio Goldsmith . . . . Carol
- • 0:09 - Topless and buns, getting out of bed in train to look out the window. Dark.
- • 0:12 - Brief topless in bathroom mirror when Serge peeks in.

- •• 0:19 - Full frontal nudity in the bathtub.
- •• 0:20 - Nude, sitting on the floor with Serge's head in her lap.
- •• 0:21 - Buns, lying face down on floor. Very brief topless. A little dark. Then topless sitting up and drinking out of bottle.
- • 0:22 - Right breast, in gaping robe sitting on floor with Serge.
- • 0:24 - Partial left breast consoling Serge in bed.
- • 0:25 - Topless sitting on chair on balcony, then walking inside. Dark.
- • 0:56 - Topless walking from bathroom and getting into bed. Dark.
- • 0:57 - Brief right breast, while on couch with Guy Marchand.
- •• 0:58 - Topless getting dressed while Serge is yelling.

Guy Marchand. . . . . .Max

Heaven's Gate *(1980)*

Jeff Bridges. . . . . John
Isabelle Huppert. . . . . Ella
- •• 1:10 - Nude running around the house and in bed with Kris Kristofferson.
- ••• 1:18 - Nude, taking a bath in the river and getting out.
- • 2:24 - Very brief left breast getting raped by three guys.

John Hurt. . . . . .Irvine
Kris Kristofferson . . . . Averill
Terry O'Quinn . . . . Captain Minardi
Sam Waterston. . . . . Canton

Heavenly Bodies *(1985)*

Jo Anne Bates . . . . Girl in Locker Room
Sugar Bouche. . . . . .Stripper
- • 0:16 - Topless doing stripper gram for Steve.

Cynthia Dale . . . . Samantha Blair
- • 0:30 - Brief topless fantasizing about making love with Steve while doing aerobic exercises.

Laura Henry . . . . .Debbie
- • 0:46 - Brief topless making love while her boyfriend, Jack, watches TV.

The Heavenly Kid *(1985)*

Jason Gedrick. . . . . Lenny
- •• 0:31 - Brief buns, in clothing store when Bobby magically dresses him in better looking clothes.

Nancy Valen. . . . . Melissa

The Heist *(1989; Made for Cable Movie)*

Pierce Brosnan . . . . Bobby Skinner
Wendy Hughes . . . . .Susan
- • 0:52 - Very brief side view of right breast making love in bed with Pierce Brosnan.

Hell Comes to Frogtown *(1987)*

Sandahl Bergman. . . . . Spangle
Suzanne Solari . . . . Runaway Girl
Kristi Somers . . . . Arabella

Cec Verrell . . . . Centinella
  •• 0:19 - Topless taking off her blouse and getting into sleeping bag with Roddy Piper. Brief topless again after he throws her off him.

Hell High *(1989)*
Karen Russell. . . . . .Teen Girl
  •• 0:04 - Topless in shack with Teen Boy while little girl watches through a hole in the wall.

Hellhole *(1985)*
Lamya Derval . . . . Jacuzzi Girl
  ••• 1:08 - Topless (she's on the right) sniffing glue in closet with another woman.
  ••• 1:12 - Full frontal nudity in Jacuzzi room with Mary Woronov.
Terry Moore .Sidnee Hammond
Ray Sharkey. . . . . Silk
Dyanne Thorne. . . . . .Chrysta
Pamela Ward. . . . . Tina
Edy Williams . . . . Vera
  ••• 0:22 - Topless on bed posing for Silk.
  ••• 0:24 - Topless in white panties in shower, then fighting with another woman.
  ••• 1:03 - Topless in mud bath with another woman. Long scene.
Mary Woronov . . . . .Dr. Fletcher

Hello Again! *(1987)*
Corbin Bernsen . . . . Jason Chadman
Gabriel Byrne . . . . .Kevin Scanlon
Shelley Long . . . . Lucy Chadman
  • 0:58 - Brief buns, in hospital gown, walking down hallway.

Hellraiser *(1987)*
Clare Higgins . . . . Julia
  • 0:17 - Very, very brief left breast and buns making love with Frank.
    1:10 - In white bra in bedroom putting necklace on.

Hellraiser II—Hellbound *(1988)*
Catherine Chevalier. . . . . Tiffany's Mother
Clare Higgins . . . . Julia
  • 0:20 - Very, very brief right breast, lying in bed with Frank. Scene from *Hellraiser*.

Henry & June *(1990)*
Maria De Medeiros . . . . Anais Nin
  • 0:50 - Brief right breast, popping out of dress top.
  •• 0:52 - Topless lying in bed with Richard E. Grant.
  •• 1:13 - Topless in bed with Fred Ward, buns getting out. Right breast standing by the window.
  ••• 1:31 - Topless in bed with Brigitte Lahaie.
    1:37 - Nude under sheer black patterned dress.
  •• 1:43 - Close up of right breast as Ward plays with her.
  •• 2:01 - Left breast, then topless after taking off her top in bed with Uma Thurman.
Richard E. Grant . . . . Hugo

Brigitte Lahaie . . . . Harry's Whore
  •• 0:23 - Brief buns and topless under sheer white dress going up stairs with Fred Ward.
  •• 1:22 - Topless in sheer white dress again. Nude under dress walking up stairs.
  ••• 1:23 - Topless and buns making love with another woman while Anais and Hugo watch.
  • 1:31 - Topless in bed with Anais. Intercut with Uma Thurman, so hard to tell who is who.
Uma Thurman . . . . .June Miller
Fred Ward . . . . .Henry Miller
  ••• 1:39 - Buns, twice, making love with Maria de Madeiros.

Hider in the House *(1989)*
Rebekka Armstrong . . . . Attractive Woman
  • 0:47 - Brief topless in bed with Mimi Roger's husband when she surprises them.

The High Country *(1980; Canadian)*
Timothy Bottoms. . . . . .Jim
  • 1:19 - Buns, walking into the pond with Linda Purl.
  • 1:24 - Buns, pulling underwear on after getting out of sleeping bag.
Linda Purl. . . . . .Kathy
    1:03 - Brief buns taking a shower in the waterfall.

High Season *(1988; British)*
Jacqueline Bisset. . . . . Katherine Shaw
  • 0:56 - Brief topless doing the backstroke in the water with Rick, then left breast while lying down. Hard to see, everything is lit with blue light.
Kenneth Branagh. Rich Lamb
  • 0:56 - Buns, putting a wrap around Jacqueline Bisset after they fool around in the water.

High Stakes *(1989)*
Maia Danziger . . . . Veronica
Sally Kirkland . . . . .Melanie "Bambi" Rose
  • 0:01 - In two piece costume, doing a strip tease routine on stage. Buns in G-string, then very, very brief topless flashing her breasts.
    1:11 - In black bra cutting her hair in front of a mirror.

Higher Education *(1987; Canadian)*
Lori Hallier . . . . Nicole Hubert
  • 0:44 - Right breast, twice, while making love with Andy in bed.
Jennifer Inch. . . . . Gladys/Glitter
Isabelle Mejias . . . . Carrie Hanson

Highlander *(1986)*
Clancy Brown. . . . . .Kuragan
Roxanne Hart. . . . . .Brenda Wyatt
  • 1:30 - Brief topless making love with Christopher Lambert. Dark, hard to see.
Christopher Lambert . . . . .Conner MacLeod
  • 1:30 - Buns making love with Roxanne Hart.

The Hitchhikers (1971)
Misty Rowe . . . . .Maggie
- 0:00 - Brief side view of left breast getting dressed.
- 0:17 - Very brief topless getting dress ripped open, then raped in van.
- 0:48 - Brief right breast while getting dressed.
- 1:09 - Left breast, making love with Benson.
- 1:10 - Brief topless taking a bath in tub.
- 1:13 - Very brief right breast in car with another victim.

Hollywood Boulevard (1976)
Candice Rialson . . . . Candy Wednesday
- 0:29 - Topless getting her blouse ripped off by actors during a film.
- 0:32 - Topless sunbathing with Bobbi and Jill.
- 0:45 - Brief topless in the films she's watching at the drive-in. Same as 0:29.

Tara Stromeir . . . . .Jill McBain
- 0:00 - Topless getting out of van and standing with film crew.
- 0:31 - Silhouette of breasts, making love with P.G.
- 0:32 - Topless sunbathing with Bobbi and Candy.
- 0:33 - Topless acting for film on hammock. Long scene.

Mary Woronov . . . . Mary McQueen

Hollywood Boulevard II (1989)
Ginger Lynn Allen . . . . Candy Chandler
- 0:33 - Topless in screening room with Woody, the writer.

Maria Socas . . . . .Amazon Queen
Lynn Theel . . . . .Ann Gregory

Hollywood Chainsaw Hookers (1988)
Esther Alise . . . . .Lisa
- 0:25 - Topless playing with a baseball bat while a John photographs her.

Michelle Bauer . . . . Mercedes
- 0:09 - Nude in motel room with a John just before chainsawing him to pieces.

Linnea Quigley . . . . Samantha
- 0:32 - Topless, dancing on stage.
- 1:02 - Topless, (but her body is painted) dancing in a ceremony.

Dawn Wildsmith . . . . Samantha

Hollywood Hot Tubs (1984)
Becky LeBeau . . . . Veronica
- 0:49 - Topless changing in the locker room with other girl soccer players while Jeff watches.
- 0:54 - Topless in hot tub with the other girls and Shawn.

Donna McDaniel . . . . Leslie Maynard
Remy O'Neill . . . . .Pam Landers
- 1:00 - Brief right breast in hot tub with Jeff.

Katt Shea . . . . .Dee-Dee
- 0:21 - Topless with her boyfriend while Shawn is working on the hot tub.

Jewel Shepard . . . . Crystal Landers

Edy Williams. . . . . Desiree
- 0:26 - Topless, trying to seduce Shawn while he works on a hot tub.
  1:26 - In black lingerie outfit in the hallway.
- 1:30 - Partial topless with breasts sticking out of her bra while she sits by hot tub with Jeff.
- 1:32 - Topless in hot tub room with Shawn.
- 1:38 - Topless again in the hot tub lobby.

Hollywood Hot Tubs 2—Educating Crystal (1989)
Tally Chanel . . . . Mindy Wright
Dori Courtney . . . . Hot Tub Girl
- 1:00 - Topless stuck in the spa and getting her hair freed.

Bob Garrison . . . . Billy "Derrick" Dare
- 0:53 - Buns, running up to hot dog stand.

Remy O'Neill . . . . Pam Landers
  0:57 - Swinging tassels on the tips of her belly dancing top.

Jewel Shepard . . . . Crystal Landers
  0:38 - In white slip during Gary's fantasy.
- 1:12 - Brief left breast, while lying down, kissing Gary.

Holocaust 2000 (1978)
Agostina Belli . . . . .Sara Golen
- 0:50 - Topless in bed making love with Kirk Douglas.

Kirk Douglas. . . . . Robert Caine
- 0:52 - Buns, during nightmare sequence. Long shots, hard to tell it's him.

Honey (1980; Italian)
Clio Goldsmith. . . . . .Annie
- 0:05 - Nude kneeling in a room.
- 0:20 - Nude getting into the bathtub.
- 0:42 - Nude getting changed.
- 0:44 - Nude while hiding under the bed.
- 0:58 - Nude getting disciplined, taking off clothes, then kneeling.

Honky (1971)
Elliot Street. . . . .
Brenda Sykes . . . . Sheila Smith
- 0:42 - Topless with her boyfriend, making love on the floor.
- 1:22 - Brief topless several times getting raped by two guys.

Horror Planet (1980; British)
a.k.a. Inseminoid
Jennifer Ashley . . . . Holly
Stephanie Beacham . . . . .Kate
Judy Geeson. . . . . Sandy
- 0:31 - Brief topless on the operating table.
- 0:37 - Same scene during brief flashback.

Victoria Tennant. . . . . Barbara

Hospital Massacre (1982)
Barbi Benton . . . . Susan Jeremy
  0:29 - Undressing behind a curtain while the Doctor watches her silhouette.
  ••• 0:31 - Topless getting examined by the Doctor. First sitting up, then lying down.
  ••• 0:34 - Great close up shot of breasts while the Doctor uses stethoscope on her.

Hostile Takeover (1988; Canadian)
a.k.a. Office Party
Jayne Eastwood . . . . Mrs. Talmage
Cindy Girling . . . . Mrs. Gayford
Kate Vernon . . . . Sally
  • 0:35 - Very brief, left breast undressing in office with John Warner. Dark.
  •• 0:39 - Right breast, turning over in her sleep, then playing with the chain.

Hot Blood (1989; Spanish)
Robert Case . . . . Ricardo
  •• 1:20 - Buns, with Alicia in stable.
Sylvia Kristel . . . . Sylvia
  • 0:44 - Buns, getting molested by Dom Luis.
Alicia Moro . . . . Alicia
  • 0:00 - Buns and lower frontal nudity in stable with Ricardo. Long shot.
  • 0:06 - In bra and panties with Julio, then buns and topless. Looks like a body double because hair doesn't match.

Hot Bodies (1988)
Sara Costa . . . . herself
  ••• 0:00 - Nude, dancing on stage. Long scene. Dancing with a big boa snake.
  ••• 0:04 - Topless and buns in G-string.
Venus de Light . . . . herself
  •• 0:22 - Topless, dancing and taking off dress.
  ••• 0:24 - Nude in large champagne glass prop.
  ••• 0:27 - Nude dancing on stage.
  ••• 0:47 - Topless and buns in G-string stripping in nurse uniform.
  ••• 0:49 - Topless and buns on hospital gurney.
  ••• 0:52 - Topless and buns dancing with a dummy prop.

The Hot Box (1972)
Margaret Markov . . . . Lynn Forrest
  • 0:12 - Topless when bad guy cuts her swimsuit top open.
  •• 0:16 - Topless in stream consoling Bunny.
  • 0:21 - Topless in the furthest hammock from camera. Long shot.
  ••• 0:45 - Topless bathing in stream with the other girls.
Rickey Richardson . . . . Ellie St. George
  •• 0:16 - Topless cleaning herself off in stream and getting out.
  • 0:21 - Topless sleeping in hammocks. (She's the second one from the front.)
  • 0:26 - Topless getting accosted by the People's Army guys.

  ••• 0:43 - Full frontal nudity making love with Flavio.
  ••• 0:45 - Topless in stream bathing with the other three girls.
  • 1:01 - Topless taking off top in front of soldiers.
Laurie Rose . . . . Sue
  •• 0:16 - Topless cleaning herself off in stream and getting out.
  •• 0:21 - Topless sleeping in hammocks. (She's the first one from the front.)
  • 0:26 - Topless getting accosted by the People's Army guys.
  ••• 0:45 - Topless in stream bathing with the other three girls.
  • 0:58 - Full frontal nudity getting raped by Major Dubay.

Hot Child in the City (1987)
Leah Ayres-Hamilton . . . . Rachel
  0:38 - In braless white T-shirt walking out by the pool and inside her sister's house.
  • 1:12 - Very brief topless in the shower with a guy. Long shot, hard to see anything.
Shari Shattuck . . . . Abby

Hot Chili (1985)
Victoria Barrett . . . . Victoria Stevenson
  • 0:55 - Very brief close up shot of right breast when it pops out of her dress. Don't see her face.
Bea Fiedler . . . . The Music Teacher
  •• 0:08 - Topless playing the cello while being fondled by Ricky.
  0:29 - Buns, playing the violin.
  •• 0:34 - Nude during fight in restaurant with Chi Chi. Hard to see because of the flashing light.
  ••• 0:36 - Topless lying on inflatable lounge in pool, playing a flute.
  ••• 0:43 - Left breast playing a tuba.
  ••• 1:01 - Topless and buns dancing in front of Mr. Lieberman.
  • 1:07 - Buns, then right breast dancing with Stanley.
Katherine Kriss . . . . Allison Baxter
  ••• 0:56 - Topless getting out of the pool talking to Ricky.
  • 1:09 - Buns and side view of left breast lying down and kissing Ricky.
Louisa Moritz . . . . Chi Chi
  0:06 - Brief buns turning around in white apron after talking with the boys.
  •• 0:34 - Nude during fight in restaurant with the Music Teacher. Hard to see because of the flashing light.
Taaffe O'Connell . . . . Brigitte
  ••• 0:21 - Topless lying on the bed. Shot with lots of diffusion.
  • 0:30 - Brief topless playing the drums.
  • 1:11 - Brief topless in bed making love with Ernie, next to her drunk husband.
Joe Rubbo . . . . Arney
  • 0:24 - Brief buns getting whipped by Brigitte.

Hot Dog... The Movie (1984)
David Naughton . . . . Dan
Crystal Smith. . . . . .Motel Clerk
- •• 0:10 - Nude getting out of spa and going to the front desk to sign people in.
Shannon Tweed . . . . Sylvia Fonda
- ••• 0:42 - Topless getting undressed, then making love in bed and in hot tub with Harkin.

Hot Moves (1985)
Monique Gabrielle . . . . Babs
- • 0:29 - Nude on the nude beach.
- •• 1:07 - Topless on and behind the sofa with Barry trying to get her top off.
Gayle Gannes . . . . Jamie
- •• 1:09 - Topless in bed with Joey.
Debi Richter . . . . .Heidi
- • 0:29 - Topless on nude beach.
- ••• 1:09 - Topless in bed with Michael.
Jill Schoelen. . . . . .Julie Ann

Hot Resort (1984)
Victoria Barrett . . . . Jane
Dana Kaminsky . . . . Melanie
- •• 1:02 - Topless taking off her white dress in a boat.
Debra Kelly . . . . .Liza
Linda Kenton. . . . . Mrs. Geraldine Miller
- • 0:11 - Very brief right breast, while in back of car with a guy.
- • 0:16 - Right breast, while passed out in closet with a bunch of guys.
- • 0:24 - Brief upper half of right breast, while on boat with a guy.
- • 0:46 - Brief topless in Volkswagen.
- • 0:51 - Brief topless in bathtub with Bronson Pinchot.
- • 1:24 - Brief topless making love on a table while covered with food.
Cynthia Lee. . . . . .Alice
- • 1:08 - Topless in the bathtub.

The Hot Spot (1990)
Debra Cole . . . . Irene Davey
- • 1:26 - Topless sunbathing next to Jennifer Connelly at side of lake. Long shot.
- •• 1:27 - Topless talking with Connelly some more.
Jennifer Connelly. . . . . Gloria Harper
- 1:01 - In black bra and panties walking out of lake with Don Johnson.
- 1:26 - Buns, lying next to Irene next to lake. Long shot.
- ••• 1:27 - Topless, talking to Irene next to lake. Wow!
Don Johnson. Harry Madox
- •• 0:41 - Brief buns, pulling up his underwear, talking to Virginia Madsen.
- • 1:17 - Buns, undressing to go swimming with Madsen.
- • 1:18 - Buns, getting out of the water. Long shot.
Virginia Madsen . . . . Dolly Harshaw
- • 0:41 - Side view of left breast while sitting on bed talking to Don Johnson.

- • 0:47 - Tip of right breast when Johnson kisses it.
- •• 1:16 - Buns, undressing for a swim outside at night. Topless hanging on rope.
- • 1:18 - Buns, getting out of water with Johnson. Long shot.
- • 1:21 - Left breast when robe gapes open while sitting up.
- 1:23 - Brief lower frontal nudity and buns in open robe after jumping off tower at night.
- 1:24 - Topless at bottom of hill with Johnson. Long shot.
- 1:45 - Nude, very, very briefly running out of house. Very blurry, could be anybody.
William Sadler . . . . Frank Sutton
Charlie Martin Smith . . . . .Lon Gulick

Hot T-shirts (1980)
Corinne Alphen . . . . .Judy
- 0:55 - In braless T-shirt as a car hop.
- • 1:10 - In yellow outfit dancing in wet T-shirt contest. Brief topless flashing her breasts at the crowd.

Hot Target (1985)
Simone Griffeth . . . . .Christine Webber
- •• 0:09 - Topless taking off top for shower, then topless and brief frontal nudity taking shower.
- ••• 0:19 - Topless in bed after making love with Steve Marachuck.
- •• 0:21 - Buns, getting out of bed and walking to bathroom.
- •• 0:23 - Topless in bed with Marachuck again.
- • 0:34 - Topless in the woods with Marachuck while cricket match goes on.

House of the Rising Sun (1987)
Jamie Barrett . . . . Janet
- • 1:04 - Very brief topless making love with Louis.
James Daughton . . . .

The House on Carroll Street (1988)
Jeff Daniels. . . . . Cochran
Kelly McGillis . . . . Emily
- • 0:39 - Brief topless reclining into the water in the bathtub.
Kenneth Welsh. . . . . Hackett

House on Sorority Row (1983)
Eileen Davidson . . . . Vicki
- •• 0:16 - Topless and buns in room making love with her boyfriend.
- 0:19 - In white bikini top by the pool.
Harley Jane Kozak. . . . . .Diane
Kate McNeil. . . . . .Katherine

The House on Straw Hill (1976; British)
Linda Hayden. . . . . Linda Hindstatt
- • 0:28 - Topless getting undressed in her room.
- ••• 0:47 - Topless, masturbating in bed.
- •• 1:06 - Right breast, in bed with Fiona Richmond.
Karl Howman. .Small Youth
- •• 0:36 - Buns, raping Linda Hayden in a field, while his friend holds a gun.

Fiona Richmond . . . . Suzanne
- ••• 0:05 - Buns and topless undressing and getting into bed and making love with Udo Kier.
- •• 0:56 - In black bra, then topless undressing in front of Kier.
- ••• 1:00 - Topless in bedroom, then making love with Kier.
- 1:03 - Brief buns, lying on Linda's bed.
- 1:05 - Buns, lying on Linda's bed.
- •• 1:06 - Right breast, in bed with Linda.
- •• 1:07 - Topless in bed with Linda.
- • 1:09 - Buns and side of left breast getting up from bed.
- • 1:11 - Full frontal nudity, getting stabbed in the bathroom. Covered with blood.

House Where Evil Dwells (1985)
Edward Albert . . . . Ted
- • 1:00 - Very brief, upper half of buns, making love with Susan George on the floor.
Susan George . . . . Laura
- ••• 0:21 - Topless in bed making love with Edward Albert.
- •• 0:59 - Topless making love again.

Housewife (1972)
Yaphet Kotto. . . . . Bone
Joyce Van Patten . . . . Bernadette
- • 0:46 - Topless and buns on pool table getting attacked by Yaphet Kotto. Probably a body double, don't see her face.
- 1:04 - Most of left breast getting on top of Kotto. In side view, you can see black tape over her nipple.
- • 1:05 - Brief side of right breast under Kotto's arm several times after she falls on the floor with him.

How Funny Can Sex Be? (1973)
Laura Antonelli . . . . Miscellaneous Personalities
- • 0:01 - Brief topless taking off swimsuit.
- • 0:04 - Brief topless in bathtub covered with bubbles.
- 0:13 - Lying in bed in sheer nightgown.
- 0:18 - Lying in bed again.
- • 0:26 - Topless getting into bed.
- • 0:36 - Topless making love in elevator behind frosted glass. Shot at fast speed.
- • 1:08 - In sheer white nun's outfit during fantasy sequence. Brief topless and buns. Nice slow motion.
- 1:16 - In black nightie.
- • 1:24 - In black bra and panties, then topless while changing clothes.

How to Beat the High Cost of Living (1980)
Richard Benjamin . . . . Albert
Dabney Coleman . . . . Jack Heintzel
Jane Curtin . . . . Elaine
- 1:28 - In pink bra, distracting everybody in the mall so her friends can steal money.
- • 1:29 - Close up topless, taking off her bra. Probably a body double.
Sybil Danning . . . . Charlotte
Jessica Lange. . . . . Louise

How to Get Ahead in Advertising (1988)
Sean Bean . . . . Carry Frisk
Richard E. Grant. . . . . Bagley
- • 0:19 - Brief buns wearing apron in kitchen all covered with food. Brief buns again talking with Rachel Ward at top of stairs.
Jacqueline Pearce . . . . Maud
Rachel Ward. . . . . Julia

How to Seduce a Woman (1973)
Alexandra Hay . . . . Nell Brinkman
- • 1:05 - Brief right breast in mirror taking off black dress.
- ••• 1:06 - Topless posing for pictures. Long scene.
- • 1:47 - Topless during flashback. Lots of diffusion.
Angel Tompkins . . . . Pamela
- 1:28 - In bra and panties for a long time getting a massage in bedroom.

The Howling (1981)
Belinda Balaski . . . . Terry Fisher
Elizabeth Brooks. . . . . Marsha
- •• 0:46 - Full frontal nudity taking off her robe in front of a campfire.
- • 0:48 - Topless sitting on Bill by the fire.
Christopher Stone . . . . R. William "Bill" Neill
- • 0:48 - Brief buns, rolling over while making love with Elizabeth Brooks in front of a campfire.
Dee Wallace Stone . . . . Karen White

Howling II (1984)
Sybil Danning . . . . Stirba
- • 0:35 - Left breast, then topless with Mariana in bedroom about to have sex with a guy.
- • 1:20 - Very brief topless during short clips during the end credits. Same shot repeated about 10 times.
Marsha A. Hunt . . . . Mariana
- •• 0:33 - Topless in bedroom with Sybil Danning and a guy.

Howling IV: The Original Nightmare (1988)
Lamya Derval . . . . Elanor
- •• 0:32 - Brief left breast, then topless making love with Richard. Nice silhouette on the wall.
Romy Windsor . . . . Marie

Howling V (1989)
Elizabeth Shé . . . . Mary Lou Summers
- • 0:33 - Buns and side view of right breast getting into pool with Donovan.
- • 0:36 - Very brief full frontal nudity climbing out of pool with Donovan.
Mary Stavin . . . . Anna
- •• 1:09 - Topless three times drying herself off while Richard watches in the mirror. Possible body double.

Humanoids from the Deep (1980)
Denise Galik. . . . . Linda Beale
Linda Shayne . . . . Miss Salmon
- • 1:06 - Topless after getting bathing suit ripped off by a humanoid.

Lynn Theel . . . . Peggy Larsen
- 0:30 - Brief topless getting raped on the beach by a humanoid.
- 0:51 - Brief topless, dead, lying on the beach all covered with seaweed.

Humongous *(1982; Canadian)*
Janit Baldwin . . . . Carla Simmons
Joy Boushel . . . . Donna Blake
- •• 0:09 - Topless looking out the window. More topless in the room in the mirror.
- 0:48 - Topless undoing her top to warm up Bert.
Janet Julian . . . . Sandy Ralston

Hundra *(1983)*
Laurene Landon . . . . Hundra
- 0:29 - Very brief topless, several times, riding her horse in the surf. Partial buns. Blurry.

The Hunger *(1983)*
David Bowie . . . . John
Catherine Deneuve . . . . Miriam
- 0:08 - Brief topless taking a shower with David Bowie. Probably a body double, you don't see her face.
Ann Magnuson . . . . Young Woman from Disco
- 0:05 - Brief topless in kitchen with David Bowie just before he kills her.
John Pankow . . . . 1st Phone Booth Youth
Susan Sarandon . . . . Sarah Roberts
- ••• 0:59 - In a wine stained white T-shirt, then topless during love scene with Catherine Deneuve.

Hurricane *(1979)*
Timothy Bottoms . . . . Jack Sanford
Mia Farrow . . . . Charlotte Bruckner
- 0:39 - Brief left breast in open dress top while crawling under bushes at the beach.

Hussy *(1980; British)*
Helen Mirren . . . . Beaty
- •• 0:22 - Left breast, then side of right breast lying in bed with John Shea.
- ••• 0:29 - Nude, making love in bed with Shea.
- •• 0:31 - Full frontal nudity in bathtub.
John Shea . . . . Emory
- •• 0:29 - Buns making love with Helen Mirren in bed. Half of lower frontal nudity when she rolls off him.

Hustle *(1975)*
Eileen Brennan . . . . Paula Hollinger
Catherine Deneuve . . . . Nicole Britton
Sharon Kelly . . . . Gloria Hollinger
- 0:12 - Brief topless several times getting rolled out of freezer, dead.
- 1:03 - In pasties, dancing behind curtain when Gloria's father imagines the dancer is Gloria.
- 1:42 - In black lingerie, brief buns and side views of breast in bed in film.
Burt Reynolds . . . . Lieutenant Phil Gaines
Patrice Rohmer . . . . Linda (Dancer)
- 1:03 - In pasties, dancing on stage behind beaded curtain. Buns in G-string.

I Love N.Y. *(1987)*
Scott Baio . . . . Mario Colone
- 1:19 - Brief, upper half of buns, getting out of bed. Dark, hard to see.

I Love You *(1982; Brazilian)*
Sonia Braga . . . . Maria
- ••• 0:34 - Full frontal nudity making love with Paulo.
- •• 0:36 - Topless sitting on the edge of the bed.
- 0:49 - Topless running around the house teasing Paulo.
- •• 0:50 - Brief nude in strobe light. Don't see her face.
- 0:53 - Topless eating fruit with Paulo.
- ••• 0:54 - Topless wearing white panties in front of windows with Paulo. Long scene.
- 1:03 - Left breast standing talking to Paulo.
- 1:10 - Left breast talking to Paulo.
- ••• 1:23 - Topless with Paulo during an argument. Dark, but long scene.
- •• 1:28 - Topless walking around Paulo's place with a gun. Dark.
- •• 1:33 - Various topless scenes.

I Love You to Death *(1990)*
Phoebe Cates . . . . Uncredited Girl in Bar
William Hurt . . . . Harlan
Victoria Jackson . . . . Lacey
Michelle Joyner . . . . Donna Joy
Kevin Kline . . . . Joey
- 0:10 - Buns, wearing an apron walking from the bedroom in Victoria Jackson's apartment.

I Never Promised You a Rose Garden *(1977)*
Bibi Andersson . . . . Dr. Fried
Jeff Conaway . . . . Lactamaeon
Kathleen Quinlan . . . . Deborah
- 0:27 - Topless changing in a mental hospital room with the orderly.
- 0:52 - Brief topless riding a horse in a hallucination sequence. Blurry, hard to see. Then close up of left breast (could be anyone's).
Susan Tyrrell . . . . Lee

I Spit on Your Grave *(1978)*
(Uncut, unrated version.)
Camille Keaton . . . . Jennifer
- 0:05 - Topless undressing to go skinny dipping in lake.
- •• 0:23 - Left breast sticking out of bathing suit top, then topless after top is ripped off. Right breast several times.
- 0:25 - Topless, getting raped by the jerks.
- 0:27 - Buns and brief full frontal nudity, crawling away from the jerks.
- 0:29 - Nude, walking through the woods.
- 0:32 - Topless, getting raped again.
- 0:36 - Topless and buns after rape.
- 0:38 - Buns, walking to house.
- 0:40 - Buns and lower frontal nudity in the house.
- 0:41 - More topless and buns on the floor.
- 0:45 - Nude, very dirty after all she's gone through.

- 0:51 - Full frontal nudity while lying on the floor.
- 0:52 - Side of left breast while in bathtub.
- •• 1:13 - Full frontal nudity seducing Matthew before killing him.
- ••• 1:23 - Full frontal nudity in front of mirror, then getting into bathtub. Long scene.

Gunter Kleemann . . . . .Andy
- 0:33 - Buns, raping Jennifer.

Richard Pace . . . . .Matthew
- 0:42 - Buns, undressing in the house to rape Jennifer.
  1:15 - Silhouette of penis while getting hung (by the neck) by Jennifer.

Erin Tabor . . . . Johnny
- 0:25 - Buns, undressing to rape Jennifer.
- 1:20 - Buns, undressing at gun point.

I, the Jury (1982)

Corinne Bohrer . . . . .Soap Opera Actress
Bobbi Burns . . . . Sheila Kyle
Barbara Carrera . . . . Dr. Charolette Bennett
- ••• 1:02 - Nude on bed making love with Armand Assante. Very sexy.
- 1:46 - Brief topless in hallway kissing Assante.

Lee Anne Harris . . . . 1st twin
- ••• 0:48 - Topless on bed talking to Armand Assante.
- 0:52 - Full frontal nudity on bed wearing red wig, talking to the maniac.

Lynette Harris . . . . .2nd twin
- ••• 0:48 - Topless on bed talking to Armand Assante.
- 0:52 - Full frontal nudity on bed wearing red wig, talking to the maniac.

Laurene Landon . . . . Velda

Iced (1988)

Debra De Liso . . . . .Trina
- 0:11 - In a bra, then brief nude making love with Cory in hotel room.

Elizabeth Gorcey . . . . Diane
Joseph Alan Johnson . . . . Alex
- 0:46 - Brief buns in bathtub reminiscing about making love with a girl.

Ron Kologie . . . . Carl
- 0:39 - Buns, in bathroom snorting cocaine.

Lisa Loring . . . . Jeanette
- 0:46 - Brief left breast in bathtub.
- 0:53 - Buns and brief right breast in bathtub.
- •• 1:05 - Brief lowe nudity getting into hot tub. Topless just before getting electrocuted.
- •• 1:13 - Full frontal nudity lying dead in the hot tub.
- 1:18 - Brief full frontal nudity lying dead in the hot tub again.

If Looks Could Kill (1987)

Bob Fitzpatrick . . . . Doorman
- ••• 0:18 - Buns, undressing and getting into bed with the maid.

Jane Hamilton . . . . .Mary Beth
Jeanne Marie . . . . Jeannie Burns
- •• 0:06 - Topless taking off her robe and kissing George.

Sharon Moran .Madonna Maid
- •• 0:17 - Full frontal nudity after Laura leaves.

Ilsa, She Wolf of the S.S. (1974)

Dyanne Thorne . . . . .Ilsa
- •• 0:00 - Buns, then topless making love in bed.
- ••• 0:01 - Topless taking a shower.
- •• 0:29 - Buns and topless in bed with the American.
- •• 0:49 - In bra, then topless undressing. Right breast while lying in bed.

The Image (1990; Made for Cable Movie)

Marsha Mason . . . . Jean Cromwell
- 0:08 - Two brief side views of left breast standing in bathroom after Albert Finney gets out of the shower.

Images (1972)

Susannah York . . . . .Cathryn
- 0:59 - Brief lower frontal nudity, then right breast lying on the bed.
  1:38 - Brief buns in the shower.

Imagine: John Lennon (1988)

John Lennon . . . . Himself
- 0:43 - Nude in B&W photos from his White Album.
  0:57 - Brief frontal nudity of album cover again during interview.

Yoko Ono . . . . Herself
- 0:43 - Nude in B&W photos from John Lennon's White Album.
  0:57 - Brief full frontal nudity from album cover again during an interview.
  1:27 - Almost topless in bed with Lennon.

Immortalizer (1990)

Rebekka Armstrong . . . . .June
- 0:16 - Topless getting blouse taken off by nurse.
- ••• 0:29 - Topless when a worker fondles her while she's asleep.

Raye Hollitt . . . . .Queenie

Impulse (1989)

Jeff Fahey . . . . .Stan
Theresa Russell . . . . .Lottie
- •• 0:37 - Left breast, making love with Stan in bed.

Impulse (1984)

Tim Matheson . . . . Stuart
- 0:17 - Buns, getting out of bed with Meg Tilly.

Bill Paxton . . . . .Eddie
Sherri Stoner . . . . .Young Girl
Meg Tilly . . . . .Jenny
  0:58 - In wet red swimsuit in photograph, then topless in B&W photograph (don't see her face) when Tim Matheson looks at photos.

In Harm's Way (1965; B&W)

Barbara Bouchet . . . . Liz Eddington
- 0:05 - Very, very brief right breast waving to a guy from the water.

Kirk Douglas . . . . Paul Eddington
Paula Prentiss . . . . Bev

In Praise of Older Women (1978; Canadian)

Tom Berenger . . . . Andras Vayda
- • 0:32 - Buns, in bed with Karen Black (seen in mirror). Long shot.
- •• 1:04 - Buns, rolling off Susan Strasberg. Kind of dark.
- •• 1:07 - Very brief lower frontal nudity three times, standing up and picking up Strasberg.
- • 1:20 - Very brief frontal nudity turning over in bed waiting for Alexandra Stewart.
- • 1:23 - Very, very brief blurry frontal nudity turning over in bed after getting mad at Alexandra Stewart.
- ••• 1:42 - Buns, undressing with Helen Shaver. Very brief balls.

Karen Black . . . . Maya
- •• 0:35 - Topless in bed with Tom Berenger.

Michael Kirby . . . .
Marilyn Lightstone . . . . Klari
- • 0:45 - Left breast, twice, on floor with Tom Berenger before being discovered by Karen Black.

Marianne McIssac . . . . Julika
- •• 0:23 - Topless and buns, getting into bed with Tom Berenger.

Helen Shaver . . . . Ann MacDonald
- ••• 1:40 - Blue bra and panties, then topless with Tom Berenger.
- ••• 1:42 - Nude lying in bed with Berenger, then getting out and getting dressed.

Alexandra Stewart . . . . Paula
- •• 1:21 - Topless in bed with Tom Berenger.
- •• 1:23 - Nude, in and out of bed with Berenger.

Susan Strasberg . . . . Bobbie
- •• 1:03 - Left breast, while making love in bed with Tom Berenger.
- ••• 1:04 - Topless in bed after Berenger rolls off her.

Alberta Watson . . . . Mitzi
- •• 0:51 - Topless sitting in chair talking with Tom Berenger, then more topless lying in bed. Long scene.

In Search of the Perfect 10 (1986)

(Shot on video tape.)

Lois Ayer . . . . Perfect Girl #2
- ••• 0:08 - In swimsuit, then topless exercising by the pool.

Michelle Bauer . . . . Perfect Girl #10
- ••• 0:53 - In yellow outfit stripping in office. Topless and buns in G-string bottom.

Iris Condon . . . . Perfect Girl #6/Jackie
- ••• 0:37 - Topless (she's the blonde) playing Twister with Rebecca Lynn. Buns in G-string.

Rebecca Lynn . . . . Perfect Girl #7/Ellen
- ••• 0:37 - Topless (she's the redhead) playing Twister with Iris Condon. Buns in G-string.

Heidi Paine . . . . Perfect Girl #8
- ••• 0:45 - Brief topless pulling down her top outside of car.

Teri Lynn Peake . . . . Perfect Girl #9
- ••• 0:47 - Buns and topless taking a shower.

Gail Thackray . . . . Perfect Girl #5
- ••• 0:31 - Topless and buns trying on all sorts of lingerie in dressing room.

In the Cold of the Night (1989)

Jeff Lester . . . . Scott Bruin
- • 0:05 - Very brief buns, rolling over to strangle Shannon Tweed.

Shelley Michelle . . . . Model 3
Adrianne Sachs . . . . Kimberly Shawn
- ••• 0:52 - Buns and topless in shower, then making love with Scott. Long, erotic scene.
- • 0:59 - Brief topless in outdoor spa.
- •• 1:06 - Topless making love on Scott's lap in bed.

Marc Singer . . . . Ken Strom
Shannon Tweed . . . . Lena
- • 0:02 - Right breast while making love with Scott.

In the Spirit (1990)

Peter Falk . . . . Roger Flan
- •• 0:17 - Buns, three times while standing up, a little embarrassed, talking to Crystal.

Melanie Griffith . . . . Lureen

Incoming Freshman (1979)

Georgia Harrell . . . . Student
Al Nazario . . . . Mooner
- • 0:44 - Buns, mooning Professor Bilbo during his daydream.
- • 0:56 - Buns again during Bilbo's daydream.
- • 1:19 - Buns, during end credits.

An Indecent Obsession (1985)

Wendy Hughes . . . . Honour Langtry
  0:32 - Possibly Wendy topless, could be Sue because Luce is fantasizing about Wendy while making love with Sue. Dark, long shot, hard to see.
- •• 1:10 - Left breast, making love in bed with Wilson.

Bruno Lawrence . . . . Matt Sawyer
Richard Moir . . . . Luce Daggett
- • 0:31 - Buns at the beach with his pals. Don't see his face.

The Inheritance (1978; Italian)

Dominique Sanda . . . . Irene
- •• 0:18 - Full frontal nudity getting undressed and lying on the bed with her new husband.
- ••• 0:37 - Full frontal nudity lying in bed with her lover.
- • 1:19 - Very brief right breast, while undoing top for Anthony Quinn.
- ••• 1:22 - Left breast, lying in bed. Full frontal nudity jumping out of bed after realizing that Quinn is dead.

Inhibition

Ilona Staller . . . . Anna
- ••• 0:08 - Nude taking a shower with Carol.
- • 0:43 - Brief full frontal nudity getting out of swimming pool.
- ••• 0:55 - Topless making love in the water with Robert.
- ••• 1:00 - Full frontal nudity getting disciplined by Carol.

Innerspace (1987)

Fiona Lewis . . . . .Dr. Margaret Canker
Dennis Quaid . . . . .Tuck Pendleton
- •• 0:08 - Buns, standing naked in the street as taxi drives off with his towel. Kind of a long shot.

Meg Ryan . . . . Lydia

The Innocent (1976; Italian)

Laura Antonelli . . . . Julianna
- ••• 0:41 - Topless in bed with her husband.
- ••• 0:53 - Full frontal nudity in bed when her husband lifts her dress up.

Innocent Victim (1988)

Peter Firth. . . . . Terence
Paul McGann . . . . .Barry
Helen Shaver. . . . . Benet Archdale
- • 1:05 - Very brief side of left breast on top of a guy in bed.

Inserts (1976)

Veronica Cartwright . . . . .Harlene
- •• 0:16 - Topless sitting on bed with Richard Dreyfus.
- ••• 0:31 - Nude on bed with Stephen Davies making a porno movie for Dreyfus. Long scene.

Stephen Davies . . . . .Rex
- •• 0:31 - Buns and balls, on bed with Veronica Cartwright, making a porno movie for Richard Dreyfus.

Jessica Harper . . . . .Cathy Cake
- ••• 1:15 - Topless in garter belt and stockings, lying in bed for Richard Dreyfus. Long scene.

Instant Karma (1990)

Rebekka Armstrong. . . . . Jamie
Craig Sheffer. . . . . .Zane Smith
- • 1:15 - Brief buns on top of Penelope. Don't see his face.

Internal Affairs (1990)

Richard Gere. . . . . Dennis Peck
Faye Grant . . . . .Penny
- • 0:50 - Right breast, while straddling Richard Gere while on the telephone.

Nancy Travis. .Kathleen Avila
- • 0:38 - Side view of left breast when Raymond opens the shower door to talk to her.

Into the Fire (1988)

Susan Anspach . . . . Rosalind Winfield
- •• 0:22 - Left breast, under trench coat when she first comes into the house, briefly again in the kitchen.
- •• 0:31 - Topless in bedroom standing up with Wade.

Olivia D'Abo . . . . Liette
0:07 - Very, very brief silhouette of left breast in bed with Wade.
- •• 0:32 - Topless on bed with Wade. A little bit dark and hard to see.
- •• 1:10 - Topless in the bathtub. (Note her panties when she gets up.)

Into the Night (1985)

David Bowie. . . . . .Colin Morris
Sue Bowser . . . . .Girl on Boat
- •• 0:24 - Topless taking off blouse with Jake on his boat after Michelle Pfeiffer leaves.

Jeff Goldblum. . . . . Ed Okin
Kathryn Harrold . . . . Christie
Tracey E. Hutchinson . . . . Federal Agent
Michelle Pfeiffer . . . . .Diana
- • 0:27 - Buns and very brief side nudity in her brother's apartment getting dressed. Long shot, hard to see.

Peggy Sands . . . . .Shameless Woman
- • 0:43 - Topless putting dress on after coming out of men's restroom stall after a man leaves the stall first.

Invasion of the Bee Girls (1973)

Anitra Ford. . . . . .Dr. Susan Harris
- ••• 0:47 - Topless and buns undressing in front of a guy in front of a fire.

Susan Player Jarreau . . . . Girl
Beverly Powers. . . . . Harriet Williams
- • 1:14 - In white bra and panties, then right breast and buns taking off her clothes for her husband.

Victoria Vetri . . . . .Julie Zorn
- • 0:30 - Brief topless getting molested by jerks.
- ••• 1:19 - Topless in the bee transformer, then brief buns getting rescued.

Invasion of the Body Snatchers (1978)

Brooke Adams . . . . Elizabeth Driscoll
0:49 - All covered in pod gunk in her bedroom when Donald Sutherland discovers her. Don't really see anything.
- •• 1:43 - Brief topless behind plants when Sutherland sees her change into a pod person. Hard to see because plants are in the way.
- • 1:48 - Topless walking through the pod factory pointing out Sutherland to everybody. Long shot, hard to see.

Veronica Cartwright. . . . . Nancy Bellicec
Jeff Goldblum. . . . . .Jack Bellicec
Donald Sutherland. . . . . Matthew Bennell

The Invisible Kid (1988)

Karen Black . . . . .Mom
Jay Underwood . . . . Grover Dunn
- • 0:27 - Brief buns running around the school halls after becoming visible with his friend.

Wally Ward . . . . .Milton McClane
- • 0:27 - Brief buns running around the school halls after becoming visible with his friend, Grover.

Invisible Maniac (1990)

Dana Bentley . . . . Newscaster
- • 1:22 - Brief topless on monitor doing the news.

Debra Lamb. . . . . .Betty
- • 0:21 - Buns and very brief side view of right breast in the shower with the other girls.
- ••• 0:43 - In bra, then topless and buns standing on the left in the locker room with the other girls.

- 0:44 - Buns and brief topless in the shower with the other girls.
- • 0:56 - In bra, then topless getting killed by Dr. Smith.
- 0:58 - Brief topless, dead.

Melissa Moore. . . . . .Bunny
- 0:21 - Buns in shower with the other girls.
- • • 0:43 - In bra, then topless sitting with yellow towel in locker room with the other girls.
- 0:44 - Topless in shower with the other girls.
- • • 1:09 - In bra, then topless making out in Principal's Office with Chet. Long scene.

Shannon Wesley . . . . .Vicky
- 0:21 - Buns and very, very brief side of left breast in the shower with the other girls.
- 0:33 - Right breast covered with bubbles.
- • • 0:43 - In bra, then topless and lots of buns in locker room with the other girls.
- • 0:44 - Buns and left breast in the shower with the other girls.
- • • 1:04 - Undressing in locker room in white bra and panties, then topless. More topless taking a shower and getting electrocuted.

Ironweed (1987)
Carroll Baker . . . . Annie Phelan
Jack Nicholson .Francis Phelan
Meryl Streep . . . . Helen
Margaret Whitton . . . . Katrina
- • 1:19 - Full frontal nudity leaving the house and walking down steps while young Francis brushes a horse.

Irreconcilable Differences (1984)
Dana Kaminsky . . . . Woman in Dress Shop
Ryan O'Neal . . . . Albert Brodsky
Sharon Stone . . . . Blake Chandler
- • 0:56 - Topless lowering her blouse in front of Ryan O'Neal during film test.

Isadora (1968; British)
James Fox . . . . Gordon Craig
Vanessa Redgrave . . . . Isadora Duncan
0:47 - Brief glimpses of topless and buns dancing around in her boyfriend's house at night. Hard to see anything.
- 2:19 - Very brief topless dancing on stage after coming back from Russia.

Ishtar (1987)
Isabelle Adjani . . . . Shirra Assel
- 0:27 - Very brief left breast flashing herself to Dustin Hoffman at the airport while wearing sunglasses.
Warren Beatty . . . . Lyle Rogers
Dustin Hoffman. . . . . Chuck Clarke
Carol Kane . . . . Carol
Jack Weston . . . . Marty Freed

The Island (1980)
Angela Punch McGregor . . . . Beth
- • 0:45 - Topless taking off poncho to make love with Michael Caine in hut after rubbing stuff on him.
0:50 - Braless under poncho walking towards Caine.

Island of 1000 Delights
Bea Fiedler . . . . .Julia
- • 0:25 - Full frontal nudity washing herself in bathtub, then nude taking off her towel for Michael.
- • 0:27 - Topless lying on floor after making love, then buns walking to chair.
- • 0:46 - Full frontal nudity taking off her dress and kissing Howard.
- • 0:50 - Topless in white bikini bottoms coming out of the water to greet Howard.
- • • 1:06 - Topless sitting in the sand near the beach, then nude talking with Sylvia.
- • • 1:17 - Right breast (great close up) making love with Sylvia.
- • • 1:18 - Topless above Sylvia.
Scarlett Gunden . . . . Francine
- • • 0:02 - Topless on beach dancing with Ching. Upper half of buns sitting down.
0:20 - Dancing braless in sheer brown dress.
- • 0:44 - Full frontal nudity getting tortured by Ming.
- 1:16 - Topless on beach after Ching rescues her.
Olivia Pascal . . . . Peggy
- • 0:16 - Topless, tied up while being tortured by two guys. Upper half lower frontal nudity.
- • 0:23 - Full frontal nudity lying in bed, then buns running out the door. Full frontal nudity running up stairs, nude hiding in bedroom.
0:33 - In braless black dress.
- • • 0:57 - Nude, taking off her clothes in shower with Michael.
- 1:26 - Brief topless running on the beach with Michael.

It's My Turn (1980)
Jill Clayburgh . . . . Kate Gunzinger
- 1:10 - Brief upper half of left breast in bed with Michael Douglas after making love.
Michael Douglas . . . . Ben Lewin
Daniel Stern . . . . Cooperman

Jackson County Jail (1976)
Marciee Drake . . . . Candy (David's Girlfriend)
- 0:04 - Brief topless wrapping towel around herself, in front of Howard Hessman. Long shot.
Tommy Lee Jones. . . . . Coley Blake
Yvette Mimieux . . . . .Dinah Hunter
- 0:39 - Topless in jail cell getting raped by policeman.
Patrice Rohmer. Cassie Anne
Betty Thomas . . . . .Waitress
Mary Woronov. . . . . Pearl

Jacob's Ladder (1990)
Perry Lang . . . . Jacob's Assailant
Elizabeth Peña . . . . .Jezzie
- 0:14 - Side view of right breast taking off robe and getting into shower with Tim Robbins.
- • • 0:16 - Topless several times opening dress and putting pants on. Then in black bra.
- • 0:31 - Very, very brief topless in bed with Robbins, then left breast a lot. Dark.

Tim Robbins . . . . Jacob Singer
•• 0:40 - Buns, twice in bathroom getting ready for ice bath.

Jakarta (1988)
Sue Francis Pai . . . . Esha
• 1:01 - Brief right breast, while making love in the courtyard with Falco.
1:13 - Brief side of right breast while kissing Falco.
•• 1:13 - Side view of right breast, then brief topless twice, making love under a mosquito net with Falco. Hard to see her face clearly.

James Joyce's Women (1983)
Fionnula Flanagan . . . . Molly Bloom
• 0:48 - Brief topless getting out of bed.
••• 0:56 - Topless getting back into bed.
••• 1:02 - Full frontal nudity masturbating in bed talking to herself. Very long scene—9 minutes!

The January Man (1988)
Harvey Keitel . . . . Frank Starkey
Kevin Kline . . . . Nick Starkey
Mary Elizabeth Mastrantonio . . . . Bernadette Flynn
• 0:40 - Topless in bed with Kevin Kline. Side view of left breast squished against Kline.
••• 0:42 - Topless after Kline gets out of bed. Brief shot, but very nice!
Susan Sarandon . . . . Christine Starkey

Jessi's Girls (1976)
Regina Carroll . . . . Claire
•• 0:58 - Topless and buns in hay with Indian guy. Don't see her face.
Sondra Currie . . . . Jessica
• 0:02 - Nude in water cleaning up, then brief left breast getting dressed.
• 0:07 - Topless getting raped by four guys. Fairly long scene.
• 0:37 - Topless kissing Clay under a tree. Hard to see because of the shadows.
Ellen Stern . . . . Kana
••• 1:10 - Left breast, then topless in bed with a guy.

Jezebel's Kiss (1990)
Katherine Barrese . . . . Jezebel
•• 0:36 - Full frontal nudity washing herself off in kitchen after having sex with the sheriff.
• 0:42 - Brief buns, going for a swim in the ocean. Dark.
••• 0:48 - Topless taking off her robe in front of Hunt, then making love with him.
• 0:58 - Brief right breast and buns while Malcolm McDowell watches through slit in curtain. Long shot.
• 1:09 - Right breast and buns getting undressed. Long shot. Closer shot of buns, putting robe on.
••• 1:12 - Topless making love with McDowell. More topless after.
Meg Foster . . . . Amanda Faberson
Malcolm McDowell . . . . Benjamin J. Faberson
• 1:12 - Buns, making love with Jezebel.

The Jigsaw Murders (1988)
Laura Albert . . . . Blonde Stripper
••• 0:19 - Topless and buns in black G-string, stripping during bachelor party in front of a group of policemen.
Michelle Bauer . . . . Cindy Jakulski
0:20 - Brief buns on cover of puzzle box during bachelor party.
• 0:21 - Brief topless in puzzle on underside of glass table after the policemen put the puzzle together.
• 0:29 - Very brief topless when the police officers show the photographer the puzzle picture.
• 0:43 - Very brief topless long shots in some pictures that the photographer is watching on a screen.
Catherine Case . . . . Stripper #2
• 0:27 - Brief topless in black peek-a-boo bra posing for photographer.
Michelle Johnson . . . . Kathy DaVonzo
0:51 - Posing in leotards in dance studio.
1:07 - Posing in lingerie on bed.
1:20 - In light blue dance outfit.
1:27 - Posing in blue swimsuit.
Yaphet Kotto . . . . Dr. Fillmore
Brinke Stevens . . . . Stripper #1
• 0:28 - Very, very brief topless posing for photographer in white bra and panties when camera passes between her and the other stripper.

Jo Jo Dancer, Your Life Is Calling (1986)
Tanya Boyd . . . . Alicia
Wings Hauser . . . . Cliff
Paula Kelly . . . . Satin Doll
0:26 - Doing a strip tease in the night club wearing gold pasties and a gold G-string.
Richard Pryor . . . . Jo Jo Dancer/Alter Ego
•• 0:06 - Buns, walking naked out of the hospital waiting for the limousine.
Barbara Williams . . . . Dawn

Jock Petersen (1974; Australian)
a.k.a. Petersen
Belinda Giblin . . . . Moira Winton
•• 0:21 - Left breast several times, under a cover with Jock, then buns when cover is removed.
Wendy Hughes . . . . Patricia Kent
••• 0:12 - Topless in her office with Tony.
• 0:13 - Topless making love with Tony on the floor.
•• 0:44 - Nude running around the beach with Tony.
•• 0:50 - Nude in bed making love with Tony.
• 1:24 - Full frontal nudity when Tony rapes her in her office.
Anne Pendlebury . . . . Peggy
Jack Thompson . . . . Tony Petersen
••• 0:13 - Buns, making love with Wendy Hughes.
••• 0:20 - Frontal nudity under tarp with Moira during protest.
• 0:22 - Buns in bed with Suzy.
•• 0:44 - Nude running around the beach with Hughes.
•• 0:50 - Frontal nudity undressing, then buns lying in bed.

370

Jacki Weaver . . . . Susie Petersen
••• 0:01 - Full frontal nudity lying in bed with Jock.

Joe (1970)
Peter Boyle . . . . Joe Curran
Susan Sarandon . . . . Melissa Compton
• 0:02 - Topless and very brief lower frontal nudity taking off clothes and getting into bathtub with Frank.

Johnny Handsome (1989)
Ellen Barkin . . . . Sunny Boyd
Elizabeth McGovern . . . . Donna McCarty
•• 0:47 - Right breast in bed with Mickey Rourke.

The Josephine Baker Story (1991; Made for Cable Movie)
David Dukes . . . . Jo Bouillon
Lynn Whitfield. . . . . Josephine Baker
• 0:00 - Topless dancing during opening credits. Slow motion.
•• 0:13 - Topless taking off her dress top for the French painter.
••• 0:14 - Topless in the mirror and dancing with the painter after making love. Nice. Dancer doing splits looks like a body double.
0:16 - Brief buns, in wet dress.
••• 0:31 - Topless on stage doing the Banana Dance.
••• 0:33 - Topless some more, doing the Banana Dance.
• 2:02 - Brief topless dancing during flashback.

Joy (1983; French/Canadian)
Nancy Cser . . . . unidentified
Jeffrey Kime. . . . . Helmut
Claudia Udy . . . . Joy
•• 0:11 - Nude, undressing, getting into bath then into and out of bed.
••• 0:14 - Nude in bed with Marc.
••• 0:31 - In swimsuits, posing for photos, then full frontal nudity.
•• 0:54 - Topless sitting with Bruce at encounter group.
• 1:04 - Buns and topless getting into bathtub.

The Joy of Flying
Olivia Pascal . . . . Maria
•• 0:39 - Topless wearing panties, in bedroom with George, then nude.
•• 0:46 - Nude with George in bathroom.
Ajita Wilson. Madame Gaballi
•• 1:20 - Full frontal nudity undressing for George.
•• 1:23 - Topless, making love on top of George.
• 1:25 - Left breast, while in bed with George.

Joyride (1977)
Melanie Griffith. . . . . Susie
• 0:05 - Topless in back of station wagon with Robert Carradine, hard to see anything.
•• 0:59 - Brief topless in spa with everybody.
• 1:11 - Brief topless in shower with Desi Arnaz, Jr.
Anne Lockhart. . . . . Cindy
•• 0:59 - Brief topless in the spa with everybody.
••• 1:00 - Topless, standing in the kitchen kissing Desi Arnaz Jr.

Joysticks (1983)
Corinne Bohrer. Patsy Rutter
John Diehl . . . . Arnie
Erin Halligan. . . . . Sandy
•• 1:08 - Right breast, then topless in bed with Jefferson surrounded by candles.
Becky LeBeau. . . . . Liza
Kym Malin . . . . Lola
• 0:03 - Topless with Alva showing a nerd their breasts by pulling their blouses open.
••• 0:18 - Topless during strip-video game with Jefferson, then in bed with him.
• 0:57 - Topless during fantasy sequence, lit with red lights, hard to see anything.
• 1:02 - Brief topless in slide show in courtroom.
Lynda Wiesmeier . . . . Candy

Julia (1974; German)
Ekkhardt Belle . . . . Patrick
• 1:01 - Very brief buns in bed with Terry.
Peter Berling . . . . Alex Lovener
0:12 - Brief buns, playing the piano outside on the dock.
Gisela Hahn . . . . .Miriam
•• 0:12 - Topless tanning herself outside.
• 1:14 - Brief topless sitting in the rain.
Sylvia Kristel . . . . Julia
0:23 - Brief topless in the lake.
•• 0:25 - Topless on deck in the lake.
• 0:28 - Brief topless changing clothes at night. Long shot.
•• 0:34 - Topless on boat with two boys.
•• 0:42 - Topless taking off her towel.
• 1:12 - Topless on tennis court with Patrick.

Julia and Julia (1987; Italian)
(This movie was shot using a high-definition video system and then transferred to film.)
Sting . . . . Daniel
•• 1:11 - Buns, sleeping in bed when Kathleen Turner leaves. Don't see his face very well.
Gabriel Byrne. . . . . Paolo
Kathleen Turner . . . . Julia
••• 0:32 - Topless making love in bed with her husband.
••• 1:08 - Topless, then right breast making love in bed with Sting.

Jungle Warriors (1985)
Ava Cadell . . . . Didi Belair
• 0:50 - Brief topless getting yellow top ripped open by a bad guy.
Sybil Danning . . . . .Angel
0:53 - Buns, getting a massage while lying face down.
Louisa Moritz . . . . Laura McCashin

Just Before Dawn (1980)

Jamie Rose. . . . . Megan
    0:33 - Topless in pond. Long shot.
- 0:34 - Brief topless in pond, closer shot.
- • 0:36 - Brief upper half of left breast, then brief topless several times splashing in the water.
- 0:37 - Topless getting out of the water.

Just One of the Guys (1986)

Sherilyn Fenn . . . . Sandy
Joyce Hyser . . . . Terry Griffith
    0:10 - In two piece swimsuit by the pool with her boyfriend.
- • 1:27 - Brief topless opening her blouse to prove that she is really a girl.

Just Tell Me What You Want (1980)

Leslie Easterbrook . . . . Hospital Nurse
Ali MacGraw. . . . . Bones Burton
- • 0:16 - Topless getting dressed in her bedroom.
- • 1:26 - Brief topless in bathroom getting ready to take a shower.

Peter Weller. Steven Routledge

Just the Way You Are (1984)

Kaki Hunter. . . . . Lisa
Kristy McNichol. . . . . Susan
- 0:50 - Very brief left breast showing her friend that she's not too hot because there is nothing under her white coat. Medium long shot.

Michael Ontkean. .Peter
Alexandra Paul . . . . Bobbie

Justine

Koo Stark . . . . Justine
- • 0:09 - Topless getting fondled by a nun.
- 0:16 - Topless getting attacked by a nun.
- 0:57 - Topless in open dress getting attacked by old guy.
- ••• 1:00 - Topless getting bathed, then lower frontal nudity.
- 1:28 - Right breast and buns taking off clothes, then brief full frontal nudity getting dressed again.
- 1:32 - Topless getting thrown in to the water.

Kandyland (1987)

Sandahl Bergman . . . . .Harlow Divine
Catlyn Day . . . . Diva
- ••• 0:50 - Topless wearing pasties doing strip routine.
- 1:06 - Brief topless talking on the telephone in dressing room.
- 1:12 - Brief topless during dance routine with the other girls.

Kim Evenson. . . . . .Joni
    0:26 - In purple bra and white panties practicing dancing on stage.
- ••• 0:31 - Topless doing first dance routine.
- • 0:45 - Brief topless during another routine with bubbles floating around.

Kangaroo (1986; Australian)

Judy Davis . . . . .Harriet Somers
Colin Friels . . . . Richard Somers
- • 1:08 - Buns, running into the ocean.
- 1:09 - Frontal nudity walking towards Judy Davis. Long shot, hard to see anything.

Katie's Passion (1978; Dutch)

Rutger Hauer . . . . .Dandy
- 1:12 - Buns seen through torn pants while he is kneeling on the floor.
- • 1:15 - Brief frontal nudity getting out of bed.

Monique Van De Ven. . . . . .Katy
    0:38 - Brief buns when guy rips her panties off.
- • 0:45 - Topless in hospital when a group of doctors examine her.
    0:50 - Left breast a couple of times talking to a doctor. Brief buns sitting down.
    1:12 - Buns, getting into bed.
- •••• 1:18 - Nude burning all her old clothes and getting into bathtub.

The Keep (1983)

Gabriel Byrne. . . . . Kaempffer
Scott Glenn . . . . Glaeken Trismegestus
Alberta Watson . . . . Eva Cuza
- 0:59 - Very brief topless making love with Scott Glenn, then brief lower frontal nudity.

Kentucky Fried Movie (1977)

Uschi Digard . . . . .Woman in Shower
- • 0:09 - Topless getting breasts massaged in the shower, then squished breasts against the shower door.

Marilyn Joi . . . . .Cleopatra
- 1:11 - Topless in bed with Schwartz.

Lenka Novak . . . . Linda Chambers
- 0:09 - Topless sitting on a couch with two other girls.

Tara Stromeir. . . . . Girl
- • 1:16 - In bra, then topless making love on couch with her boyfriend while people on the TV news watch them.

Donald Sutherland. Clumsy

The Key (1983; Italian)

Stefania Sandrelli . . . . Teresa
- ••• 0:31 - Nude when Nino examines her while she's passed out. Long scene.
- •• 0:42 - Full frontal nudity in bathtub while Nino peeks in over the door.
- •• 1:04 - In lingerie, then topless and buns, undressing sexily in front of Nino.
- •• 1:16 - Left breast, sticking out of nightgown so Nino can suck on it.
- ••• 1:19 - Topless and buns making love in bed with Laszlo.
- •• 1:21 - Topless and buns getting up and cleaning herself.
- •• 1:28 - Topless sitting in bed talking to Nino.
- ••• 1:30 - Nude, getting on top of Nino in bed.

Key Exchange (1985)

Brooke Adams..............................Lisa
   0:10 - Nude on bicycle with her boyfriend, but you can't see anything because of his strategically placed arms.
   • 0:45 - Very brief right breast getting into the shower with her boyfriend, then hard to see behind the shower curtain.
Sandra Beall ....Marcy
   ••• 1:14 - Topless on bed taking off her clothes and talking to Daniel Stern.
Daniel Stern .... Michael

Kidnapped (1986)

Barbara Crampton .... Bonnie
   0:35 - In white bra and panties in hotel room.
   ••• 0:37 - Topless getting tormented by a bad guy in bed.
   •• 1:12 - Topless opening her pajamas for David Naughton.
   •• 1:14 - Topless in white panties getting dressed.
Kim Evenson...........................Debbie
   • 0:25 - Right breast in bed talking on the phone. Long shot, hard to see.
   0:30 - In blue nightgown in room.
   ••• 1:28 - Topless getting her arm prepared for a drug injection. Long scene.
   ••• 1:30 - Topless acting in a movie. Long shot, then close up. Wearing a G-string.
David Naughton .... Vince McCarthy

Kill Crazy (1989)

Danielle Brisebois .... Libby
   •• 0:39 - Topless taking off top to go skinny dipping with Rachel.

Killer Workout (1987)

a.k.a. Aerobi-Cide
Marcia Karr...........................Rhonda
   1:03 - Topless, opening her jacket to show the policeman her scars. Unappealing.
   1:12 - Topless in locker room, killing a guy. Covered with the special effects scars.
Teresa Vander Woude.................... Jaimy
   •• 0:43 - Topless in locker room with Tommy during his nightmare.

Killing Heat (1981)

Karen Black....................... Mary Turner
   •• 0:41 - Full frontal nudity giving herself a shower in the bedroom.

The Killing Kind (1973)

Sue Bernard .... Tina
   • 0:00 - Topless during gang rape.
   • 0:19 - Topless again during flashback.
   • 1:12 - Brief topless again several times during flashbacks.

John Savage....................... Terry Lambert
   • 0:00 - Upper half of buns when other guys pull his shorts down during rape of girl.
   •• 0:58 - Buns in shower when Mrs. Lambert opens the curtains to take a picture.

The Killing of Sister George (1968)

Susannah York ....Alice McNaught
   0:19 - Topless under sheer blue nightgown.
   0:59 - In black bra and panties.
   1:45 - In black bra and panties getting undressed.
   •• 2:07 - (0:09 into tape 2) Topless lying in bed with another woman.

King David (1985)

Richard Gere ....David
Alice Krige .... Bathsheba
   •• 1:16 - Full frontal nudity getting a bath outside at dusk while Richard Gere watches.
Cherie Lunghi ....Michal
   •• 0:28 - Topless lying in bed with Richard Gere. (Her hair is in the way a little bit.)

King Kong Lives! (1986)

Linda Hamilton .... Amy Franklin
   • 0:47 - Very, very brief right breast getting out of sleeping bag after camping out near King Kong.
Brian Kerwin....................... Hank Mitchell

King of New York (1990)

Ariane ....Dinner Guest
Vanessa Angel ...., British Female
Paul Calderon........................Joey Dalesio
Janet Julian.......................... Jennifer
   • 0:26 - Very brief left breast, standing in subway car kissing Christopher Walken. Don't see her face.
Phoebe Légerè................... Bordello Woman

King of the Gypsies (1978)

Danielle Brisebois.....................Young Tita
Annette O'Toole........................Sharon
Annie Potts......................... Persa
Eric Roberts .... Dave
Susan Sarandon .... Rose
   • 0:49 - Brief right breast during fight with Judd Hirsch.
Brooke Shields .... Tita

The Kiss (1988)

Céline Lomez........................ Aunt Irene
Joanna Pacula.......................... Felice
   •• 0:49 - Side view topless making love with a guy. Intercut with Meredith Salenger seeing a model of a body spurt blood.
   • 0:57 - Topless covered with body paint doing a ceremony in a hotel room.
   •• 1:24 - Brief right breast, while making love with a guy on bed while Salenger is asleep in the other room.

Klute (1971)
Rosalind Cash . . . . Pat
Jane Fonda . . . . Bree Daniel
- • 0:27 - Side view of left and right breasts stripping in the old man's office.

Donald Sutherland . . . . John Klute
Dorothy Tristan . . . . Arlyn Page

Knightriders (1981)
Ed Harris . . . . Billy Davis
- • 0:01 - Buns, kneeling in the woods. Long shot, hard to see.
- • 1:51 - Upper half of buns, standing in a pond doing something with a stick.

Amy Ingersoll . . . . Linet
- • 0:00 - Very brief left breast, while lying down, then sitting up in woods next to Ed Harris.

Patricia Tallman . . . . Julie
- • 0:46 - Brief topless in the bushes in moonlight talking to her boyfriend while a truck driver watches.

Kramer vs. Kramer (1979)
Jane Alexander . . . . Margaret Phelps
Iris Alhanti . . . .
Dustin Hoffman . . . . Ted Kramer
Meryl Streep . . . . Joanna Kramer
JoBeth Williams . . . . Phyllis Bernard
- • 0:45 - Buns and brief topless in the hallway meeting Dustin Hoffman's son.

L'Annee Des Meduses (1987; French)
Caroline Cellier . . . . Claude, Chris' Mother
- •• 0:02 - Topless taking off top at the beach.
- •• 0:56 - Topless on boat at night with Romain.
- •• 1:06 - Topless on the beach with Valerie Kaprisky.
- • 1:14 - Left breast, lying on beach with Romain at night.

Valerie Kaprisky . . . . Chris
- •• 0:06 - Topless pulling down swimsuit at the beach.
- ••• 0:24 - Full frontal nudity while taking off dress with older man.
- ••• 0:42 - Topless walking around the beach talking to everybody.
- •• 0:46 - Topless on the beach taking a shower.
- ••• 1:02 - Topless on the beach with her mom.
- ••• 1:37 - Nude dancing on the boat for Romain.
- •• 1:42 - Topless walking from the beach to the bar.
- •• 1:43 - Topless in swimming pool.

L.A. Bounty (1989)
Sybil Danning . . . . Ruger
Wings Hauser . . . . Cavanaugh
Lenore Kasdorf . . . . Kelly Rhodes
Maxine Wasa . . . . Model
- • 0:07 - Right breast while posing for Wings Hauser while he paints. Left breast, getting up. Long shot.
- • 0:26 - Left breast while posing on couch for Hauser.
- •• 0:38 - Topless lying on couch again.

L.A. Story (1991)
Iman . . . . Cynthia
Cheryl Baker . . . . Changing Room Woman
- • 0:18 - Brief topless in dressing room, when Steve Martin sees her.

Richard E. Grant . . . . Roland
Marilu Henner . . . . Trudi
Victoria Tennant . . . . Sara

La Bamba (1987)
Elizabeth Peña . . . . Rosie Morales
- • 0:06 - Brief side view of right breast taking a shower outside when two young boys watch her from a water tower. Long shot, hard to see.

La Cicala (The Cricket) (1983)
Barbara De Rossi . . . . Saveria
- •• 0:39 - Nude swimming under waterfall with Clio Goldsmith.
- •• 0:43 - Topless undressing in room with Goldsmith.
- • 0:57 - Brief right breast changing into dress in room.
- • 1:05 - In wet white lingerie in waterfall with a guy, then in a wet dress.
  1:26 - Very brief buns in bed with Anthony Franciosa.
- •• 1:28 - Topless in bathroom with Franciosa.
- • 1:36 - Brief right breast making love with trucker.

Clio Goldsmith . . . . Cicala
- •• 0:26 - Nude when Wilma brings her in to get Anthony Franciosa excited again.
- •• 0:39 - Nude swimming under waterfall with Barbara de Rossi.
- ••• 0:43 - Full frontal nudity undressing in room with de Rossi.

La Lectrice (1989; French)
a.k.a. The Reader
Miou-Miou . . . . Constance/Marie
  1:06 - Making love with a guy while reading to him in bed.
- • 1:18 - Full frontal nudity lying in bed. Close-up pan shot from lower frontal nudity, then left breast, then right breast.
- • 1:20 - Very brief right breast, then lower frontal nudity getting dressed.

Maria De Medeiros . . . . Silent Nurse

Lady Beware (1987)
Diane Lane . . . . Katya Yarno
  0:10 - Walking around in her apartment in a red silk teddy getting ready for bed.
  0:14 - Lying down in white semi-transparent pajamas after fantasizing.
  0:24 - In black bra in apartment.
- ••• 0:46 - Topless in her apartment and in bed making love with Mack.
- •• 0:52 - Brief topless during Jack's flashback when he is in the store.
- •• 0:59 - Brief side view topless in bed with Mack again during another of Jack's flashbacks.
- • 1:02 - Very brief topless in bed with Mack.

1:06 - Brief topless lying in bed behind thin curtain in another of Jack's flashbacks.
Michael Woods . . . . Jack Price
•• 0:43 - Buns, lying down in Diane Lane's bed.

Lady Chatterley's Lover (1981; French/British)
Nicholas Clay . . . . .Oliver Mellors (The Gardener)
••• 0:21 - Nude, washing himself while Sylvia Kristel watches from the trees.
Sylvia Kristel . . . . Constance Chatterley
•• 0:25 - Nude in front of mirror.
• 0:59 - Brief topless with the Gardener.
• 1:04 - Brief topless.
••• 1:16 - Nude in bedroom with the Gardener.

Lady Cocoa (1974)
Lola Falana . . . . Coco
• 0:45 - Left breast lying on bed, pulling up yellow towel. Long shot, hard to see.
••• 1:23 - Topless on boat with a guy.

The Lady in Red (1979)
Christopher Lloyd . . . . Frognose
Pamela Sue Martin . . . . Polly Franklin
• 0:07 - Right breast, while in bedroom with a guy clutching her clothes.
••• 0:20 - Topless in jail with a group of women prisoners waiting to be examined by a nurse.
Francesca "Kitten" Natividad. . . . . uncredited Partygoer
• 0:39 - Brief topless outside during party.
Mary Woronov . . . . Woman Bankrobber

Lady Jane (1987; British)
Helena Bonham Carter . . . . Lady Jane Grey
• 1:19 - Topless kneeling on the bed with Guilford.
• 2:09 - Side view of right breast and very, very brief topless sitting by fire with Guilford.
Cary Elwes. Guilford Dudley
• 1:19 - Brief buns, getting out of bed.

Lady on the Bus (1978; Brazilian)
Sonia Braga. . . . .
• 0:11 - Brief left breast.
••• 0:12 - Topless, then buns, then full frontal nudity in bed getting her slip torn off by her newlywed husband. Long struggle scene.
•• 0:39 - Right breast standing with half open dress, then topless lying in bed, then getting into the pool.
••• 0:48 - Topless and buns on the beach after picking up a guy on the bus.
• 0:54 - Brief topless in bed dreaming.
• 1:02 - Brief topless in waterfall with bus driver.
•• 1:05 - Topless in cemetery after picking up another guy on the bus.
• 1:13 - Topless on the ground with another guy from a bus.
• 1:16 - Left breast sitting on sofa while her husband talks.

Laguna Heat (1987; Made for Cable Movie)
Harry Hamlin . . . . .Tom Shephard
• 0:50 - Buns, walking into the ocean with Catherine Hicks.
Catherine Hicks . . . . Jane Algernon
•• 0:50 - Topless and buns, running around the beach with Harry Hamlin.
•• 1:05 - Brief topless in bed making love with Harry Hamlin, having her head hit the headboard.
Rip Torn. . . . .

The Lair of the White Worm (1988; British)
Sammi Davis . . . . Mary Trent
Amanda Donohoe . . . . Lady Sylvia Marsh
• 0:52 - Nude, opening a tanning table and turning over.
• 0:57 - Brief left breast licking the blood off a phallic-looking thing.
• 1:19 - Brief topless jumping out to attack Angus, then walking around her underground lair (her body is painted for the rest of the film).
• 1:22 - Topless walking up steps with a large phallic thing strapped to her body.
Linzi Drew . . . . Maid/Nun
Tina Shaw . . . . Maid/Nun

Lassiter (1984)
Lauren Hutton . . . . Kari Von Fursten
• 0:18 - Brief topless over-the-shoulder shot making love with a guy on the bed just before killing him.
Belinda Mayne. . . . . Helen Boardman
••• 0:06 - In bra then topless letting Tom Selleck undress her while her husband is in the other room.
Tom Selleck . . . . Lassiter
• 1:00 - Buns, getting out of bed after making love with Lauren Hutton.
Jane Seymour . . . . .Sara
0:10 - Buns and brief side view of right breast lying on stomach on bed with Tom Selleck.
Jane Wood . . . . Mary Becker

The Last American Virgin (1982)
Steve Antin. . . . . Rick
Diane Franklin . . . . .Karen
••• 1:06 - Topless in room above the bleachers with Jason.
•• 1:17 - Topless and almost lower frontal nudity taking off her panties in the clinic.
Louisa Moritz . . . . .Carmela
••• 0:42 - Topless and buns in her bedroom with Rick.
Brian Peck . . . . Victor
• 0:20 - Buns, during penis measurement in boy's locker room. Don't see his face.
Tessa Richarde . . . . .Brenda
•• 0:15 - Brief topless walking into the living room when Gary's parents come home.
Kimmy Robertson. . . . . Rose
Joe Rubbo . . . . .David
• 0:45 - Buns, in bed making love with Carmilla while his buddies watch through the key hole.

Last Call *(1990)*

Crisstyn Dante . . . . Hooker
William Katt . . . . .Paul Avery
- ••• 0:29 - Buns, on floor with Shannon Tweed.
- • 0:41 - Brief buns, getting up from bed and putting his pants on.
- • 1:02 - Brief buns, in bed with Tweed.

Stella Stevens . . . . .Betty
 0:52 - Very brief left nipple popping out of black lingerie top while making love with Jason on a pool table.

Shannon Tweed . . . . Cindy/Audrey
- • 0:12 - In black body stocking, dancing on stage. Topless and buns in G-string underneath.
- •• 0:29 - Right breast, on the floor with William Katt.
- •• 0:39 - Brief buns, rotating in chair with Katt. Topless leaning against column.
- • 0:40 - Topless on stair railing.
- • 1:01 - Left breast, while leaning against column and kissing Katt.
- • 1:02 - Left breast in bed with Katt.
- ••• 1:05 - Topless making love on roof with Katt.

The Last Detail *(1973)*

Nancy Allen . . . . .Nancy
Carol Kane . . . . Young Whore
- • 1:02 - Brief topless sitting on bed talking with Randy Quaid. Her hair is in the way, hard to see.

Jack Nicholson . . . . Buddusky
Randy Quaid . . . . Meadows

The Last Embrace *(1979)*

Janet Margolin . . . . Ellie "Eva" Fabian
- • 1:10 - Brief topless in bathtub with Bernie, before strangling him.
- •• 1:14 - Right breast, while reaching for the phone in bed with Roy Scheider.
- • 1:20 - Left breast in photo that Scheider is looking at with a magnifying glass (it's supposed to be her grandmother).
 1:22 - Almost topless in the shower talking to Scheider.

The Last Emperor *(1987)*

Joan Chen . . . . Wan Jung
Jade Go . . . . .Ar Mo
- • 0:10 - Right breast in open top after breast feeding the young Pu Yi.
- • 0:20 - Right breast in open top telling Pu Yi a story.
- • 0:29 - Right breast in open top breast feeding an older Pu Yi. Long shot.

Last Exit to Brooklyn *(1990)*

Maia Danziger . . . . Mary Black
 0:10 - Out of focus buns and right breast taking off her slip.
- • 0:12 - Very brief topless making love with Harry. Topless after.

Jennifer Jason Leigh . . . . Tralata
- •• 1:28 - Topless, opening her blouse in bar after getting drunk.

- • 1:33 - Topless getting drug out of car, placed on mattress, then basically raped by a long line of guys. Long, painful-to-watch scene.
- • 1:35 - Topless lying on mattress when Spook comes to save her.

The Last Innocent Man
(1987; Made for Cable Movie)

Ed Harris . . . .
Roxanne Hart . . . .
- ••• 1:06 - Topless in bed making love, then sitting up and arguing with Ed Harris in his apartment.

The Last Married Couple in America *(1980)*

Priscilla Barnes . . . . Helena Dryden
Richard Benjamin . . . . Marv Cooper
Sondra Currie . . . . Lainy
- •• 1:32 - Topless taking off her clothes in bedroom in front of Natalie Wood, George Segal and her husband.

The Last Picture Show *(1971; B&W)*

Sam Bottoms . . . . Billy
- • 0:41 - Brief buns, after falling out of car with Jimmy Sue.

Timothy Bottoms . . . . Sonny Crawford
Eileen Brennan . . . . Genevieve
Jeff Bridges . . . . .Duane Jackson
Gary Brockette . . . . Bobby Sheen
- • 0:36 - Upper frontal nudity and buns, getting out of pool and greeting Randy Quaid and Cybill Shepherd. More buns, getting back into the pool.

Ellen Burstyn . . . . Lois Farrow
Kimberly Hyde . . . . Annie-Annie Martin
- •• 0:36 - Full frontal nudity, getting out of pool to meet Randy Quaid and Cybill Shepherd.
- • 0:37 - Topless several times, sitting at edge of pool with Bobby.
- • 0:38 - More topless, sitting on edge of pool in background.

Randy Quaid . . . . Lester Marlow
- • 0:38 - Very brief frontal nudity jumping into pool after Cybill Shepherd jumps in.

Cybill Shepherd . . . . Jacy Farrow
- •• 0:37 - Undressing on diving board. Very brief left breast falling onto diving board. Brief topless tossing bra aside.
- •• 0:38 - Brief left breast jumping into the water.
- ••• 1:05 - Topless and buns in motel room with Jeff Bridges.

Sharon Taggart . . . . .Charlene Duggs
- •• 0:11 - In bra, then topless making out in truck with Timothy Bottoms.

Last Resort *(1985)*

Brenda Bakke . . . . Veroneeka
- •• 0:36 - Topless in the woods with Charles Grodin.

William Bumiller . . . . Etienne

Last Rites (1988)

Tom Berenger . . . . Michael
Robert Corbo . . . . Gino
- 0:03 - Buns and frontal nudity in a room with Daphne Zuniga just before getting caught by another woman and shot.

Anne Twomey . . . . Zena Pace
Daphne Zuniga . . . . Angela
- 0:04 - Very brief topless running into the bathroom to escape from being shot. Covered with blood, don't see her face. Very brief right breast reaching for a bathrobe. Don't really see anything.
  0:40 - Buns, behind a shower door.
  0:50 - Buns, getting out of bed and standing in front of Tom Berenger.

Last Tango In Paris (1972)

(X-rated, letterbox version.)
Marlon Brando . . . . Paul
- 1:59 - Brief buns, pulling his pants down to moon a woman at a dance.

Maria Schneider . . . . Jeanne
- 0:15 - Lower frontal nudity and very brief buns, rolling on the floor.
- 0:44 - Topless in jeans, walking around the apartment.
- •• 0:53 - Left breast, lying down, walking to Marlon Brando, then topless.
- ••• 0:55 - Topless, kneeling while talking to Brando.
- 0:56 - Side of left breast.
- 0:57 - Topless, rolling off the bed, onto the floor.
- •• 1:01 - Right breast, in bathroom. Topless in mirror.
- 1:03 - Brief topless in bathroom with Brando while she puts on makeup.
- ••• 1:04 - Nude, in bathroom with Brando, then sitting on counter.
- 1:27 - Brief lower frontal nudity, pulling up her dress in elevator.
- 1:30 - Topless in bathtub with Brando.
- ••• 1:32 - Nude, standing up in bathtub while Brando washes her. More topless, getting out. Long scene.

The Last Temptation of Christ (1988)

David Bowie . . . . Pontius Pilate
Willem Dafoe . . . . Jesus Christ
Leo Damian . . . . Person in Crowd
Andre Gregory . . . . John the Baptist
Barbara Hershey . . . . Mary Magdelene
- 0:16 - Brief buns behind curtain. Brief right breast making love, then brief topless.
  0:17 - Buns, while sleeping.
- •• 0:20 - Topless, tempting Jesus.
- 2:12 - Brief tip of left breast, lying on ground under Jesus.
- 2:13 - Left breast while caressing her pregnant belly.

Harvey Keitel . . . . Judas

The Last Warrior (1989)

Gary Graham . . . . Gibb
- 0:07 - Brief buns, taking off his towel when he sees a ship.

Maria Holvöe . . . . Katherine
- •• 1:24 - Right breast, after the Japanese warrior removes her dress.

The Last Winter (1983)

Yona Elian . . . . Maya
- •• 0:48 - Topless taking off her robe to get into pool.
  0:49 - Buns, lying on marble slab with Kathleen Quinlan.

Kathleen Quinlan . . . . Joyce
- •• 0:48 - Brief side view of left breast taking off her robe and diving into pool Very brief buns.
  0:49 - Buns, lying on marble slab, talking with Maya.
  0:50 - Very brief right breast sitting up. Long shot, hard to see.

Laura (1979)

a.k.a. Shattered Innocence
Maud Adams . . . . Sarah
Dawn Dunlap . . . . Laura
- 0:20 - Brief side view of left breast and buns talking to Maud Adams, then brief side view of right breast putting on robe.
- ••• 0:23 - Nude, dancing while being photographed.
- ••• 1:15 - Nude, letting Paul feel her so he can sculpt her, then making love with him.
  1:22 - Buns, putting on panties talking to Maud Adams.

Maureen Kerwin . . . . Martine
- 0:03 - Brief full frontal nudity getting out of bed and putting white bathrobe on.

Left for Dead (1978)

Cindy Girling . . . . Pauline Corte
- •• 0:19 - Nude, taking off shirt in bedroom.

Elke Sommer . . . . Magdalene Krushcen
- •• 0:38 - Left breast, while posing for photographer.
- 0:39 - Very brief left breast in B&W photo.
  0:58 - Buns and topless when police officers lift her up to put plastic under her. Covered with blood, can't see her face.
- 1:09 - Very brief left breast in B&W photo.

Lenny (1974; B&W)

Dustin Hoffman . . . . Lenny Bruce
Valerie Perrine . . . . Honey Bruce
  0:04 - Doing a strip tease on stage down to pasties and buns in a G-string. No nudity, but still nice.
- ••• 0:14 - Topless in bed when Dustin Hoffman pulls the sheet off her then makes love.
- •• 0:17 - Topless sitting on the floor in a room full of flowers when Hoffman comes in.
  0:24 - Left breast wearing pastie doing dance in flashback.
- 0:43 - Right breast with Kathryn Witt.

Kathryn Witt . . . . Girl
  • 0:43 - Right breast with Valerie Perrine while Dustin
  Hoffman watches.

Less than Zero *(1987)*
Robert Downey, Jr. . . . . Julian
  1:22 - Very brief blurry buns in bedroom with anoth-
  er guy when Andrew McCarthy discovers them.
Andrew McCarthy. . . . . Clay
  • 0:03 - Very brief buns getting out of bed to answer
  the phone.
John Yurasek . . . . .Naked Man
  • 1:22 - Brief buns standing up when Andrew Mc-
  Carthy discovers him with Robert Downey, Jr.

Lethal Obsession *(1987)*
Tahnee Welch. Daniela Santini
  0:14 - Buns, putting on robe after talking to John on
  the phone.
  • 0:15 - Half of left breast, taking off coat to hug John
  in the kitchen.
  0:16 - Sort of left breast, in bed with John. Too dark
  to see anything.
  1:16 - Buns, getting an injection.

Lethal Persuit *(1989)*
Blake Bahner. . . . . Warren
Mitzi Kapture . . . . Debra J.
  •• 0:32 - Topless in motel shower, then getting out.
  (You can see the top of her swimsuit bottom.)
  0:47 - In wet tank top talking with Warren.

Lethal Weapon *(1987)*
Cheryl Baker . . . . Girl in Shower #1
Terri Lynn Doss . . . . Girl in Shower #2
Mel Gibson . . . . .Martin Riggs
  ••• 0:06 - Buns, getting out of bed and walking to the refrigerator.
Jackie Swanson . . . . Amanda Huntsacker
  •• 0:01 - Brief topless standing on balcony rail getting
  ready to jump.

Lethal Weapon 2 *(1989)*
Mel Gibson . . . . .Martin Riggs
Patsy Kensit. . . . . Rika Van Den Haas
  •• 1:15 - Right breast lying in bed with Mel Gibson.
  •• 1:19 - Topless in bed with Gibson.

Lethal Woman *(1988)*
Robert Lipton . . . . Major Derek Johnson
  • 1:05 - Brief buns in the water on the beach with
  Shannon Tweed.
Adrienne Pearce . . . . Trudy
Shannon Tweed . . . . Tory
  ••• 1:04 - Topless at the beach with Derek. Brief buns in
  white bikini bottom.
Merete Van Kamp . . . . .Diana/Christine

Letters to an Unknown Lover *(1985)*
Andrea Ferreol. . . . . Julia
Cherie Lunghi . . . . Helene
  0:40 - In white slip in her bedroom.

Mathilda May. . . . . Agnes
  • 0:43 - Upper half of breasts in bathtub when Gervais
  opens the door.
  ••• 0:58 - Buns and topless taking off her robe in Gervais'
  room.

Lies *(1984; British)*
Miriam Byrd-Nethery . . . .
Ann Dusenberry . . . . .Robyn Wallace
  •• 0:10 - Topless opening the shower curtain in front of
  her boyfriend.
  • 0:11 - Right breast while kissing her boyfriend.

Lifeforce *(1985)*
Peter Firth . . . . .Caine
Emma Jacobs . . . . Crew Member
Mathilda May. . . . . Space Girl
  • 0:08 - Full frontal nudity in glass case upside down.
  • 0:13 - Topless, lying down in space shuttle. Blue
  light.
  ••• 0:16 - Topless sitting up in lab to suck the life out of
  military guard. Brief full frontal nudity.
  •• 0:17 - Topless again in the lab.
  •• 0:19 - Topless walking around, then buns.
  ••• 0:20 - Topless walking down the stairs. Brief nude
  fighting with the guards.
  •• 0:44 - Topless with Steve Railsback in red light during
  his nightmare.
  • 1:10 - Brief topless in space shuttle with Railsback.
Steve Railsback . . . . Carlsen
  • 1:26 - Buns, standing with Mathilda May after he
  stabs her with the sword. Surrounded by special effects.

Lifeguard *(1975)*
Anne Archer. . . . . Cathy
  • 1:04 - Very brief nipple while kissing Sam Elliott.
  Need to crank the brightness on your TV to the maximum. It appears in the lower right corner of the
  screen as the camera pans from right to left.
Sharon Clark . . . . .Tina
  • 0:07 - Brief side view of right breast undressing and
  getting into the shower.
  • 0:08 - Buns and brief topless wrestling with Sam Elliott on the bed.
Kathleen Quinlan . . . . .Wendy

Link *(1986)*
Elizabeth Shue . . . . .Jane Chase
  • 0:50 - Brief right breast and buns, side view of a body
  double, standing in bathroom getting ready to take
  a bath while Link watches.

Lionheart *(1990)*
Jean-Claude Van Damme . . . . Lyon
  ••• 0:47 - Buns, putting on robe after getting out of bed.

Lipstick *(1976)*
Margaux Hemingway. . . . . .Chris McCormick
  •• 0:10 - Brief topless opening the shower door to answer the telephone.

•• 0:19 - Brief topless during rape attempt, including close-up of side view of left breast.
0:24 - Buns, lying on bed while rapist runs a knife up her leg and back while she's tied to the bed.
•• 0:25 - Brief topless getting out of bed.
Mariel Hemingway . . . . Kathy McCormick
Perry King . . . . Steve Edison
Chris Sarandon . . . . Gordon Stuart
•• 0:50 - Buns, standing in his studio talking to Margaux Hemingway on the telephone.

Listen to Me (1989)
Christopher Atkins. . . . . Bruce Arlington
Christopher Rydell. . . . . Tom Lloynd
Nancy Valen . . . . .Mia
• 0:06 - Very, very brief left breast in bed with Garson when Kirk Cameron first meets him.

Lisztomania (1975; British)
Roger Daltrey . . . . .Franz Liszt
• 0:01 - Brief buns standing on bed tying a sheet to make some pants. Dark, don't see his face.
Anulka Dziubinska . . . . Lola Montez
•• 0:08 - Topless sitting on Roger Daltrey's lap, kissing him. Nice close up.
• 0:21 - Topless, backstage with Daltrey after the concert.
• 0:39 - Topless, wearing pasties, during Daltrey's nightmare/song and dance number.
Fiona Lewis . . . . .Countess Marie
•• 0:00 - Topless in bed getting breasts kissed by Roger Daltrey to the beat of a metronome.
• 0:01 - Brief topless swinging a chandelier to Daltrey.
•• 0:03 - Brief topless and buns running from chair (long shot). Brief topless catching a candle on the bed.
•• 0:04 - Brief left breast when her dress top is cut down. Left breast, sitting inside a piano with Daltrey.

Little Darlings (1980)
Krista Errickson . . . . Cinder
Kristy McNichol. . . . . Angel
Tatum O'Neal . . . . Ferris
• 0:35 - Very, very brief half of left nipple, sticking out of swimsuit top when she comes up for air after falling into the pool to get Armand Assante's attention.

The Little Drummer Girl (1984)
Sam Frey. . . . . Khalil
Diane Keaton . . . . Charlie
Moti Shirin . . . . Michel
•• 1:07 - Nude, in a prison cell when Diane Keaton looks at his scars.

Little Nikita (1988)
Loretta Devine. . . . . .Verna McLaughlin
• 1:03 - Very brief left breast in bed after Sidney Poitier jumps out of bed when River Phoenix bursts into their bedroom.

The Little Thief (1989; French)
a.k.a. La Petite Voleuse
Simon De La Brosse . . . . .Raoul
• 1:07 - Very brief buns and frontal nudity jumping into bed (seen in mirror).
Charlotte Gainsbourg. . . . . .Janine Castang
•• 0:41 - Topless twice, taking off blouse in bedroom with Michel.

Little Vera (1988; U.S.S.R.)
Natalya Negoda. . . . . .Vera
0:15 - Very brief topless and buns getting dressed. Dark, hard to see.
••• 0:50 - Topless making love with Sergei.
•• 1:05 - Topless taking off her dress in the kitchen.

The Living Daylights (1987)
Maryam D'Abo. . . . . Kara Milovy
Virginia Hey . . . .Rubavitch (Colonel Pushkin's girlfriend)
• 1:10 - Brief side view of left breast when James Bond uses her to distract bodyguard.
Catherine Rabett . . . .

Living to Die (1990)
Rebecca Barrington . . . . Married Woman
• 0:23 - In red bra, blindfolded and tied to a lounge chair, then topless while getting photographed.
• 0:27 - Topless in chair when Wings Hauser talks to her.
Darcy De Moss. . . . . .Maggie Sams
0:11 - Taking off clothes to white bra, panties, garter belt and stockings in hotel room with a customer.
• 0:32 - Buns, getting out of spa while Wings Hauser watches without her knowing.
0:33 - Buns, in long shot when Hauser fantasizes about dancing with her.
••• 0:56 - In black bra, then topless and buns making love with Hauser.
• 1:20 - Topless in mirror taking off black top for the bad guy.
Wings Hauser. . . . . Nick Carpenter
Wendy MacDonald . . . . Rookie Policewoman

Loaded Guns (1975)
Ursula Andress . . . . .Laura
0:32 - Buns, lying in bed with a guy.
••• 0:33 - Topless and buns getting out of bed. Full frontal nudity in elevator.
•• 0:40 - Nude getting out of bed and putting dress on.
••• 0:48 - Nude getting into bathtub, topless in tub, nude getting out and drying herself off.
1:00 - Buns while getting undressed and hopping into bed.
• 1:02 - Brief side view of right breast while getting dressed.

Logan's Run (1976)
Jenny Agutter. . . . . Jessica
• 1:05 - Very brief topless and buns changing into fur coat in ice cave with Michael York.
Farrah Fawcett . . . . Holly

The Lonely Guy (1983)

Lamya Derval . . . . One of "The Seven Deadly Sins"
Robyn Douglass . . . . Danielle
• 0:05 - Upper half of right breast in sheer nightgown in bed with Raoul while talking to Steve Martin. Great nightgown!
0:33 - In sheer beige negligee lying on couch talking to Martin on the phone.
• 1:03 - Very, very brief peek at left nipple when she flashes it for Martin so he'll let her into his party.
Marie Laurin . . . . One of "The Seven Deadly Sins"
Julie Payne . . . . Rental Agent

Lonely Hearts (1983; Australian)

Wendy Hughes . . . . Patricia
• 1:05 - Brief topless getting out of bed and putting a dress on. Dark, hard to see.
Norman Kay . . . . Peter
• 1:03 - Buns, getting out of bed. Very brief frontal nudity.
Kris McQuade . . . . Rosemarie

The Lonely Lady (1983)

Glory Annen . . . . Marion
• 0:07 - Brief left breast in back seat of car with Joe. Dark, hard to see.
Bibi Besch . . . . Veronica
Joseph Cali . . . . Vincent Dacosta
• 1:05 - Buns, near pool table and walking around the house with Pia Zadora.
Carla Romanelli . . . . Carla Maria Peroni
•• 1:10 - Brief topless taking off her top to make love with Pia Zadora while a guy watches.
Pia Zadora . . . . JeniLee Randall
• 0:12 - Brief topless getting raped by Joe, after getting out of the pool.
•• 0:22 - Brief topless, then left breast, while making love with Walter.
•• 0:28 - Side view topless lying in bed with Walter.
•• 0:44 - Buns and side view of left breast taking a shower.
• 0:46 - Very brief right breast, in bed with George.
•• 1:05 - Left breast, then brief topless making love with Vinnie.

Looker (1981)

Donna Kei Benz . . . . Ellen
Randi Brooks . . . . Girl in Bikini
Pamela Jean Bryant . . . . Reston Girl
Ashley Cox . . . . Candy
Susan Dey . . . . Cindy
0:28 - In white one piece swimsuit shooting a commercial at the beach.
• 0:36 - Buns, then brief topless in computer imaging device. Topless in computer monitor.
Melissa Prophet . . . . Commercial Script Girl
Lori Sutton . . . . Reston Girl
Leigh Taylor-Young . . . . Jennifer Long
Jeana Tomasino . . . . Suzy

Terri Welles . . . . Lisa
• 0:02 - Brief topless getting photographed for operation. In black bra and panties in her apartment a lot.
Vanna White . . . . Reston Girl
Kathryn Witt . . . . Tina Cassidy
0:17 - In beige lingerie undressing in her room.

Looking for Mr. Goodbar (1977)

Tom Berenger . . . . Gary
Richard Gere . . . . Tony
•• 1:00 - Buns, on Diane Keaton's floor doing push-ups, then running around in his jock strap.
Caren Kaye . . . . Rhoda
Diane Keaton . . . . Theresa
•• 0:11 - Right breast in bed making love with her teacher, Martin, then putting blouse on.
• 0:31 - Brief left breast over the shoulder when the Doctor playfully kisses her breast.
•• 1:04 - Brief topless smoking in bed in the morning, then more topless after Richard Gere leaves.
••• 1:17 - Topless making love with Gere after doing a lot of cocaine.
• 1:31 - Brief topless in the bathtub when James brings her a glass of wine.
2:00 - Getting out of bed in a bra.
•• 2:02 - Topless during rape by Tom Berenger, before he kills her. Hard to see because of strobe lights.

Loose Shoes (1977)

Louisa Moritz . . . . Margie
Misty Rowe . . . . Louise
Betty Thomas . . . . Biker Chick #1
• 0:02 - Brief topless right breast dancing on the table during the *Skateboarders from Hell* sketch.
Susan Tyrrell . . . . Boobies

The Lost Empire (1983)

Angela Aames . . . . Heather McClure
••• 0:31 - Topless and buns taking a shower while Angel and White Star talk to her.
Deborah Blaisdell . . . . Girl Recruit
Raven De La Croix . . . . White Star
••• 1:05 - Topless with a snake after being drugged by the bad guy.
•• 1:07 - Topless lying on a table.
Anne Gaybis . . . .
Angelique Pettijohn . . . . Whiplash
0:29 - In a sexy, black leather outfit fighting in prison with Heather.
Linda Shayne . . . . Cindy Blake

Loulou (1980; French)

Gérard Depardieu . . . . Loulou
• 0:07 - Brief buns, getting out of bed after it breaks. Dark.
•• 0:36 - Buns, lying in bed with Isabelle Huppert.
Isabelle Huppert . . . . Nelly
• 0:06 - Very, very brief topless leaning over in bed.
• 0:18 - Brief topless getting out of bed.
• 0:27 - Brief topless turning over in bed.

•• 0:36 - Topless lying in bed talking on phone. Mostly right breast.

• 0:40 - Lower frontal nudity and buns taking off panties and getting into bed.

•• 0:59 - Left breast in bed with André, then topless taking him to the bathroom.

Guy Marchand . . . . André

•• 0:59 - Buns, getting out of bed with Isabelle Huppert.

Love Child (1982)

Amy Madigan . . . . Terry Jean Moore

• 0:08 - Brief side view of right breast and buns taking a shower in jail while the guards watch.

•• 0:53 - Brief topless and buns, making love with Beau Bridges in a room at the women's prison.

Margaret Whitton . . . . Jacki Steinberg

Love Circles Around the World (1984)

Sophie Berger . . . . Dagmar

••• 0:38 - Topless in women's restroom in casino making love with a guy in a tuxedo.

••• 0:43 - Topless in steam room wearing a towel around her waist, then making love.

Josephine Jaqueline Jones . . . . Brigid

•• 0:18 - Topless, then nude running around her apartment chasing Jack.

• 0:30 - Topless, making love with Count Crispa in his hotel room.

John Sibbit . . . . Jack

• 0:06 - Very brief frontal nudity pulling his underwear down and getting into bed.

•• 0:19 - Buns, trying to run away from Brigid after she yanks his underwear off.

Timothy Wood . . . . Michael

•• 1:29 - Frontal nudity, lying in bed with Jill after making love while video taping it.

A Love in Germany (1984; French/German)

Marie-Christine Barrault . . . . Maria Wyler

• 0:23 - Right breast, in bed with her lover when Pauline peeks from across the way.

•• 0:28 - Right breast in bedroom with Karl. Very brief lower frontal nudity getting back into bed. Long scene.

••• 0:43 - Topless in bedroom with Karl. Subtitles get in the way! Long scene.

Gerard Desarthe . . . . Karl Wyler

• 0:28 - Buns, lying in bed with Maria.

Hanna Schygulla . . . . Pauline Kropp

Love Letters (1984)

Jamie Lee Curtis . . . . Anna Winter

••• 0:31 - Topless in bathtub reading a letter, then topless in bed making love with James Keach.

• 0:36 - Brief topless in lifeguard station with Keach.

••• 0:44 - Brief topless admiring a picture taken of her by Keach.

••• 0:46 - Topless and buns in bedroom undressing with Keach.

• 0:49 - Topless in black and white Polaroid photographs that Keach is taking.

1:02 - In white slip in her house with Keach.

• 1:07 - Right breast, sticking out of slip, then right breast, while sleeping in bed with Keach.

Sally Kirkland . . . . Hippie

Amy Madigan . . . . .Wendy

Love Lust and Ecstasy

Ajita Wilson . . . . .Sara

•• 0:02 - Nude taking a shower and getting into bed with an old guy.

•• 0:04 - Nude making love with a young guy.

•• 0:17 - Topless in bathtub, then making love on bed.

•• 0:22 - Topless making love in a swimming pool, in a river, by a tree.

•• 0:26 - Nude getting undressed and taking a shower.

•• 0:35 - Full frontal nudity changing clothes.

••• 0:54 - Full frontal nudity making love in bed.

The Love Machine (1971)

Madeleine Collinson . . . . Sandy

•• 1:22 - Topless in shower with Robin and her sister when Dyan Cannon discovers them all together. Can't tell who is who.

Mary Collinson . . . . Debbie

•• 1:22 - Topless in shower with Robin and her sister when Dyan Cannon discovers them all together. Can't tell who is who.

Alexandra Hay . . . . Tina St. Claire

• 0:34 - Brief topless in bed with Robin.

• 0:38 - Brief topless coming around the corner putting blue bathrobe on.

Claudia Jennings . . . . Darlene

Love Scenes (1984)

Tiffany Bolling . . . . .Val

•• 0:01 - Side view of left breast in bed with Peter.

••• 0:06 - Topless getting photographed by Britt Ekland in the house.

• 0:09 - Brief topless opening her bathrobe to show Peter.

• 0:12 - Topless in bathtub with Peter.

••• 0:19 - Topless lying in bed talking with Peter, then making love.

•• 0:43 - Topless acting in a movie when Rick opens her blouse.

•• 0:57 - Nude behind shower door, then topless getting out and talking to Peter.

•• 0:59 - Topless making love tied up on bed with Rick during filming of movie.

•• 1:07 - Topless, then full frontal nudity acting with Elizabeth during filming of movie.

•• 1:17 - Full frontal nudity getting out of pool.

•• 1:26 - Topless with Peter on the bed.

Britt Ekland . . . . .Annie

Monique Gabrielle . . . . Uncredited

••• 1:11 - Full frontal nudity making love with Rick on bed.

Julie Newmar . . . . Belinda

Lovers Like Us (1975)
a.k.a. The Savage
Catherine Deneuve . . . . .Nelly
- • 1:06 - Brief left upper half of left breast in bed with Yves Montand. Dark.
- ••• 1:09 - Topless sitting up in bed.

The Loves of a French Pussycat (1976)
Sybil Danning . . . . Andrea
- ••• 0:18 - Topless dancing with her boss, then in bed.
- •• 0:24 - Topless and buns in swimming pool.
  - 0:40 - In sheer white bra and panties doing things around the house. Long sequence.
- • 0:46 - Topless in bathtub with a guy.
- • 1:03 - Left breast sticking out of bra, then topless.

The Loves of a Wall Street Woman (1989)
Private Screenings.
Tara Buckman . . . . .Brenda Baxter
- • 0:00 - Topless taking a shower, opening the door and getting a towel.
- •• 0:06 - Topless changing clothes in locker room in black panties. Nice legs!
- ••• 0:18 - Topless in bed making love with Alex.
- •• 0:31 - Topless in bed with Alex making love.
- •• 0:40 - Topless in black panties dressing in locker room.
- • 0:46 - Brief topless lying in bed, talking to her lover, side view of buns. Long shot.
- ••• 1:16 - Topless making love in bed with Alex.

Lunch Wagon (1981)
Pamela Jean Bryant . . . . .Marcy
- •• 0:04 - Topless changing tops in room in gas station with Rosanne Katon while a guy watches through key hole.
- • 0:55 - Left breast, several times, in van with Bif.
Rosanne Katon . . . . .Shannon
- • 0:01 - Brief topless getting dressed.
- • 0:04 - Brief side view of left breast changing tops in room in gas station with Pamela Bryant while a guy watches through key hole.
- •• 0:10 - Topless changing again in gas station.
Debra Kelly . . . . Diedra
- •• 0:53 - Topless under sheer robe, then topless on couch with Arnie.
Louisa Moritz . . . . .Sunshine
- • 0:37 - Topless in spa.

Lust for a Vampire (1970; British)
Yutte Stensgaard . . . . Mircalla
- ••• 0:19 - Topless, three times, getting a massage from another school girl.
  - 0:22 - Very, very brief full frontal nudity while diving into the water. Long shot, don't see anything.
- •• 0:53 - Topless outside with Lestrange. Left breast when lying down.
- • 0:58 - Topless during Lestrange's dream.

M*A*S*H (1970)
Sally Kellerman . . . . Margaret "Hot Lips" Houlihan
- • 0:42 - Very, very brief left breast opening her blouse for Frank in her tent.
- • 1:11 - Very, very brief buns and side view of right breast during shower prank. Long shot, hard to see.
- • 1:54 - Very brief topless in a slightly different angle of the shower prank during the credits.
Donald Sutherland . . . . Hawkeye Pierce

Made in Heaven (1987)
Ellen Barkin . . . . Lucille
Timothy Hutton . . . . Mike Shea/Elmo Barnett
- •• 0:08 - Buns, standing in a room when he first gets to heaven.
Kelly McGillis . . . . .Annie Packert/Ally Chandler
Mare Winningham . . . . Brenda Carlucci

Made in U.S.A. (1988)
Judy Baldwin . . . . Dorie
Adrian Pasdar . . . . Dar
- • 0:12 - Buns, walking to sit down at the laundromat when he washes all his clothes with Christopher Penn.
Christopher Penn . . . . Tuck
- • 0:12 - Buns, walking to sit down at the laundromat when he washes all his clothes with Adrian Pasdar.
Lori Singer . . . . .Annie
- • 0:26 - Brief left breast and very brief lower frontal nudity in the back of a convertible with Dar at night.
  - 0:44 - In white, braless tank top talking to a used car salesman.

Magic (1978)
Ann-Margret .Peggy Ann Snow
- ••• 0:44 - Right breast, lying on her side in bed talking to Anthony Hopkins.

Magnum Force (1973)
Clint Eastwood. .Harry Callahan
Hal Holbrook .Lieutenant Briggs
Tim Matheson . . . . Sweet
Suzanne Somers. . . . . .uncredited Pool Girl
- •• 0:26 - In blue swimsuit getting into a swimming pool, brief topless a couple of times before getting shot, brief topless floating dead.

Maiden Quest (1972)
a.k.a. The Long Swift Sword of Siegfried
Private Screenings.
Lance Boyle . . . . Siegfried
- •• 0:24 - Buns, during orgy scene.
Sybil Danning . . . . .Kriemhild
- • 0:02 - Topless in bath, surrounded by topless blonde servants.
- • 0:04 - Topless in the bath again.
- ••• 0:10 - Nude in tub surrounded by topless servant girls.
- ••• 0:12 - Topless on bed, getting rubbed with ointment by the servant girls.

- •• 0:35 - Topless while in bed with Siegfried.
- • 1:00 - Topless in bed with Siegfried.
- ••• 1:19 - Topless in bed with Siegfried.

Major League *(1989)*
Tom Berenger . . . . Jake Taylor
Corbin Bernsen . . . . .Roger Dorn
- • 0:58 - Brief buns running in locker room to cover himself with a towel when Rachel comes in to talk to the team.
Margaret Whitton . . . . Rachel Phelps

Malibu Beach *(1978)*
James Daughton . . . . .Bobby
- • 0:32 - Buns, running into the ocean with his friends.
Kim Lankford. . . . . Dina
0:32 - Buns, running into the ocean.
- • 0:34 - Brief right breast getting out of the ocean.
- • 1:16 - Right breast on beach at night with boyfriend.
- • 1:19 - Brief topless at top of the stairs.
- •• 1:20 - Brief topless when her parent's come home.
- • 1:21 - Topless in bed with her boyfriend.
Michael Luther . . . . Paul
- • 0:32 - Buns, running into the ocean with his friends.
Susan Player Jarreau . . . . Sally
- • 0:28 - Side view of left breast with boyfriend at night on the beach. Long shot.
0:32 - Buns, running into the ocean with her two male friends.
0:33 - Brief side view of left breast in water. Long shot.
- • 0:34 - Brief topless in the ocean, then topless by the fire getting dressed.
Tara Stromeir . . . . Glorianna
- • 0:08 - Topless kissing her boyfriend at the beach when someone steals her towel.

Malibu Express *(1981)*
Sybil Danning . . . . Countess Luciana
- • 0:13 - Brief topless making love in bed with Cody.
Barbara Edwards . . . . May
- •• 0:10 - Topless taking a shower with Kimberly McArthur on the boat.
- •• 1:05 - Topless serving Cody coffee while he talks on the telephone.
Darby Hinton . . . . Cody Abilene
- • 0:08 - Brief buns, taking a shower on his boat.
Kimberly McArthur . . . . Faye
- •• 0:10 - Topless taking a shower on the boat with Barbara Edwards.
Lorraine Michaels . . . . Liza Chamberlin
- ••• 0:23 - Topless in the shower making love with Shane, while camera photographs them.
Shelly Taylor Morgan . . . . Anita Chamberlain
- • 0:22 - Topless doing exercises on the floor.
- •• 0:26 - Topless making love with Shane in bed while being video taped. Then right breast while standing by door.

Suzanne M. Regard . . . . Sexy Sally
- • 0:50 - Brief topless talking on the telephone.
- •• 1:06 - Topless talking on the telephone.
Lori Sutton . . . . Beverly
- ••• 0:54 - Topless and buns, making love in bed with Cody.
Lynda Wiesmeier . . . . June Khnockers
- •• 0:04 - Topless in locker room taking jumpsuit off.
- • 1:16 - Topless leaning out of racing car window while a helicopter chases her and Cody.

Malibu Hot Summer *(1981)*
a.k.a. Sizzle Beach
(*Sizzle Beach* is the re-released version with Kevin Costner featured on the cover. It is missing all the nude scenes during the opening credits before 0:06.)
Terry Congie . . . . .Dit McCoy
- • 0:02 - Side view of right breast, while on floor during opening credits.
0:39 - In bra, taking off her blouse in front of her drama class.
- •• 0:45 - Topless in front of fireplace with Kevin Costner. Side view of right breast.
Kevin Costner . . . . John Logan
Roselyn Royce . . . . .Cheryl Rielly
- •• 0:15 - On exercise bike, then topless getting into bed.
- ••• 0:16 - Topless sitting up in bed, buns going to closet to get dressed to go jogging.
0:26 - In pink two piece swimsuit running to answer the phone.
- •• 0:52 - Topless on boat with Brent.
Sylvia Wright . . . . Actress at Party
- •• 0:01 - Nude, standing up during opening credits.
- ••• 1:07 - Topless fixing her hair in front of mirror, then full frontal nudity talking to Howard.
- • 1:09 - Topless on top of Howard.

Malicious *(1974; Italian)*
Laura Antonelli . . . . .Angela
- • 1:14 - Topless after undressing while two boys watch from above.
- •• 1:27 - Topless, undressing under flashlight. Hard to see because the light is moving around a lot.
- • 1:29 - Topless and buns running around the house.

A Man for Sale *(1982)*
Ajita Wilson . . . . .Dancer/Model
- • 0:02 - Topless several times posing for photographer with another model.
- • 0:26 - Topless and buns, dancing in an erotic ballet show.

A Man in Love *(1987)*
Jamie Lee Curtis . . . . Susan Elliot
Greta Scacchi. . . . . Jane Steiner
- ••• 0:31 - Topless with Peter Coyote.
- •• 1:04 - Buns and left breast in bed with Coyote.
1:10 - Brief side view topless, putting black dress on.
- • 1:24 - Brief topless in bed.

The Man Who Fell to Earth (1976; British)
(Uncensored version.)
David Bowie . . . . Thomas Jerome Newton
     0:58 - Brief buns, turning over in bed with Candy Clark.
     1:56 - Frontal nudity and brief buns in bed with Clark. Don't see his face.
Bernie Casey . . . . Peters
   • 1:42 - Buns, getting out of swimming pool during a black and white dream sequence.
Candy Clark . . . . Mary-Lou
   •• 0:42 - Topless in the bathtub, washing her hair and talking to David Bowie.
   •• 0:55 - Topless sitting on bed and blowing out a candle.
   ••• 0:56 - Topless in bed with Bowie.
   ••• 1:26 - Full frontal nudity climbing into bed with Bowie after he reveals his true alien self.
     1:56 - Nude with Bowie making love and shooting a gun.
Claudia Jennings . . . . uncredited Girl by the Pool
   • 1:42 - Topless, standing by the pool and kissing Bernie Casey.
Rip Torn . . . . Nathan Bryce

The Man Who Loved Women (1983)
Julie Andrews . . . . Marianna
Jennifer Ashley . . . . David's Mother
Kim Basinger . . . . Louise "Lulu"
Jill Carroll . . . . Sue the Baby Sitter
Denise Crosby . . . . Enid
Cindi Dietrich . . . . Darla
Marilu Henner . . . . Agnes Chapman
   •• 0:18 - Brief topless in bed with Burt Reynolds.
Sharon Hughes . . . . Nurse
Burt Reynolds . . . . David Fowler
   •• 1:25 - Brief buns, chiseling a statue after making love with Julie Andrews.
Tracy Vaccaro . . . . Legs

The Man Who Wasn't There (1983)
Vincent Baggetta . . . . Riley
   • 0:23 - Buns, lying on the floor after fighting with the other guys.
Steve Guttenberg . . . . Sam Cooper
   ••• 0:54 - Buns, dropping his pants in office with three other men.
   • 1:46 - Brief buns, while kissing Cindy during their wedding ceremony.
Lisa Langlois . . . . Cindy Worth
   •• 0:58 - Nude running away from two policemen after turning visible.
   ••• 1:08 - Topless in white panties dancing in her apartment with an invisible Steve Guttenberg.
     1:47 - Very, very brief upper half of left breast throwing bouquet at wedding.
Brinke Stevens . . . . Nymphet
   • 0:45 - Buns and brief topless in the girls' shower, when she gets shampoo from an invisible Steve Guttenberg.

The Man with Two Brains (1983)
Randi Brooks . . . . Fran
   •• 1:11 - Brief topless showing Steve Martin her breasts in front of the hotel. Buns, changing in the hotel room, then wearing black see-through negligee.
Kathleen Turner . . . . Dolores Benedict
   • 0:08 - Right breast when Steve Martin is operating on her in the operating room.
     0:22 - In sheer lingerie in bedroom with Steve Martin, teasing him and driving him crazy.
   • 0:36 - Buns, in hotel room with a guy about to squeeze her buns when Steve Martin walks in.

Mandingo (1975)
Susan George . . . . Blanche
   • 1:36 - Brief topless in bed with Ken Norton.
Perry King . . . . Hammond
   •• 0:17 - Frontal nudity walking to bed to make love with Dite.
Debbi Morgan . . . . Dite
   • 0:17 - Topless in bed talking to Perry King.
Ken Norton . . . . Mede
   •• 1:36 - Buns, standing in bed with Susan George. More buns making love with her.
Brenda Sykes . . . . Ellen
   • 0:58 - Topless in bed with Perry King.

Maniac Cop 2 (1990)
Claudia Christian . . . . Susan Riley
Laurene Landon . . . . Teresa Mallory
Leo Rossi . . . . Turkell
Paula Trickey . . . . Cheryl
   •• 0:41 - In orange two piece swimsuit on stage, then topless and buns in G-string.

Manifesto (1988)
Simon Callow . . . . Police Chief Hunt
Svetozar Cvetkovic . . . . Rudi
Rade Serbedzija . . . . Emile
   • 0:18 - Buns, under sheet and getting out of bed.
Eric Stoltz . . . . Christopher
   • 1:16 - Buns, helping Camilla unroll Emile in the rug.

Manon of the Spring (1987; French)
Emmanuelle Béart . . . . Manon
   • 0:11 - Brief nude dancing around a spring playing a harmonica.

Marathon Man (1976)
Dustin Hoffman . . . . Babe
   •• 1:09 - Buns, getting out of the bathtub and putting some pajamas on while someone lurks outside the bathroom.
Marthe Keller . . . . Elsa
   •• 0:42 - Topless lying on the floor after Dustin Hoffman rolls off her.

Maria's Lovers (1985)
Keith Carradine . . . . Clarence Butts
Nastassja Kinski . . . . Maria Bosic
     0:59 - In a black bra.

• 1:12 - Brief right breast, while looking at herself in the mirror.

Anita Morris . . . . Mrs. Wynic

Vincent Spano. . . . . Al Griselli

The Marilyn Diaries (1990)

Private Screenings.

John Altamura. . . . . Frankie
- • 0:13 - Buns, in hall after Marilyn Chambers takes his sheet away.

Tara Buckman. . . . . Jane
- •• 0:53 - Topless and buns, taking off robe and getting into bathtub. Left breast, in tub reading diary.
- •• 0:54 - Topless in and getting out of tub. Very brief lower frontal nudity.
- •• 1:27 - Topless in bathtub talking with John.

Marilyn Chambers. .Marilyn
- •• 0:02 - Topless in bathroom with a guy during party.
- •• 0:26 - In bra and panties in Istvan's studio, then topless.
- ••• 0:27 - Topless in panties when Istvan opens her blouse.
- •• 0:45 - Topless in trench coat, opening it up to give the Iranian secret documents.
- • 0:47 - Topless when the Rebel Leader opens her trench coat.
- • 0:48 - Topless with Colonel South.
- •• 0:57 - Topless opening her top for Hollywood producer.
- • 1:10 - In swimsuit, then topless with Roger.
- ••• 1:13 - In black lingerie, then topless making love with Chet.
- • 1:19 - Left breast, in flashback with Roger.
- •• 1:25 - In slip, then right breast, then topless with Chet.

Marked for Death (1990)

Leslie Danon. . . . . Girl #1

Joanna Pacula . . . . Leslie

Elena Sahagun . . . . Carmen

Teri Weigel . . . . Sexy Girl #2
- • 0:39 - Brief topless on bed with Jimmy when Steven Seagal bursts into the room. (She's the brunette.)

Married to the Mob (1988)

Matthew Modine . . . . .Mike Downey

Michelle Pfeiffer . . . . Angela de Marco

Nancy Travis. . . . . .Karen Lutnig
- • 0:15 - Buns and brief side view of right breast, with Tony in hotel room. Brief topless in the bathtub.

Mary, Mary, Bloody Mary (1975)

Cristina Ferrare . . . . .Mary
- •• 0:07 - Brief topless making love with some guy on the couch just before she kills him.
- ••• 0:41 - Topless when Greta helps pull down Ferrare's top to take a bath.

  1:12 - Bun and brief silhouette of left breast getting out of bed and getting dressed.

Helena Rojo . . . . .Greta
- • 0:42 - Buns and brief topless getting into bathtub with Cristina Ferrare.

Masquerade (1988)

Kim Cattrall . . . . Mrs. Brooke Morrison
- ••• 0:04 - Topless in bed with Rob Lowe.

  0:47 - In white teddy after having sex with Lowe.

Rob Lowe. . . . . .Tim Whalen
- ••• 0:04 - Buns, getting up from bed with Kim Cattrall.
- •• 0:30 - Buns, making love with Meg Tilly in bed.

Meg Tilly . . . . Olivia Lawrence

  0:55 - In pink nightgown in bedroom.

Massacre at Central High (1976)

Kimberly Beck . . . . Theresa
- • 0:32 - Nude romping in the ocean with David. Long shot, dark, hard to see anything.
- •• 0:42 - Topless on the beach making love with Andrew Stevens after a hang glider crash.

Steve Bond. . . . . .Craig

Derrel Maury . . . . .David
- • 0:32 - Buns, romping around in the ocean with Kimberly Beck. Dark, long shot. Hard to see anything.

Lani O'Grady . . . . .Jane
- ••• 1:09 - Topless walking out of a tent and getting back into it with Rainbeaux Smith and Robert Carradine.

Cheryl Smith . . . . Mary
- • 0:27 - Brief topless in a classroom getting attacked by some guys.
- ••• 1:09 - Nude walking around on a mountain side with Robert Carradine and Lani O'Grady.

Andrew Stevens . . . . Mark

Masterblaster (1986)

Tracey E. Hutchinson . . . . Lisa
- ••• 0:57 - Topless taking a shower (wearing panties).

Kari Whitman. . . . . Jennifer

Mata Hari (1985)

Christopher Cazenove . . . . . . Captain Karl Von Byerling

Derek De Lint. . . . . Handsome Traveler

Sylvia Kristel . . . . Mata Hari
- ••• 0:11 - Topless making love with a guy on a train.
- •• 0:31 - Topless standing by window after making love with the soldier.
- • 0:35 - Topless making love in empty house by the fireplace.
- •• 0:52 - Topless masturbating in bed wearing black stockings.
- •• 1:02 - Topless having a sword fight with another topless woman.
- •• 1:03 - Topless in bed smoking opium and making love with two women.

Matador (1986; Spanish)

Antonio Banderas. .Angel

Nacho Martinez . . . . Diego Montes
- ••• 0:29 - Buns making love with Eva in bed.

Assumpta Serna . . . . Maria Cardinal
- • 0:03 - Topless taking off wrap and making love with a guy just before she kills him.
- ••• 1:38 - Topless on floor with Diego. Long shot, hard to see. Topless in front of the fire.
- • 1:41 - Brief topless making love with Diego.
- • 1:43 - Topless lying on floor dead.

Mausoleum (1983)
Bobbie Bresee . . . . Susan Farrell
- ••• 0:25 - Topless and buns wrapping a towel around herself in her bedroom.
- •• 0:26 - Topless on the balcony showing herself to the gardener.
- • 0:29 - Topless in the garage with the gardener. Brief, dark, hard to see.
- • 0:32 - Brief left breast, while kissing Marjoe Gortner.
- • 1:10 - Topless in the bathtub talking to Gortner. Long shot.

The Mean Season (1985)
Mariel Hemingway . . . . Christine Connelly
- •• 0:15 - Topless taking a shower.
Kurt Russell . . . . Malcolm Anderson

Mean Streets (1973)
Jeannie Bell . . . . Diane
- • 0:07 - Topless dancing on stage with pasties on.
- • 1:00 - Topless backstage wearing pasties.
David Carradine . . . . Drunk
Robert De Niro . . . . Johnny Boy
Harvey Keitel . . . . Charlie

Meatballs III (1987)
Patrick Dempsey . . . . Rudy
- •• 0:19 - Buns, in the shower when first being visited by Sally Kellerman.
Sally Kellerman . . . . Roxy Du Jour
Isabelle Mejias . . . . Wendy
Shannon Tweed . . . . The Love Goddess

Medium Cool (1969)
Peter Boyle . . . . Gun Clinic Manager
Robert Forster . . . . John
- •• 0:36 - Nude, running around the house frolicking with Ruth.
Mariana Hill . . . . Ruth
- • 0:18 - Close-up of breast in bed with John.
- •• 0:36 - Nude, running around the house frolicking with John.

Melanie (1982)
Don Johnson . . . . Carl
Glynnis O'Connor . . . . Melanie
- • 0:08 - Very brief right breast, while turning over in bed next to Don Johnson.
- • 0:09 - Topless, while sitting up and putting on a T-shirt, then getting out of bed.

Melody in Love (1978)
Wolf Goldan . . . . Octavio
- • 1:14 - Buns, while making love in bed with Rachel and Angela.
Scarlett Gunden . . . . Angela
- ••• 0:17 - Full frontal nudity taking off dress and dancing in front of statue.
- ••• 0:50 - Nude with a guy on a boat.
- •• 0:53 - Topless on another boat with Octavio.
- •• 0:59 - Buns and topless in bed talking to Rachel.
- •• 1:12 - Full frontal nudity getting a tan on boat with Rachel.
- • 1:14 - Topless making love in bed with Rachel and Octavio.
Sascha Hehn . . . . Alain
- •• 1:08 - Buns with Melody outside. Very brief erect penis under covers.
- • 1:16 - Buns, twice while making love with Melody near an erupting volcano.

Melvin and Howard (1980)
Martine Beswicke . . . . Real Estate Woman
Dabney Coleman . . . . Judge Keith Hayes
Denise Galik . . . . Lucy
Mary Steenburgen . . . . Lynda Dummar
- •• 0:31 - Topless and buns, ripping off barmaid outfit and walking out the door.

The Men's Club (1986)
Penny Baker . . . . Lake
- •• 1:13 - Topless in bed with Treat Williams.
David Dukes . . . . Phillip
Ann Dusenberry . . . . Page
- •• 1:05 - Topless lying in bed after making love with Roy Scheider.
Marilyn Jones . . . . Allison
- •• 1:21 - Topless wearing gold panties standing in bedroom talking to Harvey Keitel.
Harvey Keitel . . . . Sully
- • 1:22 - Buns, getting up off the bed to talk to Allison.
Jennifer Jason Leigh . . . . Teensy
Cindy Pickett . . . . Hannah
Craig Wasson . . . . Paul
Gwen Welles . . . . Redhead
Treat Williams . . . . Terry

The Mephisto Waltz (1971)
Jacqueline Bisset . . . . Paula Clarkson
- • 0:48 - Very brief right and side view of left breast in bed with Alan Alda.
  - 1:36 - Sort of left breast getting undressed for witchcraft ceremony. Long shot side views of right breast, but you can't see her face.
- •• 1:45 - Very brief topless twice under bloody water in blood covered bathtub, dead. Discovered by Kathleen Widdoes.
Barbara Parkins . . . . Roxanne
- • 1:26 - Left breast, while kissing Alan Alda during witchcraft sequence.
Kathleen Widdoes . . . . Maggie West

Meridian (1989)
a.k.a. Kiss of the Beast
Sherilyn Fenn . . . . Catherine
- •• 0:23 - White bra and panties, getting clothes taken off by Lawrence. Then topless.
- ••• 0:28 - Topless in bed with Oliver.
- •• 0:51 - Topless getting her blouse ripped open lying in bed.
  1:11 - Briefly in white panties and bra putting red dress on.
Charlie Spradling. . . . . Gina
- •• 0:22 - Topless getting her blouse torn off by Lawrence while lying on the table.
- ••• 0:28 - Topless standing next to fireplace, then topless on the couch. Hot!

Metamorphosis (1989)
Laura Gemser . . . . Prostitute
- • 0:37 - Very brief topless several times in Peter's flashback.
- • 0:43 - Very brief topless in flashback again.

Miami Blues (1990)
Martine Beswicke . . . . Noira
Jennifer Jason Leigh. . . . . Susie Waggoner
  0:07 - Very brief upper half of right breast, while changing clothes behind Alec Baldwin.
- ••• 0:10 - Topless in panties, taking off red dress and getting into bed.
  0:24 - Very, very brief half of right breast while taking a bath. Long shot.
- • 0:33 - Topless making love with Baldwin in the kitchen.
Fred Ward. . . . . Sergeant Hoke Moseley

Midnight (1989)
Kathleen Kinmont. . . . . .Party
Lynn Redgrave . . . . Midnight
Karen Witter . . . . Missy Angel
- • 0:32 - In bed with Mickey. Nice squished breasts against him, but only a very brief side view of left breast.
  0:48 - In two piece swimsuit, going into the pool.
  0:58 - In nightgown, walking around with lots of makeup on her face.

Midnight Cowboy (1969)
Dustin Hoffman. . . . . Ratso
Brenda Vaccaro. . . . . Shirley
- •• 1:28 - Brief topless in bed with Jon Voight.
Jon Voight. . . . . Joe Buck
- • 0:20 - Very brief buns, walking into bedroom and jumping into bed with Cass.
- • 1:28 - Buns, in bed with Brenda Vaccaro.

Midnight Crossing (1988)
Kim Cattrall. . . . . Alexa Schubb
  0:39 - In wet white blouse, arguing in the water with her husband.

Crisstyn Dante . . . . Body double for Kim Cattrall
- • 0:29 - Brief left breast making love on small boat, body double for Kim Cattrall.
Faye Dunaway . . . . Helen Barton
John Laughlin. Jeffrey Schubb

Midnight Dancer (1987; Australian)
a.k.a. Belinda
Mary Regan . . . . .Crystal
- •• 0:29 - Topless in dressing room, undressing and rubbing makeup on herself.
- •• 0:56 - In bra, then topless in panties, changing clothes and getting into bed.
Kathryn Walker. . . . . .Kathy

Midnight Express (1978; British)
Brad Davis . . . . Billy Hayes
- • 0:12 - Buns, standing naked in front of guards after getting caught trying to smuggle drugs.
John Hurt. . . . . .Max
Irene Miracle . . . . .Susan
- •• 1:39 - Topless in prison visiting booth showing her breasts to Brad Davis so he can masturbate.
Randy Quaid . . . . Jimmy Booth

Mike's Murder (1984)
Kym Malin .Beautiful Girl #1
Debra Winger. . . . . Betty
- • 0:26 - Brief left breast in bathtub.

The Misadventures of Mr. Wilt (1990)
Griff Rhys Jones . . . . .Henry Wilt
- • 0:34 - Sort of buns, while naked and tied to inflatable doll.
- • 0:36 - More buns, up on balcony. Long shot.
Diana Quick. . . . . .Sally

Mischief (1985)
Doug McKeon . . . . Jonathan
- • 0:56 - Brief buns, putting on his underwear after making love with Kelly Preston.
Terry O'Quinn . . . . .Claude Harbrough
Kelly Preston . . . . Marilyn McCauley
- ••• 0:56 - In a bra, then topless making love with Doug McKeon in her bedroom.

Miss Right (1987)
Karen Black . . . . .Amy
- • 0:47 - Brief topless jumping out of bed and running to get a bucket of water to put out a fire.
Dalila Di'Lazzaro. . . . .
Clio Goldsmith. . . . .
Margot Kidder . . . .
Marie-France Pisier . . . . Bebe
- •• 0:07 - Topless in open top dress when the reporter discovers her in a dressing room behind a curtain.
William Tepper. Terry Bartell
- • 0:47 - Buns, jumping out of bed with Karen Black when the bed catches fire.

Missing in Action (1984)
Lenore Kasdorf . . . . Ann
  • 0:41 - Very brief topless when Chuck Norris sneaks
    back in room and jumps into bed with her.
M. Emmet Walsh . . . . Tuck

Mission Manila (1989)
Tetchie Agbayani . . . . Maria
Maria Isabel Lopez . . . . Jessie
  • 0:22 - Brief right breast several times in bed while
    Harry threatens her with knife.

Mo' Better Blues (1990)
Tracy Camilla Johns . . . . Club Patron
Joie Lee . . . . Indigo Downes
  •• 1:06 - Right breast while in bed with Bleek.
  • 1:08 - Very, very brief right breast while pounding
    the bed and yelling at Bleek.

Mob Boss (1990)
Jasaé . . . . Bar Girl
  •• 0:46 - Topless serving drinks to the guys at the table.
Dori Courtney . . . . Kathryn
  ••• 0:31 - In black bra, talking with Eddie Deezen, then
    topless. Nice close-up. Long scene.
Morgan Fairchild . . . . Gina
Sherri Graham . . . . Bar Girl
  •• 0:46 - Topless and buns, dancing on stage. Medium
    long shot.
Debra Lamb . . . . Janise
Tamara Landry . . . .
Karen Russell . . . . Mary
Brinke Stevens . . . . Sara

Modern Love (1990)
Robby Benson . . . . Greg Frank
  •• 0:35 - Brief buns running out of room after finding
    out he's going to be a father.
    0:36 - Long shot of buns, standing on roof of house
    yelling the good news to the world.
Burt Reynolds . . . . Colonel Parker

Modern Problems (1981)
Dabney Coleman . . . . Mark
  ••• 1:09 - Buns, taking off towel in front of Patti
    D'Arbanville.
Patti D'Arbanville . . . . Darcy
  • 0:48 - Very brief right breast in bed after Chevy
    Chase has telekinetic sex with her.

Modern Romance (1981)
Kathryn Harrold . . . . Mary Harvard
  • 0:46 - Very brief topless and buns taking off robe and
    getting into bed with Albert Brooks.
    1:05 - In pink lingerie opening her blouse to undo
    her skirt while talking to Brooks.
Bruno Kirby . . . . Jay

The Moderns (1988)
Genevieve Bujold . . . . Libby Valentin
Keith Carradine . . . . Nick Hart
  •• 1:17 - Buns, walking into bathroom with Linda
    Fiorentino.
Geraldine Chaplin . . . . Nathalie de Ville
Linda Fiorentino . . . . Rachel Stone
  • 0:40 - Topless sitting in bathtub while John Lone
    shaves her armpits.
  • 0:41 - Right breast while turning over onto stomach
    in bathtub.
  •• 1:18 - Topless getting out of tub while covered with
    bubbles to kiss Keith Carradine.

Mondo New York (1987)
Phoebe Légerè . . . . Singer
    0:01 - On stage, singing "Marilyn Monroe." Buns
    and most of lower frontal nudity while writhing on
    stage in a mini-skirt.
Ann Magnuson . . . . Poetry Reader
Annie Sprinkle . . . . Model/Performer
  • 0:17 - Nude, painted body with other models during
    "Rapping & Rocking" segment.

Monkey Shines: An Experiment in Fear (1988)
Jason Beghe . . . . Allan Mann
  • 0:01 - Side view of buns while on the floor, stretching
    to go running.
Kate McNeil . . . . Melanie Parker
  • 1:07 - Brief upper half of right breast, making love
    with Allan. Dark, hard to see anything.
John Pankow . . . . Geoffrey Fisher
Patricia Tallman . . . . Party Guest and Stunts
Janine Turner . . . . Linda Aikman
    0:01 - Side view of buns, lying in bed when Jason Be-
    ghe wakes up. Don't really see anything.
Joyce Van Patten . . . . Dorothy Mann

Monsignor (1982)
Genevieve Bujold . . . . Clara
  ••• 1:05 - Topless getting undressed and climbing into
    bed while talking to Christopher Reeve.

Montenegro (1981; British/Swedish)
Susan Anspach . . . . Marilyn Jordan
  •• 1:08 - Full frontal nudity taking a shower.
  • 1:28 - Right breast making love with Montenegro.
Svetozar Cvetkovic . . . . Montenegro
  ••• 1:07 - Frontal nudity taking a shower while Susan
    Anspach watches.

Monty Python's Jabberwocky (1977)
Deborah Fallender . . . . The Princess
  • 0:56 - Buns and brief full frontal nudity in bath when
    Michael Palin accidentally enters the room.
    0:57 - Topless under sheer white robe.

Monty Python's Life of Brian (1979)

Graham Chapman . . . . Brian Called Brian
- ••• 1:03 - Buns before opening window, frontal nudity opening window and being surprised by his flock of followers, buns putting clothes on. Funniest frontal nude scene.

Moon 44 (1990)

Lisa Eichhorn. . . . . Terry Morgan
John March. Moose Haggerty
- • 0:43 - Brief buns in shower room. (Sort of see frontal nudity through grating in the shower divider.)

Malcolm McDowell. . . . . Major Lee

Moon in Scorpio (1987)

Donna Kei Benz. . . . . Nurse Mitchell
Britt Ekland . . . . Linda
Jillian Kesner . . . . Claire
- •• 0:39 - Topless sitting on deck of boat with bathing suit top down.

April Wayne . . . . Isabel
- • 0:32 - Brief right breast in bed with a guy.
- • 0:35 - Brief topless putting bathing suit on in a bathroom on a boat when a guy opens the door.

Moontrap (1989)

Leigh Lombardi. . . . . Mera
- •• 1:08 - Topless with Walter Koenig in moon tent.

The Morning After (1986)

Jeff Bridges . . . . Turner
Jane Fonda . . . . Alex Sternbergen
- • 1:08 - Brief topless making love with Jeff Bridges.

Raul Julia. Joaquin Manero
Rick Rossovich . . . . Detective

Mortal Passions (1989)

Michael Bowen . . . . Burke
- • 0:42 - Brief buns, on top of Adele.

Krista Errickson . . . . Emily
- •• 0:08 - Brief topless in bed with Darcy, while tied to the bed. Topless getting untied and rolling over.
- • 0:11 - Very brief right breast, rolling back on top of Darcy.
- ••• 0:40 - Topless after dropping her sheet for Burke, then making love with him.
- •• 0:46 - Topless getting into bed with her husband.

Sheila Kelley . . . . Adele

Moscow on the Hudson (1984)

Maria Conchita Alonso . . . . Lucia Lombardo
- •• 1:17 - Topless in bathtub with Robin Williams.

Motel Hell (1980)

Nina Axelrod. . . . . Terry
0:58 - In wet white T-shirt, tubin' with Ida.
- •• 1:01 - Topless sitting up in bed to kiss Vincent.
- • 1:04 - Very brief topless in tub when Bruce breaks the door down, then getting out of tub.

Rosanne Katon . . . . Suzi

Mountains of the Moon (1989)

Richard E. Grant. Oliphant
Anna Massey . . . . Mrs. Arundell
Fiona Shaw . . . . Isabel
- •• 0:33 - Topless and very brief lower frontal nudity letting Patrick Bergin wax the hair off her legs.
- •• 1:43 - Topless in bed after Bergin returns from Africa.

Ms. Don Juan (1973)

Brigitte Bardot . . . . Joan
- • 0:19 - Left breast in bathtub.
- •• 1:19 - Topless through fish tank. Buns and left breast, then brief topless in mirror with Paul.

Jane Birkin . . . . Clara
0:58 - Lower frontal nudity lying in bed with Brigitte Bardot.
1:00 - Brief topless in bed with Bardot. Long shot.
- •• 1:01 - Full frontal nudity getting dressed. Brief topless in open blouse.

Mugsy's Girls (1985)

Ken Norton . . . . Branscombe
Darcy Nychols . . . . Madame Antoinette
Kristi Somers . . . . Laurie
- • 0:15 - Brief topless several times while mud wrestling.
- •• 0:29 - Topless and buns in bathtub on bus.
- • 0:34 - Brief topless holding up sign to get truck driver to stop.

Murder Weapon (1989)

Michelle Bauer . . . . Girl in Shower on TV
- • 1:00 - Brief left breast on TV that the guys are watching. Scene from Nightmare Sisters.

Linnea Quigley. . . . . Dawn
- • 0:08 - Buns and very brief side of left breast walking into shower. Long shot.
- •• 0:40 - Topless taking off her top in car.
- •• 0:48 - Topless and buns taking off her top in bedroom.
- ••• 0:50 - Topless in bed on top of a guy. Excellent long scene. Brief buns, getting out of bed.

Karen Russell . . . . Amy
- ••• 0:05 - Topless in bed with a guy after taking off her swimsuit top, then making love on top of him. Long scene.
- • 0:34 - Brief topless in shower.
0:58 - In black bra and panties in bedroom.

Brinke Stevens . . . . Girl in Shower on TV
- • 1:00 - Brief left breast on TV that the guys are watching. Scene from Nightmare Sisters.

Murderers Among Us: The Simon Wiesenthal Story (1989; Made for Cable Movie)

Ben Kingsley. . . . . Simon Wiesenthal
- •• 0:27 - Buns and brief frontal nudity standing in and leaving a line in a concentration camp.

Reneé Soutendijk . . . . Cyla

Murphy's Law (1986)
Leigh Lombardi...................... Stewardess
Teri Lynn Peake.............................
Carrie Snodgress................... Joan Freeman
Angel Tompkins .... Jan
- 0:19 - Topless doing a strip routine on stage while Charles Bronson watches.
- 0:27 - Brief topless doing another routine.

Murphy's Romance (1985)
Sally Field .... Emma Moriarity
Brian Kerwin .... Bobbie Jack Moriarity
- •• 0:55 - Brief buns walking into the bathroom.

My Beautiful Laundrette (1985; British)
Daniel Day-Lewis........................ Johnny
Rita Wolf .... Tania
- •• 0:15 - Topless holding blouse up, showing off her breasts outside window to Omar.

My Best Friend's Girl (1984; French)
a.k.a. La Femme du Mon Ami
Isabelle Huppert .... Vivian Arthund
- 0:40 - Brief left breast peeking out of bathrobe walking around in living room.
  1:00 - Buns, making love with Thierry Lhermitte while his friend watches.

My Chauffeur (1986)
Cindy Beal............................Beebop
Vickie Benson .... Party Girl
Jeannine Bisignano .... Party Girl
Leslee Bremmer...................... Party Girl
Sam J. Jones .... Battle
- •• 0:44 - Buns, running around the park naked.
Sheila Lussier........................ Party Girl
Darian Mathias ....Dolly

My Father's Wife (1981; Italian)
Carroll Baker .... Lara
- 0:03 - Right breast making love in bed with her husband, Antonio.
- •• 0:06 - Topless standing in front of bed talking to Antonio.
- ••• 0:18 - Topless kneeling in bed, then getting out and putting a robe on while wearing beige panties.
Cesare Barro ....Claudio
- 0:52 - Buns, bringing Patricia champagne.

My First Wife (1985)
Wendy Hughes .... Helen
  1:00 - Brief topless and lower frontal nudity under water during husband's dream. Don't see her face.
- •• 1:08 - In bra, then topless on the floor with her husband.
- •• 1:10 - Topless in bed lying down, then fighting with her husband. A little dark.
Anna-Maria Monticelli.....................Hillary

My Man Adam (1986)
Veronica Cartwright....................Elaine Swit
- 1:09 - Side view of right breast lying on tanning table when Adam steals her card keys. Long shot, hard to see.

My Pleasure is My Business (1974)
Jayne Eastwood .... Isabella
- 1:16 - Topless in bed trying to get His Excellency's attention.
- •• 1:28 - Topless sitting up in bed with blonde guy.
Xaviera Hollander........................Gabriele
- •• 0:14 - Full frontal nudity in everybody's daydream.
- •• 0:39 - Topless sitting up in bed and putting on a blouse.
- •• 0:40 - Topless getting back into bed.
- ••• 0:59 - Topless and buns taking off clothes to go swimming in the pool, swimming, then getting out.
- •• 1:09 - Topless, buns and very brief lower frontal nudity, underwater in indoor pool with Gus.
- 1:31 - Buns and very brief side view of right breast, undressing at party.
Michael Kirby............................. Gus
- 0:41 - Brief buns while making love with Xaviera Hollander.

My Therapist (1983)
Shot on video tape.
Marilyn Chambers ....Kelly Carson
- •• 0:01 - Topless in sex therapy class.
- •• 0:07 - Topless, then full frontal nudity undressing for Rip. Long scene.
- ••• 0:10 - Topless undressing at home, then full frontal nudity making love on couch. Long scene. Nice. Then brief side view of right breast in shower.
- •• 0:18 - Topless on sofa with Mike.
- •• 0:21 - Topless taking off and putting red blouse on at home.
- ••• 0:26 - Nude in bedroom by herself masturbating on bed.
- ••• 0:32 - Topless exercising on the floor, buns in bed with Mike, topless in bed getting covered with whipped cream.
- •• 0:41 - Left breast and lower frontal nudity fighting with Don while he rips off her clothes.
- •• 1:08 - Topless and brief buns in bed.
  1:12 - In braless pink T-shirt at the beach.
Danielle Martin .... Francine
- •• 0:29 - In bra, garter belt, stockings and panties, then topless in room with Rip.
David Winn ....Mike Jenner
- •• 0:19 - Buns, making love with Marilyn Chambers in bed.

My Tutor (1983)
Caren Kaye.......................... Terry Green
- •• 0:25 - Topless walking into swimming pool.
- •• 0:52 - Topless in the pool with Matt Lattanzi.
- ••• 0:55 - Right breast, lying in bed making love with Lattanzi.

Matt Lattanzi. Bobby Chrystal
Graem McGavin . . . . Sylvia
 ••• 0:21 - In white bra, then topless in back seat of a car in a parking lot with Matt Lattanzi.
Shelly Taylor Morgan .Louisa
Francesca "Kitten" Natividad. . . . . .Anna Maria
 ••• 0:10 - Topless in room with Matt Lattanzi, then lying in bed.
Katt Shea . . . . Mud Wrestler
 • 0:48 - Brief topless when a guy rips her dress off.
Jewel Shepard . . . . Girl in Phone Booth
 • 0:40 - Brief left breast in car when Matt Lattanzi fantasizes about making love with her.

The Naked Cage (1985)

Lucinda Crosby. . . . . .Rhonda
Leslie Huntly . . . . Peaches
Lisa London. . . . . .Abbey
 •• 0:22 - Topless in S&M costume with Angel Tompkins.
 •• 0:38 - Left breast making out in bed with Angel Tompkins.
Valerie McIntosh . . . . .Ruby
 ••• 0:24 - Topless and buns in infirmary, then getting attacked by Smiley. Brief lower frontal nudity.
 • 0:28 - Topless, hanging by rope dead.
Shari Shattuck. . . . . Michelle
 •• 0:42 - Buns and topless in shower, then getting slashed by Rita during a dream.
 •• 1:00 - Left breast getting attacked by Smiley in jail cell, then fighting back.
 1:28 - In panties, during fight with Rita.
Angel Tompkins . . . . .Diane Wallace
 •• 0:22 - In lingerie, then topless with Abbey.
 • 0:38 - Brief right breast, in bed with Abbey.
Christina Whitaker. . . . . .Rita
 ••• 0:08 - Topless in bed with Willy.
 • 0:55 - Brief topless in gaping sweatshirt during fight with Sheila.
 1:28 - Panties during fight with Shari Shattuck.
 1:29 - Sort of left breast in gaping dress.

Naked Warriors (1973)

a.k.a. The Arena
Pam Grier . . . . .Mamawi
 •• 0:08 - Brief left breast, then lower frontal nudity and side view of right breast getting washed down in court yard.
 ••• 0:52 - Topless getting oiled up for a battle. Wow!
Lucretia Love. . . . . Deidre
 • 0:07 - Brief topless getting clothes torn off by guards.
 •• 0:08 - Brief nude getting washed down in court yard.
 1:08 - Brief buns, bent over riding a horse.
Margaret Markov . . . . Bodicia
 • 0:07 - Brief topless getting clothes torn off by guards.
 • 0:13 - Topless getting her dress ripped off, then raped during party.
 • 0:19 - Brief left breast, on floor making love, then right breast and buns.

 0:45 - In sheer white dress consoling Septimus, then walking around.
 • 0:52 - Brief topless sitting down, listening to Cornelia.

A Name for Evil (1973)

Robert Culp . . . . John Blake
 •• 0:52 - Frontal nudity running through the woods with a woman.
 • 1:07 - Buns, going skinny dipping. Lots of bun shots underwater.
Samantha Eggar. Joanna Blake
 • 0:42 - Very brief topless turning over in bed with Robert Culp. Dark, hard to see.
Sheila Sullivan . . . . Luanna Baxter
 • 0:51 - Full frontal nudity dancing in the bar with everybody.
 • 0:54 - Topless while Robert Culp makes love with her.
 • 0:56 - Topless getting dressed.
 • 1:17 - Nude, skinny dipping with Culp.

The Name of the Rose (1986)

Christian Slater. . . . . Adso of Melk
 • 0:48 - Buns, making love with The Girl in the monastery kitchen.
Valentina Vargas. . . . . The Girl
 ••• 0:46 - Topless and buns making love with Christian Slater in the monastery kitchen.

Nashville (1975)

Karen Black . . . . Connie White
Keith Carradine . . . . .Tom Frank
 • 0:47 - Buns, sitting on floor after getting out of bed.
Geraldine Chaplin . . . . Opal
Shelley Duvall. . . . . L.A. Jane
Scott Glenn . . . . Glenn Kelly
Jeff Goldblum. Tricycle Man
Cristina Raines . . . . Mary
Gwen Welles . . . . Sueleen Gay
 •• 2:09 - In bra singing to a room full of men, then topless doing a strip tease, buns walking up the steps and out of the room.

National Lampoon's Animal House (1978)

Karen Allen. . . . . Katherine "Katy" Fuller
 1:21 - Brief buns putting on shirt when Boone visits her at her house.
James Daughton . . . . Greg Marmalard
Sarah Holcomb . . . . Clorette DePasto
 •• 0:56 - Brief topless lying on bed after passing out in Tom Hulce's bed during toga party.
Sunny Johnson. . . . . .Otter's Co-Ed
Bruce McGill . . . . D-Day
Martha Smith. . . . . Babs Jansen
Mary Louise Weller. . . . . Mandy Pepperidge
 ••• 0:38 - In white bra, then topless in bedroom while John Belushi watches on a ladder through the window.

National Lampoon's Class Reunion (1982)
Misty Rowe . . . . .Cindy Shears
- 0:37 - Very brief topless running around school stage in Hawaiian hula dance outfit.

National Lampoon's Vacation (1983)
Beverly D'Angelo. . . . . .Ellen Griswold
- •• 0:18 - Brief topless taking a shower in the motel.
- 1:19 - Brief topless taking off shirt and jumping into the swimming pool.

John Diehl. Assistant Mechanic
Eugene Levy . . . . Car Salesman
Randy Quaid. . . . . Cousin Eddie

Naughty Nymphs (1972; German)
a.k.a. Passion Pill Swingers
Sybil Danning . . . . .Elizabeth
- ••• 0:21 - Nude taking a bath while yelling at her two sisters.
- 0:30 - Topless and buns throwing Nicholas out of her bedroom.
- •• 0:38 - Full frontal nudity running away from Burt.

The Naughty Stewardesses (1978)
Donna Desmond. . . . . Margie
- •• 0:12 - Topless leaning out of the shower.

Tracey Ann King . . . . .Barbara
- •• 0:56 - Topless dancing by the pool in front of everybody.

Necropolis (1987)
LeeAnne Baker . . . . Eva
- 0:04 - Right breast, dancing in skimpy black outfit during vampire ceremony.
- 0:38 - Brief topless in front of three evil things. (Before she has special make up to make it look like she has six breasts).

Adriane Lee. . . . . Cult Member

Neon Maniacs (1985)
Alan Hayes . . . . Steven
Susan Mierisch . . . . .Young Lover
- 0:07 - Very brief upper half of right breast while kissing her boyfriend at night.

Network (1976)
Faye Dunaway. . . . . .Diana Christensen
- 1:10 - Brief left breast twice, taking off clothes in room with William Holden.

Never Cry Wolf (1983)
Charlie Martin Smith. . . . . .Tyler
- 0:32 - Buns warming himself and drying his clothes after falling through the ice.
- 1:18 - Very brief frontal nudity running and jumping off a rock into the pond.
- 1:20 - Buns running in meadow with the caribou.
- 1:23 - Brief silhouette of lower frontal nudity while scampering up a hill. More buns when chasing the caribou.

Never on Tuesday (1988)
Claudia Christian . . . . .Tuesday
- 0:43 - Brief side view of right breast in the shower with Eddie during his fantasy.

Never Too Young to Die (1986)
Vanity . . . . .Donja Deering
0:25 - In white bra in the kitchen with John Stamos while he tends to her wounded arm.
- 1:04 - Wearing a bikini swimsuit, putting on suntan lotion. Brief topless in quick cuts making love with John in a cabin bedroom.

Tara Buckman . . . . Sacrificed Punkette

New Jack City (1991)
Eek-A-Mouse . . . . Fat Smitty
- 0:15 - Buns, when Nino holds a gun to his head and makes him walk nude outside.

Tracy Camilla Johns . . . . Unigua
0:40 - Buns, while dancing in red bra, panties, garter belt and stockings.
- 0:53 - Buns and right breast in bed with Nino.

New Year's Evil (1981)
Teri Copley . . . . Teenage Girl
- 0:48 - Brief right breast in the back of the car with her boyfriend at a drive-in movie. Breast is half sticking out of her white bra. Dark, hard to see anything.

Grant Cramer. Derek Sullivan

New York Nights (1983)
Corinne Alphen . . . . The Debutante
- •• 0:10 - Topless, making love in the back seat of a limousine with the rock star.
- ••• 1:38 - Topless dancing in the bedroom while the Financier watches from the bed.

Bobbi Burns . . . . The Authoress
- •• 0:16 - Topless on the couch outside with the rock star, then topless in bed.

Cynthia Lee . . . . .The Porn Star
- •• 1:15 - Topless in the steam room talking to the prostitute.
- ••• 1:26 - Topless in office with the financier making love on his desk.

Missy O'Shea. . . . . .The Model
0:30 - In white bra in restroom making love with the photographer.
- •• 0:37 - in black bra, panties, garter belt and stockings then topless taking off bra and getting into bed.
- •• 0:40 - Topless on floor when the photographer throws her on the floor and rips her bra off.
- ••• 0:41 - Full frontal nudity putting bathrobe on.
- 0:44 - Topless standing in front of a mirror with short black hair and a moustache getting dressed to look like a guy.

New York's Finest (1988)
John Altamura . . . . Brian Morrison
Ruth Corrine Collins . . . . Joy Sugarman
- • 0:04 - Brief topless with a bunch of hookers.
- • 0:36 - Topless with her two friends doing push ups on the floor.
- •• 1:02 - Topless making love on top of a guy talking about diamonds.

Jennifer Delora . . . . Loretta Michaels
- • 0:02 - Brief topless pretending to be a black hooker.
- • 0:04 - Brief topless with a bunch of hookers.
- • 0:36 - Topless with her two friends doing push ups on the floor.

Jane Hamilton . . . . Bunny
Heidi Paine . . . . Carley Pointer
- • 0:04 - Brief topless with a bunch of hookers.
- • 0:36 - Topless with her two friends doing push ups on the floor.

Denise Torek . . . . Hooker #2
Miriam Zucker . . . . Mrs. Rush

Next Year if All Goes Well (1983; French)
Isabelle Adjani . . . . Isabelle
- • 0:27 - Brief right breast, lying in bed with Maxime.

Thierry Lhermitte . . . . Maxime

Nickel Mountain (1985)
Brian Kerwin . . . . George
Heather Langencamp . . . . Callie
- ••• 0:24 - Topless in bed lying with Willard.
- • 0:29 - Side view of left breast and brief topless falling on bed with Willard.
- 0:29 - In white panties, peeking out the window.

Night Angel (1989)
Linden Ashby . . . . Craig
- • 1:22 - Buns, kneeling down to pick up picture. Don't see his face.

Karen Black . . . . Rita
Debra Feuer . . . . Kirstie
- • 0:46 - Brief side of left breast. Dark.

Night Breed (1990)
Catherine Chevalier . . . . Rachel
- • 1:12 - Topless in police jail, going through a door and killing a cop.

Craig Sheffer . . . . Boone

Night Call Nurses (1972)
a.k.a. Young LA Nurses 2
Patti T. Byrne . . . . Barbara
- •• 0:59 - Topless several times in bed with the Doctor.

Alana Collins . . . . Janis
- •• 0:12 - Topless in bed with Zach.
- 0:24 - In white two piece swimsuit on boat.
- •• 0:28 - Topless and buns on bed with Kyle.
- • 0:52 - Brief right breast twice in shower with Kyle.

Lynne Guthrie . . . . Cynthia
- • 0:00 - Topless on hospital roof taking off robe and standing on edge just before jumping off.

Dixie Lee Peabody . . . . Robin

- •• 0:35 - Topless taking off clothes in encounter group.
- • 0:39 - Brief topless in Barbara's flashback.

Night Eyes (1990)
(Unrated version.)
Stephen Meadows . . . . Michael Vincent
- • 0:27 - Buns and balls in bed with Tanya Roberts while Andrew Stevens watches on monitor.

Tanya Roberts . . . . Nikki
- 0:18 - In white one piece swimsuit by the pool.
- • 0:20 - Side view of left breast getting dressed while sitting on bed.
- 0:25 - In white lingerie, making love in bed with Michael.
- 0:30 - Repeat of last scene on TV when Andrew Stevens brings the video tape home to watch.
- 0:55 - Making love with Stevens. Don't see anything, but still steamy. Bubble covered left breast in tub with Stevens.
- ••• 1:09 - Topless giving Stevens a massage, then making love. Nice! Buns and left breast in the shower making love.
- • 1:27 - Buns, making love with Stevens in a chair.

Andrew Stevens . . . . Will
- ••• 1:11 - Buns in the shower.
- ••• 1:26 - Side view of buns with Tanya Roberts seen through a window.

Night Force (1986)
Linda Blair . . . .
Claudia Udy . . . . Christy Hanson
- •• 0:07 - Topless making love in the stable with Steve during her engagement party.
- ••• 0:10 - Nude, fantasizing in the shower.

Night Game (1989)
Karen Young . . . . Roxy
- 0:02 - In white slip with Roy Scheider.
- • 0:06 - Right breast, while in bed with Scheider after he answers the phone.

Night Games (1980)
Joanna Cassidy . . . . Julie Miller
- 0:44 - Buns, skinny dipping in the pool with Cindy Pickett.
- •• 0:45 - Brief full frontal nudity sitting up.

Cindy Pickett . . . . Valerie St. John
- •• 0:05 - Brief topless getting scared by her husband in the shower.
- • 0:45 - Buns and topless by and in the swimming pool with Joanna Cassidy.
- 0:46 - Topless in sheer blue dress during fantasy sequence with Cassidy.
- •• 0:48 - Brief full frontal nudity getting out of the pool, then topless lying down with Cassidy.
- 1:03 - Dancing at night in a see through nightgown.
- ••• 1:14 - Full frontal nudity standing up in bathtub, then topless during fantasy with a guy in gold.
- ••• 1:18 - Topless getting out of pool at night.
- ••• 1:24 - Topless sitting up in bed and stretching.

A Night in Heaven (1983)
Christopher Atkins. . . . . Rick
- • 1:03 - Very brief frontal nudity when he pulls down his pants in hotel room with Leslie Ann Warren.
- • 1:15 - Brief buns on boat with Leslie Ann Warren's angry husband.

Sandra Beall . . . . Slick
- • 1:09 - Brief close up of left breast in shower with Christopher Atkins.

Veronica Gamba. . . . . .Tammy
Rose McVeigh . . . . .Alison
Carrie Snodgress. . . . . Mrs. Johnson

Night Moves (1975)
Susan Clark. . . . . Ellen
- • 1:09 - Brief topless in bed with Gene Hackman.

Melanie Griffith. . . . . .Delly Grastner
- • 0:42 - Brief topless changing tops outside while talking with Gene Hackman.
- • 0:46 - Nude, saying "hi" from under water beneath a glass bottom boat.
- • 0:47 - Brief side view of right breast getting out of the water.

Jennifer Warren. . . . . Paula
- •• 0:56 - Topless in bed with Gene Hackman.
- • 0:57 - Right breast after making love in bed with Hackman.

James Woods . . . . Quentin

Night of the Creeps (1986)
Suzanne Snyder . . . . .Lisa
Jill Whitlow . . . . .Cynthia Cronenberg
  0:31 - In bra and panties taking off sweater.
- • 0:33 - Brief topless putting nightgown on over her head in her bedroom.

Night of the Demons (1987)
Cathy Podewell. . . . . Judy
  0:06 - Brief buns, changing clothes while talking on the phone.
  0:07 - In white bra taking off her sweater.

Linnea Quigley . . . . Suzanne
- •• 0:52 - Topless twice, opening her dress top while acting weird. Pushes a tube of lipstick into her left breast. (Don't try this at home kids!)
  0:56 - Lower frontal nudity, lifting her skirt up for Jay.

Jill Terashita. . . . . .Frannie
- •• 0:57 - Topless making love with her boyfriend in a coffin.

Night of the Living Babes (1987)
Michelle Bauer . . . . .Sue
- •• 0:44 - Topless chained up with Chuck and Buck.
- ••• 0:46 - More topless chained up.
- • 0:50 - Topless getting rescued with Lulu.

Louis Bonanno . . . . .Buck
Teri Lynn Peake. . . . . .Vesuvia
- ••• 0:25 - Topless and buns in G-string, dancing in front of Chuck and Buck. Long scene.

Jean Poremba. . . . . Mondo Zombie Girl Darlene
- ••• 0:12 - Topless wearing dark purple wig and long gloves, with the other Mondo Zombie Girls.
- ••• 0:16 - More topless and buns in bed with Buck.
- • 0:50 - Topless on the couch with the other Zombie Girls.
- • 0:52 - Topless on the couch again.

Connie Woods. . . . . .Lulu
- • 0:46 - Topless and buns in lingerie, in a cell with Buck.
- ••• 0:48 - More topless in cell with Buck.
- • 0:50 - Topless getting rescued with Michelle Bauer.

Night Patrol (1985)
Linda Blair . . . . Sue
- • 1:19 - Brief left breast, in bed with The Unknown Comic.

Francesca "Kitten" Natividad . . . . Hippie Woman
- •• 1:01 - Topless in kitchen with Pat Paulsen, the other police officer and her hippie boyfriend.

Lori Sutton. . . . . Edith Hutton
- ••• 0:47 - In white bra, panties, garter belt and stockings, then topless three times taking off bra in bedroom with the Police officer.

The Night Porter (1974; Italian/U.S.)
Charlotte Rampling . . . . .Lucia
- •• 0:11 - Side nudity being filmed with a movie camera in the concentration camp line.
- • 0:13 - Nude running around a room while a Nazi taunts her by shooting his gun near her.
- ••• 1:12 - Topless doing a song and dance number wearing pants, suspenders and a Nazi hat. Long scene.

Night School (1980)
Rachel Ward. . . . . Elanor
- • 0:24 - In sheer white bra and panties, taking off clothes to take a shower. Topless taking off bra. Hard to see because she's behind a shower curtain.
  0:28 - Buns, when her boyfriend rubs red paint all over her in the shower.

Night Shift (1982)
Kevin Costner. . . . . Frat Boy #1
Ashley Cox. . . . . Jenny Lynn
Dawn Dunlap. . . . . Maxine
Monique Gabrielle . . . . Tessie
- • 0:56 - Brief topless on college guy's shoulders during party in the morgue.

Shelley Long . . . . Belinda Keaton
  0:20 - In black teddy and robe talking to Henry Winkler in the hallway.
  0:37 - In panties, socks and tank top cooking breakfast in Winkler's kitchen.

Ola Ray . . . . Dawn
K.C. Winkler. . . . . Cheryl
Robbin Young . . . . Nancy

Night Visitor (1989)
Shannon Tweed. Lisa Grace
Teresa Vander Woude . . . . Kelly Fremont

Teri Weigel . . . . Victim in Cellar
- 0:50 - Brief out of focus topless changing tops in the cellar.
- 0:55 - Right breast, during ceremony. Very brief topless just before being stabbed.

Night Warning (1982)
Julia Duffy . . . . Julie Linden
    0:44 - Upper half of left breast.
- 0:46 - Brief topless when her boyfriend pulls the sheets down.
- • 0:47 - Brief topless when Susan Tyrrell opens the bedroom door.
Susan Tyrrell . . . . Cheryl Roberts
- 0:17 - Left breast, sticking out of dress just before she stabs the TV repairman.

The Nightcomers (1971; British)
Stephanie Beacham . . . . Miss Margaret Jessel
- 0:13 - Brief left breast lying in bed having her breasts fondled.
- • • 0:30 - Topless in bed with Marlon Brando while a little boy watches through the window.
- • • 0:55 - Topless in bed pulling the sheets down.
Marlon Brando . . . . Peter Quint
    0:30 - Looks like you can see something between his legs, but most of his midsection is hidden by bed post.

Nightfall (1988)
Andra Millian . . . . Anna
- 0:12 - Very brief topless making love with David Birney.
- 0:41 - Very brief topless making love in front of a fire.
    0:58 - Same scene in a flashback while the guy is talking to another woman.

Nightmare at Shadow Woods (1983)
a.k.a. Blood Rage
Jane Bentzen . . . . Julie
    0:38 - In red lingerie, black stockings and garter belt in her apartment with Phil.
Chad Montgomery . . . . Gregg
- 0:52 - Brief buns, making love with Andrea on diving board just before getting killed.

A Nightmare on Elm Street 4: The Dream Master (1988)
Hope Marie Carlton . . . . Pin-Up Girl
- 0:21 - Brief topless swimming in a waterbed.
Linnea Quigley . . . . Soul from Freddy's Chest
- 1:23 - Brief topless twice, trying to get out of Freddy's body. Don't see her face clearly.

Nightmare Sisters (1987)
(This is the best video tape for viewing all three "Scream Queens.")
Michelle Bauer . . . . Mickey
- • • 0:39 - Topless standing in panties with Melody and Marci after transforming from nerds to sexy women.
- • • 0:40 - Topless in the kitchen with Melody and Marci.

- • • 0:44 - Full frontal nudity in the bathtub with Melody and Marci. Excellent, long scene.
- • • 0:47 - Topless in the bathtub. Nice close up.
- • • 0:48 - Still more topless in the bathtub.
- • • 0:53 - Topless in bed with J.J.
Sandy Brooke . . . . Amanda Detweiler
Matthew Phelps . . . . J.J.
- • • 0:53 - Buns, taking off his pants and getting into bed with Michelle Bauer.
Linnea Quigley . . . . Melody
- • • • 0:39 - Topless standing in panties with Mickey and Marci after transforming from nerds to sexy women.
- • • • 0:40 - Topless in the kitchen with Mickey and Marci.
- • • • 0:44 - Topless in the bathtub with Mickey and Marci. Excellent, long scene.
- • • • 0:46 - Topless in the bathtub. Nice close up.
- • • • 0:48 - Still more topless in the bathtub.
- • • • 0:55 - Topless dancing and singing in front of Kevin. Long scene.
- • • 0:57 - Topless on the couch with Bud.
Brinke Stevens . . . . Marci
- • • • 0:39 - Topless standing in panties with Melody and Mickey after transforming from nerds to sexy women.
- • • • 0:40 - Topless in the kitchen with Melody and Mickey.
- • • • 0:44 - Nude in the bathtub with Melody and Mickey. Excellent, long scene.
- • • • 0:47 - Topless in the bathtub. Nice close up.
- • • • 0:48 - Still more buns and topless in the bathtub.

Nights in White Satin (1987)
Kim Waltrip . . . . Stevie Hughes
    0:37 - In white wig, bra, panties, garter belt and stocking during photo session.
    0:39 - Brief side view of left breast in black slip during photo session.
- 0:53 - Topless in bathtub with Walker. Out of focus, hard to see.

The Nightstalker (1987)
Tally Chanel . . . . Brenda
- 0:54 - Brief frontal nudity lying dead in bed covered with paint. Long shot, hard to see anything.
Joan Chen . . . . Mai Wong
Lydie Denier . . . . First Victim
- • • 0:03 - Topless making love with big guy.
Ola Ray . . . . Sable Fox
Diane Sommerfield . . . . Lonnie Roberts
- 0:35 - Side view of right breast lying dead in morgue.

Nightwish (1988)
Alisha Das . . . . Kim
- • • 1:09 - Brief topless, then left breast in open dress caressing herself while lying on the ground.
- 1:10 - Braless under see-through purple dress.
Elizabeth Kaitan . . . . Donna
- 0:04 - In wet T-shirt, then brief topless taking it off during experiment. Long shot.

Ninja Academy (1990)
Michele Burger . . . . Nudist
Becky LeBeau . . . . Nudist
•• 0:26 - Nude, carrying plate, then going to swing at nudist colony. Then playing volleyball (she's the first one to hit the ball).
Bonnie Paine. . . . . Nudist
• 0:26 - Brief buns and topless playing volleyball. (She's the second blonde on the far side of the net who misses the ball.)

No Small Affair (1984)
Judy Baldwin. . . . . Stephanie
••• 0:36 - In white bra, panties and garter belt, then topless in Jon Cryer's bedroom trying to seduce him.
Elizabeth Daily. . . . . Susan
Demi Moore. . . . . Laura
• 1:34 - Very, very brief side view of left breast in bed with Jon Cryer.
Tim Robbins . . . . Nelson

No Way Out (1987)
Iman. . . . . Nina Beka
Kevin Costner . . . . Lt. Cmdr. Tom Farrell
Sean Young. Susan Atwell
0:11 - In black stockings, garter belt & corset in love scene in back of limousine with Kevin Costner.
••• 0:13 - Side view of left breast, then brief right breast, going into Nina's apartment with Costner.
0:21 - In bed in pink lingerie and a robe talking on telephone when Costner is in Manila.
0:31 - In corset and stockings with garter belt in bathroom talking to Costner.

Nomads (1986)
Pierce Brosnan . . . . Pommier
• 0:56 - Buns, taking his pants off by the window. Kind of dark, hard to see.
Lesley-Anne Down . . . . Flax
Anna-Maria Monticelli. . . . . Niki
• 0:57 - Left breast, making love in bed with Pierce Brosnan. Dark, hard to see anything.
Mary Woronov . . . . Dancing Mary

North Dallas Forty (1979)
Peter Boyle . . . . Emmett
Mac Davis. . . . . Maxwell
• 0:53 - Brief buns getting a can of Coke in the locker room.
Dayle Haddon. Charlotte
Nick Nolte. Phillip Elliott
• 0:49 - Brief buns, pulling down underwear to get into whirlpool bath in locker room.
Savannah Smith . . . . Joanne
• 0:27 - Very brief topless in bed tossing around with Nick Nolte.

Not of This Earth (1988)
Ava Cadell. Second Hooker
•• 0:41 - Topless in cellar with Paul just before getting killed with two other hookers. Wearing a gold dress.

Monique Gabrielle . . . . Agnes
Roxanne Kernohan. . . . . Lead Hooker
••• 0:41 - Topless in cellar with Paul just before getting killed with two other hookers. Wearing a blue top.
Becky LeBeau. . . . . Happy Birthday Girl
••• 0:47 - Topless doing a Happy Birthday stripper-gram for the old guy.
Traci Lords . . . . Nadine
•• 0:25 - Buns and side view of left breast drying herself off with a towel while talking to Jeremy.
0:27 - In blue swimsuit by swimming pool.
•• 0:42 - Topless in bed making love with Harry.
0:46 - Walking around the house in white lingerie.
Taaffe O'Connell . . . . Damelia
• 0:04 - Brief topless and buns from *Galaxy of Terror* during the opening credits.
Rebecca Perle. . . . . Alien Girl
0:53 - In black swimsuit wearing sunglasses.
Cynthia Ann Thompson . . . . . Third Hooker (black dress)

Not Quite Paradise (1986; British)
a.k.a. Not Quite Jerusalem
Joanna Pacula. . . . . Gila
• 1:04 - Left breast, lying in bed with Sam Robards.

Nowhere to Hide (1987)
Amy Madigan . . . . Barbara Cutter
• 1:04 - Brief side view of right breast taking off towel to get dressed in cabin. Long shot, hard to see.

Obsession: A Taste For Fear (1987)
Virginia Hey . . . . Diane
• 0:04 - Buns and very brief side view of right breast dropping towel to take a shower.
•• 0:14 - Brief right breast in bed when sheet falls down.
• 0:38 - Topless lying down, wearing a mask, while talking to a girl.
••• 1:03 - Topless waking up in bed.
••• 1:17 - Topless in hallway with Valerie.
• 1:19 - Brief lower frontal nudity and right breast in bed with Valerie, then buns in bed.
••• 1:20 - Topless getting dressed, walking and running around the house when Valerie gets killed.
• 1:26 - Topless tied up in chair while Paul torments her.

The Octagon (1980)
Carol Bagdasarian . . . . Aura
• 1:18 - Brief side view of right breast, while sitting on bed next to Chuck Norris and taking her blouse off.
Karen Carlson. . . . . Justine
Kim Lankford . . . . Nancy

Of Unknown Origin (1983; Canadian)
Jennifer Dale . . . . Lorrie Wells
Shannon Tweed. . . . . Meg Hughes
• 0:00 - Brief side view of right breast taking a shower.
Peter Weller . . . . Bart Hughes
Kenneth Welsh. . . . . James

Off Limits (1988)
Woody Brown . . . . Co-Pilot
Willem Dafoe . . . . Bud McGriff
Scott Glenn . . . . Colonel Dexter Armstrong
Tuy Ann Luu . . . . Lanh
  •• 0:48 - Topless dancing on stage in a nightclub.
Fred Ward . . . . Dix

Off the Wall (1982)
Rosanna Arquette . . . . Pam
Roselyn Royce . . . . Buxom Blonde
  • 0:35 - Left breast kissing an inmate in visiting room
    while the guards watch.
  •• 0:51 - Left breast again, kissing inmate through bars
    while the guards watch.

An Officer and a Gentleman (1982)
Lisa Blount . . . . Lynette Pomeroy
    1:25 - In a red bra and tap pants in a motel room
    with David Keith.
Richard Gere . . . . Zack Mayo
David Keith . . . . Sid Worley
John Laughlin . . . . Troy
Debra Winger . . . . Paula Pokrifki
  ••• 1:05 - Brief side view of right breast, then topless
    making love with Richard Gere in a motel.

The Offspring (1986)
Martine Beswicke . . . . Katherine White
Miriam Byrd-Nethery . . . . Eileen Burnside
  • 0:26 - Topless in bathtub filled with ice while her hus-
    band tries to kill her with an ice pick.
    0:29 - Very brief right breast, dead in bathtub while
    he is downstairs.
Susan Tyrrell . . . . Beth Chandler

Oh, Alfie! (1975; British)
a.k.a. Alfie Darling
Minah Bird . . . . Gloria
Joan Collins . . . . Fay
    0:28 - In white bra and panties, running to answer
    the phone, then talking to Alfie.
  ••• 1:00 - Topless lying in bed after Alfie rolls off her.
Patsy Kensit . . . . Penny
Rula Lenska . . . . Louise
  •• 0:12 - Topless, then left breast in bed after making
    love with Alfie.
Alan Price . . . . Alfie Elkins
  •• 0:14 - Buns washing himself off in the kitchen while
    talking to Louise's husband.
Annie Ross . . . . Claire
  •• 1:34 - Topless on top of Alfie in open black dress
    while he's lying injured in bed.
Sheila White . . . . Norma

Old Gringo (1989)
Jane Fonda . . . . Harriet Winslow
  • 1:24 - Side of left breast undressing in front of Jimmy
    Smits. Sort of brief right breast lying in bed, hugging
    him.

Jimmy Smits . . . . Arroyo
  • 1:26 - Half of his buns on bed with Jane Fonda. Long
    shot, don't see his face.

Olivia (1983)
a.k.a. A Taste of Sin
Suzanna Love . . . . Olivia
  •• 0:34 - Buns and topless making love in bed with
    Mike.
  •• 0:58 - Topless and buns making love with Mike in the
    shower.
  • 1:08 - Very brief full frontal nudity getting into bed
    with Richard. Dark, long shot.
  •• 1:09 - Buns, lying in bed. Dark. Full frontal nudity
    getting out of bed and going to the bathroom.
Jeff Winchester . . . . Richard
  • 1:17 - Buns, getting stuffed into trunk by Olivia.
    Dark.

The Omega Man (1971)
Rosalind Cash . . . . Lisa
  •• 1:09 - Side view of left breast and upper half of buns
    getting out of bed. Buns and topless sitting in bed.
  • 1:21 - Side view topless in beige underwear while
    trying on clothes.
Charlton Heston . . . . Neville

On the Edge (1985)
(Unrated version—not the R-rated version.)
Bruce Dern . . . . Wes
  • 0:52 - Brief buns, seen from below while floating in a
    pond.
Pam Grier . . . . Cora
    0:18 - In leotards, leading an aerobics dance class.
  •• 0:42 - Topless in the mirror, then full frontal nudity
    making love with Bruce Dern standing up. Then
    brief left breast. A little dark.

On the Line (1984; Spanish)
Victoria Abril . . . . Engracia
  ••• 0:16 - Topless getting undressed to make love with
    Mitch.
  • 0:29 - Very brief topless, making love in bed with
    Mitch.
    0:54 - In white lingerie getting dressed.
David Carradine . . . . Bryant
  • 0:11 - Buns, lying on a table, getting a massage by
    three women.

Once Bitten (1985)
Lauren Hutton . . . . Countess
Skip Lackey . . . . Russ
  • 1:11 - Brief buns in the school showers trying to see
    if Mark got bitten by a vampire.
Carey More . . . . Moll Flanders Vampire

Once Is Not Enough (1975)
Kirk Douglas . . . . Mike Wayne
David Janssen . . . . Tom Colt
  • 1:22 - Buns, taking off clothes and walking to the
    bathroom.
Brenda Vaccaro . . . . Linda

Once Upon a Time in America (1984)
(Long version.)
Jennifer Connelly. . . . . Young Deborah
Robert De Niro . . . . Noodles
Darlanne Fluegel. . . . . Eve
Olga Karlatos . . . . Woman in the Puppet Theatre
- •• 0:11 - Right breast twice when bad guy pokes at her nipple with a gun.

Elizabeth McGovern .Deborah
- • 2:33 - (0:32 into tape 2) Brief glimpses of left breast when Robert De Niro tries to rape her in the back seat of a car.

Treat Williams . . . . Jimmy O'Donnell
James Woods . . . . Max

One Deadly Summer (1984; French)
Isabelle Adjani. . . . . Eliane
- •• 0:21 - Brief topless changing in the window for Florimond.
- ••• 0:32 - Nude, walking in and out of the barn.
- • 0:36 - Brief left breast lying in bed when Florimond gets up.
- • 0:40 - Buns and topless taking a bath.
- • 1:41 - Part of right breast, getting felt up by an old guy, then right breast then brief topless.
- •• 1:47 - Topless in bedroom with Florimond.
  1:49 - In white bra and panties talking with Florimond.

One from the Heart (1982)
Teri Garr . . . . Frannie
- •• 0:09 - Brief topless getting out of the shower.
  0:10 - In a bra, getting dressed in bedroom.
- •• 0:40 - Side view of right breast changing in. bedroom while Frederic Forrest watches.
- ••• 1:20 - Brief topless in bed when standing up after Forrest drops in though the roof while she's in bed with Raul Julia.

Raul Julia. . . . . Ray
- • 1:20 - Very brief buns getting out of bed with Teri Garr when Frederic Forrest crashes through the ceiling.

Nastassja Kinski. . . . . Leila
- • 1:13 - Brief topless in open blouse when she leans forward after walking on a ball.

One Man Force (1989)
Maria Celedonio . . . . Maria
- • 0:30 - Brief topless, twice, hiding John Matuzak in her apartment. Long shot.

Sam J. Jones . . . . Pete

One More Saturday Night (1986)
Moira Harris . . . . Peggy
Bess Meyer . . . . Tobi
- • 1:02 - Brief topless in bed with Tom Davis.

Chelchie Ross . . . . .Dad Lundahl
- • 0:39 - Buns, squished against the car window in back seat with Moira Harris.

One Night Only (1984; Canadian)
Wendy Lands . . . . .Jane
- •• 0:36 - Topless taking a bath while Jamie watches through keyhole.
- •• 0:38 - Brief left breast in open robe.
- • 1:15 - Brief topless in bed with policeman.

Helene Udy . . . . .Suzanne
- • 0:50 - Buns and right breast in bed talking with a guy.
- • 1:12 - Over the shoulder, brief left breast on top of a guy in bed.

Lenore Zann. . . . . Anne
- •• 0:20 - Topless getting dressed in bedroom with Jamie.
- • 1:04 - Right breast in bedroom with Jamie.
- ••• 1:19 - Topless and buns making love with Jamie.

One Trick Pony (1980)
Blair Brown . . . . Marion
Joan Hackett. . . . . .Lonnie Fox
- ••• 1:21 - Nude getting out of bed and getting dressed while talking to Paul Simon.

Rip Torn. . . . . .Walter Fox
Mare Winningham . . . . McDeena Dandridge
- •• 0:14 - Topless in the bathtub with Paul Simon, smoking a cigarette. Long scene.

One Woman or Two (1986; French)
a.k.a. Une Femme Ou Deux
Zabou . . . . Constance
- •• 0:28 - Brief topless pulling up her blouse for Gerard Depardieu.

Sigourney Weaver . . . . Jessica
  1:30 - In braless white blouse.
- •• 1:31 - Very brief side view of left breast in bed with Gerard Depardieu.

The Onion Field (1979)
James Woods . . . . Gregory Powell
- •• 1:33 - Buns, taking a shower in the prison.

Open House (1987)
Adrienne Barbeau. Lisa Grant
- • 0:27 - In black lace lingerie, then very brief half of left breast making love with Joseph Bottoms on the floor.
- •• 1:15 - Brief side view of right breast getting out of bed at night to look at something in her briefcase.
- ••• 1:16 - Brief topless taking off bathrobe and getting back into bed. Kind of dark.

Tiffany Bolling . . . . Judy Roberts
Mary Stavin . . . . .Katie Thatcher

Opposing Force (1986)
a.k.a. Hell Camp
Lisa Eichhorn .Lieutenant Casey
- • 0:17 - Wet T-shirt after going through river.
- ••• 0:33 - Topless getting sprayed with water and dusted with white powder.
- •• 1:03 - Topless after getting raped by Anthony Zerbe in his office, while another officer watches.

Ordeal by Innocence *(1984)*

Faye Dunaway. . . . . Rachel Argyle
Sarah Miles . . . . Mary Durrant
Diana Quick .Gwenda Vaughn
Cassie Stuart .Maureen Clegg
  •• 1:14 - Topless in bed talking to Donald Sutherland.
Donald Sutherland . . . . Arthur Calgary

The Osterman Weekend *(1983)*

Meg Foster . . . . .Ali Tanner
  0:14 - Very, very brief tip of right breast after getting
  nightgown out of closet.
Rutger Hauer. . . . . John Tanner
Dennis Hopper . . . . .Richard Tremayne
John Hurt . . . . .Lawrence Fassett
  • 0:01 - Buns, getting out of bed and walking to the
  shower.
Chris Sarandon . . . . Joseph Cardone
Helen Shaver. . . . . .Virginia Tremayne
  •• 0:24 - Topless in an open blouse yelling at her husband in the bedroom.
  • 0:41 - Topless in the swimming pool when everyone
  watches on the TV.
Merete Van Kamp . . . . Zuna Brickman
  •• 0:01 - Topless and brief buns in bed on a TV monitor,
  then topless getting injected by two intruders.
  • 0:35 - Brief topless on video again while Rutger Hauer watches in the kitchen on TV.
  • 1:30 - Topless again on video during TV show.
Cassie Yates. . . . . Betty Cardone
  •• 0:48 - Topless getting into bed with Chris Sarandon
  while Rutger Hauer watches on TV.
  • 0:51 - Right breast, making love with Sarandon.

Other Side of Midnight *(1977)*

Marie-France Pisier . . . . Noëlle Page
  • 0:10 - Very brief topless in bed with Lanchon.
  0:28 - Buns, in bed with John Beck. Medium long
  shot.
  0:45 - In white bra, in dressing room talking to Henri.
  0:50 - Topless in bathtub, giving herself an abortion
  with a coat hanger. Painful to watch!
  •• 1:11 - Topless wearing white slip in room getting
  dressed in front of Henri.
  ••• 1:17 - Full frontal nudity in front of fireplace with Armand, rubbing herself with oil, then making love
  with ice cubes. Very nice!
  • 1:35 - Full frontal nudity taking off dress for Constan-
  tin in his room.
Susan Sarandon . . . . Catherine Douglas
  • 1:10 - Topless in bedroom with John Beck. Long
  shot, then right breast while lying in bed.
  2:18 - In wet white nightgown running around outside during a storm.

Out Cold *(1989)*

Lisa Blount . . . . Phyllis
Tom Byrd. . . . . .Mr. Holstrom
  • 0:10 - Brief frontal nudity getting out of bed with Teri
  Garr when her husband comes home.
Teri Garr. . . . . Sunny Cannald
Debra Lamb. . . . . Panetti's Dancer
  • 1:04 - Brief topless dancer in G-string on stage. Don't
  see her face.
John Lithgow . . . . Dave Geary
Bruce McGill . . . . Ernie Cannald
  •• 0:12 - Frontal nudity, opening the shower door, talk-
  ing to Teri Garr. Brief buns, putting on underwear.
Randy Quaid . . . . Lester Atlas

Out of Control *(1984)*

Cindi Dietrich. . . . . .Robin
  • 0:29 - Topless taking off her red top. Long shot.
Sherilyn Fenn . . . . Katie
  0:19 - In wet white T-shirt in pond with the other
  girls.
Martin Hewitt. . . . . Keith
Richard Kantor. . . . . Gary
  • 0:29 - Buns, pulling his underwear down during a
  game of strip spin the bottle.
Betsy Russell. Chrissie
  0:19 - In white corset and panties in the pond.
  •• 0:29 - Topless taking off her top while playing Strip
  Spin the Bottle.
  0:30 - Buns, taking off her panties.
Claudia Udy . . . . .Tina
  0:19 - In leopard skin pattern bra and panties.
  • 0:28 - In leopard bra and panties playing Strip Spin
  the Bottle, then very brief topless taking off her top.
  Long shot.
  • 0:47 - Brief left breast getting raped by bad guy on
  the boat.
  • 0:54 - Brief left breast, then right breast making love
  with Cowboy.
Jim Youngs. . . . . .Cowboy
  • 0:54 - Buns making love with Claudia Udy.

Out of the Dark *(1988)*

Starr Andreeff. . . . . Camille
Karen Black . . . . Ruth
Cameron Dye. . . . . Kevin Silver/Bobo
  • 0:32 - Brief buns when Kristi yanks his underwear
  down while he is throwing a basketball. Don't see
  his face.
Karen Mayo-Chandler . . . . Barbara
  • 0:16 - Brief topless pulling red dress down wearing
  black stocking in Kevin's studio.
  ••• 0:17 - Topless and buns posing during photo shoot.
Karen Witter. . . . . .Jo Ann

Out on Bail *(1988)*

Kathy Shower. . . . . Sally Anne
  • 1:01 - Brief topless in shower with Robert Ginty.

The Outing (1987)
Mark Mitchell . . . . Mike Daley
• 1:08 - Buns when his friend gets killed, then very brief frontal nudity sitting up.
Michelle Watkins . . . . Faylene
• 0:12 - Topless taking off her top, standing by the edge of the swimming pool, then running topless through the house with panties on.

The Outlaw Josey Wales (1976)
Sam Bottoms . . . . Jamie
Clint Eastwood . . . . Josey Wales
Sondra Locke . . . . Laura Lee
•• 1:20 - Briefly nude in rape scene.

Overexposed (1990)
Karen Black . . . . Mrs. Trowbridge
William Bumiller . . . . Hank
• 0:54 - Brief buns, taking off his pants to get into bed with Catherine Oxenberg.
Shelley Michelle . . body double for Catherine Oxenberg
•• 0:54 - Left breast several times, buns when taking off panties, lower frontal nudity while in bed with Hank. Wearing a wig with wavy hair.
David Naughton . . . . Phillip

Pacific Heights (1990)
Beverly D'Angelo . . . . Ann
• 0:01 - Sort of topless in reflection on TV screen, then right breast, in bed with Michael Keaton.
0:03 - Very brief buns, turning over on bed when two guys burst in to the house.
Melanie Griffith . . . . Patty Parker
Matthew Modine . . . . Drake Goodman

Paint It Black (1989)
Sally Kirkland . . . . Marion Easton
0:05 - Most of left breast, while sitting in bed talking to Rick Rossovich.
Rick Rossovich . . . . Jonathan Dunbar
• 0:48 - Upper half of buns getting out of bed with Julie Carmen.
Monique Van De Ven . . . . Kyla Leif

Paperback Hero (1973; Canadian)
Elizabeth Ashley . . . . Loretta
••• 0:37 - Nude in shower with Keir Dullea. Long scene.
••• 0:39 - Topless, straddling Dullea in the shower.
Dayle Haddon . . . . Joanna
0:31 - Lower half of buns, under T-shirt while standing behind a bar with Keir Dullea.

Paradise (1981)
Willie Aames . . . . David
0:42 - Buns, walking into the ocean with a fishing net. Dark, hard to see anything.
•• 1:12 - Frontal nudity swimming with Phoebe Cates under water.
Phoebe Cates . . . . Sarah
•• 0:23 - Buns and topless taking a shower in a cave while Willie Aames watches.
0:36 - In wet white dress in a pond with Aames.

• 0:40 - Very brief left breast caressing herself while looking at her reflection in the water.
0:43 - Buns, getting out of bed to check out Aames' body while he sleeps.
0:46 - Buns, washing herself in a pond at night.
•• 0:55 - Side view of her silhouette at the beach at night. Nude swimming in the water, viewed from below.
••• 1:11 - Topless making love with Aames.
••• 1:12 - Full frontal nudity swimming under water with Aames.
••• 1:16 - Topless making love with Aames again.

Paradise Motel (1985)
Leslee Bremmer . . . . uncredited Girl Leaving Room
• 0:38 - Topless buttoning her pink sweater, leaving motel room.
Gary Hershberger . . . . Sam
•• 0:33 - Buns, running away from the Coach's house.
Colleen McDermott . . . . Debbie
•• 0:24 - Topless in motel room with Mic, when Sam lets them use a room.

Parasite (1982)
Cherie Currie . . . . Dana
Demi Moore . . . . Patricia Welles
Cheryl Smith . . . . Captive Girl
•• 0:08 - Topless tied by wrists in kitchen.
•• 0:12 - Topless knocking gun out of guy's hands standing behind fence.
Tom Villard . . . . Zeke

The Park is Mine (1985; Made for Cable Movie)
Tommy Lee Jones . . . . Mitch
Yaphet Kotto . . . . Eubanks
Helen Shaver . . . . Valery Weaver
• 0:46 - Very brief topless undressing then very, very brief left breast catching clothes from Tommy Lee Jones.

Partners (1982)
Iris Alhanti . . . . Jogger
•• 0:21 - Topless in the shower when Ryan O'Neil opens the shower curtain.
Jennifer Ashley . . . . Secretary
Robyn Douglass . . . . Jill
•• 1:00 - Brief topless taking off her top and getting into bed with Ryan O'Neil.
Denise Galik . . . . Clara
John Hurt . . . . Kerwin
Ryan O'Neal . . . . Benson
•• 0:48 - Buns, in Indian outfit for photo session with Robyn Douglass. Don't see his face.

Party Camp (1987)
Jewel Shepard . . . . Dyanne Stein
••• 0:57 - In white bra and panties, then topless playing strip poker with the boys.
April Wayne . . . . Nurse Brenda

Party Favors (1987)

(Shot on video tape.)

April Dawn Dollarhide. . . . .

George "Buck" Flower. . . . . .Pop

Jill Johnson . . . . Trixie
- •• 0:04 - Topless in dressing room, taking off blue dress and putting on red swimsuit.
- ••• 0:35 - Topless in doctors office taking off her clothes.
- ••• 1:03 - Topless doing strip routine in cowgirl costume. More topless after.
- • 1:16 - Topless taking off swimsuit next to pool during final credits.

Jean Poremba . . . . Bobbi
- •• 0:04 - Topless in dressing room, taking off red top and putting on black one.
- • 0:23 - Brief topless when blouse pops off while delivering pizza.
- ••• 0:27 - Topless and buns in G-string doing a strip routine outside.
- • 0:31 - Brief topless flapping her blouse to cool off.
- ••• 1:04 - Topless doing a strip routine in a little girl outfit. Buns, in G-string. More topless after.
- • 1:16 - Nude taking off swimsuit next to pool during final credits.

Gail Thackray . . . . .Nicole
- • 0:04 - Topless in dressing room with the other three girls changing into blue swimsuit.
- • 0:11 - Brief left breast in the swimsuit during dance practice.
- • 0:12 - Topless during dance practice.
- • 0:17 - More topless during dance practice.
- •• 0:42 - Topless doing strip routine at anniversary party. Great buns in G-string shots.
- ••• 1:01 - Topless and buns in G-string after stripping from cheerleader outfit. Lots of bouncing breast shots. Mingling with the men afterwards.
- • 1:16 - Nude by the swimming pool during the final credits.

Party Incorporated (1989)

Marilyn Chambers. . . . . Marilyn Sanders
- ••• 0:56 - In lingerie, then topless in bedroom with Weston. Nice!
- • 1:11 - Brief topless on the beach when Peter takes her swimsuit top off.

Ruth Corrine Collins . . . . .Betty
- • 0:07 - Topless on desk with Dickie. Long shot.
- •• 1:08 - Topless in bed with Weston when Marilyn Chambers comes in.

Kimberly Taylor. . . . . .Felicia
- •• 0:26 - Topless shaking her breasts trying an outfit on.
- ••• 0:39 - Topless and buns in G-string in the bar with the guys.

Christina Veronica. .Christina
- ••• 0:52 - Buns and topless dancing in front of everybody at party.

Party Plane (1988)

Laura Albert . . . . .uncredited Auditioning Woman
- •• 0:30 - Topless, taking off blue dress during audition. She's wearing a white ribbon in her ponytail.

Michele Burger . . . . Carol
- • 0:31 - Topless, squirting whipped cream on herself for her audition.
- •• 0:38 - Topless doing a strip tease routine on the plane.
- ••• 1:02 - Topless mud wrestling with Renee on the plane.
- • 1:09 - Topless in the cockpit, covered with mud.
- •• 1:17 - Topless in serving cart.

Iris Condon . . . . Renee
- • 0:29 - Buns, in white lingerie during audition.
- ••• 0:48 - Topless plane doing a strip tease routine.
- ••• 1:02 - Topless on plane mud wrestling with Carol.
- • 1:12 - Left breast, covered with mud, holding the Mad Bomber.
- • 1:17 - Left breast, then topless in trunk with the Doctor.

Jill Johnson . . . . Laurie
- ••• 0:06 - Topless and buns changing clothes and getting into spa with her two girlfriends. (She's wearing a black swimsuit bottom.)
- ••• 0:11 - Topless getting out of spa.
- •• 0:16 - Topless in pool after being pushed in and her swimsuit top comes off.
- •• 0:20 - In bra and panties, then topless on plane doing a strip tease.

Jaclyn Palmer. . . . . Suzie
- ••• 0:06 - Topless and buns changing clothes and getting into spa with her two girlfriends. (She's the dark haired one.)
- ••• 0:11 - Topless again, getting out of spa.
- ••• 0:23 - In bra, then topless doing strip tease routine on plane.
- •• 0:35 - Topless doing another routine on the plane.

Renee Way. . . . . Andy
- ••• 0:01 - Topless taking off her blouse to fix the plane.
- ••• 0:06 - Topless sitting on edge of spa.
- ••• 0:11 - Topless again, getting out of spa.
- • 0:12 - Brief topless dropping her towel while talking to Tim.

Pascali's Island (1988; British)

Ben Kingsley. . . . . Basil Pascali

Helen Mirren . . . . .Lydia Neuman
- • 1:00 - Left breast, lying in bed with Charles Dance. Long shot.

Pat Garrett and Billy the Kid (1973)

Rita Coolidge . . . . .Maria
- • 1:34 - Brief right breast getting undressed to get into bed with Kris Kristofferson.

Kris Kristofferson . . . . Billy the Kid
- • 0:37 - Buns, getting into bed with a girl after Harry Dean Stanton gets out. Long shot, hard to see.

Charlie Martin Smith . . . . Bowdre

The Patriot *(1986)*
Jeff Conaway . . . . Mitchell
Simone Griffeth . . . . Sean
  •• 0:46 - Brief topless lying in bed, making love with Ryder.

Patti Rocks *(1988)*
John Jenkins . . . . Eddie
  • 1:07 - Buns, making love with Patti in bed.
Karen Landry . . . . Patti
  0:48 - Buns, walking from bathroom to bedroom
  and shutting the door. Long shot.
  • 0:48 - Very brief right breast in shower with Billy.
  •• 1:04 - Topless in bed with Eddie while Billy is out in
  the living room.
Chris Mulkey . . . . Billy
  •• 0:24 - Nude in restroom with Eddie, undressing and
  putting on underwear.

Patty Hearst *(1989)*
Natasha Richardson . . . . .Patricia Hearst
  •• 0:13 - Topless, blindfolded in the bathtub while talking to a woman member of the S.L.A.

Pauline at the Beach *(1983; French)*
Simon De La Brosse . . . . Sylvain
Arielle Dombasle . . . . Marion
  • 0:24 - Brief topless lying in bed with a guy when her
  cousin looks in the window.
  •• 0:43 - Brief topless in house kissing Henri, while he
  takes her white dress off.
  •• 0:59 - Topless walking down the stairs in a white bikini bottom while putting a white blouse on.

Payback *(1988)*
Michele Burger . . . . Laura
  • 0:08 - Brief topless sitting up in bed just before getting shot, then brief topless twice, dead in bed.
Jean Carol . . . . Donna Nathan
  ••• 0:24 - Topless opening her pink robe for Jason while
  reclining on couch.

Payday *(1972)*
Ahna Capri . . . . Mayleen
  • 0:20 - Left breast in bed sleeping, then right breast
  with Rip Torn.
  ••• 0:21 - Topless sitting up in bed smoking a cigarette
  and talking to Torn. Long scene.
Rip Torn . . . . Maury Dann
  • 1:21 - Brief buns getting up out of bed.

Payoff *(1991; Made for Cable Movie)*
Keith Carradine . . . . .Peter "Mac" MacAlister
  • 0:01 - Sort of buns, in shower, seen from above,
  looking down.

Pennies from Heaven *(1981)*
Josh Cadman . . . .
Jessica Harper . . . . Joan
  • 0:43 - Brief topless opening her nightgown for Steve
  Martin.

Penthouse Love Stories *(1986)*
Colleen Applegate . . . . Service Station Woman
  ••• 0:10 - Nude, making love in a bedroom. Long scene.
Michelle Bauer . . . . Therapist's Patient
  ••• 0:45 - Nude, making love in Therapist's office with
  his assistant.
Larry Ferris . . . . Ecstacize Man
  •• 0:32 - Frontal nudity and buns with a woman in the
  shower.
Monique Gabrielle . . . . Monique and AC/DC Lover
  ••• 0:01 - Nude in bedroom entertaining herself. A must
  for Monique fans!
  ••• 0:18 - Nude making love with another woman.
Xaviera Hollander . . . . herself
Todd Keller . . . . .Service Station Man
  •• 0:11 - Brief frontal nudity in bedroom with a woman.
Julie Parton . . . . Loveboat Woman
  ••• 0:51 - In white bra and panties in bed. Nude masturbating while the other girls watch. Nice, long,
  sweaty scene.
Barbara Peckinpaugh . . . . .Therapist's Assistant
  ••• 0:45 - Nude, making love in Therapist's office, with
  the patient.
Shana Ross . . . . AC/DC Lover
  ••• 0:17 - Full frontal nudity in bedroom with Monique
  Gabrielle.
Vicki Vickers . . . . Snapshot and Loveboat Woman
  ••• 0:37 - Nude, taking pictures of herself.
  •• 0:51 - Topless on hammock watching Julie Parton.
  •• 0:55 - Left breast, twice while lying on hammock.

Perfect *(1985)*
Jamie Lee Curtis . . . . Jessie Wilson
  0:14 - No nudity, but doing aerobics in leotards.
  0:26 - More aerobics in leotards.
  0:40 - More aerobics, mentally making love with
  John Travolta while leading the class.
  1:19 - More aerobics when photographer is shooting
  pictures.
  1:32 - In red leotard after the article comes out in
  Rolling Stone.
Marilu Henner . . . . .Sally
  0:13 - Working out on exercise machine.
Charlene Jones . . . . Shotsy
  • 0:17 - Topless stripping on stage in a club. Buns in G-
  string.
Mathew Reed . . . . Roger
  • 1:01 - Buns, dancing in a jock strap at Chippendale's.

Perfect Strangers *(1984)*
Anne Carlisle . . . . .Sally
  • 0:34 - Left breast, while making love in bed with
  Johnny.
Ann Magnuson . . . . Maida

Perfect Timing *(1984)*
Jo Anne Bates . . . . .Karen
  ••• 0:21 - Nude, getting ready to get her picture taken.

Paul Boretski . . . . Joe
- •• 0:11 - Brief frontal nudity and buns, rolling over on the bed.
- • 0:29 - Frontal nudity on the roof in the snow with Bonnie.
- • 0:35 - Buns, on bed getting slapped on the behind.
- • 0:50 - Buns, in bed with Judy.
- •• 1:03 - Brief frontal nudity on TV with Judy while he and Bonnie watch.

Nancy Cser . . . . Lacy
- 0:54 - In white lingerie, taking off clothes for Harry and posing.
- ••• 0:56 - Topless getting photographed by Harry.
- • 0:58 - Topless, making love with Harry.
- • 1:01 - Topless.

Alexandra Innes. . . . . Salina
- •• 1:06 - Right breast and buns, posing for Harry.

Stephen Markle. . . . . Harry
- • 0:58 - Buns, making love with Lacy.

Mary Beth Rubens . . . . Judy
- • 0:04 - In a bra, then topless in bedroom with Joe.
- •• 0:05 - Nude, walking to kitchen, then talking with Harry.
- • 0:08 - Left breast seen through the camera's view finder.
- • 0:10 - Nude, getting dressed in bedroom.
- 0:49 - In red bra and panties.
- •• 0:50 - Nude, in bed with Joe.
- ••• 1:00 - Nude, discovering Joe's hidden video camera, then going downstairs.

Michele Scarabelli . . . . Charlotte
- •• 1:11 - Brief buns, then topless in bed with Harry.
- • 1:18 - Topless in bed with Harry during the music video.

Performance (1970)

James Fox . . . . Chas
- • 0:00 - Very brief frontal nudity and buns making love with a woman. Don't see his face.
- • 0:02 - Buns, getting up next to his girlfriend.
- • 0:24 - Brief buns, getting roughed up by bad guys.

Mick Jagger . . . . Turner
- 0:48 - Side view of buns, getting out of bathtub.

Anita Pallenberg . . . . Pherber
- • 0:44 - Side view of left breast, in bed with Mick Jagger.
- ••• 0:47 - Topless and buns, in bathtub with Lucy and Jagger.
- • 0:50 - Buns, injecting herself with drugs.
- •• 1:20 - Right breast, while lying on the floor. Then topless and buns, in bed with Chas.

The Perils of Gwendoline in the Land of the Yik Yak (1984; French)

Zabou . . . . Beth
- •• 0:36 - Topless in the rain in the forest, taking off her blouse.
- •• 0:57 - Topless in torture chamber getting rescued by Tawny Kitaen.

- •• 1:04 - Topless after Kitaen escapes.
- • 1:11 - Buns, in costume during fight.

Brent Huff . . . . Willard
- • 0:51 - Brief buns, in G-string while wearing costume.
- •• 0:52 - Buns, in G-string, walking around with Tawny Kitaen in costumes.
- •• 0:54 - More buns, after the women realize he's a man.
- ••• 0:56 - Buns, in jail while wearing only the G-string.

Tawny Kitaen . . . . Gwendoline
- ••• 0:36 - Topless in the rain in the forest, taking off her top. More topless with Willard.
- •• 0:52 - Buns, walking around with Willard in costumes.
- • 0:55 - Buns, falling into jail cell, then in jail cell in costume.
- • 0:57 - Buns, rescuing Beth in torture chamber.
- •• 1:01 - Topless in S&M costume in front of mirrors.
- • 1:04 - Brief topless escaping from chains.
- • 1:07 - Buns, in costume while riding chariot and next to wall.
- • 1:09 - Buns, standing up.
- •• 1:11 - Buns, in costume during fight. Wearing green ribbon.
- •• 1:18 - Topless making love with Willard.

Personal Best (1982)

Patrice Donnelly . . . . Tory Skinner
- •• 0:16 - Full frontal nudity after making love with Mariel Hemingway.
- •• 0:30 - Full frontal nudity in steam room.
- 1:06 - Topless in shower.

Scott Glenn . . . . Terry Tingloff

Mariel Hemingway . . . . Chris Cahill
- •• 0:16 - Brief lower frontal nudity getting examined by Patrice Donnelly, then topless after making love with her.
- •• 0:30 - Topless in the steam room talking with the other women.

Kenny Moore . . . . Denny Stiles
- •• 1:31 - Nude, getting out of bed and walking to the bathroom.

Personal Services (1987)

Julie Walters . . . . Cynthia Payne
- • 0:21 - Very brief side view of left breast, while reaching to turn off radio in the bathtub. Her face is covered with cream.

Pets (1974)

Joan Blackman . . . . Geraldine Mills
- • 0:46 - Brief side view of left breast, while getting out of bed after making love with Bonnie.

Candice Rialson . . . . Bonnie
- •• 0:26 - Topless dancing in field while Dan is watching her while he's tied up.
- ••• 0:33 - Topless making love on top of Dan while he's still tied up.
- 0:35 - Running through woods in braless orange top.
- •• 0:40 - Topless getting into bath at Geraldine's house.

- 0:45 - Topless posing for Geraldine.
  0:54 - In black and red lingerie outfit getting ready for bed.
- ••• 1:02 - Topless taking off lingerie in bed with Ron, then making love with him.
  1:34 - Almost topless, getting whipped by Vincent.

Phantom Empire (1987)
Michelle Bauer . . . . Cave Bunny
  0:32 - Running around in the cave a lot in two piece loincloth swimsuit.
- •• 1:13 - Finally topless after losing her top during a fight, stays topless until Andrew puts his jacket on her.
Sybil Danning . . . . .The Alien Queen
Dawn Wildsmith . . . . Eddy Colchilde

Phantom of the Mall: Eric's Revenge (1988)
Morgan Fairchild. . . . . .Karen Wilton
Kimber Sissons . . . . .Suzie
Kari Whitman . . . .,. . . . Melody Austin
- •• 0:25 - Topless in bed about five times with Peter. Don't see her face.

Picasso Trigger (1989)
Cynthia Brimhall. . . . . Edy
- •• 0:59 - Topless in weight room with a guy.
Hope Marie Carlton. . . . . Taryn
  0:17 - In white lingerie on boat with Dona Speir.
- ••• 0:56 - Topless and buns in spa with a guy.
Patty Duffek . . . . Patticakes
- •• 1:04 - Topless taking a Jacuzzi bath.
Liv Lindeland. . . . . Inga
Kym Malin . . . . Kym
- •• 1:04 - Topless taking a shower.
Dona L. Speir . . . . Donna
  0:17 - In white lingerie on boat with Hope Marie Car-lton.
- ••• 0:49 - Topless and buns standing, then making love in bed.
Roberta Vasquez . . . . Pantera

Pick-Up Summer (1979; Canadian)
Joy Boushel . . . . Sally
- ••• 0:56 - Topless playing pinball, then running around.
Carl Marotte . . . . Steve
- • 0:18 - Side view of buns, hanging a B.A. out passenger window at Rod.
Helene Udy . . . . Suzy
  0:34 - Very, very brief topless when the boys spray her and she jumps up.
Michael Zelnicker . . . . .Greg
- • 0:04 - Brief buns, hanging a B.A. out the back window of the van.

Pink Floyd The Wall (1982)
Jenny Wright. . . . . .American Groupie
- ••• 0:41 - Topless backstage in back of a truck doing a strip tease dance in front of some people.

A Place Called Today (1972)
Cheri Caffaro .Cindy Cartwright
- •• 0:14 - Full frontal nudity covered with oil or something writhing around on the bed.
- • 1:21 - Brief side view of right breast undressing in the bathroom.
- • 1:23 - Brief full frontal nudity getting kidnapped by two guys.
- •• 1:30 - Nude when they take off the blanket.
- • 1:35 - Brief topless just before getting killed.
Lana Wood. .Carolyn Scheider
- ••• 0:40 - Side view of left breast, then topless lying down talking to Ron.

Planet of the Apes (1968)
Jeff Burton . . . . .Dodge
- • 0:26 - Very brief buns taking off clothes to go skinny dipping. (Guy on the right.)
Robert Gunner. . . . . Landon
- • 0:26 - Very brief buns taking off clothes to go skinny dipping. (Guy on the left.)
Charlton Heston. . . . . George Taylor
- • 0:26 - Buns, seen through a waterfall and while walking on rocks. Long shots.
- • 1:04 - Buns standing in middle of the room when the apes tear his loin cloth off.

Play Misty for Me (1971)
Clint Eastwood. . . . . Dave Garland
Donna Mills. . . . . .Tobie
- • 1:10 - Brief side view of right breast hugging Clint Eastwood in a pond near a waterfall. Long shot, hard to see.
Jessica Walter . . . . Evelyn
- • 0:13 - Very brief right breast in bed with Clint Eastwood. Lit with blue light. Hard to see anything.

Playbirds (1978; British)
Pat Astley . . . . .Doreen Hamilton
- •• 0:00 - Topless posing for photo session.
Suzy Mandel . . . . Lena
- •• 0:12 - Nude stripping in Playbird office.

Playroom (1989)
Lisa Aliff . . . . .Jenny
- •• 0:23 - Topless making love on top of Christopher.
James Purcell . . . . .Paul
- •• 0:25 - Buns, making love with Jamie Rose on a chair.
Jamie Rose . . . . Marcy

Point Blank (1967)
Angie Dickinson. . . . . Chris
  0:46 - In white slip when John Vernon opens her dress.
- • 0:51 - Topless in background putting dress on. Kind of a long shot.

Police Academy II: Their First Assignment (1985)
Julie Brown. . . . . Chloe
Colleen Camp . . . . .Kirkland
Leslie Easterbrook. Callahan
Steve Guttenberg. . . . . .Carey Mahoney

Art Metrano . . . . Lt. Mauser
- 0:39 - Buns, in the locker room after the guys put epoxy resin in his shampoo.

Porky's (1981; Canadian)
Rod Ball. . . . . Steve
- 0:18 - Brief frontal nudity sitting on bench in the cabin.
- 0:21 - Very brief frontal nudity, following Meat out the front door of the cabin, then buns, in front of the house.

Kim Cattrall . . . . Honeywell
- 0:58 - Brief buns, then very brief lower frontal nudity after removing skirt to make love in the boy's locker room.

Susan Clark . . . . Cherry Forever
Scott Colomby . . . . Brian Schwartz
Tony Ganios . . . . .Meat
- • 0:21 - Brief buns, running out of the cabin during practical joke.

Kaki Hunter. . . . . Wendy
- 1:02 - Brief full frontal nudity, then brief topless in the shower scene.

Wyatt Knight. . . . . Tommy Turner
Pat Lee . . . . Stripper
- 0:33 - Brief topless dancing on stage at Porky's showing her breasts to Pee Wee.

Dan Monahan. . . . . Pee Wee
- 0:22 - Buns, running down the road at night. Long shot.

Jack Mulcahy. . . . . Frank Bell
- 0:21 - Very brief frontal nudity, getting up from bench. Then buns in front of the cabin.

Cyril O'Reilly . . . . .Tim
- 0:21 - Very, very brief frontal nudity, getting up from bench. Then buns, in front of the cabin.

Allene Simmons . . . . Jackie
- 1:02 - Topless in the shower scene.

Jill Whitlow . . . . .Mindy
Roger Wilson. . . . . Mickey

Porky's II: The Next Day (1983; Canadian)
Rod Ball. . . . . Steve
Scott Colomby . . . . .Brian
Cissie Colpitts-Cameron . Graveyard Gloria/Sandy Le Toi
0:26 - Buns in G-string at carnival.
- • 0:39 - Topless and buns in G-string, stripping for Pee Wee at cemetery.
- • 0:40 - More topless, pretending to die.
- • 0:42 - Topless, being carried by Meat.

Kaki Hunter. . . . . Wendy
Dan Monahan. . . . . Pee Wee
- 0:39 - Buns at cemetery with Graveyard Gloria, then upper half of lower frontal nudity holding her.
- 0:40 - Upper half of lower frontal nudity when he drops Gloria.
- 0:42 - Nude, trying to hide Steve.
- • • 0:44 - Nude when guys with shotguns shoot at him.

Jack Mulcahy. . . . . Frank Bell
Cyril O'Reilly . . . . .Tim

Porky's Revenge (1985; Canadian)
Kim Evenson . . . . .Inga
- • 0:02 - Right breast, while opening her graduation gown during Pee Wee's dream.
- • 1:27 - Topless showing Pee Wee that she doesn't have any clothes under her graduation gown.

Tony Ganios. . . . . Meat
- • 0:16 - Buns, getting out of swimming pool (the fifth guy getting out). More buns running around.

Mark Herrier. . . . . .Billy
- • 0:16 - Buns, getting out of swimming pool (the second guy getting out). More buns running around.

Kaki Hunter . . . . .Wendy
1:22 - In white bra and panties taking off her clothes to jump off a bridge.

Wyatt Knight . . . . Tommy Turner
- • 0:16 - Buns, getting out of swimming pool (the first guy getting out). More buns running around.
- 0:54 - Buns, getting his underwear pulled down while trying to escape from a motel room from Balbricker.

Rose McVeigh . . . . Miss Webster
- • • 0:39 - In black bra, panties, garter belt and stockings then topless in her apartment with Mr. Dobish while Pee Wee and his friends secretly watch.

Dan Monahan . . . . Pee Wee
- • 0:02 - Buns, when his graduation gown gets accidentally torn off during a dream.
- • 0:16 - Buns, getting out of swimming pool (the fourth guy getting out). More buns running around.
- • 1:27 - Buns, getting his graduation gown town off.

Nancy Valen. . . . . .Ginger

Portfolio (1983)
Carol Alt. . . . . herself
- 0:28 - Brief right breast, while adjusting black, see-through blouse.
0:31 - Brief side view of a little bit of right breast while changing clothes backstage at a fashion show.

Kelly Lynch. . . . . Elite Model
Shari Shattuck . . . . Elite Model

Posed for Murder (1988)
Charlotte J. Helmcamp. . . . . .Laura Shea
- 0:00 - Topless in photos during opening credits.
- • • 0:22 - Posing for photos in sheer green teddy, then topless in sailor's cap, then great topless shots wearing just a G-string.
0:31 - Very brief right breast in photo on desk.
0:44 - In black one piece swimsuit.
- • • 0:52 - Topless in bed making love with her boyfriend.

Possession (1981; French/German)
Isabelle Adjani . . . . Anna/Helen
- 0:04 - Topless in bed.
- 0:16 - Topless lying in bed when Sam Neill pulls the covers over her.
- • • 0:47 - Right breast, then topless lying in bed!.
- 1:08 - Right breast, while lying on the floor with Neill, then sitting up.

The Postman Always Rings Twice (1981)
Anjelica Huston . . . . Madge
- 1:30 - Brief side view left breast sitting in trailer with Jack Nicholson.

Jessica Lange. . . . . Cora Papadakis
  0:17 - Making love with Jack Nicholson on the kitchen table. No nudity, but still exciting.
  0:18 - Pubic hair peeking out of right side of her panties when Nicholson grabs her crotch.
- 1:03 - Very, very brief topless, then very, very brief right breast twice, when Nicholson rips her dress down to simulate a car accident.
  1:26 - Brief lower frontal nudity when Nicholson starts crawling up over her in bed.

Jack Nicholson . . . . Frank Chambers
- 1:25 - Buns, lying across the bed.

Powwow Highway (1988; U.S./British)
Gary Farmer . . . . Philbert Bono
- •• 1:00 - Buns, in bedroom getting out of bed to wake up Buddy.

Amanda Wyss . . . . Rabbit Layton

Predator 2 (1990)
Maria Conchita Alonso . . . . Leona
Elpidia Carrillo. . . . . .Anna
Nick Corri . . . . Detective
Bill Paxton. . . . . Jerry
Corey Rano . . . . Ramon Vega
- 0:23 - Buns, hanging upside down several times.
- 0:26 - Nude, hanging upside down, dead.

Teri Weigel . . . . Columbian Girl
- 0:22 - Brief topless making love on bed. More topless several times being held on the floor, brief full frontal nudity getting up when the Predator starts his attack.

Preppies (1984)
Nitchie Barrett. . . . . Roxanne
- 0:11 - Brief topless changing into waitress costumes with her two friends.

Cindy Manion. . . . . Jo
- 0:11 - Brief topless changing into waitress costumes with her two friends.
- 0:44 - Topless during party with the three preppie guys.

Katt Shea . . . . Margot
- ••• 0:20 - Topless teasing Richard through the glass door of her house.
  0:54 - In bra and panties with Trini, practicing sexual positions on the bed.
- 1:07 - Brief topless after taking off bra in bed.

Lynda Wiesmeier. . . . . Trini
  0:54 - In bra and panties, practicing sexual positions on beds with Margot.
- ••• 1:06 - Topless on bed with Mark.

Presumed Innocent (1990)
Bonnie Bedelia . . . . .Barbara Sabich
Raul Julia . . . . Sandy Stern
Greta Scacchi . . . . Carolyn Polhemus
- 0:46 - Left breast, while making love on desk with Harrison Ford.
- 0:53 - Buns, lying in bed on top of Ford.

Pretty Baby (1978)
Keith Carradine . . . . Bellocq
Susan Sarandon . . . . Hattie
  0:12 - Feeding a baby with her left breast, while sitting by the window in the kitchen.
- 0:24 - Brief side view, taking a bath.
- ••• 0:39 - Topless on the couch when Keith Carradine photographs her.

Brooke Shields . . . . .Violet
- 0:57 - Topless and buns taking a bath.
- 1:26 - Topless posing on couch for Keith Carradine.
- 1:28 - Buns, getting thrown out of the room, then trying to get back in.

Pretty Smart (1986)
Julie Kristen Smith . . . . Samantha Falconwright
- •• 0:26 - Topless in bed.
- 0:40 - Topless in bed.
- 0:52 - Topless sitting in lounge by the pool.

Kim Waltrip . . . . .Sara Gentry (the teacher)
- •• 0:53 - Topless sunbathing with her students.

Pretty Woman (1990)
Judy Baldwin . . . . .Susan
Lucinda Crosby . . . . Olsen Sister
Richard Gere . . . . .Edward Lewis
Shelley Michelle . . . . .body double for Julia Roberts
  0:04 - In black panties and bra, waking up and getting dressed.

Julia Roberts . . . . Vivian Ward
- 1:30 - Very, very brief tip of left breast, then right breast, then left breast seen through head board, in bed with Gere. It's her—look especially at the vertical vein that pops out in the middle of her forehead whenever her blood pressure goes up.

The Prey (1980)
Steve Bond. . . . . Joel
Gayle Gannes. . . . . Gail
- 0:36 - Brief topless putting T-shirt on before the creature attacks her.

Priceless Beauty (1989; Italian)
Christopher Lambert . . . . Monroe
Diane Lane. . . . . .China/Anna
- •• 0:34 - Topless in bed with Christopher Lambert.
- 0:35 - Brief left breast, then side of right breast on top of Lambert.

Claudia Ohana. . . . . Lisa

Prime Cut (1972)
Janit Baldwin . . . . Violet
  • 0:25 - Very brief nude, being swung around when Gene Hackman lifts her up to show to Lee Marvin.
  • 0:41 - Brief topless putting on a red dress.
Sissy Spacek . . . . Poppy
  • 0:25 - Brief side view of left breast lying in hay, then buns when Gene Hackman lifts her up to show to Lee Marvin.
  ••• 0:30 - Topless sitting in bed, then getting up to try on a dress while Marvin watches.
   0:32 - Close up of breasts though sheer black dress in a restaurant.
Angel Tompkins . . . . Clarabelle
  • 1:03 - Very brief left breast sitting up in bed to talk to Lee Marvin.
   1:04 - Very brief back side view of left breast jumping out of bed.

The Prime of Miss Jean Brodie (1969)
Pamela Franklin . . . . Sandy
  •• 1:21 - Topless posing as a model for Teddy's painting. Brief right breast, kissing him. Long shot of buns, while getting dressed.
Maggie Smith . . . . Jean Brodie

The Prince of Pennsylvania (1988)
Bonnie Bedelia . . . . Pam Marshetta
   0:12 - In black bra in open blouse in kitchen. Long scene.
Amy Madigan . . . . Carla Headlee
  • 0:37 - Left breast and buns getting out of bed with Keanu Reeves and putting on a robe.
Dan Monahan . . . . Tommy Rutherford
Fred Ward . . . . Gary

Prison Stories, Women on the Inside
(1990; Made for Cable Movie)
Rae Dawn Chong . . . . Rhonda
  • 0:26 - Very brief right breast several times in prison shower with Annabella Sciorra.
Lolita Davidovich . . . . Lorretta
Silvana Gallardo . . . . Mercedes
Rachel Ticotin . . . . Iris
   0:07 - Brief buns, squatting while getting strip searched in jail. Don't see her face.

Private Lessons (1981)
Ed Begley, Jr. . . . . Jack Travis
Pamela Jean Bryant . . . . Joyce
  • 0:03 - Very brief right breast, changing in the house while Billy and his friend peep from outside.
Sylvia Kristel . . . . Mallow
  • 0:20 - Very brief topless sitting up next to the pool when the sprinklers go on.
  •• 0:24 - Topless and buns, stripping for Billy. Some shots might be a body double.
  •• 0:51 - Topless in bed when she "dies" with Howard Hessman.
  • 1:28 - Topless making love with Billy. Some shots might be a body double.

Private Passions (1983)
Gavin Brannan . . . . Mark
  • 1:19 - Buns, lying in bed on top of Sybil Danning.
Sybil Danning . . . . Katherine
David Siegel . . . . Toni
  • 0:29 - Buns, with Laura. Don't see his face.

Private Resort (1985)
Vickie Benson . . . . Bikini Girl
  • 0:28 - In blue two piece swimsuit, showing her buns, then brief topless with Reeves.
   1:11 - Buns, in locker room, trying to slap Reeves.
Johnny Depp . . . . Jack
  •• 0:12 - Buns, in hotel room with Leslie Easterbrook.
Leslie Easterbrook . . . . Bobbie Sue
  •• 0:14 - Very brief buns taking off swimsuit, then topless under sheer white nightgown.
Lisa London . . . . Alice
   0:51 - In beige bra and panties several times with Ben and Jack while she's drunk.
Rob Morrow . . . . Ben
  • 0:36 - Brief buns standing with Hillary Shapiro worshiping Baba Rama.
  •• 0:39 - Buns getting caught naked by Mrs. Rawlins, then more buns, running through the halls.
Hilary Shepard . . . . Shirley
  ••• 0:36 - Topless, then buns, taking off her dress in front of Ben.

Private Road (1987)
Mitzi Kapture . . . . Helen Milshaw
   0:50 - Wearing a white bra during a strip-spin-the-bottle game.
  •• 1:29 - Topless, making love in bed with Greg Evigan.

Private School (1983)
Phoebe Cates . . . . Christine
   1:21 - Brief buns lying in sand with Mathew Modine.
   1:24 - Upper half of buns flashing with the rest of the girls during graduation ceremony.
Sylvia Kristel . . . . Ms. Copuletta
   0:57 - In wet white dress after falling in the pool.
Kari Lizer . . . . Rita
  • 0:30 - Very brief left breast popping out of cheerleader's outfit along with the Coach.
Matthew Modine . . . . Jim
Julie Payne . . . . Coach Whelan
  • 0:30 - Very brief left breast popping out of cheerleader's outfit along with Rita.
Betsy Russell . . . . Jordan Leigh-Jensen
   0:02 - Taking a shower behind a frosted door.
  • 0:04 - Very, very brief right breast and buns when Bubba takes her towel off through window.
  ••• 0:19 - Topless riding a horse after Kathleen Wilhoite steals her blouse.
   0:35 - In jogging outfit stripping down to black bra and panties, brief upper half of buns.
   1:15 - In white bra and panties, in room with Bubba.
   1:24 - Upper half of buns flashing with the rest of the girls during graduation ceremony.

Brinke Stevens. . . . . Uncredited School Girl
•• 0:42 - Brief topless and buns in shower room scene.
She's the brunette wearing a pony tail who passes in
front of the chalkboard.
Lynda Wiesmeier. . . . . School Girl
••• 0:42 - Nude in shower room scene. First blonde in
shower on the left.

Prizzi's Honor (1985)
Anjelica Huston. . . . . .Maerose Prizzi
Debra Kelly . . . . .Bride at Mexican Chapel
Jack Nicholson . . . . Charley Partanna
2:05 - Buns, sort of. Viewed from above while he
takes a shower. Hard to see anything.
Kathleen Turner . . . . Irene Walker
• 0:30 - Very brief left breast making love with Jack
Nicholson on bed.

Problem Child (1990)
Jack Warden . . . . .Big Ben
• 1:07 - Buns, on TV in bar, mooning into the camera
when he doesn't know it is on. (Yes, it is him.)

Programmed to Kill (1987)
a.k.a. The Retaliator
Sandahl Bergman . . . . Samira
• 0:11 - Brief side view of right breast taking off T-shirt
and leaning over to kiss a guy. Don't see her face.

Project: Alien (1990)
Darlanne Fluegel. . . . ."Bird" McNamara
• 0:18 - Buns, getting out of bed and putting on a ki-
mono.
Michael Nouri. . . . . Jeff Milker

Prom Night (1980)
Jamie Lee Curtis . . . . Kim
Pita Oliver . . . . Vicki
•• 0:35 - Brief buns, mooning Mr. Sykes outside of ten-
nis court.
Mary Beth Rubens. . . . . Kelly
• 0:59 - Very brief right breast making out with Drew
in the locker room.
• 1:02 - Brief upper half of breasts, standing up to put
dress on. Dark.

Prom Night III (1989)
Tim Conlon. . . . . Alex
• 0:15 - Brief buns and very brief balls when the flag
he's wearing falls off.

Promised Land (1988)
Debi Richter . . . . Pammie
Meg Ryan . . . . Beverly
• 0:22 - Very brief side view of left breast in bed with
Kiefer Sutherland.

Promises, Promises (1963; B&W)
Jayne Mansfield. . . . . Sandy Brooks
0:02 - Bubble bath scene.
••• 0:04 - Topless drying herself off with a towel. Same
shot also at 0:48.

••• 0:06 - Topless in bed. Same shot also at 0:08, 0:39
and 0:40.
••• 0:59 - Buns, kneeling next to bathtub, right breast in
bathtub, then topless drying herself off.

Psycho III (1986)
Juliette Cummins . . . . Red
••• 0:39 - Topless making love with Duke in his motel
room, then getting thrown out.
Jeff Fahey . . . . Duane
Katt Shea . . . . Patsy
Brinke Stevens . . . . body double for Diana Scarwid
•• 0:30 - Brief topless and buns getting ready to take a
shower, body doubling for Diana Scarwid.

Psycho IV: The Beginning
(1990; Made for Cable Movie)
Olivia Hussey . . . . Norma Bates
•• 0:49 - Topless in motel room mirror while young
Norman, watches through peephole.

Pucker Up and Bark Like a Dog (1989)
Iris Condon . . . . Stretch Woman
Robert Culp . . . . .Gregor
Wendy O. Williams. .Butch
Lisa Zane . . . . Taylor Phillips
•• 0:52 - Topless in shower with Max. Left breast, while
in bed.

Pump Up the Volume (1990)
Samantha Mathis . . . . Nora Diniro
•• 1:13 - Topless taking off sweater on patio with Christian Slater.
Christian Slater. Mark Hunter

The Punisher (1989)
Dolph Lundgren. . . . . .Frank Castle
• 0:06 - Upper half of buns, kneeling in his underground hideout. Don't see his face.
• 1:23 - Same shot at 00:06 used again.

Puppet Master (1989)
Barbara Crampton . . . . Woman at Carnival
Irene Miracle . . . . Dana Hadley
Kathryn O'Reilly . . . . Carissa Stamford
• 0:41 - Left breast in bathtub, covered with bubbles.
• 0:43 - Brief left breast getting out of tub. Nipple covered with bubbles.
0:50 - Riding on Frank in bed. Don't see anything,
but still exciting. Very brief buns under sheer nightgown when she gets off Frank.
1:11 - Right breast under sheer black nightgown,
dead sitting at the table. Blood on her face.

Puppet Master II (1990)
Collin Bernsen . . . . Michael
•• 1:10 - Buns, while putting out fire on the bed.
Charlie Spradling . . . . .Wanda
•• 1:04 - Topless getting out of bed and adjusting her
panties.

Purgatory (1988)
Adrienne Pearce . . . . Janine
- •• 0:51 - Brief topless in shower scene with Kirsten.

Tanya Roberts . . . . Carly Arnold
- • 0:29 - Nude, getting into the shower.
- • 0:42 - Very brief topless in bed with the Warden.
  0:43 - In white lingerie in whorehouse.
- •• 0:57 - Left breast, then brief topless in bed talking to Tommy.

Purple Hearts (1984)
Annie McEnroe . . . . .Hallaway
- •• 1:23 - Brief topless coming out of the bathroom surprising Ken Wahl and Cheryl Ladd.

Cyril O'Reilly . . . . Zuma

Purple Rain (1984)
Apollonia. . . . . Apollonia
- •• 0:20 - Brief topless taking off jacket before jumping into lake.
  0:41 - In lingerie making love with Prince.
  1:06 - In black lingerie and stockings singing on stage.

Q (1982)
Bobbi Burns . . . . .Sunbather
- •• 0:06 - Topless taking off swimsuit top and rubbing lotion on herself.

David Carradine . . . . Detective Shepard
Candy Clark . . . . Joan
Mary Louise Weller . . . . .Mrs. Pauley

Q & A (1990)
Paul Calderon . . . . Roger Montalvo
- • 1:50 - Brief buns, on floor of boat, getting strangled by Nick Nolte.

Timothy Hutton . . . . .Al Rielly
Nick Nolte. . . . . Mike Brennan
Javier Rios . . . . Boat Lover
- • 1:44 - Brief buns, on boat, getting pulled out of bed by Nick Nolte.

Quackser Fortune has a Cousin in the Bronx (1970; Irish)
Margot Kidder. . . . . Zazel
- •• 1:03 - Topless undressing on a chair, then brief right, then breasts when Gene Wilder kisses her.
- • 1:05 - Side view of left breast, then buns, getting out of bed.

Gene Wilder . . . . Quackser Fortune

Quartet (1981; British/French)
Isabelle Adjani. . . . . Marya Zelli
- •• 1:06 - Topless in bed with Alan Bates.

Alan Bates. . . . . .H.J. Heidler
Pierre Clementi . . . . .Theo
Jeffrey Kime. . . . . James
- •• 0:49 - Nude, posing with two women for the pornographer.

Maggie Smith. . . . . .Lois

Quest For Fire (1981)
Joy Boushel . . . . Tribe Member
Rae Dawn Chong. . . . . .Ika
- 0:37 - Topless and buns, running away from the bad tribe.
  0:40 - Topless and buns, following the three guys.
  0:41 - Brief topless behind rocks.
- • 0:43 - Brief side view of left breast, healing Noah's wound.
- • 0:50 - Right breast, while sleeping by the fire.
  0:53 - Long shot, side view of left breast after making love.
- • 0:54 - Topless shouting to the three guys.
- • 1:07 - Topless standing with her tribe.
- • 1:10 - Topless and buns, walking through camp at night.
- • 1:18 - Topless in a field.
- • 1:20 - Left breast, turning over to demonstrate the missionary position. Long shot.
- • 1:25 - Buns and brief left breast running out of bear cave.

The Quiet Earth (1985; New Zealand)
Bruno Lawrence .Zac Hobson
- •• 0:02 - Brief frontal nudity lying on the bed.
- •• 0:04 - Brief nude getting back into bed.
- • 0:33 - Very brief frontal nudity jumping out of the ocean. Blurry, hard to see anything.
- •• 1:01 - Frontal nudity during flashback lying in bed.

Alison Routledge . . . . .Joanne
  0:49 - Brief buns, after making breakfast for Zac.
- •• 1:24 - Topless in guard tower making love with Api.

R.P.M. (1970)
Ann-Margret . . . . Rhoda
- •• 0:07 - Brief left breast and buns getting out of bed talking with Anthony Quinn.
  0:30 - In fishnet top.

Teda Bracci . . . .

R.S.V.P. (1984)
Jane Hamilton . . . . .Mrs. Ellen Edwards
Tamara Landry. . . . . Vicky
- •• 0:43 - Topless sitting in van taking top off.
- •• 0:48 - Topless making love in the van with two guys.

Suzanne Remey Lawrence . . . . Stripper
- •• 0:56 - Topless dancing in a radio station in front of a D.J.

Laurie Senit . . . . Sherry Worth
- •• 1:00 - Topless in the shower with Harry Reems.
- •• 1:06 - Topless again.

Katt Shea . . . . Rhonda Rivers
- • 0:31 - Side view of left breast, making love in bed with Jonathan.

Allene Simmons . . . . Patty De Fois Gras
- •• 0:13 - Topless taking off red top behind the bar with the bartender.
- •• 0:38 - Topless in bed with Mr. Edwards, then buns running to hide in the closet.

•• 0:41 - Frontal nudity in room with Mr. Anderson.
••• 0:51 - Topless talking to Toby in the hallway trying to
    get help for the Governor.
Lynda Wiesmeier. . . . . .Jennifer Edwards
    •• 0:11 - Topless diving into the pool while Toby fanta-
      sizes about her being nude.
    • 0:19 - Topless in kitchen when Toby fantasizes about
      her again.
    ••• 1:21 - Nude getting out of the pool and kissing Toby,
      when she really is nude.

Rabid (1977)
Marilyn Chambers. . . . . Rose
    •• 0:14 - Topless in bed.
    •• 1:04 - Topless in closet selecting clothes.
    •• 1:16 - Topless in white panties getting out of bed.

The Rachel Papers (1989)
Dexter Fletcher . . . . .Charles Highway
    • 0:58 - Very brief buns, jumping into bed with Ione
      Skye.
Ione Skye . . . . Rachel
    •• 0:58 - Topless getting undressed and into bed with
      Charles. Long shot, then topless in bed.
    ••• 1:03 - Brief topless in three scenes. From above in
      bathtub, in bed and in bathtub again.
    •• 1:04 - Left breast, making love sitting up with
      Charles.
    • 1:06 - Brief topless sitting up in bathtub.
    • 1:08 - Brief topless long shot getting dressed in
      Charles' room.
    • 1:28 - Brief topless kissing Charles in bed during his
      flashback.
James Spader . . . . De Forest

Racing with the Moon (1984)
Nicholas Cage. . . . . Nicky
Barbara Howard . . . . Gatsby Girl
Carol Kane . . . . Annie
Michael Madsen . . . . Frank
Elizabeth McGovern . . . . Caddie Winger
    • 0:45 - Upper half of breast in pond with Sean Penn.
Sean Penn. . . . . Henry "Hopper" Nash

Ragtime (1981)
Jeff Daniels . . . . .O'Donnell
Michael Jeter. . . . .
Elizabeth McGovern . . . . Evelyn Nesbit
    ••• 0:52 - Topless in living room sitting on couch and ar-
      guing with a lawyer. Very long scene.
Mary Steenburgen . . . . .Mother
Dorsey Wright. . . . .

The Rain Killer (1990)
Woody Brown. . . . . Jordan Rosewall
    ••• 0:39 - Buns, getting into bed, kneeling next to bed,
      then getting into bed with Satin. Long scene.
Maria Ford . . . . .Satin
    •• 0:29 - Nude, dancing on stage in club. Backlit too
      much.

••• 0:37 - Topless in bedroom with Jordan, taking off her
    clothes, getting tied to bed. Long scene.
• 0:41 - Topless lying on her back on bed, dead.
• 0:48 - Same scene from 0:41 when Rosewall looks at
  B&W police photo.
Ray Sharkey . . . . .Vince Capra

Rain Man (1988)
Tom Cruise . . . . .Charlie Babbitt
Valeria Golino. . . . . .Suzanna
    • 0:35 - Very brief left breast four times and very, very
      brief right breast once with open blouse fighting
      with Tom Cruise after getting out of the bathtub.
Dustin Hoffman . . . . .Raymond Babbitt
Gigi Vorgan . . . . .Voice-Over Actress

The Rainbow (1989)
Sammi Davis . . . . Winifred Inger
    ••• 0:21 - Topless and buns with Amanda Donohoe un-
      dressing, running outside in the rain, jumping into
      the water, then talking by the fireplace.
    •• 0:30 - Topless and buns posing for a painter.
    • 1:33 - Brief right breast and buns getting out of bed.
    ••• 1:44 - Nude running outside with Donohoe.
Amanda Donohoe . . . . Winifred Inger
    ••• 0:21 - Nude with Sammi Davis undressing, running
      outside in the rain, jumping into the water, then
      talking by the fireplace.
    ••• 0:43 - Full frontal nudity taking off nightgown and
      getting into bed with Davis, then right breast.
    ••• 1:44 - Nude running outside with Davis.
Glenda Jackson. . . . . .Anna Brangwen
Paul McGann . . . . Anton Skrebensky
    •• 1:30 - Buns, opening a bottle of wine in room with
      Sammi Davis.
    • 1:44 - Very brief frontal nudity and buns running up
      a hill with Amanda Donohoe.

Rainbow Drive (1990; Made for Cable Movie)
Kathryn Harrold . . . . Christine
David Neidorf . . . . Bernie Maxwell
    • 1:16 - Buns, in shower room when Peter Weller is in-
      terrogating him.
Chelchie Ross. . . . . Tom Cutter
Peter Weller . . . . Mike Gallagher

Raw Force (1981)
Camille Keaton. .Girl in Toilet
    •• 0:28 - Topless in bathroom with a guy.
    •• 0:29 - Topless in bathroom again with the guy.
    • 0:31 - Topless in bathroom again when he rips her
      pants off.
Jillian Kesner. .Cookie Winchell
Jewel Shepard . . . . Drunk Sexpot
    • 0:31 - Topless in black swimsuit, when a guy adjusts
      her straps and it falls open.

The Razor's Edge (1984)
Stephen Davies . . . . Malcolm
Catherine Hicks . . . . Isabel
- • 0:43 - Brief upper half of left breast, in bed after seeing a cockroach.
Theresa Russell . . . . Sophie

Re-Animator (1985)
(Unrated version.)
Barbara Crampton . . . . .Megan Halsey
- •• 0:10 - Brief buns putting panties on, then topless, putting bra on after making love with Dan.
- •• 1:09 - Full frontal nudity, lying unconscious on table getting strapped down.
- • 1:10 - Topless getting her breasts fondled by a headless body.
- • 1:19 - Topless on the table.

Rebel (1985; Australian)
Bryan Brown . . . . Tiger Kelly
Rainee Skinner . . . . Prostitute in bed
- • 0:37 - Brief topless sitting up in bed.

Reckless (1984)
Daryl Hannah . . . . Tracey Prescott
    0:48 - In a white bra fighting in gymnasium with Johnny then in pool area in bra and panties.
- ••• 0:52 - Topless in furnace room of school making love with Johnny. Lit with red light.
Aidan Quinn . . . . Johnny Rourke
- • 1:03 - Very brief frontal nudity and buns running into Daryl Hannah's brother's room.
- • 1:12 - Side view nude, taking a shower.

Red Blooded American Girl (1988)
Kim Coates . . . . Dennis
- • 0:01 - Buns, giving Rebecca a glass in bed.
- • 0:30 - Very brief buns, getting into bathtub.
Lydie Denier . . . . Rebecca Murrin
- ••• 0:00 - Topless in bed wearing panties, garter belt and stockings. Buns, rolling over. Long scene.
Andrew Stevens . . . . Owen Augustus Urban III
Heather Thomas . . . . Paula Bukowsky
    1:19 - Lower half of right breast when Andrew Stevens is on top of her. Very, very brief silhouette of right breast. Probably a body double.

Red Heat (1987; U.S./German)
Linda Blair . . . . Chris Carlson
    0:09 - In blue nightgown in the bedroom with her boyfriend, almost topless.
- ••• 0:56 - Topless in shower room scene.
- ••• 1:01 - Brief topless getting raped by Sylvia Kristel while the male guard watches.
Sue Kiel . . . . Hedda
- • 0:56 - Brief topless in shower room scene (third girl behind Linda Blair). Long shot, hard to see.
Sylvia Kristel . . . . Sofia
    0:23 - In red lingerie.
- •• 0:56 - Topless in shower room scene.
- • 1:01 - Brief topless raping Linda Blair.

Red Heat (1988)
Gina Gershon . . . . Cat Manzetti
Gretchen Palmer . . . . Hooker
- • 1:20 - Topless and buns in hotel during shoot out.
Arnold Schwarzenegger . . . . Ivan Danko
- •• 0:02 - Buns in the sauna and outside fighting.
Gigi Vorgan . . . . .Audrey

Red Sonja (1985)
Sandahl Bergman . . . . .Queen Gedren
Brigitte Nielsen . . . . Red Sonja
- • 0:01 - Half of right nipple through torn outfit, while sitting up.
Arnold Schwarzenegger . . . . .Kalidor

Reform School Girls (1986)
Michelle Bauer . . . . uncredited Shower Girl
- •• 0:25 - Topless, then nude in the shower.
Leslee Bremmer . . . . uncredited Shower Girl
- •• 0:25 - Brief topless in the shower three times. Walking from left to right in the background, full frontal nudity by herself with wet hair, topless walking from left to right.
Linda Carol . . . . Jennifer Williams
- •• 0:05 - Nude in the shower.
- • 0:56 - Topless in the back of a truck with Norton.
- •• 1:13 - Topless getting hosed down by Edna.
Sybil Danning . . . . Warden Sutter
Darcy De Moss . . . . Knox
Sherri Stoner . . . . Lisa
- • 1:03 - Very brief topless and buns, lying on stomach in the restroom, getting branded by bad girls.
Wendy O. Williams .Charlie
- •• 0:26 - Topless talking to two girls in the shower.

The Reincarnation of Peter Proud (1975)
Margot Kidder . . . . .Marcia Curtis
- • 1:29 - Brief topless sitting in bathtub masturbating while remembering getting raped by husband.
Cornelia Sharpe . . . . Nora Hayes
- •• 0:03 - Topless in bed with Michael Sarrazin, then buns when getting out of bed.

Remember My Name (1978)
Geraldine Chaplin . . . . Emily
- • 1:23 - Very brief left breast, lying in bed, then right breast, with Anthony Perkins.
Jeff Goldblum . . . . Mr. Nadd

Rendez-Vous (1986; French)
Juliette Binoche . . . . Anne "Nina" Larrieu
- • 0:07 - Brief topless in dressing room when Paulot surprises her and Fred.
- ••• 0:25 - Side of left breast, then topless and buns in empty apartment with Paulot.
- •• 0:32 - Full frontal nudity in bed with Quentin.
- •• 0:35 - Buns, then brief topless in bed with Paulot and Quentin. Full frontal nudity getting out.
- •• 1:08 - Topless taking off her top in front of Paulot in the dark, then topless lying on the floor.
- • 1:11 - Right breast, making love on the stairs. Dark.

Olimpia Carlisi. . . . .
Caroline Faro. . . . . Juliette
  • 0:22 - Buns, walking up stairs, then full frontal nudity
    on second floor during play. Buns, hugging Romeo
    and falling back into a net.
Lambert Wilson. . . . . Quentin
  • 0:22 - Very brief buns, falling with Juliet onto net dur-
    ing play.

Rented Lips (1988)
Robert Downey, Jr. . . . . Wolf Dangler
  • 0:01 - Buns, wearing fishnet shorts in S&M outfit
    during porno movie shoot.
  • 0:22 - Buns, through shorts again during playback of
    the film.
Edy Williams . . . . Heather Darling
  • 0:22 - Topless in bed, getting fondled by Robert
    Downey, Jr. during porno movie shoot.

Repossessed (1990)
Linda Blair. . . . . Nancy Aglet
Charlotte J. Helmcamp . . . . .Incredible Girl
Melissa Moore. Bimbo Student
  •• 0:05 - Topless pulling her top down in classroom in
    front of Leslie Nielsen.

The Return of the Living Dead (1985)
Linnea Quigley . . . . Trash
  ••• 0:05 - Topless and buns, strip tease and dancing in
    cemetery. (Lower frontal nudity is covered with
    some kind of make-up appliance).
  • 1:08 - Topless, walking out of the cemetery to eat
    someone.
Jewel Shepard . . . . Casey

Return to Horror High (1987)
Darcy De Moss . . . . Sheri Haines
  • 0:21 - Very brief left breast when her sweater gets lift-
    ed up while she's on some guy's back.
Brendan Hughes . . . . Steven Blake
Maureen McCormick . . . . Officer Tyler
Remy O'Neill. . . . . Esther Molvania
Kristi Somers. . . . . Ginny McCall

A Return to Salem's Lot (1988)
Katja Crosby . . . . Cathy
  •• 0:36 - Topless making love in bed with Joey.
  • 0:48 - Side view of right breast kissing Joey outside
    next to a stream.

Reuben, Reuben (1983)
E. Katherine Kerr . . . . Lucille Haxby
  • 0:51 - Brief left breast in bedroom, undressing in
    front of Tom Conti.
Kelly McGillis. . . . . .Geneva Spofford

Revenge (1990)
Kevin Costner . . . . Cochran
  •• 1:14 - Brief buns getting out of bed and wrapping a
    sheet around himself.
Sally Kirkland. . . . . Rock Star
John Leguizamo . . . . Ignacio

Madeline Stowe . . . . .Miryea
  0:44 - Side view of buns when Kevin Costner pulls up
    her dress to make love with her.
  0:52 - In white slip talking to Costner in bedroom.
  • 1:00 - Buns, making love with Costner in jeep. Very
    brief topless coming out of the water.
  • 1:07 - Very brief topless when Costner is getting beat
    up.

Revenge of the Cheerleaders (1976)
David Hasselhoff . . . . Boner
  • 0:28 - Buns in shower room scene.
  ••• 0:30 - Frontal nudity in shower room scene while
    soaping Gail.
David Robinson . . . . Jordan
  • 0:13 - Buns when Tish plays with him while she's un-
    der the counter.
Patrice Rohmer. . . . . Sesame
  • 0:28 - Brief topless and buns in the boys shower
    room.
Cheryl Smith . . . . Heather
  • 0:00 - Brief topless changing tops in back of car.
    (Blonde on the far right.)
    0:28 - Buns, in shower room scene.
    0:36 - Full frontal nudity, but covered with bubbles.

Revenge of the Nerds (1984)
Bernie Casey . . . . U. N. Jefferson
Anthony Edwards. . . . . .Gilbert
Julie Montgomery . . . . Betty
  •• 0:49 - Frontal nudity getting ready for a shower.
  • 1:10 - Topless in the pie pan.
Lisa Welch . . . . Suzy

Revenge of the Ninja (1983)
Ashley Ferrare. . . . . Cathy
  0:33 - In white lingerie sitting on couch with Dave.
  • 0:48 - Brief topless getting attacked by the Sumo Ser-
    vant in the bedroom.
    1:13 - In wet white tank top talking on the phone.

Rich and Famous (1981)
Candice Bergen . . . . .Merry Noel Blake
Jacqueline Bisset. Liz Hamilton
Matt Lattanzi . . . . The Boy, Jim
  ••• 1:10 - Buns, making love with Jacqueline Bisset.
Meg Ryan .Debbie at 18 years
David Selby . . . . Doug Blake

Richard's Things (1980)
Amanda Redman . . . . .Josie
  •• 0:51 - Topless, lying in bed talking to Liv Ullman.

Rikky & Pete (1988; Australian)
Tetchie Agbayani . . . . Flossie
  • 0:58 - Brief upper half of left breast in bed with Pete
    when Rikky accidentally sees them in bed.
  ••• 1:30 - Topless in black panties dancing outside the
    jail while Pete watches from inside.
Bruno Lawrence. . . . . Sonny

Risky Business (1983)

Cynthia Baker . . . . Test Teacher
Tom Cruise . . . . Joel
Rebecca De Mornay . . . . Lana
- 0:28 - Brief nude standing by the window with Tom Cruise.

River's Edge (1987)

Danyi Deats . . . . Jamie
- 0:03 - Topless, dead lying next to river with her killer. (All the shots of her topless in this film aren't exciting unless you like looking at dead bodies).
- 0:15 - Close up topless, then full frontal nudity when Crispin Glover pokes her with a stick.
  0:16 - Full frontal nudity when the three boys leave.
  0:22 - Full frontal nudity when all the kids come to see her body. (She's starting to look very discolored).
  0:24 - Right breast when everybody leaves.
  0:30 - Right breast when they come to dump her body in the river.
Dennis Hopper . . . . Feck
Leo Rossi . . . . Jim
Ione Skye . . . . Clarissa

Roadhouse (1989)

Jasaé . . . . Strip Joint Girl
Laura Albert . . . . Strip Joint Girl
- •• 0:45 - Topless and buns dancing on stage, wearing a hat.
Cheryl Baker . . . . Well-Endowed Wife
Michele Burger . . . . Strip Joint Girl
Kymberly Herrin . . . . Party Girl
Susan Lentini . . . . Bandstand Babe
Kelly Lynch . . . . Doc
- •• 1:04 - Topless and buns getting out of bed with a sheet wrapped around her.
Kym Malin . . . . Party Girl
Heidi Paine . . . . Party Girl
Jaclyn Palmer . . . . Party Girl
Patrick Swayze . . . . Dalton
- ••• 0:30 - Brief buns getting out of bed while Kathleen Wilhoite watches.
Patricia Tallman . . . . Bandstand Babe
Christina Veronica . . . . Strip Joint Girl

Roadhouse 66 (1984)

Willem Dafoe . . . . Johnny Harte
- •• 1:02 - Buns, standing up while kissing Jesse.
Kaaren Lee . . . . Jesse Duran
- •• 1:00 - Topless, taking off her top to go skinny dipping with Willem Dafoe. Dark.
Judge Reinhold . . . . Beckman Hallsgood, Jr.
Kate Vernon . . . . Melissa Duran
- 1:03 - Brief topless in back of car with Judge Reinhold. Dark.

Robot Jox (1990)

Gary Graham . . . . Achilles
- 0:32 - Very brief buns, getting dressed in his room while talking to Athena.

Anne-Marie Johnson . . . . Athena
- •• 0:35 - Buns, walking to the showers after talking to Achilles and Tex.

Roller Blade (1986)

Michelle Bauer . . . . Bod Sister
- 0:11 - Topless, being held by Satacoy's Devils.
- ••• 0:13 - More topless and buns in G-string during fight. Long scene.
- 0:16 - Brief topless twice, getting saved by the Sisters.
- •• 0:33 - Topless during ceremony with the other two Bod Sisters. Buns also.
- ••• 0:35 - Full frontal nudity after dip in hot tub. (Second to leave the tub.)
- •• 0:40 - Nude, on skates with the other two Bod Sisters. (She's on the left.)
Barbara Peckinpaugh . . . . Bod Sister
- •• 0:33 - Topless during ceremony. Cut on her throat is unappealing.
- ••• 0:35 - Full frontal nudity after dip in hot tub with the other two Bod Sisters. (She's the first to leave.)
- •• 0:40 - Nude, on skates with the other two Bod Sisters. (She's in the middle.)
Suzanne Solari . . . . Sister Sharon Cross
  0:04 - Buns, in G-string, lying in bed.
- 1:21 - Brief upper half of right breast, taking off suit. Buns in G-string.

The Romantic Englishwoman (1975; British/French)

Helmut Berger . . . . Thomas
- 1:08 - Upper half of buns, sitting at edge of pool talking to Glenda Jackson.
Nathalie Delon . . . . Miranda
Glenda Jackson . . . . Elizabeth
- 0:30 - Brief full frontal nudity outside, taking robe off in front of Michael Caine.
- 0:31 - Buns, walking back into the house.
- 1:08 - Side view of right breast sitting at edge of poll talking to Thomas.
- 1:45 - Very, very brief topless in bed talking with Thomas.
Kate Nelligan . . . . Isabel

Romeo and Juliet (1968)

Olivia Hussey . . . . Juliet
- 1:37 - Very brief topless rolling over and getting out of bed with Romeo.
Leonard Whiting . . . . Romeo
- •• 1:34 - Buns, in bed with Juliet, then getting out to stretch. Long scene.

A Room with a View (1986; British)

Simon Callow . . . . The Reverend Mr. Beebe
- 1:04 - Frontal nudity taking off clothes and jumping into pond.
- ••• 1:05 - Nude running around with Freddy and George in the woods. Lots of frontal nudity.
Helena Bonham Carter . . . . Lucy Honeychurch
Daniel Day-Lewis . . . . Cecil Vyse

Rupert Graves . . . . Freddy Honeychurch
••• 1:05 - Nude running around with Mr. Beebe and
    George in the woods. Lots of frontal nudity.
Julian Sands. . . . . George Emerson
••• 1:05 - Nude running around with Freddy and Mr.
    Beebe in the woods. Lots of frontal nudity.
Maggie Smith . . . . Charlotte Bartlett

The Rosebud Beach Hotel (1985)
Julie Always . . . . Bellhop
•• 0:22 - Topless, in open blouse, undressing with two
    other bellhops. She's the blonde on the left.
•• 0:44 - Topless, playing spin the grenade, with two
    guys and the two other bellhops. She's on the left.
Colleen Camp. . . . . Tracy
    0:07 - In white lingerie in hotel room with Peter Sco-
    lari.
    0:28 - In black one piece swimsuit on lounge chair,
    then walking on the beach.
Cherie Currie. . . . . Cherie
    1:13 - Singing with her twin sister in braless pink T-
    shirt on the beach.
Fran Drescher . . . . Linda
Monique Gabrielle . . . . Lisa
•• 0:22 - Topless and buns undressing in hotel room
    with two other girls. She's on the right.
•• 0:44 - Topless taking off her red top in basement
    with two other girls and two guys.
• 0:56 - In black see-through nightie in hotel room
    with Peter Scolari.
Dirga McBroom . . . . Bellhop
• 0:49 - Buns, then topless, standing with the other
    bell hops, outfitted with military attire. (She's the
    one at the far end, furthest from the camera.)
Julie Parton . . . . Bellhop
•• 0:49 - Buns, then topless, standing in line. Second
    from the camera.

Rosemary's Baby (1968)
Mia Farrow . . . . Rosemary Woodhouse
• 0:10 - Brief left breast in room in new apartment on
    floor with John Cassavetes. Hard to see anything.
• 0:43 - Brief close up of her breasts while she's sitting
    on a boat during a nightmare.
•• 0:44 - Buns walking on boat, then breasts during im-
    pregnation scene with the devil.

Runaway (1984)
Kirstie Alley . . . . Jackie
    1:04 - Briefly in white bra getting scanned at the po-
    lice station for bugging devices.
Tom Selleck. . . . . Ramsay
Cec Verrell . . . . Hooker
•• 0:44 - Topless in hotel bathroom while Tom Selleck
    sneaks into her room.

Running Out of Luck (1986)
Rae Dawn Chong . . . . Slave Girl
•• 0:42 - Left breast, while hugging Mick Jagger, then
    again while lying in bed with him.

•• 1:12 - Left breast painting some kind of drug laced
    solution on herself.
•• 1:14 - Right breast, while in prison office offering her
    breast to the warden.
• 1:21 - Buns and left breast, in bed with Jagger during
    a flashback.
Dennis Hopper. . . . . Video Director
Mick Jagger . . . . Himself
• 0:42 - Brief buns in mirror in room with Rae Dawn
    Chong lying in bed. Another buns long shot in bed
    on top of Chong.

Running Scared (1986)
Darlanne Fluegel . . . . Anna Costanzo
Tracy Reed. . . . . Maryann
• 0:18 - Brief buns.
• 1:30 - Very brief topless in bed with Gregory Hines.
Jimmy Smits. . . . . Julio Gonzales

Rush Week (1989)
Laura Burkett . . . . Rebecca Winters
•• 0:43 - Topless in the shower, talking to Jonelle.
• 0:55 - Brief topless getting dressed after modeling
    session.
Kathleen Kinmont . . . . Julie Ann McGuffin
• 0:07 - Brief topless several times during modeling
    session. Buns in G-string getting dressed. Long shot.

Ruthless People (1986)
Jeannine Bisignano. . . . . Hooker in Car
    0:17 - Topless, hanging out of the car. Long, long
    shot, don't see anything.
• 0:40 - Topless in the same scene three times on TV
    while Danny De Vito watches.
• 0:49 - Left breast hanging out of the car when the
    Chief of Police watches on TV. Closest shot.
    1:15 - Same scene again in department store TV's.
    Long shot, hard to see.
Laura Cruikshank . . . .
Anita Morris. . . . . Carol
Judge Reinhold. Ken Kessler
Helen Slater . . . . Sandy Kessler

S.A.S. San Salvador (1982)
Sybil Danning . . . . Countess Alexandra
• 0:07 - Brief left breast, while lying on the couch and
    kissing Malko.

S.O.B. (1981)
Julie Andrews . . . . Sally Miles
•• 1:19 - Topless pulling the top off her red dress during
    the filming of a movie.
Rosanna Arquette. . . . . Babs
• 0:21 - Brief topless taking off white T-shirt on the
    deck of the house. Long shot, hard to see.
Marisa Berenson. . . . . Mavis
•• 1:20 - Topless in bed with Robert Vaughn.
Corbin Bernsen . . . .
Gisele Lindley. . . . .
James Purcell . . . .
Gay Rowan. . . . .

The Sailor Who Fell From Grace with the Sea (1976)

Kris Kristofferson . . . . Jim Cameron
Sarah Miles . . . . Anne Osborne
- • 0:18 - Topless sitting at the vanity getting dressed while her son watches through peephole.
- •• 0:23 - Topless, fantasizing about her husband.
- •• 0:42 - Nude, making love with Kris Kristofferson.
- • 1:15 - Brief right breast, in bed with Kristofferson.

Salome's Last Dance (1987)

Linzi Drew. . . . . 1st Slave
- •• 0:08 - Topless in black costume around a cage.
- •• 0:52 - Topless during dance number.

Dougie Howes . . . . Phoney Salome
- • 1:05 - Very brief frontal nudity at the end of a dance routine when you think he's a female Salome.

Glenda Jackson . . . . Herodias/Lady Alice
Tina Shaw . . . . 2nd Slave
- •• 0:08 - Topless in black costume around a cage.
- •• 0:52 - Topless during dance number.

Salvador (1986)

Elpidia Carrillo . . . . Maria
- • 0:21 - Very brief right breast, lying in a hammock with James Woods.

Cynthia Gibb . . . . Cathy Moore
James Woods . . . . Richard Boyle

Satan's Princess (1989)

Lydie Denier . . . . Nicole St. James
- • 0:27 - Full frontal nudity, getting out of pool.
- ••• 0:28 - Full frontal nudity, next to bed and in bed with Karen.
- ••• 0:45 - Topless and buns, making love in bed with Robert Forster.

Robert Forster . . . . Lou Cherney
Leslie Huntly . . . . Karen Rhodes
- ••• 0:27 - Topless sitting on bed and in bed with Nicole.

Marilyn Joi. . . . . Hooker
Caren Kaye . . . . Leah
Debra Lamb . . . . Fire Eater/Dancer
- •• 0:23 - Topless in G-string doing a fire dance in club.
- • 0:25 - Topless, doing more dancing. Long shot.

Saturday Night Fever (1977)

(R-rated version.)
Joseph Cali . . . . Joey
Paul Pepe . . . . Double J.
- • 0:22 - Buns, while making love in back seat of car with a girl.

Saturn 3 (1980)

Kirk Douglas . . . . Adam
- • 0:57 - Brief buns fighting with Harvey Keitel, more brief buns sitting down in bed with Farrah Fawcett.

Farrah Fawcett . . . . Alex
- •• 0:17 - Brief right breast taking off towel and running to Kirk Douglas after taking a shower.

Harvey Keitel. . . . . Benson

Savage Beach (1989)

Hope Marie Carlton . . . . Taryn
- 0:06 - Almost topless in spa with the three other women.
- • 0:32 - Topless changing clothes in airplane with Dona Speir.
- •• 0:48 - Nude, going for a swim on the beach with Speir.

Patty Duffek. . . . . Patticakes
- • 0:06 - Topless in spa with Lisa London, Dona Speir and Hope Marie Carlton.
- •• 0:50 - Topless changing clothes.

Lisa London . . . . Rocky
- • 0:06 - Topless in spa with Patty Duffek, Dona Speir and Hope Marie Carlton.
- •• 0:50 - Topless changing clothes.

Michael Shane . . . . Shane Abeline
- •• 0:08 - Buns, getting out of pool.

Dona L. Speir . . . . Dona
- 0:06 - Almost topless in spa with the three other women.
- • 0:32 - Topless changing clothes in airplane with Hope Marie Carlton.
- •• 0:48 - Nude, going for a swim on the beach with Carlton.

Maxine Wasa . . . . Sexy Beauty
- ••• 0:08 - Side view of left breast, in pool with Shane, then topless getting out of pool.
- ••• 0:10 - Topless while Shane talks on the phone.

Teri Weigel. . . . . Anjelica
- ••• 0:33 - Topless taking off black teddy and getting into bed to make love.
- •• 0:47 - Topless making love in the back seat of car.

Savage Streets (1985)

Linda Blair . . . . Brenda
- ••• 1:05 - Topless sitting in the bathtub thinking.

Debra Blee . . . . Rachel
- 0:20 - In a bra in the girls locker room.

Marcia Karr . . . . Stevie
Rebecca Perle. . . . . Cindy Clark
- 0:24 - In bra and panties, fighting with Brenda in the locker room.
- •• 0:53 - Brief topless in biology class getting her top torn off by Linda Blair.

Linnea Quigley. . . . . Heather
- • 0:28 - Topless getting raped by the jerks.

Suzanne Slater . . . . uncredited
- •• 0:09 - Topless being held by jerks when they yank her tube top down.

Kristi Somers . . . . Valerie
- 0:24 - In bra and panties in the locker room.

Scandal (1989)

(Unrated version.)
Britt Ekland . . . . Mariella Novotny
- •• 0:31 - Topless lying on table with John Hurt.
- • 0:51 - Right breast talking with Hurt and Christine.

Bridget Fonda . . . . Mandy Rice-Davis
- 0:20 - Brief topless dressed as an Indian dancing while Christine tries to upstage her.
  0:54 - In white lingerie, then lower frontal nudity in sheer nightgown in room with a guy.
  1:05 - Brief buns walking back into bedroom. Long shot.
John Hurt . . . . .Stephen Ward

Scarecrow (1973)
Eileen Brennan . . . . .Darlene
- 0:27 - Brief topless in bed when Gene Hackman takes off her bra and grabs her breasts.
Dorothy Tristan. . . . . Coley

Scarface (1983)
Angela Aames . . . . .Woman at the Babylon Club
Lana Clarkson . . . . .Woman at the Babylon Club
Mary Elizabeth Mastrantonio. . . . . Gina
- 2:36 - (0:39 into tape 2) Very, very brief left breast when she gets shot and her nightgown opens up when she gets hit.
Shelly Taylor Morgan . . . . .Woman at the Babylon Club
Michelle Pfeiffer . . . . Elvira
Pepe Serna . . . . Angel
Katt Shea . . . . .Woman at the Babylon Club

Scenes from the Class Struggle in Beverly Hills (1989)
Ed Begley, Jr.. . . . . .Peter
Robert Beltran. . . . . Juan
- 1:34 - Brief buns, when his shorts are pulled down by Frank.
Jacqueline Bisset . . . . .Clare
Ray Sharkey. . . . . Frank
- 1:10 - Brief buns sleeping in bed with Zandra.
Arnetia Walker. . . . . .To-Bel
- 0:37 - Topless making love with Frank on the sofa.
- •• 1:10 - Topless in bed waking up with Howard.
- ••• 1:23 - Topless making love on top of Ed Begley, Jr. on the floor.
Mary Woronov . . . . Lizabeth
- ••• 1:06 - In black lingerie, then topless in bedroom, then in bed with Juan.

Schizoid (1980)
Mariana Hill. . . . . Julie
  0:58 - Left breast, while making love in bed with Klaus Kinski. Dark, hard to see.
Christopher Lloyd . . . . Gilbert
Craig Wasson . . . . Doug
Donna Wilkes . . . . Allison Foles
  0:12 - Topless taking off her bra in bathroom while Klaus Kinski watches. Buns, getting into the shower. Out of focus shots.
- •• 0:13 - Side view topless getting into the shower.

School Spirit (1985)
Leslee Bremmer. . . . . .Sandy
Linda Carol . . . . Hogette
Roberta Collins . . . . Helen Grimshaw

Jackie Easton . . . . .Hogette
Julie Gray . . . . Kendall
Marlene Janssen . . . . .Sleeping Princess
- •• 0:42 - Topless and buns, sleeping when old guy goes invisible to peek at her.
Becky LeBeau. . . . . .Hogette
Tom Nolan. . . . . Billy Batson
- 0:17 - Buns in open hospital smock. More buns while running up stairs.
Pamela Ward . . . . Girl in Sorority Room
- ••• 0:15 - Buns, then topless while Billy is invisible. More topless with other women in shower room.

Scorchy (1971)
Connie Stevens . . . . Jackie Parker
- •• 0:23 - Open blouse, revealing left bra cup while talking on the telephone. Brief topless swimming in the water after taking off bathing suit top.
- •• 0:52 - Side view left breast, taking a shower.
- ••• 0:56 - Brief right breast making love in bed with Greg Evigan. Topless getting tied to the bed by the thieves. Kind of a long shot and a little dark and hard to see.
- 1:00 - Brief topless getting covered with a sheet by the good guy.

Scream Dream (1989)
Melissa Moore . . . . Jamie Summers
- ••• 0:39 - Topless in black panties in room with Derrick. Then straddling him.
- •• 0:58 - Topless in dressing room pulling her top down during transformation into monster.

Screen Test (1986)
Michelle Bauer . . . . .Dancer/Ninja Girl
- •• 0:04 - Topless dancing on stage.
- ••• 0:42 - Nude, with Monique Gabrielle, making love in a boy's dream.
Deborah Blaisdell . . . . Dancer
- •• 0:04 - Topless dancing on stage.
Monique Gabrielle . . . . Roxanne
- •• 0:06 - Topless taking off clothes in back room in front of a young boy.
- ••• 0:42 - Nude, with Michelle Bauer, seducing a boy in his day dream.
- •• 1:20 - Topless taking off her top for a guy.

Screwball Hotel (1988)
Corinne Alphen . . . . Cherry Amour
  0:46 - Buns, in black outfit on bed with Norman.
Gianna Amore . . . . Mary Beth
Lori Deann Pallett. . . . . Candy
- ••• 0:26 - Topless in the shower while Herbie is accidentally in there with her.

Screwballs (1983)
Kim Cayer . . . . .Brunette Cheerleader
Alan Daveau . . . . .Howie Bates
- 1:00 - Buns, after losing at strip bowling.
Raven De La Croix . . . . .Miss Anna Tomical
- ••• 1:08 - Topless during strip routine in nightclub.

Linda Shayne. . . . . Bootsie Goodhead
••• 0:43 - Right breast, while in back of van at drive-in theater, then topless.

Season of Fear *(1989)*
Clancy Brown . . . . Ward St. Clair
Clare Wren . . . . Sarah Drummond
    0:23 - Topless in bed with Mick. Long shot, hard to see.
    0:25 - Brief silhouette, behind shower door.
• 0:42 - Side view of left breast, on top of Mick. Very, very brief left breast, turning over when they hear a noise outside.

Second Time Lucky *(1986)*
Diane Franklin . . . . Eve
    0:07 - In white bra and panties in frat house bedroom taking her dress off because it's wet.
•• 0:13 - Topless a lot during first sequence in the Garden of Eden with Adam.
••• 0:28 - Brief full frontal nudity running to Adam after trying an apple.
• 0:41 - Left breast taking top of dress down.
••• 1:01 - Topless, opening her blouse in defiance, while standing in front of a firing squad.
Roger Wilson . . . . Adam Smith
•• 0:13 - Buns, in the Garden of Eden.
•• 0:30 - Buns, standing out in the rain.

Secret Admirer *(1985)*
C. Thomas Howell . . . . Michael Ryan
Kelly Preston . . . . Deborah Anne Fimple
•• 0:53 - Brief topless in car with C. Thomas Howell.
• 1:17 - Very brief topless in and out of bed.
Leigh Taylor-Young . . . . Elizabeth Fimple
Dee Wallace Stone . . . . Connie Ryan
Fred Ward . . . . Lou Fimple

Secret Fantasy *(1981)*
Laura Antonelli . . . . Costanza Vivaldi
••• 0:16 - In black bra in Doctor's office, then left breast, then topless getting examined.
•• 0:18 - In black bra and panties in another Doctor's office. Topless and buns.
•• 0:19 - Topless getting X-rayed. Brief topless lying down.
•• 0:32 - Topless and buns when Nicolo drugs her and takes Polaroid photos of her.
•• 0:49 - Topless and buns posing around the house for Nicolo while he takes Polaroid photos.
•• 0:53 - Topless and buns during Nicolo's dream.
••• 1:12 - Topless in Doctor's office.
•• 1:14 - Topless and buns in room with another guy.
•• 1:16 - Topless on train while workers "accidentally" see her.
•• 1:20 - Topless on bed after being carried from bathtub.
•• 1:25 - Topless dropping dress during opera.
•• 1:27 - More topless scenes from 0:49.

The Secret of My Success *(1987)*
John Pankow . . . . Fred Melrose
Helen Slater . . . . Christy
Margaret Whitton . . . . Vera Prescott
• 0:31 - Very brief topless taking off swimsuit top in swimming pool with Michael J. Fox.

Secrets *(1971)*
Jacqueline Bisset . . . . Jenny
    0:49 - Very brief lower frontal nudity, putting panties on while wearing a black dress.
••• 1:02 - Brief buns and a lot of topless on bed making love with Raoul.

The Secrets of Love—Three Rakish Tales *(1986)*
Marc Legein . . . . Luke
• 0:18 - Buns, in the hay with the Weaver's wife.
• 0:24 - More buns.
Tina Shaw . . . . The Weaver's Wife
••• 0:10 - Topless in bed with Luke.
••• 0:17 - Topless in the barn.

The Seduction *(1982)*
Colleen Camp . . . . Robin
Morgan Fairchild . . . . Jamie
• 0:02 - Brief topless under water, swimming in pool.
• 0:05 - Very brief left breast, getting out of the pool to answer the telephone.
    0:13 - In white bra changing clothes while listening to telephone answering machine.
    0:50 - In white lingerie in her bathroom while Andrew Stevens watches from inside the closet.
•• 0:51 - Topless pinning her hair up for her bath, then brief left breast in bathtub covered with bubbles.
• 1:21 - Topless getting into bed. Kind of dark, hard to see anything.
Andrew Stevens . . . . Derek

See No Evil, Hear No Evil *(1989)*
Richard Pryor . . . . Wally
Joan Severance . . . . Eve
•• 1:08 - Topless in and leaning out of the shower while Gene Wilder tries to get her bag.
Gene Wilder . . . . Dave

Senior Week *(1987)*
Vicki Darnell . . . . Everett's Dream Teacher
•• 0:03 - Topless during classroom fantasy.

Seniors *(1978)*
Priscilla Barnes . . . . Sylvia
•• 0:18 - Topless at the top of the stairs while Arnold climbs up the stairs while the rest of the guys watch.
Dennis Quaid . . . . Alan

Sensations *(1988)*
Blake Bahner . . . . Brian Ingles
•• 0:10 - Very, very brief lower frontal nudity pushing the covers off the bed, then buns getting out of bed.

Jennifer Delora . . . . .Della Randall
  • 0:11 - Brief topless talking to Jenny to wake her up.
  • 0:13 - Brief topless a couple of times in open robe.
  •• 0:38 - Topless making love with a guy on bed.
Jane Hamilton . . . . Tippy
Rebecca Lynn . . . . Jenny Hunter
  • 0:11 - Topless, sleeping on couch.
  •• 0:23 - Topless talking on the telephone.
  •• 1:09 - Topless making love in bed with Brian.
Denise Torek . . . . Phone Girl #2
  • 0:23 - Topless talking on the phone sex line.
Miriam Zucker .Cookie Woman
  • 0:06 - Topless on couch making love with a guy
    while Jenny and Brian watch.

The Sensuous Nurse (1979)
Ursula Andress . . . . .Anna
  •• 0:16 - Topless and buns in bed after making love with
    Benito.
  •• 0:22 - Nude swimming in pool while Adonais watch-
    es.
  ••• 0:50 - Nude slowly stripping and getting in bed with
    Adonais.
  ••• 1:10 - Nude getting into bed.
Lucianna Paluzzi . . . .
  •• 0:20 - Topless in room, ripping off her clothes and re-
    luctantly making love with Benito.
Carla Romanelli . . . . Tosca
  •• 0:06 - Topless, then nude standing in the winery,
    then running around.
  •• 0:41 - Nude, in basement, playing army, then mak-
    ing love with bearded guy.

The Sentinel (1977)
Tom Berenger .Man at End
Beverly D'Angelo . . . . Sandra
  0:25 - Masturbating in red leotard and tights on
    couch in front of Cristina Raines.
  • 0:33 - Brief topless playing cymbals during Raines'
    nightmare (in B&W).
  1:24 - Brief topless long shot with zombie make up,
    munching on a dead Chris Sarandon.
Jeff Goldblum . . . . Jack
Sylvia Miles . . . . .Gerde
  • 0:33 - Brief left breast, three times, standing behind
    Beverly D'Angelo. Right breast, ripping dress of
    Christina Raines. B&W dream.
  1:23 - Brief topless, three times, with D'Angelo made
    up to look like zombies, munching on a dead Chris
    Sarandon.
  1:27 - Very brief right breast during big zombie
    scene.
  • 1:28 - Brief topless when the zombies start dying.
Cristina Raines . . . . .Alison Parker
  • 0:18 - Briefly in sheer beige bra, putting her blouse
    on.
  • 0:33 - Very, very brief left breast immediately after
    Sylvia Miles rips her dress off. B&W dream sequence.
Chris Sarandon . . . . Michael Lerman

Separate Vacations (1985)
Susan Almgren . . . . .Helene Gilbert
  •• 1:05 - Topless and buns in bed with David Naugh-
    ton.
Nancy Cser . . . . Stewardess
Jennifer Dale . . . . Sarah Moore
  • 0:17 - Brief right breast in bed with her husband after
    son accidentally comes into their bedroom.
  0:20 - In a bra and slip showing the baby sitter the
    house before leaving.
  •• 1:14 - Topless on the cabin floor with Jeff after having
    a fight with her husband.
  • 1:19 - Brief right breast, in bed with her husband.
Blanca Guerra . . . . Alicia
  • 0:56 - Topless on the bed with David Naughton
    when she turns out to be a hooker.
Laura Henry . . . . Nancy
Sherrie Miller . . . . Sandy
David Naughton . . . . .Richard Moore

Separate Ways (1979)
Karen Black . . . . Valentine Colby
  • 0:04 - Topless and in panties changing while her hus-
    band talks on the phone, then in bra. Long shot.
  •• 0:18 - Topless in bed, while making love with Tony
    Lo Bianco.
  •• 0:36 - Topless taking a shower, then getting out.
Pamela Jean Bryant . . . . Cocktail Waitress
Sybil Danning . . . . Mary
David Naughton . . . . Jerry Lansing

Serial (1980)
Pamela Bellwood . . . . .Carol
Sally Kellerman . . . . Martha
  ••• 0:03 - Topless sitting on the floor with a guy.
Patch Mackenzie . . . . Stella
  • 0:59 - Brief topless in mirror in swinger's club with
    Martin Mull.
Robin Sherwood . . . . .Woman
Clyde Ventura . . . . Donald

The Serpent and the Rainbow (1988)
Cathy Tyson . . . . Dr. Marielle Duchamp
  • 0:41 - Brief topless making love with Dennis. Proba-
    bly a body double, don't see her face.

The Serpent of Death (1989)
Jeff Fahey . . . . .Jake Bonner
Camilla More . . . . Rene
  •• 0:15 - Brief topless in bed with Jeff Fahey.
  •• 1:22 - Brief left breast while in bed, then topless and
    buns, getting out of bed (in mirror).

Serpico (1973)
Cornelia Sharpe . . . . Leslie
  •• 0:41 - Topless in bathtub with Al Pacino.

The Seventh Sign (1988)
Michael Biehn . . . . Russell Quinn
Demi Moore . . . . Abby Quinn
- 1:03 - Brief topless, taking off bathrobe to take a bath. She's about 8 months pregnant, so she's pretty big.

A Severed Head (1971; British)
Claire Bloom . . . . Honor Klein
- 1:10 - Topless leaning up then right beast while sitting up in bed with Richard Attenborough.

Jennie Linden . . . . Georgie Hands
0:02 - Buns, rolling over on the floor with Ian Holm.

Sex Appeal (1986)
Louis Bonanno . . . . .Tony
Tally Chanel . . . . Corinne
- 1:22 - Brief topless at the door of Tony's apartment when he opens the door while fantasizing about her.

Samantha Fox. . . . . Sheila
- ••• 1:14 - In black lingerie, then topless and buns in black G-string with Rhonda. Long scene.

Jane Hamilton . . . . .Monica
- ••• 0:58 - Topless dancing on the bed with Tony in his apartment. Long scene.

Kim Kafkaloff. . . . . Stephanie
- •• 0:29 - Buns, in G-string in Tony's bachelor pad. Topless dancing and on bed.

Taija Rae . . . . .Rhonda
- •• 1:14 - In black lingerie, then topless in black push-up teddy with Sheila.

Sex on the Run (1979; German/French/Italian)
a.k.a. Some Like It Cool
a.k.a. Casanova and Co.
Jeannie Bell . . . . Slave Girl
Marisa Berenson . . . .
1:23 - Almost right breast, while in bed with Tony Curtis when she rolls over him.

Britt Ekland . . . . .Countess Trivulsi
- 0:44 - Left breast while making love in bed with Tony Curtis (don't see her face).

Andrea Ferreol. . . . .
Sylva Koscina . . . . Jelsamina
- ••• 0:28 - Topless and brief buns dropping her top for Tony Curtis, then walking around with the "other" Tony Curtis.
- •• 1:20 - Topless talking to her husband.

Marisa Mell. . . . . Francesca
- 0:52 - Very, very brief left breast getting out of bed with Tony Curtis.
1:12 - Braless in white nightgown.

Lillian Müller. . . . . Angela
- ••• 0:15 - Second woman (blonde) to take off her clothes with the other two women, nude. Long scene.

Olivia Pascal . . . . .Convent Girl
- ••• 0:15 - First woman (brunette) to take off her clothes with the other two women, full frontal nudity. Long scene.

Sex with a Smile (1976; Italian)
Barbara Bouchet. . . . . . . "One for the Money" segment
- ••• 0:50 - Topless sitting up in bed with a guy in bed, then lying down, wearing glasses.

Edwige Fenech. .Dream Girl
- •• 0:03 - Topless tied to bed with two holes cut in her red dress top.
0:09 - Buns, in jail cell in court when the guy pulls her panties down with his sword.
- •• 0:13 - Brief topless in bed with Dracula taking off her top and hugging him.
- 0:16 - Topless in bathtub. Long shot.

Dayle Haddon . . . . The Girl
- •• 0:23 - Topless, covered with bubbles in the bathtub.
- 0:43 - Buns, taking off robe to take a shower, then brief topless with Marty Feldman.

Sydne Rome. . . . ."A Dog's Day" segment

Sexpot (1986)
Ruth Corrine Collins. . . . . Ivy Barrington
- •• 0:09 - Topless on table, taking her dress off for Phillip.
- •• 0:41 - Buns, in Damon's arms.
- •• 0:51 - Left breast, while in shower talking to Boopsie.

Jennifer Delora. . . . . Barbara
- ••• 0:28 - In bra, then topless with her two sisters when their bras pop off. (She's in the middle.)
- •• 0:36 - Topless on bed with Gorilla.
- 1:32 - Topless during outtakes of 0:28 scene.

Jane Hamilton . . . . Beth
- ••• 0:28 - In bra, then topless with her two sisters when their bras pop off. (She's on the right.)
- 1:32 - Topless during outtakes of 0:28 scene.

Christina Veronica . . . . Betty
- ••• 0:28 - In bra, then topless with her two sisters when their bras pop off. (She's on the left.)
- •• 0:46 - Topless taking off her top in boat with Gorilla.
- 0:54 - Topless lying on the grass with Gorilla.
- 1:28 - Topless during outtakes of 0:28 scene.

Shadow Play (1986)
Ron Kuhlman . . . . .John Crown
- 1:06 - Buns, standing and holding Dee Wallace in his arms.

Dee Wallace Stone . . . . Morgan Hanna
- 1:06 - Brief topless making love with Ron Kuhlman. Kind of dark and hard to see.

Shadowzone (1989)
Robbie Reves . . . . .James
0:16 - Frontal nudity long shot.
- 0:26 - Frontal nudity lying under plastic bubble.

Shawn Weatherly. .Dr. Kidwell

The Shaming (1979)
a.k.a. Good Luck, Miss Wyckoff
a.k.a. The Sin
Anne Heywood . . . . Evelyn Wyckoff
- ••• 0:49 - Right breast, then topless in open blouse after being raped by Rafe in her classroom.
0:52 - Topless on classroom floor, making love with Rafe.

John Lafayette . . . . Rafe
- •• 0:43 - Very brief frontal nudity, taking off his jumpsuit in classroom with Anne Heywood.
- • 0:52 - Buns, making love on top of Heywood in classroom.

Shampoo (1975)
Warren Beatty . . . . George
- • 0:42 - Upper half of buns with pants a little bit down in the bathroom with Julie Christie.
- • 1:24 - Buns, making love with Christie when Goldie Hawn discovers them. Long shot, hard to see.

Julie Christie . . . . Jackie
Lee Grant . . . . Felicia
- • 0:03 - Brief topless in bed sitting up and putting bra on talking to Warren Beatty. Long shot, hard to see.

Goldie Hawn . . . . Jill
Sharon Kelly . . . . Painted Lady
- • 1:17 - Brief topless covered with tattoos all over her body during party. Lit with strobe light.

Jack Warden . . . . Lester Carr

She (1983)
Sandahl Bergman . . . . She
- •• 0:22 - Topless getting into a pool of water to clean her wounds after sword fight.

She'll be Wearing Pink Pyjamas (1985; British)
Maureen O'Brien . . . . Joan
- • 0:46 - Brief topless making love in bed with Tom. Dark.

Julie Walters . . . . Fran
- ••• 0:07 - Full frontal nudity taking a shower with the other women. Long scene.
- •• 0:58 - Nude, undressing and going skinny dipping in mountain lake, then getting out. Nice bun shot walking into the lake.

Jane Wood . . . . Jude
- • 0:07 - Nude, shaving her legs in the women's shower room.

She's Gotta Have It (1987; B&W)
Tracy Camilla Johns . . . . Nola Darling
- •• 0:06 - Topless lying down in bed with Jamie.
- •• 0:58 - Topless on floor with Greer.
- •• 1:15 - Topless making love with Mars.
- ••• 1:41 - Topless in bed masturbating.

Joie Lee . . . . Clorinda Bradford
John Canada Terrell . . . . Greer Childs
- • 0:59 - Buns, making love with Nola Darling.

Sheba, Baby (1975)
Pam Grier . . . . Sheba Shayne
- • 0:26 - Side view of left breast, lying in bed with Brick.

Sheena (1984)
Nancy Paul . . . . Betsy Ames
Tanya Roberts . . . . Sheena
- ••• 0:19 - Nude taking a shower under a waterfall.
- ••• 0:54 - Nude taking a bath in a pond while Ted Wass watches.

The Sheltering Sky (1990)
John Malkovich . . . . Port
- ••• 0:32 - Frontal nudity and half of buns, getting out of bed and opening door.

Eric Vu-An . . . . Belqassim
- • 1:59 - Buns, rolling over in bed with Debra Winger. Long shot, don't see his face.

Debra Winger . . . . Kit Moresby
- 0:13 - Upper half of lower frontal nudity in open robe when John Malkovich caresses her stomach.
- 0:24 - Buns, getting out of bed.
- • 0:41 - Very brief topless grabbing sheets and getting out of bed with Tunner.
- 1:58 - Lower frontal nudity and sort of buns, getting undressed with Belqassim.

Shirley Valentine (1989)
Pauline Collins . . . . Shirley Valentine
- • 0:13 - Brief left breast giving Joe a shampoo in the bathtub.
- •• 1:17 - Topless jumping from the boat into the water in slow motion. Very brief topless in the water.
- •• 1:19 - Buns, hugging Tom Conti, left breast several times kissing him.

Joanna Lumley . . . . Marjorie

The Shout (1979)
Alan Bates . . . . Charles Crossly
John Hurt . . . . Anthony Fielding
Susannah York . . . . Rachel Fielding
- •• 0:53 - Brief topless changing from a bathrobe to a blouse in bedroom.
- • 1:02 - Brief nude in upstairs room getting ready to make love with Alan Bates.
- 1:05 - Brief buns, standing at end of hallway.
- 1:11 - Topless in bathtub with John Hurt.
- • 1:18 - Brief topless getting up from bed with Bates. Long shot, hard to see anything.

The Sicilian (1987)
(Director's uncut version.)
Christopher Lambert . . . . Salvatore Giullano
- •• 1:02 - Buns, when the Duchess yanks his underwear down. Don't see his face, but probably him.

Barbara Sukowa . . . . Camilia Duchess of Crotone
- •• 0:05 - Buns and brief topless taking a bath.
- • 0:07 - Brief right breast reading Time magazine. Full frontal nudity in the mirror standing up in the tub.
- • 0:08 - Brief right breast standing at the window watching Christopher Lambert steal a horse.
- ••• 1:01 - In bra, then topless in bedroom with Lambert. More topless, then nude. Long scene.

Sid and Nancy (1986; British)
Gary Oldman . . . . Sid Vicious
Patti Tippo . . . . Tanned and Sultry Blonde
Chloe Webb . . . . Nancy
- • 0:21 - Left breast, under Sid's arm in bed with him. Covered up, hard to see.
- •• 0:44 - Topless in bed after making love, then arguing with Sid.

Side Out (1990)

Hope Marie Carlton. . . . . Vanna
C. Thomas Howell. . . . . Monroe Clark
Harley Jane Kozak . . . . Kate Jacobs
  • 0:53 - Brief left breast, the out of focus left breast in
    bed with Peter Horton.
Christopher Rydell. . . . . Wiley Hunter

Side Roads (1988)

Ingrid Vold . . . . Bonnie Velasco
  • 0:29 - Brief topless in motel room, getting undressed
    and carried into bed by Joe.
    0:30 - In white lingerie, talking with Joe. Long scene.
    0:56 - In white bra and panties, changing clothes.
  • 1:45 - Brief topless in mirror, getting out of bed.

Siesta (1987)

Ellen Barkin . . . . Diane
  ••• 0:03 - Brief full frontal nudity long shot taking off red
    dress, topless, brief buns standing up, then full fron-
    tal nudity lying down.
    1:23 - Right nipple sticking out of dress making love
    and getting raped by taxi driver. Lower frontal nudi-
    ty then brief buns. Dark, hard to see.
    1:28 - Very brief side view of right breast putting on
    dress in bed just before Isabella Rossellini comes into
    the bedroom to attack her. Long distance shot.
Gabriel Byrne . . . . Augustine
    1:28 - Brief buns and frontal nudity, getting out of
    bed. Long shot, hard to see.
Jodie Foster. . . . . Nancy
    0:47 - In a black slip combing Ellen Barkin's hair.
    0:50 - In a slip again in bedroom with Barkin.
Isabella Rossellini. . . . . Marie
Julian Sands. . . . . Kit

Silent Night, Deadly Night (1984)

Tara Buckman. . . . . Mother (Ellie)
  • 0:12 - Brief right breast twice when the killer dressed
    as Santa Claus, rips her blouse open. Topless lying
    dead with slit throat.
  • 0:18 - Very, very brief topless during Billy's flashback.
  • 0:43 - Brief topless a couple of times again in another
    of Billy's flashbacks.
Toni Nero. . . . . Pamela
  • 0:30 - Brief right breast twice just before Billy gets
    stabbed during fantasy scene.
  • 0:42 - Topless in stock room when Andy attacks her.
  • 0:44 - Topless in stock room struggling with Billy,
    then getting killed by him.
Linnea Quigley . . . . Denise
  ••• 0:52 - Topless on pool table with Tommy, then put-
    ting on shorts and walking around the house. More
    topless, impaled on antlers.
Robert Brian Wilson. . . . . Billy at 18
  • 0:30 - Sort of buns in bed with Pamela.

Silent Night, Deadly Night, Part 2 (1986)

Tara Buckman . . . . Mother
  • 0:09 - Very brief right breast, with Santa Claus during
    flashback.
  • 0:14 - Very brief topless on ground during flashback.
  • 0:22 - Very, very brief blurry topless during flashback.
  • 0:47 - Very, very brief topless during flashback.
Elizabeth Kaitan . . . . Jennifer
    0:58 - Most of right breast, then buns, kissing Ricky.
Toni Nero. . . . . Pamela
  •• 0:22 - Topless in back of toy store in flashback from
    Silent Night, Deadly Night.
Linnea Quigley. . . . . Denise
  ••• 0:26 - Topless on pool table and getting dressed
    flashback from *Silent Night, Deadly Night.*

Silent Night, Deadly Night III: Better Watch Out! (1989)

Robert Culp . . . . Lt. Connely
Laura Herring. . . . . Jerri
  ••• 0:48 - Topless in bathtub with her boyfriend Chris.

Silent Night, Deadly Night 4: Initiation (1990)

Maud Adams . . . . Fima
Tommy Hindley . . . . Hank
  • 0:03 - Brief buns, carrying Kim onto bed.
Marjean Holden . . . . Jane
Neith Hunter . . . . Kim
  • 0:03 - Brief topless several times in bed with Hank.
  • 0:47 - Brief topless during occult ceremony when a
    worm comes out of her mouth.
  • 1:05 - Right breast, while lying on floor. Long shot.
    1:06 - Topless, covered with gunk, transforming into
    a worm.
  • 1:07 - Very brief side of right breast, while sitting up.

The Silent Partner (1978)

Gail Dahms . . . . Louise
  • 0:31 - Right breast in bathroom with another guy
    when Elliott Gould surprises them.
Michael Kirby. . . . . Packard
Céline Lomez . . . . Elaine
  • 1:05 - Side view of left breast, then topless, then
    buns with Elliott Gould.
Susannah York . . . . Julie
  • 0:38 - Very brief right breast pulling her dress back
    up with Elliott Gould.

Silk 2 (1989)

Monique Gabrielle . . . . Jenny "Silk" Sleighton
  ••• 0:27 - Topless, then full frontal nudity taking a show-
    er while killer stalks around outside.
    0:28 - Very, very brief blurry right breast in open robe
    when she's on the sofa during fight.
  • 0:29 - Brief topless doing a round house kick on the
    bad guy. Right breast several times during the fight.
  ••• 0:55 - Topless taking off her blouse and making love
    on bed. Too much diffusion!

Silkwood (1984)
E. Katherine Kerr . . . . Gilda Schultz
Bruce McGill . . . . Mace Hurley
Kurt Russell . . . . Drew Stephens
Meryl Streep . . . . Karen Silkwood
  • 0:24 - Very brief glimpse of upper half of left breast
    when she flashes it in nuclear reactor office.
Fred Ward . . . . Morgan

Simply Irresistible (1983)
(R-rated version. *Irresistable* is the X-rated version.)
Samantha Fox . . . . Arlene Brooks
  • 1:20 - In see-through white nightgown, then brief
    peeks at right breast when nightgown gapes open.

Sincerely Charlotte (1986; French)
Caroline Faro . . . . Irene the Baby Sitter
Isabelle Huppert . . . . Charlotte
  0:20 - Brief topless in bathtub. Long shot, out of fo-
    cus.
  1:07 - Very brief left breast changing into red dress in
    the back seat of the car.
  •• 1:15 - Topless in bed with Mathieu. Kind of dark.

Sister Sister (1987)
Jennifer Jason Leigh . . . . Lucy Bonnard
  •• 0:01 - Topless making love during a dream.
    0:52 - In lingerie talking with Eric Stoltz.
  •• 0:53 - Left breast, making love with Stoltz in her bed-
    room.
  • 0:58 - Topless in bathtub surrounded by candles.
Eric Stoltz . . . . Matt Rutledge

Sisters (1973)
Margot Kidder . . . . Danielle Breton
  • 0:11 - Very brief left breast, undressing while walking
    down hallway. Long shot.
  • 0:14 - Topless opening her robe on couch for her
    new boyfriend. Shadows make it hard to see.

Ski School (1990)
Ava Fabian . . . . Victoria
  ••• 0:53 - In white bra and panties, then topless making
    love with Johnny.
Charlie Spradling . . . . Paulette
Darlene Vogel . . . . Lori
  • 1:03 - Topless in bed with Johnny.

Skin Deep (1989)
Denise Crosby . . . . Angie Smith
Raye Hollitt . . . . Lonnie
  • 0:26 - Brief side view topless and buns getting un-
    dressed and into bed with John Ritter.
Heidi Paine . . . . Tina
  • 0:01 - Brief side view topless sitting on John Ritter's
    lap while Denise Crosby watches.
Brenda Swanson . . . . Emily

Slam Dance (1987)
Virginia Madsen . . . . Yolanda Caldwell
Mary Elizabeth Mastrantonio . . . . Helen Drood

Lisa Niemi . . . . Ms. Schell
  ••• 0:54 - Nude in Tom Hulce's apartment.
  • 1:00 - Topless, dead, lying on the floor in Hulce's
    apartment.

Slammer Girls (1987)
Sharon Cain . . . . Rita
  • 0:23 - Brief topless changing clothes under table in
    the prison cafeteria.
  •• 1:02 - Topless walking around an electric chair trying
    to distract a prison guard.
Tally Chanel . . . . Candy Treat
  0:57 - Doing a dance routine wearing feathery past-
    ies for the Governor in the hospital.
Samantha Fox . . . . Mosquito
  •• 0:17 - Topless in the shower hassling Melody with
    Tank.
Jane Hamilton . . . . Miss Crabapples
Kim Kafkaloff . . . . Ginny
  • 0:23 - Brief topless changing clothes under table in
    the prison cafeteria.
Sharon Kelly . . . . Professor
  • 0:23 - Brief topless changing clothes under table in
    the prison cafeteria.
  •• 0:35 - Topless squishing breasts against the window
    during prison visiting hours.
  •• 0:37 - Topless with an inflatable male doll.
Darcy Nychols . . . . Tank
  • 0:17 - Topless ripping blouse open while hassling
    Melody.

Slap Shot (1977)
Melinda Dillon . . . . Suzanne
  ••• 0:30 - Right breast, lying in bed with Paul Newman,
    then topless sitting up and talking. Nice, long scene.
Michael Ontkean . . . . Ned Braden
  •• 1:56 - Brief buns skating off the hockey rink carrying
    a trophy wearing his jock strap.
M. Emmet Walsh . . . . Dickie Dunn
Jennifer Warren . . . . Francine Dunlop

The Slasher (1975)
Sylva Koscina . . . . Barbara
  •• 0:17 - Left breast lying down getting a massage.
  •• 1:18 - Topless undressing and putting a robe on at
    her lover's house. Left breast after getting stabbed.

Slaughter (1972)
Marlene Clark . . . . Kim Walker
  • 0:11 - Very brief buns and right breast, getting
    thrown out of room by Jim Brown.
Stella Stevens . . . . Ann
  •• 0:47 - Left breast, several times in bed with Jim
    Brown.
  • 0:55 - Left breast, making love in bed with Brown
    again. Dark.
  • 0:57 - Brief right breast, in bed afterwards. Close up
    shot.
  ••• 1:14 - Buns and topless taking a shower and getting
    out. This is her best nude scene.
Rip Torn . . . . Hoffo

Slaughter High (1986)
Billy Hartman . . . . Frank
• 1:00 - Brief buns in bed with Stella.
Caroline Munro. . . . . Carol
    0:19 - Walking around her house in lingerie and a robe.
Simon Scuddamore. Marty
• 0:05 - Nude in girl's shower room when his classmates pull a prank on him.

Slaughterhouse Five (1972)
Perry King. . . . . Robert Pigrim
Ron Liebman. Paul Lazzaro
Valerie Perrine. . . . . Montana Wildhack
• 0:39 - Topless in *Playboy* magazine as a Playmate.
• 0:43 - Topless getting into the bathtub.
••• 1:27 - Topless in a dome with Michael Sacks.

Slaughterhouse Rock (1988)
Hope Marie Carlton. . . . . Krista Halpern
• 0:09 - Brief right breast, taking off her top in bedroom with her boyfriend.
•• 0:49 - Topless, getting raped by Richard as he turns into a monster.

Slave of the Cannibal God (1979; Italian)
Ursula Andress. . . . .
•• 0:33 - Topless taking off shirt and putting on a T-shirt.
••• 1:07 - Nude getting tied to a pole by the Cannibal People and covered with red paint.
    1:20 - Brief peek at buns under her skirt when running away from the Cannibal People.

Slavegirls from Beyond Infinity (1987)
Cindy Beal . . . . Tisa
    0:25 - Walking around in white bra and panties.
••• 0:36 - Topless on beach wearing white panties.
• 1:05 - Left breast leaning back on table while getting attacked by Zed.
Elizabeth Kaitan. . . . . Daria
••• 0:38 - Topless undressing and jumping into bed with Rik.
Brinke Stevens. . . . . Shala
    0:29 - Chained up wearing black lingerie.
• 0:31 - Brief side view of left breast on table. Nice pan from her feet to her head while she's lying face down.

Slaves of New York (1989)
Nick Corri . . . . Marley Mantello
Adam Coleman Howard . . . . Stash
• 1:15 - Buns, putting on his pants and silhouette of penis. Dark, hard to see.
Madeleine Potter. . . . . Daria
• 1:14 - Topless making love with Stash on chair. Mostly see left breast. Dark.
Chris Sarandon . . . . Victor Okrent

Sleepaway Camp II: Unhappy Campers (1988)
Susan Marie Snyder . . . . Mare
•• 0:08 - Brief topless lifting up her T-shirt.
•• 0:24 - Brief topless flashing in boy's cabin.
•• 0:33 - Topless in Polaroid photograph that Angela confiscates from the boys.

Sleepaway Camp III: Teenage Wasteland (1989)
Tracy Griffith . . . . Marcia Holland
Jill Terashita . . . . Arab
•• 0:16 - Topless putting sweatshirt on.

The Sleeping Car (1990)
Judie Aronson. . . . . Kim
•• 0:42 - Brief topless on top of David Naughton making love. Brief topless three times after he hallucinates.
Jeff Conaway . . . . Bud Sorenson
Sandra Margot. . . . . .19-Year Old Girl
Dani Minnick . . . . Joanne
David Naughton . . . . Jason McCree

Sloane (1984)
Debra Blee. Cynthia Thursby
• 0:15 - Very brief topless during attempted rape.
Ann Milhench . . . . Janice Thursby
•• 0:02 - Topless and buns getting out of shower and being held by kidnappers.

Slow Burn (1986)
Beverly D'Angelo . . . . Laine Fleischer
• 1:01 - Topless making love with Eric Roberts. Don't see her face. Part of lower frontal nudity showing tattoo.
Eric Roberts . . . . Jacob Asch

Slumber Party '57 (1976)
Bridget Holloman. . . . . Bonnie May
• 0:10 - Topless with her five girl friends during swimming pool scene. Hard to tell who is who.
• 0:26 - Left breast in truck with her cousin Cal.
Joyce Jillson . . . . Gladys
Janice Karman . . . . Hank
•• 1:06 - Topless, sitting watching Smitty and David make love in the stable.
Noelle North . . . . Angie
•• 0:37 - Buns, then topless in bed with a party guest of her parents.
Cheryl Smith . . . . Sherry
Debra Winger. . . . . Debbie
• 0:10 - Topless with her five girl friends during swimming pool scene. Hard to tell who is who.
••• 0:53 - Topless three times, lying down, making out with Bud.
Janet Wood . . . . Smitty
• 0:10 - Topless with her five girl friends during swimming pool scene. Hard to tell who is who.
•• 1:06 - Left breast, then topless in stable with David while his sister watches.

The Slumber Party Massacre (1982)
Debra De Liso . . . . Kim
• 0:08 - Very brief topless getting soap from Trish in the shower.
•• 0:29 - In beige bra and panties, then topless putting on a U.S.A. shirt while changing with the other girls.
Brinke Stevens. . . . . Linda
•• 0:07 - Buns, then topless taking a shower during girls locker room scene.

Slumber Party Massacre II (1987)
Juliette Cummins. . . . . Sheila
•• 0:24 - In black bra, then topless in living room during a party with her girlfriends.
Heidi Kozak . . . . Sally
Kimberly McArthur . . . . Amy

A Small Circle of Friends (1980)
Karen Allen . . . . .Jessica
• 0:47 - Brief topless in bathroom with Brad Davis. Don't see her face.
• 0:48 - Very brief topless, pushing Davis off her. Then very, very brief half of left breast turning around to walk to the mirror.
Brad Davis. . . . . Leo DaVinci
•• 1:22 - Brief buns, dropping his pants with several other guys for Army draft inspection.
Shelley Long . . . . .Alice
Jameson Parker . . . . .Nick Baxter
Daniel Stern . . . . Crazy Kid
• 1:22 - Brief buns, dropping his pants with several other guys for Army draft inspection.

Smash Palace (1981; New Zealand)
Bruno Lawrence . . . . Al Shaw
••• 0:39 - Buns in bed after arguing, then making up with Jacqui.
Anna-Maria Monticelli. . . . . Jacqui Shaw
0:21 - Silhouette of right breast changing while sitting on the edge of the bed.
••• 0:39 - Topless in bed after arguing, then making up with Bruno Lawrence.

Smile (1974)
Colleen Camp. . . . . Connie Thompson
0:47 - Side profile of right breast and buns in dressing room while Little Bob is outside taking pictures.
Melanie Griffith . . . . Karen Love
0:07 - Brief glimpse at panties, bending over to pick up dropped box.
• 0:34 - Very, very brief side view of right breast in dressing room, just before passing behind a rack of clothes.
• 0:47 - Very brief side view of right breast, then side view of left breast when Little Bob is outside taking pictures.
• 0:48 - Very brief topless as Polaroid photograph that Little Bob took develops.
• 1:51 - Topless in the same Polaroid in the policeman's sun visor.

Annette O'Toole. . . . . .Doria Houston
0:34 - In white bra and panties in dressing room.
1:06 - In white bra and slip talking to Joan Prather in bedroom.
Joan Prather. . . . . .Robin
0:47 - Brief buns in dressing room, taking off pants while Little Bob is outside taking pictures. (She's wearing a pink ribbon in her hair.)

Smoke Screen (1988)
Kim Cattrall . . . . Odessa Muldoon
0:31 - Brief half of right breast sitting in bed with sheet pulled up on her.
•• 1:16 - Topless in bed on top of Gerald.
••• 1:17 - Topless lying in bed under Gerald while he kisses her breasts.

Soft Touch (1987)
(Shown on *The Playboy Channel* as *Birds in Paradise*.)
Jennifer Inch. . . . . Tracy Anderson
• 0:01 - Full frontal nudity during the opening credits.
• 0:02 - Topless with her two girlfriends during the opening credits.
••• 0:17 - Topless exercising on the floor, walking around the room, the lying on bed. Long scene.
• 0:20 - Full frontal nudity getting out of bed.
• 0:23 - Topless in bed.
••• 0:50 - Topless sunbathing on boat with Carrie.
•• 1:01 - Full frontal nudity, sitting on towel, watching Carrie.
• 1:02 - Full frontal nudity, waving to a dolphin.
•• 1:04 - Topless at night by campfire with Carrie.
••• 1:05 - Brief left breast, then topless putting on skirt and walking around the island.
•• 1:13 - Topless in hut with island guy.
• 1:19 - Topless in stills during the end credits.

Soft Touch II (1987)
Seen on The Playboy Channel as "Birds in Paradise."
Jennifer Inch. . . . . Tracy Anderson
• 0:01 - Topless during opening credits.
• 0:02 - Topless with her two girlfriends during opening credits.
•• 0:14 - Topless dancing in Harry's bar by herself.
• 0:27 - Full frontal nudity on stage at Harry's after robbers tell her to strip.
• 0:29 - Side of left breast tied to Neill on bed.
• 0:31 - Topless tied up when Ashley and Carrie discover her.
•• 0:52 - Full frontal nudity during strip poker game, then covered with whipped cream.
• 0:57 - Full frontal nudity getting out of bed.

Soldier of Orange (1977; Dutch)
Derek De Lint. . . . . .Alex
Rutger Hauer . . . . Erik Lanshoff
Jeroen Krabbé . . . . Gus
Susan Penhaligon. . . . . .Susan
• 1:34 - Brief topless kissing her boyfriend when Rutger Hauer sees them. Medium long shot.
••• 1:36 - Topless in bed with her boyfriend and Hauer.

Sole Survivor (1982)

Anita Skinner. Denise Watson
- 0:29 - Very, very brief right breast in bed with Dr. Richardson. Brief side view of right breast when he jumps out of bed.

  1:13 - In bra, zipping up pants.

Brinke Stevens. . . . . Jennifer
- • 0:45 - In bra playing cards, then topless.

Some Call It Loving (1972)

Tisa Farrow . . . . Jennifer
- • • 1:17 - Topless in bed with Troy.

Brandy Herred. Cheerleader
- • • 1:12 - Nude dancing in a club doing a strip tease dance in a cheerleader outfit.

Richard Pryor . . . . Jeff

Some Girls (1988)

Jennifer Connelly. . . . . Gabriella

Patrick Dempsey . . . . Michael
- 0:34 - Brief frontal nudity, then buns running all around the house chasing Jennifer Connelly.

Andre Gregory . . . . Mr. D'Arc
- 1:24 - Buns, standing in the study looking at a book. Very brief frontal nudity when he turns around to sit at his desk.

Sheila Kelley . . . . Irenka
- 0:13 - Topless and buns getting something at the end of the hall while Michael watches. Long shot, hard to see.
- 1:01 - Topless in window while Michael watches from outside. Long shot, hard to see.

  1:17 - In black slip seducing Michael after funeral.

Something Wild (1986)

Jeff Daniels . . . . Charles Driggs
- • • 0:16 - Buns, lying in bed after making love with Melanie Griffith.

Melanie Griffith . . . . "Lulu"/Audrey Hankel
- • • • 0:16 - Strips to topless in bed with Jeff Daniels.
- 0:25 - Topless and buns standing in the window.

Sorceress (1982)

Lee Anne Harris. . . . . Mira
- • • • 0:11 - Topless (on the left) greeting the creature with her sister. Upper half of buns, getting dressed.
- • • 0:29 - Topless (she's the second one) undressing with her sister in front of Erlick and Baldar.

Lynette Harris . . . . Mara
- • • • 0:11 - Topless (on the right) greeting the creature with her sister.
- • • • 0:29 - Topless (she's the first one) undressing with her sister in front of Erlick and Baldar.

Bob Nelson . . . . Erlick
- 0:43 - Brief buns, just before being put to death.
- • • 0:45 - Buns, getting massaged.

Sorority Babes in the Slimeball Bowl-O-Rama (1988)

Michelle Bauer . . . . Lisa

  0:07 - In panties getting spanked with Linnea Quigley.
- • • • 0:12 - Topless brushing herself in the front of mirror while Quigley takes a shower.
- 0:14 - Brief full frontal nudity when the three nerds fall into the bathroom.

  0:33 - In black bra, panties, garter belt and stockings asking for Keith.

  0:35 - Wearing the same lingerie, on top of Keith in the locker room.
- • • • 0:40 - Topless taking off her bra.
- • • • 0:43 - More topless undoing garter belt.
- • • 0:46 - More topless in locker room.
- • • 0:47 - More topless taking off stockings.
- 1:04 - Full frontal nudity sitting on the floor by herself.
- • • 1:05 - Full frontal nudity getting up after the lights go out. Kind of dark.

George "Buck" Flower . . . . Janitor

Linnea Quigley. . . . . Spider

Brinke Stevens . . . . Taffy

  0:07 - In panties getting spanked with Michelle Bauer.
- • • • 0:12 - Nude showering off whipped cream in bathtub while talking to a topless Michelle Bauer. Excellent long scene!

Sorority House Massacre (1987)

Joe Nassi . . . . Craig
- 0:50 - Buns, running away from the killer that has just killed his girlfriend Tracy in a tepee.

Nicole Rio . . . . Tracy
- • • 0:20 - In a sheer bra changing clothes with two other girls in a bedroom.
- • • 0:49 - Topless in a tepee with her boyfriend, Craig, just before getting killed.

South of Reno (1987)

Lisa Blount . . . . Anette Clark

  1:02 - In black bra getting blouse torn open while lying down.

Danitza Kingsley. . . . . Louise

Julie Montgomery . . . . Susan
- 1:22 - Brief topless kissing Martin. Dark, hard to see.

  1:25 - In motel room wearing black top and panties, then pink spandex top with the panties.

Spaced Out (1980; British)

Glory Annen. . . . . Cosia
- • • • 0:23 - Topless talking to the other two space women. Long scene.
- 0:31 - Very brief topless changing clothes while dancing.
- • • 0:43 - Topless in bed with Willy.
- • • • 1:08 - Topless lying down.

Ava Cadell. . . . . .Partha
- •• 0:41 - Left breast making love on bed with Cliff.
- • 0:42 - Nude wrestling on bed with Cliff.
- • 0:43 - Brief left breast lying in bed alone.
- •• 1:08 - Topless sitting on bed.

Kate Ferguson. . . . . .Skipper
- • 1:07 - Brief topless making love with Willy in bed. Lit with red light.

Tony Maiden. . . . . .Willy
- • 0:38 - Buns, getting examined by Cosia.

Michael Rowlatt . . . . Cliff
- • 0:42 - Buns, getting out of bed trying to get away from Partha.

Barry Stokes . . . . Oliver
- • 0:54 - Buns, undressing to get in bed with Prudence.

Speaking Parts (1989; Canadian)

Gabrielle Rose. . . . . .Clara
- •• 0:41 - Right breast, on TV monitor, masturbating with Lance. Then topless getting dressed.

Special Effects (1984)

Eric Bogosian. . . . . Neville
- • 0:21 - Buns, while fighting with Zoe Tamerlis in bed. Medium long shot.

Zoe Tamerlis . . . . Amelia/Elaine
- 0:01 - Side view of right breast, wearing pasties during photo session.
- • 0:16 - Brief topless sitting by pool with Eric Bogozian.
- •• 0:19 - Topless getting into bed and in bed with Bogozian.
- • 0:22 - Topless, dead in spa while Bogozian washes her off.
- 0:44 - Brief topless in moviola that Bogozian watches.
- •• 1:12 - Topless making love on bed with Keefe.
- • 1:17 - Topless getting into bed during filming of movie. Brief topless during Bogozian's flashbacks.
- 1:20 - More left breast shots on moviola getting strangled.
- ••• 1:33 - Topless with Bogozian when he takes her dress off.
- • 1:35 - Topless sitting on bed kissing Bogozian. More topless and more flashbacks.
- • 1:40 - Brief topless during struggle. Dark.

Spellbinder (1988)

Alexandra Morgan . . . . .Pamela
Kelly Preston. . . . . .Miranda Reed
- ••• 0:19 - Topless in bed making love with Timothy Daly.
- 1:26 - Dancing around in a sheer white gown with nothing underneath during cult ceremony at the beach.

Rick Rossovich. . . . . .Derek Clayton

Spetters (1980; Dutch)

Toon Agterberg. . . . . .Hans
- ••• 0:35 - Frontal nudity, measuring and comparing his manlihood with his friends in the auto shop.
- • 1:21 - Buns, getting gang raped by gay guy he has been stealing money from.

Rutger Hauer . . . . .Witkamp
Jeroen Krabbé . . . . Henkhof
Reneé Soutendijk . . . . Fientje
- •• 1:12 - Topless making love in trailer with Jeff.

Maarten Spanjer. .Jeff
- ••• 0:35 - Frontal nudity, measuring and comparing his manlihood with his friends in the auto shop.
- • 1:12 - Buns climbing into bed in trailer with Reneé Soutendijk.

Hans Van Tongeren . . . . .Ron Hartman
- ••• 0:35 - Frontal nudity, measuring and comparing his manlihood with his friends in the auto shop.

Splash (1984)

Daryl Hannah. Madison
- • 0:27 - Brief right breast, swimmming under water, entering the sunken ship.
- • 0:28 - Buns, walking around the Statue of Liberty.
- • 1:26 - Brief right, then left breast in tank when Eugene Levy looks at her.
- • 1:44 - Brief right breast, under water when frogman grabs her from behind.

Amy Ingersoll. Reporter
Ron Kuhlman . . . . Man with Date
Eugene Levy. . . . . .Walter Kornbluth

The Spring (1989)

Shari Shattuck . . . . Dyanne
- • 0:00 - Nude, several times, swimming under the water. Shot from under water.
- • 0:50 - Topless and buns, swimming under water.
- •• 0:51 - Topless, getting out of the water.
- •• 0:59 - Brief topless, turning over in bed with Dack Rambo.
- • 1:05 - Standing up in wet lingerie, then swimming under water.

Spring Break (1983; Canadian)

Corinne Alphen . . . . .Joan
- 0:32 - Taking a shower in a two piece bathing suit in an outdoor shower at the beach.

Sheila Kennedy. . . . . Carla
- •• 0:49 - Topless during wet T-shirt contest.

Perry Lang . . . . Adam
- • 0:27 - Brief buns opening his towel in the shower, mooning his three friends.

Spring Fever USA (1988)

Amy Baxter . . . . Amy (Car Wash Girl)
Mark Levine. .Duke Dork
- • 1:17 - Buns, twice, in boat hallway with his skinny brother after being tricked.

Janine Lindemulder . . . . Heather Lipton
- •• 0:14 - Taking off her stockings, then brief topless undressing for bath, then taking a bath.

Cari Mayor. . . . . .Girl on Campus
Robert Moss. Dick Dork
- • 1:17 - Buns, twice, in boat hallway with his heavy brother after being tricked.

Sherrie Ann Rose . . . . Vinyl Vixen #1
Renee Shugart . . . . .Beach Beauty

Squeeze Play (1979)

Jim Harris . . . . Wes
- •• 0:39 - Buns, tied up in a room while people walking by look in through open door.

Jennifer Hetrick . . . . Samantha
- •• 0:00 - Topless in bed after making love.
- • 0:26 - Right breast, brief topless with Wes on the floor.
- 0:37 - In bra, in bedroom with Wes.

Stacey (1973)

Anitra Ford . . . . Tish
- •• 0:13 - Topless in bed making love with Frank.

Cristina Raines . . . . Pamela

Anne Randall . . . . Stacey Hansen
- ••• 0:01 - Topless taking off her driving jump suit.
- ••• 0:12 - Topless changing clothes.
- ••• 0:39 - Topless in bed with Bob.

Star 80 (1983)

Carroll Baker . . . . Dorothy's Mother

Lonnie Chin . . . . Playboy Mansion Guest

Deborah Geffner . . . . Billie

Tabitha Harrington . . . . Blonde

Mariel Hemingway . . . . Dorothy Stratten
- •• 0:00 - Topless in still photos during opening credits.
- • 0:02 - Topless lying on bed in Paul's flashbacks.
- ••• 0:22 - Topless during Polaroid photo session with Paul
- • 0:25 - Topless during professional photography session. Long shot.
- • 0:36 - Brief topless during photo session.
- • 0:57 - Right breast, in centerfold photo on wall.
- • 1:04 - Upper half of breasts, in bathtub.
- • 1:05 - Brief topless in photo shoot flashback.
- • 1:17 - Brief topless during layout flashbacks.
- • 1:20 - Very brief topless in photos on the wall.
- •• 1:33 - Topless undressing before getting killed by Paul. More brief topless layout flashbacks.

Lorraine Michaels . . . . Paul's Party Guest

Eric Roberts . . . . Paul Snider
- • 1:39 - Buns, lying dead on floor, covered with blood after shooting Dorothy, then himself.

Cathy St. George . . . . Playboy Mansion Guest

Kathryn Witt . . . . Robin

Star Slammer—The Escape (1986)

Bobbie Bresee . . . . Marai

Sandy Brooke . . . . Taura
- ••• 0:21 - Topless in jail putting a new top on. In braless white T-shirt for most of the rest of the film.
- •• 1:09 - Topless changing into a clean top.

Dawn Wildsmith . . . . Muffin

Stars and Bars (1988)

Daniel Day-Lewis . . . . Henderson Bores
- •• 1:21 - Brief buns, trying to open the window. Very, very brief frontal nudity when he throws the statue out the window. Blurry and dark. More buns, climbing out the window and into a trash dumpster.

Starting Over (1979)

Candice Bergen . . . . Jessica Potter
- 1:01 - In a sheer blouse sitting on couch talking to Burt Reynolds.
- • 1:29 - Very, very brief left breast in bed with Reynolds when he undoes her top. You see her breast just before the scene dissolves into the next one. Long shot, hard to see.

Jill Clayburgh . . . . Marilyn Holmberg
- • 0:45 - Very brief upper half of breasts taking a shower while Burt Reynolds waits outside.

Burt Reynolds . . . . Phil Potter

Daniel Stern . . . . Student 2

State of Grace (1990)

Sandra Beall . . . . Steve's Date

Ed Harris . . . . Frankie

Gary Oldman . . . . Jackie

Sean Penn . . . . Terry

Robin Wright . . . . Kathleen
- •• 0:38 - Topless making love standing up with Sean Penn in the hall. Dark.
- 1:01 - In bra on bed with Penn, than walking around while talking to him.
- • 1:58 - Brief side of right breast taking off towel and putting on blouse.

State Park (1988; Canadian)

Crisstyn Dante . . . . Blond in Net
- • 0:45 - Very, very brief left breast putting swimsuit top back on after being rescued from net by the guy in the bear costume.

Jennifer Inch . . . . Linnie
- • 0:34 - Brief right breast, undoing swimsuit top while sunbathing.
- • 0:39 - Brief topless, taking off swimsuit top while cutting Raymond's hair.

Isabelle Mejias . . . . Marsha

Stateline Motel (1975; Italian)

a.k.a. Last Chance for a Born Loser

Ursula Andress . . . . Michelle Nolton
- ••• 0:34 - Left breast, then topless on bed with Oleg.

Barbara Bach . . . . Emily

Staying Together (1989)

Melinda Dillon . . . . Eileen McDermott

Sheila Kelley . . . . Beth Harper

Tom Quill . . . . Brian McDermott
- • 0:03 - Brief buns getting out of bed with Stockard Channing. Hard to see because of the reflections in the window.

Daphne Zuniga . . . . Beverly Young
- •• 0:56 - Buns, lying in bed with Kit. Nice, long buns scene.

The Steagle (1971)

Richard Benjamin . . . . Harold Weiss

Susan Tyrrell . . . . Louise
- • 0:48 - Brief left breast twice, lying on bed with Richard Benjamin.

Stealing Heaven (1988)
Derek De Lint . . . . .Abelard
- ••• 0:47 - Brief frontal nudity taking off his shirt. Then buns, in bed making love with Kim Thomson.
  1:07 - Brief side view of buns under Kim. Long shot.
Cassie Stuart . . . . Petronilla

Steaming (1985; British)
Felicity Dean . . . . Dawn
- •• 1:12 - Topless painting on herself.
Patti Love . . . . Josie
- • 0:08 - Frontal nudity, getting undressed.
- • 0:45 - Brief topless.
- • 1:30 - Topless, jumping around in the pool.
Sarah Miles . . . . Sarah
- •• 0:23 - Topless getting into pool with Vanessa Redgrave.
- •• 0:49 - Topless getting undressed.
- •• 1:31 - Nude lying down next to pool.
Vanessa Redgrave . . . . .Nancy
- • 1:32 - Buns and brief side view of right breast getting into pool.

Steel and Lace (1990)
David Naughton . . . . Dunn
Brenda Swanson . . . . .Miss Fairweather
- •• 0:58 - Topless in lunchroom, opening her blouse in front of one of the bad guys on the table.
Clare Wren . . . . .Gally

The Stepfather (1987)
Terry O'Quinn . . . . .Jerry Blake
- ••• 0:02 - Buns, getting undressed, frontal nudity in mirror as he gets into the shower.
Gabrielle Rose . . . . Dorothy
Jill Schoelen . . . . .Stephanie Maine
- •• 1:16 - Buns and brief side of right breast getting into the shower. Topless in the shower.
Steve Shellen . . . . Jim Ogilvie

Steppenwolf (1974)
Pierre Clementi . . . . Pablo
- • 1:40 - Very brief frontal nudity, sleeping on floor with Dominique Sanda.
Carla Romanelli . . . . Maria
- ••• 0:59 - Topless sitting on bed with John Huston. Long scene.
Dominique Sanda . . . . Hermine
  1:40 - Brief lower frontal nudity, sleeping with a guy.
- • 1:41 - Very brief left breast, waking up and rolling over to hug John Huston.

Stewardess School (1987)
Sandahl Bergman . . . . Wanda Polanski
Corinne Bohrer . . . . Cindy Adams
Vicki Frederick . . . . Miss Grummet
Leslie Huntly . . . . Alison Hanover
- •• 0:46 - Topless, doing a strip tease on a table at a party at her house.
Julie Montgomery . . . . Pimmie Polk

Still of the Night (1982)
Sara Botsford . . . . Gail Phillips
Meryl Streep . . . . Brooke Reynolds
  0:22 - Side view of right breast and buns taking off robe for the massage guy. Long shot, don't see her face.

Stitches (1985)
Deborah Fallender . . . . Nurse
Rebecca Perle . . . . Bambi Belinka
- •• 0:34 - Topless during female medical student's class where they examine each other.

Stormy Monday (1988)
Sting . . . . Finney
Sean Bean . . . . .Brendan
- •• 0:37 - Buns, putting on his underwear while Melanie Griffith watches.
Catherine Chevalier . . . . Cosmo's Secretary
Melanie Griffith . . . . .Kate
  0:03 - Buns and side of right breast, behind shower door. Don't see anything because of the glass.
- • 1:11 - Very brief left breast, while making love in bed with Brendan.
Tommy Lee Jones . . . . .Cosmo

The Story of "O" (1975; French)
Corrine Clery . . . . .O
- •• 0:09 - Topless in bedroom with two women.
- •• 0:12 - Topless being made love to.
- •• 0:20 - Frontal nudity making love with two men.
- •• 0:29 - Topless taking a bath while a man watches.
- ••• 0:42 - Buns, on a sofa while her boyfriend lifts her dress up, then topless while another man plays with her, then nude except for white stockings.
- •• 0:51 - Brief topless chained by wrists and gagged.
- ••• 1:22 - Nude making love with a young guy.

The Story of "O" Continues (1981; French)
a.k.a. Les Fruits de la Passion
Arielle Dombasle . . . . .Nathalie
- • 0:17 - Brief left breast, lying on her stomach in bed with Klaus Kinski.
- ••• 0:40 - Full frontal nudity on bed, making love in front of O.
- • 1:00 - Very, very brief left breast, while grabbing her blouse out of Kinski's hands.

Straight Time (1978)
Dustin Hoffman . . . . Max Dembo
  0:38 - Very, very brief tip of penis in jail shower scene after getting sprayed by guard. Don't really see anything.
Theresa Russell . . . . .Jenny Mercer
- ••• 1:00 - Left breast, while in bed with Dustin Hoffman. Don't see her face.
M. Emmet Walsh . . . . .Earl Frank
- • 0:47 - Buns, handcuffed to fence in the middle of the road with his pants down.

The Stranger *(1986)*
Bonnie Bedelia . . . . Alice Kildee
- • 0:15 - Brief right breast sticking up from behind her lover's arm making love in bed during flashback sequence (B&W).
- • 0:19 - Brief left breast turning over in hospital bed when a guy walks in. Long shot, hard to see.
- •• 0:38 - Right breast again making love (B&W).

Straw Dogs *(1972)*
Susan George . . . . Amy
- •• 0:32 - Topless taking off sweater, tossing it down to Dustin Hoffman, then looking out the door at the workers.
- ••• 1:00 - Topless on couch getting raped by one of the construction workers.
Dustin Hoffman . . . . David

Street Hunter *(1990)*
Susan Napoli . . . . Eddie's Girl
- •• 0:40 - Topless in bed with Eddie (she's on the left, wearing white panties).

Streets of Fire *(1984)*
Ed Begley, Jr. . . . . Ben Gunn
Elizabeth Daily . . . . Baby Doll
Marine Jahan . . . . "Torchie's" Dancer
0:28 - Buns in G-string dancing in club.
0:34 - More dancing.
- • 0:35 - Very brief right breast under body stocking, then almost topless under stocking when taking off T shirt.
Diane Lane . . . . Ellen Aim
Amy Madigan . . . . McCoy
Bill Paxton . . . . Clyde
Rick Rossovich . . . . Officer Cooley

Streetwalkin' *(1985)*
Samantha Fox . . . . Topless Dancer
Melissa Leo . . . . Cookie
- •• 0:15 - Topless, stripping and taking off her top for a customer.
- • 0:18 - Brief right breast, having sex with her pimp on the floor.
Julie Newmar . . . . Queen Bee

Stripes *(1981)*
Sue Bowser . . . . Mud Wrestler
Dawn Clark . . . . Mud Wrestler
John Diehl . . . . Cruiser
Roberta Leighton . . . . Anita
- • 0:07 - Topless, wearing blue panties, while putting her shirt on and talking to Bill Murray.
Bill Paxton . . . .
Judge Reinhold . . . . Elmo
P.J. Soles . . . . Stella
Sean Young . . . . Louise Cooper

Stripped to Kill *(1987)*
Debra Lamb . . . . Amateur Dancer
Kay Lenz . . . . Cody Sheehan
- ••• 0:23 - Topless dancing on stage.
- ••• 0:47 - Topless dancing in white lingerie.
Deborah Ann Nassar . . . . Dazzle
- ••• 0:07 - Topless wearing a G-string dancing on stage with a motorcycle prop.

Stripped to Kill II *(1988)*
Jeannine Bisignano . . . . Sonny
0:06 - Buns, while wearing a black bra in dressing room.
- ••• 0:38 - Topless and buns during strip dance routine in white lingerie.
Maria Ford . . . . Shady
- •• 0:21 - Topless, dancing on table in front of the detective. Buns, walking away.
- • 0:40 - Brief upper half of left breast in the alley with the detective.
- •• 0:52 - Topless and buns during dance routine.
Marjean Holden . . . . Something Else
- •• 0:17 - Topless during strip dance routine.
Debra Lamb . . . . Mantra
- •• 0:04 - Topless during strip dance routine.
- ••• 0:42 - Topless in black lingerie during strip dance routine.
Karen Mayo-Chandler . . . . Cassandra
0:06 - Black bra and panties in dressing room.
- •• 0:18 - Topless taking off her top for a customer.

Stripper *(1985)*
Sara Costa . . . . herself
- ••• 0:16 - Topless doing strip dance routine.
- ••• 0:46 - Topless and buns dancing on stage in a G-string.
- ••• 1:12 - Topless doing another strip routine.
Venus de Light . . . . herself
- • 0:59 - Brief topless, on stage, blowing fire.
- ••• 1:07 - Topless and buns in black G-string, doing routine on stage, using fire.
Suzanne Primeaux . . . . herself
- •• 0:03 - Topless dancing on stage, kneeling on her left knee. Very brief buns in G-string.

The Stud *(1978; British)*
Minah Bird . . . . Molly
- •• 0:26 - Topless in bed when Tony is talking on the telephone.
Joan Collins . . . . Fontaine
- • 0:10 - Brief left breast making love with Tony in the elevator.
0:27 - Brief buns in panties, stockings and garter belt in Tony's apartment.
0:58 - Brief black bra and panties under fur coat in back of limousine with Tony.
- • 1:03 - Brief topless taking off dress to get in pool.
- • 1:04 - Nude in the pool with Tony.

Emma Jacobs. . . . . Alexandra
- •• 0:44 - In bra, then topless taking bra off in bedroom.
- • 0:48 - Close up of breasts making love with Tony in his dark apartment.
- • 1:14 - Topless in bed with Tony, yelling at him.

Sue Lloyd . . . . Vanessa
- • 1:04 - Topless in the swimming pool with Joan Collins and Tony.

Student Affairs (1987)

Jim Abele. . . . . Andrew Armstrong
- • 1:07 - Buns, when his friends play a practical joke on him in the shower.

Deborah Blaisdell . . . . Kelly
- ••• 0:26 - Topless sitting up in bed talking to a guy.

Louis Bonanno . . . . Louie Balducci

Jane Hamilton . . . . Veronica
- •• 0:48 - Topless changing in dressing room, showing herself off to a guy.
- • 0:51 - Brief topless in a school room during a movie.
- •• 0:56 - In black lingerie outfit, then topless in bedroom while she tape records everything.

Jeanne Marie. . . . . Robin Ready
- • 0:35 - Brief topless wearing black panties in bed trying to seduce a guy.
- ••• 0:41 - Topless making love with another guy, while banging her back against the wall.
- • 0:44 - Very brief topless in VW with a nerd.
- • 1:09 - Very brief topless falling out of a trailer home filled with water.

The Student Body (1975)

June Fairchild . . . . Mitzi Mashall
- • 0:15 - Brief topless and buns, running and jumping into the pool during party. Brief long shot topless, while in the pool.
- •• 0:21 - Topless getting into bed.

Peter Hooten. Carter Blalock

Jillian Kesner . . . . Carrie Rafferty
- •• 0:29 - Left breast, making out with Carter in the car.

Student Confidential (1987)

Corwyn Anthony. . . . . Greg
- • 1:26 - Buns, getting into bed with Susan.

Katherine Kriss. . . . . Elaine's Friend

Susie Scott . . . . Susan Bishop
- • 0:02 - Lying in bed covered with a gold sheet. Sort of right breast through her hair.
- •• 1:26 - Full frontal nudity standing in front of Greg.

The Student Nurses (1970)
a.k.a. Young LA Nurses

Karen Carlson . . . . Phred
- • 0:08 - Topless in bed with the wrong guy.
- 0:19 - In bra, on sofa with Dr. Jim Casper.
- ••• 0:50 - In bed with Jim, topless and buns getting out, then topless sitting in chair. Long scene.
- • 1:02 - Brief topless in bed.

Lawrence Casey . . . . Dr. Jim Casper
- •• 0:52 - Buns, walking to Karen Carlson to talk.

Elaine Giftos . . . . Sharon
- • 1:14 - Brief topless undressing and getting into bed with terminally ill boy. Dark, hard to see.

Barbara Leigh. . . . . Priscilla
- ••• 0:43 - Topless on the beach with Les. Long scene.

Richard Rust. . . . . Les
- • 0:43 - Buns, lying in sand with Barbara Leigh.

Pepe Serna. . . . . Luis

The Stunt Man (1980)

Barbara Hershey. . . . . Nina
- • 1:29 - Buns and side view of left breast in bed in a movie within a movie while everybody is watching in a screening room.

Steve Railsback. . . . . Cameron

Submission (1976; Italian)

Andrea Ferreol . . . . Juliet
- •• 0:43 - Topless in room with Franco Nero and Elaine.

Lisa Gastoni . . . . Elaine
- 0:28 - Lower frontal nudity on the floor behind the counter with Franco Nero.
- • 0:30 - Left breast, while talking on the phone with her husband while Nero fondles her.
- •• 0:32 - Topless and buns, making love on bed with Nero. Slightly out of focus.
- •• 0:33 - Topless getting out of bed to talk to her daughter.
- ••• 0:43 - Topless in room with Juliet and Nero. Long scene.
- ••• 0:45 - More topless on the floor yelling at Nero. 0:54 - Brief lower frontal nudity in slip, sitting on floor with Nero.
- ••• 0:57 - Left breast, while wearing slip, walking in front of pharmacy. Then full frontal nudity while wearing only stockings. Long scene.
- •• 1:00 - Topless in pharmacy with Nero, singing and dancing.
- •• 1:28 - Topless when Nero cuts her slip open. Nice close up.
- •• 1:29 - Topless getting up out of bed.

Franco Nero. . . . . Armond
- • 0:32 - Brief side view of buns when making love with Lisa on the bed.

Sudden Impact (1983)

Clint Eastwood. . . . . Harry Callahan

Sondra Locke . . . . Jennifer Spencer

Lisa London . . . . Young Hooker
- •• 1:04 - Topless in bathroom, walking to Nick in the bed.

Sugar Cookies (1973)

Lynn Lowry . . . . Alta/Julie
- ••• 0:03 - Brief topless falling out of hammock, then topless on couch with Max, then nude. Long scene. (Brunette wig as Alta.)
- 0:13 - Brief right breast in B & W photo.
- • 0:14 - Left breast on autopsy table.
- •• 0:20 - Topless in movie.

•• 0:52 - Topless taking off clothes for Mary Woronov. Topless on bed. (Blonde as Julie.)
••• 1:00 - Topless and buns with Woronov in bedroom, nude while wrestling with her.
• 1:04 - Topless with Woronov in bathtub.
••• 1:06 - Nude in bed with Woronov. Long scene.
•• 1:11 - Right breast outside displaying herself to Max.
• 1:16 - Right breast, then topless making love with Woronov.
••• 1:20 - Nude with Woronov and Max. Long scene.
Daniel Sador . . . . .Gus
  0:37 - Buns in bed with Dola, then running around.
George Shannon. . . . . Max
•• 0:14 - Buns, on top of Mary Woronov in bed.
Monique Van Vooren . . . . Helene
Jennifer Wells . . . . Max's Secretary
• 0:28 - Topless in red panties in Max's office while he talks on the phone, then lower frontal nudity.
•• 0:56 - Full frontal nudity getting dressed.
Mary Woronov . . . . Camila
••• 0:10 - Topless in bathtub, then wearing white panties exercising topless on the floor. Long scene.
• 1:04 - Topless with Julie in the bathtub.
• 1:07 - Brief topless, then left breast, making love with Julie.
• 1:17 - Brief right breast when Lynn Lowry yanks her dress up.

Summer Affair (1979)
Ornella Muti . . . . .Lisa
• 0:44 - Topless silhouette in cave by the water.
• 1:00 - Brief topless getting chased around in the grass and by the beach.

Summer Heat (1987)
Lori Singer. . . . . .Roxy
•• 0:36 - Topless in bed with Jack. Kind of dark and hard to see.

Summer Job (1989)
Amy Baxter . . . . , Susan
•• 0:10 - Topless changing in room with the other three girls. More topless sitting on bed.
  0:15 - In white bra, looking at herself in mirror.
• 0:34 - Brief topless when her swimsuit top pops off after saving a guy in swimming pool.
• 0:45 - In white lingerie, brief topless on stairs, flashing her breasts (wearing curlers).
  1:00 - Brief buns in two piece swimsuit turning around.
• 1:23 - Topless pulling her top down talking to Mr. Burns.
Kirt Earhar. . . . . Tom
• 0:30 - Buns in black G-string bikini when his swim trunks get ripped off.
• 0:43 - Buns in G-string underwear getting out of bed and going to the bathroom.
Cari Mayor . . . . Donna
• 0:10 - Brief topless twice, taking off her top before and after Herman comes into the room.

George O. . . . . .Herman
• 0:17 - Buns getting his underwear torn off by five angry women then running back to his room.
Sherrie Ann Rose . . . . .Kathy Shields
  0:25 - In bed wearing white bra and panties talking to Bruce. Long scene.
  0:52 - Buns, walking around in swimsuit and jacket.
•• 0:53 - Topless taking off swimsuit top kneeling by the phone, then brief buns standing up.
  1:15 - In yellow two piece swimsuit walking on the beach.
•• 1:24 - Brief topless taking off her yellow top on the beach talking to Bruce.
Renee Shugart . . . . .Karen
  0:15 - In lingerie reading a magazine.
• 0:42 - Topless taking off her top. Long shot, dark.
• 0:45 - In white lingerie, standing on stairs, then very brief left breast flashing.

Summer Lovers (1982)
Peter Gallagher . . . . Michael Pappas
• 0:22 - Buns, running into the water after Valerie Quennessen.
• 0:54 - Frontal nudity getting ready to dive off a rock while Daryl Hannah and Quennessen watch. Long shot, hard to see anything.
Daryl Hannah. . . . . Cathy Featherstone
• 0:07 - Very brief topless getting out of bed.
  0:17 - In a two piece swimsuit.
  0:54 - Buns, lying on rock with Valerie Quennessen watching Michael dive off a rock.
  0:56 - In a swimsuit again.
• 1:03 - Brief right breast sweeping the balcony.
Valerie Quennessen . . . . .Lina
• 0:12 - Topless on balcony.
••• 0:19 - Nude on the beach with Michael.
• 0:23 - Brief topless in a cave with Michael.
•• 0:30 - Topless lying on the floor with Michael.
  0:54 - Buns, lying on a rock with Daryl Hannah watching Michael dive off a rock.
• 1:03 - Left breast in bed.
•• 1:05 - Topless dancing on the balcony.
  1:09 - Topless on the beach.
Hans Van Tongeren . . . . Jan Tolin

Summer Night (1987; Italian)
Mariangela Melato. . . . . Signora Bolk
•• 0:26 - Topless behind gauze net over bed making love with a German guy.
•• 1:02 - Topless on the bed making love with the prisoner.
•• 1:09 - Topless again.
••• 1:13 - Buns, walking out of the ocean, then topless with wet hair.

Summer School (1987)
Kirstie Alley . . . . Robin Bishop
Ken Olandt . . . . Larry
•• 0:48 - Brief buns wearing a red G-string in a male stripper club.

Summer School Teachers *(1975)*
Candice Rialson . . . . Conklin T.
- • 0:14 - Breasts and buns when Mr. Lacy fantasizes about what she looks like. Don't see her face, but it looks like her.
- ••• 0:38 - Topless outside with other teacher, kissing on the ground.

A Summer Story *(1988)*
Imogen Stubbs . . . . Megan David
- •• 0:36 - Left breast several times, then right breast while making love with Frank in barn.
  0:41 - Very, very brief buns, frolicking in pond at night with Frank.
  1:03 - Very brief silhouette of left breast during Frank's flashback sequence.
James Wilby . . . . Frank Ashton
- • 0:08 - Buns, in creek with Mr. Garten while skinny dipping.
Susannah York . . . . Mrs. Narracrombe

Summer's Games *(1987)*
Amy Baxter . . . . Boxer/Girl from Penthouse
- •• 0:04 - Topless opening her swimsuit top after contest. (1st place winner.)
- •• 0:18 - Topless during boxing match.
Andi Bruce . . . . News Anchor
  0:12 - Brief right breast turning around to look at monitor.
- • 0:42 - Topless turning around to look at the monitor.
Lori Deann Pallett . . . . Torch Carrier
- • 0:00 - Half topless running in short T-shirt carrying torch.
- •• 0:04 - Topless opening her swimsuit top after contest. (2nd place winner.)
Teri Lynn Peake . . . . Penthouse Girl

Superchick *(1978)*
Uschi Digard . . . . Mayday
- ••• 0:42 - Buns and topless getting whipped acting during the making of a film, then talking to three people.
Joyce Jillson . . . . Tara B. True/Superchick
- • 0:03 - Brief upper half of right breast leaning back in bathtub.
- •• 0:06 - Topless in bed throwing cards up.
- • 0:16 - Brief topless under net on boat with Johnny.
- • 0:29 - Brief right breast several times in airplane restroom with a Marine.
  1:12 - Buns, frolicking in the ocean with Johnny. Don't see her face.
- • 1:27 - Close up of breasts (probably body double) when sweater pops open.
Candy Samples . . . . Lady on Boat
- ••• 0:08 - Topless in bed with Johnny on boat.

Superfly *(1972)*
Sheila Frazier . . . . Georgia
- •• 0:40 - Topless and buns, making love in the bathtub with Superfly.

Surf Nazis Must Die *(1986)*
Bobbie Bresee . . . . Smeg's Mom
Dawn Wildsmith . . . . Eva
- • 0:25 - Topless being fondled at the beach wearing a wet suit by Adolf. Mostly right breast.

Surfacing *(1980)*
Kathleen Beller . . . . Kate
  0:22 - Very brief buns, pulling down pants to change. Dark, hard to see.
  0:23 - Very brief right breast undressing. Dark, hard to see.
- • 0:24 - Very, very brief topless turning over in bed.
  0:25 - Buns, standing next to bed.
- ••• 1:23 - Topless washing herself in the water. One long shot, one side view of right breast.
Joseph Bottoms . . . . Joe
- • 0:23 - Buns, in bed with Kathleen Beller.

The Surrogate *(1984; Canadian)*
Carole Laure . . . . Anouk Vanderlin
- • 0:48 - Very brief topless when Frank rips her blouse open in his apartment.
Barbara Law . . . . Maggie Simpson
Marilyn Lightstone . . . . Dr. Harriet Forman
Shannon Tweed . . . . Lee Wake
- ••• 0:03 - Topless taking a Jacuzzi bath.
- • 0:42 - Brief topless changing in bedroom, then in bra getting dressed. Long shot.
- ••• 1:02 - Topless in sauna talking with Frank. Long scene.

Survivor *(1987)*
Sue Kiel . . . . The Woman
- ••• 0:33 - Right breast, then topless and buns making love with Survivor in hammock. Long scene.

Suzanne *(1980; Canadian)*
Jennifer Dale . . . . Suzanne
- •• 0:29 - Topless when boyfriend lifts her sweatshirt up when she's sitting on couch doing homework.
- •• 0:53 - Topless with Nicky on the floor.

Suzanne *(1973)*
a.k.a. The Second Coming of Suzanne
Suzanne has nudity in it, *The Second Coming of Suzanne* has the nudity cut out.
Sondra Locke . . . . Suzanne
- •• 0:27 - Topless sitting, looking at a guy. Brief left breast several times lying down.
- ••• 0:29 - Topless lying down.

Swamp Thing *(1981)*
Adrienne Barbeau . . . . Alice Cable
- • 1:03 - Side view of left breast washing herself off in the swamp. Long shot.

Swann in Love *(1984; French/German)*
Marie-Christine Barrault . . . . Madame Verdunn
Jeremy Irons . . . . Charles Swann

Ornella Muti . . . . Odette de Crécy
- •• 1:15 - Brief left breast, making love with Jeremy Irons.
- ••• 1:28 - Topless sitting on bed talking to Irons.

Swashbuckler (1976)
Peter Boyle . . . . Lord Durant
Genevieve Bujold . . . . Jane Barnet
- • 1:00 - Very brief side view nude, diving from the ship into the water. Long shot, don't really see anything.
- • 1:01 - Buns and brief side of left breast seen from under water.
Anjelica Huston . . . . Woman of Dark Visage
Pepe Serna . . . . Street Entertainer
Dorothy Tristan . . . . Alice
Brenda Venus . . . . Bath Attendant

Sweet Country (1985)
Jane Alexander . . . . .Anna
- • 1:39 - Brief side view of left breast after getting out of bed.
Carole Laure . . . . Eva
- •• 0:31 - Topless changing in apartment while Randy Quaid watches.
- • 0:43 - Nude in auditorium with other women prisoners.
- ••• 1:13 - Nude in bed with Quaid.
Joanna Pettet . . . . Monica

Sweet Revenge (1987)
Nancy Allen. . . . . Jillian Grey
Gina Gershon . . . . K.C.
- • 0:41 - Brief topless in water under a waterfall with Lee.
Michele Little . . . . Lee
- • 0.41 - Brief topless in water under a waterfall with K.C.

Sweet Sixteen (1982)
Steve Antin . . . . .Hank Burke
Aleisa Shirley. . . . . Melissa Morgan
- • 0:16 Side view of body, nude, taking a shower.
- • 1:11 - Topless undressing to go skinny dipping with Hank. Dark, hard to see.
- • 1:13 - Topless, getting out of the water.
Susan Strasberg. . . . . .Joanne Morgan

Sweet Sugar (1972)
Pamela Collins. . . . . .Dolores
- • 0:26 - Brief topless when doctor tears her bra off.
- ••• 0:50 - Topless in the shower with Phyllis Davis.
Phyllis Davis . . . . Sugar
- ••• 0:34 - Topless in bed with a guard.
- ••• 0:50 - Topless in the shower with Dolores.
- •• 0:57 - Brief topless in the bathroom.
Ella Edwards . . . . Simone
- • 0:58 - Topless in bed with Mojo.

Sweet William (1980; British)
Jenny Agutter. . . . . .Ann
- 0:27 - Buns, standing on balcony with Sam Waterston.
- •• 0:28 - Topless sitting on edge of the bed while talking with Waterston.
- • 0:44 - Brief left breast when Waterston takes her blouse off in the living room.
Anna Massey . . . . Edna
Sam Waterston. . . . . William
- • 0:27 - Buns, seen through a window in the door, standing on balcony with Jenny Agutter.

Swept Away (1975; Italian)
a.k.a. Swept Away...by an unusual destiny in the blue sea of august
Mariangela Melato. . . . . .Raffaela Lenzetti
- •• 1:10 - Topless on the sand when Giancarlo Giannini catches her and makes love with her.

Swing Shift (1984)
Alana Collins . . . . Frankie Parker
- 0:11 - Buns in B&W photo that Christine Lahti shows to Fred Ward. Possible photo composite.
Ed Harris . . . . Jack Walsh
- • 0:03 - Very brief frontal nudity when he sits down in chair wearing a towel around his waist.
Goldie Hawn . . . . Kay Walsh
Kurt Russell .Lucky Lockhart
Fred Ward . . . . Biscuits Toohey

The Swinging Cheerleaders (1974)
Colleen Camp . . . . Mary Ann
Sandra Dempsey . . . . 1st Girl at Tryout
Rosanne Katon . . . . Lisa
- •• 0:25 - Topless taking off her blouse in her teacher's office. Half of right breast while he talks on the phone.
Cheryl Smith . . . . .Andrea
- •• 0:12 - Topless taking off her bra and putting sheer blouse on.
- • 0:17 - Left breast, several times, sitting in bed with Ross.

The Sword and the Sorcerer (1982)
Kathleen Beller. . . . . .Alana
- • 0:54 - Side view of buns, lying face down getting oil rubbed all over her.
Shelly Taylor Morgan . . . . Bar-Bra
- • 0:54 - Brief topless when Lee Horsley crashes through the window and almost lands on her.

Sylvester (1985)
Melissa Gilbert . . . . .Charlie
- • 0:23 - Very, very brief topless struggling with a guy in truck cab. Seen through a dirty windshield.
- •• 0:24 - Very brief left breast after Richard Farnsworth runs down the stairs to help her. Seen from the open door of the truck.

Taffin (1988; U.S./British)
Pierce Brosnan . . . . Mark Taffin
Alison Doody . . . . Charlotte
 • 0:14 - Very, very brief side view of right breast when Pierce Brosnan rips her blouse open. Long shot, hard to see.
Tina Shaw. . . . . Lola the Stripper
 •• 1:04 - Topless doing routine in a club.

Tai-Pan (1986)
Bryan Brown. . . . . Dirk Struan/"Tai-Pan"
Joan Chen. . . . . May May
 0:55 - In sheer top sitting on bed talking to Bryan Brown.
 • 0:56 - Brief left breast washing herself, hard to see anything.
 1:14 - Sheer top again.
 1:30 - Sheer top again.
Janine Turner . . . . Shevaun

Take Two (1988)
Grant Goodeve . . . . .Barry Griffith/Frank Bentley
 • 0:31 - Buns, in bed with Robin Mattson.
 ••• 0:46 - Buns, getting into bed with Mattson again.
Robin Mattson .Susan Bentley
 0:21 - Exercising in yellow outfit while Frank Stallone plays music.
 •• 0:25 - Brief topless taking a shower.
 0:26 - Showing Grant Goodeve her new two piece swimsuit.
 ••• 0:29 - Topless in bed with Goodeve.
 ••• 0:45 - Right breast in shower, then topless getting into bed.
 • 0:47 - Brief topless getting out of bed and putting an overcoat on.
 0:51 - One piece swimsuit by the swimming pool.
 1:12 - In two piece swimsuit at the beach.
 ••• 1:28 - Topless taking a shower after shooting Goodeve in bed.
Karen Mayo-Chandler. . . . . Dorothy
 •• 1:17 - Brief topless on bed when her gold dress is pulled down a bit.
Suzanne Slater . . . . Sherrie
 •• 0:11 - Topless in office talking with Grant Goodeve, wearing panties, garter belt and stockings.
 • 1:00 - Topless undressing to get into hot tub wearing black underwear bottom.

Takin' It All Off (1987)
Becky LeBeau . . . . Becky
 •• 0:16 - Topless and brief full frontal nudity getting introduced to Allison.
 ••• 0:23 - In black bra and panties, then nude doing a strip routine outside.
 • 0:35 - Brief full frontal nudity pushing Elliot into the pool.
 • 0:36 - Brief topless in studio with Allison again.
 • 0:36 - Brief left breast in dance studio with Allison.
 •• 1:23 - Nude, dancing with all the other women on stage.

Francesca "Kitten" Natividad . . . . .Betty Bigones
 ••• 0:12 - Nude, washing herself in the shower.
 •• 0:39 - Nude, on stage in a giant glass, then topless backstage in her dressing room.
 •• 0:42 - Topless in flashbacks from *Takin' It Off*.
 0:46 - Topless in group in the studio.
 ••• 0:53 - Nude, dancing on the deck outside. Some nice slow motion shots.
 •• 1:16 - Topless on stage in club.
 ••• 1:23 - Nude, dancing with all the other women on stage.
Jean Poremba. . . . . Allison
 0:36 - In pink bra and G-string.
 ••• 0:49 - In white lingerie, then topless, then nude dancing.
 ••• 0:58 - Topless, dancing outside when she hears the music.
 ••• 0:59 - Nude dancing in a park.
 •• 1:01 - Nude dancing in a laundromat.
 ••• 1:03 - Nude dancing in a restaurant.
 ••• 1:07 - Nude in shower with Adam.
 •• 1:13 - Topless dancing for the music in a studio.
 ••• 1:23 - Nude dancing with all the other women on stage.
Gail Thackray. . . . . Hannah

Takin' It Off (1984)
Francesca "Kitten" Natividad . . . . .Betty Bigones
 •• 0:01 - Topless dancing on stage.
 ••• 0:04 - Topless and buns dancing on stage.
 ••• 0:29 - Topless in the Doctor's office.
 ••• 0:32 - Nude dancing in the Psychiatrists' office.
 ••• 0:39 - Nude in bed with a guy during fantasy sequence playing with vegetables and fruits.
 •• 0:49 - Topless in bed covered with popcorn.
 • 0:51 - Nude doing a dance routine in the library.
 ••• 1:09 - Nude splashing around in a clear plastic bathtub on stage.
 •• 1:20 - Nude at a fat farm dancing.
 •• 1:24 - Nude running in the woods in slow motion.
Angelique Pettijohn . . . . .Anita Little
Ashley St. Jon. . . . . Sin
 ••• 0:20 - Topless and buns doing two dance routines on stage.
 •• 0:53 - Nude, stripping and dancing in the library.

Taking Care of Business (1990)
Jill Johnson. . . . . Tennis Court Girl
Loryn Locklin . . . . Jewel
 • 0:42 - Buns and very brief side view, twice, seen through door, changing by the pool. Then in black two piece swimsuit.

Tales From the Darkside, The Movie (1990)
Rae Dawn Chong. . . . . Carola
 • 1:09 - Left breast in blue light, twice, with James Remar. Don't see her face.
Deborah Harry. . . . . Betty
Christian Slater. . . . . Andy

Talking Walls (1987)

Judy Baldwin. . . . .

Sybil Danning . . . . Bathing Beauty

Sally Kirkland. . . . . Hooker

Marie Laurin . . . . Jeanne

Steve Shellen. . . . . Paul Barton
- •• 0:58 - Buns, taking off his clothes and running down railroad tracks.

June Wilkinson . . . . Blonde
- • 0:13 - Brief left breast, in car room, getting green towel yanked off.

  0:14 - Very, very brief left breast in car room again. Dark.
- •• 1:08 - Brief topless, getting green towel taken off.

The Tall Guy (1990)

Jeff Goldblum . . . . Dexter King

  0:34 - Brief right cheek of buns, rolling around on the floor with Kate. Don't see his face.

Neil Hamilton . . . . Naked George
- •• 0:04 - Buns, walking around apartment talking to Jeff Goldblum. Brief frontal nudity (out of focus).
- • 0:06 - More buns, when getting introduced to Goldblum.
- • 1:22 - Brief buns, during end credits.

Anna Massey. . . . . Mary

Emma Thompson . . . . Kate
- ••• 0:33 - Very brief right breast, brief buns, then topless during funny love making scene with Jeff Goldblum.

Tango & Cash (1989)

Dori Courtney. . . . . .Dressing Room Girl
- • 1:06 - Topless, sitting in chair looking in the mirror in the background. Long shot.

Michael Jeter. . . . . Skinner

Roxanne Kernohan . . . . .Dressing Room Girl
- • 1:06 - Brief topless in dressing room with three other girls. She's the second one in the middle.

Tamara Landry . . . . Girl in Bar

Kurt Russell . . . . Cash
- •• 0:31 - Brief buns walking into the prison shower room with Sylvester Stallone.

Sylvester Stallone . . . . Ray Tango
- •• 0:31 - Brief buns walking into the prison shower room with Kurt Russell.

Tanya's Island (1980; Canadian)

Vanity. . . . . Tanya

  0:04 - Very brief topless and buns covered with paint during B&W segment.
- ••• 0:07 - Nude caressing herself and dancing during the opening credits.
- •• 0:09 - Nude making love on the beach.

  0:11 - Brief right breast, while talking to Lobo.
- •• 0:19 - Brief topless on the beach with Lobo, then more topless while yelling at him.
- • 0:28 - Mostly topless in flimsy halter top exploring a cave.

- • 0:33 - Full frontal nudity undressing in tent.
- • 0:35 - Left breast sleeping. Dark, hard to see.

  0:37 - Buns while sleeping.
- • 0:40 - Topless superimposed over another scene.

  0:48 - Brief buns swimming in the ocean.
- •• 0:51 - Full frontal nudity walking out of the ocean and getting dressed.
- • 0:53 - Brief topless in open blouse.
- •• 1:08 - Topless in middle of compound when Lobo rapes her in front of Blue.
- • 1:16 - Full frontal nudity running through the jungle in slow motion. Brief buns.

Target (1985)

Ilona Grubel. . . . . Carla
- • 1:12 - Brief topless in bed with Matt Dillon.

Tarzan, The Ape Man (1981)

Bo Derek . . . . Jane
- ••• 0:43 - Nude taking a bath in the ocean, then in a wet white dress.
- • 1:35 - Brief topless painted all white.
- • 1:45 - Topless washing all the white paint off in the river with Tarzan.
- •• 1:47 - Topless during the ending credits playing with Tarzan and the orangutan. (When I saw this film in a movie theater, the entire audience actually stayed to watch the credits!)

Richard Harris. . . . . Parker

Miles O'Keeffe . . . . Tarzan
- • 0:45 - Sort of buns, under loin cloth in the surf. Lots of other semi-bun shots in the loin cloth throughout the rest of the film.

  1:09 - Buns, in loin cloth at side of lake with Bo Derek.
- • 1:48 - Buns, in loin cloth wrestling with orangutan during end credits.

Tattoo (1981)

Maud Adams . . . . .Maddy
- • 0:22 - Very brief topless taking off clothes and putting a bathrobe on.
- •• 0:23 - Topless opening bathrobe so Bruce Dern can start painting.
- •• 0:25 - Brief topless getting into the shower to take off body paint.
- •• 0:58 - Brief topless and buns getting out of bed.
- •• 1:04 - Topless, knocked out on table before Dern starts tattooing her.
- ••• 1:07 - Topless looking at herself in the mirror with a few tattoos on.
- •• 1:24 - Topless lying on table masturbating while Dern watches through peep hole in the door.
- ••• 1:36 - Full frontal nudity taking off robe then making love with Dern (her body is covered with tattoos).

Bruce Dern. . . . . Karl Kinski
- •• 1:36 - Buns, while making love with Maud Adams before she kills him.

The Teacher (1974)
Angel Tompkins . . . . Diane Marshall
- ••• 0:09 - Topless on a boat taking off her swimsuit.
- ••• 0:12 - More topless on the boat getting a suntan.
- ••• 0:36 - Topless taking off her top in bedroom, then buns and topless taking a shower.
- • 0:41 - Brief right breast lying back on bed.
- •• 0:43 - Brief topless opening her bathrobe for Jay North.
- •• 0:47 - Side view of right breast lying on bed, then right breast from above.
- •• 0:52 - Topless in boat after making love.

Teachers (1984)
Lee Grant . . . . Dr. Burke
Julia Jennings . . . . The Blonde
- •• 0:05 - Brief left breast, while sitting up in bed with Nick Nolte.

Nick Nolte . . . . Alex
JoBeth Williams . . . . Lisa
- • 1:39 - Brief topless taking off clothes and running down school hallway yelling at Nick Nolte.

Teen Lust (1978)
Kirsten Baker . . . . Carol Hill
- • 0:45 - Brief side view of left breast changing clothes in her bedroom.

Perry Lang . . . . Terry
- • 0:01 - Buns in jock strap getting his pants pulled down while he does pull ups.

The Tempest (1982)
Raul Julia . . . . Kalibanos
Susan Sarandon . . . . Aretha
- 0:58 - In braless white tank top washing clothes with Molly Ringwald in the ocean.
- 1:53 - In wet white T-shirt on balcony during rainstorm with Jason Robards and Raul Julia.
- 1:55 - In wet white T-shirt on the beach.
- • 1:57 - Brief right, then left breasts in open T-shirt saving someone in the water.

Terminal Choice (1985; Canadian)
Teri Austin . . . . Lylah Crane
- 0:14 - Full frontal nudity, covered with blood on operating table. Long shot.
- 0:21 - Right breast, on table being examined by Ellen Barkin. Dead, covered with dried blood.
- 0:26 - Very brief left breast under plastic on table, hard to see.

Ellen Barkin . . . . Mary O'Connor
Joe Spano . . . . Frank Holt
- ••• 0:34 - Buns, taking off towel and getting dressed in locker room while talking to Anna.
- • 0:49 - Buns, making love in bed with Anna. Long shot, don't see his face.

Diane Venora . . . . Anna
- 0:44 - In lingerie, talking to Frank.
- • 0:48 - Brief left breast, making love in bed with Frank. Don't see her face.

Cheryl-Ann Wilson . . . . Nurse Fields

Terminal Entry (1986)
Barbara Edwards . . . . Lady Electric
- ••• 0:05 - Topless taking a shower and getting a towel during video game scene.

Jill Terashita . . . . Gwen

Terminal Exposure (1988)
Tara Buckman . . . .
Hope Marie Carlton . . . . Christie
- ••• 1:11 - Topless in bathtub licking ice cream off a guy.

Ava Fabian . . . . Bruce's Girl
Luann Lee . . . . Bruce's Girl
Nicole Rio . . . . Hostage Girl

Terminal Island (1973)
Phyllis Davis . . . . Joy Lange
- ••• 0:39 - Topless and buns in a pond, full frontal nudity getting out, then more topless putting blouse on while a guy watches.

Marta Kristen . . . . Lee Phillips
Barbara Leigh . . . . Bunny Campbell
- ••• 0:22 - Topless and buns undressing in room while Bobbie watches from the bed.

Tom Selleck . . . . Dr. Norman Milford
Clyde Ventura . . . . Dillon
- •• 0:42 - Buns, taking off pants with Phyllis Davis, then covered with honey and bees, then running to jump into a pond.

The Terminator (1984)
Michael Biehn . . . . Kyle Reese
- • 0:06 - Side view of buns after arriving from the future. Brief buns running down the alley. A little dark.

Linda Hamilton . . . . Sarah Connor
- •• 1:18 - Brief topless about four times making love on top of Michael Biehn in motel room.

Bill Paxton . . . . Punk Leader
Rick Rossovich . . . . Matt
Arnold Schwarzenegger . . . . The Terminator
- ••• 0:03 - Buns, kneeling by garbage truck, walking to look at the city and walking toward the three punks at night.

The Terror on Alcatraz (1986)
Sandy Brooke . . . . Mona
- • 0:05 - Right breast on bed getting burned with a cigarette by Frank.

Alisa Wilson . . . . Clarissa
- • 1:14 - Brief topless opening her blouse to distract Frank, so she can get away from him.

Terror Train (1980; Canadian)
Vanity . . . . Merry
Joy Boushel . . . . Pet
- •• 0:49 - Topless wearing panties in sleeper room on train with Mo.

Jamie Lee Curtis . . . . Alena

Tess (1979; French/British)
Arielle Dombasle . . . . Mercy Chant
Peter Firth . . . . Angel Clare
Suzanna Hamilton . . . . Izz

Nastassja Kinski . . . . Tess Durbeyfield
- • 0:47 - Brief left breast, opening blouse in field to feed her baby.

Texas Detour (1977)
Priscilla Barnes . . . . Claudia Hunter
- ••• 1:03 - Topless, changing clothes and walking around in bedroom. Wearing white panties. This is her best topless scene.
- • 1:11 - Topless sitting up in bed with Patrick Wayne.

Lindsay Bloom . . . . Sugar McCarthy

That Cold Day in the Park (1969)
Suzanne Benton . . . . Nina
- • 0:38 - Side view of left breast putting top on. Long shot.
- • 1:05 - Topless taking off her clothes and getting into the bathtub. Another long shot.

That Obscure Object of Desire
(1977; French/Spanish)
Carole Bouquet . . . . .Conchita
- ••• 0:53 - Topless in bedroom.
- ••• 1:01 - Topless in bed with Fernando Rey.

Angela Molina . . . . .Conchita
- • 0:53 - Brief topless in bathroom.
- •• 1:20 - Nude dancing in front of a group of tourists.
- • 1:29 - Brief topless behind a gate taunting Fernando Rey.

There Was a Crooked Man (1970)
Jeanne Cooper . . . . Prostitute
- • 0:18 - Brief left breast trying to seduce the sheriff, Henry Fonda, in a room.

Kirk Douglas . . . . .Paris Pitman, Jr.
- • 0:11 - Brief upper half of buns leaving bedroom wearing only his gun belt.
- •• 1:09 - Brief buns and balls, jumping into a barrel to take a bath in prison.

Lee Grant . . . . Mrs. Bullard
Pamela Hensley . . . . Edwina
- • 0:12 - Very brief left breast lying on pool table with a guy.

There's a Girl in My Soup (1970)
Christopher Cazenove . . . . Nigel
Gabrielle Drake . . . . Julia Halford-Smythe
- • 0:09 - In beige bra with Peter Sellers, brief left breast in bed with him. Might be a body double.

Goldie Hawn . . . . Marion
- • 0:37 - Buns and very brief right side view of her body getting out of bed and walking to a closet to get a robe. Long shot.

Geraldine Sherman . . . . Caroline
- •• 0:43 - Topless in bed, then getting out after Goldie Hawn splashes water on her.

They're Playing with Fire (1984)
Sybil Danning . . . . .Diane Stevens
0:04 - In two piece swimsuit on boat. Long scene.
- ••• 0:08 - Topless and buns making love on top of Jay in bed on boat. Nice!

- •• 0:10 - Topless and buns getting out of shower, then brief side view of right breast.
0:43 - In black bra and slip, in boat with Jay.
- •• 0:47 - In black bra and slip, at home with Michael, then panties, then topless and buns getting into shower.
- ••• 1:12 - In white bra and panties in room with Jay then topless.

Thief of Hearts (1984)
(Special Home Video Version.)
Barbara Williams . . . . Mickey Davis
- • 0:46 - Right breast in bathtub when her husband comes in and tries to read her diary.
- ••• 0:53 - Topless making love with Steven Bauer in his condo.

Romy Windsor . . . . Nicole
- ••• 0:12 - Full frontal nudity with Steven Bauer getting dressed.

Thieves of Fortune (1989)
Michael Nouri . . . . Juan Luis
- • 0:57 - Buns, taking a shower outside. Long shot.

Claudia Udy . . . . Marissa
Shawn Weatherly . . . . Peter
- • 1:09 - Brief topless several times, taking a shower (while wearing beard and moustache disguise).
- ••• 1:21 - Topless in white panties distracting tribe so she can get away.

Things are Tough all Over (1982)
Evelyn Guerrero . . . . .Donna
Richard "Cheech" Marin . . . . Mr. Slyman
- • 0:21 - Buns in the laundromat dryer.

Third Degree Burn (1989; Made for Cable Movie)
Virginia Madsen . . . . .Anne Scholes
Treat Williams . . . . Scott Weston
- • 0:43 - Brief buns taking off his robe with Virginia Madsen in his bedroom.

Those Lips, Those Eyes (1980)
Glynnis O'Connor . . . . .Ramona
- • 0:37 - Left breast in car with Tom Hulce. Dark, hard to see.
- •• 1:12 - Topless and buns on bed with Tom Hulce. Dark.

Threshold (1983; Canadian)
Jeff Goldblum . . . . .Aldo Gehring
Donald Sutherland . . . . Dr. Vrain
Mare Winningham . . . . .Carol Severance
- • 0:56 - Brief full frontal nudity, lying on operating table, then side view of left breast getting prepped for surgery.

Thrilled to Death (1988)
Rebecca Lynn . . . . Elaine Jackson
- • 0:01 - Topless twice when Baxter opens her blouse.
- •• 0:31 - Topless in locker room talking to Nan.

Christine Moore . . . . Nan Christie
0:31 - In bra in women's locker room.
••• 0:38 - Topless in office with Mr. Dance just before killing him.
Christina Veronica. . . . . Satin
•• 0:33 - Topless talking to Cliff during porno film shoot.

Thumb Tripping *(1972)*
Meg Foster . . . . Shay
• 1:19 - Very, very brief topless leaning back in field with Jack. Long shot.
• 1:20 - Topless at night. Face is turned away from the camera.
Mariana Hill. . . . . Lynn
• 1:14 - In black bra, then very, very brief left breast when Jack comes to cover her up.
• 1:19 - Topless frolicking in the water with Gary.
1:20 - In white swimsuit, dancing in bar.

Thunder Alley *(1985)*
Clancy Brown . . . . Weasel
Melanie Kinnaman . . . . .Star
• 0:52 - Brief topless under water in pool talking to a guy.
• 1:14 - Topless and buns making love on bed and getting out.
Jill Schoelen. . . . . Beth
Roger Wilson. . . . . Richie

Thunderbolt and Lightfoot *(1974)*
Jeff Bridges . . . . Lightfoot
Clint Eastwood . . . . John "Thunderbolt" Doherty
June Fairchild . . . . Gloria
• 0:20 - Very brief right breast getting dressed in the bathroom after making love with Clint Eastwood.
Leslie Oliver. . . . . Teenager
•• 1:16 - Brief topless in bed when robbers break in and George Kennedy watches her.
Luanne Roberts . . . . .Suburban Housewife
• 0:57 - Brief full frontal nudity standing behind a sliding glass door tempting Jeff Bridges.

Tie Me Up! Tie Me Down! *(1990; Spanish)*
Victoria Abril . . . . .Marina Osorio
••• 0:24 - Full frontal nudity playing with a frogman toy in the bathtub.
• 0:34 - Buns and brief side of right breast, getting dressed.
•• 0:44 - Topless changing clothes, then on TV while Maximo watches.
••• 1:09 - Topless changing clothes.
••• 1:16 - Right breast, then topless in bed making love with Ricky.
Antonio Banderas . . . . .Ricky
• 1:17 - Buns in mirror on ceiling, making love with Victoria Abril. Long shot.

A Tiger's Tale *(1988)*
Ann-Margret . . . . Rose
• 0:45 - Side view of left breast in bra, then topless jumping up after fire ants start biting her. Brief buns running along a hill. Long shot, probably a body double.
C. Thomas Howell . . . . Bubber Drumm
• 0:38 - Upper half of buns getting undressed in bedroom while Ann-Margret changes in the bathroom.
Leigh Lombardi . . . . .Marcia
Kelly Preston . . . . Shirley
•• 0:03 - Topless in the car, letting C. Thomas Howell open her blouse and look at her breasts.
Angel Tompkins . . . . .La Vonne

Tigers in Lipstick *(1979)*
Ursula Andress . . . . The Stroller and The Widow
0:02 - In black bra, panties and garter belt and stockings opening her fur coat to cause an accident.
0:48 - In slip posing for photographer.
• 0:50 - Very brief topless when top of slip accidentally falls down.
• 0:51 - More topless with the photographer.
Laura Antonelli. . . . . The Pick Up
0:24 - In brown lingerie lying in bed, then getting dressed.
0:34 - In same lingerie, getting undressed, then in bed.
Sylvia Kristel . . . . The Girl
0:04 - Topless in photograph on the sand.
0:06 - Braless in sheer nightgown lying in bed.
•• 0:09 - Topless lying in bed with The Arab.
•• 0:16 - Lying in bed in red lingerie, then left breast for awhile.

Tightrope *(1984)*
Randi Brooks .Jamie Cory
••• 0:20 - Topless taking off her robe and getting into the spa.
0:24 - Buns, dead in the spa while Clint Eastwood looks at her.
Genevieve Bujold . . . . .Beryl Thibodeaux
Clint Eastwood. . . . . Wes Block
• 0:33 - Buns, on the bed on top of Becky. Slow pan, red light, covered with sweat.
Margaret Howell .Judy Harper
• 0:44 - Brief left breast viewed from above in a room with Clint Eastwood.
Rebecca Perle. . . . . Becky Jacklin
Jamie Rose . . . . Melanie Silber
0:07 - Buns, lying face down on bed, dead.

Till Marriage Do Us Part *(1974; Italian)*
Laura Antonelli. . . . . Eugenia
•• 0:58 - Topless in the barn lying on hay after guy takes off her clothes.
•• 1:02 - Full frontal nudity standing up in bathtub while maid washes her.

438

•• 1:07 - Right breast with chauffeur in barn.
•• 1:36 - Topless surrounded by feathers on the bed while priest is talking.
Karin Schubert . . . . Evelyn

Time Walker (1982)
Nina Axelrod. . . . . Susie
Greta Blackburn . . . . Sherri
Melissa Prophet. . . . . Jennie
• 0:27 - Brief topless putting bra on while a guy watches from outside the window.
1:17 - Very, very brief right breast in shower when the mummy comes to get the crystal.
Allene Simmons . . . . Nurse
Jason Williams . . . . Jeff

Tintorera (1977)
Jennifer Ashley. . . . .
Priscilla Barnes. . . . .
• 1:12 - Very brief topless dropping her beer into the water.
• 1:14 - Topless, on the beach after the shark attack (on the left).
Andres Garcia . . . . Miguel
• 0:41 - Very brief frontal nudity in boat kitchen with Susan George and Steve.
•• 0:42 - Nude, picking up George and throwing her overboard.
Susan George . . . . Gabriella
• 0:42 - Very brief topless waking up Steve.
Fiona Lewis . . . . Patricia
0:20 - Side view of left breast in silhouette. Long shot, hard to see. Nude swimming under water just before getting eaten by a shark. Don't see her face.

To Die For (1988)
Steve Bond . . . . Tom
Eloise Broady. Girl at Party
Ava Fabian . . . . Franny
Brendan Hughes . . . . Vlad Tepish
• 1:13 - Buns, making love with Kate.
Remy O'Neill. . . . . Jane
Amanda Wyss . . . . Celia Kett

To Kill a Clown (1971)
Blythe Danner. . . . . Lily Frischer
• 1:10 - Side view of left breast sitting on bed talking to Alan Alda. Hair covers breast, hard to see. Buns, getting up and running out of the house.

To Live and Die in L.A. (1985)
Debra Feuer . . . . Bianca Torres
• 1:47 - Brief topless on video tape being played back on TV in empty house, hard to see anything.
Darlanne Fluegel. . . . . Ruth Lanier
•• 0:44 - Brief topless and buns, in bed when William Petersen comes home.
1:29 - In stockings on couch with Petersen.
• 1:50 - Very brief topless on bed with Petersen in a flashback.

John Pankow . . . . John Vukovich
• 1:06 - Buns, changing in the locker room.
William L. Petersen. . . . . Richard Chance
• 0:44 - Brief frontal nudity, but hard to see anything because it's dark.

The Tomb (1987)
Michelle Bauer . . . . Nefartis
Sybil Danning . . . . Jade
Francesca "Kitten" Natividad . . . . Stripper
••• 0:19 - Topless and buns in G-string dancing on stage.
• 0:21 - Brief topless again.
Dawn Wildsmith . . . . Anna Conda
••• 0:54 - Topless taking off robe in room with Michelle Bauer, then getting pushed onto a bed full of snakes.

Tomboy (1985)
Jerry Dimone . . . . Randy Star
•• 0:59 - Buns, making love with Betsy Russell in the exercise room.
Betsy Russell. . . . . Tomasina "Tommy" Boyd
•• 0:44 - In wet T-shirt, then brief topless after landing in the water with her motorcycle.
•• 0:59 - Topless making love with the race car driver in an exercise room.
Kristi Somers . . . . Seville Ritz
•• 0:14 - Topless taking a shower while talking to Betsy Russell.
• 0:53 - Brief topless stripping at a party.
Cynthia Ann Thompson . . . . Amanda
• 0:23 - Brief right breast getting out of car in auto repair shop.
•• 1:02 - Topless delivering drinks to two guys in the swimming pool.

Too Hot To Handle (1975)
Cheri Caffaro . . . . Samantha Fox
•• 0:06 - Topless wearing a black push-up bra and buns in black G-string.
• 0:13 - Full frontal nudity lying on boat.
••• 0:39 - Topless making love in bed with Dominco.
••• 0:55 - Full frontal nudity taking off clothes and lying in bed.
• 1:06 - Brief left breast in bed with Dominco.
Aharon Ipalé. . . . . Dominco de la Torres
• 0:39 - Buns, in bed with Cheri Caffaro. Dark, hard to see.

The Toolbox Murders (1978)
Marciee Drake . . . . Debbie
•• 0:09 - In wet blouse, then topless taking it off and putting a dry one on.
Evelyn Guerrero . . . . Maria

Total Exposure (1991)
Jeff Conaway . . . . Peter Keynes
Deborah Driggs . . . . Kathy
••• 0:08 - Topless dancing in front of Jeff Conaway, then making love in bed with him. Long scene.
• 0:22 - Brief side view topless in B&W photos that Conaway looks at.

- 0:24 - Brief buns in black G-string and side of right breast changing clothes in locker room.
- •• 0:25 - Topless and buns, trying to beat up Season Hubley.

Season Hubley . . . . Andi Robinson
0:07 - Buns, getting into hot tub. Probably a body double.
Michael Nouri . . . . Dave Murphy

The Touch (1971; U.S./Swedish)
Bibi Andersson . . . . Karen Vergerus
- 0:31 - Topless in bed with Elliott Gould.
- ••• 0:56 - Topless kissing Gould.
  1:13 - Very, very brief right breast washing Gould's hair in the sink.

Tough Guys (1986)
Kirk Douglas . . . . Archie Long
- 1:36 - Buns, standing on moving train, mooning Charles Durning.
Darlanne Fluegel . . . . Skye Foster
- 0:47 - Very brief side view of right breast, leaning over to kiss Kirk Douglas.
Lisa Pescia . . . . Customer #1
Hilary Shepard . . . . Sandy

Tough Guys Don't Dance (1987)
Wings Hauser . . . . Regency
Ryan O'Neal . . . . Tim Madden
Isabella Rossellini . . . . Madeleine
Debra Sandlund . . . . Patty Lareine
- •• 1:24 - Topless ripping her blouse off to kiss the policeman after they have killed and buried another woman.

The Toxic Avenger: Part II (1988)
John Altamura . . . . Toxic Avenger
Phoebe Légerè . . . . Claire
- 0:31 - Brief right breast, while caressing herself while making out with the Toxic Avenger.

Toy Soldiers (1983)
Terri Garber . . . . Amy
- 0:18 - Brief right breast taking off her tank top when the army guys force her. Her head is down.
Tim Robbins . . . . Bean
Tracy Scoggins . . . . Monique

Track 29 (1988; British)
Sandra Bernhard . . . . Nurse Stein
Colleen Camp . . . . Arlanda
Christopher Lloyd . . . . Henry Henry
- 0:34 - Very brief side view of his buns lying in the hospital getting spanked by Sandra Bernhard.
Gary Oldman . . . . Martin
- 1:24 - Buns, holding onto Christopher Lloyd and stabbing him.
Theresa Russell . . . . Linda Henry

The Tracker (1988; Made for Cable Movie)
Kris Kristofferson . . . . Noble Adams
Mark Moses . . . . Tom Adams
- •• 0:35 - Buns, getting out of the river after washing himself, then getting hassled by some bandits.

Tracks (1977)
Dennis Hopper . . . . Sgt. Jack Falen
- •• 0:58 - Frontal nudity running through the train. Long scene.
Sally Kirkland . . . . uncredited
Taryn Power . . . . Stephanie
- 0:32 - Brief side view of right breast changing in her room on the train. Don't see her face.
- 1:15 - Brief left breast making love with Dennis Hopper in a field.

Trading Places (1983)
Jamie Lee Curtis . . . . Ophelia
- ••• 1:00 - Topless in black panties after taking red dress off in bathroom while Dan Aykroyd watches.
- ••• 1:09 - Topless and black panties taking off halter top and pants getting into bed with a sick Aykroyd.

Traveling Man (1989; Made for Cable Movie)
John Lithgow . . . .
- 0:48 - Brief buns, trying to get the VCR away from Mona in her living room.

Traxx (1988)
Priscilla Barnes . . . . Mayor Alexandria Cray
Gwendolyn Hajek . . . . Playmate
Suzanne Primeaux . . . . Hooker #1
- •• 0:37 - Topless, dancing on stage while wearing a mask.

Tropical Snow (1989)
David Carradine . . . . Oskar
Nick Corri . . . . Tavo
- •• 0:11 - Buns in bed with Madeline Stowe.
- •• 0:44 - Buns, standing naked in police station.
Madeline Stowe . . . . Marina
- 0:05 - Very brief side view of left breast putting red dress on.
- 0:11 - Buns, lying in bed. Very brief right breast sitting up. (I wish they could have panned the camera to the right!)
- •• 0:24 - Topless in mirror putting red dress on.
  0:32 - Buns, lying on top of Tavo in bed.
- 0:54 - Brief topless making love in the water with Tavo. Then buns, lying on the beach (long shot.)
  1:22 - Long shot side view of right breast in water with Tavo.

Trouble in Mind (1986)
Genevieve Bujold . . . . Wanda
Keith Carradine . . . . Coop
Kris Kristofferson . . . . Hawk
Lori Singer . . . . Georgia
- 1:01 - Very brief left breast, in bed with Kris Kristofferson.

The Trouble with Dick (1986)

Susan Dey. . . . . Diane
Elaine Giftos . . . . Sheila
Elizabeth Gorcey. . . . . Haley
- • 0:13 - Very brief left breast in gaping T-shirt while she lies on bed, plays with a toy and laughs.
  0:26 - Lower half of buns under robe on sofa with Dick.
  0:27 - Half of right breast on top of Dick in bed.

Tom Villard . . . . Dick Kendred
  0:30 - Side view of buns, leaving Haley's room.
- • 0:58 - Buns from under his shirt, getting out of bed to open the door.

Truck Stop Women (1974)

Uschi Digard. . . . . .Truck Stop Woman
- •• 0:18 - Topless getting arrested in the parking lot by the police officer, then buns and topless getting frisked in a room.

Claudia Jennings. . . . . Rose
- • 0:27 - Brief topless taking off blouse and getting into bed.
  0:48 - Brief side view of right breast in mirror, getting dressed.
- • 1:10 - Brief topless wrapping and unwrapping a towel around herself.

True Blood (1989)

Jeff Fahey .Raymond Trueblood
Sherilyn Fenn . . . . Jennifer Scott
- • 1:22 - Very brief right breast in closet trying to stab Spider with a piece of mirror.

True Love (1989)

Al Juliano. . . . . Male Stripper
- • 0:43 - Buns in G-string dancing on stage in a club.

Tuff Turf (1984)

Robert Downey, Jr. . . . . Jimmy Parker
Kim Richards. Frankie Croyden
  1:07 - In black lingerie getting dressed.
- • 1:29 - Brief topless supposedly of a body double (Fiona Morris) in bedroom with James Spader but I have heard from a very reliable source that it really was her.

James Spader . . . . Morgan Hiller

The Tunnel (1987)

Jane Seymour . . . . Maria
- • 0:29 - Very brief left breast in bed with Peter Weller when the sheet is pulled down.
- •• 0:44 - Brief right beast getting dressed, throwing off her robe.

Peter Weller. . . . . Juan Pablo

Turkish Delight (1974; Dutch)

Rutger Hauer. . . . . Erik
- ••• 0:01 - Brief nude walking around his apartment talking to a woman he has just picked up.
- • 0:04 - Buns, in bed (covered with a sheet), then very brief frontal nudity throwing another girl out.

- •• 0:36 - Frontal nudity getting up to answer the door with flowers.
- •• 1:12 - Frontal nudity lying in bed depressed.
- •• 1:16 - Buns, making love with Olga in bed.

Monique Van De Ven. . . . . Olga
- •• 0:24 - Topless when Rutger Hauer opens her blouse, then nude on the bed.
- •• 0:27 - Topless, waking up in bed.
- ••• 0:33 - Topless on bed with Hauer, then nude getting up to fix flowers.
  0:42 - Buns, with Hauer at the beach.
- •• 0:46 - Topless modeling for Hauer, then brief nude running around outside.
- •• 0:54 - Topless in bed with open blouse with flowers.
- • 1:04 - In wet T-shirt in the rain with Hauer, then brief topless coming down the stairs.

Tusks (1990)

Lucy Gutteridge. . . . . Micah Hill
- •• 0:23 - Topless in tub taking a bath.

Twice a Woman (1979)

Bibi Andersson. . . . . .Laura
- • 0:05 - Topless taking off her bra and putting a blouse on.
- • 0:06 - Brief side view of left breast, getting into bed, brief left breast lying back in bed.

Sandrine Dumas. . . . . .Sylvia
- • 0:06 - Topless, kneeling on the bed, then more brief topless in bed with Bibi Andersson.
- ••• 0:47 - Brief right breast, then topless in bed with Andersson. Long scene.
- • 1:15 - Left breast, lying in bed with Anthony Perkins. Long shot.
- ••• 1:23 - Topless with Andersson.

Twice Dead (1989)

Charlie Spradling . . . . .Tina
- •• 1:11 - Topless taking off jacket next to bed.
- ••• 1:14 - Topless making love with her boyfriend in bed.
- • 1:18 - Brief topless dead in bed.

Jill Whitlow. . . . . Robin/Myrna
  0:27 - In white slip, getting ready for bed, then walking around the house.

Twins of Evil (1971)

Madeleine Collinson. . . . . .Freida Gelhorn
- •• 1:07 - Right breast, then brief topless undoing dress, then full frontal nudity after turning into a vampire in bedroom.

Mary Collinson. Maria Gelhorn

The Twist (1976)

Ann-Margret . . . . Charlie Minerva
- • 0:24 - Left breast when Claire daydreams someone is sticking a pin into Ann-Margret's breast. A little bloody. Body double.
- • 1:24 - Very, very brief left breast during Bruce Dern's daydream. Seen from above, body double again.

Sybil Danning . . . . Jacques' Secretary
•• 1:24 - Brief topless sitting next to Bruce Dern during his daydream.
Bruce Dern . . . . William
•• 0:45 - Buns, taking off his clothes and walking onto stage during a play. Long shot.
Sydne Rome . . . . Nathalie

Twisted Justice (1990)
Karen Black . . . . Mrs. Granger
Bonnie Paine . . . . Hooker
•• 0:11 - Topless in black panties and stockings, getting photographed.
Tanya Roberts . . . . Secretary
Shannon Tweed . . . . Hinkle

Two Moon Junction (1988)
Sherilyn Fenn . . . . April
••• 0:07 - Topless taking a shower in the country club shower room.
•• 0:27 - Brief topless on the floor kissing Perry.
•• 0:42 - Topless in gas station restroom changing camisole tops with Kristy McNichol.
• 0:54 - Brief topless making love with Perry in a motel room.
••• 1:24 - Nude at Two Moon Junction making love with Perry. Very hot!
• 1:40 - Brief left breast and buns in the shower with Perry.
Kristy McNichol. . . . . Patti Jean
•• 0:42 - Topless in gas station restroom changing camisole tops with Sherilyn Fenn.
Richard Tyson . . . . Perry
• 0:58 - Very, very brief buns wrestling with April in a motel room. Dark, hard to see.

Two to Tango (1988)
Adrianne Sachs . . . . Cecilia Lorca
•• 0:29 - Side of left breast and buns in bedroom with Lucky Lara. More left breast while Dan Stroud watches through camera.
•• 0:59 - Topless and buns in bed with Dan Stroud.
Alberto Segado . . . . Lucky Lara
• 0:29 - Buns on top of Adrienne Sachs, making love with her in bed.

The Unbearable Lightness of Being (1988)
Juliette Binoche . . . . Tereza
0:22 - In white bra in Tomas' apartment.
• 1:33 - Brief topless jumping onto couch.
1:36 - Buns, sitting in front of fire being photographed, then running around, trying to hide.
• 2:18 - Left breast in The Engineer's apartment.
Daniel Day-Lewis. Thomas
Derek De Lint . . . . Franz
Lena Olin . . . . Sabina
•• 0:03 - Topless in bed with Tomas looking at themselves in a mirror.
0:17 - In black bra and panties looking at herself in a mirror on the floor.
1:21 - In black bra, panties, garter belt and stockings.

•• 1:29 - Topless and buns while Tereza photographs her. Long shots, hard to see.
• 1:43 - Very brief left breast, in bed with Tomas. 2:32 - Brief topless in B&W photo found in a drawer by Tomas.
Stellan Skarsgard . . . . The Engineer
• 2:18 - Buns, making love with Tereza.

Under Cover (1987)
David Denney . . . . Hassie Pearl
• 0:43 - Brief buns walking around boy's locker room wearing his jock strap.
Jennifer Jason Leigh . . . . Tanille Lareoux

Under the Gun (1989)
Sam J. Jones . . . . Braxton
• 0:41 - Brief buns, taking a shower at Vanessa Williams place. Don't see his face.
Vanessa Williams . . . . Samantha Richards

Under the Volcano (1984)
Anthony Andrews. . . . . Hugh Firmin
Jacqueline Bisset. . . . . Yvonne Firmin
Albert Finney . . . . Geoffrey Firmin
••• 0:49 - Buns and brief frontal nudity in bathroom with Jacqueline Bisset and Anthony Andrews when they try to give him a shower.
•• 0:52 - Buns and very brief frontal nudity, putting on his underwear.

The Underachievers (1987)
Edward Albert . . . .
Barbara Carrera . . . . Katherine
Becky LeBeau . . . . Ginger Bronsky
••• 0:40 - Topless in swimming pool playing with an inflatable alligator after her exercise class has left.
Jewel Shepard . . . . Sci-Fi Teacher
• 0:27 - Topless ripping off her Star Trek uniform when someone enters her classroom. Dark, hard to see.
Susan Tyrrell. . . . . Mrs. Grant

Unfaithfully Yours (1984)
Nastassja Kinski . . . . Daniella Eastman
• 0:37 - Topless and buns in the shower.
Dudley Moore . . . . Claude Eastman
Cassie Yates . . . . Carla Robbins

The Unholy (1988)
Jill Carroll . . . . Millie
• 1:10 - Very brief upper half of left breast talking in the courtyard with Ben Cross.
Hal Holbrook . . . . Archbishop Mosley

An Unmarried Woman (1978)
Alan Bates . . . . Saul
Jill Clayburgh . . . . Erica
0:05 - Dancing around the apartment in white long sleeve T-shirt and white panties.
•• 0:12 - Brief topless getting dressed for bed, kind of dark and hard to see.
•• 1:10 - In bra and panties in guy's apartment, then brief topless lying on bed.

The Unnameable (1988)

Laura Albert . . . . .Wendy Barnes
- •• 0:46 - Left breast while lying on floor kissing John, then brief buns when he pulls her panties down.

Until September (1984)

Karen Allen . . . . .Mo Alexander
- •• 0:41 - Topless in bed making love with Thierry Lhermitte.
- •• 1:13 - Topless and buns walking from bed to Lhermitte.
- • 1:25 - Brief topless jumping out of bathtub.

Christopher Cazenove. Philip
Maryam D'Abo . . . . Nathalie
Thierry Lhermitte . . . . Xavier de la Pérouse
- •• 0:43 - Buns, after making love with Karen Allen.
- 0:53 - Almost frontal nudity getting out of bathtub.

Up 'n' Coming (1987)

(R-rated version reviewed, X-rated version available.)
Marilyn Chambers. . . . . .Cassie
- ••• 0:01 - Nude, getting out of bed and taking a shower.
- •• 0:08 - Topless making love in bed with the record producer.
- • 0:30 - Brief topless in bed with two guys.
- •• 0:47 - Full frontal nudity getting suntan lotion rubbed on her by another woman.
- •• 0:55 - Topless taking off her top at radio station.

Lisa De Leeuw . . . . .Altheah Anderson
- • 0:33 - Very brief topless by the pool when her robe opens.
- • 0:48 - Brief topless walking around the house when her robe open.
- •• 0:49 - Left breast talking with a guy, then topless walking into the bedroom.

Monique Gabrielle . . . . Boat Girl #1
- • 0:39 - Topless wearing white shorts on boat. Long shot.
- • 0:40 - More brief nude shots on the boat.

Up the Creek (1984)

Tim Matheson. . . . . Bob McGraw
Dan Monahan. . . . . Max
Julie Montgomery . . . . .Lisa
Tom Nolan . . . . Whitney
Lori Sutton . . . . .Cute Girl
- • 0:40 - Brief topless pulling up her T-shirt to get the crowd excited while cheerleading the crowd.

Jeana Tomasino. . . . . Molly

Up! (1976)

Russ Meyer film.
Raven De La Croix. . . . . Margo Winchester
Francesca "Kitten" Natividad. . . . . Greek Chorus
Candy Samples . . . . The Headsperson

Used Cars (1980)

Cheryl Rixon . . . . Margaret
- •• 0:29 - Topless after getting her dress torn off during a used car commercial.

Kurt Russell . . . . Rudy Russo
- • 1:04 - Very brief buns putting on red underwear.

Betty Thomas. . . . . Bunny
- 0:37 - Dancing on top of a car next to Kurt Russell wearing pasties to attract customers (wearing a brunette wig).

Jack Warden. . . . . Roy L. Fuchs/Luke Fuchs

Valentino Returns (1988)

Veronica Cartwright. . . . . .Pat Gibbs
- ••• 0:33 - Topless sitting in bed with Frederic Forrest. Fairly long scene.

Barry Tubb. . . . . .Wayne Gibbs
- •• 1:15 - Buns, fighting two other guys after skinny dipping with Jenny Wright at night. Very, very brief, blurry frontal nudity after getting hit and rolling into the water.

Jenny Wright . . . . Sylvia Fuller

Valley Girl (1983)

Michael Bowen . . . . Tommy
Nicholas Cage . . . . Randy
Colleen Camp . . . . .Sarah Richman
Elizabeth Daily . . . . .Loryn
- •• 0:16 - In bra through open jumpsuit, then brief topless on bed with Tommy.

Cameron Dye. . . . . .Fred
Deborah Foreman . . . . .Julie
Joyce Hyser . . . . .Joyce

The Vals (1982)

Tiffany Bolling . . . . .Valley Attorney and Parent
Gina Calabrese. . . . . .Annie
- • 0:04 - Topless changing clothes in bedroom with three of her friends. Long shot, hard to see.
- • 0:15 - Right breast making love with a guy at a party.
- 0:32 - In black bra with her friends in a store dressing room.

Jill Carroll . . . . .Sam

Vampire at Midnight (1988)

Esther Alise. . . . . Lucia Giannini
- ••• 1:01 - In black lingerie, then topless and buns while taking off clothes to wish Roger a happy birthday.

Barbara Hammond. . . . . Kelly
- •• 0:07 - Topless and buns, getting out of the shower and drying herself off.
- • 0:16 - Left breast, dead, in Victor's car trunk. Blood on her.

Jeanie Moore . . . . .Amalia
- •• 0:32 - Topless getting up to run an errand.

Christina Whitaker . . . . Ingrid
Jason Williams . . . . .Detective Roger Sutter

Vampire Cop (1990)

Melissa Moore . . . . .Melanie Roberts
- ••• 0:46 - Topless in bed with the Vampire Cop.
- •• 0:51 - Right breast, sitting in bed talking with Hans.
- • 1:21 - Right breast, in bed on the phone during end credits.

443

Vampire Hookers *(1979)*
Lenka Novak . . . . Suzy
    0:22 - In sheer green dress getting into coffin.
    0:33 - In sheer green dress again.
    0:45 - In sheer green dress again.
  •• 0:51 - Topless in bed during the orgy with the guy and the other two Vampire Hookers.

Vampire Lovers *(1970; British)*
Ingrid Pitt . . . . Marcilla/Carmilla
  •• 0:32 - Topless and buns in the bathtub and reflection in the mirror talking to Emma.
Madeline Smith . . . . .Emma
  •• 0:32 - Topless trying on a dress in the bedroom after Carmilla has taken a bath.
  • 0:49 - Topless in bed, getting her top pulled down by Carmilla.

Vampire's Kiss *(1989)*
Maria Conchita Alonso . . . . Alva
    0:47 - In white bra, ironing her clothes in her living room.
    0:59 - In white bra getting attacked by Nicholas Cage.
Elizabeth Ashley . . . . Dr. Glaser
Jennifer Beals . . . . Rachel
    0:14 - Almost topless in bed with Nicholas Cage. Squished left breast against Cage while she bites him. In one shot, you can see the beige pastie she put over her left nipple.
    0:27 - In bed again with Cage.
    0:41 - In black lingerie taking her dress off for Cage.
Nicholas Cage . . . . Peter Loew
Kasi Lemmons . . . . Jackie
  •• 0:05 - In black bra and panties, then topless in living room with Nicholas Cage.

Vampyres *(1974)*
Murray Brown . . . . .Ted
  •• 0:22 - Buns, making love in bed with Fran.
  • 0:56 - Buns, falling into bed.
Anulka Dziubinska . . . . Miriam
  • 0:00 - Brief full frontal nudity in bed with Fran, kissing each other before getting shot.
  • 0:43 - Topless taking a shower with Fran.
  ••• 0:58 - Topless and buns in bed with Fran, drinking Ted's blood. Brief lower frontal nudity.
Sally Faulkner . . . . Harriet
  • 1:14 - Side of left breast, partial buns, then right breast while making love with John in the trailer.
  •• 1:22 - Full frontal nudity getting her clothes ripped off by Fran and Miriam in the wine cellar before being killed.

Vanessa *(1977)*
Olivia Pascal . . . . Vanessa
  ••• 0:08 - Nude undressing, taking a bath and getting washed by Jackie. Long scene.
  ••• 0:16 - Buns, then full frontal nudity getting a massage.
  • 0:26 - Topless getting fitted for new clothes.

  • 0:47 - Full frontal nudity when Adrian rips her clothes off.
  ••• 0:56 - Full frontal nudity on beach with Jackie.
  ••• 1:05 - Nude making love with Jackie in bed. Nice close up of left breast.
  •• 1:19 - Full frontal nudity lying on the table.
  •• 1:27 - Topless in white panties, garter belt and stockings shackled up by Kenneth.

Vanishing Point *(1971)*
Gilda Texter . . . . Nude Rider
  • 1:17 - Topless riding motorcycle.
  ••• 1:19 - Topless riding motorcycle and walking around without wearing any clothes. Long scene.

Vice Academy *(1988)*
Ken Abraham . . . . .Dwayne
Ginger Lynn Allen . . . . Holly
    1:20 - Buns, in white lingerie outfit when graduation robe gets torn off.
Linnea Quigley . . . . Didi
  ••• 0:45 - Topless making love with Chuck while he's handcuffed.
Karen Russell . . . . Shawnee
  •• 0:09 - Topless exposing herself to Duane to disarm him.
  •• 1:13 - Topless pulling her top down to distract a bad guy.

Vice Academy, Part 2 *(1990)*
Ginger Lynn Allen . . . . Holly
  • 0:44 - Buns in black bra, panties, garter belt and stockings.
  •• 1:04 - Buns in G-string, then topless dancing with Linnea Quigley on stage at club.
Scott Layne . . . . Petrolino
  • 0:49 - Buns, in men's locker room twice when Linnea Quigley and Ginger Lynn Allen come in.
Melissa Moore . . . . .Glaze
Linnea Quigley . . . . Didi
  •• 1:04 - Buns in G-string, then topless dancing with Ginger Lynn Allen on stage at club.

Video Vixens *(1973)*
Sandra Dempsey . . . . .Actress
  •• 0:05 - Full frontal nudity, lying down getting make up put on.
George "Buck" Flower . . . . Rex Boorski
  •• 0:52 - Frontal nudity taking off his pants, then buns in bed with actress during filming of a movie. In B&W.
Robyn Hilton . . . . .Inga
  •• 1:18 - Topless, opening her top in a room full of reporters.
Kimberly Hyde . . . . Claudine
Marius Mazmanian . . . . Psychiatrist
  •• 0:42 - Buns and balls from behind, frolicking on couch with his patient. In B&W.
Bernie Scorpio . . . . Turnip Twin
  ••• 1:05 - Frontal nudity standing next to his identical twin brother after their trial.

Lennie Scorpio . . . . Turnip Twin
•• 1:03 - Frontal nudity, then buns on top of victim in bed.
••• 1:05 - Frontal nudity standing next to his identical twin brother after their trial.
Cheryl Smith. . . . . Twinkle Twat Girl
••• 0:24 - Full frontal nudity doing a commercial, sitting next to pool.

Videodrome (1983; Canadian)
Deborah Harry .Nicki Brand
•• 0:16 - Topless rolling over on the floor when James Woods is piercing her ear with a pin.
0:22 - In black bra, sitting on couch with James Woods.
James Woods . . . . .Max Renn

Vindicator (1986; Canadian)
a.k.a. *Frankenstein '88*
Teri Austin. . . . . .Lauren Lehman
• 0:30 - Very brief left breast and buns in mirror getting out of the bubble bath covered with bubbles. Long shot, hard to see anything.
Pam Grier . . . . Hunter

Violets Are Blue (1986)
Bonnie Bedelia . . . . Ruth Squires
Kevin Kline . . . . Henry Squires
• 1:02 - Brief buns, standing up and putting on his shorts, on island with Sissy Spacek.
Sissy Spacek . . . . .Gussie Sawyer

Virgin High (1990)
Michelle Bauer . . . . Miss Bush
Linnea Quigley . . . . .Kathleen
•• 0:24 - Topless, nonchalantly making love on top of Derrick.
•• 0:55 - Brief topless several times on top of Derrick, then topless.
• 1:21 - Topless in photo during party.

Visionquest (1985)
Madonna . . . . .Nightclub singer
Linda Fiorentino . . . . .Carla
Matthew Modine . . . . .Louden Swain
• 1:29 - Very brief buns taking off underwear to get weighed for wrestling match.
Daphne Zuniga. . . . . Margie Epstein

Vital Signs (1989)
Diane Lane . . . . Gina Wyler
••• 1:11 - In white bra, then topless making love with Michael in the basement.
Adrian Pasdar . . . . .Michael Chatham
1:11 - Upper half of buns, with his pants partially down in basement with Diane Lane.
Jimmy Smits . . . . Dr. David Redding
Gigi Vorgan. . . . . Nell

W. B., Blue and the Bean (1988)
a.k.a. *Bail Out*
Linda Blair. . . . . .Nettie

David Hasselhoff .White Bread
Debra Lamb. . . . . Motel Clerk
• 0:42 - Full frontal nudity opening door in motel to talk to David Hasselhoff.

Wall Street (1987)
Michael Douglas . . . . .Gordon Gekko
Daryl Hannah. . . . . .Darian Taylor
Hal Holbrook . . . . Lou Mannheim
Annie McEnroe. . . . . .Muffie Livingston
Sylvia Miles . . . . .Realtor
Suzen Murakoshi . . . . Girl in Bed
• 0:13 - Brief full frontal nudity getting out of bed and walking past the camera in Charlie Sheen's bedroom (slightly out of focus).
Martin Sheen . . . . .Carl Fox
Monique Van Vooren . . . .
Sean Young . . . . Kate Gekko

Warlords (1988)
Michelle Bauer. . . . . .Harem Girl
••• 0:14 - Topless, getting her top ripped off, then shot by a bad guy.
David Carradine. . . . . Dow
Greta Gibson . . . . .Harem Girl
•• 1:05 - Topless in tent with the other harem girls. Holding a snake.
•• 1:09 - Topless again.
Debra Lamb. . . . . .Harem Girl
••• 0:14 - Topless, getting her blouse ripped off by a bad guy, then kidnapped.
••• 0:17 - Topless in harem pants shackled to another girl.
Brinke Stevens . . . . Dow's Wife
Dawn Wildsmith . . . . .Danny

Warm Summer Rain (1989)
Kelly Lynch. . . . . .Kate
• 0:03 - Brief topless and side view of buns in B&W lying on floor during suicide attempt. Quick cuts topless getting shocked to start her heart.
•• 0:23 - Full frontal nudity when Guy gets off her in bed.
•• 0:24 - Side view of right breast in bed, then topless.
••• 0:58 - Buns then topless, getting washed by Guy on the table.
••• 1:07 - Brief buns making love. Quick cuts full frontal nudity spinning around. Side view of left breast with Guy.
••• 1:09 - Nude picking up belongings and running out of burning house with Guy.
Barry Tubb. . . . . .Guy
•• 0:23 - Lower frontal nudity getting off Kelly Lynch in bed.
0:25 - Side view of buns dreaming in bed.
•• 0:58 - Frontal nudity kneeling on floor and behind the table while washing Lynch.
• 1:00 - Buns while getting washed by Lynch.
• 1:07 - Brief buns making love with Lynch. Quick cuts.
••• 1:09 - Nude picking up belongings and running out of burning house with Lynch.

The Warrior and the Sorceress (1984)

David Carradine . . . . Kain
Maria Socas. . . . . Naja
••• 0:15 - Topless wearing robe and bikini bottoms in room with Zeg. Sort of brief buns, leaving the room.
•• 0:22 - Topless standing by a wagon at night.
•• 0:27 - Topless in room with David Carradine. Dark. Most of buns when leaving the room.
• 0:31 - Topless and buns climbing down wall.
• 0:34 - Brief topless, then left breast with rope around her neck at the well.
• 0:44 - Topless when Carradine rescues her.
• 0:47 - Topless walking around outside.
• 0:57 - More topless outside.
• 1:00 - Topless watching a guy pound a sword.
• 1:05 - Topless under a tent after Carradine uses the sword. Long shot.
• 1:09 - Topless during big fight scene.
• 1:14 - Topless next to well. Long shot.

Warrior Queen (1987)

Tally Chanel . . . . Vespa
••• 0:09 - Topless hanging on a rope, being auctioned.
••• 0:20 - Topless and buns with black slave girl.
•• 0:37 - Nude, before attempted rape by Goliath.
•• 0:57 - Topless during rape by Goliath.
Sybil Danning . . . . Berenice
Samantha Fox. . . . . Philomena
Josephine Jaqueline Jones . . . . Chloe
••• 0:20 - Topless making love with Vespa.

Watchers II (1990)

Irene Miracle. . . . . .Sarah Ferguson
0:28 - In pink leotard, going into aerobics studio.
••• 0:40 - Side view in black bra, then topless a few times in the bathtub.
Tracy Scoggins .Barbara White
Marc Singer . . . . .Paul Ferguson
Mary Woronov . . . . Dr. Glatman

We're No Angels (1989)

Robert De Niro . . . . Ned
Bruno Kirby. . . . . Deputy
Demi Moore . . . . Molly
• 0:18 - One long shot, then two brief side views of left breast when Robert De Niro watches from outside. Reflections in the window make it hard to see.
Sean Penn. . . . . Jim

A Wedding (1978)

Geraldine Chaplin. . . . . .Rita Billingsley
Mia Farrow . . . . Buffy Brenner
••• 1:10 - Topless posing in front of a painting, while wearing a wedding veil..
Lauren Hutton. . . . . Florence Farmer

Weeds (1987)

Nick Nolte. . . . . .Lee Umstetter
•• 0:51 - Buns, getting out of bed and putting his pants on.

Weekend Pass (1984)

Sara Costa . . . . Tuesday Del Mundo
••• 0:07 - Buns in G-string, then topless during strip dance routine on stage.
Graem McGavin. . . . . .Tawny Ryatt
Valerie McIntosh . . . . Etta
Hilary Shepard . . . . .Cindy Hazard
•• 1:05 - In red bra, then topless taking off bra.
• 1:07 - Buns and topless getting into bathtub.
Ashley St. Jon . . . . .Xylene B-12
•• 0:13 - Topless dancing on stage.

Weekend Warriors (1986)

Monique Gabrielle . . . . Showgirl on plane
•• 0:51 - Brief topless taking off top with other show-girls.
La Gena Hart . . . . Debbie (car hop)
Brenda Strong . . . . Danny El Dubois
• 0:44 - Topless, lit from the side, standing in the dark.
Tom Villard . . . . .Mort Seblinsky

Weird Science (1985)

Judie Aronson. . . . . .Hilly
Robert Downey, Jr. . . . . .Ian
Kelly Le Brock. . . . . Lisa
0:12 - In blue underwear and white top baring her midriff for the two boys when she is first created.
1:29 - In blue leotard and grey tube top gym clothes to teach boy's gym class.
Kym Malin . . . . Girl Playing Piano
• 0:55 - Brief topless several times as her clothes get torn off by the strong wind and she gets sucked up and out of the chimney.
Bill Paxton . . . . Chet
•• 0:30 - Buns taking off towel to give to his younger brother in the kitchen.
Renee Props . . . . One of The Weenies
Suzanne Snyder . . . . .Deb
Wally Ward . . . . .A Weenie
Jill Whitlow. Perfume Salesgirl

Welcome to 18 (1986)

Mariska Hargitay . . . . .Joey
• 0:26 - Buns, taking a shower when video camera is taping her.
0:43 - Watching herself on the videotape playback.

Welcome to Arrow Beach (1973)

a.k.a. Tender Flesh

Meg Foster. . . . . Robbin Stanley
0:12 - Buns and brief side view of right breast getting undressed to skinny dip in the ocean. Don't see her face.
•• 0:40 - Topless getting out of bed.
Joanna Pettet . . . . Grace Henry

Welcome to L.A. (1977)

Keith Carradine . . . . Carroll Barber
Geraldine Chaplin . . . . .Karen Hood
•• 1:28 - Full frontal nudity standing in Keith Car-radine's living room.

Lauren Hutton . . . . Nora Bruce
- • 0:56 - Very brief, obscured glimpse of left breast under red light in photo darkroom.

Harvey Keitel . . . . Ken Hood
Sally Kellerman . . . . Ann Goode
Sissy Spacek . . . . Linda Murray
- •• 0:51 - Brief topless after bringing presents into Keith Carradine's bedroom.

Wet Water T's (1987)
Amy Baxter . . . . herself
- ••• 0:33 - Topless in black lingerie bottoms, then buns in G-string, dancing on stage in a contest.
- •• 0:38 - Topless during judging.
- •• 0:39 - Topless during semi-finals.
- ••• 0:40 - Topless dancing with the other women during semi-final judging.
- ••• 0:43 - Topless during finals.
- •• 0:47 - Topless during final judging.
- ••• 0:48 - Topless dancing after winning first place.

Teri Lynn Peake . . . . herself
- ••• 0:13 - Topless and buns, dancing on stage in white G-string, in a contest.
- •• 0:36 - Topless again during judging.
- •• 0:39 - Topless during semi-finals.
- ••• 0:40 - Topless dancing with the other women.
- ••• 0:43 - Topless dancing during finals.
- •• 0:46 - Topless during final judging.

Wetherby (1985; British)
Suzanna Hamilton . . . . Karen Creasy
    0:42 - In white lingerie top and bottom.
    1:03 - In white lingerie getting into bed.
    1:06 - In white lingerie, fighting with John.
Richard Harris . . . . Sir Thomas
Vanessa Redgrave . . . . Jean Travers
Joely Richardson . . . . Young Jean Travers
- •• 1:10 - Topless in room with Jim when he takes off her coat.

Where the Heart Is (1990)
Suzy Amis . . . . Chloe McBain
- • 0:08 - Topless during her art film. Artfully covered with paint, with a bird. Topless again in the third segment.
- • 0:09 - Topless during the film again. Hard to see because of the paint. Last segment while she narrates.
Joanna Cassidy . . . . Jean McBain
Dabney Coleman . . . . Stewart McBain
David Hewlett . . . . Jimmy
- • 0:56 - Buns, walking around the hall in an angel costume.
Sheila Kelley . . . . Sheryl
Uma Thurman . . . . Daphne McBain
- • 0:08 - Topless during art film, but her entire body is artfully painted to match the background paintings. The second segment.
    0:40 - More topless with body painted posing for her sister. Long shot.
    1:16 - In slide of painting taken at 0:40.
    1:43 - Same painting from 0:40 during end credits.

Where's Poppa? (1970)
Ron Liebman . . . . Sidney Hocheiser
- • 0:45 - Buns running across the street, then in front of door in hall, then brief buns leaving George Segal's apartment.

Whispers (1989)
Chris Sarandon . . . . Detective Tony
Victoria Tennant . . . . Hilary Thomas
- • 0:43 - Buns and side of right breast getting into bathtub. Long shot, looks like a body double (the ponytail in her hair changes position).
- • 0:44 - Buns and brief topless running down the stairs. Looks like the same body double.

White Mischief (1988)
Geraldine Chaplin . . . . Nina
John Hurt . . . . Colville
Sarah Miles . . . . Alice
Jacqueline Pearce . . . . Idina
- •• 0:07 - Topless standing up in the bathtub while several men watch.
Greta Scacchi . . . . Diana Broughton
- •• 0:16 - Topless taking a bath while an old man watches through a peephole in the wall.
- •• 0:24 - Brief topless in bedroom with her husband.
- •• 0:29 - Brief topless taking off bathing suit top in the ocean in front of Charles Dance.
- •• 0:30 - Topless lying in bed talking to Dance.

White Palace (1990)
Eileen Brennan . . . . Judy
Barbara Howard . . . . Sherri Klugman
Rachel Levin . . . . Rachel
Susan Sarandon . . . . Nora Baker
- ••• 0:28 - Topless on top of James Spader. Great shots of right breast.
- • 0:38 - Topless on bed with Spader.
James Spader . . . . Max Baron
- •• 0:38 - Buns, taking off clothes and getting into bed with Susan Sarandon. Don't see his face.

Whose Life Is It, Anyway? (1981)
Janet Eilber . . . . Patty
- •• 0:30 - Nude, ballet dancing during B&W dream sequence.
- • 1:13 - Very brief side of left breast when her back is turned while changing clothes.
Kaki Hunter . . . . Mary Jo

The Wicked Lady (1983; British)
Glynnis Barber . . . . Caroline
- ••• 0:58 - Topless and buns making love with Kitt in the living room. Possible body double.
Alan Bates . . . . Jerry Jackson
Faye Dunaway . . . . Barbara Skelton
Marina Sirtis . . . . Jackson's Girl
- ••• 1:06 - Full frontal nudity in and getting out of bed with Alan Bates.
- ••• 1:20 - Topless getting whipped by Faye Dunaway during their fight during Bates' hanging.

Wicked Stepmother *(1989)*
Colleen Camp . . . . Jenny
Barbara Carrera . . . . Priscilla
- 1:14 - Very, very brief upper half of right breast peeking out of the top of her dress when she flips her head back while seducing Steve.

Laurene Landon . . . . Vanilla

The Wicker Man *(1973; British)*
Britt Ekland . . . . Willow
- ••• 0:58 - Topless in bed knocking on the wall, then more topless and buns getting up and walking around the bedroom. Long scene.

Lorraine Peters . . . . Girl on Grave
- • 0:22 - Side view of right breast sitting on grave, crying. Dark, long shot, hard to see.

Ingrid Pitt . . . . Librarian
- •• 1:11 - Brief topless in bathtub seen by Edward Woodward.

Wifemistress *(1977; Italian)*
Laura Antonelli . . . . Antonia De Angelis
0:50 - In lacy nightgown in her bedroom.
1:22 - Brief upper half of left breast in bed with Clara and her husband.
1:25 - In sheer lacy nightgown leaning out the window.
1:29 - Almost right breast making love with a guy in bed.

Olga Karlatos . . . . Miss Paula Pagano, M.D.
- •• 0:42 - Topless undressing in room with Laura Antonelli. Right breast and part of left breast lying in bed with Marcello Mastroianni.
- • 0:46 - Brief topless in bed with Mastroianni and Clara.

Wild at Heart *(1990)*
Nicholas Cage . . . . Sailor
Willem Dafoe . . . . Bobby Peru
Laura Dern . . . . Lula
- ••• 0:07 - Topless putting on black halter top.
- •• 0:26 - Left breast, then topless sitting on Nicholas Cage's lap in bed.
- •• 0:35 - Topless wriggling around in bed with Cage.
- • 0:41 - Brief topless several times making love with Cage. Hard to see because it keeps going overexposed. Great moaning, though.

Sherilyn Fenn . . . . Girl in Accident
Isabella Rossellini . . . . Perdita
Mia M. Ruiz . . . . Mr. Reindeer's Resident Valet #1
- •• 0:32 - Topless standing next to Mr. Reindeer on the right, holding a tray. Long scene.

Charlie Spradling . . . . Irma
- •• 0:40 - Brief topless in bed during flashback.

The Wild Life *(1984)*
Michael Bowen . . . . Vince
Sherilyn Fenn . . . . Penny Hallin
Tracey E. Hutchinson . . . . Poker Girl #2
- • 1:23 - Brief topless in a room full of guys and girls playing strip poker when Lea Thompson looks in.

Leigh Lombardi . . . . Stewardess
Francesca "Kitten" Natividad . . . . Stripper #2
- ••• 0:50 - Topless doing strip routine in a bar just before a fight breaks out.

Christopher Penn . . . . Tom Drake
Randy Quaid . . . . Charlie
Ashley St. Jon . . . . Stripper #1
- ••• 0:47 - Topless and brief buns doing strip tease routine in front of Christopher Penn and his friends.

Eric Stoltz . . . . Bill Conrad
Lea Thompson . . . . Anita
0:38 - In bra and panties putting body stocking on.
Jenny Wright . . . . Eileen
- •• 0:22 - In bra and panties, then topless changing in her bedroom while Christopher Penn watches from the window.

Wild Man *(1988)*
Ginger Lynn Allen . . . . Dawn Hall
- •• 0:24 - Topless taking off her dress in front to Eric, then making love with him.

Michelle Bauer . . . . Trisha Collins
1:02 - In sheer white lingerie with Eric. Buns also.
- ••• 1:06 - Topless on couch making love with Eric. Brief lower frontal nudity.

Jeanie Moore . . . . Lady at Pool

Wild Orchid *(1990)*
Jacqueline Bisset . . . . Claudia
1:21 - Dancing in braless white tank top during carnival.
Bruce Greenwood . . . . Jermone McFarland
- •• 1:02 - Buns, in room with Carré Otis.

Carré Otis . . . . Emily Reed
- •• 0:51 - Left breast in mirror looking at herself while getting dressed.
- ••• 1:01 - Topless when a guy takes off her dress while Mickey Rourke watches.
- ••• 1:02 - Right breast, then topless on the floor with Jerome.
- • 1:31 - Brief topless in flashback with Jerome.
- • 1:42 - Topless opening her blouse for Rourke.
- ••• 1:44 - Nude making love with Rourke. Nice and sweaty.

Jens Peter . . . . Volleyball Player
- ••• 1:29 - Bun, in room with Jacqueline Bisset and Carré Otis.

Assumpta Serna . . . . Hanna
- ••• 0:39 - Topless at the beach and in the limousine. Very erotic.

Wildcats *(1986)*
Goldie Hawn . . . . Molly
- • 0:30 - Brief topless in bathtub.

Bruce McGill . . . . Dan Darwill
M. Emmet Walsh . . . . Coes

Wildest Dreams *(1987)*
Deborah Blaisdell . . . . Joan Peabody
- • 1:10 - Brief topless during fight on floor with two other women.

Ruth Corrine Collins . . . . Stella
- ••• 0:22 - Topless wearing panties in bedroom on bed with Bobby.
- • 1:10 - Brief topless fighting on floor with two other women.

Jane Hamilton . . . . Ruth Delaney
Jill Johnson . . . . .Rachel Richards
- •• 0:51 - Topless on bed underneath Bobby in a net.
- • 1:10 - Brief topless during fight with two other women.

Jeanne Marie. . . . . .Isabelle
- •• 0:35 - Topless in panties in bedroom with Bobby.

Susan Napoli. . . . . Punk #4
- • 0:21 - Brief left breast, leaning backwards on couch with her boyfriend.

Angela Nicholas . . . . .Claudia
- •• 1:01 - Topless typing on computer doing Bobby's book keeping.

Heidi Paine . . . . .Dancee
- • 0:23 - Topless in the arms of a gladiator in Bobby's bedroom.

Miriam Zucker. . . . . Customer

Wilding, The Children of Violence (1990)
Catlyn Day . . . . Officer Breedlove
Karen Russell. . . . . Cathy
- •• 0:20 - Topless in bedroom when Wings Hauser pulls her lingerie down.

Wimps (1987)
Jim Abele. . . . . .Charles Conrad
Deborah Blaisdell . . . . .Roxanne Chandless
- • 1:22 - Brief topless and buns taking off clothes and getting into bed with Francis in bedroom.

Louis Bonanno . . . . Francis
- • 1:13 - Buns, running into a restaurant kitchen.

Jane Hamilton . . . . Tracy
- • 0:40 - Lifting up her sweater and shaking her breasts in the back of the car with Francis. Too dark to see anything.
- •• 0:44 - Topless and buns taking off sweater in a restaurant.

Jeanne Marie. . . . . Janice
- •• 0:20 - Topless in bed taking off top with Charles.

Annie Sprinkle. .Head Stripper
- •• 1:12 - Topless on stage with two other strippers, teasing Francis.

Winter Kills (1979)
Belinda Bauer . . . . Yvette Malone
- •• 0:46 - Topless making love in bed with Jeff Bridges, then getting out of bed.
- • 1:25 - Topless, dead as a corpse when sheet uncovers her body.

Jeff Bridges . . . . Nick Kegan
- •• 0:50 - Buns, getting dressed after making love with Belinda Bauer.

Tisa Farrow . . . . Nurse Two
Candice Rialson. . . . . .Second Blonde Girl

Winter of Our Dreams (1981)
Bryan Brown . . . . Reb
- • 0:48 - Brief buns falling into bed with Judy Davis.

Judy Davis . . . . Lou
- • 0:19 - Brief left breast sticking out of yellow robe in bed with Pete.
- • 0:26 - Very brief side view of left breast taking off top to change. Long shot.
- •• 0:48 - Topless taking off top and getting into bed with Bryan Brown, then brief right breast lying down with him.

Witchboard (1987)
Tawny Kitaen. . . . . .Linda
- • 1:26 - Topless, nude, brief full frontal nudity stuck in the shower and breaking the glass doors to get out.

Witchcraft II: The Temptress (1989)
Mia M. Ruiz . . . . .Michelle
- • 0:27 - Brief topless several times making love with a guy on the floor during William's hallucination.

Delia Sheppard . . . . Dolores
- •• 1:20 - Brief topless several times with William.

Witchcraft III: The Kiss of Death (1991)
Lisa Toothman . . . . .Charlotte
- •• 1:02 - Buns and topless in shower with Louis while William has a bad dream.
- •• 1:12 - Left breast on bed with Louis, against her will.

Witchfire (1986)
Vanessa Blanchard . . . . Liz
- •• 0:52 - Brief topless in bed and then the shower.

The Witching (1983)
a.k.a. Necromancy
Sue Bernard . . . . Nancy
- • 1:03 - Brief topless in bed with Michael Ontkean.

Pamela Franklin . . . . Lori
- •• 0:38 - Topless lying in bed during nightmare.
  0:46 - Partial right breast, tied to a stake. Flames from fire are in the way.
- • 1:07 - Brief topless putting on black robe.
- • 1:17 - Brief topless in several quick cuts.

Anne Gaybis. . . . . Spirit
Michael Ontkean . . . . .Frank
Barbara Peckinpaugh . . . . Jennie
- ••• 0:02 - Topless and buns in open gown during occult ceremony. Brief full frontal nudity holding a doll up.

Laurie Senit . . . . Witches Coven
Brinke Stevens . . . . Black Sabbath Member

Witchtrap (1989)
Linnea Quigley. .Ginger O'Shey
- ••• 0:34 - Nude taking off robe and getting into the shower.
- •• 0:36 - Topless just before getting killed when the shower head goes into her neck.

Witness *(1985)*
Kelly McGillis. . . . . Rachel
- ••• 1:18 - Topless taking off her top to take a bath while Harrison Ford watches.

Wolf Lake *(1978)*
a.k.a. Survive the Night at Wolf Lake
Robin Mattson . . . . Linda
- • 0:54 - Brief full frontal nudity during rape in cabin. Dark.
- • 0:55 - Brief topless afterwards.

The Woman in Red *(1984)*
Kelly Le Brock . . . . Charlotte
  0:02 - Wearing the red dress, dancing over the air vent in the car garage while Gene Wilder watches.
- • 1:13 - Brief right breast, getting into bed. Too far to see anything.
  1:15 - Brief lower frontal nudity getting out of bed when her husband comes home. Very brief left breast, but it's blurry and hard to see.
Gene Wilder . . . . Theodore Pierce
- • 1:15 - Side view of buns getting back into bed with Kelly Le Brock after getting out to take his underwear off the lamp.

Women & Men: Stories of Seduction
(1990; Made for Cable Movie)
Melanie Griffith. . . . . Hadley
Elizabeth McGovern . . . . Vicki
  0:18 - In white lingerie in train car with Beau Bridges.
- ••• 0:22 - Topless when Bridges takes her top off when she lies back in bed.
Peter Weller. . . . . Hobie
James Woods . . . . Robert

Women in Love *(1971)*
Alan Bates. . . . . Rupert
- • 0:25 - Buns and brief frontal nudity walking around the woods rubbing himself with everything.
- • 0:50 - Buns, making love with Ursula after a boy and girl drown in the river.
- ••• 0:54 - Nude fighting with Oliver Reed in a room in front of a fireplace. Long scene.
Glenda Jackson . . . . Gudrun Brangwen
- ••• 1:20 - Topless taking off her blouse on the bed with Oliver Reed watching her, then making love.
- •• 1:49 - Brief left breast making love with Reed in bed again.
Jennie Linden . . . . Ursula Bragwen
- • 0:38 - Brief topless skinny dipping in the river with Glenda Jackson.
- • 1:11 - Brief topless in a field with Alan Bates. Scene is shown sideways.
Oliver Reed . . . . Gerald Crich
- ••• 0:54 - Nude, fighting with Alan Bates in a room in front of a fireplace. Long scene.

Working Girl *(1989)*
Melanie Griffith . . . . Tess McGill
  0:08 - In bra, panties, garter belt and stockings in front of a mirror.
  0:32 - In black bra, garter belt and stockings trying on clothes.
  0:43 - In black bra, garter belt and stockings getting out of bed.
  1:15 - In white bra, taking off her blouse with Harrison Ford.
- • 1:18 - Very, very brief right breast turning over in bed with Ford.
- • 1:20 - Topless, vacuuming. Long shot seen from the other end of the hall.
Sigourney Weaver . . . . Katherine Parker
  1:22 - In white lingerie, sitting in bed, then talking to Harrison Ford.
Elizabeth Whitcraft. . . . . Doreen DiMucci
- •• 0:29 - Topless on bed on Alec Baldwin when Melanie Griffith opens the door and discovers them.

The Working Girls *(1973)*
Elvira . . . . Katya
  0:18 - Dancing in a G-string on stage in a club.
- ••• 0:20 - Topless, dancing on stage.
Lynne Guthrie . . . . Jill
- ••• 0:43 - Topless, dancing on stage at club.
- •• 0:48 - Topless in swimming pool with Nick.
Laurie Rose. . . . . Denise
Bob Schott . . . . Roger
- • 0:07 - Buns, getting out of bed to meet Honey.

Working Girls *(1987)*
Roger Babb . . . . Paul
- • 1:18 - Frontal nudity with Molly.

World According to Garp *(1982)*
Glenn Close . . . . Jenny Fields
John Lithgow . . . . Roberta
Jenny Wright . . . . Curbie
- •• 0:33 - Brief topless behind the bushes with Robin Williams giving him "something to write about."

The World is Full of Married Men *(1979; British)*
Carroll Baker . . . . Linda Cooper
- • 0:19 - Brief left breast sitting up in bathtub covered with bubbles.

Xtro *(1982)*
Maryam D'Abo. . . . . Analise
- ••• 0:25 - Topless making love with her boyfriend on the floor in her bedroom.
- •• 0:56 - Brief topless with her boyfriend again.

Yanks *(1979)*
Lisa Eichhorn . . . . Jean Moreton
- • 1:48 - Brief topless in bed with Richard Gere.
Richard Gere . . . . Matt
Vanessa Redgrave. . . . . Helen
- • 1:25 - Brief side of left breast and buns, taking off robe and getting into bed.
Annie Ross . . . . Red Cross Lady

The Year of the Dragon (1985)
Ariane.................................. Tracy Tzu
- 0:59 - Very brief topless when Mickey Rourke rips her blouse off in her apartment.
- 1:14 - Nude, taking a shower in her apartment.
- 1:18 - Topless straddling Rourke, while making love on the bed.

You Can't Hurry Love (1984)
Bridget Fonda ....Peggy
Sally Kellerman .... Kelly Bones
Danitza Kingsley .... Tracey
Kristy McNichol.........................Rhonda
David Packer........................... Eddie
- 0:59 - Buns, in store taking his pants off while people watch him from the sidewalk.
Jean Poremba ....Model in Back
- 0:05 - Topless posing in the backyard getting photographed.
- 0:48 - Nude in backyard again getting photographed.
Kimber Sissons .... Brenda
0:48 - Partial side of right breast in open shirt, bending over to pick up her bra off the coffee table.
Merete Van Kamp ....Monique

Young Doctors in Love (1982)
Jaime Lyn Bauer .... cameo
Ed Begley, Jr..................Young Simon's Father
Dabney Coleman ....Dr. Joseph Prang
Kimberly McArthur .... Jyll Omato
- 0:58 - Topless in front of Dabney Coleman after taking off her Santa Claus outfit in his study.
Tessa Richarde.......................Rocco's Wife
Janine Turner .... cameo
Sean Young.................. Dr. Stephanie Brody
0:48 - In white panties and camisole top in the surgery room with Michael McKean.

Young Einstein (1989; Australian)
Glenn Butcher................... Ernest Rutherford
- 0:56 - Buns standing in front of sink when Marie comes to rescue Einstein. (He's the one on the left.)
Warren Coleman.................Lunatic Professor
- 0:55 - Buns in Lunatic Asylum taking a shower.
- 0:56 - More buns standing in front of sink when Marie comes to rescue Einstein. (He's the one on the right.)
- 0:58 - Brief buns crowding into the shower stall with the other Asylum people.

Young Guns (1988)
Emilio Estevez .... William H. Bonney (Billy the Kid)
- 1:19 - Brief buns standing up in the bathtub.
Pat Lee .... Janey
Terry O'Quinn.................... Alex McSween

Young Guns II (1990)
Ginger Lynn Allen ....Dove
Tom Byrd............................ Pit Inmate
Emilio Estevez .... William H. Bonney (Billy the Kid)
- 1:00 - Buns, getting up out of bed, putting his pants on.
William L. Petersen.....................Pat Garrett
Christian Slater.............Arkansas Dave Rudbaugh
Jenny Wright .... Jane Greathouse
- 1:07 - Buns, taking off her clothes, getting on a horse and riding away. Hair covers breasts.
- 1:38 - Buns, walking down stairs during epilogue.

Young Lady Chatterley (1977)
Lindsay Freeman ....Sybil (light-duty maid)
Harlee McBride ....Cynthia Chatterley
- 0:19 - Nude masturbating in front of mirror.
- 0:41 - Nude in bathtub while maid washes her.
- 0:52 - Nude in car while the chauffeur is driving.
- 1:03 - Nude in the garden with the sprinklers on making love with the Gardener.
Ann Michelle ....Gwen (roommate)

Young Lady Chatterley II (1986)
Wendy Barry .... Sybil "Maid in Hot House"
- 0:12 - Topless in hot house with the Gardener.
Sybll Danning ....
- 1:02 - Topless in the hut on the table with the Gardener.
Alexandra Day .... Jenny "Maid in Hut"
- 0:06 - Topless in hut on the bed with the Gardener.
- 0:28 - Topless taking bath with Harlee McBride.
Monique Gabrielle .... Eunice
- 0:15 - Topless in the woods with the Gardener.
- 0:43 - Topless in bed with Virgil.
Harlee McBride.................Cynthia Chatterley
- 0:20 - Topless getting a massage with Elanor.
- 0:28 - Topless taking a bath with Jenny.
- 0:35 - Topless in library seducing Virgil.
- 0:50 - Topless in back of the car with the Count.
- 0:58 - Topless in the garden with Robert.

Young Nurses in Love (1987)
John Altamura ....
Jennifer Delora .... Bunny
Jane Hamilton ....Franchesca
- 1:05 - Topless on top of a guy on a gurney.
Jeanne Marie .... Nurse Ellis Smith
- 0:31 - Brief side view of left breast in mirror with Dr. Riley.
- 1:09 - Topless in panties, getting into bed with Dr. Riley.
Sharon Moran ....Bambi/Bibi
Annie Sprinkle ....Twin Falls
- 0:23 - Topless getting measured by Dr. Spencer.

The Young Warriors (1983; U.S./Canadian)
John Alden . . . . Jorge
- 0:16 - Dropping his pants in a room during pledge at fraternity.

Anne Lockhart. . . . . Lucy
- • 0:42 - Topless and buns making love with Kevin on the bed. Looks like a body double.

Jimmy Patterson . . . . "Ice Test" Monty
- 0:14 - Buns, dropping pants and sitting on a block of ice during pledge at fraternity.

Linnea Quigley . . . . Ginger
- 0:05 - Nude in and getting out of bed in bedroom.

Randy Woltz . . . . "Brick Test" Frank
- 0:16 - Dropping his pants in a room during pledge at fraternity.

Youngblood (1986)
Fionnula Flanagan. . . . . .Miss McGill

Cynthia Gibb . . . . Jessie Chadwick
- 0:50 - Brief topless and buns making love with Rob Lowe in his room.

Rob Lowe . . . . Dean Youngblood
- • • 0:16 - Buns, standing in hallway in jockstrap and walking around while Cindy Gibb watches.

Patrick Swayze . . . . Derek Sutton

Jim Youngs . . . . Kelly Youngblood

Your Ticket is No Longer Valid (1982)
Jennifer Dale. . . . . Laura
- • • 0:27 - In black panties, then topless when her husband fantasizes, then makes love with her.
  - 1:23 - Left breast in bed with Montoya, then sitting, waiting for Richard Harris.

Richard Harris . . . . Jason
- 1:19 - Buns, taking off robe and sitting on the floor.

Winston Reckert . . . . Antonio Montoya
- 1:24 - Buns, in bed with Jennifer Dale.

Zandalee (1991)
Erika Anderson . . . . .Zandalee Martin
- • • • 0:02 - Nude, taking off robe and dancing around the room.
- • • • 0:21 - Nude, undressing, then in bed with Judge Reinhold. Long scene.
- • • 0:30 - Right breast, then topless making love in bed with Nicholas Cage.
- • • 0:32 - Topless as Cage paints on her with his finger.
- • • • 0:45 - Left breast, then topless and lower frontal nudity on floor with Cage.
- • • 0:47 - Nude, getting massaged by Cage with an oil and cocaine mixture.
- 0:48 - Brief topless getting into bed with Reinhold. Slightly out of focus.
- • • 1:09 - Topless opening her dress for Reinhold while lying on a river bank, then making love with him at night in bed.

Nicholas Cage . . . . Johnny Collins
- • • 0:30 - Buns, making love in bed with Zandalee.

Judge Reinhold. . . . . Thierry Martin
- • • • 0:21 - Buns in bed with Zandalee.
- 0:23 - Upper half of buns, standing by the window.

Zapped! (1982)
Willie Aames. . . . . .Peyton

Scott Baio. . . . . .Barney

Corinne Bohrer. . . . . Cindy

Rosanne Katon. . . . . Donna

Jewel Shepard . . . . uncredited Girl in Car
- 0:39 - Brief topless after red and white top pops off when Scott Baio uses his Telekinesis on her.

Heather Thomas. . . . . Jane Mitchell
- 0:20 - Brief open sweater, wearing a bra when Scott Baio uses telekinesis to open it.
- 1:28 - Body double, very, very brief topless in photo that Willie Aames gives to Robby.
- 1:29 - Body double brief topless when Baio drops her dress during the dance.

Zardoz (1974; British)
Charlotte Rampling . . . . .Consuella
- 1:44 - Very brief right breast feeding her baby in time lapse scene at the end of the film.

Zombie (1980)
Tisa Farrow. . . . . Anne Bolles

Olga Karlatos . . . . Mrs. Menard
- 0:40 - Topless and buns taking a shower.

Zombie Island Massacre (1984)
Rita Jenrette . . . . Sandy
- • • • 0:01 - Topless taking a shower while Joe sneaks up on her. Topless in bed with Joe.
- • • 0:10 - Brief right breast with open blouse, in boat with Joe. Left breast with him on the couch.

OTHER SOURCES

An excellent magazine that you should definitely check out is *Celebrity Sleuth*. In it, you'll find photographs of many celebrities that don't or won't do nudity for video tapes. People like Jackie Onassis, Karen Lynn Gorney, Deidre Hall, Carey Lowell and Caroline Munro are featured in various issues of *Celebrity Sleuth*. If you can't find it at your local newsstand or you need back issues, contact:

> Celebrity Sleuth
> P.O. Box 273
> West Redding, CT 06896

Drive-in film critic, Joe Bob Briggs, publishes a weekly newletter, *We Are the Weird*. He writes a humorous column and reviews a movie in each edition. The movies he reviews are usually the type that are destined for inclusion in *The Bare Facts Video Guide*. It costs $35.00 for 52 issues. His address is:

> We Are the Weird
> P.O. Box 2002
> Dallas, TX 75221

If you can't find the video tapes listed in *The Bare Facts Video Guide* for rent at your local video tape rental stores, an excellent source for purchasing video tapes is *Movies Unlimited*. Their catalog costs $7.95 plus $3.00 shipping, but you get a $5.00 credit voucher to use on your order. The address is:

> Movies Unlimited
> 6736 Castor Avenue
> Philadelphia, PA 19149

Back issues of *Playboy* magazine can be purchased through *The Playboy Catalog*. Their catalog is free by calling 1-800-345-6066. They have a large assortment of *Playboy* magazine back issues from the 1960's to the present in addition to *Playboy* Video Magazines, Becky LeBeau's *Soft Bodies* series and other video tapes.

Another source for locating hard to find video tapes is *Critic's Choice*. Their catalog is free by calling 1-800-544-9852. They have over 2,300 video tapes for sale. They also have a Video Search Line that operates Monday through Friday, from 9 a.m. to 5 p.m. EST. Their phone number is 1-900-370-6500. The cost is $1 for the first minute and $.50 for each additional minute. They will research your request and call you back within 1 to 2 weeks. The decision to buy—or not to buy—is yours.

The book I use to help locate adult film stars is called, *The Blue Guide to Adult Film Stars*. It is published every January and is available for $19.95 (plus $2.55 for shipping and handling. New Jersey residents add 6% sales tax.) from:

The Blue Guide
Box 16
Ogdensburg, NJ 07439
(201)-729-3022

If you are interested in writing to your favorite actor or actress to get an autograph or ask a question, you might want to purchase the book *Celebrity Access—The Directory*. The cost is $21.95 (plus $2.50 for shipping and handling. California residents add 7.25% sales tax.) and is available from:

Thomas Burford
20 Sunnyside Avenue, Suite A241
Mill Valley, CA 94941
(415) 389-8133

If you are interested in viewing the Rob Lowe video tape that he accidentally made in 1989, you can purchase it from Al Goldstein, publisher of *Screw* magazine. His New York cable TV show, *Midnight Blue*, showed some of the footage on show #672. The cost is $29.95, you need to specify VHS or Beta. Contact:

Media Ranch, Inc.
P.O. Box 432
Old Chelsea Station
New York, NY 10013

Since all of the descriptions in *The Bare Facts Video Guide* are listed by minutes, you should have a VCR that uses a real-time counter. VCR's made by *Mistubishi* and *Sony* do this as well as S-VHS models from most all the manufacturers.

REFERENCES

Books:

Bowker's Complete Video Directory 1990
  R. R. Bowker, 1990

The Complete Actors' Television Credits, 1948–1988, Second Edition
  Volume 1: Actors and Volume 2: Actresses
  James Robert Parish and Vincent Terrace
  The Scarecrow Press, Inc., 1990

The Complete Directory to Prime Time Network TV Shows, 1946–Present
  Tim Brooks and Earle Marsh
  Ballantine, 1988

Halliwell's Film Guide, Seventh Edition
  Leslie Halliwell
  HarperPerennial, 1990

HBO's Guide to Movies on Videocassette and Cable TV 1991
  Daniel Eagan
  Harper & Ross, 1990

Leonard Maltin's TV Movies and Video Guide, 1991 Edition
  Leonard Maltin
  Signet, 1990

The Motion Picture Guide (1984 through 1991 editions)
  Stanley Ralph Ross and Jay Robert Nash
  Baseline II, 1991

Movies on TV and Videocassette, 1991–1992
  Steven H. Scheuer
  Bantam Books, 1990

Movies Unlimited catalog
  Various catalogs from 1987-1991
  Movies Unlimited, 6736 Castor Avenue, Philadelphia, PA 19149

Roger Ebert's Movie Home Companion 1991 Edition
  Roger Ebert
  Andrews and McMeel, 1990

Russ Meyer—The Life and Films
  David K. Fraiser
  McFarland & Company, Inc., 1990

Video Movie Guide 1991
  Mick Martin and Marsha Porter
  Ballantine, 1990

The Blue Guide to Adult Film Stars—1990 Edition
  FD Enterprises, 1990

MORE REFERENCES

Periodicals:

Entertainment Weekly magazine
  Various issues from 1990–1991
  Entertainment Weekly Inc., 1675 Broadway, New York, NY 10019

Playboy magazine
  Various issues from 1972–1991
  919 North Michigan Avenue, Chicago, IL 60611

Penthouse magazine
  Various issues from 1980–1991
  1965 Broadway, New York, NY 10023-5965

Premiere magazine
  Various issues from 1987–1991
  Premiere Publishing, 2 Park Avenue, New York, New York 10016

The San Jose Mercury News newspaper
  Various issues from 1987–1991
  750 Ridder Park Drive, San Jose, CA 95190

TV Guide magazine
  Various issues from 1987–1991
  Triangle Publications, Inc., 100 Matsonford Road, Radnor, PA 19088

We Are the Weird newsletter
  Various issues from 1990–1991
  Joe Bob Briggs, P.O. Box 2002, Dallas, TX 75221

ABOUT THE AUTHOR

Craig Hosoda is a Software Engineer. He grew up in Silicon Valley, California, then went to the University of California at Berkeley where he graduated with a B.S. degree in Electrical Engineering and Computer Science. After graduation, he worked at Hewlett-Packard for two years before getting a programming job at Industrial Light and Magic, George Lucas' special effects division of Lucasfilm Ltd. (Craig's film credits can be found in *The Golden Child*, *The Goonies* and **batteries not included*.)

While working at ILM, the seeds for *The Bare Facts Video Guide* were planted during a casual conversation one day with his friend, Marty Brenneis. While working on the film, *Howard the Duck*, Marty asked Craig about Lea Thompson's film credits. When Marty didn't know about her nude scene in *All the Right Moves*, Craig thought, "There should be a book that lists this type of important information in one place..."

After returning to Silicon Valley in 1987 to raise a family with his wife, he began research for the book during the evenings while working as a software engineer during the day. Unfortunately, it was difficult to balance a full-time job, work on *The Bare Facts* and have time for his family, so in July 1990, he quit his regular job to devote his life to uncovering the bare facts.

HOW THIS BOOK WAS CREATED

This book was published using the latest in database publishing techniques on an Apple Macintosh IIci computer. A custom ACIUS *4th Dimension* database was created to keep track of the data. An export module was written in *4th Dimension* that outputs the information with *FrameMaker* format tags into a text file. The text file was read into Frame Technology's *FrameMaker* and cleaned up a bit. Camera-ready copy was printed on an Apple Personal LaserWriter, then sent to the book printer.